DU PONT
DYNASTY

DU PONT DYNASTY

by Gerard Colby

Lyle Stuart Inc.   Secaucus, New Jersey

Published by Lyle Stuart Inc.
Published simultaneously in Canada by
Musson Book Company,
A division of General Publishing Co. Limited
Don Mills, Ontario

Queries regarding rights and permissions should be
addressed to: Lyle Stuart, 120 Enterprise Avenue, Secaucus, N.J. 07094.

Manufactured in the United States of America

Library of Congress Cataloging in Publication Data

Colby, Gerard, 1945-
    Du Pont dynasty.

    Rev. ed. of: Du Pont. 1974.
    Includes bibliographical references and index.
    1. Du Pont family.   2. E. I. du Pont de Nemours &
Company—History.   3. Chemical industry—United
States—History.   4. United States—Social conditions.
5. United States—Economic conditions.   I.   Colby, Gerard,
1945-   Du Pont.   II.   Title.
HD9651.9.D8C65   1984   338.7'66'00922   [B]   84-2619
ISBN 0-8184-0352-7

This 1984 edition is dedicated

To Charlotte Dennett, for her rare courage and dedication to justice and the people's right to know,

To the memory of my mother, Veronica Colby Zilg, for her inspiration and belief,

And to the people of Delaware and employees of Du Pont, for sacrifices untold and their continuing struggle for human dignity and true democracy.

CONTENTS

Foreword
and
Acknowledgments

One may easily see history as only a succession of chances or conjectures—but, if so, there is nothing to study, there are no correlations to be made between events, and in fact there is only a rope of sand, a series of non sequiturs which one can do nothing but narrate. . . .

But it is the optical illusion or the occupational disease of the research student to imagine that only the details matter, and that the details are all of equal value—that the statesman has no cohesive purpose but is merely a bundle of contradictions—and that everything is under the rule of chance, under the play of absurdly little chances—history reducing itself at the finish to an irony of circumstance.

Herbert Butterfield, 1959

This is a great "How" age. But "Why" remains unanswered, and will doubtless in due course again claim attention.

Malcolm Muggeridge, 1958

For better or worse, this book is an attempt to answer the question "Why?" For too long, in this writer's opinion, biography, and particularly Du Pont biography, has been locked in the subject's own preoccupation with "How" and reduced to the usual melodrama of autobiography. *Du Pont Dynasty,* however, has been written with the conviction that biography cannot stand outside history.

Footnotes are included to answer the demands of our skeptical and technocratic age. But "History," William Appleman Williams once wrote, "is simply not the arithmetic total of footnotes." A full bibliography for such a book as this would be meaningless. Each source of a single quotation is without value unless seen within the context of related documents and books on the era concerned.

This, of course, involves a question of methodology in analyzing the past. Although authors have the benefit of historical hindsight, their choice of emphasis is inevitably influenced by their own value system—despite any claims to the contrary. Admitting this is the first, necessary step toward honesty with oneself as a writer, with one's work, and with readers. It is also a prerequisite for approaching a true science of social affairs, for one's own mental tools must be recognized as a variable in the creative process of research and writing; men and women, try as they may through mental gymnastics, do not stand outside themselves. Having acknowledged that, the author can then proceed more cautiously and accurately with the task of searching for the historical trends that lie within the mountains of data accumulated through empirical investigation. Beyond the superficial shell of opinions, including those of the subject—in this case the Du Pont family—as well as those of the author, lies the kernel of reality in motion, unfolding the history of not only one family, but of the country and times that shaped their story. By this method of searching for the meaning within behavior, *Du Pont Dynasty* was completed after five years of research, including three years of writing.

Any man's work is the sum total of his previous experience. In that sense, this book owes much to my personal and intellectual friendship with Dr. Robert Carson of the Department of Economics at State University College at Oneonta, New York. Through his lectures and seminars, Carson's students have been offered a solid foundation for future endeavors in economic history. I am also indebted to Martin J. Sklar of the History Department of Northern Illinois University. Sklar's groundbreaking theory of the disaccumulation of living labor power from the point of production was an invaluable insight into the Twenties when evaluating the role of the Du Ponts and John J. Raskob in that decade, as well as their inability to comprehend Roosevelt's policies as the response of corporate liberalism to the crisis of disaccumulation in the Thirties. Finally, Professor William Appleman Williams of the History Department of Oregon State University is owed more than can ever be repaid. For his comprehensive writings, which deserve study and restudy, Williams stands as a giant among historians.

As for the Du Ponts specifically, much information was accumulated from many interviews during my one-year stay in Delaware. Most of those people who were interviewed have elected to retain their anonymity. This is understandable if one is at all familiar with Delaware. Although I had researched the influence of the Du Pont family on that state before my arrival, I was totally unprepared for my discovery of its actual pervasion. At the Delaware Historical Society, pictures of Du Ponts, legally in the Society's control, were refused republication for "moral" reasons—as if it were moral for an institution supposedly dedicated to historical investigation to prevent the public from sharing its possessions. But as one of the librarians put it: "We depend upon their cooperation and we wouldn't want to do anything to jeopardize that." His assistant, somewhat embarrassed, tried to offer an explanation that only succeeded in being more candid: "This is a small state," she explained. "We don't want to do anything that will get us into trouble." At the University of Delaware, where buildings named after Du Ponts abound, another strange coincidence: of all the records of congressional hearings stacked in the library, one was notably missing when I visited there in 1970—the 1934 Dickstein–McCormick hearings on the aborted plot for an armed coup against Roosevelt. At the Eleutherian Mills–Hagley Foundation Library, a tax-free institution to which the Du Pont family donates its correspondence and records, post-1933 manuscripts were abruptly seized after a librarian gave them to me for my research. A "mistake" had been made, she hurriedly explained, since those manuscripts involved people who were still living; I was subsequently barred from all post-1933 manuscripts.

The obstacle of Du Pont influence also extended beyond Delaware. In New York, for example, an attempt to secure pictures of Du Ponts originally published in *Life* magazine would be refused, according to a representative of Magnum Photos acting as a go-between, "if the book was in any way unfavorable to the family." So much for freedom of the press in the most liberal of American cities. Similarly, in Jacksonville, Florida, the willingness of *Times-Union* photo librarians to cooperate evaporated overnight. When I returned the next morning to pick up a photograph of Epping Forest, the princely estate of the late Alfred I. du Pont, I was told that the newspaper had changed its mind and would not sell the photo without the permission of Mr. du Pont's brother-in-law, Edward Ball.

With regard to interviews with Du Ponts, formal invitations were either declined or ignored. Inroads were made into some Du Pont households, however, usually through employees. For most of these people, personal courage was fortified by a genuine commitment to an open society.

Delaware's "Garden Day," when many Du Pont estates are opened to the public, also proved helpful. The inclusion of my name as a sponsor of 1971's Garden Day along with those of many Du Ponts provided, besides an amusing touch of irony, an opportunity to actually see how residing on a Du Pont estate would feel.

Despite the hindrances mentioned above, much valuable information was collected over the years through the cooperation of others. In Delaware, special acknowledgment must be given to the research records of David McCorquedale. Thanks are also due to the library staffs of the Wilmington *News-Journal* and the Delaware *State News*. Despite the restriction already referred to, the staff of the Eleutherian Mills–Hagley Foundation Library, including its director, Richmond D. Williams, genuinely tried to be as cooperative as possible within the limitations imposed on them. In Jacksonville, the librarian of the *Times-Union* was particularly helpful, opening its files and providing copying services free of charge. In New York, I am indebted to the librarians of the Fifth Avenue Public Library (particularly its economics division), Columbia University, and City College for extensive use of their facilities and services. I am also indebted to the North American Congress on Latin America for information on pre-revolutionary Cuba.

Herbert Alexander of the Citizen's Research Foundation at Princeton, New Jersey, was very helpful in obtaining information on Du Pont political donations. At Hyde Park, New York, Francis Seager, librarian, and J. C. James, director, enabled me to secure copies of Du Pont–Roosevelt correspondence from the Franklin D. Roosevelt Library. The National Action/Research on the Military Industrial Complex in Philadelphia was kind enough to allow me access to their research facilities for investigating war contracts. In Washington, D.C., the cooperation of Mr. W. Moore and Mr. Roberts of the Library of Congress and Lt. Colonel Audrey E. Thomas of the Directorate for Defense Information is also noted.

Thanks are also in order for the tireless services of the staffs of the Philadelphia Public Library, the Wilmington (Delaware) Public Library, the Charleston (South Carolina) Public Library, the Jacksonville (Florida) Public Library, the Miami Public Library, the New Orleans Public Library, the Kansas City Public Library, and the Los Angeles Public Library—all of whom put up with far too many demands by this author during his visits to their facilities.

The responsibility for the interpretation and emphasis of material used in this book, including its arguments and textual errors, however, is solely the author's.

In that regard, it seems appropriate to offer a special comment on my use of the term Black. I have capitalized Black just as I would Afro-American, Irish-American, Hungarian-American, or any proper name used to designate a particular segment of the American people. Beyond that point, it could also be argued that Black people constitute one of many nationalities that populate the United States. While Irish-Americans, for example, may well have been transformed, through assimilation, from a nationality to a hardly identifiable ethnic grouping by the third generation, Afro-Americans, due to four hundred years of economic and political discrimination, have been fused into a national identity which endures as long as the oppressive conditions that shaped its origins and development. Thus, it has been argued, the distinction due a national grouping is a main reason for capitalizing its name.

Finally, for providing the financial lifeline that kept this project from foundering under an angry sea of debts, I would like to thank those personal friends who offered assistance when I was too proud to ask. To the Author's League Fund and the Carnegie Fund for Authors, which provided personal aid without queries about what I was writing, acknowledgment is also due.

Foreword
and
Acknowledgments
to 1984 Edition

Esse non videri
—Roman adage ("Be, but do not be seen")

On September 8, 1983, a twin engine propeller plane suddenly appeared over the international airport at Nicaragua's capital, Managua, and began dropping bombs. Hit by ground fire, the mystery plane screamed to a crash at the base of the airport's control tower.

Sandinista forces found the two pilots dead but recovered a Panamanian customs declaration indicating that the plane, a Cessna 404, had been flown from Panama City to San José, Costa Rica; other documents contained instructions for making secret contact with an American official at the United States Embassy there. CIA officers had been working out of the embassy, supplying Nicaraguan rebels of the Revolutionary Democratic Alliance with intelligence, money, arms—and recently, five light airplanes specially fitted in the United States with bombs and machine-guns. The Cessna 404 was one of those planes.

The CIA's covert operation was in direct violation of United States law. Congress had refused to authorize any monies for the CIA to overthrow the Nicaraguan government and some Congressmen were furious that the Reagan administration had gone ahead anyway and ordered the CIA into action, backed by thousands of U.S. troops in Honduras.

An investigation was launched by the *New York Times* into the illegal CIA supply operation, and the trail led through a dummy Panamanian company, Servicios de Mar, Aire y Tierra (Sea, Air and Land Services) back to the Washington, D.C., area and a company called Investair Leasing Corporation. Investair's general manager, Edgar L. Mitchell, it was discovered, had previously been vice-president and treasurer of a CIA-owned Arizona company, Intermountain Aviation, from 1966 to 1975. Investair's marketing director, Mark L. Peterson, had been secretary and treasurer of another CIA airline, Air America, infamous for its involvement with the heroin trade of CIA mercenaries in Laos.

But the trail did not end there. It led further on, to Delaware, where Investair had been incorporated, as have scores of other CIA proprietaries.

And it led to the Du Ponts.

The Cessna 404 that the CIA had used to bomb the Managua airport had been converted to carry bombs and guns by a small Middletown, Delaware, company named Summit Aviation. Unknown to most Americans, it is a source of whispers in Delaware, a small state with a small-town atmosphere.

Airplanes with foreign markings had been seen for years at Summit's airfield and recently the firm had contacted the Federal Aviation Administration on plans to extend its asphalt runway to accommodate larger aircraft. Summit, according to sources familiar with its financial affairs, had scored a large secret contract with a federal agency. The purpose of the contract was the conversion of business planes for clandestine military operations by the CIA. Of ten multi-engine civilian aircraft reportedly outfitted for such use, six have virtually disappeared, untraceable from FAA records which list no owners; three others were leased from companies in other states and are probably in CIA service abroad; the other was the Cessna which bombed Managua's International Airport.

Where was the CIA getting the money to pay for the conversions? How much was Summit profiteering off illegal military operations conducted in direct violation of the will of Congress? And who, besides President Reagan and CIA officials, was involved?

Delaware's U.S. Senator Joseph Biden, a member of the Senate Intelligence Committee, has launched his own investigation into Summit in response to complaints by at least one Delaware citizen. He has so far released no findings. But one man obviously is involved and knows about the illegal arms deals: Summit's president, Richard C. du Pont.

Du Pont? That is a name more commonly associated with paint and nylon and chemicals. But spy planes, illegal arms deals, and the CIA?

To many Americans, Du Pont is a corporation; and there is a vague awareness that there is a Du Pont family involved with the company. Few know of the darker side of the Du Pont Company. Three hundred and twenty-seven public relations and marketing employees, $128 million yearly in advertising, and $5 million devoted to prime time television spots make sure, along with publicist and former comedian Marty Ingels, that America sees only the Du Pont image of perfection and "Better Things for Better Living." One hundred and thirty thousand Du Pont employees get an added propaganda injection through a plethora of company magazines, newsletters, and video displays.

That people with the Du Pont name might be involved in secret arms deals and illegal CIA operations would seem as far-fetched to many Americans as the fact that a Du Pont vice-president was the secret backer of the blatantly neo-fascist *Freeman* magazine published in upstate New York during the McCarthy witchhunts of the 1950's or that a Du Pont subsidiary in Czechoslovakia supplied the Nazi war machine with artificial rubber.

Whether it is Du Pont's quietly keeping tabs on employees whose government connections might someday become useful, or Chairman Irving Shapiro's approaching President Carter's Commerce Secretary to get him to drop an investigation into Du Pont's alleged violation of laws prohibiting compliance with the Arab boycott of Israel, or Irénée du Pont's use of a Cuban holding company, Penas de Hicacos, to secretly buy up German municipal and utility bonds during the 1920's, the real story of the Du Ponts—their activities behind the scenes—doesn't fit their popular image.

I first became interested in the Du Pont family while I was working as press secretary for Congressman John Dow of New York. Dow was an opponent of the Vietnam war when it was not yet popular to be so. I was looking into the influence of war profiteers on political elections and policies. My research led me to the 1934 Senate munitions hearings which revealed that the Du Ponts had made over $250 million in profits off World War I.

What really captured my interest was the Dickstein-McCormick House Investigating Committee's findings that a plot existed to seize the White House with a Mussolini-type march on Washington by veterans who were to be armed by the Du Ponts. The bizarre report included corroborating testimony from Paul Comely French of the Philadelphia *Record*, National Commander of the Veterans of Foreign Wars James Van Zandt, and former Commandant of the Marine Corps General Smedley Butler, who had been twice decorated by Congress with the Congressional Medal of Honor.

I was aware that the Du Ponts considered President Roosevelt "a traitor to his class," but it was hard to believe they would go that far. Federal Judge Charles Brieant, currently of the Southern District of New York, also thought the report was preposterous during his trial of my suit against Du Pont Company, and dismissed it and the credibility of the 1974 edition of this book out of hand. I, however, investigated, and after five years I had learned to believe that such dismissals reveal not only a dangerous naïveté about power, and the extent to which those who have it will go to protect their power, but also a disturbing bias in favor of such "pillars of society."

Such revelations as the House Committee's should have aroused any historian's attention, but they have been overlooked in textbooks, and drowned in a sea of denials, derision and secrecy.

That was 16 years ago. Since then, I have been taken on a long odyssey in pursuit of the truth, including a year of residence and many subsequent visits to Delaware, the Du Ponts' home called "the company state" by Ralph Nader's investigators. I cannot claim that I wasn't disturbed by what I encountered there, and that is reflected in the tone of the 1974 edition of this book, which so upset the Du Ponts and their sympathizers.

It has been ten years since the first edition of this book was published and, in the words of Judge Brieant, "privished." That is the term often used in publishing's higher circles to describe the way a worrisome book is "killed off:" to "*priv*ately publ*ish*," rather than *pub*licly, by deliberately shortening the life span of a book by cutting off its lifelines to promotion, advertising and distribution. It has happened to many authors. In my case it happened after Du Pont Company officials, responding to the concerns expressed by Du Pont family members, made a series of phone calls to Book-of-the-Month Club (BOMC) to persuade it to reconsider its Fortune Book Club's contract with my publisher, Prentice-Hall.

The almost immediate (and reportedly unprecedented) cancellation by BOMC of a book under such circumstances would have a chilling impact on most publishers, and Prentice-Hall, a conservative house with a weak position in the trade book market, was certainly no exception. Prentice-Hall drastically slashed its print run and advertising budget, despite the book's having met its advance sales target and won wide acceptance in reviews across the country. (A notable exception were writers from northern Delaware and Philadelphia who personally knew the Du Ponts, admired them to some extent, and placed reviews in such key opinion-molding sources as the *Wall Street Journal*, the Philadelphia newspapers and the *Harvard Business Review.*)

Du Pont Company also launched an investigation of the *New York Times* reviewer, placed internal company critiques in the hands of reviewers with instructions not to acknowledge Du Pont as the source of their information, and criticized reviewers in personal letters to editors, who are always sensitive to the threat of lost advertising.

Prentice-Hall allowed the book to go out of stock while demand for it remained high, and ultimately let it go out of print altogether.

I learned these facts only because journalist Charlotte Dennett, my wife, and I decided to risk our time and money to launch a federal court suit against Du Pont and Prentice-Hall. Federal suits give a wide berth in discovery proceedings that allow you to subpoena records and take sworn depositions. The process, however, is lengthy and extremely expensive, especially if you are paying your lawyers a flat hourly rate, as we were. When we ran out of money, friends and relatives and many others concerned about the freedom of the press came through, although we have now been left with considerable debt.

We won much, in the sense of new friends and insightful information about publishing. We also lost much, including our crucial right to trial by jury, thanks to the failure of our first attorney, Michael Standard of Rabinowitz,

Boudin and Standard, to simply file our jury request on time. That we ever made it to trial at all is due largely to Charlotte's investigative and paralegal work and to the brilliance and dedication of our second attorney, Ronald De Petris.

A Republican and former Assistant U.S. District Attorney, De Petris was concerned enough about the freedom of the press and contract law to accept a partial contingency and defend the rights of an admitted left-of-center writer, even though he knew he would quite possibly be facing the hostility of conservative judges. He believed in equality before the law.

This may be especially difficult to obtain in Delaware. There, even the population's understanding of the very history of their state is dominated by Du Pont interests: the Historical Society of Delaware counts at least six Du Pont family relations on its board of trustees (J. Bruce Bredin, Mrs. Henry B. du Pont, Pierre S. du Pont III, Mrs. Walter J. Laird, Mrs. Willard Speakman III, and Jane Richards Roth, wife of Senator William Roth), as well as Du Pont loyalists such as Dr. Walter J. Hecock of the family foundation library (the Eleutherian Mills-Hagley Foundation Library), William Poole (a family foundation trustee), and Dr. Carol Hoffecker of the Du Pont-endowed University of Delaware.

The Delaware population's perception of what their rights are and what is legally possible is also dominated by Du Pont interests. The Delaware Bar Foundation's board of directors includes, for example, Du Pont Company's former chief counsel, Charles Welch, Victor Battaglia, former city solicitor under Mayor Harry Haskell (son of a Du Pont executive), Edmund N. Carpenter II, a Du Pont son-in-law and personal lawyer and former campaign finance manager for Pierre S. du Pont IV, Delaware's current governor, O. Francis Biondi, a lobbyist for New York banks who helped draft Governor du Pont's banking laws which have adversely affected the credit card balances of millions of Americans—and made him a multimillionaire through real estate deals for banks and other financial institutions moving into Wilmington.

But the problem of perception is not limited to Delaware. European bankers who greeted Governor du Pont's lieutenant governor (and would-be heir apparent) Michael Castle and representatives of Delaware's Chamber of Commerce in 1981 during their visit to invite foreign banks into Delaware, knew more about the enormous implications of Governor du Pont's new tax laws than most Americans. In the same vein, many Americans are unaware of what Du Pont Company's profits off pesticides and fertilizers have to do with "the green revolution" of larger (but often less nutritious) food plants promoted by the U.S. Agency for International Development (AID), or Elise du Pont's promotion of American corporate investment abroad as head of AID's Bureau of Private Enterprise, or Senator William Roth's bill to destroy the Commerce

Department and set up a new Department of International Trade and Investment.

Certainly, such issues have little to do with the late Sam Hallock du Pont's $1 million coin collection, or Mrs. Martha (Muffin) du Pont's auctioning off of her 220 dolls (one alone was worth $12,000) to "simplify her life," or John du Pont's closing of his pool to young Olympic aspirants because he can no longer afford its upkeep with his estimated $125 million fortune. But there is a social meaning here too, when one recalls Muffin du Pont's valiant efforts to reform Delaware's overcrowded prisons and the disdain with which her concern for the less fortunate (from which she hails) was held by the rest of the Du Pont clan.

There is a political lesson, also, in the values through which the Du Ponts view life in the insistence by heirs of Marion du Pont Scott that her $400 million will be confirmed by the courts before they will honor her last request that they give or sell the historic home of James Madison, Montpelier, to the National Trust for Historic Preservation. There are lessons too in the minimum $180,000 the Du Pont's give Republican candidates every two years, and Governor du Pont's putting forth a reduced budget for "lean times" while he cuts taxes for the rich and vetoes a Democratic-backed bill to allow public funding of Delaware's political campaigns with less money than it cost the state each year to maintain the governor and his household. There is even something to be learned in the little-known firing by Du Pont Company of Annie Oakley (recorded as Mrs. Frank E. Butler on the payrolls) in 1920 after 31 years of testing and promoting Du Pont sporting gunpowder. She received no pension.

In the Du Pont story, each of these are unified in social meaning with such better known Du Pont events as the exploding of the atomic bomb or the greatest corporate merger of its time, Du Pont's acquisition of Conoco.

For that reason, this book does not delve into many of the tangential scandals that would titillate prurient tastes, or wallow in the trivia that dominates other books on the Du Ponts. Instead, I have tried, with admittedly humble resources, to explain what the Du Ponts and their extraordinary history mean for American society, its past and its future. From the facts a pattern emerged and a hypothesis was put to the test. Many of the predictions about the Du Ponts set forth in the 1974 edition, including the growing ties to Rockefeller family interests (such as Chase Manhattan Bank and Continental Oil Company, Conoco) and a reawakening of right-wing politics on the national arena, have since been confirmed. From that hypothesis a theory has been developed that has become the thesis of this book: that the Du Ponts are unique as a sociological and anthropological phenomenon in American history, at the same time as they are representative of the corporate interests for which they have for so long been leading proponents. It is precisely the tension between that uniqueness and that representative quality which creates the Du Pont drama.

In the year 2000, the Du Ponts will celebrate their 200th year in America. Barring the nuclear war which they, like most of the super-rich *Forbes* magazine surveyed in 1983, see very little danger of, the Du Ponts will celebrate the anniversary of their arrival on these shores as either common citizens of a republic which has passed through the trial and emerged onto a higher democratic stage, or as a financial dynasty within a new corporate hierarchy that has chosen to rely more on police and prisons than on justice.

This is a conclusion drawn from the history of the Du Ponts themselves. If such facts and conclusions so painfully challenge our preconceptions, it is only because we have been prevented from being exposed to them for too long.

My thanks first to Charlotte for her magnificent support and help, to Bernie, Vic, Jerry, Jack, Ted, Jake, Freida, Don and all those in Delaware who risked so much to bring in vital information, to friends who came through in the difficult final hours of this edition's writing, especially Rose and Lou, Ed and Mary Anne, and those friends in Texas who dared to believe: Ann, Steve and Jim.

Finally, readers of the 1974 edition should note that over the years I have adopted my middle name, Colby, as my pen name. It is infinitely more pronounceable than Zilg and, bequeathed by my mother, equally as close to my heart.

January, 1984

Introduction

In the front lobby of the Nemours Building in Wilmington, Delaware, covering the wall above its ever-revolving doors, is an immense mural that has startled more than one visitor.

On the left it shows a frontier family of four climbing up the hill from their log cabin, the father carrying a bundle of wood, one piece of which he is using to test the softness of the ground for planting. They are all serious and stern.

On the right another, more modern family of five, perhaps of the 1940's, is also climbing up the hill, but a large steaming factory has replaced the log cabin in the background. With picnic basket in hand, they are all happy and strong looking.

In the middle, surrounded by a brilliant sunlike glow of gold, is Chemistry, springing forth in all his silver splendor, much like the resurrected Christ, with book in one hand, holding up a testing glass in the other. Chemistry is an awesome god; his silver face betrays no emotion, no human warmth. He is only power, the power that fuses both families together, connecting them through time, transforming the first (the past) into the second (the present) with the magic words, "Better things for better living through Chemistry."

This is no small interpretation of history, merely frightening in its distortion of humanity into silver abstraction. Nor is it a world outlook that can merely be dismissed for its myopic vision. It will not allow itself to be so easily dismissed. It is real. It is alive. For it is that view of life as seen through the living eyes of those who summoned it into existence—the richest family on earth, a family with a corporate empire that stretches over six continents of the world, penetrating almost every nation in the "free" world, influencing directly or indirectly the life of every human being on earth. From behind their nylon curtain, they are actively shaping the course of human destiny.

They are the Du Ponts of Delaware.

Greenville Center, Inc. 1 DIRECTOR	Terminal Warehouses, Inc. 1 DIRECTOR	Bancroft Mills 1 DIRECTOR	Dunhaven, Inc. 1 DIRECTOR	Remington Arms Co. (DU PONT)
Jacksonville Terminal, Inc. 1 DIRECTOR	Red Devil, Inc. 1 DIRECTOR	Bredin Realty Co. 1 DIRECTOR	Rancho San Andreas, Inc. 1 DIRECTOR	
St. Joseph Land & Development Company 1 DIRECTOR	Block Blight, Inc. 2 DIRECTORS	Rockland Corporation 3 DIRECTORS (Wilmington Trust)	Henry Clay Village 1 DIRECTOR	Garrett Corporation 1 FORMER DIRECTOR
Silver Glenn Springs, Inc. 1 DIRECTOR	Downtown Wilmington, Inc. 2 DIRECTORS	Longwood Airport 1 DIRECTOR	Glenden Land Co. 1 DIRECTOR	Dukane Corporation 1 DIRECTOR
Jacksonville Properties, Inc. 1 DIRECTOR	Wiltruco Realty, Inc. 1 DIRECTOR	Dutch Village, Inc. 1 DIRECTOR	Spruce Building Corp. 1 DIRECTOR	National Computer Analysts, Inc.
Florida National Realty Co. 1 DIRECTOR	Ballynahinch Castle, Inc. 1 DIRECTOR	Old Brandywine Village, Inc. 1 DIRECTOR	Woodlawn Associates	
Rodney Real Estate, Inc. 2 DIRECTORS	Wakulla Edgewater Company, Inc. 1 DIRECTOR	Weymouth Properties, Inc. 1 DIRECTOR		
Brandywine Valley Associates	Delaware Wild Lands, Inc.	Chesapeake Inn 1 DIRECTOR		

REAL ESTATE

ARMS AND DEFENSE INDUSTRIE & COMPUTERS

DU PONT FAMIL
Total Selected Assets of Companies on Cha $270 Billion

General Motors Corporation 7% COMMON $18,000 MILLION	Continental Can Corp. 1 FORMER DIRECTOR	Apalachicola Northern Railroad 100% COMMON	du Pont Aerospace 100%
Europa Corporation 100%	Thorton Fire Brick Company 1 DIRECTOR	Port St. Joe Dock & Terminal Company 100% COMMON	du Pont Aero Finance 100%
St. Joe Paper Co. 100% COMMON	New England Nuclear (Du Pont Co.)	J. E. Rhoads, Inc. 1 DIRECTOR	Orlando Aviation Services 100%
Comedy Center 100%	Baymond Corporation 1 DIRECTOR	Marine Construction Company of Wilmington 1 DIRECTOR	New Garden Aviation 100%
Bradford, Inc. 1 DIRECTOR	Florida East Coast Railroad 1 DIRECTOR $91 MILLION	Delaware (Raceway) Park, Inc. 1 DIRECTOR	DelAair, Inc. 100%
Speakman Company 2 DIRECTORS	Keystone Sand Co. 100% COMMON	Metrox Corporation 1 DIRECTOR	North American Rockwell
Nemours Corporation 1 DIRECTOR	Mavibel International Corporation 1 DIRECTOR	Garrett- Miller Co. 1 DIRECTOR	Vetrol Aircraft Corporation 1 DIRECTOR
George B. Du Pont, Inc. 1 DIRECTOR	Mulco Products, Inc.	Niront Corporation 1 DIRECTOR	All American Industries 2 DIRECTORS

MISCELLANEOUS

Continental Aviation 1 DIRECTOR

Swearington Aircraft 1 DIRECTOR

Atlantic Aviation 1 DIRECTOR

Dumod Corporation 1 DIRECTOR

Boeing Aircraft Corporation 1 DIRECTOR $2400 MILLION

AVIATION

Hercules Chemicals Corporation 1 FORMER DIRECT $1.09 BILLION

Tetraetilo De Mexico, S.A. 49% COMMON (Du Pont Co.)

Toyo Products Co., Ltd. 50% COMMON (Du Pont Co.)

Mitzui Polychemicals Co., Ltd. 50% COMMON (Du Pont Co.)

Uniroyal Corporation 18% COMMON 1 DIRECTOR $1300 MILLION

Mitzui Fluoro- Chemicals, Co., Ltd 50% COMMON (Du Pont Co.)

CHEMICALS ANI

Delmarva Power & Light Company
1 DIRECTOR
$1.4 BILLION

Diamond State Telephone
1 DIRECTOR
$388 MILLION

St. Joseph Telephone & Telegraph
1 DIRECTOR

UTILITIES

Phillips Petroleum (FORMER DIRECTOR)
2·6% COMMON
$3100 MILLION

Mid-Continent Petroleum

Oil Associates, Inc.
1 DIRECTOR

Chanslor-Western Oil

Ardee Oil, Inc.
3 DIRECTORS

Mill Creek Oil Company
1 DIRECTOR

Ridgely, Inc.,
1 DIRECTOR

Continental Oil Company (Du Pont)

Crown Central Petroleum
$546 MILLION

Charter Oil Company (19%)

OIL

Coca-Cola International
1 DIRECTOR
$1300 MILLION

United Foods
1 DIRECTOR

Delaware (Liquors) Importers, Inc.
2 DIRECTORS

Artesians Water Co.
1 DIRECTOR
(Wilm. Trust)
$13 MILLION

Coca-Cola Bottling Co. (Maine)
1 DIRECTOR
1 FORMER DIRECTOR

FOOD INDUSTRY

Chemical Bank New York Trust Company
1 DIRECTOR
$48.2 BILLION

Delaware Trust
5 DIRECTORS
$721 MILLION

Artesians Savings Bank
1 DIRECTOR

Wilmington Savings Fund Society
3 DIRECTORS
(Du Pont Co.)

Merchants & Farmers Bank of Franklin, Va.
1 DIRECTOR

Girard Bank of Delaware
1 DIRECTOR
$341 MILLION

Girard Trust Company
6% PREFERRED
$32.9 BILLION

Mellon National Bank
7% COMMON

Bank of Delaware (Du Pont Company)
$930 MILLION

Florida National Banks
10% COMMON
$1300 MILLION

Wilmington Trust
14 DIRECTORS
$1.4 BILLION

Citicorp
1 DIRECTOR
$129 BILLION

American Guaranty and Trust Company (Del.)

BANKS

WHYY-TV
1 DIRECTOR

Rollins (Broadcasting)
$114 MILLION

Wilmington Suburban News

COMMUNICATIONS MEDIA

E I du Pont Nemours & Co.
19%
7 DIRECTORS
$24.3 BILLION

Ducilo S.A.
72% COMMON
(Du Pont Co.)

Showa Neoprene K.K.
50% COMMON
(Du Pont Co.)

Atlas (Powder) Chemicals
1 FORMER DIRECTOR

Electric Hose & Rubber Co.
1 DIRECTOR
$27 MILLION

RUBBER

Claymont Insurance Corporation
1 DIRECTOR

United Investors Life Insurance Company
2 DIRECTORS

Farmers Mutual Insurance Co.
2 DIRECTORS

Liberty Mutual Insurance Company
1 DIRECTOR

Continental American Life Insurance Co.
2 DIRECTORS
$319 MILLION

INSURANCE

---

du Pont Laird Securities

Delfi Capital Sales
1 DIRECTOR

Waddell & Reed, Inc.
24% COMMON

Delaware Fund, Inc.
$287 MILLION

Decatur Income Fund
$448 MILLION

Delta Trend
1 DIRECTOR
$20 MILLION

Sigma Government Securities Fund

Sigma Exchange Fund

Sigma Trust Shares
2 DIRECTORS
$23 MILLION

Sigma Tax Free Fund

Delfi Management, Inc.
2 DIRECTORS

Andelot, Inc.
1 DIRECTOR
$10 MILLION

W. H. du Pont Associates, Inc.
1 DIRECTOR

United International Fund

Almours Securities
1 DIRECTOR
Not Available

Sigma Venture Shares
1 DIRECTOR
$34 MILLION

Delfi American Corporation

Sigma Investment Shares
4 DIRECTORS
$50 MILLION

Sigma Money Market Fund

Laird, Inc.
2 DIRECTORS
$32 MILLION

United Funds (Del.) Inc. (Waddell & Reed)
$400 MILLION

Sigma Capital Shares
4 DIRECTORS
$28 MILLION

Broseco Corporation
1 DIRECTOR

Laird Bissell & Meeds
4 DIRECTORS

Wilmington Research Corporation
1 DIRECTOR

Sigma Special Fund

Nemours Corporation

Laird & Company
$3 MILLION

CAPITAL INVESTMENTS

DU PONT COMPANY HOLDINGS IN THE UNITED STATES

$17.9 billion in assets
Over 130,000 blue- and white-collar workers

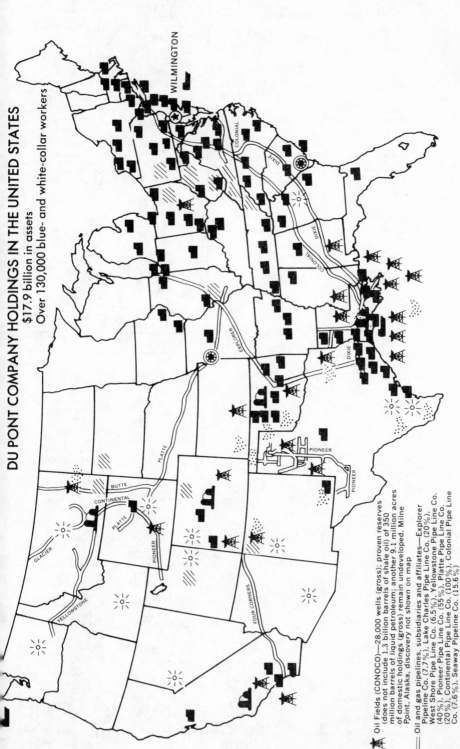

Oil Fields (CONOCO)—28,000 wells (gross); proven reserves (does not include 1.3 billion barrels of shale oil) of 350 million barrels of liquid petroleum; another 9.1 million acres of domestic holdings (gross) remain undeveloped. Milne Point, Alaska, discovery not shown on map

Oil and gas pipelines, subsidiaries and affiliates—Explorer Pipeline Co. (7.7%), Lake Charles Pipe Line Co. (20%), West Shore Pipe Line Co. (6.5%), Yellowstone Pipe Line Co. (40%), Pioneer Pipe Line Co. (55%), Platte Pipe Line Co. (20%), Continental Pipe Line Co. (100%), Colonial Pipe Line Co. (7.6%), Seaway Pipeline Co. (15.6%).

Other holdings: Louisiana Gas System, Inc. (100%), Butte Pipe Line Co. (12.5%), Four Corners Pipe Line Co. (10%), Wabash Pipe Line Co. (25%), Glacier Pipeline Co. (100%), Dixie Pipeline Co. (4%), Crude Oil Pipeline Co. (100%)

Gas Fields (CONOCO)—4000 wells (gross); 2.3 billion cubic feet of natural gas

Uranium Mining or Exploration (CONOCO)—455,000 gross acres of uranium-prospective lands; Texas, New Mexico, Nevada, Utah, Washington, Wyoming, Montana, Georgia

Oil refineries (CONOCO)—Brands: CONOCO, Kayo, Fast Gas, Econo, Jet, Fasgas; 282,000 barrels of oil refined each day

Coal holdings (Consolidated Coal Co.)—32 underground mines; 18 surface mines; 11.8 billion tons of recoverable coal (includes 1.2 billion tons leased from U.S. Gov't). (65% of total coal resources are in excess of Clean Air Act's emissions standards for sulfur content of .1 bb per million)

Du Pont plant sites and CONOCO natural gas processing plants—over 80 plant sites in 20 states and 15 natural gas processing plants in Texas, Oklahoma, Louisiana, Colorado, Wyoming, New Mexico

Du Pont-run U.S. Government plants (Aiken, S.C.—Savannah River Nuclear Operations of Department of Energy

Tanker and ship terminals owned by Du Pont (Baltimore Md.; Lake Charles, La.; Vancouver, Canada)

Sources: Du Pont 1983 Annual Report; *International Petroleum Encyclopedia*—1983, Pennwell Publishing (Tulsa); U.S. Dept. of Energy; *Moody's Industrial Manuals*, 1983 and 1980; Du Pont—CONOCO Offer and Proxy Reports, July, 1981; Mar., 1983.

One

BARONS OF
THE BRANDYWINE

In a chair overlooking the night-enshrouded city of Wilmington, a middle-aged man sat amidst the sound of tinkling glasses as waiters drifted by winking to each other in clandestine code. He looked like any businessman, dressed in a simple suit with a tie striped a bit too broadly, his brown hair swept back from a broad brow in the no-nonsense style typical of his family, his face florid but friendly. Only the nervous deference paid his presence gave any hint of the extraordinary. But Edward du Pont* was no ordinary man. And this night, in Wilmington's newest private club, he was observing the promise of a most unusual summer.

His dark eyes pierced the glass of the picture window, scanning the constellation of the city below. From it shot a blazing blue line that traced a lone highway reaching toward a southern horizon lost in shadow, where seas thundered pristine shores, stirring dreams of gilded tourist meccas. For generations, southern Delaware had been renowned for a rare tranquility, its isolation on a peninsula jutting between the Delaware and Chesapeake Bays leaving it untrammeled by the strains of urban life. Even his family's construction of this highway to the world's largest nylon plant at the lower end of the state had not disturbed the area's pre-industrial ambience, and southern Delaware retained its curious fragrance as the backyard of Virginia colonial gentility blended with the raw pungency of the tideland. Although most Du Ponts were Unionists during the Civil War, the practical task of rule had led them to compromise with the region's Dixiecrat legacy, and his family had seen fit to manipulate the social forces history had handed them in order to secure a hundred years of political stability. Even the nylon plant at Seaford, when its huge shining steel came into operation shortly before World War II, seemed to point westward, toward the ships and rails of

---

*Since the original E.I. du Pont, who signed his name with a small "d" in deference to his father, Pierre S. Du Pont, "du Pont" has been mostly used for family signatures. However, when referring to the family as a whole, as well as to its company, E.I. du Pont de Nemours, Du Pont is used.

Baltimore, rather than back toward Delaware, and the goods that did travel north on the highway raced past the quiet villages, leaving them untouched and intact.

Now all that was changed. Seaford, once the crown jewel of Du Pont's textile empire, had been belted by winds of technological change it itself had generated. Having conquered and pillaged the markets of natural fibers during the 1970's, polyester had reached the point of overproduction, idling the Seaford plant far below capacity, leaving it a tarnished relic of an age gone by when his family could rely on textile profits to keep control of their company and their own destiny. It was an era now eclipsed by revived world competition and its attending displays of tensions, uncertainty, and weaponry, all symbolized by the giant armored birds that settled each day to roost some sixty miles to the north at Dover's mammoth air force base.

Near there, in the stately colonial halls that mark Delaware's capital, Edward's cousin, Governor Pierre S. du Pont IV, rules in absentia while pursuing his all-but-announced race for the 1988 Republican presidential nomination. His ambition for the White House—well-placed, since he is chairman of GOPAC, a major dispenser of funds to local Republican candidates around the country—complements the needs of the rest of Edward's family as they confront the crisis of transition from their position as America's oldest industrial family to the assumption of leadership in the world of high finance. Responding to that crisis and Governor du Pont's interest in courting the financial powers who are the kingmakers of Republican national politics, a crack team of loyal lieutenants is working hard these days in Dover, conferring regularly with Edward's allies and New York bankers to remake not only Delaware, but America.

Already, the national ramifications of what they have done have been felt by millions of Americans across the country. Thanks to favorable laws, large banks are now free to use Delaware like a Bahamas tax haven and charge credit card customers around the nation whatever interest they like, even retroactively. They may also foreclose on homes to collect credit card debts and can charge unlimited fees for credit card usage. Other state legislatures, fearful of losing any more bank resources to Delaware, are feeling the pressure of bank lobbyists to change their laws too, all in violation of the intent of federal laws such as the Glass-Steagal Act, passed during the Depression to stop precisely such compromising overlapping of interests through over-concentration and dangerous credit overextension by the large central banks. As the states gut the New Deal safeguards, the Federal Reserve System is also feeling the pressure to accept changes in national law by Congress just to keep some sense of financial order through national banking standards.

The impact on American society will be enormous, raising the spectre of another 1929 of feverish speculation in the domestic money markets as banks attempt to compensate for the reduction of capital coming in from abroad because of diminishing control by American industry over world markets and growing defaults on foreign loans (with the Third World now replacing Weimar Germany's role during the 1920's), spurring financial chaos and setting the stage for eventual collapse.

Dover, however, is unperturbed by such long-term lessons from history. What counts now are short-term political and financial fortunes, and Wilmington is enjoying an unprecedented influx of bank capital; thirteen major banks from New York and Maryland, in fact, have joined the Computer Corporation of America from Detroit, which manages the credit card business of 90 banks in the Midwest, and the nation's third largest retailer, J.C. Penney, in resettling in Delaware since Governor du Pont's bills, drafted by New York bankers and former Du Pont Chairman Irving Shapiro, were rushed through an obliging legislature which is ranked by the Citizens Conference on State Legislatures as one of the nation's worst.[1]

It is not surprising, then, that the only major road from Dover leads back to Wilmington, the real capital of Delaware. Nor that it is named Du Pont Highway. It scrapes its way north through the flat rich farmland and past the handsome stables where champions are bred for the purses offered by the raceway owners, who are often, as exemplified by the Du Ponts, the same families who own the stables.

Ten miles or so past the burgeoning state prison at Smyrna, where severe overcrowding sparks strikes by mostly Black and Hispanic inmates against the Du Pont Administration in the shadow of a restored gallows, and just a few miles north of the chaotic tinsel strip that runs through the helpless town, the automobiles filling Du Pont Highway flow within the emergency evacuation zone of the Salem nuclear power generating plant.

The Salem plant's facilities have been plagued by structural cracks, leaks of radioactive water, faulty equipment and the charges of a nuclear engineer who resigned in protest of designs he claimed would result in over-pressurization. Incidents of over-pressurization have since been reported. The nuclear plants also rest precariously on a mound of dredged sand in the Delaware River, a part of New Jersey appropriately christened Artificial Island. Although a serious seismic disturbance would turn the sand to jelly, the nuclear station does not rest on bedrock, which is hundreds of feet beneath the sand. A geological fault, with 75 earthquakes of varying degrees recorded over the last 200 years and increased activity reported recently, runs right down the middle of Salem's four reactors and two more reactors once proposed for Summit, Delaware, by the Delmarva Power and Light Company, a co-owner of the Salem plants.[2]

Governor du Pont's Public Service Commission had given Delaware the green light to proceed with environmental studies as the first steps in construction of the Summit plants; Northern Delaware still has the dubious distinction of having the greatest concentration of nuclear power plants per capita in the world. Over 440,000 people live within 20 miles of the sites, a population expected to double over the next 15 years.

Here the governor has graciously stretched the law beyond its snapping point—this time federal law—so that nearby Wilmingtonians and those Du Pont relatives feverishly immersed in the area's real estate speculation can be spared the deflationary anxiety of being included in the governor's nebulous evacuation plan. New Jersey has admitted it does not even have an evacuation plan for anyone beyond five miles of the Salem complex.[3] The Nuclear Regulatory Commission, on the other hand, has given the time estimates in New Jersey's evacuation plan and Governor du Pont's plan, which encompasses a ten-mile radius, a "poor" confidence rating.[4] This fact is ignored in du Pont's introduction to a slick brochure in which he assures area residents "maximum protection in the case of a radiological accident."[5]

But then there are big plans for Delaware, and for Delmarva Power and Light, one of the nation's highest utility rate chargers,[6] on whose board the powerful Du Pont family patriarch, Irénée du Pont, Jr., sat until recently. Also, one must consider the sensitivities of Bechtel Corporation, from which Reagan cabinet members Schultz and Weinberger hail, and whose paid consultant is the governor's business mentor, Du Pont's Irving Shapiro.[7] Finally, as always in Delaware, there is Du Pont Company itself. The Du Ponts have a big stake in nuclear power. Their chemical company helped make the atomic and hydrogen bombs for the government, operates the nation's only processor of heavy water, tritium and weapons grade plutonium, and uses, along with its subsidiary, New England Nuclear Corporation, radioactive materials in hundreds of products. For years Du Pont has been one of the government's largest nuclear contractors,[8] and its recently acquired oil subsidiary, Conoco (Continental Oil Company), owns one of the largest uranium reserves and processing mills in the United States.[9]

So, despite the fact that some of the population of the Wilmington metropolitan area happen to find themselves within the last five miles of the ten-mile evacuation zone,[10] and despite the fact that the Nuclear Regulatory Commission recommends in such cases that the adjoining metropolis be fully informed and included in evacuation plans with adequate provision for public notices,[11] Wilmingtonians remain uninformed, busy with their shops or jobs and predictably fatalistic in their powerlessness.

Du Pont Highway continues northward until it spans the Chesapeake
Canal and descends into the sulphur-polluted air of the nearby Getty oil
refinery. Now, clearly, you are in northern Delaware, industrial Delaware.
Getty's tongue of firelight licks hungrily at the dark, the beneficiary of
Governor du Pont's regulatory largesse[12] and his refusal to support county
collection of taxes on industrial fixtures as mandated by the state's
constitution.[13] The governor is the owner of considerable blocks of oil
stock,[14] a source of income which he did not allow to interfere with his
lobbying for amendments to Delaware's Coastal Zone Act to allow shore
support facilities and pipelines for oil companies drilling off the Delaware
coast. Despite the obvious violation of Delaware's conflict-of-interest law,[15]
the Du Pont family's leading politician has braved the potential
embarrassment with a disarming smile and look of sincerity. But then there
are other commitments than mere oaths of office. There is always "progress"
and "growth."

Evidence of this can be seen a few miles down the highway. At Tybouts
Corner in New Castle, the federal Environmental Protection Agency has
identified one of the nation's most hazardous land fills.[16] Du Pont is listed as
one of the companies which have dumped toxic wastes at the site.[17] To the
west of the highway, at the Newport Du Pont plant, the EPA has also
conducted tests for water pollution. They indicate that DuPont's chemical
and radioactive wastes stored at Newport have contaminated the Potomic
Aquifer, the main source of drinking water for half a million Delawareans,
threatening its survival.[18]

A few minutes beyond New Castle, Du Pont Highway crosses the
Wilmington city line, racing brightly through still another tinsel strip
bordering the Greater Wilmington Airport, championed a few years back by
Irénée du Pont, Jr., and Edward's father, Henry B. du Pont. Part of the
airport's grounds is devoted to Atlantic Aviation Corporation, one of the
nation's largest outfitters of executive aircraft, founded by Henry and now
run by Edward. Atlantic also outfits foreign military aircraft.

From the lofty air-conditioned hush of the new Rodney Square Club above
Wilmington, Salem's ponderous string of warning lights can be seen, and
before it, the sparkling blue-white arc of the Delaware Memorial Bridge. The
giant span is proof of the iron resolve of Edward's clan (in this case in the
persons of the late Francis V. du Pont, former Federal Commissioner of
Highways, and in-law Bayard Sharp) to get things done with federal funding
and lucrative tax-free bonds when they set their minds to it. Twin, red-
pulsing spires support the Du Pont extension of their domain into southern
New Jersey where, next to the languid black waters of the Delaware,
Edward's family built their largest manufacturing complex. Deepwater is a

vast blazing city swollen with lights, over 400 buildings, some 6,000 proud men, and 60 years of infamy since it first made headlines in the 1920's when the U.S. Surgeon General closed it down for poisoning its workers. Deep within its bowels, embedded in plants and buildings, uranium oxide residue left behind by Du Pont's involvement in producing the first atomic bombs for the Manhattan Project[19] slowly penetrates the lives of thousands of workers who are either unsuspecting or too terrified of unemployment to allow themselves to wonder. Other chemical poisonings of workers at Deepwater have already contributed to New Jersey's Salem County's having the highest bladder cancer death rate in the nation.[20] Deepwater, nevertheless, is billed in Wilmington as a model for occupational safety and health.

On the Delaware side of the river the bridge disgorges cars onto Interstate 95, another result of Du Pont lobbying. Below, to the right, is Cherry Island, another Du Pont toxic waste dump where the EPA found unacceptable arsenic, chromium and lead levels in tests of underground water. I-95 crosses Du Pont Highway and winds north past Richard C. du Pont's large All-American Industries, a major defense contractor and aviation specialist, and heads toward the cluster of skyscrapers that stand castle-like on the crest of a hill. Beneath Wilmington's towers, along the streets of what is known as "The Valley," there is little evidence that progress has touched the lives of Hispanic and Black residents; homes remain tattered and in dire repair as tenants with brush and pail strive for some measure of human dignity. But just a few blocks up the hill fashionable shops blossom into a downtown mall, a splendid example of how real estate fever and entrepreneurial spirit can shamelessly mate with the drive for social justice alleged to have motivated the urban renewal programs of President Johnson's War on Poverty. Sponsored by the Greater Wilmington Development Council (the brainchild of Edward's late father, Henry, and his successor at the helm of civic affairs, Irénée du Pont, Jr.), the boom in downtown real estate centered around a group of Du Pont family insiders and local politicians organized together as the Rockland Corporation. Rockland was led by W.W. "Chick" Laird and Eleuthère I. du Pont, organizer of the Sigma Group of mutual funds, of whose sweet waters the current governor has partaken. Rockland became so successful that after the federal trough was appropriately drained of its public monies and a corporate spirit moved across the land preaching the return to individual self-reliance, its lucrative holdings were promptly consumed by the Du Ponts' major holding bank, the Wilmington Trust Company.

In most American cities, all roads lead to local replicas of Rome's Palatine Hill, and Wilmington is no exception. The local Appian Way is called Market Street, a main street passing humbly between monuments to Du

Pont power: to the right, the Delmarva Power and Light headquarters, Governor du Pont's huge new state office building looming a block behind, and finally the family-founded Delaware Trust bank; to the left, the headquarters for the Du Pont-founded *News-Journal* papers and modern steel and glass towers that house the Du Pont-controlled Bank of Delaware, the once-Du Pont-controlled Farmers Bank (now owned by Philadelphia's Girard Trust, in which the Du Ponts have a sizable holding) and the Wilmington Trust Company.

When you have finished climbing Market Street and find yourself at the square on the crest of the hill, you have arrived at the heart of the Du Pont empire. Clustered about the square are the pinnacles of command in the state: Continental American Life Insurance, the largest insurance firm in Delaware, which Eleuthère du Pont has guided into a merger with Crown Central Petroleum, a major producer of domestic oil; City Hall, its once ardent affair with Henry du Pont's GWDC having been cooled by a Democratic mayor yet to muster the courage to confront his city's first family; the Wilmington Library, its pre-Hitler swastikas still boldly emblazoned in stone above its front doors, and its public funds still controlled by Edward du Pont's private Wilmington Library Institute; the mammoth Du Pont International Headquarters, backed in a row by two equally massive structures, the Nemours and the fortress-like Brandywine buildings; and, finally, the newest Goliath on the square, the Wilmington Trust Center, the Du Pont family's new headquarters since the chemical industry's volatile performance and declining numbers of the clan in the top management of the Du Pont Company forced the family to dissolve the holding firm that controlled the company founded by them over 180 years ago.

Here is the center of the family's financial power and its hopes for the future. Approaching it is like visiting an ancient Roman temple. Clusters of globes, swollen with lurid white light, flank the wide stone steps of the Romanesque former U.S. Post Office, modern flambeaux begging illusions of grandeur. The federal government has been obliterated from the portico and replaced by giant letters cut in stone spelling the name inspired by the Du Ponts' major bank: WILMINGTON TRUST CENTER; a huge war eagle is perched above the main entrance, its head cocked in the traditional imperial pose, a baleful eye pointed at would-be intruders in its nest. Behind and above the entrance towers a modern steel Goliath that seems to mount the older public building. It is an amazingly brash celebration of power.

Inside the main doors, as if in guilty homage to a more tasteful earlier generation, murals adorn adjacent walls, on the left showing 19th century workers mixing a broth of chemicals with crude tools in front of a windmill;

on the right, workers of the 20th century busy at sundry tasks, one even protected by a respirator, while in the middle a white-robed scientist holds up the sacred vial promising a magic elixir for profit margins and better living through chemistry. Yet the mural's populist style seems out of place in the crisply modern interior. The lobby is cavernous. Its cold sparsity is broken only by a computerized security center commanding the middle of the floor and guarding access to the elevators and the inner sanctum of Du Pont family power: the bank's trust department.

Wilmington Trust, with $1 billion of its own assets, is not a very large bank; but its multibillion-dollar trust department ranks among the top in the country. The reasons can be summed up in one word: Du Ponts.

Of some 1,600 living Du Ponts, only 250 constitute the inner circle. Of these, only about 50 make up the all-powerful inner core of the family. Together, these 50 Du Ponts control or share control over $211 billion worth of assets, greater than the annual Gross National Product of most nations. They own huge or controlling interests in over 100 multimillion-dollar corporations and banks, including some of the world's largest, to say nothing of their 180-year-old pet project, E.I. du Pont de Nemours & Co.

The Du Ponts of Delaware own more personal wealth and control more multimillion-dollar corporations than any one family in the world. They employ more servants than Britain's royal family, own more yachts, cars, swimming pools, planes, and estates than any family in recorded history.

Residing comfortably on some 24 country estates surrounding Wilmington, the Du Ponts enjoy the good life. Many of their homes rival Europe's finest palaces, some even containing whole rooms brought over intact from French and German castles. Decorating their walls are some of the world's greatest masterpieces of art. After spending the day riding to the hounds over private green pastures or racing some of their many thoroughbreds, like their world-famous Kelso, they may drink rare wines and dine on lobster flown in live from Maine. Or they may quietly spend the evening watching colored lights play upon their dancing fountains and botanical gardens, or hosting fashionable fêtes and charity balls. Their dinner guests are among the world's most powerful political and business personalities, all of whom pay homage to the barons of the Brandywine.

But most of all, the elder Du Ponts like to devote their time to their global empire. Irénée's cousin Lammot du Pont Copeland, Sr., was a typical example. Besides enjoying his 1,500-acre estate covered with acres of rare flowers, Lammot tinkered with a variety of titles. Until 1972 he was chairman of the board of directors of E.I. du Pont de Nemours and was a director of the Chemical Bank of New York, Wilmington Trust Company (the family holding bank), and the Christiana Securities Company (the family holding company). He had been a director of General Motors, Pennsylvania Railroad, and U.S. Rubber Company. He had been a trustee of the University of Pennsylvania, a member of the Board of Overseers of Harvard University, a member of the National Republican Finance Committee, and was trustee of at least four family foundations. He was worth well over $200 million when he died in 1983.

Copeland was not exceptional in the Du Pont family. The late William du Pont was worth $350 to $400 million. When Henry B. du Pont II died in 1970, he too was worth $200 million. George P. Edmonds, whose wife is a Du Pont, is worth a similar amount. And the names of Du Pont multimillionaires go on and on.

The center of Du Pont wealth has of course been the corporations and banks in which they have had huge blocks of stock, if not controlling interests. Some of these are household names: E.I. du Pont Co., Continental Can Corporation, Uniroyal (U.S. Rubber Co.), Remington Arms Co., Phillips Petroleum (Phillips 66), General Motors Corporation (despite claims to the contrary), Penn Central Railroad, Philadelphia Baseball Club (Phillies), W.T. Grant, Hercules Chemical, Atlas Chemicals, Boeing Aircraft Corporation, Samuel Bronstein Productions, United Fruit Company (Chiquita Bananas, etc.), American (Domino) Sugar Refining Company, Mid-Continent Petroleum Corporation, Continental American Life Insurance Co., United Investors Life Insurance Co., All-American Industries, United Foods, Inc., First National City Bank of New York (now Citibank), Chemical Bank of New York, Coca-Cola International, National Computer Analysts, Delaware Life Insurance, Artisan Savings Bank, Bank of Delaware, Farmers Mutual Insurance Co., Garrett Miller Co., Liberty Mutual Insurance Co., Atlantic Aviation, Summit Aviation, Continental Aviation, North American Rockwell, Florida National Bank, Florida East Coast Railroad, St. Joe Paper Company, Diamond State Telephone Co., Garrett Corporation (Calif.), Life Insurance Company of Virginia, Merchants and Farmers Bank of Virginia, Dumod Corporation, Electric Hose and Rubber Co., J.E. Rhoads, Inc., Laird, Inc., Mulco Products, Inc., Oil Associates, Inc., Speakman Co., Laird & Co., Chanslor-Western Oil Co., A.V.C. Corp., Niront Corporation, Newport News Shipbuilding and Drydock Co., Guaranty Reinsurance, Delta Trend, WHYY-TV (Wilmington), Nemours Corporation, W.H. du Pont Associates, Inc., Wilmington Trust Co., Marine Construction Company (Wilmington), Farmers Bank of Delaware, Rockland Corp., Dutch Village, Inc., Piasecki Aircraft, Christiana Securities Company, Dukane Co. (Illinois), Symington Wayne Corp. (Dresser Industries, Inc.), Delmarva Power and Light Company, Delaware Trust Co., Delfi Management, Inc., Sigma Trust Shares, United International Fund, Sigma Capital Shares,

Waddell & Reed, Inc., Rodney Real Estate Associates, News-Journal Company, Delaware Importers, Inc., Decatur Income Fund, Sigma Investment Shares, Inc., Laird, Bissell & Meeds, Downtown Wilmington, Inc., Delaware Park, Inc., Old Brandywine Village, Inc., Ardee Oil Co., Thorton Fire Brick Co., D. Van Nostrand Co., Mill Creek Oil Co., Baymond Company, Bradford, Inc., Bredin Realty, Artesians Water Co., Wilmington Suburban News, Rollins, Inc., Metrox Corp., Crucible Steel, Ridgely, Inc., Terminal Warehouses, Inc., Sci-Tek, Delaware Chemical Engineering Corp., Claymont Insurance Corp., Wiltruco Realty Inc., Wilmington Savings Fund Society, Maribal International Corp., The Broseco Corp., Board of New York Air Brake Company (now a division of General Signal Company), Greenville Center, Inc., National Publishers Service, Inc., Glenden Land Co., Spruce Building Corp., Dunhaven, Inc., Endo Pharmaceutical, Great Western Publishing Co., Calamet Publishing, San Fernando Valley Times and Standard Register. In the last decade the Du Pont family has added to their holdings Continental Oil (Conoco), New England Nuclear, Crown Central Petroleum, Du Pont Aerospace, Du Pont Aero Finance Inc., Orlando Aviation Services, American Guaranty and Trust Company (Del.), Commuter News Digest, Craft Reports, Report on Credit Unions, the Comedy Center, du Pont Laird Securities, National Liberty Corporation (Pa.), Rancho San Andreas Inc. (Cal.), Fox Min Enterprises (Pa.), Henry Clay Village (Del.), Europa Corp. (Fla.), Sigma Money Market Fund, Sigma Exchange Shares, Sigma Government Securities Fund, Sigma Special Fund, and New Garden Aviation.

In addition, Du Pont Company now provides interlocking directorships with Texas Instruments, Bank of America, Bethlehem Steel, Bell Canada, AT&T, Dart-Kraft, IBM, International Harvester, United Airlines, Toronto-Dominion Bank, Champion International, John Hancock Mutual Life Insurance, Federated Department Stores, Haskins Laboratories, American Security Bank, General Reinsurance Corporation (a major investor in Delaware state bonds), Stanley Works, Hart Schaffner, and Marx, Harvey Hubbell Inc., American Stores Company, and J.P. Morgan and Company and Morgan Guaranty Bank. The Alfred I. du Pont Estate also is the largest single shareholder in the Charter (Oil) Company, which owns a large share of Florida National Banks, Inc.

While the Du Ponts' direct personal wealth has been computed at $7.629 billion,[21] a very conservative estimate, and more recently by *Forbes* Magazine at $10 billion, the worth of their fortune is best measured in the $211 billion in assets in which they have controlling interests or at least a great resounding influence over major decisions in the boardroom.

Edward du Pont is senior vice-president and a leading member of the board of directors of the Wilmington Trust Company. The bank's trust department is his purview. Edward is personally a very rich man. He and his immediate family directly own or have control over $72,000,000 worth of Du Pont common; he shares control with three other family members over another $58,000,000 worth of Du Pont common.[22] He is also chairman of Atlantic Aviation, which in 1982 did over $7 million worth of business with Du Pont Company alone.[23] But the source of his great power is the bank's trust department and his succession to the mantle of civil leadership once worn by his father, Henry B. du Pont II, and until recently by his elder cousin, Irénée du Pont, Jr.

Irénée had been a familiar sight around Wilmington, chugging along in his old Volkswagen, a self-styled trademark of folksy potential preferable to the connotations associated with limousines, which he employed only rarely. Yet such quiet claims to humility did not protect him from a classical gaffe in September, 1966, when he travelled into the slums of Wilmington's east side to address a crowd of several hundred mostly Black students with the promise, "You don't have to get to the top of the ladder to find satisfaction."[24]

Some who remember that day found it hard to take from a man who lives on one of America's grandest estates, Granogue, with a four-story 70-room mansion surrounded by formal gardens, greenhouse and over 514 rolling green acres. But no one doubted that Irénée du Pont was dead serious.

Edward du Pont is a serious man also, with personal ambitions perhaps much greater than Irénée's. He has been active in the Republican Party, serving on the state finance committee (a post once held also by his cousin, Governor Pierre du Pont) and was Republican state treasurer until 1971, when he fully assumed the family obligations bequeathed by his father's death the year before. Despite a scandal over embezzlement of public funds by his top aide at his Library Institute, Edward's reputation and his ideological commitment to private contractual control over public money remain unshaken.

Modest in tone and appearance and only 49 years of age, he is already a leader in family affairs. As an officer of Christiana Securities, the $2 billion family holding company, he helped Irénée work out the fantastic deal with Du Pont Company's C.B. McCoy and Irving Shapiro that allowed Christiana's merger into Du Pont at a substantial gain to the family. He then joined Du Pont's board of directors, while keeping an open ear at Wilmington Trust to the desires of other family members to pursue their goal of diversifying their investments beyond chemicals. His academic credentials suggest rigorous financial training; he is a graduate of Yale and Harvard's Graduate School of Business.

Edward's commitment to helping the Du Pont clan successfully complete their transition from being America's oldest industrial family to becoming a financial power in their own right is reflected in his support for Irving Shapiro's expressed wish to make Delaware the nation's "first state in financial services." He also acts as if he is in full support of the efforts of his cousin, Governor Pierre "Pete" du Pont, to make that goal a reality through unprecedented tax breaks to lure large banks to Delaware. And he appears ready to support Pete's presidential ambitions. As the leading Du Pont in the trust department of Wilmington Trust Company, Edward du Pont has become the keeper of the keys to the family's enormous financial power, a frightening power whose full potential is yet to be felt by America. In dissolving Christiana Securities and unlocking the family's chain to Du Pont Company, Irénée and Edward may be unleashing furies from a Pandora's box.

The Du Ponts own the state of Delaware. They exercise inordinate influence over its major newspapers (a legacy of their former ownership), they control its state and local government, radio and TV stations, university and colleges, and its largest banks and industries, with four exceptions: Getty Oil, Phoenix Steel, and the Chrysler and General Foods plants, and even with these they've made profitable deals. The Du Pont company alone employs more than 11 percent of Delaware's labor force, and when the family's other holdings and dependent businesses are included, the percentage rises to over 60 percent. Throughout the United States over a million Americans work to increase the Du Pont fortune, and tens of thousands more work overseas at lower wages. Through one or more of their corporations, the Du Pont family touches every nation in the "free" world with its silver hand.

Predictably, the long arm of Du Pont can also be found in Washington, D.C. Du Pont family members have represented Delaware in both houses of Congress. In the last 40 years Du Pont lieutenants have served as representatives, senators, U.S. Attorney General, secretaries of defense, directors of the CIA, and even Supreme Court justices.

With this power, "the Armorers of the Republic," as they like to call themselves, have helped drive America into world wars,[25] sabotaged world disarmament conferences,[26] built deadly arsenals of atomic weapons and nerve gas,[27] flirted with Nazis,[28] and, according to charges brought by, among others, a former commandant of the U.S. Marine Corps before the Dickstein-McCormick House Investigating Committee, once were even implicated in an attempt to overthrow the United States government[29]—at the same time managing to avoid paying their fair share of taxes.[30] A family ambition that was once limited to a total monopoly over America's gunpowder industry has now been extended to every corner of the world. As Edward and Irénée personify it, the power of the Du Pont family is purposely subtle and quiet, but enormously effective.

That style is reflected in the hushed tones of the Rodney Square Club. Bearing the august name of Delaware's signer of the Declaration of Independence as well as the square which portrays his galloping statue in front of the Du Pont Headquarters, the Rodney Club is still another brainchild of the ubiquitous Irving Shapiro. Founded in June, 1983, the club's board of governors may not read like the Philadelphia Social Register one associates with the Du Ponts, but it is a competent list of Who's Who among Delaware's political powerbrokers, including everyone from former Mayor Harry Haskell's city solicitor, Victor Bataglia, and former New Castle County Executive Mary Jornlin Theisen to current County Executive Richard Collins and bank lobbyist O. Francis Biondi.

Shapiro, searching for a less stuffy means of organizing the power elite than through the formal decorum of dinners at Du Pont country mansions or their exclusive Wilmington or University and Wist Club, and recognizing that a leadership restructuring was needed if Wilmington was to both follow and help the Du Pont metamorphosis, used his formidable influence to bring political activists and power brokers together with local business leaders. The list of names on the business side of this local roundtable is equally impressive and far-ranging, drawing on liberals as well as conservatives for credibility and political breadth. It includes Du Pont's former chairman C.B. McCoy and current chairman Edward Jefferson, University of Delaware president E.B. Trabant and Pontiac dealer Tony Ursomarso, Du Pont family lawyer E. Norman Veasey and Wilmington Trust chairman Bernard Taylor, and even some Du Ponts, including Jane Roth, the wife of Republican U.S. Senator William Roth, of Kemp-Roth tax cut fame, former state senate majority leader Reynolds du Pont (the Governor's uncle) and, of course, Edward du Pont.

Here, high above the city, amid pseudo-posh trappings that mix vinyl with neo-Victorian and stark modern walls with elegant drapery drawn and tethered, business deals and political pacts can be probed without first having to run the gauntlet of Du Pont family whims and personal fancies and their clubs' ethnic and sexual discrimination. It facilitates lobbying, concentrates networks, institutionalizes alliances. In that sense, the Rodney Club was a reorganizing of Wilmington's power around more flexible, modern themes than the rigid, almost feudal social heirarchy of the Du Pont elders. With their passing from both the company management and life itself, the way was open to fill the vacuum with a new approach that more accurately reflected the political realignments that followed demographic changes in northern Delaware over the last two generations. Thanks to Shapiro, the man who so ably guided the company through the political and market storms of the Seventies, Wilmington has at last "arrived"; like the great cities of America, it, too, now has its own exclusive social club with an identifiable presence as an institution of the corporate class.

Governor du Pont, as of August, 1983, had yet to make an appearance at the Rodney Square Club, wisely avoiding any semblance of personal collusion with such an easily identifiable well-heeled clique. And the club's governors, also wise to the ways of public posturing, seem not concerned. They are confident in Pete's willingness to carry out their wishes in the future with the same eager dedication he has shown in the past.

Edward, on the other hand, is free to openly accept the club as a means of widened social contact that could extend the reach of the family's power beyond Du Pont Company even as many lament its decline. He, like most powerful Du Ponts, allows others the illusion they need, the belief that the power of the Du Ponts is dissipating and America becoming more democratic. Looking down from the club's 12th floor window, however, Edward knows a simpler reality: Wilmington is simply changing once again with his family.

In the distance to the north, beyond the thousands of scientists toiling at Du Pont's vast research complex in search of patents to make Edward's family even richer, is the 300-acre Nemours estate of the late Alfred I. du Pont, marked by the tall carillon that guards Alfred's and his wife's graves. Nemours offers the promise of not only a large new hospital but also the surprising return of Alfred's huge fortune to the family fold after a Florida exile of half a century. If Alfred's grandson, Alfred du Pont Dent, finally succeeds in his decade-long effort to wrest control of the estate from the Floridian cronies of his grandfather's late brother-in-law, Ed Ball—and he probably will—the planned selling of the estate's $2 billion assets will result in the Du Pont family controlling one of the largest foundations in the world. No one needs to remind Edward or Dent what worldwide influence a large endowed foundation gave another family, the Rockefellers, heralding their similar transition some 70 years ago from an industrial dynasty to the most potent financial and political force of their time.

Beyond Nemours and the Alexis I. du Pont High School in the suburbs, beside the creek called Brandywine, lies the cultural soul of the family, symbolized by the old gunpowder mills along the Brandywine and the original home of the company's founder, the first Eleuthère I. du Pont. It is a restless soul, troubled by the end of an era. Beyond the family graveyard gouged out of the hill above, the family stirs from its 50-year slumber in the rolling hills of "chateau country," awakened by the discomfort of change and the challenge of a new age. "There lies a sleeping giant," Napoleon warned of China. "Let him sleep! For when he awakes, he will move the world." If the alteration of the face of Delaware attending the rise of Governor Pete du Pont is any harbinger of the future, it is enough to make any Napoleon shudder in his grave.

Who these Du Ponts and their lieutenants are and how they arrived at all this wealth and power is the 180-year story of the Du Ponts of Delaware.

If you travel through northern Delaware, through "Du Pont country," past such Gallic names as Nemours, Chevannes, Bois-des-Fosses, Guyencourt, Montchanin, and Granogue, you might think you were passing through a slice of France. And in fact you are. For that is where the Du Pont story began over two hundred years ago—in the doomed halls of that very corrupt monarch in eighteenth-century Europe, Louis XV, King of France.

TWO

BUILDING A COMPANY

1. THE RISE OF PIERRE DUPONT

France's King Louis XV was a serious man, some said the most serious in Europe. He wore his crown heavily, reminding those around him "After me, the deluge." Louis knew about deluges. He had brought a deluge of graft, corruption, and mistresses into his court. He also brought a deluge of debts and death to the people of France.

France in 1764 was trying to recover from Louis's latest war with his economic rival, England. He had gambled everything in that contest and almost lost his entire empire. He lost also the respect of his people. Seven long years of war had ravaged the countryside and depleted France's reserve of gold and human life. Starvation and disease replaced Louis as ruler in the cities, the common man falling as common victim.

When Louis had finally called a truce the year before, sighs of relief were heard throughout the nation as the French people paused to take stock of their losses and begin the task of rebuilding the economic strength and competition that had caused the war in the first place. The increasing needs of a growing population and economy brought their accompanying increase in demands, and throughout most of France feudal life gave way to the industrial revolution of capitalism, factories increasingly becoming the centers of wealth's accumulation. It was one of those great ages of change; the entire French people stirred with expectation of the new, while feudal lords clung stubbornly to the old, and everyone, king and peasant alike, seemed to suspect what was coming.

What came first was a challenge of ideas from the new middle class of industrialists, the bourgeoisie. As in all social revolutions, the bourgeoisie's unconscious challenge for authority by their accumulation of wealth eventually took the more conscious form of deliberate agitation of ideas favoring their economic interests. It was this war of ideas that was prelude to the inevitable armed war of revolution.

In the warm month of April of that year Jacques Turgot, a baron turned financier and leader of France's capitalists, came across a newly published economic essay on grains, "Reflections on the Wealth of the State." It was written in a dry, technical style, despite its more lively dedication to its financial benefactor, Madame de Pompadour, the King's former mistress. Yet it was a skillful attempt to master the new ideas of landed capitalism, an ambitious flaunting of the theories of the Physiocrats. Turgot was impressed. He decided to contact its young author, Pierre Samuel Dupont.

Pierre was only 25 at the time, although his round, pudgy face made him look older. A collar of fat stretched from ear to ear beneath his cleft chin, matching the contours of his wide nose. His small brown eyes were weak, like his lips, lending an unimpressive appearance. He was and looked the son of a small-town watchmaker, Sam Dupont, and Anne Montchanin, member of an impoverished noble family.

Pierre's mother had never quite been able to accept her family's diminished status, and she openly hoped her son would be the family's messiah. She pushed Pierre to acquire an education and had her cousin Jancourt introduce him into the circle of Physiocrats. Pierre soon caught some of his mother's fire. As he became more impressed with the lavish wealth and extravagances of Versailles's class of powdered men and aloof ladies, Pierre found less that was praiseworthy in the wretched lives of average Parisians. Inspired by the increasing power of the bourgeoisie he had met, he learned all he could of their Physiocrat theories. He abandoned the plays he had been writing and instead began to compose pamphlets on these more fashionable, rewarding topics. Eventually one of his pamphlets found its way to Turgot.

Turgot took Pierre under his wing and within a year named him editor of the monarch's new *Journal of Agriculture, Commerce, and Finance*. At 26, Pierre had his first regular salary, and celebrated by marrying his childhood sweetheart, Marie Le Dee. On October 1, 1767, Marie gave birth to their first child, Victor Marie. Three years later Pierre asked his benefactor, Turgot, to act as godfather to his next child. "Yes, certainly, my dear Dupont," replied Turgot. "If it is a boy, will you not call him Eleuthère Irénée in honor of liberty and peace?"[1]

On June 24, 1771, Eleuthère Irénée, founder of the Du Pont empire, was born.

Throughout the next decade and a half, Pierre Dupont loyally served the corrupt French throne, holding various offices, including Inspector General of Commerce under Louis XVI, who succeeded his grandfather in 1774. With Vergennes, his new benefactor, Dupont was involved in the preliminary negotiations that led to the peace treaty of 1783 between France's ally, the new United States, and her archenemy, Britain. In return for this latter service, King Louis rewarded Pierre in December 1783 with nobility. The coat of arms Pierre selected was characteristically modest: ostrich plumes, a lion, an eagle, and the motto "Rectitudine Sto" ("By Uprightness I Stand").

After the death of his wife in September 1784, Pierre assumed the responsibility of grooming his sons at his Bois-des-Fosses estate at Nemours.

Victor didn't enjoy grooming. He was more inclined to be a dilettante. A handsome, brown-haired giant, Victor failed at every job ever given him. He failed as a junior secretary in Pierre's own Department of Commerce. As an investigator, he was instructed to travel throughout the provinces and send back commercial reports; the reports turned out to be excellent descriptions of fetes and dinner parties. Victor also gave outspoken descriptions of individuals—which were sometimes not only embarrassing, but politically dangerous for his family. Something had to be done with him. Perhaps a long voyage overseas. In 1787 Pierre had Victor appointed secretary to the first French minister to the new United States, Comte de Moustier. There was only one problem. The government refused to pay Victor a salary.

Pierre's younger son, Irénée, was just the opposite of Victor. Irénée was smaller in size. Although he had his father's cleft chin and weak lips, his dark eyes were much stronger in appearance, peering coldly from behind a long-sharp nose. Serious about practical matters, especially serious about himself, Irénée was extremely restrained in his emotions. At the young age of 16, he cut an aloof figure worthy of any self-respecting middle-aged nobleman. It may seem a paradox that one could later be so successful in the business world as Irénée and yet always have such difficulty befriending anyone who was not family. Once, in a brief glimmer of self-reflection, Irénée himself damned his unnatural "coldness" toward people. Yet it may have been that very fearful, lamed personality that drove this younger son of Père Dupont to such ruthless pinnacles of success.

Irénée showed little interest in matters of human relations; his absorption in science prompted Pierre to send him to study under an old friend, Lavoisier, chemist and head of the French monarch's gunpowder mills. At Essonne, Eleuthère Irénée, named for "peace and liberty," was trained in the instruments of war for the powder-making role he would later play on the American stage of history.

2. REFUGEES FROM REVOLUTION

In 1788, popular rebellion finally erupted, sharpened by widespread hunger, the King's heavy taxes, and his use of foreign mercenaries to protect his wealthy court. To consider the emergency, Louis convened the Estates-General of clergy, lords, and commoners, and Pierre had himself elected a member of the supposedly non-nobility Third Estate, representing Nemours, where his country estate was located. The following year the bourgeoisie led the Third Estate in a seizure of power, and not to resist the irresistible, Pierre joined the tide, even serving at different times as secretary and president of the new Constituent Assembly.

As the nation moved further to the political left, however, Pierre remained stubbornly on the right. With Lafayette, then commander of the National Guard, Pierre founded the short-lived Societé de 1789, an organization made up of the most conservative wing of the bourgeoisie which favored a constitutional monarchy. Shorn of his 30,000-franc annual salary and allowances by the Jacobins, the radical party of the petite bourgeoisie (shopkeepers, etc.), Pierre began attacking the Jacobins in the Constituent Assembly with long conservative orations, always bowing in great delight whenever someone in the galleries managed to clap in agreement. During one particularly loud and enthusiastic speech, the Guard had to save Pierre from his outraged colleagues, who wanted to throw him into the Seine. Undaunted, Pierre, with his son Irénée, continued to unleash reactionary broadsides from his newly acquired publishing house in Paris. Increasingly isolated, Pierre only aggravated the situation when he and Irénée led their sixty-man private guard to defend the King's palace on August 10, 1792, from a Jacobin assualt that was demanding an end to monarchy. The Duponts, in fact, were the only Frenchmen still willing to physically defend the rulers of France.

After that episode, from which he and Irénée only narrowly escaped their own end, Pierre was driven into hiding while his publishing house was wrecked by crowds of angry Parisians. Both Irénée and Victor, who had returned from America, tried to assume republican pretensions. Irénée, now married to Sophie Dalmas, granddaughter of a royalist general, worked at Lavoisier's Essonne managing the saltpeter factory for the new republican government and published a newspaper, *Le Republican,* to sing his new revolutionary tune. Victor became a gendarme to avoid the draft, even participating in raids on royalists. Only his marriage in 1794 to a royalist, blue-eyed Josephine de Pelleport, brought enough pangs of conscience to end this career and renew suspicions as to his political leaning.

Finally, just a year and a half after King Louis's head fell to the guillotine, and two months after his friend Lavoisier suffered a similar fate, Pierre was arrested on July 13, 1794. Dupont would undoubtedly have also met the guillotine had not the bourgeoisie, now satisfied that their revolution was complete and irreversible, asserted control over the revolution from the petits-bourgeois radicals that month. Robespierre, leader of the Jacobins, was wounded by an assassination attempt and on July 29, 1794, was executed along with twenty-one of his lieutenants. On August 25 Pierre Dupont was allowed to return to his estate a free man.

With the overthrow of the radicals, more fortunate times returned to the Duponts. Victor was reappointed to government, while Pierre, who remarried, returned to Paris as a member of the new Council of Ancients, the lawmaking body of the French Directory. It wasn't long, however, before Pierre's prejudice against "that Corsican," Napoleon Bonaparte, led him back into trouble.

"Don't you know what Corsicans are?" he wrote Reuball, a high government official, opposing Napoleon's appointment as commander-in-chief of French forces in Italy. ". . . These people should always be kept subordinates, even when they are capable and honest. . . . Are there no Frenchmen left?"[2] Despite Pierre's attacks, Napoleon's military victories won him constant promotions.

Pierre launched a new paper, *L'Historien,* as the organ for revived royalism and attacks on the five Directors, but when he was elected president of the Council of Ancients, the bourgeoisie struck, backing Napoleon's coup. Both Pierre and Irénée soon found themselves again in prison. Through a friend who was a member of the commission that prepared lists for deportation, Pierre luckily regained their freedom under a plea of senility. But he had to pledge to leave France. It took little persuasion.

By 1799 Pierre had secured financial commitments to the tune of millions of francs to back his investment plans for a colony, "Pontiania," in America. To embellish his image to prospective investors, he also separated and capitalized the two syllables of his name, Du and Pont. Thus was born the "Du Ponts."

To prepare the way, Pierre sent to America his new royalist wife, Francoise Robin Poivre, along with her son-in-law Bureaux de Pusy and her granddaughter Sara de Pusy. Madame Du Pont would buy a large house, while Bureaux de Pusy, a former army engineer, would see about prospects for land speculation.

On October 2, 1799, with the wrath of the revolution spurring them on, the thirteen remaining Du Ponts, including Pierre, Irénée and his family, and Victor and his family, boarded an American ship, the *American Eagle,* bade France adieu, and set sail for America under the Du Pont banner. Right from the beginning of their American adventure, the Du Ponts made sure that Americans understood their feeling about their wealth. Wary of the American crew, through the entire three month journey they guarded their many crates of clothes and furniture, even their grand pianos, with drawn swords.

3. THE BIRTH OF DU PONT

In the gray wintry eve of January 1, 1800, a Newport, Rhode Island, family just leaving their home for the New Year's church service noted a strange shadow moving in the nearby sea. There, a lone dark ship was slowly entering the harbor, its tall sails torn and shredded, its sides bristled with barnacles, its deck bruised and battered by the high seas. None of that small group hurrying off to their devotion could have suspected that that ship carried a family destined by historical forces to affect their lives and those of their posterity; for into the harbor of Newport that night flew the banner of Du Pont de Nemours.

The somber shore, with its barren docks devoid of welcomers, did not quash Père Du Pont's enthusiasm for his first step on American soil. Unlike his grandchildren, Du Pont did not expect 21-gun salutes when their ship finally pulled into an American port. In fact, he was greatly relieved that they had even reached land. For ninety-three days the *American Eagle* had wandered about the ocean like some lost child of the sea, more than half that time flying the flag of distress. Lacking adequate provisions, the noble Du Ponts had been reduced to consuming a soup of boiled rats that they had trapped in an old tub, and twice they had had to hail passing English ships for food and water. The Du Ponts were literally at sword's end with their crew when land was sighted. After ninety-three days, almost a month longer than it took Columbus to cross the Atlantic three centuries before, the Du Pont journey with the wandering *American Eagle* was finally over.

Landing amid the harsh New England winter, Père Du Pont led his shivering clan to the first lit house they saw. The elder Du Pont rapped heavily on its door, but failed to summon any answer. Instead, through the windows teased a full dinner neatly laid out on a table awaiting the return of the family that had gone to their worship, as was the custom of church-goers of that time. While the American family unsuspectingly folded their fingers in humble worship of their God of Wrath, the Du Pont family broke into their home and ate their entire meal.[3] A new age arrived on that first day of the nineteenth century. The Du Ponts had entered American history—in their own peculiar way.

Unlike most immigrants to America, the Du Ponts were no paupers. They arrived with large wooden crates bulging with furniture, clothes, books, and some 241,000 francs. Moreover, a million more francs were committed to be on the way. Unlike the early immigrants, who had to build their own homes or find some temporary refuge, the thirteen Du Pont arrivals had waiting for them a large, comfortable house at Bergens Point, New Jersey; Pierre named it Goodstay.

Soon after his arrival, Pierre journeyed to the bustling little city of New York, setting up expensive offices at 61 Pearl Street and then at 91 Liberty Street. From his office, Pierre released a prospectus in which the backgrounds of himself, Victor, and son-in-law Bureaux de Pusy were portrayed in all their glory. Shy Irénée, on the other hand, was rendered only one meager sentence: "E. I. du Pont* has had much experience of business methods in France in agriculture, in manufactures, and the useful arts."[4] Small promise for the man who would soon found the world's greatest gunpowder company!

Pierre promptly celebrated his newfound liberty by purchasing slaves for his wife. On June 21, 1800, for 70 pounds Paul Mersereau sold to Mrs. Du Pont de Nemours, as described in the contract, "One negro woman being a slave (called Jeen) and a young female child (called Lydia)"[5] for fourteen years of slavery, after which time freedom must be granted. Only five years later, Pierre would suddenly understand the yearn for freedom. "I need to be free," he would write to Jefferson.[6] Even then, however, Jeen and her children remained slaves in the House of Du Pont.

At Goodstay, Père Du Pont elaborated to his sons and daughters on his plans for his private empire, "Pontiania," and the family bustled with excitement. Pierre proposed purchasing American lands and reselling them to small farmers at inflated prices.[7] However, an old friend from his diplomatic days in Paris, Thomas Jefferson, now Vice-President, answered one of Pierre's letters by cautioning about land speculators who had already infiltrated western lands and driven up prices. Apparently, Jefferson's warning flags guided the Du Ponts from the rocks of land speculation, but Pierre only came up with other fantastic schemes, including smuggling gold into Spain. Finally, after months of failure and desertions in the family ranks, Victor came to the rescue, proposing that Pierre dissolve his New York firm and let Victor establish his own company with loans from France. "On the condition that I am in absolute control of it," he said in a burst of smugness, "I will assume entire responsibility for the consequences."[8]

Not overly impressed with the business aptitude of either his father or his brother, Irénée began to speculate on other ways to maintain his family's high standard of living. In light of his past training under Lavoisier, one alternative stood out—gunpowder.

American powder plants in those days were few in number and poor in

---

* Pierre's sons, in deference to their father, spelled their last names with a small "d."

quality, and it took only one visit to the largest American powder plant, at Frankford, Pennsylvania, to convince Irénée of his true vocation. Americans simply did not know how to make gunpowder, and as Adam Smith would have said in that age of free enterprise, where there is a demand there will be a supply. Irénée determined he was going to be the supplier.

In February 1801 Irénée and Victor arrived at the French port of Le Havre full of expectation and a passion for the coin of their homeland. By June, while Victor was drowning his own mission in a sea of parties, Irénée was already returning home laden with favors. Napoleon's astute foreign minister, Talleyrand, had reasoned that giving aid to E. I. du Pont would destroy forever England's monopoly over the American powder market. He was right. Besides machinery at cost, Talleyrand offered mechanical designs by government draftsmen and the newest secret improvements in making powder, including speedier methods of refining saltpeter, an essential ingredient. The French regime even drew up the original legal papers for Irénée's company on April 21, 1801, assigning "citizen" Irénée a salary of $1,800 a year as director, and assigning twelve of eighteen $2,000 shares to Père Du Pont's firm in Paris. Thus was achieved the capital birth of Du Pont.

After Irénée's return to America, his attempt to buy the Frankford Mills met with a stone wall of refusal. Then, upon his father's advice, he tried to find a suitable site for his gunpowder mills somewhere in the hills surrounding Federal City (later, Washington, D.C.), his biggest prospective customer. But that too failed. After traveling by horseback for weeks, looking for a place that would meet his needs, Irénée was openly contemptuous of America and its people. "The country, the people, the locations are all worthless,"[9] he wrote his father in disgust. Then he rode into Wilmington, Delaware, and into history.

Here flowed the Brandywine Creek, actually a swift river that could easily power the wheels of a powder mill. Here Irénée found Frenchmen, men who shared his culture, his language, and even his political conservatism, being refugees from the successful slave revolt of Santo Domingo. Here was a community tailored to his needs, a community of men who would gladly work for him at lower wages than most Americans. At the nearby up-for-sale Broome farm there was even an unused cotton mill ready for conversion to powder-making and a hillside of timber from which to burn charcoal. And here also was personal friendship, Alexandre Bauduy, a Santo Domingo refugee who had long been a friend of Victor du Pont.

But above all, here was money, the money of Peter Bauduy, Alexandre's brother, offered as financial support if Irénée would agree to settle on the

Brandywine. It was an enticement Irénée could not resist. On April 27, 1802, Irénée and Bauduy bought the Broome farm, from which would spring the country's largest powder plant within a decade.

4. KEYSTONES OF AN EMPIRE

Today the name Du Pont summons visions of nylon stockings and dacron shirts, of paint and waxes, photographic film and antifreeze, of cellophane wrappers and atomic energy, of social omnipotence and an almost intoxicating wealth.

But in 1802 Pierre Samuel Du Pont could never have foreseen such a future for his name in America. After a series of family desertions, business failures, and the shock of finally being cut out of the family firm by his son Victor, Pierre Du Pont was lost in melancholy. Prodded by his wife's desire to return to her homeland, Pierre agreed to sail for France, but not before he left Victor with a $78,000 "loan" and signed over Jeen and her child Lydia for ten years of slavery[10] to Irénée. Irénée must have enjoyed the slavery of these hapless people for the full ten years, as there is no record of his ever having voluntarily set them free. In fact, in September of that year he acquired yet another slave: Jeen gave birth to a beautiful little girl.

In France Pierre resumed his business activities and even engaged in secret negotiations with Napoleon over the Louisiana Purchase on behalf of Thomas Jefferson. Du Pont had known Jefferson for over twenty years, ever since Jefferson was minister to the royal court of Louis XVI. "You have never had but one Vice," punned Du Pont to Jefferson on the latter's ascension to the presidency. "I compliment your country and both hemispheres that you have at last lost it."[11] When, however, Pierre Du Pont wrote Jefferson of his plan to return to France, the Sage of Monticello answered in a more serious vein, requesting Pierre to travel to Washington City for a special conference. As his date of departure was close at hand, Pierre declined. It was then that Jefferson wrote Du Pont a long letter, asking him to undertake a strange mission in his behalf, one that would set the course of American—and Du Pont—expansion right up to the present day.

". . . impress on the Government of France," Jefferson asked, "the inevitable consequences of their taking Louisiana."[12] The new president was determined that France should not occupy Louisiana, which she had just acquired from Spain. Jefferson's whole political thesis on the future of his country centered around the belief that democracy and prosperity depended on the ability of free men to move onto free lands; the West, including Louisiana, was an integral part of this belief. As for the Indian peoples who happened to dwell on these "free lands," he urged settlers "to press upon them."[13] Along these lines, Jefferson drew up the Ordinance of 1784, opening the trans-Appalachian west to settlement, carving out ten relatively large territories that would immediately be entitled to self-government. Statehood would be theirs as soon as each territory was filled with a population equal to that of the smallest of the thirteen original states. And as that population grew, so also would the market for agricultural and industrial goods. In this way, Jefferson's thesis helped to shape American industrial, and Du Pont, history.

By 1790, a mere ten years before the Du Ponts' arrival, a million people had settled in these valleys or to the west.[14] "[Our success] furnishes a new proof of the falsehood of Montesquieu's doctrine that a republic can be preserved only in a small territory," Jefferson proudly announced in 1801. "The reverse is the truth."[15] "New frontiers," he argued, were what were needed to prevent disputes between "factions,"* or classes, that Madison, his teacher in expansionist mercantilism, had warned about. "Extend the sphere," Madison had explained in 1787, "and you take in the greater variety of parties and interests; you make it less probable that a majority of the whole will have common motive to invade the rights of other [wealthy] citizens; or if such a common motive exists, it will be more difficult for all who feel it to discover their own strength, and to act in unison with each other."[16] By 1804 Jefferson was in full accord with Madison. "The larger our association, the less it will be shaken by local passions."[17]

Indeed, by 1801 the passions were there. A burgeoning population of small farmers and a growing export trade even from western lands like Tennessee and Mississippi were forcing Jefferson to seek again new "free lands" as a vent for social pressure between classes, as well as to find a market for investment and trade. Jefferson was aware that within five years of that date Kentucky, Indiana, Michigan, and Ohio would be shipping surpluses down the Mississippi, reemphasizing the importance of having the port of New Orleans open to American export trade.

This question of export markets was extremely important to Jefferson, so important that he was willing to risk war with France for New Orleans. As early as 1786 he had worked out an explanation of the social forces that caused Shays' Rebellion that year, a popular uprising against the special privileges enjoyed by property holders. That populist rebellion in Massa-

---

* "Faction" meant an economic interest or grouping (which in some cases included various contending classes) in Madison's *Federalist Papers:* ". . . a landed interest, a manufacturing interest, a moneyed interest, and many lesser interests" (which included most of the country's population).

chusetts, crushed by troops, destroyed any illusion about a theoretical "voluntary association of government" and became the spur for the creation of a strong centralized government at the Constitutional Convention the following year. The cause of the Massachusetts rebellion, Jefferson explained, lay in the lack of enough export markets that would have enabled small farmers to sell their goods and pay their taxes and debts. "Open the Mediterranean,"[18] Jefferson then prescribed (and later did in his undeclared war against Tripoli and other North African city-states), and class tensions would be reduced with returning prosperity.

To Jefferson and to most Americans as the crisis deepened, the western frontier became a utopia, an escape that allowed evasion of the task of building a truly harmonious society. But for the lower classes of free farmers and uneducated who could never hope to live like aristocrats such as Jefferson, the frontier replaced formal education; a kind of nonintellectual learning by survival and succeeding became an ingrained part of the American psychology. Edward Everett, Massachusetts' delegate to the Constitutional Convention, summed it up as early as 1787 when he remarked that expansion "is the principle of our institutions,"[19] and it was the driving force behind Jefferson's letter to Du Pont de Nemours in 1802.

"This measure will cost France, and perhaps not very long hence, a war which will annihilate her on the ocean,"[20] wrote Jefferson to Du Pont, and he asked his French friend also to deliver a letter to Robert Livingston. To Livingston, Jefferson was more blunt. "The day that France takes New Orleans we must marry ourselves to the British fleet and nation."[21]

Pierre was shocked. He knew that if he presented Jefferson's ideas to Napoleon as they were written, the French emperor would consider them an open challenge and declare war. He immediately wrote back to Jefferson proposing another alternative. Why not promise to help France regain Canada? Surely a French neighbor to the south is better than a British neighbor to the north, but if Louisiana must be yours, why not offer Canada in exchange? Why not say "Give us Louisiana and at the first opportunity we shall restore Canada to you."[22] Old Pierre Du Pont harbored a good memory, recalling one of the French designs behind his government's alliance with the American colonies during their revolution: keep Canada open for possible repossession by France in the future. Now that day when France could regain her Quebec may have come, a big enough feather for any returning emigré to wear in his cap when looking for a government position. Of course, Pierre was little concerned with the fact that his suggestion meant war between Britain and the United States over Canada.

Jefferson wouldn't stand for it. As far as his government was concerned, France had given up all rights in America with the Treaty of Ghent almost twenty years before. Desperately searching for other alternatives, Pierre finally had a brainstorm: why not offer to buy Louisiana? Jefferson again refused. But war, Pierre retorted, suddenly carrying the palm of peace, "will cost your commerce, agriculture, and nation ten times as much."[23] Jefferson stubbornly disagreed and fired off a letter to Livingston warning him about Du Pont's misconceptions.

There was little doubt that Père Du Pont was full of misconceptions as he left America. In fact, his mind was completely confused as he boarded the ship, *Virginia Packett,* even leaving behind important notes which he had planned to use to draw up a commercial report to his stockholders. This loss increased his apprehension about explaining his firm's collapse and his rather large gift to Victor, but he hoped to allay enough suspicions to allow him to keep his Paris firm open and active. Always resourceful, even in the middle of the Atlantic Ocean, Pierre compensated by spending his idle hours writing an abstract essay called "Instinct."

It is unclear how much effect Pierre had on the final settlement of the Louisiana crisis. The President was still bellowing threats of war when he asked an excited Congress on January 18, 1803, to allocate funds for the Lewis and Clark expedition "to provide an extension of territory which the rapid increase of our number will call for."[24] Jefferson was proposing expansion across the Mississippi with or without a peaceful settlement with France. But the President was at least frank about his real goal: Pacific trade. "The interests of commerce place the principal object within the constitutional powers and care of Congress," he said, "and that it should advance the geographic knowledge of our own continent cannot but be an additional gratification."[25]

Despite Livingston's pessimistic but accurate reports of Napoleon's unwillingness to negotiate, Pierre's more optimistic reports probably did help to stay any definite move toward war, Jefferson obviously having decided to avoid a conflict if at all possible. On January 11 he ordered James Monroe to France, supposedly to assist Livingston, but actually to make an offer of $2 million to Napoleon—and he secretly authorized more if necessary, without any confirmation from Congress.[26] If France wanted war, then Monroe and Livingston were to cross the channel and invite Britain into an alliance with the United States.

Then the impossible happened. On April 10, 1803, Napoleon called in his ministers and ordered them to sell all of Louisiana for 60 million francs. Although Pierre did not know it, Napoleon actually had no alternative. Militarily occupying Louisiana required the island of Santo Domingo as a supply base. In 1802 Napoleon's brother-in-law, General Leclerc, did successfully invade the island, crush the Black revolutionary government that had been established there, and, through betrayal at a peace conference, capture its heroic leader, Toussaint L'Ouverture. But the pattern of deception soon loses its character of surprise, and the combined onslaught of yellow fever and the valiant guerrilla war carried on by L'Ouverture's followers brought ultimate defeat to the French invaders. Leclerc and 50,000 other Frenchmen were buried that year in the warm soil of San Domingo, and with them died also Napoleon's plans for occupying Louisiana and reestablishing a French empire on the North American continent. By the time another expedition could be gathered, rumblings of approaching war with Britain forced the emperor to retain his troops in Europe. Now, not only would he be unable to occupy Louisiana, but his treasury's need for funds for the coming conflict required him to sell Louisiana entirely. On May 8, 1803, Louisiana was sold to the United States for 60 million francs, or approximately $15 million. One week later, Britain declared war on France.

On the other side of the ocean the Louisiana Purchase doubled the size of the United States, carrying Jefferson's stars and stripes from the mouth of the Mississippi to the Rocky Mountains. At the year's end, bursting with pride and relief, Jefferson wrote Du Pont of his gratitude. "I congratulate you on having lived to give those aids in a transaction replete with blessings to unborn millions of men, and which will mark the face of a portion of the globe so extensive as that which now composes the United States of America."[27]

Though the blessings to the unborn may be debatable, the Louisiana Purchase was a very real blessing to Pierre's second son, Irénée. In terms of long-range benefits, the Louisiana Purchase widened western markets for Du Pont explosives for generations to come. But there was an immediate boon as well. The spring of 1803 brought Irénée news of his father's role in the Louisiana Purchase, and on July 20 he wrote to Jefferson requesting special government patronage. Shortly thereafter, the United States government became Irénée's first customer, awarding him a contract for refining government-owned saltpeter.

By then, Irénée had moved his family to the Brandywine and was completing construction of his gunpowder mills. Sophie moved happily into her new home, called Eleutherian Mills. Five bays wide and two rooms deep, with a large central hall, the two-story stone mansion was an imposing sight perched gray and aloof on the green hillside. Nearby stood Irénée's small stone office, and below, the Brandywine with three new mills, two new buildings, a new race for the mills, a drying place for the gunpowder, a magazine for storing it, and quarters for the workers.

Most of these first workers were men from the French community along the Brandywine. Irénée also used indentured servants, sometimes sent over from France by Père Du Pont.[28] These men worked for nothing but their keep until their passage to America was paid off, and they were often obliged to remain in Irénée's employ as an original condition for their passage.

Thus, cheap labor and government patronage joined an ever-expanding market as keystones in the construction of a profitable Du Pont Company in its earliest days, keystones which Du Pont never abandoned but has used to build its empire right up to the present day.

From his hilltop office overlooking the Brandywine, Irénée now watched his mills churn out hundreds of pounds of powder daily, powder that found a ready market, thanks to war. Some 22,000 pounds of Du Pont powder were used by U.S. warships in the undeclared war against Tripoli and the other North African city-states. Sales jumped threefold in the first year, from $10,000 in 1804 to $33,000 in 1805. On July 4, 1805, Jefferson's Secretary of War, Colonel Henry Dearborn, announced that Irénée's company would do all the government's powder work. Napoleon's puppet government in Spain also ordered 40,000 pounds, much of which was used to crush rebellions by the oppressed Spanish population. But to Irénée du Pont there were no victors, no losers, no oppressors or oppressed, and above all, no causes—just rows of wooden casks filled with black powder, and a mounting family treasure.

5. THE ATLANTIC BREWS A STORM . . .

The Brandywine was the scene of family festivities in 1809 when Victor du Pont and his family returned from his latest business disaster in Genesee, New York. Victor had gone there after his commercial firm collapsed in 1809, to engage in land speculation. There was only one problem—he found no buyers. Donning the role of family savior, Irénée announced that he was building his brother a regency mansion and buying him a business, a wool factory provided with fleece from herds sired by his own Don Pedro, a ram of unusual virile qualities that Irénée had brought back with him from France.

The financial and labor source for both ventures was, of course, the powder company. Describing this, the acrid letters of Irénée's partner, Peter Bauduy, complaining of Irénée's business methods, were brewing a tempest of trouble across the ocean. In fact, by now the European stockholders were in an uproar over Irénée's personal appropriations and the expenses for Victor while their own profit-sharing had been suspended by him.

To calm the storm, Irénée was forced to release Du Pont Company's first statement in 1810, showing a profit over six years of over $43,000 on some $243,000 in sales—a return of almost 20 percent! The statement fulfilled its purpose, reducing shouts to grumbles while the mills continued to grind out their profits: in 1810, $30,000; in 1811, $45,000, more in one year than was made in the entire first six years of business. That year was a turning point not only for Du Pont Company, but also for the country as a whole: E. I. du Pont de Nemours & Co. was now the largest producer of gunpowder in the United States.

Such a monumental feat would probably have quieted the occasional clamor from Europe had not Père Du Pont been stirring his own cauldron of mischief. When his Paris firm collapsed in the French panic of 1811, Pierre surrendered to his creditors his firm's twelve $2,000 shares in Irénée's powder company. These creditors, in turn, now began pressing claims for immediate payment. Irénée for the most part ignored these claims through the years, even when the desperate widow of his dead stepbrother, Bureaux de Pusy, came to America to see about her husband's investment. Arriving in October of 1813, by August 1, 1814, she still had no stock report from Irénée, despite his previous assurances.

"You assured me so positively last June," she wrote, "that the accounts of the Powder Company were almost finished. . . . I believed you and waited all that month, but for the twentieth time you have failed me. . . . Do you want to buy my shares in your establishment?" she asked desperately. "I enclose here a last offer to sell them to you at a price that seems fair to us both; but in God's name answer. . . ."[29]

Irénée did. He said no . . . politely, of course.

6. . . . AND WAR

With the arrival of the War of 1812, Du Pont Company won its own victory over the balance sheets. In the autumn of 1811 the thunder of approaching war had forced the federal government to order 50,000 pounds of Du Pont powder. In 1812, with hostilities actually begun, Washington hiked the order to 200,000 pounds; in 1813, to 500,000 pounds, forcing Irénée to double the company's capacity with the new Hagley mills nearby. With additional orders from the Navy, Du Pont sold more than a million pounds of powder to the government during the war.

Only Du Pont had the capacity to fill the huge powder needs of the government, and the government paid well for the delivery. Although

Washington supplied its own saltpeter, Du Pont still charged the highest[30] price up to that time for powder: 58 cents per pound. In the first year of war alone, Du Pont showed gross sales of $148,597.62, the crucial margin of success for the young company. Du Pont powder was soon carried by coastal schooners and powder wagons as far north as Boston, as far south as Charleston, and as far west as Pittsburgh. Even John Jacob Astor's trappers and hunters in the West consumed 25,000 pounds of powder every year.

The Brandywine suffered few losses during the war. Although given special exemption from military duty, Du Pont workers, mostly Frenchmen, were formed into two companies of militia by the Du Pont brothers. It was with these men that the Du Pont family in the election of 1813 engaged in their first experiment in America in para-military means to gain their own political ends. Assembling both companies in full uniform on October 5, 1813, Irénée and Victor marched on the polls to forcibly register alien votes for Irénée's pro-war party, the Democratic-Republicans. Crowds of angry Delaware voters, however, became incensed at such strong-arm tactics and chased the Du Pont companies back to the Brandywine.

Charges were brought against the Du Pont brothers and confirmed by an official investigation.[31] Although the brothers were never brought to trial, the citizens of the state were so enraged over the affair that the following year Delaware's legislature was compelled to prohibit the raising of private militia by employers. Reluctantly, Irénée disarmed his men. It was not to be the last time the Du Ponts would raise a private army, but it was Irénée's last personal spat with the law.

In fact, both Du Ponts became exemplary American citizens after the war.

In 1815 Victor du Pont was elected to Delaware's House of Representatives from the Brandywine, already called "Du Pont country," and in 1820 he entered the state Senate. Here, in Dover, the state capital, Victor was at home, swaggering in the familiar world of perfumed ladies and formal balls. For three years he reveled in dancing and drinking, finding between games of whist even the infrequent debates over roads and bridges a welcome relief from the austere Irénée and his meticulous payment of notes.

Irénée was resourceful in more than pecuniary ways. In 1816 Sophie, at the age of 41, gave birth to their seventh child, Alexis Irénée. Now there were Alfred, Victorine, Evelina, Henry, Eleuthera, Sophie, and Alexis. With three sons, Irénée would indeed have no lack of heirs to carry on his life's work. And Irénée had taken measures to insure that the powder company would be his and his alone.

The death of Victorine du Pont's husband, Ferdinand Bauduy, two years earlier had dissolved the last ties to his partner, Peter Bauduy. "May this sorrow unite us," Bauduy had written Irénée after his son's death. "Be my friend, for I have just lost the best one I had."[32] It was a futile request. Little more than a year passed before Bauduy was forced out of the firm.

Thus Bauduy missed the war profits of the previous August of 1814, when Irénée sold 1,840 barrels to the government. In November another 156,000 pounds of powder brought Irénée $70,000. From then to the peace in February 1815, when he forced out Bauduy, Irénée sold an additional 687 barrels, worth $13,740. With peace, on one hand came sales to the Spanish Captain-General of Cuba, and on the other, demands for payment again from Irénée's European shareholders. When one of these backers, banker Jacques Bidermann, sent his son Antoine to America to check out his investment, Irénée's lovely daughter, Evelina, so charmed the lad that he stayed, married her, and ended up in Peter Bauduy's old job.

Helping Irénée in this last maneuver was none other than Père Du Pont. At first so enraged with Irénée's ignoring of his responsibilities to his European shareholders that he called him "unnatural," Pierre quickly buried the family hatchet in 1815 when Napoleon escaped Elba and marched on Paris. Pierre, it seems, as secretary of the new provisional government, had earlier signed Napoleon's abdication and ordered his banishment to Elba to make way for the monarch's short-lived restoration. Napoleon reentered Paris just as Pierre was hurriedly sailing for America, abandoning his sick wife.

Two years later, after a long illness in America, this most colorful of the Du Ponts entered a coma from which he never emerged. On August 7, 1817, with Irénée and Victor at his bedside, Pierre Samuel Du Pont de Nemours ended his turbulent career with a simple, final sigh.

Pierre Du Pont, the knighted nobleman of Louis XVI and the founder of America's first industrial family, was buried beneath a simple slab of stone in the middle of a lonely place, called Sand Hole Woods, overlooking the Brandywine. Since that day, the Du Ponts have buried their dead at Sand Hole Woods, transforming that simple graveyard into the world's most exclusive cemetery of industrial royalty, the final resting place of the House of Du Pont.

Six months after the death of his father, Irénée du Pont suffered another, and for the company, greater loss. On March 19, 1818, the old Upper Yards' five mills exploded, one after another, leaving behind thirty-six dead. Only eight of the dead were identifiable, pieces of human flesh being found everywhere: in the flower gardens of Irénée's mansion, on the lawn of Victor's Louviers estate across the creek, even perched on the treetops like some ghastly fruit of death. Irénée's brother-in-law, Charles Dalmas, and Irénée's wife Sophie were both wounded, Sophie with an injury from which she would never recover.

Despite this setback, by 1824 the Du Ponts of Delaware were entering a new bracket of wealth and power in America. Irénée was appointed a member of the board of directors of the Bank of the United States, which held a monopoly over U.S. currency and was a notorious center of fraud and corruption.* He was to hold that post until 1829, two years before a congressional investigation revealed that institution's use of bribes to win renewal of its charter.

Since 1814, Irénée had also been a director of the Farmers Bank of the State of Delaware and had even invested in toll roads and a ferry line across the Delaware River.

Victor also was enjoying himself. When he retired from the state Senate in 1824, he too became a director of the Farmers Bank. In 1826 Victor du Pont joined his brother on the board of directors of the Bank of the United States.

Victor could also be proud of his son, Charles I. du Pont. Charles would soon invest in the Union Bank of Delaware and the Columbia Insurance Company and pursue a successful law practice separate from the family business. Acceding to his father's seat in the state Senate, he would eventually run for governor. One of his first steps toward achieving that ambition was his marriage first to Dorcas Van Dyke, daughter of U.S. Senator Nicholas Van Dyke, and later to Anne Ridgely, daughter of State Senator Henry M. Ridgely.

7. A PASSING OF CROWNS

The Brandywine turned festive on January 1, 1827, with dinner and brandies and the innumerable toasts of Victor du Pont. Victor, patting his

---

* In its fight to renew its charter, the Bank of the United States paid out $30 million in the form of nonmercantile "loans" (see Senator Thomas Benton's *Thirty Years in the Senate*, II, 365–66). Congress, which renewed the charter, had many of its members on the Bank's payroll (see Reports Nos. 460–65, First Session, 22nd Congress, 1831). By 1841, $76 million in assets had vanished from the Bank. Its long-time president, Nicholas Biddle, paid out $1,018,000 for which no vouchers were ever found. Its cashier, John Andrews, embezzled $426,930.67; its second assistant cashier, Joseph Cowperthwaite, defaulted in the sum of $55,081. Both Biddle and Andrews were sued for $400,000 for restitution in 1836; in 1844, after Biddle's death, a Pennsylvania court settled the case favorably for the claimants. Among the famous names who acted as counsel for the Bank during these years of fraud were Daniel Webster, Supreme Court Chief Justice Salmon Chase, and Richard Blatchford, father of Supreme Court Justice Samuel Blatchford.

jolly corporation, even bought a New York lottery ticket, saying he felt lucky that year.

Thirty days later he was dead. Years of spirited living and third helpings had finally caught up with Victor's 60-year-old heart. Suffering an attack on the streets of Philadelphia, he was carried to his room in the United States Hotel, where he died within two hours.

Some time later, his family was informed that Victor's ticket had won, returning $850. For once Victor had finally had some luck.

Irénée took his brother's passing very hard. Victor had been a tonic of cheer for Irénée's lonely life of bills and empty profits. With Victor's death went the family's last connection with the grand societies of France and America. After his burial, the family grew increasingly clannish, reserved, and totally absorbed in profit-making.

The next year Irénée suffered his third great loss—his wife. Sophie had long declared a wish to return to France, and only months before her death Irénée had finally promised her "soon." Sophie never made it. "Mrs. du Pont is so ill today," Irénée wrote on August 5, "that I hardly know what I am writing."[33] She died on November 27, 1828, at the age of 53.

After Sophie's death Irénée sank deeper into his melancholia. He was now a man of 57 with streaks of gray running through his hair and sad eyes reflecting a deep, anguished loneliness. For months he could be seen staring into space for long periods of time. Then his eyes would turn back on his greatest love, the Brandywine. What had once been only a means to make his family rich now became an end in itself, and Irénée drowned his sorrows in the deluge of company affairs. Widowed Victorine tried to take her mother's place in running Irénée's home for him, while 30-year-old Alfred, his oldest son, helped out in the mills by taking on greater responsibility. But nothing could fill the void Sophie left. Eleutherian Mills was now an empty mansion for Irénée, with his second son Henry about to enter West Point as a cadet, and frail Alexis Irénée away at prep school.

Fortunately, the powder company absorbed most of Irénée's time. Du Pont Company by this time had a capacity of over 800,000 pounds annually, about one-seventh of the total U.S. output. By 1832 it had exported 1.2 million pounds of explosives, a big chunk of its 13.4-million-pound grand total output for almost thirty years of business. Du Pont powder was now shipped all over the world, even to the West Indies and South America.

On June 27, 1833, Irénée saw his daughter Sophie Madeleine marry her first cousin, Lieutenant Samuel Francis du Pont, U.S.N., the youngest son of Victor. It was a small, private affair, the first of many intermarriages that would someday make the Du Ponts the most inbred family in the

United States. Watching this legal union of his blood with Victor's, Irénée must have recalled the promise he once made to Victor when his brother expressed feelings of guilt about the debts he owed him. "We are bound to each other," he reassured Victor, "like twins of whom both would die if one did."[34]

On October 29, 1834, only a month after he married off the last of his unwed daughters, Eleuthera, to Dr. Thomas McKie Smith, Irénée du Pont was struck down in the streets of Philadelphia by a heart attack. Carried to his room at the United States Hotel, he died there at 3:00 A.M. on Friday, October 31, 1834. Irénée, dead at 63, had survived his brother by seven years, yet had died in the same manner, the same city, and even the same hotel—"like twins. . . ."

Eleuthère Irénée du Pont, named for "liberty and peace" and founder of the greatest gunpowder industry the world has ever known, was lowered into a simple grave at the Du Pont family cemetery in Sand Hole Woods. As Irénée's three black-suited sons nervously stood by, piles of dirt were thrown down on the coffin, burying forever the man who had guided the firm for thirty-two years from its struggling birth to its present grandeur. Nearby, to the right, was the grave of Père Du Pont, and to *its* right was that of Victor, as the elder son. To this day, Du Ponts bury their dead to the right or left of Père Du Pont, according to the "line" from which they are descended.

8. ALFRED THE MEEK

In the seven generations of Du Ponts that have stood in the golden flow of the Brandywine, it has been the rarest of the species who did not at some time crave command of the family enterprise. For the Du Ponts, the company has been a passion that borders on the fanatic, a prize that has often torn family binds to shreds. True, most in the family have been unwilling to invest the time and work required to win such an august role, and even some who did have deferred for reasons of health or other personal obsessions, like running for Congress. But none that devoted his life to the family firm and remained long enough to partake of the sweet pleasures of its economic power has ever rejected the family crown when it was offered—none, that is, save Alfred du Pont.

Alfred, in this as in other ways, was as unlike his father as a son could be. Broad-shouldered and powerfully built, Alfred looked more like just another honest powderman than the son of shrewd Irénée du Pont. Alfred seemed a rather kind individual, more interested in his chemical experiments than in a profit sheet. Irénée could not inject into his son his own secular religion for profits and business management. Alfred frankly hated business affairs and lacked his father's ruthless ability to build. Instead, powder-making was more to his liking.

It was precisely for this reason that Alfred insisted he did not wish to take the family helm at the time of his father's death. As his younger brothers, Henry and Alexis, were too young and inexperienced to captain the country's largest gunpowder company, the family was swept by panic only hours after Irénée's death.

The Du Ponts solved the problem by initiating an institution that survived for 140 years: an interim presidency held by an in-law. Antoine Bidermann, Irénée's son-in-law and close friend for over twenty years, became acting chief on November 1, the day after Irénée died.

With over twenty years of experience in the company's sales, Bidermann proved an excellent administrator, helped, of course, by the company's own great capacity for generating profits, now over a million pounds of black powder per year. For the next three years, while Alfred familiarized himself with the firm's gears, the company grew to the point where Antoine was able to fulfill Irénée's final wish: he paid off the last of the European shareholders. In 1837 he sailed to France and returned with the last of the nonfamily stocks. Then he announced his retirement, his mission accomplished for his dead friend. On April 1, 1837, 39-year-old Alfred reluctantly took his father's seat by the small wooden desk.

Now that his father was gone, Alfred was frankly frightened by his new responsibility. To alleviate his situation, he insisted that his younger brothers join him in a new partnership. Henry and "Aleck" agreed, establishing the precedent for future Du Pont generations, of three partners serving as a kind of executive committee, with no offices such as president or treasurer, the senior partner being the final authority on all decisions. It was a tradition that would endure as long as the company remained a partnership, over sixty years.

Another precedent was established at this time. Victor's children were excluded from leadership in the firm, an ostracism perhaps spurred by their careers outside the firm. Although Victor's youngest son, Samuel Francis, did have a small voice in the company through his cousin-wife, Sophie, Victor's side of the family was never allowed to play a commanding role. Irénée's sons were determined to keep a tight rein.

By the time of Alfred's ascension to power, industrial capitalism was in full bloom in America. It was the Machine Age, the age of inventions, of Morse's telegraph, Goodyear's vulcanized rubber, and Hoe's rotary printing press. Sewing machines made their appearance along with thousands of cheap-labor immigrants from war-blighted Europe. The black billows of factories were rising all across young America, and with them the smoke of steamboats cruising down rivers and plowing through canals, and competing for the transportation market, the steam engine puffed over 2,000 miles of operable track.

Then the bottom fell out again. Speculation had overextended the resources of the country's banks. New York banks finally suspended specie payments and the economy's boom swung characteristically back into its infamous bust. One-third of the country's workers were thrown out of work, and the streets of American cities filled with children begging for bread. Hundreds of people died of cold and starvation in those cruelest of days. A brief recovery in 1837 emboldened hope, but then the economy slipped back into seven more years of depression. By 1841, 33,000 businesses went under, with losses estimated at $440 million, and a full one-third of Ohio's banks failed.

"We have seen within the last four years many sudden and heavy changes in money matters," Alfred du Pont warned in February of that year, "but the crisis of the last week exceeds anything of the kind it has been our lot to experience."[35]

Actually, in the midst of all this poverty and ruin, Du Pont Company was doing quite well. In fact, the plant was working at full capacity. The skirmishes along the Mexican border in 1836 and along the Canadian Quebec–Niagara border in 1838–1840 had brought in a steady stream of government orders. But more important was the cry, "Go west, young man!" as western expansion continued and the unemployed raced in long, endless trains of battered wagons toward hidden promises of the setting sun to meet their fate with hungry packs of land speculators.

Orders for Du Pont powder kept pouring in to dig the Ohio and Mississippi canals to the Great Lakes, to blast out stumps for midwestern farmers. Railways and roads carved their way through the Rockies, iron and coal mines were discovered, silver mines were blasted, and lawmen brought a strange kind of justice to the West—all with Du Pont powder. The U.S. government used Du Pont powder to kill American Indians, drive them from their lands, and force them into disease-ridden "reservations," and the discovery of gold in the West helped keep the powder demand constant.

But what was good for Du Pont was not necessarily good for the country. Starvation and unemployment continued to gnaw at the country's defenseless population. Bread riots broke out in the East, recalling to Alfred memories of his father's tales of class war in revolutionary France.

"Our political dissensions are such," he wrote, "that it would require the enemy at our doors to induce us to make proper preparations for defense."[36]

Alfred was not the only one thinking of such a solution. In May of 1846 the United States provoked hostilities and then declared war on Mexico. Mexico was then the titular ruler of California, the whaler's paradise and harbor for China trade. And with war, prospects of an expanded market and the 1848 discovery of gold came full economic recovery. Alfred agreed with one young congressman, Abraham Lincoln, that the war was immoral and provoked, but Du Pont never refused government contracts. In fact, Du Pont Company sold one million pounds of powder to the government during the war. To keep up with the huge volume of orders, Alfred was forced to build more powder mills, the Lower Works, below the Hagley Yard and across the creek.

Armed with Du Pont powder, American armies swiftly invaded Mexico, smashing into the countryside as General Taylor swept south from Texas and General Scott attacked Mexico City, the capital. At Chapultepec Hill an American army surrounded and massacred hundreds of young cadets, most of them mere children, from a nearby military academy. It was Mexico's own "day of infamy," but she received little sympathy in concrete terms. When, for example, Du Pont received a 200,000-pound order from Havana for the desperate Mexicans, Alfred immediately raced to Washington to display his patriotism. He returned to the Brandywine laden with the sorrow of duty to country and lucrative government contracts. "However unjust our proceeding may be," he wrote the Havana agents, "and however shameful our invasion of Mexican territory, we cannot make powder to be used against our own country."[37]

And against our own family, Alfred might have added. His cousin (and brother-in-law) Captain Samuel F. du Pont was commander of the warship U.S.S. *Cayane* at the time, clearing the Gulf of California of Mexican ships to facilitate the invasion of Mexican territory, destroying thirty vessels in all and seizing La Paz in Lower California. Sam even led a military expedition into the Mexican mainland after occupying the city of Mazatlán in November 1847. As for qualms of conscience, Captain du Pont seemed free of that too human burden. "They [the Mexicans] are not worthy of your sympathy," he wrote his wife, Sophie, "because I doubt if there is a virtuous man in the nation."[38]

When "virtuous" United States dictated its terms of peace to Mexico, Sam was not satisfied with the American conquest of more than half the total territory of Mexico (Nevada, New Mexico, Arizona, Colorado, and California), a domain greater in area than France and Germany combined.

"The folly of not including Lower California is hard for us to get over,"[39] he grumbled.

There were other losses that were hard for Du Ponts to get over during those days of war and conquest. In 1847 an explosion tore up the Upper Yards and the lives of eighteen men. Anne du Pont, wife of Charles, described to her cousin the scene from Louviers: "The shrieks of the wives and children so soon made widows and orphans rose in sad succession to the preceding horror. Human heads, arms, and feet were found on that peaceful-looking bank of the Brandywine where you and I have walked."[40]

Alfred du Pont never got over it. Perhaps because he felt guilt-ridden about the wartime speedup in production that always raises risks to the men's safety, perhaps because he was already so fatigued by the heavy load of responsibilities, the explosion shattered Alfred's already frayed nerves.

Once, Alfred would have surrendered his responsibilities right then and there. But by now he had become, like his father, obsessed with the drive for profit-making, a creature driven by the insatiable needs of private enterprise. Alfred struggled on for two more years, still continuing to increase the workers' rate of production. In 1849 Du Pont workers boosted the previous year's production by 400,000 pounds. They made 10,000 pounds of powder every day, the mills running twenty-four hours a day, fourteen by lamplight. Alfred also introduced some improvements in shipping techniques. He brought coopers and machinery to the Brandywine to manufacture kegs on the premises, standardizing their size and quality and ensuring their availability. Next, he had a pier and magazine built on the Delaware River at Edge Moor, three miles above Wilmington, to load ships more easily. Now bad weather would not prevent loading, as it had when wagons brought powder to the ships directly from the yards.

Finally, in 1850, Alfred's health could take no more and he resigned from the company. Now an invalid, he would last six more years before dying as he was born, within earshot of the grinding mills.

9. HENRY THE CONQUEROR

Most men when they are "called to duty" leave business and go to war. For the Du Ponts, the opposite is often the rule: they leave war and go into business.

Such was the case with Alfred's successor and younger brother, Henry. Three months before Irénée's death, when he became concerned about Alfred's lack of enthusiasm for the business side of the company, Henry was called home from his participation in the U.S. Army's massacre of the Creek Indians.

Henry du Pont was a graduate of West Point, and looked it. Standing straight as a board, he had fiery red hair and beard that flared in contrast to his black suit and matching high hat, his cold blue eyes giving the finishing touch to the commanding appearance he so relished. And Henry not only looked like a commander; he was determined to be one. Alfred's resignation now left Henry to fulfill his ambitions.

With a battle cry of economy and expansion that sent the entire gunpowder market into a flurry of excitement, Henry collected thousands of dollars in outstanding debts, fired some agents and hired new ones, and soon expanded Du Pont's market across the country.

When mills 7 and 8 exploded in 1852, killing two men, Henry proved he was no Alfred. Chomping on his "Henry Clay" cigars (as with his father, Henry chose this apologist for chattel slavery as his idol), Henry traced down the cause to an alleged mistake by one worker, William Cowan. Henry abruptly fired the man, publicly charging him with negligence. Less than a year later, Cowan, still unemployed and hounded by charges of guilt, hanged himself.

Henry was hungry for markets; no market was too far from his grasp. When Du Pont's contract to deliver powder to Czarist Russia during the Crimean War was hindered in 1854 by a blockade by the British royal navy, Henry had his young nephew Lammot du Pont, the tall, lanky son of Alfred, run the blockade outside Chesapeake Bay. Through Gibraltar and into the Mediterranean steamed Lammot, a fleet of angry British warships in hot pursuit. It was perhaps the greatest single naval manhunt of the nineteenth century, yet to be given its proper place in recorded history. Successfully passing through Bosporus and into the Black Sea, Lammot was just nearing the besieged Russian lines at Sebastopol when British warships challenged and then fired two broadsides into his ship. Still he managed to steam ahead, steering between huge, hazardous rocks before finally beaching safely behind Russian lines. The result for Du Pont was a cool $3 million.[41]

This success, however, did not prevent Henry from also selling gunpowder to the British.

With the Crimean War profits, Du Pont easily weathered the 1858 depression. Unfortunately for Henry, that year marked yet another explosion, which killed three men and, for the first time, a Du Pont—Alexis I. du Pont. "Aleck," the fatalist of the family, had seldom seriously considered his work personally dangerous. "I did not think it would happen this way,"[42] he said between prayers, and died.

The soft, warm earth of the Brandywine had no sooner covered Alexis du Pont than Henry announced a successor to the departed's seat at the exalted table of partners. Lammot du Pont, champion of Sebastopol, brightest among the rising stars in the Du Pont celestial globe of 24 grandchildren of the company's founder, was chosen for good reason. Lammot had just perfected a method that allowed Du Pont to use Chilean and Peruvian nitrate.

Previously, Peruvian nitrate (salt of soda or sodium nitrate) contained impurities that quickly made powder damp, with poor firing results. For this reason, E. I. du Pont had rejected its use. Lammot, using his grandfather's calculations, solved the problem with a unique formula: 72 parts Peruvian nitrate, 12 parts sulphur, and 16 parts charcoal. This allowed a higher percentage of oxygen and nitrogen in the mixture and kept the powder dry. Glazed with sulphite, it even poured more freely. American gunpowder would no longer be dependent on India's potassium nitrate (salt of potash), which was expensive to ship.

Lammot's formula lowered costs and increased demand so much that the Du Ponts were forced to build mills in Pennsylvania that they could not personally supervise. Du Pont also drove the market price for powder down to 18 cents a pound by 1859, cutting the ground out from under its competitors and increasing even further demand for its own powder. Lammot's new "soda powder" was the first innovation in gunpowder in hundreds of years, for the first time separating blasting powder from powder used in firearms.

By 1859 the "Red Fellow," as the men called Henry, was beaming like a torch, but beneath his joy lurked a nagging fear. Across the vast American market the question of a slave economy being able to coexist with free-labor capitalism had reached the boiling point after over half a century of simmering rivalry.

As a Whig, Henry insisted that the slavery of Black people was not an issue for whites to have to fight over. Instead, he supported Henry Clay's attempts to reach a compromise between the two completely hostile economic systems. But the march of history would no longer be waylaid by compromise. Northern industrialists, if they were to expand into new western territories, could not afford to allow southern production to profit by slave labor, and the southern planters could not afford to lose the slaves upon which their very existence as a privileged class depended.

Only such deep economic contradictions could swell to the surface moral clarions loud enough to sway the hearts and minds of millions, and clarions there were and millions were moved. And in the midst of it all, sitting in a state that had both slave and free labor, both slavemaster and abolitionist, Henry du Pont easily surmised that armed conflict might be inevitable. In 1858 he sent Lammot to Europe for three months to study plants and improved production methods in England, France, and Belgium. The next year Lammot began to rebuild the Pennsylvania mills to enable them to produce his new soda powder. But just as the conversion neared completion, history moved faster than Lammot. The lightning before the storm had at last kindled the thunder of drums.

Three

HARVEST OF GOLD

1. A HOUSE DIVIDED NEED NOT FALL

"I think it is miserable that Lincoln's elected," Ellen du Pont angrily wrote her brother, Henry Algernon du Pont, at West Point. "Whenever I think of our having such a President from such a party, it makes me feel like tasting green persimmons does to the children. . . . I wish the Republicans and the abolitionists were in the Atlantic, when we would be at rest."[1]

Ellen was no exception in the Du Pont household, for there is no doubt that the first family of Delaware had strong southern sympathies and made little effort to hide them. In fact, a branch of the family were themselves slaveholders in South Carolina. Père Du Pont's great uncle, Abraham Dupont, had settled his roost there in 1695. It was his son, Gideon Dupont, who brought the flooding technique to rice growing in Carolina, and these southern cousins now reigned as proud slavemasters over a huge plantation in St. James Parish, Goose Creek. The Du Ponts of Delaware were not particularly eager to be forced into a war against kin over an issue with which they were not necessarily in disagreement and which, they correctly surmised, had been endorsed by the Constitution since the founding of the federal union.

Did not Henry du Pont—charged some Delaware abolitionists—the chief of the Delaware clan, openly support John Bell, compromise candidate of the slaveholders? And did not Charles I. du Pont, state senator and Whig candidate for governor of Delaware, vigorously endorse the pride of white racism, John C. Breckinridge?

Of course, there *was* Sam, the thorn in Delaware's Dixie hearts.

No one with the wildest imagination could claim Captain Samuel F. du Pont to be a friend of the South since Sam Houston of Texas had assailed him in the halls of the U.S. Senate in December 1855. Sam Houston, a figure of national prominence since ripping Texas from Mexican hands two decades earlier (for which Houston, the slaveholder, is portrayed today as liberator, and Santa Ana, leader of the last stand of Mexicans who had abolished slavery, is condemned as a dictator), delivered one of the severest tongue lashings ever to echo in those hallowed halls, condemning Du Pont for his role on the controversial Naval Efficiency Board. Du Pont had been the hatchetman of that unofficial tribunal, chopping down the careers of over seventy officers and publicly branding several hundred other officers with charges of incompetency. Senator Houston's attack in response was razor sharp, and bleeding Sam du Pont never forgot it.

Although a firm opponent of slavery, this first cousin of Henry du Pont was no abolitionist. Like all the Du Ponts, Sam stood opposed to John Brown's valiant effort to free slaves by force of arms at Harper's Ferry. Captain du Pont heartily approved of Brown's hanging in 1859, even as the abolitionist's Virginian executioners, Colonel Robert E. Lee and Virginia Governor Jefferson Davis, were plotting more monumental treachery of their own against established government. But when the tense country drew closer to its violent climax with the 1860 presidential election, Sam surprised no one when he supported the candidate of northern capital, a corporation lawyer named Abraham Lincoln. For the first time since their landing at Rhode Island, the Du Ponts were not politically united, and everyone in the state seemed to know it.

A few hundred anxious people gathered in Wilmington after the polls closed on election night, and for Delaware's slaveholders the state's completed tally brought sweet victory. Breckinridge, the candidate of slavery and constitutional tradition, had overwhelmingly carried the state, while Lincoln received less than one-fourth of Delaware's vote. Only in the Brandywine and Christiana hundreds did Lincoln receive clear majorities, the gunpowder workers giving "Boss Henry's" endorsement of Bell a surprisingly bold rejection. While the Du Pont workers' returns may well have embarrassed Henry, he could excuse the vote as merely reflective of the North as a whole as labor organizations from Ohio to Maine endorsed and worked for the candidate of wage labor.

The returns brought another personal embarrassment for the family, however. Charles I. du Pont lost the election for governor, despite his admitted slaveholding leanings. It seems Charles had made one fatal mistake—he had supported the Catholic's right to organize his church as he saw fit. That his sister, Amelie du Pont, was a Catholic may have had some bearing on his position and, ultimately, his defeat. In any case, more than one Du Pont of "Irénée's side" of the family winked in intimate assurance that Victor du Pont's strain for failure had at last surfaced in the successful lawyer.

Those who did engage in such mischief may well have winced with disappointment of their own, however, when the national returns finally came in, for defeat had extended its heavy hand beyond Charles to most of the family. While losing Delaware, the Wilmington telegraph office reported, Lincoln had won the country and been elected the sixteenth president of the United States.

There were varied kinds of mourning that night along the Brandywine. Charles fumed quietly, while the Red Fellow stormed about Eleutherian Mills like an enraged bull. A month passed and the snows of December were just cooling Henry's temper when South Carolina announced its secession from the Union, soon followed by most of the slaveholding states. For Henry and most of the family, confusion reigned supreme, no one sure where to land a safe foothold. It was a time of bewilderment—and fateful decision.

In February 1861, after Lincoln's own inauguration, Jefferson Davis was inaugurated President of the Confederate States of America and the following month ordered the raising of a 100,000-man army under the command of General Robert E. Lee. From both sides of the Potomac went feelers to Delaware inquiring on which bank its first family would pledge their allegiance. As late as April 29, 1861, after Fort Sumter had been fired upon and the Civil War begun, Charles du Pont Bird of Dover sent an urgent letter to rebellious Virginia assuring that "some of the du Ponts are friendly to the South."[2] For no small reason, the message was considered important enough to find its way into the hands of the Confederate commander-in-chief, General Robert E. Lee.

2. FATTENING THE WALLET

As angry Carolina batteries pounded Fort Sumter into dead silence, a long train of anxious Delawarians filed up to Eleutherian Mills only to find its master absent from his usual duties. Henry du Pont had slipped out of the state, igniting a wildfire of rumors. Perhaps to Virginia, some speculated, or Maryland? All Delaware was soon ablaze with excitement over the prospect.

But this shrewdest of Irénée du Pont's sons was no fool to private emotions. Du Pont Company's wealth, he well understood, didn't depend on slave labor, but on a strong, doling Washington, and Lincoln had made contact months before the outbreak of war. Like his father and brother before him, Henry's heart ultimately followed his wallet, and he suspected it would soon be fattened by a pledge of allegiance.

No sooner had the first Confederate cannon roared than Henry du Pont was seen scurrying about Washington, loudly pledging his undying loyalty to the flag and scooping up vast mounds of war contracts in the process. Between the first hostilities of April 11, 1861, and the year's end, Henry sold over $2.3 million worth of cannon and musket powder to the U.S. government,[3] the greatest boom in sales Du Pont had ever known. This ended forever the previous suggestion of his nephew, E. I. du Pont II, that the mills close down for a while, laying off five hundred workers. Instead, the mills were now worked day and night.

But even the Brandywine's vast reservoir of black powder wasn't enough to meet the war's needs. New kinds of weapons, 14-, 15-, and 20-inch naval guns, for example, needed a more powerful powder to propel huge projectiles. Black powder blasted instead of propelled. In tests using the best Du Pont powder, the big guns burst like bombs. What was needed was a powder that would produce a progressively burning propellant that would apply its energy in the barrel and not suddenly in the breech.

Captain Thomas J. Rodman, U.S.A., assisted by young Lammot du Pont, had labored on this problem before the war, and in 1859 developed what Rodman called "Mammoth Powder." This powder was composed of grains ranging in sizes from walnuts to baseballs, depending on gun caliber. The larger grains burned at a slower rate of combustion, allowing the generated energy time to take the line of least resistance—the open barrel. With Rodman's discovery, Lammot du Pont was able to separate propellant and disruptive lines of powder in Du Pont's mass production. Thus, when the war broke out, Lammot du Pont was the only man familiar enough with Rodman's work who also had the manufacturing ability to put Mammoth Powder into mass production for battle use. It was this Du Pont powder that gave the North's naval guns crucial superior firing power during the war.

Other crises arose for Du Pont Company during these early years of the war. By the end of 1861 the government's supply of Indian saltpeter was already running low and Lincoln feared that British sympathies for the South (and its cotton) might close the British East Indies market of saltpeter to the Union. One day Lammot du Pont, still in his twenties, was summoned to Washington. There, in the midst of a war-bustled White House, Lammot quietly listened to the words of a worried president. When at last his ears deciphered their meaning, he stood with mouth agape.

He was being asked to sail to England and singlehandedly corner the world's saltpeter market in the name of Du Pont Company. Five hundred thousand dollars in U.S. gold bullion would be sent him in London on the next American steamer after he arrived. Would he do it? Swallowing a stammer with a loud gulp, Lammot fingered his close-cropped beard and agreed, but on one condition: Du Pont Company must be awarded the government contract to refine the saltpeter. Even at such a tense moment emerged the Du Pont instinct to squeeze every drop of profit out of an opportunity. It was just such an ability to exploit history that would someday make Du Pont a name known on six continents.

3. ROBBING THE GOLDEN FLEECE

On the brisk fall morning of November 19, 1861, a tall, lanky man with an American accent and a black fringe beard, and wearing a black suit and top hat stepped ashore in England. Immediately, because of his resemblance to Abraham Lincoln, he caused quite a stir. Within days, however, the local stir grew into a national uproar.

Traveling throughout the markets of London, Liverpool, and Greenock, within nine days this man quietly bought up all the saltpeter in Britain. Everywhere, from the House of Rothschild to the Bank of England, he became a mysterious overnight legend. As the market became depleted, his buying soon drove up prices for saltpeter and he, in turn, was suddenly pressed by his creditors for prompt payment. If he didn't procure the necessary funds quickly, he was told, he would lose everything he had so masterfully captured.

A few mornings later the office of Barings, Brown, Shipley & Company, an agent for Du Pont Company, had a visitor, a young man claiming to be Lammot du Pont of Delaware and asking for a "small" loan of half a million dollars. The numbed agents gathered their nerve and courteously showed their visitor to the door. A day or so later, when Peabody & Company announced it had advanced Lammot du Pont the money, cries of anguish emanated from Barings, Brown, Shipley & Company, while that tall man whom they did not believe met the arrival of the third steamship from America since his arrival, carrying in its hold $500,000 worth of gold bullion.

Hardly had Lammot paid off his creditors and begun loading the saltpeter than the London *Times* suddenly fired another bombshell, publicly opposing the shipment. Bewildered, Lammot read that the U.S. warship *San Jacinto* had forced a British ship, the *Trent,* to stop on the high seas as it left Havana. After firing a shot across her bow, federal troops had boarded the *Trent* and seized James Mason and John Slidell, commissioners from the Confederate states on their way to England. With the enthusiastic approval of a jubilant Congress, the southern emissaries were then imprisoned in Boston. England immediately issued a note of protest, correctly charging that the boarding was a violation of international rights since the *Trent* was in international waters flying the British flag. With the cool tenacity of an English bulldog, London demanded Slidell and Mason's safe return. Until this was done, the *Times* now insisted, the Union should be prevented from purchasing the saltpeter.

Beneath all the legal platitudes the paper bellowed, Lammot knew that the London *Times* spoke for Britain's economic rulers and guessed his time was running out. He quickly finished chartering his ship and crew and was just loading the last of the cargo when a British customs officer appeared at the dock demanding to inspect the owner's credentials. Lammot handed them over, hoping that would be all, but the officer then requested that Lammot accompany him to the customs house. With a wink to his crew, Lammot agreed, but actually the tall, bearded American had other ideas. As he left the dock following the customs officer, Lammot whispered to the captain of his ship to prepare to sail at a moment's notice.

Now, one might suppose a normal procedure in such circumstances would be to dispose of these small affairs of state as quickly as possible and renew his efforts to escape with his prize. But such was not the way of Lammot du Pont. An insatiable appetite to learn the hidden intricacies of state maneuvers had been the secret of the Du Ponts' ability to harvest the rich fields of government patronage since Versailles, and this great-grandson of Pierre Du Pont had learned well the family's skill.

On the way to the customs house, Lammot induced the doltish officer to share lunch with him. Sated with food, wine, pleasantries, and flattery, the officer soon blurted out that it was actually the British Prime Minister, Lord Palmerston, who had ordered Lammot's ship docked as part of a new British embargo on all shipments to America. It was all the sad confirmation that Lammot needed.

Later, rid of his official chore at the credentials house, Lammot returned to his ship and quietly ordered the captain to sail at high tide, 4:00 A.M. the next morning. London, however, was no Sebastopol when it came to eluding the will of the British stock market. A file of armed redcoats on the wharf the next morning saw to that.

As silently as he came, Lammot then took leave of England alone on another ship, and returned to Washington. There, in his characteristically unassuming way, Lammot quietly suggested to Lincoln that he threaten Britain with war. And just as quietly, Lincoln agreed, ordering Secretary of State Seward to draw up young du Pont's credentials. All this, however, was only a toothless bluff to rescue the tattered vestiges of the Union's pride. A few days before, Lincoln had received an ultimatum from London threatening war itself unless Slidell and Mason were immediately released. At the same time, reports came in that thousands of British troops had sailed for Canada. Faced with the dilemma of war on two fronts, Lincoln surrendered to compromise, releasing the southerners with full apologies. On January 1, 1862, Slidell and Mason boarded ship to resume their journey to England.

On that day also, from another ship, Lammot du Pont watched the

American shore dip into a watery horizon. A few weeks later he arrived in London and four times pressed his name at 10 Downing Street only to be rebuffed each time. Indeed, it was the kind of treatment a Du Pont was unused to, and Lammot finally decided to literally grip destiny by the throat.

While waiting there for an appointment one day, Lammot suddenly bolted from a chair and rushed past attendants right into Lord Palmerston's private office. Before a startled but amused ruler of the world's largest empire, Lammot du Pont then laid down his own ultimatum: saltpeter or war. Clearly agitated by the whole affair, the Prime Minister promised to have a decision by the afternoon. But Lammot fired back that that was impossible and concluded that war seemed the only alternative. He would sail for the United States the next day, he explained, and left.

That evening, while not exactly enjoying his last dinner at Morley's Hotel, Lammot had a surprising visitor—the Prime Minister. Lord Palmerston joined him at a table and whispered that his permit would be granted the next day; the British Empire was bending, although a bit amusedly, to a Du Pont. But Lammot, as stubborn as ever, insisted one be rendered on the spot. Palmerston, although embarrassed by the youth's impulsiveness, scribbled off a permit and commented that he was at liberty to state confidentially to Mr. Lincoln that scarcely for any cause now would England go to war with America. He did not, however, mention why—the opposition, as Senator Hoar of Massachusetts would later put it in 1879, of "workers of Lancashire."

By February 2, Lammot's shipment of 4 million pounds of saltpeter was sailing over the ocean bound for America. It was an important and prosperous victory for the family, fully supplying the North's (and Du Pont's) war effort for an entire year. Thereafter, relaxed tensions between Britain and the United States allowed easier purchases, and, for Du Pont, easier profits.

4. ADMIRAL SAMUEL F. DU PONT—THE PRIDE AND DISGRACE

Lammot du Pont was not the only member of his family who prominently served the federal government during the Civil War. The very blockade of southern ports that had indirectly caused the capture of Slidell and Mason and jeopardized Lammot's mission was the work of none other than Lammot's colorful cousin, Rear Admiral Samuel F. du Pont.

If family legend would have its way, Sam was an old, whiskered sea warrior when he received his commission as a midshipman in the U.S.

Navy at the age of 12. In fact, Sam rose steadily into the Navy's upper ranks through a passion for both service and connections. His very first commission had been arranged by his grandfather, Père Du Pont, as a personal favor from President Thomas Jefferson. The second break for this elder son of Victor du Pont came during the Mexican War, when, given command of the warship U.S.S. *Cayane,* Commander du Pont ravished the Gulf of California and won his first official recognition. Typically, Sam's superior at that time was Commodore William Shubrick, an in-law through his cousin and sister-in-law Julia du Pont. After that Sam was appointed a member of the board to organize the Naval Academy, winning for himself the title of "Father of Annapolis." From there, Sam joined the Lighthouse Board and then the infamous Naval Efficiency Board, where he made a notorious name for himself as a butcher of naval careers.

In July of 1857, Samuel (now Captain) du Pont was given not only one of the Navy's finest ships, the U.S.S. *Minnesota,* but also one of its most important duties up to that time: the William B. Reed diplomatic mission to China. Again, "A long friendly acquaintance with the Minister," Sam admitted, "doubtless assisted in getting me the command."[4] It was a fortunate, artful coincidence in the finest of Du Pont traditions.

Although it proved to hold little historical weight against the gigantic drama unfolding between the states, the Reed Mission was considered important at the time of its launching. The United States was interested in opening new markets for products from its growing industries. Europe, long the consumer of most of America's exports, was simply not enough of a profitable market by the 1850's, and the movement to the Pacific Coast was induced partly by lucrative trading prospects with China's huge population—a tremendous market for American shirts, tobacco, and manufactured goods. As early as 1800, twenty-three United States vessels had visited Canton with $2.5 million in cargo. By 1832 seven firms and twenty U.S. merchants were regularly trading with China, and by 1850 furs (particularly sealskins) from the Northwest had also found their way to the besieged giant of the East.[5]

The economic motivations for the mission, however, held little interest for Captain du Pont. What did interest Sam almost to the point of fatigue was his ship and crew. Captain du Pont especially was alarmed about the caliber of seamen under his command. On September 7, 1857, he reported to the Secretary of Navy that his crew was below mediocrity. But Sam had a broad solution to the whole problem. "As seamen are so inferior to what they formerly were," he wrote the Secretary, "the landsmen should be selected with more care and should not all of them be taken from our large cities from which we get some of the most vicious and worthless of their population."[6] Instead, the snapping obedience of a naïve country boy was closer to Sam's heart.

Du Ponts were seldom impressed by anything—not even a country—not connected with their firm, and Captain Samuel du Pont was certainly no exception. China, bleeding giant of hundreds of millions, was regarded by Sam with a Western arrogance familiar to conquerors. What did impress Sam upon his arrival in China was not China, but the European, and particularly British, warships patrolling its waters. In fact, Sam was downright jealous. These invading forces had just completed a successful war against the Chinese Imperial regime to win Britain's "right" to continue dumping her $17 million annual Indian opium trade on China, despite a Chinese edict of prohibition since 1838.

China had suffered heavy losses in that joint European attack of 1842 and was subsequently forced to allow her population to become addicts for British profits. In addition, the cities of Canton, Amoy, Foochow, Ningpo, and Shanghai were opened for "trade" with other European powers, and the port of Hong Kong permanently ceded to the London Stock Exchange.

Then, in 1856 and 1857, the people of Canton rose in rebellion and began burning down foreign factories, the very essence of their exploitation. The British imperialists immediately waged war for more trade concessions and were joined by the Russian Czar and the new French Republic, both lusting for profitable treaty "revisions." Russia and France, for varying reasons, then invited the United States to join as a treaty power, spurring the Reed Mission. The United States, however, wanted to remain neutral in the fighting now taking place between the attacking Europeans and the resisting Chinese. Such neutrality, Washington reasoned, might result in more friendly relations with Peking and greater trade dividends than joining in the attack would return.

Sam du Pont disagreed. No sooner had he arrived and witnessed the piracy of the European warships than he developed a sudden passion for China's economy. With the cavalier attitude of a Brandywine aristocrat, Captain du Pont demanded that Washington allow him to join in the looting. "Our present neutrality does not enhance us in the slightest degree in their [Chinese] good opinion or good will," he wrote Delaware's Senator Bayard on November 24. "In short, they do not reason by our standard of ethics or anything else, and it seems quite absurd to judge them the same."[7]

Sam didn't get his wish; the orders stood firm: no United States participation. Sam had to resign himself to pining away aboard the *Minnesota*, listening to foreign cannon roar against the harbor, watching enviously from his ship as European forces successfully attacked fort after fort, finally hammering the city of Canton into submission in December. Canton's provincial viceroy, Yeh, was seized by the British and kidnapped to Calcutta, India, where he was imprisoned.

Yeh may have been one of the lucky ones. Canton became a hellhole for its Chinese population during the British occupation. British seamen looted, raped, and started fights that sometimes resulted in murder of Chinese. The Western forces heaped a barrage of violence on the defenseless population, treating them with open racist contempt. Indeed, it was surprising to no one that the people of Canton were hostile to the foreign invaders—no one, that is, except Captain du Pont. Sam was infuriated that the Cantonese were not cloaked in the slick veneer of politeness known to the upper-class Mandarins. "They [the Cantonese] are a stiff-necked people by themselves," he wrote in a huff, "and will have to be treated as such."[8] Apparently, Reed agreed. "The powers of Western civilization must insist on what they know to be their rights and give up the dream of dealing with China as a power to which ordinary rules apply."[9]

Nothing sparked Sam to action like defending American business interests overseas. When it was feared that the oppressed Chinese population of Macao might rise in an insurrection that would endanger U.S. investments there, Sam charged his warship across the sea to the rescue, occupying the port from December 30, 1857, to February 27, 1858. By March 24 he was again in the Chinese interior, prowling along the Yangtze River, this time forcibly intervening for a white merchant faced with revolt by his Chinese crew. For Samuel du Pont, the interests of civilization and white supremacy were synonymous. This position would remain unchanged even during the bitterest hostilities against southern slaveholders during the Civil War.

Days of Pride

Slowly, with an uneasy gait, the blue-uniformed soldiers rode through the streets of Baltimore, and as they filed past the rows of houses with their tall, white marbled steps, crowds of white residents began to form along the side. The shouts soon came—"Damned Yankees!"—but the men from Massachusetts looked straight ahead, trying to get their regiment of militia through the city as quickly as possible and on to the endangered capital, trying not to notice what had become the mounting fury of a racist mob. Suddenly, the venom that had been so strengthened by the Confederate attack on Sumter only a week before, spilled out onto the streets, and the entire regiment was under attack. Before it was over, a number of Union soldiers had been killed or wounded.

A few hours later, a hundred miles to the north, Captain Samuel du Pont, commander of the Philadelphia Naval Yard since his return from

China, received word that all railroad communications between the nation's capital and the North had been cut. Only Annapolis, Maryland, still had a line open to Washington. Captain du Pont immediately assumed responsibility for restoring communications and fired off a series of orders to all the forces of the Yard under his command. Soon Union ships were steaming between Philadelphia and Annapolis, opening a vital sea line of contact between the North and the endangered seat of government.

As reward for his quick initiative, Samuel du Pont was appointed president of the commission delegated to select a permanent naval base in the South for a proposed Union blockade off the southeastern coast. Port Royal, South Carolina, one of the finest and deepest harbors in America, was chosen as the target, and Sam du Pont was given command of the attack.

As Commodore of the South Atlantic Blockading Squadron, Samuel du Pont commanded the largest fleet in U.S. naval history up to that time: 75 ships, including 25 Army transports, and 14,000 troops under Brigadier General Thomas West Sherman. All these forces gathered at Hampton Roads, Virginia, a vast armada spreading out before Sam's astonished eyes. It was a huge responsibility, but as Sam well knew, also a huge opportunity to enhance his naval career. On October 29, 1861, Commodore du Pont cast his die of ships to the fortune of the sea.

It almost proved a disaster. As the fleet advanced down the coast, nature rose to render Sam some justifiable fears. A thick, dark storm suddenly rolled over the sky and hit the fleet with hurricane winds. Throughout the entire tempest, as rain and sea lashed against his flagship, the *Wabash,* Sam could do nothing but trust his junior officers to keep the fleet together. When the rain finally lifted, he was heartsick: not a ship was in sight, just the choppy waves of a hungry sea. By November 3 at 8:00 P.M. he could see only seven ships from his flagship, and he was beginning to fear the worst. But within twenty-four hours Sam's eyes widened gleefully as twenty-five ships anchored off Port Royal, many more dotting the horizon.

As his fleet flocked around him once more, Sam ordered the dangerous shoal outside Port Royal buoyed and breached by the lighter vessels, those under 18 feet of draft. Then, as silently as cats moving in on their prey, the heavy gunboats slipped over, and finally the *Wabash.* "The responsibility of hazarding so noble a frigate was not a light one," Du Pont wrote with characteristic modesty in his official report. "Over a prolonged bar of over two miles there was but a foot or two of water to spare, and the fall and rise of the tide is such that if she had grounded she would have sustained most serious injury from straining, if not become a total loss. Too much, however, was at stake to hesitate and the result was entirely successful. . . .

The safe passage of this great ship over the bar was hailed by gratifying cheers from the crowded vessels."[10] The credit for the skillful maneuver, however, did not really belong to Sam but, as his own biographer points out, to the careful examination and calculation by Captains C. H. Davis and C. O. Boutell, U.S.N.[11] In effect, all Sam had to do was sail across the shoal when instructed to by his junior officers.

With the bar crossed, the attack began in earnest. By circling in constant motion, the Union ships were able to avoid serious damage from the shore batteries while levying a furious barrage of their own. Soon, some excellent Du Pont Mammoth Powder reduced the rebel forts to silence, and Port Royal was in Union hands. Sam did not attend to the Union occupation. Commander Charles Henry Davis, his Chief of Staff, and Commander John Rodgers were the ones who actually went ashore in a raiding party, discovered that the forts had been abandoned, and hoisted the Union banner. Meanwhile, Sam was busy writing his formal reports to Washington. "The two, Rodgers and Davis, are off on the other side to see the Bay Point occupation and forts," he wrote his wife, "and I am going to set to work on my reports."[12]

It was Du Pont's greatest victory, the circular motion tactic winning him an unqualified reputation as a skilled professional warrior. But Sam's claim to fame was almost immediately challenged as stolen from his Chief of Staff, Charles Davis. Davis's son and biographer years later claimed that "the tactics of the battle, which were Davis's own, were masterful."[13] Sam howled in outrage to his wife about the accusations, but they were later supported by Secretary of Navy Gideon Welles, who reported that Rear Admiral Sylvanus W. Godon had told him that "the attack by sailing in a circle was not part of the original plan (of Du Pont), but an expedient, an afterthought, when it was found more convenient to move from under fire than to remain."[14] Davis, according to Welles, was indeed the author of the circling tactic, not Samuel du Pont.*

---

* There are some questions that must be raised as to the fairness of this serious charge of fraud. First, Welles was no friend of du Pont, as we shall see later; second, Welles' charges were not made until two years after du Pont's death, although there were other charges from other individuals earlier. Nevertheless, charges are not restricted to being made by friends in order to be acceptable to either a court of inquiry or a curious historian, and the Secretary's delayed timing of his charges may well have been an act of kindness to an already disgraced du Pont following his disaster at Charleston. More likely, there may have been a political motive for the delay: discrediting the fame of du Pont might have affected morale during these difficult early days of the war when such exhilarating victories as Port Royal were infrequent against the barrage of defeats plaguing the Union cause. Moreover, Welles' charges against du Pont and his reference to Admiral Godon were made in 1867, while Godon was still alive. In the next twelve years of his life, Godon never

Nevertheless, it was Samuel du Pont who proudly wore the wreath of Port Royal's conqueror, receiving the gratitude of a relieved Congress on February 22, 1862, and being appointed Rear Admiral, a new title given to the highest naval officers. Delawarians even presented their hero with a silver sword. Sam had never been able to feign humility. He was ecstatic.

After Port Royal, Admiral du Pont intensified the southern blockade in hope of cutting off the population of the rebellious states from needed supplies. Then he attacked northern Florida, occupying Jacksonville and capturing control of the St. John's River. This effectively sealed off blockade runners. Sam also captured control of the Savannah River. At this time, had Sam landed troops, he might have been able to take Charleston and Savannah. But he didn't, because of his own hesitancy as well as that of Secretary of War Edwin Stanton. Within a short while the opportunity was lost as Confederate General Robert E. Lee moved some of his forces into the area.

Still another opportunity was lost when Du Pont's junior officers, Commanders Davis and Rodgers, seized the initiative and moved their gunboats up the Savannah River to seal off Fort Pulaski from the city of Savannah. This accomplished, they then fired upon and seized the fort. Admiral du Pont then intervened and ordered them to relinquish their prizes, claiming Savannah had little strategic value and that he had not enough troops to hold it. It was to prove to be one of the most serious naval blunders of the Civil War, a key factor in the Admiral's first and last defeat and the U.S. Navy's worst disaster up to that time.

---

denied them, nor does the ship's log or any naval document substantiate du Pont's claim that the successful tactics were his own. In fact, the charges were so strong within the months after the battle that du Pont was forced on May 5, 1867, to reassure his cousin-wife of his veracity. "The essential idea that the ships must not anchor was mine,"[15] he wrote, claiming to have instructed Commodore Davis, Captain John Rodgers, and Captain C. R. P. Rodgers (fleet captain) as the battle approached. This claim, however, went unsubstantiated by either C. R. P. Rodgers or John Rodgers, and in fact was contradicted by Davis and Secretary Welles. Du Pont also saw fit never to make this particular claim public.

Instead, years later Samuel du Pont's nephew, Colonel Henry A. du Pont, wrote Sam's biography, attempting to bury the charges of fraud by merely referring to the Admiral's letter to his wife, and by remarking that in 1875, during Henry's visit with Admiral Godon in Paris, Godon "spoke in the most warm and appreciative terms of Admiral du Pont."[16] In the biography, Henry strove to create the impression that no rift existed between Godon and his uncle. It was a needless, confusing point, for the fact that no rift may have existed between Godon and du Pont does not in any way answer the charges of Davis and Welles, since it was not Godon, but Davis, who allegedly had his rewards stolen from him by du Pont and had cause for personal antagonism. Whether Henry even brought up the charges during his visit with Godon is unknown, for no comment is made of them; Henry was not able to even comment that Godon had denied them.

Crisis at Charleston

In the cold early weeks of March 1862 a huge, bizarre form was seen moving in the waters of Hampton Roads. It was a strange, ugly monster bellowing steam and covered with a thick, gray skin of armor. The ironclad *Virginia,* formerly the frigate U.S.S. *Merrimac,* was entering history.

Quickly, the *Virginia* crushed two federal vessels as if they were made of paper, and the entire future success of Admiral du Pont's blockade looked jeopardized. A ripple of panic swept through the Union naval ranks as the Confederate ironclad overnight became lord of the eastern seaboard. Its reign, however, was short-lived, for soon an even stranger ironclad, described by Confederates as "a cheesebox on a raft," steamed into Hampton Roads to challenge the *Virginia* for supremacy of the seas. It was the *Monitor*.

On March 9, 1862, the two ships clashed for hours, the *Virginia*'s broadsides bouncing off the iron suit of its adversary while the *Monitor* delivered blow after decisive blow from its swivel-turreted gun fired with the newest burning hell from the Brandywine: Du Pont Mammoth Powder. Ultimately, the *Monitor*'s maneuverability and high-powered cannon won the edge of victory. The Union's blockade was saved, sealing the fate of the Confederacy.

With the battle of the *Monitor* and the *Virginia* dawned a new age of metal ships, eclipsing forever the wooden world of the old Navy. Emboldened by the military and propaganda prospects of ironclads, Lincoln ordered many more built, not only to strengthen the blockage but also to turn the Union's naval strategy toward taking the offensive. On January 6, 1863, Secretary of the Navy Gideon Welles ordered monitors to be sent to Admiral du Pont's fleet for use in an attack on Charleston, South Carolina. "The capture of this most important port rests solely upon the success of the naval force," Welles wrote Du Pont, "and it is committed to your hands to execute."[17] These were fateful words, shaping the doomed strategy of an overzealous naval commander only too eager to impress his superiors.*

---

* For over a century now the Du Ponts have waged a relentless publicity campaign trying to hide this most dishonored of their family skeletons. They have had biased biographies of the Admiral published and speeches made that rewrite history in the light that most protects and favors the family name. Even Congress has fallen into line by reinstalling the name of Samuel du Pont among the country's naval heroes, naming a circle in Washington, D.C. after this first son of Victor du Pont.

Ask any Du Pont today about Admiral du Pont's defeat at Charleston and his forced resignation in disgrace, and they will point accusingly at Secretary of Navy Gideon Welles. Du Pont's defeat at Charleston, they insist, was caused by Welles'

Sam du Pont's first move of genius was to leave behind most of his fleet. The *Canandaigua, Housatonic, Unadilla, Wissahickon,* and *Huron,* all

alleged insistence on purely a naval victory, barring the use of troops and wooden ships.

History, however, stands in refutation. On January 28, 1863, Admiral du Pont answered Welles' original orders with the comment that the use of troops was necessary "to secure success."[18] In all the ensuing months of communication, Welles never contradicted this suggestion. Nor did du Pont ever make a specific request for *more* troops. If protocol prevented this on the part of a naval officer (as the Admiral's biographer insists[19]), du Pont could easily have written to the regional military commander attached to his command and inquired of the general's plans and opinion as to whether the Army had enough troops at its disposal in the event of the necessity of military assistance in the attack. But this was never done. Nor did du Pont object when General Hunter, commanding the Union troops in the campaign, evacuated his forces from James Island, an impregnable base of operations against Charleston. Du Pont remained silent and cheerful, despite objections from more farsighted (and perhaps courageous) subordinate officers like Captain Percival Drayton, U.S.N. On July 2, 1862, Drayton felt compelled to write du Pont that "I for one do not believe that Charleston can be taken except through James Island."[20] Drayton's opinion should have been given more weight by the Admiral: the Captain was from South Carolina and knew Charleston extensively.

Contrary to du Pont's later claims, Secretary Welles did not order nor expect a purely naval attack on Charleston by du Pont, although he doubted how much the Army would be able to assist. "This Department," he wrote du Pont on May 13, 1862, "has determined to capture Charleston as soon as Richmond falls, which will relieve the iron boats *Galena* and *Monitor.* . . . The War Department sent instructions today to General Hunter with whom you will cooperate fully, unless the move should be purely naval, when we will render you every assistance."[21] Six months went by and there is no record that the latter option was ever entertained by Washington. On January 6, 1863, Welles informed du Pont that "General Hunter will be sent to Port Royal with about ten thousand men to act as shall be deemed best, after consultation with yourself."[22]

Throughout the fourteen months of planning the attack, du Pont's communiques were very vague, either for reasons of a careerist's fear of his superiors or in order to keep his superiors in the dark about his plan for a purely ironclad attack that he believed would win him Washington's accolade, or perhaps simply because du Pont's plans were themselves vague. For some reason, no request for additional troops was ever made. Nor did du Pont ever advise Welles of the extent of Confederate troop and battery strength along the river. Welles even remarked with concern on January 31, 1863, "The Department is not acquainted with the harbor obstructions constructed by the rebels and therefore cannot advise with you in regard to those obstacles."[23]

Instead of requesting additional troops, du Pont complained to Welles about not having enough *wooden* ships. Welles explained that only ironclads were available, as the blockade's spare wooden ships were pursuing the Confederates' *Florida* and *Alabama* in the West Indies. "The Department does not desire to urge an attack on Charleston with inadequate means," Welles cautioned du Pont, "and if, after careful examination, you deem the number of ironclads insufficient to render the capture of that post reasonably certain, it must be abandoned."[24]

Nevertheless, with the opportunity for glory and duty beckoning, Admiral du Pont, commanding the U.S.S. *New Ironsides,* led eight ironclads into the greatest disaster in the history of the United States Navy up to that time.

warships of considerable effectiveness but of the wooden variety, were left in reserve outside the harbor bar. Sam also left behind the huge *Wabash* and four other gunboats, the *Vermont, Paul Jones, Sebago,* and *Marblehead,* to protect U.S. Army positions at Hilton Head and Beaufort. Of course, this all would have been unnecessary had Sam instead decided to use those 10,000 troops to help his attack on the well-fortified southern harbor.

The streets of Charleston were filled with gray-uniformed Confederate troops in that April of 1863. Horses, pulling their loads of cannon and ammunition, raced up and down the main thoroughfares, charging the residents with a mood of anticipation. Yet, the normal business of the "peculiar institution" went on undisturbed: wagons brimming with Black faces scarred with fear and angry frustration rolled into the auction place to constitute Carolina's most lucrative trade—slavery. Along the daisied walks in front of the huge white mansions of the city strolled dainty southern belles, colorful parasols shading their bleached-white skin. Indeed, Charleston seemed a smug little town, gilded with the trappings of stolen wealth and labor, sure of the perpetuity of its existence.

Only when strange thunderclaps broke into the quiet noon of April 7, only when Admiral Samuel du Pont had fired his mammoth cannon into the sweet spring air, did the city sense the frightening imminence of what had so proudly been hailed as war.

Sam's ship, the U.S.S. *New Ironsides,* was positioned in the middle of the battle formation and protected by surrounding ironclads so "signals could be better made to both ends of the line."[25] But the hazy weather of the South's spring had stopped their advance and the Admiral elected to wait another day. At noon on April 7, the attack—and the chaos—began.

"I made signal to the vessels to weigh anchor," Sam later reported, "having previously ordered them not to reply to the batteries on Morgan Island, but reserve their fire until they could pass Fort Sumter, in case there were no obstructions, and attack its northwest face."[26] For Du Pont to assume there were no obstructions was amazing. It reveals his unconcern about informing Secretary Welles of such an important battle aspect earlier. Obstructions were there, all right: rows of casks strung from piles extending from none other than James Island, a strategic position previously abandoned by the Union army with the full concordance of the Admiral.

It was a catastrophe. Snagged like a trapped school of tuna, the fleet could only endure the murderous fire poured down on them from Fort Moultrie and all the Confederate batteries on Sullivan's Island, Morris Island, and Fort Sumter. The positioning of the Admiral's boat (ostensibly to facilitate communications) proved disastrous when the monitors' line found the *New Ironsides* clumsily blocking their attempts to maneuver.

Sam meanwhile refused to return fire at Fort Sumter "without great risk," he believed, "of firing into them" (his own ships). It was total chaos, with Sam bumbling in the middle. As a final self-inflicted injury, he even crashed his own ship against two of the other ironclads.

Within forty minutes after the battle began, five of the ironclads were disabled and all had been hit. In anticipation of easy victory, Sam had allowed Henry Villard, a reporter from the New York *Tribune,* on board the *New Ironsides* for a coloring of glory. The publicity stunt backfired. Even inexperienced Villard, who tried his best to be generous in his account, could see that the Father of Annapolis and conqueror of Port Royal had stumbled into the deadliest of traps. "As the forts and batteries like so many vomiting craters of volcanoes sent forth one torrent of destruction after another," he reported, "my heart failed and panged with fear of seeing the little monitors shivered into atoms."[27]

Apparently, Villard wasn't the only man on board who panged with fear. Without his *New Ironsides* having fired more than a single round, although she was but 1,000 yards from Sumter's batteries, Sam sounded the retreat for both his attack and his career.

Days of Disgrace

As Villard feared, Du Pont's fleet of monitors did indeed come close to being shivered into atoms. The *Keokuk,* for example, was hit over ninety times, its armored body punched with gaping holes. Even the *New Ironsides,* which suffered no real material damage—because of its position in the middle of the formation, it was shielded by the other monitors—was hit sixty to seventy times.

"During the evening," the Admiral later reported, "the commanding officers of the monitors came on board my flagship and, to my regret, I soon became convinced of the utter impracticability of taking the city of Charleston by the force under my command."[28] Actually, Sam needed little convincing. In fact, contrary to the impression conveyed in his official report, Sam hadn't even asked his junior officers for their opinions. The *Tribune* reporter was present at the time and recorded that "The Admiral quietly received their reports, but did not ask for their opinion."[29]

Ignoring the unused remainder of his fleet, Du Pont still considered using only ironclads that had already been engaged in a disastrous battle. "I had hoped that the endurance of the ironclads would have enabled them to have borne any weight to which they might have been exposed," he wrote, "but the weight of the Confederate batteries' firing power had been too great."[30] Du Pont's fleet altogether fired only 139 projectiles, the turret guns of the monitors being able to fire only once every seven or ten minutes. In contrast, the rebels fired 2,220 projectiles, according to the most conservative estimate. The Philadelphia *Public Ledger* of April 14, 1863, reported 3,500 shots fired from 400 to 500 rebel guns.

The next morning the *Keokuk* sank. Again, Du Pont refused to consider the rest of his fleet for a renewal of the attack. "The reserved squadron of wooden vessels referred to in my general order of battle under Captain J. F. Green of the *Canandaigua* was always in readiness," he reported, "but their service in the engagement was not called into action."[31] As far as Sam was concerned, the attack was over.

Unfortunately for the hero of the Brandywine, the President of the United States disagreed.

On April 13 President Lincoln telegraphed Du Pont ordering him to stay within the bar at Charleston and prevent the rebels from erecting batteries on Morris Island. Du Pont defiantly refused, claiming the ships, because of poor anchorage, were endangered by an easterly gale.

On April 14 Lincoln tried again, ordering Du Pont and General Hunter to take the batteries on Morris and Sullivan Islands. "We still hope," wired Lincoln, "that by cordial and judicious cooperation you [Du Pont and Hunter] can take the batteries on Morris Island and Sullivan's Island and Fort Sumter. But whether you can or not, we wish the demonstration kept up for a time for a collateral and very important object."[32] The meaning of Lincoln's order as Commander-in-Chief was obvious: continue the attack even as only a diversion for a military assault being planned elsewhere.

Du Pont again refused, now belatedly claiming he needed more troops. General Hunter was furious. He suggested another attack immediately, employing his 10,000 troops. Still Du Pont refused.

By now Hunter was desperate. On May 22 he wrote Lincoln charging that the Admiral had ignored his troops both during the attack and now, after the attack. "I fear Admiral du Pont distrusts the ironclads so much that he has resolved to do nothing with them this summer, and I therefore most earnestly beg you to liberate me from those orders to cooperate with the Navy which now tie me down to share the Admiral's inactivity."[33]

Hunter proposed a daring invasion of Georgia. He promised to raise an army of freed Black slaves, commission their officers, and begin a march burning the plantations of slaveholders. Hunter's abolitionist colors were showing, and Lincoln would have no part of it. In Colonel Henry A. du Pont's words, it was "a plain violation of the laws of civilized warfare," but not too uncivilized for General Sherman to receive permission to do exactly the same thing a year later. What made the crucial difference was Hunter's plan to arm the Black slaves. That, Lincoln felt, was too radical an approach toward war against slavemasters. The "Great Emancipator" had limits to emancipation.

Immediately after his refusal to renew the attack, Admiral du Pont came under public criticism, first from Secretary Welles and then from his own lieutenant-commander on the *New Ironsides,* George E. Belknap, a relation of W. W. Belknap, then serving in a high post in the War Department and later Secretary of War under Grant. But when critical remarks also flew from his chief engineer, Alban Stimers, Sam struck back. Whereas Belknap was related to circles of power, Stimers was a mere chief engineer, whom any admiral could handle. Stimers was promptly arrested and put on trial for insubordination. Luckily for the engineer, Secretary Welles intervened and rescued him from the Admiral's storm of vengeance.

Most northern newspapers handled Du Pont's defeat diplomatically and generously; most, that is, except one. On April 15 the Baltimore *American* carried an account of the battle under the title, "HOW NOT TO DO IT." Its editor, Charles C. Fulton, who as a reporter was at the Ogeechee River in the warship *Bibb* just before the Charleston attack, declared that "the operation against Charleston had been entrusted to incompetent hands."[34] Exactly one week later Sam asked the Navy Department to publicly intervene and reject the *American*'s condemnation, especially since Fulton's reports had received the censored approval of Assistant Secretary of the Navy Gustavus Fox.

As was usual by now, the Admiral's cries of outrage were poorly received in Washington. The Department simply replied that releasing Du Pont's official report would hurt U.S. morale because it was full of charges of the weaknesses of the ironclads. "What public benefit, let me ask, could be derived from its publicity," Welles asked Du Pont on May 15. "You had received both from the President and myself communications enjoining you to continue to menace Charleston in view of operations in other quarters."[35]

While Du Pont felt he had been unjustly criticized, one question haunted Washington: why didn't the Admiral suggest alternative plans for an attack on Charleston if, as he now claimed, the monitors were to blame? The answer was even more condemning than the Baltimore newspaper's charge of military incompetence: careerism. Right after the attack, already under criticism, Du Pont complained to his wife Sophie that "If consulted from time to time, if my opinion had been asked, I would have spoken freely."[36] Fearing the bad favor of Secretary Welles and other superiors, Sam had elected to remain silent and risk the lives of the men under his command. "Had you at any time expressed an opinion against the expediency of an attack," Welles wrote Du Pont on May 14, "or a belief that it would be disastrous, such was my confidence in you, and my respect for your intelligence and capability, that I should certainly have reviewed the subject, and not unlikely an entirely different arrangement of our forces would have been projected."[37]

Meanwhile, another defeat fell on our hapless hero. Sam had allowed the sunken *Keokuk*'s guns to fall into enemy hands.

The Admiral had given a monitor to Chief Engineer Edward Robie to blow up the wreck and then neglected the responsibility of seeing to the task's fulfillment. Although Robie failed in his attempt to use torpedoes to destroy the *Keokuk*, Du Pont had little concern for the successful carrying out of that task until it was too late. Under the cover of night, rebel divers removed the ship's guns.

By now, Welles had taken all his patience would endure. On April 16 Sam had written him a letter dripping with self-righteous honor. "I have to request," Du Pont had crowed, "that the Department will not hesitate to relieve me by any officer who, in its opinion, is more able to execute that service in which I have had the misfortune to fail—the capture of Charleston."[38] Welles decided to take Du Pont at his word. On June 3 he ordered Rear Admiral Andrew H. Foote to take over command of the South Atlantic Blockading Squadron. Later, Welles made a more explicit explanation for his decision by censuring Du Pont. "The duty of destroying the *Keokuk*, he angrily wrote the bewildered Delawarian, "and preventing her guns from falling into the hands of the rebels, devolved upon the commander-in-chief rather than on Chief Engineer Robie."[39]

Foote never lived to take command, much less take Charleston. He died en route from New York on June 26, and was replaced by Rear Admiral John A. Dahlgren, who took over Du Pont's command on July 6, 1863— but not before Admiral du Pont managed to engage in one final act of publicity piracy.

On June 10 the Confederate ironclad *Atlanta* was seen approaching Wassaw Sound on its way to attack the Union blockade. Sam ordered the monitors *Nahant* and *Weehawken,* commanded by the ever reliable Captain John Rodgers, to do battle. Seven days later, on June 17, the *Atlanta* appeared, accompanied by two wooden steamboats filled with gay southern spectators eager to see the hated Yankees get beaten at last.

Rodgers lost no time in spoiling their day. As soon as he was in range, he fired his cannon at the *Atlanta* four times, each time achieving a hit, forcing the battered warship to run aground and surrender. The two steamboats turned about and fled with their horrified passengers. It was one of the South's last great junkets.

The *Atlanta* had been taken, but the credit for the prize graced not the name of John Rodgers, but that of Samuel F. du Pont. "All look to it," he wrote triumphantly to Sophie, "as a special providence in my behalf."[40] His biographer claimed "the capture of the *Atlanta* by the *Weehawken* was primarily due to Du Pont's good judgment and to the promptitude with which he put his decisions into effect."[41]

Neither the public nor Congress was as impressed, however. On December 17, 1863, the Senate began an official inquiry into Admiral du Pont's conduct at Charleston. On January 13, 1864, the House of Representatives did likewise. As far as the public and the government were concerned, Samuel du Pont had led the U.S. Navy into the worst defeat of its history.

Admiral du Pont, his health broken by his forced retirement in complete disgrace, spent the next two years in seclusion at Louviers, his father's mansion on the Brandywine. Only here, by the familiar, constant grinding of the powder mills, was he able to find refuge from Congressional investigations and public damnation. Here, a man once considered as a possible future presidential nominee ended his life like his father—a failure. On June 23, 1865, at the age of 62, Samuel Francis du Pont died, of a broken heart, the family claimed. They were probably right.

5. HENRY A. DU PONT, HERO OF THE BRANDYWINE

In those terrible days of mass slaughter, the countryside of Virginia was covered with the human residue of battle. Thousands of men, their bodies torn and bleeding, would be laid side by side in an open field. There, each man would wait to die, lullabied to endless sleep by the low hum of a thousand lonely groans surrounding him and blending into a choir of death.

Such was the somber scene following the battle of Piedmont in June of 1864 when a thin federal officer waded silently through a vast blue lake of fallen compatriots, his eyes never lowering but fixed stright ahead, his black shiny boots never pausing in their gait but rising and falling; even after the blue sea of uniforms turned to gray, they still continued, stepping among the dead and dying, stopping only when they found the polished boots of a fellow officer.

There lay Colonel William H. Browne of the Confederate infantry, now a wounded prisoner, and now, as in the past at West Point, a good friend of Captain Henry A. du Pont, U.S.A., son of Henry du Pont, Sr. For a while, the two men talked the mutual language of aristocracy, expressing their anticipation of seeing each other during Browne's captivity. Finally, as he rose to leave, Henry asked his former classmate if he had any money. No, Browne replied, whereupon Du Pont reached into his pocket and drew out a ten dollar bill, and left.

Henry never saw Browne again. The Confederate officer died that night of his wounds and was deposited in a hollow Virginia grave the next morning. Years later, Henry would remark that his "most intimate and devoted friends were Southerners."[42]

Although it may seem strange that Henry A. du Pont fought so gallantly for the Union cause while harboring strong southern sympathies, the answer lies in the stronger bonds he felt toward the family code of hierarchy.

Henry du Pont had always wanted his son, Henry Algernon, to be the career soldier that family duty and company crisis had prevented him from becoming. From his earliest days, Henry Algernon just assumed that his military career was inevitable, and after his appointment to the Military Academy he more than satisfied his father's ambitions. When he graduated on May 6, 1861, Henry was first in his class. Not surprisingly, this oldest son of the de facto ruler of Delaware was also a first-class snob, considering West Point not aristocratic enough for a descendant of Pontius Cominius, the legendary Roman ancestor of the Du Ponts. During his tenure as a cadet, Henry's letters reveal that he had more in common with schoolmates from the southern planter class than with northerners, not merely because Delaware was also a slave state with common problems, but because of common aristocratic airs.[43]

Eventually, Henry found his father's stern aristocratic training useful on the battlefield. Put in command of an artillery unit, he quickly rose to the position of Chief of Artillery of the Department of Virginia and later of the Army of Virginia, holding the rank of brevet Captain. In 1864 he commanded Light Battery B of the Fifth U.S. Artillery at the Battle of New Market. Later, at the Battle of Winchester, his horse was shot from under him but, according to reports, he cheered his men on to press the attack. At the Battle of Fisher's Hill, Captain du Pont countered a flank attack by rallying his guns while insisting on riding on his clearly visible, and for his men inspirational, white horse. Bullets whistled around him, as did afterwards the praise of his superiors. Henry's rank was raised to brevet Major in September—then, after another brilliant performance at the Battle of Cedar Creek, to brevet Lieutenant Colonel the following month. But thirty years would have to pass before the government would, for opportune reasons, choose to award Henry the Congressional Medal of Honor "for gallant and meritorious conduct."

Henry's conduct, however, was not always so gallant or meritorious.

His description of General Franz Seigal, United States Volunteers, for example, reveals a haughty class arrogance. Seigal, like many thousands of immigrants who had volunteered willingly to fight against slavery, had participated in the 1848 workers' revolution that swept Europe and threatened the rule of capitalists. Because of the general's background, Henry's limited toleration for taking orders from anyone was further strained, no doubt aggravated by Seigal's questionable competency and his failure to credit Henry for delaying an enemy advance on a strategic bridge during the Battle of New Market on May 15, 1864.

According to Du Pont family legend, Henry gallantly refused General David Hunter's order to bomb the Virginia Military Academy in June 1864. His own memoirs testify,[44] however, that he executed the order with speed and deadly efficiency. When the Union demolition was completed, VMI, including its famed, extensive library, was left a gutted ruin, burned to the ground, while Henry was left mending his wounded conscience. Decades later, as a United States senator, Henry would introduce a bill for payment of compensation.

6. THE CONQUEST OF DELAWARE

While his son was in the field conquering new glory for the family name, "Boss Henry" du Pont was beset with dangers closer to home. Delaware at the outbreak of the war was still a slave state, and there were many grumblings of support for the Confederacy. In Dover the state legislature refused to vote its loyalty to the Union, and the downstate counties of Kent and Sussex, ruled by slaveholders, openly expressed allegiance to the South.

Because of Henry's personal pledge of loyalty at the White House, Lincoln had Governor Burton of Delaware appoint him Major General of the state's armed forces. The first order Henry gave in this office was to forcefully collect as many guns in the state as possible for "inventory." Then he ordered every Du Pont employee to take an oath of loyalty to the federal government. Those who refused were immediately fired; those who remained were given a bonus and drafted into two companies of state militia captained by Lammot and Charles du Pont. With his mills now guarded, Henry felt free to order every officer and man in the Delaware state militia to take the loyalty oath. However, unlike the Brandywine workers, not all Delawarians were yet accustomed to unilateral decrees from Henry du Pont. Many refused outright.

Faced with the prospect of armed insurrection, Henry lost no time in telegraphing the federal commander in Baltimore, General John A. Dix, and within days long blue files of federal troops were marching down the streets of Wilmington. With the state's largest, and actually only, city securely in his hands, "General" Henry, as he was by now called, marched his forces into southern Delaware, crushing any spirit of resistance that flickered in the area. From that day on, Du Pont control of the entire state of Delaware has been complete. Nor did Henry ever try to hide this awesome power. In 1868, 1876, 1880, 1884, and 1888 he was Delaware's proudest presidential elector in the Electoral College.

7. PROFITS FROM TRAGEDY

The war rolled back and forth across the continent like some giant whirlwind of death, twisting and tearing everything in its path, setting thousands of brothers and friends at each other's throats. In Delaware, too, the war caused its hardships. Sophie du Pont, wife of Rear Admiral Samuel du Pont, for example, complained of having "no society whatever but Irishmen."[45] Her next most frequent complaint was of Lincoln, whom she, like many of her kin, intensely disliked.

Indeed, the war was hard on the social life of the Brandywine, and as is often the case when idleness has only worry for companion, the Du Pont women became deeply religious, their hours of pious devotions exceeded only by the hours spent discussing newfound aches and pains. For a short while, young Alexis Irénée II relieved some of their boredom by offering pistol lessons to the younger women. Then he and his pistols enlisted in the Union cause, and the church services increased in frequency.

Only once during the war did the Du Pont girls have some color brought into their drab lives. After the firing on Fort Sumter, federal troops were sent to guard the mills. Sporting their brightest parasols and finest lace dresses, the girls often traveled to Camp Du Pont, where they were treated to parades and even serenades by members of the band. Eventually, propositions were made to the women by soldiers whose class intimidated spines had been well starched with alcohol. At that point, Henry drew the class line, ordering a sundown curfew on all the family's women.

Delaware was a lonely state for not only Du Ponts, but most of its women. One out of every eight men, Black and white, was sent to war, the state soon being depleted of its best manpower. At one point available men became so scarce that Henry requested the use of fifty Confederate prisoners from Camp Du Pont to fill vacancies in the artillery company guarding his mills.[46]

Henry's powdermen were exempt from the draft on his own insistence.[47] Henry's mills, however, could be as dangerous as the worst of battlefields. Between 1861 and 1865, eleven explosions ripped through the mills, killing forty-three men and injuring scores more. Henry blamed the explosions on "unknown causes," insinuating sabotage, but most Delawarians conceded that a decline in the mills' safety standards caused by the General's production speed-up was probably more to blame.

Henry ran the mills day and night. He had lost about $150,000 when his southern inventories were seized by the Confederates (some of which were compensated for after the war), and also lost much business, but the war had been more than a soothing balm. Before the bloodshed began, Du Pont Company had never sold more than $752,000 worth of powder in a year. The second half of 1861 more than tripled that amount from just government sales alone, excluding other business the war economy stimulated. In 1862 Henry raked in another $661,000 from government contracts; in 1863, $527,000 more; in 1864, $444,000; between January of 1865 and the peace in March, another $65,000.[48] In terms of the present dollar's buying power, Du Pont made tens of millions of dollars out of the Civil War.

But with long hours of work and the danger of frequent explosions inherent in the mills, Henry was forced to provide a plentiful supply of inducements to keep his workers producing. His special draft exemptions weren't attractive enough, especially with the revival of labor militancy in the North after 1863. Grudgingly, he conceded to raise wages by 75 percent during the war. It was a good investment. The men kept identifying with the name of Du Pont rather than with those of labor organizers like Bill Sylvis.

Labor organizations, which had risen during the late 1850's only to volunteer whole locals as companies in the fight for free labor, began to make a comeback after 1863. This revival was spurred by industrialists who refused to raise wages although they were richer than ever from war profiteering. The industrialists had little hesitation about raising prices, however. While wages for the worker rose on a national average by 43 percent, they could not keep up with a 117 percent hike in the general price index.

The anger over inflation and unemployment finally broke out into rioting in New York in 1863, when the Draft Act was passed, although much of the insurrection was marred by ugly racist overtones and, in some cases, even southern sympathy. By the thousands, however, workers went to die in a fiery holocaust while young industrialists like Andrew Carnegie, Philip Armour, James Hill, John D. Rockefeller, Jay Gould, Jim Fisk, and J. P. Morgan, all in their draftable twenties and all destined to become luminaries in American business history, managed to buy replacements for their numbers in the draft lottery for only $300—a small price, many a buyer conceded, when he saw his number in the morning papers listed among the dead. Meanwhile, these "new nobility" raised the price of pig iron on the New York market from $20 a ton in 1860 to $80 a ton in 1864, until 29-year-old Carnegie was in ecstasy, softly repeating to himself, "Oh, I'm rich! I'm rich!"[49] James Mellon perhaps exemplified the new wealth being created when he wrote to his father admiringly of friends who made millions through speculation in wheat. "They continue growing richer," he explained, "and don't care when the war ends."[50]

Du Pont Company, of course, was not to be left behind. In December of 1862 Henry's price for black powder was 18 cents per pound, up 2 cents from the market price of a year before. Henry justified the price hike by pointing to the rise in prices of materials used in making powder, but this was only partly true. During the war, charcoal's price did rise 50 percent, sulphur 80 percent, cooper work 90 percent, saltpeter 135 percent; but what Henry didn't bother to mention was that Du Pont Company did not buy charcoal or cooper work—it provided its own. And, thanks to Lammot's trip to England, the federal government furnished Du Pont with saltpeter throughout the war. In fact, Lammot's trip had netted the company a contract that brought in another $384,000 for refining 11,542,000 tons of government saltpeter.[51]

Desperately, but futilely, Lincoln's administration tried to fight back. In March of 1863 the federal government passed a tax of one cent per pound on the sale of gunpowder.

The tax passage was Lammot du Pont's first defeat in political circles. The young chemist had traveled south to Washington to lobby against the proposed tax among his political contacts. The effort, by and large, was a failure. It seems the political climate in the city at the time was not conducive to openly condoning war profiteering. The country's capital by now had been turned into one huge hospital. For the last two years Washington had been menaced by Confederate armies attacking from Virginia, the fighting and dying showering the surrounding countryside with blood. More than once Lammot had to wade through a vast sea of stretchers to get into the polished white government buildings—perhaps even passing by the poet Walt Whitman, who was also there at the time and who has handed down to us perhaps the most graphic recorded description of the city's climate during the war. Unlike any Du Pont, Whitman was working day and night caring for the wounded, his hair and beard already white at the age of 42.

"In one of the hospitals," he wrote in his diary, "I find Thomas Haley, 4th New York Cavalry. He is a fine specimen of youthful physical manliness, shot through the lungs and inevitably dying. Next to him is Thomas Lindy, 1st Pennsylvania Cavalry, shot very badly. . . . Poor young man, he suffers horribly, has to be constantly dosed with morphine, his face ashy and glazed bright young eyes. . . . Opposite, an old Quaker lady is sitting by the side of her son, Amer Moore, 2nd U.S. Artillery, shot in the head. He will surely die. I speak and he answers pleasantly."[52]

And as Amer Moore lay dying outside, inside the marbled halls of corruption Lammot du Pont, young, strong, and healthy, spoke also, sometimes quietly, sometimes booming, but always lobbying. Lammot's campaign to destroy the powder tax did fail, but it succeeded on a far more important front of the battle for profits: the idea of government-owned powder plants was killed, the willingness of members of that Congress to take bribes having become legendary.[53]

No man's death diminishes a Du Pont, it has been said, unless it is that of another Du Pont, and certainly nothing diminished the fiery vehemence with which the clan demanded its share of the war's booty. With each new tax that Lincoln's desperate government passed, Henry du Pont would sadly shake his head and raise his prices, sometimes not even needing taxes for an incentive. In November 1863 Du Pont's price for powder was 26 cents per pound, up almost 70 percent in one year. The government then raised duties another one-half cent per pound, but while it was winning battles against Lee's armies, it was losing the war with the Du Ponts. By April 1864 Henry had again raised the price of Du Pont powder to 30 cents per pound. The U.S. Treasury was now so depleted that it was unable to make immediate payment, so Henry was forced to exercise an uncharacteristic patience. Between April and July the government was able to remit only $360,000 to the Du Ponts; by August it still owed the family $350,000 from the Army alone, to say nothing of the Navy's debt for Du Pont Mammoth Powder.[54] By the war's end, Washington was paying Du Pont's highest price since the war began—33½ cents per pound—and without complaint. "There has never been a case in any country in the world," Henry had answered his critics, "where a nation at war has had its powder so cheaply as the United States have [*sic*] had it since the breaking out of the Rebellion."[55]

Upon examining the price for powder that the Confederate government was paying, one can see why Lincoln didn't publicly complain. The non-profit Confederate mills at Augusta, Georgia, operated at a cost of $1.08 per pound of powder when it began operations, and by the war's end the South, depleted of resources like saltpeter, was paying up to $3 per pound. Throughout the war the Confederacy had only two small mills, the largest capable of producing only 500 pounds per day. In the four years of the war, Davis's regime could not supply its infantry with more than ninety rounds of ammo per man.

Du Pont on the other hand, furnished between 3.5 and 4 million pounds of powder to the federal government during the war, averaging over 2,700 pounds per day and exceeding the output of the Confederate mills at Augusta by over one million pounds. Obviously, Lincoln was glad to have the powder. But not so obviously, he was also glad to encourage the growth of northern industries with fat war contracts, for industrialization and its concurrent social organizational changes were shaping a new country—in fact, through the federal government, creating a national identity. Before the war there was really no Union to save because there actually was no nation-state in the modern sense of the term. This became Lincoln's great task—to create a nation-state in the North in order to enforce a union with the South and destroy a slavery-based economy that retarded the growth of industrial wage-labor.

As Lincoln succeeded in this task, so also did the Du Ponts, making a profit of over $1 million from the Civil War. As new markets were found in the West, Du Pont Company relied more and more on transporting its powder over great distances. Lammot du Pont had a railroad spur built from nearby Montchanin to Wilmington, connecting the mills directly with the national railway network for the first time. Henry often requested and received special exemptions from the government prohibition on transporting powder, shipping Du Pont powder across Iowa to the mines of Nebraska and gold fields of Pike's Peak, even across the ocean to European colonialists busy at the time conquering and dismembering the continent of Africa.

8. THE DARK BRANDYWINE

Throughout the Civil War the great war-making powers of the Du Pont mills made them a choice target for Confederate military strategy. Once, two southern spies were caught on their way to blow up the gunpowder plant. Paranoia ran deep through the Brandywine Valley during these fearful days, neatly serving Du Pont Company's efforts to exclude "outside troublemakers" such as labor organizers. One day this policy almost resulted in murder. A stranger was seen walking in the vicinity of the mills. "A spy! A spy!" shouted a hysterical mob as it swept down on the man with clubs. Among them was Lammot du Pont, who, after discovering the stranger was only a harmless tramp, let the man go.

There were other, more valid causes for fear during the war, however. Three times the mills were a target for possible Confederate attack.

In September 1862 Henry and Lammot du Pont were called to Washington and informed that General Robert E. Lee had moved his army into Maryland on the way to attack Harrisburg, the capital of Pennsylvania.

Three thousand of Lee's cavalry, they were told, had been ordered to make a lightning raid on the mills. Feverishly, the Du Ponts made preparations to meet the onslaught, but on September 17 Lee's advance was beaten back at the Battle of Antietam, and the mills escaped danger.

The second peril came in June of 1863. Lee's army had invaded the North as far east as the Susquehanna River near York, Pennsylvania. Two hundred Du Pont workers and other Delawarians rode west under the command of Lammot and Eugene du Pont, son of the late Alexis du Pont, to protect the Philadelphia-Baltimore Railroad. Charles I. du Pont took direct leadership of Delaware's militia, massing them along the state's western border. Independence Day, usually a time of celebration and fireworks on the Brandywine, was spent in hushed silence. Then the Wilmington telegraph clicked the news of Lee's defeat at Gettysburg. A sigh of relief, it was said, was clearly audible throughout the valley; then the area rocked with belated, and grateful, holiday festivities.

The last and greatest scare came in July 1864. Confederate general Jubal Early was marching north for another attack. Uneasiness throughout the Wilmington area turned to outright fear when false reports came in that Washington had fallen. Then fear turned to horror when further reports claimed Baltimore had also succumbed. The Brandywine was almost in a panic when a train between Baltimore and Wilmington was actually stopped by Confederate raiders. A huge crowd had gathered around the telegraph office when word finally came that Early had actually been repulsed at Washington.

But the dying went on. Delaware alone sent 13,651 of its men into the slaughter; many of them never returned. Throughout the four years of war, church bells tolled sadly in Wilmington and along the Brandywine whenever a casualty train passed through. Sometimes the people of Wilmington would board the trains and offer refreshments to wounded soldiers. New casualty lists bordered in black kept appearing, and the people of Wilmington grieved.

The Du Ponts also suffered their war casualties, although not on the battlefield.

Since hostilities had begun, beautiful Charlotte Shepard Henderson du Pont felt like she was trapped behind enemy lines, and indeed she was. Charlotte was from one of the leading families of Virginia, and like every good, gentle southern belle, she defended slavery with that particularly bold ferocity known only to slaveholding aristocracy. Married to E. I. du Pont II, son of Alfred, she remained unconsoled by the fact that abolitionists were neither members nor welcome guests of the Du Pont family. Du Pont powder made by her husband's family, she knew, was killing her gray-uniformed relatives and friends by the score. Her southern sympathies were further aggravated by the self-righteousness of her mother-in-law, Margaretta du Pont. Margaretta was a bossy, strong-willed woman, too strong for Charlotte's war-frayed nerves. Charlotte finally suffered a nervous breakdown from which she never fully recovered, dying years later in a mental asylum in Philadelphia. Irénée never forgave his mother for Charlotte's mental collapse. He refused to speak to her right up to his death in 1877 only a few months after the burial of his wife.

The war years brought another death to the family—Victorine du Pont, the first child of Irénée and Sophie du Pont and the tragic widow of young Ferdinand Bauduy. In poor health at the age of 68, Victorine was fading quickly, and soon her life was flickering on its deathbed. Her brother Henry suggested sending for Reverend Brinckle, her dear friend "Mr. B."

"Oh, not tonight," she said. "I should like to see Mr. B. very much, but wait till morning."

Just before dawn she opened her eyes to see the doctor taking her pulse.

"How is it?" she asked.

"Very low. I can scarcely feel it."

"I thought so," she whispered, and died.

"Mr. B." finally joined her two years later, a victim of a typhoid epidemic that swept through Wilmington and dipped its deadly finger also into the Brandywine. Yet, even during this plague, the mills kept turning, grinding out their black gold into the dark of night.

When the sun finally rose on April 10, 1865, the nightmare of war was but a few hours over. Across the tired land a sweet stillness filled the air, and again it was spring. Throughout the North there was celebration, even on the Brandywine, especially on the Brandywine, where coffers brimmed with gold and stately mansions rose triumphantly to a new order, a new age. For where one era of the Du Pont saga ended, another began, bringing one of the most determined and ruthless campaigns of empire-building ever recorded.

Four

BUILDING A MONOPOLY

1. THE NEW NOBILITY

In northern Delaware, around Wilmington and the Brandywine, a dense veil of humidity often hangs over the countryside, clothing trees and people alike with an unseen weight, steeping lungs and tiring arms, burdening any effort at labor. Especially if there is a hot summer sun and the rolling green hills are filling the air with their heavy sweet scent. Especially if you've been working since dawn, putting in your daily twelve hours of labor as Du Pont workers did in the nineteenth century. Once in a while the men would lay down their tools and take a break—perhaps, if they were masons, would even doze a few moments under a tree or by the stone walls they were endlessly building for Henry du Pont.

And more than once the masons would be startled to their feet by the thunder of charging hoofs and the barks of huge hounds brought by Henry "to wake you fellows up."[1] As the men had come to learn, "Boss Henry" took work seriously. They seldom objected to such treatment for it was a privilege, they believed, to be a Du Pont worker. They would jump back to work—that is, until the president of Du Pont Company was seen riding away over a distant hill. Then the men would get their break, forced to steal it like thieves.

"General" Henry daily inspected Du Pont farmlands like some medieval warlord reviewing his conquered territories. As he rode tall and straight, his red hair and beard blazing in the sunlight, Henry's cold blue eyes would beam like molten steel as he proudly watched more and more of Delaware's open fields disappear behind his stone walls. The master of every detail of Du Pont Company, the unchallenged chieftain of the Du Pont clan, Henry was the most powerful man in Delaware. But that was not enough. In terms of powder-making, Henry wanted to be the most powerful man in America.

Henry had company. Other men also wanted to be lord masters of their respective fields of investment—John D. Rockefeller in oil, Andrew Carnegie in steel, Philip Armour in meatpacking, Jay Cooke and J. P. Morgan in banking, Jay Gould in railroads, and many more in a circle of power that was becoming smaller and smaller. All had avoided the draft during the Civil War. All had reaped fortunes from the slaughter. J. P. Morgan made millions out of Union defeats which depressed the nation's currency and drove up the price of gold he had hoarded through specula-tion. Young Jay Cooke raked in $20 million in commissions for bank loans he arranged for the Union's million-dollar-a-day expense account. Philip Armour bought pork for $18 a barrel and sold it to the Union army for $40, amassing a fortune of $2 million before the war ended. John Rocke-feller bought his way out of the draft and stalked safely through the fields of western Pennsylvania hunting his dream of oil and world estates. From corrupt Congress and state governments, over 325 million acres of some of the most fertile land in America—common land belonging to all the American people, and worth close to a billion dollars—were given as gifts to Jay Gould and other railroad magnates for their own profit.

All this, while 600,000 young workers and farmers died in war, their bodies piled in trenches five or six deep, 400,000 more maimed, burned, or crippled. No fortunes were reaped for these less fortunate. Harriet Tubman, the black "Moses of her people" serving as a scout for the Union army, described the fortunes of the dead and dying Black soldiers she saw in front of Fort Wagner after one of the bravest assaults in American military history. "And then we saw the lightning," she said, "and that was the guns; and then we heard the thunder and that was the big guns; and then we heard the rain falling and that was the drops of blood falling; and when we came to get in the crops, it was dead men that we reaped."[2]

But for the new nobility of industrialists and bankers, the harvest was pure gold. After the war was over, it was they who sat in the seats of power, who held the reins of the new Republican Party, who plundered the nation's natural and human resources. Nothing could be denied them, and they made sure nothing was. It was as if the great war for freedom, with all its sacrifice and suffering, had been for them. And, in fact, it was.

Among them were the Du Ponts. While Lammot du Pont was demand-ing of Washington less taxes on his family's increasing wealth, his Uncle Henry was counting his gold and scoffing that, as far as gunpowder was concerned, America never had it better.

Neither had the Du Ponts. They had profiteered to the extent of over $1 million from the slaughter. Whatever misgivings Henry may have had about freeing Black people from slavery, he couldn't argue with cold cash.

After Lee's surrender, Henry combined a public display of patriotism with a shrewd eye for private profit. On Washington's request, he cancelled all unfilled war contracts. At public auction he bought back most of the powder he had sold the government during the war for 33 cents a pound. But now the price for surplus government powder was only 5 cents per pound, less than the cost of producing new powder for his customers. For six years Henry bought surplus government powder made by Du Pont and other companies. Du Pont even privately exchanged one pound of good powder for four pounds of condemned surplus. This maneuver kept black powder prices up, and was profitable besides: for less than the cost of producing new powder, Henry bought old powder, reworked it, and sold it back to customers. By 1890 Du Pont Company was still reworking Civil War powder.

This ruse, plus Lammot's newly patented horizontal press for compression of powder, and the company's mound of Civil War profits, allowed Henry to undersell his smaller competitors. And then, almost as if sent by some intimate providence, came the postwar depression. Henry watched as smaller companies went under, while Du Pont, buttressed by its war profits, captured more and more control of the gunpowder market. By scrambling about the country in search of new markets, Henry expanded Du Pont beyond Delaware, competing with powerful rivals like Hazard Powder, Laflin and Rand, and California Powder. As early as 1858 Henry had opened a plant in the coal-mining district of Wapwallopen Creek in Luzerne County, Pennsylvania. By 1869 Henry had added another Pennsylvania concern and five more mills. A new New York agent, F. L. Kneeland, added his own brand of promotion wizardry. Yet, for all these gains, competition from the stronger of Du Pont's rivals remained stiff and troublesome, especially from California Powder on the Pacific Coast.

Henry never got over the loss of the West Coast market during the war. Gold miners had raised $100,000 to start their own California Powder Company when Du Pont and other eastern companies couldn't make regular large deliveries during the fighting. By 1865 California was producing more than 500,000 pounds of blasting powder a month. After the war was terminated, California Powder increased its profits by using Chinese labor, paying the immigrants extremely low wages.

Henry was hopping mad. He wanted those profits and was prepared to wage a ruthless trade war till he got them.

2. THE POWDER TRUST

It was in answer to the chaos of competition after the war that Henry took his first step toward monopoly. No longer did Adam Smith's balancing "hidden hand" seem evident in the marketplace of free enterprise; to many bigger industrialists, including Henry du Pont, a more forceful approach toward the economic anarchy of *laissez-faire* capitalism seemed necessary. And here, as in other areas in the future, it was Du Pont that led the way. In 1872 Henry sent out letters to his biggest competitors, inviting them to a special conference at Du Pont's New York office at 70 Wall Street. Why not end our price wars, he suggested, and stabilize the market under our joint domination. With visions of empire dancing in their heads, representatives from Laflin and Rand, Hazard, Oriental Powder, and Austin Powder showed up to meet Henry and Lammot du Pont's warm handshakes. Two others, American Powder and Miami Powder, sent their full endorsements. It was an embrace of bitter enemies, all determined sooner or later to crush the others; but for the time being it was the birth of the Gunpowder Trade Association, commonly called the Powder Trust.

At that historic meeting Lammot du Pont, Henry's brilliant nephew chemist, was elected president, and votes in the council were distributed according to each company's size. Du Pont was accorded ten votes, as were Laflin and Rand, and Hazard. Oriental received six votes; Austin, American, and Miami each got four votes. Uniform prices were established and a fine of $1 per keg was set for violations of the Trust's rates. The United States was sliced up like a birthday cake, cut into trade territories for each member, and the market banquet was topped off with a free-for-all "neutral belt" in the area of Utah, Wyoming, Montana, Colorado, and New Mexico, where the members could let loose their natural inclinations and tear each other apart to their hearts' content. As for California, Lammot had plans of his own.

Lammot was soon wielding his new Trust ax with deadly accuracy. He attacked the three largest independent powder companies, concentrated in New York and the Ohio Valley, cutting the cost of rifle powder from $6.25 a keg to $2.25. Blasting powder was also cut from $2.75 to $.80. It was too much for the smaller firms to match: two of them sold out; the other joined the Trust, agreeing to its terms and leadership.

Du Pont was riding high, expanding along with the country. The postwar period had brought a frenzy of profit-making for the new industrial nobility. In the ten years between 1860 and 1870, 22,000 miles of railway had been laid. The total value of manufactured products increased by over 100 percent during that period, from $1.9 billion to $4.2 billion. Fixed capital invested in industry rose from a little over $1 billion in 1859 to $1.695 billion in 1869, up over 60 percent. Not surprisingly, however, corruption and graft penetrated every circle of power. Jay Gould cheated old Cornelius Vanderbilt of $6 million through the sale of counterfeit Erie bonds. The U.S. Ambassador to England, Robert Schenck, was contributing to international relations in his own unique way by defrauding his

English friends of $50,000 through the sale of phony stock. In New York, Boss Tweed was openly sacking the city treasury of an estimated $200 million. Even the presidential cabinet was not immune. Both Secretary of Treasury W. A. Richardson and Secretary of War W. W. Belknap were forced to resign in 1876 for taking bribes. Vice-President Schuyler Colfax was also found to be involved in similar deals, as was President Grant's brother-in-law, Abel R. Corbin. Senator Patterson of New Hampshire, Representative Oaker Ames of Massachusetts, and James Garfield, future U.S. President, were all involved in bribe-taking in connection with the fraudulent construction of the transcontinental Union Pacific Railroad.

Of course the real victim was the average working American. Great slums grew with great fortunes, pangs of hunger with mountains of imported French wines and pastries. "Millions lived in abject poverty in densely packed slums," writes historian Foster Rhea Dulles. "They struggled merely to maintain their families above the level of brutal hunger and want . . . the great majority [working] such long hours for such little pay that their status was a tragic anomaly in the light of the prosperity generally enjoyed by business and industry."[3]

Then the bottom fell out. Private business, in the quest for greater profits, had produced too much—too much machinery, iron, and lumber; too much textiles, cotton, and wheat; too much of everything—while the American population had too little. By constantly attacking labor organizations as "un-American," the new business class, aided by the federal and state governments they controlled, kept wages down. But here was the rub. By doing so, they also kept down the American people's ability to buy and consume the products they were producing for the new industrial nobility. With no new markets, business stagnated and nervous creditors called in their debts as thousands rushed on the banks. On September 18, 1873, the great Philadelphia banking house of Jay Cooke & Co. closed its doors, signaling general financial collapse. The humming of woolen looms and the clatter of machinery suddenly stopped. Everywhere, it seemed, there was panic.

Everywhere but on the Brandywine. The only panic Henry felt was over how to deal with all the competitors falling into his lap. In 1873, using the firm's name, Henry had bought 500 shares of Sycamore Mills near Nashville, Tennessee. By May 1876 Sycamore had been "absorbed" by the Trust. That was the same year Henry secretly acquired majority control over Hazard, thereby holding twenty of forty-two votes in the Powder Trust. That year he also bought a controlling one-third of the stock of Austin Powder Company, gaining four more votes. "More than half the powder machinery in this country," the "General" wrote in 1877, "has been lying idle since the panic of 1873."[4] He merely intended to get them moving again, he claimed, under the name of "Du Pont."

Against those firms already moving toward success, General Henry waged a war that made Sherman's march look like a Sunday stroll. He crushed the Lake Superior Powder Company for committing the crime of keeping its prices low. Then Hercules Torpedo Company, Hecla Powder Company, and Hercules Powder Company, one by one, fell. Like a red-bearded Nordic conqueror, Henry, with his financial sword, cut under the prices of the Great Western Powder Company. Quick to destroy any potential rival for his throne, Henry strangled the young and growing Marcellus Powder Company in its crib. And even that wasn't enough for Henry's appetite. It wasn't long before he teamed up with Laflin and Rand to consume their old ally, Oriental Powder. Now Henry held twenty-seven votes in the Trust.

When underselling didn't work, other, more persuasive methods did. In the tradition of his older brother, Alfred du Pont, Henry held his own in an age of bribery. He broke no tradition of family honor: since at least 1843, and probably before, it had been company policy to offer bribes to employees of other companies for information on rival production techniques and marketing practices.[5] Sometimes mysterious explosions rocked rival mills. By 1881 Du Pont had seized control of 85 percent of the nation's black powder industry through the Trust, even buying into its greatest competitor, Laflin and Rand. As Henry once put it, "We do our own dictating."[6]

3. LAMMOT'S BLASTING OIL

Perhaps Henry's greatest pleasure was bringing to its knees that king of the Pacific, California Powder. It was also to be the precursor of his only defeat.

In 1875, after a relentless campaign of underselling, Lammot du Pont bought a 43½ percent interest in California Powder. On taking over in 1876, however, Henry found one thing he didn't like. Over $1 million of California's capital was invested in the production of "Hercules" dynamite.

Henry had never been impressed with this "blasting oil," as he called it. Black powder was good enough for him, and what was good enough for him was good enough for the country. The country disagreed. So did his nephew, Lammot du Pont.

Lammot had been interested in dynamite's development since his youth, when Professor Ascanio Sobrero invented nitroglycerine at the University of Turin in Italy. On the invention of guncotton, an earlier step toward dynamite, Alfred du Pont had commented, "The discovery is brilliant and such as to create astonishment but the introduction of guncotton in common use must be the work of time."[7] Much time, insisted his brother Henry.

Fortunately for technological progress, Alfred Nobel of Sweden came along. With his invention of blasting caps, nitroglycerine suddenly became very popular. On railroads and ships, salesmen casually carried the "blasting oil" to all parts of Europe and then to the United States.

"All hell will pay for this!" Henry angrily warned. "Wait!"[8]

A series of explosions that soon followed seemed to bear Henry out. Then Nobel's own plant in Europe blew up and everywhere the cry went out against nitroglycerine. Ships and railroads refused to carry it and agents around the country cancelled their orders. Henry's blue eyes twinkled. "We think that will be the end of Nitro-Glycerine in this continent."[9]

But Nobel was not finished yet. Back to his lab he went, trying to reduce nitroglycerine's sensitivity by absorbing it into a porous, insensitive substance. He first tried charcoal, then sawdust, then brick dust, and finally the solution! Kieselguhr—powdered earth! He found that when he saturated powdered earth with nitroglycerine it became a puttylike substance. He found he could knead the substance and pack it into cartridges. He could also knead it into short round sticks, which he wrapped in tough waxed cartridge paper. It was very safe from shocks, yet easily set off by fuses, and still had twenty times the explosive power of black powder. He called the sticks "dynamite."

Nobel began producing dynamite in 1866 when Du Pont was the largest producer of black powder in the world. Henry's reaction was predictable. "They are all vastly more dangerous than gunpowder," he still charged in 1871, "and no man's life is safe who uses them."[10]

The country, however, was more impressed with dynamite than with Henry, and again, so was Lammot du Pont. As the brilliant inventor of "soda powder," Lammot was always looking for ways of bettering high explosives, and dynamite seemed to be proving itself. It was quickly used in blasting the zinc, lead, and silver mines of the West. It tunneled sewers in New York and uprooted stumps in Ohio. Dynamite blasted iron and coal and furnished tons of limestone for flux to be used in smelting iron ore for the new Bessemer process of making steel. It drained Louisiana swamps and even sank new oil wells for John Rockefeller.

Lammot was convinced of its threat as a competitor to black powder, but when he approached Uncle Henry about producing dynamite he got a resounding "No!" "We have sent circulars to all our agents," said Henry, "cautioning them against allowing any such to be stored in our magazines."[11] That was in 1873. Change did not come easily to Henry. In fact, in the forty years of his presidency of the company, he had refused to allow a single desk or chair in his office to be moved. The floor remained bare, devoid of rugs, as it had been in his father's day. He still insisted on writing his 600 letters a year with an old quill, refusing to allow a type-writer in the office, until the day his chief clerk brought one in on his own initiative.

But Lammot was undaunted by his uncle's rejection. The tall chemist had the unusual ability to turn crisis into patient good humor. Once, while paymaster at the Wapwallopen Mills in Pennsylvania, he stopped at a hotel for an overnight stay, carrying the monthly payroll. Late at night, as he lay in bed, he heard footsteps at his door. He pretended to be asleep. A lantern's yellow light peeked through the door and slowly crossed the room, creeping closer until it finally rested under Lammot's bed, where he kept his traveling bag. Suddenly Lammot jumped out of bed, swept up the intruder in a bundle of bedclothes, and bodily threw him down the stairs with a gusty laugh. Lammot laughed even harder the next morning when he heard that the landlord had disappeared during the night. He visited that hotel frequently during the coming months, continuing to enjoy the landlord's marked absence whenever he stayed.

Lammot knew his Uncle Henry and had won battles with the old fellow before. When his family showed an ugly prejudice against his Jewish fiancée, Mary Belin, Lammot simply ignored their pleas and married her. He knew he was too important to the firm to be shut out forever. Sure enough, on New Year's Day, 1866, following the family tradition of male members visiting female members bearing gifts, Uncle Henry showed up at Lammot's door to greet his nephew's new bride. By that visit, Henry reluctantly broke the family ice and officially welcomed Mary as a Du Pont.

Now Lammot played the waiting game again, while Henry ranted in anger over that "blasting oil." Throughout the bust days of the 1870's when $750 million worth of business collapsed, Du Pont still produced twenty-four varieties of gunpowder and seventeen different grades of blast-ing powder. That kind of business was hard to argue against, despite dynamite's growing popularity. Henry even tried to stop the Pennsylvania Railroad from removing its ban on dynamite, despite Lammot's gentle suggestion for its production by Du Pont. And still Lammot waited.

So when the case of Lammot's taking over a major dynamite investment in California Powder finally came up in 1876, old Henry had more than cause for suspicion. When Lammot explained that California owned a valuable new patent for dynamite called "White Hercules," Henry became furious. One million dollars invested in dynamite! But the General was licked; that was too much to throw away. With a reluctant grunt, he approved the continued dynamite production.

It was only the beginning of Henry's frustration, however. The Union Pacific Railroad announced that, because of accidents, it was refusing to allow any shipping of dynamite to the Midwest. Again with the utmost reluctance, Henry was forced to allow the building of another dynamite plant at Cleveland. To his surprise, the plant tripled its output of dynamite within three years. As profits rolled in, Henry was weakening, and Lammot knew it. Then eastern agents clamored for dynamite and Henry was forced to approve their adding Hercules dynamite to Du Pont's list of products. By 1880, the General was in full retreat.

That year, after almost fifteen years of patient strategy, Lammot struck with his demands. In a meeting with his uncle, he insisted Du Pont go directly into the dynamite business. Not surprisingly, Henry still refused. But this time Lammot had the upper hand. Shortly thereafter he quietly induced his fellow Powder Trust partner, Laflin and Rand, to join with him in a common venture: the production of dynamite. Then he had Laflin and Rand contact his uncle about the deal. Lammot was threatening to set up his own company! Even more insulting, he had induced Henry's own son William to join him! The General tore up a storm. When Lammot took an option for land near Wilmington for the dynamite mill site, his uncle was incensed—and defeated. "We are going into the high explosives business," he proclaimed, still in shock. "That is, we are forming a company which we are heavily interested to manufacture the same, and have not as yet fully determined on the name."[12]

Henry needn't have bothered. Lammot already had a name: Repauno Chemical Company, after the Repaupo River in New Jersey, where Lammot had already decided on a site far from the Brandywine, to Henry's relief. Within five months the plant was built and daily producing 2,000 pounds of "Atlas" dynamite.

By then Lammot du Pont was 49 years old. His mustache and thin, short-cropped beard had become streaked with gray, and years of working in the laboratory and counting his gold by candlelight had forced him to wear steel-rimmed glasses. "Uncle Big Man" to the family's children, Lammot now could stretch his long legs over his own desk as president of his own dynamite company. Someday, the family reasoned, he might even be president of Du Pont as well.

It seems Henry agreed to that prospect. When Lammot installed the first plant telephone system in 1882, Henry did likewise not too long after. When Lammot planned a clubhouse for his workers, Henry too came up with the idea of donating one of his homes as a clubhouse after his death, to be later called the Du Pont Country Club. Henry also began to like dynamite—or at least its profits. He took a second one-third interest in Lammot's company in 1883, making his nephew the second richest Du Pont, and it was no surprise to anyone when California Powder, under Henry's control, sold its huge Cleveland plant to Lammot for a scant $30,000.

Lammot took up residence in Philadelphia, the first Du Pont in more than seventy-five years to live away from the Brandywine. He enjoyed it there, even when he came under heavy criticism by neighboring shad fishermen for polluting the Delaware with his plant's production waste, beginning the extermination of the river's fish population. Lammot insisted that any attempt at controlling this pollution had to be within the margin of profit by turning waste into saleable chemicals. Within a few decades, the Delaware would be a current of death.

On March 30, 1884, Lammot was in the Repauno office with Walter Hill, plant superintendent, and A. S. Ackerson of Laflin and Rand's St. Louis sales office when suddenly a worker burst in reporting trouble in the N.G. (nitroglycerine) house. Lammot and Hill ran into the mill and found the nitroglycerine mixture boiling and about to explode. Lammot ordered the workers to get out, ignoring their pleas that he also leave. Then he quickly tried to dilute the mixture by transferring it into an adjoining water tank. It should have worked. It didn't. What Lammot didn't know was that some nitroglycerine from the previous day had been allowed to stand overnight. It was impossible to stop the reaction.

Lammot and Hill finally gave up and ran out of the N.G. house, falling behind an earthen bunker built for such a danger. But for once in his life Lammot had miscalculated. He had built the bunker only ten feet from the house. It was a fatal mistake. When the building exploded, it fell on top of them.

Lammot's multilated body was later found under tons of earth beside Hill's. Five other men also died, including Ackerson. Tired of waiting, the sales agent was approaching the building when the 2,000 pounds of nitroglycerine exploded. His neck was instantly broken.

That tragic night Mary Belin du Pont pulled the shades down low in her Philadelphia home. Pierre Samuel, her oldest son, stepped forward. "Let me do that, Mother," he insisted. "I'm the man of the family now."[13] From that day on, 14-year-old Pierre was called "Dad" by his younger brothers, Henry Belin, William, Irénée, and Lammot, Jr. Years later, he would be called the "father of the modern corporation."

4. A SWORD IS SHEATHED

Lammot's untimely death was a terrible blow to the family. The Du Ponts had always gotten along better with the kindly "Big Man" than with stern Uncle Henry. Through the years, Henry had evoked the family's resentment by his constant land grabbing, often putting titles in his own name while refusing to allow any Du Pont homes to be individually owned. Also, Henry's piracy did not end at the family's doorstep. He took home more profits every year than all the other partners combined.

An even bigger gripe, however, was Henry's refusal to allow young Du Ponts to move up the ladder of authority. Of titles and jobs he gave plenty—under his direction, of course; but of power he gave nothing. Eugene, the eldest son of Alexis, had joined the partnership at the end of the Civil War. But there were no new partners until 1871, when another son of Alexis, Francis Gurney du Pont, chemist and amateur astronomer, also joined the firm. Then E. I. du Pont II, son of Alfred, died of consumption at the age of 48 in 1877. Irénée's was the forty-fifth Du Pont grave dug among the trees of Sand Hole Woods, but only four of those graves contained men who had known power in Du Pont Company: E. I. du Pont, Alexis I., Alfred V., and Irénée II.

The next year Henry made his sons, William and Henry A., partners in the firm. This nepotism caused justifiable resentment in the family. William was totally inexperienced, just out of M.I.T., and his brother Henry A. had never made powder in his entire life. This latter and favorite son of Henry had resigned his army commission in deference to the demands of his wife Pauline, and was quickly placed in a prominent company position by his father. Given the lucrative job of negotiating with railroads for rebates and drawbacks, "Colonel" Henry developed contacts that would later aid him in becoming president of the Wilmington and Northern Railroad. Soon he was made Du Pont's sales manager, traveling everywhere.

Some other Du Ponts had already left the company, however, disgusted with Henry's compulsive domineering. Lammot's brothers, Alfred Victor (Uncle Fred) and Bidermann du Pont, in 1854 moved to Louisville, Kentucky, where they successfully invested in paper manufacturing, street cars, utilities, and eventually coal mines. But most of the Du Ponts stayed in Delaware with the company. It wasn't easy, since Henry, through the company, actually owned the roofs over their heads and seldom let them forget it. During those thirty-odd years, Lammot was the cement that bound the family together, acting as compromiser, adviser, and often comforter of the defeated.

With Lammot, then, also died Henry's mediator. The General remained his conservative self. True, electric lights were installed in the yards on the insistence of his best customer, the U.S. Army. And oil lamps and steel pens were permissible for his five overworked clerks; but three candles and a quill still served him fine. Like a broken record, Henry still performed the thirty-year-old ritual every night of blowing out first the tall new candle on the left, then the used middle candle, and then the short one on the right; then he would remove the smallest, move the others down one position, and place a new candle on the left.

Henry had other daily rituals. Fully indulging in his passion for stone walls, he still insisted on inspecting his lands every day, although he did trade in his horse for a buggy, in which he carried a trowel to dig up loathsome weeds and daisies. He also kept up his peculiar sport of waking sleeping workers with greyhounds. Henry still wore his old silk top hat on weekdays and a new one on Sunday. The old man and his top hat had become a way of life along the Brandywine. One night, that hat finally came to some practical use. While making one of his nightly surprise inspections by lantern, Henry discovered that a shaft in a glazing mill had become overheated. He quickly ran to the race, scooped up a hatful of water, and ran back to douse the shaft, preventing a likely explosion.

By 1886 Henry's fiery red beard was graying and he had exchanged his boots for carpet slippers. Beneath his desk almost forty years of work had left a hole worn in the wooden plank, much like a cobbler's seat. Then, in January of 1888, Sophie, the wife of the late Rear Admiral and the adored aunt of the family, died as she had lived, an invalid. Her passing marked the rapid decline of the second generation of American Du Ponts.

On August 8, 1889, on his seventy-seventh birthday, Henry blew out his last candle. He died in his home after an illness which began the previous June. The General had survived Lammot but six years. "Boss" Henry's death brought to an end an iron reign of thirty-nine years. He left behind a Powder Trust that monopolized 92½ percent of all American powder, a personal fortune of tens of millions, and a long series of graves, broken lives, and smashed powder companies. Henry also left behind a fittingly modest epitaph:

"Mark the perfect man and behold the upright; for the end of that man is Peace."

Even in death Henry insisted on being "Boss."

Five

CRISIS IN THE KINGDOM

1. CALM BEFORE THE STORM

As Henry du Pont was being lowered into his grave, many of his family cast a worried glance at the clear blue horizon. More than one Du Pont suspected that Henry, the infamous foe of change, had actually planted the economic seeds that would transform every life on the Brandywine. Beyond that clear horizon, they feared, brewed a storm of change. They were wrong. The turbulence stirred by Henry's Powder Trust would be no mere storm. It would be a hurricane.

Right then, however, all the Du Ponts were immediately concerned with was preserving the only life they had known, and for a short while it actually seemed that life along the Brandywine might continue as it had for almost ninety years.

Francis G. du Pont regularly waddled down to his private homemade pond, wearing a rubber raincoat and boots to hide his bathing suit from the bees and mocking eyes he suspected were everywhere. This self-consciousness, however, never got in Frank's way when he wanted personal errands done by men who had been hired to make gunpowder. In fact, he used company workers to dig his pond, as well as to occasionally clean it out.[1] Free of such drudgery, Frank found time to develop his hobby of astronomy, even building a revolving roof on one of his three observatories. For hours, he would wiggle his mustache and peer through an arsenal of telescopes, looking for something meaningful in his life beyond powder.

The Du Ponts enjoyed other pleasures as well. As they had done for over seven decades, they continued to fish in the Brandywine for the trout they were so fond of. Occasionally they held fishing parties to which everyone would bring peaches and huge lunch baskets. Everyone, that is, who was rendered that most precious of Wilmington boons—a Du Pont invitation—and to the Du Ponts, "everyone" was family and only the closest of business friends.

Du Pont workers, meanwhile, even with Henry gone, were forced to continue to steal those precious breaks by hiding in the Hagley Yard's boring shop. This small shed was used for varnishing kegs and cutting labels. The trimmings that accumulated there were the closest thing the workers had to a chair on which to rest. The Du Ponts were well aware of this secret refuge, but apparently had decided it was wiser to let the workers believe they were getting away with something. It improved morale and, besides, the men also worked more efficiently if allowed to take occasional breaks. Company discipline, however, ruled that the breaks must never enjoy official sanction, but were to be a privilege stemming from the generosity of the individual foreman, rather than a right of the workers. Before his death, for example, Eleuthère Irénée II would often rout the workers out of the boring shop by making a fuss with the thumb latch as if it were stuck. This ruse gave the men a chance to hide. Then he would walk away to allow the men to sneak back to work as if they were thieves. Such tactics effectively kept the workers' self-confidence and respect at a low— and for the Du Ponts, controllable—level.

There were elements on the Brandywine, other than the humid weather, that could make it difficult to keep one's mind on work. While the workers kept the Brandywine mills churning out profits, members of the Du Pont family would occasionally hold boat races down the river. Canoes would be hauled to Montchanin station on the family-owned Wilmington and Northern Railroad and then moved upstream above the mills. The railroad would even provide a private coach or caboose for Du Ponts who went along as spectators. With a yell, young Du Ponts would mount their canoes in the Brandywine and speed twenty miles downstream to the mills, their shouts and carefree laughter within easy earshot of the toiling workers.

Most of the workers, however, were accustomed to such antics. Du Pont employment was lifetime for the faithful, a legacy handed by workers to their children as in the days of serfdom. No man at the Brandywine had ever seen another powder mill. That had been one of Irénée du Pont's first rules.[2] In this way, Du Pont workers were denied any standard outside the Brandywine's from which to judge their working conditions or salaries, which were actually, in Alfred du Pont's own words, only "average" for powder-making,[3] although the men were led to believe otherwise. Except for millwrights and machinists employed to make repairs, the four foremen's $1 a day was the highest pay at Du Pont, and in those times the men were required to work an average of sixty hours a week. As these were also days of high unemployment in the country, Du Pont workers unsurprisingly valued their jobs, especially when they were restricted under contract from taking any powder knowledge or experience gained at Du Pont with them to other employers.

Because of these and other conditions imposed by the Du Ponts, the workers saw little of the outside world. Even on occasions of such disasters as epidemics and explosions, the Du Ponts refused to allow help from Wilmington to come into the Brandywine valley, employing their own fire, police, and medical resources. They even had their own coroner. To make everything legal, a formal report would be sent to Wilmington authorities by a Du Pont lawyer.

Du Pont workers spent most of their lives in the powder mills, while their wives sat on the stoops of their homes whittling away years with the willows for the Du Pont charcoal house, contributing to the rent they had to pay the company for their homes.

If the workers were like serfs, the Du Ponts certainly fulfilled the role of paternalistic feudal lords. They set up a kind of workmen's compensation for the loyal and humble. If a worker was permanently maimed on the job, he was given his first official break by the Du Ponts: he would be assigned light work for the rest of his life. If he was killed, which was always a likely prospect, his widow and children might get as much as $10 a month. With a "suitable" education at the Brandywine Manufacturer's Sunday School, set up by the Du Ponts, the boys could look forward to working all their lives for the Du Ponts, replacing their dead fathers as soon as they were old enough. The girls, on the other hand, could look forward to spending their lives as maids or cooks in Du Pont mansions, or, if they preferred, to providing themselves as obedient wives for the powdermen with whom they grew up. Suited to Du Pont's needs, and not those of its pupils, the Sunday School did its job and the Du Ponts were very proud of it indeed.

Still, during the Civil War when explosions were most frequent, Eleuthera du Pont could not get over her habit of calling the Irish families "ignorant" and "uncivilized."

The Du Ponts also had a smothering concern for the religious "well-being" of their workers daily facing eternity for Du Pont profits. In addition to Episcopalian Christ Church, erected in 1841, the Du Ponts also built a Catholic church, St. Joseph's on-the-Brandywine, bringing in a good Irish priest as the first rector. Most of the French workers had by now been supplanted or replaced by Irish immigrants, all devout Catholics. This did not faze those among the Du Ponts with anti-Catholic sentiments. In fact, they rather liked it that way. Catholicism, Alfred I. du Pont would later explain, was "ideal" for Du Pont powdermen. It was strict and authoritarian, making a disciplined work force that would follow orders unquestioningly. And it was also fatalistic, putting all the burden for a powderman's safety on an invisible God rather than on the very visible Du Ponts.

Significantly, it was not long before St. Joseph's harbored a large cemetery in front of its doors. Fatal explosions on the Brandywine killing at least three workers occurred on an average of once every fourteen months and were so gruesome that the Du Ponts took to whitewashing the mills' walls to hide the stains of splashed blood. By 1880 the cemetery was brimming, including the graves of 154 persons who had been killed in fifty-four accidents since 1815,[4] some of them buried only as human fragments. This accident record, made by Frank du Pont, is admitted to be incomplete.

Religion, it is obvious, was only the gilded paint on the economic cement that fused the Brandywine into a social form akin to feudal society. Like the lords of the manor, the Du Ponts ruled the valley with an uncontested will. Concern for protecting their secret methods of powder production made inevitable their cloistered aloofness to outsiders. The language barrier of the first, French-born generation of Du Ponts and their workers, of course, helped, but perhaps most evident of all was the class barrier that the Du Ponts erected, their snobbery having become legendary.

Next to themselves, the Du Ponts loved most their wealth. And since the time of their founder, they had a unique way of combining their first love with their second. "The marriages that I should prefer for our colony," Père Du Pont had written, "would be between cousins. In that way, we should be sure of honesty of soul and purity of blood."[5] Years of gold-diggers and the narrow confines of such a small community of elites made Du Pont intermarriages if not natural, at least normal. By the third generation in America, there would be ten such matings.

In the nineteenth century the Brandywine was a world all its own, one difficult for outsiders to understand. The employees of the Brandywine and their families called the Du Ponts by their first names: "Mr. Alfred" and "Miss Eleuthera." The Du Pont youngsters even spoke with their own peculiar accent. A kind of vestigial feudalism was the social structure by which even the Du Ponts lived. No Du Pont owned his own home or land; everything was the common property of the family as a whole. No Du Ponts in the company drew salaries; instead, each withdrew what he needed for living expenses, which could run quite high but in most cases did not.

Yet, despite its social isolation and backwardness, the Brandywine's economic base was perhaps the most modern in America, a contradiction that would someday burst the tiny community from its social jackets.

Despite the workers' belief that they were privileged individuals, the local merchants still regarded them as credit risks. Once, when E. I. du Pont II, plant superintendent, tried to make out a check in a Wilmington store, he was stopped. The merchant feared that his check would not be honored. "But you should know me," the superintendent said. "I'm Irénée du Pont." The merchant looked at Irénée's black powder stains and work clothes and laughed. "If you're a Du Pont," he answered, "I'm General Grant." Irénée, at first puzzled, finally looked at himself in a mirror and joined in the laughter. Of course!

2. AN APPRENTICE NAMED ALFRED

Up the hill from St. Joseph's on a bluff overlooking the Brandywine was the private Du Pont cemetery. By 1877 there were forty-five graves there, the latest occupant being E. I. du Pont II. In 1884 Lammot du Pont joined his younger brother. It was this latest death that shocked a young playboy at M.I.T. into joining his family's business. This young man, the eldest son of deceased E. I. du Pont II, was destined to become the vital link between the past and the future grandeur of the name of Du Pont.

When Alfred I. du Pont's name was added to the employee list in October of 1884, the Du Pont mills were being run almost as they had been when his great-grandfather started the company. Sporting and military powder was still made with saltpeter. Explosives used Lammot's less expensive soda powder.

The first step Alfred learned about powder production was the making of saltpeter at a refinery by boiling soda and potash. Charcoal was produced at the coalhouse by carbonizing wood; for sporting and military powder, willow was used; for blasting or soda powder, any wood would do. Because both the refinery and the coalhouse required open fires, they were located far up the bank in the Upper Yard to avoid the danger of sparks setting off the powder and triggering explosions.

The second step was the production of black dust at the composition house. Charcoal and sulphur were ground and mixed in fixed proportions. The grinders were powered by water wheels turned by water pouring down races that were built parallel to the Brandywine. Shafting was set on piers three feet above the ground; the grinding of gears when the shafting changed direction was the loudest and most familiar sound at the mills, and sung many a Du Pont worker to eternal sleep.

One water wheel supplied power to a number of mills through this shafting. When the Brandywine water level was in a very high or low stage, a steam plant, Frank's suggestion to General Henry, was operated far up on the hill.

Hagley had twenty rolling mills, built on the brink of the Brandywine, much like cannon muzzles pointing across the creek. Sometimes that's exactly what they were. Explosions would blow both men and machines across the creek, sometimes as far as the flower gardens of Du Pont mansions. Each mill was small enough so that a blast would not directly set off the other mills. Supposedly.

At the mills, saltpeter or soda, depending on the type of powder produced, was added to black dust from the composition room. Here it was pulverized and mixed by two slowly revolving ten-ton iron wheels. And here was the danger of death. One piece of metal in a mixture was all that was needed to set off an explosion. There were other dangers. Of those who escaped "going across the creek" more than one "natural" death was caused by tuberculosis and various lung diseases caused by breathing in the fine black dust. Of those who contracted such diseases at Du Pont, according to company records, over a third died.

A run of gunpowder took three to four hours; blasting powder one hour. Usually the powdermen went into the mills only to start or stop machinery for a run or to add water to the mixture, which had to be done every hour. In between these times, the men would sometimes stay in a "night shanty." No smoking was allowed, so most powdermen chewed tobacco bought at the company store.

In the pressroom the fine dust from the mills was pressed into two-by-one-inch thick slabs weighing 3,000 pounds per square inch. Then cutting machines broke the slabs into pieces. Here was the most dangerous job in the mills. More workers died working at this job than any other. Between 1815 and 1907, of 393 workers killed, 138 were pressmen.[8]

From the pressroom, the broken presscakes went to the graining mill, where they were crushed by corrugated rollers into grains of various desired sizes. Then they were packed in 50-pound bags and sent to the glazing mills. There the bags were emptied into the glazing barrels (revolving hollow cylinders), where graphite was added. The graphite smoothed and polished the grains, filling their pores. Sent to the packing house, the finished powder was sealed in bags, branded, and stored in the magazine in the Upper Yard, ready for shipment. The whole process was connected by a miniature railroad of carts drawn by horses or workers.

This generally was the process that made Irénée's first gunpowder sellable, although it took war and continental expansion to provide a buyer.

Alfred knew all this when he started with the company. He also knew that his lowly job as powderman's apprentice was only a temporary position and that he was destined by name to become a partner in the firm. Of course, his aspirations were stimulated by a starting salary of $83 a month, almost two and a half times the average starting monthly wage of $34 a month. In fact, his starting monthly salary as an unskilled worker was higher than the powdermen's $40, the teamsters' $42, the millwrights', wheelwrights', and mechanics' $45 to $60, and even that of his immediate boss, the powder foreman, who was paid $60 a month. Only the boss millwrights, wheelwrights, and mechanics received more, and only by $7.

Alfred worked his way up. After twenty-one months, he became what few Du Pont workers could hope to become in a lifetime: assistant superintendent. His salary was now $1,500 a year. Alfred also received an annual allowance of $480 from his father's estate. And on May 12, 1885, when he turned twenty-one, he had been handed his cash legacy—$100,000.

Now Alfred began to enjoy life. His mansion, Swamp Hall, was the first house in Delaware to have electricity. Although, like most Du Ponts, he had few intellectual pursuits beyond some books on technology and dreams of ways to make more money, Alfred did manage to own Delaware's first automobile. He also set up his own musical band, called the Tankopanicum Band, after a local Indian name. Ironically, Alfred directed while his younger cousin Pierre, the eldest son of Lammot du Pont, played. Within a few decades it would be Pierre who did the directing for a much larger Du Pont organization, while Alfred would blow his horn futilely in the background.

3. THE FAMILY REBEL TURNS TO ESPIONAGE

By the time he came of age, Alfred had already gained a reputation in the family for being somewhat of a rebel, as much as that is possible for a Du Pont. As a young orphan, he had stood with shotgun in hand in defense of his home and brothers and sisters when the family elders threatened to split up the five children of deceased E. I. du Pont II. Because of this show of determination, the family decree was reversed and the children were allowed to remain together at Swamp Hall. Uncle Henry seemed to like Alfred's spunk, it was said, and this was probably true. On his death in 1889, the General left Alfred $25,000. Needless to say, Alfred also liked his Uncle Henry.

The family, however, was constantly worried during his childhood. Always in trouble in grammar school, Alfred carried his reputation to Phillips Academy at Andover, Massachusetts. Once, he was attending an unauthorized party when the school superiors burst in. "Dupie," as his friends called him, refused to be caught and leaped out a window into the waiting arms of a policeman. This would normally be the end of the story, but Alfred was no normal boy. As he was being marched off to jail, the lad began sadly to profess that he was getting what he deserved. When the constable was sufficiently duped into relaxing his guard, Alfred tripped him and raced off to freedom.

Again, at the Massachusetts Institute of Technology, Alfred majored in mischief. During his stay there, gambling and drinking bouts with the

DU PONT CONSANGUINE MARRIAGES

"The marriages that I should prefer for our colony would be between cousins. In that way, we should be sure of honesty of soul and purity of blood." — Pierre Samuel du Pont de Nemours

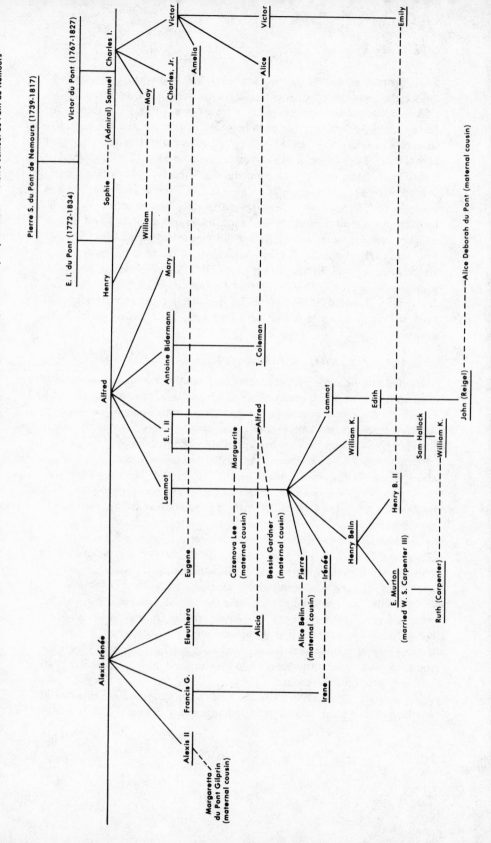

famed boxer John L. Sullivan had his family in a frenzy. With his cousin, T. Coleman du Pont, as roommate and advisor, Alfred carelessly squandered away an allowance of $30 a month, when most Americans couldn't earn that much by working. The turning point in Alfred's life came during those M.I.T. days when Lammot du Pont, whom Alfred had always considered the ablest Du Pont, was killed. Undoubtedly, the personal shock was great on the young man. Sobered by the death, he left M.I.T. within six weeks to join the family firm and begin his long, fabulous career.

Throughout his life Alfred never lost his rambunctious behavior. In fact, it was his trademark until his death some four decades later, often shaking the social foundations of not only Delaware's first family, but Delaware itself. Even in those early days at the firm, Alfred made himself disliked. No sooner, for example, was Alfred on the Brandywine when tensions rose between him and Coleman for the hand of their cousin, Alice du Pont. Coleman won (in those days he seldom lost), marrying a cousin like many Du Ponts of his generation. On another occasion, Alfred showed up at a family wedding at the bride's house—in a police wagon. It was to the family's relief, then, that Alfred finally decided to marry and settle down. No one could believe it; not even Alfred himself.

In May of 1886 Alfred's brother Louis du Pont brought home from Yale a blonde, attractive coed, Bessie Gardner. Bessie was young and gay and charming, with all the right credentials, including family: she was a cousin. Alfred was enchanted, deciding right then and there to relieve his brother of the burden of having a girl friend. After Bessie's return to school, Alfred wrote her regularly, suddenly developing so strong an affection for his younger brother that he found frequent visits to Yale necessary. By Christmas, Alfred had won his prize and announced his engagement to Bessie. Louis was shocked. "You are not going to marry Bessie Gardner?"[7] he asked in bewilderment. "Why, yes, I am," Alfred answered confidently and returned to Wilmington, his task completed and his brother heartbroken.

On January 4, 1887, Alfred and Bessie were married and took off for a honeymoon in Bermuda. When they returned, Bessie went right to work bringing fresh air into the Brandywine valley. She bought tasteful furnishings for Swamp Hall and brought culture into Alfred's life for the first time, although Alfred may not have shown much appreciation. But there was happiness again at Swamp Hall after almost a decade of loneliness, and in October 1887 a baby was born, much to the entire family's delight.

As he seemed to be proving his stability, Alfred was given more responsibility in the company. When the U.S. Army asked Henry to get information on the new European invention, smokeless powder, the General at first ignored them. Black powder was good enough, he insisted. However, the Army—which was Du Pont's best customer—persisted, and finally Henry decided to send Alfred to Europe.

In March of 1889 Alfred arrived in Paris with an enthusiastic smile and a letter of introduction from Secretary of State James Blaine. Both failed to impress the Paris officials, however. The French government was understandably uneasy about turning over military secrets to foreigners. In fact, the French government was just generally uneasy, especially about the French people. Paris was still smoldering from the workers' revolt and Paris Commune nineteen years before. The current regime was the same one that had accepted Prussian arms and crushed that revolt, killing 20,000 Communards in a mass slaughter that made the much-publicized 1,500 aristocratic deaths of the "reign of terror" look amateurish in comparison. Workers still massed in Paris every year to commemorate that struggle, and the bourgeoisie and their restored government were frightened for their lives. New weapons are very important to regimes that must rely on terror. In fact, smokeless powder was considered so precious a secret to the French "republic" that it was manufactured in different stages in four different parts of France, far from the vengeful hands of the revolutionary working class of Paris.

During his talks in Paris, Alfred did find out one valuable fact. Two and a half grams of this smokeless powder would put a bullet through a target that five grams of Du Pont powder could only dent. That was enough to inspire any Du Pont's curiosity.

Still another small fact unearthed by Alfred opened the door that was destined to change the countenance of Du Pont. Alfred discovered that Belgium's Coopal & Company also produced smokeless powder, Quickly slipping into Belgium and covering the countryside with a shower of bribes, Alfred managed to have himself smuggled into Coopal's yards disguised as a laborer. There, keeping his mouth shut and eyes open, Alfred spied on production performances and stole secret patented information to bring back to the Du Pont firm in America. As if this were not enough, Alfred then marched into the Coopal office and confronted its startled officials with his knowledge. Either sign royalty contracts with Du Pont, Alfred warned, or Du Pont will produce smokeless powder on its own volition, and from across the ocean Coopal will be unable to collect anything. The Belgians, bewildered as to how Alfred acquired their secret information, and without means of proving espionage, realized they were trapped. Coopal signed.

Alfred then set sail for America, stopping in England along the way. Chilworth Powder Company, he had heard, was planning to manufacture the new brown prismatic powder in America. That, Alfred felt, would never do. Using similar methods, he persuaded Chilworth to abandon their plans and also sign royalty contracts with Du Pont. Through Alfred, Du Pont had gone international; but more important, Du Pont now had both smokeless and brown prismatic powders. Both were to prove fateful prizes for both Du Pont and the U.S. Army.

4. THE STORM ARRIVES

When Alfred returned to America laden with treasures and family praise, he found Henry du Pont dying. By August, the General was dead.

After some deliberation, the family chose Eugene, the trim, red-bearded son of Alexis du Pont, to assume the company leadership. For over a decade thereafter Eugene tried to wear Henry's royal mantle, but couldn't—his shoulders just weren't broad enough.

Eugene du Pont was a somber man who spoke little but had a cool head in a crisis. It was this quality that was noted and appreciated by the family during the thirty-odd years he had worked in the company. Having served also as Lammot du Pont's assistant, Eugene seemed to have all the Du Pont qualifications, even a Du Pont cousin, Amelia, as wife.

But it was only with Henry's absence that the full weight of his burden became clear to the rest of the family. Henry had been "General" on every marketing and production front of Du Pont's war of conquest, and it soon became obvious that Eugene was no Henry du Pont. The amount of work completely overwhelmed Eugene and he began to delegate important responsibilities to regional directors. It was this need of assistance that probably prompted him also to break with the family tradition of starting at the bottom and to bring in his son, Eugene, Jr., to help with administrative affairs in the office. His brother, Dr. Alexis I. du Pont II, who had no powder experience but plenty of executive ability, also became a new partner. A new office building was completed in Wilmington five times bigger than the old five-room office on the Brandywine. Eugene filled it with typewriters, phones, secretaries, clerks, stenographers—any one or thing he could get to help him rule Henry's empire.

The overall effect was that Eugene streamlined Du Pont Company, cutting here, chopping there. Railroads replaced the mule teams hauling carts along the mills. Then, in 1889, Eugene chopped masons and carpenters from the Du Pont payroll. Men who had devoted their lives to Du Pont were suddenly cut out of the only means to a living they had ever known. That was when the trouble began.

That Christmas, Frank du Pont's barn was mysteriously set afire and burned to the ground. A week later another Du Pont barn blazed against the night. In the following months two more barns burned. Barns, the symbol of Du Pont domination over thousands of acres of Delaware land, had become a target of probably the very men who had built so many miles of stone fences for Henry du Pont's land grabbing. The Du Ponts' honeymoon with their workers was over.

It was in the midst of this tension that on October 7, 1890, the greatest single powder explosion in the history of the world occurred in Du Pont's Upper Yard. Twelve people died in the disaster, including a woman and her baby when her cottage collapsed, and the fires of a hysterical public were soon fanned by company officials.

Disclaiming any company responsibility for the accident, Eugene charged that the explosion was the work of saboteurs. An investigation disputed this, proving that an overheated solder iron was to blame, but Eugene was not to be stopped now. Using the explosion for its own end, the company obtained the conviction in a Delaware court of four people, including two former masons, for the barn burnings. As the so-called arsonists were being jailed, another fire broke out on a Du Pont farmland. Despite Eugene's insistence on the guilt of the imprisoned people, the fires continued for three more years.

The family grew nervous. The storm they had feared since Henry's death was at last approaching. Before the decade was out, the seed of wealth planted by Henry's Trust would bear bitter fruit for the entire family, souring even its traditional feeling of unity.

The first blow to this family unity came from Henry's son, William du Pont. It was no secret among the clan that William's marriage to his cousin May du Pont was not a happy one, but the family was nevertheless shocked when William became the first Du Pont to obtain a divorce. As if that wasn't bad enough for the family's public image, William then married another divorcée, Anne Rogers Zinn of New Castle. May du Pont, in turn, refused the role of martyr and married her childhood sweetheart and lawyer for her divorce proceedings, Willard Saulsbury. Predictably, the gossip ran wild in Delaware.

The Du Ponts were enraged. Through Bishop Leighton Coleman, Eugene's brother-in-law, they drove the minister who performed the Saulsbury ceremony right out of the country. The hapless clergyman finally found refuge from Du Pont wrath in the Swiss mountains. Then the family turned its ire on William, demanding he immediately resign from the company. He did, but not before splitting his 20 percent share as a partner between two younger Du Pont executives, Alfred I. du Pont, now superintendent of the Hagley Yard, and Charles I. du Pont III, assistant superintendent of the Upper Yard. It was William's second act of rebellion against the family elders, and many of the younger Du Ponts clucked in approval.

It had become clear by now to most of the clan's youth that Eugene's changes in the company were merely of form, not substance. Eugene still held the reins as tightly as Henry had in keeping the family youth from advancing in authority. In reaction, Alfred and Charles had demanded a share in the business for the substantial responsibilities they held. Now each had a 10 percent share bequeathed by William, and Eugene had no choice but to agree to make them partners. But at partnership meetings the elder Du Ponts continued to ignore brash young Alfred as well as Charles of the exiled Victor line, not realizing that the crisis of youth was really a growing crisis of the company as a whole.

William was also forced to resign his presidency of the Repauno dynamite company, a position he had taken over successfully after Lammot du Pont was killed. Now forced into exile on secluded Montpelier, the former Virginia estate of James Madison, William bred racing horses and watched from a lonely distance as his job was handed to his former subordinates, J. Amory Haskell and Hamilton M. Barksdale. Both men were destined for higher roles in the Du Pont saga, Barksdale ensuring that role by marrying Charles du Pont's sister Ethel. The family, of course, had no objections, continuing the Du Pont tradition since Antoine Bidermann of absorbing brilliant lieutenants into the clan.

Just when a calm seemed to be returning to the Brandywine, however, a thunderstorm struck again. Alfred's brother Maurice ignored the family's confidence and secretly married Margery FitzGerald during a trip to Cork, Ireland. What made this bad for the family's self-image was that Margery was a barmaid. The marriage hit the Delaware newspapers first, and then the Du Ponts. When Maurice returned with his bride, only Alfred welcomed him home, deliberately snubbing his proud family. Alfred's example may have melted some ice, because the clan then decided to forgive their prodigal son and offered Maurice a job in the family firm—only to be again shocked by Maurice's refusal and resumption of his travels. The family was very upset, a condition which Alfred's defense of his brother only irritated.

By now Alfred was definitely beginning to make enemies, a handicap that would someday shake the foundations of the company and lead to his downfall.

In December of 1892, through no act of his own, Alfred made even more enemies in the clan. His brother Louis had never gotten over losing Bessie Gardner to him. After her marriage, Louis lost interest in his studies and spent three consecutive senior years unable to graduate from Yale. In fact, he never graduated. Instead, he took to heavy drinking and partying in New York—all of which was amply publicized, to his family's deep mortification. Louis, however, seemed amused. He finally decided to give the smug clan a real shock. On December 2, 1892, Louis du Pont walked into the Wilmington Country Club, took out a revolver, and fired a bullet through his brain.

After this tragedy, Alfred found few sympathetic family ears. Even Swamp Hall became increasingly tense as Louis's shadow constantly fell over his marriage, Bessie growing more estranged from her husband. It was soon apparent to both Alfred and Bessie that their marriage was just as doomed as poor Louis.

With all this ugly publicity, the Du Ponts seemed almost glad to hear of the death of "Uncle Fred" in Louisville, Kentucky, the following May. Now here at last was a Du Pont who was a credit to his name. An industrialist and honored citizen of Louisville, Fred owned the pride of the city—a fine estate and mansion he called Central Park. Fred du Pont had left the Brandywine and the company—an action usually considered a capital crime in the family court—because of Henry's tight control. What was worse, he dressed shabbily, unbefitting a member of a proud old family like the Du Ponts. One Du Pont was said to have once complained, "Lord! You'd think the man was a beggar." Fred looked the role and acted it. Despite his huge estate, he continued to live most of the time in his single old room at the Galt Hotel.

But now all was forgiven. When he died, supposedly of a heart attack, Fred du Pont was the richest man in Kentucky. He had also done his family duty: "Uncle Fred" had been the careful guardian of the estates of his brothers E. I. du Pont II and Lammot du Pont, watching over the children of both families for years.

The clan was immensely pleased with itself. They took Fred's body home for an honored funeral on the Brandywine. His huge, handsome nephew, T. Coleman du Pont, solemnly presided over the whole affair.

Then the Cincinnati *Enquirer* broke the shocking truth: Fred had not died peacefully. He had been murdered—in a bordello no less. On Tuesday morning, May 16, according to the *Enquirer,* a doctor was called to the scene of a shooting in Maggie Payne's bordello on West York Street. A death certificate was made out for one James Johnson of Bowling Green, Kentucky. The hearse that picked up the body, however, never went to Bowling Green. Instead it raced to the Du Pont mansion at Central Park.[8]

Lies! claimed the Louisville *Courier-Journal* the next day. "The *Courier-Journal*," wrote its editor, Marse Henry Watterson, "has made a thorough investigation of all the incidents in connection with the case, and unhesitantly states its unqualified belief that there is no foundation whatever for the belief that Mr. A. V. du Pont came to a violent end."[9] It was later revealed that Mr. A. V. du Pont owned a considerable interest in the *Courier-Journal* and that Watterson was heavily in Fred's debt.

Today most Du Ponts quietly admit that Fred was killed by a desperate woman who wanted financial support for the child she claimed she had borne him. Fred had refused, it was learned, but his killer was never arrested. The long hand of Fred's nephew, Coleman du Pont, had silently moved Kentucky authorities and Marse Watterson to cover up the lurid death.

The family was glad to see the last of 1893. In the four years since Henry's death, the Du Ponts had received more shocks and bad publicity than in all their previous ninety years on the Brandywine. With the opening of the new smokeless powder plant at Carney's Point, New Jersey, some Du Ponts hoped a new, more peaceful age for the family had arrived. They couldn't have been more wrong.

5. THE SLAUGHTER OF THE SMALL

Since 1880 the Powder Trust had been having problems. Smaller companies had been constantly breaking Henry's rules and resorting to competition among themselves. While alive, Henry had tried to stop it. The minutes of the Gunpowder Trade Association show that between 1881 and 1883 there were 230 cases of violation of price agreements tried by the Trust.[10] Nevertheless, the violations continued.

When Eugene took over, he decided the best way to deal with violators was simply to destroy them. If independents and even loyal Trust members could also be devoured by Du Pont at the same time, so much the better for the Brandywine.

One of Eugene's first acts as Du Pont president was to order F. J. Waddell, a Du Pont sales agent, "to put the new Chattanooga Powder Company out of business by selling at lower prices."[11] On Eugene's orders, Waddell bribed the railroad agent at Ooltewah, Tennessee, to obtain weekly statements of Chattanooga's powder shipments, including the number of kegs, destination, and consignee's name.[12] That was in 1890. Within five years, Du Pont and Laflin and Rand had control of 55.41 percent of Chattanooga's stock.

Similar piracy brought down the Phoenix Powder works. Another company, the Southern Powder Company, elected to put up a hard fight, but after it too went under, Eugene decided to use it as an example for the rest of the gunpowder industry: he dismantled it completely. Gone forever was Henry's pretext of trying to get idle powder machinery "going again."

At first, these kinds of terror tactics weren't successful. Companies didn't surrender en masse as Eugene had expected, so the ruthless campaign was continued. Between 1896 and 1902 Du Pont attacked the Birmingham Powder Company. Through bribery, Eugene gained control of railroad freight rates out of Birmingham. He set an extortionate price of 70 cents per keg on powder and added freight charges to the locations of Birmingham's customers. "It was, perhaps," testified Waddell, "a year until they died."[13]

In 1897 Eugene turned his attention to the new Indiana Powder Company. He set up the Great Northern Supply Company in the vicinity of Terre Haute where Indiana sold powder to miners. After all, said Eugene, there's nothing wrong with competition. It was a price slaughter. He undercut Indiana's $1.75 price per keg to $1.25. Early in 1902 Indiana sold out to Du Pont and Laflin and Rand.

Two other new independents, North Western Powder Company and Fairmount Company, were also strangled by similar methods. And many more, including the Equitable Powder Co., the Dittmar Powder and Chemical Co., Peyton Chemical, American Ordinance, and the Chamberlain, Cartridge & Target Co., were forced to their knees. Between 1896 and 1899 Du Pont also pillaged the nation's high explosives industry, Du Pont-controlled Eastern Dynamite Company gaining control of New York Powder Company, United States Dynamite Co., Clinton Dynamite, Mt. Wolf Dynamite, The American Forcite Powder Manufacturing Company, and several others.[14]

By 1897 the American market was too small to hold the Du Pont giant. Eugene wanted to branch out across the world, and the growth of the United States as a world power was a big lever with which to wrench open foreign cartels. Through the Jamesberg Agreement, Eugene took his first big step abroad and Du Pont and European powder giants carved up the world. Du Pont was given the United States and all its territories and possessions, present and future, as well as Mexico, Guatemala, Honduras, Nicaragua, Costa Rica, Colombia, and Venezuela.[15] The rest of South America and the non-Spanish Caribbean Islands were considered free-for-all areas. Canada and the Spanish islands were not to be affected, although Du Pont soon gained control also of these. Du Pont was now international, and Eugene smiled at the prospect of even greater profits from abroad. He was right. Within sixty years, Du Pont would be an international name spreading a vast industrial empire across six continents.

In 1897, with profits and companies pouring into their family treasury, the Du Ponts decided they needed a better way to concentrate their new holdings. Colonel Henry du Pont suggested the new corporation form of business organization. But there was one big obstacle—Delaware's constitution. It failed to offer all the corporate favors the Du Ponts preferred.

Henry came up with an idea that only a Du Pont could dare suggest. Why not change Delaware's constitution? The family quickly agreed. After all, it was only a formality.

Under Colonel Henry's direction, a state constitutional convention was called. No one alive could remember when the last one had been held. That's all right, Henry explained, Delaware needs fresh air—fresh business air. When the convention was adjourned, Delaware had a new constitution which gave special tax favors to corporations, as well as making it very simple to set one up. The Du Ponts quickly took advantage of the situation. By the end of 1903 the 95-year-old partnership was dissolved and a new Delaware Corporation, E. I. du Pont de Nemours & Co., Inc., was born. But almost twenty years would pass before Du Pont Company would structurally be transformed into what we know now as a modern corporation, and not without the bitterest of family feuds, extending into national politics and even international intrigue. Meanwhile, as Du Pont had gone through crisis, so also had American capitalism, and as Du Pont had gone international, so also, forced by crisis, had the United States and its most prestigious business center, Wall Street.

6. FOLLOWING THE TURNING TIDE . . .

While the Du Ponts of Delaware were growing richer during the 1890's, most Americans were growing poorer. The economy had boomed, all right, in the 1880's with Du Pont Company riding the wave of prosperity for big business. Coal production in 1870 had been 33 million tons; by 1890 American industry was using Du Pont powder to blast out more than 157 million tons. Iron production quadrupled. Silver production increased fivefold; copper output was nine times greater. Then American capitalism simply ran out of a continent. Based on the existing technology at the time, there were no more new markets. The problem again became a surplus of capital and goods. In 1893 the economy swung back to that cyclical partner of the boom: the bust.

That year 400,000 men were unemployed. By midsummer of 1894, the figure rose to four million. Five hundred banks closed their doors and 15,000 businesses failed. A public outcry rose against the nation's industries being controlled by a few giant private corporations. Du Pont wasn't the only company having labor problems those years. More than thirty strikes rocked the nation, including the Pullman strike, as workers tried to fight back against the arbitrary rule of corporate giants. Coxey's Army of unemployed marched on Washington, only to be quickly scattered by armed federal troops, but it was a serious warning for the future. The corporate elite fought back with every violent means at their disposal— private armies of armed Pinkerton detectives, police, even federal troops— but the workers of the country continued marching. Big business massacred strikers at Holmstead and Coeur d'Alene, jailed thousands of rank-and-file workers, hanged the innocent Haymarket Four in an attempt to stop the organizing of labor, tried Knights of Labor on "conspiracy" charges, had Black workers lynched in the South by the hundreds—and still the march of blue collars continued. In 1894 businessman F. L. Stetson stood nervously in the long shadow of Karl Marx's prediction of capitalist collapse as he warned his fellow businessmen, "We are on the eve of a very dark night unless a return to commercial prosperity relieves popular discontent."[16] Senator William Frye was more frank. "We must have the market (of China) or we shall have revolution."[17] The country's corporations, like Du Pont, had outgrown the American marketplace.

James Madison had predicted just such a plight in 1829. When the economy ran out of a continental market, he had warned, America would face a major economic crisis. The crisis had come and most of the business class agreed on Frye's solution—continued expansion, but this time overseas. Theodore C. Search, president of the new National Association of Manufacturers, chimed in: "Many of our manufacturers have outgrown or are outgrowing their home markets, and the expansion of our foreign trade is their only promise of relief."[18] The American Asiatic Association and the Pan-American Society rose in chorus.

Even the populists joined in, shaking off their previous call for a complete economic reorganization toward some form of planned economy and social ownership of the means of production—in a word, socialism. "We are being driven from the market of the world," cried radical Jerry Simpson on behalf of western farmers. Simpson viewed high tariffs as a protective government subsidy to manufacturers at the cost of the American farmer. But he missed recognizing overseas expansion as just another side of the same gold coin.

Expansion meant military expansion, and rumblings of war clouds could be heard in the distance. Senator Nelson Aldrich, a Rockefeller relative, demanded a "bitter conquest" for "industrial supremacy" in the world. The yellow press of Hearst and Pulitzer began to call war "good for business," as William McKinley stated, "We want our own markets for our surplus products."[19] "American factories are making more than the American people can use," exclaimed Senator Albert Beveridge in 1897. "American soil is producing more than they can consume. Fate has written our policy for us; the trade of the world shall and must be ours."[20]

By that year, military targets had become more specific. "We have a record of conquest, colonization, and expansion unequaled by any people in the nineteenth century. We are not to be curbed now," boasted Senator Henry Cabot Lodge. "For the sake of our commercial supremacy in the Pacific we should control the Hawaiian Islands and maintain an influence in Samoa."[21] The revolution in Cuba, said Grover Cleveland, was "deranging the commercial exchanges of the island, of which our country takes the predominant share."[22] Japanese expansion in the Far East, propelled by its own growing industries, also "deserves our gravest consideration," said Cleveland, "by reason of its disturbance of our growing commercial interests."[23] Theodore Roosevelt met with McKinley and recommended that "we take and retain the Philippines."[24] Encouraged, Lodge was soon "recommending that the United States add Canada, the Nicaraguan Canal, Hawaii, and Samoa to its dimensions. "We shall have at least one strong naval station," he explained, "and when the Nicaraguan Canal is built, the island of Cuba will become to us a necessity."[25] McKinley took office calling for a pacification of Cuba, while William Jennings Bryan blended racism with Christian fundamentalism with the assertion "the Filipinos cannot be citizens without endangering our civilization."[26]

Bryan was echoed by a host of intellectual apologists who stepped forward to provide a philosophy that would justify this emerging overseas American imperialism. Frederick Jackson Turner recalled Jefferson's demand for "new frontiers," while economist William Graham Sumner underlined *laissez-faire* individualism as the dynamo behind expansion, ignoring that his economy had already replaced the *laissez-faire* businessman with monopolies in the seat of power. Brooks Adams in *America's Economic Supremacy,* later paraphrased by Professor Woodrow Wilson, insisted that expansion was the key to wealth and called for America to accept its historical destiny as the new center of empire and make the Pacific and Asia its colonies. Alfred Thayer Mahan agreed, calling on the federal government to accept "The White Man's Burden" by building a large navy that would forcibly bring the white, Anglo-Saxon, Protestant God and civilization to the heathen world. Mahan's writings were said to have found strong endorsement by Acting Secretary of Navy Theodore Roosevelt, who later as president built up the American Navy in six years from a force of seventeen battleships in 1901 into the second largest sea power in the world.

On March 15, 1898, a special federal agent was sent to New York to ascertain the feelings of the new business nobility, including William Rockefeller, Thomas Ryan, John Jacob Astor, and J. P. Morgan. Wall Street was "feeling militant," he reported back, with nothing but war talk.

As John D. Rockefeller explained a year later, "Dependent solely upon local business we should have failed years ago. We were forced to extend our markets and to seek for export trade."[27]

And seek they did. Acting Secretary of Navy Teddy Roosevelt took it upon himself to send unauthorized orders to Commodore Dewey to sail troops to the Philippines and stand by, ready to take the islands. McKinley refused to countermand the order; one night during prayers, he explained, the Lord came and advised him to annex the Philippines because it would be cowardly, dishonorable, and bad business not to. "And then I went to bed, and to sleep, and slept soundly."[28]

On April 11, 1898, President McKinley demanded and received from Congress army and navy forces "to secure a full and final determination of hostilities between the Spanish governor and the people of Cuba." What he did not tell Congress was that the Spanish governor, counseled by the Vatican, had already announced a cessation of hostilities with the Cuban revolutionaries. To this day, many Cubans hold that they had already won their independence when the United States intervened to crush not only the Spanish but also the Cuban revolution that threatened over $50 million in American investments already there.

The Spanish-American War had begun, but it was actually a war against indigenous revolutions in overseas lands that American capitalists wanted and Spanish colonialists were unable to defend. Cuba was seized in an invasion by 200,000 U.S. troops and placed under a U.S. military rule that was later succeeded by a government whose constitution openly allowed U.S. intervention at Washington's slightest whim. That year the Virgin Islands and Puerto Rico were seized and annexed, as was Hawaii, Wake, and Guam, the "manifest destiny" of the Monroe Doctrine having been extended now to the Pacific. By 1899, 60,000 American troops were busily crushing the Filipino revolution, occupying the island and massacring its defenseless women and children in many predecessors to Vietnam's My Lai, having destroyed the antiquated Spanish fleet along the way.

That same year the Monroe Doctrine touched the Asian mainland under a new name: The Open Door Policy. The new policy was heralded in the *Philadelphia Press:* "As important as the Monroe Doctrine has been for America in the past century. It protects the present, it safeguards the future"[29] of American capital expansion into a China being raped by European and Japanese capitalist powers. The *Boston Transcript* was more blunt: "We have an infinitely wider scope in the Chinese market than we should have had with a sphere of influence in competition with half a dozen other spheres."[30] Many Europeans caught on. A Berlin paper summed it up in one sentence: "The Americans regard, in a certain sense, all China as their sphere and orbit."[31] By the turn of the century, 2 percent of all U.S. trade went to China, American companies were setting up factories there, and U.S. troops had marched into Peking to protect U.S. investments—and loot.[32]

This emphasis on "spheres of interest" in Chinese markets was the source of President Theodore Roosevelt's sudden turn toward humanitarianism a few years later when he helped negotiate the peace treaty that ended the Russian-Japanese War. A balance of power in Asia was necessary to prevent one power from acquiring dominance over China and thus threatening American capitalism's own economic penetration. The age of U.S. imperialism had arrived.

By 1900 the United States had temporarily satisfied its appetite for expansion. For maintaining control and for making future conquests, a permanent General Staff was created, the Navy enlarged, and the Army raised to a standing force of 100,000 troops.

The economy, injected with new markets for capital investments and products, made a comeback and soon its industries were again booming. Despite cries of moral protest from socialists, a few labor groups, and Mark Twain and his Anti-imperialist League who wanted to spoil it all with their consciences, the American business class managed to enjoy themselves at the new territorial banquet. Teddy Roosevelt bellowed "Bully!" Wall Street, symbolized by J. P. Morgan, contentedly patted its stomach, and everyone who was anyone seemed to be happy—including the Du Ponts.

7. ALFRED'S POWDER FIGHTS A WAR

When Frank gave up his beloved astronomy to experiment in smokeless powder at the new Carney's Point plant, the family was more than enthusiastic. The son of deceased Lammot, Pierre Samuel du Pont, joined Frank. This Pierre was just the opposite of his turbulent great-great-grandfather, the first Pierre Samuel. He was small and quiet, but determined and very efficient in everything he did. Pierre caused no waves at a time when calmness was a precious commodity in selling oneself to Du Pont elders. Everyone agreed he had a marvelous future, especially when he and Frank produced the first Du Pont powder for shotguns. In 1895 Du Pont landed a contract for making smokeless powder for U.S. artillery and rifles.

Young Alfred, however, although a partner, did not share in Pierre's popularity. His youthful ambition ruffled the feathers of his elders. They had even rejected his Belgian and British deals for producing smokeless and brown prismatic powder, but finally complied when the U.S. government agreed to pay the royalties due the Europeans. Although Frank and

Eugene were upset about giving Alfred a victory, profits came first. Alfred was soon producing brown powder based on the British formula for the U.S. Navy.

Alfred tried his best to make peace in the family. After his Swamp Hall, the second and third homes in Delaware to be wired with electricity were those of the Du Pont elders Eugene and Frank—and they were done by Alfred. Then Alfred brought his electric good cheer to Aunt Mary, widow of Lammot, Great Aunt Louisa, widow of Henry, then to the homes of spinster cousin Mary, Dr. Alexis I., Colonel Henry, and Colonel Henry's sister, Mrs. Antoine L. Foster. Alfred even wired Christ Church and St. Joseph's Church, including the convent, the rectory, and the school.

But electricity, marvel though it was, could not make up for what Alfred lacked: tact. The elders continued to ignore him at partnership meetings. Alfred grew more estranged and soon began spending more and more time at his hunting hideaway, Cherry Island, on the eastern shore of Virginia. Finally he stopped attending partnership meetings altogether.

With the coming of war in 1898, Alfred suddenly found himself in demand. The government was in short supply of brown prismatic powder and wanted 20,000 pounds a day. Could Du Pont fill the order? The elders turned to Alfred. The Brandywine was only producing 3,000 pounds a day, but Alfred insisted his men could meet the order. They did—within sixty days.

Alfred worked his men eighteen hours a day. Every day, for 18 cents an hour, "Long John" Thompson burned 300 pounds of charcoal from 500 pounds of wood, Alfred giving him "1 percent to come and go on" in deviance with the 3 from 5 ratio. Alfred helped by inventing a faster type of press for making powder grains. Every twenty-four hours saw 800 square, zinc-lined boxes, each holding 25 pounds of brown powder, delivered to Colonel Henry's Wilmington and Northern Railroad.

The Du Ponts were always a class-conscious family. They knew that their mills' production and their wealth ultimately depended on the labor of their workers. During the Spanish-American War, therefore, it was common family practice to keep a tight paternalistic eye over the workers' private lives, and this included religion.

As nonreligious E. I. du Pont had explained, religion served to quell the fears of powdermakers every day facing eternity. Young Du Ponts were taught this fact as part of their executive training in psychological class warfare; Alfred was no exception. He knew St. Joseph's was an important weapon in the Du Pont arsenal of control. Once, Alfred stopped a worker, Charles Deery, whom he thought was straying from St. Joseph's flock. "Deery," he grimly warned, "I'll have to speak to Father Bermingham. A pretty note, your turning Presbyterian."[33] Deery, in fact, had never thought of such a thing. He loved the Church as he did the Du Ponts. He had worked for them for forty years, ever since an explosion had burned the eyes out of his father, also a Du Pont worker. He had even named his two daughters Madelaine and Bessie, after "Mr. Alfred's" little girls. It must be his wife's sewing circle in the Presbyterian Church! By evening, as Alfred left the plant, he was met by Kate Deery at the gate, who pleaded her case for some innocent sewing and promised that she, Charlie, and her daughters would forever be good standing members of St. Joseph's. Alfred assured her he was pleased to hear it.

Nor was Alfred concerned when Italian Catholics came to work at the Brandywine. Like fatalistic Irishmen, he explained to his partners, like fatalistic Italians. "Moreover, an Italian will do what he is told," he added, "whereas an Irishman is apt to get to 'thunkin' of some way to do it better. When an Irishman on a powder line gets to 'thunkin,' it's time to begin to look for him on the other side of the creek."[34]

Meanwhile, other American workers and farmers marched in uniforms across more distant creeks singing "There'll be a hot time in the old town tonight" to a splendidly mismanaged war. The cavalry had no horses, the horses had no saddles, and the infantry had no shoes. Sometimes the men had no food and sometimes what food they had killed them. Rations put in tin cans gave whole companies ptomaine poisoning. Troops in the tropical heat of Cuba found themselves clad in woolen uniforms. Yellow fever sliced its way through 200,000 troops in Cuba. For every man killed in action, thirteen men died of disease.

Yet, as Secretary of State Hay claimed, it was "a splendid little war" for the heroes who commanded the troops and the "yellow press." Teddy Roosevelt's Rough Riders had no horses at San Juan Hill, but they did have an enthusiastic reporter, Richard Harding Davis. And "Long John" Thompson may have made only 18 cents an hour, but in four months Du Pont delivered 2.2 million pounds of brown prismatic powder to the government at 33 cents a pound and Alfred was declared an unsung hero of the war. What also went unsung was the fraud the Du Ponts were committing. The powder they sold the government at 33 cents a pound cost them only 8 cents a pound to produce. That was 320 percent profit, extortion in anyone's book.[35]

The Du Ponts made over half a million dollars from that short war. Others, however, were not so fortunate. In 1898 two explosions rocked Carney's Point, killing one worker. On December 9, 1898, one day before the peace treaty was signed, the overworked Brandywine was also hit with a series of explosions that killed five workers.

Even with the war ended, Du Pont continued wartime production, having increased plant capacity by nine times the prewar days. Frank and Pierre ran into problems with their smokeless powder plant. In March of 1899 an explosion killed three workers and wounded many others, including Francis I. du Pont, son of Francis G., and Alexis I. du Pont III. In April, Captain Sidney Stuart and five workers were loading a 13-inch shell with guncotton. Suddenly there was an explosion and the shell, the men, and the ground they were standing on disappeared. Pierre was visibly shaken, and from that time on his interest strayed from production to the safer subject of finances.

In September, Pierre finally left his family's firm. The elders had decided to incorporate the firm but allowed no room for younger Du Ponts on the new board of directors, the only family members allowed to hold stock. Disgusted, Pierre decided to move on to the greener fields of Kentucky and join his cousin, T. Coleman du Pont.

But Pierre's disappointment was no match to that of his more erratic cousin, Alfred. All the partners of the old firm had been named to the board of directors and all had been given offices—except him.

Alfred was visibly hurt and confused. "I think the old company may need you sometime, I just have that feeling,"[36] his father, E. I. du Pont II, had said to Alfred on his deathbed. Those words found little meaning to him now. In 1899 there was no way Alfred I. du Pont could have foreseen that Du Pont Company was approaching the greatest crisis of its existence, a crisis that would propel him into a decade of personal tragedy with the family title "Savior of the Du Ponts."

Six

THE NEW ORDER

1. APPEARETH THE "SAVIOR"

On January 21, 1902, Eugene du Pont, 62-year old president of Du Pont Company, failed to appear at his office. He had a cold, it was reported. One week later he was dead.

Eugene's death from pneumonia was more than just a personal shock to his family. It was also a business crisis, perhaps the greatest the family had ever faced. Decades of failing to bring young Du Ponts into the seats of power now came back to haunt the elders in their time of greatest need. Eugene's younger brother Frank, the next in line of succession, was too ill to take over the firm. In fact, he would join his dead brother at Sand Hole within two years. Eugene's other brother, Dr. Alexis, was also ill. He too would die within weeks of Frank. Their cousin and fellow partner, Charles I. du Pont, although still in his thirties, was also failing. He would be dead before the year was out. In all, Du Pont's board of directors was a round table of dying knights unable to rule or save the family's industrial kingdom.

Desperate, the elders turned to Colonel Henry A. du Pont, the only remaining director, but Henry had deeply involved himself in Delaware politics. For years he had been following to the point of obsession the quest for the political holy grail of his life: Delaware's seat in the U.S. Senate. Because of a bitter personal feud with one John "Gas" Addicks over political control of the state, his obsession had reached the point of blind fanaticism. With an election approaching, he refused to tie himself down with the enormous responsibilities of captaining the corporate armada called Du Pont.

It was cruel irony for the Du Ponts. Henry du Pont, who had devotedly given the company fifty toilsome years of his life, had actually started this crisis with his policy of keeping the family youth out of positions of power and favoring his own sons for succession. Now with one son, William, scandalously exiled, his last remaining and favorite son, Henry, refused to lead the company at its time of greatest need.

Some in the family looked to Alfred. "Too young," cautioned Frank,[1] and too impulsive. With just such a remark, Frank summarily doused what family fires may have been kept burning for that eldest son of E. I. du Pont II. Alfred was hurt, of course, but surprisingly kept his opinions to himself. He suspected what was about to happen and for once in his life kept a cool head in front of his family, then secretly took a train to New York to visit its leading banks.

While Alfred scrambled about Wall Street, the elders announced the predictable decision. No one in the family, they felt, had the qualifications to run the company. They were trapped into the most unfortunate of alternatives: sellout. Why lose a family fortune by turning the company over to inexperienced youth, they reasoned, and their reasoning was indeed sound. We must sell the company to Laflin and Rand, they explained, the only firm with enough capital to buy us out at our own price. Actually, it wasn't as bad as it sounded at first. Although supposedly a competitor, the Du Pont family actually held a substantial interest in Laflin and Rand. In fact, Laflin's president, J. Amory Haskell, had been an employee and lieutenant of Lammot du Pont and had helped Ethel du Pont's husband, Hamilton Barksdale, take over Repauno Chemicals after William du Pont's exile. Haskell had been transferred to Laflin and Rand after Du Pont became the largest, although still minority, stockholder. With Haskell running the show, nothing would actually change but the name of the firm, and perhaps, with persuasion, that might also remain.

But it was still a terrific blow to the family's pride. Sadly they met at a stockholder's meeting to write the formal obituary to E. I. du Pont's powder company. They would ask $12 million from Laflin and Rand, Frank explained. After some discussion, Colonel Henry rose to formally move for the record that the company's assets be offered for sale to Laflin and Rand, and that Hamilton Barksdale serve as negotiator. Alfred had been quiet during the meeting, clad in grimy work clothes from the yards. When Henry made his motion, Alfred closed his eyes, perhaps to help his failing hearing. Then he rose to offer an amendment: that they be sold "to the highest bidder." Only a harmless formality, the elders felt, and Henry accepted the amendment as "friendly" and the motion was passed. Then the meeting was adjourned, the Du Ponts breathing a sigh of relief that Alfred had not made a scene. They sighed too soon.

Alfred suddenly threw himself in front of the door, blocking it. "Gentlemen," he exclaimed, "I'll buy the business!"[2] Frank's long face became drawn and irritated. He said that was impossible. "Besides, it's cash, you know."[3] Alfred became furious. The confrontation with Frank, delayed for years, had finally come. "Why not?" he exploded. "If you can't run the company, sell it to someone who can!"[4] His voice rising and becoming more shrill, Alfred admonished the elders for holding back the family youth and declared the company to be his birthright. "I pointed out to him [Frank] the fact that the business was mine by all rights of heritage; that it was my birthright. I told him that I would pay as much for the business as anybody; that furthermore I proposed to have it. I told him I would require one week to perfect the necessary arrangements looking toward the purchase of the business, and asked for that length of time."[5] Who was better qualified? Alfred demanded. For the first time in years, Frank was silent.

Colonel Henry had felt guilty during the whole affair. Alfred's stand gave his conscience and political ambition a way to redeem themselves.

"All right, I'm with you,"[6] he said, slapping a long hand on Alfred's broad shoulder. "Gentlemen, I think I understand Alfred's sentiment in desiring to purchase the business. I wish to say that it has my hearty approval. I shall insist that he be given the first opportunity to acquire the property."

Alfred had won the first battle, but not the war. Frank du Pont considered it just another of Alfred's scenes, making the whole transaction more difficult for everyone. In the tradition since Antoine Bidermann, a phone call was made to the talented Du Pont in-law Hamilton Barksdale. Barksdale was an able executive and, as far as the elders were concerned, a good choice for president pro tem. Dr. Alexis offered him the job.

Barksdale, catching the scent of family feud, wisely declined. "In my opinion," he told Dr. Alexis, "it would be a great misfortune for the company to place anyone at the head of the concern until you have exhausted all efforts to secure a man of your own name to take the helm."[7] It was obvious that all efforts had not been exhausted. Alfred still had one week to make good his challenge.

Alfred used every minute of that week. He knew his executive abilities were lacking and, as his efforts at Wall Street had failed, he needed help in financing his project. Only one man he had ever known could provide the talents he needed. He hopped into his automobile and drove through the streets of Wilmington until he came to 808 Broome Street, the home of his cousin and former schoolmate, T. Colemen du Pont.

2. APPEARETH THE KENTUCKY KING

Thomas Coleman du Pont was from the Kentucky branch of the family where Uncle Fred, Alfred's guardian, had ruled. The son of Bidermann du Pont, Uncle Fred's brother, Coleman had been Alfred's roommate at M.I.T. But he was more than just a roommate to his younger cousin. He was Alfred's teacher and hero. A huge, dark, handsome man, Coleman was

6 feet, 4 inches of charm and solid muscle. At Urbana College in Ohio he had captained the football and baseball teams, stroked the crew, and ran the hundred-yard dash in ten seconds flat. Coleman could drink, fight, and play the role of he-man better than anyone Alfred had ever met, with the possible exception of John L. Sullivan. After finishing M.I.T., he rivaled Alfred for the hand of their cousin Alice du Pont, called "Elsie" in the family. Typically, Coleman won and carried his bride off to Central City, Kentucky, where his father owned coal mines, and his uncle just about everything else.

Coleman had a reputation for having a big heart. When his father discovered a rich deposit of coal, for example, Coleman celebrated Thanksgiving by sending each coal miner just what he needed most—a free bag of coal. When he installed the first tub with running water in that part of Kentucky, he proudly let in the poor people who had come from miles around to see and marvel. Coleman could flash the biggest smiles at times like that.

Like Alfred, Coleman worked his way up in business. Starting as a mining apprentice, he was soon superintendent and chief engineer. He even joined the Knights of Labor to try to get a feeling for the workers and their thinking. Apparently, Coleman's class background prevented him from understanding much. He couldn't comprehend why the miners were angry about his father's paying them only $1.25 to $1.75 a day for their hazardous labor. He also could not understand why the Knights of Labor finally struck his father's mines in 1884.

His past membership notwithstanding, Coleman crushed the Knights' strike by using convicts as strikebreakers. Pulling strings in political circles, he forced the prisoners to march under armed guard from the stockade at Shegog Crossing to his mines, crossing the angry picket lines. There, under the barrels of shotguns, the prisoners mined for the Du Ponts as slave labor till dusk and then were marched back to prison. Finally one prisoner was shot to death trying to escape; Coleman remained his usual cool and indifferent self, but that death was too much for the miners. Faced with starvation in their homes and the likelihood of more prisoners dying, they gave in. With a bellowing laugh, Coleman lit up one of his huge cigars in celebration and flashed that famous grin.

In retaliation for lost profits, Coleman then decided to teach the workers who was boss. Miners in those days were paid by the tonnage of coal remaining on top of screens. Coleman changed the size of the screens' holes from $1\frac{1}{2}$ inches to 2 inches. Thus less coal stayed on top of the screen, returning fewer dollars to the miners for their labor, forcing the workers to labor twice as fast and hard to make the same wage per day. Coleman's scheme was an obvious attack on the workers, an effective wage cut and speed-up. Again the miners tried to fight back with another strike in 1887, and again Coleman used scabs to crush the strike. The 2-inch screens remained. Coleman celebrated by buying control of Central City's major newspaper, *The Argus,* and renaming it the *Central City Republican.*

Six years later, in 1893, Coleman ran for public office, aspiring to be Central City's second mayor. The campaign issue at the time was labor, its rights and its needs. Predictably, he was defeated, and just as predictably, Coleman couldn't understand why. "I won't stay in a place where that's all they think of me,"[8] he complained, his ego hurt. In 1895 T. Coleman du Pont left Central City, never to return and never to be missed.

Coleman went to Johnstown, Pennsylvania, to join his friends J. Moxham and Tom Johnson and take the post of general manager of their Johnson Company, later to become Lorain Steel and a part of J. P. Morgan's U.S. Steel. Soon "Coly" was the driving force and president of a score of companies, always promoting new deals with his huge size, gusto, and growing management reputation. When he bought Johnstown's street railway, he profited so well that he branched out into speculating with its properties, buying low here, selling high there.

In 1900 Coleman moved to Wilmington following his latest acquisition—a local button factory. For one reason or another, the factory failed to produce a single button, and Coleman, eager to avoid any tarnish on his image as a financial soldier of fortune, dropped the company like it had the plague. Instead, he involved himself again in land speculation and bought a mansion at 808 Broome Street, which he later turned into a country club for his children and many friends, reigning like a king over weekly dances.

It was here that Alfred went to see Coleman about his plan to buy the family business.

"Al, it's a big thing," Coleman said. "I'll have to talk to Elsie."[9] Alfred left while Coleman the Giant ran to his tiny wife for advice. Elsie du Pont, it seemed, was Coleman's real source of strength. He completely relied on her, for behind the powerful bulk of Kentucky steel was a secret weakness—Coleman was frankly a scared little boy. He was frightened to death of failure. Often he would suffer severe fits of nervous indigestion during business trips, and Elsie constantly kept a bag packed in case Coleman telegrammed for help. In such times only Elsie could shore him up and pull the deal through.

After Coleman explained Alfred's proposal, Elsie's face wrinkled into a frown. "You know what it is to be in business with your relatives,"[10] she warned. Du Ponts do not make good business partners: each thinks his way is divinely superior. In this regard, however, Coleman was no exception in the family. "I won't go in," he finally resolved, "unless I get a free hand."[11] "A free hand" meant the presidency. Alfred could be the vice-president and general manager, a role close to the mills and one which perfectly suited Alfred. But Coleman also had one more condition. He wanted his cousin, Pierre du Pont, to join them as treasurer. Alfred agreed. He knew Pierre's qualifications. Since leaving the Brandywine, Pierre had become president of the Johnson Company and had worked closely with Coleman on many other deals. He had an excellent mind for finances and his calculated caution would be a good balance to Coleman's boldness. Too good, as time would prove. Alfred would later regret this decision.

United in common purpose for the present, the cousins then met with the elders. With the prestige of victory that always bowled over his opposition, Coleman displayed his best as a slick promoter. Tall and powerfully built, his eyes flashing with emotion as his body made sweeping gestures, he was an impressive sight and soon dominated the gathering like any good showman. In a deep booming voice, he proposed to pay *more* than the minimum $12 million the elders wanted. The exact amount, he assured them, would depend on a survey of the company's assets. With his elders obviously pleased, Coleman then slipped in his plan. He suggested the sellers accept notes worth $12 million with 4 percent interest plus 28 percent of the common stock in the new corporation in exchange for their stock. "You wouldn't want to cripple our plans by tying up all our cash,"[12] he said in a deep, calm voice. The elders looked at each other for a moment and nodded agreement. Within a few hours it was all over. For a mere $3,000 in cash, the legal cost of setting up the new company, the three cousins had acquired the largest gunpowder trust in the history of the world.

3. COLEMAN'S FIREWORKS DISPLAY

While Coleman was signing contracts that would bring new life and a new age to Du Pont, a new age of wonders had also been born to the world—the twentieth century. Electricity brought light and teletypes, X rays and radio. The Flatiron Building rose twenty stories into the Manhattan sky, dwarfing the gilded automobiles of the rich and the taxicabs that sputtered about at its base.

But it was also an age of continued poverty for most Americans. By 1899, 250,000 Americans owned most of America's wealth, while 50 million earned only $1.50 a day. Prices fell, but so did wages.

The average family needed $800 a year to survive, yet most unskilled jobs paid no higher than $500.[13] Starvation forced over a million women into the factories at even less pay than their male counterparts earned,[14] 80 percent of them receiving less than $16 a week.[15] Even with both parents working there wasn't enough to meet the basic needs of most American families. The solution was agonizing. Working-class families were forced to see their children leaving school to work for ten hours a day in a sweatshop or a factory. In 1900 the census recorded 1,750,178 "gainfully occupied children aged ten to fifteen."[16] By 1910 almost two million children,[17] or 18 percent of the nation's total labor force, toiled for the "fat cats" of Wall Street. Working conditions were horrible,[18] and the federal government knew about them.[19] In fact, the Supreme Court had openly refused to intervene in child labor. The right of property was blatantly held more important than the right of life. Some children were killed, many were maimed for life, and many more were cheated. "At the Marble Coal Company," for instance, "twelve-year-old Andrew Chippie's forty cents a day was regularly credited against the debt left by his father, killed four years before in a mine accident."[20] The debt was to the inevitable company store. Meanwhile, coal mine owners like the Du Ponts of Kentucky were enjoying their most profitable year yet as the United States became the leading industrial nation in the world. Glass output, for example, rose by 52 percent since the depression of the 1890's. No one but the parents noticed the ten-year-old children who tied stoppers on 300 bottles a day.

And no one could understand why anyone would want to shoot such a kindly old imperialist like President William McKinley. Portly McKinley had just completed a visit to the 1901 Pan-American exposition at Buffalo, where the promoters presented a breath-taking display of fireworks called "Our Empire," filling the sky with exploding stars and rockets representing Cuba, Puerto Rico, and the Philippines. "I killed President McKinley because I done my duty," exclaimed his radical assassin. "I didn't believe one should have so much service and another man should have none. . . . I don't believe we should have any rulers."[21] Now what was that madman raving about? cried the rulers. The "public opinion" of the rulers' yellow press just couldn't understand. Neither did the Du Ponts.

In fact, Coleman du Pont was too busy building his own empire to even care. Right after he assumed the presidency, he disappeared from sight. Two weeks later he reappeared at a director's meeting in Wilmington and dumped a bag on the table. "There's control of Laflin and Rand,"[22] he boasted. The Du Ponts were startled. Coleman explained how he had approached John L. Riker, a major stockholder in Laflin and Rand, and unfolded his plan to consolidate all powder companies in the United States. Riker became infected with Coleman's enthusiasm and the possible returns, and finally agreed to exchange Laflin shares for those of the new Du Pont corporation. Coleman fiananced the deal through bonds of new front names, Delaware Investment Co. and Delaware Securities Co.[23] As part of the deal, he also bought the Moosic Powder Co.

Du Pont now held control of the very company to which the elders would have sold out.

But more than Laflin and Rand was at stake. Coleman's decision to absorb Du Pont's largest competitor implicitly meant that he intended to destroy the Gunpowder Trade Association and absorb also the entire Powder Trust into Du Pont Company. It was a chilling move for what independent powder firms remained; chilling for them, but for the Du Ponts, breathtaking.

Coleman now controlled fifty companies strung out across the country, each with its own manufacturing, administrative, and marketing operations. Coly quickly tore into them, dissolving each operation and binding them together into one Du Pont International Corporation; J. Amory Haskell of Laflin and Rand was made vice-president. Any minority stockholders were bought out by a new dummy company, the E. I. du Pont de Nemours Powder Co. Among those new companies absorbed were the California Vizorit Powder Co. (high explosives), the American E. C. & Schultz Gunpowder Co., and the International Smokeless Powder & Chemical Co.

Then Coleman, paying $240,000 to shake off price and trade agreements, simply walked out of the Gunpowder Association, leaving behind a hollow shell. And just as simply, the Powder Trust fell apart—mostly into Du Pont hands. Gone now were the secret trade pacts and ownerships. The Du Pont Empire was now open for all to see.

Big, roistering Coleman now basked in the limelight of Du Pont attraction. Family praises fed his vanity; he felt he deserved them, and he did. He had done the impossible. Spending about $8,500 in cash, he had acquired through the issue of stock $35,955,000 in new assets. When the firm's books had been accounted by Pierre and his small, tight-lipped secretary from Ohio, John J. Raskob, the company's assets were found to be worth over $24 million. That made the new total $59,955,000. (Pierre later certified this amount on December 31, 1905.)

Even the elders, who had received only $15 million in new stocks for the old company, were more than pleased. That is, Colonel Henry was, for he was the only one of the old school still alive.

4. ADVANCING WITH "CIVILIZATION"

By 1905 "Coleman's Company," as it was increasingly being called among the family (to Alfred's growing concern), was directly manufacturing 64.6 percent of all U.S. soda blasting powder, 80 percent of all salt-peter blasting powder, 72.5 percent of all dynamite, 75 percent of all black sporting powder, 70.5 percent of all smokeless sporting powder, and 100 percent of all military smokeless powder.[24]

This last product, military smokeless powder, was a gift from the United States government. Du Pont, despite the experiments by Pierre, Frank, and Frank's son, Francis I. (and despite present claims to the contrary), had never discovered a perfected smokeless powder. The U.S. government did. Patents covering the manufacture of Navy and Army smokeless powder were all filed on the discoveries of men hired by the government. Patent No. 489,684 was issued to Professor Charles E. Munroe, under the employ of the Navy Department, on January 10, 1893. Its exclusive rights to manufacture, however, were awarded to Du Pont with no available reason given. Patent No. 550,472 was issued to Lieutenant John B. Bernadou and Captain George A. Converse of the U.S. Navy on November 26, 1895. Their discovery had been developed at the U.S. Torpedo Station Laboratory at Newport, Rhode Island. Patent No. 586,586 was issued to Lieutenant Bernadou on July 20, 1895, as were Patents No. 652,455 and 652,505 on June 26, 1900, and Patent No. 673,377 on May 7, 1901.

The first patent by Professor Munroe could not be used by the Du Ponts, however, its specifications differing from those ordered by their greatest customers, the U.S. Army and Navy. The second patent, filed by Lieutenant Bernadou and Captain Converse, was more suitable to Du Pont needs because it used alcohol-ether and colloid instead of Munroe's Metro-benzine colloid. Unfortunately for Du Pont, this patent was purchased by International Smokeless Powder Company, which partly explains Cole-man's swiftness between 1903 and 1904 in completely buying out Inter-national. For the other patents, Coleman slipped Bernadou $75,000. The Navy and Army, which actually controlled the patents, were also very helpful. Navy and Army officers were given large blocks of International Smokeless Powder stock. Lieutenant Meigs, inspector at Bethlehem Steel for the U.S. Navy, for example, was given 1,000 shares worth $100 each, a total value of $100,000.[25] Brigadier General James Reilly[26] and General Ryan,[27] U.S. Army, were also large stockholders.

Military officers weren't the only friends the Du Ponts had. Patrons for their deadly art were everywhere in Washington, particularly in the White House. President Theodore Roosevelt's Corollary to the Monroe Doctrine was met with great approval on the Brandywine. That American warships would protect the Du Pont monopoly over Caribbean and Central Ameri-can powder markets solidified the international cartel arrangements made a decade earlier.

Roosevelt's Big Stick came down mercilessly in that area, paving the way for future American business expansion. In 1903 alone, Roosevelt landed U.S. troops in Honduras, the Dominican Republic, and Panama (as well as Syria). His greatest concern, however, was in Panama. There he intended to build a canal linking the Atlantic and Pacific naval and merchant fleets. That Panama was a territory of Colombia presented a problem at first. Attempts to pressure the Colombian senate to pass the Hay-Herrán Treaty giving the United States 100-year rights to the proposed canal met with defeat. Apparently the Colombian senate didn't scare easily. Roosevelt's response was typically Kiplan.

"Those jackrabbits—contemptible little creatures of Bogotá preventing the advance of civilization."[28] Within months he was writing to agents in Panama. "How are things going on that revolution in Panama?"[29] Secretary of State Hay joined in by assuring Varilla, head of the Panama Canal Company, "The United States will not allow a revolution to fail."[30] It didn't.

Soon Du Pont powder was blasting its way through Panama, and treasurer Pierre du Pont was chalking up higher and higher sales volumes. In the Caribbean, as in America, Du Pont had a monopoly, and the digging of the Canal was not made any cheaper by noncompetitive prices for black powder and dynamite paid at taxpayers' expense.

Between July 1905 and July 1906 the War Department presented the Du Ponts with another token of their esteem: an order for 5,947,820 pounds of smokeless powder. The Delaware family showed its appreciation by charging 70 cents per pound for powder costing only 32 cents per pound to produce. Over $2.2 million was netted in profits.

Then another gift was laid on doorsteps along the Brandywine: an order for 300,000 pounds of powder for 32-caliber weapons. The powder had a net cost of 44 cents a pound, the Du Ponts charged 84½ cents per pound, profiteering another $230,000.

Such fraud, the Chicago *Chronicle* explained, "is greater than any profit ever derived by any seller of any product of staple sold in one year to the government in the history of the republic."[31] But that wasn't all. "The monopoly carrying on the business," the *Chronicle* added, "was at the same time contracting with foreign nations to furnish ammunition with which they could attack American merchant men on the high seas."

Where there is a demand, Coleman would say, there will be a supply. E. I. du Pont I would have been proud.

In 1906 Secretary of War William Howard Taft announced that the United States needed a reserve of 30 million pounds of powder to be adequately prepared for war. No one asked which war he was referring to, but one point was obvious: The Indian Head plant built by the government produced only one million pounds a year, all of it consumed in Navy target practice. Unless more government mills were built that could produce powder at cost (35 cents per pound) the War Department would have to pay Du Pont's price of 75 cents a pound. The Family would run off with a huge net profit of $12 million. One-tenth that amount would in one year build government factories that could produce the Secretary's reserve at one-half the cost. Would the Secretary agree to build the plants? Taft gave his answer at the year's end: He announced that the War Department had bought 6 million pounds of powder from the Du Ponts that year.

Coleman's head was swimming with power. In 1904, 50 cents was paid per common share of Du Pont's stock; in 1905, $3.50; in 1906, $6.50. One by one, Coly began to kill off the last independent competitors in America. First, American Powder: in 1909 it made $288,500; by 1907 it pulled in barely $30,000. The Lakeside Powder drew $60,000 in sales in 1905; by 1907, $23,500.[32] Then the Burton Powder Company fell under his financial blows; then the Cressona Powder Company; then Connell Powder. Coleman even turned on a member of his own family, Anne Ridgely du Pont, daughter of Eugene. Anne had married William Peyton, President of the Peyton Chemical Company of California. Over her protests, Coleman bought 3,000 of the company's 6,500 shares and grabbed over $230,000 worth of Peyton's bonds. Then he used the courts to win his claim of control. Soon Peyton was out of a job and a family rift began that was healed only by the salve of enormous profits under new management. Finally, only the Buckeye Powder Company of Peoria, Illinois, was left. That's when Coleman's troubles began.

5. ROBERT THE GIANT KILLER

The president of Buckeye was Robert S. Waddell. For twenty years Waddell had served Eugene du Pont well as a sales agent, rising to become Du Pont's general sales director. Because of his own shortcomings, Eugene gave a lot of independence to individual department heads. But with Eugene's death, the company drastically changed. Waddell found the new president didn't want men, but "puppets dancing on strings," puppets that sometimes were pitted against each other. Coleman swaggered into the company molding everything in his own image, slashing here and building there, all the while maintaining his characteristic insensitivity to employees.

Waddell was disgusted. As early as March 11, 1902, Coleman was disputing with his sales director, trying to force the stubborn old-timer under his thumb.[33] But Waddell was not a man to bend to anyone, even T. Coleman du Pont. On November 25, 1902, after twenty years of efficient service with Du Pont, Waddell resigned. "A definite policy for the conduct of the business along fair and just lines might have evolved," he wrote Coleman. "Instead of this, your letter indicates that it is the purpose to thrust the heads of departments, like roosters, into a pit to fight for supremacy. The stakes are too small. I have never been involved in such a disgusting condition of business."[34] Waddell insisted that he would not become "an automaton in a business machine."

Waddell established his own powder company, the Buckeye Powder Company in Peoria, Illinois. Coleman, of course, was not very happy about this turn of affairs. First he tried to buy into Waddell's company. Waddell refused. Then Coleman hired lawyers, detectives, and spies to harass Waddell's young firm. Waddell filed his first formal complaint with the U.S. Department of Commerce and Labor on October 19, 1903. "I have no desire to assume the role of a reformer," he wrote Secretary George Cortelyou, "and have refrained from presenting this matter until it has become a necessity in defense of our business."[35] But the harassment continued. Coleman sent agents to stir up the Peoria community against Waddell's plant, spreading rumors that it was dangerous to the town. On March 3, 1905, Waddell filed another complaint against Coleman's monopoly. "Mr. T. C. du Pont represents the American manufacturers," he wrote Labor Commissioner James Garfield on Du Pont's trade agreements, "and furnishes the pooling data for associates."[36] This complaint reached the Department's Bureau of Corporations, but still no aid was given the beleaguered firm.

In 1906 Waddell's firm, after two years of profitable business, finally began to falter as Du Pont tightened its stranglehold, choking off capital reserves from Buckeye. Waddell then decided to fight back with bigger guns than complaints to government bureaucracies.

On June 16, 1906, Waddell published an open letter to the President and members of Congress exposing the Du Ponts for their price fraud on brown and smokeless powder sold to the government. "Here is an absolute and exclusive monopoly," he wrote, "superior to the government, intrenched at the Capitol, with its representatives in the House, Senate, and Departments. . . . It is not safe to intrust this Du Pont monopoly with the most essential article for national defense, nor is it right to rob the people to build up this monopoly and fatten millionaries."[37] No one could argue with that. Even Alfred had to admit he had put on a few pounds.

But Waddell's language and facts grew stronger. "The market for the Government is cornered by a single group of conspirators,"[38] he said. If the government wants powder, Waddell pointed out, it must accept the bid of the Du Pont Trust. "The welfare of the nation is in the balance against the Du Pont Trust," he concluded. "Our inquiry is personable and reasonable. Are you with the Powder Monopoly or the people?"[39]

Apparently, Congress and the President couldn't make up their minds. By the time 1907 rolled around, Waddell's plant was slipping fast, his sales plunging from 1905's $200,000 to $98,500.[40] One of the big factors in this decline was a mysterious explosion that destroyed Waddell's plant.

Waddell was being ruined and he wanted revenge. Now no throne of power was too high to challenge—not even the President of the United States. Waddell turned the light on Theodore Roosevelt's 1904 campaign closet and found a $70,000 Du Pont skeleton. "If a $70,000 campaign contribution is sufficient," he announced, "to obligate the executive and legislative department of the government to take $12 million from the taxpayers of the country and give it to the millionaires of this gigantic powder monopoly, the independent powder companies and voters of the country want to know it now."[41]

The earth on Capitol Hill began to tremble. On January 24, 1907, J. Amory Haskell, vice-president of Du Pont International, was called to testify before the House Appropriations Committee to explain Du Pont control over foreign patents that were available to the government only at prices set by Du Pont. Haskell was perfectly composed as he suggested that Du Pont had purchased foreign rights on a "secret process" powder to protect the United States government. What Haskell did not suggest but the Congressmen already realized was that Du Pont control over those patents actually restricted the government from their use except under Du Pont dictates. "To my mind," Waddell later commented, "it represents imbecility, corruption, or collusion between the Government and the Powder Monopoly."[42]

Waddell blasted the Du Ponts again on February 2, calling for government-owned plants to break the government's curious habit of providing charity for one of the country's richest families. He charged that the Du Ponts were frauding the government of over $2 million a year by charging 75 cents a pound for smokeless powder that only cost 31 cents to manufacture. It hit like a bombshell. The country's headlines screamed his charges about Du Pont donations to Roosevelt. Something had to be done.

On February 4, 1907, a mere two days after Waddell's attack had rocked the sacred temple on the hill, Congress passed House Joint Resolution 224, directing the Secretary of Commerce and Labor to "investigate and report to Congress what existing patents have been granted to officers and employees of the Government of the United States upon inventions, discoveries, or processes of manufacture or production upon articles used by the Government of the United States, and how and what extent such patents enhance the cost or otherwise interfere with the use by the Government of articles or processes so patented."[43]

The government tried every method of placating Waddell. On February 20, Acting Commissioner of the Federal Trade Commission's Bureau of Corporations, Herbert Knox Smith, even wrote a personal letter of appreciation to Waddell.

But Waddell was not to be placated, especially since his firm had finally collapsed. There were now no independent powder companies in America. Waddell's hated enemy, Coleman du Pont, was in absolute control.

Ironically enough, it was the Du Ponts who then came to Waddell's aid by imprudently trying to seize control of the National Rifle Association at its annual convention at Sea Girt, New Jersey. The convention broke up under charges of corruption, which tarnished the Du Pont public image. Nevertheless, when it reconvened at the 71st Regiment Armory in Chicago, the battle, with all its slanderous charges and countercharges, erupted again and finally elected was James A. Drain of Olympia. Drain was reportedly the candidate of the Du Pont Trust.[44]

By mid-1907 a national furor had arisen against the Du Pont monopoly. But Coleman still wasn't worried. After all, he knew the federal government was no trust-buster, despite the Sherman Anti-Trust Act. This was the greatest merger era of all times, when mergers horizontal (same market) and vertical (different markets of production) were taking place at a rate of 500 per year. Roosevelt, in his eight years of office, despite all his verbalism about a "Square Deal," initiated only forty-four legal actions, only twenty of which were strong enough to win indictments. Of these twenty, the Roosevelt administration produced only one anti-trust conviction, against American Tobacco Company, which was allowed to continue as a monopoly anyway using interlocking directorates.

The Justice Department accepted "the rule of reason" in court, holding that not all monopolies were bad. In fact, it contended, some were good. Competition was recognized as an increasing problem of instability and more and more of the new business nobility were coming to agree with J. P. Morgan that industrial stability must replace *laissez-faire* capitalism. In popular literature, Horatio Alger with his hard work, puritan ideas, and inevitable success became the hero of the age; individualism was no longer self-sufficiency but domination over others. J. P. Morgan became the exceptional individual, given the right to rule by God, a sort of new "divine right" of industrial kings. In social philosophy, social Darwinism warped the theory of evolution into a justification for political domination at home and abroad, and the United States became understood as a unique, higher expression of man's values, a position that gave support to its "manifest destiny" to control a large portion of the globe.[45] Thus, both monopolies at home and imperialism abroad received the theological and philosophical icing necessary for popular consumption.

"Progress is our most important product" advanced the notion of the business corporation working for the common good, in an effort to improve the poor reputation of the business elite.[46] The individual *can* manipulate the economy for the common good, monopolists explained. There was nothing wrong now with government and business cooperating to stabilize the economy for the common good, even if that usually meant only Wall Street's common stock returns.

Roosevelt understood progressivism for what it really was—an instrument of conservatism. It was the rationalization of the old order to meet the needs of a new monopolistic order. Like all American presidents, Roosevelt was no foe of business interests. Even as governor of New York, he stifled an investigation of insurance companies that involved political and business associates. Roosevelt favored an informal détente between corporations and their government to iron out wrinkles in the system. When Upton Sinclair's *The Jungle* raised a national outcry over the filthy and dangerous working conditions in the nation's meatpacking plants, the Pure Food and Drug Act was written in a form acceptable to both Armour and Swift, while providing restrictions that eventually eliminated smaller, fly-by-night competitors. Federal meatpacking regulations, therefore, served the interests of monopoly rule in the long run; workers were soon working in clean white gowns and aprons that were no doubt a victory for them in improving their working conditions, but still went home to tubercular shanty towns.

Often, however, Roosevelt found that not all big businessmen shared Swift's or Armour's level of consciousness as a class with a sense of history, consciously adjusting philosophically and politically to the changing needs of industrial growth under private ownership. To develop order and stability in the domestic market, formal regulation sometimes had to take the place of informal détente. The formation of the Interstate Commerce Commission was a conscious attempt to regulate the nation's railroad system to the benefit of the general corporate order and Roosevelt's call in 1904 and 1905 for firmer control over rates produced the Hepburn Act of 1906. The functioning of the Federal Trade Commission was along these lines. Its purpose was (and is) to inform business on future contours of domestic economic policy. Some corporations took its advice seriously. Some didn't. One of these was Du Pont.

The Du Ponts were Neanderthals when it came to understanding Roosevelt's corporate "liberalism." They were not against a well-organized society; it was just that their only understanding of benevolent despotism was primitive, or rather, medieval in character, like their social-feudal colony on the Brandywine. Although they fully accepted their "right" to monopolize their respective industry, and fully identified as a class with those who did likewise, they were nevertheless the happy, greedy victims of their own *laissez-faire* propaganda, embracing the very individualism they used to deter their workers from considering labor unions. It's not surprising, therefore, that they didn't respond to Roosevelt's corporate therapy. In fact, they fought it all the way.

Roosevelt was in a dilemma. He was faced with Du Pont obstinacy just when he needed flexibility most from them. Public sentiment had been stirred against the Powder Trust and workers were again in the streets because of a new economic depression. Charges of corruption against his War Department were being raised in the halls of Congress. Even he had been linked to these charges by the exposure of the $70,000 Du Pont contribution to his 1904 campaign. The President was frankly embarrassed by the whole affair. He had to act.

He did. On July 30, 1907, Roosevelt's Justice Department filed suit against the Du Ponts and their companies for violation of the Sherman Anti-Trust Act.

Coleman du Pont was in a foam. Roosevelt's Attorney General, Charles Bonaparte, had promised to allow Du Pont lawyers to present their case before a government suit was initiated, but the Attorney General had pressed ahead on Roosevelt's orders. "We then knew from actual experience," wrote Coleman in a company memorandum, "that the Attorney General was not to be depended upon and placed no more confidence in his department."[47] At least, *that* Attorney General. Under the next administration, Coleman would find the Attorney General's office very dependable. He would also receive the valuable services of the Chairman of the Senate Committee on War Department Expenditures, Colonel Henry A. du Pont.

6. THE JUNKER OF DELAWARE

It has been said that of all the Du Ponts, none made such an impact on the political life of the state of Delaware as Henry Algernon du Pont. The son of "General" Henry du Pont, the president of Delaware's largest railroad, the rewriter of the state constitution, Henry was above all the Junker of Delaware.

Henry was one of those vain men who loved military titles and insisted on being called "Colonel" even after he retired from the Army in 1875 and joined the family firm. With his silver-rimmed glasses and carefully waxed Van Dyke beard, he looked as stern and stiff as the high collars he wore. A military man in posture since his West Point training, he took his talents for command with him into the family firm.

Henry's first job with his father's company was to demand rebates from railroads which freighted Du Pont products. These railroads were at the mercy of their largest customers along their lines, the monopolies, including Du Pont. When such giants of industry as Du Pont demanded rebates, the rails had little choice but to bend. Henry was particularly good at whipping his swagger stick, so good that he even became president of the Wilmington and Northern Railroad and from 1898 to 1913 served on the Board of Directors of the Philadelphia and Reading Railroad.

With these railroad and Du Pont offices, Henry inherited his father's political power in Delaware. He made good use of it, apparently, for by 1889, the year of his father's death, he was already casting his eyes on Dover, the state capital, where the legislature was then arguing over who was going to be the next U.S. Senator, popular election of senators not having been introduced yet. It was at this time that Henry first crossed swords with his lifelong foe, John Edward O'Sullivan Addicks.

John "Gas" Addicks was the son of a minor Philadelphia politician. Born in 1841, he quit school at the age of 14 to go to work. But Addicks developed an energy and cunning that soon made up for his wooden spoon. At the age of 19, he went to work for a Philadelphia flour mill merchant, Levi Knowles. Within two years, he was Knowles's partner.

Addicks was as clever as he was ruthlessly ambitious. It was he who introduced Minnesota Spring wheat to eastern farmers. From profits he accrued and political favors for local political ward-heeling, he was rewarded with gas franchises in Boston, Brooklyn, Jersey City, and Chicago. John Addicks then went into the illuminating gas business, from whence came his nickname, "Gas." By watering stocks and manipulating contracts, he grew rich and maintained an eight-acre estate near Claymont, Delaware. He sold this estate in 1888, three years after moving to Boston.

The next year "Gas" Addicks rediscovered Delaware. Back from Europe, where he made millions from Siberian railroad stock, he used $25,000 to buy Dover legislation that netted him a return of $2 million.[48] Now this was the kind of state he liked! Unfortunately, he didn't know that it was already claimed turf—Du Pont turf.

Addicks was a big man. At least he looked big, with his expensive clothes and huge pearl stuck in his ascot tie. With a broad forehead and jutting brow, he was as impressive a character as ever walked into the sleepy town of Dover. Soon Addicks was a big name in Delaware. What he didn't know as he announced his candidacy for the U.S. Senate was that another name was even bigger—Du Pont.

When the 1892 election rolled around, Addicks offered $10,000 per legislature vote. He wanted the Du Pont man, Anthony Higgins, out. Spending over $100,000, he gained control of the Republican organizations in the downstate counties Kent and Sussex. Only New Castle remained as solidly opposed as Henry du Pont's stone walls. Colonel Henry had been at work. He even wrote a letter to President Benjamin Harrison requesting that Watson Sperry, editor of the Wilmington *Morning News*, be given a federal appointment that would take the independent editor out of Delaware politics.[49] Sperry had been supporting another Republican by the name of Massey for senator. Such a factional dispute could hurt Higgins just when Addicks was mounting his attack. Harrison, a Republican, took the hint. Sperry became a special envoy on a secret mission to Persia. The long arm of Du Pont can take one very far. Higgins, meanwhile, was reelected.

In 1895 a new senator had to be picked by the legislature. These were the days when U.S. senators were chosen by state legislatures. It would be almost twenty years before the Seventeenth Amendment would give this power to the people, and until then, Delaware's legislators jealously guarded their prerogative. (In fact, the Seventeenth Amendment was rejected by the legislatures of only two states: Utah, the dominion of conservative Mormons and Guggenheim copper interests, and Delaware, the Duchy of Du Pont.)

Addicks now controlled six votes, not enough to elect him but enough to check a clear Republican majority and prevent anyone's election. Higgins was then made to step aside and Colonel Henry du Pont announced his candidacy, expecting Addicks's house of money to collapse. To Henry's surprise, Addicks's camp suffered only one desertion. It was still a deadlock. Henry was furious and just as stubborn as Addicks—and richer. At this point, either Henry or Addicks—depending on whom one takes as source—but probably Addicks, made a statement that would resound in infamy through Delaware's history to this day: "Me or nobody!" Delaware got nobody. The personal feud between two individuals would keep Delaware from being fully represented in the U.S. Senate for twelve long years. One, and only one, each insisted, would be the victor; as it turned out, in either case Delaware was the loser.

After thirty-five ballots, the Speaker of the Senate, William T. Watson, declared no election and adjourned the legislature. Henry was outraged, insisting he would have his election. He got the Speaker of the House to declare that Watson's decision was invalid. The grounds were amazing. During the balloting, Governor Marvel had died and Watson, as Speaker of the Senate, succeeded him under the state constitution. But the constitution did not prohibit Watson from continuing on as Speaker of the Senate and he did, casting his ballots during the election. At no time was his vote ever challenged. But after his ruling, Du Pont forces, including the Speaker of the House, declared Watson had no right to rule as Speaker of the Senate and declared both his ruling and right to vote invalid. That gave Henry the majority he needed. The Speaker of the House issued a certificate of election and Henry moved to Washington demanding the Senate seat him.

Delaware was shocked by Du Pont's dishonesty. The Wilmington *Every Evening* repeated Watson's right to vote.[50] The country was shocked also. The Philadelphia *Public Ledger* reiterated the position of the Wilmington paper,[51] and even the *New York Times* charged that Watson's voting rights and ruling were "according to the state constitution and laws of all precedents in the state."[52] Apparently the U.S. Senate agreed. On May 15, 1896, the Senate voted to refuse to seat Henry and sent him packing.

Colonel Henry returned to Wilmington a bitter man. For ten more years he waged a relentless war for the Senate seat. In 1898 his image was boosted when he was awarded the Congressional Medal of Honor for his heroism in the Civil War. The medal was a little late—thirty-four years, to be exact. But it was noted that this was a time when newspaper headlines were warning, "WAR IS NOW INEVITABLE," and the government needed good relations with the Du Ponts to prepare munitions at "reasonable" rates for war with Spain and expansion overseas. Nevertheless, Henry proudly wore his medal at all public appearances.

The following year Addicks controlled twenty-one of fifty votes in the Legislature; Henry du Pont held only eight. But the Colonel had inherited his father's stubbornness; now it was definitely Henry who cried "Me or nobody!" In 1901 Addicks had twenty-two votes but again Henry denied Delaware its right to Senate representation. In fact for the next two years Delaware had no representative at all in the U.S. Senate. By 1903 Delaware had become a national scandal; under Theodore Roosevelt's pressure, compromise senators James Frank Allee and L. Heister Ball were selected for remaining Senate terms. By 1905, however, the feud was renewed for one of the seats and still a deadlock persisted. The stubborn Junker of Delaware refused to surrender, especially when he was about to bring up his biggest gun, the president of Du Pont Company.

With Coleman du Pont, Addicks finally met his match. Coly's first move was to smash Addicks's machine by luring his hacks away with bribes. Henry gave thousands to Sussex County Republicans.[53] Coleman then had

George Kennan, the old secretary for deceased Lammot du Pont, write a now-famous article in *Outlook* magazine charging Addicks with "Holding Up a State."

Coleman was as efficient in organizing the campaign as he was ruthless in his threats. Henry felt things were going so well, he sailed off on a European cruise to relax his nerves. In June, Addicks announced he was pulling out in the interest of the Republican Party, his twelve-year hold on the party smashed in one short year by T. Coleman du Pont. On June 12 the Republican caucus nominated Henry by a vote of twenty to ten. On June 13, 1906, he was elected U.S. Senator.

Eight hours before, Addicks boarded a Dover train bound for New York. He never returned. The copper market soon fell as the 1907 depression began, and Addicks's fortune disappeared. As Henry sat in the halls of federal government, the government began to hound Addicks right out of business. A legal fight arose out of his gas deals and resulted in a federal court awarding $4 million against him.

Addicks was reduced to hiding from subpoenas, living in poverty. Still the hunt went on. Two years after his defeat in Delaware, process servers found him in a dreary Hoboken tenement, living under an assumed name, his gas and light turned off for nonpayment by a company he had once owned. For eleven more years the harassment went on, "Gas" Addicks finally dying in the slums of New York on August 7, 1919, a forgotten and broken man.

For Delaware, as for Du Pont Company, Coleman's "new order" had arrived.

Seven

DU PONT CIVIL WAR

1. ROUND ONE—THE BATTLE OVER OPERATION

All was not victory for Coleman du Pont in the first few years of his reign over Du Pont Company. In fact, the 1907 federal suit against the company would make these first years with Du Pont his only years. But perhaps his greatest thorn was his cousin and vice-president, Alfred I. du Pont.

Right from the beginning of the new order under the three cousins, differences arose between Coleman and Alfred. Coleman wanted to close the Brandywine mills. Alfred objected. Coleman wanted to move the company's headquarters to New York. Alfred again objected. In both cases, Alfred won.

Alfred, in turn, was worried about Coleman's increasing power in the firm. Frank, Charles I., and Dr. Alexis were all dead. Colonel Henry had left for Washington. To replace them, Coleman brought his western clerk, Lewis L. Dunham, and his father's friend, Arthur J. Moxham, into the company. Furthermore, Moxham joined the board of directors, as did J. Amory Haskell, former president of Laflin and Rand, and L. R. Beardslee and James G. Reilly, both from companies which Coleman had bought out, as well as Henry F. Baldwin, Coleman's brother-in-law, and Hamilton Barksdale, Mrs. Coleman du Pont's brother-in-law. Baldwin, Haskell, Barksdale, and Moxham were all given bonuses to make them shareholders, and Moxham, Barksdale, and Haskell were appointed to the executive committee as vice-presidents.

Pierre also brought his brothers into this circle, Irénée taking the post of assistant treasurer, and Henry Belin, William Kemble, and Lammot donning overalls for the powder works. J. Amory Haskell also brought in his brother, Harry Haskell, and his trusted assistant, Charles Copeland, later to marry Pierre's sister Louisa.

Alfred was relieved that Francis I. du Pont, Frank's son and Delaware's single tax pioneer, headed the Carney's Point plant and joined him on the executive committee. But there were many new young Du Ponts that Coleman was bringing into the company whose first loyalty seemed to be to the big man from Kentucky: A. Felix du Pont, second son of deceased

Frank; Eugene, Jr. and Alexis I. du Pont III, sons of deceased Eugene; Eugene E. du Pont, son of Dr. Alexis; Victor du Pont, Jr., of the exiled Victor line; and Colonel Henry's son, Henry Francis du Pont. And the newest addition to the Board, fat and lazy Victor du Pont, Sr., was no help whatsoever. Clear warning flags flew when Coleman set up his Delaware Securities Co. and Delaware Investment Co. Of each, Moxham was president, Coleman vice-president, and Pierre treasurer. Alfred had been left out.

Alfred was worried. He knew about Coleman's infamous card tricks. He did not want to deal with a man who held a stacked deck, which is what the board of directors and junior executives were beginning to appear to be.

Other disputes arose. Alfred and Coleman debated over the eight-hour work day, the cause célèbre of the rising labor unions. Coleman felt it was better to take the steam out of labor organizers approaching Du Pont plants by voluntarily instituting the eight-hour day. Alfred bitterly opposed Coleman's plan. In 1904 an eight-hour bill was before Congress. On November 2 Alfred wrote the Secretary of Commerce and Labor of his opposition and hope that the workers' bill would be killed in Committee and never reach the floor for a vote. Alfred's argument was typically patronizing. He insisted that he, not the workers, knew what was best for them. All the stale arguments were aired again, including the "right" of the worker to work as long as he liked. (The bill did not rule out compulsory overtime, however.) But his chief argument was from his class side of economics: it would necessitate costly reorganization, force Du Pont to raise prices and employ more men in the mills, increase the chance of accidents (true only if Du Pont increased its line speed-up—which, of course, it did as Alfred knew it would), and finally—the real point—it would "abridge the right of the employer to offer labor such terms and wages as he saw fit."[1]

Coleman and his directors disagreed, believing the eight-hour law would cut unemployment while still allowing the employer to extract through speed-up ten hours worth of labor in eight hours. Eventually, Du Pont voluntarily decreased its ten-hour work day to eight hours, but not before Alfred had been forced out of control over the company's production.

Another contention was a new invention by Alfred, a steel glazing barrel. Naturally, Alfred was very enthusiastic about it. The barrel cut the cost of a 25-pound keg of black powder from 84 cents in 1907 to 78 cents in 1910. It also cut workers to pieces when it exploded, as it was much more dangerous than the old wooden barrels. After four accidents, Coleman abandoned the barrel despite Alfred's voiced disappointment.

By 1909 Alfred's worth to the company was quickly fading. In 1902, when he rose to prominence in the firm, Alfred's black powder was king. But for the next eight years, dynamite sales increased 300 percent while black powder's sales rose by only 25 percent. By 1909 dynamite sales topped those of black powder by ten million pounds. Black powder had reached its all-time high in 1907 and now was declining.

So was Alfred. With no dynamite experience, he was becoming less indispensable to the firm and was increasingly irritating to Coleman now reigning in his new four-story offices in Wilmington. And what family ties had bound Alfred to the company were now quickly being frayed over the issue of Alfred's marriage and his relationship with another young Du Pont cousin, Alicia Heyward Bradford, the daughter of Eleuthera du Pont and Judge E. G. Bradford.

By 1902 Alfred and Bessie were seldom speaking. For one thing, Louis's suicide had soured their marriage. Further, Bessie's rudeness to Alfred's sister Marguerite, and her cold manner to Alfred, kept his relatives away from Swamp Hall, effecting an isolation that Alfred resented. Then Alfred's hearing failed in 1904 and he had to give up his amateur band. Drifting from ties in Wilmington, he began spending more time writing to and visiting with the Ball family, particularly young Jessie Ball. An old Virginian family, the Balls were friends who lived near his private hunting retreat at Cherry Island. It was there in November of 1904 that Alfred suffered his second physical blow within a year.

He was hunting with Bill Scott, superintendent of Du Pont's Pennsylvania mills, and some other friends. The men were spread out on the trail of game, Alfred and a friend on one side of a hedge, Scott thirty yards away on the opposite side. Suddenly Scott thought he heard something and wheeled and fired at the hedge. Alfred's friend ducked, and as he did, he saw Alfred's hat fly off. Then Alfred dropped his gun and fell, blood pouring from his face.

He was rushed to the University of Pennsylvania, where surgeons performed an operation on his left eye. Bessie hurried from Europe with their daughter, Maddie, but the visit was not a happy one for Alfred. While Maddie weeped at her father's bedside, Bessie just stared at him coldly. Understandably, Alfred grew depressed.

When he returned to Swamp Hall, the family threw a Christmas party to cheer him up. It only made matters worse. He suffered a relapse and had to return to the hospital. There, Alfred had his eye removed and replaced with a glass one.

By September 1905 Alfred had left Swamp Hall and made financial arrangements with Bessie. Although he was by then a millionaire, his settlement for his wife and children was not generous: only $24,000 a year. A $600,000 trust fund for his four children, Alfred Victor, Maddie, Bessie, and Victorine, was set up, Alfred choosing a Philadelphia lawyer for his trustee. Bessie chose Pierre du Pont. It was to be the beginning of a long friendship between the two, as well as the opening shot of the greatest civil war in the history of the clan.

As early as 1901, Alfred had begun seeing Alicia Bradford and they in turn were seen on picnics together. Rumors started to fly along the Brandy-wine. Alicia's mother was Eleuthera du Pont, daughter of the original Alexis I. Alicia's father was the stern judge of the U.S. Circuit Court, Edward Green Bradford. The Judge got wind of the meetings and became furious. He wanted them stopped—immediately! Alfred was still a married man, and if he wasn't, that was worse: then he was a divorced man!

Alicia became very frightened. Her father was a domestic tyrant who ruled over her life. "As a child," she said years later, "I was frightened all the time—terrified of everything. Suddenly it came to me that my father was the cause of this. He had wanted me to be a boy."[2] Alicia could not see Alfred, at least not this way.

Alfred then introduced Alicia to George A. Maddox, a handsome but not too bright boy employed by Du Pont Company. Over the Judge's objections, he arranged clandestine meetings for her and Maddox. Sud-denly they shocked the family with their announcement of plans to marry. Alfred made all the arrangements, even setting up the Christ Church for the wedding. After the ceremony, he gave them a Du Pont home, Louviers, the estate of Admiral Samuel du Pont. When word came that Alicia was almost immediately pregnant, the whispers along the Brandywine flew faster than the river itself.

Alfred immediately rewarded Maddox with a promotion. He became regional superintendent of black powder plants in the Midwest, jumping over more experienced men in line for the job. This position kept Maddox away from Alicia most of the time. But Alicia was seldom alone. Alfred became a constant visitor.

In 1903, the year Bessie gave birth to Alfred's fourth child, Victorine, Alicia Maddox also gave birth to a daughter. She was named Alicia, and reportedly had unmistakable Du Pont characteristics, obviously from her mother's side.

For the next three years, while Maddox was usually hundreds of miles away, Alicia continued playing hostess to Alfred. In April 1906 Alicia lost her second child, a boy. The death must have been a shattering blow to her. She publicly drew ever closer to Alfred. It must have also affected Alfred.

Within a month, moved out of pity for Alicia's unhappiness, he filed for divorce.

In December Alfred's divorce from Bessie was granted on the grounds of mental cruelty. From that day, Coleman grew less tolerant of his troublesome cousin. Then Maddox suddenly handed Coleman his resignation. A Philadelphia newspaper later reported that he was bringing suit against Alfred, but that he suddenly withdrew the suit before filing a bill of particulars.

The mystery grows deeper. Alicia suddenly disappeared. Far from prying family eyes, she was secluded in a mansion in Carlisle, Pennsylvania. She had secretly filed for divorce from Maddox and was awaiting its approval. On October 8, 1907, her waiting was ended. One week later Alfred and Alicia were in New York together. There they were married. The indefatigably improper Maurice du Pont was the best man.

The news hit the Brandywine like a blockbuster. "Al, now you've done it," Coleman warned his cousin when he returned. "The family will never stand for this. Don't you think you'd better sell out to me and get away from here?"[3]

"I'll see the family in hell first!" replied Alfred.

That kind of talk was family treason. As if that wasn't bad enough, Alfred also turned his back on the company. He announced that he would not stand by the firm or accept any responsibility for it in the coming U.S. federal suit. Instead, he filed a motion to have his individual case separated from the company's and dismissed. He denied knowing anything of the Gunpowder Trust, of Coleman's companies, Delaware Securities and Delaware Investment, of any wrongdoing—of which the government was proving there was plenty. After three days of testimony, Alfred's case was dropped by the government.

Coleman and Pierre were speechless. Although Coleman had also taken leave, claiming illness, and never appeared in court, at least he didn't separate his claim of innocence from that of the company. In retaliation, Alfred was soon dropped from the company's finance committee, allegedly for his deafness. Coleman's in-law, Hamilton Barksdale, took Alfred's place, while Pierre was made acting president during Coleman's absence.

"The Count," as Alfred was called by the family, was not through yet. After marrying Alicia, he refused to visit his children at Swamp Hall, probably at Alicia's encouragement. Alfred's daughter Maddie finally left Swamp Hall to join her father at his new Brandywine estate, Rock Farms. But Maddie didn't stay long. She soon eloped to France with a Princeton undergraduate, John Bancroft, Jr., son of a wealthy textile manufacturer in

Wilmington. Despite a hurried announcement of her pregnancy, Maddie's marriage didn't work out. Her husband soon threatened to sue her for divorce on the grounds of her admitted adultery with a young German student, Max Heibler, during their honeymoon. Bancroft cited Maddie's newly born infant as a co-defendant named Max Heibler, Jr. Alicia, anxious to avoid scandal, intervened with promises of treasure and threats to "rip the hinges from any Delaware closet, Du Pont cabinets among them." Bancroft's adultery suit was suddenly amended to desertion, and subsequently withdrawn. But by the arrival of a second child, Bancroft could take no more. A divorce was applied for and granted. Maddie remained in Germany, eventually marrying Max Heibler.

Somehow, Maddie's letters on her marriage woes reached Coleman's hands. It is not known whether he immediately turned them over to Alfred, but when he did, Alfred was furious, believing the letters had run the family gauntlet.

Alfred's relations with Coleman deteriorated even further after that. By 1911 the two cousins were bidding against each other for property along the Brandywine. Coleman, as usual, won.

Alfred realized his grip on the company was slipping fast, but he was helpless to stop it. His previous indispensability in the firm continued to decrease with the decline of black powder. In 1910, despite the fact that black powder sold 500,000 pounds less than in 1904, Alfred built a half million dollar plant at Welpen, Minnesota. It was a triumph of monumental vanity and stupidity. At this point only the ties of family could hold him in the firm, and those he had literally told to go to hell.

Awaiting his inevitable fate with the company, Alfred contented himself with buying a new yacht, which he named "Alicia." Then he halted his donations to the Wilmington Symphony Orchestra because of a snub to Alicia by Wilmington society circles. As a result, the orchestra was forced to disband.

Ugly rumors began to float around about Alicia's previous marriage, causing Alicia to cringe and Alfred to grow frantic in rage. He traced them all down to two people, Mrs. Mary Bush, a widow of a Wilmington manufacturer, and Alicia's stout aunt of 57 years, Elizabeth Bradford du Pont. Then Alfred did the unthinkable. He publicly filed legal suit against both women for slander. It wasn't long before Philadelphia papers picked up their hottest "society" story of the year. The Philadelphia *North American* called it "The Women's War that convulses Delaware."[4] Even the New York *World* reported that the rumors about Alicia du Pont "are of such a nature that they cannot be published."[5] The New York *Sun* exposed the family's futile efforts to hold off Alfred, and named more Du Pont women who could be expected to become involved: Victorine du Pont Foster, sister of Senator Henry A. du Pont; Alice du Pont Oritz, Elizabeth Bradford du Pont's daughter; Eugenie Roberts, niece of Elizabeth Amy du Pont, spinster daughter of the late Eugene; and Mrs. Henry A. Thompson.[6]

There was a family outcry. Alfred had gone too far. Elizabeth was the widow of the late Dr. Alexis du Pont, and Mrs. Bush's adopted son had also married Alicia's younger sister, Joanna du Pont Bradford. Alfred had involved the whole clan and it could not stand by and allow him to publicly drag the name of Du Pont through the gutter. Private rumors were one thing; public suits were quite another.

Alicia's aunt ran to her son-in-law, attorney Thomas F. Bayard, Jr., of an old distinguished family that had placed four of its members in the U.S. Senate. Bayard, a Democrat, wanted to be number five, but he needed Du Pont support. He took the case gladly.

Mrs. Bush ran to May du Pont's husband, attorney Willard Saulsbury. Although Saulsbury was no friend of "that tribe" which Coleman, Colonel Henry, and Pierre represented, he agreed to take the case. Saulsbury, it seems, also had designs on a Senate seat.

The case dragged on for months, and still Alfred filed no bill of particulars. The newspapers were slaughtering the carefully cultured Du Pont image, which didn't help build popular sympathy for the clan's defense against the government's anti-trust suit. The family begged Alfred to come to reason, to think of the family as a whole. When that didn't work, they tried threats, Finally, Bayard and Saulsbury wrote to Alfred's lawyer, J. Harvey Whiteman, warning him that unless a bill was filed within thirty days, the defense would move for nonprosecution.

Whether Alfred had proof or not will never be known. Four days later he withdrew the suit in the interest of "family honor."

But Alfred had his personal revenge. He moved into Nemours, his new $2 million palatial estate of five square miles. It included sunken gardens, greenhouses, and two grilled gateways of bronze, one from Wimbledon Manor in England, the other from the Russian Imperial Palace of Catherine the Great. But the center of attraction was the mansion itself. Built of limestone, an architectural blend of French chateau and Southern plantation, it stood three stories high, had seventy-seven rooms, and housed scores of servants. Art treasures were scattered throughout. The drawing room alone, for instance, had a seventeenth-century rug worth $100,000. In the basement, "the Count" kept an arsenal of weapons, including a machine gun and a small cannon. As if that were not enough to discourage unwelcome visitors, Alfred surrounded the entire estate with a nine-foot-high stone wall at the top of which were embedded pieces of sharp broken glass "to keep out intruders, mainly of the name of Du Pont."[7]

The family took the hint and stayed away. But Alfred had just begun to take his personal revenge. As he moved into Nemours, he evicted Bessie and the children from Swamp Hall. Then he had their home completely demolished. Alfred, of course, met his family obligation. He increased Bessie's annuity by $1,200 to cover the rent for a home in Wilmington, a very generous offer, he believed, from a man then grossing over $400,000 every year from his holdings in Du Pont Company alone.

The clan was appalled. Never had such ruthlessness been seen within the family since the original Irénée had cheated his stepsister. The family feared it was plunging to new lows.

Not low enough, as far as Alfred was concerned. When the federal anti-trust case ended with a conviction after four years and sixteen volumes of testimony, Alfred refused to agree to an appeal.

It was the final act of family heresy. Family feuds could always be healed, but company rifts required deliberate action. The appeal went on, but not Alfred. In a prearranged meeting of the executive committee in January 1913, Alfred was relieved of all operating duties as general manager and vice-president. Crushed, "the Count" sailed for France to lick his wounds.

2. A SMALL CIRCLE OF FRIENDS

Coleman and Pierre were now in absolute control of the firm, but the federal conviction had jeopardized what that control actually meant. Since the government had filed suit in 1907, the Du Ponts had stalled the case, hoping for a more lenient administration under William Howard Taft.

They had good reason to hope. After distinguishing himself with his anti-labor decisions on the Ohio bench, Taft became head of Roosevelt's War Department in 1904. It was he who showered Du Pont with such profitable contracts. When this great admirer of John D. Rockefeller ran for the presidency in 1908, T. Coleman du Pont offered a donation of $20,000. Taft, however, decided not to repeat Roosevelt's mistake and risk the possibility of bad publicity, but assured Coleman of his sincere friendship with the Delaware family.

Coleman was more than a friend. He was the national director of the Republican Party's Speaker Bureau and a member of the executive committee of the Republican National Committee. When criticism arose over his affiliation because of the anti-trust case, Coleman prudently handed in his resignation to Taft on September 22, 1908. Six days later he wrote Taft of his full support in the coming election. Coleman's support meant something. "The General," as he was later called because of his appointment as general of the Delaware National Guard, controlled Delaware politics like a feudal lord since he became Colonel Henry's campaign manager in 1906.

After his election, Taft showed his appreciation by offering the office of Secretary of State to a Du Pont lawyer, John C. Spooner. The former senator from Wisconsin decided to decline, the Du Ponts bowing to the demands of John Rockefeller and Andrew Mellon, who wanted to put in their own man, Senator Philander Knox. Instead, the office of Attorney General was given to George W. Wickersham, the very Du Pont lawyer who had counseled the building of the Powder Trust.

President Taft and Colonel Henry du Pont were close political colleagues. When Taft was campaigning for president, it was Colonel Henry who hosted a dinner in Delaware in Taft's honor attended by many Du Pont luminaries. Henry, a supporter of high tariffs that would protect industries like Du Pont, felt no hesitation about writing Taft at Hot Springs, Virginia, right after the election explaining his position on reciprocity.[8] Henry even enjoyed occasional music and dinner at the White House.[9] When the old Junker of Delaware was maneuvering for reelection in 1911, Taft feared another national scandal and suggested that it would be "very advantageous" to Henry if his aides were to pay a visit to that maker of presidents and public image, Senator Mark Hanna, so that Henry's candidacy would be handled "in the proper light."[10]

The visits were made but the light was not very proper. Henry bought the election and everyone knew it. "It is common testimony that in all the shameful history of the State," wrote the New York *Evening Post,* "money was never used more freely and more openly about the polls than this year. . . .

"The only person who had the most at stake in the election of a Republican Legislature in Delaware is Senator Henry A. du Pont who is a candidate for reelection, and the only Republican candidate whose name will go before the Legislature, so far as is known. The only known reason for spending large sums of money to elect a Republican Legislature is to insure the choice of a Republican for U.S. Senator.

"Who is so interested," the *Post* went on, "in the choice of a Republican for Senator as the candidate upon whom the choice will fall? That is why one hears such bitter talk in the State about the way money was used to buy votes to make Republican the next legislature which, barring the unforeseen, will reelect Senator du Pont."[11]

Beverly Robinson, a niece of Henry's, was in New York at the time this article appeared. She was a lawyer with the Wall Street firm of Mason and Nichols. Embarrassed, she wrote her uncle suggesting he sue for libel. Henry chose not to take her advice.

Instead, Henry launched a purge in Delaware's Republican Party, ousting all but the most loyal. One of those less fortunate was R. Layton, U.S. Treasury Department auditor for the state records. Henry told Layton the party could frankly do without him.[12] President Taft didn't mind this attack on a government official, especially when the Delaware platform carried such praise for the President. For this support Henry received Taft's personal gratitude.[13] On Henry's reelection, Taft wrote him a warm note of congratulations.[14]

But the Colonel's woes were not over with his reelection. His crude methods during the campaign inspired the founding of the Anti-Bribery League after the election.

The Du Ponts were worried. Charges of corruption and federal suits were flying around their heads. It had to stop. A new public image had to be built about them, one that would bring them respect, the kind of respect that protects wealth.

Coleman had already begun the campaign. On February 11, 1910, he wrote Bessie, Alfred's divorced wife, for information that she might have for the company's publicity.[15] Colonel E. G. Buckner, Du Pont's military salesman, wrote Coleman on March 21 regarding the company's efforts to supply propaganda to the press concerning the country's munitions build-up. "I think you should be very guarded in giving anyone the impression that Admiral Evans was being in any way coached by you or any member of the Company."[16] Buckner knew that if Coleman's name was associated with Evans' article, it wouldn't be used.

Coleman liked a professional job, so he hired the public relations firm of James J. Archibald. "We have tried to develop a plan," wrote Archibald's L. B. Lewis to Vice President Haskell, "that would result in getting into the general newspaper field, and have made headway. We have in mind a proposition that would, if carried out, comprise about 1,500 newspapers, through which avenues we would be able to reach the public with such matters as would be of general newspaper interest and of benefit to the Company."[17]

By May 13, 1910, the campaign was underway. Coleman wrote instructions to his public relations firm on an article by Admiral Evans, former Commander-in-Chief of the Atlantic Fleet and its famous tour of the world in 1907–8. The article, entitled "Preparedness," was complimentary to Du Pont Company and stressed the need for having military supplies like Du Pont powder constantly available in huge stockpiles. Coleman affirmed that

Admiral Evans should be subsidized for his efforts and then listed specific magazine targets for its publication: *Harpers, Century, Hampton, World's Week,* and *Scribners.*[18] Although the article was never printed, it is an example of Du Pont's method of manipulating its public image.

Du Pont was a pioneer in corporate deception of the public. In 1915 Pierre asked Bessie to write a complimentary history of the company.[19] She complied.

Coleman's publicity campaign probably bolstered Taft's inclination to go easy on Du Pont in the anti-trust case. Taft wanted to basically continue the progressivism of Roosevelt and frowned on the thought of formal regulation completely replacing informal détente between monopoly's collective government and individual monopolies. Taft preferred cooperation, and this extended to the Du Pont case.

On June 12, 1911, the U.S. District Court in Delaware (with Du Pont in-law Judge Bradford markedly in absentia) found the Du Ponts guilty of violating the Sherman Anti-Trust Act. But the court offered the first family of the state a back door. It emphasized that since over a hundred corporations had been taken over by Du Pont, "the impossibility of restoring original conditions in the explosives trade narrows the field of operation of any decree we may make."[20] The decree was indeed narrowed. It directed the government and the family to jointly decide how the Trust should be reorganized. That meant that the Du Ponts would be allowed to decide their own sentence!

Coleman perhaps chose not to tip his hand and applaud the verdict. Actually, he was genuinely angry about being found guilty. He still could not see anything illegal about the Powder Trust. In a memorandum to company employees, he handed down the company line, charging Taft and the federal courts with corruption. "The Courts are human beings with ambitions and desiring to go forward. Their only chances of going forward are two, first, by popularity getting a nomination in a good political position, second, by being appointed to a higher judicial position. Neither of these would be possible if a decision was rewarded in opposition to the policy of the administration or in opposition to the popular cry against corporations."[21] Coleman claimed the court hadn't even read the evidence[22] and charged that Waddell was really a blackmailer who left the company in order to force Du Pont to buy him out at a profit.[23] Waddell's letter of resignation showed another kind of man, however, a man who was simply disgusted with Coleman's heavy-handed policies. And Coleman's charge did not belie the fact that Waddell had refused to accept Coleman's offer to buy into Waddell's Buckeye Powder Company.

Coleman cooled his temper, however, long enough to meet Taft's

Attorney General at the wealthiest, most fashionable and prominent social club in Washington. Both Coleman and George Wickersham were members of the Metropolitan Club at 17th and H Street. There, they conversed on the case, Coleman even handing his former employee the company's legal position.[24]

That done, Coleman next wrote a letter to his businesss partner in building the McAlpin Hotel in New York—Charles P. Taft, the President's brother. "I feel so morally certain that your brother does not want to do an injustice to anybody and if he was morally certain that the rectifying of an injustice could be of the greatest benefit to him as well as to ourselves. . . . my judgment is that it would be of great help to him in the future."[25]

Indeed, Coleman was a great help in the coming year's presidential election. He geared the political machine he had built in Delaware to absolute support for Taft and, as a Republican national committeeman, personally endorsed him for renomination.

The President, however, was not interested in publicly endorsing Coleman du Pont. To Senator Frank Allee he denounced "the General" as "slippery as an eel and crooked as a ram's horn."[26] He had good reason to feel this way. The latest episode of Du Pont corruption had been written in the halls of the Senate just a month before.

In a public blast against "that tribe," Willard Saulsbury had charged Senator Henry A. du Pont with buying votes during the 1910 election. Colonel Henry had selected a Sussex County Republican, Cornelius Swain, as U.S. Marshal; Saulsbury claimed that Swain had used Du Pont money to buy votes. The charges, coming in the wake of the previous electoral scandals and Du Pont's monopoly conviction, were splashed across the nation's headlines. Now it was all out, and just when Henry was thinking of another ocean cruise.

A subcommittee of the Senate Committee on Privileges and Elections investigated, as Henry broke into a cold sweat. Witness after witness took the stand, including Senator Frank Allee, testifying under oath that on November 5, 1909, Henry gave Kent and Sussex County Republicans $53,000 for illegal use in the state elections the following Tuesday. At a meeting at Du Pont offices in Wilmington, according to the testimony, Swain was handed his $3,000 share by Coleman du Pont and Caleb Layton.

Swain's attorney, Daniel O. Hastings, admitted that his client was given the money. But Swain himself never testified. A secret conference between Colonel Henry and Attorney General Wickersham resulted in Swain's being allowed instead to submit a written defense claiming he wasn't aware of the contents of the package Coleman had given him.[27] Henry, in turn, admitted giving the money, but claimed ignorance as to the purpose for which it was used.[28] Coleman never testified and the case was dropped.

On February 23 an enraged Senator James Reed of Missouri called for a more thorough investigation of Henry's election. He repeated his demand on February 28, but the "Senate Club" was not to be moved. The honor of the Senate itself was now at stake. Reed finally gave up.

President Taft found little comfort in Senator Reed's defeat. White-washes can be politically dangerous, particularly when they protect a leading member of the infamous Powder Trust. He wanted no part of a suggested secret meeting with the Powder Trust's president and rumored briber, Coleman du Pont. Senator Allee was in sympathy with the President's fears and, after consultation with Pierre, who was wiser than Coleman about effecting a settlement with the government, suggested a meeting with Alfred du Pont instead. With the government-Du Pont recommendation due in court in two months, Taft had little choice.

Alfred arrived at the White House looking fully the role of the economic power elite. Splendidly attired in a silk hat and morning coat, Alfred was out to do what most businessmen were doing to William Taft: bluff him into submission. With former Du Pont lawyer Wickersham on hand as Taft's Attorney General, Alfred took his seat in a conference room, looked firmly into the President's eyes, and calmly threatened to throw a million people out of work unless Du Pont was permitted to keep its 100 percent monopoly on military smokeless powder.

"Do you mean to threaten the United States government?"[29] thundered Taft.

Of course not, replied Alfred quietly, and then calmly repeated his threat of closing the plants the nation depended upon for commercial explosives. Taft's resistance collapsed; he never dared to mention the possibility of government intervention to reopen Du Pont plants as it had reopened the country's railroads during the Pullman strike. The Dollar Diplomacy of armed intervention was *for* Big Business, not against it. The government of the United States, which could invade whole countries in Latin America, was simply no match for the Du Ponts of Delaware. Within a few hours it meekly surrendered.

Supplemental court hearings then began for Du Pont's reorganization. It was a colorful circus with Alfred as ringmaster. A long line of army and navy officials paraded before the Court, including Admiral Knight, President of the Joint Army and Navy Board on Smokeless Powder; Admiral Twining, Chief of the Navy Ordnance Bureau; General Crozier, Chief of Ordnance of the Army; and many reputed Du Pont stockholders clothed in brass—all demanding that Du Pont be allowed to continue its monopoly over smokeless powder.

Coleman, with victory within his grasp, was still not satisfied. While shying away from the court (and therefore by legal necessity, the company), he still insisted that Du Pont had a right to be a monopoly, Sherman Anti-Trust Act be damned. Taft by now felt Coleman should be damned. Twice before the Court's decision, on April 15 and June 10, he tried to reassure Coleman with the favor of special exemptions for Du Pont from the official prohibition on exports to Mexico, which was torn at the time by revolution inspired by contending American and British interests. In both cases, shipments of Du Pont fuses for dynamite were excused as "not to be used in promoting conditions of domestic violence which I have found to exist in Mexico."[30] But Coleman still wasn't satisfied.

"The businessmen are fools," Taft wrote angrily to his brother Charles, "like some of the voters. For a time they don't see their real interest; they don't have the power of discrimination. That man T. Coleman du Pont is one such man. I have no use for him whatsoever. They do not see beyond their noses. They only think of their own particular interest and don't take a broader view. They are in favor of special privilege in the sense of having themselves favored and everybody else prosecuted. That is the attitude of Gary and Perkins* and Du Pont and others."[31]

On June 13 the Court handed down its final decree, called by one family historian "one of the outstanding farces of American judicial history."[32] Du Pont, the Court held, would be broken up into three separate companies: Du Pont, Atlas, and Hercules. The two new companies were given plants for general explosives, but Du Pont was allowed to keep its entire monopoly on military smokeless powder. Coleman's trust had all but survived the ordeal unscathed. In fact, Atlas and Hercules were new in name only. Du Pont executives filled their ranks from top to bottom. Du Pont family members still controlled the stocks and bonds of both companies. Alfred du Pont, for example, alone held $757,000 worth of Hercules' 6 percent bonds. Atlas and Hercules even set up their central offices in Wilmington, right across the street from Du Pont headquarters.

It was an exemplary step in the pattern of progressivism: keeping companies separate does not necessarily mean competition.[33] Through government and business cooperation the marketplace is temporarily stabilized through overseas expansion which allows a modicum of domestic rationalization. Taft understood this when two days before the Du Pont

---

* Elbert H. Gary, President of U.S. Steel; George W. Perkins, partner of J. P. Morgan & Company.

decision he wrote that "operations are sometimes necessary to save the life of the patient."[34]

Generally, though the family disagreed, the patient certainly was healthy. Du Pont's assets in 1810 were some $109,000. Now they were well over $81 million with sixty plants in twenty-two states, and all at the bargain cost of over four hundred workers killed, thousands more maimed or wounded. Dividends reached $12 per share in 1910 and remained so for the next three years.

3. WILMINGTON'S GOLDEN DAYS

Wilmington had never been merrier. The new twelve-story Du Pont Building had been completed, containing 2,000 rooms and a 300-room hotel—Du Pont Hotel, of course. With its stores along the street front and a playhouse in its court, Du Pont Building stuck out like an elephant against the small red brick houses of Wilmington. At dusk, no one could doubt that the Du Ponts were clearly overshadowing the people of Delaware.

Parties and formal balls with French champagne flowing became frequent occasions for the Du Ponts in their hotel's rathskeller. Even Alfred agreed that this was more like Berlin than sleepy Wilmington. Alfred was actively back in the firm now as a member of the finance committee, his reward for the Taft negotiations. Coleman, having purged the company of Alfred's followers, now felt that his cousin raised no real threat to his rule. Meanwhile, Alfred quietly bought the Wilmington *Morning News* and six downstate papers for the final battle he considered inevitable.

Coleman outpaced all the other Du Ponts when it came to lavish spending in those "golden days." His gallstone operation in 1910 had kept him "sick" and out of court for two years. But as soon as the case was over, Coleman emerged as healthy as a bull. He immediately hit New York and set up a command post in a penthouse on top of his 21-story McAlpin Hotel. Coleman became a big man in the world's biggest town. He and Charles Taft began building other hotels, including the famous Waldorf-Astoria. His penthouse became the scene of frequent wild parties, often filled with the entire chorus of a Broadway play. As for Elsie, his wife and former adviser, Coleman discarded her. "One never sees her, never hears of her,"[35] commented a New York newspaper. Once, when a manager showed him to a hotel suite, Coleman handed him two fetching negligees left by a former occupant and told him, "Take these out and have them filled."[36]

Every New Year's Eve "the General," as he became known, rode about the city in his plush limousine handing out $20 gold pieces to policemen for keeping order in an age of poverty and rebellion. Coleman was even made New York's honorary police commissioner.

Coly was having a grand time. Sometimes he liked to share his good cheer by embarrassing others. He kept a box of loaded cigars on his desk for just such occasions. Sometimes he served flannel cakes to guests with genuine pieces of flannel in them. Once, during a vacation at his estate on the southerly marshes of Maryland, a New York banker friend complained that the privy at Coleman's shooting box was too cold. Later the banker was startled when he sat on what he thought was some wild animal. Coleman had had the privy seat lined with genuine fur. Coleman's jokes even extended to his family. Lammot du Pont, not the brightest member of the family, once arrived in New York only to realize he had forgotten who he was to meet. "Have forgotten name my 4:00 appointment," he wired Coleman. "Please advise." "Name your 4:00 appointment—J. P. Morgan," Coleman replied. "Your name Lammot du Pont."[37]

But Coleman knew where his bread was buttered. "I exist in New York," he explained, "but I live in Delaware."[38] Wilmington was Coleman's political base, and his ego could not be confined to the largest city in the world. "I'm going to build a monument one hundred miles high," he boasted, "and lay it on the ground."[39] The result was a 200-foot-wide highway smashing through Delaware's farms from Wilmington to the border of Maryland, bringing the lower part of the "first state" under heavier Du Pont influence. Coleman merely wrote it off his taxes as "charity" but years later that charity would greatly benefit the family's attempt at centralizing the state and connecting the company's nylon plant at downstate Seaford with the major eastern highways.

Colonel Henry also found Delaware to be a good political base. After the court's 1912 decision, Henry more openly served his family's company in the U.S. Senate. That year, Henry was one of the Senate's leading opponents against a bill proposing that the Army and Navy build their own powder plants to supply their needs at cost. In 1913 Senator du Pont's committee struck out a provision in a bill that would have placed a ceiling on the amount the government would pay for Du Pont powder, while later establishing a $100,000 allotment for the crude beginning of an American air force.

In June 1914 Henry voted for exemption for American ships from Panama Canal tolls, in direct violation of the original canal treaty with Great Britain still legally in effect at the time. Clearly, Henry's first allegiance was to the company, not to international legal rights. A fleet of Du Pont ships used the canal as the main gateway to Chilean nitrate resources. Since the first Lammot du Pont had discovered soda powder, Du Pont had been extensively involved in exploiting Chile's nitrate. Du Pont works were set up about eight miles inland from the port of Taltal, and by 1912 Du Pont imported 77,578 tons of Chilean nitrate of soda.[40] Henry's vote and influence were important to the company's profits. Through its use of Chilean nitrate, Du Pont had captured a monopoly on fertilizer in America. The government exemption on canal tolls was a subsidy to that monopoly.

In 1916 a revenue bill was pending that sought to raise $26 million partly by taxing the profit of munitions manufacturers. It wasn't long before the Junker of Delaware was angrily snapping his riding whip. First he tried to have the bill killed in committee. When that didn't work, he launched a vicious attack on July 24 on the Senate floor against those unpatriotic enough to support the bill; he forced a reduction in the tax.

Henry du Pont, of course, denied any connection with Du Pont Company. When the federal anti-trust suit named him as a co-defendant, he moved to have his case dismissed because he had resigned from the company a year earlier to take his Senate seat. The Delaware court granted his motion, despite the fact that Colonel Henry had been on Du Pont's board of directors since the 1870's and was a director at the time of Coleman's incorporation of January 1906. Even Coleman's attorneys admitted that Henry had "attended meetings of the Board of Directors of said Company from time to time."[41] Henry didn't even deny his knowledge of the Powder Trust; he merely claimed the Trust hadn't intended to monopolize the powder market.[42] It was just an accident.

Some people weren't fooled. As early as June 17, 1906, the Wilmington *Sunday Star* asserted "the powder trust knows the new senator intimately, as a child knows its father, and he knows the powder trust."[43]

Such revealing light made Henry wince. In 1912 he turned the light off. He bought a controlling interest in his journalistic critic. The *Sunday Star* was never critical again.

But other Delawarians were not to be silenced. Henry should have gotten wind of the national tempo in 1912. That year, two Du Ponts, Alfred and Coleman, headed the Delaware delegation to the Republican convention that renominated their friend William Taft. Taft, however, was no match for Woodrow Wilson. Upset by Taft's incompetence, William Rockefeller had deserted Taft for an alliance with Wilson's supporters from the National City Bank: Cleveland Dodge, J. P. Morgan, Jr., J. Armour, James Stillman, and Jacob Schiff of Kuhn, Loeb, & Co. Morgan forces also backed Roosevelt's Progressive Party, which cut into Taft's vote.

Taft's support from the Mellons and Carnegie was simply not enough.

The Du Ponts, although definitely among the social elite, were not yet in the same superleague as Rockefeller or Morgan.

Colonel Henry disliked Wilson for being one of those "progressives." Henry was proud to point to his record as being one of the least progressive in the history of the U.S. Senate. He was a violent opponent of women's suffrage, voting against a proposed constitutional amendment in 1913. When women suffragettes asked to see him in Wilmington, he refused. Finally, in January 1914 he consented to honor them with an audience in Washington. After traveling all the way from Delaware, the women were greeted by the Junker's icy stare and cold remark that he was firmly opposed to giving the vote to two million illiterate women.

But what Henry did not mention was that most of those women worked in factories, and Senator Henry, like most Du Ponts, was no friend of the working class. As president of the Wilmington and Northern Railroad, he had forced railroad workers to toil for only a dollar a day if they wanted a job at a time when unemployment was high and starvation seen everywhere. Henry voted against many supposedly pro-labor bills, including the Clayton Anti-Trust Bill of 1914 and the eight-hour day of the Adamson Bill of 1916. Instead, Senator du Pont helped draw up the Volunteer Army Act of 1914 that paved the way for universal conscription of working-class youth into the Army. A rigid hawk, Henry had vigorously supported McKinley's war in 1898, the "Big Stick" of Roosevelt, and the "Dollar Diplomacy" of Taft. When war broke out in Europe, this key member of the leading munitions family in America was as pro-war as anyone in the halls of Congress.

The country's population wanted peace, however, especially the workers, and 1916 was a bad year for Du Pont political ambitions. Wilson was reelected. Henry, now required by the Seventeenth Amendment to face election by the people, was not.

Henry's machine had easily won him the nomination on the Republican ticket. By stuffing ballot boxes, shipping repeaters from one polling place to another, and intimidating independent voters at the polls, Henry's forces captured a majority of the primary's delegates to the Dover convention. There, his Committee on Credentials refused to seat fourteen independent Republicans from Kent County and the convention gave Henry the nomination. It also gave the people of Delaware nausea.

"WHAT HAS H. A. DU PONT EVER DONE FOR THE LABORING CLASSES?" asked one Delaware newspaper.[44] Another announced that it could no longer support Henry's "Du Pont or nobody" philosophy.[45] Then the anti-war Wilmington *Every Evening* revealed that Henry's record of absenteeism in the Senate was the highest of any senator in the country running for reelection.[46] That year Henry bought control of the *Every Evening,* changing its position overnight from dove to hawk.

But other forces joined in on the attack, including labor unions. The Central Union and four brotherhoods of trainmen denounced Henry as "labor's enemy."[47] When the electoral returns finally came in, Henry's ambitions had been thoroughly swamped by a tidal wave of rejection. But even more shattering to Henry was his belief that his defeat had been engineered by a member of his own family—Alfred I. du Pont.

He was right.

4. ROUND TWO—THE BATTLE OVER CONTROL

Since 1912, when he was reappointed to the company's finance committee, Alfred du Pont realized that it was only a matter of time before the family feud renewed itself. The control of the Du Pont Trust was at stake and no trust can have more than one master. Now there were three masters: he, Coleman, and Pierre, each talented in his own field, all equally ambitious, and each believing himself superior to the others. Eventually one would have to emerge as lord and master, and most likely that would be the one who was closest to the firm's direct operations. Alfred knew that, of the three, his position was the weakest in this regard. He feared, therefore, that he might be the first to be eliminated. As the Du Pont saga unfolded, his fears were proven justified.

The Triumvirate Splits

Perhaps Alfred's greatest weakness was in his personal ties to the clan, ties constantly strained by his own family problems. It seemed to the clan that Alfred's family woes never ended, even with his new marriage to Alicia Bradford. Tragedy seemed to hover over the couple. Alicia's first pregnancy by Alfred ended in a miscarriage that left her in poor health. Her second pregnancy produced a child who lived only long enough to be christened. Then Alicia's eyesight failed, resulting in a social setback in the tightly knit world of Wilmington society. Her vanity prevented her from wearing her thick eyeglasses on the streets, and she passed many friends by without even a nod. Misunderstandings soon arose which only added to her social ostracism in Wilmington.

Alicia's life grew sadder. Because of her failing eyesight, Alicia also was forced to give up her favorite pastime of riding thoroughbreds. Probably from all this, she had a bitter quarrel with Maddie, who then eloped to Germany. To add to the embarrassment, it was Coleman's wife, Elsie, who paid for her passage.

Alfred also grew increasingly bitter, especially over the death of his last infant. He turned his wrath onto his son, Alfred Victor. He demanded Victor be sent to the Hallock School in Massachusetts, which Alfred had helped establish with a Morgan deputy, Charles Mellen, president of the New Haven Railroad. Bessie objected, but as Alfred was Victor's guardian under Delaware law, the boy was sent.

With Victor out of Delaware, Alfred then began a secret campaign in Dover. There, in the sleepy House of Representatives, only the name of Du Pont ever seemed to raise an air of excitement. This time it was an uproar.

Alfred had Democratic boss Thomas Bayard Heisel quietly support a bill to change Victor's name to Dorsey Cazenove du Pont, hinting that Bessie was guilty of infidelity. Representative Swain of Delaware City and bribery fame rammed the bill through the Miscellaneous Committee and the House, assured by Alfred that there would be no opposition. "The Count," however, had made one mistake: he underestimated his former wife. Bessie got word of Alfred's action and frantically began contacting the Du Ponts. The family was furious and, as if by some magic Du Pont hand, the bill was recalled from the Senate to the House Miscellaneous Committee for hearings. In February 1913 Alfred du Pont appeared and testified that he believed his son would "bring disgrace" to his name, but refused details. The Committee was not moved by his arguments, especially when Bessie read a heartbreaking letter from Victor at school asking why his father was doing this to him. Alfred remained obstinate and forced the bill to the House floor for a vote, where it was finally defeated 17 to 15. Alicia's brother, Representative Edward Bradford, Jr., was the only Republican who voted for it. Defeated, Alfred returned to Wilmington and the ire of the entire Du Pont family.

Through this whole ugly affair, Coleman and Pierre had been Bessie's staunchest defenders, but it was an uneasy alliance. Friction was beginning to build up between the talented cousins, for while Coleman was partying in New York, Pierre was facing the courts and was building the company as acting president in Wilmington. Then another point of friction arose in the person of William du Pont.

Willie, now shaggy in middle age, wearing a walrus mustache and gold-rimmed glasses, had been out of the firm since his divorce and second marriage, but he was still one of its largest stockholders and was entitled by all rights to a seat on the Board of Directors. Perhaps at Alfred's urging, he requested that seat in 1911. Pierre flatly turned him down. Willie then appealed to Coleman. Coleman, always eager to show his heavy hand and generosity to family, agreed to support his claim.

It was a bad mistake for Coly. He was acting like an absentee landlord, countermanding Pierre's decision in his typically insensitive manner. His brother-in-law, Hamilton Barksdale, objected strongly and as a result of this quarrel he and Coleman were never close again. Pierre, knowing that Coleman would win, diplomatically chose the role of mediator. Pierre liked to side with winners, even if he didn't agree with them. Willie was seated.

Three years later, like a modern King Richard returning from unholy crusades along Broadway, Coleman decided to journey to Wilmington and claim his throne. Pierre had actually been running the company for over six years by then, and he was soon at odds with his older cousin. Within a few months, relations between the two grew very tense. "In the summer of 1914," Pierre later wrote, "T.C. [Coleman] suggested sale of his entire holdings in the Powder Company to me. The conversation leading to this suggestion had, as subject, the organizing of the company. He and I differed in our estimate of the value of some of our men and in our opinion as to the method of handling the company's affairs. Without an intention to overestimate the situation, I might say that relations in regard to the company's affairs were and had been somewhat strained . . . he evidently, in fact, openly did not desire to sell but explained his opinion that it was best under the circumstances."[48]

Coleman held off these plans when war broke out in Europe in 1914, feeling his organizational ideas were now crucial. Pierre disagreed, but Coleman went ahead with his restructuring anyway. His first target was the firm's executive committee. Coleman felt that with an average age of 52, the committee needed younger blood. He suggested an incentive for younger Du Pont executives. He would offer to sell to them 20,700 shares of his common stock at $160 a share. There was a reason other than company interest that compelled this move by the company president. Coleman needed cash for another of his big deals—the largest office structure in the world. Looming forty stories high over New York's streets, the Equitable Building would have 2,300 rooms, according to Coleman's plans, and it would cost over $30 million.

On December 10, 1914, Coleman put his offer in writing. By then Du Pont stock had risen to 163 from November's 127, with more rises expected in the next year with the war's continuance. Coleman made his offer to the finance committee, also reorganized by him. Under Coleman's new program, this committee now bypassed the executive committee, reporting directly to the board of directors. Control of the purse strings, Coleman explained, meant control of the company and that should always be in the hands of directors, not executives. He, Pierre, and Alfred were its members, and Coleman also added William. This shift left Barksdale, a member of the old executive committee who had now fallen out of Coleman's favor, slated for green pasture. Barksdale had only one recourse: to support Pierre's next series of moves to seize complete control of the company.

Pierre's Coup

When Coleman originally made his offer, he wrote Pierre: "I have, as you know, always thought well of common stock and put a higher figure on it than you have. I think it well worth 185 today and think it will go up to 190 or 200 before the year 1915 is many months old."[49] Coleman was right. By March 31, 1915, Du Pont stock was quoted at 298 bid, 302 asked.

Coleman soon expected to have cash from Du Pont Company, so he severed negotiations for the Equitable loan with his New York banker friends. Since his health was deteriorating, however, Coleman decided to leave the matter in the hands of the finance committee while he went to the Mayo Clinic for lung tests. "As I am going away today," he wrote Pierre on December 14, "and do not know how long I will be gone, I have left the matter in Mr. L. L. Dunham's hands."[50] Dunham was Coleman's secretary.

Quietly, his ambition whetted by opportunity, Pierre watched Coleman's departure like a hawk after prey. Already, he knew, wheels had been set in motion. Between the date of Coleman's offer and his departure, Pierre had his brother Irénée offer to buy Coleman's stock for $125 a share before the finance committee could meet. Coleman refused, but Pierre may well have foreseen Coleman's rejection and may have only wanted Alfred to get wind through the family grapevine of the price he had offered.

At any rate, on December 23, a fateful day in Alfred du Pont's life, the finance committee met to consider Coleman's offer. Alfred introduced a resolution to accept Coleman's offer but to advise "that we do not feel justified in paying more than $125 per share for this stock at this time."[51] On an $8 dividend basis (which the company had paid to shareholders that year), Alfred pointed out that this was little more than a 6 percent return on investment. He did not think a smaller yield was attractive to the men, he explained; he considered the war's duration uncertain and refused to stake everything on its continuation. Willie agreed, while Pierre craftily chose to vote negatively, as if he really wanted the company to purchase the stock and knew nothing of Irénée's offer.

After the meeting, Pierre wired Coleman news of the two-to-one vote and his sentiment of support. He failed, however, to mention the all-important words of the resolution: "at this time." This gave Coleman the impression that the offer had been turned down permanently. He also left the words out of the official minutes of the meeting, and skillfully managed to have them signed by Alfred and William unnoticed. The coup was under way.

> Dear Coleman,
>   I have been intending to write you about the reception of your proposition by the Finance Committee. Unfortunately, Alfred, who approved the plan before you went away, got somewhat crosswise in the meeting and I think it best to let the matter rest for the moment, preferably until I can see you, before taking another step.[52]

This was no confirmation of a "definite rejection" by the committee, as Pierre later claimed. Nor did Pierre mention Willie's position in agreeing with the temporary rejection. Instead, only Alfred, who was already in bad straits with Coleman, was mentioned.

Pierre's report from the finance committee to the board of directors also never implied a final rejection. "The committee expressed the feeling that we were not justified in paying more than $125 per share and asked Mr. P. S. du Pont to take the matter up with Mr. T. C. du Pont further."[53]

On January 6 Coleman had replied that he was disappointed with Alfred's position and charged that "Alfred has some ulterior motive in mind"[54] and suggested withdrawal of his offer to the younger executives. Always appearing the model of integrity before Coleman, Pierre had written back on January 9 that Coleman should wait until he had a chance to talk with Willie.[55] Finally, at that point, Pierre did mention Willie, but only to secure enough time to gather financial support from Morgan banks for the purchase of Coleman's stock. Although Coleman had agreed to wait,[56] Pierre never contacted Willie, who had left town for a few weeks, believing the matter would not be settled until Coleman returned.

On January 15, Coleman again offered to withdraw unless Pierre had talked to Willie and was already committed.[57] With his financial backing and Du Pont securities now set up as a holding company for the coup, Pierre replied on January 18 that he had done neither.[58] Pierre then waited for Coleman to finalize the withdrawal to the executives and drop control of the company into his lap. He must have broken into a cold sweat when Coleman wrote back on January 20 that he should wait until he returned East "when I am sure we can work out some plan."[59]

Pierre immediately stepped up the operation. Pierre unleashed phase two of his coup. With Coleman's offer to the company effectively stalled, Pierre now needed only some "emergency" to prod Coleman into selling to him.

At about this time a rumor began circulating around Wall Street that a prominent Du Pont stockholder was about to sell his entire holdings to

Germany. As Du Pont was a major supplier to the British war effort, it was not long before Nobel, the great British explosives manufacturer (now called Imperial Chemicals), sent word to Pierre that one of its officials, a Mr. Kraftmeier, was en route for a secret meeting with him in New York.

On January 23 Pierre and Irénée met Kraftmeier at his New York hotel. With a personal discipline that would have swelled his great-grandfather, E. I. du Pont, with pride, Pierre managed a straight face as Kraftmeier explained that British Secret Service had uncovered plans to sell Du Pont to German interests through Kuhn, Loeb, & Co.

Pierre told the Englishman he was mistaken and assured him of Du Pont's loyalty to the British cause. Two weeks later, however, on February 5, Pierre wrote to Coleman du Pont that the company was willing to sell munitions to Germany.

Pierre was also already aware that in the fall of 1914 one Captain Fritz von Rintelin, a German agent, had approached J. Amory Haskell, a major Du Pont stockholder and director, to see if Du Pont could be bought out. Haskell had rejected the offer.

Such belated rumors, however, were a great opportunity to throw suspicion on Alfred. Now Pierre could explain to Irénée why he wanted Coleman's stock by any means. In the interests of patriotism to clients, he also contacted Coleman and informed him of the grave meeting with Kraftmeier. He never mentioned the Haskell affair; instead, he asked Coleman to sell his entire holdings for $200 a share to prevent Alfred either from buying another director's holdings or perhaps from selling his to the Germans. Coleman, alarmed by Pierre's warnings, gave his consent to a complete divestiture of his stocks.

Why did Coleman agree to sell out? Originally, he had only intended to sell 20,000 to 40,000 common shares. Pierre later claimed that Coleman was in financial need. But that seems hardly the case. The Equitable Building was *not* a crucial matter to Coleman's finances. Pierre had used some 14,000 preferred and 54,000 common shares as collateral for Morgan's $8.5 million loan. Coleman could easily have done likewise. In fact, 26,400 of that 54,000 common used by Pierre as collateral was Coleman's.

The answer lies in an obscure letter from Coleman to Pierre, held by the younger cousin until its release on April 2, 1947. In this letter, dated March 17, 1915, Coleman wrote that Pierre was "in the saddle running things possibly against some opposition." What opposition? Alfred's? Undoubtedly, but Coleman realized he himself had opposed Pierre on many decisions. Pulling out was best for both the company and his own health. Probably all this was speeded along by Pierre's hint that Alfred might be buying stock or dealing with the Germans to sell his stock. Coleman must have had more than a little doubt as to where Alfred's sympathies lay. After all, Alfred's daughter *was* in Germany and her husband *was* fighting for Germany, and Alfred *had* allied himself with anti-war forces in the Democratic Party. Besides, Alfred was always out to wrong him, Coleman commented at the time. Alfred and William "were after the stock," he wrote Pierre. Pierre must have smiled.

On February 10 the finance committee met. As the meeting drew to a close, Alfred asked, almost as an afterthought, "How are the negotiations for the Coleman du Pont stock progressing?"

"Why, they are all off," Pierre replied.

Alfred was shocked. "Since when?"

"They were called off shortly after you and Willie turned down the offer in December."

Alfred exploded. "But they were not turned down! There was merely a difference of opinion as to price, and it was my understanding that you were to convey to T.C., through Mr. Dunham, that we believe the price of $160 a share excessive, and we suggested $125 as a proper price at that time."

"That was not my understanding," said Pierre calmly. "My understanding was that you turned down T.C.'s offer definitely."[60]

Willie then agreed that Pierre was mistaken and Alfred suggested that Pierre correct the mistake immediately. Pierre complied. Alfred then asked for copies of Pierre's letters to Coleman on the matter.

Predictably, Alfred never received the letters. What Alfred had no way of knowing was that his younger cousin had made no simple mistake, but had acted with cold deliberation. Pierre had already set up his holding company, Du Pont (Christiana) Securities, with which he planned to purchase Coleman's stock and buy the loyalty of company executives with pieces of Coleman's pie.

Instead of the Coleman stock letters, Pierre sent Alfred some of the letters pertaining to the Kraftmeier meeting. Alfred repeated his request, but Pierre never sent them. The draft of his January 4, 1915, letter to Coleman shows why: Pierre's manicured fingers had clearly been planting the seeds of Alfred's downfall. Pierre's tight-lipped treasurer, J. J. Raskob, was hurriedly finalizing the arrangements for the sale, while Pierre and his associates, his brother-in-law R. R. Carpenter, his brothers Irénée and Lammot du Pont, and one or two others landed a $8.5 million loan from J. P. Morgan & Company. On February 20 Pierre was able to telegram Coleman affirming the purchase of all of Coleman's stock, 63,300 common, 14,600 preferred, for $13.9 million: $8 million in cash, $5.9 million in notes payable. On February 22 Coleman replied with his own final confirmation.

On February 28 Alfred du Pont opened his morning newspaper to receive the shock of his life. "Coleman du Pont sells out to P. S. du Pont and others in company." Pierre had seized control of the firm.

The "others" were executives that Pierre had frankly bribed with $125,000 pieces of the Coleman du Pont pie. These men, Harry F. Brown (smokeless powder manager), Harry G. Haskell (high explosives), William Coyne (nonmilitary sales), W. G. Ramsey (engineering), and F. G. Tallman (purchasing), joined Pierre, Irénée, Lammot, and J. J. Raskob in forming the Du Pont (Christiana) Securities Company. Also on hand as members were Robert Ruliph (Ruly) Morgan Carpenter, Pierre's brother-in-law, and Alexis Felix du Pont, brother of Francis I.

Alfred spent that Monday at his desk anxiously waiting to hear from Pierre. Finally, when no contact had been made by 4:00 P.M., Alfred telephoned Pierre and asked him to walk down to his office. Pierre arrived calm and composed.

"Pierre du Pont," Alfred exclaimed, "don't do this thing . . . It is wrong!"

Pierre quietly asked why.

"Because you have accomplished something by virtue of the power and influence vested in you as an officer of the company . . . For that reason the stock which you have acquired does not belong to you but to the company which you represent. I therefore ask you to turn this stock over to the company."[61]

Pierre calmly refused and left.

Alfred was not the only Du Pont shocked by news of the purchase. Willie du Pont discovered the news a day after Alfred did and he wired Pierre from his Georgia home: "Paper states you have purchased Coleman's stock. I presume for the company. Any other action I should consider a breach of faith."[62] Faith or not, Pierre was sticking to his financial guns.

Francis I. du Pont called a meeting of all family members not in Pierre's syndicate for March 4 at Alfred's office. That night, Francis, Alfred, William, Eugene E., Henry F., Philip F., and Alexis I. du Pont were present. Soon, however, two uninvited callers walked in—Pierre and Irénée. After politely asking if they could be seated, they began a friendly chat on trite family affairs with their astonished relatives. For almost an hour this small talk went on, Alfred losing the initiative over the meeting's direction. In despair, he disconnected his hearing box and stared at the ceiling. Pierre then suddenly asked Willie to explain his allegation of bad faith. Willie stated that Pierre's use of the company name was in bad faith. Alfred and Francis supported Willie's claim. Pierre obviously did not, despite the fact that all but one of the fourteen banks associated with Morgan Company in floating the $8.5 million loan to Pierre were depositories of Du Pont Company, and that right after the loan the banks enjoyed increased Du Pont deposits of over $7.4 million. But then, as Pierre later explained, any new injection of funds into Du Pont's treasury would result in a rise in bank balances.

In desperation, Alfred asked Pierre if he would sell the stock to the company. Pierre calmly replied that he would not and asked if there were any further charges against him. The room was silent, too silent for Alfred. Feeling he had the upper hand, Pierre added a touch of drama to the occasion by warning his relatives not to say behind his back what they could not say to his face. Then, as quietly as he had come, he left.[63] From that moment on, it was clear to all who was in the seat of power.

Two days later, trying to appear fair, Pierre announced he had decided to reverse his previous refusal to sell the stock. But at the following directors' meeting, the offer was jeopardized by an alleged—and undoubtedly calculated—legal technicality. At a prearranged time, it seems, in walked John P. Laffey, the company lawyer, with a marked law book in hand and pockets bulging with a $100,000 share in Coleman's stock. The lawyer explained that he considered it illegal for the company to invest more than its surplus of $7.5 million. For that remark, Laffey was soon rewarded with a director's seat. Then William Coyne, his pockets likewise bulging, added insult to Alfred's injury by insisting the board give a full vote of confidence to their leader, Pierre Samuel du Pont. It was unanimous. Alfred left the room in complete disgust.

Pierre's offer was referred to the finance committee for a final decision. Only now the finance committee had a newly appointed member, Irénée du Pont. When Alfred and William moved to accept Pierre's offer, Irénée blocked it. A clear majority of the complete four-man committee was necessary and Pierre, as seller, had abstained. It was all over. Pierre's coup was now complete.

Alfred and Willie knew it was only a matter of time before it would be all over for them. Pierre had already replaced Coleman officially as president and had bought control of the board of directors. He even lured Henry F. and Eugene du Pont and three other in-laws, Charles Copeland, William Winder Laird, and Hugh Rodney Sharp, into his camp. In all the scrambling for Coleman's power, Pierre's shrewdness had put him on top.

Alfred's Revenge

After his cousin's coup became apparent, Alfred, never one for concession, decided to continue the battle on the legal front. He had Philip du
Pont contest Pierre's acquisition in federal court. This was the final futile
chapter in the greatest feud that ever tore the Du Pont family. It was also
the end to Alfred's role in the company. He, Francis, and William were all
purged from the board of directors and replaced by members of Pierre's
syndicate: Ramsey, Tallman, and Henry F. du Pont, the deserter. At the
annual stockholders' meeting a short while later a motion was carried
endorsing Alfred's ousting and applauding Pierre. "I don't like to admit it,
Doc," Alfred told his family physician, "but this is the most humiliating
thing I've ever had happen to me."[64]

Alfred's cause won over quite a few members of the family. William,
Francis I., Paul, Archibald, Ernest, Eleanor du Pont Perot, and Philip all
lined up on Alfred's side and all were to share his permanent exile from
the family firm.

Alfred and William also continued the battle on fronts other than the
courts.

To rival Pierre's Wilmington Trust Company, they set up the Delaware
Trust Company and built an office building in Wilmington across the street
from Du Pont Building. It was two stories higher so that Alfred and
William could cast an aloof eye down on their hated neighbor. The buildings still stand to this day, both banks dominating northern Delaware's
finances.

Next, Alfred heard that Coleman was planning to run for President of
the United States. The press, he read, had found Coleman at his new office
in the Equitable Building at 120 Broadway. "I have received thousands of
letters from small businessmen and farmers," he said with all due modesty,
"asking that I permit my name to be used."[65] Two weeks later the Business Men's Presidential League opened its lavish offices at Coleman's
Waldorf-Astoria, announcing that T. Coleman du Pont was one of
America's great businessmen and a likely presidential candidate. Coleman
agreed. In June 1916 one of Delaware's senators rose in Congress to make
a speech calling for Coleman's presidency. Coly, as humble as ever, was
delighted.

At first, Alfred was confused. Could Coleman really believe he was a
serious contender? Alfred considered Coly's ego and answered in the
affirmative. Yet there had to be another angle, one where Coleman could
get something out of the campaign besides probable defeat.

The answer came on the wind of rumors that 78-year-old Colonel Henry, if reelected in 1916, would serve only half his Senate term and then have his hand-picked governor appoint Coleman in his stead. "That was my chief reason for throwing the Colonel out," Alfred later explained.

If Alfred lacked cleverness in business, he was amply endowed when it came to politics. In alliance with J. Frank Allee, he button-holed twenty of the thirty-five New Castle caucus members at the Richardson Hotel in Dover and captured the election as National Republican delegate from New Castle County.

Colonel Henry was virtually caught with his pants down. He had been so sure of that election for himself that he hadn't even bothered to attend. He left everything to Coleman, who was there to make sure the caucus sent its delegate to vote for his own nomination at the national convention. When Coleman threatened to take the fight to the Dover convention's floor, Allee used the General's presidential ambitions against him. Make it a floor fight, he told Coly, and you lose New Castle's vote at the national convention.

Coleman retreated, but he failed to capture Alfred's vote anyway. Alfred had the caucus's resolution of "instruct" for Coleman changed to "endorse." When Alfred went to the convention as New Castle's delegate, he claimed the resolution's wordage was too vague to be binding and voted instead for Theodore Roosevelt. Coleman received only 13 of 987 votes at the convention. "Bang! T. C. du Pont's boom blows up!" ran the headline on Alfred's *Morning News*. Coleman's Business Men's Presidential League closed its doors at the Waldorf, never to reopen.[66]

Alfred used the same tactic to split the Republican Party on the state level and crush Colonel Henry's reelection bid. He fully endorsed Theodore Roosevelt right up to the Republican national convention. Then he switched "loyalty" to the Democratic nominee for Henry's Senate seat, Josiah Wolcott. Alfred was actually not too happy about Wolcott. He had proposed Alicia's first cousin, Thomas F. Bayard, Jr., husband of Elizabeth Bradford du Pont, for the Democratic nomination. Instead, Wolcott, a supposed friend of labor, won. Faced with the choice of Wolcott or Colonel Henry, Alfred easily chose the former.

Almost at once, Alfred began feverishly writing a steady stream of checks for Wolcott's campaign. His seven newspapers constantly played up union charges that Henry was "labor's enemy," and local labor leaders like railroad brakeman Ed Davis stomped through Delaware factories and churches repeating the question: "What has H. A. du Pont ever done for the working class?" To further split the Republican vote on which Henry's machine was counting, Alfred raised the Progressive Party banner and ran Ed Bradford for Congress and Dr. R. R. Burton of Lewes for Henry's seat in the Senate.

On election night Alfred invited family and friends to his Nemours estate to hear the returns. The first results came from Wilmington, Henry's stronghold. The Colonel was having a hard time, a clear indicator of his impending doom statewide. By the last tallies it was clear that Wolcott had won, 25,416 votes to Henry's 22,925. Burton pulled in 2,361 votes, but they weren't even necessary to beat the old Colonel. Every Republican endorsed by Alfred's Progressive Party won; all opposed by Alfred lost.

Nemours broke into celebration. Champagne popped and Alfred lit up one of his 50-cent cigars. "Nothing like a great occasion for turning over a new leaf. This is the last cigar I'm ever going to light."[67] It was.

It was also one of Alfred's last great victories in Delaware. For while Alfred was turning over a new leaf, cousin Pierre, undaunted and untouched, was turning the family business into a new order that was to dominate Delaware's economy—and its politics—for most of the next sixty years. Building from Coleman's careful blueprint, Pierre streamlined the company's organization according to his own liking now, erecting one of America's first modern corporations while racing to prepare Du Pont for its crucial role in that worldwide orgy of mass slaughter known as World War I.

Eight

MERCHANTS OF DEATH

1. TIES TO A WINDFALL

In the spring of 1914 a cold chill swept over Europe with the news of the assassination of Archduke Franz Ferdinand, pretender to the ancient Hapsburg throne of Austria-Hungary. Within hours, the cold war of intrigue and market rivalry that had gripped the capitals of Europe in fear and suspicion for over a decade heated up with stormy ultimatums that flashed like lightning over the breadth of the continent, turning its landscape into fiery holocaust. Only after five years of firestorms and mass murder would ten million bewildered refugees finally emerge from the poisoned smoke, wandering in shock over the shattered continent, groveling in rubbled craters that once were cities, stumbling into bloody trenches where ten million more of their friends and brothers, once strong young men, now silently lay, unable to hear the wail of their five million widows and nine million orphans. And carrying that wail, winds rose and swept over the scarred countryside, trying desperately, and also futilely, to bring fresh air to a stale, diseased civilization.

From this global tragedy emerged a total of 23 million dead and, in the United States alone, 20,000 new millionaires—one new American millionaire for every six American boys killed. Among these new Croesuses were the Du Ponts.

Of all the Du Ponts, only the direct family of Alfred I. du Pont suffered any personal danger from the war. Alfred's son Victor saw combat in France. Alfred's wife, Alicia, almost did likewise, although, unlike Victor, not by choice.

Alicia had sailed to France in the spring of 1914 with her brother, Ed Bradford, in the hope of improving her health and spirits. She was pregnant again, desperately trying to give Alfred a son. The trip would do her good, Alfred had thought, and it did. Letters returned to Nemours describing delightful tours through France's wine-growing regions and Alicia's improving condition.

Then the impossible but inevitable finally occurred, shattering forever

Alicia's lazy afternoons. As declarations of war hurled across Europe in the last week of April 1914, German armies smashed through Belgium and rumbled into France toward Paris. Alfred was nearly frantic when he learned that the war's outbreak had caught Alicia separated from her brother. She was stranded alone, trapped between the ocean and the approaching war, prevented by the hysteria from returning to America as the French army crumbled before the German advance. Unable to book passage to France, Alfred kept the cables to Europe burning with advice to his pregnant wife. Finally, to Alfred's relief, Ed found his sister and they managed to buy passage on a ship to America in September.

Back in the palatial peace of Nemours, Alicia gave birth on October 21 to a son, Samuel. Alfred was overjoyed, but the baby lived only one day. At Nemours, beside his infant sister, Samuel was buried along with Alfred's last hope, for it was Alicia's last pregnancy. With tragedy hovering over his second marriage, Alfred's face took on a hardened, icy look, which his glass eye only accentuated.

For other Du Ponts, however, times were more fortunate, especially for Alfred's cousin, Pierre du Pont. At the time of the Ferdinand assassination Pierre was abroad also, in London, signing international trade agreements with German and British munition makers.[1] With the outbreak of hostilities between countries of two parties to the agreement, Pierre considered the new treaty in abeyance. He knew that this was a different kind of war, a war of trenches and heavy fortifications, requiring more high explosives for assaults than probably either the English or German parties could provide. And Du Pont was only too happy to oblige.

Pierre and his syndicate were deep in World War I long before the United States was. They executed the largest powder contracts in history through credit extended to the British government by J. P. Morgan & Company, Pierre's friend in the purchase of the Coleman du Pont stock. Between August and December 22, 1914, 21,621,300 pounds of explosives were ordered from Du Pont by Britain and her allies. When the war broke out, Du Pont had the capacity to produce 8.4 million pounds of smokeless powder per year; within six months Pierre had contracted to supply thirteen times that amount.

Most of the cost for the required plant expansion by Du Pont in those early years of the war was paid by the British. "The United States is not in the war, gentlemen," Du Pont's vice-president in charge of military sales, Colonel E. G. Buckner, told the Allies. "We can produce the explosives you need and we think we can produce in time, but only if you assume the financial risks of an emergency expansion. . . . I repeat, it's your war, and the risks must be yours!"[2] In 1915 the British paid the Du Ponts $100 million through J. P. Morgan & Company to expand the plant capacity of their explosives division. That year, Du Pont's annual smokeless powder capacity, which had been 8.4 million only a year before, reached 200 million pounds; by 1916 it was 290 million pounds; by 1918 it grew to an astronomical 455 million pounds.

World War I was a windfall for the Du Ponts. By February 1915 the money value of Allied contracts had already exceeded $59 million. And higher profits meant higher dividends to the shareholders, especially the family. The split-up of the company had reduced the common stock dividend in 1913 from $12 to $8, but the war more than made up for lost ground. "We were not taking any chances of the war ending in six months," recalled Colonel Buckner. "We asked the Allies one dollar a pound of powder. . . . Our demand was a cash payment of 50%. . . . Our demand was finally agreed to."[3] One year later, in 1915, the Du Ponts lowered their price to 97½ cents per pound, a questionable generosity when one considers that smokeless powder cost them only 31 cents a pound to produce. That year Du Pont's net earnings reached an all-time high of $57.4 million. Within one year, net earnings would jump to $82.1 million, although, with increased volume in sales, the elimination of capital construction costs through Allied funding, and other factors which mitigated many of the rising costs of raw materials, Du Pont was able to reduce its price per pound to 51.3 cents by May 1917, thus spurring demand even further. As one historian noted, "It was, therefore, the confirmation of Pierre's hard bargain with the Allies, together with the unexpectedly long duration of the war, that was the key to big profits for the Du Pont Company."[4]

Such unprecedented earnings were quickly reflected in Du Pont's rising stock value. In the summer of 1914 a common share of Du Pont stock sold for $160. By the following April the price was quoted at $390. By June it hit $670; in September, $775, at which time Pierre split the company's common stock, issuing two new shares for every old one. But by October, Du Pont stock had climbed to $430—or $860 under the former reckoning!

During all this time, the Du Ponts tried to keep their financial alliance with the British a secret from the U.S. government. Since 1908, after the government filed its anti-trust suit against Du Pont, no government representatives had been allowed entrance into a Du Pont plant without signing a secrecy pledge. In 1909 Pierre issued a decree that no information was to be given to anyone by any employee without specific approval from Du Pont headquarters in Wilmington.

These restrictions were further tightened when the war broke out and Pierre, with the family's full approval, rejected a plea from the U.S. Secretary of War for information on his contractors. The United States was certainly concerned then that a financial entanglement might draw America into the war; and, as Wilson was particularly concerned with Germany as a potential rival to U.S. market expansion, he was anxious to know whether Du Pont munitions were finding themselves in German hands.

Such was not the case, but Washington certainly had cause for suspicion. Pierre du Pont himself wrote Coleman on February 5, 1915, that if the Germans "came forward with orders in quantity similar to the orders of the Allied nations we would be willing to sell."[5] This, despite promises to British Imperial's Kraftmeier to the contrary two weeks earlier. To Pierre, World War was just a matter of profitable business. That year, when Congress was considering a bill prohibiting U.S. munitions sales to belligerents, the Du Ponts considered opening a plant in Canada, and eventually did.

In 1917, two months after the United States entered the war, the Du Ponts again refused the government information on their trade secrets. A similar but more urgent request in 1918 from the War Department was also turned down. Finally, an angry personal demand from Secretary of War Baker for information on Du Pont's TNT plant drew an informative reply from Wilmington, but only after the government placed its first TNT order with Du Pont.

Congress's declaration of war on Germany was a day for which some Du Ponts had worked for years. As revealed by a Congressional investigation in 1919, T. Coleman du Pont in 1915 established with other leading industrialists and bankers the infamous National Security League to promote America's entry into the war. For two years before the declaration of war, the League, aiming to draw America into the conflict, published vicious attacks on congressmen who opposed entering the slaughter. When German submarine warfare threatened Du Pont munitions shipments, the League demanded that America defend her right to "freedom of the seas" and the right to sell military aid to Germany's enemy.

It was precisely this "aid" that moved Coleman and Pierre to be staunch supporters of Britain's war effort. In 1915 Du Pont held more than $46 million worth of British one-year notes in partial payment for Du Pont powder. $9.2 million worth of French credit was also in Du Pont hands, along with Anglo-French bonds worth $36,350,000, and $19,350,000 worth of other Allied obligations.[6] By 1919, the Du Pont family held Allied credit worth $111.6 million.[7]

The best explanation for Du Pont concern for these credits came from Pierre himself. "If the war had ended we would have been in a bad condition," he testified years later, "because I know that there was one case in which we owed $100 million. We were obligated to return that $100 million to the Allies who furnished the money to go ahead with our contract. We had spent the $100 million and about $60 million more in plants and furnishing money for materials, and our company would have gone broke if we had been compelled to return that money."[8]

The only alternative was the war's continuation, and the only way that could be accomplished successfully by Britain was through America's intervention, breaking the battlefield deadlock and dipping the scales in favor of Allied victory. To this end, the Du Ponts made no small contribution.

2. MARCHING AS TO WAR . . .

In June 1916 the cobblestoned streets of Wilmington shook with beating drums and marching feet. It was as if war had come to Delaware months before any formal declaration from Washington. And, in fact, it had.

Pierre du Pont—inspired by Allied profits and by vivid descriptions of French suffering and urgent appeals from two French cousins, Madeleine de Tregomain and Marguerite Bidermann—had been moved late in 1915 to send $1,000 to French war relief. But more than Pierre's personal inclinations were involved. For what was personal policy for the president of Du Pont soon became unofficial, albeit persuasive, company policy. Publicly, Pierre never endorsed Coleman du Pont's warmongering National Security League, but privately he did not frown on marching Du Pont employees down the main street of Wilmington in one of Coleman's pro-war "preparedness" parades.

Such parades had become part of a national hysteria after the sinking of the *Lusitania* a month before by German submarines. But Du Pont support for the war, because of their vulnerability to criticism, remained covert. Officially, Du Pont Company took no position. Yet charges were made publicly in the New York *World* on October 18, 1915, that the company prohibited its workers from wearing Wilson buttons; Pierre denied the reports. But no one denied that the Du Pont family was deeply involved in the preparedness movement, including Coleman's pro-war National Security League, nor that the Du Ponts openly gave financial support to the pro-war Republican presidential candidate, Charles Evans Hughes. There was more than a grain of truth to the charges of Senator Robert La Follette in the Milwaukee *Journal* of August 28, 1916, that pro-war propaganda was being paid for by the "Maxims and the Du Ponts." Three years later a congressional investigation into the National Security League confirmed the charges.

Pierre's denials did receive support from another U.S. senator—Henry A. du Pont. Like Pierre, Henry denied his family's involvement in the preparedness movement. Yet when Coleman set up the National Security League, the senator wrote Coleman of his approval and stated that such an organization should have been founded even sooner.[9] There is no doubt that Henry was in favor of a declaration of war against Germany, and he voiced his opinion openly in the Senate.

Henry was a bitter opponent of anti-war senators La Follette and William J. Stone. Taking time off from his check-writing for the French government, in 1916 he helped defeat the Gore Resolution, which would have warned Americans to stay off armed ships of foreign nations. When, in 1916, a tax on munitions profits was proposed in Congress, Senator du Pont was among those who led the attack against it, eventually forcing a modest reduction in the tax. Pierre, like his father Lammot du Pont during the Civil War, also lobbied against the tax on behalf of the company. All of this, of course, did not help to dampen the Du Ponts' dislike of Woodrow Wilson with his claims for peace.

Pro-war sentiment was by no means confined to the Du Ponts, however. By 1917 war hysteria had been whipped to a fever pitch. Coleman du Pont was not alone in setting up the National Security League. Joining him were other economic royalists: John D. Rockefeller, George W. Perkins of U.S. Steel, William K. Vanderbilt, Nicholas F. Brady of New York Edison, Henry H. Rodgers of Rockefeller's Standard Oil, Simon and Daniel Guggenheim of the copper trust, and, predictably, J. P. Morgan.

"What do Morgan and Schwab [the head of Bethlehem Steel] care for world peace," cried Senator La Follette, "when there are big profits in world war? The Schwab properties which stood at a market value of seven millions before they began supplying the Allies are today given an aggregate value of forty-nine millions!"[10]

It was a futile cry. The President, who had been reelected on the platform of "He kept us out of war," was now trying to put Americans into the war. "Our industries have expanded to such a point," Wilson had explained in 1912, "that they will burst their jackets if they cannot find a free outlet to the markets of the world. . . . Our domestic markets no longer suffice. We need foreign markets."[11] Wilson was right. In 1913 the U.S. economy again sank into a frustrated depression that threatened to be worse than that of the 1890's. Even Du Pont suffered a drop in sales in 1914. Then the European war came to the rescue, a war which involved rising Germany, the very power Wilson saw as America's main competitor for the economic empire of overseas markets needed to pull the country out of depression.[12]

By 1916 Wilson had forced the resignation of Secretary of State William Jennings Bryan because of Bryan's objection to official government sanction of U.S. munitions trade to European belligerents, including that of the Du Ponts.

The man who replaced Bryan was Robert Lansing, Bryan's assistant. Lansing, after a conference with an officer from the National City Bank on October 23, 1914, had convinced Wilson to change his position from Bryan's "true spirit of neutrality" to one based upon "strict legality" and allow Wall Street to grant short-term credits to European governments so they could purchase American supplies and thereby help stimulate the depressed economy.[13] After Lansing replaced Bryan, Wall Street's short-term loans became long-term loans, H. P. Davidson of J. P. Morgan convincing Wilson's son-in-law, Secretary of Treasury McAdoo, that "to maintain our prosperity we must finance it."[14] By 1917 Wilson was chiming, "The world must be made safe for democracy,"[15] never managing, however, to explain how the British Empire's rule over India and Ireland, the French Empire's rule over Indochina and Central Africa, the Russian Empire's rule over Poland, or the Italian regime were any more "democratic" than the German Empire. As Wilson himself admitted to the pro-war American ambassador to Britain, Walter Hines Page, "England owned the earth and Germany wanted it."[16] At that time the American business community also wanted it. "Perhaps our going to war" cabled Page to Washington, "is the only way in which our present prominent trade position can be maintained and a panic averted."[17] Just one month later Wilson demanded a declaration of war from Congress, and got it.

When the war was over and the American dead had been forgotten amid the glee of domestic prosperity, Wilson no longer needed to explain the war in terms of democracy. "Why, my fellow citizens," he could wearily admit, "is there any man here, or any woman—let me say, is there any child here—who does not know that the seed of war in the modern world is industrial and commercial rivalry."[18] Only once, in 1913, had Wilson been more frank. "Suppose you go to Washington and try to get at your Government," he had explained. "You will always find that while you are politely listened to, the men really consulted are the men who have the biggest stake—the big bankers, the big manufacturers, the big masters of commerce . . . the masters of the Government of the United States are the combined capitalists and manufacturers of the United States."[19]

So the Du Ponts, the Rockefellers, the Morgans, and the rest of "the big bankers, the big manufacturers, the big masters of commerce" got their war, but not without objections from many Americans. Some brave individuals pointed out that U.S. political alliances only followed the economic alliances of monopoly capital. The crusade against German submarine warfare made mockery of reason, they felt, when no such crusade was made against Britain's deadly mining of the North Sea. British mines had established a blockade of food and medical shipments that was inflicting heavy casualties among the German civilian population and blocking American ships from using international waters, in violation of international law. Yet Wilson insisted that "the present German submarine warfare against commerce is a warfare against mankind."[20] "The only difference," protested Senator Morris two days later, "is that in the case of Germany, we have persisted in our protest [of violations against neutrality on the sea], while in the case of England we have submitted. . . . We are going into war upon the command of gold. . . . By our act we will make millions of our countrymen suffer, and the consequences of it may well be that millions of our brethren must shed their lifeblood, millions of broken-hearted women must weep, millions of children must suffer with cold, all for the commercial right of American citizens to deliver munitions of war to belligerent nations."[21]

And millions did suffer, horribly. Some 3,700,000 Americans were sent into the slaughter; 130,274 never returned. Of those that did, 203,460 came back with wounds. The American loss was light compared to the rest of Europe: 10 million soldiers dead, 20 million more maimed, crippled, burned, or otherwise injured. Another 13 million civilians died.

For years, life, such as was possible, was carried on in endless miles of trenches that stretched over the face of Europe like diseased scars. For all, it was a nightmare of terrified eyes plunging forward behind deadly steel bayonets, of thundering distant cannons and the deafening answer of batteries nearby, of flashing bombs showering a fiery rain of shrapnel, of towering barbed wire ripping into a muddy flight from the steady, murderous clatter of machine guns, of enormous machines that chased and crushed men under their spiked treads, of bullet-spitting biplanes swooping down and dropping their load of explosives, and finally, of enormous lakes scooped out of the muddy landscape by falling bombs where, if it rained hard enough, the dead could be silently buried at sea hundreds of miles from any ocean. John Dos Passos perhaps conveyed it all in one sentence: "The blood ran into the ground, the brains oozed out of the cracked skull and were licked up by trench rats, the belly swelled and raised a generation of bluebottle flies."[22]

3. A BANQUET OF GOLD

Pierre du Pont's belly also swelled during the war, but from cakes and wines. Because of the war, he was now drawing an annual income of over $1 million after taxes, as were many of his Du Pont brethren. Even Alfred raked in over $3 million in 1915 on his Du Pont holdings alone. In the first half of 1916 he reaped another $3.8 million, although $2.8 million of it was tied up in Anglo-French bonds.

For the Du Ponts, World War I was a great banquet of gold: over $1 billion in gross income was raked in by them during the war. Public criticism of Du Pont profiteering was typically brushed aside, Colonel Buckner candidly explaining, "I am proud to admit we have made millions of dollars. I, for one, am ashamed of our conduct for remaining out as long as we did."[23]

Now few at Du Pont felt any reason for shame. In fact, corporate pride was the order of the day. Pierre du Pont, for example, celebrated his new fortunes of war by building one of America's largest and most extravagant estates, Longwood, near Kennett Square, Pennsylvania, just seventeen miles north of Wilmington. Worth over $15 million, Longwood encompassed over a thousand carefully tended acres of Japanese waterfall, flowered pools, and sunken gardens, including six glassed acres of greenhouses for rare tropical flowers and exotic fruits.

Longwood had many features that were unparalleled among America's great estates. One was an open-air theatre capable of seating 1,200 guests, completely equipped with a stage and a curtain of dancing colored fountains. Another was a huge authentic Norman bell tower imported from Europe. Still another were the immense multileveled fountains that gushed hundreds of feet into the air as colored lights played on them, spraying a rainbowed veil to the accompaniment of a ten-thousand-pipe organ which, according to *Fortune* magazine, was capable of filling three cathedrals with melody and took 14 railroad cars to transport. Pierre hired Firmin Swinnen, former organist at the world-famous Antwerp Cathedral, as its attendant. Another feature at Longwood were the magnificent trees—hundreds of them—and flowers that were to make the estate one of the horticulture wonders of the world. Within this splendor Pierre contentedly settled in a 30-room mansion at the center of the estate, staffed by over one hundred servants who carefully looked after the bald-headed bachelor.

One of these servants was a dark, handsome lad named Lewis Mason. Lewis had come to work for Pierre as a young boy of 17. Faithful, gentle, and always humble, Lewis was particularly close to Pierre, so close that rumors began to fly along the Brandywine. The boy ate with Pierre, slept at the mansion, and never wore a uniform. Although he did serve as Pierre's chauffeur, Lewis was much more to him, serving as a constant companion, even on long trips.

In June 1913 Pierre suffered what may have been the greatest loss of his life—his mother. Without her, Pierre, now a middle-aged man, suddenly seemed lost. Plagued by loneliness that even his close companion Lewis was unable to resolve, Pierre gave his mother's estate, St. Amour, to his brother Lammot and took up a suite of rooms at the Hotel Du Pont for weekdays when he did not wish to return to Longwood. Sometimes he attended dinner at Lammot's and at the home of his sister Isabella and her husband Rodney Sharp. There, he developed a close relationship with a frequent house guest and old friend, Alice Belin. Alice, who was some years younger than Pierre, came from a wealthy family in Scranton, Pennsylvania. Her father, Henry Belin, Jr., was head of Du Pont's Pennsylvania operations and president of Scranton's Trader's National Bank. But Henry Belin was more than just wealth—he was family, the brother of Pierre's mother. It was only natural, then, that in June 1915 Pierre asked Alice to be his wife. Unfortunately, Alice could not be married from her home: Pennsylvania law forbade the marriage of first cousins. They were quietly married instead in New York on October 6, 1915, at the home of Alice's brother, Ferdinand Lammot Belin. Pierre was 45.

Alice showed no resentment toward Lewis when she moved into Longwood and, in fact, apparently grew genuinely fond of the boy. In 1918, caught in the influenza epidemic that swept across the country, Lewis Mason died. Lewis's passing deeply depressed Pierre.

He never had a child by Alice, but years later he tearfully laid the cornerstone for the $1.2 million Chester County/Memorial Hospital at West Chester, Pennsylvania, in his memory. As long as Pierre lived, he never forgot Lewis.

Nor did other Du Ponts ever forget Pierre for the wealth he brought them during the war.

With World War I, Du Pont Company moved from a tertiary to a primary American industry, producing 40 percent of all explosives shot from Allied cannons. The Du Ponts didn't flinch a muscle when Secretary of War Baker called them "a species of outlaws." They just kept counting their $1.011 billion in military contracts, the equal of 276 years of previous military business and 26 years of regular business from all Du Pont commodities. In one year, 1915, Du Pont war contracts totaled $347 million. That year Pierre wrote Coleman that "The march of the smokeless powder business is going on uninterruptedly."[24]

Besides powder, Du Pont also made such pleasantries as poison gas. This was the work of a scientist from Du Pont-endowed Johns Hopkins University, Charles Lee Reese, who became Du Pont's chemical director. Du Pont also made 87,000 demolition outfits for troops and 8,000 smoke boxes for screening ships at sea, and provided one-half of America's dynamite and black powder used for domestic chores.

Everything was done on a gigantic scale. Whole cities of shanty shacks

Eleuthére Irénée du Pont (1771–1834), founder of Du Pont
Company. (WIDE WORLD PHOTOS)

Pierre Samuel du Pont de Nemours, founder of the Du Pont family. Among other titles, Du Pont was also Inspector of Commerce under King Louis XVI of France and president of the Council of Ancients. As secretary of the provisional government, he signed the order for Napoleon's exile to Elba. (ELEUTHERIAN MILLS HISTORICAL LIBRARY)

E. I. du Pont meeting with Paul Revere, Secretary of War Henry Dearborn and President Thomas Jefferson. Jefferson gave Du Pont its first business: refining government saltpeter. (WIDE WORLD PHOTOS)

E. I. du Pont's original gunpowder mills along Brandywine Creek had only three stone walls; the fourth wall was made of wood to vent explosions that threw men and machinery across the creek, but left the structure still standing. (GERARD COLBY)

Brandywine Manufacturers' Sunday School, where children of Du Pont workers got their education, now houses the main building of the Hagley Museum. (GERARD COLBY)

Alfred du Pont, the "Reluctant Prince" who was Du Pont president during the Mexican-American War. Du Pont opposed the war as "shameful," but supplied the invading U.S. armies. (ELEUTHERIAN MILLS HISTORICAL LIBRARY)

Rear Admiral Samuel F. du Pont, "Father of Annapolis." (U.S. NAVY)

Henry du Pont, "The General," conquered Delaware for the Union during the Civil War; later he conceived the Gunpowder Trust. (WILMINGTON *News-Journal*)

Eugene du Pont, Henry du Pont's successor as company head, incorporated Du Pont and engaged in international cartels. (ELEUTHERIAN MILLS HISTORICAL LIBRARY)

Alfred I. du Pont, "the Savior of the Du Ponts," was thrown out of the company by archrival Pierre du Pont II during the family's most bitter feud. (UNITED PRESS INTERNATIONAL)

Colonel Henry Algernon du Pont (right), the "Junker of Delaware" who became a U.S. senator and chairman of the Senate Railroad and Military Affairs committees, shaking hands with another old soldier at re-enactment of famous Civil War battle of New Market. (UNITED PRESS INTERNATIONAL)

Three who made an empire. Du Pont triumvirate included, left to right, Irénée du Pont, Pierre S. du Pont II and Lammot du Pont II, all sons of inventor, also organizer of the Gunpowder Trust, Lammot du Pont, whose portrait is above them. (WIDE WORLD PHOTOS)

"General" T. Coleman du Pont, who absorbed the Gunpowder Trust into Du Pont, is flanked by Republican Party
leaders W. Murray Crane of Massachusetts and Gordon
Ramsey. Through "Delaware's Dirty Deal," Coleman du
Pont became a U.S. senator and reigned as a backroom national leader through the administrations of Harding and
Coolidge. (UNITED PRESS INTERNATIONAL)

Du Pont brothers testifying at Senate munitions probe,
September 14, 1934. In the first row beyond the table are
Irénée du Pont, Pierre du Pont, Lammot du Pont and cousin
A. Felix du Pont. (UNITED PRESS INTERNATIONAL)

Du Pont women pursuing one of their favorite hobbies during the Thirties. Left to right: Mrs. A. Felix du Pont, Jr., Mrs. Esther du Pont Weir, Mrs. Phyllis du Pont, Mrs. Pauline du Pont Dean, Mrs. A. Felix du Pont, Sr.

A feud is ended. Newlyweds Ethel du Pont and Franklin Roosevelt, Jr., pose in 1937 with parents: left, Eleanor and President Franklin D. Roosevelt; right, Mr. and Mrs. Eugene du Pont, Jr. After bearing Franklin Jr. two sons, Eleanor divorced him, remarried, divorced again, and ended in suicide. (WIDE WORLD PHOTOS)

were raised for workers. The construction and engineering departments alone raised their manpower from 800 to 45,000. The water-pumping capacity for all Du Pont plants exceeded the daily water supply of Philadelphia and Boston combined. Refrigerating apparatus generated 9 million pounds of ice a day, equal to all of Chicago's ice consumption. The world's largest guncotton plant was built at Hopewell, Virginia, financed mostly by the British government; the world's largest smokeless powder plant at Old Hickory, Tennessee, was financed by the U.S. government. Du Pont sold 125 million rounds of special ammo for airplanes, 206 million black powder pellets for loading in shells, and 90 different varieties of powder. Profits in 1916 alone reached over $80 million and there seemed no end to the dizzying shower of gold and blood. The 1918 Annual Report summed it up in one sentence: "It is difficult to imagine a more satisfactory result."[25]

By the time this report was released in 1919, the war's end was in sight. Du Pont by then had raked in $237 million in net profits, an amount unparalleled in those times for four years of business. Of $140,983,000 distributed to stockholders, the bulk went to the Du Pont family. This was a dividend of 458 percent of the stock's par value.

Pierre couldn't have been more popular along the Brandywine, giving many Du Ponts an annual income of over a million dollars. Even Alfred enjoyed an annual income of over $3 million. Many Du Ponts bought additional vast country estates in the hills surrounding Wilmington. Colonel Henry enlarged his estate, Winterthur, to include hundreds of acres of botanical gardens and a mansion of 150 rooms, including 40 bedrooms, each furnished in priceless antiques of a different period. Pierre's brilliant little secretary and now treasurer of Du Pont, John J. Raskob, built a fifty-room Italian Renaissance mansion equipped with an electrically lighted tennis court and an organ on which with a single finger he pecked such tunes as "There'll Be a Hot Time in the Old Town Tonight," obviously unaware of the historic link that the tune conveyed of World War I as an economic (European market) extension of the Spanish-American War for overseas (Caribbean and Asian) markets.

Alfred was also building an enormous mansion, called White Eagle, on a 250-acre plot at Sands Point, Long Island, that he had purchased to satisfy a whim of his wife, Alicia. White Eagle was an expensive whim, costing Alfred $236,000, but Alicia wanted to be close to her husband, who was busy in New York setting up a new company, the Nemours Trading Corporation.

Alfred was trying to do a little profiteering of his own from the war. He billed his new company as a merchandising business organized to supply war-torn Europe with desperately needed supplies—for a price, of course.

Alfred took insurance against any possible ugly publicity by leasing his Grand Central Palace Hotel in New York to the government as a hospital for wounded soldiers. Behind this veil of patriotism Alfred performed his tricks of financial wizardry. His Nemours Trading Corporation soon engendered over forty different departments which exported to Europe, and mostly France, everything from shoes and chemicals to food and automobiles. At first, Alfred's enterprise seemed destined to set new records in profits; it enjoyed invaluable assistance, in obtaining orders, from Myron T. Herrick, a member of the board of directors and an old friend of Alfred's. Herrick had a more important asset, however. He happened to be the U.S. ambassador to France.

4. ALFRED'S *COUP DE GRACE*

Like his business ventures in New York during the war, Alfred du Pont's continued court struggle in Delaware against his cousin Pierre looked like it might have some prospects for success. In court, Pierre looked nervous for the first time in all the years Alfred had known him, the bald-headed president of Du Pont warily eying Alfred's counsel: William A. Glasgow, Jr., former anti-trust prosecutor for the Justice Department; and John J. Johnson, a highly reputable corporation lawyer who had a distinguished record in fighting the anti-trust suits against Standard Oil, American Tobacco, and Northern Securities, and now hoped to save his capitalist soul by establishing a legal precedent for minority stockholders.

Such a formidable legal battle on top of recent ugly publicity about Du Pont's war profits alarmed Pierre, especially when Johnson raised the point of privileged information that should have been open to all shareholders. "These men," Johnson bellowed with his characteristic flamboyancy, "played with marked cards. They were blinded by the gigantic fortunes before them. When Raskob went to New York to begin negotiations with the Morgans for the $8.5 million . . . he knew that he could not have obtained any such loan if it had not been for his connections with the Du Pont Company and the Morgans' knowledge of the vast profits that were in sight for the company."[26]

"He double-crossed the powder company," argued Glasgow, "and he double-crossed Coleman who was selling the stock . . . there was no question about the ability of the company to buy it . . . [but] Pierre had never made a legitimate offer to sell the stock which he had purchased [and he knew] J. P. Laffey, the counsel for the powder company, was ready with an opinion that the company could not legally make the purchase. This Your Honor is what you would call a lead pipe cinch."[27]

Six days after the United States declared war, Judge J. Whitaker

Thompson finally handed down his decision on the *Philip F. du Pont vs. Pierre S. du Pont* case. Thompson declared Pierre guilty of fraudulent transactions. The company's rejection of Coleman's stock was never final, the court held, but only temporary, and Pierre should have consulted the stockholders before purchasing the stock for himself. The court ordered a special stockholders meeting to allow the purchase of Coleman's stock.

Although he had already had Alfred, William, and Francis I. thrown off the Board of Directors, Pierre was nevertheless worried: the judge had barred voting with any of Coleman's stock now held by Pierre's syndicate. An appeal, Pierre reasoned, based on profitable leadership during the war, had to be made to shareholders. He fired off a quick letter to all stockholders claiming that the company's leadership had not been found "in bad faith, betrayal of trust, or wrongdoing," in effect, calling the court a liar. Judge Thompson couldn't let this attack go by, and forced Pierre under threat of penalty for contempt of court to send a second letter withdrawing his previous claims. For a short while, at least, it looked like Alfred might be vindicated.

Whatever such hopes Alfred may have held were soon dimmed. He heard rumors that Pierre had secretly warned the Justice Department that any bad decision in the case would hurt Du Pont's war effort. The first concrete sign, however, that things were not going so well for Alfred after all was Thompson's appointment of Daniel G. Hastings, a political hack for Coleman, as special master for the stock meeting. Alfred protested, but to no avail.

Pierre was calmly preparing Alfred's coup de grace. He needed 230,717 of 461,432 shares (excluding Coleman's holdings) to win a majority control. His syndicate held 100,000; blood relatives, another 50,000; and directors whom he had installed, another 14,000. That made a total of 164,000 shares, not nearly enough. But Pierre had one great advantage over Alfred: he was the active president of the company. Against company employees, high and low, who held another 30,000 shares, Pierre turned on the pressure. Using the company's resources, he also began putting the squeeze on defenseless independent pensioners and other stockholders, emphasizing that a defeat for him would be a repudiation of the company management that had brought dividends worth 183 percent of par value within fifteen months.

Pierre used every angle imaginable. Friendship, threats, he even frantically waved the flag of patriotism, hiring Charles Evans Hughes (and his reputation as a former Justice of the U.S. Supreme Court) to write a booklet that attempted to legally justify Pierre's maneuvers. Pierre had the booklet widely distributed throughout Delaware and among stockholders across the country. It was rumored that Hughes received a "fee" of $50,000 for that little gem. But one fact that is indisputable concerning Hughes was that he won the Republican presidential nomination that year with the full support of the Delaware delegation and later received his largest single campaign donation—over $92,000—from none other than Pierre du Pont. Mrs. T. Coleman du Pont, in a personal gesture of support for the pro-war candidate, donated another $2,000.[28]

Alfred soon found himself swamped with desertions. By the time of the stock meeting, he held only 140,842 shares, including William du Pont's 27,994. Pierre grossed 312,507 shares for a smashing victory; Judge Thompson dismissed Alfred's bill of complaint. Alfred, "the savior of the Du Ponts," was left with his moral victory. Pierre, never too concerned with such matters, wasn't impressed. He preferred power.

5. THE HOME FRONT

In 1916 only twelve states in the United States had a greater illiteracy rate than Delaware. Yet, because of the enormous wealth concentrated in the small circle of Du Ponts around Wilmington, Delaware ranked fourth in the country in per capita income. While the Du Ponts lounged royally on their lavish estates, one-fourth of the state still remained under marsh.

During World War I, draft examinations in southern Delaware showed that 20 percent of youths under 21 could not even write their own names.[29] Yet corporate leaders such as Henry A. du Pont, who served on the Senate Committee on Military Affairs during the 1916–17 hearings on universal military training, fully endorsed the drafting of these hapless youths. These were the men who were forced to fight and die in muddy trenches thousands of miles from their homes while Alfred du Pont light-heartedly explained his war service between cocktails. "My war record," he wrote his brother Maurice, "consisted in staying home and trembling for fear I would be eaten by a Boche. I believe I [did] less than nothing for the war."[30] Alfred was being modest. He did manage to smuggle funds into Germany to his daughter Maddie, while her husband was fervently fighting for the Kaiser.

The rosters of active service from Delaware always show a marked deficiency of Du Pont names, and World War I was no exception. Only one Du Pont saw active service in that war. Alfred Victor du Pont, the son whom Alfred thought would bring disgrace to his name, enlisted in the U.S. Marine Corps as a private and eventually saw combat. Only years later would Alfred learn of his son's wartime activity.

Du Pont "soldiers" on the home front didn't have it much easier than their brothers overseas. While a dozen Du Ponts enjoyed an annual income of over $1 million during the war, workers at Du Pont plants were paid only $1 an hour. With the depression and starvation of 1914 still fresh in their minds, 100,000 men, women, and even children swarmed into the plants, willing to risk violent death, injury, or chemical poisoning for that precious one dollar. Sixty thousand of them were housed in shanty barracks, dorms, boardinghouses, or Du Pont-built "hotels." Working conditions were even worse. In Du Pont's Deepwater, New Jersey, plant across the river from Wilmington, workers died from poisonous fumes of the lethal benzol series, their bodies turning a steel blue. At the Penns Grove, New Jersey, plant workers were called "canaries": picric acid had actually dyed their skins yellow. Picric acid poisons the mucous membranes of the respiratory tract, attacks the intestinal tract, and destroys the kidneys and nerve centers.

Throughout most of Du Pont's high-explosives war plants, deadly fulminate of mercury was generated. Du Pont didn't bother to take any statistical tests, but a contemporary British study reported that 40 percent of all workers who handled it suffered dangerous chemical poisoning. There were other criminal dangers. Nitroglycerine, the essential ingredient in dynamite production, gives off fumes that cause permanent damage to the lungs and heart. Inhalation of smokeless powder dust also causes lung diseases, including tuberculosis. According to Du Pont's own statistics, of those workers who contracted TB, 30 percent died; most never recovered.

But perhaps they were the lucky ones. There were 347 workmen killed in Du Pont plants during the war, a figure that Pierre's production speed-up no doubt contributed to. There is no record of the number injured.

Du Pont workers were not protected by labor unions, and for a very good reason: the Du Ponts did not allow unions. Nor did they allow strikes. Both were considered "un-American" and both Du Pont prohibitions were backed up by the full force of federal law (the Espionage Law of 1917 and the Violent Sedition Act of 1918) and armed troops. To keep their workers intimidated, the Du Ponts hired a 1,400-man private police force trained by the former police commissioner of Washington, D.C. This force was supposedly established to prevent sabotage, although in the two years of war there was not one recorded case of attempted sabotage, or plans for sabotage, at Du Pont. The real purpose of the police force lay in an elaborate spy system set up by Ruly Carpenter. Hundreds of secret agents were planted in Du Pont factories; no worker could be sure a Du Pont spy was not working right next to him, supposedly looking for German agents. And, of course, anyone who expressed dissent with the war or dissatisfaction with Du Pont wages or conditions risked being branded a German spy, Russian Communist, or some other "foreign" brand of "inhumanity."

Du Pont workers were expected to rank among America's model patriots, and Pierre later proudly displayed a chart showing that his employees bought over $1 million worth of Liberty bonds during the war. Some workers like those at the Du Pont plant at Newburgh, New York, were clothed in red, white, and blue costumes and paraded down main street like feudal serfs, bearing the crest of their lord and master: "Du Pont."

A cold terror swept through Longwood in October 1917. The success of the Russian workers and their Bolshevik Party was a threat to every capitalist in the world. Herbert Hoover wrote that the fear of the new revolutionary Soviet Union hung like a pall over every conversation at Versailles. It was also a personal blow to the Du Ponts. Since the Crimean War over fifty years earlier, Czarist Russia had been one of Du Pont's best customers. In fact, the Czar had been their very first customer in World War I, ordering 960,000 pounds of TNT on October 8, 1914. As late as August 1917 the capitalist government of Kerensky, still pursuing the unpopular war and licking its wounds from a popular insurrection a month before, ordered 20 million pounds of Du Pont powder. As Du Pont had an overabundance of war contracts, Kerensky's order could not be accepted, although it gave Pierre hope of even more profitable contracts in the future. Then came the Bolshevik insurrection in October to spoil it all, socialists and workers' factory councils (soviets) replacing Kerensky's corrupt regime.

Overnight, the Du Ponts lost millions of dollars in contracts and bonds simply because the Russian people dared to demand an end to a slaughter that had become endless.* In retaliation, the "Armorers of the Republic" fully endorsed the American armed invasion of Russia from 1919 to 1922 in the futile but bloody attempt by Allied armies to overthrow the soviet government of Lenin.

The Du Ponts, however, were not prepared for the popular support given the soviets in Russia, nor for the organized efficiency of the Bolshevik Party. They fully anticipated quick victory with the strategy of intervention. Their confidence was no doubt bolstered by recent success in a similar, though more covert, intervention in Hungary. There, the workers' government of Bela Kun was overthrown by conservative forces financed and

---

* Remington Arms, destined to become part of the Du Pont empire in the Thirties was another company that lost millions because of the Russian Revolution. During the war Remington had contracted with the Czar to make one million rifles. In a rare show of courage, Kerensky repudiated the contract after the capitalist revolution of February 1917 deposed the Czar. This left Remington with 750,000 completed guns and an apparent loss of over $10 million. Only Wilson's request for a declaration of war and his War Department's subsequent purchase of 600,000 of the Russian rifles saved Remington from bankruptcy.

armed by the European and American governments. Key in weakening that government was the manipulation of International Red Cross and the U.S. relief commission's food shipments by Herbert Hoover, then head of the U.S. Food Administration, and later Secretary of Commerce and President of the United States. Hoover's maneuvers caused thousands of people in Hungary to starve to death. His right-hand man in that crime was William Glasgow, the former Assistant Attorney General under Taft who helped preserve Du Pont's continued monopoly of smokeless powder, and later Alfred I. du Pont's lawyer and close consultant.

Glasgow's role was echoed in the U.S. Senate by Willard Saulsbury, for a time president pro tem of that body and an in-law of the Du Ponts. Saulsbury, despite his personal differences with Colonel Henry du Pont, took up the role of guardian of the clan's interests. Alfred du Pont wasn't satisfied, wanting one of his own hand-picked men, Dr. Lewis Ball, in Saulsbury's seat. It wasn't that Alfred considered Saulsbury a poor senator. Alfred admitted privately that his in-law was actually quite proficient at protecting the interests of munitions makers. It was just that Alfred wanted a puppet, which Saulsbury refused to be. In the election of November 1918 that refusal cost Saulsbury his job.

That year brought victories also to Pierre, although of a more financial nature. On July 2, near Nashville, Tennessee, Du Pont completed construction of the largest smokeless powder and nitrating plant in the world. Called Old Hickory, it was also the largest fraud in the world.

6. FRAUDS AND FIRINGS

Six months after the United States entered the war, the U.S. government asked Du Pont Company to submit a proposal for building government plants. Du Pont's capacity, which in 1917 was close to fifty-four times that of 1914, was simply not enough to meet U.S. needs. Pierre du Pont must have known this because he was expecting the request. Within only five days Du Pont's proposal was on a desk in Washington: $90 million for construction, $187 million more for operating expenses.

Robert S. Brookings of the War Industries Board studied Pierre's proposal and decided it was outrageous. According to Brookings, the Du Pont plan would realize for Du Pont a net profit of 15 percent or $13.5 million on construction, and $30 million on the operation of completed plants—a total haul of $43.5 million!

Brookings immediately warned Secretary of War Newton Baker, who, in turn, appealed to Pierre to lower his estimate. But the wily Du Pont was adamant. Patriotism is fine for the workers, but after all, the Du Ponts had all the men, the experience, the engineering and research facilities . . .

Secretary Baker called the Du Ponts "a species of outlaws," but his breath was wasted. If the government wanted to build powder plants to meet its war needs it would have to surrender some profits for Du Pont. When the contract was finally signed, a gross profits ceiling of $2 million was agreed upon, far below the original profit calculated by Brookings. This estimate, however, proved to fall far short of final costs. It also proved to be a source of national scandal.

According to the contract, five plants were to be constructed: two in Virginia, one in Wisconsin, one in Pennsylvania, and one in Tennessee. The last, Old Hickory, was supposed to be built by Du Pont on a cost-plus basis, the Wilmington company charging a fee of only $1. Du Pont estimated its cost at $75 million when ground was broken in March. By the beginning of operation in July, the cost had risen to $90 million. When it was later sold by the government, however, its value was placed at only $3.5 million. Someone, it was clear, had made a huge profit, and many sources agreed that that "someone" went by the name of Du Pont.

In 1921 a Special House Investigating Committee headed by Representative William Graham of Illinois found that Old Hickory wasn't even needed during the war. The United States had an abundant supply of nitrate stockpiled all during the war. "The committee finds that there has been expended for construction upon the Government's nitrate program to the present time the sum of $116,194,974.37 and that *this expenditure produced no nitrates prior to the armistice, and contributed nothing toward winning the war.*"[31] Old Hickory was an "enormous waste and extravagant expenditure of public funds not in any way justified and . . . the ones primarily responsible for these things very properly merit the disapproval and condemnation of the people of the country in this and upcoming days of the Republic."[32]

Pierre's pockets may not have been hurting, but his pride may have suffered some reversals. After the charges of the Graham Committee, any Du Pont propaganda dealing with Old Hickory lauded the company's "sacrifice" and efficiency in its construction. Pierre agreed with Bernard Baruch's declaration that the $90 million plant was necessary because of the threat of German submarines cutting off the Chilean nitrate supply. The Graham Committee, however, specifically held that argument unjustified, since the U.S. Navy had firm control of the Panama Canal and the lower Atlantic.

Then the Graham Committee exposed another Du Pont fraud. Du Pont, which at the beginning of the war priced its powder at 50 cents per pound to the U.S. government, lowered its price to the U.S. by only one cent per pound during the entire war, although it increased its volume by over 54 percent by 1918. If that wasn't bad enough, the committee also found out that Du Pont powder cost only 33 to 36 cents per pound to produce. At the least, that meant a profit of 33 percent per pound for the Du Ponts. The profit was even higher from Allied customers. "Theretofore the plants built by the Du Ponts," concluded the Congressional committee, "had been paid for out of the profits of contracts made with the Allied nations before we entered the war."[33]

But the government wasn't the only party claiming to have been cheated. Other charges were made that Du Pont had committed terrible irregularities in paying wages. One more incredible charge accused the company of cheating dead victims of the influenza epidemic out of burials and stealing their personal belongings.[34] Pierre, as always, was patient, calmly counting his money while government investigations were lost in the mire of postwar administrations rife with scandal, first under Harding's Attorney General, Harry M. Daugherty, an intimate of T. Coleman du Pont—who donated tens of thousands of dollars to Harding's presidential campaign[35]—and later under John G. Sargent, Attorney General under Calvin Coolidge, also the proud recipient of a $10,000 campaign donation by Irénée du Pont, the president of Du Pont Company.[36]

"And doesn't it make you feel 'chesty,' " boomed Colonel Buckner to his conscience-smitten salesmen in 1918. *"I am proud I am a Du Pont man* . . . Great God! And some of you are in doubt, some of you have lost sight of all these *Great, Big, Magnificent* things your Company is doing for our country and the world—and can only hear the voice of some measly little fice barking at your heels. Stamp the life out of the brute, hold your head erect, expand your chest and be *proud* that you belong to an organization that the world knows can *do things!"*[37]

And do things they did. Gunpowder, explosives, and poison gas were produced at an unprecedented rate. Production problems were worked out in the Experimental Station and the Smokeless Powder Department. Water drying replaced air drying of powder, for instance, cutting drying time from sixty to ninety days down to eight days. The men worked fourteen hours a day at the plant with no time and a half for overtime after the regular eight-hour shift.

While Du Pont workers risked their lives to work in the grime of black powder and guncotton, Pierre always amazed visitors by appearing cool and calm, greeting everyone in a fresh clean suit and polished head as if he had just stepped out of a bubble bath. In fact, he had. Longwood satisfied his every whim with its acres of colorful flowers and refreshing pools and fountains. Seldom delving into high society, Pierre found Longwood to be a peaceful refuge from the noise of the office's paper shuffling. But as 1918 drew to a close, the end of the profitable war was in sight. Eighty-five percent of Du Pont's business was involved in the slaughter, holding over a hundred war contracts. Between sips of a cool drink in Longwood, Pierre realized all good things must come to an end. Something had to go. Something did. That Christmas week Pierre laid off over 37,000 workers.

This curious gift of season cheer startled the entire country, but Pierre remained his cool, calm self. The remaining workers who were loyal Americans and bought their Du Pont-sponsored Liberty bonds were appropriately rewarded at the war's end—Pierre fired close to 70,000 more. This hatchet job chopped Du Pont's plant force down from 85,600 to 18,000 within only seven weeks. It wasn't that Pierre wasn't fond of the workers. After all, their sweat had generated over $237 million in profits. It was just any good businessman's way of saying thanks when you're no longer needed.

7. COMETH THE REPRESSION . . .

In 1919, after two years of soaring prices and a government ban on strikes, 4 million hungry workers hit the streets in picket lines, fighting to raise wages to the level of prices. The cost of living had doubled since 1914, yet real wages were 14 percent less in 1919 than in 1914. The government, backing the "open shop" drive of the National Association of Manufacturers, answered the strikes with the armed intervention of troops and veterans. Du Pont fully supported the heavy government repression of strikers under the guise of stopping "creeping Communism." Ruly Carpenter's army of spies began looking for the Red Terror under every worker's lunch pail.

The Du Pont witch hunt did not confine itself to company plants. A large percentage of the American work force, and perhaps the most militant, were immigrants, who had always been an important pool of cheap labor for the owners of industry. Now these workers became scapegoats for government repression. Thousands, including whole families, suffered overnight arrest and detention in barbed wire camps in a nationwide terror raid conducted by Attorney General Mitchell Palmer. Thousands were deported, their civil rights totally denied. Those who escaped the raids were subjected to further intimidation from foreign-language newspapers which constantly tiraded against socialism and everything else "un-American." For most immigrants—and there were millions of them—these were the only newspapers they could read.

In 1920 Colonel William Boyce Thompson, testifying before Senator Kenyon's Privileges and Elections Committee, exposed the fact that the American Association of Foreign Language Newspapers acquired 400 foreign-language newspapers with a circulation of 5 million, in order to promote "Americanism." The necessary $400,000 fund, he explained, had been established under the leadership of T. Coleman du Pont, former president of Du Pont Company and a leader of the National Security League. But Coleman was not alone. Joining him were some of the leading businessmen of the day: financier Cleveland H. Dodge, Andrew Mellon, copper magnate Daniel Guggenheim, John T. Pratt of Standard Oil, and Francis Sisson of Morgan Guaranty Trust Company.

The Du Ponts were also a leading force in the creation of the Boy Scouts of America, at that time conceived of as the nationalistic, para-military alternative to alleged socialist "corruption" of youth. The early Scout Law required unyielding loyalty "to the President, and to his officers, and to his parents, his country, and *his employer*." Coleman du Pont was on the Scouts' first National Council and remained a member until 1915, when the Boy Scout organization endorsed Coleman's "preparedness" movement with its "Be Prepared" slogan.* In 1925, Coleman's son, Francis V. du Pont, resumed the Du Pont presence on the National Council. The Du Ponts also had a hand in the early days of the American Legion, a veterans organization originally founded by Wall Street interests in 1915 and reestablished by Theodore Roosevelt II in 1919 and used against strikers after the war. Later, the Legion would allegedly be included in even more reactionary plots by the Du Ponts during the 1930's.

To the Du Ponts, "Americanism" was, frankly, capitalism, and capitalism was Du Pont. Those who dared to challenge Du Pont were, as Colonel Buckner put it, "little fice barking at your heels." "You will find their names are forgotten," Buckner boasted, "but Du Pont Company lives on, growing bigger and bigger and grander and grander with each day of its existence. Ashamed of Du Pont? No! And so long as Pierre S. du Pont is at its head and has the power to shape its policies you shall never have reason to. . . . I am *proud* to admit we have made millions of dollars."[38]

And so was Pierre. "I am firmly of the opinion," he stated, "that we have now reached another turning point in the conduct of affairs of E. I. du Pont de Nemours & Co."[39] In April 1919 Pierre, not yet 50, resigned as president, turning the company over to the "next line of men," namely his brother Irénée. Pierre did not leave the company, however. He stayed on as chairman of the Board of Directors and retained the presidency of the

---

* Among the leading corporate figures involved in organizing and financing the Boy Scouts of America were T. Coleman du Pont, John D. Rockefeller, George Pratt, Mortimer Schiff, J. P. Morgan, Andrew Carnegie, and a score of generals and admirals, including Admiral George Dewey. Pratt was even National Treasurer of the Boy Scouts for many years.

family holding company, Du Pont Securities, renamed Christiana Securities in 1919.

. . . And Expansion

Pierre had already begun the turning point for Du Pont. Early in the war Pierre realized that Mars would someday end his rain of gold. With the advice of his new Development Department headed by Ruly Carpenter and his brother, Walter S. Carpenter, Pierre bought into the chemical field during the war, diversifying the company's interests. In 1915 Du Pont purchased the Arlington Company, maker of lacquers, pyroxylin plastics, and enamels; in 1916, the Fairfield Rubber Company, maker of rubber-coated fabrics; in 1917, Harrison Brothers & Company, producer of dyes, paints, varnishes, and heavy chemicals. From 1917 to the end of the war in 1919 Pierre bought out five more chemical firms: the Beckton Chemical Co., Cawley Clark & Co., Bridgeport Wood Finishing Co., Flint Varnish and Color Company, and New England Oil, Paint and Varnish Company.

But this was only the first step, a base on which to build the greatest chemical empire the world has ever known. With $90 million in surplus profits from over $1 billion in gross income during the war, the Du Ponts could easily ignore their newly won title, "the merchants of death." While millions of weary Americans were trying to adjust to the ways of a peacetime economy, Pierre was casting his eyes over the financial world, searching for new markets, new frontiers to conquer, facing a decade of international intrigue and even greater treasure that would make his family one of the richest in the world.

Nine

BUILDING OF THE EMPIRE

1. THE DYNAMO

The 1920's were in many ways the formative years of modern American society. In that decade the country became truly urban in its economic base, and subsequently in its way of thinking, its ideals, and its heroes.

For some, it was a desperate age, when men wished only to soothe their wounds and forget their scars, to leave to nightmares the madness of World War I. For others, it was a futile age, of attempting to pick up the pieces of a world shattered by the war no one wanted yet everyone endured. For all, it was a frenzied age, with Victorian morals overwhelmed by raccoon coats and the dancing heels of the wild Charleston, the speakeasy's "rap three times and walk in slowly" becoming the hallmark of America's Roaring Twenties.

And roar it did, propelled by an industrial expansion that met no competition from war-exhausted Europe. It was an age of flourishing technological innovation: mechanical coal-loaders and mine locomotives, power shovels, pneumatic drills, continuous strip-sheet rolling, the Gammer machine for glass tubing, the Ross carrier for lumber, automatic cigar-makers—all of which increased the volume of production. This was the time when the Czech term "robot" was integrated into the American language, and for good reason.* Greater productivity meant lower labor costs, and these were reflected in prices. Goods became cheaper, for the first time available to the common man who, if he escaped technological unem-

---

* During the Twenties, with better technology, the number of man-hours required per unit of output declined by 30 percent in manufacturing alone.[1] Mechanization was the keynote of the decade, with horsepower per worker in manufacturing shooting up 50 percent from 1919 to 1929, in the mines and quarries 60 percent, in the steam railroads 74 percent.[2] Subsequently, from 1919 to 1929 output per man-hour rose 72 percent in manufacturing, 41 percent in mining, and 33 percent in railroads.[3] In turn, production volume for raw materials, manufacturing, construction, and agriculture climbed 34 percent from 1922 to 1929, a startling 4.1 percent average per year.[4] *The Twenties mark the first time when production volume rose not at the cost of more labor time, but less, expanding leisure time and dawning a whole new social era in American history.*

ployment, enjoyed a gain of 10.9 percent in average real earnings from 1923 to 1928.[5]

Lower prices for goods provided a higher standard of living, among the highest in the world, and the assembly-line techniques of one of the decade's most prominent anti-Semites, Henry Ford, made the Model T available for the first time to an expanding mass market, making masses of people mobile to an extent not known since early migratory pioneers, and generating not only the expansion of roads and suburbs, but ways and institutions sharply different from those of a more sedentary population.

With the rise of mass production came also the rise of the modern consumer society. Everything from the Sears Mail Order Catalog to the traveling salesman encouraged the spending of the dollar, even in the rural countryside. The radio industry, in 1920 a feeble wireless telegraph service, by 1930 was a billion-dollar industry with practically all its revenue dependent on corporate advertising, spreading the new urban culture throughout the land. Advertising flooded newspapers, doubling the paper volume consumed by the population. The Post Office was also drafted into the search for consumer markets: 80 percent of all mail was ads. Concrete mixers, dump trucks, and highway-finishing machines pushed roads through remote areas, and close behind them came the migratory hordes of the motorized urban middle class. New privately owned service industries—from restaurants to Hollywood studios to record companies—rose to profit from the increased "free time" available to millions. Government expenditures also rose for libraries, parks, and, to meet the needs of advanced industrial society for a literate but socially disciplined work force, corporate-controlled education. In thousands of schools, only those texts were used that were approved by corporate publishers and state and local school boards, all dominated by the business ethic and its myopic view of history and social goals.*

Resting on the solid security of an expanding economy and leisure time, the Twenties became an age of flourishing arts in which Gershwin brought America into the musical world, Hemingway completed *The Sun Also Rises,* while playwright Eugene O'Neill captured the anxious, frantic, suicidal impulses of the mechanical consumer age in his *Dynamo.* Unheeded and to this day unrecognized, young intellectuals like Waldo Frank, Van Wyck Brooks, Harold Stearns, and George Doran fired broadsides of social critique that penetrated into the fog of the American soul.

Great fortunes rose overnight with great skyscrapers, as American capi-

---

* For a review of the history of American education, see Herbert Gintis, Sam Bowles, *The Capitalist System* (Englewood Cliffs, N.J.: Prentice-Hall, Inc.), 1970.

talism zoomed to seemingly endless heights. American corporations, their market needs not misled by government rhetoric about "isolationism," expanded direct overseas investment from $94 million in 1919 to $602 million in 1929. Between 1922 and 1929 the undistributed earnings of American corporations averaged more than $2.5 billion a year.[6] Dividends rose a phenomenal 110 percent from $3 billion in 1922 to $6.3 billion in 1929,[7] the new market quotation ticker clicking madly in attempt to keep up with the profit boom. It was an age that made the richest families, including the Du Ponts, dizzy with gold and self-confidence.

Services, if they had been measurable, probably climbed at a higher rate than manufacturing in the Twenties, and with the new private and government service industries there rose a new urban "middle class." These were unlike the old middle class of the self-employed and professionals. Rather, this was a nonmanual, white-collar work force, not actually a middle class but a new strata of the working class that was increasing at a faster rate (38.1 percent) than the manual work force (7.9 percent). While still in the minority—14.5 million white-collar workers as compared to 30 million blue-collar workers—the white collar workers yet constituted a reliable bedrock of political conservatism, identifying in values and life styles with their corporate employers in private industry or in government's highest circles. As such, they politically supported corporate leaders in their struggles against both the reactionary rural right and the radical urban left. But just as important, their purchasing power played a crucial role in fueling the developing consumerism of American capitalism.

The employed manual work force was also infused with the new corporate ideology, and with wages steadier than ever before, collective bargaining had little impact. Trade unionism went into decline, while installment buying made consumer durables available for the first time to many with small cash resources. The push for spending encouraged acceptance of overtime for wages, workers often sacrificing the leisure time made available by labor-saving and time-saving technology.

"I think the most striking thing about labor in America," wrote an Australian visitor, "is that it has become the slave of the paymaster. In Australia, men value their hours of leisure too highly to sell them for any wages. In America, men can be got to work . . . for almost any hours if it means extra pay."[8]

No doubt inflation, the cheap-labor pool, and employers' demands played important roles, but the overwhelming factor in employees' willingness to work overtime was undoubtedly the honest desire to participate in the new higher standard of living. This meant, in effect, accepting the values that went with that standard of living, the values of the new corporate ideology that defined people by externals—their home, their dress, and the quantity of new, shiny products they owned. And it was this ideology that led the worker into the constant debt that disciplined him in the workplace. In this way, the worker's product returned through the marketplace to enslave him.

Indeed, the Twenties were not golden for most Americans. Dazzling, yes, but made more of tin than gold. The Brookings Institution records that of 27,474,000 families of two or more people, over 21 percent had incomes of less than $1,000 a year, 42 percent had less than $1,500 a year, and 71 percent (nearly 20 million families) made less than $2,500 a year. The *combined* incomes of the bottom 42 percent equaled the incomes of merely .01 percent of the rich families at the *top* of the scale. Further, 78.4 percent had no aggregate savings at all, while 0.9 percent (only 24,000 families) possessed 34 percent of the total savings in the country. With rising mechanized productivity came also rising unemployment—4 million workers idled during the Twenties as compared with 1 million before the war, a startling hike of 300 percent, much of it reflecting increasing *technological* unemployment. This, along with workplace abuses, unresolved grievances and resentments, the teeming population growth in the cities (helped by farm mechanization and rural migrations), and the crime and corruption of prohibition, all made a social powder keg ready to be ignited by a Black Thursday.

But until that day, the Twenties were a materialist Eden, whose God was Profit. Faith in business as a way of life became a religion and was even accepted in universities as a science justifying an assortment of special degrees. The University of Pennsylvania had opened the first College of Business in 1881, but it was not until the Twenties that the Business School rose to prominence throughout the country. In 1929 Stanford opened the first graduate school of business in the West, rivaling Harvard's leadership in the East, and soon a variety of "business degrees" spewed forth across the land.

In the midst of all this, people with leisure time indulged in an assortment of time-consuming nonsense and games, from flagpole sitting to Mah-Jongg and crossword puzzles. Spectator sports blossomed: in one year there were over 17 million admissions to college football games, 27 million attending major league baseball. Participatory sports grew also, two million golfers playing on 89 municipal golf courses around the country, and over half a million tennis players. It is not surprising that it was in sports that Americans found heroes to identify with, in contrast to their own mass anonymity in the factory production line, the sterile business world, and their memories of mass deaths on the battlefield. Here were Bobby Jones in golf, Babe Ruth in baseball, Red Grange in football. There was also a decent "all-American" boy named Charles Lindbergh, who was honored for integrity as well as aerial daring, and was greeted on his return by Secretaries Wilbur, Davis, and Charles Evans Hughes and a host of admirals and generals and given a ticker-tape parade in Manhattan. For millions, these figures were in sharp contrast to the "national leaders" in the White House, Harding and Coolidge, who seemed to sit silently doing nothing while others, including their cabinet members, made millions.

And as much as it was a new age—when old habits and patterns of thought were broken down and replaced with a *mass* culture of consumerism, of changing moral standards and the breakdown of the old marriage and family ties, of the liberated "Flapper," of bathing beauty contests and shorter dresses, and women as consumer objects—it was also an age when the old society fought back—an age of cultural and legal conflicts between religion and science, between the old morality and the new, between the large, tightly knit family and the "nuclear" family; of conflicts over prohibition, race, and immigration; of the "old-time religion" of Holy Rollers and the infamous Scopes "Monkey" trial; of the resurgent Ku Klux Klan and "Jim Crow" union policies and the lynchings of hundreds of Black Americans. It was an age when Sacco and Vanzetti could go to their execution innocent and generally unheard, while people seriously listened to Chicago's king of crime, Al Capone, harangue that "Bolshevism is knocking at our gates. . . . We must keep the worker away from red literature and red ruses." In the golden insanity of stock speculation and overnight fortunes, who had time to notice that industrial speed-ups, according to the Federal Bureau of Labor Statistics, were killing 25,000 workers, permanently disabling another 100,000, and injuring some 3 million workers *every year?*

It was in the midst of all this that the Du Ponts of Delaware built the greatest industrial empire known to history, an empire that encompassed everything from chemicals to automobiles, from politics to culture, from war to peace.

The Twenties were the years the Du Ponts made their greatest impact on American society. Though not capturing the headlines as often as in the decade that followed, the Du Ponts during the Twenties set the course for their future. To a great extent, they became a symbol of the new age and directly contributed to the development of some of its most important aspects.

In technology, the Du Ponts secured dye patents and processes that stimulated the clothing and paint industries to new heights. Their attractive and practical "Duco" lacquers encouraged the growth of the automobile industry, as did their tetraethyl lead for high compression gasoline. Their organization of General Motors charged Chevrolet forward eventually to outpace Ford's Model T. Their cellophane stimulated the market volume of the food industry. Their Pyralin plastic increased radio sales and helped develop shatterproof glass for auto windshields. Their rayon and synthetic leather boosted both the fabrics and women's apparel industries.

In consumerism, it was the Du Ponts who pioneered the way for installment buying with Pierre du Pont's G.M. Acceptance Corporation. In advertising, the Du Pont Company developed the most imaginative and efficient publicity bureau in American business history. "Du Pont Magazine" was a pioneer in corporate propaganda.

Du Pont produced one of the first cheap motion picture cellulose films for Hollywood during the Twenties.

Du Pont was one of the first large companies to help in the industrialization of the South that began in the Twenties.

Henry B. du Pont, Richard C. du Pont, A. Felix du Pont, and A. Felix, Jr., were all pioneers of the aviation industry.

Pierre S. du Pont was considered by many during the Twenties as the "hero of education." His secretary and treasurer, John J. Raskob, was called the "Wizard of Wall Street."

Alfred I. du Pont was hailed as the hero of pensions.

T. Coleman du Pont, founder of the National Highway Association, was known as the hero of roads.

When it came to financing the erection of the tallest building in the world, the Empire State Building, again it was the Du Ponts.

When it came to the fraudulent land boom in Florida, again the Du Ponts were on hand.

During the Twenties it seemed the Du Ponts were everywhere and into everything. And, in fact, they were.

Whether in the halls of Congress or the halls of Versailles, the hushed rubber fields of Malaya or the loud Big Board of Wall Street, the name of Du Pont was heard and, in most cases, feared.

The Twenties were the golden years for the Du Ponts. And as much as they contributed to the development of the Second Industrial Revolution in the Twenties, they were more aided by it. While they directed the labor of others, they themselves did little actual production or work. In that real sense, the closing of the Brandywine powder works in 1920 was the symbolic end of the first half of the Du Pont saga, for it marked the family's move from the grime of industrial production to the polished sterility of the financier-industrialist's office. From this corporate Olympus, the Du Ponts directed their financial legions into areas of investment, carving out a market from conquest only to find that it had created another market need, and so on it went, from powder to chemicals and dyes, from chemicals and dyes to General Motors, from General Motors to U.S. Rubber, tetraethyl lead gasoline and Phillips Petroleum, from powder to Remington Arms Company, from chemicals to synthetic textiles. Each was a building block for the next, each driven by market needs through economic and political conquests. This is the fifty-year second half of the Du Pont saga, a saga which began with the conquest of chemicals.

2. THE CONQUEST OF CHEMICALS

For one hundred years the Du Ponts had displayed little interest in venturing into nonexplosive chemicals. Then, in 1908, in the storm of publicity over an anti-trust suit, Washington raised the threat of establishing its own government plants for the manufacture of gunpowder. This threat was apparently taken seriously in besieged Wilmington, prompting the Du Ponts to consider other fields of investment that could also serve as outlets for their nitrocellulose, a nitrated cotton which was the principal raw material in Du Pont's manufacture of smokeless powder.

A search for such outlets uncovered the requirement of nitrocellulose in the manufacture of lacquers, celluloid, artificial leather, and artificial silk (rayon). It was not surprising, then, that the Du Ponts took their first step outside gunpowder that year by purchasing the Fabrikord Company, then the largest manufacturer of artificial leather in the United States. Later, in 1913, the new acquisition was absorbed directly into the parent and reorganized as a Du Pont company. By then, however, the government's threat seemed less pressing, especially as war loomed on the European horizon.

World War I with its enormous powder orders temporarily interrupted Du Pont's expansion program, but soon provided the additional capital needed for capturing other markets for nitrocellulose: in 1915 the Arlington works, one of the country's largest celluloid manufacturers, and from 1917 to the war's end five more manufacturers of paints, varnishes, and acids. This was the family's first step into chemicals.

To protect these newly acquired paint and lacquer markets, as well as to open a new market for benzol and toluene, the basic ingredients of their TNT, TNX, and picric acid industries, the Du Ponts endeavored to capture the synthetic dye industry. Toluene and benzol are both coal-tar crudes, and such coal-tar derivatives were the basis of the entire synthetic dyes industry.

Before World War I, German corporate interests had captured a monopoly of the dyes industry through secret patents and processes for superior dyes. During the war the United States was starved of these dyes, first by a British naval blockade, and then by President Wilson's declaration of war. To add to their concern for their own markets, the Du Ponts were also encouraged into the dyes industry by cries for dye intermediates from other textile, paper, and leather firms. For the Du Ponts, the war presented an opportunity no blood relative of E. I. du Pont could resist.

In February 1917 Irénée du Pont's executive committee appropriated $600,000 for the construction of a synthetic indigo plant at Deepwater, New Jersey, just across the river from Wilmington. Later, that plant would be the center of death and a national scandal.

Irénée set up the company's first Organic Chemicals Division, putting his younger brother, Lammot du Pont, in charge. "We ought to be as smart as the Germans," declared Irénée. "Let's see if we are."[9]

They weren't. Du Pont scientists had begun experiments in the previous March, but their inability to crack the secrets of German processes led Du Pont in September to send agents to England. The government there had seized a German-owned indigo works and handed it over to Levinstein, Ltd., the largest chemical combine in Great Britain. As the major supplier of gunpowder and explosives to wartime Britain, Du Pont was in a strong position to pressure the British for access to German-patented manufacturing processes. The result was predictable: a contract by which Du Pont provided capital for the plant facilities in exchange for manufacturing information. More than one Briton must have noted the irony of seeing badly needed British capital, paid to the Du Ponts for war materials, returning to Britain at the price of its newly acquired scientific know-how. Soon, Du Pont engineers and technicians were in Britain taking notes and gathering experience and, according to later charges by the British, Levinstein's customers. Meanwhile, Irénée allocated an initial $7 million for investment in dyes.

The alliance between Britain's largest chemical combine and the United States' largest powder combine caused only applause in Washington. But the U.S. entry into the war brought Du Pont an even greater boon.

In 1918 Congress passed the Trading-with-the-Enemy Act, and the federal government seized all German-owned property in the country. All German patents subsequently fell under the jurisdiction of the office of the Alien Property Custodian, A. Mitchell Palmer, and his successor, Francis P. Garvin. Eventually, however, these patents came under the jurisdiction of Du Pont. How this remarkable feat was carried out has become the tale of one of the great public thefts in American history.

Through the long hand of Wilmington, Alien Property Custodian Garvin was crowned president of the Chemical Foundation, a company set up by Du Pont and some smaller chemical interests. Then, in April 1919, a full five months after the Armistice ended the war, Alien Property Custodian Garvin began to sell hundreds of secret German patents to Chemical Foundation President Garvin, and through the Foundation to Du Pont,[10] which had set aside $12.5 million of its war profits for investment in the new field.[11] In this quick and bloodless coup, Du Pont acquired the secret patents that became the key to its growing monopoly on dyes. Government records later revealed that some 5,700 German patents were sold by the Alien Property Custodian for the paltry sum of $271,000.[12] Most of them went to the Chemical Foundation.

Du Pont's helping hand extended even to Versailles. There, alongside Wilson at the great peace conference table, sat Bradley Palmer. On the first day of Garvin's patent sales, Palmer received an urgent cable from Washington, in which Garvin encouraged the U.S. Mission to destroy the German chemical industry. He asked that all imports of German dyes, which Wilson had arranged as part of Germany's harsh reparations payments, be handed over to the Chemical Foundation to protect the higher-priced American dyes. To underscore his position, Garvin then laid down an open threat. "Doubtful," he wired, "if any dyes will be used even if imported. You may face a new tea party."[13] If the President undertook to arrange for such importation, he might well face, as one federal prosecutor later charged, "a new revolution in the United States."

A month later, on May 20, Wilson clarified his position for the American chemical corporations by urging Congress to legislate protection for dyestuffs and related industries. Then, in June, Wilson and his allies incorporated into the final draft of the Versailles Treaty certain provisions for the break-up of the German chemical monopoly.

But Wilmington had won only half the battle. Despite these gains in the realm of law and scientific formulas, and despite Wilson's additional calls for dye tariffs in December of 1919 and 1920, the Du Ponts still lacked the most important ingredient in dye-making—practical know-how. Without German experience, most of the newly acquired German patents were indecipherable. The Du Ponts decided to resolve this problem by dealing directly with the Germans. In November 1919, Du Pont agents met secretly in Zurich, Switzerland, with representatives from Badische-Anilin und Soda Fabrik Co., one of Germany's largest chemical firms and later part of the I.G. Farben monopoly.

The negotiations, of course, were weighted in favor of Du Pont right from the start. The German corporation realized it lacked the power to stop Washington's sale of their patents to the Chemical Foundation. But to weaken its adversary even more, Du Pont threatened crucial economic leverage against the Germans through its ability to turn the regulatory screw of the American tariff on German chemical imports. At first, the Germans reacted defensively, then they retreated prudently, finally they capitulated shamelessly to Du Pont terms, agreeing to surrender the practical secrets of the Bosch-Haber ammonia process in exchange for a share of the world market. Du Pont, in turn, agreed to set up a multinational corporation, controlling about 25 percent of its stock, and to put up its working capital.[14]

But the Du Ponts were to gain more than a process for cheap ammonia production. "A successful ammonia arrangement," explained Du Pont agent Charles A. Meade, "certainly would lead at once to a dye exchange."[15] As one irate member of a Senate Investigating Committee charged years later, "At the moment when you were showing the country here that it was very important to take over the control of the chemical monopoly, to take it away from Germany and get a well-developed chemical industry in this country, you [Du Pont] were dealing with the Germans over there."[16]

All would probably have gone well "over there" for the Du Ponts if they had not been so rash. But the thirst for practical knowledge apparently led to corporate espionage and bribery, and ultimately the seduction of German scientists from their homeland to Wilmington. This was too obvious a show of bad faith for the insulted Germans, and the entire pact was scrapped and negotiations terminated. Eventually even the top Du Pont negotiator, Eysten Berg, resigned in protest. But Du Pont agents did succeed in smoothing some ruffled German feathers for future deals. "We parted as good friends,"[17] remarked one Du Pont official.

By now, however, the Du Ponts had decided they had no friends in Germany, only competitors. Moreover, the legal gains won for them by Wilson in the Versailles Treaty were lost as new deals were struck between French and German corporations. Clearly, the French government was impairing the Reparation Commission's ability to demand the opening of the sealed German manufacturing processes.

Wilmington was enraged.

In desperation, the Du Ponts turned again to the U.S. government for a tariff wall to pressure the Germans into submission. To bring Congress into tow, the Du Ponts launched the greatest international publicity drive the world has ever seen.

In 1920, Charles K. Weston, Du Pont's dapper publicity head, was dispatched to London. There he was cabled by M. R. Poucher, head of Du Pont's dye sales, that "Disarmament is a farce while Germany retains organic chemical monopolies."[18] Poucher's cable became, with the endorsement of Chairman Pierre S. du Pont, the official company line that was soon incorporated in scores of articles carried in hundreds of American newspapers. Dashing between London (where he saw the British bill restricting German dyes imports through Parliament) and Paris, Weston succeeded in reversing popular opinion that had been overwhelmingly against the use of poison gas in war. This was done by developing a public hysteria over alleged German control over poison gas production through the dyes industry. By December 10, 1920, he was able to send the Du Ponts a glowing report:

My mission seems to be going fairly well; I have met a number of our American newspaper correspondents, and have I think succeeded in selling them our ideas. One cannot tell, of course, until the results begin to appear in American newspapers.

The correspondents in Paris report to the offices here, so it is apparent that if the men in London get the right angle, it will be wonderfully helpful.

In Paris I shall devote my energy very largely to bringing the correspondents in contact more closely with American sources of news, at the same time trying to give them the proper angle so that they will appreciate the importance of the news.[19]

Appreciate they did. Within a few months one of Du Pont's top executives, J. J. Byrne, wrote back to Weston:

Recently there have appeared a number of dispatches in the American papers along the lines that are very desirable to us. These look to me as if they have been cabled to this country as a result of your visit to the other side:

1. The *Boston Transcript* of December 21, 1920, carried a fine story on "Britain Foresees Gas Warfare," dated from London.

2. The *Washington Herald* had a cable dispatch written by Wythe Williams from Paris about German dye plots against the U.S. This was taken up by the *Manufacturers Record* and made the subject of a splendid full page editorial.

3. The *Evening Bulletin* of Philadelphia had a dispatch from London talking about the importance of British action passing the dye bill and its relation to American affairs.

4. The *Public Ledger* of January 8, 1921, had a dispatch from Paris about "Germany Sets Dye Trade Trap."

These dispatches are syndicated in many cases to appear in different places throughout the country, so that the publicity on these four items I mentioned must have been considerable.[20]

Weston hired a newspaperman, Ben A. Raleigh, to run the Paris end. "Guy Martin and the articles which he wrote for the Paris edition of the *New York Herald Tribune* and the *Chicago Tribune* throw an interesting sidelight on my visit," Weston wrote Du Pont's Charles Meade. "They were written by Ben A. Raleigh, an old newspaper acquaintance whom I left on guard in Paris. He assumed the name of Guy Martin for publication purposes. . . . He as my agent will carry out any suggestion."[21]

It was this Mr. Raleigh who, on January 25, 1921, also reported:

> The Associated Press carried a cable on the substance of an interview I had with Prof. Blondell. . . . The *Public Ledger* Syndicate and the *Chicago Tribune* Syndicate papers are to be supplied with a story I have arranged which will point out that the French Government, upon confidential information from its investigators in Germany regarding a coming great German dump of goods, will further increase its coefficient tariff rates on dyestuffs, chemicals, etc. . . . This story should bring out some editorials in the American press, and it might be possible to have it suggested to some of the newspapers that editorial treatment of the cable would be of public service. . . .
>
> I sent you a cable yesterday notifying you of the coming appearance of the stories for the *Public Ledger* Syndicate and the *Chicago Tribune* papers. I hope to get some more material over the Associated Press wires shortly. . . .
>
> By the way, I suppose that an occasional luncheon, etc., in the furtherance of the project would not be objected to, but I should like authorization. In this case Dr. Chapin paid for the lunch, but I want to be in a position to come back at him and the other people who we want to cultivate, including such men as [Wythe] Williams of the *Public Ledger,* Roberts of the Associated Press . . . Floyd Gibbons of the [Chicago] *Tribune.*
>
> Carl Ackerman, who dropped into the *Ledger* Bureau while I was there, over on a visit from London, requested me to remember him to you. . . .[22]

(Roberts was then head of Associated Press; Carl Ackerman later became head of Columbia University's School of Journalism.)

More than luncheons were involved. From 1918 to 1925 Du Pont doled out over $130,000 to organizations participating in the publicity campaign.[23] Two of Washington's leading firms, Thomas R. Shipp & Co. and Bronson Batchelor, Inc., handled Du Pont's newspaper publicity on this side of the Atlantic. Speaking campaigns were launched to address conventions and civic and service clubs, while personal interviews were arranged with prominent businessmen. Government officials were also enlisted in the

Du Pont campaign, employing the very willing War Department and the Chemical Warfare Service. Irénée du Pont became the country's leading spokesman for "preparedness," wrapping his case for a dyes monopoly in the U.S. flag. The textile industry, in which Du Pont was also becoming involved, was also recruited for appeals to Congress. Finally, Du Pont pressure was brought to bear directly on the electoral arena. And here, in the person of Senator William S. Kenyon, Delaware's first family met their greatest political challenge since Frank Waddell's vengeful campaign brought on the 1907 anti-trust indictment.

Senator William Kenyon first came on the Du Pont scene in 1919. That year the National Security League's championing of the Du Ponts' "preparedness" theme, urging huge armaments expenditures, turned briefly into press attacks on Congress, and Kenyon led an angry investigating committee in retaliation. The result was an embarrassing light thrown on the League's chief financial backer, former Du Pont president T. Coleman du Pont.

This revelation came when other events were also bearing down on the Du Pont golden image—charges of war profits, of the "Old Hickory" fraud, of dye patent bribery and political machinations, of huge campaign donations and cheating on contracts with British allies. From 1920 to 1923 Senator Kenyon's forces took up all these charges and launched penetrating searches into Du Pont family closets. His second target, after Coleman's League, was Du Pont's dyes campaign.

On May 7, 1920, Senator Kenyon read before the Senate an extraordinarily blatant letter from Du Pont's Charles Weston to Senator Moses of New Hampshire. In it, Weston threatened to withhold support from the candidacy of General Leonard Wood for the Republican presidential nomination unless Senator Moses, Wood's campaign manager in the East, ceased his opposition to Du Pont's bill calling for a 20 percent tariff on foreign dyes. Dated April 16, 1920, Weston's letter was directed against Moses' proposed amendment to the bill.

> The amendment which you have offered and your active opposition to the preparedness features of the dye bill seem to some of us to be not in accord with your fervent appeals to us to support him [Wood] because of his stand for national preparedness.
>
> Personally, I want to support General Wood, but I find it difficult to reconcile the two attitudes of one of his important campaign managers—the one on the floor of the Senate and the other one on the public platform—sufficiently to have full faith in his cause.
>
> I am outlining a publicity campaign to inform the public concern-

ing the present status of the proposed dyes legislation. May I ask you to set me straight as to the apparent contradiction in your attitude on the dyes bill as that I may be perfectly accurate in what I write?[24]

"We have," exclaimed Kenyon angrily, "the remarkable spectacle of a U.S. Senator who is engaged in managing a presidential campaign practically threatened as to what may happen to that campaign if he does not withdraw his opposition to this bill."[25]

This was no small threat. Pierre du Pont had been the Republican Party's largest contributor in the last presidential election in 1916, donating $92,500, and thus carried great weight in the party.

Irénée immediately released a statement claiming the letter was only a personal one desiring information. On the very next day, however, the *New York Times* revealed that after Weston's letter was sent to Moses, Richard Sylvester, former Washington chief of police and then Du Pont confidential agent, approached General Wood while he was campaigning in Indiana and asked him to pressure Moses to stop his opposition to the dyes bill.[26]

Congress was in an uproar. Debate on the Dye Tariffs Bill was in full heat. Senator Thomas of Colorado, in the dramatic moment of the day, read the terms of a contract between Du Pont and Levinstein, Ltd., of Manchester, England, for a world monopoly of dyes. Interestingly enough, Thomas had acquired the contract from the Boston court where Levinstein had filed suit against Du Pont for a breach of faith.

"If I am correct in this," he charged, "I believe the purpose of this bill to be little short of infamous. The nature and support of the Du Ponts is known as well to other Senators as to me. That letter and this contract seem to me almost positive proof of the interests and influences behind this bill which drew up its provisions and which counted it as an asset for carrying out this purpose."[27]

The bill was killed by a filibuster. For once, it seemed the Du Ponts had lost.

The dyes tariff defeat, however, was only a temporary setback for the family, one that egged them on into even deeper involvement in national politics.

General Wood—the first imperial governor of the new U.S. colonies, Cuba and the Philippines, the personal leader in the U.S. crushing of national independence movements in both lands, and the darling of all militarists—suddenly found himself abandoned. At the eleventh hour premature publicity by the Kenyon Committee of his financial backers sent legions over to the camp of Warren G. Harding, and waiting there, in charge of the Republican Finance Committee's alleged $10 million slush fund, was T. Coleman du Pont.

"The Republican Party has picked a pair of winners," Coleman declared. "Delaware is for the ticket, I know. Our delegates left me on the third ballot and when the time came to go Harding they went solid."[28] Coly was right. Delaware, or Du Pont, was solid. Both he and his wife, along with Alexis I. du Pont, were listed by the Kenyon Committee among those who gave $1,000 each from two to twelve times.[29] Years later it was revealed that Coly gave an additional $25,000.[30] Irénée gave $14,722 (on top of the $8,110 he had donated only the year before), while Pierre gave $12,378.[31] Harding, the Standard Oil Man from Mark Hanna's Ohio machine, who enjoyed universal toleration by all the major families of America, had full Du Pont endorsement. Even old Colonel Henry A. du Pont christened Harding as "our magnificent candidate."[32]

Harding, history records, was anything but "magnificent." In fact, the most generous description that has been rendered his tenure in the White House was that he "did nothing" at all except play poker and drink. With Mellon seated as king of the Treasury and Morgan and Standard Oil/Sinclair Oil representatives filling the rest of his "Black Cabinet," Harding was left to his sublime idleness.

The country had Coleman du Pont, among others, to thank for Warren Harding's presidency. After Harding's nomination Coleman was among the top party officials who gathered at the Marion Club in Ohio (where Harding's office was located) to plan the campaign. Arriving too early, the politicians found no chef on hand, whereupon Coleman charged into the Club's kitchen, donned an apron, and cooked the entire party a breakfast of eggs and meat. It was typical Coleman.

Harding's Democratic opponent, Governor James Cox of Ohio, was unable, despite his partnership in the Pure Oil Company, to pull his fellow plutocrats over to his side.

An espouser of Wilson's League of Nations, Cox enjoyed the support of only a few major business leaders, one being J. P. Morgan & Company partner Thomas W. Lamont. But even in Lamont's circles, many Morgan colleagues simply saw no reason to play games. Abandoned on all sides, having an unknown with only a magic name, Assistant Navy Secretary Franklin D. Roosevelt, as his running mate, Cox had no real prospects for victory. In desperation, he repeated the charges of Montana's Senator Walsh that Coleman du Pont had been put in charge of the Republican Finance Committee in Washington to raise a $10 million slush fund. Then on October 16 he launched, with evidence, a direct attack on Coleman's slur campaign among salesmen, that new breed of "traveling men."

"I hold in my hand," he stated dramatically before a hushed audience in Cleveland, "the letter and circular issued by Coleman du Pont as Chairman of the Traveling Men's Bureau of the Republican National Committee. I think that everyone knows that Coleman du Pont is not a traveling man and that he has no great public interest in this campaign. I can understand how he would undertake to organize groups and stir up prejudices to encompass my defeat, because Coleman du Pont, as the Krupp of America, a member of a great munitions family, knows what it means should I be elected and secure the ratification of the Treaty of Peace and the League of Nations.

"This family has grown financially fat and insolent on the profits of the war. When men bleed and die on the battlefield, the munition makers receive dividends, and the League of Nations definitely provides against this sort of profiteering in the future.

"Not only is the League of Nations designed to make peace permanent, but it provides for taking away the agencies of war for a general disarmament and war prevention, it declares against the manufacture of munitions in any event by *private concerns,* because such concerns inspire and invite war.

"No wonder Coleman du Pont is interesting himself in behalf of the reactionary candidate whose motto is 'scrap the League of Nations.' "[33]

It was a new "devil theory" that simplistically ignored the reality that one did not have to be a munitions maker to profit from war. Indeed, Cox's own Pure Oil Company had benefited from the war mobilization. The key difference was in the interpretation of the League's potentiality. Cox, like Wilson, saw it as a way of enforcing a preservation of the existing world order. Their opponents, including most of the Du Pont and Morgan families, saw the League as a *restraint* on the freedom of American business and its political flexibility in foreign affairs.

"I would keep America as she has been," explained Senator Henry Cabot Lodge, a Morgan protégé, "not isolated, not prevent her from joining other nations for these great purposes—but I wish her to be master of her own fate."[34] Certainly the Du Ponts had concern regarding their manufacture of arms, but more likely their opposition to the League stemmed from their fear of the reciprocal trade relations it might involve, relations that could remove their infant dye industry from its tariff incubator before it was strong enough to face the world of competition. But even with munitions, Cox erred in his facts, opening himself to a lashing from Pierre's sharp tongue.

As chairman of Du Pont, Pierre leaped to Coleman's defense, characterizing Cox's charge of war profiteering as a "gross injustice." Coleman had severed ties with the company before the U.S. entry into the war, Pierre pointed out; he also asserted the "untruth" of any connection between his cousin and any "corruption fund of $10 million." Meanwhile, Coleman remained cool and confident, lounging on his new lavish estate on the Hudson, Nevis, the former home of Alexander Hamilton.

Two weeks later Warren G. Harding was elected President of the United States.

While the Du Ponts cultured their political gardens, they kept up the steady barrage of company propaganda calling for the dyes tariff in the interest of "patriotism and national security." Newspapers across the country reprinted the articles prepared by Weston's publicity bureau and marveled at Du Pont's patriotic fervor.

"Fulfilling the largest Federal war contract of the kind ever given," ran one of the most circulated articles, ". . . this corporation served the country so well that not one complaint was recorded by Government officials." Even contemporary evidence showed this to be graphically untrue, there having been many complaints about prices by government officials, including Secretary of War Baker. As Colonel Buckner, Du Pont's military sales director, joyously calculated in 1918, if only military business was considered, then the world war orders amounted to 276 years of Du Pont business. As the Graham investigating committee pointed out in 1921, for Du Pont, patriotism ended with the pocketbook.

Nevertheless, the Du Ponts were displayed by Weston's articles as titans of family integrity, worthy of study and admiration by all Americans. "The disintegration of American home life," the same article contended, "could be largely arrested by a national study of how to make a family a thinking, working unit like that of the du Ponts." Again, Weston was careful to avoid the deluge of divorces that had swamped the family in recent years, spilling over in feuds that tore the family asunder.

More than one of Weston's publicity employees must have winced at the claims of their own department that "It is the business of a corporation to tell the public what it is doing, and why; giving out the information regularly, freely, widely, accurately, forcefully. We maintain a Publicity Bureau whose sole function it is to tell the truth about our business, apart from any advertising or press agent considerations."

This claim, however, did not prevent Weston's bureau from integrating the same article into the campaign for Du Pont control over German dyes. "Not until the Du Ponts perfected standardization of dye colors was it possible to match a tint or shade of any but German dyes. When you wanted a certain blue, for example, you could not order by a catalogue number with any likelihood of getting the hue desired—unless the maker of the dye was a German. The Du Ponts now have such control of the pigment processes that the outcome is identical, for shade and wear, strength and delicacy, evenness and density, with the highest class German products."[35]

Yet, one of the most important factors in the development of Du Pont dyes was the company's luring of German scientists to Wilmington with bribes. Finally, in February of 1921, a bizarre set of circumstances led to the swearing out of warrants in Cologne, Germany, for the arrest of four leading German scientists. The scientists, Dr. Joseph Hachslander, Heinrich Jordan, Otto Runge, and Max Engelmann, all former "old and trusted" employees of Friedrich Bayer & Company of Leverskursen, had all secretly accepted jobs with Du Pont. Working with a Dr. Kunze of Zurich, the scientists were charged with "illegally appropriating valuable recipes, formulae, etc.," and were allegedly smuggling the documents and drawings across the German-Dutch frontier in a truck which, by pure accident, had been discovered by Dutch officials, impounded, and returned to Cologne.

Two of the scientists subsequently disappeared. Two others, Runge and Hachslander, were later found in Wilmington happily tinkering away in their new Du Pont labs with handsome salaries of $25,000 per year. Irénée interpreted it simply as an example of company integrity and innocence. "The Du Pont Company has not violated any law or any business principle," he explained, "and these accusations made by the German kartel are simply another move in its campaign to prevent the development of an industry here. They are in line with the propaganda against the passage of protective legislation in the United States which it has been spreading since we began to seriously threaten the German monopoly.

"In the absence of any formal answer which may be made to the charges, it is only justice to the accused German chemists to say that the Du Pont Company employed Dr. Hachslander and Dr. Runge as the best experts it could find to interpret and help put into practical operation the processes and formulae covered by the German patents which were seized and made available to American manufacturers when this country went to war with Germany."[36]

Case closed.

Five months later the Du Pont Company received a boon almost as important politically as the German scientists were technically—a U.S. senator. Almost immediately, it became known around the country as "Delaware's Dirty Deal."

Delaware's Dirty Deal

Coleman du Pont had wanted to be a U.S. Senator for a long time, possibly since helping his cousin, Colonel Henry A. du Pont, in his twelve-year struggle to defeat "Gas" Addicks for the senatorial seat. And Coleman's hardheaded persistence, along with his renowned financial power, usually got him what he wanted.

In 1916, however, his ambition was thwarted through the intervention of his vengeful cousin, Alfred I. du Pont. Coly's scheme was to run a presidential campaign to gain some national prominence that could justify his appointment to the Senate later that year; old Colonel Henry was rumored to be ready to resign. This plan was smashed by Colonel Henry's defeat in his bid for reelection—a defeat engineered by Alfred. By 1920, when Coleman was neck-deep in national Republican politics, both senatorial seats were occupied by Alfred's protégés, Josiah Wolcott and L. Heisler Ball. If not economically, Alfred was at least politically Baron of Delaware. Believing Coleman's defeat secured, on January 24 of that year Alfred told his political lieutenant, Frank Allee, of his decision "to give up the political game altogether,"[37] and asked him to pass the word on.

Again, as in his maneuvers for leadership in the Du Pont Company, Alfred had been overconfident and had not weighed the timing of his announcement. It was a critical mistake.

Fear swept the ranks of the Republican Party. Most erroneously suspected that Alfred's financial well had run dry. Rumors had begun to leak out in the past year of Alfred's very real pecuniary difficulties. The Nemours Trading Corporation, which Alfred had formed during the war to sell badly needed American goods to Europe at high prices, had been the victim of his usual economic miscalculations, for Alfred had ignored in Europe the inevitable result when anything is bled white. With its factories destroyed, profitable markets lost, and currencies depreciated, Europe's finances—and his company's prospects—collapsed. Alfred suddenly found himself besieged by calls for more money. In addition, in October 1919 he was sued for his takeover of Allied Industries and the French-American Construction Corporation through Nemours Trading. Charging that their property had been made valueless, five Allied stockholders demanded $270,000 in compensation. To add to his problems, Alfred was also hit by a government demand for $1,576,000 owed on his 1915 income taxes. Insult was then added to injury. On March 6, 1919, the Court of Appeals ruled on Alfred's 1916 Du Pont Company stock defeat to Pierre. Not only did the three-judge panel agree with the lower court's dismissal of Alfred's suit, but it dissented with every criticism the lower court had made of Pierre's conduct during the struggle for control.

But much worse was to come for Alfred. His wife's illnesses were growing more frequent, becoming a pattern of steady decline. That summer Alicia was bedridden at her new Long Island estate, White Eagle, occupying her time by writing a book on wine making.

By fall, both Alicia and Nemours Trading Corporation were disintegrating before Alfred's eyes. In November Alfred made out his final check to Nemours Trading for $300,000, raising his total investment to close to $5 million. "That will have to last,"[38] he told its president. It didn't.

Alicia's spirits picked up around Christmas time, and Alfred took the opportunity for a vacation from his woes. He decided to visit his old friends, the Balls, who had moved to California. Old Captain Ball was dead now, and his widow lived there with two sons and a daughter, Jessie, who was probably the main reason for the compulsive 3,000-mile "visit." Alicia insisted on seeing him to the station, and on the platform she waved good-bye as the train pulled out. She never saw him again.

Four days later, on January 7, Alfred arrived at the San Diego station, where he was met by Miss Ball. But no sooner had plans been made for a luncheon the next day, when Alfred received a telegram: Alicia was dead. She had accompanied Francis du Pont and his wife to Charleston to attend a debutante party for a young relative. The trip was too much, and after an attack during the night, she died the next day at a nearby hospital.

Alfred buried Alicia at Nemours beside her infant daughter and son. It was the final, demoralizing blow. The fighting spirit seemed gone. He abandoned White Eagle, his business, everything.

Two weeks later, on January 21, he wrote the president of Nemours Trading Corporation, James Dashiel, that "I have decided to liquidate the Nemours Trading Corporation." He expected a loss of some $5 million. Before it was all settled, Alfred found himself in debt to the tune of $10 million.

The announcement of the firm's collapse shook Dover's politicians out of their characteristic slumber. Then came the thunderbolt of January 24, merely three days later. "There is nothing in [politics] but wear and tear, mudslinging and an awful lot of expenditure,"[39] Alfred explained.

Alfred's brother-in-law, Ed Bradford, Jr., warned of the possible rout of the Republicans into the camp of Coleman du Pont's "Bazaza & Company." "I do not think your fears well founded," answered Alfred. "Bazaza and Company are just about as near dead ducks in this state as anything above ground could be."[40] Alfred was simply too busy setting his financial house in order to bother with Coleman. Coleman, for his part, had sent condolences to Alfred on Alicia's death (as Alfred did likewise ten days later when Coleman's youngest son suddenly died), and had even offered financial assistance, which Alfred, fearing such a personal obligation, had politely refused. Rumors may well have spread, however, that family differences were being bridged, rumors fanned by Alfred's sale of the *Morning News* and six weeklies, which eventually found their way into the hands of Pierre du Pont. Abruptly, the *Morning News*'s editorials reversed gear and called for the seating of Coleman du Pont in the U.S. Senate.

These rumors about Alfred now ran rout through the ranks of his old political allies, allies who were more the product of financial generosity than political conviction, and room was soon made on the 1920 state slate for a young insurance broker named William D. Denney. This man, with absolutely no public record to speak of, was chosen to run for governor. It was not long before Alfred began to suspect the obvious, that behind Mr. Denney pushed the invisible hand of Coleman du Pont.

No sooner was Denney in office in 1921 than whispers began to fly of a deal involving Coleman. That May, Coleman paid a visit to Senator Josiah Wolcott in Washington, and Dover buzzed in anticipation. On May 6 Alfred wrote his sister Marguerite:

> I understand there is a scheme to put Coleman in the Senate by Governor appointment. The plan is to get the present Democratic Senator, Wolcott, to resign by offering him the Chancellorship of the State, which appointment is made by the Governor next month, and then to have the Governor appoint Coleman in his stead. While it is merely a rumor, it comes from a good source and I do know that Coleman was in Washington the other day and saw Wolcott. Coleman has recognized for some time that he has no chance of being elected to the Senate by the people as long as I was alive and kicking. . . . [In 1916] when the Colonel tried to make the grade and I threw him out, there was a distinct understanding, or so I am told, between the Colonel and Coleman that the Colonel would serve only one half the time and resign, and have the Governor appoint Coleman instead. That was really my chief reason for throwing the Colonel out. I do not see how to meet this new threat of having the state represented by Coleman. Possibly the rumor was invented. . . .[41]

On May 24 Governor Denney himself confirmed it wasn't by announcing that Josiah Wolcott was his appointee for the highest judicial office in Delaware. Alfred came out of political retirement to try to stop the tidal wave of desertions, but Wolcott expressed his willingness to resign. The other senator, Lewis Ball, who also owed his position to Alfred, gave an interview to the *Morning News* in which he praised Coleman. Protest, however, burst like a storm. Ten members of the New Castle bar petitioned against Wolcott's confirmation by the state legislature. Even Colonel Henry, his sense of moral dignity outraged, had his *Evening Journal* voice its opposition. But it all came too late, too disorganized. On July 7, amid a wild tumult, the legislature confirmed Wolcott's appointment by a mere three votes.

"You will regret this to the end of your life," was Alfred's bitter comment to a former follower who tried to justify his vote. "You have chosen and there is no turning back, as you will find out."[42]

Coleman, meanwhile, had steered clear of all the mudslinging by "vacationing" in Colorado. He had already suffered the indignity of close fighting with Senator Kenyon over his controversial stand on immigration. Since the Russian Revolution of 1917, Congress had established laws that discriminated against immigrants from peasant and poor working-class backgrounds, most of whom came from southern and eastern Europe, where socialism was widely accepted. The war's end brought a flood of strikes and the promise of a flood of immigration, and in 1921 Congress limited immigration from any nation to 3 percent of its national residents in this country in 1910, a provision particularly favorable to British, German, and Scandinavian immigrants.

Coleman openly opposed this policy as chairman of the Inter-Racial Council, "an organization of more than 1,200 of the leading industrial establishments,"[43] and published articles in national magazines in 1920 that called for nonrestrictive laws. "Will the shutting off of immigration afford protection against ultra-radicalism, as so many seem to think," he asked, "or will it threaten our commerical supremacy?"[44] Listing the number of key basic industries in which immigrants made up the majority of workers—coal, steel, iron, clothing, cotton and woolen goods, sugar refining, and railway maintenance—and citing the $25 billion worth of goods they created and the savings they accumulated for use by bankers, Coleman warned that literacy tests could result in a shortage of cheap labor. He warned of the 275,000 immigrants, mostly able-bodied men, who were returning to their homelands, taking with them $550 million earned in the United States. "We are losing at both ends, our entrances and our exits— the women and children coming in, the able-bodied males going out."[45]

Women and children were not Coleman's concern; cheap labor was.

"Our native-born workmen [meaning the AFL leadership] do not realize that without immigrants for our unskilled grades of work, there would be little work available for the skilled American workers. . . . The need for unskilled immigrant labor in industry has even now not been met. . . . That need is mentioned in order to emphasize the importance of the immigrant to industrial expansion and to show how industry is vitally concerned with the stabilization and assimilation of our immigrants and with so fundamental a thing as our attitude toward the immigrant on his arrival.

"Receive the immigrant with a smile," advised this financial fox. "Next, we might offer him a little protection, if not for altruistic purposes, then for the selfish purpose of building up a national reputation that will attract the best immigrants.

"The immigrant must feel that he is protected. He must be inspired with confidence in our form of government and in our institutions. He must be attracted to citizenship; for citizenship, if it is to mean anything, must be sought after, not thrust upon the immigrant."[46]

In this interest, he encouraged "spontaneous Americanization which, by indirect methods, can be delicately but effectively stimulated." All this could be done, Coleman suggested, while a federal board of assimilation "distributed immigrants to industrial centers to meet the manpower needs of the owners of industry." Coleman disclaimed the "red hysteria." "Only 1% of the foreign-language newspapers have shown a tendency toward communism," he noted, "a much lower percentage than among the English-language newspapers." That same year a Senate investigating committee, led by Coleman's indomitable foe, Senator Kenyon, explained why this was so: Coleman du Pont controlled about 90 percent of the foreign-language newspapers in the United States. Through his American Association of Foreign Language Newspapers, Coleman pushed "by indirect methods" his particular brand of "Americanism," which was indeed "delicately but effectively stimulated."

"Day by day the money-masters of America become more aware of their danger," wrote an angry Upton Sinclair that year; "they draw together, they grow more class-conscious, more aggressive. The war has taught them the possibilities of propaganda; it has accustomed them to the idea of enormous campaigns which sway the minds of millions and make them pliable to any purpose. They have been terrified by what happened in Russia and Hungary, and they propose to see to it that the foreign population of America is inoculated against modern ideas. They form the 'Publishers' Association of the American Press in Foreign Languages,' whose purpose it is 'to foster unswerving loyalty to American ideals'—that is to say, to keep America capitalist. Then a group of our biggest exploiters, headed by Coleman du Pont of the Powder Trust, buy the

'American Association of Foreign Language Newspapers.' They give a dinner to the heads of all the newspaper advertising agencies, at the Bankers Club of New York, and explain that in the future all advertising must be placed through this great association. So the massed advertising of American corporations is to be wielded as a club, to keep the newspaper columns of foreign language newspapers free from radicalism. So when there is a strike anywhere in the 'Powder barony,' and Poles and Hungarians are being bayonetted and shot, the powder barons will know that the Polish and Hungarian newspapers are printing no news of the shooting and giving no encouragement to the strike."[47]

Needless to say, such attacks by the famous muckraker did not make Coleman's day. Nor did his grilling before Kenyon's committee on September 25, which made front-page news in the *New York Times* the next day. Coleman was receiving too much notoriety for many of his business partners. Besides, many of them simply disagreed with his immigration campaign. The problem, they explained, was growing unemployment, which the unskilled immigrant would only make worse. Industrial expansion, moreover, was no longer tied to employing more and more workers, but rather fewer, through mechanization, which reduced the cost of labor while producing more, thus reducing prices and thereby opening new consumer markets. What cheap labor was needed could easily be acquired by the millions of rural people 19,436,000 between 1920 and 1929 who would soon leave the farms as the new trucks, tractors, and combines replaced agricultural jobs and reduced farm prices. These people, bringing the conservatism and individualism of the rural mind, would help business in its fight against socialism, while immigration laws that restricted any other growth of the unskilled labor pool would shore up workers' wages generally and narrow the gap in wage differentials.

As usual, Coleman's thinking was simply behind the times. To avoid any further embarrassment or antagonisms, in February 1921 he resigned his chairmanship of the Inter-Racial Council. That year the 1917 restriction on immigration was further tightened, as it would be again three years later. Coleman's campaign had clearly collapsed. He never raised its banner again.

It was only three months later, then, that Denney made his appointment of Wolcott to the Chancellory, and Coleman was safe in Colorado, far from the flying sparks and ugly slurs. On July 7 Denney wired Coleman at Colorado Springs of his appointment to the United States Senate.

"As you know," Coleman telegraphed back to Denney, "I have never cared for any political ambition, but when called to duty by one's State or country, there is but one thing to do—give the best in you. This I will do.

There are men in the State who could fill the position more brilliantly and with greater credit, but there are none who would work harder for the good of the nation and for Delaware. I hope to show you and the good people of Delaware my appreciation of this great honor by acts rather than words."[48]

Brave words indeed for someone who as a senator became best known for his absenteeism.

National magazines, such as *Outlook,* termed Coleman's appointment "peculiar." The Philadelphia *Record* called it "Delaware's Shameful Deal." Across the country it became known as "Delaware's Dirty Deal."

Dirty or not, Coly wore his senator's toga with distinct pride when he came to Washington in November, becoming a frequent visitor to the house of Harding's largest pre-convention contributor and now attorney general, Harry H. Daugherty, the dispenser of favors in the administration. When a public furor arose over the Graham Committee's exposure of Du Pont fraud on World War I powder prices and the useless Old Hickory plant, Attorney General Daugherty refused to prosecute, even after it was revealed in April 1922 that the selling of Du Pont's war plants had netted $14 per share for the stockholders in Pierre's dummy Du Pont Chemical Company, and even under the threat of Daugherty's impeachment voiced in Congress on April 11 by Representative Woodruff.

Coleman's cousins, meanwhile, launched their final drive for their dyes bill. In 1921 Du Pont stock had been dragged down with the general stock decline of the post-war recession. Not wishing to cut into profit margins or dividends, Irénée had rectified the situation temporarily by slashing the wages of all employees by 10 percent. This, of course, hurt the average Du Pont worker most, but as the company was not unionized, there was little the individual workers could do but voice impotent complaints.

All three cousins realized that this was only a temporary expedient, however, and put their long-range hopes on capturing the dyes monopoly and other areas of investment. The dyes campaign fell under the personal direction of Irénée and Lammot, the latter being in charge of the organic chemicals division. But it was lean, spectacled Irénée who, as president, mapped the strategy and led the struggle.

Irénée was a man obsessed with business, precisely because it was *his* business. Years ago, as a lower executive, even his play was business oriented. Every Thursday night he, John J. Raskob, and three other minor executives would play at being the executive committee dealing with the company's major problems. Occasionally, they even produced a good idea, which they dutifully passed on to higher executives.

Disliking press agentry and cant, Irénée disliked the new income tax system even more, and he was very willing to employ the former to defeat the latter. A man who loved his microscope and other laboratory tools like a craftsman, he was also a great negotiator in company circles, tending, it was often remarked, to encourage the company's efficiency and success "by picking the most feathers with the least squawk." It was these talents that he used to pick the feathers of the German dye monopoly till it was bare. But German corporations could squawk. When they did—as when in September 1921 Dr. Beckmann of the Chemical and Pharmaceutical Association charged Du Pont with industrial theft and commercial bribery—Irénée simply ignored them. When he was called to testify before a Senate committee the following March, Irénée adopted his elder brother's renowned pose of calm and confidence, and denied any intention of a monopoly over dyes, while almost in the same breath he admitted to directing a strong lobbying campaign. "We have been here," he smiled, "frankly and openly."[49]

Coleman was also there, "frankly and openly" close to Harry Daugherty's Alien Property Custodian, Thomas B. Miller. During Miller's tenure, with Charles Weston's publicity bureau showering "public opinion" on Washington, the Du Ponts managed to buy up most of the important German dye patents remaining under Miller's custody. Miller eventually wound up in the Atlanta Penitentiary for taking a $50,000 bribe. Coleman never paid him a visit.

Wrapping their case in the U.S. flag, the Du Ponts continued a barrage of mounting pressure on Congress in 1922. Senator T. Coleman du Pont, when he could spare time from his financial speculation in such fields as professional boxing, did his part, writing Irénée that "Senators Watson, Frelinghuysen, Pepper, and one or two others will defend the Du Pont Company."[50] The result was a complete victory for the Du Ponts in the 67th Congress: the passage of House Resolution 2435, the Tariff Act of 1922.

By then the Du Ponts had $40 million invested in dyes and related chemicals, building on their first wartime expansion when they committed 60 percent of their total investment of commerical properties and equipment in chemicals.[51] Now, armed with German patents and scientists, and protected from foreign competition by a tariff shield, the Du Ponts became the Number One dyemaker in America. Eventually they produced over 500 different dyes and extended their chemical holdings across the country: in 1924, the Viscoloid Company, maker of Viscoloid, a pyroxylin material much like Du Pont's Pyralin (originally made by the acquired Arlington Company), and Lazote, Inc., which made synthetic ammonia; in 1925, the Eastern Alcohol Corporation was formed with the Kentucky Alcohol

Corporation as partners to make ethyl alcohol from West Indies molasses; in 1926, the National Ammonia Company; in 1928, a 50 percent interest in the Bayer-Samesan Corporation, maker of seed disinfectants, and the Grasselli Company, since 1839 a leading manufacturer of acids, and a 50 percent interest in the Pittsburgh Glass Company (sold later); in 1929, a 70 percent interest in the Krebbs Pigment and Chemical Company, maker of lithopone, and Capes-Viscose, Inc., maker of cellulose caps and bands; in 1930, the Roessler and Hasslacher Chemical Company, specialists in electrochemicals, peroxides, and insecticides, and a 51 percent interest in Kinetic Chemicals, Inc.; in 1931, the Commercial Pigments Corporation, maker of titantium pigments, and the Newport Company, compounder of dyes and synthetic organic chemicals; for $834,000, an interest in the Bakelite Corporation; for $2 million, a one-third interest in the Niacet Chemical Corporation; for $250,000, a 50 percent interest in the Old Hickory Company; and a 62 percent controlling interest in Acetol Products, Inc.

It was just like the old gunpowder trust days, as the Du Pont Company quietly grew into the world's largest chemical empire through a hearty diet of smaller entrepreneurs. As Irénée once put it, "It's nice to be friendly with competition."[52]

Not only the domestic market, but also the foreign market succumbed to Du Pont's demands. But it was not the Germans who were the first to be pressured by the tariff wall into releasing their technical secrets, as had been anticipated; it was the French.

Rayon

The French signed their first agreement with the Du Ponts in 1920, under the shadow of rabbled cities and the first American tariff bill on chemicals (doomed to defeat that year). With a 60 percent investment, Wilmington formed the Du Pont Fibersilk Company with France's largest manufacturer of viscose rayon, Comptier de Textiles Artificiels, and bought up the patent rights for North America. Under the guidance of French technicians, the Du Ponts set up the country's first rayon plant at Buffalo, New York, and soon thousands of pounds of wood pulp were being turned into millions of skeins of artificial silk fiber.

Rayon's success was almost immediate, creating for textiles the greatest revolution since the cotton gin, although not exactly appreciated as much by the cotton industry. In fact, Du Pont's rayon competition was one factor in the decline in cotton textiles after 1924 and the resultant layoff of thousands of workers. But rayon's success was assured, and the Du Ponts quickly bought out the French, allowing Comptier's president, Edmond Gillet, a seat on the Du Pont Board of Directors. It was a small price to pay for what the National Resources Committee would classify in 1937 as one of the six outstanding technical achievements of the twentieth century, ranking with the telephone, automobile, airplane, motion picture, and radio in importance.

Establishing the "rayon" name in 1924, the Du Ponts moved its production into the South, escaping the North's protective legislation enforcement, unionism, and decent wages. Thriving in an area where wages were 43.6 percent lower than in the North,[53] cotton and rayon mill owners easily controlled state and local governments. From here, representatives were sent to Congress " to protect Southern industry" by hostilely opposing any proposed child labor laws or protective legislation for women that might interfere with the hiring of keen young eyes and nimble fingers held so dearly (and paid for so cheaply) by the textile industries. The old, who were unemployable in these industries, became a burden assumed by the younger relatives, rather than by the employer. It is not surprising, then, that Du Pont Company consistently opposed social security insurance throughout the Twenties.

The Du Ponts built three rayon plants in this decade. All were in the South: near Richmond, Virginia; at the Old Hickory plant site in Tennessee; and at Waynesboro, Virginia, the site of eight production units worth $46 million and employing 6,400 workers, all non-union. From the Richmond (actually, Ampthill, Virginia) site, the Du Pont Engineering Company built a special concrete roadway to the Richmond-Petersburg Turnpike to facilitate the marketing of manufactured rayon. By 1927, rayon workers in the South were producing one-third of Du Pont's total income. Du Pont's $3.3 million in research was soon returning over $5 million in profits every year.[54]

Cellophane

A year before Du Pont established its "rayon" name, it entered into an alliance with the same French firm, Comptier de Textiles Artificiels, to establish a cellophane plant in Buffalo. Again, Du Pont used French technicians, including cellophane's inventor, J. E. Brandenberger. French salesmen were sent over to Wilmington to push the product and train Du Pont salesmen. No sooner were the plant and training completed than the Du Ponts followed their previous pattern and bought out their French partners.

Cellophane was originally marketed as an attractive eye-catcher in packaging, without any practical use. Predictably, no one would touch it. But Chairman Pierre was not to be beaten. While pontificating about "A principle laid down one hundred years ago by Du Pont: the sound way to success is in filling needs,"[55] Pierre encouraged an expansion of the company's advertising department to create those needs. It was only after repeated attempts at selling Du Pont cellophane had failed that stubborn Pierre finally agreed to pour money into research to find some practical use for his product. Eventually, in 1927, after 2,000 experiments, cellophane's moisture-proof practicality was developed, and by 1931 was being applied to packaging everything from cigarettes to bread. Within a decade of their first investment in 1924, cellophane was grossing over $5 million every year for the Du Ponts,[56] with four out of seven factories, again, in the South.

Film and Ammonia

Two other big money-makers also came from the market-hungry French. One was photographic film. With Pathé Exchange, Inc., which manufactured a cellulose plastic for photographic film, Du Pont secured a 51 percent majority interest in establishing the Du Pont Film Manufacturing Company. Again, they soon bought out their French partners, while Du Pont Film supplied booming Hollywood with 40 percent of all its negative film and one-fifth of all its positive film.

The other lucrative product was synthetic ammonia. In 1924 the Du Ponts purchased rights of the Claude Process for the fixation of nitrogen out of the air, a method that was an improvement over the German process for which Du Pont Company had negotiated in Switzerland in 1919. Using this as a basis for the production of ammonia, the Du Ponts launched a high-pressure synthesis plant at Belle, West Virginia. From here, spewed forth ammonia for refrigeration; light clear plastics for aircraft and for other uses; urea for fertilizers and medicines; and alcohols and solvents for anti-freeze solutions.

All of these investment areas (dyes, cellophane, rayon, ammonia, cellulose film, etc.) supplied markets for Du Pont's original powder-making ingredients, particularly nitrocellulose. But all, in turn, demanded their own markets. It was this search for markets for their new chemical acquisitions that led the Du Ponts to their greatest treasure house of all: General Motors.

3. THE G.M. GIANT

Few investments in the history of world capitalism have returned such pure gold as the Du Ponts' involvement with General Motors. From an initial $43 million contribution to G.M.'s treasury sprang Du Pont Company's greatest market. Over $20 million in dividends were reaped every year, to say nothing of family dividends and salaries and fees as G.M. executives and directors, the market it provided for other companies (such as the family-controlled U.S. Rubber Company), and the enormous economic and political power such control carried. Clearly, the history of Du Pont in the twentieth century is closely tied to the history of G.M.

The Du Ponts, however, were only the godparents of G.M. While they were important in recognizing its potential and guiding its growth, the origins of General Motors were in the imagination and drive of Detroit's "Little Giant," William Crapo Durant.

The grandson of wealthy Henry H. Carpo, Michigan's lumber magnate and governor, short, stocky, Billy Durant, backed by his financial leverage and prestigious name, was one of the fastest talking promoters Michigan ever saw. As a young man, Durant took his first successful plunge into carriage manufacturing, cheating a mechanic out of a valuable patent for $50. With his profits he set up the Durant-Dort Carriage Company, employing expert designers and skilled workers who made him a millionaire by the age of 40.

In 1904, after testing its luxury product on every imaginable road, 43-year-old Billy Durant bought the financially troubled Buick Motor Company. Within ten months, by enlisting the financial aid of New York bankers, he had increased Buick's initial $75,000 capitalization twentyfold. Soon Durant was building more plants, hiring more labor, increasing production, and selling the fashionable Buicks by the hundreds to wealthy clients. By 1908 his firm was producing 8,000 cars a year, earning him the title "the Little Giant."

That year Durant organized his life's great love, the General Motors Corporation, as a holding company. Within two years, swaggering about Michigan with his firm's $12 million capitalization, Durant began buying out his less fortunate smaller competitors in a series of lightning maneuvers: Cadillac, Oldsmobile, Oakland Motor Companies, Northway Motors Company, Weston Mott Company, and fifteen others. Except for the hesitancy of his nervous bankers, he would also have bought out Henry Ford, then the leading auto manufacturer.

This enormous expansion drained Durant's working capital, however, and with a sales drop in the 1910 recession, he was forced that year to surrender control to Boston and New York bankers for a contracted period of five years in exchange for a badly needed $15 million loan. It had become typical of the new industrial age that the financiers, through their control of the purse strings, dictated to the industrialist.

With only five years to raise $15 million to restore his control over General Motors, Durant thought he had hit pay dirt with the Chevrolet, his medium-priced answer to Ford's Model T. While forming the $20 million Chevrolet Company in Delaware, where tax laws and fees were more favorable, "the Little Giant" was unaware that he was being quietly watched by a bigger giant in that state, the Du Pont family.

Pierre du Pont's wry little secretary, John J. Raskob, was convinced by February 1914 that General Motors, with an enormous plant capacity and economies of scale, would double its earnings within a year. That month he bought 500 shares of G.M. common at $70 a share; Pierre bought 2,000 at $82 out of G.M.'s 65,000 total. Raskob proved to be right. G.M.'s stock rose to $200 by the summer of 1915, to $350 by September.

By then, about half of Pierre's stock portfolio (besides his Du Pont holdings) was filled with G.M. shares. The interest of the president of Du Pont was very real and very obvious.

Apparently, a business acquaintance of Pierre's, Lewis G. Kaufman, caught wind of this. Kaufman was the president of New York's Chatham & Phoenix Bank, and had once asked Pierre to join its board. More importantly, however, Kaufman was also a member of the Board of Directors of General Motors and an ally of Durant. Durant's showdown with the bankers was approaching, and what more formidable ally could Durant have than the Du Ponts? Perhaps he could use the Du Ponts. An invitation was extended to Pierre to attend the G.M. board meeting in New York on September 16, 1915. Would he come? Certainly, Pierre replied. But it was not the Du Ponts who were to be used.

Pierre and Raskob arrived at the meeting and immediately grasped the situation. G.M. and Chevrolet had netted enough income to enable Durant to pay off the bankers, but regaining control was another matter. Both sides were deadlocked on the composition of a new board of directors, and as Pierre's control of about 3,000 shares made him the largest minority stockholder, both sides immediately intrigued to win him over. Following Raskob's sound advice, Pierre ignored all temptations, insisting on remaining a neutral. It was a shrewd move. This peacemaker role soon resulted in one of the great coups of corporate history: Pierre was invited to assume the chairmanship of General Motors as a neutral arbiter! And he was also asked to name three other associates to serve as neutral directors between the two warring camps! Twinkling his blue eyes with all due humility, Pierre accepted, naming Raskob, Du Pont Vice President J. Amory Haskell, and cousin and brother-in-law Henry Belin. Du Pont had its foot in G.M.'s door.

Pierre was no sooner in office than he began a whirlwind tour of Detroit, making contacts both within and outside of G.M., always encouraging the adoption of Du Pont's centralized corporate structure as essential in tying together the vast G.M. empire under one leadership. But for this proposal one problem consistently emerged—Billy Durant.

Durant naturally wanted to regain control over the company he had founded and organized. But when he voiced that desire at the November 12 board meeting, he received a chilling silence from the Du Ponts. Pierre, in fact, wrote that he was "disturbed"; but being preoccupied with Du Pont's wartime profiteering, he was unable to devote much time to directing G.M. operations or organization. He was also unable to stop Durant's surprise takeover in December. Through a syndicate that used the proceeds from a sale of Chevrolet stock to buy up a controlling block of G.M., Durant regained control, but not for long.

Throughout 1916 "the Little Giant" did pretty much what he wanted as president, despite a constant struggle with the Du Ponts over their suggestions for modernizing the corporate structure into a more efficient system like that of their own company. His only concession that year came in December, when he agreed to allow another in-law of Pierre's, Hamilton Barksdale, to take a seat on the board of Chevrolet, which was marked for eventual merger into G.M. Otherwise everything seemed under control— that is, until Wilson went to war.

While the war proved a windfall for the Du Ponts, it was a disaster for Durant. Suddenly G.M. stock plummeted to new lows. Speculators, uneasy about the threat of curtailment in wartime supplies and diminished demand for automobiles, unloaded their G.M. holdings by the thousands, sending the stock's value down to $75. With Raskob's eager assistance, Durant foolishly began buying up all the unloaded shares he could find in an attempt to shore up its price. It was a futile gesture, at best, and Durant eventually had to turn to Wilmington for additional capital. It was then that the Du Ponts made their historic move.

"Our interest in the General Motors Company," Raskob explained to his Du Pont chieftains on December 19, 1917, "will undoubtedly secure for us the entire Fabrikord, Pyralin, paint, and varnish business of these companies, which is a substantial factor . . . it is the writer's belief that ultimately the Du Pont Company will absolutely control and dominate the whole General Motors situation."[57] Two days later, the Du Ponts authorized the purchase of $25 million worth of G.M. stock.

There was a specific incentive for this investment. By then, Du Pont had bought six large chemical companies from the $90 million expansion fund it had set aside out of war profits. These firms were all markets for Du Pont's nitrocellulose and related chemicals. But they, in turn, could use

General Motors as a market for their own products: lacquers, paints, varnishes, Pyralin, and artificial leather (Fabrikoid). One company, Fairfield Rubber (purchased in 1916), even made rubber-coated fabrics for auto and carriage tops as its chief product. Durant's misfortune provided a rare opportunity. There was still $50 million left in the investment purse. It was into this that the family reached to pull out their G.M. prize.

Pierre's first move was to establish his own way of doing things in G.M. Using Du Pont Company as a model, he set up a modern centralized corporate structure with a financial committee dominated by himself, Raskob (who assumed the chair), Pierre's brother Irénée, his cousin Henry F., and J. Amory Haskell. Durant, of course, was also a nominal member, but he had few doubts about his own stature there. His realm, rather, was the Executive Committee, where he presided over other representatives from the major managing divisions. But Durant was not left alone in G.M. management as president. Haskell was also on hand to watch over things and report back to Pierre.

Meanwhile, Pierre frankly explained the acquisition to Du Pont's stockholders: "The motor companies are very large customers of our Fabrikoid and Pyralin as well as paint and varnishes."[58]

Between 1917 and 1919 Du Pont bought another $24 million worth of G.M. stock. In the space of two short years the Du Ponts had completed a $49 million investment in G.M. and controlled 23 percent of its stock. It was a commanding position. "The large engineering and construction forces of the company," Pierre explained in the 1918 *Annual Report,* "the development, legal and accounting department facilities, coupled with the demands of the motor industry for talent of that kind, has furnished a connecting link which seems desirable in all investments. The consumption of paints, varnishes, and Fabrikoid in the manufacture of automobiles gives another common interest."[59]

Furthering this "common interest" became the direct responsibility of Vice President Haskell, Du Pont's sales manager, who was shifted over to G.M. in charge of its operations committee. There, he watched what products were used, pushed Fabrikoid as a substitute for genuine leather, and sponsored the use of Du Pont Pyralin. "It is not pure imagination," commented the Supreme Court some forty-five years later, "to suppose that such surveillance from that source made an impressive impact upon purchasing officials. It would be understandably difficult for them not to interpret it as meaning that a preference was to be given to Du Pont products."[60] Haskell's presence did its job. As early as 1918, when he first appeared on the G.M. scene, other chemical companies "saw the handwriting on the wall." Flint Varnish and Chemical Works, an old associate of

G.M., was probably the first to capitulate. Its president showed up one day to state to Durant that he "knew du Pont had bought a substantial interest in General Motors and was interested in the paint industry." He did not wish to lose his greatest customer, he explained, and eventually be ruined. Perhaps he should be bought out instead? He was. Later, Du Pont dissolved his company and absorbed its plants.

Du Pont control over finances quickly undermined what remaining control over operations Durant enjoyed. In 1919 Chevrolet was absorbed, increasing G.M.'s capitalization to over $1 billion. A huge Cadillac plant was built in Detroit, which also was the site of a new $20 million office building. With acquisition of Fisher Body Company and other firms, G.M.'s profits from its 86,000 employees and thousands of consumers topped $60 million. Additionally, over $50 million had been invested in unconsolidated companies, $47 million for new property and plants, and $12.7 million more in properties had been acquired through consolidation. That year, also, since the wartime burdens of Du Pont had lessened, Pierre and Raskob gave up their Du Pont positions to devote their full attention to the company's investment in General Motors. This move produced quick results, including $60 million worth of G.M. plant design and construction business to Du Pont's engineering department. Meanwhile, to pay for all this expansion, Pierre invited two old friends to join the board of G.M. as sources of capital: Nobel, Du Pont's powder ally in England, and J. P. Morgan. This weakened Durant's hold even further, but it was the enormous expansion program that finally backfired on G.M. when the post-war recession of 1920 hit—and Billy Durant was the victim.

That year, dealers returned cars by the score and G.M. machinery soon lay idle, choked with $84.9 million worth of unsold inventory. It was a classic case of overproduction clashing head on into an economic contraction of government wartime spending. G.M. stock lost its attractiveness and, in the press for working capital for other investments, was sold by speculators. On a single day in July, 100,000 G.M. shares were suddenly dumped on the market and the rout was on. G.M.'s price broke to $20½.

It was a desperate Billy Durant who again tried his ruse of buying up dumped G.M. shares. And it was an even more desperate Billy Durant who, swamped by the deluge of selling that had further broken the stock to $12 a share, found that his funds had run out and began borrowing on his own General Motors holdings. It was a foolish move—and a fatal one.

When the market closed on November 18, Durant found himself in urgent need of $940,000 before the market reopened the following morning. Without that sum he would be unable to meet his creditors' demands for additional collateral and would be ruined. As a last resort, he phoned

J. P. Morgan & Company and asked them to buy 1.1 million shares of his G.M. holdings at $12, the day's closing price. Then he informed Pierre and Raskob.

What ensued was Durant's undoing. Pierre met with the Morgan partners before their meeting with Durant. All agreed the situation was very dangerous for the entire stock market, for if Durant suddenly defaulted to the brokers who carried his loans, they in turn might be forced to close their doors, triggering a general financial collapse. Quickly, a plan was outlined. Durant would be bailed out, but only if he sold his control and resigned from the presidency. Then they laid their ultimatum on Durant, offering to buy $27 million worth of his stock at $9½ per share, well below the market price, Durant had little choice but to surrender, a broken man. By having J. P. Morgan float a $35 million bond issue, Du Pont Company completely bought Durant into corporate oblivion.

Two weeks later, on December 1, 1920, Pierre du Pont assumed the presidency of General Motors, occupying both the top executive job and the chairmanship with no more than a quip about coming into "a receivership of our own."[61] The conquest of G.M. was complete.

4. ALFRED'S LAST BATTLE

The warm balmy air of Miami Beach in the winter of 1922 greeted Delaware's "baron," Alfred I. du Pont, and his new bride, Jessie Ball.

Only three months after his wife Alicia died, Alfred had begun seeing Jessie, and no sooner had the first anniversary of Alicia's death passed, ending the proper year of mourning for his marriage out of pity, than he joined Jessie in wedlock. Immediately, Alfred's life became calmer, his composure more stable, his actions less erratic. Jessie, who had taught Alfred to combat his growing deafness with sign language, brought a new peace to Alfred, a peace which had taken him three marriages to find.

Alfred's financial condition improved with his disposition. Relatives offered help, including Willie du Pont, his partner in the Delaware Trust Bank, who agreed to write off a $300,000 investment in Nemours Trading. But when it came to cousin Coleman's offer to help, Alfred answered with a polite refusal. That would be going too far, indeed.

Curiously enough, rumors of a $6 million loan from Pierre, or arranged by him, have persisted through the years and been recorded in many family biographies, but have absolutely no base in reality. Instead, under the legal guidance of William Glasgow, Alfred paid his debt entirely by his own effort. He sold out the goods of his Nemours Trading for $1 million, which he gave to J. P. Morgan who, in turn, lowered the 9 percent interest rate on the remaining $3 million debt to 7 percent. By hypothecating half his total Du Pont stock holdings, worth $12 million, he secured loans. He sold all his Liberty bonds and, worst of all woes, laid up his beloved yacht. In November 1921 a Federal District Court dealt another blow, deciding in a test case against Alfred's attempt to avoid paying back income taxes owed for 1915.

"I shall have to pay $2 million more," he wrote his sister Marguerite du Pont Lee, "not a pleasant prospect with the obligations which I have already to bear. . . . If I refuse to pay, they may issue a distraint warrant . . . [and] grab Nemours and everything else they can lay their hands on. . . ."[62] Alfred met this crisis the following month by simply locking up Nemours himself and moving with Jessie into Hotel Du Pont.

Yet, in spite of all this, Alfred still managed the luxury of personal satisfactions only a plutocrat could enjoy. He completed the construction of his fourteen-story Delaware Trust Building in Wilmington, relishing the feeling of looking down at the twelve-story Du Pont Building across the street. In May, after failing to interest J. P. Morgan in buying his entire 75,000-share holding in Du Pont (Morgan suggested he sell to Irénée who offered only $82 a share), he sold 20,000 shares at $100 each, bringing in $2 million. Then a federal court order allowed Alfred to put off paying his back taxes until a Supreme Court reviewed his case. Meanwhile, the value of his remaining Du Pont stocks climbed higher with the end of the recession. By June, his financial crisis was over.

Through all this, Jessie had been Alfred's sole source of strength. "The Brid [one of his names for her], I must confess . . . is a million times more wonderful than I hoped. Think of spending one whole year with a girl and never a cross word or having the slightest misunderstanding or receiving anything but constant loving, thoughtful emotion!"[63] Alfred wrote that little testimony on the eve of his first wedding anniversary. It was a month later, in February 1922, that he took her for that winter vacation in Miami, and there met the surprise that began his last great political battle in Delaware.

One day, Alfred and Jessie were playing cribbage in the swank lobby of Miami's Flamingo Hotel, when Jessie noticed a tall man approach and stand over them. Alfred finally looked up. "Hello, Coly," he said without enthusiasm. He did not accept his cousin's offered hand. "I want you to meet Jessie." "Cousin Jessie," greeted Coleman in his typically pretentious manner, and drew up a chair. A friendly chat ensued, the first in years. But Jessie did manage to voice her lack of enthusiasm for Coly's card tricks. She had learned them all, she explained, while still in her teens. Yet family ice had been broken.

In May, apparently on Coleman's suggestion, Democrat John Raskob sent Alfred an invitation to a buffet party he was throwing to launch Coly's Republican senatorial campaign. Coleman wished to run in November not only for the remaining six months of Wolcott's term in the Senate, but also for the regular six-year term beginning in March. Alfred returned the invitation, curtly wishing Raskob "a very pleasant evening."[64] Coleman's fortune became not so "pleasant," however, when cousin Alfred appeared on Memorial Day at the formal opening of the Washington Memorial Bridge in Wilmington. Alfred had organized and chaired the commission that built the bridge spanning the Brandywine, and had attracted that day a large gathering of his former political followers. Coleman suspected such a gathering boded him no good, and he was right.

Two rural newspapers, the Newark *Ledger* and Dover *State News,* began firing stinging attacks at Coly and eyebrows raised along the Brandywine. These newspapers had belonged to Alfred, but the *Ledger* had been recently given to Ed Davis and the *State News* to the son of Frank Allee. Both Davis and Allee were chief lieutenants of Alfred du Pont, and suspicions especially arose when it was revealed that Alfred was meeting the *Ledger's* enormous deficits. Alfred publicly disclaimed any political role "that might split the Republican Party,"[65] only to seize control of the New Castle County Republican organization the following week, throwing out most of Coleman's supporters. The first shot had been fired, and the war was on.

The state's leading newspapers, controlled by Pierre, unleashed a counterattack, while William G. Taylor, the banker Alfred had made the reform mayor of Wilmington, deserted his former ally and led a victory parade for Coleman.

Meanwhile, Alfred came out publicly for the Democratic candidate, Thomas Bayard, as did Willard Saulsbury. It was the height of political hypocrisy, with Bayard and Saulsbury, both wealthy Du Pont in-laws, loudly trumpeting for control by "the people." "Shall Delaware belong to the Du Ponts? Are we a free people, or shall we permit ourselves to be crushed under the weight of Du Pont wealth?"[66]

Coleman's greatest liability, however, was probably himself. His own record in the Senate, marred by absenteeism and a vote against the bonus bill for World War I combat veterans, provided fuel for his adversaries. During the campaign Coleman even supported President Harding's veto of the bonus bill, although it is unclear how Coly reconciled the President's opposition to this "class legislation" with Harding's own giveaways to the oil industry or his own lobbying for Du Pont's dyes tariff bill that year. Coleman may well have succeeded in this feat of logic to his own satisfaction, but thousands of voters in Delaware remained unconvinced, especially when on October 28, only a little more than a week before the election, the federal government filed suit in Wilmington against the dyes monopoly held by the Du Pont-controlled Chemical Foundation.

At noon on November 9 the canvassing board in Wilmington showed Bayard ahead in both elections. Coly immediately filed a protest, but the final tally two days later proved that Bayard had won both terms, the short term by 60 votes, the long term by 325 votes.

Only the most naïve believed a new "people's day" had come to Delaware with the election, for Bayard was little different in his prejudices than his father, a former U.S. senator and secretary of state. And it came as no surprise to anyone when it was revealed that of the $6,125 Bayard had received in donations, all but $25 had come from his mother-in-law, Elizabeth Bradford du Pont, widow of Dr. Alexis du Pont, Coleman's cousin, and the very woman whom Alfred had sued years before for slandering his now deceased Alicia. Alfred too, it seems, was not immune to the rule that politics makes strange bedfellows.

His thirst for family revenge quenched, Alfred now began to consider leaving all the bitterness behind by leaving Delaware behind. That year he began building the new 125-foot steam yacht that was soon to take him to a new life, and family empire, in Florida.

5. IRÉNÉE'S SECRET WAR

In Du Pont's transition from powder to chemicals as its major product, the Twenties were the key years, years of a process of change which was not without its financial pains.

In 1919, despite its great diversification into chemicals and automobiles, Du Pont Company was still in possession of a multimillion dollar investment in powder-making capacities, factories which produced munitions requiring markets. With peace threatening to curtail the domestic market for war explosives, Pierre and Irénée cast their eyes abroad in search of overseas markets. Before the ink was even dry on the Versailles peace treaty, Du Pont had established its first arms export company.[67] Colonel William Taylor was put in charge of European sales, and ordered to contract agents throughout the continent. Europe, its face scarred by the war, was not to be left in peace.

Three years later, the same year Du Pont hired its first military sales agent in Poland, the Allies held the first of their many postwar disarmament conferences amid fevered rumors of German rearmament. And to Irénée's dismay, one of the central questions to be discussed was government control of the world chemical industry and trade.

C. K. Weston, Du Pont's publicity chief, was immediately dispatched to the capital. There, Weston succeeded in contacting Dr. Edgar Fahs Smith, whose name appeared on the list of delegates as a member of the technical staff in regard to chemical warfare. Weston soon was reporting back to Irénée that, as far as advisers to the disarmament commissioners were concerned, the situation was "well in hand."[68] By December, when the conference was in full session, Weston was working with Smith daily in handling publicity favorable to Du Pont interests,[69] and the central issue of government control was soon dropped by a conference subcommittee as "inadvisable." Not surprisingly, many delegates joined England's Lord Balfour in noting that the conference had sublimely accomplished nothing.[70]

By 1924 Du Pont had military sales agents in Sweden as well as Poland, while Taylor worked out of an office in Paris. Business, however, was still not up to Irénée's standards, for the Germans were already successful competitors of Du Pont's smokeless powder division in Europe. "A German-English group," reported Taylor years later, "were attempting to control the military supplies in Europe with a view to large profits through the future rearmament of the European nations which was destined to take place."[71]

The "German-English group" mentioned by Taylor were the great chemical firms Koln Rottweiler, A.G., and Nobel, Ltd. Irénée was familiar with both of these companies. As far back as 1897, Du Pont had signed the Jamesberg Agreement with these companies, dividing up the world munitions market like so many pieces of cake. In 1907 both companies were parties to another cartel agreement with Du Pont. Irénée was indeed familiar with these firms. In fact, the Du Ponts owned substantial blocks of stock in both of them.

On April 22, 1924, Taylor wrote Du Pont's vice-president for military sales, Major K. K. V. Casey, confirming German rearmament. This rearmament was in direct violation of Article 170 of the Versailles Treaty, which forbade the manufacture or importation of arms of any kind. The United States, although not a signer of the treaty, had included Article 170 by reference in its own peace treaty with Germany, stating that "Violation of articles 170 and 198 [which forbade Germany any military, naval, or air forces] by Germany would constitute, therefore, not only a violation of Germany's obligations to the other parties of the Treaty of Versailles, but also a violation of its treaty obligations to the United States."[72] The Du Ponts never officially informed the U.S. government of the German violations, for as annoyed as they were over the German competition, they were even more alarmed by new political developments in Geneva.

Taylor's letter was apparently not the only report of German rearmament. Rumors had grown so strong that the League of Nations felt compelled to announce plans for another disarmament conference the following year in Geneva. Irénée was well aware that the Geneva Conference, if successful, could undermine the entire world munitions market for all private corporate enterprise, including Du Pont. Clearly, this was not the time to squabble publicly and provide the peacemakers with ammunition. Instead, as this was an election year, this was the time to give over $34,000 in Du Pont family donations to the incumbent Republican administration.

Fortunately for the Du Ponts, this was one of the rare occasions when their characteristically narrow concerns about their own company coincided with the long-range vision of others in Washington for a more powerful United States. Led by Senator Henry Cabot Lodge, these political forces had more than one disagreement about a disarmament conference that would attempt to stop the arms race, set arms limitations, and thereby freeze the status quo of economic and military power in favor of Europe (which collectively would enjoy control over more arms and markets) rather than America. Such reservations were also held by many of the corporate "liberals" who controlled the scandal-rife White House of Harding and his equally incompetent successor, Calvin Coolidge. Next to Secretary of Treasury Andrew Mellon, magnate of banking, steel, and oil, the most powerful man in this circle was the secretary of commerce, Herbert Hoover.

Hoover saw the Geneva Conference as a possible impediment to the market expansion of American arms manufacturers. If American disarmament negotiators were to protect the market interests of American industry, they must be informed of corporate opinion. And what better way than to hear it from the war horse's mouth?

"You are invited," wrote Hoover to American arms manufacturers, "to send a representative to an informal preliminary conference to discuss the economic phases of the forthcoming Geneva Conference for the control of the International Trade in Arms, Munitions, and Implements of War. . . . It is important that the American representatives at Geneva be fully posted as to the views of American manufacturers of sporting arms and ammunitions, so that he may be able to safeguard their interests."[73]

Irénée was probably not surprised by this invitation. Although the Geneva Conference was supposed to be a secret, news of it had been leaked to him before the general public was told. But more importantly, the name of the secret U.S. delegates had also been leaked. Even before the formal announcement was made, Du Pont's lobbying machine had already been unleashed on Washington. K. K. V. Casey, Colonel Aiken Simons, A. Felix du Pont's maternal cousin, and W. J. Kinsman—all Du Pont executives

—had already had conferences with Admiral Andrew Long, Major General Ruggles, and the State Department's Allen Dulles, delegates to the Geneva Conference. General Ruggles had been approached a full eighteen days before his appointment was officially made. "As directed, I called on General G. L. Ruggles, Assistant Chief of Ordnance, who is to go to Geneva," reported Simons of his March 25 visit. "General Ruggles stated that the United States was committed on the policy of cooperation in the limitation program, and that the following license plan seemed to be the most harmless. . . . The War Department would take care that the Department of State protected such American industries . . . to which I replied that this had not been done heretofore. . . . General Ruggles then suggested that the license be put under the Department of Commerce [Hoover], which I agreed was better."[74]

Years later, at the Munitions Hearings, Irénée explained the company's preference for Hoover. "I should think that the Department of Commerce would be more competent to handle a commercial transaction, probably, than would the State Department";[75] the State Department was in favor of disarmament as part of a general strategy to win its political and economic objective without recourse to war. (The Du Ponts did not know that this was a design also held by Hoover.)

"Does it strike you as singular," Senator Clark asked Irénée at the same hearings, "that a delegate to the Geneva Conference, whose appointment was considered as being very secret, should be in close conference with your representative on the subject two weeks before his appointment was announced by the State Department?"

"All I can say," Irénée answered, "is that apparently he did."[76]

The April 1925 pre-conference in Washington was attended by every major arms manufacturer in the country. "The meeting was called to order by Secretary Hoover," Du Pont representatives reported back to Irénée, "who suggested that the representatives present express their views and that these views be put in writing and a committee be appointed to represent the interested industries at a later meeting, at which, it was hoped, that the delegates appointed by our government to attend the Geneva Conference would be present. . . . It was the unanimous opinion of the representatives of the industry that there were grave objections to the proposed draft in its present form."[77] "Mr. Hoover [was] very sympathetic and helpful throughout," recalled Simons three years later, "and with his assistance a call was sent to 36 other industries. . . . Resolutions were drafted showing the objections of the American manufacturers to the proposed international agreement. . . . It is believed by the action of Mr. Hoover in appointing this committee and the committee's subsequent work, the

Geneva Conference was prevented from adopting international agreements which would have been burdensome to American manufacturers, and so far as I know the committee has never been dissolved."[78]

Hoover was indeed helpful, pledging to the arms manufacturers that "he intended to have a system whereby all United States customs commissioners would have absolute instructions to issue licenses automatically upon presentation of a consular visa and that every effort would be made by the United States Government to eliminate red tape, delay, or hindrance. In the case of some large and purely military materials such as heavy guns, battleships, etc., it might be necessary to refer the matter to Washington but even then every effort would be made to eliminate delay or annoyance to the manufacturer."[79] Gone was any pretension about "sporting arms and ammunition." Now the subject was clearly in the area of big guns and battleships.

Gone also were any pretensions about preventing German rearmament. Allen Dulles, chief of the State Department's Near Eastern Division (and later head of the CIA), made it clear that in the control of arms traffic, the draft convention would have to ignore Germany's violations. "Coming to the article 32 which defined what countries should ratify the convention in order to make it effective, Mr. Dulles stated that notwithstanding the fact that it was known that Germany was exporting arms and munitions, it was not possible, from a diplomatic standpoint, to mention Germany or any of the Central Powers in this connection since they were supposed to abide by the treaties which put an end to the World War."[80] "Clearly," explained the Senate report on munitions in 1936, "the inference was that in order to swell the reparations fund, the Allies were winking at the German treaty violation."[81]

Although Du Pont and other American arms manufacturers were concerned about German arms competition, there was nothing that could be done to prevent it if Germany was to acquire the capital fuel to keep up its reparation payments to the Allies. Therefore, the State Department advised, U.S. arms manufacturers had better fend for themselves and protect their own economic ambitions now being threatened by the Disarmament Conference. To this cause, they were assured, the State Department would lend its assistance.

Predictably, the Disarmament Conference held two months later in Geneva was a complete failure. The real issue of government control of the world's chemical industry and trade was dropped, a subcommittee terming it "inadvisable." Hoover, urging a modification of regulations "too drastic and too unenforceable,"[82] had established a committee which put the views of the Du Ponts and other arms manufacturers into writing and then into the hands of U.S. delegates to the Geneva Conference. "These views," reported the Senate Munitions Committee in 1936, "were in large measure written into the Treaty for the supervision of trade in arms, signed at Geneva on June 17, 1925, and ratified 9 years later by the U.S. Senate."[83] The Senate needn't have bothered. By then it was too late. The nailed boots of fascism were already on the march.

"The munitions industry is on record that it [the disarmament accord] is a workable agreement," commented the Senate Munitions Committee, "and one that does not seriously interfere with its business."[84] It was a contradiction in terms.

"In reference to our conversation regarding the International Convention on the Trade in Munitions," Simons wrote in a company memorandum right after the Conference, "it may be of interest to you to hear that on my recent visit to Washington I saw a copy of the convention finally signed at Geneva, and it is not nearly as bad as we thought it might be. There will be some few inconveniences to the manufacturers of munitions in their export trade, but in the main they will not be hampered materially. . . ."[85] Significantly, Commerce Secretary Hoover was given the licensing power for such military trade with full Du Pont endorsement.

In 1929 Irénée contracted another sales agent in Europe, this one in Latvia. He also fought a secret price war with Dynamite Aktien Gesellschaft, later part of I. G. Farben, the giant German chemical combine, over a slice of the powder business in Mexico. As usual, Du Pont won. But Irénée had decided to win even if he lost this market to the Germans: in order to profit from German rearming and soften its market aggressiveness in Latin America, he invested $1,785,522 in I. G. Farben,[86] bought up 7.9 percent of the stock of both Dynamite Aktien Gesellschaft and Koln Rottweiler Pulverfabrikey, A. G., and with Britain's Nobel, set up an alliance with Badische Anilin to produce and sell his newest success—and scandal—tetraethyl gasoline.

6. DEEPWATER'S SILENT TERROR

On the southern edge of New Jersey, situated along the banks of the Delaware, was one of the strangest cities in the United States. Although nightly it cast a vast 6-square-mile panorama of blinking lights, this city had no mayor, no legal government at all. Although it was one of the country's busiest ports, it was not listed on nautical maps. Press releases were issued in its name, yet it had no post office.

This was Deepwater, a Du Pont "dyes" plant that had, not dyes, but poison gas as its main product. For some of its workers, however, between 1923 and 1925 its main product was death.

Deepwater was the result of a collaboration between Du Pont and General Motors, or, to be more precise, Irénée du Pont, president of Du Pont, and Pierre du Pont, president of General Motors and chairman of both companies. In 1922 General Motors researchers discovered that tetra-ethyl lead, when added to gasoline, could supposedly make one gallon do the work of two. But before G.M. even filed its patent application, Pierre informed Irénée of the discovery. By October 6 the brothers had signed an exclusive contract handing over the manufacture of its no-knock compounds to Du Pont, which was already producing the appropriate gases. Deepwater, publicly billed as a dye works, had become a complex of poison gas plants, producing phosgene and chlorine gases and the deadly benzol series. Already, strange rumors had begun to circulate in the area of "the House of Butterflies," the five-story brick building where workmen drew pictures of winged insects on the walls and paused to snatch at the empty air. On September 2, 1923, these rumors were capped by terror. Frank Durr, a 37-year-old man who had worked for Du Pont since he had been a lad of 12, suddenly died at his home in nearby Penns Grove, New Jersey. Listed by Du Pont as a "dyeworker," he, like many of his co-workers, had been recently plagued by frightful nightmares, and he died in a straight-jacket like a madman.

Yet there was silence, the kind of silence known only in a company town. Durr's wife was given a small $17 a week pension for only four years and Deepwater continued its deadly production without interruption, constantly striving to keep up with the new demands of Standard Oil's Bayway plant to the north.

Standard Oil joined Pierre's General Motors to form the Ethyl Gasoline Corporation in 1924. A fifty-fifty alliance, Ethyl Gasoline marketed the new "no-knock" power fuel treated with tetraethyl lead supplied by Du Pont. This arrangement created a boom in Du Pont's tetraethyl lead production. Just as Pierre was anticipating profits from the new firm, he was hit in October by screaming headlines. Five workers in Standard Oil's Bayway plant had suddenly gone violently insane, dying in raving delirium. Their deaths were attributed to fumes from Du Pont's tetraethyl lead, which the newspapers promptly condemned as "looney gas."

Efforts were quickly made to point out that only the year before the Bureau of Mines had given tetraethyl a clean bill of health. Then, to Pierre's embarrassment, it was revealed that General Motors had financed the Bureau's investigation. Furthermore, the deaths by poisoning of two workers at G.M.'s Canton, Ohio, plant were also exposed.

The country was in a furor. New York City health authorities forbade all ethyl gasoline sales, and cities across the country followed suit. Yet the spotlight fell only on Bayway and the Standard Oil/G.M. alliance. Deepwater, although the subject of many queries, escaped exposure. But when the discoverer of tetraethyl lead, Thomas Midgely, commented that "The Du Ponts have been having trouble, too," Irénée decided a statement was in order. "Tetraethyl lead is poisonous," he conceded, "and its manufacture involves risk, but no more so than many chemicals manufactured and used in enormously greater amounts. The Du Pont Company, during the experimental period, experienced much trouble with men becoming poisoned, even to the extent of fatalities. During the past year of production, when more than 100 men have been employed continuously, the difficulty has diminished steadily. In the past several months, under full production, only slight difficulties have been encountered."[87]

Irénée's "slight difficulties" assertion came just one week after the third death at Deepwater in three months: Joseph Cianci, a 24-year-old "dyeworker" and operator, had died on July 30, 1924; Frank Hanley, a 28-year-old "dyeworker," had died on August 12; and Sim Jones, a 47-year-old janitor, died on October 20. All died with the same "looney gas" symptoms; all died in Salem Memorial Hospital, which was only a 20-minute ambulance run from Deepwater.

Yet word of the deaths was not publicized until the following year. Wilmington's three daily newspapers, all owned by Pierre and Irénée's Christiana Securities, failed to report the deaths. Salem also was silent. The editor of its major newspaper was also the president of Salem Hospital, which, while being a public tax-free institution, owed its electric laundry system and a good part of its revenue to the Du Ponts. The Du Ponts made donations annually and often paid for the treatment of patients from Deepwater three times as much as the hospital received from the Salem city budget; the budget, in turn, allegedly received as much as 50 percent of its tax revenue from the Du Ponts. No one in Salem, therefore, questioned why a Du Pont executive from Deepwater was also on Salem Memorial's Board of Managers. Nor did anyone question why no coroner's inquest was ever held about Deepwater's strange deaths. Dr. E. C. Lyon, Salem's county physician, between praises of the Du Ponts' care for their men, explained why to a national magazine writer: "No, it was not an accident. It was an occupational disease and there is no occasion to call in the coroner."[88]

Another such case of "occupational disease" was John Demesse. Demesse, a plumber, died with "looney gas" symptoms at Delaware Hospital in Wilmington after doing some work in the Deepwater plants. The hospital listed the death as typhoid. Mrs. Mary Casey, a cousin, who spoke with the attending doctor, recalled that "He said there were typhoid germs in the body, but that John's lead poisoning didn't help him any."[89] Efforts by *Nation*'s investigating reporter to reach the physician, Dr. Lawrence J. Rigney, were futile. Curiously enough, it was not he, but a member of the hospital staff, Dr. John Russo, who signed the death certificate. Russo, when questioned, claimed to have no recollection of the case and reported later that he could find no record of it in the hospital. The death certificate, furthermore, gave no contributory cause of death, nor was the question, "Where was disease contracted if not at place of death?" ever answered. The space was left blank.

Another case was that of Charles Hendricks, a painter, who became delirious and tried to kill himself by jumping off a ferry crossing the Delaware between Deepwater and his Delaware home. Still another was Harry Baker, who jumped out of a window at Salem Memorial after being taken there from Deepwater. Baker was caught and returned to bed. But, for once, publicity got out, and he was whisked off to a private sanitarium at Gladwyn, Pennsylvania, his bills paid by the Du Ponts and his wife given a small allowance.

Still, Irénée had his ever-willing publicity director, C. K. Weston, insist that "illnesses have gradually decreased since the early stages of the work."[90] The reality, however, was the opposite. "To scores of poisonings at Bayway," reported Silas Bent, *Nation* writer, "there had been hundreds at Deepwater. A physician who worked there during but half of the period of production told me he himself handled hundreds of cases."[91] Many had actually been poisoned only to be treated and sent back to the poorly ventilated plant to be poisoned again and again.

On February 13 Frederick DeFiebre, a 21-year-old "dyemaker," became the fourth of Irénée's "slight difficulties" to die at Salem Memorial. Nothing was said about it. Three days later another "dyemaker," Robert Huntsinger, died in a straightjacket, grinning and gritting his teeth, at Cumberland County Hospital for the Insane at Bridgeton, New Jersey, his home. This time, far enough from Deepwater's curtain of silence, the news was carried even in the New York papers, and Weston was forced to concede the death in a twelve-line item printed in the Wilmington papers.

Then, only a week later, on February 28 Loring M. Boody, a 53-year-old carpenter, died at Carney's Point, New Jersey, an industrial town of one-story cottages owned and policed by the Du Ponts. Dr. Lee, a Du Pont Company physician, attributed Boody's death partly to uremic poisoning. But at this point no one believed it, especially since Boody's friend and co-worker, James Connell, had come down with "looney gas" symptoms only the day before Boody's death. Connell never returned to Deepwater. A month later, on March 27, he too died.

By this time the deaths had become too blatant to ignore. Deepwater was closed. Du Pont headquarters released a statement mentioning that the deaths of Boody and Connell had inspired the company "to make modifications to insure greater manufacturing safety," while news items reported "some difficulties in the experimental stage" but "none within the past few months." Actually, the plant had been ordered closed by New Jersey's Labor Commissioner, Dr. Andrew McBride. After five weeks of "mechanical readjustments," including a new $60,000 ventilating system, McBride allowed the plant to reopen only to see it closed shortly thereafter pending a federal investigation by the U.S. Surgeon General. With 300 million gallons of ethyl gasoline already having been distributed throughout twenty-eight states, and after the highly publicized strange death of a garage mechanic in Weston, West Virginia, federal intervention was necessary to avoid a national panic.

Altogether, in eighteen months over 300 Du Pont workers had been stricken, not including those slightly poisoned and cases of hysteria from anxiety. Eight workers had died, four of them in Salem Memorial Hospital, three in a single month. Although there were some cries of voluntary manslaughter and murder, no charges were pressed against Du Pont management. Instead, the case went to the inner circle of Coolidge, the recipient only two years before of over $34,000 in election donations from Irénée and Lammot du Pont, and the acknowledged guardian of corporate interests. Surely the billion dollar industry was the subject of much concern.

In January 1926, a year after the last Deepwater deaths, now a distant memory, Coolidge's Surgeon General, Hugh S. Cumming, released his report. Although labeled an occupational hazard, tetraethyl gasoline was okayed for use as a motor fuel. Four months later Irénée reopened the Deepwater plant. His faith in the Republican Party upheld, he also wrote out a personal check for $37,500 to its campaign treasury. According to the Senate Munitions Committee's *Report* in 1936, his was the only Du Pont donation that year.

The embarrassed withdrawal of Standard Oil from the tetraethyl production during the investigation left the field to Du Pont. Du Pont continued its production of tetraethyl lead, and through the Ethyl Corporation, the Du Ponts policed the pricing of all gasoline companies (except Sun, which had its own process) through a monopoly of the anti-knock compound that it sold to refiners. Among the conditions for a franchise or license, for example, was the maintenance of a two-cent differential on the sale of so-called "premium" gasoline over regular. The monopoly was effective up to 1940.[92]

And what of Deepwater's silent terror? The company's annual report of 1936 explained that the Deepwater deaths were "no sudden holocaust, due to the neglect of precautions," but rather the "slow and gradual toll which humanity has always paid, and perhaps must always pay, for the conquest of new and dangerous ground." By then, tetraethyl lead production was returning $3.5 million in clear profit every year.

Meanwhile, "the House of Butterflies" continued its output of other deadly gases, seldom releasing its casualty reports. As one former Du Pont physician once remarked, "But why make all this fuss about tetra lead? The Du Ponts make other poisons in there in even greater quantity which kill a man like that!" (He snapped his fingers.) "And those plants are still going full blast."[93]

7. THE GOLDEN DECADE

Except perhaps for the decade of 1952–1962, the Twenties remain the golden years of the Du Pont saga; and the five years from 1924 to 1929, despite the tragic scandal of Deepwater, were perhaps the most rewarding half-decade that Delaware's first family ever experienced. These were the years when their political power almost equaled their enormous economic power, making the Du Ponts—perhaps for the first and last time—even seem progressive, raising the family's national prestige to new heights.

For Pierre's intimate circle, these were the years of legal victories in the courts and elected offices in Delaware. First, Wilmington's Judge Hugh Morris in January 1924 dismissed the weak federal challenge against the Chemical Foundation, Du Pont's conduit for obtaining German dye patents. Morris even praised the Foundation's officers for their conduct during "the test of actual trial," and concluded that "the evidence is overwhelming that they [the patents] were and are without substantial value to American citizens."[94] How Morris reconciled this statement with Irénée's cries that national security was at stake and the patents' worth of $17 million remains one of the great mysteries of U.S. judicial history. "The sale was in effect to America and its citizens," Morris held in his circle of contradictions, "not to those then engaged in chemical and allied industries."[95]

This, of course, was the government's argument for public ownership; but according to Morris's "Delaware reasoning," where "public" is synonymous with "Du Pont Company," this was an argument for Du Pont ownership. Francis Garvin, the former federal Alien Property Custodian who had handed over the bulk of the 5,700 patents to the Du Pont's Chemical Foundation, of which he was also president, saw defeated Germany behind the U.S. government prosecution. "I and my associates are very much gratified. But this is only one more victory in a struggle which has been going on now for six years and will go on for many years more before our country has become chemically independent. Germany does not intend, even though this decision is a setback, to give up her attempts to regain her world monopoly. . . . This is a bitter, many-fronted battle for the national defense, industrial progress, and freedom from diseases of our children and our children's children."[96] Thus, by this reasoning, the U.S. government, victorious conquerors of Germany in war, had become pawns of the defeated nation in peace, and by one stroke of Judge Morris's hand, the Du Ponts became the champions of American progress and the world's sick. It was judicial absurdity without historical parallel.

While Pierre had much to celebrate, his arch foe and cousin, Alfred, was not so fortunate with the courts. Alfred had tried to avoid paying income taxes on additional stock gains from Pierre's profitable 1915 reorganization of the company. Having filed his return before March 15, 1915, and not having been assessed for the stock until the Bureau of Internal Revenue caught up with him in December 1919, Alfred claimed that the three-year period for additional assessment had already expired. He stubbornly fought the case through all the federal courts, right up to the Supreme Court. There, he met the scowling face of an old adversary—William Taft.

As President, Taft had been humbled by Alfred in 1911 during negotiations over Du Pont's anti-trust conviction. A year later he lost many of Delaware's votes when Alfred first opposed his renomination at the Republican Convention and then bolted to the Democratic Party's slate in Delaware.

After his presidential defeat to Wilson in 1912, Taft had returned to his law practice. In 1921 Harding's Attorney General, Harry Daugherty, urged Taft's appointment as Chief Justice of the Supreme Court in order to reorganize the courts to facilitate the government's prosecution of the labor movement, at that time rising in response to the post-war recession. Daugherty's arguments fulfilled Taft's long-held judicial dream, and as Chief Justice, the ex-president led the court in a swing to the right, invalidating many labor laws.

Alfred had few friends in Washington when his case finally came before the Court in 1923, but he had an ample supply of enemies. In the Court, the maverick Republican faced Taft and three other Harding appointees. He also had to confront Charles Evans Hughes, now in the powerful office of secretary of state; Hughes had backed Pierre's legal struggle against Alfred in 1915 with a pamphlet, allegedly in return for $50,000 worth of Pierre's gratitude. Alfred had also not done much to win Coleman's favor, helping in his election defeat the previous year, and Coleman was a member of Harding's powerful inner circle. Alfred justifiably suspected his cousin would "do everything he can to prevent a revision [in my favor] and I am not sure that [Senator Lewis] Ball is not working with him."[97]

The decision was predictable. On May 22, 1923, Taft ordered Alfred to pay $1,576,015 in taxes and sue for recovery afterwards, if he preferred. Alfred waived the meaningless right to a futile recovery suit in exchange for the Treasury's writing off of $200,000 worth of interest. His final payment came to $1,694,207. Fortunately, by then his Du Pont stock and other corporate holdings had risen in value with the new prosperity, securing his fortune. Yet the Court decision may well have been one factor in Alfred's resigning from active politics in Delaware and leaving the field free to his ever-watchful and ever-ambitious cousin, T. Coleman du Pont.

"P.S., Irénée, and Company," commented Alfred, "seem to forget that their day is past and that no individual . . . can dictate to the people. My work is bearing its natural fruit. Of course, the vote of Delaware is always close and they may be able to spend enough money to divide the Republican ticket, but that is about all."[98] With scandals ripping through the Republican administration and Harding's mysterious death, Alfred never thought Coleman would be audacious enough to run again on a Republican ticket. He was wrong, as usual underestimating his wily kin.

Through Colonel Henry's persuasions on weak Calvin Coolidge, the new President, Coleman retained his position as Republican National Committeeman. Then Coly was given the senatorial nomination, while the Democrats picked one of his supporters to remove the "Dirty Deal" of 1921 as a campaign issue. In November 1924 Coly rode the Coolidge landslide into his long-sought goal—the U.S. Senate. Irénée wrote Alfred that the result reflected his nonparticipation in the contest. Alfred replied that he hoped this could mend old family ties. After almost twelve bitter years, Alfred was finally tiring of feuding.

"Dear Alfred," wrote an appreciative Coleman, "I would like you to feel that, if there is anything I could do for you or for your interests in Washington, you will not hesitate to call on me."[99]

A little more than a year later Alfred received a check for close to $2 million from the Treasury Department of Andrew Mellon. The Internal Revenue Bureau, upon Alfred's request, was refunding $1,461,979 of his 1918 tax returns, plus $499,618 in interest. For the first time, Alfred was enjoying the wind blowing in from Washington.

The generator of this new wind was Andrew Mellon, the secretary of treasury appointed in 1921 by Harding and continued by Coolidge. Mellon was no mere appointee of financial-industrial wealth. Rather, as much as John Rockefeller, he *was* that wealth—the wealth of the Aluminum Company of America (which paid a dividend of 1,000 percent in 1921); the wealth of Mellon National Bank, one of the largest in the country; the wealth of Gulf Oil Company, one of the largest oil firms in the world. More than the White House, it was Mellon's Treasury Department that was the core of domestic government in the early and middle Twenties. Until his appointment, wholesale tax rebates were unheard of. Under Mellon, remissions, rebates, and reductions amounted to over $6 billion, filling eight folio volumes totaling 10,000 pages. While failing to block any tax loopholes and actually reducing by 60 percent the tax revenue taken in from incomes of more than $300,000, Mellon also used the plea of stopping tax evasion to pass his Revenue Act of 1921. This law totally eliminated the excess profits tax passed during the war, saving corporate stockholders another $1.5 billion a year. Mellon gave $27 million back to U.S. Steel (in which he had large stock holdings), $91,472 to the Mellon banks in Pittsburgh, and even $404,000, his second largest personal refund (John D. Rockefeller got $457,000), to himself. During his tenure, over $7 million in Treasury refunds went to Mellon's personal account, $14 million to his Aluminum Company.

Under Mellon's encouragement, the maximum surtax on incomes from $2 million upward was reduced in 1921 from 65 percent to 50 percent. In 1924 he introduced another bill, proposing a further reduction to 25 percent. This was too much even for a subservient Congress, and a Senate investigation was launched, headed by Senator James Cousens of Michigan. Coolidge, under Mellon's tutoring, drafted a letter of rebuke to the Senate, and a storm of protest broke. As recipients of Mellon's favor, the Du Ponts leaped to his defense.

"Their recent actions are as bad as anything in red Russia," Irénée told the *New York Times* while boarding the luxury liner *Aquitania* for a European cruise. "It is time to call a halt. The idea that the Senate should take exception to President Coolidge's note and even suggest that it be expunged from the record is the most preposterous thing that has happened in Washington."[100]

Pierre also jumped into the act, supporting Mellon's contention that great wealth in America is not dangerous as it is in other countries, since inheritances do not go to single individuals, but are spread out throughout families. There are 160 Du Ponts, Pierre claimed, and he denied published reports that his cousin, Alexis I. du Pont, was worth over $30 million when he died in 1921. Pierre, of course, failed to mention that of those 160 Du Ponts, only he, his two brothers, and cousins Alfred and Coleman possessed the real power of the family fortune. Wealth, the Du Pont family's own history had shown, did not break up, but tended to aggregate.

Mellon's bill was defeated that year. The House even threatened to include an amendment raising the inheritance tax on great wealth. "Carried to an excess," the Secretary angrily retorted, "they differ in no way from the methods of the revolutionists in Russia."[101]

Saved from "the perils of socialism," Mellon's tax policies played a large role in fueling the dangerous speculative boom of 1924–1929, releasing many funds for which there was no constructive economic outlet.

The Du Ponts, however, found imaginative ways to spend their money. Some sixty Du Pont households in and around Wilmington turned Delaware into their private playground. Roaring through towns and countryside in speedy roadsters or swooping overhead in colorful airplanes, these 300 Du Ponts totally dominated the state's social life. Under the urging of Senator T. Coleman du Pont, "the hero of roads" who founded the state's highway department, Delaware became the site of an extensive paved-road building program.

Many of those roads led to the twenty-four Du Pont estates that surrounded Wilmington. Here was Bessie Gardner du Pont's "Chevannes," Eugene's "Owl's Nest," Francis I.'s "Louviers," Victor's "Guyencourt," Edmond's "Centerville," and Irénée's magnificent "Granogue." Here were the estates of Ernest du Pont, A. Felix du Pont, S. Hallock du Pont, Mrs. Philip du Pont, and many others, including those of in-laws, the Copelands, Lairds, Bayards, Carpenters, Sharps, and Mays.

Here old Colonel Henry tinkered away in his 180-room Winterthur, writing on the subject that fascinated him most, his own family. During the Twenties, Colonel Henry wrote four books: *Story of Huguenots* (1920), *Early Generation of the Du Ponts and Allied Families* (1923), *Campaign of 1864 in Valley of Virginia* (1925), *Rear Admiral Samuel F. Du Pont, U.S.N.* (1926)—before dying at the age of 88 in his 35-room Washington mansion facing Massachusetts Avenue, on December 31, 1926.

His son, Henry F., who was at his deathbed, got the bulk of Colonel Henry's estate. Two years later William du Pont, Jr., reaped the bulk of *his* father's estate also. Old Willie had survived the Colonel's bitter threat to keep him out of the family cemetery, and now his bones rest next to those of his kin at Sand Hole Woods.

Here also in the outskirts of Wilmington was Alfred's reopened Nemours, ready for the "Count" 's occasional visits, its glass-chipped walls as foreboding as ever to Pierre's kin. And here, of course, was Pierre's 200-room Longwood, the envy of Europe's royal houses, built atop the site of the old Anvill Tavern, in whose cellar was carried on a thriving bootleg slavery trade. Now six acres of land were housed under glass, where peaches, apricots, nectarines, and melons thrived that would honor a king's banquet. In these winter gardens, warmth was provided for Pierre's flourishing South African violets, his exotic kumquats, banana and guava plants, papaya, Indian mango, Arabian coffee bush, and even coconut palms.

It was from these regal heights that Pierre accepted Alfred's public challenge that "our whole school system is archaic and lifeless from lack of funds."[102] In fact, Black children were being taught in sheds, suffering from a law on Delaware's books since after the Civil War that prohibited taxing whites to build schools for Black children. White schools were little better in terms of quality education. Twenty percent of all Delaware youths, both black and white, could not even write their own names.

Pierre had himself appointed to the State Board of Education and revised the school code, curbing local powers which controlled funds and the selection of texts. He then demanded that local districts pay half the cost of a new construction program. "What does Du Pont care if you go bankrupt," thundered the opposition. These adversaries, made up mostly of rural landowners who still needed large tenant families to work their lands, were no competition for the industrial-financial power which Pierre represented. The needs of Delaware's high-technology chemical companies for a literate working class would not be frustrated by rural landlords who were fighting a losing battle to preserve the old agricultural society. That way of life was already being smashed by Coleman du Pont's roads and farming machines that increasingly eliminated field jobs and sent the unemployed to Wilmington in search of work. Nor would the Du Pont family—living in a precarious luxury surrounded by growing poverty and restlessness, and depending on Wilmington's atmosphere of social stability for the smooth functioning of their executives—be denied their measure of social control through a rationalized educational system they could dominate.

The school districts were forced to bend, while Pierre personally paid out over $4 million to replace 100 dilapidated schools. He became a national sensation as "the hero of education." Pierre enjoyed the title and merely took the sum off his taxes.

Cousin Willie was not so fortunate in the tax area. He spent huge sums to construct not schools, but Bellevue, his palatial estate near Wilmington complete with two private race tracks and a stable of some of the country's finest mounts. As if that were not enough, Willie had three other estates: one at Newton Square, Pennsylvania; his Hopeton plantation near Brunswick, Georgia; and Montpelier, the estate of James Madison, in Virginia. Willie was Delaware's number one taxpayer in 1924 at $250,000.

Right behind him in second place was his cousin Coleman du Pont, at $160,000. Both learned the hard way Pierre's lesson that it was better to give than to have to pay.

It was in response to this tax burden that Pierre assumed an even greater political role. In 1925 Coleman had his crony, Governor Robinson, appoint Pierre to the post of income tax collector. Under Delaware law, all income taxes went to Pierre's pet project, the public school system. *Outlook,* a national magazine secretly financed by James Stillman, president of National City Bank, hailed this coalition of power between school builder Pierre and his cousin Coleman, "the exponent of good roads in the state": "It will be a case of expert knowledge both in school matters and road building, and of business genius applied to collecting taxes, which up until now have never been satisfactorily gathered. . . . The eyes of education all over the country have been on Mr. du Pont for some time, and this will increase the interest felt in his plans and methods."[103]

Pierre's methods were more than "satisfactory"—tracking down tax delinquents, including many poor in the state who simply couldn't afford to pay, and hauling them into court. By Pierre's third term as tax collector, Delaware ranked tenth in the country in literacy rate, Du Pont-controlled schools providing the hope for upward social mobility that helped dissipate social unrest and labor militancy in the state. "In Delaware schools," reported one contemporary biographer, "the children chirp George Washington, Abraham Lincoln, and Pierre du Pont in the same breath."[104] Pierre's compulsory education had made its mark.

Not everyone was caught by Pierre's tax witch hunts however. One of those who escaped was his own cousin, Alfred. In fact, between 1920 and 1926 Alfred paid no income tax at all. Then he left the state.

Alfred, it seems, was trying to bridge old family rifts, not only to Coleman and others, but also to his immediate family. In April 1927 Jessie arranged a triumphant reunion at Nemours between him and his daughter Victorine and son Alfred Victor.

Alfred V. had never forgiven his father for the charges of infidelity laid on his mother, Bessie Gardner du Pont. Despite being disinherited for siding with his mother, young Alfred V. was still his father's son. During a summer vacation from Yale, he took his very first job—as a strikebreaker for the Pennsylvania Railroad, on whose board his cousin Pierre sat as a director. After graduation from Yale, Irénée gave Alfred V. a manager's post at the Du Pont works at Louviers, Colorado. There he married Marcella Miller, Denver society belle and sister of Helen Edward Stokes of New York fame and fortune. In April 1927 while serving in Wyoming at Du Pont's Barksdale Mills, he traveled to Wilmington to confront cousin

Lammot with a demand for greater opportunity. Lammot turned him down, and he resigned from Du Pont convinced that he had inherited his father's curse from the family.

It was then that young Alfred sought and got a reconciliation with his father. Three years later, when he established an architectural firm in Wilmington with a young gifted French partner, Gabriel Massena, his first commission came from his father. This was no small gift. Alfred V. was to build an elaborate sunken garden for Nemours that would rival that of Versailles. By then, Alfred V. was also enjoying a $12,000 annual income from a bequest of some of Dad's stocks.

The same month that he reconciled with his family, Alfred, Sr., decided to leave Delaware. With the shrewd help of Jessie's brother, Ed Ball, Alfred's finances were now solid. He had lost over $12 million by refusing to enter his Nemours Trading Corporation into bankruptcy. But now his conscience was clear to enjoy the rest of his money in other speculations.

One of these was Florida. As early as 1923 his interest had been captured by Jessie's purchase of a $33,000 beach-front property in Miami Beach. Despite his prophecies of doom over the Florida land boom, Alfred tinkered with the idea of purchasing a million dollar estate at Coconut Grove, but was dissuaded by Jessie. Occasionally, he would come across Coly, who was also involved in the land boom, and these encounters may well have whetted his appetite for speculation.

Finally, in January 1926, the sales frenzy began to slow and the speculative dynamo began to grind to a halt. Jessie sold her property in time, reaping a $132,000 profit. Then came the Florida crash in March, prices collapsing, money scarce, banks failing, speculators unable to pay for land they had not intended to keep. About a month later, on April 5, Alfred ended his waiting.

Alfred bought four river-front lots on the St. John's River for $100,000 and began the construction of a mansion that was described at the time as "one of the most pretentious in the Jacksonville area."[105] Named Epping Forest, after an old Ball family Virginia homestead, the two-story mansion was a seven-bedroom hacienda complete with fountains and docks for Alfred's boats and yacht. From there, Alfred could travel twenty miles up the river to the busy port of Jacksonville, where his new office was located in the Barrett National Bank Building.

By then Alfred had quietly bought up 66,081 acres of timberland in northern Florida, and 800 lots in the fishing village of Carrabelle. At the depressed prices of the crash, the total cost was only $808,311. The following year he bought control of the Florida National Bank of Jacksonville, the first in a series of banks that would eventually dot the map of Florida.

"You will doubtless be surprised at my taking this step," he wrote Delaware tax commissioner P. S. du Pont of his renunciation of Delaware citizenship, "but . . . I had no other course left to pursue. The golden tentacles of the wealthy class have been quietly laying hold of the whole state of Delaware. They have managed to control every office, both in the state and in the city of Wilmington."[106]

Soon Florida too would be held in the grasp of golden tentacles—those of Alfred du Pont. But the story of the Du Pont empire in Florida—a story encompassing the modern history of Florida—will be recounted later.

Alfred was not the only Du Pont to enter new fields of investment or move beyond the Brandywine. The adventurous Coly was rumored to be a heavy speculator in Mexican oil lands. Gentle-natured Francis I. du Pont used his experience in explosives to set up three firms, the Delaware Chemical Engineering Company, the Ball Grain Explosives Company (manufacturing fuses for military explosives), and the U.S. Flashless Powder Company, in which he was joined by Ernest, Archibald, and E. Paul du Pont. Paul du Pont took to automobiles, manufacturing a car which he appropriately named the "Du Pont"; as he was unable to secure finances from Alfred or any other source, his venture could not stand up to the competition from such giants as Pierre's Chevrolet and soon folded. Later, E. Paul du Pont would have better luck as president of the Indiana Motorcycle Company, anticipating and capturing a market that grew out of a popular fad of the Thirties.

Many of the Du Ponts took apartments in Paris, Rome, and New York. New York was Coleman's roosting place. Here he rode like a king through the teeming streets of the world's largest city in a chauffeured limousine which bore the prestigious "P.D." (police department) license plate. This license plate, one of 250 issued to bankers, millionaires, contractors and corporation heads, allowed the General to enjoy special traffic privileges in a city where most of the working population had just enough to eat, never mind privileges. When an investigation was launched into this undemocratic practice in 1925, the Delaware Senator explained that he had been a Special Deputy Police Commissioner for the last five years and had "taken an active interest in police affairs during that time," including the study of "European police systems with a view to improving conditions in New York."[107]

Coleman's privileges and studies continued throughout the Twenties. Despite his famous habit of distributing gold coins to New York's "finest," it seems Coleman du Pont, a director of Bankers Trust Company, was taking no chances on retaining armed state power in the most efficient manner possible.

Besides Coleman, who had a new estate on the Hudson River, only a few Du Ponts actually bought estates outside Wilmington and these usually served as only seasonal homes away from their Wilmington estates. Lammot du Pont, to whom Pierre gave his mother's Wilmington estate, St. Amours, also bought a summer estate on fashionable Fisher's Island off Long Island, paneling it with thousands of dollars worth of woodwork from the finest old homestead mansions of the Eastern shore of Maryland. His brother Irénée bought a winter estate on the north coast of Cuba's Mananzas Province, which he named Xanadu, after the fabled kingdom of Coleridge's "Kubla Khan." Soon the Du Pont Xanadu was to have legends of its own.

Not only estates, but also yachts were a symbol of the Du Ponts during the Twenties. The Delaware family owned more of them than any other family in America. Irénée owned the 60-foot-long *Icacos;* Lammot, his 76-foot *Nemea;* A. Felix, Jr., his 73-foot *Orthia;* E. Paul, his 58-foot *Theano;* Ernest, his 74-foot *Edris* and 38-foot *Ponjola;* Eugene E., his 50-foot *High Tide;* Henry B., his 54-foot *Nor' Easter;* Henry F., his 35-foot *Sea Urchin;* Coly, his *Tech I, Tech II,* and *Tech III;* his son Francis V., his 84-foot *Tech Jr.;* and Alfred, his 125-foot *Nenemoosha* and the 101-foot *Gadfly,* the last one for scurrying over Florida swamps. Du Pont in-laws also steamed through the high seas, Donaldson Brown of G.M. in his 149-foot *Oceania,* Ruly Carpenter in his 121-foot *Galaxy,* and his brother, Walter Carpenter (then Du Pont treasurer and married to a former Du Pont governess) in his 65-foot *Grey Gull.*

During the Twenties, major newspapers often ran stories of the gay times enjoyed by the rich on their yachts. In 1924, for example, Coleman du Pont's fishing trip with his son and two friends off the Florida coast was duly carried by the *New York Times,* as if Coly's landing of a 600-pound shark rivaled in heroics and importance the world-shaking events of the day. Again, in 1927, when E. Paul's wife slipped off a bobbing yacht into the Delaware River and had to swim to shore, her feat was recorded by history.

Some of the family were infected with the aviation craze sweeping the country since Lindbergh's flight and became early pioneers of the new industry. Henry B. du Pont owned the first private plane licensed by the Department of Commerce. Richard C. du Pont, son of A. Felix du Pont, was so fascinated with soaring planes that he became one of the country's leading experts on gliders, while his brother, A. Felix, Jr., casually flew by plane every day to work in Camden, New Jersey, where he inspected aviation finishes in the paint department.

In 1927 Henry B. opened the Du Pont Airport just outside Wilmington, and rumors soon reached New York that Giuseppe M. Bellanca, one of the world's foremost designers of monoplanes, was being lured to Wilmington from his Staten Island plant. The Du Ponts were offering a landing field with 1,100 feet of Delaware River frontage and a complete factory on 350 acres of land only fifteen minutes from the Du Pont Hotel. By the following January the rumors were confirmed with the announcement that the Italian-born designer, after failing to interest Henry Ford, had accepted the presidency of a $1 million company established by Henry B. du Pont. "Businessmen here," commented the *New York Times,* "consider it significant that members of the group so closely identified with General Motors, the greatest rival of Henry Ford, should be following him into the aircraft industry."[108] "Significant" was an understatement. Henry B.'s Atlantic Aviation became the largest business aircraft sales and service organization in the world, spurring Henry's substantial investments in helping develop Trans World Airlines, North American Aviation, and Bendix Aviation.

Henry B. du Pont's airport often became a center of suspense in the late Twenties. Once in 1928 A. Felix, Jr., who had joined the Army Air Corps, was overdue in a flight home from his Texas training camp. A mist had developed near Wilmington, and, as these were the days before electronic guidance systems, the waiting Du Ponts were frantic with worry. Finally, Felix's father could stand the suspense no longer; he mounted a plane and flew off into the clouds in search of his son. High above the field, Felix peered through the clouds, anxious over added dangers that would come with night. Then just as dusk approached, the white and gold plane of young Du Pont was sighted.

Another incident, although of a less personal nature, occurred a year later. Charles Lindbergh, the famous "lone eagle," flew in for a secret conference with the Du Pont Company. The subject was a revolutionary new idea—rocket power. At the Du Pont headquarters Lindbergh explained that black powder could be used in solid-propellant rockets. He tried to capture their interest by suggesting some immediate practical application. "Now, we could develop a rocket that could be attached to a plane for the purpose of giving it one minute of thrust in case of engine failure on takeoff, thus avoiding having to land it in a city or in trees."[109]

The Du Ponts were openly dubious, expressing the opinion that there seemed no future in rockets connected with airplanes. A month later Lindbergh received a final letter of rejection, which claimed that "to equal the thrust of one minute of a Wasp engine would require about 400 pounds of black powder, and the heat would be so intense that the powder would have to be burned in a fire-brick combustion chamber."[110]

What escaped the Du Ponts, however, was the possibility of *liquid* propellant, which needed a metal lining only 1/32 of an inch thick. Goddard, "the father of modern rocketry," knew this and, after talking with Lindbergh, visited Wilmington the day before Thanksgiving and was interviewed by three Du Pont laboratory men.

"I realized soon," he wrote shortly thereafter, "that the object of this questioning was . . . to find every last detail of the rocket I have developed during the last nine years, and after I saw this I avoided further questions as to these construction details, as much as possible."[111] "All Goddard took away from it was the conviction," wrote one author, "that the Du Pont people, far from being interested in underwriting his work, were only interested in picking his brain."[112] Goddard left Wilmington, turning instead to the Guggenheims for support.

This loss due to crude greed was perhaps the only economic opportunity missed by the Du Ponts during the presidency of Lammot du Pont. Stern and somber Lammot had succeeded to Irénée's position in 1926, when the company's structural reorganization had been completed to meet its expansion into new fields of chemicals, following Pierre's formula of management-decentralization/financial-centralization.

Although his abruptness had not made him renowned for popularity among his subordinates, Lammot still possessed a talent for detecting the crucial point in any proposition, and he applied this talent to his market concern for General Motors as well as Du Pont.

Soon after Lammot's succession, the Du Ponts fully indulged in the speculative craze distinguishing that period. Although most of their speculation was for long-term investment purposes relating to the company's market needs, one situation was the exception. In 1926 the Du Ponts harvested $44 million in G.M. business.[113] Then in February 1927 Pierre sold $25 million worth of G.M. preferred stock. The unloading of so much stock on the market triggered criticism from angry brokers, analysts, and even G.M. stockholders.

Pierre, however, was also buying as well as selling. Pierre's concern for his immediate family's ability to retain control of the country's gunpowder business prompted him to spend $2 million in 1922 for 16,500 shares of Atlas Powder, one of the 1911 spin-off companies in which cousin Coleman had also invested. Pierre used his Christiana Securities for this investment, and the following year, knowing that he would be without an heir, transferred 49,000 shares of Christiana and 24,000 shares of Du Pont to a new holding company, Delaware Realty and Investment Corporation, the stock of which he divided into eight equal shares among his brothers and sisters. Still, Pierre's fear of Coleman urged him on to further Atlas investments.

By 1923 Christiana Securities—in which his immediate family owned a 60 percent interest and thereby 30 percent of Du Pont and 35 percent of G.M.—controlled 49,500 out of Atlas's 261,438 outstanding stock. Of this, however, 33,000 was nonvoting stock, and Pierre continued to worry over Coleman's share of this prosperous company. His concern eased in April 1927, when Coleman, tired of business, agreed to sell him 21,071 shares at $60 apiece. Thus, in 1927, 70,000 shares of Atlas Powder was firmly in Du Pont hands.

During that year the Du Ponts spied another prize—United States Rubber Company, the country's largest producer of industrial rubber. Irénée, W. W. Laird, Sr., Henry Dowds, and eleven other family members or company directors purchased 97,750 shares of U.S. Rubber's stock. The following June a second Du Pont syndicate, which included Pierre, bought an additional 154,750 shares. By then the Du Ponts held, through personal syndicates and the Du Pont Company, a total 18 percent of U.S. Rubber's common (324,516 shares) and 11 percent of its preferred (75,619). Wilmington Trust was named as the trustee for 150,425 shares held by Irénée, Lammot, and Henry B.

With this 29 percent control, the Du Ponts installed one of their own company executives, Francis B. Davis, as U.S. Rubber's president and chairman to watch over an international rubber empire that stretched from the Malaya forests to the hills of Dutch Java and included thousands of de facto slave laborers.

In 1910 U.S. Rubber had secured a concession from the Dutch colonial regime in Sumatra. By 1928 it owned 104,000 acres throughout the Dutch East Indies and another 30,821 acres in Malaya; of these, 87,000 acres were planted and harvested by Indonesian or Malayan labor at slave wages. In 1927, the year of the first Du Pont investment, U.S. Rubber produced 25,677,000 pounds of the 35,484,997 total grown production of American corporations.[114] U.S. Rubber eventually became an important market for Du Pont's neoprene. General Motors, in turn, became a captive market for U.S. Rubber's tires. In January 1931 G.M. signed a contract that provided for half of its tires to be bought from U.S. Rubber in return for rebates.

The Du Ponts made other investments:

. . . in American Sugar and Refining Company (Domino Sugar),[115] which had substantial sugar cane plantations in Cuba, Puerto Rico, and other parts of Latin America, paying slave wages.

. . . in United Fruit Company,[116] which maintained banana republics throughout Latin America. During the late Twenties United Fruit imported into Cuba 9,600 Blacks from Haiti and Santo Domingo to work on plantations not far from Irénée's estate. The company paid the Cuban government $25 per man as a bond, promising to return them home. As it was cheaper to forfeit the bond than ship them home and hire new workers, United Fruit made it a habit of breaking its promise, stranding the workers in a foreign land. "These companies," wrote one contemporary author, "intensify the chronic unemployment on the island by importing Negro laborers—under slave terms—from Haiti and Santo Domingo. These are kept in semi-military compounds, guarded by troops and denied every civil liberty."[117] In 1928, 1,500 men, women, and children, employees of United Fruit, were murdered by troops in Santa Marta, Colombia, for striking in protest of receiving only 60 percent of their promised wages. The survivors were imprisoned on the banana plantation and flogged, while two U.S. warships were anchored nearby in readiness to intervene if necessary.

. . . in United States Steel, long a supply target for G.M.'s automaking. In June 1927 Du Pont Company acquired 114,000 shares of U.S. Steel common at an average $122.80 price.

It was this last investment that began the reaction by the business community, particularly the Morgan interests, to the Du Ponts' unbridled power grabbing. Within a few hours, news of this $14 million investment sparked a flurry of activity on Wall Street, causing U.S. Steel's stocks to advance 5¼ points, appreciating over $1 million. When the market closed, Du Pont's investment had made $600,000 in one day, and rumors began circulating that a Du Pont was soon to replace recently deceased E. W. Gary as chairman of the giant combine.

On July 29 the Federal Trade Commission informed Du Pont that it was investigating the U.S. Steel acquisition as a possible "community of interest among these three corporations (Du Pont-G.M.-U.S. Steel)." "I think it is their opportunity to satisfy public curiosity or suspicion as to what they are doing," declared F.T.C. Commissioner A. F. Myers. "Will General Motors buy all of its steel from the Steel Corporation and all its paint from the Du Ponts, and if so, what would be the effect on other sellers?"[118]

Pierre, as chairman of G.M., quickly responded two days later to reports of closer ties between G.M. and U.S. Steel. "There is no basis for the report,"[119] he assured the press, while Irénée, as chairman of Du Pont, reported that out of a total 7,116,235 common shares of U.S. Steel, Du Pont's holdings were only 114,000.

The government remained unimpressed. Although controlled by Morgan interests, the federal administration was also concerned with an economy that had a balance of interests among the controlling financial groups in the country.

Hardly a few months after J. P. Morgan, Jr., was elected U.S. Steel's new chairman, the Du Ponts were forced to sell their steel stock. "The Du Pont interests are now looked upon as the largest single stockholding group in the country," the *New York Times* explained. "As long ago as last autumn it was reported in the financial district that the government would frown upon any additional purchases which would give the Du Pont interests anything like a controlling voice in any of the large corporations of the country."[120]

It was a blow to the Du Ponts, but one cushioned by the fact that their acquisition had caused such feverish speculation that the price of U.S. Steel stock had risen from $120 to $160.50. When they sold their 114,000 shares in March, they reaped a golden harvest of $2.6 million in profits.

Such market prices, inflated only by the exchange floor's rumor and the speculator's expectation of a quick killing, of course did much to overvalue securities and prepare the way for the bottom's falling out the following year. But worse was yet to come.

Three days after Lammot dropped 114,000 U.S. Steel shares on the market, John J. Raskob, Pierre's former tight-lipped secretary and now G.M. director, dropped a speculative bomb. Sailing for Europe, Raskob commented to reporters that G.M. would be selling at not less than twelve times earnings; "All former records will be broken by production in 1928."[121]

The market's investors, with fantasies of G.M. stock dancing in their heads from its present 187 to 225 predicated on Raskob's prediction, became rabid. Wall Street broke into pandemonium, handling 1,989,500 shares in two hours, a large part bought and sold around G.M.'s post. As the *New York Times* put it, such was "the magic of his name," that it put the market into a speculative boil. When it was over, G.M.'s stock was worth an additional $47,850,000, up to $3.3 billion, the highest value ever recorded for any American industrial security up to that time.

The magic of John Raskob, of course, was also the magic of Pierre du Pont. Ever since he had quit his first stenographer's job after being refused a raise, and landed a job through a friend as Pierre du Pont's personal secretary in Ohio, Raskob's star had risen with Pierre's. First, showing an aptitude for financial transactions, as treasurer of Pierre's streetcar railway in Texas, then as treasurer and vice president of Du Pont, Raskob was always at Pierre's side, encouraging his boss's original investment in G.M., then accompanying him when Pierre moved from Du Pont to G.M. in 1919 to protect Du Pont's investment in the troubled auto company.

G.M. rode on the boom of 1922–1929, and Raskob rode on G.M., serving on the board's executive committee and as chairman of its all-important finance committee. It was in this latter role that Raskob's words were noted by the market over the decade, especially as G.M. grew into the largest auto maker in the country, surpassing Henry Ford's company in 1926.

The automobile was remaking America, widening it, spreading the city out with suburbs linked by paved roads. To further stimulate the mass market for G.M.'s low-priced Chevrolet, Raskob fathered the G.M. Acceptance Corporation, pioneering the way for buying on the installment plan—buying now, paying later soon became G.M.'s answer to Wall Street's dreams of unlimited consumption. To further management incentive, and consolidate Du Pont control over G.M., Raskob assisted Pierre's founding of the Management Securities Company, which bought $33 million worth of G.M. common. By 1928 the eighty G.M. executives who took interests in this company were all millionaires. In a few years, Raskob had made more millionaires than Andrew Carnegie had in a lifetime.

The rise of G.M. was also the rise of Du Pont, and when Du Pont made $41,113,968 in profits in 1927—a 10 percent increase over 1926—it was noted that nearly half came from General Motors dividends. After ten years of Pierre's first investment, the Du Ponts were realizing a 100 percent return in annual dividends on their total G.M. investment. Raskob, as the leading financial figure on the board of both companies, was credited with the fact that a $1,000 investment in Du Pont in 1921 returned an average 1,000 percent profit in six years. Heralded by *American Review of Reviews* in 1928 as "the financial genius of the Du Pont Company," Raskob was by then a director not only of Du Pont and General Motors, but also Bankers Trust, Curtis Airport Corporation, Lawyers County Trust Company, and the Missouri Pacific Railroad. As a director of corporations which employed over 300,000 people and on which at least one million Americans directly depended for their livelihood, this shy, small man had a commanding influence on the life of one out of every hundred Americans.

At the age of 49, John Raskob was reputedly worth $100 million,[122] owning a baronial estate near Wilmington called Archmere, a farm in Maryland, and a residence in New York City. Even the popes had honored Raskob, appointing him to the Knights of the Order of St. Gregory the Great for his gifts to the Hospital of Infant Jesus in Rome, for which Raskob responded with a $1 million pledge to the Catholic Diocese of Wilmington for "the advancement and preservation of the Catholic faith."

Such was the financial flesh to the "magic of Raskob's name." But there is always a weak link in the chain of money. Raskob's own functioning within Du Pont and G.M. underscored that weakness as being a lack of markets to absorb each company's surplus of goods. Throughout the decade Raskob strove to create new markets by promoting installment buying, modern technology which could create cheaper goods, and the purchase of other companies in related industries. Like many of his class, Raskob recognized that such corporate expansion rested on the political foundations of the government they controlled; *unlike* many of his class, Raskob also recognized that those foundations were becoming increasingly unstable. Crime, he realized, is no mere act of individual aberration, but has social origins and political implications that undermine respect for the existing political order and its laws, especially those laws protecting the privileges of propertied interests like himself.

It was in response to this widespread flouting of existing law that Raskob began to enter directly into the political arena in 1926. It was the beginning of a struggle with leaders of his own class that was to take him out of the Republican Party and propel him to the highest post in the Democratic Party, earning him the title of its "savior."

And here, again, Raskob followed the lead of Pierre du Pont.

8. THE GREAT CAMPAIGN

"What is the greatest thing," an interviewer once asked Irénée du Pont during the Twenties, "that chemistry could do for humanity as a whole?"

Eliminate sickness? Prevent death or control the aging process? Or perhaps discover a perpetual fuel? No, none of these was the primary concern of the president of the world's largest chemical company. "The man who puts into words some of the things he believes chemistry will do," Irénée answered, "would seem a fit subject for an insane asylum," and then proceeded accordingly.

"I think it is likely that material will be found which, taken into the human system, will accomplish the results of eight hours of sleep. This will change the active existence of a man from sixteen hours a day to twenty-four hours a day and, incidentally, make extraordinary changes in our everyday life."

One of the most important changes that would result from a cure for sleep, Irénée proposed, would be the "re-agent" "which enables a young man to work long hours and withstand fatigue which cannot be withstood by men who have reached their mental prime of life."[123]

Irénée, as usual, saw squeezing every possible ounce of labor out of a worker as "the greatest thing chemistry could do for humanity as a whole."

Irénée's answer, stated in a national magazine in 1923, created a furor of protest, even from some of his own business associates who preferred vaguer, more sophisticated ways of saying the same thing. But what was even more significant than the blunt crudity of such a statement from a leading industrialist, was the fact that it reflected the basic business belief of the age—that increased productivity, increasing a man's output, since it increases the volume of production and lowers the cost of goods, is always progressive. The more there is of something the better it is for everyone. As this generated business prosperity, few questioned this rule of quantity over quality, over *what* was produced. And certainly no sound businessman, especially such a free enterpriser as Irénée du Pont, ever thought to question whether increased productivity under the existing private-profit values and social order may have a bad side as well as a good, that technology could harm as well as benefit. If it works, the pragmatist reasoned, then it was good. Increasing the output of each worker was, in the eyes of business leaders, synonymous with "progress."

This pragmatic bias, of course, was incorrect, as its legacy of pollution and lack of social planning in the cities and automobile-created suburbs has long since attested. But even more appalling than the inability of most business leaders to foresee in the Twenties the obvious problems developing for the future, was their inability to comprehend the real economic and social causes of the problems and social forces developing before their eyes. Perhaps the most glaring of these new social forces was the urbanizing of the country's population—a force which the Du Ponts had a hand in shaping, and which eventually led Pierre du Pont and John Raskob out of the Republican Party.

The Crisis of the Cities

Despite the legal curtailment of immigration and a decline in the national birth rate, the populations of American cities were continuing to swell during the Twenties. One of the chief causes of this was the mechanization of agricultural labor that both increased output per man and decreased the number of farm workers needed to sow, cultivate, and reap a harvest. Between 1920 and 1930 the number of trucks on farms rose from 139,000 to 900,000 (Pierre's G.M. being a leading seller) and the number of tractors from 246,000 to 920,000. In 1920, 3,000 harvesting combines were sold; in 1929, 20,000.[124]

The result was a mass migration to the cities. Lured by the city's wages, opportunities, and glamor, 19,436,000 people left the farm between 1920 and 1929. After 1921 the cities' populations were swollen by 2 million rural migrants every year.[125] Inured to farm income levels, and divided by a racism that pit the white majority against the 1.2 million Blacks that had migrated to the cities between 1915 and 1928,[126] these migrants accepted low wages. Since they also competed with European immigrants for jobs, a vast cheap labor pool, politically weak and internally divided against itself, became available to industrialists who could use the crisis to stabilize wages and retard job turnover.

By 1924 a labor supply equilibrium was reached and unemployment began to rise even in the face of an expanding economy. This was *a new kind of unemployment, a technological unemployment* created by mechanization of industry that replaced even highly paid craftsmen. Although the government kept no statistics, it has been estimated that unemployment rates averaged 13 percent for 1924 and 1925, 11 percent for 1926, 12 percent for 1927, and 13 percent for 1928.[127] Millions wandered the city streets while most businessmen and government officials during the Harding and Coolidge administrations continued to rest on their old thesis that unemployment existed only in bad times, that men who really wanted work could find it and, besides, the only ones who suffered were those too thriftless to save.

One who did not hold to this view was Secretary of Commerce Herbert Hoover. Hoover pushed for active federal intervention to coordinate labor union/management collaboration and mitigate unemployment with public works projects. President Calvin Coolidge, buttressed by images of "self-made man" Horatio Alger, summed it all up in a single, short statement: "The business of America is business."

Perhaps the most obvious result of the crisis of the cities was the increase in crime. "It is a dangerous thing," the president of the Baltimore and Ohio Railroad, Daniel Willard, explained to a Senate Investigating Committee in 1928, "to have a large number of unemployed men and women—dangerous to society as a whole—dangerous to the individuals who constitute society. When men who are willing and able to work and want to work are unable to obtain work, we need not be surprised if they steal before they starve. Certainly I do not approve of stealing, but if I had to make a choice between stealing and starving, I would surely not choose to starve—and in that respect I do not think I am unlike the average individual."[128] And too often the powerless, unable to challenge the powerful, turn on themselves.

And aggravating this already explosive situation was "the greatest experiment of the Twentieth century"—and perhaps the most foolish—prohibition.

Prohibition, although enjoying the religious fervor of the Woman's Christian Temperance Union, did not really challenge the flourishing liquor business until the businessmen of the South and West supported the Anti-Saloon League in the interests of labor efficiency and regularity. Total abstinence pledges were not requested by the League, only an unremitting war on the saloon—the local workman's club and, in those days of ward healers, the political meeting place of the working class.

With World War I, came not only the suppression of grain as a food (and liquor) supply, restricting the saloon, but also a national hysteria of "Americanism" that in 1917 swept the Volstead Act through Congress. It took three more years and the deliberate bypassing of most of the industrial city governments and all of the original "Puritan" states of New England to ratify the law, but on January 16, 1920, the Eighteenth Amendment went into effect. The amendment was essentially a victory of large business interests and the middle-class traditions of small town and farming areas, over the new urban culture and its industrial working class. But it was also an extreme victory, going beyond saloons in its prohibition of the manufacture and sale of all intoxicants. As such, it was a victory that soon turned on itself, creating a dangerous reversal of its original purpose of furthering labor discipline and social stability.

As an unenforceable law, prohibition undermined respect for the government. Even the business class showed its disregard, always able to replenish its stock of wines and liquor with ease. Alfred I. du Pont's Nemours estate, for example, had a $100,000 cellar which Alfred enjoyed openly. Government officials were also not immune to lawbreaking. In 1920, for example, the sale of liquor was prevalent at both the Republican and Democratic conventions, and even President Harding, officially a "dry," was known for his substantial unofficial "wetness." Corruption in politics, business, and labor unions became widespread, blackmail and bribery used against city officials, state legislators (some of whom were also involved in speculation in illegal brewing), and even IRS agents. Courts were bribed, as smuggling grew into a nationwide system. Redistillation generated deaths, while city "night clubs" generated fortunes, and with it all rose organized crime and hired guns. Racketeering, backed by murder and bombings, sold "protection from competition" in every city neighborhood, "protecting" businessmen from strikes.

It was not surprising, then—given their commitment to the new technological innovations, increased productivity, and urbanized culture—that Irénée and Pierre du Pont should pragmatically look no further than prohibition for the cause of increased crime in the cities. Although they had strictly enforced a dry rule in their own plants during the war, holding that a Du Pont manager may "properly decline to employ a man who uses intoxicants at any time on or off the job,"[129] the dangerous folly of unenforceable legislation nationwide was immediately recognized by Pierre, who initiated pressure to ease Delaware's law.

As the crisis of the cities intensified in the Twenties, Pierre began to see a repeal of the Eighteenth Amendment as a panacea, often appearing on Delaware radio shows and at public meetings. But Pierre also had a more direct, personal reason for proposing repeal—taxes. Irénée explained that one of his companies alone would save $10 million in corporation taxes if the country had, say, the British tax on beer.[130]

By 1926, a year after Du Pont went into the production of industrial alcohol, Pierre had involved his wife Alice, his brother Irénée, and his friend John J. Raskob, in the Association Against the Prohibition Amendment, a national "wet" organization he was heavily financing. In December *Current History* carried Pierre's "Commendable Features of the Quebec Plan," which pointed out that 75 percent of the country drank, that deaths by alcoholism were not decreasing, and that arrests were not meaningful because they were seldom enforced. Prohibition was a failure, he declared, and suggested Quebec's plan of state regulation.

One of those who could not have agreed more was Alfred E. Smith, New York's Tammany governor. A graduate of the city streets who had never been to college, Smith was a symbol of the new urban political force in the Democratic Party that was friendly to organized labor and advocated public welfare. As a fellow "wet" and a Catholic, Raskob took an immediate liking to Smith when they met during the governor's 1926 reelection campaign. Apparently, the liking was so strong that it merited a $50,000 donation from Raskob.[131]

The Raskob-Smith ties thickened. One day, one of Smith's friends, James J. Riordan, president of County Trust Company of New York, had a meeting with actor Eddie Dowling, a friend of Raskob, about the need of his bank for huge corporate depositors. "Eddie," Riordan explained, "your friend has $3 million of General Motors and Du Pont money in deposit in New York City. If I can get him to put it in the County Trust Company, my bank will jump from a $2 million bank to a $5 million bank."[132] Raskob got the word. Soon afterwards County Trust was the proud recipient of $3 million in deposits from General Motors and Du Pont Company, and an additional $5 million from Raskob's G.M. Acceptance Corporation. Raskob joined County Trust's board of directors. At the same time, County Trust elected a new chairman of the board— Alfred E. Smith. As Dowling later put it, "That was the beginning of Al's desertion of the 'sidewalks of New York.' "[133]

Two years later at the Democratic convention in Houston, Al Smith was nominated for the presidency by a crippled Franklin Roosevelt. It was the second time Roosevelt had done this for Smith, having nominated him also at the 1924 convention. At that time, in a packed Madison Square Garden, the old forces of WASP and rural traditions (namely southern and western middle-class interests and the Ku Klux Klan) locked horns with the new urban forces of the Catholic and Jewish ranks of the working class aligned with liberal financiers and industrialists. That battle, fought to an agonizing draw, finally resulted in the doomed compromise nomination of John W. Davis, attorney for J. P. Morgan Company.

Now, in 1928, Al Smith came back stronger and more organized than ever, backed by millionaire contractor William F. Kenney, Harry Payne Whitney of Standard Oil, Wall Street stock manipulator M. J. Meehan, copper magnates W. A. Clark and John Ryan, candy manufacturer George W. Loft, Bernard Baruch, Thomas Fortune Ryan, and Francis P. Garven, and of course, John J. Raskob, who dramatically endorsed Smith on the eve of the convention.

Smith won easily, and even as the votes were being tallied at the convention hall, nearby in Kenney's private railroad car Raskob secretly was arguing against a "dry" vice-presidential candidate. Raskob wanted an all-wet slate. For once, the man with the magical name lost.

Despite this minor setback, Smith's triumph was also "Johnny" Raskob's glory. Raskob was immediately picked to be Smith's campaign manager and assume the post of National Chairman of the Democratic Party.

"It is not enough to be wet and popular," commented the *New Republic*. "The business support is absolutely essential in those [eastern industrial] states, and Smith knows it. That is why Raskob was picked."[134]

Raskob's appointment, however, backfired. "There is a certain amount of resentful comment in business circles," the *New Republic* noted, "largely based on the fact that Raskob is, and has been, connected with the stock end of General Motors rather than the constructive end."[135] The term "resentment" was generous, at best.

G.M. officials, who did not know of Raskob's intentions until they saw the headlines, were among the war party—and for good reasons. As soon as Raskob took over Smith's campaign, G.M.'s stock sagged. If one man's word could create wealth, the market reasoned, it could also depreciate it.

Detroit stirred uneasily, as did G.M.'s Morgan interests, who were backing Herbert Hoover, the Republican nominee. Pressure soon mounted on Raskob to resign either his political post or the chair of G.M.'s finance committee. Raskob was shocked, but the ultimatums came anyway. Pierre leaped to his defense, publicly endorsing the Democratic ticket and privately threatening to resign if the attacks on Raskob did not end. But this only aggravated further the demands of Pierre's bitter enemies—the Fishers.

As soon as Fisher Body came into G.M. in 1920, Pierre began having problems securing Du Pont orders from their division. Durant's purchase gave G.M. control of 60 percent of their stock, but also allowed a voting trust by the five Fisher brothers, which enabled them to retain broad powers of management. When the Du Ponts took control of G.M. and began using the auto giant as a market for Du Pont products, only the Fisher brothers stubbornly held out.

In August 1921 Pierre, then chairman of both Du Pont and G.M., asked his brother Lammot, "whether General Motors was taking its entire requirements of Du Pont products from Du Pont."[136] As Du Pont vice president, Lammot replied that four out of G.M.'s eight divisions bought their entire requirements of paints and varnishes from Du Pont; five divisions, their entire requirements of Fabrikoid (artificial leather); four, their entire requirements of rubber cloth; and seven, their entire requirements of Pyralin and celluloid. Lammot also included a chart showing: G.M. divisions, "okay"; Fisher Body, "None."

Pierre ordered a drive for Fisher business, which finally culminated on October 22, 1922, in a personal letter from Lammot to Fred Fisher. "In view of the stock ownership relations between Fisher Body Corporation, Flint Varnish and Color Works [owned by Du Pont], General Motors Corporation, and Du Pont Company, it would seem that Flint Varnish and Color Works should enjoy a large part, if not all, of Fisher Body's paint and varnish business, unless there is some good reason for not having it."[137] Still the Fishers resisted, even in the face of a Du Pont admonition in 1926 that G.M. would receive a super discount only if Fisher started buying.

Amid such a campaign of mounting pressure, then, the Fishers saw the 1928 election as their last chance to get rid of Raskob and perhaps even Pierre Du Pont. They anticipated getting the support of Morgan interests on G.M.'s board. What came more as a surprise was the support they received from Alfred Sloan, the G.M. executive Pierre had installed in the presidency.

Sloan had been retained after the Du Pont acquisition for his organizational talents, and he was soon pushed to the top. Childless, uninterested in books or art, an abstainer from sports, smoking, or drinking, lean and homely, Sloan was a firm believer in the Puritan ethic, often repeating, as if in prayer, "Work hard, there is no shortcut." This partially deaf man's total devotion to his work at G.M. had won him the admiration of all parties involved in G.M.'s ownership, as well as a seat on Du Pont's Board of Directors. Sloan's insistence, then, that Raskob resign for the purpose of "making it unmistakably clear that the corporation takes no part in political affairs,"[138] came as a real blow.

It has sometimes been insinuated that Sloan's move to oust Raskob was based partly on personal reasons; Raskob had opposed Pierre's intention to put Sloan on the Du Pont Board in 1923, but only in concern for the morale of G.M. executives and their fear of the "Du Pont stamp on General Motors."[139] But it is more likely that Sloan's opposition came from a genuine desire, as he later put it to Pierre, "to protect the corporation's interests as I see it."[140] And Raskob's own recent "magic words" in March to the stock market hadn't done much to protect G.M.'s stock from inflating artificially to 199 only to fall again within a few weeks and spur the panic of June 12. That date was the largest trading day in history up to that time, when over 5 million shares changed hands, dragging even radio down 23 points, and prompting a New York newspaper to report forebodingly, "Wall Street's bull market collapsed yesterday with a detonation heard around the world"[141]—and around G.M.'s Board table.

Facing a united opposition of Sloan, Fisher, and Morgan interests, Raskob resigned his finance post on August 9, 1928. Irénée, concerned over Pierre's threat to resign also, insisted to the other board members that "It is of the utmost importance that the other resignation be not accepted." Pierre's motivation, he explained, was "loyalty to a friend rather than the necessity of the case."[142]

During all his years with G.M., Pierre had had only one other disagreement with Sloan, over Pierre's support of the copper-cooled engine. That disagreement had convinced Pierre to resign the presidency and give it to Sloan. This one convinced him to resign the chairmanship, turning the Du Pont watchdog role over to his brother Lammot, the president of Du Pont, and Walter Carpenter, the brother of Ruly Carpenter, who had replaced Raskob as treasurer of Du Pont. Both Pierre and Raskob, however, remained on G.M.'s Board with Pierre's other relatives, Irénée, Henry F. du Pont, and Donaldson Brown. Raskob also resigned as an executive committee member of Missouri Pacific Railroad and shed his directorships in Texas and Pacific Railroad, Gulf Coast Lines, and Denver and Rio Grande Western Railroad, all part of the Missouri Pacific system.

Pierre took his leave of G.M. seriously, but he took prohibition, crime, and taxes even more seriously. Just the April before, he had written in *Current History* magazine that prohibition's crippling of liquor commerce is not the answer to drunkenness, nor was the loss in tax revenues. "England has taught us another lesson in regard to alcoholic beverages. While reducing the consumption of alcohol to one-half of what it was before the World War, the government has incidentally provided itself with important revenues. The total income from alcoholic drink during the years 1923–1926 has averaged about 134,000,000 annually. With a population at about 42 million this means £3,200,000 each year from one million inhabitants. For the United States, such a tax would return $1,850,000,000 each year. As our average income tax collections for the years 1923–1926 from individuals and corporations were $1,817,000,000, resulting in a considerable surplus, it is fair to say that the British liquor policy applied to the United States would permit the total abolition of the income tax both personal and corporate."[143] The fact that Pierre's family was the largest personal source of tax revenue in Delaware was only one motivation. Pierre's appeal was also directed to others of his class who, like his friend Raskob, sat in the plush lounge of the Union League of Philadelphia and sweated over ways to cheat the government of their own making out of its legal due.

As a leader of the National Association Against Prohibition, Raskob, too, denounced the prohibitionists as modern inquisitors, but as late as June 11 he had doubted if his class understood the economic ruin they were causing. "My judgment is that both parties will dodge this whole liquor question by inserting some innocuous plank in their respective platforms at the June Convention."[144]

But now, as Democratic Chairman, Raskob could push the prohibition question to the fore, using his business reputation to appeal for corporate support of the Smith campaign. "He is no experiment," Raskob tried to reassure a troubled Wall Street. "Business, big or little, has nothing to fear."[145] Business, big or little, did not believe him. When Raskob lost his G.M. finance position, his name also lost its magic. By September, a month after his G.M. finance resignation, it was clear that Raskob had failed in his mission. Smith's original backers remained firm, with Raskob personally donating an enormous $110,000 and Pierre another $50,000, but the majority of the country's wealthiest families—the Eastmans, the Rockefellers, the Guggenheims, the Schwabs, the Firestones, Bakers, Chryslers, and Mellons—all supported J. P. Morgan's candidate, Herbert Hoover, a mining millionaire in his own right and a Secretary of Commerce respected by the entire business community, which had much to be grateful for in these boom years.

Alfred Sloan, who had demanded Raskob's resignation on the basis of his involvement in "political affairs," gave Hoover's campaign $25,000, while the five Fisher brothers donated $25,000 and their Fisher Bodies Corporation, a G.M. division, put up an additional $100,000.[146] Other G.M. directors who voted against Raskob also gave huge sums to the Republican cause: George F. Baker, Jr., $27,000; George Whitney, $2,750; and Alfred H. Swayne, $15,000. The Republican treasury came to over $9 million, almost $2 million more than Smith's.

Pierre was not even able to hold his own family together on the elections. In fact, divisions within the family over prohibition were so severe that in August, Coleman's son, Frank du Pont, and Ruly Carpenter, jointly announced a family truce. No Du Ponts, the chairman of the Republican National Committee was assured, would oppose Hoover in Delaware, where there was family agreement on the Republican Party. The only split occurred over prohibition, they explained, and Pierre would support Smith only nationally.

Irénée, who in July had blasted the prohibitionists for "their one great success" of leaving "a trail of unparalleled corruption and lawbreaking,"[147] remained loyal to Hoover, donating $22,000.[148]

Lammot, who also disagreed with prohibition, nevertheless did not feel "that all other questions, out of deference to it, should go by the board or be left to settle themselves. I do not believe that prohibition is of paramount importance." Lammot more sensibly concluded that economic welfare, tariffs, farm relief, federal reserves, railway regulation, and government ownership were the primary major issues and, in a note of frankness about the business-oriented ideology of both parties, explained that "there is no radical difference in principle between the two parties. The difference is more in the elaboration of the principles or putting them into effect."[149] For Lammot, it was merely a question of tactics in preserving corporate rule. He gave $42,300 to Hoover's campaign.[150]

Other Du Ponts followed suit: Ruly Carpenter, $15,000; Walter Carpenter, $3,000; William du Pont, Jr., $2,500; Charles Copeland, $500; and A. Felix du Pont, $1,000 to $5,000.[151] Even Alfred and Coleman found themselves on the same side for once, Alfred donating $25,000 from his Florida command post, and Coleman, as Republican Senator from Delaware, $10,000.[152] Even a Du Pont director, Grasselli, gave Hoover $2,000.

As *World's Work* put it at the time, "The experiment of linking one of the biggest posts in American industry to one of the biggest in American politics had failed signally."[153] Perhaps shrewd Johnny Raskob was the one most surprised.

Raskob continued devoting his full attention to the campaign, but always remained his shy and reserved self, blushing under questioning, often retreating to the inner sanctums of corporate offices. Always assuming a calm, self-assured poise, only his constantly moving hands betrayed the insecurity pulsing beneath the mask of confidence. From his frequent and genuine smiles emerged almost inaudible tones, requiring listeners to strain to hear. With his slight 5'7" stature and warm brown eyes, the balding Democratic Chairman appeared more bookish than a man of the hard political world. Politicians with itchy palms would line up by the droves in his New York office with rash promises to deliver a state, a city. And Raskob may well have believed them, stating, amid rumors that he was to be the next Secretary of Treasury and Pierre the next Secretary of State, that "I believe that there is a divinity which shapes our ends. I'm positive it was so in my case."[154]

Unfortunately for Raskob, his manifest destiny was not to find its star with Al Smith. Raskob had expected salty Al, with his uncouth East Side accent, to turn the laugh on serious Herbert. But the country's working population was more concerned with the serious issue of continued prosperity than with laughs. Hoover understood this and geared his well-financed campaign accordingly.

HARD TIMES
Always come when Democrats try to run the nation
ASK DAD—HE KNOWS!
Take No Chances!
Vote a Straight Republican Ticket!![155]

Such Republican campaign cards were directed at the 17 million potential new voters who were children of immigrants and migrants to the cities. Hoover ignored the endorsement that labor union leaders had given Smith, and zeroed his appeal in one the employed workers' reverence of the almighty dollar and on their middle-class aspirations. Although the great majority were destined to remain workers all their lives, many were sustained by a hope of rising to a higher class. Hoover put himself forth as the symbol of that middle class, an Iowa farm-born Quaker and WASP of Main Street battling the foreign and flashy legions of immoral Broadway.

Encouraged by such provincial facades, rural forces, backed by large financial interests, came to the fore, led by Smith's old enemy, the Ku Klux Klan. With prohibition and Smith's Catholicism as issues, it became a campaign of prejudices, not of principles, for on principles both parties were in fundamental accord. Smith, while raging about Teapot Dome and other Republican scandals, carefully avoided any attack on the stock speculation boom or Mellon's tax rebates to the rich.

With its large working class internally divided, the revolt of the cities was broken. Raskob, anxious to stamp out intolerance toward Roman Catholics like himself, on the eve of the election unleashed a furious attack on Republican slurs; but it came too late, and may have generated a backlash often handed to losers. And Smith did lose, gathering only 14,981,000 votes to Hoover's unprecedented 21,385,000.

"I've just licked Pierre and Raskob and made Florida Republican," Alfred proclaimed from Epping Forest, "and I am reeking with gore."[156] Like most of the South, Florida had gone for Hoover, by some 44,000 votes, and the victory belonged mostly to Alfred's Hoover Democratic Committee. Alfred du Pont, who called Black people "coons,"[157] had made his entrance into Florida politics—by allying with the Ku Klux Klan. "By virtue of your success," he wrote Hoover the day after the election, "our country has been preserved from a threatened catastrophe the result of which one does not care to contemplate. Every inhabitant of the United States may now feel assured of even greater prosperity. . . ."[158]

9. THE CRASH OF THE HOUSE OF CARDS

Shortly after the election of Hoover, a story goes, Irénée du Pont threw a party at his hilltop manor, Granogue. Scores of guests were invited, and as each couple appeared at the front door they were handed the keys to a brand new roadster in which they were invited to ride about the area until the sports car ran out of gas or crashed. Both alternatives, the story claims, were accomplished that night.

There seems little doubt that the Du Ponts were certainly wealthy enough during the Twenties to afford such an extravagance. Only a day after Hoover won the election, G.M.'s directors announced a 150 percent dividend and paid out $43.5 million in cash, over a quarter of that going to Delaware's first family. In addition, their own Du Pont Company reaped $30,129,000 in only the first six months of 1928, a profit of $11.32 (or 50 percent) on each share. Twenty million dollars of that came from G.M., and another $2.6 million from the U.S. Steel divestiture.

Many members of the family sat on the boards of the country's leading banks: Pierre du Pont was a director of Bankers Trust, Detroit National Bank, Wilmington Trust, and Philadelphia National Bank. Lammot du Pont was a director of Fidelity Philadelphia Trust, Wilmington Trust, and Chemical Bank, which had over $12 million in undistributed earnings. Walter S. Carpenter, Jr., was a director of Chase National Bank. His brother, R. R. M. (Ruly) Carpenter, was a director of Girard Trust. Donaldson Brown was also a director of National Bank of Detroit, while John J. Raskob continued to serve on Al Smith's favorite bank, Lawyers County Trust. And finally there was the indomitable Alfred du Pont, who in February 1929 assumed the presidency of Florida National Bank.

The Du Ponts seemed the first in everything—the first in number of large mansions (about 30), the first in yachts (22), the first in cars (over 500), the first in personal wealth, and the first in bodily numbers. They

controlled the world's largest chemical company, the world's largest automobile company, and the world's largest industrial rubber company.

Pierre's $7 million life insurance policy, which required him to abstain
from flying his own airplane, was the largest in the country. Nevertheless,
he found its annuities lower in yield than his own personal stock holdings,
too low in fact to support his style of living or to keep up the value of his
enormous estate. New inheritance laws and concern that his immediate
family retain control of Du Pont presented other dilemmas. His Delaware
Realty and Investment Corporation solved the problem by setting up a
lifetime guaranteed annuity for him and his wife to the tune of $900,000 a
year. With this and other corporate salaries and dividends, he needn't have
thought twice about his decision to spend $29,000 to have a single bush
brought to his Longwood Gardens.

Irénée was not only the second largest life insurance policy holder in the
country—at almost the same amount as Pierre—but also a director and one
of the largest stockholders in Coleman's former Equitable Life Assurance
Company. He was also supreme lord over a vast ocean-front estate at
Varadero Beach in Cuba, where he occasionally fished with "the butcher of
Cuba," President Machado. Irénée enjoyed other, more peculiar sports as
well, including the breeding and training of vicious iguanas; and often,
with a gusty laugh, he would slip over the wrists of his women guests bracelets of solid gold, which he appropriately called his "slave bracelets."[159]

Other Du Ponts were just as extravagant. Henry F. du Pont wore custom-
tailored suits from Twyeffort's, which cost $225 apiece; Alfred du Pont,
worth $100 million in 1928, seldom went anywhere with less than $500 in
his pocket as "loose change"; and cousin Henry B. du Pont collected
airplanes like a child collects toys.

Of course, the family had its embarrassments, including a rash of elope-
ments and divorces, and some much publicized objections from Massachusetts conservation officials over a Du Pont-sponsored crow-shooting contest.
Morgan interests also continued their pressures, forcing in one year (1928)
not only the U.S. Steel divestiture and the Pierre and Raskob ousting from
G.M. activity, but also in November, the sale of Pierre's 70,000 share
holdings in Atlas Powder. Atlas, it seems, was expanding into the market
of Canadian Explosives, Ltd., owned jointly by Nobel, Ltd. (allies of the
Morgans) and Du Pont. Under pressure from CXL's president and
familiar rumors of another anti-trust action, Pierre let Atlas go in the
interest of good Du Pont business and to preserve English and Morgan
friendships.

But the family, cushioned by its featherbed of golden fleece, always
managed to move on to bigger and better diversions from boredom. Samuel

Hallock du Pont, son of Pierre's brother William Kemble du Pont, continued to prowl his estate, Henry Clay, hunting stray cats with his rifle, or practiced knife throwing at his other estate, appropriately named Squirrel Run.[160] Sam's antics seemed harmless enough until one day he began using his wife as a target for his knife-throwing hobby. She left that night, complaining of knives and of Sam's many bathroom mirrors, securing a quick divorce. Sam, undaunted, later entered into marriage again and a surprisingly calmer life. Philip du Pont was different. Old "Fireman Phil" liked to chase fire engines, finding rest for his troubled mind only by taking long quiet walks through Delaware's forests quietly reading and writing poetry, happily shooting down singing birds between poems.[161]

Such eccentricity did not stop at the lower ranks of the Du Pont family. Lammot, for example, although a multimillionaire, was the family's fanatic on thrift, often carrying his own luggage in order to avoid having to tip. Throughout his tenure as president and chairman, Lammot was a familiar sight bicycling through the street of Wilmington, saving carfare by pedaling to work as head of the largest chemical company in the world.

Irénée had his frightening fantasies, some of which shocked the world, coming as they did from one of its most powerful personalities. In a speech to the American Chemical Society, for example, he advocated a race of "supermen" created by mind-stimulation drugs. But he did not end on that disturbing note. He also insisted that "by injecting proper compounds into an individual, we can make his character to order"[162] and increase not only a worker's productivity, but also his spending. "Such a discovery," he told the chemical industrialists, "could add some 50 percent to both our hours of production and our hours of pleasure, and by its complete accomplishment would greatly decrease the cost of housing and the capital per unit of production of all those factories which today do not operate on a twenty-four hour schedule."[163]

Here, Irénée did not display the grasp of corporate economics that his eldest brother possessed. Pierre well understood the relation between what Veblen termed "leisure time" and capitalism's need, as John Keynes later put it, to constantly increase aggregate demand for its products. As early as 1928 Pierre was described by one national magazine as believing "that the key to national prosperity lies in high wages, which finance consumption." "The trouble with Europe," he told an interviewer, "is that they don't want enough." "Mr. du Pont explained that he did not believe that long hours were needed to finance the higher standard of living, pointing out that the average man required leisure to enjoy the use of things if his wants are to increase."[164]

Pierre's statements only reflected the economic realities of the new industrial age of machines increasingly replacing men, lowering costs of products, and creating the modern consumer society. But it was left to his able lieutenant, John Raskob, to integrate the new spending patterns of the wage earner into the needs of the marketplace for liquid capital. In promoting this integration, John Raskob, as one of the great bulls of Wall Street, was a pioneer of corporate co-optation of the workman, paving the way *economically* for the union-management collaboration in maintaining the status quo that had already been promoted by Hoover, first as Secretary of Commerce and now as President, and was to find its political culmination under the administration of Franklin Roosevelt.

Raskob's role in this milestone development of the American social order was crucial. His General Motors Acceptance Corporation was the first attempt by a large corporation to raise demands for its products and capture the liquid capital of the wage-earning middle and working classes through the lure of installment buying. Following in the footsteps of T. Coleman and Pierre du Pont's policies in their own company, Raskob introduced not only bonus payments and stock-sharing to G.M.'s executives, but also introduced, with Pierre's endorsement, bonuses and stock-sharing to the company's work force. G.M. workers earning $5,000 or less were allowed to buy up to ten shares of 6 percent debenture stock on which an extra dividend of $3 a share annually for five years was given as a special distribution to employees by the owners. By encouraging "ownership management" and the worker's limited ownership of "income-producing property" (stock), Raskob's policies tried to create a "small-capitalist" mentality that would build identity with corporate management and "loyalty to the company." And, in fact, his policies did tend to reduce turnover during the Twenties and undercut labor troubles and strikes.

Along these lines, in May 1929 Raskob announced his most ambitious scheme yet, a plan for a great securities investment trust to sell stock to the common man with loans for purchases. The proposal, coming in the midst of a furious boil of speculation on Wall Street, and a resultant dangerous need of liquid capital, received great publicity and almost universal acclamation. Even the Roman Catholic Church's *Commonweal* endorsed this scheme of one of its most beloved members as a fulfillment and extension of the rule of private property.[165]

Three months later Raskob published one of the most famous articles of the Twenties, "Everybody Ought to Be Rich," in *Ladies Home Journal*. The title amply portrays Raskob's unbridled enthusiasm for speculation, suggesting that with a mere $15 per month investment everybody not only ought to be, but *could* become rich—$80,000 rich in twenty years. Needless to say, thousands of unfortunates took his advice.

Raskob's greatest contribution to corporate liberalism, however, came in November with his endorsement of the forty-hour, five-day week, then the clarion call of organized labor. What was truly unique for its time was Raskob's comprehension of how the five-day week would fit not only into a rationalized consumer society ruled by monopolies, but into a society being shaped by that most explosive of technological forces—automobiles. As such, it stands today as a landmark in the development of the corporate liberalism that found fruition under Roosevelt and now is the ideological mainstream of big business.

"The latter text," he wrote in the prestigious *North American Review,* after explaining the five-day case, "is the justification of the five-day week, and not in any sentimental spirit, but from the standpoint of good business. Put briefly and frankly, the reason for proposing that industrial production be limited to five days a week is to give the workers additional time and opportunity to function as consumers of what they produce. We have got production geared up to such speed and efficiency in this country that we are faced with something more than the beginnings of a problem of getting the goods we are making consumed. Every manufacturer, every capitalist concerned with financing industry, knows this. Our sometimes frantic selling efforts and our elaborate science of advertising bear witness to the fact. Yet we could easily make half as much again as we are making. We have to keep the production machinery throttled down. We dare not develop its latent potentialities. Our recent progress in the export market has been great, but world conditions limit that progress.

"Now the American workingman, in all the chief industries, is paid a high wage—and it is steadily going higher. In the mass, he has a tremendous buying power. That buying power has been multiplied by the extension in every direction of the deferred payment or installment system. Nowhere in the world is the standard of living so high or the demand for conveniences and luxuries so insistent. The trouble must be lack of sufficient time and opportunity to buy, and to use the things bought. It is a typically American situation, and it requires a solution as boldly American as high wages, mass production and installment selling.

"The five-day week is such a solution. Machinery and machine tools used in the productive processes are the only classes of goods which will not at once begin to be consumed more rapidly when we have an extra day of leisure, and even they will be consumed more rapidly in the end. Every other sort of goods will at once feel the stimulus of increased consumption, for leisure time is consuming time."[166]

With remarkable perception, Raskob envisioned a world of expanding consumption and tourism. "The mileage travelled by automobiles on

American roads any fair Sunday must pretty nearly equal the mileage covered on the other six days of the week. What would happen if to a full Sunday holiday we add a full Saturday holiday? There will be an immediate and tremendous increase in the use, which is to say in the consumption, of automobiles, tires, gasoline, oil—and roads. The effects of that increased consumption will flash like an electric impulse back to the factories, the iron mines, the glass works, the oil field and the cement mill.

"With two full play days ahead of them people will start out Friday evening or Saturday morning on longer trips than they can take under present conditions. More good roads will have to be built. More hotels and tourist camps will be called for, to the benefit of the construction industries, particularly the lumber trade, as well as the furniture, chinaware, glassware, cutlery, cooking equipment, tent and blanket industries and many others. People moreover will need extra suits and dresses, camping equipment, fishing tackle, sports goods. Those who do not travel will largely spend their extra leisure participating in or watching sports. . . . Many people, it may be supposed, will sit around home. But just the same they will consume more goods . . . or they will read more magazines and newspapers and use, that is consume, their radio equipment more intensively.

". . . The proponents of the five-day week are satisfied that psychologically and practically the extra half day will be equal to an extra full day of leisure. They believe, in fact, that the plan will purchase extra consumption for a full day at the price of only a half day of production." Explaining that workers' productivity is not high on Saturday morning because their mind is not on their jobs, and that workers' consumption of products is actively hurt by their tiredness after work, Raskob concluded that "It is seriously questionable whether the amount of work done on Saturday mornings under the present system is worth while—worth what it costs" (in wages and cutbacks on consumption).

". . . Retail trade profits by the Saturday half-holiday, but it would profit immensely more if all of Saturday were at the disposal of the mass of industrial workers to spend, buy, and consume. Of course the retail trades and public services which would be called on to serve extra on Saturdays would have to provide their workers with compensatory leisure, giving them a five-day week also, which in turn would make them better customers and consumers."

Even holidays fitted into Raskob's consumption plan; he suggested "the celebration of all holidays except Christmas on Monday. Everyone knows how the fixture of Labor Day on Monday increases travel and the indulgence in sports. Whenever the Fourth of July, Memorial Day, Columbus

Day or any other holiday happens to fall on a Monday, the same phenomenon occurs. Patriotism and sentiment would suffer no injury if these holidays were always celebrated on the nearest Monday; production would halt less than it does now when a holiday falls in the middle of the week; but consumption would be powerfully stimulated. With Saturday, Sunday, and Monday ahead of them, people would really start out to do things.

". . . I am firmly convinced—and so are others who have studied the matter—that the worker would probably produce not only as much, but more, in five days, even with only the present equipment. The knowledge that he had two days out of the seven in which to enjoy life and family companionship would make every ambitious worker in the land more efficient. But, in addition, modern machinery, methods and power have already developed a vast margin of unused production capacity, and there is literally no limit at present to be foreseen to further progress in this direction. In other words, America is in shape to produce in five days all she can consume in seven, with a lot left over for export. That being so, the five-day week, in my judgment, should become the rule in America with as little delay as possible." Since foreign markets were not adequate to absorb America's surplus, Raskob's emphasis was on further developing the domestic consumer market.

Raskob then directly addressed Wall Street's need for liquid capital, explaining that much consumer ability was presently tied up in savings banks. "Here in short is a vast fund of capital which is not entering the arteries of production and trade in the most efficient way." Raskob then repeated his earlier remedy—an investment company to promote workers' investing in "sound common stocks," providing loans for marginal purchasing. "It may be along the lines of an investment trust, issuing its own securities against selected holdings, or it may serve chiefly by guiding the small investor in his selection of securities. It may operate along both of these lines. The important thing is that this is the way to help the worker."

This, in fact, was the way to ruin the worker, to wipe out his life's savings. For marginal trading (buying stocks with borrowed money), stock specialists now understand,[167] is never "sound," but extremely risky. It was exactly such speculation that had led to the overpricing of stocks during the Twenties, their quotes backed not by money but by paper pledges on margin. The rise of stock values like Du Pont's no longer reflected the slower rise of real earning power generated by cost-saving (particularly labor-saving) technology, consuming markets, and cheap labor markets here and abroad, but had advanced far beyond that, beyond the capacities of the market to increase earned profits at annual percentages high enough and constant enough to keep attracting and holding investors.

The competition of speculators to purchase valuable stock had driven up the price of stocks, so that a stock's attractiveness, not its real or prospective earnings, became the determination of value, a false inflated value.

In 1924 the *New York Times* averages of the prices of twenty-five representative industrial stocks stood at 110. By 1925 they had eased up to 135, and despite some mild setbacks in 1926 and 1928, the advance was steady, the *Times* commenting on November 21, 1928, that "for cyclonic violence yesterday's stock market has never been exceeded in the history of Wall Street." At the close of trading on January 2, 1929, the averages had soared to 338.

Du Pont shared in this stock balloon, helped by the heady wind of triumph over the Chemical Foundation's futile suit to recover from Du Pont German patents used in chemical processes. In one year, 1928, Du Pont stock jumped from 310 to 525. In January 1929, Pierre, who had already engineered one split during the decade, did so again, this time $3\frac{1}{2}$ to 1. This made one Du Pont share bought in 1922 now worth the equivalent of seven shares.

Not content with millions made from their own Du Pont yields, many Du Ponts joined Raskob in the firestorm of speculation sweeping the market. The Federal Reserve System, which in 1927 had spurred the market's furious pace by lowering interest rates on loans for marginal buying, became frightened enough in 1928 to reverse its position and raise rates by 1 percent. It was a futile gesture, and from the spring of 1928 to the spring of 1929 the total of brokers' loans doubled.

In January 1929 the F.R.S. released a public warning that succeeded in scaring some commercial banks into pulling back and refusing to under-write loans, sending up call money for stocks on margin to 20 percent. But the leading financiers would have none of that; National City Bank's Charles E. Mitchell abruptly threw $25 million into the money market and the blaze was rekindled. When Paul R. Warburg, a banker and founder of the Federal Reserve System, in March denounced "unrestrained specula-tion," warning that it would "bring about a general depression involving the whole country," he was accused of "sandbagging" prosperity.

Raskob's County Trust, Pierre's Bankers Trust, and Lammot's Chemical Bank, the latter two solidly within the Morgan sphere, all threw money into the call market. It was like throwing gasoline on the speculative fires, and brokers' loans and marginal buying soared even higher. Lammot, as chairman of General Motors, even threw $25 million in G.M. funds into the call money market to back the brokers who could barely keep up with the orders. Pierre personally had $32 million of cash in the market.[168] Albert H. Wiggin, president of Chase National (of which Walter S.

Carpenter and Alfred Sloan were directors), even borrowed from his own bank to speculate on its stock—selling it short! By the summer of 1929, brokers' loans to carry the margined stocks were increasing at the rate of $400 million a month.

Some brokerage houses, to increase their influence and attract needed capital, distributed to "insiders" shares in companies at far below their current price, in effect swindling the public. In July 1929 stocks of Standard Brands, Inc., were offered to "insiders" at $10 below the market. One of the insiders was John J. Raskob, who quickly snatched up 500 shares worth of instant profit. Six months earlier, in January, he had similarly bought 2,500 shares of United Corporation at $75 apiece.[169] Years later a Senate investigation revealed that both Raskob and Sloan were on J. P. Morgan's "Preferred List" of professional speculators.

In 1922 loans to brokers to underwrite margined stocks amounted to $1.9 billion; by 1929 they totaled $8.5 billion. In the heat of speculation, only a few voices were heard warning that stock values did not truly reflect real earnings. Alfred du Pont's warning in 1928 to his son Alfred V. not to buy on margin seems the only record of any member of the Du Pont family questioning the speculation boom. "In the matter of investments," he wrote, "a young man like you should be guided, in my opinion, by the dividend return principally."[170]

By then, however, the ability of the domestic American market to consume the commodities of its own industries was exhausted, despite the new "consumer society" and its installment buying. With 71 percent of the population still receiving wages and salaries averaging less than $2,500 a year, and over 90 percent earning less than $40 a week, "Capital," as banker Frank Vanderlip admitted, "kept too much and labor did not have enough to buy its share of things."[171] By 1929 the United States was using only 80 percent of its productive capacity.[172]

Only a few of the leading industrialists and politicians understood the magnitude of approaching disaster. Some, in their search for markets to generate real earnings, cast eyes abroad to foreign lands. Since the 1890's, foreign markets had been the traditional outlet for goods and the source of profitable cheap labor and resources. "We must finance our exports by loaning foreigners the wherewithal to pay for them," warned Wall Street lawyer John Foster Dulles in 1928. "Without such loans we would have the spectacle of our neighbors famishing for goods which were rotting in our warehouses as unusable surplus."[173]

Herbert Hoover, although differing with Dulles over government control of such loans, agreed with his general principle, stating openly that "We must find a profitable market for our surpluses."[174] As early as 1924, as

Secretary of Commerce, he had warned that the "export market becomes of peculiar importance to us in maintaining a stable and even operation of our domestic industries. It has an importance in that regard far beyond the percentage of our exports to our total production."[175]

But by 1929, $602 million in annual direct U.S. investments abroad were simply insufficient to help maintain the "stable and even operation" of domestic industries, and real earnings were unable to keep pace with the meteoric rise of stock prices inflated by speculation. "Sooner or later," stated economist Roger Babson in September 1929, "a crash is coming, and it may be terrific."[176]

It was. Du Pont's stock reached its high of 231 that month. Then the market broke rather badly, recovered, and broke again. Du Pont ended the month at 188. The market steadied, but with a nervous shudder.

On October 18 fear was renewed as the *New York Times* industrials declined 7 points; the next day 12 more points were lost (Du Pont lost 5) and everyone could only sigh with relief that the Big Board would close for Sunday. The reprieve was brief. On Monday things got worse; they steadied on Tuesday, worsened on Wednesday, the late ticker only adding to anxieties in brokerage offices across the country. Then on Thursday, October 23, came the deluge: with one tremendous crash, the bottom dropped out of the whole market. It was a panic of selling, 16,410,000 shares were dumped on the market, 2,600,000 in the last hour alone, breaking the *Times* industrials 43 points. A flood of calls went out from brokers for more collateral on marginal stock, and the crash of 1929 began. "Du Pont was selling at 80," Alfred wrote his son, "and the ragman was looking for our certificates. Candidly, I think Du Pont is not worth much more than par. I never did. . . ."[177]

John Raskob disagreed, stating almost at the same time, "Prudent investors are now buying stocks in huge quantities and will profit handsomely when this hysteria is over."[178] Such brave words, however, would not prevent thousands of his "common man" followers from losing some $25 billion, marking "the slaughter of innocents." Nor was there now much meaning in Pierre's "optimistic" feelings after attending President Hoover's management conferences during the year, or Alfred Sloan's assurance only a few days before the crash that "business is sound." G.M., incidentally, after declaring a 150 percent dividend in 1928 and climbing to 78 in 1929, broke to 33. *Times* industrials closed at 175 average on Black Thursday; by July of 1932, when they hit 58, no one dared claim business was sound. The industrial world acknowledged it was in the grip of a terrible depression.

For most, the crash brought total disaster, wiping out a whole lifetime of fortunes and savings. Suicides of prominent businessmen only added to the panic. In New York the body of a merchant was dragged out of the Hudson, his pockets holding only $9.40 in change and a few margin calls. In Manhattan, a story goes, two men jumped hand in hand from a high window in the Ritz Hotel; they had a joint account. The head of Rochester Gas and Electric Company used his own facilities and took gas. James J. Riordan, president of County Trust—whom Raskob had persuaded to help write off the campaign deficit of their friend and co-director, Al Smith, with a $50,000 check—went home and blew his brains out. Raskob and salty Al shared the job of pallbearer. And in ironic contrast to all this, from his Pocantico Hills estate old John D. Rockefeller issued his first public statement in many years: "Believing that fundamental conditions of the country are sound . . . my son and I have for some days been purchasing sound common stock." Eddie Cantor, describing himself as "comedian, author, statistician, and victim," said later, "Sure, who else had any money left?"[179]

The Du Ponts. In fact, to have his tax return show fictitious "losses" that year, Pierre had to illegally exchange $4.5 million worth of securities with Raskob. As income tax laws permitted deductions of capital losses from income received from stock, Pierre simply bought $4,606,000 worth of Raskob's stock in November and sold $4,582,750 worth of his own stock to Raskob. Both sold at a loss and claimed so on their tax returns. In January, after the tax year was over, they then simply bought back each other's stock; Pierre on January 6 gave Raskob a check for $5,254,125, which Raskob deposited on January 8. Then, on the same day, Raskob wrote out his own check to Pierre for $5,289,500.

Pierre saved over $600,000 in taxes through this scheme. But he still had to pay the highest tax in the country that year; over $4.5 million. This meant that in 1929, despite the Crash, Pierre's income was an estimated $31.5 million.[180] The wide range of securities involved in the swindle also underscored Pierre's sweeping role as a stock manipulator: Warner Brothers, Sun Petroleum, Checker Cab, Bank of United States, National Cash Register, Otis Elevator, Anaconda Copper, Kennecott Copper, Baltimore and Ohio Railroad, and, of course Du Pont and General Motors.

Other Du Ponts also fared well that year. Only one suffered, his fall shaking the family harder than the crash—Senator Coleman du Pont.

Coleman's first real troubles began, like the market's, in 1928. In February a Senate investigating committee uncovered his name in connection with the Teapot Dome scandal.

Teapot Dome remains one of the milestones in American history, depicting the depth of Washington's corruption by big business. Since 1922 very

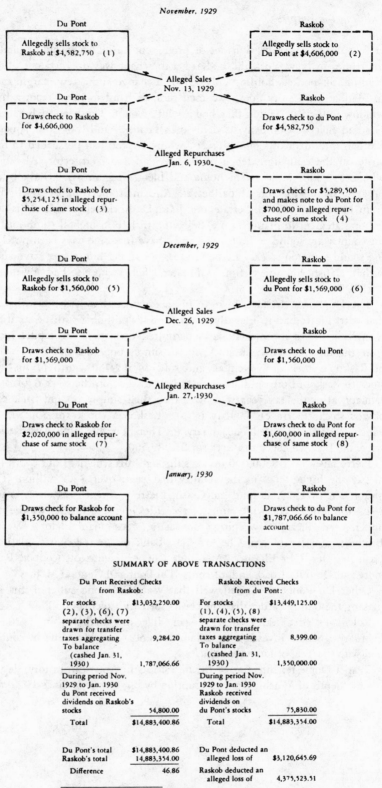

November, 1929

Du Pont	Raskob
Allegedly sells stock to Raskob at $4,582,750 (1)	Allegedly sells stock to Du Pont at $4,606,000 (2)

Alleged Sales
Nov. 13, 1929

Du Pont	Raskob
Draws check to Raskob for $4,606,000	Draws check to du Pont for $4,582,750

Alleged Repurchases
Jan. 6, 1930

Du Pont	Raskob
Draws check to Raskob for $5,254,125 in alleged repurchase of same stock (3)	Draws check for $5,289,500 and makes note to du Pont for $700,000 in alleged repurchase of same stock (4)

December, 1929

Du Pont	Raskob
Allegedly sells stock to Raskob for $1,560,000 (5)	Allegedly sells stock to du Pont for $1,569,000 (6)

Alleged Sales
Dec. 26, 1929

Du Pont	Raskob
Draws check to Raskob for $1,569,000	Draws check to du Pont for $1,560,000

Alleged Repurchases
Jan. 27, 1930

Du Pont	Raskob
Draws check to Raskob for $2,020,000 in alleged repurchase of same stock (7)	Draws check to du Pont for $1,600,000 in alleged repurchase of same stock (8)

January, 1930

Du Pont	Raskob
Draws check for Raskob for $1,350,000 to balance account	Draws check to du Pont for $1,787,066.66 to balance account

SUMMARY OF ABOVE TRANSACTIONS

Du Pont Received Checks from Raskob:		Raskob Received Checks from du Pont:	
For stocks (2), (3), (6), (7) separate checks were drawn for transfer taxes aggregating	$13,032,250.00 9,284.20	For stocks (1), (4), (5), (8) separate checks were drawn for transfer taxes aggregating	$13,449,125.00 8,399.00
To balance (cashed Jan. 31, 1930)	1,787,066.66	To balance (cashed Jan. 31, 1930)	1,350,000.00
During period Nov. 1929 to Jan. 1930 du Pont received dividends on Raskob's stocks	54,800.00	During period Nov. 1929 to Jan. 1930 Raskob received dividends on du Pont's stocks	75,830.00
Total	$14,883,400.86	Total	$14,883,354.00

Du Pont's total	$14,883,400.86	Du Pont deducted an alleged loss of	$3,120,645.69
Raskob's total	14,883,354.00		
Difference	46.86	Raskob deducted an alleged loss of	4,375,523.51

* Franklin D. Roosevelt Library, PPF226

high government officials, including Secretary of Interior Albert B. Fall, were exposed as having illegally sold rich oil lands owned by the public to private oil interests, particularly to the Sinclair Oil Company. Five members of Harding's cabinet and many other officials were forced out of office over the scandal. Years later, Fall was sent to jail for his role in the scheme, which included accepting some $50,000 in bribes.

To widen Wall Street's participation in the conspiracy, Henry F. Sinclair had set up a dummy corporation, the Continental Trading Company. Sinclair, however, made one mistake: when rumors began to circulate about Teapot Dome, he passed around traceable Liberty bonds registered in the company's name to top Republicans in Washington, ostensibly to help defray the party's 1920 campaign deficit. In 1928 Senate investigators traced these bonds to many leading Republicans: Will H. Hays, Republican National Chairman and Postmaster General; John Weeks, Secretary of War; Andrew Mellon, Secretary of Treasury; and Delaware's own favorite Senator, T. Coleman du Pont.

Coleman, it was shown, had accepted $75,000 worth of Continental's Liberty bonds directly from Harry Sinclair to reimburse Coleman for his part in liquidating the 1920 Republican Party deficit. It was further revealed that the Continental Trading Corporation had been set up to purchase 3.3 million barrels of oil at $1.50 a barrel and resell them to promoters at $1.75 a barrel, without reporting the profits to the Internal Revenue Bureau. The company had used the Liberty bonds in its transactions and bribes, and implications involving Coleman's position as a top Republican Senator in Harding's "inner circle" were obvious. Even to Coleman. He resigned from the Senate in December 1928, before being called for questioning by the investigating committee. The charges against him were allowed to go unanswered. Coleman never testified.

No sooner was this allowed to rest, however, than Coleman's name came up again with regard to Florida land frauds. On April 4, 1929, ninety-three small investors sued Coleman and his business partners for a loss of $1.45 million in a Boca Raton real estate fraud. In one of the most voluminous complaints ever filed in New York Supreme Court—370 pages of documents and legal arguments—the investors charged that Coleman, as a director and member of the finance committee of the Mizner Development Corporation, had "with notice and knowledge" permitted false advertising which promised an increase in land value with a program of development which never existed but was used only to "excite the interest and play upon the imagination of the public."

Indeed, it was strange that someone of Coleman du Pont's corporate experience would, if he was sincere about the "development corporation," allow it to be run by Addison Mizner, an architect without any real estate experience, and his brother, Wilson Mizner, a writer and playwright with little experience in business at all. Nevertheless, on December 7 the stockholders lost the most valuable of their three points in the suit. Justice Peters held that false advertising was not the issue per se, as the "defendants were under no obligation to persons who were neither stockholders nor officers of the corporation."[181] Coleman had won again.

But it was a bitter victory for Coleman, whose rapidly deteriorating health bespoke of cruel irony. For years the huge, 6′ 4″, 210-pound athlete, the cigar-chomping "General" with the broad smile and sweeping gestures, had been the very symbol of Du Pont power. From captaining the greatest gunpowder trust known to history, to building the National Security League which led America into World War I, Coleman had been a national giant.

Now, Coleman ended his life a broken man, his hair white and his face pallid, reduced to amusing himself by fingering fine laces and watching mechanical toys, able to speak only by means of an artificial larynx connected by a tube through a hole in his cancerous throat. "Can't talk, can't eat, hardly breathe," he croaked to callers. "Better dead." The General finally got his wish on, of all days, November 11, 1930—Armistice Day.

"Yes, poor T.C. has cashed in at last," wrote Alfred, who had befriended his old foe on his deathbed. "How long and how hard did he work for his end!"[182]

Having distributed most of his fortune to his heirs before his death, Coleman left behind only $17 million. But as he was lowered into Sand Hole Woods, the General also left behind a very disturbed family. Even the confident leader of the clan, Pierre, stood by his cousin's grave with a worried look creasing his brow. For the fall of Coleman du Pont foreshadowed a dark decade ahead, indeed the darkest, most dangerous years of the family's history, years through which the Barons of the Brandywine would try every legal—and illegal—means possible to preserve their new empire and keep millions of hungry, jobless Americans from sharing their fabulous wealth.

Ten

DECADE OF DESPAIR

1. THE FRUIT OF DROUGHT

The crash of 1929 released a virtual Pandora's box of stored-up economic ills. And in their wake, like a terrible plague spreading across the land, into every factory and every home, came the Great Depression.

The initial reaction from Wilmington and Washington was one of mixed alarm and disbelief. President Hoover, holding that one does not encourage a sick man to recover by reminding him of his illness, cheerily attempted to allay the population's mounting fears with bedside manner and false obituaries over the dead body of the Depression.

"I don't see how such a shrinkage in [stock] value," wrote an irritated Alfred du Pont, "totalling, I presume, several billions of dollars, can take place, involving a proportinate shrinking of credit, without causing a period of depression."[1] That was in January of 1930, when the number of jobless had already soared from 450,000 at the time of the crash to over 4 million. By the following October the unemployed topped 5 million. "Millions of men going around with empty dinner kettles," Alfred noted. "One can never tell what social upheaval may be imminent."[2]

In this crisis Herbert Hoover, despite popular belief to the contrary, was a man lacking neither purpose nor resolve. In his foreign trade policies as Secretary of Commerce, he had been a vigorous expansionist, and although he saw the real preservation of domestic prosperity in the development of foreign markets, Hoover had also been a strong advocate of labor-management cooperation, government economic regulation, and public works spending in the domestic field.

As early as 1921 Hoover had encouraged a program of collaboration between union leaders, chiefly William Green and Sidney Hillman, and corporate leaders, and proposed a regular policy of federal intervention in the areas of unemployment, welfare, and labor distribution. His Conference on Unemployment that year, over which he was the presiding and guiding force, endorsed planned public works. The following year, in 1922, Hoover founded with Franklin Roosevelt the American Construction

Council to plan the construction industry as a trade association, denouncing rugged individualists and unbridled profit seekers as mavericks dangerous to the balanced order of giant corporate trusts.

A sponsor of a series of federal labor-management conferences, Hoover supported the drive to end the twelve-hour day in steel and backed the Railway Act of 1926. He also helped found the American Association of Labor Legislation, the decade's most important organization of developing corporate liberalism, bringing together such financial celebrities as Bernard Baruch, G.E. president Gerard Swope, banker Frank Vanderlip, and Standard Oil's George Pratt.

Although his 1928 victory was billed as a triumph of the WASP middle class, Hoover's whole record was clearly a commitment to the business aristocracy. "America is not yet dominated by its great cities," hailed the St. Paul *Pioneer Press* at the time of his election. "Control of its destinies still remains in the smaller communities and rural regions, with their traditional conservatism and solid virtues. . . . Main Street is still the principal thoroughfare of the nation."[3] Nevertheless, it was from Wall Street, not Main Street, that Hoover selected his cabinet: Secretary of State, Henry Stimson, a Roosevelt administration relic related to two partners of Morgan's Bonbright & Company; Commerce, Robert Lamont, president of American Steel Foundries and a Morgan protégé; Treasury, Andrew Mellon, succeeded by gold magnate Ogden Mills; Navy, Charles Adams, director of A.T. & T. and father-in-law of J. P. Morgan's son Henry.

It was in this spirit, then, that Hoover invited Pierre du Pont, Alfred Sloan, Henry Ford, and other leading industrialists to a special manufacturers' conference in November 1930. By that time, with unemployment up to 6 million, the deepening crisis had moved Hoover to conclude that the economic problems of the country could not "work themselves out" without some initiative and coordination on the national level. The result was a pledge by Pierre and his industrial brethren "on their individual behalf" not to initiate any "movement for wage reduction." In return, labor leaders including John L. Lewis, John Frey, and William Hutcheson, pledged that "no movement beyond those already in negotiation should be initiated for the increase of wages."[4] To further break down the dam of corporate fears holding back capital investment and to stimulate jobs, on November 23 Hoover wired the country's governors to encourage their state and county governments with the "energetic yet prudent pursuit of public works."

In many ways, Hoover laid the groundwork for the future New Deal by initiating the steps toward federal involvement in many areas of the economy, including welfare, public works, stock market regulation, farm subsidization, and oil price support (by encouraging state laws restricting the tapping of resources and therefore oil volume). But in each area, Hoover failed to take the necessary step toward a highly centralized state capitalism. He did establish the Federal Farm Board in 1929, with Alexander Legge—Baruch's protégé and president of International Harvester—as chairman of a committee of other large agricultural industrialists with a direct stake in the new price-support program; but he was yet unwilling to restrict the volume of food production. Although he encouraged local and state public works projects, Hoover was unwilling to establish a massive $1 to $3 billion federal works program along the lines proposed by the National Unemployment League or his own Emergency Committee on Unemployment, settling for a small $150 million appropriation. Again, while he established the Federal Employment Service to help the states mitigate unemployment, Hoover also vetoed the Wagner Bill, which would have replaced the FES's twenty-four independent offices with a grants-in-aid system conforming to minimum federal standards. Still again, with regard to relief, although he encouraged expanded state and local programs, Hoover was reluctant to move toward direct federal aid and regulation.

In each area, Hoover was hesitant to resolve the need of a national economy of huge trusts for a rationalized economic *system* through a centralized political state, relying instead on inadequate local and private resources to solve a national crisis. While he grasped the economic and social implications of industrialization probably before many others even suspected their existence, Hoover lacked the necessary personal character to initiate adequate measures in the face of substantial corporate opposition (including that of Lammot du Pont) that had earlier endorsed his candidacy.

Yet, it was just this deficiency in action that stirred some corporate desertions from his ranks. "Hoover," wrote Alfred du Pont in Florida, "is not handling the situation with the force it needs. The emergency is much more drastic than we were facing during the war."[5] Alfred's concern was shared by many of his relatives in Wilmington, particularly Irénée and Pierre, who well understood that an irate labor movement was indeed more of a threat to America's established order and property values than any foreign enemy.

When unemployment reached 8 million in January 1931, doubt rose over the feasibility of Hoover's "voluntary" wage maintenance policy. But when the number of jobless workers topped 9 million in October, its failure was unquestionable. In December 1929, corporate leaders had imposed "only" twenty-three wage cuts on the working class; by August 1931, wage cuts had climbed to 221, among them, Du Pont-controlled

U.S. Rubber. Between wage cuts and layoffs (which hit recently migrated Blacks from the South hardest because of discrimination and their relegation to the most expendable unskilled jobs), starvation racked the cities. Pennsylvania, for example, recorded a 25 percent rise in cases of undernourishment among its school children. Ford Motor Company's medical department reported that workers were increasingly catching infections because of malnutrition, while Henry Ford disclaimed any responsibility for public welfare. Bread lines lengthened, and the number of street beggars and apple sellers doubled and redoubled until the avenues of the cities were so filled with poverty and humiliation that the rich took to ocean voyages to escape the miserable scene.

With unemployment and resultant starving families came despair, soon leading to a mass of emotional breakdowns and even suicides. In 1929 the suicide rate was 14 per 100,000 people; in 1930, 15.7; in 1931, 16.8; in 1932, 17.4—an increase of 24 percent since the depression had begun.

Families, lacking an economic base on which to survive, deteriorated by the hundreds of thousands, as over 2 million men became transients, riding the rails in a futile search for jobs. Southern Pacific alone reported ejecting 683,457 staggering transients from its trains in 1932.

Hoover's response to this crisis was totally inadequate. Although he helped Wagner enact the Employment Stabilization Act of 1931, the law's effectiveness was largely contingent on the quality of its administration, quality which Hoover's appointments undermined. The FES board became an impotent statistical body, a fate which Hoover's own Committee on Recent Economic Changes also shared.

One of the leading members of that committee was Du Pont director John J. Raskob. Disturbed by Hoover's failure to act on its findings, Raskob was also concerned over Hoover's increasing attacks against the New York Stock Exchange. Throughout the Coolidge years Hoover had been critical of stock manipulation and the market's drain on credit. In 1930 he turned his wrath on speculators like Raskob, threatening the Exchange with federal regulation unless it "voluntarily" restricted credit for short selling. Here was the nailed fist beneath the velvet glove of Hoover's famous (and often misunderstood) "voluntarism." But by 1932 Hoover's demand for a "rational" market had become hysterical: he charged that the continuing fall of stock prices was the result not of the fall in earnings, but "sinister" forces. This prompted a Senate investigation that resulted in still further restraints on speculation. But here again, Hoover stepped back from taking the plunge into federal regulation. That would have to wait until later, with FDR's founding of the Securities Exchange Commission (which, by the way, also won Raskob's ire).

Despite their concern over Hoover's lack of dynamic leadership, Raskob and Pierre initiated no direct reform on their own with regard to assistance to the unemployed. Delaware's workers had no unemployment insurance, nor were there any relief laws. Du Pont Company, which did give loans to employed workers, refused to provide these loans or any assistance to its workers once they were laid off and needed help most. And Lammot, despite pledges to Hoover's wage maintenance policy, had fired 20 percent of Du Pont's work force, over 7,000 industrial workers and hundreds of chemists and engineers, in order to keep up Du Pont's traditional 10 percent profit yield on invested capital. In 1932, when scores of other firms were struggling under the threat of bankruptcy, Du Pont showed a $26 million profit.

On the national front, Pierre served on Hoover's Committee for Employment. The committee's title exemplifies Hoover's concern with presenting a positive appearance—in effect, ignoring negative realities. The committee's role in aiding the racist suppression of jobs for Filipino and Mexican-American agricultural workers in California was a dramatic display of the bankruptcy of its "positive" approach in practice.

Of all the Du Ponts, only Pierre's archenemy, Alfred, took any direct action. "They [the Republicans] are not willing to obligate the government to take care of those out of employment, when it is patently their duty to do so," he wrote angrily. In Florida, Alfred took up what Hoover hesitated to do, using his personal fortune for what he believed should be paid by public taxes. Every morning he sent a string of trucks through Jacksonville which gathered up jobless men, white and black, to put them to work maintaining parks and other public places. Alfred paid each man a daily "survival" wage of $1.25. For two years Alfred continued this $400 a day project, until the New Deal took over with a more realistic program. Alfred was active also in Delaware, where the new governor, C. Douglas Buck, Coleman du Pont's son-in-law and political protégé, appointed him chairman of the state's Old Age Welfare Commission in exchange for Alfred's willingness to mail every month 800 personal checks averaging $16 each. By 1931, when the state legislature passed an old age pension bill, Alfred had spent some $350,000, and, as vice president of the American Association for Old Age Security, was also personally directing a national crusade.

Alfred's doles, however, were not merely humanistic, but humanism seen through a sophisticated class perspective. "If capitalism is not to fall by the wayside," he explained, "then it must work out some plan which will secure the laboring man against all economic conditions. This, in my opinion, can be readily done, provided a fair and comprehensive plan of profit-sharing could be worked out so as to provide a surplus to be devoted to the welfare and maintenance of the working class, just as there is now a surplus devoted to the interests of invested capital."[6]

Although Lammot du Pont was definitely opposed to profit-sharing, his brothers were close to Alfred on this question of the need for some comprehensive plan. Such a plan had been proposed in 1931 by G.E. president Gerard Swope to the convention of the National Electrical Manufacturers Association. Swope proposed a compulsory cartelization of all major American corporations into federally controlled trade associations for each industry. Each association would regulate both production and prices, keeping the former down while keeping the latter up. Codes for "fair practices" would be enforced by the government, and central planning would be implemented by a national economic council of corporate leaders and "responsible" union leaders.

The Swope Plan was recognized at the time as an obvious flirtation with the economic order of fascism that had already been established in Italy by Mussolini and was then being proposed by Hitler in Germany, and Hoover accurately denounced it as such. Fearful of so far-reaching a step, Hoover stepped back from the abyss, while others, including John J. Raskob and Pierre and Irénée du Pont, stepped forward.

The Swope Plan, in many ways the child of Hoover's own encouragement of trade associations throughout the Twenties, won wide acclaim in the business community, particularly from three powerful organizations, the National Association of Manufacturers, the U.S. Chamber of Commerce, and the National Industrial Conference Board. The Du Ponts were active in all three, particularly the NICB, whose economist, Dr. Virgil Jordan, solemnly declared that American business was ready for an "economic Mussolini."[7] Significantly, the chairman of the National Industrial Conference Board was none other than Irénée du Pont.

Irénée was in no way alone in his enthusiasm for such "planning." From a poll of its members in 1932, the U.S. Chamber of Commerce reported that 90 percent of its members favored national planning of some sort. The American Legion's 1931 national convention proposed a "national defense council" for the purpose of immediate concentration and utilization of the resources of the nation. In the summer of 1932 Owen Young, chairman of General Electric, backed Swope with a call for "strong government." C. T. Revere, Wall Street broker, was a bit more candid, writing: "If any country in continental Europe were confronted by a crisis of the character indicated in the United States today, there would be a demand for a dictator. Unless conditions improve—and improve very soon—we are not certain that we ourselves may not be involved in a situation that may call for just such a step."

"Give the President," spoke financier Henry I. Harriman in May 1932 "so far as it can constitutionally be done, the right, when Congress is not in session, to suspend the operation of existing laws and to provide for emergency measures required by public welfare." Harriman, who was elected president of the U.S. Chamber of Commerce later that month, called for a reorganization of the Federal Trade Commission "so as to enlarge the power of the trade associations and to permit them to adopt fair basic rules governing the conditions under which each trade shall be carried on." Echoing Swope, Harriman suggested that "business itself establish its economic council to consider the fundamental problems that affect all business." The myth of anti-trust was fully discarded; the trusts were now nakedly visible for all to see.

Even Alfred du Pont enjoyed his personal fantasies in this controversy over political regimentation. "Were I a dictator of the United States today," he wrote to a relative, "the first thing I would do would be to cancel or repeal every bonus and every pension that might be termed unearned, giving only to such as have suffered by injury or old age in the service. . . . I would put every dollar to work in the country and in addition to that, I would put every son of a gun, or daughter of a gun, back of that dollar and make them work."[8] Alfred even dreamed of an island prison surrounded by vicious sharks where he would imprison, among others, some of his relatives. For people like Pierre and Raskob he reserved a special treat: he would have them shot.

Pierre and Raskob's political protégé Al Smith, had more serious proposals, suggesting in October 1931 that "to say the least, a mild form of dictatorship, honestly operated, honestly intentioned, must be set up, or else we will simply have the promise of relief on paper."[9]

Smith by then had reversed his earlier "retirement" from politics and was openly reseeking the Democratic presidential nomination, backed again by Pierre du Pont and John J. Raskob. And it was within this tense political atmosphere that Du Pont, merely a month earlier, made its first investment in Remington Arms, the second largest gun manufacturer in the country, which, in turn, was also negotiating to buy an interest in Winchester Repeating Arms, then in receivership. This Du Pont investment, made mainly for a gunpowder market, was charged three years later before a Senate committee with having other, more military designs. But more on that later.

Pierre's public political activities, however, centered around his continued campaign for prohibition repeal and liquor taxes as a source of government revenue. In this campaign he was joined by Raskob and Smith, both of whom were directors of his National Association Against Prohibition.

On April 23, 1930, Pierre appeared before the House Judiciary Committee with a thick volume of categorical replies to all the "dry" arguments. It was his finest hour. "The people were surprised at the ratification of the Eighteenth Amendment," he claimed. "They may be surprised in a year or so by finding it repealed." Then he delivered the committee a stern warning, which, coming from a former chairman of Du Pont and General Motors, struck a chord of concern throughout the hearing room. "No one should refuse to submit questions to a vote by the people. To refuse is to invite reference to that court of last resort referred to in the Declaration of Independence, in these words of unmistakable meaning: 'Whenever any form of government becomes destructive of these ends [the security of the rights of the people], it is the right of the people to alter or to abolish it.' "

A stir swept the room, but Pierre continued, citing violation of the Constitution by Congress and the executive branch, the embarrassment of the Supreme Court, and the experience of liquor legislation in England, including statistical evidence. While giving perhaps the most comprehensive testimony against prohibition ever delivered before Congress, Pierre also spoke in ominous terms.

"If there were such agitation over any other amendment as there is over this one," he said, "I would favor reconsideration of it, too."

"Or reconsideration of the Constitution itself?" asked Kansas's Congressman Sparks.

"Yes," Pierre answered, looking straight at Sparks, "the Constitution itself."[10]

Such statements may seem strange in their force of conviction when they are considered against the more burning questions of those days; they serve to demonstrate the limitations the "liberal" Du Ponts imposed on themselves through their extreme caution in making public statements in these early years of the Depression, and their unwillingness to commit themselves ideologically to either the Hoover camp (which they saw as feeble) or the Swope camp (which they mildly distrusted).

For Pierre, prohibition represented the only clear safe ground on which to publicly stand in the political whirlwind, agreeing with Colonel Grayson M. P. Murphy (a Morgan banker and broker who later allegedly played a crucial role with the Du Ponts in a more dangerous political conspiracy) that prohibition was harmful to industry. But even there, on the secure turf of prohibition, the Du Ponts were subject to mild discomfort. On the same day of Pierre's testimony, in one of the few perceptive remarks of her teetotaling life, Dr. Mary Harris Armor addressed the National Conference of the Women's Christian Temperance Union, charging that "big business" sought to bring back liquor so that "the poor man will drink the liquor to pay their taxes."[11] Although Dr. Armor never expressed much active concern for the plight of the poor whites and blacks that constituted the majority of her own state of Georgia, nevertheless, even Pierre couldn't argue with her point, having long advocated a liquor tax to replace the tax on corporate incomes. In this regard, Hoover's National Law Enforcement Commission, which tried futilely to find some solution to "the entire question of law enforcement and organization of justice," lent weight to Pierre's cause, issuing a report which thoroughly destroyed the notion that prohibition had reduced crime; in fact, it proved that prohibition had created more widespread evils than ever. The commission, headed by former Du Pont lawyer and U.S. Attorney General George Wickersham, submitted its report to President Hoover, who promptly filed it away, his dry convictions unshaken.

More effective than either Pierre or Wickersham was John Raskob: while others talked, Raskob organized. What Raskob was organizing was to prove to be the most formidable force in American politics for twenty years—a "new" Democratic Party.

2. RASKOB, THE PARTY BUILDER

Perhaps more than anyone else, John Raskob grasped the essence of the 1928 election—the revolt of the cities.

In 1920 the Republican candidate, Harding, had carried all twenty-seven of the nonsouthern cities; in 1928 the Democratic candidate, Smith, won over eight of those cities and made considerable gains in sixteen more. As Smith's campaign manager and Democratic National Chairman, Raskob had geared the Democratic appeal to the new immigrant and migrant population that made up the bulk of the unskilled industrial work force of the northern cities. The results of this strategy were conclusive: for the first time since Wilson, the Democratic Party had won majorities in Boston, New York, Jersey City, Providence, New Haven, Milwaukee, St. Louis, and San Francisco.

Torn by internal divisions and "Coolidge prosperity," that revolt of Catholic and Jew, of unskilled immigrants and dispossessed Anglo-Saxon farmers, had failed. But Raskob was well aware that the *social* revolt of the teeming masses in the cities would continue and intensify, and he was determined that its political form should remain and develop within the confines of the Democratic Party, where liberal business reformers could use it for their own purposes. With the Crash and growing social discontent, the importance of confining the urban revolt within the Democratic Party was made even more paramount. After 1929 the revolt of labor and the dispossessed became the driving motor for a party steered by corporate leaders like Raskob, Pierre du Pont, Bernard Baruch, and Gerard Swope, who all realized the necessity of structural reform in order to save the basic system of private ownership and corporate control.

Raskob's first move in this direction was to write off some of the 1928 Democratic deficit with a personal contribution of $150,000. Pierre also helped, writing a check for $25,100. These and an additional $735,000 in donations from Smith supporters, including financiers Herbert Lehman, Bernard Baruch, and William F. Kenney, helped soothe the party's anger over the fact that the National Chairman, in his enthusiasm for his friend, had overspent the National Committee's $4 million authorization by some $3 million. John J. Raskob, "the man who made eighty millionaires," had left the party broke.

Criticisms of Raskob continued throughout 1929, particularly from Dixie Democrats, many of whom had bolted to the Hoover campaign banner in 1928. This crack in "the solid South" had been engineered by the resurgent Ku Klux Klan, whose anti-Catholicism was not exactly appreciated by such a papal favorite as John Raskob. During the last days of Smith's campaign, KKK bigotry had so enraged Raskob that he exploded in a public attack that many claimed lost Smith the election. Raskob, however, was not a man to attack a force that was not a challenge: it was the fact that the Klan had already been successful in its anti-Smith drive that prompted Raskob to drop his usual calm demeanor. The election, it was clear, had already been lost.

After Smith's defeat, Raskob correctly saw the Klan's backwardness as the major obstacle to his moving the Democratic Party forward and rebuilding it into an urban-based organization. What complicated matters for the chairman was the rich financing the Klan enjoyed from many of Raskob's fellow businessmen, providing the financial backbone for a mass rural alternative to Raskob's own plans for the party. It was this rural strength that gave the Klan its danger as a powerful organization of the Right with many analogies to European fascism: its backward ideological roots were deep in country and village folk; its financial backing by the business class; its rabid anti-communism and opposition to the labor movement; its use of minorities as scapegoats; its stress on nationalism and racial "purity"; its hostility to many manifestations of the new urban culture of industrial society; its calls for a return to mystical visions of the past; its "Spartan" opposition to sensual and indulgent living in the cities; and its demand for a new social discipline, a new order to return to the ancient mystical virtues of the "old pioneer" stock and its "Protestantism."

It was this force, guided by the southern agricultural aristocracy who made up the bulk of the Dixie bloc in Congress, that challenged Raskob's leadership by demanding his resignation. That Raskob was able to resist such pressure reflected the strength of new urban forces in the Democratic Party. It was in the cities that the party had made solid gains, cutting 900,000 votes from the Republican 1924 victory in New York alone.

After the crash the southern assaults intensified, reaching their peak in April 1930 in the Senate. There, Senator Robinson, ranking Republican member of the Senate Lobby Investigating Committee investigating the anti-prohibition lobby, called the Democratic National Chairman before the committee in revenge for attacks by Democratic committee members on Claudius Huston, Republican National Chairman. But Robinson had another, more deadly motive: he was hoping to exacerbate dry-wet divisions within the Democratic Party. Raskob, by affirming his $65,000 contribution to the National Association Against Prohibition, gave the Republicans exactly what they wanted.

Thunderous demands broke out from Dixie for Raskob to resign. "Mr. Raskob's own testimony before the Senate Committee," declared North Carolina's Senator Simmons on the floor of the Senate, "disclosed that the money he and others are contributing to the Association is being used, or is to be used, for the defeat of dry Democrats who are opposed by wet Republicans."[12]

From amid this storm, Raskob emerged calm and unmoved. "I have no intention of resigning,"[13] the little Du Pont lieutenant quietly told Washington correspondents, and he dug in, waiting for the barrage to end and the 1930 campaign to begin.

The election of 1930 strengthened Raskob's hold on the party by providing new leadership from the "wet" cities of the North. On a pledge of unemployment insurance, Franklin Roosevelt was reelected governor by 750,000 votes, twice the plurality rolled up by Governor Al Smith in 1922 when he set the Democratic record. Republican states like Ohio and Illinois also elected Democrats, and unemployment insurance became the battle cry of the Democratic organizations in New Jersey, Rhode Island, New Hampshire, Nebraska, Idaho, and of course, Delaware. Vilified for months, the National Chairman now became referred to as "canny, soft-spoken little Raskob."[14]

For Raskob, the question of unemployment insurance was entwined with the question of how to finance it. Always, this returned him to the battle against prohibition, an issue which he saw as an opportunity to both strengthen his hold on the "wet" North and purge his "dry" enemies in the South. He became determined to push rural southern forces into a confrontation.

At the Democratic National Committee meeting in Washington, D.C., the following March, Raskob submitted Pierre's "home-rule" liquor plan, warning that if it were rejected, "we must squarely face the fact that our party is really divided into two parties"[15] of the rural "dry" South and the urban "wet" North. Boos, jeers, hisses, yells, and cheers filled the hall which, according to one report, "bordered on the riotous." Worried over a split which would hurt the party's election chances in 1932, Franklin Roosevelt, then the front runner for the presidential nomination, sided with the South, holding that only the National Convention could voice party policy. Roosevelt was obviously consolidating his position for the nomination. The Raskob-Roosevelt feud was on.

Raskob walked out of the National Committee meeting empty-handed, only to pursue his campaign the following month. In April he sent out a memorandum asking every member of the National Committee to send in his individual position on major issues, particularly prohibition. The results, he explained, would be tabulated and submitted to the National Convention.

Again an uproar. "The best service that Mr. Raskob can render the Democratic Party," cried the Raleigh *News and Observer*, "is to pay up the debts he contracted and get out of the chairmanship."[16] The Republican press had a heyday. The New York *Herald Tribune*, organ of the Republican Mills-Reid family, printed a cartoon showing Raskob forcing the Democratic mule's face into a barrel of whiskey, while saying, "If you don't want to drink, all right, but at least *say* so." Likewise, the Ford-controlled Detroit *News* showed Raskob at a restaurant table bellowing for a beer, while a teetotaling "Miss Democracy" held her head in mortification.

But Raskob's letter was in reality a shrewd call for a vote which had been denied him at the Washington meeting. As one admiring national magazine put it, "For 'an amateur in politics,' Mr. Raskob seems to be getting things he wants and to want things worth getting."[17] The vice president for the National Association Against Prohibition had the "drys" and their rural southern power on the run.

Raskob's next move was to centralize the Democratic Party. He put up $122,000 to open a permanent national headquarters in Washington for *daily* work, abandoning the previous approach of a national presence only four months every four years. There, Raskob placed as head Jouett Shouse, a popular wet Missourian; he held a dinner in Shouse's honor, mentioning only his own intention not to resign before slipping away to leave Shouse in the limelight and everyone with the impression that he had delegated his authority to another. Hardly.

Through Shouse and his $25,000 publicity assistant, Charles F. Michelson, Raskob worked silently and unseen, enjoying his anonymity. While publicly dismissed as "the man who puts up the dough," Raskob moved deftly behind the scenes, building his organization in the cities, bringing in the labor movement, particularly the Teamsters Union. In the South he supported challenges of party loyalty against Dixiecrats who had abandoned Smith in 1928. Purges occurred in South Carolina, Virginia, Alabama, and North Carolina. Although everywhere bolters were forced out through well-financed primaries or challenges that put them into the political isolation that set them up for the chopping block, nowhere was the hand of the little butcher from Wilmington publicly seen. By the end of the year, Johnny Raskob had consolidated the Democratic Party from a battered, incoherent organization into a party moving faster and faster toward assuming a positive urban character.

As the national spokesman for the Democratic Party, Raskob offered proposals that reflected this new power base, suggesting old age and unemployment insurance and his old favorite, a five-day week without a diminution of weekly wages, a sharp contrast with Hoover's "share-the-work" policy which encouraged accompanying wage cuts. "The last [the five-day week] we have, in eminently good company," Raskob stated, "been urging as a solution for the present unemployment caused by the improvement of machinery, and for the depression of business caused by the falling off in buying power because of unemployment. Old age and unemployment insurance, we believe to be the bulwarks for the capitalist system against communism. With the capitalist system effectively producing abundant wealth, it should be able to assure these human minimums to all its people. These are the greatest fears, old-age pauperism and unemployment, which if left unsatisfied might drive the masses to put their faith in another social order."[18]

Raskob backed Swope's protégé, U.S. Steel president Owen D. Young, in his presidential ambitions. But like Hoover, he also stepped back from endorsing the Swope Plan's call for a formal move toward a centralized state capitalism. Government should stay out of business, Raskob felt, "except to safeguard the public by regulation against monopoly and unfair trade practices." Beyond this tongue-in-cheek concession by a Du Pont-

G.M. director to political expediency, Raskob's corporate intentions were clarified by a proposal "that citizens contemplating a business merger may beforehand obtain by the decision of a federal commission an assurance not only that their labor shall not have been in vain, but also that they will not be subject to criminal prosecution under the terms of the Sherman Law. Businessmen, we believe, will favor these suggestions as being helpful and fair."

Many did. But some, like Swope and Baruch, felt Raskob's suggestions were also inadequate. Already, John Garner, Speaker of the House, was proposing that Congress give the President almost dictatorial powers, while Roosevelt, who had enjoyed backing in 1930 from Baruch and Young, expressed interest in Swope's proposals. Subsequently, Young endorsed Roosevelt.

Then Raskob made one fatal mistake. His personal crusades, whether in the form of prohibition or his friendship with Al Smith, prompted him to launch a prohibition poll of 90,000 contributors to the 1928 war chest, most of whom were wets. As this put Roosevelt in an awkward position as a "moderate wet" between anti-prohibitionists and the southern support he had won by his noncommital stand at the Republican National Committee meeting, the poll would definitely hinder Roosevelt's nomination chances.

"It is unfair," Raskob answered, "to suggest that I am using my position as National Chairman to help or hinder any candidate."[19] Yet it was clear that Roosevelt opposed any plank which would read out of the party anyone who wished to be prohibitionist in his local election. Raskob's credibility as National Chairman began to slacken among his former northern liberal supporters. When Raskob joined Garner in supporting the Republican proposal for a federal sales tax, the battle lines were drawn. Roosevelt made his appeal for the "forgotten man," and Al Smith came back fighting. "I will take off my coat and fight to the end," retorted the crusty little banker, "against any candidate who persists in any demagogic appeal to the masses of the working people of this country to destroy themselves by setting class against class and rich against poor."[20] Raskob announced his support of Smith and the battle was on.

Actually, it had already begun. In January 1932, soon after Raskob's prohibition poll, ugly reports began appearing in the national press connecting the party's debts to Raskob's control. The influential *New York Times* charged that the National Chairman "has soaring ideas about the tariff and prohibition, which, *through merit acquired by his generosity*, and a steadfastness in bleak Democratic weather, he hopes to get into the party platform."[21] In response, Raskob could only hurl charges of religious bias at those who raised the issue of the party's debts.

Yet the attacks continued; the liberal *New Republic* called for an end to his "one-man control" of a national political party by the whip hand of money and credit: "He, on his part, tempted by the prospect of dictating a platform, naming a candidate, and perhaps running an administration, has connived rather than protested at the rising [debt] obligation.

"The Democratic Party's debt to Mr. Raskob is now the largest known political commitment in our history. It is nearly three times as large as the Republican 'debt of gratitude' that gave us Teapot Dome. Nor is it an outright gift, one that might, for theory's sake, leave the party free. Mr. Raskob has given his party some money, but this is a living loan, an indeterminate mortgage—the sort of debt that reeks of obligation. . . . The debts that Chairman Raskob was influential in incurring, Banker Raskob has taken up."[22]

So stinging an attack would normally draw a heated response. But there was none. Nor could there be, since Chairman Raskob was indeed Banker Raskob. After the 1928 disaster a $400,000 note in the party's name was left in the hands of the County Trust Company of New York. The late James J. Riordan, Al Smith, W. F. Kenney, and Raskob himself had all contributed to Smith's campaign and were also all directors of County Trust. Curiously enough, the Democratic note was underwritten by Democratic officials Riordan, Kenney, and Raskob. By March of 1932, when the *New Republic* article appeared, $33,766 had been added by the bank to the debt as accrued interest.

Raskob's new Washington headquarters, likewise, had cost $10,000 a month to operate. By January 1, 1932, the party owed Raskob $354,250 for this alone, raising the grand total of notes held by Raskob to $779,106.[23] Although Pierre's $5000 in 1930 and $12,500 and other contributions in 1931, and Raskob's own $125,000 donation in 1932 (accompanied again by a check from Pierre for $27,000), helped eliminate much of this debt,[24] the publicity damage had already been done.

The publication of these facts did not enhance Raskob's image among the party's new urban rank and file, nor did his endorsement of Al Smith, who had lost most of his New York power base to his successor, Governor Franklin Roosevelt, the creator of the country's first comprehensive system of unemployment relief and a strong proponent of public power works. By the time of the convening of the National Convention in Chicago late in June 1932, it was apparent Smith could not win. Pierre, Raskob, and Baruch then convinced Smith to throw his support over to former Secretary of War Newton Baker in an effort to block Roosevelt's nomination. "I was four years ahead of my party," a dejected Al Smith told the convention, "and look what happened to me."

Between the candidacy of Baker and that of Texas's John Garner (who was backed by newspaper magnate William Randolph Hearst, William McAdoo, and the Ku Klux Klan), Raskob had succeeded in preventing Roosevelt from gathering the two-thirds vote necessary for nomination. By the fourth ballot, only pressure from Louisiana's Huey Long prevented the Mississippi delegation from beginning a desertion from the Roosevelt camp that might have turned into a disastrous rout.

Fortunately for Roosevelt, Smith had made many enemies. William McAdoo, who controlled the large California delegation, held a deep grudge against Smith for preventing his own nomination in 1924 by similar means. Nor were Klan forces from the South any friend of "the happy warrior" or Raskob, and Hearst hated the internationalist Baker almost as much as he did Smith. The outcome of this animosity toward the Smith camp came late in the evening when lean William McAdoo mounted the speaker's platform to announce that California was casting its 44 votes for Roosevelt. The Smith galleries jeered, but the dam had burst. Within minutes, riding a flood of endorsements, Franklin D. Roosevelt was the Democratic nominee for President.

A master compromiser, Roosevelt selected Garner as his running mate while also moving quickly to placate the Du Pont forces. A. Mitchell Palmer, the Attorney General under Wilson who had secured German dye patents for the Du Ponts, was asked to draft the nominee's platform. A conservative document, Palmer's platform ignored unemployment and Roosevelt's "forgotten man." In their stead, prohibition was raised as the main issue of the campaign. Raskob continued as National Chairman, and his labor lieutenant, Irish Catholic Dan Tobin, head of the Teamsters, was named head of the Democratic Labor Committee.

Roosevelt received substantial aid from Pierre and Raskob. Pierre donated $15,000 and Raskob $23,000.[25] But the greatest boon for Roosevelt was Raskob's national party machine, based in Washington with political strings to every American city. Without it, campaign manager Jim Farley would have been hard put to wage an effective unified campaign capable of turning out the vote in such large numbers as was done.

Roosevelt's was a low-keyed campaign, completely avoiding any statement on collective bargaining (despite a plea by John L. Lewis), deficit spending, the NRA, federal housing, or increased income taxes on the wealthy, and in fact it was often contradictory. Roosevelt contented himself with attacks on Hoover's expenditures, while he advanced unemployment-aid and public works that would require huge sums of government spending. He called for an end to growing centralization of power in Washington, yet proposed planning and federal regulation of utilities and the stock market. In all this, his tone was low and even at times discordant, allowing public animosity toward Herbert Hoover to win his vague case for him.

Hoover's image had already suffered a crushing blow by the Depression. Industrial production was down 50 percent, according to the Federal Reserve Board; iron and steel, 85 percent; lumber, 77 percent; cement, 65 percent. Factory payrolls had been slashed 65 percent, employment 44 percent. Over 13 million workers were jobless and over 4,000 banks had failed.

But the *coup de grâce* to Hoover's career was delivered in June 1932, by his own hand. A "bonus army" of thousands of tired, unemployed veterans and their families arrived that month in Washington demanding a federal bonus promised them by law, but not payable until the 1940's. They had traveled thousands of miles in battered jalopies, trucks, and wagons; many had even walked. And when Hoover wouldn't even receive them, they pitched tents, erected shacks, and slept in the capital's parks to petition Congress. As soon as Congress adjourned after refusing to grant the marchers any relief, Hoover made a show of force. On July 28 a police attempt to evict some of the squatters resulted in the killing of two veterans. Hoover then called in the Army. Army Chief of Staff General Douglas MacArthur, who described the marchers as "a mob . . . animated by the essence of revolution,"[26] delayed the use of troops only long enough to have his swagger stick and medal-covered uniform arrive from a nearby fort.

Aided by Colonel Dwight D. Eisenhower and Major George Patton, MacArthur ordered tanks, four troops of cavalry with drawn sabers, and a column of steel-helmeted infantry with fixed bayonets to enter downtown Washington and advance on the unarmed veterans. From Pennsylvania Avenue, MacArthur's proud army marched across the Anacostia Bridge, thousands of veterans and their wives and children fleeing before them, and advanced on their shanty village, lobbing tear gas bombs and setting its shacks and tents afire. An infant died from the tear gas, an 11-year-old boy was blinded for life, and many veterans were wounded. MacArthur, responding to a reporter's claim of having seen a cavalryman use his saber to slash off a veteran's ear, explained, somewhat amused, that that was quite impossible. "You don't slash with a saber," he told the press, "you lunge,"[27] and, striking the correct pose for photographers, he demonstrated the proper thrust.

That night, from the windows of the White House's Lincoln Room, Hoover watched the red glow from the burning camps in the southeast and retired. The next day the press was informed that "the President was pleased."[28]

Such crude brutality only spurred desertions already underway in Hoover's ranks, even among some leading Republicans. After Roosevelt privately expressed interest in the Swope Plan, corporate desertions mounted. Finally, Henry Harriman, president of the U.S. Chamber of Commerce, confronted Hoover with the fact that FDR had agreed to the Swope Plan's enactment. If the President persisted in his opposition, he warned, he would lose the support of many leaders in big business.

Hoover persisted, and many of the most "enlightened" corporate leaders, particularly in the light-goods industries who suffered most immediately from the loss of retail sales, decided to throw their full weight behind Roosevelt. Among Roosevelt's top supporters were W. N. Reynolds (R. J. Reynolds Tobacco), William K. Vanderbilt, Cyrus McCormick, Edward Harkness, Edward Guggenheim, Jesse Straus (R. H. Macy Co.), Harry Warner (motion pictures), and Mrs. Harry Payne Whitney. Many were registered Democrats; others, including Republican senators Robert La Follette, Jr., Hiram Johnson, George Norris, Smith Wildman Brookhart, and Bronson Cutting, were not. Additionally, rumors persisted of secret Rockefeller contributions despite their public donations to the Republican ticket, their traditional stronghold.

Other than Pierre, most of the Du Ponts were publicly for Hoover, although many with some private reluctance. "We may not yet be coming out of this depression," Lammot du Pont told some 400 Buick dealers convened in New York, "but we are on the verge of coming out of it."[29] Publicly, Lammot backed his convictions with a $30,000 donation to the Republican treasury; privately, he voted for Roosevelt. R. R. M. Carpenter gave $19,600, Walter Carpenter gave $2,000, William du Pont, Jr., gave $5,500, and Irénée, $10,200.[30] (Irénée also voted secretly for Roosevelt.) In the Republican camp they were joined by most of the richest families: the Morgans, Bakers, Carnegies, Fords, Pratts, Mellons, Firestones, most of the Guggenheims, and ever reliable Alfred Sloan. Many of these, however, may have noted the temper of the country and, like Lammot and Irénée, saw Hoover's cause as already lost.

The White House, sensing the inevitable, was a palace of gloom. "If you put a rose in Hoover's hand it would wilt,"[31] remarked sculptor Gutzon Borglum. "Down with Hoover, slayer of veterans!" was Hoover's only greeting on a campaign visit to Detroit. Thousands of auto workers lined the streets of that city as he passed by, but they remained sullen and silent. When the President finally arrived at the speaker's platform, his face was ashen, his hands trembling. Hoover looked a pathetic, beaten man. A "hero" only four years before, Hoover was now the national villain.

Election day came almost as an anticlimax, Roosevelt's 22.8 million votes totally overriding Hoover's 15.75 million. Roosevelt's victory was clearly a city return based on the vote of labor and the rural disinherited. Roosevelt swept thirty-two of the thirty-six largest cities. For the first time since before World War I, a Democratic candidate had won majorities in Cincinnati, Indianapolis, Cleveland, Chicago, Detroit, Pittsburgh, Baltimore, Minneapolis, Kansas City, Salt Lake City, Denver, Seattle, Portland, Oakland, and Los Angeles. Two hundred and eighty-two counties were won that had never before gone Democratic. The South, based on the returns in its cities, had again become reliably "solid." Miners of the six Appalachia states also joined the Democratic landslide, giving Roosevelt 39 of 45 counties. Many Blacks abandoned their traditional loyalty to the party of Lincoln, a desertion no doubt aided by their increasing migration from rural Dixie to the industrial cities of the North.

It was the most dramatic electoral reversal in American history, and Roosevelt owed much of it to the Democratic National Chairman's four-year effort to build an urban-based party. It was Raskob who had financed the party through its difficult transition years. It was Raskob who had formulated the grand urban strategy and forged a coherent, centralized organization. And it was Raskob who had grasped the lightning of the urban revolt and put it in the Democratic machine to power it to victory. As Charles Michelson, Democratic Party publicity director, put it two months after the election, Raskob was "the man who saved the Democratic Party."[32]

3. THE HONEYMOON

On a particularly hot New England day in the summer of 1931 a flashy new automobile was speeding along the Osterville-Hyannis road, when, rounding a curve, it sideswiped a car operated by Miss Ethel Howard, forcing her to crash head-on into another, oncoming car. Screeching to a halt, the driver, Henry B. du Pont, surveyed the accident he had caused and found a young teacher, Miss Julia Avila, badly hurt. Three days later Julia died in Cape Cod Hospital.

Whatever pangs of conscience Henry may have had privately, he showed none in public. When Julia's father, Manuel Avila, sued for the loss of his daughter, Henry, true to family tradition, claimed innocence and for six months fought the suit in court. The jury, however, was not convinced and finally ordered him to pay Julia's family $11,168.

Such a sum was a small fortune in those grim days of the Depression, when children went to school in shoes soled with cardboard and some witnessed their unpaid teachers passing out in the classroom from lack of food. Yet for the Du Ponts, $11,000 was an expendable pittance from a financial reservoir grown even larger since 1929. For, despite its bitter bequest to most Americans, the Depression had been kind to the Du Ponts. In fact, in terms of the competition it destroyed and the avenues for cheap investments it provided, the Great Depression had been very kind, indeed.

Alfred I. du Pont, for example, continued collecting failing banks in Florida, complaining that he had to tighten his belt and was able to spend "only" $300,000 to have the new architectural firm of his son Alfred Victor complete America's rival to the sunken gardens of Versailles: Nemours.

Likewise, William du Pont, Jr., began designing the Delaware Race Track, the first of twenty-five such ventures around the world, while directing the $50 million investment of the American Horse Shows. Meanwhile, Anthony Drexel, the husband of Francis G. du Pont's granddaughter, rode the green as a leading player of that most aristocratic of sports, polo.

Henry F. du Pont pursued his epic wanderings through the country's shops and auctions in search of antiques for his Winterthur mansion, now expanded to 180 rooms. In 1930 he lent his art experts to police to track down fraudulent dealers who had undermined the market. Ernest du Pont, whose home was robbed of $50,000 to $75,000 worth of jewelry in 1931, engaged in a similar hunt, only to be shocked with the revelation that the thief was his own maid.

The Depression, like previous panics, also provided the bankruptcies and credit shortage of which empires are made, and the Du Ponts used the crisis to expand their holdings into many new fields of investment.

With land prices plummeting, Maurice du Pont became president, treasurer, and director of Realty Accumulating (sic!) Company and the Great Hills Improvement Company. Francis I. du Pont joined the New York Cotton Exchange and became a director of the Missouri-Kansas Pipeline Company. Raskob increased his financial holdings, adding American Surety Company, Emigrant Industrial Savings Bank, and American International Corporation to his Du Pont, G.M., Missouri Pacific Railroad, and County Trust directorships. Donaldson Brown, Du Pont in-law and G.M. director, also became a director of the St. Louis-San Francisco Railway. Walter Carpenter, Jr., joined the board of Bell Telephone of Pennsylvania.

Du Pont executives also followed Du Pont investments. Vice President Jasper Crane joined the board of D. Van Nostrand Company; Harry Haskell, Sr., the boards of Noranda Mines, Ltd., International Mining Corporation, Triplex Safety Glass Company, and Equitable Trust of New York; Leonard Yerkes, the board of Seabord Air Line, a firm many naïve stock investors had mistaken during the Twenties for an airline with growth prospects. William P. Allen became chairman of Childs (Restaurants) Company of New York, and Francis B. Davis, settling into his new post as head of U.S. Rubber, also served as the president of Sampson Corporation and director of New York Trust Company, Malayan-American Plantations, Ltd., Meyer Rubber Company, Nangatuck Chemical Company, Dominion Rubber, Ltd., Rubber Plantations, Ltd., Columbus Rubber Company, Ltd., and U.S. Rubber Plantation Products.

Irénée du Pont joined the board of the troubled Reading Railroad (which he left in 1935), while Eugene du Pont invested heavily in Phillips Petroleum, Inc., and the Delaware Motor Sales Company. Eugene's life was not all pleasant during these days, however, for his was the only Du Pont home in which tragedy struck during the decade. One day, while decorating a chair in the studio of her Dogwood estate, his wife forgot that she had left the car running in the closed garage that was directly below. After a while, she grew drowsy and fell asleep; she never awoke.

Besides that unhappy experience, the Du Ponts ran a streak of luck in the early Thirties. Alfred, on a trip to Cairo, stopped in a curio shop and bought for $17.50 a vase in which he found a strange mineral formation. Later his chemists uncovered a fortune in gold and silver coins dating back to Ptolemy, 300 B.C. His cousin and fellow exile, William, Jr., received a boon of a more traditional nature. Wilmington's federal judge ruled that four transfers of his father's amounting to $6,433,000, which had been made to old Willie's children two years before his death, were not made "in contemplation of death," and ordered the Internal Revenue Service to begin repaying Junior the taxes paid on his father's estate.

A more personal treasure came to Richard C. du Pont in 1932—his life. While he was cruising in the West Indies with his cousin Victor du Pont and friends Thomas Laffey and Scott Townsend, Richard's sloop, the *Nahma,* disappeared. Frantic, the Du Ponts made a special appeal to the U.S. Coast Guard to spare no expense in a search. A. Felix, Sr., was already in Norfolk organizing an expedition to save his son when an Army transport reported finding the sloop foundered off the Carolina coast, all hands alive and well. The ship carried the young men to Panama where, like proper Du Ponts, they refused the pauper's aid of the Salvation Army and headed for home assuring all they could care for themselves. They did.

This harrowing experience did not diminish Richard's flare for danger one bit. He continued his glider flying, which won him world distance records and the National Soaring Championship in 1934, 1935, and 1937. In that last year he also won the $1,500 Silver Evans Trophy for flying his glider into two thunderheads and riding them successfully for the first time in history. His father, A. Felix du Pont, Sr., and brother, A. Felix, Jr., were also airplane buffs. Felix du Pont, Jr., even built a cradle in his plane for his 4-month-old son Felix III. All these Du Ponts managed to crash occasionally, but always without serious injury. A. Felix, Jr.'s 19-year-old wife, the former Eleanor Hoyt (who was Lindbergh's 16-year-old pilot after his triumphant return from Paris), also skimmed the brink of aerial disaster. Flying home to Wilmington in her familiar scarlet monoplane, she encountered a blinding fog over Staten Island and dropped down, trying to fly beneath the clouds. The mist was so bad she was barely able to sight an open field, and she decided to try to land. As she approached the ground, the plane suddenly hit a high wire fence and crashed. Fortunately, she was neither far from Seaview Hospital nor seriously hurt, and later was whisked away by private ambulance to her mother's luxurious home in Manhattan.

None of these incidents dimmed the Du Pont craze for airplanes, Henry B. du Pont increasing his holdings in Trans World Airlines (over which he reigned as chairman), Bendix Aviation, and North American Aviation (which also owned Eastern Airlines until 1938, when it was sold to Kuhn, Loeb, & Co. and Smith Barney & Co., Wall Street brokers). Apparently, the only serious aerial casualty the family suffered during the Thirties was a year-old heifer. Peacefully grazing on Coleman du Pont's Irvington-on-the-Hudson estate, the heifer dropped dead from fright as a roaring U.S. Army air armada swooped overhead toward New York City.

Coleman's son Frank had less aerial ambitions. Francis V. du Pont succeeded his father as president of the Equitable Trust Company of Wilmington and managed Coleman's substantial investments in McHenry Coal Company, Jellico Mountain Coal Company, Louis Sherry, Inc., and Savarin Restaurants. By 1937, while others had gone bankrupt, Frank had expanded into Empire Trust Company, Continental American Life Insurance Company, and Prudential Investors.

Pierre du Pont's holdings also increased. He became a director of the Pennsylvania Railroad, largest railroad in the country, and joined Raskob in building the Empire State Building, tallest building in the world—all this while retaining directorships in Du Pont, Wilmington Trust, and General Motors.

Du Pont control of General Motors was further intensified in 1931 when their arch foes, the Fishers, were bought out. Subsequently, the Fisher Body Division bought increasing amounts of paint, varnish, and imitation leather from Du Pont. In addition, that same year G.M. signed a contract with the Du Ponts' U.S. Rubber Company, agreeing to buy one-half of its tires from U.S. Rubber at market value in exchange for rebates. By 1934 these rebates amounted to $1,437,087 to the Chevrolet Division alone. The following year showed a $1,044,516 rebate, all in violation of anti-trust laws.[33] Du Pont had other areas of G.M. locked up as well, as General Robert E. Wood, president of Sears, Roebuck and Company, discovered when he wrote Du Pont Vice President W. F. Harrington in 1938 for permission to use Freon gas. "Very much to our surprise, we find that the [G.M.] Frigidaire Company has an exclusive arrangement for the use of this gas from [Du Pont] Kinetic Chemicals, Inc. We know this has always been contrary to the policy of the Du Pont Company—as a matter of fact, it is contrary to government policy."

"I am appealing to you," wrote Wood, reminding Du Pont that Sears "has been a very large customer of the Du Pont Company for many years and has maintained the most friendly relation with the Du Pont Company."[34] To no avail.

While other companies foundered, Du Pont, with as much as 30 percent of its income coming from G.M. dividends, grew stronger during the Thirties, no doubt helped by its lack of outside funded debt, a trait characteristic of the chemical industry in general. In 1929, when the national average of eighteen of the largest companies earned 15.1 percent on their investments of capital, Du Pont earned 17.3 percent. In 1930 the national average of 10.3 percent was still below Du Pont's 10.6 percent. By 1931 the national average had slipped to 7.8 percent, Du Pont, still 10 percent; in 1932, 4.6 percent, Du Pont 5.2 percent; in 1933, 7 percent against Du Pont's 7.8 percent; in 1934, 9.1 percent, Du Pont 9.4 percent. From 1929 to 1931, in the depths of the Depression, Lammot still paid handsome dividends of at least $4.00 a share. Only in 1932 and 1933, when earnings slipped as low as $1.81, did he cut dividends to $2.75, only to raise them again in 1934 to $3.10, leaving over $115 million in working capital.[35] Key to this success, of course, was labor peace, which the vast reserve of unemployed in the labor market helped to enforce.

In 1931—the year the family installed the world's largest oval table (30′ by 72′ of solid Brazilian mahogany) in their Du Pont board meeting room—another "Du Pont" company of national impact appeared on the scene: F. I. du Pont & Co. No sooner had the pillars of Wall Street stopped shaking from the Crash, than Francis I. du Pont jumped into the frozen investment waters, gambling that its low quotes would soon heat up again. Opening a brokerage house on Wall Street when the Dow-Jones Industrial Average was stagnating below 42 was a big risk. "I remember one day in 1934," his son Edmond recalled years later, "when total volume on the New York Stock Exchange came to only 274,000 shares. My father tore off a section of the stock tape with that figure and handed it to me. But he was a scientist. He wasn't downhearted by the Stock Market. He felt that corrective forces already were at work then at a time when the future looked black."[36]

Francis was not alone in this belief in "corrective forces." Pierre, looking beyond the tired Hoover excuses that the market was only "shaking out" its overvaluation, had developed an enthusiasm for the Swope Plan and its dramatic enactment through Roosevelt's NRA. The National Industrial Recovery Act, drafted mainly by Swope and Henry Harriman as a quick response to Senator Black's thirty-hour-week bill, was one of the milestone laws that came out of Roosevelt's 100-day "honeymoon" with Congress. It was also the hallmark of Roosevelt's short-lived honeymoon with the Du Ponts. Black's thirty-hour week bill had been endorsed by AFL's William Green as one that struck "at the root of the problem—technological unemployment," and had been passed by the Senate. Swope, meanwhile, had already been working on a scheme of trade associations based on his experience with industrial mobilization and the War Industries Board during World War I. Presented as a compromise, and endorsed by labor legislator Senator Robert Wagner as "the first step toward a nationally planned economy," the bill became law.

Pierre joined Swope on the NRA's Industrial Advisory Board, and in December was elected chairman. "I feel that the result of the National Labor Board's efforts will do away with strikes,"[37] he enthusiastically told the American Arbitration Association a month later. The NLB was Pierre's darling, a way by which huge corporations like Du Pont could enforce labor peace through arbitration, while at the same time burdening their smaller rivals with enforceable codes. Small industries correctly recognized this legalized discrimination of *capabilities* to meet organized labor's needs as a further step by monopoly capital toward consolidation of power. As chairman of the Industrial Advisory Board, Pierre responded to their complaints by admonishing them: when they've "learned to settle their grievances in the proper way," he explained, "and not by strikes and refusing to abide by their codes, there would cease to be these talks about hardships."[38] This was not only corporate power speaking; it was the tone of history, of increasing and inevitable economic concentration.

For the first year of the New Deal, Roosevelt received general support from Du Ponts. His public works program for the Tennessee Valley, the TVA, was fully endorsed by E. Paul du Pont: "Nothing, I believe, could be a better plan for recovery."[39] Pierre, in addition to joining the NRA and its National Labor Board, also accepted appointment to the Business Advisory and Planning Council of the Department of Commerce. Irénée, despite his Supreme Court conviction for trying to evade taxes on $150,000 for 1924–1926 through trust funds for his wife and children, also gave

Roosevelt his endorsement and a check for $5,000. When FDR, respond-
ing to the domestic rush of bank deposits and the international rush on
gold, ordered a Bank Holiday and called for private hoarders to turn over
their gold to government reserves, Irénée cheerfully surrendered the many
gold pieces he had accumulated as director fees over the past twenty years—
to his own Wilmington Trust. "On my return from Cuba yesterday," he
announced to the press, "Mrs. du Pont asked me to deposit them in your
institution. She feels it is her duty to get them into the government's gold
reserve, which I understand will be accomplished by this deposit."[40] That
year he donated $5,000 to the Democratic Party.[41] When FDR finally had
to depreciate the dollar, even Lammot announced his approval, claiming
that "Nothing can be more important to business than absolute certainty as
to the basis of money, which is the medium of exchange in all commercial
transactions."[42] Roosevelt was balancing the budget, and the Du Ponts
were ecstatic.

What in Italy and Germany required violent coups and fascist parties to
achieve, Roosevelt accomplished bloodlessly in his first 100 days, pushing
through the new Democratic Congress an enormous federal, and particularly executive, centralization and regulation for the country's political
economy: The NRA, a $500 million unemployment relief bill, a farm
subsidy bill (he would later restrict farm production), a railroad regulation
bill, a Federal Deposit Insurance Corporation to shore up failing private
banks, a public power bill (TVA), a Home Owners Loan Act, and the
beer bill.

In December 1933 the twenty-first Amendment was ratified and prohibition ended. Pierre became Delaware's first Liquor Commissioner, happily
collecting the revenues he thought would soon replace the income tax. But
in some ways it was a bitter victory. The man most responsible for giving
the American people the chance for voting on prohibition and its repeal,
John J. Raskob, the man who had built the Democratic Party into an urban
power, had been summarily deposed by Roosevelt right after his election.
From that day on, Raskob's suspicion of "radical" Roosevelt grew.
Throughout 1933 he watched the presidential drama with cautious support,
waiting to judge the results and how they would affect the Du Pont-
Roosevelt honeymoon. His wait was not long.

4. DESERTING THE SHIP OF STATE

When the Du Ponts arrived in this country in 1800, they brought not
only their wealth, but also their European customs and attitudes. Most of
these faded away over succeeding generations, but one remained, nourished
by the spring of ongoing private enterprise. This was their patriarchal

relationship with their employees, a relationship which, through the hierarchical journeyman structure of powder-making in those early days, closely
resembled the master-apprentice traditions of the European guild.

For over 100 years this patriarchal relationship was the labor foundation
of the company's stability and growth. It was a hierarchical tradition which
the Du Ponts strove to maintain, not only because it represented what they
considered the best and only way to make powder, but also because it gave
them a double *social* power: on the one hand, it gave them influence over
the entire life of their workers from their religion to the way they dressed;
and on the other, because the male Du Ponts were physically on the job
with their employees and were familiar to them, a real bond held these
workers together and separated them from workers of other companies.
This, and the fact that Du Pont workers were bound to the existing order
by their simple interest in becoming managers or lower-echelon bosses
themselves, effectively diminished their capabilities of self-realization as
members of a working *class*, thereby retarding the development of their
class consciousness.

It was this patriarchal attitude that guided Du Pont's labor policies
throughout the reigns of E. I. du Pont, Alfred du Pont, "Boss" Henry du
Pont, Eugene du Pont, and T. Coleman du Pont. As late as 1920, Coleman,
an advocate of piecework, could maintain that an employee who needed a
raise should put his trust in his boss's good judgment. "If he has the right
stuff in him," he said, "and if he isn't afraid to expend plenty of body or
brain sweat to make himself a bigger and broader man, the matter of salary
will work itself out quite satisfactorily in the end. As I said, I never asked
for a salary raise in my life."[43] Few believe Coleman du Pont ever needed to.

There had begun to be changes by then, however, symbolized by the
closing of the old Brandywine powder works. Now Du Ponts no longer
worked with their men, but exchanged their blue overalls for a white shirt
and tie. Mechanization and the assembly line was revolutionizing manufacturing, and the economic base for the hierarchical journeyman structure
had been eliminated with the flood of unskilled labor into new Du Pont
plants during the war.

In the chemical industry, as in most other industries, mechanization
enabled the unskilled worker to produce as much and more than the skilled
journeyman. Whereas a skilled worker was capable of annually producing
$3,239 worth of products in 1899, by 1929 an unskilled worker was able
to produce $11,850 worth of products.[44] In 1931 the chemical worker's
output was 40 percent higher than in 1929, a mere two years earlier. This
increase lowered the cost of labor, in chemical products, and while wages
were increased to $23.40 a week in 1933 (higher than the $17.60 average

for eighty-nine manufacturing industries), these wage increases barely kept up with the increase of chemical workers' productivity. In fact, as its output increased, labor was getting a smaller and smaller piece of the pie. In 1919 wage costs amounted to 17.1 percent of the value of products; by 1933 they were only 12.4 percent.[45] The difference between the 17 percent and 12 percent was lost to the worker and went to the stock owners of the chemical corporations, the biggest of which was Du Pont.

Such facts were proudly made known to Du Pont stockholders but never released to Du Pont workers, and they were the kind of facts a union would have brought to them. Du Pont management knew this and enforced a strict anti-union policy.

The foundation of this policy was the preservation of the hierarchical work situation that separated their employees from each other. Although the economic rationale for the skilled journeyman had been generally eroded by mechanization, Du Pont kept the hierarchical workplace structure for its social control benefits. Journeymen became integrated into the management ranks as foremen. On these men the Du Ponts built the Works Council, a company union composed of management and workers, as a buttress against any organizing drive by independent outside unions. In an attempt to maintain the personal patriarchal relationship between management and worker, the Du Ponts encouraged identification with the firm: a proud "You are a Du Pont man" approach, reinforced by a stock investment plan. Du Pont was the first company to develop a course on HOBSO (How Our Business System Operates) to inoculate blue-collar workers against creeping socialism. Capitalism, to the Du Ponts, was civilization itself, and as such, had to be defended at all costs. Otherwise, as Irénée warned in the early Twenties, "a dark age" would befall mankind.

Pierre du Pont at first was confident that the NRA would not disturb an organization of labor so fundamental to the profit-generating efficiency of the entire chemical industry, and particularly Du Pont. The NRA's chemical industry codes, after all, had been drafted by Du Pont and other manufacturers. Minimum wages were set in 1933 at 35 to 40 cents per hour, and that year the industry was already paying $56\frac{1}{2}$ cents, and 61.9 cents in 1934. Hours also should have required no further adjustments in Pierre's mind; a 40-hour week was set in 1933, when the industry's average was already down to a 41-hour week, and the week was further reduced to $38\frac{1}{2}$ hours early in 1934. Neither wages nor hours, Pierre believed, were issues that outside unions could use for an organizing drive. But to further protect Du Pont, Hercules, Atlas, and other chemical manufacturers from such a possibility, they installed in the collective bargaining codes for the industry a provision giving management the right "to engage, promote, or release employees."[46] Pierre was confident that everything was under control. "The Recovery Act," he said in January 1934, "has provided an opportunity to deal with strikes in the way labor wants to deal with them, so eventually I think strikes will disappear."[47] Pierre had reason to feel that way. Already, in September 1933, the National Labor Board had broken strikes at Weirton Steel Company and Ford Motor's Edgewater, New Jersey, plant, leaving grievances unresolved.

This concern for dealing with strikes "in the way labor wants to deal with them" reflected the collaboration given to Swope's NRA by labor leaders such as John L. Lewis and Sidney Hillman. These were leaders of unions in industries (mining and garment) whose conditions were far different from those of the better paid chemical industry; they represented the majority of the country's industries. In order to alleviate the deplorable working conditions and low wages that were prevalent, Lewis, Hillman and others readily agreed to the suspension of anti-trust laws that would have blocked the codes of the trade associations that the NRA made law. Industrial leaders like Baruch and Swope, in return, also accepted the necessity of majority rule for a "closed shop" in order to give union leaders like Hillman and Lewis control over an otherwise uncontrollable labor rebellion. Most corporate members of the National Labor Board, which reviewed labor-management disputes, understood union policing was necessary to their own business interests if corporate stability was to be maintained. They accepted the New Deal concept of labor as an "interest group" in its own right, one which cannot be coerced but can be controlled through enticements. Only one member of the Board, whose immediate industry was not faced with labor rebellion, could not understand this "big picture"—Pierre du Pont.

On March 2, 1934, Pierre filed the NLB's first dissenting opinion. It was over the right of majority rule in deciding a plant's unionization. Pierre opposed this interpretation of Section 7A of the National Industrial Recovery Act (which had guaranteed collective bargaining), insisting on the right of minorities and individuals to negotiate separately with the company, a position which would have effectively made unions impotent. The specific case involved a company which refused to deal with a railway union after it had been elected into the plant. Instead, it "bargained" with its own "employees committee," a company union. The analogy to Du Pont's own Works Council was obvious. In fact, soon after, in order to preserve the "legality" of the Works Council, the Du Ponts had to permit the withdrawal of management's 50 percent participation. Company control, however, remained firm, although in other Du Pont-controlled companies, which yielded Du Pont over 40 percent of its income in 1933, company unions were not as strong and were soon challenged by rank-and-file labor. With these challenges, the anxiety of the Du Ponts grew.

March 2, 1934, marked the end of the Du Pont-Roosevelt honeymoon. Within a short period, Pierre resigned from both the NLB and the NRA's Industrial Advisory Board.

Actually, by then Pierre was the only Du Pont who hadn't already abandoned the Roosevelt ship of state. Three months earlier, in January, Lammot had blasted Roosevelt for going too far in his reforms. "The year 1933," he stated, "has witnessed an adventurous attack by the administration upon the political, social, and economic ills of the country."[48] Lammot announced he was being forced to discontinue Du Pont's stock investment plan for its employees because the burden of restrictions of the Securities Act of 1933 was "so onerous."[49] This "onerous" law, drafted by Sam Rayburn and future Supreme Court Justice Felix Frankfurter, had required each new stock issue to be accompanied by a statement fully disclosing relevant financial information for public inspection, and held corporate directors like Lammot criminally and civilly liable in case of any misrepresentation.

Roosevelt passed other bills in 1934 that prodded increasing corporate desertions:

Stock manipulators like Raskob and Pierre were disturbed by the Securities Exchange Act, which created the Securities and Exchange Commission (SEC) to regulate the securities market.

The Air Mail Act, which stipulated rigid controls in awarding federal contracts, forced the dissolution of Henry B. du Pont's General Aviation Corporation, 48.5 percent of whose stock was held by General Motors. General Aviation had owned 300,311 shares of Henry's North American Aviation, and Lammot had invested G.M. funds also in North American, buying over one million shares, a 30 percent interest, and another 13 percent interest in Transcontinental and Western Air, Inc. The passage of the act caused losses and General Aviation's distribution of its North American holdups, followed by dissolution.

The Communications Act, which created the Federal Communication Commission (FCC), was an attempt to regulate the airwaves and stabilize and cartelize the radio, telegraph, and cable industries, but was looked at suspiciously in Wilmington as a step toward "radical" government control.

The Railroad Retirement Act, which required pensions for railway workers, also did not warm the hearts of railroad directors like Pierre, Irénée, Donaldson Brown, and Raskob. Moreover, FDR's abandonment of a balanced budget in favor of huge government spending projects marked a new step toward making deficit spending a permanent feature of federal financial policy. Lammot had opposed such tendencies during the Hoover administration, even though Hoover's $6 billion deficit had been incurred in salvaging banks, railroads, and insurance companies through his Reconstruction Finance Corporation. Now, with most of these funds going for public relief, mostly to dispossessed farmers and unemployed workers, Lammot was fuming with anger.

Lammot simply did not understand the economic realities of his age. Technology, by increasing productivity, was altering the entire social fabric of the United States. For, while the absolute numbers of industrial workers had increased due to industrial development, the number of workers it took to produce a given volume of products decreased. The rate of increase of employment relative to production volume was decreasing. For the first time in history, mechanization was reversing the time-old pattern of accumulating living labor power in order to increase production and meet needs; now, a pattern of *dis*accumulation—and with it, mounting technological unemployment—was developing. Roosevelt's economic advisors understood this as a key factor in the unusual severity and length of this Depression. This was no usual cyclical bust, but a different kind of depression, with a whole new, complicating factor of technological unemployment, requiring the intervention of the government to provide income and consumer ability—through publicly financed work projects such as the WPA or post office expansion, even at the cost of bureaucratic waste.

The Du Ponts displayed an increasing mistrust of the new Democratic Congress. The shock of the House's rejection of a sales tax in March 1933, and its imposition, instead, of higher taxes on large incomes and inheritances, had only begun to wear off when in February 1934 Senator Gerald Nye attacked munition makers as the main cause of World War I. One month after Pierre's futile support of the "open shop" on the National Labor Board, the Senate, acting on the impetus of a *Fortune* article which verified many of Nye's contentions, authorized Nye to form an investigating committee. This was in April 1934, when a book attacking munition makers like Du Pont, *The Merchants of Death* by Englebrecht and Hanighen (described even by *Business Week* as an "exhaustive presentation of the facts"[50]), became a best seller.

The Du Ponts prepared for civil war, convinced that a major socialist upheaval was imminent. This delusion was enhanced by the stormy atmosphere in which they were trying to maintain old values and older profits: strikes were sweeping across the country from southern textile mills to the northeast to San Francisco, where a general strike, led by Communists, strove to right economic injustices but actually had little political intent or consequence. Self-proclaimed "radical" mayors and a governor, responding to the desperation of the times, were threatening "big business" with taxes and controls. The membership of the AFL, enjoying a revival protected by the NRA's collective bargaining clause, jumped from 2.2 million in 1933 to over 4 million in 1934, and Lewis, breaking with the AFL's "skilled labor" prejudices, led an organizing drive among the unskilled millions of industrial workers which was soon to develop into the Congress of Industrial Organizations.

"Many people," Ruly Carpenter wrote Raskob in March 1934, were confused as to why Roosevelt was "doing many things." People were unaware of "much of the truth" of Roosevelt's aims, and unaware that the President was strangling free press and speech. "Thousands of men," he claimed, were leaving jobs for better pay with the government. "Five Negroes on my place in South Carolina refused work this spring . . . saying they had easy jobs with the government. . . . A cook on my houseboat at Fort Myers [Florida] quit because the government was paying him a dollar an hour as a painter. . . ."[51] Perhaps Raskob could go to Washington for an explanation?

Raskob rejected Carpenter's proposal, replying on March 20 that he was "entirely out of politics since July 1932, and I am anxious to keep out."[52] Raskob withdrew from personal activity shortly after the Democratic Convention nominated Roosevelt, performing only his functional duties as National Chairman. During that period, he wrote Democratic official Jouett Shouse that "when one thinks of the Democratic Party being headed by such radicals as Roosevelt, Huey Long, Hearst, McAdoo, and Senators Wheeler and Dill, as against the fine, conservative talent in the party as represented by such men as you, Governor Byrd, Governor Smith, Carter Glass, John W. Davis, Governor Cox, Pierre S. du Pont, Governor Ely, and others too numerous to mention, it takes all one's courage and faith not to lose hope completely."[53] Apparently, by the time of Ruly's letter in 1934, the Twenty-first Amendment had severed the last anti-prohibition ties to Roosevelt. In 1934, $400 million in liquor taxes went into the Treasury, yet the cut in income taxes the Du Ponts had expected never materialized. By March 1934 Raskob had lost all hope in the New Deal Democrats, and suggested to Ruly an alternative—an independent political organization "encouraging people to work, encouraging people to get rich, showing the fallacy of communism in its efforts to tear down our capital structure, etc."

Raskob encouraged Carpenter, who had organized the Du Pont spy system during the war, to head the new organization. "You haven't much to do," he wrote, "and I know of no one that could take the lead in trying to induce the Du Pont and General Motors groups, followed by other big industries, to definitely organize to protect society from the suffering which it is bound to endure if we allow communistic elements to lead the people to believe that all businessmen are crooks, not to be trusted, and that no one should be allowed to get rich." Then Raskob became more specific about power. "The reason I say that you are in a peculiarly good position to do this is that you are young enough to undertake the work, you have the time, you are wealthy enough to not have to depend upon a job or salary for a living, and are in a position to talk directly with a group that controls a larger share of industry through common-stock holdings than any other group in the United States. When I say this I mean that I believe there is no group, including the Rockefellers, the Morgans, the Mellons, or anyone else that begins to control and be responsible for as much industrially as is the Du Pont Company."[54]

Five months later, on August 15, 1934, the District of Columbia issued a charter to a new organization pledged to "combat radicalism"—The American Liberty League. Founded to "uphold the Constitution" and "to preserve the ownership and lawful use of property when acquired," with a greater emphasis on property rights than civil rights, Irénée, Raskob, Al Smith, and Shouse made up four of its six officers.

The League's national executive committee included John W. Davis of U.S. Steel, Sewell Avery, president of Montgomery Ward and director of U.S. Steel, and Grayson M.-P. Murphy, a director of Guaranty Trust Company. These and six other corporate leaders represented Morgan interests which were upset by Roosevelt's abandonment of the gold standard, the handling of J. P. Morgan before a Senate committee investigating nonpayment of two years of taxes, and the passage of the Glass-Steagall banking act, which was supported by and favored Rockefeller banking interests. Rockefeller interests were also on hand in the League, but did not play leading roles. President Alfred Sloan and Vice President William Knudsen, both Du Pont protégés, represented General Motors.

The League's Advisory Council completed the sketch of total Du Pont defection from the Roosevelt camp: there, prominently displayed, appeared the name of Pierre S. du Pont and his wife Alice. But it was Irénée who was now the voice of Du Pont, denouncing Roosevelt for "doling out other people's money for relief."[55]

The legitimacy of the new government system itself was called to question as "unconstitutional." The federal government, Irénée said, "apparently believes it can tax those who have and hand it to those who have not, but that act is clearly unconstitutional."[56]

Roosevelt chided the League as an organization formed to uphold two of the Ten Commandments. Apparently, he didn't take the League seriously. He was soon to learn how much he was mistaken.

Du Pont reaction to the administration was not limited to the Liberty League. In the same month that the League's founding was announced, Pierre also used his membership on the Department of Commerce's Business Advisory and Planning Council. Joining William Harriman, chairman of Union Pacific, and Walter Gifford, president of A.T. & T., on August 20 he denounced the protection of small investors in legally requiring uniform accounting and reporting in corporate financial reports. The following year he resigned also from this agency.

The Du Ponts did more than protest. They also took direct and forceful measures, hiring an army of Pinkertons and other private detectives to infiltrate the labor ranks of Du Pont and General Motors as company spies.[57] In May 1934 the Wilmington headquarters of the Delaware State Police sent fifty revolvers to company gun men at the Du Pont Hopewell plant for possible use in a textile strike.[58] Federal Laboratories, with which Du Pont shared a joint agency and in which Atlas Chemical Company had a substantial holding (with Lammot and Pierre du Pont as large shareholders),[59] sold various vomiting and tear gases to corporations and police departments throughout the country. Among its corporate clients were General Motors and Pacific R & H Chemical, a Du Pont-owned corporation.

The tense year of 1934 was also when the Du Ponts suddenly bought a 56 percent interest in Remington Arms, the manufacturer of small arms and one-third of the country's "sporting" ammunition. This investment secured a market for Du Pont gunpowder, as well as Remington's additional asset as the largest producer of steel knives in the country. Soon afterward, Du Pont also acquired the Charles Packer Company, one of the country's largest makers of shotguns, the Peters Cartridge Company, and the King Powder Company of Ohio.[60] These were all market-related acquisitions, but, according to charges before a Senate committee later that year, may also have been marked for more illegal purposes.

For in these same summer months of 1934, Remington Arms, the treasurer of the American Liberty League, and the name "Du Pont" were all implicated in one of the most bizarre plots in American history, a plot confirmed by the Dickstein-McCormick House Investigating Committee, to forcibly overthrow the Roosevelt administration and with it, the government of the United States.

5. THE MACGUIRE AFFAIR

In the summer of 1934 Gerald MacGuire, a lawyer in the Morgan brokerage office of Grayson M.-P. Murphy and an official of the American Legion, visited General Smedley Butler at his home in Newton Square, Pennsylvania. Butler, former Commandant of the Marine Corps and holder of two Congressional medals of honor, had ended his 33-year career in the Marines three years earlier amid a storm of diplomatic protest over his public description of Italian dictator Benito Mussolini as "a mad dog about to break loose in Europe." The General had stubbornly rejected Hoover's demand for a retraction and had retired from the service a proud but bitter man. But he was also probably the most popular soldier in America. As such, he was an attractive prize for any movement, and it was for this reason that MacGuire, mistakenly banking on the General's personal bitterness and the then frequent brandings of Roosevelt as a "dictator," paid the old soldier a call.

America, MacGuire told Butler, was in great danger from a "communist menace," and needed a complete change of government. Then MacGuire made his pitch. A "militantly patriotic" veterans' organization, like the fascist Croix de Feu operating in France, was the only kind of organization that could force a change in Washington; he suggested Butler lead such an organization in "a march on Washington." "We have three million dollars to start with on the line," he told Butler, "and we can get three million more if we need it."[61]

"To be perfectly fair to Mr. MacGuire," Butler testified some months later, "he didn't seem bloodthirsty. He felt such a show of force in Washington would probably result in a peaceful overthrow of the government. He suggested that 'we might even go along with Roosevelt and do with him what Mussolini did with the King of Italy.' . . . Mr. MacGuire proposed that the Secretary of State and Vice President would be made to resign, by force, if necessary, and that President Roosevelt would probably allow MacGuire's group to appoint a Secretary of State. Then, if President Roosevelt was 'willing to go along,' he could remain as President. But if he were not in sympathy with the fascist movement, he would be forced to resign, whereupon, under the Constitution, the Presidential succession would place the Secretary of State in the White House. . . . He told me he believed that at least half of the American Legion and Veterans of Foreign Wars would follow me."[62]

Butler was amazed at MacGuire's plan but played along to uncover details. "Is there anything stirring yet?" he asked MacGuire.

"Yes, you watch," the broker replied. "In two or three weeks, you will see it come out in the papers. There will be big fellows in it. This is to be the background of it."[63]

Exactly two weeks later, on August 23, the American Liberty League publicly announced its existence, with MacGuire's employer, Grayson M. P. Murphy, as its treasurer.

Butler knew MacGuire spoke for certain financial interests, mostly those of J. P. Morgan & Company. A year before, in July 1933, MacGuire and another Legion official, William Doyle, had payed him a similar visit to ask him to lead a well-financed "rank-and-file" movement to oust the Legion's autocratic leadership at the Chicago convention that autumn. To assure Butler of backing, MacGuire showed him two entries in a bank deposit book, for $42,000 and $64,000. Butler's suspicions grew—"Soldiers don't have that kind of money," he said later—but he suggested he be given some time to think it over. "I wanted to get to the bottom of this thing and not scare them off."[64]

MacGuire took the bait and at a second meeting presented information that nine very wealthy men were doing the financial backing, one being Grayson M.-P. Murphy. "I work for him," MacGuire assured the General, "I'm in his office."[65]

"What has Murphy got to do with this?"

"Well," answered MacGuire, "he's the man who underwrote the formation of the American Legion for $125,000. He paid for the field work for organizing it and has not gotten all of it back yet."

"That is the reason he makes kings, is it?" remarked Butler. "He has still got a club over their heads."

"He's on our side," insisted MacGuire. "He wants to see the soldiers cared for."[66]

What Murphy really wanted, as did most of Morgan's "sound money" circle, was a reversal of Roosevelt's abandonment of the gold standard. Only on the solid arbiter of gold, reasoned Morgan, could the economy recover. Butler suspected this when MacGuire handed him a drafted speech to be read at the convention, calling for a resolution urging that the United States return to the gold standard. MacGuire tried to mask the request in terms of the veterans' interests. "We want to see the soldiers' bonus paid in gold. We don't want the soldiers to have rubber money or paper money."[67]

Butler insisted on meeting some of "the principals" involved, and shortly afterwards the General had another caller—Robert Sterling Clark, Wall Street broker who had supported Al Smith's 1928 campaign with a $35,000 donation.[68] Clark identified himself as one of the men interested in seeing the General become the Legion's new National Commander. "Our group is for you," he remarked, but "the Morgan interests say that you cannot be trusted, that you are too radical, and so forth, that you are too much on the side of the little fellow. . . . They are for Douglas MacArthur." After Clark mentioned that the "gold speech" "cost a lot of money,"[69] Butler remarked: "It looks to me as if it were a big business speech. There is something funny about that speech, Mr. Clark."

Clark's answer was calm but blunt. "I've got thirty million dollars," he explained. "I don't want to lose it. I am willing to spend half of the thirty million to save the other half. If you get out and make that speech in Chicago, I am sure that they will adopt the resolution and that will be one step toward the return to gold, to have the soldiers stand up for it."

At that, the General dropped his pretense and flatly refused. Undismayed, Clark asked to use the phone and called MacGuire long distance. "You've got forty-five thousand dollars," he told MacGuire, "You'll have to do it that way,"[70] and left.

Butler, then, was obviously aware of MacGuire's contacts when he was visited again the following year by MacGuire. He was also aware that at the Legion Convention in October 1933 a gold standard resolution had been passed. But what the General did not know was that MacGuire had been subsequently sent to Europe in the spring of 1934 on "business" which amounted to a survey of the role played by veterans in Mussolini's Fascisti, in Germany's Nazi Party, and in France's fascist Croix de Feu movement. "The Croix de Feu is getting a great number of recruits," he wrote Clark from Paris, "and I recently attended a meeting of this organization and was quite impressed with the type of men belonging. These fellows are interested only in the salvation of France, and I feel sure that the country could not be in better hands. . . ."[71]

MacGuire's favorable impressions of European fascism did not exist in a social vacuum, however. Many business leaders, including those in the Du Pont camp, and even some liberals for a time, had been infatuated with the fascist movement. General Motors' William Knudsen, for example, on his return from Europe, described Hitler's Germany to a reporter as "the miracle of the twentieth century." Even Alfred I. du Pont's daughter Madeleine had contracted the fascist epidemic during her stay in Germany, and her third marriage to Friedrich Hermann Ruoff had spawned three young Nazi zealots. In America many openly fascist organizations had sprung up, including the Khaki Shirts, the Blue Shirts, the White Band, the Nationalists, and the Silver Shirts. Lawrence Dennis emerged as the "theoretician" of American fascism, and *The American Guard* magazine appeared, published by the "Swastika Press." More home-grown brews also were stirred, including the racist Southern Committee to Uphold the Constitution, the Crusaders, the para-military Minute Men and Women of

Today, and the anti-Semitic Sentinels of the Republic, all financed, and some even created, by the Du Ponts' American Liberty League.

Colorful Smedley Butler, however, was not made of this stuff. Appalled by MacGuire's offer, he contacted a crusading reporter for the Philadelphia *Record*, Paul Comly French. "The whole affair smacked of treason to me," Butler remarked, and French decided to travel to New York. On September 13, 1934, French visited Gerald MacGuire at the brokerage firm of Grayson M.-P. Murphy Company and, posing as a sympathizer trusted by Butler, won MacGuire's confidence.

"The whole movement is patriotic because the Communists will wreck the nation unless the soldiers save it through fascism," MacGuire reportedly told French. "All General Butler would have to do to get a million men would be to announce the formation of the organization and tell them it would cost a dollar a year to join."[72]

"At first he suggested that the General organize this outfit himself," French later told the House Investigating Committee, "and ask a dollar a year dues from everybody. We discussed that, and then he came around to the point of getting outside financial funds, and he said it would not be any trouble to raise a million dollars. He said he could go to John W. Davis or Perkins of the National City Bank, and any number of persons and get it. . . . Later, we discussed the question of arms and equipment, and he suggested that they could be obtained from the Remington Arms Company on credit through the Du Ponts. I do not think at that time he mentioned the connections of Du Ponts with the American Liberty League, but he skirted all around it. That is, I do not think he mentioned the Liberty League, but he skirted all around the idea that that was the back door. One of the Du Ponts is on the board of directors of the American League and they own a controlling interest in the Remington Arms Company. . . . He said the General would not have any trouble enlisting 500,000 men."

MacGuire then showed French a letter of support: "It's from Louis Johnson, the former National Commander of the American Legion." "He said that he had discussed the matter with him," French related, "along the lines of what we were now discussing, and I took it to mean that he had discussed this fascist proposition with Johnson, and Johnson was in sympathy with it."

On November 20, 1934, General Butler revealed the whole ugly scheme by testifying before a private session of the Special House Committee on Un-American Activities. He suggested that if the Committee wanted to get to the bottom of this, they question the biggest interests involved: Grayson M.-P. Murphy, General Douglas MacArthur, Hanford MacNider, ex-

National Commander of the American Legion, and leaders of the American Liberty League.

The Committee called none of these, but it did have James Van Zandt, National Commander of the Veterans of Foreign Wars, and Gerald MacGuire testify under oath. Van Zandt corroborated Butler's testimony and admitted knowing of the plot. MacGuire, on the other hand, would admit only that he had met occasionally with Butler, but claimed that he had been "misunderstood." French's testimony, however, corroborated Butler's and Van Zandt's. But the Committee, perhaps frightened of the implications, refused to delve further into the conspiracy, suppressing much of the most incriminating testimony in its official report to the House on February 15, 1939. Nevertheless, the report confirmed a plot to overthrow Roosevelt with a fascist *coup d'état:*

"In the last few weeks of the Committee's official life it received evidence showing that certain persons had made an attempt to establish a fascist organization in this country. . . . There is no question that these attempts were discussed, were planned, and might have been placed in execution when and if the financial backers deemed expedient.

"This committee received evidence from Major General Smedley D. Butler (retired), twice decorated by the Congress of the United States. He testified before the Committee as to conversations with one Gerald C. MacGuire in which the latter is alleged to have suggested the formation of a fascist army under the leadership of General Butler.

"MacGuire denied these allegations under oath, but your Committee was able to verify all the pertinent statements made by General Butler, with the exception of the direct statement suggesting the creation of the organization. This, however, was corroborated in the correspondence of MacGuire with his principal, Robert Sterling Clark, of New York City, while MacGuire was abroad studying the various forms of veterans' organizations of fascist character."[73]

Despite the Committee's report, no indictments were handed down. Corporate leaders who were implicated in the conspiracy by sworn testimony, including the Du Ponts, were never even called for questioning. "The Congressional Committee investigating un-American activities has just reported that the Fascist plot to seize the government . . . was proved," observed lawyer Roger Baldwin, head of the American Civil Liberties Union, "yet not a single participant will be prosecuted under the perfectly plain language of the federal conspiracy act making this a high crime. Imagine the action if such a plot were discovered among Communists! Which is, of course, only to emphasize the nature of our government as representatives of the interests of the controllers of property. Violence, even to the seizure of the government, is excusable on the part of those whose lofty motive is to preserve the profit system."[74]

Indeed, Butler's testimony was at first subjected to a shower of ridicule. Even the *New York Times*, which had described the Liberty League's founding as having "a real chance to be useful"[75] hurriedly dismissed the "so-called plot of Wall Street interests" as having "failed to emerge in any alarming proportion," while *Time*, the leading anti-New Deal publication of J. P. Morgan's trusted friend and journalist protégé, Henry Luce, called it a "plot without plotters . . . no military officer of the United States since the late tempestuous George Custer has succeeded in publicly floundering in so much hot water as Smedley Darlington Butler. . . . Thanking their stars for having such sure-fire publicity dropped in their laps, Representatives McCormick and Dickstein began calling witnesses to expose the 'plot.' But there did not seem to be any plotters. . . . Mr. Morgan, just off a boat from Europe, had nothing to say but partner Thomas Lamont did: 'Perfect moonshine! Too utterly ridiculous to comment upon!' "[76]

Significantly, among *Time*'s leading stockholders at the time was Luce's college chum, Henry P. Davison, like Lamont, a partner of J. P. Morgan & Company.[77] Morgan's friend Grayson M.-P. Murphy derided Butler's charges as "a joke—a publicity stunt" and received wider coverage than Butler's own testimony or Van Zandt's and French's corroboration. Then a curtain of silence fell. When the House Committee released its report, there was little comment from the press. Of all the country's large newspapers, most of which were (and are) controlled by well-financed syndicates, only the liberal New York *Post,* French's Philadelphia *Record,* and two New Jersey papers printed the details of the conspiracy and the corroborating testimonies. Not a word of the plot was printed in Delaware's Du Pont-controlled press, and the "MacGuire Affair" slipped into the fog of unrecorded history.

Beyond the superficial rationale of class allegiance, many reasons have been put forth as to why Roosevelt may have shied away from pressing further into the "MacGuire Affair" investigation. There is little doubt that hearings and indictments against such leaders of finance would have precipitated a national crisis, and probably an international one as well. Economically, such a course of action would only have tottered an already weakened public faith in the prevailing economic system Wall Street represented and Roosevelt was pledged to preserve. Legal proceedings against such powerful interests, also, would have precipitated a political crisis, not only for the Roosevelt administration, but for the private enterprise essence of the state as a whole and its property values of government. Apparently, the initial exposure had also sent the wolves into hiding, so that no more was really needed than the Committee Report's verbal hand-slapping that "Armed forces for the purpose of establishing a dictatorship by means of Fascism . . . have no place in this country."[78]

Such gestures seem impotent if viewed in a historical vacuum. But the Dickstein-McCormick Committee was conducting its investigation in the shadow of another, more publicized spectacle which already had the country spellbound and the forces of reaction in full retreat—the Senate munitions hearings.

6. REARMING THE WEHRMACHT

The invasion of Japanese armies into Manchuria and the reemergence of bellicosity among the European powers boded no good tidings for international peace, and the American people felt the chill of war approaching from both sides of the continent. Their immediate reaction was a healthy revulsion, and in their traditional pragmatism, they chose the most visible manifestation of war, munitions, rather than its most basic cause, economic markets, as an immediate target. It was a pragmatism shared by all, including New Dealers like Senator Gerald Nye, which allowed an ignoring of the question of *system* while searching for suitable *personal* villains. This pragmatic attitude, as old as the Pilgrims, had been the basic theme of American social thought since the early colonial days, and had guided free enterprisers like the Du Ponts in disjointedly building American capitalism. Yet, neither Irénée du Pont nor Gerald Nye ever perceived its functioning in unfolding events and historical decisions, nor even within the workings of their own minds.

To Irénée, villainizing munitions makers could only be the seedy work of the Communist Third International, and on July 7, 1934, he said so. But even then Irénée was only continuing the family's line of personally desiring peace while, in the course of following good business principles, officially promoting war.

Pierre tried to deal with this contradiction as early as 1930. "The popular conception of a munitions maker," he wrote to Merle Thorpe, editor of *Nation's Business*, "is a sinister individual with a deep hatred for peace and a contempt for the pursuits thereof. He is pictured as doing all in his power to fan the flames of distrust between nations and to delight in the conflicts that ensue, since they create enormous and immediate profits for his corporation. I called this the popular conception of the munitions maker; in reality, it is the popular misconception.

"No munitions concern can live by war alone. During the 139 years of the existence of the United States as a nation there were four major conflicts before the World War. They lasted 10 years in all, or about 7% of the time. How could any independent corporation keep itself alive for 139 years by turning out a product that was only wanted 10 years of the time?"[79] Not war preparations, insisted Pierre, but peacetime products, occupied the intervening time and gave Du Pont stability.

Pierre's contentions on their own terms were unquestionable, but they ignored a basic theme throughout the history of his own company: in each period of the company's expansion, profits from a previous war were the foundation and, in many cases, the crucial determining factor for sustaining that growth. The Napoleonic wars and U. S. government contracts kept Du Pont Company alive through its first fledgling years. The War of 1812 provided the funds necessary for the company's growth in the next two decades, enabling it to survive such disastrous internal setbacks as frequent explosions; the same was true of the roles of the Mexican War and the Crimean War in the 1840's and 1850's. The Civil War funded the firm's trust building after 1865, helped by panics which weakened smaller competitors, underscoring also the importance of capital concentration and its large labor and productive resources to the rise of Henry du Pont's Powder Trust. And the Spanish-American War was the strongest impetus to Du Pont's building its smokeless powder plants and subsequent monopoly in that field.

There is little doubt that the company's own efficiency and technological innovation, as well as the powder needs of an expanding young continental power, were stabilizing factors for Du Pont. But Pierre totally ignored the crucial role played by war profits throughout his firm's growth. "In the case of the Du Pont Company," Pierre wrote, "taxes paid to the U.S. government during the recent war not only absorbed the entire profit of the company on powder sold to our government, but in addition, they wiped out all of the profit made on these powders during the preceding 20 years."[80] Later, the Senate munitions hearings, using Du Pont's own records, proved this allegation false. In fact, World War I generated $250 million in profits for Du Pont, more than 126 years' worth of previous peacetime business, providing the $90 million surplus fund used to expand into the chemical and automobile industries.

These facts were known especially to Pierre, who directed that expansion. Yet the fear of being villainized prompted their suppression, especially as the world's governments of private enterprise were gathering in another of their many desperate disarmament conferences, trying to serve their own market interests while attempting at the same time to stop their inevitable bloody result. "I consider the calling of the London naval conference a long step in the right direction," Pierre wrote at the time.

"Sentiment against war has always been strong; added to this sentiment now is the crushing burden of taxation, and a disarrangement of all the orderly channels of domestic and international commerce."[81]

There is little evidence that Pierre did not really believe his own words. Yet, even as he wrote them, Du Pont's arms export company was busily fueling the fires of war and corrupting foreign governments in the process.

As early as 1925, Du Pont had illegally been smuggling arms to Mukden warlords in Manchuria, who paid well for Du Pont's willingness to violate an imposed embargo. In 1928 a contract with Poland for 300 tons of powder per year for twelve years was landed only through bribes, politely termed "commissions." "In order to get this," Colonel Taylor, Du Pont's European salesman, advised the Wilmington headquarters, "we will have to pay 7% commission, of which 2% must be paid in its entirety the day of the signing of the contract."[82] Two weeks later, on February 3, the home office replied: "You may be sure, in the event that you conclude a deal along the lines indicated in your letter of January 18, that I will promptly remit by cable the amount involved to pay the 2% commission, so that there will be no delay."[83]

Five months later a Du Pont agent in Poland by the name of Klawe, landed a $1.8 million sale. Du Pont executive O'Gorman ecstatically wrote Taylor from Wilmington: "Mr. Klawe's commission on the 1,000-ton order contract was 7 percent, or approximately $126,000. Upon signing the contract, even before we received the Polish notes, we made advance payment on commission to Klawe of $30,000. . . . You are fortunate to have Mr. Klawe as agent, as he is a man who is very well connected and thoroughly understands what must be done in order to secure business."[84]

In China Du Pont powder was sold to Chiang Kai-shek's forces in similarly soiled circumstances. "N. E. Bates would suggest we do not pay any other commission except 7.5%, Preston Wilk, Dyestuffs, Wilmington," Du Pont headquarters cabled Taylor on September 23, 1929. "Du Pont dyestuffs office, Shanghai, China, Will advance all prices at plant 5% for distribution as follows: 4%, Chinese Army, Nanking. . . ." The "commission" was settled at "4% Chinese Army, Nanking; 1% Colonel de Fremery," a Dutch mercenary. ". . . We will advise Bates to settle definitely on the basis quoted."[85] In Shanghai, also, bribes were paid. Dr. Noelting, head of Du Pont offices there, cabled: "Anyway, presents will have to be given to various parties in China New Year, and the overprice we get can be used for this purpose."[86]

By 1929 Du Pont had full-time powder agents in Estonia, Holland, Latvia, Poland, Sweden, Denmark, and Norway. In 1932 they contracted agents also in Belgium and Lithuania.

During the early Twenties nitrocellulose powder was sold in Spain, Poland, Czechoslovakia, and other parts of Europe. A. Felix du Pont and Harry Haskell rejected Nobel Ltd.'s protests, but Pierre, not wishing to anger his G.M. partners, surrendered the TNT and nitroglycerin market.[87] Thereafter, Du Pont, in conjunction with Nobel Ltd. (which merged in 1926 as Imperial Chemicals Industries, Ltd.), had military sales agents sprinkled throughout Latin America, in Argentina, Bolivia, Chile, Brazil, Colombia, Ecuador, Paraguay, Uruguay, and Venezuela. Other agents were located in Europe's Bulgaria and Romania, and throughout southern Europe.[88]

Through their partnership, Du Pont-I.C.I. sold nitrocellulose powder to Britain in 1929, 1930, 1931 and 1934; to Belgium in 1931; Estonia in 1929, 1931, and 1934; Greece in 1935; Bulgaria in 1935; Holland in 1929 and 1933; Latvia in 1929 and 1934; Lithuania in 1930, 1932, and 1934; Poland in 1930; Romania in 1934; and Turkey in 1934.

Smokeless powder was sold to Yugoslavia in 1929, 1931, and 1934; Romania in 1929 and 1934; Turkey in 1930 and 1935; Latvia in 1934; Holland in 1934; Belgium in 1934; Estonia from 1930 to 1933; and Finland from 1932 to 1934.

None of these munitions sales were in violation of any American law. In fact, such exports had the full support of Herbert Hoover during his eight-year tenure as Secretary of Commerce and four-year term as President. Hoover, unlike Wilson, placed less emphasis on the political aspects of foreign policy, and great emphasis on developing a system of overseas *economic* expansion, a system that included government regulation of credit to foreign nations and its relation to exports as "part of our domestic progress, both socially and economically."[89] This meant not only providing credit to a foreign government so it could purchase American goods as a commodity market, but also investments by American corporations and loans by American banks to develop a capital market. "In stimulating our exports," Hoover observed in 1923, "we should be mainly interested in development work abroad such as roads and utilities which increase the standards of living of people and thus increase the demand for goods from every nation, for we gain in prosperity by a prosperous world, not by displacing others."[90] This was the essence of corporate liberalism.

Although this analysis conflicted with the necessity for American corporations to keep wages in their overseas factories low, Hoover was impressed by its sophistication and the long-range need of corporate profit for social stability and order, and thus released his anti-interventionist *Memorandum on the Monroe Doctrine* in 1928, holding that "confidence in that [noninterventionist] attitude is the only basis upon which the

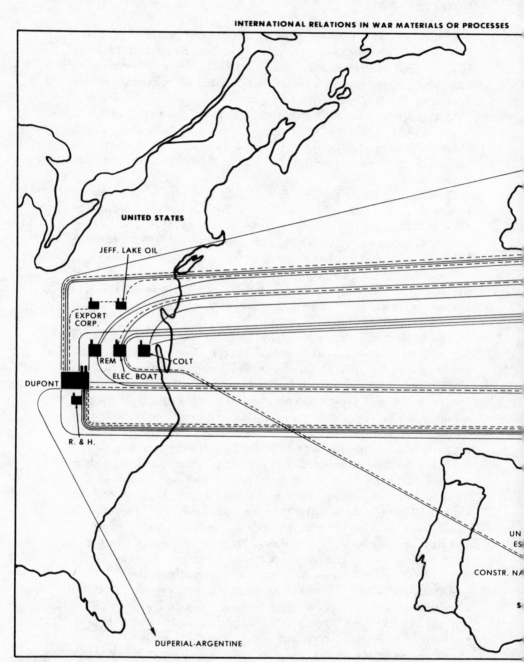

UNITED STATES

JEFF. LAKE OIL

EXPORT
CORP.

REM

ELEC. BOAT

COLT

DUPONT

R. & H.

DUPERIAL-ARGENTINE

UN
ES

CONSTR. NA

S

CONTINUOUS LINE: FINANCIAL ARRANGEMENTS FOR SALES AND/OR PART OWNERSHIP OR PRICES OR TERRITORY.
DOTTED LINE: INTERCHANGE OR SALE OF CHEMICAL OR OTHER PATENT INFORMATION ON IMMEDIATE OR CONVERTIBLE
WAR MATERIALS OR PROCESSES

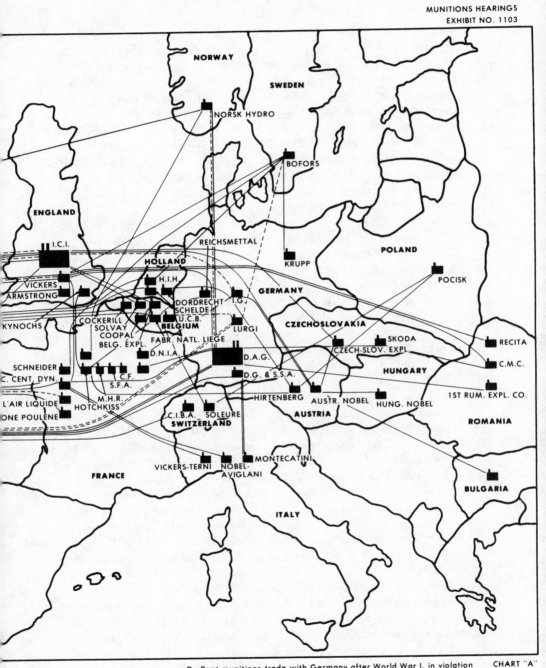

Du Pont munitions trade with Germany after World War I, in violation
of the Versailles Treaty and U.S. - Germany Treaty.
Source: Senate Munitions Hearings, Exhibit #1103
Report, 1936.

economic cooperation of our citizens can be welcomed abroad."[91] Throughout his presidency, Hoover rejected the gunboat diplomacies of his predecessors, including Coolidge, and avoided any foreign interventions or any direct government participation in an economic program overseas which could lead to political confrontation with a foreign power. Hoover shared the feeling of most corporate leaders after World War I, that war primed the pump of revolution, especially during a depression. Both as Secretary of Commerce and as President, Hoover encouraged *private* corporate expansion, consulting with the Du Ponts particularly over any disarmament program which threatened embargoes that would restrict their commodity or capital markets, even informing Colt Arms of the latest results in the arms race sweepstakes.

The Du Ponts took full advantage of this policy, developing not only an export market, but an overseas capital market as well. In Mexico they invested $312,000 and bought a 50 percent interest in Compañia Mexicana de Explosivos, S.A. In Argentina they invested $788,000 and, with a 51 percent holding, set up the E. I. du Pont de Nemours & Cía Argentina, S.A., which included Industrias Químicas Argentina de Perial, S.A., Industrial y Comercial. They also bought for $313,000 a 35 percent interest in Société Francaise Duco, S.A., and for $789,000 a 42.4 percent interest in Compañía Sud America de Explosivos, S.A.

In close, safe, and stable Canada the Du Ponts made their biggest investment, pouring $10,180,000 into Canadian Industries, Ltd., for a 46.8 percent holding. In mother England, in exchange for "Duco" patents and processes, they acquired 49 percent of Nobel Chemical Finishes, Ltd., and bought a $819,000 interest in Leather Cloth Proprietory, Ltd. In 1930 they made another large sale of processes to Nobel Finishes. England was also the site in 1925 of General Motors' acquisition of Vauxhall, the auto firm. A year later Pierre expanded General Motors directly overseas, opening an assembly plant in South Africa to slip behind the Commonwealth's tariff barriers and also exploit the cheap wages enforced by its racist white Afrikaner government. In 1926 the Du Ponts also bought a 22.9 percent interest in Société Francaise Fabrikoid, which controlled the Fabrikoid markets in French North African colonies of Algeria, Tunisia, and Morocco.

The rising Axis powers also proved to be good business prospects. Mussolini's well-ordered Italy looked so attractive to the Du Ponts that they invested over a million dollars in its chemical industry, buying 70 percent of Societa Italiana della Celluloide and 90 percent of Societa Amonima Mazzucchelli. Japanese militarists, too, benefited from Du Pont's perfectly normal business ethics. Their invasion of Manchuria in 1931, the actual beginning of World War II, was looked at sympathetically by President Hoover, whose noninterventionist policy never considered a war against Japan, which would create instabilities hindering to business. "There is something on the side of Japan," he announced. "Ours has been a long and deep-seated friendship with her and we should in friendship consider her side."[92] U.S. investments were few in the area, and most were unaffected by the Japanese invasion. European interests did not fare as well there, and in 1932 the League of Nations finally proposed sanctions. Hoover, however, dissented. "I have insisted upon the aloofness of the United States from the League of Nations in that the sanctions of the League are those of force either economic or military, whereas the United States could not and would not enter into force sanctions."[93] Hoover proposed instead a policy of nonrecognition, to buy time in protecting U.S. interests in Asia. "The whole doctrine of nonrecognition," he explained, "is not alone a method of involving world opinion but it is equally important in the phase that it avoids precipitant action and allows time to work out proper solutions."[94]

With such attitudes emanating from their own government, it was not surprising that the Du Ponts entered into a profitable agreement with Japanese interests that year. Shortly after Secretary of State Stimson condemned Japan's attack on Manchuria, Japanese executives from the Mitzui Chemical combine met with Du Pont executives in Wilmington and handed over $900,000 in exchange for Du Pont's ammonia explosive formula, a process for manufacturing cheaper munitions. The State Department, despite Stimson's public oratory, privately gave the Du Pont sale its full approval.

But the most startling overseas business in which the Du Ponts were engaged was their role in rearming Germany.

Hamburg was too preoccupied celebrating the New Year to notice that Du Pont executives arrived there on January 1, 1926. At this German port, in a secret meeting, Du Pont signed a "gentleman's agreement" with representatives from two of the largest explosives manufacturers in Germany— Dynamit Aktien Gesellschaft (D.A.G.), and Köln Rottweiler, both soon after absorbed into I. G. Farben, German capitalism's answer to Du Pont. By this agreement, each company was to get the first option of any new processes and products developed by the other. This included black powder, disruptive explosives, smokeless propellants for "sporting" purposes, detonation, safety fuses, powder fuses, and "generally all devices for initial detoxication or ignition."[95]

Everything was open to the German militarists, including all patents and secret inventions covering commercial explosives.[96] As to acrylic products, Du Pont agreed to sell this plastic to commercial molders for 85 cents per pound, but to dentists for 45 cents an ounce (or $7.20 per pound). In order to circumvent the legal complications involved if dental associations were somehow to discover this ruse, Du Pont simply exercised its free enterprise by adding an additional ingredient, usually 1 percent of a dangerous poison such as arsenic, to the product sold to commercial molders, making it unemployable for dentures.[97]

The interchangeability between commercial explosives and military explosives was obvious, and later noted by many experts in the Senate munitions hearings.[98] This made Du Pont's agreement, as the Senate Investigating Committee politely put it, "incompatible" with the Versailles Treaty which forbade German rearmament of any kind, or importation of information or arms for such. The Du Ponts were well aware of the military danger of such an agreement. A letter found in their files attested that I. G. Farben had an explosives capacity comparable to "a large, rapidly mobilizable force, or a large number of guns, or a fleet."[99]

Later that year Du Pont and Nobel prevented Köln Rottweiler from assisting the Argentine government in building its own powder plant, setting bids so high that the Argentine government was forced to withdraw. To soothe German nerves, Nobel agreed to "wink" at German contracts with Turkey, and Köln Rottweiler stole Turkish business amounting to 120 tons of rifle powder from Du Pont, while Nobel sold TNT to Turkey through Austria's Philip. The German sales were in open violation of the Versailles Treaty. "I would regret," wrote a disturbed Taylor to Wilmington on October 27, 1926, "to see the Du Ponts winking at German treaty violations. It would be a great shame."[100]

Shame or not, wink they did. Convinced that protest was futile and U.S. intervention in German rearmament "improbable," Colonel Aiken Simons, head of Du Pont's military sales, wrote Du Pont Vice President Casey and gave the State Department's Allen Dulles as the authority officially confirming the U.S. policy of allowing German arms smuggling to "swell" the reparation fund. Actually, acknowledged the Senate Munitions Committee, Dulles had made this policy clear at the pre-Geneva meetings of 1925. Accordingly, "the Du Pont company did not call this to the attention of the United States government."[101] Such an official protest would have won them no new friends in Washington, which was anxious to keep the lid on.

The Du Ponts apparently were so impressed with German expansion recovery and rearmament that they decided to invest in promising German companies themselves, purchasing 49 percent of Duco, A.G., and 3.5 percent of Deutsche Gold and Silber Scheideanstalt. This, with their holdings in I. G. Farben and its subsidiaries, D.A.G. and Köln Rottweiler, gave the Du Ponts a $3 million investment in the German arms industry. In 1929 they signed another "agreement" with I. G. Farben, while in the same year G.M. chairman Lammot du Pont made the Du Pont stake in Germany even higher by acquiring 80 percent of Adam Opel, A.G., Germany's biggest auto maker. This $25,957,000 investment was increased by another $7,395,000 in 1931, giving G.M. a 100 percent investment.

Lammot's decision to endorse a 100 percent investment in Germany's biggest auto company must be considered in its historical context, for 1931 was a tumultuous year in German history. A rising labor movement, led by mutually hostile (and thus divided) Social Democrats and Communists, was being answered by a rising fascist movement led by Hitler and supported by many of Germany's largest financial and industrial interests, including Georg von Schnitzler, a leading director of Du Pont's trade partner, I. G. Farben.[102] Lammot du Pont and other Du Ponts on G.M.'s finance committee (Henry F. du Pont, Irénée du Pont, Donaldson Brown, and Walter S. Carpenter) showed no particular dissatisfaction over Hitler's gain in the 1930 elections that might have dissuaded them from deeper commitments in the German economy; their 1931 investment was clearly a display of confidence in its future.

A year later, Du Pont's European sales agent, Colonel William Taylor, again reported to Wilmington of German rearmament, including the smuggling of American arms to Nazis by way of the Dutch rivers that flow into Germany. "There is a certain amount of contraband among the river shippers," he wrote, "mainly from America. Arms of all kinds. . . . The principal arms coming from America are Thompson submachine guns and revolvers. The number is great."[103] Significantly, the only American firm licensed to manufacture and sell the Thompson submachine gun was Federal Laboratories, with which Du Pont shared joint sales agencies. In January 1933 Taylor sent another excited report of Dutch gunrunning to Nazis in the Cologne area.[104] Within a month, Du Pont made its decision to take a direct plunge into the German munition smuggling.

On February 1, 1933, A. Felix du Pont, Sr., the suave, young-looking head of Du Pont's foreign sales, along with Vice President K. K. V. Casey, secretly met with two Hitler agents, Jungo Giera and Count Westarp. Westarp was the more easily identifiable of the two; he was a representative of the German General Staff.[105] Giera, however, kept his real identity to himself. Actually, he was Peter Brenner, a former German spy in the United States during World War I who had become a counterspy to avoid U.S. prosecution. After the war Brenner continued his sleuthing, selling his talents to at least thirteen different nations.

Although Felix and Casey did not know Giera's real name, they were familiar with his background. During the Senate munitions investigations a year later, Senator Clark questioned Casey about this knowledge. "Did you know that he was an international spy?" asked the Senator.

"Yes," replied Casey openly, "I knew that. He told me so himself. I knew him as Jungo Giera, and he told me that he engaged in spy work in thirteen countries."

"Did he tell you that before we entered the war he was a spy for the Germans in this country, acting under the direction of von Papen and Boy-Ed, the military and naval attachés of the German embassy in Washington?"

"Yes," answered Casey, "I also received that information."[106]

Despite Giera's seedy background, or perhaps because of it, Felix signed a contract with him on February 1, 1933, naming him Du Pont's agent "for the Kingdom of Holland and as its exclusive agent for the Republic of Germany, to negotiate the sale of military propellants and military explosives to purchasers (other than the government of Holland and its colonies) located in said territories."[107] That Holland was the source of much of the smuggling into Germany reported by Colonel Taylor was considered by the Senate Committee a year later to be "most significant," for the rearming "Republic of Germany" then had as its new chancellor Adolf Hitler. The presence of Count Westarp of the German General Staff left little doubt as to whose hands Du Pont munitions were intended for.

Felix's contract, of course, was an open violation of the arms embargo of the Versailles Treaty and, by reference, the U.S.-German peace treaty, and was noted as such the following day, February 2, 1933, when Lammot convened his Du Pont Executive Committee. The legal problems of the contract were realized immediately, and Lammot nullified it, ordering Felix to draw up another. On February 15 Felix and Giera signed another contract, confirming Giera's sales to the government of Germany, actually Hitler, with "approval or consent of the United States government." This provision, the Senate Munitions Committee later implied, was a mere legal technicality to protect the company, as such consent would have been impossible unless the U.S.-German peace treaty was openly scrapped. Yet, the Du Ponts were well aware of the State Department's past "winking" policy, as explained to them by Allen Dulles as far back as 1925, and since the U.S.-German treaty referred only to the Versailles Treaty, they may well have thought a new interpretation of it and such "consent" were a real possibility.

Du Pont never got a chance to sell its wares directly to Hitler, however, for it was stopped by its own cartel partner, Imperial Chemicals. Lammot had written Imperial's Sir Henry McGowan on February 9, informing him of the Giera contract. Lammot's letter drew a quick reply from McGowan questioning the agreement's feasibility in light of expected treaty revisions by Hitler that would allow home manufacture and export by revived German militarism. "I think that any future negotiations would tend to become more difficult," he warned Lammot, "and the Germans would probably consider that as we each reserve to ourselves orders from our respective governments, they should be entitled to do likewise."[108]

Faced with Imperial's disapproval, and possibly even stronger reaction from its other cartel partner, I. G. Farben, Lammot canceled the Giera contract one month later, on April 14. Giera was angered over this reversal and threatened to sue Du Pont publicly for his expenses. Although the company legally owed Giera nothing, Du Pont paid $25,000 to keep his favor. As Lammot explained a year later to the Senate Investigating Committee, Giera's infamous character was no problem as far as the Du Ponts were concerned. In fact, they needed him to handle arrangements with another customer—Japan.[109]

The Giera affair did not lessen Du Pont's interest in German sales. In January 1934 Taylor reported his attempt to arrange a deal directly with a top smuggler, Beno Spiriro. "The contraband of ammunition is increasing tremendously," he wrote Du Pont headquarters from Paris. "I.C.I. [Imperial Chemicals] have received continuous inquiries for delivery to the free port of Hamburg from Magnus and Beno Spiriro (they are two of the rather shady dealers mentioned in the last letter). We have invited Beno Spiriro to meet us this week in Paris, but he refused to come. We are going further into this matter."[110]

While there is no evidence to suggest that Taylor succeeded in securing the services of Spiriro for Du Pont, there is no question that the wily salesman had better results in other areas. In 1934 Du Pont had financial and market dealings in war materials or processes with Norway's Norsk Hydro, Holland's H.I.H., Switzerland's C.I.B.A., France's Rhone Paulene, and Germany's D.G., S.S.A., and D.A.G.[111] In addition, Du Pont had arrangements for interchange or sale of chemical and other patent information on immediate or convertible war materials and processes with both Germany's Lurgi, A.G., and France's L'air Liquide.[112] By then, 4 percent of Du Pont's total sales were exports. Du Pont had explosives companies in Chile and Mexico and, according to one report, was contemplating still another plant in Czechoslovakia.[113] When business inquiries were made on the arms embargo, Du Pont simply referred them to Imperial Chemicals. Together, Du Pont and Imperial owned 20 percent of one of Hitler's largest munitions makers, D.A.G.,[114] part of the I. G. Farben combine.

Du Pont's purchase of Remington Arms also brought involvement in

German rearmament. Remington had cartel agreements with a number of German munitions companies. In 1929, 1932, and 1933 Remington paid $55,000 in royalties to Rheinisch Westfalische Sprengstoff for use of its patents including those for priming in bullets. In 1931 and 1932 Remington also signed contracts for interchange of chemical information with Hydrierwerke, A.G., and in 1933 and 1934, with Lurgi, A.G. Lammot du Pont later claimed he knew nothing of these contracts, yet it was when Remington was already under Du Pont control, in January 1934, that it signed still another military ammunition patents agreement with D.A.G. Under this contract, D.A.G. succeeded to the rights of Rheinisch West-falische Sprengstoff. Subsequently, Remington paid $16,745 in royalties within the first six months for Remington's sale of D.A.G. cartridges to the U.S. government.[115] "In other words," commented the Senate Munitions Committee in its report, "though the German munitions companies cannot sell abroad, American companies can sell for them, and to our own government at that."[116]

With Hitler's triumph, German munitions companies were flooded with war orders as rearmament began full blast, and any new Du Pont chemical discoveries, under its cartel agreements, became immediately available to the Nazi war machine. One Du Pont discovery that was particularly priceless was neoprene—synthetic rubber. Under the patent agreement, this 1931 discovery was open to I. G. Farben's inspection and subsequent use. Not surprisingly, in 1933 I. G. Farben also "discovered" neoprene, and was free to set up manufacturing plants like Du Pont's Deepwater Point plant. "After 1933," William Shirer reports in *The Rise and Fall of the Third Reich*, "the Nazi government gave I. G. Farben the go-ahead with orders to raise its synthetic oil production to 300,000 tons a year by 1937. By that time the company had also discovered how to make synthetic rubber from coal and other products of which Germany had a sufficiency, and the first of four plants was set up at Schkopau for large-scale production of buna, as the artificial rubber became known. By the beginning of 1934, plans were approved by the Working Committee of the Reich Defense Council for the mobilization of some 240,000 plants for war orders. By the end of the year rearmament, in all its phases, had become so massive it was obvious that it could no longer be concealed from the suspicious and uneasy powers of Versailles."[117]

Such was the tense global atmosphere that brewed the stormy Senate munitions hearings of 1934. Irénée's denunciation of the investigation as a plot of the Communist Third International appeared in the papers on July 8, but it fell on deaf ears. For that same day, Hitler launched his bloody Brown Shirt purge, an annihilation of his own party zealots, which now made clear to the whole world that it was not some new depression-frenzied movement of the German middle class that was in charge and encouraging rearmament, but actually the same familiar militarists, financiers, and industrialists who had prodded the German people into World War I. Inevitably, it was this war, its causes and aftermath, that became the center of national attention as the Senate Committee called before it the country's greatest munitions family—the Du Ponts—to give them some of the most embarrassing moments in their lives.

7. THE MUNITIONS HEARINGS

Almost from the very first day of their appearance on September 10, 1934, a little more than two weeks after the founding of the Liberty League, the Du Ponts captured the imagination of the country. The swift series of exposés that emerged from the hearings—billed by the press as an investigation of "the Krupps of America"—seemed indeed to verify the "devil theory" about war and its origins. Evidence was provided from Du Pont's own files, which had been seized by the Senate Committee, that World War I represented a business gain for the family of 1130 percent over pre-war years and "that one member of the War Industries Board signed for the government contracts totaling more than $49 million with the Du Pont Corporation, in which he was a stockholder."[118] Du Pont's $100 million contracts with Britain, which were financed by loans from J. P. Morgan & Company, were also exposed, as was the fact that Du Pont, claiming losses for a shift to peacetime production, had paid absolutely no taxes in 1919 and 1920, the period of their G.M. acquisition.

Through it all, the Du Ponts tried to retain a pose of aristocratic serenity. Pierre, dressed in a medium-colored suit, looked like any stout, balding old grandfather, his kindly blue eyes peering shyly through glasses perched on his nose. Felix, in his flashy light suit, looked the essence of handsome respectability, while Lammot and Irénée, smartly dressed in conservative black suits, calmly puffed on their pipes amid quiet denials of just about every charge that was made against them.

They denied having any foreign cartels. Then evidence was produced, along with Irénée's admission, of trade pacts with Britain's Imperial Chemical Industries for dividing the world's trade and sharing each other's patents.

They denied profit as their sole motive, claiming their patriotism. "Why," declared Felix, "if it had not been for the service that the Du Ponts performed for the cause of the Allies before and after the United States entered the World War, the United States today would be a German colony."[119] Despite the obvious sincerity of Felix's enthusiastic claim to glory, the Committee then produced evidence of not only Du Pont refusal to cooperate with the War Department before and during the war, and its price bargaining, but also prewar and postwar cartel agreements with German munitions makers that were now arming Hitler, and in which Du Pont held blocks of stock. The Giera contract, signed by Felix himself, was also brought forth, as well as evidence that Du Pont's knowledge of German rearmament extended as far back as 1924.

They denied any control of General Motors. Pierre even denied any substantial personal holdings. "Have you not held considerable private personal interests in General Motors?" asked one Senator. "No," replied Pierre, "nothing considerable."[120] Then he was reminded that he had sold $33 million worth of G.M. stock in 1929, and Pierre suddenly found himself with a memory.

They denied any engagement in bribery. Then the Committee produced evidence of the payment of "commissions" to Chinese and Polish officials.

They denied any lobbying, Irénée in particular disputing any influence over the Geneva Disarmament Convention of 1925. Then evidence was produced proving that Du Pont executives K. K. V. Casey, Aiken Simons, and W. J. Kinsman had lobbied in conferences with the State Department's Allen Dulles, Admiral Andrew Long, and Major General Ruggles, all delegates to the Geneva Convention. A recent letter was also produced containing a suggestion by Walter Carpenter, Jr., that a Du Pont sales office in Washington, D.C. should be used for lobbying purposes. "The sales office," wrote Carpenter, "would be a good hiding place for the legislation if it were necessary to have one."[121] Irénée and Carpenter, abandoning previous denials of lobbying, quickly explained that the correct word in the letter should have been "hiving," not "hiding."

Even more incriminating was evidence proving lobbying attempts by the Du Ponts to prevent the Senate Committee's own investigation. "Had a talk with Colonel Brabson of Military Intelligence," Casey had written some months before, "and drew attention to the Nye resolution. As Colonel Brabson comes from Tennessee and is very close to Secretary [of State] Hull, he will discuss this matter with him, so that when the matter is referred to the State Department, at least they will be familiar with the situation and the possible disadvantages from the viewpoint of the Army."[122] The attempt, obviously, had failed. Roosevelt even turned over files to the Senate Committee to help in its investigation, aiming to use its publicity to stir popular anger toward the strongest opponents of his reform program. The Du Ponts were aware of this, and the name of Franklin Roosevelt was entered in the social black book of Wilmington.

Of the four Du Ponts, Pierre was the only one who succeeded in never once dropping his calm demeanor throughout the hearings. Felix sometimes played an almost comical role. Once, when diplomatically embarrassing cables from a Du Pont agent, Antonio Carames, were produced proving that Du Pont had blocked Köln-Rottweiler from building a powder plant for the Argentine government, the senators struck the cables from the public record. "I agree," Lammot hastily added, "that they should not go into the record." Senator Raushenbush, however, pushed the matter further. "You took out the German competitor for the powder plant," he summarized, "and Argentina probably didn't know until the cables today why it never got its powder plant."

Lammot, refusing to admit anything, took his curved-stemmed pipe from his mouth and calmly waved it in disagreement.

Raushenbush was infuriated. "How can you say that, in view of all the evidence we have introduced?"

Felix interposed. "We'd rather sell powder than build powder plants,"[123] he tactlessly explained. The next day, Argentina's government was described by news reports as "furious."

Felix never had been known as the genius of the family. Once, Alfred I. du Pont recalled, "Coleman du Pont said to me one day: 'Alfred, I think we will have to raise Felix's salary.' I naturally inquired, 'Why?' 'Well,' Coleman answered, 'this morning he made a bright remark.' It afterward turned out that the remark was not original so his salary was not raised."[124] After his performance during the munitions hearing, Felix rose no higher in the company, having to content himself with playing baritone horn for the Wilmington Police Band.

The Du Pont munitions revelations triggered a wave of angry protests from around the world. When a Mexican general was mentioned in the hearings, Mexico delivered a strong note of protest to Washington. International spy Giera successfully resisted calls for his appearance, claiming from his Monticello estate that his testimony would start another global war. "The world is going to see the need for curbing these merchants of death and their business," thundered Senator Nye. "There is a large effort being made to slow up the investigations. There is talk to the effect that the revelations being brought to light are quite apt to start a war. One can guess where this talk and other like it comes from."[125]

Major K. K. V. Casey was another burden for the three brothers. During his testimony on December 5, Senator Vandenberg read a letter written to him by Colonel Taylor, Du Pont's overseas salesman. Dated April 22, 1924, the letter laid the growth of German rearmament to

"Jews." Ignoring the obvious anti-Semitism, Vandenberg asked Casey for verification: "This would indicate that in 1924 it was apparently known to European governments as well as munitions makers that a substantial German rearming plan was underway."

"Yes," replied Casey uneasily, "it would seem to indicate that."

Alarmed by such an admission, Irénée dropped his calm appearance and, jumping to his feet, shouted that the letter meant nothing of the kind. "You put that in Casey's mouth!"[126] he charged.

Whereupon, Vandenberg read other letters from Taylor dated 1926, affirming German rearmament violations of the Versailles Treaty.

"Why, in your opinion," the Senator then asked Casey, "was Nobel reluctant to act?"

"I do not know," replied Casey.

Again Irénée jumped up, claiming that any assertion that the munitions people could have hindered German rearmament was "rank nonsense."

"If so," replied Vandenberg, "it's Major Casey's rank nonsense, not mine."[127] Casey, like Felix, was also to rise no higher in the company hierarchy.

But Irénée was not all fire and brimstone during the hearings. Sometimes he was outrageously amusing. Once, when asked who was the "Fletcher" referred to in Carpenter's letter as a possible lobbying agent, Irénée replied that he thought he was a former ambassador to Chile.

"What is he doing now?" asked Senator Clark.

"Hasn't he some sort of position in the Republican organization?" Irénée countered.

The crowd in the hearing room roared with laughter. Harry P. Fletcher was chairman of the Republican National Committee, the recipient of over $55,000 in Du Pont family donations that year.

Other times, Irénée was more alarming. When asked what he thought of conscripting wealth as well as manpower, he replied, "We would have a hell of a time." Then he added his own deep regard for democracy. "To wage a successful war, you need an absolute monarch. I have yet to hear of a democracy or republic waging a successful war."[128] Irénée, like many others, was apparently not convinced that America was a democracy during its successful engagement in World War I. Lost in the world of the technocrat, Irénée then predicted that fleets of airplanes carrying poison gas and incendiary bombs would wipe out the civilian populations of whole cities. A decade later Irénée's predictions would come true, with his own company supplying most of those weapons, including the most horrendous of all, the atomic bomb.

"The only way to prepare for war," Irénée assured the senators, "is to prepare in advance; otherwise, as I have said before, you are going to have a hell of a time. If we are well enough prepared, we will never have another war."

"Wasn't Germany prepared for the World War?" asked Senator Nye.

"Yes," replied Irénée, "that is true, and she was prepared for the purpose of starting war and not for defense. We ought to be prepared for any attacks that could be piled on us. I am talking now about defensive warfare, not world conquest, but if it's conquest you want, then you will need an absolute monarch."

"When would you bring in the monarch," asked Senator Pope, "now or when the war starts?"

"I think we are pretty near that already,"[129] Irénée answered with a smile, and even the committee could not avoid joining in the laughter that followed.

Irénée's antics betrayed a proud arrogance. Occasionally he would even casually blow smoke rings from his pipe in front of the committee. Caught by photographs and news accounts, such behavior was interpreted by millions as an aristocratic contempt for democracy. Lammot's statements, like Irénée's, did little to counteract this belief. "I would rather have a form of democratic government," he announced during the hearings, "but the way matters now stand I think our Constitution is on the verge of going into the scrap basket, and that's why I have joined the Liberty League."[130] Unlike Irénée with his glib manner, however, Lammot spoke always in the gravest tones, leaving little doubt that he meant exactly what he said.

For three months, in September and December 1934 and January 1935, the Senate centered its spotlight on the Du Ponts. Yet throughout the hearings it became increasingly clear that the Du Ponts were no devils. In fact, as one writer accurately reported, they looked like men who could pass the plate at Sunday service without incurring a second look. These were not men who sought blood, but successful businessmen who were only practicing accepted business methods. Du Pont's ammo agreements with German companies were described by them as simply as if they were exchanging facts on a new light bulb. The only way they differed from the average businessman was not in ethics, but in the commodity. And even here, the Du Ponts were not unique. Other American companies had also done business with the Nazi regime. United Aircraft Corporation, for example, sold twenty-nine airplane engines to Hitler in 1933, increasing their German business from $6,000 in 1932 to $272,000; by 1934 the figure was $1,445,000. Curtis Wright, Douglas Aircraft, and Sperry Gyroscope all provided airplane equipment easily adaptable to wartime use.[131] And

General Electric, Alcoa, and Standard Oil of New Jersey (now Exxon) all maintained patent agreements with companies of Nazi Germany.

Some of Hitler's largest suppliers were American, British, and French corporations, all eager, like any private businessman, to land a profitable sale. F. B. Nichols, vice-president of Colt Firearms, was not unique when he commented on the flood of Hitler's war orders. "Man, it makes my mouth water, and here we are, over here, prepared to produce material par excellence and getting nothing."[132] Indeed, the crimes of the Du Ponts could only be described as the crimes of private enterprise itself, and, such being the case, the Du Ponts remained immune from federal prosecution, for their ethics presumed certain basic principles of political economy shared by everyone in Washington, including those in the White House.

At the end of the hearings, Pierre emerged unscathed and as polite as ever, even teasing the committee as to its impotent role. "May I add my expression of appreciation for your courtesy," he told the senators as he prepared to leave, "and wish that instead of waiting for twenty years before we have these reunions, we might have them once or twice a year?"

"Like this?" Senator Nye asked. "Yes, like this," Pierre replied with a deriding smirk. "Do not let us waste twenty years, but have one every year. We will not need so much time to rehearse."[133]

Irénée offered his own form of charm. On Christmas he sent Nye and the other senators a special gift—a book attacking the Soviet Union.

8. A CLIMACTIC DEFEAT

Since the arrival of Alfred I. du Pont in Florida, residents along the St. John's River had learned that the state's sunsets not only could be beautiful, but also could roar. Every evening the six-pound cannon mounted outside Alfred's mansion would boom across the river, and with all proper pomp and ceremony, the Stars and Stripes would be lowered from a nearby pole.

On Sunday, April 28, 1935, Alfred's neighbors heard no cannon and suspected something was amiss. Something was—Alfred.

Alfred, now 71 and failing, had suffered a massive heart attack the previous Wednesday, then improved, only to endure another on Sunday evening at 8:00 P.M. Seeing an oxygen tent being rolled in, Alfred murmured, "So it's come to this. Too late, too late," and turning to Jessie, "It's no use, Jessie, it's no use." He lost consciousness at 10:00 P.M., but an hour later he opened his eyes. "Thank you, doctors," he said, "thank you, nurses. I'll be all right in a few days."[134] Less than an hour and a half later he was dead.

On May 3 Delaware's largest clan gathered at Nemours and watched, amid incantations of the Episcopal Bishop of Delaware and songs by the choir of the Cathedral of St. John, as Alfred was buried. A few years later Alfred's body would be removed from its temporary grave and placed beneath the towering bell tower he had designed before his death. Although neither Pierre nor Bessie, Alfred's first wife, were there, they would never escape Alfred's presence, not even after his death. Above his tomb, Alfred's 210-foot-high clarion had thirty-two bells to remind them daily of the greatest and most persistent rebel in the history of their family.

Pierre refused to attend Alfred's funeral. The presence of Roosevelt's Secretary of War, George Dern, signified how deep the breach between Pierre and Roosevelt had become. Dern had been a close friend of Alfred's, but as a member of Roosevelt's official family he was not held dearly by Pierre's wing of the clan. In fact, the rubbing of shoulders at the funeral by Dern and Irénée was one of the great ironies of the decade. Only four days later, Irénée joined Henry Ford in a complete denunciation of Dern's boss. "The demagogue's hypocritical cry of 'divide the wealth,' " Irénée boomed, "if followed would take away incentive not only of future progress but also of further production so that there would be in the future continually less to divide."[135] That speech, made at a Dearborn, Michigan, dinner of industrialists hosted by the Fords, marks the beginning of the greatest assault ever launched on the New Deal. It was also to be the Du Ponts' greatest failure.

Although the munitions hearings had failed to return a single indictment against the Du Ponts for their many sworn statements subsequently proven false, its spotlight had succeeded in forcing them to withdraw from more ambitious adventures, perhaps more MacGuire affairs. Instead, their political efforts against Roosevelt were channeled into the more legal electoral arena, and particularly into the Republican Party.

The munitions hearings had revealed some of these deepening ties: Harry Fletcher, a contemplated Du Pont lobbying agent, became Republican National Chairman. William J. Donovan, former Assistant Attorney General and the man picked by the Republicans to oppose Herbert Lehman—Roosevelt's benefactor and political protégé—for the New York governorship in 1932, became the Du Ponts' lawyer during the munitions hearings. The *New York Times* in 1934 also took note of the visit of A. Felix du Pont and his sister Alice to the Brazilian plantation of Henry Ford, the Republican Party's strong man. A Nazi sympathizer since 1923, when Hitler personally accorded him special praise, in August 1938 Ford would accept from Hitler the first Grand Cross of the German Eagle ever awarded to an American. This was the man to whom the Du Ponts were drawn in increasing political ties. The main vehicle the Du Ponts used for control over the Republican Party was their American Liberty League. Although its president, Jouett Shouse, had declared at its founding that "as prescribed by its charter, the League is to be absolutely nonpartisan in character. We do not intend to enter the election,"[136] most of the League's 1935 Congressional program was incorporated into the 1936 Republican platform.

The League undoubtedly owed the first sixteen months of its existence to the Du Ponts. Pierre, Irénée, S. Hallock du Pont, Henry B. du Pont, William du Pont, Jr., Charles Copeland, Ruly Carpenter, and Donaldson Brown each gave $5,000. By December 1935 Du Pont associates contributed another $152,622, $38,000 donated outright as gifts. The balance, in the form of Du Pont loans to the League, amounted to a staggering $114,000, $79,750 from Irénée alone.[137] This included contributions to not only the League, but also its more provocative auxiliaries.

With these funds, full-time organizers established League chapters at twenty-six colleges and universities; 100 pamphlets were written and printed, and several million copies distributed; a speakers' bureau was established and the League sponsored many nationwide radio addresses, all echoing Lammot's demand that "all government regulation of business, as such, and as distinguished from other forms of activity, should be abolished."[138] From its 31-room office manned by a staff of fifty people (larger than the GOP's seventeen-man staff in a twelve-room headquarters), press releases spewed forth constant attacks on the New Deal, relief, and the proposed thirty-hour week. Payment of war veterans' adjusted compensation bonus was described as an "extravagance," as were the Social Security Act and all "burdensome taxes imposed upon industry for unemployment insurance and old age pension." Most of the major newspapers of the country fell in line, printing releases or carrying favorable news articles on the League's positions. Even the *New York Times* gave the League front-page billing thirty-five times between August 1934, and November 1936.[139]

Besides press releases, the League also created or subsidized a host of auxiliary anti-democratic organizations:

American Federation of Utility Investors
American Taxpayers League
Crusaders
Farmers Independence Council
League for Industrial Rights
Minute Men and Women of Today
National Economy League
New York State Economic Council

Irénée du Pont, blowing smoke rings while facing Senate committee during munitions hearings.

Pierre du Pont (left) and John J. Raskob, "the Wizard of Wall Street," at Liberty League dinner, January 1936. Raskob, Pierre du Pont's private secretary, rose to become Du Pont treasurer and chairman of General Motors' all-powerful finance committee. Raskob was an early advocate of consumer spending. Both he and Du Pont were later convicted of joint fraud on 1929 tax returns. (UNITED PRESS INTERNATIONAL)

Richard C. du Pont, Jr., director of All-American Industries and president of Summit Aviation. (COURTESY DELAWARE TRUST COMPANY)

Reynolds du Pont, once Delaware's leading state senator (c. 1972), is still a powerful force in state and national Republican circles. (DELAWARE *State News*)

Irénée du Pont, Jr., director of Du Pont Company and past director of Delmarva Power and Light Company and Christiana Securities, is still the most powerful single Du Pont (DELAWARE *State News*)

Sentinels of the Republic
Southern Committee to Uphold the Constitution
Women Investors in America, Inc.[140]

The most important of these organizations was the Southern Committee to Uphold the Constitution, whose chairman was Texas oil magnate and former National Association of Manufacturers president, John H. Kirby. Its goal was the creation of a mass movement of whites in the South, in the hope of robbing Roosevelt of his Dixie vote and also, through stirring up anti-Black racism, attacking the organizing drives of CIO unions from the North. As a first step in this direction, in July 1936 the Southern Committee sponsored a "grass roots" convention at Macon, Georgia, to begin Governor Talmadge's campaign for the Democratic presidential nomination. At this gathering, Vance Muse, editor of *The Christian American* and right-hand man of John Kirby, circulated what the *New York Times* described as "a picture of Mrs. Roosevelt going to a Negro meeting with a Negro escort on either side of her."[141] "From now on," Muse said of the New Deal's labor policies, "white women and white men will be forced into organizations with black African apes whom they will have to call 'brother' or lose their jobs."[142]

The Macon convention had found its greatest support in Wilmington. Pierre and John Raskob, now fully won over to Lammot's ultra-conservative position, both donated $5,000 to help defray expenses. Lammot gave $2,500; Henry B., $500, Irénée, $50, and Alfred Sloan, $1,000.[143] Other contributions came from leading executives of some of the country's largest corporations, including Continental Can and Standard Oil.

The second most important of the League's auxiliaries was the Sentinels of the Republic, an anti-Semitic organization which constantly warned the country of "the Jewish-Communist" menace. In 1936 the Senate Lobbying Committee released correspondence from the Sentinels' files that revealed its fascist sympathies. "I think, as you say, that the Jewish threat is a real one," wrote its president, Boston banker Alexander Lincoln to W. Cleveland Runyon of Plainfield, New Jersey. "My hope is in the election next autumn, and I believe that our real opportunity lies in accomplishing the defeat of Roosevelt." Runyon replied that the people were crying for leadership. "The Sentinels should really lead on the outstanding issue. The old line Americans of $1,000 a year want a Hitler."[144]

Although the Sentinels got most of their $160,000 treasury from the Pitcairn (Pittsburgh Plate Glass Company) family, Irénée and Du Pont vice-president A. B. Ethols found it in their hearts to manage small goodwill contributions.[145]

Of all the Du Ponts, Irénée was the moving spirit in the Liberty League. In 1935, when 40,000 national guardsmen were called out in nineteen states to put down strikes, he lashed into Roosevelt's unemployment relief and farm subsidy policies. "Instead of its having its policies on rewarding a man for what he does, the Roosevelt Administration goes in exactly the opposite direction," he charged in December, "having adopted the policy of rewarding a man for what he does not do. It practices the socialistic maxim 'work like hell so that the parasites may get the benefit of your labor.' "[146]

Even as Irénée spoke, cousin Henry F. du Pont, G.M. director, was preparing for his four-and-a-half-month cruise around the world. Taking along his wife Ruth and daughter Pauline, Henry gaily sailed from New York the following week on the Cunard Line's *Franconia*—in a $36,000 suite. Other Du Ponts fared as well. Du Pont Company enjoyed $55,676,-000 in earnings in 1935, a 19 percent increase over 1934, paying the family $7.5 million in dividends just in the first half of the year. Ocean trips like Henry's, then, were not uncommon. Pierre took a European cruise in 1935, as did Lammot. Lammot's trip covered a six-week tour of Germany, Belgium, and France; although declining any comment on the growing European arms race, he did say that business prospects looked good.

Lammot's trip to Germany came just before Hitler's Italian ally, Mussolini, attacked Ethiopia and a world war looked inevitable. The following January, Roosevelt decided to use the situation of mounting European tensions to not only announce the continuation of Hoover's nonintervention policy, but also launch his own reelection campaign with a declaration of war on America's leading munition makers, the Du Ponts.

Before an unprecedented joint session of Congress in the House Chamber on January 3, 1936, Roosevelt introduced his "Neutrality Act," establishing an arms and ammunition embargo, as well as an embargo on the export of all commodities that might be used for war purposes. Then, abandoning his previous underplaying of their significance, the President attacked his critics in the Liberty League. "They steal the livery of great national ideals to serve discredited special interests," he charged. "This minority in business and industry . . . engage in vast propaganda to spread fear and discord among the people. They would gang up against the people's liberties." He leveled a broadside attack on the League's anti-labor policies. "They seek the restoration of their selfish power. They offer to lead us back round the same old corner into the same old dreary street."

Before the astonished minority of Republican Congressmen, Roosevelt attacked the League for trying to "hide their dissent in a cowardly cloak of generality."

"Our resplendent economic aristocracy does not want to return to that individualism of which they prate, even though the advantages under that system went to the ruthless and the strong.

"They realize that in thirty-four months we have built up new instruments of public power. In the hands of a people's government this power is wholesome and proper. But in the hands of political puppets of an economic aristocracy such power would provide shackles for the liberties of the people.

"Give them their way and they will take the course of every aristocracy of the past—power for themselves, enslavement for the public . . . their weapon is the weapon of fear."[147]

The shock of Roosevelt's dramatic counteroffensive made the entire country reel. Democrats applauded it, Republicans condemned it. "It was a great bid for reelection," derided Delaware's Senator Townsend. The League was more clangorous, charging the President with "fermenting class hatred," and in a real way they were right. Roosevelt was quite willing to use the popular anger against the League's wealthy strikebreakers in order to beat back their challenge and continue the program of reform he believed necessary if American capitalism were to endure.

In this crusade, he had the continued support of light manufacturing enterprises and business dependent upon the retail market. These included Joseph E. Davies of General Foods, Henry Doherty of Cities Service, C. E. McCann of Woolworth, the Straus family of R. H. Macy, R. J. Reynolds and Mrs. Doris Duke Cromwell of the tobacco industry, Pabst, Ruppert, Busch, and Feigenspan of the brewing industry, Harold McCormick of International Harvester, Vincent Bendix (aviation), Herbert Swope of R.K.O., and Sosthenes Behn of I. T. & T. Financial interests were also represented by Cornelius Vanderbilt Whitney of New York, Mary and Margaret Biddle of Philadelphia, William Harriman, Joseph Kennedy of Boston, Floyd Odlum, Texas's Jesse Jones, and California's A. P. Giannini. These individuals personally provided over $220,000 for Roosevelt's war treasury. Labor unions donated another $770,000, and Chase National, Manufacturer's Trust, and the United Mine Workers together loaned over $250,000. Lammot even suffered some desertions in G.M. ranks: James Mooney, president of G.M.'s Export Corporation donated $5,000, while the Du Ponts' old enemy, Fred Fisher, gave $10,000.[148]

One of Roosevelt's greatest allies, however, was Roy Howard, head of the largest newspaper chain in the country and the United Press International Wire Service. As early as January 9, 1935, UPI ran an article by Herbert Harris charging that ". . . the only liberty the League fosters is the liberty to water stock, rig the market, manipulate paper, and pyramid holding companies to the stratosphere. . . . It is the liberty to pay starvation wages and break strikes with hired thugs. . . . It is the liberty to warp the minds and bodies of children in textile mills and on sharecropping farms. It is the liberty to buy opinions of the pulpit and the press. It is the liberty which leads to death."[149]

When the Senate Lobby Investigating Committee released a list of the Liberty League's leading corporate contributors in January 1936, the United Press headlines screamed, "Liberty League Controlled by Owners of $37,000,000,000." Again, when the Treasury Department, on January 9, charged Pierre and Raskob with tax evasion for their fraudulent 1929 exchange of $4.5 million worth of stocks, the UPI gave the news top billing.

These charges brought before the Board of Tax Appeals were of enormous value to Roosevelt's campaign. The *New York Times* on January 12 revealed that Roosevelt had personally planned the Treasury's "John Doe" probe of the Raskob-Du Pont 1929 tax returns, keeping the Treasury Department in the dark on the famous names involved. When the Treasury discovered the fraud and laid its evidence before the President, Roosevelt carefully outlined an anonymous "John Doe" approach so that it would not appear to have political motivations. Pierre's tax machinations might well have gone undetected except that he chose to contest the additional $600,000 tax assessment. It was a foolish mistake. By doing so, Pierre handed Roosevelt a loaded gun. Now Roosevelt could choose the time to fire. In January, with his attack on the "economic Royalists" just underway, the time seemed ripe.

"Tyranny!" retorted Raskob on January 12, two days after the Treasury filed its suit. "Fortunately, even the government, let alone a few administration heads politically interested, is not strong enough to destroy by slander or otherwise the reputation of Mr. du Pont—a really great and fine character and a citizen whose integrity, honor, and love of country have become firmly established in the hearts and minds of his fellow citizens through nearly fifty years of active life in industry, philanthropies, and political and social welfare of his state and country."[150]

Such verbal cheerleading did not faze Washington. The next day, Secretary Morgenthau countered that it was not the government, but Pierre who entered the public eye by contesting what was owed. Raskob's charges of "cheap politics," Morgenthau claimed, simply did not stand up to the fact that the first Treasury notice on the fraud came on December 8, 1932, when Hoover was still President, and that there had been many continuances since, all of them ignored. Morgenthau did not explain, however, why the suit was suddenly now being pressed.

Roosevelt had them running and he knew it. When it was announced that Al Smith might appear at an upcoming Liberty League dinner, Democratic Senator Schwellenbach, the Democratic Senator from Washington who had become the administration's "hatchet-man," made a stirring appeal to Smith on the Senate floor not "to give way to the temptation of following the advice of J. Pierpont Morgan, John J. Raskob, and Pierre du Pont and all the rest of these rascals and crooks who control the American Liberty League. I say that Governor Smith ought first to remember that no man can successfully turn his back upon a friend," meaning Roosevelt. Pierre and Raskob, the Senator warned, should share the fate of "racketeers in our great cities who were finally put in the penitentiary because of the fact that they evaded their income taxes."[151]

The League dinner turned out to be the most famous political gathering of American industrialists and financiers in the twentieth century. It was the type of affair, held in Washington and dangling the lure of limelight, that Al Smith, now an embittered enemy of Roosevelt, could not ignore. On January 25, 1,500 dinner-jacketed businessmen from most of the country's largest banks and corporations crowded into the Mayflower Hotel's flag-draped main ballroom and applauded the appearance of their guest of honor, the man who only two years before had condemned legislation against child labor: Alfred E. Smith. And salty Al gave them what they wanted to hear.

"There can be only one capital, Washington or Moscow," the crusty banker rasped. "There can be only the clear, pure, fresh air of a free America, or the foul breath of communistic Russia. There can be only one flag, the Stars and Stripes, or the flag of the godless union of Soviets. There can be only one national anthem, the Star Spangled Banner, or the International." To Smith, the American way of life was private enterprise, Americanism was capitalism, and he expressed no "possible faith in the capacity of political management to provide either stability or progress, if it should set out to operate the agencies of wealth creation, particularly industry."[152] Roosevelt, claimed Smith, was marching Marx and Lenin under the guise of Jefferson and Jackson.

Particularly pleased were the Du Ponts. Over a dozen members of the family were on hand to lead the standing ovation: A. Felix, Jr., Alfred V. and his young wife, Marcella, Emile F., Eugene E., Octavia, Henry B. and his wife Emily, Irénée and his wife Irene, and Pierre and Alice. "It was perfect," Pierre told reporters. "He gave a splendid definition of democracy," added Raskob.

Across the country the opposite sentiment prevailed. The Dallas *Morning News*'s editorial, "They will get little by standing on a platform that demands a return to the old order," probably spoke for most of the country's voting population. Yet there was little doubt that many of the public attacks on the League's dinner were directed by the Democratic camp. Secretary of State Cordell Hull, for example, drew up notes, approved by the President, for an attack on the dinner by Democratic Senator Robinson.[153] Robinson made his attack in Congress, although Hull's notes came too late to be used.

But in the closed circle of Du Pont social life, none of this dissent was taken seriously. Raskob's enthusiasm could not be dampened by so minor a factor as public opinion, and he publicly resumed his political career, on January 30 releasing an appeal, on his private stationery, to corporate leaders on behalf of the League. "As a property owner, stockholder and director in several corporations, I hope you will not think me presumptuous in calling on you and your friends to unite with others in issuing a clarion call to join the American Liberty League . . . which is doing everything possible to root out the vicious radical element that threatens the destruction of our government."[154]

While Raskob and Irénée appealed for money, Roosevelt's forces vied for public support. UPI kept up its favorable articles, and other newspapers, including the New York *Post* and the Baltimore *Sun,* joined in the attack on the League. "The brood of anti-New Deal organizations spawned by the Liberty League," wrote the *Post,* "are in turn sponsoring fascism."[155] The Southern Committee to Uphold the Constitution also came under fire. "This is a hybrid organization financed by northern money," charged the Baltimore *Sun,* "but playing on the Ku Klux Klan prejudices of the South. When Raskob, a Roman Catholic, contributed $5,000, he was told his money would be used to stir up the KKK and also to finance a venomous attack on Mrs. Roosevelt." The *Post* article disclosed that at the Macon "grass roots" convention it was the Southern Committee that circulated the picture of Mrs. Roosevelt being escorted by Blacks to a meeting, and that the leaflet read, "President Roosevelt has . . . permitted Negroes to come to the White House banquet table and sleep in the White House beds." The exposure of such ugly racism lowered the Du Pont family's image to its worst depths, especially when the Southern Committee's Vance Muse stated that the Du Ponts never showed disapproval of publication of the picture. Later it was revealed by the press that following the Macon convention and the publication of Muse's leaflet, Henry B. du Pont and Alfred Sloan still made donations of $500 and $1,000 respectively.[156] Then, on July 18 the committee investigating the munitions industry released its damaging report.

Against this mountain of public opinion, the Republican standard-bearer, Kansas Governor Alfred Landon, rode on a wave of Du Pont cash. By September Lammot had contributed $105,000; Irénée, $95,000; Pierre, $84,000; A. Felix, $15,000; Henry B., $17,000. Additional donations of up to $1,500 each were made by Pierre, Pierre S. III (Lammot's son), William Kemble du Pont, William, Jr., H. Fletcher Brown, Ruly Carpenter, Charles Copeland, his son Lammot du Pont Copeland, M. W. Carpenter, Walter S. Carpenter, Jr., and Du Pont executives Harry Haskell, W. F. Harrington, and T. S. Grasselli. In the $1,000 bracket were Du Pont directors Jasper Crane and C. R. Mudge.

The Republican ticket also received the general support of most of the heavy manufacturing and financial interests.

Ohio and Maine received special attention from the Du Ponts. Irénée, Lammot, and Pierre each gave $5,000 to the unsuccessful Ohio Republican machine. In Maine, holder of the slogan "as Maine goes, so goes the country," Irénée had donated $5,000, helping the Republicans win the governorship and three congressional seats in the December 1935 elections. Now Landon was calling it a "victory parade" that would move on to sweep out the New Deal in the national elections in November. In Delaware's "chateau country," Du Ponts toasted the name of Landon— and a few, a very few, even expected him to win.

He didn't. Against so popular a President and dynamic a campaigner as Roosevelt, he never even stood a chance. Wherever Roosevelt went during the campaign, cheering thousands lined the streets to pay homage to the man they credited with returning jobs and incomes. On November 2 Roosevelt was reelected on the largest landslide in history, carrying every state but Maine and Vermont. Again, as in 1932, the millions in the cities endorsed the Roosevelt ticket, including for the first time wholesale desertions of the GOP by Black wards. Of the cities with a population over 100,000, Roosevelt captured 104, Landon 2. New York City alone gave him a 1.3 million plurality. Listening to returns at Roosevelt's Hyde Park estate, campaign manager Jim Farley aptly summed up the Republican disaster: "As Maine goes, so goes Vermont."

It was the greatest political defeat ever suffered by the Du Ponts. As even Delaware delivered most of its votes to Roosevelt, a pall of gloom descended over the mansions along the Brandywine. Over $855,520 donated by some eighteen Du Ponts to the Republican banner had been lost, a total of $116,100 from Irénée alone.[157] Another $500,000 raised through the Liberty League had also been to no avail.

The League had been a total failure. When it was founded in 1934, a membership of 4 million had been projected. By the time of the Mayflower dinner in January 1936, 70,000 members were claimed. Yet in March the

League filed with the House Committee a list of only 22,433 "contributing members." The summer of 1936 brought a maximum of 124,856 members, whose only criterion for membership was sending in their name and address for the League's mailing list. As it spoke only to the interests of businessmen and bar associations, the League never became a mass organization. "Liberty League speakers sought to appeal to audiences which were largely composed of college educated people, businessmen, and professional people," wrote George Ziegelmueller. "At no time did one League speaker ever address a local audience which consisted primarily of working class people."[158] The League became a hated name throughout America. Even the defeated Landon bitterly described the League's support as a "kiss of death."

The League's subsidiaries suffered a similar fate. The Farmers Independence Council, for example, had been a total failure: no real farmers joined. Again, over $350,000 in donations to these right-wing subsidiaries had been rendered futile. This was a crushing blow to the family's morale, for support of these fascist tendencies was quite widespread throughout the family. This assertion can probably be more accurately documented if individual Du Pont donations to each organization are reviewed, as filed with the Senate Lobby Investigating Committee:[159]

American Liberty League
Donaldson Brown—$20,000
R. R. M. Carpenter—$20,000
Walter Carpenter, Jr.—$4,834
Charles Copeland—$15,000
A. M. L. du Pont—$5,000
Henry B. du Pont—$20,000
Irénée du Pont—$86,750
Lammot du Pont—$15,000
Pierre S. du Pont—$5,300
Sam Hallock du Pont—$20,000
William du Pont, Jr.—$20,000
A. B. Ethols, Du Pont V.P.—$575
William Knudsen, G.M. V.P.—$10,000
Alfred Sloan, G.M. Pres.—$20,000
John J. Raskob—$20,000

Southern Committee to Uphold the Constitution
John Raskob—$5,000
Alfred Sloan—$1,000
P. S. du Pont—$5,000
Lammot du Pont—$3,000

Irénée du Pont—$100
Henry B. du Pont—$500

Economists National Committee
Walter Carpenter, Jr.—$100
Lammot du Pont—$1,000

Crusaders
Irénée du Pont—$10,000
Lammot du Pont—$1,000
Alfred Sloan—$10,000
A. B. Ethols—$75

Farmers Independence Council
Lammot du Pont—$5,000
Alfred Sloan—$1,000

Sentinels of the Republic
Irénée du Pont—$100
A. B. Ethols—$25

American Federation of Utility Investors
A. B. Ethols—$250

New York State Economic Council
Lammot du Pont—$1,000

Minute Men and Women of Today
Irénée du Pont—$1,400

In addition, the Delaware branch of the Liberty League received $10,357 from Ernest, Eugene, Eugene E., Irénée, and Alice (Mrs. P. S.) du Pont, and Ernest May, Mrs. Ernest du Pont May, Crawford Greenewalt, and Marianna du Pont Silliman. Lammot also contributed to Repeal Associates, another child of the Liberty League.

Never before had one family so singly dominated a political campaign. Hence, the crushing defeat of the Republican ticket in 1936 was also a crushing rejection of the Du Ponts. Symbolized by Taylor Caldwell's *Dynasty of Death* and *The Eagles Gather,* Du Pont was probably the most hated name in America. Pierre and Irénée du Pont and John Raskob all gave up politics, never again to mount a national platform. The League and most of its subsidiaries were abandoned, although Lammot continued to support the League until 1938, when the United Press reported that "the American Liberty League today listed contributions of $13,332 during the last two months, including $5,000 from Lammot du Pont of Wilmington,

Delaware."[160] It was Lammot's last recorded donation to the League, which soon after dissolved.

The 1936 election marked the end of the political careers of a whole generation of the Du Ponts, but it was not the end of their struggle against the New Deal. Thereafter, with Lammot assuming the family's active leadership, the Du Ponts concentrated their effort against the tide of unionization that was sweeping the country and threatening even their own General Motors. Working through the National Association of Manufacturers and other, less respectable organizations, the Du Ponts now engaged in a futile but bloody attempt to stop history.

9. THE FINAL BATTLE

Room 3115 at 30 Rockefeller Plaza in New York City looked like any business office during the Thirties. On the door was inscribed a perfectly respectable title: "Edward S. Cowdrick, Consultant in Industrial Relations." From all its modest appearance, no stranger would have ever guessed that here was the national headquarters of one of the most powerful secret organizations in the United States, the Special Conference Committee.

Even if some crusading reporter had caught rumors of its existence, he would have had a hard time tracing them to this office: the Special Conference Committee had no telephone listing; it had no letterheads, and all its records were marked STRICTLY CONFIDENTIAL. His only lead might have been if he had learned that Mr. Cowdrick was the SSC's secretary.

Yet once every year, behind that door gathered some of the leading industrialists in America, secretly meeting to discuss ways to crush what one member, J. M. Larkin, vice-president of Bethlehem Steel, described as "a drive against the open shop."

Du Pont interests were well represented on the Committee: Lammot du Pont, Du Pont president and chairman of General Motors; Donaldson Brown of Du Pont and G.M.; Willis R. Harrington, Du Pont vice-president; Alfred Sloan, president of G.M.; Harry W. Anderson, G.M.'s labor relations director; and Cyrus S. Ching, U.S. Rubber's industrial and public relations director.

Founded in 1919 in the heat of postwar strikes, the Special Conference Committee was revived in 1933 when Gerard Swope, as Chairman of the Commerce Department's Business and Advisory Council, appointed some of the SSC's members to the Council's Industrial Relations Committee and made Cowdrick its secretary. By the time of the 1936 elections, many of the Committee's members had withdrawn from activity in the Roosevelt administration, backing the Du Pont-sponsored Landon candidacy and being particularly alarmed by "continued governmental legislation and the aggressive pressure of union leaders."[161] In preparing a line of action, the Committee, described by Senator Elbert Thomas of Utah as "the secret General Staff of big business," studied various fascist organizations, including the anti-Semitic Sentinels of the Republic, for possible use in breaking strikes. One prominent member, A. H. Young, vice-president of U.S. Steel, even proposed to the Committee a piece of legislation obtained, as Young explained it to Cowdrick, "from an officer of the German government." Young's legislation was almost a duplicate model of Hitler's Act for the Organization of National Labor, which had destroyed Germany's trade unions.

But the most immediate concern of the Committee was a new labor tactic to win union recognition—the sit-down strike. When rubber workers successfully used the sit-down for the first time in Akron, Ohio, a wave of fear swept corporate board rooms across the country. In a Committee memorandum, part of the "informational service" encouraged by U.S. Rubber's Cyrus Ching, Cowdrick described and praised the attempt by Goodyear to end the plant occupation by inspiring vigilante groups to back the company's open-shop policy. That scheme had failed to break the Akron strike, and workers around the country saw a potent tactic to use against speedup and the open shop.

But corporate executives did not give up the tactic of vigilante groups, and on June 1, 1936, Cowdrick wrote Harry Anderson, G.M.'s labor relations director, to ask his opinion of the Sentinels of the Republic. Anderson was apparently unaware of Irénée du Pont's support of this organization, but offered his own home-brew alternative. "With reference to your letter of June 1 regarding the Sentinels of the Republic," he replied a few days later, "I have never heard of the organization. Maybe you could use a little Black Legion down in your country. It might help."[162]

The "Black Legion" Anderson referred to was indeed a great help to General Motors in its struggle to prevent auto workers from unionizing. With members wearing black robes and slitted hoods adorned with white skull and crossbones, the Black Legion was the terror of Michigan and Ohio auto fields, riding like Klansmen through the night in car caravans, bombing union halls, burning down homes of labor militants, and flogging and murdering union organizers. The organization was divided into arson squads, bombing squads, execution squads, and anti-communist squads, and membership discipline on pain of torture or death was strictly enforced. Legion cells filled G.M. factories, terrorizing workers and recruiting Ku Klux Klansmen.

Since 1933 the Black Legion's power had permeated police departments and high places in city, county, and state governments. They were intimately connected with G.M. company unions and the Republican Party. G.M. foremen were actually seen donning black robes inside a G.M. plant in Flint, Michigan, in preparation for a raid.[163] One of these raids resulted in the death of a Detroit WPA worker named Charles Poole. Later, Poole's sixteen murderers were brought to trial—all were Black Legion members, five of them leading members of Detroit's powerful Wolverine Republican League. Defending them was Wolverine director Harry Z. Marx, head of the American Legion's Americanization Committee, counsel for Detroit's notorious anti-labor chief of police, Heinrich Pickert, and a supporter of Michigan's ex-governor, Wilbur M. Bruckner. In fact, only two days before Poole's murder, Bruckner had announced his candidacy for the U.S. Senate at a meeting sponsored by the Wolverine Republican League.

"A reputable national organization," wrote Lou Wedemar of Hearst's *Universal Service,* "numbering among its members some of America's most distinguished statesmen and financiers, was regarded by the Black Legion, terrorist cult, as an ally in its plots of wholesale murder. . . . It was established further that several members of the Legion murder party which recently shot to death a doomed victim were also members of this same highly regarded organization, and that certain Black Legionnaires believed their memberships in the two bodies overlapped."[164]

The Poole murder trial blew the lid off the Black Legion's backers. "An important section of the membership consisted of substantial citizens," reported Will Lissner of the *New York Times.* Captain Ira H. Marmon of the Michigan State Police testified that at least fifty unexplained "suicides" from 1933 to 1936 were probably the work of the Black Legion. One murder was described as a "thrill" by a former Black Legion member, Dayton Dean. It seems Colonel Harvey Davis, after a drinking bout with several Legionnaires, "wanted to know what it felt like to shoot a Negro." The result was the sadistic murder of one Silas Coleman. Such violent racism was openly admitted by the Black Legion's national commander, Virgil R. Effinger. "I belong to the Ku Klux Klan," he was reported saying, "am proud of it and don't care who knows it."[165] In disgust, *New Republic*'s Forrest Davis described the Black Legion as a "depraved Ku Klux Klan."[166]

But Black Legionnaires were no mere "depraved" racists. The list of murder victims charged to their hands reveals an anti-UAW motive of cruel, deliberate reasoning. John Bielak, UAW organizer in the Hudson plant, was given "warnings" by a Black Legionnaire, Isaac White; on March 15, 1934, Bielak's body was found riddled with bullets beside a lonely country road near Monroe, Michigan. Only three months earlier, on December 22, 1933, another auto union organizer, George Marchuk, was also found dead with a bullet through his head. Marchuk, like many UAW organizers in its early struggling days, was a communist, and it was no surprise three years later to discover it was the Legion that was responsible for the bombing of the Communist Party's Detroit offices. Indeed, among the Legion's own principles revealed to new members at initiation was: "We regard as enemies of ourselves and our country all aliens, Negroes, Jews and cults and creeds believing in racial equality and owing allegiance to any foreign potentate."

By the fall of 1935, with the bombing of strike headquarters and workers' homes during the Motor Products strike, a public outcry had arisen in Michigan. Charles Poole's murder in 1936 raised the outcry to a veritable roar, spurring the arrest of some fifty Black Legionnaires. Michigan requested the extradition of Virgil Effinger, but Ohio officials allowed his disappearance before he could be brought across state lines. Then the Detroit *News* discovered that Detroit's Wayne County prosecutor, Duncan McCrea, was himself an admitted member of the Black Legion, and his chief investigator, Charles Spare, was a founder of the Michigan branch of the Ku Klux Klan. Desperate, some Michigan citizens, pointing out that the Legion had crossed state lines, requested a federal probe. In response, Minnesota's Senator Elmer A. Benson introduced a resolution calling for a federal investigation of the Black Legion, which the anxious Senate quickly buried in committee. On May 28, 1936, Roosevelt's Attorney General, Homer S. Cummings, admitted that the Justice Department had "known of the Black Legion for about a year," but that a federal probe was impossible since "no federal law had been violated."

Pennsylvania's Governor George H. Earle was one of the enraged many who saw the long arm of Du Pont working behind the scenes. "I charge that this organization," he stated on June 8, 1936, "is the direct result of the subversive propaganda subsidized by the Grand Dukes of the Duchy of Delaware, the Du Ponts, and the munition princes of the American Liberty League.

"I was United States Minister to Austria in 1933–34. I saw for myself how fascism and Nazism are born furtively, in the dark; how they develop through just such organizations as the Black Legion, distorting prejudices, rousing passions, making a mockery of the truth, finally bursting forth into violence and bloodshed. . . . The Black Legion is the first fruit of their campaign for fascism."[167]

The Du Ponts never answered Earle's charges, which went ignored by most of the press. The New York *World-Telegram,* however, did offer its own condemnation of the Legion two months later. "The Black Legion's crimes are part of a larger picture of intolerance in America," read its editorial. "They are cut from the same piece of teachers' oaths, anti-red forays into campuses, vigilante and lynching mobs, anti-labor terrorism and the other manifestations of special-interest racketeering wrapped in the garb of patriotism."[168]

The Black Legion reputedly had a membership of some 40,000 in Michigan and 75,000 nationally. It was never successfully rooted out, posing under a variety of names in General Motors company towns throughout Michigan, Indiana, and Ohio. As late as March 2, 1938, the New York *World-Telegram* reported that the Black Legion was operating in Macomb County, Michigan, under the name of the Patriotic Legion of America. But by then the Black Legion had lost its momentum. Although the Klan still did, and does, thrive in Michigan, the Black Legion's effectiveness ended with the defeat of its main objective—the crushing of the United Auto Workers. That objective failed with the victory of the Great Flint Strike of 1936–1937.

The Great General Motors Sit-Down Strike

The Flint Strike brought to General Motors what the Special Conference Committee had feared most, the sit-down strike. And yet it was Lammot du Pont and Alfred Sloan's own policies that brought it on.

By 1936 General Motors was the country's largest manufacturer and the world's largest corporation, with a net annual profit of $225 million. Lammot du Pont's own salary that year was over $100,000;[169] President Alfred Sloan and vice-president "Speedup King" William Knudsen received $375,000 each in 1935. In 1936, 350 of G.M.'s officers and directors were paid $10 million in salaries and bonuses. G.M. officials lounged on twenty-four privately owned yachts and were provided with their own railroad cars for traveling in privacy and luxury.

In contrast, the lives of G.M. workers were miserable. In 1935, when the federal government declared $1,600 as a minimum income possible for a family of four to live decently, the average G.M. worker took home $900. Style changes resulted in layoffs for three to four months out of every year, with no unemployment insurance provided. Company speedups to increase productivity were appalling, forcing the men to work like fiends. One worker told the *Atlantic Monthly* that the constant deafening noise of the factory had once made him so dizzy he couldn't recall where his car was when he left the plant. Men became sick, vomiting their lunches, their skin described as having a "jaundiced color" like tuberculers, and when temperatures soared above the hundreds in July 1936, workers died in G.M. plants by the scores. Yet the speedups continued, enforced by foremen who could fire at will. The terrible threat of being unemployed during a depression had succeeded in intimidating the men for years. "The fear of layoff is always in their minds," reported a federal NRA investigation in 1935, "even if not definitely brought there by the foremen. The speedup is thus inherent in the . . . lack of steady work and an army of unemployed waiting outside . . . insecurity, low annual earnings, inequitable hiring and rehiring methods, espionage, speedup, and displacement of workers at an extremely early age. . . . Unless something is done soon, they intend to take things into their own hands to get results."[170]

Such seething sentiments were well known to the Du Ponts. In 1934, when the United Auto Workers demanded negotiations according to the NRA law, Lammot refused. Roosevelt, fearing that Du Pont intransigence would lead to a conflict, offered a "compromise" which included proportional representation for the company union, the Works Council, and provided for an Auto Labor Board that would decide which union would represent the workers. Later, the UAW discovered that labor's representative on this board was a member of the Black Legion.

This G.M. policy was not due simply to Lammot's principled obstinacy. Rather, General Motors was too important a keystone in the whole Du Pont empire to be placed in the hands of an independent trade union with any power at all. By 1935 G.M. had surrendered $250 million in dividends to Du Pont since its original investment. That year alone, G.M.'s dividends represented 30 percent of Du Pont's income, another 13 percent coming from other corporate investments. In that very real sense, G.M. represented not only Du Pont's largest investment and greatest customer, but also the very symbol of the future of Du Pont investments in many other industries as well. This, in effect, meant the future of Du Pont itself. Du Pont's 19 percent increase in earnings over 1934, for example, was partly a result of the profits generated by G.M.'s hapless workers. "A factor contributing importantly to the increase," stated the 1935 *Annual Report*, "was the action of the automotive industry, which consumed directly and indirectly the company's products, in advancing the fall of 1935 the introduction of new models. . . ." Although average prices had fallen 36 percent since the Depression began, G.M.'s dividends, $22.4 million in 1935 alone, kept up Du Pont's profit margin.

To keep this empire intact, Lammot spent $994,855 between 1934 and 1936 for "detective work" in G.M. plants, including arms and gas; $419,850 went to the infamous Pinkerton Agency.[171] This spy system was, as the La Follette Committee explained, "a gigantic commercial enterprise in which employers collaborate with professional spies in assaulting citizens because they exert their lawful right to organize for collective bargaining."[172] Even government officials were not immune to Pinkerton harassment from G.M. Sent to Toledo in 1935 to act as conciliator during a strike at the Chevrolet plant there, Assistant Secretary of Labor Edward F. McGrady was constantly shadowed by G.M. agents. That September, in anticipation of a strike, Chevrolet bought $1,000 worth of tear gas for the police department of Flint, Michigan, site of G.M.'s biggest plants. A year later, that gas was used in the greatest battle of organized labor.

The United Auto Workers finally won its autonomy inside the conservative American Federation of Labor in May 1936, and the following month it sent one of its crack organizers, Vice-President Wyndham Mortimer, into the G.M. heartland. Arriving in Flint, a total company town, Mortimer secretly visited homes of workers, signed people up, sent records to the UAW national headquarters, and soon was publishing a weekly newsletter to 7,000 workers. In a short while he had organized a core of workers in Fisher Body No. 1 plant, knowing that the Fisher and Chevrolet plants were the crucial links in G.M.'s chain of production. Mortimer was then recalled by the AFL leadership, which was frightened by his success; but he arranged for Robert Travis, an experienced organizer, to take his place, and the union continued to grow.

The defeat of the Du Pont-sponsored Republican ticket in November played a catalyst role in encouraging labor militancy at Flint. G.M. had openly endorsed Landon, but the workers had voted Roosevelt back into office. The week following the election, the emboldened auto workers in Fisher No. 1 fought another speedup and wage cut with seven work stoppages. On November 9 Travis met with forty union members, key men in each department, to plan a sit-down. Three days later striking workers forced the rehiring of two men, and the union grew further. On December 30, G.M.'s attempt to shift dies by rail from Flint to another plant where the union was weak finally touched off the beginning of the greatest strike in labor history. "Shut her down!" came the cry through the plant, and the occupation of G.M. was underway. By January 7, 100,000 G.M. workers were idle across the country.

G.M.'s management made every attempt to break the strike. First it tried to demoralize the workers by directing attacks through the press, charging "ultimatums" and "dictatorship," and by organizing its own vigilante Flint Alliance. The strikers ignored the slurs and organized themselves in the plant to handle everything from sanitation to security, labor classes to sports and theatre, all governed by two daily meetings of 1,200 workers. The strike captured the imagination of the country, and financial and cultural help poured in. Charlie Chaplin donated his current movie, *Modern Times*. Dramatic groups put on plays. All the while, Lammot du Pont fumed.

The Du Ponts tried to stamp out this rising national support for the Flint strikers through another one of their arms, the National Association of Manufacturers. "The refusal to abide by the will of Congress on the part of leading members of the National Association of Manufacturers," reported the Senate Civil Liberties Committee three years later, "spurred by the legal opinion distributed by the Assocation, was one of the principal reasons for the inability of the NLRB to establish peaceful collective bargaining in situations such as the General Motors strike in January and February, 1937."[173] NAM waged a nationwide propaganda war against unions and the Flint strikers and secured court injunctions against the NLRB that was designed, according to the Senate committee, to "nullify the administration of the National Labor Relations Act, impairing the successful operation of the law." Significantly, the committee noted that "the largest contributor during this period (1932–1937) was E. I. du Pont de Nemours & Co. with $118,600, most of which was donated in 1936 and 1937. The rising interest of this company in the Association's activities is indicated by the increase in its contributions from $725 in 1933 to $55,000 in 1937." General Motors, at $66,250, was NAM's second largest contributor.

On January 11, G.M. called in the Flint police to evict the strikers. The police launched repeated assaults, firing shotguns and revolvers. Although fourteen workers were wounded, the strikers beat back the attack with bottles and water hoses.

Then G.M. pressured Michigan's Governor Frank Murphy, a long-time correspondent of John J. Raskob, to intervene with the National Guard, but Murphy hesitated. The contingent of 3,000 troops sent were filled with workers who wore their own union buttons, and their reliability was in question. Besides, Murphy did not want the reputation of his office or the Democratic Party damaged by a bloodbath. On January 13 he called G.M. and the UAW together and succeeded in hammering out a compromise that called for evacuation in exchange for recognition of the UAW as the sole bargaining agent.

In the midst of evacuations, however, UAW officials were handed a prepared G.M. press release by UP reporter Bill Lawrence, announcing the scheduling of a meeting with the Flint Alliance after the evacuations were completed to discuss "representation." What was the union's reaction? the reporter asked.

The evacuations immediately stopped. But the nonstriking plants had already been reopened, and the union's position would be further weakened each day. Something had to be done. On February 1 the auto workers seized Chevy No. 4, G.M.'s largest plant.

Murphy responded angrily by ordering 4,000 troops with fixed bayonets, machine guns, and 37-mm. howitzers to surround Chevy 4. An injunction was served, and tensions rose. Thousands of workers poured in from around Michigan, some armed. Plans were formulated by veterans to seize Flint's city hall and free the strikers if they were arrested. Roosevelt, who had been secretly encouraging Murphy to intervene if necessary (while lying reassurances to a worried John L. Lewis),[174] then reversed his position and backed off, fearing a widened class conflict, and perhaps aware that Mortimer had already defined the struggle in class terms. "This thing is deeper than most people realize," the UAW vice-president had told the Flint strikers. "Behind G.M. is the Steel Institute. Behind the Steel Institute are the Du Ponts. It is a fight between the American working class and the tap root of American capitalism."[175] Mortimer later stated that Roosevelt constantly pressured the negotiating committee to settle on G.M.'s terms.[176]

When Roosevelt's efforts were resisted by the strikers' determination, pressure shifted onto Alfred Sloan and G.M. vice-president, William Knudsen, one of Pierre du Pont's G.M. protégés who was directly handling the renewed negotiations. Lacking the active support of federal and state troops, fearing the damage to machinery, production, and retention of markets, fearing a possible widened class conflict and the ugly name G.M. would be given by bloodshed, General Motors surrendered on Thursday, February 11, 1937. The workers marched out of the plants in triumph, and Knudsen retired from the scene to sulk (despite smiles for cameramen) over G.M.'s first labor defeat.

The historic UAW–G.M. agreement was signed not by the chairman, Lammot du Pont, but by Du Pont in-law Donaldson Brown, G.M. vice-president. Brown was chairman of G.M.'s finance committee and also served on Du Pont's finance committee. As such, he was the living symbol of the marriage between Du Pont and General Motors. Within three months, however, this marriage lost its management dynamic, such was the impact of the Flint defeat. Lammot resigned the chair, giving it to Sloan who, in turn, passed the presidency on to Knudsen in reward for his Flint negotiations. Donaldson Brown was the only Du Pont who remained in management, becoming vice-chairman.

The G.M. cabinet shake-up represented a general withdrawal by Du Pont and Morgan interests from G.M.'s active management. Pierre's old order, the executive and finance committees, was abolished and replaced by a policy committee (which included Lammot and Walter S. Carpenter, Jr.)

and an administration committee of G.M. executives. In the process, leading Du Ponts (Henry F., Pierre, Irénée, and John Raskob) and Morgans (Junius S. Morgan, George F. Baker) were dropped.

The Great Flint Strike stands as a turning point in Du Pont history, for the brave determination of the auto workers convinced many of the family that a new age had dawned on the American political economy, an age when the rigid habits of *laissez-faire* could no longer meet the needs of corporate capitalism. Along the corridors of Du Pont headquarters, through the mansions along the Brandywine, a new awareness was gradually seeping into the Du Pont mentality that ownership per se did not guarantee claims for control, but that in the era of strong industrial unions, control must be made an area of its own *political* concern; government regulation, and through it, the union leadership, must be used in a policing role to maintain labor peace and submission. But few Du Ponts agreed with New Dealers that militant unions such as the UAW could eventually be used for this purpose. This is probably because their shortsightedness on profits prevented them from foreseeing the enormous mellowing influence on union leadership that legal recognition, the binding contract, the narrow "interest-group" mentality, and legally established channels sanctioned by a flattering government could have.

Be that as it may, another dynamic was already developing that would forge a Du Pont-Roosevelt truce. For as the Flint Strike forced the Du Ponts to move, reluctantly but necessarily, closer to New Deal labor policies, so also the 1937 economic collapse and growing fears of foreign market losses to Axis aggression were forcing Roosevelt to move closer to the Du Ponts. Since the President's commitment to private enterprise ruled out wholesale nationalization of any major industry, including the arms industry, the approach of possible war made the Du Ponts no family to ignore. In fact, it necessitated a shocking alliance.

Eleven

THE NEW DEAL GROWS OLD

1. ROOSEVELT COMES TO TERMS

On a warm, sunny Delaware afternoon in June 1937 hundreds of Du Ponts and guests buzzed with excitement in front of Christ Church. There, on a lush green hill overlooking the original Brandywine Mills, cameras whirred and bulbs flashed as the formally dressed crowd began mounting the Church's old stone steps, recording the innumerable Du Pont cleft chins lifted in anticipation of seeing the wedding of the century. Inside, filed between polished wooden pews, rows of famous faces watched the tall, thin tuxedoed groom anxiously await the arrival of his bride, Ethel du Pont. But the real star attraction of the day was the groom's illustrious parents, Mr. and Mrs. Franklin D. Roosevelt.

Of all possible events, this union of the House of Du Pont and the White House was probably one of the least expected by the public. Only a year before, the Du Ponts were at virtual war with President Roosevelt, both sides firing broadsides of political tirade. Yet, as the strange scene of Irénée and Lammot du Pont toasting Franklin D. Roosevelt, Jr., unfolded, it became clear that past Du Pont-Roosevelt rivalries were only the internal feud of a class as to how best to rule.

This is not to imply that the clash between the Du Ponts and Roosevelt was not real. In fact, it had become so bitter that the President abstained from most correspondence with Delaware's first family. That was left to his wife, Eleanor, who ably played the role of diplomatic liaison for this courtship of her son to the house of the enemy.

Franklin, Jr., and Ethel had been seen together since April 1934, when at a Philadelphia wrestling match Franklin smashed the camera of a hapless reporter who was too intent on capturing the scene of the President's son dating the daughter of Eugene du Pont, Jr. Two months later, while Eleanor mitigated the President's "refuse" to a more subtle "regret," Franklin, Jr., was among the 1,000 who attended Ethel's debut at her father's Greenville estate, Owl's Nest. Eleanor made up for the occasion, however, by having Ethel join her on the presidential yacht, *Sequoia*, to watch Junior row futilely against Yale's crew. In December Ethel was a holiday guest at the White House.

By the following spring Ethel had become a regular companion to the Roosevelts at Junior's crew races, and Eleanor, assuming the chaperone's responsibility of writing Ethel's parents, seemed to have grown genuinely fond of her.

While Franklin, Jr., pursued his amorous campaign, relations between the two families remained strained. Yet it is interesting that while both sides publicly denounced each other in the harshest terms—"dictator," "economic royalists," etc.—privately they maintained correspondence on a friendly first-name basis. "Dear Eleanor," writes Ruth, wife of Henry F. du Pont, protesting a cartoon against "a blameless citizen," banker J. P. Morgan. "I think the matter should be brought to the attention of the President. He may already have seen these attacks and have taken steps to have them stopped. . . . Affectionately yours, Ruth."[1] Eleanor, who confided to her secretary that she didn't agree with the "blameless citizen," wrote back on November 20, 1934: "Dear Ruth, I gave the cartoon to the President and he says that people in prominent positions, such as Mr. Morgan and himself, must expect articles and cartoons of this nature—only that most of them are ten times worse! Affectionately, Eleanor."[2]

Again, half a year later, when Winterthur informed the White House of its "unqualified admiration"[3] of the President's veto of the Bonus Bill for veterans, "delighted" Roosevelt gave the "usual" first-name reply: "It is indeed pleasing to know that you and Harry approve. . . ."[4] To a similar "appreciation" from Pierre du Pont, however, the President had a terse formal note sent that he was "particularly gratified to know that you approve the message. It was indeed kind of you to take the trouble to tell me so."[5] Obviously, at a certain point, or person, lines were drawn.

Despite this public brawl between their families, the private love affair of Ethel and Franklin, Jr., went along handsomely, and no sooner had the dust of the 1936 elections settled, than on November 14 the couple astounded the country by announcing their engagement.

In feverish expectation, newspapers announced June 30 as the wedding date. To plan and run the whole affair, the Du Ponts hired a social legend of the time, Mrs. Edward J. MacMullen. "Mrs. Mac" was, in her own words, "the ringmaster of the Philadelphia social circus,"[6] and the Du Pont-Roosevelt wedding was the greatest three-ring circus yet. Over 1,300 people were invited, too many for even the "chateau country" of two dozen big Du Pont mansions to house. Fortunately, the Vicmead Hunt Club, owned by Victor and Ellen du Pont Meeds, came to the rescue.

Everything, of course, was fairy-tale perfect, and the press tent, filled to the brim, recorded every historic moment. The President and Mrs. Roosevelt arrived in Delaware in the morning, parked their private railroad car at a siding at Montchanin Station, and guarded by a small army of state troopers, secret servicemen, and soldiers from Fort Du Pont, entered the church. At the prearranged strike of an organ key, down the aisle came the bridesmaids, each wearing a star sapphire clip given by the bride. Then, on Eugene's arm, floated Ethel, literally wearing a fortune. Her gown was made of shimmering white tulle, with a tight V-neck bodice trimmed with orange blossoms, which also circled her tiny waist. The sleeves were puffed and full, and five inches below the waist the skirt was shirred, flaring widely at the bottom. As she gracefully approached the altar crowned with a Juliet cap of miniature orange blossoms, a 12-foot-long, three-tiered lace veil followed in her wake. But despite the enormous expenditure obviously involved, Ethel's gown, like the waves of her brown hair, spoke of the simple elegance that comes with established wealth. The ceremony itself reflected this bearing, with the word "obey" omitted from Ethel's vows, as was the groom's usual statement of endowing the bride with all his worldly goods. Clearly, here also lines were drawn.

When it was over, Franklin, Jr., led his new bride back up the aisle to the reception at Owl's Nest and the veritable treasure of gifts, including the eleven dozen sets of silver from New York's Woodside Sterling given by the President and stamped with the Du Pont crest. The Du Pont-Roosevelt union was now a reality. But even as Franklin and Ethel left Christ Church, dark thunderclouds suddenly rolled over the Delaware sky, lashing the party with winds and rain. It was an ominous symbolic beginning for a marriage doomed to failure and divorce.

Despite the marked absence of Pierre from the wedding, Ethel du Pont's marriage to FDR, Jr., was a turning point in relations between the two most powerful families in America. But in itself the marriage, like Du Pont Company's hiring the year before of Theodore Roosevelt III, grandson of Teddy, was only a personal icebreaker. Greater, more earth-shaking events propelled the President toward a political truce.

The country's uneasy "recovery" since 1934 had been, as Lammot du Pont accurately described it, "artificial,"[7] based on a program of deficit spending that, through the construction industry, fueled the pumps to keep the ship of state afloat. By 1937 Roosevelt, never a titan in Keynesian economics, began listening closely to suggestions by Treasury Secretary Henry Morgenthau to give business a chance now that the emergency was "over." Business, meanwhile, beset by sit-down strikes for CIO recognition, expressed concern about the political rise of CIO head John L. Lewis and about reports of his intention to form a labor-farmer alliance for a presidential bid in 1940.

In June, the month of his son's wedding, Roosevelt responded by making two dramatic steps toward a reconciliation with the business community. The first was his historic rebuff of Lewis over the South Chicago steel strike, a tense struggle in which ten workers had already died from unprovoked police attacks recorded in a Paramount newsreel that was never released to the public. Roosevelt, always a firm believer in the rights of private property, had never been happy with the militant sit-down tactic and Lewis had already been disillusioned by Roosevelt's deceptions over possible National Guard use during the Flint G.M. strike. The President, having nothing to lose now with Lewis, put the hapless strikers on the same level as their corporate oppressors with the pious charge of "a plague on both your houses" during the Chicago massacre. This constituted both a slap in the face to his former supporters, and an attempt to nip both labor militancy and Lewis's political ambitions in the bud.

His second move was economic. A student of the classical economic school, Roosevelt had developed enough concern about mounting inflation to adopt Morgenthau's position. Hoping to encourage private business to invest again by easing their fears of government competition, he slashed federal spending, cutting Harry Hopkins' WPA budget, and all but ending Ickes's PWA. There was only one problem. Corporate leaders were still too uncertain about the government's labor and tax policies and business conditions in general to risk new investments.

The result came merely two months later: the most brutal drop in industrial stocks in the country's history. From August on, Roosevelt began sharing the fate of his predecessor: the Depression was becoming known as "Roosevelt's depression." When the President called Congress into special session in November, he found opposition from not only his old CIO allies, but also the middle-class which had backed him as long as he kept the economy afloat. Congress, in open rebellion, repudiated his "sound" economic policies and passed legislation authorizing deficit spending. The President's own bills failed to pass. By December the crash had wiped out all the stock market's gains made since 1935. Two million men had been thrown out of work since Labor Day and Roosevelt, like Hoover, found himself alone.

But it was an isolation short-lived. For that month Roosevelt found new allies. And it was one of history's great ironies that they spoke through the lips of his arch-rival, Lammot du Pont.

Before 1,000 of the country's largest employers gathered for a luncheon at the Waldorf-Astoria as the Congress of American Industry of the National Association of Manufacturers, a thin, grave Lammot du Pont slowly mounted the podium to give the keynote address—and shocked the country.

"When the future is uncertain, business is uncertain," Lammot declared, and with a calm, deliberate voice he compared industrial leaders to a driver who is blinded by "a fog of uncertainty" and has to slow down to avoid a crash. The analogy was obvious.

"Uncertainty rules the tax situation, the labor situation, the monetary situation, and practically every legal condition under which industry must operate. Are taxes to go higher, lower, or stay where they are? We don't know. Is labor to be union or nonunion, is the AFL or the CIO to dominate it? It is impossible to even guess at the answers. Are we to have inflation or deflation, more government spending or less? Industry is without a scrap of knowledge on either subject. Are new restrictions to be placed on capital, new limits on profits? Industry does not know. The whole future is a gigantic question mark."

Lammot was hitting at Roosevelt's weakest point—his pragmatic flip-flops in policy, and he was laying corporate hesitancy right on the White House doorsteps.

This was nothing new. But what he said next was.

"I say this in criticism of nobody. Perhaps the uncertainties of the recent past, which were, in part at least, the outgrowth of world conditions beyond one nation's control, justify and excuse the uncertainties of the present. That is for history to decide. What has been done, wisely or unwisely, is behind us. Let us leave it there. It is no time for post mortems."

A stir flashed around the hall. This was no usual Du Pont tirade, but a new line of conciliation. This was a Lammot du Pont who offered the olive branch rather than the usual hatchet.

"Give industry a reasonable degree of certainty upon which it can count in planning current and future operations," Lammot continued. "In short, lift the fog and let us see the road we must travel."

Then the Du Pont chairman made an unprecedented set of concessions to Roosevelt, but from each dangled its favorite snare.

"At this juncture, the stabilization of tax rates over a definite period, plus a simplification of the tax structure, may be almost more important than the actual level of taxes. . . . The present fear that we face a rapidly ascending tax scale, as well as new taxes, the nature of which nobody can guess, stands like a wall in the path of industrial expansion."

The meaning was obvious. Replace the graduated income taxes and surtaxes on corporate profits with a "simple" across-the-board rate similar to the single tax championed by Francis I. du Pont. Stop any further taxes on corporate profits and capitalists will stop holding back capital for investment. Then Lammot turned to labor.

"The labor situation should be stabilized . . . the stabilization of fair conditions over a definite period may be more important even than the details of wage rates and hours or the precise form of labor legislation."

For Lammot, labor stability meant also legal stability, especially with regard to the sit-down strike's violation of the laws of private property ownership. "As long as the lawmaking mills grind, the fog of uncertainty mocks the industrial planner." The legal conditions of private industry, he insisted, must be "finally determined."

Then Lammot made his bid for national headlines, calling for a $25 billion program for capital investing to employ the 4 million unemployed. How? By "vastly broadening the market for existing products through lowering their cost and by maintaining a rule of fair return for all effort, not excepting capital effort."[8]

Of course much of this was old-hat, including Lammot's free-enterpriser belief in the self-healing properties of the internal market and the glory of chasing the dollar. But his $25 billion proposal for finding 4 million jobs made the front page of the *New York Times*. And of even greater interest to the White House was du Pont's willingness to accept unions into Roosevelt's grand scheme for labor peace. This was a far cry from the old feudal attitude of refusing to accept labor as a legitimate interest group in its own right. Lammot's statement revealed a new maturity in the corporate mentality about the systematic needs of rationalizing a corporate state through "interest group" politics that essentially divided the working class against itself.

But even more revealing was Lammot's recognition of "world conditions beyond one nation's control" as being a key factor in creating the Depression. Although Roosevelt would not accept NAM's call for "recognition of the open shop as well as collective bargaining," he would turn increasingly to world affairs for a market solution to domestic ills. And key to this shift in policy emphasis was the cultivating of business cooperation. Significantly, every major point made by Lammot concerning taxation, labor peace, and legal stability became an integral part of Roosevelt's policy over the next four years.

The day after Lammot's speech, the Brookings Institution endorsed a modification of the federal levy on corporate profits, while the *New York Times* quoted William B. Warner, president of McCall Corporation: "We as manufacturers are opposed to communism. . . . America must ask itself, 'If not the private enterprise system, what system?' " Pressure was building on the New Dealers.

Two days later, on December 10, Roosevelt welcomed a guest no New Dealer would ever have guessed would be seen at the White House—Alf Landon. "I guess you got the best of it," admitted the President, and then Roosevelt announced his opposition to nationalizing the country's railroads. "A national system of adequate economic and solvent railroads, privately owned and privately managed," reported a relieved *New York Times,* "was outlined by the President as the goal toward which the transportation policies of his Administration were directed." This account by the *Times,* following a gleeful description of the disappointment of nationalization "agitators," was undoubtedly accurate. Neither Roosevelt's intentions nor basic policy had moved to the right; actually, only his rhetoric had ever been on the left, and he now discarded that.

Other New Dealers, however, did not. In two speeches later that month, Secretary of Interior Harold Ickes charged Lammot du Pont and other corporate leaders with threatening America with "big business fascism."[9] Assistant Attorney General Robert Jackson, who had endorsed Roosevelt's refusal to nationalize railroads as "frank and realistic," was a bit milder, knocking the monopolists for their "strike of capital." But the crusading days of the New Deal were over. At a Jackson Day dinner on January 8, 1938, Roosevelt asked for the confidence of the business community, and the next day endorsed cartels along the line of the original NRA. Corporate leaders such as Myron Taylor of U.S. Steel began having a series of conferences with the President. "The President," Ickes wrote disgustedly in his diary, "after letting Jackson and me stick our necks out with our anti-monopoly speeches, is pulling petals off the daisy with representatives of big business."[10]

Lammot du Pont remained cool and calm throughout these attacks, not wishing to force Roosevelt back into a crusade against big business. When called before the Senate Committee on Unemployment in December, he cautiously refused to discuss his views on unemployment insurance or aid to the aged indigent. On the normally explosive issue of taxation of profits, he declared he had "not thought through" the arguments. It was a far cry from the recent past.

"One of the greatest requirements of the present situation is industrial peace," he explained quietly. "Government and business should take counsel together in a spirit of forebearance and cooperation." Gone forever was *laissez-nous faire*!

Some of the senators were not enthused over Lammot's deliberate diplomacy. "You are unwilling," thundered Senator Byrnes, "to express an opinion about the business of Congress, but in a speech that you made you did undertake to say some things about taxes. Have you forgotten that?"

"No," Lammot replied, "but I was not talking to a group of senators then."[11]

The Du Pont-Roosevelt rapprochement progressed steadily. In January 1938 Eugene filed a suit contesting over $63,000 in back taxes for 1933 to 1935 on his children's trusts, claiming the technicality that his income went to them, not him. He won the case two years later. The wait was worth it. He got $20,000 above what he asked.

In September Roosevelt's probe of Pierre and Raskob's 1929 tax fraud resulted in a conviction ordering them to pay $2.1 million in back taxes. "One could secure no better illustration of the tyranny which a government bureau can inflict on a citizen," Raskob had claimed when the charges were first made. Pierre had been no less adamant, claiming the case was "part of a scheme to injure me and to force a compromise of claims in a manner amounting to extortion." The tax board remained unmoved. In 1938 it ruled: "Men do not conduct themselves and accomplish the end as did these parties toward each other and attain an end so advantageous to their fortunes without a common understanding. The design was too complete to be without a designer. The record before us bares its transparency." Which, one report commented, was a polite way of saying cheating, lying, and trickery. Yet, there was no Du Pont outcry in 1938. And these men would receive no penalty, not even a fine. In fact, they did not even fully pay back what they owed. In December, hidden in the back pages of the *New York Times,* was an item reporting that Pierre and Raskob struck a deal with the government, agreeing to pay only $586,369 and $1,473,202 respectively.

The *Times's* poor coverage was not exceptional. Throughout the trial, the case was ignored by the press. "One astonishing feature of this affair," the *Christian Century* observed, "has been the slight attention paid to it by most of the press." What if it was James Roosevelt or John L. Lewis? the magazine asked. "But when the men involved are outstanding champions of reactionary social and political views, and masters of far-reaching industrial enterprises, the press apparently is ready to say as little as possible about the matter, and to forget it as soon as possible."[12]

Meanwhile, in October, Lammot had also sued to recover $5 million paid in federal taxes in 1934. Again the Du Ponts won, Lammot awarded a full refund on March 19, 1939. The government had merely made a mistake . . . a very big mistake.

On May 10, 1939, Irénée, too, got a refund. This one was for $27,999.

In June Lammot had Wilmington Trust sue to recover $223,000 paid in 1935 on thirteen Du Pont family trusts. This, too, was honored.

That same month, Pierre admitted "mistakes" in twenty previous stock reports, falsely recording acquisitions outweighing sales. Again, the SEC exonerated him of "any willful wrongdoing." In 1940 the government again convicted him for $172,000 in taxes owed for 1931.

On November 10, 1939, the Board of Tax Appeals handed Lammot another $222,701 by dropping its claims for back taxes owed for 1935, citing an "agreement by attorneys of du Pont and the government."

Clearly, a new day had dawned on Du Pont-government relations, the Roosevelt administration completely reversing its earlier tax crusades. "It knocks the whole base from under the New Deal structure," Interior Secretary Ickes commented in 1940 on FDR's corporate compromises and tax breaks. "We are running up the white flag."[13]

Sometimes the white flag took on a more personal character. On February 8, 1938, FDR's son and private secretary, James, arrived in Cuba. After visiting the Cuban secretary of state with the U.S. ambassador, he then flew on to the beautiful Varadero Peninsula to see the second most important American on the island, Irénée du Pont. Roosevelt stayed overnight as the honored guest of Xanadu.

On June 26, when the Du Ponts were celebrating the tercentenary of the Swedish landing in America, on hand again was President Roosevelt. Arriving in flag-draped Wilmington by train, the President immediately stepped into an awaiting limousine and headed north toward "chateau country." With the roar of escort motorcycles breaking the rural quiet of Owl's Nest, the presidential caravan drove up the tree-lined approaches to Eugene's mansion, where he was greeted by Mr. du Pont and his wife. The next afternoon, after ceremonies in Wilmington with the Prince of Sweden, the President returned to Owl's Nest and dropped off his military aide, Colonel Watson, with Mrs. du Pont. Then Eugene climbed into the back seat with FDR. "Serious conversation apparently engrossed the President and his host as the car drove off,"[14] noted the *New York Times*.

Although knowledge of the exact nature of that "serious conversation" went with Messrs. Roosevelt and du Pont to their graves, there were certainly enough subsequent developments in Du Pont Company alone to merit its attention.

The Revenue Act of 1938 repealing the tax on undistributed profits was before Congress. Only a month before, on May 21, before the American section of the International Chamber of Commerce, Lammot had called for a release of venture capital from taxes and regulation. "There is no such thing as an unreasonable profit if the risk is great enough," Lammot had stated to the press. Roosevelt's anti-monopoly stance would not allow the

President to endorse the new bill, yet he would not oppose it when it was passed by Congress.

Of all the country's corporations, Du Pont had probably suffered least from the profits tax. "Statistically," commented *Fortune* reviewers in 1937, "Du Pont is not exciting; it is breathtaking."[15] Profits had climbed from $26 million in 1932 to almost $90 million in 1936, far surpassing the golden $78 million year of 1929. Stockholders earned $7.53 a share, a 16.6 percent return on investment; over $6 of that had been paid out as dividends. Dividends such as these, of course, were Du Pont's big story. Since 1925, Du Pont had earned over $627 million and paid out $555,224,000 in dividends. Yet, its capital construction continued mostly unabated, registering $644 million in assets in 1937. Between 1929 and 1939 investment doubled and overall employment rose by 6,500 to 41,000 workers.

There were four basic reasons for this phenomenal success in the midst of depression.

The first reason, of course, was General Motors, which annually provided from 20 percent to 30 percent of Du Pont's income through stock dividends and purchases of Du Pont fabrics and finishes. G.M. was Du Pont's largest customer. Through "stock and management interlocks," a report to the Senate Anti-trust Committee in 1974 asserted, G.M. was able to keep its sales high during the Thirties by engineering conversions in urban mass transit systems from electric to G.M. buses and diesel locomotives.

The second reason was Du Pont's own work force. Through modern machinery and other forms of technology, and forced speedups, the productivity of Du Pont workers rose 33 percent in the decade from 1926 to 1936.[16] Discipline was enforced through the absence of independent unions, the presence of company unions, and an elaborate security system which included Pinkerton spies. Certain minor concessions also helped undercut labor militancy, such as the introduction in May 1937 of disability insurance payments, providing full pay for a three-month maximum, and a six-week maximum for pregnancy.

Through Roosevelt's first term NRA labor policies had little effect on Du Pont work conditions or pay. In fact, when the original NRA was declared unconstitutional by the Supreme Court in 1935, Du Pont was one of the few companies that could state that it was not affected by the ruling and intended to continue the good relationship that it had always maintained with its employees.

With New Deal retreats accompanying Roosevelt's second term, Du

Pont's labor situation froze. The few labor rebellions that did erupt were easily crushed by management, in some cases with federal assistance. The test case came in 1939, when the CIO's United Mine Workers brought an unfair labor practices charge against Du Pont for interfering with its membership drive at the rayon plant at Belle, West Virginia, and for sponsoring activities of a management-controlled "employee association." The West Virginia AFL, notorious for sweetheart contracts, backed Du Pont's claim of "neutrality" before the NLRB trial examiner in Cincinnati. On December 3 the CIO's charges were dismissed.

The third reason was sales. Next to their own efforts through General Motors, no corporation outdid the Du Ponts in developing their sales market. The capture of the General Motors market was only part of this campaign. Across the country, from rayon ladies' apparel to Pyralin radio dials, Du Pont's name was advertised among corporate buyers with unparalleled vigor by one of the most efficient publicity bureaus in the world. Key to this advertising campaign was Du Pont's originating of "impulse buying" surveys in 1935. These studies monitored the buying habits of shoppers across the country for the purpose of discovering methods of psychological manipulation. The color of packages, uses of printing techniques, and see-through cellophane were all studied as a behaviorial science to promote consumption and sales, and also to provide a huge market for Du Pont's cellophane. Such workable schemes to increase demand brought a profitable response from market-starved companies during the Depression, and it is no accident that out of these dark years emerged Du Pont's famous slogan, "Better things for better living . . . through Chemistry."

Du Pont's promotion was not only economic during the Thirties, but also political, reflecting the conservative values of the family neatly wrapped in the flag. The new mass media was used extensively, and in October 1935 the Du Ponts began their famous radio series, "Cavalcade of America." Once a week, at prime time, 8:00 to 8:30 P.M., Du Pont-approved scripts were read over CBS by leading actors.

The broadcast of May 25, 1938, at a time of strikes and mounting political militancy by labor, was typical in its politics, repeating the family's version of its history. "If they will but listen to reasonable minds here in France, like yours, 'Sieur du Pont!'"[17] Jefferson was quoted saying to King Louis's Commerce Minister; this was followed by sounds of the "horror" of starving French peasants in revolt. Irénée, with drums beating in the background, clings to his gentle wife from behind barred doors. "Bloodshed is all they think of!" he cries, "Bloodshed! I will hate it all my life! Listen to them. They are like wolves!" Safe and far from the wolves, Irénée pours forth his patriotic fervor for his new American homeland. "I love this new country. I am only waiting for the day when they will grant me citizenship. . . ." Irénée's long delay in becoming a citizen is thus dutifully explained: He loved America. He had faith in it, and to prove this he joined the board of the Bank of the United States. "I know what it is to be a debtor," the aristocrat informs his depression-racked audience. "I have been familiar with poverty, debt, imprisonment. . . . I can sympathize with you." Chained like a slave to his profitable gunpowder mill, poor Irénée describes his life as "a prisoner on parole." "You see, Monsieur," explains wife Sophie, as she gently tears historical fact to pieces, "it was not only the money for the mills, but he has taken care of all the families of his workmen. He has built them new homes and pensioned them." And collected rent in a company town. Now here is a liberal company ahead of its time! It is not surprising, then, the narrator asserts, that Du Pont workers would not associate regularly with other workers in the area. After all, is the implication, who needs a union anyway when workers have the Du Ponts!

Such was one of 141 national broadcasts of Du Pont's "Cavalcade of America."

The fourth reason for Du Pont's success during the Depression was research. Few companies in the world spent more on research than Du Pont. Every day Du Pont's experimental research center near Wilmington buzzed like a beehive as thousands of scientists and assistants busily searched for new products at cheaper costs. From here came "Dulux" enamels, Orlon, Dacron, and neoprene, the artificial rubber which revolutionized the tire and hose industries. From here came moisture-proof cellophane, which revolutionized the baked goods market, and Lucite, the symbol of the new age of plastics. And from here came Du Pont's greatest money maker, nylon.

In 1935 Dr. Wallace C. Carothers, a Harvard chemist lured to Du Pont by Lammot's pecuniary bait, developed a man-made fiber which was strong, tough, elastic, water-resistant, and capable of withstanding high temperatures. "Here is your synthetic textile fiber," Carothers said as he walked into the Du Pont management office. This "superpolymer" was the *first* truly synthetic fiber, the result of $27 million and seven years of Carothers' life. Carothers was not through yet, however. He spent the next two years in applied research in Wilmington, trying to adapt his discovery to Du Pont's commercial needs. Finally, on September 21, 1938, Du Pont announced the production of a "new silk," nylon. At Seaford, Delaware, the first (and still largest) nylon yarn plant in the world began turning out the new nylon stocking, and nylon was soon being used in shower curtains, undergarments, hairbrushes, toothbrushes, surgical sutures, musical strings, and even fishing tackle. Carothers, however, saw none of this. A year before, on April 29, 1937, after producing over fifty patents for discoveries under Du Pont, he committed suicide.

"Told here is what is right with the country," Lammot declared at the opening of Du Pont's exhibit at the 1939 New York World's Fair, "in contrast with the emphasis over the last decade on what is wrong with it." But even here amid the "Wonder World of Chemistry" some things went wrong. Two experimental "tricks" failed right in front of Lammot, Henry B., and William du Pont's eyes; a glass rabbit that was supposed to vanish out of a glass top hat remained stubbornly visible, and a soapless soap machine refused to produce soap at all. Through it all, Lammot kept his humor, although the commissioned mural for the exhibit did cause a rise. "That one, where two blue men are diving into a muddy pool," he remarked, "I couldn't figure out quite what it meant." "Neither could I," confessed another executive, shaking his head. Not all went wrong, though. The World's Fair debut of the nylon stocking scored a smashing hit. For Lammot, it signified the need for "freer opportunity," which he defined as "no interference with the free flow of capital."[18]

Yet, as Lammot well knew, "the free flow of capital" required the removal of political obstacles to fertile markets. Roosevelt, considering the New Deal reforms basically completed, had removed most of the domestic obstacles: the undistributed earnings tax, anti-trust prosecutions; even the pump primer, the deficit spending program, was hastily renewed in the spring of 1938. But the economic reverses of 1937 persisted; the economy remained sluggish. In desperation, Roosevelt began to return to the emphasis of his predecessor—foreign markets. And here he found Japan's growing threat to the Open Door in China, and German corporate infiltration of Latin America.

The Du Ponts themselves had tried to meet these threats with cartel agreements. By 1938–1939, however, it was apparent even to Wilmington that more powerful forces than trade pacts were in motion. Franco was crushing the Spanish Republic, Japan's armies were smashing into China, and Hitler's panzer divisions were massed on the Czech border. The world was teetering on the brink of a new holocaust.

For the Du Ponts, political forces were developing that would deliver them to a new golden age.

2. DEFENDING THE ECONOMIC FRONTIERS

On September 12, 1939, three days after Hitler's blitzkrieg of Poland began World War II, two special trains arrived at the New York World's Fair from Wilmington. From the station, 1,200 well-dressed Delawarians, led by Lammot du Pont, Mrs. Alfred V. du Pont, and Governor Richard C. McMullen, marched to the Delaware State exhibit to celebrate Delaware Day. And no reporter was surprised when the day's keynote address was delivered not by the state's governor, but by Lammot du Pont.

With the fear of war heavy in the air, Lammot talked directly to what was on people's minds. A quarter of a century before, he opened, United States industry was near panic when war cut off its supplies. "Today, in sharp contrast, every important American industrial and medicinal need is being filled by American factories on American soil, whatever the emergency stemming from the present European conflict."[19]

Lammot, of course, was implying that Americans should be grateful for Du Pont's capture of German dye formulas after World War I and its demands for the high tariff wall that protected its venture into chemicals. Du Pont, he was explaining, was ready for war if it came.

But, contrary to popular polemics, the Du Ponts in no way wanted war. They feared it not only as the disrupter of stable market conditions abroad, but also as the midwife of revolution. "The stability of business in this country," declared Lammot on January 1, 1940, "is dependent in no small degree upon the establishment of a just and permanent peace throughout the world."[20] Three weeks later, before the Michigan Manufacturers Association, vice-president Henry B. du Pont again warned of the temptation of war profits. Our job is at home, he stated, despite the temporary profits of war. The economic and political aftermath of war "will be a headache. . . . Merely to regain and maintain the old standard of living reached during the 1920's, as measured by per capita production and consumption, would necessitate the operation of our factories and mines during the next ten years at an average rate of activity far higher than we have known."[21]

The Du Ponts were not alone in this belief. Most of the large manufacturing and financial interests were also opposed to war, as illustrated by NAM's opposition to entering into the conflict. Most still hoped their needs for foreign markets could be solved short of actual war.

Roosevelt shared this sentiment, endorsing Chamberlain's Munich appeasement of Hitler's ambition for Czechoslovakia. But as far back as his tenure as Wilson's Assistant Secretary of the Navy, Roosevelt had maintained a firm commitment to defend America's overseas trade routes, fully accepting Wilson's belief that "our economic frontiers are no longer coextensive with our territorial frontiers." During his first term in the White House Roosevelt increasingly saw the need of a *system* of corporate expansion overseas as the basic means of economic recovery. Pressured by business interests and his own sense of reality, he recognized the Soviet

Union and helped organize the Export-Import Bank to handle the anticipated trade boom. Encouraged by his own aristocratic sense of *noblesse
oblige,* he announced the Good Neighbor Policy to encourage Latin
American resistance to German corporate trade and investment. By
imposing economic sanctions and by sending thirty Navy warships around
Cuba to harass the nationalist government of President Grau San Martín,
however, Roosevelt emphasized that good neighbors do not rock the boat,
especially where $3 billion of U.S. corporate investment is concerned.
When it came to Bolivia's and Mexico's seizure of Standard Oil concessions, again U.S. economic sanctions were imposed, and in 1937 Roosevelt
sanctioned the bloody suppression of the Puerto Rican independence
movement when 171 people were shot down by police as they peacefully
assembled for a pro-independence parade.

In 1935, two years before the "recession," Roosevelt explained his
foreign policy: "The full measure of America's high productive capacity is
only gained when our businessmen and farmers can sell their surpluses
abroad. . . . Foreign markets must be regained if America's producers are
to rebuild a full and enduring domestic prosperity for our people. There is
no other way if we would avoid painful economic dislocation, social
readjustment, and unemployment."[22] That this was nothing but a continuation of American policy since the Spanish-American War was
underscored by Assistant Secretary of State Francis B. Sayre's reflection on
the market crisis of the 1890's and his quote of President McKinley: "The
expansion of our trade and commerce is the pressing problem."[23]

With the economic collapse of 1937, Roosevelt returned increasingly to
Hoover's emphasis on foreign markets as the solution to domestic stagnation. Roosevelt had already considered the New Deal's domestic program
completed, and always dismissed any consideration of abandoning private
corporate ownership in favor of nationalization and a self-contained
economy. Committed to the rule of private interests, and concerned with its
reform only for the sake of efficiency, he was bound to their needs for
profitable foreign markets. Throughout the Thirties this position led to
increasing antagonisms with the expanding Axis powers. "We're just
going to wake up and find inside of a year," declared Treasury Secretary
Morgenthau in December 1937, "that Italy, Germany, and Japan have
taken over Mexico." The State Department's Adolph Berle was already
involved in economic warfare with German airlines in Mexico, explaining
that, "We initiated a campaign to clear these lines out."[24]

Through this entire debate, the Du Ponts remained publicly indifferent
to the rise of fascism. Franco's attack on the Spanish Republic may have
divided the country, but not the House of Du Pont (with the sole excep-

tion of Zara du Pont, Coleman's sister). So glaring was the Du Pont position on Spain that it was even used by Republicans during the 1936 election. Colonel Latham Reed, Republican leader of Suffolk County in New York, drew the line in attacking David Dubinsky, head of the Ladies' Garment Union who had abandoned the Socialist Party to campaign for Roosevelt. "The question is whether you are for Dubinsky or Du Pont. While the Du Ponts have been furnishing labor more jobs . . . Dubinsky has been soliciting funds to finance the Communists in Spain."[25]

That same day Toledo fell to Franco's fascist armies. Although Du Pont had earlier violated arms embargoes on Germany and China, through the entire Spanish Civil War, it refused to honor any powder order from the besieged Republic. But Du Pont's position was only consistent with Roosevelt's own policies, drafted in fear of conflict with both Hitler and the vote-controlling hierarchy of the Catholic Church which supported Franco.

Japan's renewed attack on China in July 1937, however, was another matter entirely. Here the entire Open Door policy was at stake. China was already buying more and more goods and services from American corporations, and future prospects, according to financier W. Cameron Forbes, were "considered especially bright. Never before has China offered greater promise for its future trade, industry, and general economic progress than . . . just prior to the outbreak of the present hostility."[26] By 1935 American corporations had outscored Japanese companies by $25 million in trade with China. The Japanese attack of 1937, then, threatened not only the last great market frontier, China, but also the whole of Asia, the source of 51.5 percent of the U.S.'s raw and crude material imports, 85 percent of its tungsten, 99 percent of its jute, and 98 percent of its shellac—all essential to American industry.

At the same time, the deepening Rome-Berlin ties were seriously alarming Washington. In October 1937 Roosevelt took the first step toward war with his "Quarantine the Aggressor" speech, and two months later he began his rapprochement with NAM, then led by the largest munitions makers, the Du Ponts. In January 1938 he submitted a $7 billion budget with a $1 billion deficit for a bigger Navy to protect trade routes. "There can be no military disarmament without economic appeasement," explained Secretary of State Hull. "Only healthy international trade will make possible a full and stable domestic economy."[27]

Hull's economic rationale was too obvious. "The reason for all this battleship and war frenzy is coming out," declared Democratic Representative Maurey Maverick on March 6. "The Democratic administration is getting down to the condition that Mr. Hoover found himself. We have pulled all the rabbits out of the hat and there are no more rabbits."[28]

On October 11, 1938, Congress appropriated $300 million more for armaments. In December the United States loaned China $25 million. By then, Britain, America's largest trade partner, had already been granted "most favored nation" status, marking the first U.S. policy change with Britain since 1812.

When Hitler launched a pogrom of German Jews so vicious that it forced such luminaries as Albert Einstein, Thomas Mann, and Kurt Weill to flee to America, popular sympathy was so strong that Pierre du Pont had to deny any connection with the anti-Semitic offsprings of his American Liberty League—"I have never entertained any prejudice that would mark me with disfavor to any race or people. I have one-eighth Jewish blood in my veins that I am not ashamed of"—and promised to publicly withdraw support from the League if there was "one trace" of race-hate propaganda. There were many "traces," some even led to the doorstep of his brother Irénée, who contributed to the anti-Semitic Sentinels, but Pierre did not withdraw.

Still, despite its horror of Hitler, the American population wanted peace, and it was a strange alliance of fears that moved John L. Lewis and the Du Ponts to support the same candidate in 1940. Labor justifiably feared the war preparation, primarily because Roosevelt and his new corporate allies could control the labor market and its conditions through the draft and defense contracts. "Unless substantial economic offsets are provided to prevent this nation from being wholly dependent upon the war expenditures," warned Lewis, "we will sooner or later come to the dilemma which requires war or depression."[29]

Most of the Du Ponts, on the other hand, agreed with Bernard Baruch's fear that war would mean "the institutions of government, as we have known them, would fall down . . . and that the whole moral attitude of the world would change."[30]

Enjoying their new détente with Roosevelt, the Du Ponts denied making any contribution to the Republican ticket in 1940. "A spokesman for the Du Ponts," reported the *New York Times* in 1939, "said today the company is not taking an active part in politics. The making of contributions is a thing of the past, he said."[31] Again, in a letter to the Senate Campaign Expenditures Committee, Lammot disavowed making any contributions. "Please be advised that since the Hatch Act [which forbade large corporate donations] last July 1, I have made no contributions. . . ."[32] But the Gillette Senate Investigating Committee did produce records that $68,350 was donated by the Du Ponts to Willkie's campaign, $40,000 alone from Lammot. When the grand total was finally released in Congress in 1944, the Du Pont figure had jumped to $186,780.[33]

Although the Du Pont contribution was the largest in the Republican treasury, it was a long way from their $855,000 investment of four years earlier. It represented a more realistic analysis in Wilmington of both Roosevelt's policies and Willkie's chances.

"I have said this before, but I shall say it again," Roosevelt assured the country during the campaign. "Your boys are not going to be sent into any foreign wars." What Roosevelt did not mention, however, was that as far back as 1937, the same year the Neutrality Act was passed, he had unveiled to his cabinet the secret Industrial Mobilization Plan, contemplating that "no less than 20,000 factories [including Du Pont's] should be earmarked for production of war materials,"[34] laying the germ of the future military-industrial complex that emerged from World War II.

By January 1939, French pilots were being trained in California, in July Secretary Hull notified Japan of possible tariff warfare, and in September Roosevelt asked for and received a repeal of the arms embargo. In June 1940, frightened by Hitler's blitzkrieg, Congress voted a $17 billion arms program while Roosevelt, speaking at Charlottesville, publicly pledged support to Britain; in September fifty U.S. destroyers were given to Britain in exchange for naval and air bases in the Caribbean.

"I am fighting to keep our people out of foreign wars," Roosevelt pledged, "and I will keep on fighting." Undoubtedly he meant it. But Roosevelt also knew that if overseas corporate markets were to be protected and developed, the chances for peace on his terms were slim indeed. If American corporations were ever to employ 10 million jobless Americans, if economic recovery was ever to be achieved, those markets, he was convinced, must be held, protected, and expanded. But the country was not privy to Roosevelt's cabinet meetings, nor privy to his beliefs. Accepting his word as fact, they elected him to an unprecedented third term.

By the 1940 election, the Du Ponts, like Roosevelt, had accepted the inevitable. Nylon was already seen by Japan as a direct threat to her chief source of export income, the silk industry. "It was said to be even possible," reported the *New York Times* Tokyo correspondent, "that the introduction of the new yarns may be so great as to result in further depression of the value of the yen."[35] In their desperation, Japanese industrialists even toyed with the idea of better breeding of cocoons for improving the quality of silk. But the most significant decision was to use the coal of conquered Manchuria to go into nylon itself in order to combat Du Pont. Japan had already done this with rayon in 1936, rising to become Du Pont's leading competitor. Soon it was also to do the same with nylon, sparking propaganda attacks from Wilmington.

Toward Nazi Germany, the Du Ponts took a more friendly position. As late as 1938, G.M.'s vice-president, J. D. Mooney, had accepted a medal from Hitler, and G.M. president William Knudsen, greeted by Goering, returned with glowing reports of Nazi Germany as the "miracle of the twentieth century." Du Pont troubles with German competition dated back to the late 1890's, but most of these had been successfully mitigated through mutually profitable cartel agreements. With war approaching in 1939, Du Pont signed its last price-fixing and trade pact with I. G. Farben, known then to be Hitler's largest financial backer, while reports were sweeping across continents of I.G.'s complicity in Hitler's "final solution to the Jewish problem."

In 1940 I.G. set up a synthetic alcohol and neoprene plant near the infamous Auschwitz concentration camp. There, Hitler's SS provided Polish slave labor who were worked to exhaustion before meeting their "final solution" at the nearby ovens of extermination plants. I.G. made the poison gas for this and other death camps. When the gas ran out, children were hurled alive into Auschwitz's furnaces. Children were tortured in front of their mothers, wives in front of their husbands, while I.G. conducted drug experiments on women, most of whom died.

That same year Du Pont officials were still negotiating secret trade pacts with I.G. Du Pont's foreign relations department reported to the executive committee on February 9, 1940: "The Du Pont Company informed I.G. that they intend to use their good offices after the war to have the I.G. participation restored."[36] Later that year a Du Pont official wrote Britain's Imperial Chemical Industries: "I think we have all agreed that there is a moral commitment, if and when circumstances permit, for these former shareholders to become shareholders again but the basis on which this may be done will have to be discussed at that time."[37] Some of I.G.'s Nazi directors couldn't participate after the war, however. They were put on trial as war criminals.

While German bombers screamed over London, Du Pont refused to turn over I.G. secrets to Imperial Chemicals.[38] This was not primarily a matter of personal sympathies, but merely good business. The Du Ponts wanted to protect their status as neutrals, and for very good reasons. G.M. still owned Opel, A.G., Germany's largest car manufacturer, which was now doing a thriving business mobilizing Hitler's Wehrmacht. And although they hurriedly sold their remaining I.G. Farben and D.A.G. stock in 1940, they still considered I.G. a business partner for the future.

In April 1941, with war looming over America, the Du Ponts passed a resolution declaring that patent exchanges with I.G. "remain suspended until the termination of the present international emergency. . . . Nevertheless, both parties agree to reassign all assigned patents and patent applications at any time."[39]

Other obligations, such as market areas, however, remained in force. With its cartel complications cleared away, the Du Ponts now readied themselves for their greatest, and most profitable, venture yet—World War II.

3. THE WAR OF WARS

At the annual convention of the Youth Congress on February 11, 1940, its star lecturer, Mrs. Eleanor Roosevelt, was asked by one youth if Du Pont Company, "which had made huge profits out of the last war," wanted the United States to enter the war.

"No," she replied, "I don't think so, because they are making plenty of money now. Of course one can't be sure about any corporation if a huge sum of money should be placed before it."[40]

Such words accurately reflected the anti-corporate sentiments of the time, but the First Lady was quite correct: the Du Ponts did not want American entry into the war. Yet, almost two years before Pearl Harbor, they were already in it.

Seeing that "huge sum of money," the Du Ponts had submitted estimates for a smokeless powder plant to Britain and France as early as January 1940. On June 4 the Allies approved the estimate and signed a contract, agreeing to finance the entire project through the Tennessee Powder Company.

A month later Roosevelt followed suit, ordering $20 million worth of smokeless powder from Du Pont. To produce it, Du Pont was commissioned with $25 million to build and run a plant at Louisville, Kentucky, which would triple the country's powder output. Signing the contract as Secretary of War was an old friend of Wilmington, Henry L. Stimson, who had been Secretary of War under Taft and Secretary of State under Hoover.

It took another year, however, before war came. In April 1941 Roosevelt allowed Navy warships patrolling the Atlantic to pass on the whereabouts of German submarines to the British Royal Navy. In July U.S. troops occupied Iceland. All Japanese assets in the United States were frozen. On September 11 Roosevelt ordered U.S. warships to fire on German submarines on sight. Through all these provocations, Roosevelt insisted to his cabinet that the American people would support a war only if the other side fired "the first shot."[41] In November he forced Japan's hand by having Secretary of State Hull deliver an ultimatum to Tokyo calling for complete Japanese withdrawal from Indochina and China to preserve the Open Door. The first offer for negotiation by the Japanese Prime Minister was rebuffed by the President, and even before Japanese negotiators arrived in Washington, on December 3, 1941, the U.S. Navy had decoded the Japanese "winds" message calling for "war with the United States, war with Britain."[42] Four days later came the Pearl Harbor attack.

Armed with a core of 300 powder experts it had kept on the payroll since the last war, Du Pont swung into war production, ready and willing. Lammot had anticipated the conversion as early as 1935. "Plants which are engaged in the peacetime activity of manufacturing chemicals," he had stated on April 24, 1935, "could be converted quickly into the manufacture of materials used for explosives, poison gases, and other materials of importance in war." Now Lammot had his reins on the greatest munitions industry in the world, and he was more than willing to help the war effort—for a price.

"Deal with the government and the rest of the squawkers the way you deal with a buyer in a seller's market!" he explained at NAM's resolutions committee meeting in New York in 1942. "If the buyer wants to buy he has to meet your price. 1929–1942 was the buyer's market—we had to sell on their terms. When the war is over, it will be a buyer's market again. But this is a seller's market."[43]

This was in September 1942, while American marines were fighting back Japanese onslaughts against Guadalcanal, and Stalingrad was being besieged by Hitler's 6th Army. Lammot, however, had more important concerns. "They want what we've got. Good. Make them pay the right price for it."

They did.

Fifty-four new plants at thirty-two locations around the country were built by Du Pont with $1 billion of taxpayers' money, the company investing only 5 percent.[44] "Today," wrote President Walter Carpenter in the 1942 *Annual Report*, "the company has performed for the government in two years nearly twice as much engineering design and construction work as it did for itself and its clients on all commercial projects between the close of the first world war and the outbreak of this one." For one plant, the $350 million Hanford Engineer Works near Pasco, Washington, Du Pont's construction fee was only $1, a feat of generosity which it heralds to this day. What Du Pont rarely mentions is that from the other plants it reaped over $680,000 in construction fees alone, and operation fees ran into the millions.

The real money, of course, was not in the construction of plants, but in the powder sales they generated, and here Du Pont had more than adequate compensation for its troubles. The company produced 4.5 billion pounds of explosives, about 70 percent of the entire country's total output during the war and three times Du Pont's World War I output. More TNT was produced than ever before anywhere, totaling 1.5 billion pounds. Smokeless powder, Du Pont's old money maker, was another 2.5-billion-pound gold mine, production volume rising to a ton a minute. One plant in Indiana alone produced over one billion pounds, almost as much as Du Pont's total output during the golden days of World War I. By June 1943 Lammot was able to boast that Du Pont was producing more explosives than were being made in the entire country at World War I's peak of production in 1918. In one day, every day, Du Pont produced more explosives than it made for the Union throughout the four years of the Civil War.

In nonexplosives Du Pont production and operating profits were even larger. Throughout the war Wilmington proudly claimed that Du Pont's production of explosives was a smaller percentage (25 percent) of its total output than in the last world war (80 percent). But much of its nonexplosive production also went to feed the face of the god Mars. Du Pont nylon replaced Japanese silk in parachutes, took the place of Chinese pig bristles in paintbrushes, and was used in everything from glider tow ropes to tropical mosquito screens. Du Pont paints coated the hulls of whole naval fleets, Du Pont dyes were used in uniforms, Du Pont antifreeze kept army trucks going in winter, and Du Pont cellophane wrapped rations, drugs, and supplies. A single Du Pont factory turned out eighty-six products that went into the Superfortress bomber alone. The war economy consumed 50,929 miles of Du Pont 35mm film, 38 million miles of nylon parachute yarn, 92.9 million pounds of cellophane, and 11 million pounds of DDT, Du Pont's insecticide wonder that has since been linked to cancerous tumors.

For four hectic years Du Pont's nylon plants, given over exclusively to military purposes for government contracts, produced at full capacity. Artificial rubber also enjoyed a boost: by May 1941 Du Pont was producing 6,000 tons of neoprene each year; 168 million pounds of "Cordura" rayon found a new market in tires for bombers and heavy trucks. Whole new series of products were made after Pearl Harbor: insecticides; food preservatives; fire extinguishing fluids; transparent plastic hoses for aircraft; camouflage paints that could not be detected by infrared photography; explosive rivets for aircraft to speed up production; cellophane wrapping for dehydrated foods; smoke screens; adhesives to replace rubber cement; preservatives for wood, textiles, and metal; even cold- and heat-resistant clothing that would keep a heavy man afloat in water.

In the boom year of 1941 Du Pont cleared $77 million in profits. The

1942 *Annual Report* announced the largest sales volume in the company's 140-year history, $498 million, generating a profit of $55 million. Then, as now, friends in Washington helped. Former G.M. vice-president Edward R. Stettinius was federal Commissioner for Industrial Materials, while Alfred V. du Pont was consultant to the Joint Chiefs of Staff. James V. Forrestal, Navy Undersecretary, testified before the House Naval Affairs Committee in June 1943 that Du Pont had one Army contract that guaranteed a net profit of 16 percent. When the committee voiced objections, he offered that the figure might seem smaller if compared with Du Pont's capital and prewar rate of profit.

Again, Wilmington was the happy recipient of $5.3 million in returned federal taxes. Individual Du Ponts, meanwhile, continued their honeymoon with the Treasury. In May 1942 the Treasury Department acknowledged a $137,258 tax refund for Ruth, wife of Henry F. du Pont. A month later Eugene also received his $86,223 refund.

But the real bonanza was netted by General Motors. G.M. grossed $14 billion in contracts from the War Production Board, which was chaired by none other than G.M.'s own president, William Knudsen, and had Du Pont in-law George P. Edmonds as adviser. The board awarded G.M. one-twelfth of all its contracted funds, and much of this found its way to Wilmington. In 1941 alone Du Pont raked in $37 million in G.M. dividends and millions more in sales to its favorite market. Despite Donaldson Brown's flag-waving, all was not so patriotic with G.M. For months in the crucial year of 1942 G.M. refused to convert to tanks and planes, the Du Ponts blocking the standardization of tank engines. "To our own cartels," reported Assistant Attorney General Thurman Arnold, "we owe the failure to expand American industry prior to Pearl Harbor. To the interests of these cartels in stabilizing prices and restricting production we owe our present scarcity in all basic materials."[45]

Arnold's accusation came in the heat of a federal anti-trust case against Du Pont. On recommendation of the War Department, Roosevelt had the case stayed because of the war effort. Another trust suit, however, resulted in the conviction of Du Pont, Atlas, and Hercules, and cost the Du Ponts a minor $40,000 fine. No injunction was issued against the price fixing because it was ostensibly a criminal case. Yet no restraint was put on the trust practices of the directors. The suit generated sufficient propaganda to force the Du Ponts into line, but Lammot didn't serve a day.

There were other incidents. On July 29, 1943, federal investigators charged Du Pont with overpricing by charging a company $111,186 for film processing. Again, on July 16, 1945, the Du Ponts were fined $122,500 for anti-trust violations on acid sales during the war effort. As

Lammot put it in 1941, "The modern idea is that competition should not only be recognized but welcomed—if it is fair."[46] And during a war only the Du Ponts would decide what was fair.

Lammot's only defeat during the war came not from government prosecutors, but from Rockefeller interests. Promoted by Winthrop Aldrich, chairman of Chase National Bank, and Nelson Rockefeller, the Trade Agreements Act had been introduced in Congress to grant broad treaty-making powers to the President. After the war the private corporate system "will be definitely on the spot again," Senator Walter George, chairman of the Senate Finance Committee and the special postwar planning committee, warned the U.S. Chamber of Commerce. Jobs for 55 million workers must be provided, requiring a $155 billion Gross National Product, which in turn requires consumer spending ability. Unemployment that would turn millions of people to the government again for action "must be forestalled." Senator George predicted that "the government will become a continuous borrower of the savings of the people and will use these savings on various kinds of projects for the purpose of creating employment and continuous national income."[47] And domestic industry required a system of foreign markets secured by quick presidential action.

Lammot took no issue with George's thesis; his only concern was the method—the "New Deal" White House. Speaking for the Manufacturing Chemists Association, Lammot opposed a Rockefeller resolution calling for support of the Act on the ground it would create a "rubber-stamp Congress." Finishing his statement, Lammot asked for a voice vote, which was uncertain. Then he asked for a show of hands. The Resolution Committee held its breath, but Aldrich's forces held the day, winning 34 to 11. This was an important sign of how powerful the Rockefellers had become in financial circles since Roosevelt's SEC restrictions on Morgan's monopoly of Wall Street.

In 1913 the Federal Reserve System, promoted by Senator Nelson Aldrich, a Rockefeller relation, replaced Morgan as the banker's banker with the government. In 1934 the Banking Act, promoted by Winthrop Aldrich, forced the split-up of Morgan interests into commercial and savings banks. In 1940 another law, backed by Roosevelt, established competitive bids by investment banks for clients, undercutting control by the Morgan Stanley Investment Bank. In all cases, the Rockefellers and their allies were the major beneficiaries.

Concerned over possible regulatory encroachment and even further "munitions" charges by New Dealers after the war was over, Lammot saw the need for a tremendous publicity campaign to improve Du Pont's image. "It took the country twelve years to throw out prohibition," he declared on

May 9, 1943. "It took eight years for a reaction by vote to set in against the New Deal, but national polls show that now is a favorable time to begin educating the public in the need for free enterprise."[48]

Du Pont's propaganda program intensified during the war. In 1942 William Dutton, a Du Pont public relations executive, published his *Du Pont—One Hundred and Forty Years* through Charles Scribner's Sons in New York. Billing his biography as "an effort toward a better understanding of one American corporation," Dutton drew almost totally from "the patient assistance that has been given me by my numerous collaborators in the Du Pont Company. More than fifty executives of the company, including members of the Du Pont family, have contributed in the form of suggestions. The result is the Du Pont Company as seen by Du Pont men."[49] So much for history.

Lammot himself took to the airwaves to speak by WBOS shortwave to American forces abroad. "Better yet cheaper homes," he promised, "finer and less costly automobiles, radios, and refrigerators; more nourishing food, superior medicines—a greater abundance of almost everything that adds to the comfort and satisfaction of living—all of these will be awaiting the homecoming soldier when the war is won."[50] To those sons of the Depression, it sounded like heaven on earth. Lammot even played candid tribute to the war. "Spurred to extraordinary efforts by the extraordinary needs of the past two years, we have gone ahead thirty or forty years as measured by the old rate of development in many fields." Significantly, Lammot was the fourth of a series of NAM speakers arranged through NBC to address the fighting GI's.

That year Du Pont also produced its first film drama, "Soldiers of the Soil." Prepared with Hollywood slickness, the forty-minute film was designed "to help the war effort with emphasis upon food production, and to aid the farmer by outlining the abundance of scientific methods and equipment made during the past ten or fifteen years,"[51] especially Du Pont accomplishments, and particularly Du Pont fertilizers.

For some younger Du Ponts, the war was not just good business; it was their lives. Lammot du Pont, Jr., Ernest T. du Pont, Jr., C. Douglas Buck, Jr. (Coleman du Pont's grandson), and Reynolds du Pont (who was wounded) joined the Navy, while A. Felix du Pont, Jr., pursued his aerial passions by flying combat missions in the Air Corps as did Hugh R. Sharp, Jr., son of Isabella du Pont. J. Simpson Dean, husband of Polly du Pont, sleuthed in the OSS, forerunner of the CIA. All were officers, befitting their class backgrounds, and all returned to their Delaware mansions after the war, safe and proud heroes of the family.

But the clan did suffer one casualty—Richard C. du Pont, son of A. Felix, Sr. Richard had been one of the world's top fliers. He was the national glider champion in three separate years during the Thirties, sweeping through the sky like a great silent eagle, hopping from one fleecy cloud to the next, sometimes for over 150 miles, breaking world distance records in 1935, 1936, 1937, and 1938. In 1939, as head of All-American Aviation Co., he landed a government contract to begin air mail service and air express to 155 cities and towns in six eastern states, using pickup systems similar to those of trains, without alighting.

When the war broke out, Richard was appointed special assistant to General Henry Arnold, Chief of the U.S. air forces. In Sicily he proclaimed "great possibilities for airborne operations in combat areas. Gliders are being used to land large numbers of troops and equipment in enemy territory where power planes cannot get, as they do not depend on an airport. For a glider, there is no such thing as a restricted area."[52]

On September 12, 1943, at March Field, California, Richard took his last flight. A new glider he was testing with five other pilots suddenly wavered as it attempted to land. Two of the men immediately jumped out of the plane and parachuted to safety. Richard tried this also, but after jumping out, he found his chute wouldn't open, and he plunged to his death below. Some days later the family bore its greatest aviator to Sand Hole Woods. There, to the sobs of his wife Allaire and relatives, Richard finally met his "restricted area."

Despite this loss, the family survived the war handsomely. Richard's widow and Walter Carpenter watched over the growth of All-American Aviation, which increased its net profit from $27,000 in 1943 to over $188,000 the following year. Henry B. du Pont's North American Aviation grossed millions in government contracts, while paying employees the minimum 40 cents per hour wage, 10 cents less than an unskilled laborer's relief wage through the WPA. His Inglewood, California, plant paid less than the average of all Southern California's aircraft plants. In June 1941 its workers peacefully picketed the plant, asking for 75 cents per hour minimum and a 10-cent increase for all. Henry's answer, with Roosevelt's concurrence, was the tip of federal bayonets.

With the protection of Roosevelt's "stay at work" and wage-freeze policies, corporate prices rose 45 percent during the war, while wages remained frozen at 15 percent above the 1941 level. In Du Pont, "no-strike" pledges policed the factory. Although it did not have an independent union to worry about, Du Pont backed up its no-strike policy by fingerprinting some 800,000 applicants, screening out union organizers, labor militants, and other "undesirables." Accordingly, Du Pont suffered no major strike or act of sabotage and reaped a 60 percent increase in operating profits, from $100 million in 1940 to $160 million in 1944.[53]

The war resulted in a further concentration of capital holdings, and the Du Ponts were primary examples. In 1941 A. Felix du Pont, Jr., became vice-president and director of the Ballanca Aircraft Corporation before entering the service. In 1942 George T. Weymouth, a Du Pont in-law, became vice-president of General Analine and Dye, the American subsidiary of I.G. Farben, a position which fit well into his duties as chief of the Industrial Salvage Section of Knudsen's War Production Board. In 1943 Du Pont Company acquired the Patterson Screen Company, producer of X-ray and fluoroscope screens. Edmond, son of the decreased Francis I. du Pont, expanded his Wilmington Chemical Company to enable it to make synthetic rubber. About that time, the family began buying into Boeing Corporation, one of the largest war contractors, and the next year Alfred I. du Pont's estate in Florida bought its fifteenth bank, the American National Bank, bringing its total resources up to $259 million.

Remington Arms, staffed by some 450 Du Pont supervisors and technicians, also thrived off the war, expanding production to a peak 25 million cartridges a day, while operating five other small arms ammunition plants for the government. Remington turned out over a million rifles for the Army, and to this Du Pont darling can be attributed the introduction of one of the most deadly weapons in history: incendiary ammunition.

With Henry B.'s North American Aviation, perhaps the family's most spectacular gains were scored. North American's net sales increased from $36 million in 1940 to $718 million in 1944. Operating profits rose from $10 million to $87 million, total assets climbing from $54 million to $203 million.[54]

U.S. Rubber, too, made a fortune, occasionally allowing its own directors to purchase special stock options, such as the $150,000 bonanza of President Francis Davis. Finally, with stockholders pressing suit against Du Pont domination, in December 1944 a federal court had to set ceilings on annual bonuses U.S. Rubber's officers could award themselves. By then, U.S. Rubber's net sales had doubled since 1940 to $450 million, boosting net profits from operations from $19 million to $52 million.

While the family's holdings chalked up new profit records, Du Pont Company's own international holdings also returned yields, even in Nazi-occupied Europe. After the war Du Pont received $520,000 in wartime dividends on their investments in French industries and patent royalties. It seems the Nazis had been considerate enough to deposit these profits in two French banks. For the Du Ponts, business friends endured even in war.

Racing to fill the mounting war demands, Du Pont's own operating profits jumped from $100 million in 1940 to $158 million in 1941, a startling 58 percent increase in profits in one year. During the four years of war production, from 1941 to 1945, Du Pont cleared $741 million in operating profits, three times greater than the World War I figure which won the family its "merchants of death" title. In addition, Du Pont Company collected $137.5 million in dividends from General Motors, and the family reaped millions more from personal holdings. Du Pont paid out over $288 million in dividends to its stockholders, much of that again going to the family. Dividends were reduced from an average $7 per share in 1939–1941 to $4.25 in 1942–1943 and $5.25 in 1944–1945 to allow a doubling of the company's net current assets from 1941's $149 million to $284 million by 1945, and a 40 percent rise in earned surplus from 1942's $235 million to 1945's $365 million. Surprisingly enough, although these figures are from Du Pont's own records published in Moody's *Industrial Manuals* (1945–1946), they previously have gone either unnoticed or ignored.

The demands of running such a gargantuan enterprise took its toll of older Du Pont executives during the war, making room for the next generation. In 1940 Lammot handed the presidency over to 52-year-old Walter S. Carpenter, Jr., head of the finance committee, and assumed Pierre's chairmanship. Two years later Charles Copeland and Francis B. Davis, Jr., resigned from the Du Pont board and were replaced by Charles's son, Lammot du Pont Copeland, destined for business tragedy, and Crawford Greenewalt, Irénée's son-in-law. In 1944, the same year Pierre left General Motors, A. Felix du Pont, Sr., was succeeded by Francis I. du Pont's second son, Emile, whose management fortunes had risen with nylon.

Of all these new stars in the Du Pont galaxy, the brightest was young Crawford Greenewalt. An M.I.T. graduate who began his successful career as a Du Pont chemist, Crawford had made technological contributions over the years that earned him the notice of Du Pont directors and introduction into the family's social life. But it was his easy way and disarming charm that in 1926 won for this slim, handsome chemist the greatest boost to his career, the boss's daughter. He married Margaretta, Irénée du Pont's offspring, and from then on he could only go up.

Through these years, Crawford's outstanding attribute, besides his personal charm and technical skills, was his devotion to the study and photography of hummingbirds. Crawford would travel anywhere, California, Cuba, even the jungles of Ecuador and Brazil, to capture the image of his many feathered friends. Once an associate mentioned seeing a nest of scarlet tanagers on his estate in Greenville. A week later the same friend found Crawford perched on an elaborate 20-foot-high tree platform, zeroing in on the tiny family, happily snapping up the milestones of tanager history.

For all his technical talents, however, Crawford's sense of practicality sometimes fell amiss. Once, in the workroom of his rambling mansion, he and his son David built a boat and its engine. Unfortunately, Crawford forgot one thing—room for pilot or passengers. To run it, he had to hang alongside in a canoe.

Late in 1942 Crawford got his big break. General Leslie Groves, head of the top-secret Manhattan Project, asked Du Pont to build and operate a plant to mass-produce material for a mysterious new weapon. The government specified only two conditions: (1) no direct Du Pont profits could be accrued, and (2) all patent rights were to go to Washington. Sensing the potential of a new atomic industry, the Du Ponts accepted, assigning E. B. Yancy of the Explosives Department and Roger Williams to head the venture. Crawford was made a member of the board of directors and assigned to personally represent the Du Pont leadership as head of the Development Department.

Some weeks later, Enrico Fermi removed the cadmium control rods from a radioactive pile under the University of Chicago's Staff Field Stadium. There, worriedly looking on, was Crawford Greenewalt. At 3:20 P.M. the chain reaction began. Years later Crawford admitted doubting that he or the city of Chicago would ever survive that day. But as the radioactivity built up, Fermi shut down the pile, his case for atomic power proven beyond doubt. The date, December 2, 1942, marks the beginning of the Atomic Age. It also marks the beginning of Crawford's meteoric rise to the presidency. From that day on, the job of actually building the world's first atomic bomb became mostly the responsibility of Du Pont. The Manhattan Project, in effect, became the Du Pont project.

According to Henry D. Smyth's official report on the atom bomb, *Atomic Energy for Military Purposes,* the Du Ponts generally ran the show. They built all the facilities for the bomb's production, designing and constructing a small-scale plant at Oak Ridge, Tennessee, and a big plutonium plant at Hanford, Washington, which they also operated. Du Pont scientists and engineers became members of the project's research and engineering staffs. The Metallurgical Lab in Chicago was stocked with key Du Pont men "on loan." All significant research data on plutonium, the fissional matter, was reported to Wilmington. Labs were instructed to provide any additional information Du Pont wanted. Du Pont men were not only involved in plant research and production, but also in producing pure uranium from the oxide and in the development of catalysts and new coolants and lubricants needed for the chain-reacting pile where fission of the atom is induced and controlled.

Behind barbed wires, the production plants were secretly constructed and the bomb put together. Du Pont executives enjoyed top clearance, while investigating U.S. senators were barred. Once, a story goes, one Senator demanded of a guard, "What are they making in there?" The guard answered with a deadpan face: "Bubble gum."

For Du Pont, the Manhattan Project provided priceless information and, later, good publicity. Although the patents went to the government, the know-how went to the Du Ponts, and as their experience with German dyes had taught them, patents without know-how are worthless. In the most costly phase of experimentation and production, Du Pont Company acquired priceless knowledge at no expense. Knowledge, it has been said, is power, and for the Du Ponts, atomic knowledge could be the basis of extending personal wealth through control over a new, powerful technology. As the new atomic industry grew over the postwar decades, these assumptions turned into operating profits.

Two and a half years after Crawford Greenewalt anxiously witnessed the first controlled atomic reaction in history, Du Pont's efforts finally bore their deadly fruit. In two blinding flashes through the skies of Japan, the cities of Hiroshima and Nagasaki and 70,000 people disappeared in rising mushrooms of ugly black smoke.

The bomb and the coinciding Soviet attack on Japan ended the Second World War. But for two long years Roosevelt had delayed in relieving the besieged Soviets with an attack on Hitler's western European front. Many in the administration were openly worried about the possible loss of European markets to a postwar social revolution backed by a strong Soviet army, and some agreed with Harry Truman's earlier proposal to let Nazi Germany and the Soviet Union fight it out. "We cannot go through ten years like the ten years at the end of the Twenties and the beginning of the Thirties," Assistant Secretary of State Dean Acheson asserted to Congressmen in 1944, "without having the most far-reaching consequences upon our economic and social systems. . . . We have got to see that what the country produces is used and sold under financial arrangements [profits] which make its production possible. . . . My contention is that we cannot have full employment and prosperity in the United States without the foreign markets."[55]

It was a sentiment with which most Du Ponts heartily concurred. With the Wehrmacht crumbling before Soviet forces, German corporate and military leaders, more frightened of socialism than American or British occupation, threw the bulk of their forces, averaging 180 German divisions, on the eastern front to try to hold back the Soviet advance of 225 infantry divisions and 22 armored corps on Berlin, while only 37 Anglo-American divisions advanced steadily from the west.[56]

Roosevelt, fearing a separate German-Soviet peace and needing the Soviets to help clear Japan from Asia, made concessions to the Soviet concern for an East European buffer zone as a defense against possibly revived German militarism in the future. As the Soviets had already endured 20 million deaths and the complete destruction of a land area comparable in the United States to an expanse from New York to Chicago, the Soviet concern carried a strong logic. Since eastern Europe was also the conduit for supplies for the Soviet troops advancing on eastern Germany, and the political contours of the area reflected the imposing reality of Soviet armed presence, both Roosevelt and Churchill felt their position weak and reluctantly acquiesced at Yalta.

The War Department and corporate leaders like the Du Ponts were dismayed over these developments, and probably with small justification. For Roosevelt had avoided any commitment to withdraw U.S. troops in eastern Germany or to offer reconstruction aid to the Soviets, seeing both moves as possible diplomatic levers against the Russians in the future. Germany's surrender, coupled with the successful Los Alamos testing of the atom bomb, removed the key obstacles to corporate desires to hold onto East European and Asian markets. And Roosevelt's untimely death removed what personal hesitations may have previously plagued the White House in considering a break with the Russian allies.

In July, President Harry Truman, guided by State Department policy-makers like Dean Acheson and W. A. Harriman, met Stalin and other Soviet leaders at Potsdam and demanded a reversal of the Yalta agreements in Poland, threatening to exclude the Soviet Union from any reconstruction aid such as later developed under the Marshall Plan. American market concern for Asia, particularly China and Indochina, made them even more adamant the following month. Ignoring Japanese peace approaches, as well as requests by Fermi that the potency of the atom bomb be first demonstrated openly to give Japan a chance knowledgeably to surrender, Truman ordered the dropping of the atom bomb. "Our dropping of the atomic bomb on Japan," the President later observed, "had forced Russia to reconsider her position in the Far East."[57]

Indeed it had. The Soviet Union—fearing the return of colonialist and conservative regimes hostile to its social system, as had already been allowed by the U.S. in Italy (and later in Indochina, India, and Western Germany), and already concerned about American corporate expansion in the Middle East—entered the war against Japan, attacking occupied Manchuria and joining the Korean guerrilla forces led by Kim Il Sung in their assault on Japanese occupation forces. While the Soviets carefully avoided any conflict with the atomic-armed United States, their presence in Eastern Europe and Asia encouraged the forming of communist governments which were understood per se by Washington as detrimental to the Open Door policy of corporate expansion abroad. "Democracy" had little meaning beyond propaganda for the State Department, as anti-communist dictatorships were embraced in Asia, the Middle East, and Europe. Talk of a crusading war for "free enterprise" democracy was widespread in the highest government circles. By then Truman had summed up America's posture toward her former Soviet ally in one startling statement: "They could go to hell."[58]

One "hot" world war for America's economic frontiers had come to an end, only to have another "cold" world war begin. And out of it all, the Du Ponts would build an even larger empire. For these were the historical forces that propelled Wilmington to extend its own frontiers abroad, until the "Du Pont" brand name was stamped on every continent on earth.

Twelve

COLD WARRIORS FROM WILMINGTON

1. THE ICEMAN COMETH

In 1953 Irénée du Pont was asked by reporters if he thought the New Deal would ever come back. "I hope I'll be thoroughly tucked away in the family cemetery before then,"[1] the old industrialist replied.

Irénée needn't have worried. His own remarks served as fitting confirmation that the anti-Du Pont days of the New Deal were as much buried in the past as their august creator. In many ways it was a symbolic twist of history that only one year after Franklin Roosevelt's death, the War Department gave the late President's private yacht, the *Potomac,* to Maryland's fisheries fleet in exchange for another reconverted yacht, *The Du Pont.*

Wilmington's relations with Washington certainly underwent a dramatic change for the better in the postwar era. The Cold War administrations of both Truman and Eisenhower were filled with former Du Pont lieutenants and allies. Tom Clark, a former Texas lobbyist for the Du Pont-owned Ethyl Gas Corporation, charged in the 1930's with unethical practices by a Texas Senate Investigating Committee, became Truman's Attorney General in May 1945. Dean Acheson, lawyer for the Du Ponts, became Secretary of State. Lewis M. Douglas, a G.M. director, was chosen for the important post of ambassador to Great Britain. Louis Johnson, one of the key American Legion figures allegedly involved with Du Ponts in the abortive 1934 coup, was made the second Secretary of Defense in 1949, after the suicide of James Forrestal. Four years later G.M. president Charles Wilson, who had earlier won the hearts of Wilmington with his purchase of G.M. tires from Du Pont-controlled U.S. Rubber, became Eisenhower's Secretary of Defense. Eisenhower's CIA director was Allen Dulles, a Du Pont confidante as far back as the 1920's and president of United Fruit, in which the Du Ponts held a substantial block of stock.[2]

These appointments reflected the two main concerns of major corporate interests at that time: labor pacification and international expansion. The achievement of both was essential to corporate leaders if the rebellious nightmare of the Depression was not to be repeated. And the answer for both has become known as the Cold War.

On the domestic front the Du Ponts, like most corporate leaders, were beset by labor almost immediately after the war. Workers across the country, restrained during the war by a federal wage freeze and Roosevelt's clarion calls for patriotism, now hit the bricks, demanding relief from inflation and speedups. Like many corporations, G.M. felt 1946 was not the year for the decisive battle against a militant labor movement, and after forcing a bitter strike, granted a raise of 18½ cents per hour. But even as that was done, the Du Ponts were joining other members of the National Association of Manufacturers in preparing the greatest repression known to American labor.

The Du Ponts and other NAM members had never given up their opposition to the Wagner Act and other New Deal laws. In 1944 the Du Ponts had futilely donated over $109,000 to the Republican attempt to defeat Roosevelt.[3] After this failure, the Du Ponts saw the need of organizations outside of NAM to widen its base of support.

The two main nongovernment organizations used by the Du Ponts for this campaign were American Action, Inc. and the National Economic Council. Both were designed to build bipartisan support for NAM's anti-labor crusade and lead a purge of New Dealers who had survived Roosevelt in Congress.

Of the two groups, American Action was the most obvious successor to the Liberty League mantle. In 1946 Lammot du Pont and John Raskob joined high-ranking officials from the American Legion and Veterans of Foreign Wars, and corporate leaders like Ernest Weir (steel) and Joseph Pew (Sun Oil) in backing American Action, Inc. "to fight communism, defeat communist-backed candidates for Congress, and rally to this job anti-communist voters all over the country."[4] Lammot and John Raskob both made large donations to support the seed of reaction.[5]

The Chicago *Sun*'s headlines amply explained the purpose of the new organization. "BIG FINANCIERS AID MOVEMENT—MILLION RAISED FOR PURGE OF 187 CONGRESSMEN." A week later, on October 28, the most notorious anti-Semite of the Thirties, Gerald L. K. Smith, requested "all people associated with the America First Crusade" to cooperate with American Action. Significantly, one Wisconsin Republican candidate who enjoyed particular support from American Action was none other than Joseph R. McCarthy, the decade's grand inquisitor. In South Dakota another reactionary, Senator Harlan J. Bushfield, received $4,000 from Lammot du Pont. The Great Witch-Hunt had begun, accompanied by a chorus of headlines echoing the State Department's growing bellicosity toward the Soviet Union and "Godless communism." Truman's Secretary of Navy, Francis P. Matthews, chairman of the Securities Acceptance Corp., joined other members of the Chamber of Commerce's Committee on Socialism and Communism in producing a series of hysterical anti-communist pamphlets and films.

It was through a celebration by industrialists of their Congressional victories in November 1946 that the population was introduced to the second organization used by the Du Ponts, the National Economic Council. The NEC gathered for a dinner at the Waldorf-Astoria to pay homage to Upton Close, a red-baiting radio commentator who had three times been driven off the air by popular protests. And there, sitting proudly at the head table, were Lammot du Pont and John J. Raskob.

While American Action scored victories in the heat of campaigns, the NEC was designed to succeed in more covert, whispered struggles in the halls and lobbies of Congress. Many of the NEC's proposals failed precisely because they were so outrageously bold: the removal of the Supreme Court on the grounds of its alleged socialism, or a constitutional amendment that would limit the government's power to levy taxes and place a ceiling on income taxes. But other suggestions, such as aid to Franco's fascist regime in Spain and the surrender of oil-rich federal tidelands to the more manipulatable state legislatures, eventually became law. The NEC's greatest victory, however, was the Taft-Hartley Act.

Written, according to charges by eighteen representatives and five senators,[6] by NAM leaders William Ingles, a G.E. lobbyist, Theodore Isserman, legal counsel for Chrysler, and corporate lawyers Mark Jones and Jerry Morgan, and introduced by Republican Senator Robert Taft and Representative Hartley, the Taft-Hartley Act effectively repealed the Wagner Act, the Norris-LaGuardia Anti-Injunction Law, and the Fair Labor Standards Act. Supported by the Du Ponts and their NEC and NAM allies, the act outlawed the closed shop, industry-wide bargaining, jurisdictional strikes, and strikes by government employees. The court injunction was restored as a strikebreaking weapon against unions, and union rights for federal mediation were withdrawn from any union whose officers failed to sign non-communist pledges. At the law's passage in June 1947, *Business Week,* the voice of the U.S. Chamber of Commerce, accurately described it as "A New Deal for America's Employers." The campaign to break the independent will of organized labor now had legal sanction. Soon, thousands of the most militant rank-and-file leaders of unions, most of them not communists, were purged or smeared as "Russian Reds," and the way paved for anti-socialist bureaucrats to strangle rank-and-file democracy and seize control of most of the country's unions. Within a few years, the weakened CIO, through a merger, was brought under the control of the conservative AFL leadership from which it had broken earlier in the Thirties.

Although polls recorded no popular demand for the act's passage or retention, the Taft-Hartley Act has remained the guide of federal labor policy to this day. In content, the Taft-Hartley Act was not an aberration of federal policy, however, but merely the culmination of what had been corporate-government design all along, ever since the New Deal's NRA—institutionalized control of labor.

On August 7, 1947, Truman chose Cyrus Ching of DuPont-controlled U.S. Rubber as Director of Federal Mediation and Conciliation Service. In this post, Ching administered the new law as chief arbitrator in major labor-management disputes. Meanwhile, Attorney General Tom Clark carried out Truman's order that all government employees be forced to take a loyalty oath. Clark set up the Loyalty Board, which became a smoke screen for the smashing of left-wing trade unions, and drew up the infamous "subversive organizations" list that became the bible of every Cold War inquisitor.

With these victories under its belt, the NEC continued its hate campaign across the country. "We have already covered the states of Michigan, Ohio, and Indiana, and most of Illinois," reported NEC President Merwin Hart to Lammot du Pont, "so far as libraries and colleges are concerned, as well as certain other sections."[7] Again, after the 80th Congress adjourned, Hart wrote Irénée: "We have definite evidence in a number of instances that our work with respect to measures before Congress had been decisive in the disposition of these measures. All we need, in order to be a conclusive influence on a substantial number of measures, is the funds to get additional personnel and to meet other necessary costs."[8] Irénée obliged, sending Hart a check for $21,000, bringing Irénée's total contributions to the NEC to $31,513.[9] Lammot and Raskob also made large tax-deductible gifts. Through these and other corporate donations, the NEC continued its campaigns against federal aid to education, displaced persons legislation, public housing, immigration, federal civil rights bills, rent and price controls, increased social security, the United Nations, and even U.S. ratification of the Geneva Convention.

Not only were laws influenced, but also talented personnel were recruited by the Du Ponts from these witch-hunts. One prime example was Irving Shapiro, now Du Pont chairman. His story is one of success through persecution and disgrace.

Emboldened by the government's attack on labor and communists, many right-wingers openly assaulted "Reds" and "pinko" liberals after the war.

Even former Vice-President Henry Wallace's 1948 presidential campaign was marked by physical beatings, pelting with eggs and debris, and attacks by fascist bands while police often looked the other way. President Truman himself once remarked at a press conference, "Why doesn't Wallace go back to Russia?" This was the atmosphere in which a series of events led to the rise of Irving Shapiro into the highest Du Pont circles.

When Irving S. Shapiro joined Du Pont in 1951 he was in his middle thirties. To anyone familiar with the backgrounds and personalities of the organization's top executives, there could hardly have been a more unlikely candidate for the chairmanship of the company. Yet he reached that post after only a little more than twenty years of service.

For example, Shapiro is a Jew, a lawyer, a Democrat, and not even remotely related to any Du Pont or any relative of a Du Pont. Yet, here he is top man of the company. As a boy of eight, Shapiro began working in the Minneapolis dry-cleaning shop of his father, a Lithuanian immigrant to the United States. One of Shapiro's brothers still runs that plant, but another deserted to set up his own carpet company. Irving's career took him even further afield. After getting his LL.B. with honors from the University of Minnesota Law School in 1941, Shapiro headed for the nation's capital and the O.P.A., where he worked alongside another young lawyer, who was to become even more prominent, much sooner, Richard Milhous Nixon.

In 1943, Shapiro, who was kept out of service by an asthmatic condition, joined the Justice Department. He soon impressed his superiors in the criminal division and in 1948 was named an assistant prosecutor in one of the most controversial trials of the time, that of eleven top leaders of the United States Communist Party on the charge of advocating the overthrow of the government. The trial, a raucous one that went on for nine long months, was presided over by Judge Harold S. Medina, a former corporate lawyer who had also been a professor at Columbia Law School. The communist leadership were convicted. They appealed. Shapiro handled the appeal for the government and he won. The law under which the communists were convicted was the Registration Act, a repressive law which Harvard Law School's Professor Zachariah Chafee described as "the most drastic restriction on the freedom of speech ever enacted by the United States during peace. . . ."[10] "The Communist Party is on trial only so far as free speech itself is on trial," declared a statement issued by Utah's Chief Justice, James Wolfe, Charles Houston of Harvard Law School, and Arthur Garfield Hays of the ACLU. "Such a decision would, in fact, outlaw the Communist Party and other left-wing groups in the United States in a manner hardly to be distinguished from the outlawing of the

Communist Party by Hitler, Mussolini, or Franco."[11] It was a futile cry. Only many years later, when the witch-hunting extended even to the hallowed liberal U.S. Senators, would the inquisitions be exposed for their lies and demagoguery and brought to an end.

Irving Shapiro never relented on these sorry days. In fact, they made his career. In 1951 his reputation won him the post of legal counsel to the Du Ponts in fighting their anti-trust suits, and he did so well that he steadily reaped the rewards of Du Pont Company management. In 1965 he was appointed assistant general counsel for Du Pont. In 1970 Shapiro became vice-president in charge of finance. Three years later he was appointed chairman and now sits contentedly at the Du Pont board of directors, guiding its acquisitions and price deals, charting its labor strategies, and steering the firm clear of the rocks of anti-trust prosecutions.

The anti-communist crusade was not left only to hirelings. Irénée and Henry B. du Pont were both among the country's most outspoken headhunters. To these multimillionaires, American capitalism was Utopia and dissidents were heretics bewitched by a foreign ideology. "A century ago," stated the company's public relations department in its 1950 *Autobiography,* "Karl Marx dreamed and wrote of a Utopia where the people would own the tools of production and share in their output. His dream has come true, not in the Communist state founded on the theories he propounded so ardently, but in capitalist America."[12]

By that date, however, Du Pont's utopian "capitalist America" was again suffering from its chronic disease, overproduction. Despite their public ridicule of Marx's theories on overproduction, privately in the board room of the Wilmington headquarters the Du Ponts had always paid the greatest attention to the market problems of overproduction. Ideologically they preferred to describe this chronic ailment as a "lack of aggregate demand," the Keynesian's semantic substitution for "underconsumption," the classical economic term used by Marx. But no matter how it was expressed, it essentially came out the same thing—the need for expanding markets.

During the Fifties Du Pont's 2,500-man advertising department tackled the need for an expanded consumer market with mass media promotion and its "impulse-buying" surveys. The latter were used to inform corporate customers of the consumer's psychology and encourage the use of Du Pont products as a means toward manipulating it. "Cellophane packages have a special appeal for children shopping with their families," a Du Pont pamphlet explained to retailers. "The sight of candy stimulates appetite appeal, influences more 'Store Decisions' and builds profitable candy volume. . . . Cellophane bags emphasizing special holidays and printed cellophane holiday overwraps increase sales." This conclusion in 1954 was the result of Du Pont's fifth impulse-buying survey, which tested the attitudes of 5,338 shoppers in 250 supermarkets in 35 cities throughout the United States. "Does she [the shopper] plan to buy candy in advance or decide in the store? Here are the facts from the survey. . . . Nine of ten decisions to buy candies are made in the store." Cellophane increased the sales of potato chips, pretzels, macaroni, and baked goods such as bread, rolls, and pies, explained Du Pont. Showing a picture of a little girl pointing at cookies, the company summed it all up: "She sees them. They look good. *Then* she decides to buy."[13]

Although a crucial role was played by this new advertising field, the consumer market remained inadequate. To keep up its traditional 10 percent rate of return on invested capital, the family inevitably returned to the two keystones on which the Du Pont Company had originally been built—the cheap labor market and government patronage.

At first Du Pont's postwar move toward areas of cheap labor was primarily domestic, in the southern United States. This move had already been initiated as far back as the Twenties, when Du Pont opened its first rayon and cellophane plants in Tennessee, Virginia, and West Virginia. Following the textile drift below the Mason-Dixon, in the late Thirties Lammot du Pont constructed the first nylon plants in Belle, West Virginia, and in Seaford, located in southern Delaware. But it was only after Crawford Greenewalt replaced the interim-presidency of Walter Carpenter in 1948, that Du Pont really began its full-scale Dixie invasion.

"We have linked our destiny to the South . . . ," explained D. F. O'Conner of Du Pont's Explosives Department in 1951. "Of greatest significance is the expansion program which has taken place since the end of World War II."[14] Eight new plants had been built in the South by then, making a total of twenty Du Pont plants in nine southern states, nearly half of the company's total investments and inventories. Thirty thousand workers produced neoprene rubber in Louisville, Kentucky, plastics in Parkersburg, West Virginia, agricultural chemicals in La Porte, Texas, sulphuric acid in Richmond, Virginia, Orlon in Camden, South Carolina, nylon "salts" in Orange, Texas, nylon intermediate chemicals in Victoria, Texas, and nylon in Chattanooga, Tennessee. Maryland, Missouri, and Alabama were also dotted with Du Pont plants. Within three years after Greenewalt took over the presidency, the Chattanooga nylon plant tripled its capacity, while Du Pont financial agents were busily selling stock to local wealth in Virginia, Texas, and Florida, securing the support of the South's richest states.

It is worthwhile to note the South's political atmosphere at the time of Du Pont's Dixie expansion. In what was to prove a successful attempt to check rising labor militancy and strangle the CIO's postwar union-organizing drive, southern wealth had generated some of the most rabid anti-communism and racist hysteria in the region's history. In this campaign, the rulers of the South found enthusiastic allies in northern corporations. The Southern States Industrial Council was one offspring of this corporate mating. Founded during the Thirties to fight the NRA, unions, and "government regulation," the Southern States Industrial Council was one of the most influential forces in the postwar South. Through the dedicated efforts of its vice-president, Thurman Sensing, the SSIC built a highly effective propaganda apparatus to influence over 1,000 weekly newspapers across the South. But the SSIC owed its effectiveness largely to the generosity of its largest contributor, Du Pont, which donated four times as much money as its nearest contender for first place, the Chesapeake and Ohio Railroad Company. Other major contributors were General Motors, Firestone, General Electric, and Household Finance Company.

The red-baiting defeat of Florida's New Deal senator, Claude Pepper, probably the most eloquent voice for liberalism in the South, was financed and organized by Alfred I. du Pont family interests. This defeat was a symbol that the entire region was being dragged back into the dark ages of bigotry and reactionary narrow-mindedness that many southern New Dealers had hoped would never again return. But return it did, and in its grim wake came northern industry, led by Du Pont.

During this expansion Du Pont was understandably touchy on the question of cheap labor. "This is another ghost that should be laid to rest so far as the chemical industry is concerned," said O'Conner. "The ratio of skilled operators to unskilled in this industry is very high and the wages paid to chemical operators are among the highest of any industry, North or South."[15] Yet, despite that ratio, Du Pont did not come to the South for its higher-paid skilled labor. In fact only 17 percent of the Ph.D.'s, M.A.'s, and B.A.'s hired by Du Pont came from the South. Du Pont's real interest in the South lay in its *un*skilled labor, who were paid as much as 20 percent lower than their northern counterparts. With this boon, and the availability of petroleum, water power, coal, and other raw and crude material sources, Dixie represented the most valuable capital market for Du Pont in the Fifties.

By the 1960's Du Pont had constructed even more plants in the South: at Kingston, North Carolina, to produce the new wool-like Dacron, and at Memphis, Tennessee, to produce sodium cyanide and hydrogen peroxide. As one South Carolina businessman remarked, "The question is whether Du Pont is out to buy up the South."[16] For Wilmington, there was no question about it.

In the marbled corridors of Washington, Du Pont found the second means to wider markets. Behind its Cold War policies, the federal government was engaged in supporting a massive investment program overseas by American corporations. In Africa, the Middle East, and Asia, American business interests increasingly replaced the war-exhausted European colonialist, while in devastated Europe, the Marshall Plan encouraged U.S. corporate control over the industries and markets of electronics, automobiles, synthetic rubber, petroleum, and farm machinery. "Economic stability" continued as the hallmark of U.S. foreign policy—as Assistant Secretary of State Dean Acheson put it, "chiefly as a matter of national self-interest"— and where the dollar went soon followed the flag. To pursue George Kennan's "containment policy" of anti-revolution through anti-communism, a large military arsenal of armaments and overseas bases was built and the "red scare" propagated, while a U.S. Navy document secretly pointed out the real issue: "Realistically, all wars have been for economic reasons. To make them politically palatable, ideological issues have always been involved. Any possible future war will undoubtedly conform to historical precedent."[17]

The first conflict grew out of U.S. intervention in Japan's former colony, Korea. After occupying southern Korea in 1945, U.S. troops under the command of General Hodges forcibly dissolved the Korean Provisional Congress in Seoul, and Syngman Rhee was flown in from Washington to establish a regime of pro-western military leaders and landlords. With U.S. encouragement, Rhee declared the 38th parallel to be a permanent border dividing Korea, and began liquidating all opposition, particularly trade unions and intellectuals. Over a quarter-million people were massacred. In the midst of a contrived "election" (which was boycotted by most political parties and organizations in the south), riots broke out against the new Rhee dictatorship. As full-scale civil war erupted, the legitimacy of Rhee's regime was further undermined by new elections held throughout the south and north which established the Democratic People's Republic of Korea. The alternate government based its capital north of the 38th parallel, where Korean forces who had fought the Japanese guaranteed safety under the communist leadership of Kim Il Sung.

One of the D.P.R.'s first acts was to request the withdrawal of all Allied occupying forces. In December, 1948, the Soviet commander obliged. The U.S. command in Seoul refused, and as Rhee's position deteriorated in the south with his defeat in the May 1950 elections, skirmishes along the 38th parallel increased. On June 17, John Foster Dulles arrived at the 38th parallel and assured Rhee's troops that the time was "not far off" when they would be able to display their "prowess." On June 25 war broke out between Rhee's forces and D.P.R. troops stationed along the parallel. In a burst of enthusiasm, Rhee promised his regime in Seoul that Pyongyang, the D.P.R. capital, would be occupied by his forces within three days. Three days later D.P.R. troops were in Seoul. Rhee was in Tokyo with his American wife, having fled with the country's gold reserves.

Washington was enraged. Backed by a resolution it rammed through the United Nations to restore the U.S.-imposed status quo only in the south, the United States landed troops at Inchon and also invaded the north. Levelling the countryside with jet bombers, General Douglas MacArthur marched U.S. troops right up to the Chinese border, threatening attack on the new communist government of Mao Tse-tung, even suggesting the use of the atomic bomb. At this point, China intervened, pushing MacArthur's armies back into southern Korea.

Wilmington was enraged also. Irénée du Pont called for increased aid to the dictatorship of Chiang Kai-shek "to help run the Reds out of China, instead of just sending more American boys to Korea."[18] Apparently, Irénée had forgotten that it was Chiang who had already been run out of China. Truman's memory was a little better, and although the U.S. did intervene in the Chinese civil war by protecting Chiang on Taiwan with the Seventh Fleet, he avoided Irénée's suggestion of an attack on China.

Besides the more important aspect of defending the new Asian economic frontier and traditional "Open Door" foreign policy, the Korean War also proved good business for the new Military-Industrial Complex that had emerged out of World War II. Du Pont, of course, was one among many giants who took the bulk of government war orders. Years later Henry B. du Pont would admit in a public statement that the lion's share of military orders and profits during the Korean War and the armaments race went to the biggest corporations.[19] In 1950 Du Pont scored one of its highest annual profits, 13.3 percent.[20] G.M. reaped an even higher return. During the war years of 1950–1952 G.M. averaged an annual profit rate, before taxes, six times that of the 1929 boom year. From July 1950 to June 1952 G.M. grossed $5.5 billion in war contracts.

The Korean War may have ended, but the armaments race did not. Eisenhower continued the traditional Open Door policy of foreign markets being the key to continual corporate profit expansion and domestic prosperity. "For all our material might," declared the new President in his Inaugural Address, "even we need the markets in the world for the surpluses of our farms and factories. Equally we need for these same farms and factories vital materials and products of distant lands."

Helping arm for Pax America as Ike's new Secretary of Defense, was G.M. president Charles E. Wilson. "What is good for America is good for General Motors," he once exclaimed at his confirmation hearings, "and vice versa." It is an amusing footnote to Wilson's successful government career that it began so embarrassingly. On his way to Ike's Inaugural Ball his shiny new G.M. Cadillac broke down. Again, when the first cabinet meeting was held later that week, the first empty chair was Wilson's, his absence reported as the result of a similar breakdown. Apparently, in these cases, what was financially good for General Motors was not even good for Charles Wilson, much less America.

Under Wilson's reign the Defense Department was good also for Du Pont. Although only 5.3 percent of the chemical industry's output went to the military, by 1960 over 20 percent of its total expenditures for research and development was financed directly by the Defense Department, with Du Pont receiving a generous portion.[21] Additionally, defense contracts to Du Pont customers for nonexplosive material, from paint to nylon, spurred Washington's sales.

Du Pont itself did not heavily diversify into the defense sector, but the family found the arms race profitable in other spheres of holdings. As a director, Irénée du Pont's son-in-law, Colgate Darden, watched over the family's holding in Newport News Shipbuilding and Dry Dock Company, one of the country's largest shipbuilders, which grossed over 80 percent of its income from war contracts. North American Aviation (with Henry B. du Pont as the controlling stockholder) and Boeing Aircraft (of which Crawford Greenewalt became a director) were both big money makers. By 1957, North American and Boeing were reaping profits of 19.9 percent and 21.3 percent, respectively.[22] On the basis of return on investment, only five of the top fifty companies in sales in 1957 were among the top fifty in profits. These five firms happened to be exactly the five with the largest amounts of new defense contracts that year. And among the five were North American Aviation and Boeing.

Henry's company, a leader in missile frames and rocket engine technology, was undoubtedly the most active Du Pont interest in war contracts during the Fifties, and probably the boldest. On May 7, 1959, for example, North American ran a large ad in the *Wall Street Journal* offering high-level employment to a top-ranking officer of the Air Force or Navy, preferably with experience with the Joint Chiefs of Staff. This job, explained the ad, required giving information about the Department of Defense's "product development strategy" and "weapons system requirements," as well as personally assisting in military sales. It was too blatant to be left ignored. "You are trying," said Representative Edward Hebert of the Armed Services Committee to a North American witness, "to buy not only an individual's ability, but also knowledge he acquired in a high echelon position where secret planning was done."[23] Henry's executives merely shrugged and continued their policies. After all, went the reasoning, they were only doing what was common business practice. By 1969, 2,072 officers with the rank of Colonel or Navy Captain or above were employed by the ninety-five leading military contractors,[24] North American proudly being one.

Phillips Petroleum was another Du Pont interest in the arms race of the Forties, Fifties, and Sixties. Since Phillips' founding in 1917, Eugene E. du Pont was guardian of the family's stock holding in this sphere,[25] and personally served on the board of directors until 1954. During his postwar tenure, Phillips was extremely aggressive, increasing its assets from $332 million to $1.3 billion and its net income from $23 million to $95 million. Phillips was attracted particularly to new oil resources. In southeastern Alaska, for example, it secured an operating agreement on nearly one million acres of land. For $39 million, it acquired over 200,000 acres of offshore holdings.

Phillips often joined with other Du Pont family interests in big deals. With Henry's North American Aviation, it formed Astrodyne, Inc., to develop solid fuels for missiles and space rockets. After the Rubber Act of 1948 ended government ownership of a number of synthetic rubber plants, Phillips joined Du Pont-owned U.S. Rubber (in which Henry B. was also a major personal stockholder) and other oil and rubber giants in buying up the government's general-purpose synthetic rubber and butyl industrial capacity. Eisenhower sold twenty-six plants for $285 million, which was above their net value, yet these plants yielded $166 million in profits from 1951 to 1955 alone. At the time of the sales, five dissenters on the Senate Banking and Currency Committee correctly but futilely argued that the government could have reaped more in operational profits in four to five years than the total amount of the sales.

Phillips had other legislative boons during the Fifties. As the largest seller of natural gas to interstate pipelines, it was the sole supplier to the Michigan-Wisconsin Pipe Line Company. Since the war, helpless consumers found their gas rates climbing higher and higher. State officials and the pipeline company stood helpless as Phillips claimed its need for a 12 percent profit. When the Federal Power Commission refused to regulate the rates in 1951, the Wisconsin Public Service Commission went to court, while a Phillips official warned that if the case persisted "the people of Wisconsin could freeze . . . they would never get another cubic foot of natural gas."

The Wisconsin PSC won its case before the Supreme Court, which ordered the FPC to review and regulate Phillips's rates. But the FPC's Eisenhower appointees, while publicizing their opposition to Phillips, moved slowly in implementing the court's decision. Then, in 1955, the

Harris-Fulbright bill freed gas producers from public regulation. A 5- to 10-cent increase per 1,000 cubic feet quickly ensued, producing a gain for the industry of up to $3 billion a year. As the second largest holder of gas reserves in the United States, Phillips got the lion's share.

These and other defense contracts to Remington Arms and U.S. Rubber comprised the bulk of the Du Pont family's profits from the Cold War during the Fifties.

For Du Pont Company itself, the most direct sustained contact with the arms race was its work in developing the most terrifying weapon on earth—the hydrogen bomb.

In August 1950 a very lean, relaxed Crawford Greenewalt appeared before the Congressional Joint Committee on Atomic Energy. By the end of the day he walked out with an Atomic Energy Commission contract to develop the hydrogen bomb and operate its plant production. Although Crawford boasted to the press of Du Pont's agreeing to a $1 a year fee, he did not bother to mention that two other companies, G.E. and Sandria Corporation, had done likewise. Nor did he mention that Du Pont was to be one of four big contractors who would together receive an AEC "compensation" of over $2.5 billion yearly.

For the Du Ponts, it was a symbolic contribution to their celebration of the 150th anniversary of their landing on the lucrative American shore.

2. YEARS OF TRIUMPH

Old Man Winter brought his usual holiday tidings to Delaware in January 1950, with freezing winds racing south along the Brandywine, chilling everything in their path. But a few miles to the north, just across the Pennsylvania border, a tropical fantasy unrolled before the eyes of scores of Du Pont children eating bananas fresh from flourishing banana plants and darting between bougainvillea-covered marble columns. Behind the steamed glass walls of Longwood's conservatory, over 400 well-dressed relatives strolled along 3½ lush acres of alleys lined with poinsettias, roses, and orchids, listening to the melodies a hidden organist played on Pierre du Pont's $250,000 organ, or inspecting a collection of family relics (wedding dresses, E. I. du Pont's original European furniture, letters from Lafayette and Jefferson) gathered in honor of this 150th anniversary of the landing of the Du Ponts in America.

From every part of the United States, and four European countries, 632 Du Ponts gathered on this New Year's Day for the first family reunion in half a century. Over half of them did not have far to travel, however, living nearby on the two dozen Du Pont estates that filled the hills surrounding Wilmington. Of those present, 75 percent were blood descendants of the

French nobleman, Pierre Du Pont de Nemours, the rest were kin by marriage. Many didn't even know their relatives. Each was given a name card on arrival, the color of which designated to which of six branches of the family he or she belonged. But the centrifugal force was the name of E. I. du Pont; the image of his original residence, Eleutherian Mills, was stamped on every ashtray at the dozens of round tables.

Half of the seventy-four members at the 1900 reunion were there, and their palates may have sensed that little had changed in Du Pont taste since then. Pierre hired the same caterer, Holland's of Philadelphia, to serve a similar menu: seafood cocktail, green salad, claret wine, filet mignon with mushrooms, potato balls, string beans, game pie (a heavily spiced dish made from a variety of wild animals), terrapin stew, coffee, champagne, pudding, and the old family favorite, johnnycake, to commemorate the first Du Pont meal in America on January 1, 1800—the meal that had been stolen by their newly arrived ancestors from the house of a colonial family gone to church (accounts differed as to whether old Père Du Pont left behind a few gold pieces in compensation). But this time Pierre made sure the family paid its own way: he assessed each member 50 cents for each year of age. At 80, Pierre paid the highest tab.

Amid popping flashbulbs of photographers from such national magazines as *Life,* the Du Ponts royally ate their historic midday meal. There was no head table. There were no speeches. This day the whole family basked in glory. Some, of course, had more glory than others: Crawford Greenewalt, for example, who collected a salary of over $138,000 the previous year and another $300,000 in cash and stock bonuses, for a total $438,000 "compensation" for the same year the average annual wage of a Du Pont worker was $3,430. Or Henry B. du Pont, his broad face flushed with the triumph of $300,000 in salaries and bonuses from Du Pont alone, never mind his other holdings in U.S. Rubber and North American Aviation. Nearby sat Emile F. du Pont, his always busy mind ticking away behind his bushy brows, counting the $65,000 in Du Pont salary and bonuses he would reap that year and the millions returning their yield from stock speculations. But the most contented of all was old Pierre. Flanked by his aging brothers Lammot and Irénée, Pierre saw this day's gathering through the eyes of a financial conqueror. General Motors, Du Pont, U.S. Rubber, Remington Arms, all part of a vast corporate empire, were now safely in his family's hands. If anyone had the right to swell in triumph, it was he.

Ironically, Pierre's greatest day came on the eve of his greatest defeat, a defeat which would kick a crucial keystone—General Motors—out of the Du Pont empire.

The family's troubles in G.M. began in 1948, the year of Du Pont's biggest sales record yet, $968 million. In November Lammot was called before a federal hearing to testify on Du Pont interests in General Motors, U.S. Rubber, Ethyl Gasoline, Bendix Aviation, and a host of other firms. Although accompanied by so esteemed a counsel as Dean Acheson, former Undersecretary of State, Lammot still had his difficulties. "I made a bad showing at the end of the session," he admitted to reporters as he emerged from the hearing. "I testified that I had not written a certain letter and then the government pulled the letter out of the files. It was very embarrassing." Yet the impending blow remained unforeseen. "We still don't know what it's all about,"[26] Lammot said.

Six months later, he found out. Attorney General Tom Clark, moving on the government's desire to preserve some balance among corporate interests and prevent the total domination of G.M. by the Du Pont family, filed an anti-trust suit in Chicago's District Court to break up "the largest single concentration of power in the United States."[27] Over 100 defendants were named, including the family holding companies, Christiana Securities and Delaware Realty and Investment Corporation. But the real target was Du Pont Company's $560 million investment in General Motors. In a 65-page complaint, the government charged that Du Pont controlled the selection of G.M. officers, directors, and policies. The G.M. bonus plan operated to make executives more responsive to Du Pont's wishes, since Du Ponts dominated the committee that gave out the bonus incentives. Citing these as violations of the Sherman and Clayton anti-trust laws, the complaint asked for the cancellation of all G.M.-Du Pont contracts, and the sale of all Du Pont holdings in U.S. Rubber, G.M., and Kinetic Chemicals (refrigerants).

This was no *laissez-faire* "free market" approach by the government. Since the Justice Department's "rule of reason" fifty years earlier, the government had abandoned any pretense toward turning back the clock and restoring a private enterprise system free of trusts. The G.M. suit merely represented the opinion that General Motors was now simply too large an economic force to allow its domination by any one family or financial group. Rather, control over the largest corporation in the world would have to be shared jointly by many financial groups.

The reaction in Wilmington was a mixture of shock and suspicion: shock that the suit had come, and that it was pressed by Clark, a former Du Pont lobbyist who was believed friendly to the company's interests; and whispered suspicion that behind this move was the hand of Morgan interests in G.M. and Truman's need for a corporate scapegoat to mitigate his anti-labor image.

"An unjustified attack," responded Greenewalt, promising the stockholders, "your company will fight."[28] His first step was to give the real meaning to his claim of public support by requesting a change of venue to

Wilmington. This was denied, but Henry B. du Pont had already outlined the next step in responding to public attacks on the growing power of big business. "These criticisms have in the main come from the lips of many people in politics, bureaucrats, irresponsible labor elements, and unfortunately, also from many well-meaning but uninformed people, and they have been fanned by the radical section of the press and radio."[29] Accordingly, the Du Ponts expended most of their energies the following year in the political arena, Du Pont's public relations department grinding out the proper image.

The Korean War and the hydrogen bomb contract cooled the administration's crusading fires for a while. Then the Justice Department's scoring of the family's use of its minors as holding companies reopened the battle in 1952. The government filed a class action suit against 186 Du Ponts related by blood or marriage to Pierre, Irénée, and Lammot. "Evidence in the record in this case," stated the government brief, "shows it is the practice and policy of senior members of the class and their defendant representatives to distribute during their lifetimes a substantial portion of their stock holdings to minors in the family, usually by setting up trusts of stock."[30]

It took Irénée 701 pages to explain his denial of the government's charges. But the one most upset by this attack on the very lifeblood of Du Pont inheritance was Lammot, bitterly describing it as "another indication of the lengths to which the government's prosecution of anti-trust cases has led it."[31] Lammot was infuriated, but this was one fight he would have to pass up.

In July 1952, 225 lineal or marital descendants of E. I. du Pont and 6,000 of their employees gathered on the banks of the Brandywine to celebrate the sesquicentennial of his founding of the powder company. Across the country, 80,000 workers in seventy-one Du Pont plants were given a special holiday. A national radio broadcast followed the dramatic reenactment of the founding of the original Eleutherian Mills and tours were given by fourteen Du Pont ladies in specially designed dresses of the period. Speeches were given by Crawford Greenewalt and Henry B. du Pont. But one familiar, grim face was conspicuously absent: that of Lammot du Pont.

Lammot had been stricken with a heart attack the previous week while vacationing at his summer mansion at Fisher's Island, New York. He had long suffered from an arteriosclerotic heart ailment—this was one reason for his resignation from General Motors in 1946—but worries over maintaining control of the Motors firm returned to haunt him in the government's anti-trust prosecution, agitating the convulsion of his 71-year-old heart a week before the anniversary celebration. In the morning of July 24 Lammot suffered a second attack, this one from a massive pulmonary embolism. The doctor arrived at his bedside just a few minutes before his death at 7:00 A.M. Although Lammot had gone through four wives, breeding ten children, not one was at his bedside. In a great sense, he died as he lived—alone.

A few days later Pierre and Irénée watched with the rest of the clan as Lammot was buried at Sand Hole Woods. It was only too obvious that the fifth generation of Du Ponts was dying out. A. Felix, Sr., was already lying there, having died in 1947 at the age of 69. So were his brothers Ernest, who died in 1944, and E. Paul du Pont, who died of a heart attack in 1950. Ethel Hallock du Pont, wife of Pierre's dead brother William K., had died in 1951; Bessie, Alfred's first wife, in 1949; Pierre's sister Isabella, in 1946. Later that year cousin Julia, sister of Eugene, Jr., would die, and Henry B. would lose his mother Eleuthera the following year. Of the three famous brothers, Irénée was over 70, Pierre over 80, and now Lammot was gone. Having already distributed most of his fortune to family trusts and foundations, Lammot left behind only a $70 million estate.

Death spared Lammot from taking the witness stand in the G.M. case, but his ghost haunted the trial. His words ironically spoke across decades in correspondence, proving the government's charge of Du Pont control. "It seems that Du Pont has always assumed the responsibility for the financial direction of G.M.,"[32] Lammot wrote Sloan in 1923 on G.M.'s board and finance committee composition. The full meaning of such responsibility, the government contended, was that in 1941 G.M. took 93 percent of Du Pont's automobile Duco production. The Du Ponts retorted that they acquired G.M.'s business because their products were superior, but the government only countered that better quality products by Du Pont were in the company's interest of protecting its 23 percent investment in G.M.

In 1945 Sloan had written Du Pont president Walter S. Carpenter, Jr., on the prospects of inviting General George Marshall onto the G.M. board, "recognizing the position he holds in the community and among the government people."[33] But it was Lammot who answered three days later: "My reasons for not favoring his membership on the board are first, his age; second, his lack of stockholdings; and third, his lack of experience in industrial business affairs."[34] With those words, the idea was squashed.

Du Pont control over the board's membership was absolute. In 1943 the Du Ponts opposed allowing any more bankers on the G.M. board, and Alfred Sloan followed suit. In 1947, after the Du Ponts expressed favorable reaction to the idea of bankers, Sloan completely reversed his policy.

In February 1953, 76-year-old Irénée took the stand, his lean figure now topped with a crown of white hair. The old industrialist remained his amiable self, at times even apologetic for his failing hearing. At one point, he finally gave up his hearing aid and cupped a hand to each question. "These things are very badly made," he commented; "the Du Pont Company ought to go into the business."[35] The courtroom, crowded with business executives from a nearby convention, rang with laughter.

But it was old, bald and pouchy Pierre who gave the most important testimony. While his younger brother watched proudly from the spectators' bench, the 83-year-old owlish financial giant wiggled his bushy white mustache with answers that showed he was as sharp as ever under questioning. From behind the bright blue eyes a keen memory worked, recording a sweeping grasp of developments since 1890. Du Pont's involvement in World War I was an act of patriotism, Pierre contended, as was his seizure of control of the company from Alfred. Claiming to have been tipped by British Intelligence through Imperial Chemical's Kraftmeier that the Germans were about to buy up a large bloc of Du Pont stock, Pierre admitted he had encouraged Coleman to sell his stock to him. After this testimony, however, the government produced a 1915 letter from Pierre to Coleman stating that "if they [the Germans] come forward with orders in quantity similar to the order of the allied nations, we would be willing to sell." And one government witness, Sir William Wiseman, head of British Intelligence in the United States during World War I, testified that "I can state definitely that Mr. Kraftmeier was never at any time connected with the British Intelligence Service."[36] The "patriotism" motive by itself simply did not stand up.

Despite a volume of evidence against him, Pierre managed to deftly dodge any attempt by the government to make him admit G.M. control. The potential market "had no connection whatever with my opinion of the G.M. purchase or my vote,"[37] he insisted, branding the government's charge of building a $5 billion empire against the law as "false." For days on end, Pierre recorded the whole history of the company's growth, as he saw it. Some said it was his finest hour. Whatever the opinion, it was also his last.

One year later Pierre joined his brother Lammot at Sand Hole Woods. Pierre had just finished one of his dinners at his Longwood estate when he was struck by severe abdominal pain. He had ruptured a blood vessel. Rushed to Wilmington Memorial Hospital, he died within hours, Irénée and Margaretta, the sister who married Ruly Carpenter, at his bedside. Although childless, Pierre, unlike his very prolific brother, died among friends.

In one way, though, Pierre's death was like Lammot's—its financial outcome. Pierre had also divested the bulk of his estate among family trusts long before he died. What was left, $80 million, was willed to his tax-free Longwood Foundation for the upkeep of his vast gardens.

Pierre's passing at 84 in 1954, and Eugene's death at 81 the same year, were expected by the family. But the autumn chill of the following September brought a real shock: 21-year-old David Flett du Pont, Lammot's youngest son, was fatally injured in an auto crash on Fisher's Island while visiting his mother; he died in the same hospital as his father did three years earlier.

These were not all bad times, however, for the family did succeed in the anti-trust case. First, the government retreated from its attack on the family as a whole, dropping charges against all but seven individuals. Then, in December 1954, Judge Walter La Buy ruled that the government had not proved the family had *intended* to create a monopoly when they bought into G.M. It was merely a historical accident. "We were confident that this would be the result,"[38] declared a jubilant President Crawford Greenewalt, standing beside his grinning father-in-law, Irénée du Pont, and his predecessor, Walter Carpenter, Jr. Indeed, a million dollars can buy a lot of legal confidence. That day, Du Pont's stock rose 4½ points.

But the real battle had been won before the case even went to trial. From the very first day the government filed its suit, Du Pont's public relations department took up the brunt of the counterattack. On taking office, Crawford Greenewalt had been advised by Walter Carpenter to make public relations his most important concern. Fully agreeing, Crawford now handed the job of defending the company to his two top public relations officers, Harold Brayman, former president of the National Press Club and the prestigious Gridiron Club, and his assistant, Glen Perry, formerly of the New York *Sun*.

Brayman went right to work, adopting the position that the government's charges were an attack on "bigness" per se, and correctly countering that only bigness could have provided the capital for the original research and plant investment for everything from nylon to atomic energy. Brayman's argument carried infallible logic—greater concentration of capital and resources *was* superior to the disjointed economy of the *laissez-nous faire* nostalgists. But as logical as it was, his case lacked emotional appeal for the public.

For the first three years of deliberations, Brayman and Perry continued their campaign, waiting for the opportunity for an emotional appeal to appear. Brayman reversed Du Pont's traditional fear of press probes and sought instead to use them to the company's advantage. This change in policy stemmed from Brayman's "precinct" publicity concept, a term that reflected his many years spent in observation of political organizations.

Under this concept, publicity was directed to three key audiences: (1) employees, customers, stockholders, suppliers, business associations, and towns where plants were located; (2) writers, the press and media, and campus intellectuals; and (3) government officials. By centering on these, all of whom already had an interest in the company, Brayman estimated that a ripple of "public" opinion started by the company's usual broad releases would become a wave.

He was right. When *Fortune* approached the firm for information for an article on the company, a special office was set up in Du Pont headquarters and its writers and researchers were given exclusive interviews and details from the company's viewpoint. The result was an article favorable to Du Pont. Other magazines were soon attracted to Wilmington. *Newsweek* had already run a cover story, "Is It Bad to Be Big," with Crawford's picture on the cover. In April 1951 *Time* did likewise.

Crawford made a rare appearance before the National Press Club. Vicepresident Harry Haskell, Sr., made another speech in Maine, and Lammot du Pont Copeland, then secretary, also spoke publicly. All these speeches were distributed by Brayman to every newspaper editor in the country. But still the emotional impact was missing.

The solution came in 1952. The government charged that the Du Pont children, through their trust funds, were being used as holding companies by their parents. Seizing the opportunity, Brayman then published a photo of Alletta du Pont Bredin, "a hardened conspirator of eight months," sitting in her playpen. The picture made the government's case look absurd. Hardly a newspaper in the country failed to print it.

A month later, on April 14, Brayman made his report to Du Pont management that "it seems reasonable to say that the picture appeared in more than 1,200 American newspapers. . . ." Of 376 clippings received, "With only two exceptions, all of it was critical of the Department of Justice and favorable to Du Pont." "An impression was created in the minds of millions of people," Brayman later recalled, "which won the case for us with the public—if we could keep it won when the case came to trial."[39]

To help at the Chicago end, Brayman appointed Robert Curtin, Delaware correspondent for the *New York Times,* to get to know personally the correspondents, wire service reporters, and media men covering the trial in the Windy City. To add a human touch to Du Pont's staid image, Pierre and Irénée were encouraged to be present at the early days of the proceedings and grant their rarest of gifts, pictures and interviews. Articles favorable to the Du Pont executives' image were persistent throughout the trial, while many large corporations, cautiously sympathetic to Du Pont's line that the case represented an attack on all big business, lent their support in government and elsewhere.

By the time La Buy delivered his juryless decision, it was obvious that Du Pont had won a political battle as well as an economic one. Brayman's precinct technique used the press agentry of political parties. In that important sense, the favorable ruling was a political triumph precisely because Du Pont's public relations department had become a *political* organization, molding and organizing public beliefs on an essentially political issue—trust-busting.

The La Buy decision only confirmed Crawford's convictions about public relations. Already Du Pont's radio and TV experiment with "Cavalcade of America" had produced excellent results. In 1937 the Psychological Corporation's survey had reported to the Du Ponts that fewer than half of the 10,000 people questioned had a favorable opinion of the company, and 16 percent had a downright hostile view of the munitions makers. Through twenty-two years of award-winning plays written by such quality writers as Arthur Miller and Stephen Vincent Benét, Du Pont changed its image. Its 781 radio episodes and 202 TV network shows stressed the company's "Better Things for Better Living . . . Through Chemistry" line. The merchants of death became a foggy memory, replaced by the smiling chemist. In 1958 the Psychological Corporation found that 79 percent of those tested thought well of Du Pont Company; less than 3 percent were unfavorable. Satisfied, the Du Ponts ended the annual surveys that year.

Euphoria filled the air along the Brandywine mansions these days. Grateful for this Eisenhower era, the Du Ponts gave $248,000, the highest amount contributed to the Republican campaign in 1956, to defeat liberal Democrat Adlai Stevenson. This was a huge increase over their $74,000 investment in Eisenhower in 1952, but it represented the family's feelings that political dividends had been amply returned. Once, when asked by a reporter if he disliked 'Ike,' Irénée gave him a dollar. Why? the astonished reporter queried. "Because you ought to have your head examined,"[40] Irénée answered.

Eisenhower's administration had already protected many companies in which the Du Ponts had interests. In 1954, for example, United Fruit was spared the indignity of having to surrender 400,000 acres of unused land to the Guatemalan government for redistribution to peasants. The Guatemalan government was willing to provide compensation and 3 percent interest. A U.S. arms embargo followed, backed finally by an open invasion from Honduras given air cover by F-47 bombers flown by the CIA. The United Nations protested and the Security Council authorized the sending of an emergency peace-keeping force to guarantee Guatemala's borders, but the temporary president of the Security Council, who happened to be the U.S. ambassador, failed to give the Secretary-General the needed order. The Guatemalan government was overthrown. The head of the CIA, General Walter Bedell Smith, then joined the board of United Fruit, while United Fruit's president, Allen Dulles, became CIA Director.

Less covert was Du Pont's support of the new oil depreciation allowance. Besides Du Pont's own direct involvement with the oil industry through the production of synthetic rubber and its Ethyl Gasoline Corporation, the family had invested personal funds in Phillips Petroleum, Chanslor-Western Oil, Ardee Oil (in Texas and Montana), and Oil Associates (in Louisiana and Texas). By the 1960's, Lammot du Pont Copeland's Delaware Fund would hold huge blocks of stock in Universal Oil, Standard Oil of New Jersey, Royal Dutch Petroleum, Occidental Petroleum, and Gulf Oil; E. I. du Pont's New England Fund would be a large stockholder in Mobil and Texaco; and Emile F. du Pont's Blue Ridge Mutual Securities in Continental Oil, Atlantic Richfield, Cities Service, and Union Oil of California.

But probably the greatest incentive for Du Pont's production of the film "It Never Rains Oil" was its heavy investment in the automobile industry, particularly General Motors. Sponsored by the leading oil associations, Du Pont's film presented the case for the depreciation allowance, a curious logic that argues that a business should be paid by the taxpayer for selling its product on the market. According to the minutes of the National Petroleum Council in 1953, Deputy Petroleum Administrator Joseph La Fortune, on leave as vice-chairman cf Gulf's Warren Oil Corporation, "furnished the information as to the money expended by Du Pont for having the film made in Hollywood, its fine possibility as education mediums for use in colleges, high schools, etc., availability and cost to those interested in showing the film."

At this meeting of the biggest oil companies, La Fortune tried to propose standby pipeline facilities on the East Coast in case of an energy crisis. The president of Sinclair Oil objected: "The surpluses in our industry are an anathema," he explained, "but I think we are particularly sensitive to it, or at least I feel that way about it. Surpluses not handled or controlled are an anathema, because they have a way of destroying price structures, they have a way of breaking down progress, and they can destroy an industry. . . . I am talking particularly here about standby pipeline facilities. It applies with equal force to standby tanker facilities, standby refining facilities, standby storage, and if you please, standby production. . . ."

"I assure you," answered La Fortune, "that our government is not trying to ask you to do something that is unprofitable or would be unsuccessful.

They are trying to bring up something here that they think will be helpful to our country in the event of an emergency.

"If it is unpractical, gentlemen, you can forget about it."

They did.[41]

Such easy victories as these and the domination of the "free" world's business by American finance and industry produced a general feeling of omnipotence among corporate leaders in the Fifties, and the Du Ponts were no exception. Their lawyer in the anti-trust proceedings of the Thirties and Forties, Dean Acheson, became Secretary of State. The new postwar dispenser of government favors, the Department of Defense, was headed by a G.M. president, Charles Wilson. The U.S. Commissioner of Roads from 1953 to 1955 who initiated the huge road-building campaign (and subsequent decline in mass transit planning for the future) was Francis V. du Pont. The lawyer who had successfully argued their case before La Buy, John Harlan, was soon after rewarded with a Supreme Court robe, and thousands of copies of La Buy's decision itself were reprinted by Du Pont and distributed triumphantly to the country's newspapers.

Then in 1955, less than a year later, the Du Ponts made their most dramatic announcement of the decade—they were investing another $75 million in General Motors. In their triumph, they had lit the fuse of destruction.

3. END OF AN ERA

Du Pont's announcement of its new $75 million investment in General Motors set off a chain reaction from Washington to New York. To many in the capital, it was seen as a direct slap in the government's face, an act of tightening economic domination by one family too bold to be ignored.

Wall Street stirred anxiously, including the offices of the Morgan group. G.M.'s management had increased its membership on the board of directors with full Morgan approval after the war and the directorship of Richard King Mellon of Mellon National Bank had also been allowed. This injection of another power group reflected G.M.'s need for more outside capital to finance domestic and overseas plant expansion after World War II, plus, many hoped, a new willingness on the part of the Du Ponts to allow other financial interests in G.M. As the Mellons had often been considered rivals of the Du Ponts, the appearance of R. K. Mellon was taken by many as a sign that the Morgan hand was strengthened, especially as no one from Wilmington had replaced Lammot du Pont when he retired in 1946. This power change was also accompanied by a 10 percent drop in G.M.'s business with Du Pont Company. Now, however, with this new massive injection of capital from Wilmington, the Du Pont yoke about G.M. looked stronger than ever.

But this time the family had gone too far; they had chosen the wrong time for so bold a move. Du Pont's attempt to even further dominate the world's largest corporation stood in the face of a general business trend, encouraged by corporate circles in power in Washington, toward *joint* control in the larger corporations by several financial groups, a trend toward financial diversification in many fields that could prevent the pitfalls of concentrating holdings in one or two areas of an unstable marketplace and act as a breaker against the threat of a general "dominos" contraction in the capital market which could trigger a depression. This trend had been encouraged by Roosevelt and Rockefeller interests and been endorsed by Congress in its 1950 amendment to the Clayton Anti-trust Act, an amendment that allowed vertical expansion but not single-group monopoly.

With the Du Pont family's open rejection of this trend (possibly in fear of eventually losing exclusive control over their own firm in exchange for being allowed entrance into other corporations), the corporate and financial leaders in government now had to demonstrate the necessity of legal enforcement. Thus the Du Pont-G.M. prosecution represented a major trial case.

On June 3, 1957, in one sweeping decision, the Supreme Court's corporate liberals undid all that the Du Ponts had built over fifty years. Although Eisenhower's Justice Department did not contest La Buy's 1954 denial of any market conspiracy in its appeal, the Warren Court, with Harlan and Tom Clark abstaining as interested parties, reversed the La Buy decision by a 4 to 2 opinion. "It is not requisite," held the Court, "to the proof of a violation of Section 7 [of the Clayton Anti-trust Act] to show that restraint or monopoly was intended."[42] Commercial and financial domination by *one* family, a less tolerable aspect of monopoly to the Court than financial domination by many groups, had been proved. It is worthy to note that of the four justices who comprised the majority, Black and Douglas were both New Deal appointees who shared Roosevelt's concern over single-group concentration that had spurred his TNEC probe, and the other two, Eisenhower appointees, Warren and Brennan, had both been New Deal sympathizers who understood the need to encourage diversification.

The news hit Wall Street like a thunderbolt, sparking the busiest activity of the year. Du Pont's stock gyrated up and down aimlessly before ending the day up 1 point. The boards of G.M. and U.S. Rubber, meeting at the time, refused comment, but Crawford did manage to remark that he was "naturally disappointed." The power of the state, it was clear, was being imposed to bring industrial mavericks like the Du Ponts into line. Meanwhile, the case was returned for "equitable relief" to La Buy, who avoided a decision in the ensuing election year.

The Du Ponts did not sit idly by and await their fate. In 1958 they joined Eisenhower and Vice-President Richard Nixon in supporting the gubernatorial candidacy of Senator William E. Knowland, the "open-shop" candidate of California's big corporations. The labor unions saw Knowland, a proud holder of a long anti-labor record in Washington, as part of the nationwide campaign of candidacies and bills being directed by NAM. "California has been chosen as a battleground to test 'right to work,'"[43] charged C. J. Hagerty, secretary-treasurer of California's State Federation of Labor. These suspicions were subsequently confirmed with Knowland's support for Proposition 18, which would have outlawed a union shop. But the most explosive tip-off was Knowland's use of a Du Pont-sponsored pamphlet written by Joseph Kamp, who was described by the *New York Times* as a "veteran pamphleteer of extreme right-wing causes." Kamp was notorious for his opposition to the liberal Supreme Court of Earl Warren, who also had no friends in Wilmington.

Kamp's pamphlet, "Meet the Man Who Plans to Rule America," was a rabid attack on AFL-CIO vice-president Walter Reuther; it was fully endorsed by Mrs. Helen Knowland, the Senator's wife, as "a powerful message which could actually swing the pendulum in California if it could be gotten into the hands of millions of people."

Helping in this endeavor were Du Pont directors Pierre S. du Pont III, son of Lammot, and Du Pont in-law Donaldson Brown, former vice-chairman of G.M. Brown, in fact, was so enthusiastic about Kamp's tirades that he not only contributed generously, but also provided Kamp with a list of names to whom his name could be mentioned when donations were requested.

The Du Pont involvement was all Knowland's opponent, Attorney General Pat Brown, needed to lock up the election. Asserting that Knowland's campaign had been directly linked with "fascistic anti-Semitic forces in the East supporting his drive to take over the governorship of this state," Brown rode the angry labor tide to victory. Meanwhile, a spokesman for Pierre asked the people to "let the facts speak for themselves."[44] On election day the facts did speak—with an eloquence even Pierre du Pont III could not ignore.

The Knowland campaign was the last time for over a decade that the Du Ponts publicly involved themselves in a political campaign, and for good reason. In an era of declining witch-hunts, the linking of Du Pont with right-wing causes threatened to undermine the "Better Things for Better Living . . . Through Chemistry" image that had been so carefully nurtured since the turbulent Thirties. Now the brand of Du Pont was again being used by Democrats attacking Republican candidates. Only a few weeks after Brown's charges in California, Tammany Boss Carmine De Sapio described the Rochester, New York, Republican state convention as dominated by Irénée du Pont, Richard Nixon, and Rockefeller interests. "These men were the phantom delegates to the Republican state convention in Rochester who determined its course, who chose its candidates, who wrote its platform and who dedicated its philosophy to the greater glory of big business."[45]

No doubt De Sapio's charges carried more than a grain of truth. The convention had indeed been controlled by Winthrop Aldrich, George Champion, president of Chase Manhattan, and former New York governor Thomas Dewey. Aldrich's nephew, Nelson Rockefeller, did emerge as the gubernatorial candidate. And Nixon and Irénée du Pont did indeed have a great voice in the national Republican apparatus. But the picture of a Tammany Boss charging the Republicans with being bossed did not inspire anger, but an impotent cynicism that only further crippled any effort to stop Rockefeller's triumphant march to Albany.

That the word "Du Pont" could again be used against the family's interests, almost as effectively as their use of "communist," was disquieting to many Du Ponts. Not since the Thirties had such a tactic against them been so successful. For the Du Ponts, 1958 marked the beginning of a decade of extreme political caution, of working unseen in the wings of the political arena to try to determine government policy, while at the same time striving to keep their famous name out of political print.

Undoubtedly the greatest immediate reason for this low-key political profile was General Motors. Crawford, Irénée, and the others still hoped to emerge from the courtroom debacle with most of their G.M. treasure. Wilmington had worked out a scheme to keep its G.M. stock but surrender the voting rights of the company to individual Du Pont stockholders, effectively preserving the family's control.

In October 1959, after hearing testimony by Du Pont witnesses (including Neil H. Jacoby, dean of UCLA's Graduate School of Business Administration and later chairman of President Nixon's Pay Board as a "neutral representative of the public"), Judge La Buy accepted the company's plan, declaring complete divestiture by the family "unnecessarily harsh and punitive." But La Buy had another reason for this ruling: the "severe impact" on the stock market, another echo from Du Pont's public relations campaign. From the bench the judge read a letter of a 90-year-old woman who was concerned with the case because her only income came from G.M. stock. "The Court will not assume the responsibility of such a risk,"[46] declared the judge, himself a resident of Chicago's exclusive Lakeshore Drive area appropriately dubbed "the Gold Coast."

"We are gratified,"[47] responded Crawford humbly. "A victory," hailed the stock market. "It is favorable to the Du Pont family group because they avoid an enormous tax confiscation," commented Gerald Loeb, partner of E. F. Hutton & Company. "Other Du Pont stockholders are protected from varying amounts of taxes. The decision is favorable to corporations in general which have stock in other companies." Loeb's own firm, of course, was one of these holders of G.M. stock. But perhaps the most penetrating remarks came from stockholder Jacques Coe: "You can quote me as saying 'the mountain labored and brought forth a mouse.' "

Two months later, on December 7, Donaldson Brown, Walter S. Carpenter, Henry B. du Pont, and Lammot du Pont Copeland resigned from G.M.'s board. It is interesting to note what interests were allowed to replace them immediately on the finance and bonuses committees: Lloyd Brace, trustee of the Rockefeller Foundation, director of A.T. & T., Gillette, and John Hancock Mutual Life Insurance, and chairman of First National Bank of Boston; and General Lucius Clay, chairman of Continental Can (in which the Du Ponts held a substantial block of stock)— symbolizing G.M.'s ties in the Military-Industrial Complex. Both men, although enjoying association with Morgan interests, were intimate with the Rockefellers.

Du Pont dropped all joint consultants with G.M. It dropped G.M. executives as transfer agents for its stock, assigning Chemical Bank (a bank now jointly held by Rockefeller-Morgan interests) and surrendering the company's voting rights to individual stockholders, meaning the family. Everyone was happy. Judge La Buy was happy. The Du Pont family was happy. Rockefeller interests, with their first foothold in G.M.'s door, were happy.

The Supreme Court, however, was not. On May 22, 1961, the high court ruled, by the same majority of liberals, that Du Pont Company must also yield its 63 million shares of G.M. stock, worth over $3.5 billion, within ten years. "We think the public is entitled to the surer, clearer remedy of divestiture," explained the Court.

The impact of the decision was sharp. A selling flood of Du Pont stock ensued with bids one-eighth off the last sale. Du Pont closed $5\frac{1}{2}$ points down; G.M., $2\frac{3}{8}$ points down.

But the real concern of the family was taxes. Existing income tax laws could collectively cost individual family stockholders well over a billion dollars. This was because distributing G.M. shares to Du Pont's share-holders was the only feasible way of divesting most of Du Pont's G.M. holdings. Du Pont couldn't sell all its holdings openly on the market. The average daily volume of General Motors on the New York Stock Exchange was only 28,100 at the time. Du Pont's sale of 63 million shares of G.M. stock over ten years would mean selling 25,100 shares daily, doubling the market's volume. The market was unable to absorb this sale and still keep G.M.'s stock prices from falling. By the same token, secondary distribu-tions on the market were deemed unwise, as most stock purchasers would not buy at the high prices of the first distribution, but would wait for the cheaper prices of the second distribution. The only recourse left was a distribution to Du Pont's 210,840 shareholders. Each shareholder of 100 Du Pont shares would receive 137 shares of G.M. To pay the resultant increase in income taxes, stockholders in upper income levels would have to sell G.M. shares.

This was the company's main concern—as it had always been—the family. "We hope the present Congress will move promptly to protect these shareholders . . .,"[48] Crawford told the press on hearing of the decision. The *New York Times* understood the meaning of his words. "Legislation on the tax problem," it commented, "is expected to have a much better chance in Congress as a result of the decision."

Lending his helping hand in Congress was Delaware's own Democratic Senator, J. Allen Frear. Frear introduced a bill that not only changed the designation of the divestiture from "ordinary" income to "capital gains," but "modified capital gains," and allowed Christiana's divestiture of 18 million shares to be tax-free up to their original purchase value. This would save Du Pont's stockholders a total $530 million. Later Frear would be appointed to a vice presidency of Wilmington Trust, the Du Pont family bank, and a seat on the board of Diamond State Telephone.

The bill found friends everywhere. Conservatives endorsed it as a protec-tion of property rights. Liberals such as Senator Eugene McCarthy warned that failure to pass the bill "might have the effect of distorting operations of the two corporations, and of distorting the investment portfolios of holdings of many persons or corporations."

But the biggest surprise was the support of President Kennedy. The Du Ponts had opposed his candidacy in 1960, backing Vice-President Richard Nixon with the largest contribution of his campaign, $125,000.[49] Yet an aura of good feelings had developed between Washington and Wilmington during the Cold War, and this extended into the new Kennedy administra-tion. In May 1961, the same month the Supreme Court handed down its final decision, Jacqueline Kennedy was seen at Winterthur being hosted by Henry F. du Pont (Henry, in fact, was appointed chairman of the White House's Fine Arts Committee because of his expertise on antiques). But the real reason for the President's support was the activity of Du Pont lobbyist Clark Clifford.

For a cool $1 million (some Washington insiders insist the fee was closer to $2 million) the Du Ponts bought the services of this leading Washington lobbyist. It was an investment that soon paid high dividends.

While encouraging Crawford Greenewalt to personally lobby more than sixty Congressmen and administration officials, Clifford brought his own personal pressure down on the White House. This was no light matter for Kennedy. Clifford was one of the most powerful men in the country. He had married into the Kimball Arms Company, and his star had risen since his wartime association with Missouri banker Jack Vardaman landed him the post of special assistant to Vardaman's old crony, President Harry Truman. One of the administration's strongest opponents of the United Mine Workers' strike, Clifford also drafted the Military Unification Plan of 1947, which concentrated power in the secretary of the renamed War Department, the Department of Defense. Through the next thirteen years, Clifford was one of the strongest proponents of the Cold War's armaments race, and he was offered the directorship of the CIA (which he also played a central role in establishing in 1946) by President Kennedy after the CIA's invasion of Cuba ended in humiliating defeat. This was a man whose corporate clients included I.T. & T., G.E., Hughes Tool (Howard Hughes), Phillips Petroleum, and the Pennsylvania Railroad. As a consequence, he enjoyed the confidence of Congressmen and Presidents, including Kennedy.

One day, while Greenewalt and his Du Pont lieutenants prowled the legislative halls, Clifford led a corporate cortege into the Treasury Department's legal offices. There, Clifford had just begun presenting his case to Robert Knight, the Treasury's general counsel, when a secretary interrupted: "Mr. Knight, the President is calling."

Clifford turned to his assistants and advised, "I think it would be appropriate for all of us to leave the room."

"Oh, but the call isn't for Mr. Knight," explained the secretary, "it's for Mr. Clifford!"[50] Calls from the President, joked the others, follow Mr. Clifford at such opportune moments.

On February 3, 1962, President Kennedy signed the Du Pont bill into law.

A month later Judge La Buy paid the Du Ponts his final service. On March 1 he ruled that thirty-five of the seventy-five Du Pont defendants would be allowed to receive their portion of 18 million G.M. shares held by Christiana Securities. In addition, all members of the family would be permitted to directly purchase G.M. shares then and in the future. La Buy also refused a government request for a permanent injunction against future Du Pont-G.M. interlocking directorships and other related activities, insisting that only a ten-year ban applied.

This ruling was in direct violation of the administration's own public posture and the Supreme Court's intention. "It should be clearly understood," President Kennedy had said to reporters when signing the tax-relief bill, "that neither the Congressmen nor I have approved a divestiture which will permit the stock of General Motors to pass through Christiana to the stockholders of Christiana. If the pass-through occurred, a large percentage of General Motors stock would be acquired by members of the Du Pont family. This, it is argued, would mean that the Du Pont family would still effectively control both Du Pont and General Motors."[51] La Buy's decision allowed the family through its private trusts and in-laws to retain an estimated 17 percent holding,[52] well over the 5 percent defined later as a "controlling interest" by the House Banking Committee.[53] In opposition to this position, on March 10 Senators Paul Douglas and Albert Gore made public a letter they had sent to Attorney General Robert F. Kennedy, warning that La Buy's "wholly inadequate" ruling would nullify the Supreme Court's decision. At the time, even government prosecutors warned that the family would be able to retain a holding of at least 6 percent.

The Kennedy administration, however, refused to appeal.

La Buy's ruling settled the case, but not Clifford's lobbying. The Du Pont bill had allowed Christiana Securities to distribute its G.M. holdings as a "return of capital," which simply meant getting your money back, a tax-free transaction. But the legislation stipulated this tax-free bonus only insofar as the value of the G.M. stock returned to the shareholders equaled what the shareholders paid for Christiana stock. Any value above that was naturally taxable as a capital gain.

By 1964, when the last 8.5 million G.M. shares were to be distributed, this tax-free limit had already been exhausted by the two previous distributions. And since G.M.'s stock price had nearly doubled since 1961, from $45–55 a share to $100 a share, the Du Ponts were facing almost twice the capital gains taxes they would have had to pay for the same shares in 1961.

Again Clifford silently worked his way into the highest circles, this time of the new Johnson administration, most of whom were still Kennedy appointees. On July 4, 1964, he met with Treasury Secretary C. Douglas

Dillon and argued for a change in the tax rules to permit a tax-free non-pro-rata distribution. In this way, younger Du Ponts and recent buyers of Christiana could get distributed G.M. stock tax-free, since Christiana stock in recent years had sold high enough to absorb the additional G.M. stock value. Older, longer-term holders of Christiana, who had bought their Christiana stock years before at lower prices, would simply not participate in the distribution, thus avoiding any capital gains tax.

The greatest opposition to this proposal came from the tax lawyers of the Treasury, who honestly questioned why the Du Ponts should be given special relief. Again Clifford exerted pressure. In the early fall he visited the Treasury's legal offices, where Fred Smith had replaced Robert Knight as general counsel. And again he pulled his "call to the President" routine (Clifford's closeness to the President is exemplified by the fact that he was later appointed Secretary of Defense by Johnson), specifically asking Smith if he could use his private office to make the call. The pressure was on.

A few days later Robert Knight received a phone call at his Wall Street law office, Shearman and Sterling. It was Clark Clifford. "He asked me," Knight later testified before the Senate Finance Committee, "whether the fact that his clients produced a lot of revenue was the kind of factor that would permit a reconsideration"[54] of a disproportional distribution. Clifford warned that Secretary Dillon might be calling Knight back soon for a consultation on the subject. A request from so powerful a financial figure as C. Douglas Dillon, heir of the founder of Dillon Read & Co., Clifford knew, could not be ignored by any ambitious Wall Street lawyer such as Knight.

On November 2 Dillon did just that, and two days later Knight was in Washington being briefed by Clifford. By the following week, on November 10, Knight was in a joint meeting with Treasury and Christiana lawyers, and ten days later he publicly reversed his 1962 decision, recommending the Clifford plan. In December the Treasury Department announced that it, too, was reversing its previous policy. The Du Ponts had won.

Almost immediately, challenges arose. Senator Albert Gore demanded and got a public hearing. Dillon hurriedly claimed it was his policy to avoid personal knowledge of specific tax cases. Knight explained that the original ruling was based on Congress's anticipation of a specific tax collection of $450 million based on G.M.'s $55 a share. The doubled G.M. value, he explained, would still produce this amount, despite the tax-free decision. Gore, among others, countered that Congress had not specified any amount. The $450 million estimate was, in fact, based on updating an earlier estimate of $350 million, when G.M. stock was only $45. Knight's claim simply did not stand up to the record of the Congressional debate over the Du Pont bill at the time. Moreover, what if G.M.'s stock had fallen? Had Congress ever intended to tax additionally to collect its full $450 million estimate? Never. The Treasury's ruling, charged Gore, was "negotiated and issued in secrecy and contrary to the clear intent of Congress."[55]

Yet it was not changed. "Very frankly," said Senator Douglas, "it seems to me this has been a heads-I-win, tails-you-lose ruling—heads Du Pont wins, tails the government loses."[56] The government, in fact, lost an additional $56 million to $100 million to the Du Ponts.

All told, the Du Ponts saved an estimated $2 billion in taxes. Clifford certainly earned his famous fee.

In 1965 the Du Pont Company completed its divestiture. Twenty-three million G.M. shares had been distributed in 1962, 17 million in 1964, and now the last 23 million. At the stockholders meeting on April 12, 1965, Lammot du Pont Copeland, who was the new president, proudly announced that owners of distributed G.M. stock were now getting a higher combined income from both stocks than they had formerly received through just Du Pont. What he did not mention was that this was partly due to G.M.'s spurt of growth after being relieved of Du Pont's commercial yoke.

Du Pont, meanwhile, tried to prevent selling of its stock by increasing dividends from $7.50 in 1961 to $7.75 in 1962. Its net income actually rose during these early years of the divestiture, from $418 million in 1961 to $472 million in 1963, a 12 percent rise. There are reasons for this rise, reasons that had much to do with Lammot du Pont Copeland's emphasis on expanding overseas investment where consumer markets, cheap labor, and lower taxes reside, reasons that also had much to do with Copeland's emphasis on building a direct consumer market in the United States. The early success of these shifts marked Copeland's rise within the family and his assumption of the presidency in 1962. But the decline in earnings that the company consistently suffered from 1963 on was in good part due to the loss of G.M. dividends—by 1965, more than $300 million worth. Copeland was undoubtedly right about individual family shareholders earning more through their variety of stocks, but the company itself had suffered what chairman Crawford Greenewalt aptly described to the stockholders as "the end of an era."[57]

4. THE YOUNG CHARLEMAGNES

Amid a white cloud of smoke from eighty smoldering candles, spectacled old Irénée du Pont gaily took the knife offered by his daughter Irene and began the long deep cut down eight tiers of frosted cake. When he finally reached bottom with a triumphant smile, the largest birthday party in Delaware's history began.

Some 300 formally dressed Du Ponts, including seven of Irénée's eight children and most of his thirty-five grandchildren, gathered in the shimmering Grand Ballroom of Hotel Du Pont to pay homage to the clan's Grand Patriarch on his 80th birthday. While magazine photographers recorded the rare assembly for the entire country, the Du Ponts danced, filled themselves with cake, and drank chilled champagne. Irénée seemed the happiest of all, puffing on his cigar as he made the rounds, amusing Walter Carpenter, Jr., and Mrs. A. Felix, Jr., at their table, joking with son-in-law Bruce Bredin on the dance floor. As spry as ever, old Irénée whirled through almost every dance during the evening. Finally, at 1:30 A.M. a daughter told him the party was over. "Oh," he countered with a grin, "I thought it had just begun."[58]

That remark probably best depicts Irénée's general outlook on life. He once described his main contribution to the company as "optimism, when it was needed."[59] To a man so wealthy as Irénée du Pont, such an attitude was not difficult to maintain, even in his waning years.

From Granogue, his magnificent hillside mansion outside Wilmington, Irénée daily kept close tabs on Du Pont Company developments, often being consulted as a patriarch should be, by his son-in-law, Du Pont president Crawford Greenewalt. But it was at Xanadu, his vast Cuban estate, that Irénée spent the most enjoyable months of his last years.

Xanadu was Irénée's own private empire in a foreign land, a 450-acre ocean-front estate carved out of the Cuban jungle, complete with a nine-hole golf course.

Irénée's interest in Cuba extended back to the Twenties, when the Florida land boom sparked interest also in Cuban real estate. Irénée chose one of the most beautiful areas on earth, the northern coast of Cuba's Matanzas Province, for the materialization of his dream of "Xanadu," the mythical kingdom of Coleridge's "Kubla Khan." Soon bulldozers were clearing away the palm trees and workers were putting in the first sewer system of the region, later to be known as one of the most exclusive resort areas of the world, Varadero Beach. To guard the boundaries of the estate, a tall stone wall was built in the gunpowder-making architectural tradition of Delaware's first family. Outside the wall were lined rows of stone houses for Xanadu's fifty servants, who were undoubtedly some of the best-paid Cubans on this island of poverty and de facto American colonialization.

The only break in Xanadu's stone wall was a huge iron gate, through which Irénée would ride his limousine when returning from tours of the island or trips to Havana, then the "fun city" of American corporate leaders. Through these gates Irénée would enter his estate and ride along his private two-lane paved road, traveling over hundreds of hilly acres of manicured green grass and swaying palm trees, until finally his limousine climbed up the last high hill, on which stood his imposing twenty-room mansion.

Irénée's hacienda was one of the most elegant pieces of architecture in Cuba. Floored with Italian marble, paneled with mahogany woodwork, and roofed with Spanish tiles, the mansion became the scene of dinner parties for some of the most famous and privileged people of the world. At any moment, Irénée might arrive unannounced with furred and jeweled guests, emerging from his plane on the estate's private landing strip or walking off his 60-foot yacht *Icacos*. Although Irénée's parties were often unanticipated, Xanadu would always be ready to entertain his and his guests' slightest whim. The rambling house, although furnished in poor taste with cheap shoddy furniture, was four stories high, the first with an 18-foot-high ceiling designed to make Irénée seem powerful and others seem small. It worked.

Here Irénée was undisputed lord and master, residing in Cuba four months out of every year, having his cigars lit by Cuban servants, fishing with Cuban dictators Machado and Batista, swimming while wearing prescription-lensed goggles so he could enjoy the details of underwater coral life in a country where most of the population that needed glasses went without.

But the most bizarre of Irénée's pastimes was his large collection of iguanas. Irénée spent thousands of dollars to breed, feed, and keep these crocodile-like lizards in specially constructed pens. Some of these tough, vicious lizards grew to 3 feet in length under Irénée's loving care, and more than once the old industrialist was seen marching about with one of these ugly beasts crawling next to him on a leash. Irénée derived a peculiar kind of pleasure from these lizards. By barking a command, he could make them all come out of their pens and surround him, standing at attention. He had trained them, on another command, to attack a target to kill. It was an appalling example to the Cubans of the degeneracy of the idle rich. In a moment of the bizarre captured for history, a *Life* photographer in 1957 recorded old Irénée feeding his iguanas papaya from a jar at a time when most of the Cuban population was suffering from malnutrition.

Next to the U.S. ambassador, Irénée was probably the most powerful American in Cuba. When James Roosevelt visited Cuba on an official mission for his father in 1937, his first visit was to the Cuban Secretary of State; his second, and last, was to Xanadu. Once, the story goes, Irénée even had the Cuban president, General Fulgencio Batista, denied entrance to the estate. Yet such haughty insults didn't prevent the Cuban dictator from awarding the old industrialist with the medal of the Order of Carlos Manuel de Céspedes in 1954. Irénée, too busy to attend the honors personally, proudly accepted from afar.

In 1957 the Master of Xanadu played host to sons-in-law Crawford Greenewalt and Colgate Dardin, the latter a Du Pont director and president of the University of Virginia, while at the very same time, some miles away, Fidel Castro and Che Guevara fought a desperate guerrilla war against Batista's armies. Two years later Castro triumphantly entered Havana and Irénée's reign over Xanadu came to an end. Today Xanadu is "Casa du Pont," a public restaurant and museum where Cubans see for themselves how American corporate leaders once lavishly lived in their land.

Although Cuba's new revolutionary government refused to give Irénée compensation, the U.S. Congress did. Delaware's Senator John Williams, the "conscience of the Senate," sponsored an amendment to a tax bill that allowed a $2.1 million tax write-off for the family.

Xanadu was not Irénée's greatest loss, however. Irene, his cousin-wife, died in 1961, leaving her octogenarian husband heartbroken. Two years later Irénée followed her to Sand Hole Woods. He was 86.

Most of Irénée's $400 million fortune had been distributed among family trusts and foundations before he died. Control over the remaining $40 million estate was given to three trustees, Crawford Greenewalt, Irénée du Pont, Jr. (his only son), and son-in-law Ernest May (who subsequently lost control, in a bitter suit against the others). Of the three, lean, serious-minded Irénée, Jr., who had succeeded to his father's seat on Du Pont's board in 1959, clearly emerged as the rising new power in the family. But it was not Irénée, Jr., who held the spotlight when the family gathered at Sand Hole Woods to bury the old patriarch. Rather, it was his cousin, Lammot du Pont Copeland, the new president.

The son of Du Pont director Charles Copeland and Irénée's sister Louisa, Copeland did not make the most impressive of appearances; his round, pudgy face and short black hair were in sharp contrast to his trim, handsome predecessor, Crawford Greenewalt. Only the sharp, penetrating eyes shrewdly peering with a touch of humor from behind light-rimmed glasses betrayed the analytical mind that had propelled Copeland to the top among a score of able relatives in the company. Imbued with a complete devotion to the company, and a pleasant personality, Copeland had risen steadily in the company, first as successor to his father's post as secretary, where he headed the new stockholder's relation program, then as finance committee chairman (the traditional stepping-stone), and finally president in 1962.

Copeland's personal wealth no doubt added to his stature. Enjoying the benefits of many inheritances, Copeland was one of Du Pont's largest stockholders by the time of his ascension to the presidency; he held 190,941 shares of Du Pont common and 338,348 of Christiana Securities, making, with other corporate holdings, his total worth somewhere between $200 million and $400 million. Residing in Mt. Cuba, his luxurious 3,000-acre estate outside Wilmington, Copeland avidly collected the works of such painters as Charles Baskerville and was a member of the exclusive Walpole Society (an organization of American antique connoisseurs, whose membership was limited to thirty), president of Henry F. du Pont's Winterthur (Museum) Corporation, and treasurer of the family's Eleutherian Mills-Hagley (Library) Foundation. To anyone familiar with Du Pont wealth, this seemingly shy hunter and fisherman was no financial lightweight.

Yet what most marked Copeland's rise was his ability to listen attentively and answer forthrightly, often with a humorous approach. And during the Fifties the man he listened to most was president Crawford Greenewalt. "Mr. Greenewalt and I look at life from a similar point of view,"[60] he commented after his appointment as president—and one of Greenewalt's foremost projects in the late Fifties had been overseas expansion.

Living off the fat of General Motors and its own earnings, Du Pont was late in joining the tremendous postwar surge of corporate investment abroad. The embarrassment of its cartel agreements with I. G. Farben, despite its fervent denials of their existence, forced Du Pont to release "exclusive" rights on I. G. Farben nylon patents to the Alien Property Custodian in 1947. These patents, however, were described by one official as "not of importance and of pretty foggy" utilization. In other words, Du Pont really lost nothing.

On September 28, 1951, Du Pont and Remington Arms had been convicted of conspiring with Britain's Imperial Chemicals, Ltd. to divide the wartime markets in munitions, chemicals, and small arms. On the basis of the 1939 agreement, the government also named West Germany's I. G. Farben as an accomplice, but not a defendant. Throughout the trial, Lammot du Pont, Walter Carpenter, and Charles Davis claimed that their innocence rested on their acting as corporate executives under the direction of the Du Pont board. But the image of Lammot du Pont being a puppet for anyone was simply unconvincing. Although federal judge Sylvester Ryan found "that the nylon agreement of 1939 was illegal because it was part of a licensing scheme, accomplished by concerted action of Du Pont and I.C.I. for allocation of territories and pooling of patents embracing the whole of the nylon manufacturing industry and the whole of the nylon technology,"[61] Lammot, Carpenter, and Davis received no penalties. "Their acts were not calculated to bring them direct personal gain," the judge held, while in the same breath admitting, "any profit which they might have received came through stock ownership (and of this we have no proof)."

To settle this case so happily, Du Pont agreed to release nylon patents for free. The newspapers gleefully reiterated the government's contention that this would break Du Pont's nylon monopoly. Actually, nylon production processes were no secret, but its operation required huge investments which up to then had scared away most everyone but the giant from Wilmington. To avoid another anti-trust suit, Du Pont allowed a small company in Florida, Chemstrand, to take a license for nylon production. Then Chemstrand was bought by a larger chemical firm, Monsanto, which was willing to borrow enough capital to give Du Pont a run for its money with improved technology. By 1967, twenty-three other companies had joined the nylon race.

Six years followed the severing of profitable arrangements with I.C.I. before Du Pont adopted a serious program of capital expansion overseas. By then Du Pont was the tortoise in the chemical industry's hot race to go abroad after World War II. Although the leader in exports, Du Pont lagged in foreign plant investment, and rising U.S. taxes and inflation were making it more and more difficult to generate the traditional 10 percent yield on domestic plant investment. In contrast to Du Pont, Monsanto increased its overseas assets from $57 million in 1953 to $160 million in 1959, reaping the high profits of cheap foreign labor and the revived European market, and becoming a leading competitor.

Du Pont's growing move abroad paralleled its growing legal defeats in attempting to hold onto G.M.'s annual dividends. In 1957, the year of the Supreme Court divestiture decision, Du Pont established its first wholly owned foreign subsidiary in Holland and began construction on a $30 million neoprene plant in Derry, Northern Ireland. This move was an attempt to break into the Common Market, where revived European industry and other American corporations threatened the markets Du Pont sought. By having a toehold inside Europe, the Du Ponts expected to be able to cash in on the elimination of tariff walls inside the Common Market.

The company by then had set up a new style of overseas operation, shifting from the previous emphasis on technological exports it had maintained under the I.C.I. agreement, to more profitable and direct product exports. From 1953 to 1957 this export trade sharply grew from $100 million to $146 million. With foreign and American competition threatening these new markets, Wilmington increasingly saw the need to protect them. The impending loss of G.M. earnings made this concern even more paramount.

In 1958 Du Pont made its first full commitment to major overseas expansion. W. Sam Carpenter III, the ruggedly handsome middle-aged son of Walter Carpenter, Jr., was made general manager of the new International Department. The International Department was no mere revitalized Foreign Relations Department. Its scope was wider and its concern more direct and detailed, because Du Pont was now to be physically present in foreign lands. In recognition of this prospect, Carpenter's department was put on a level with the industrial department in the company hierarchy, responsible directly to the executive committee for management and financial returns on all Du Pont foreign enterprises.

As the International Department had no technological resources of its own, Carpenter had to rely on specific industrial departments for know-how and technically trained personnel to run the plants abroad. In return, Carpenter advised the industrial divisions on the best use of foreign markets for their export sales. In this way, Du Pont's capital market aided the commodities market in a coordinated system of exploitation.

Probably most revealing of Wilmington's foreign ambitions, however, was the worldwide scope of the new department's concerns. Two geographic divisions were immediately set up, one covering all of Latin America, and the other, Europe. For each manager stationed overseas to run the plant operations, Carpenter had a deputy manager in Wilmington who integrated the domestic departments with overseas activities. Carpenter also set up two smaller staff divisions concerned with future overseas business: (1) the Development Division, to handle the administrative details of licensing and to find further opportunities for Du Pont ventures overseas; and (2) the Foreign Trade Division, to maintain representatives who searched for markets in areas where there was not sufficient volume to warrant a manager for each of Du Pont's products.

It was a complex operation, but a necessary one.

Undaunted by 200 Irish construction workers carrying placards reading "Du Pont: the dictators of 1958" and "Freedom before Du Pont domination," striking over the arbitrary dismissal of a shop steward, Carpenter pushed through the completion of the Derry plant and customer service lab for Great Britain in 1959. By then Du Pont had a finishes plant in Venezuela; Freon refrigerant plants in Brazil and Argentina; a paint plant in Cuba (subsequently lost to the revolution); a finishes plant in Belgium; an Orlon plant in the Netherlands; and a key sales subsidiary in Switzer-

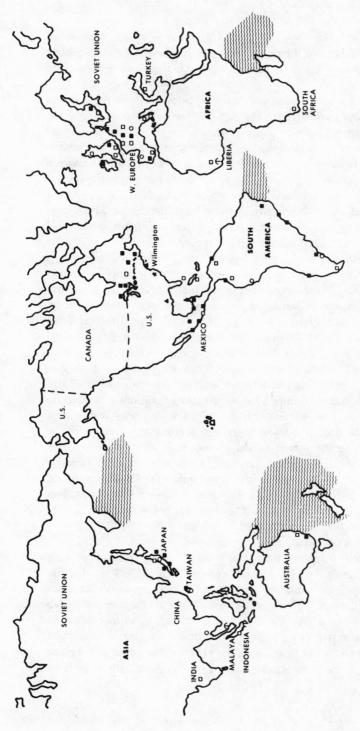

DuPont World Empire

★ Du Pont International Headquarters: Wilmington, Delaware

▲ Du Pont International Design & Engineering Offices - Houston, Texas; Plainview, Long Island, N. Y.

■ Du Pont Plants (including subsidiaries) - Canada, England, West Germany, Belgium, Holland, Luxembourg, Sweden, Spain.
Mexico, Colombia, Venezuela, Brazil, Chile, Argentina, Australia, Taiwan, Japan

○ Du Pont Foreign Sales Offices - Bangkok, Thailand; T'aipei, Taiwan; Lima, Peru; Paris, France; Milan, Italy; Geneva, Switzerland; Tokyo, Japan; Buenos Aires, Argentina

⬆ UNIROYAL Plantations - Indonesia, Malaya, Liberia

◻ UNIROYAL Plants - India, Malaya, Indonesia, Japan, Australia, South Africa, Liberia, Turkey, Italy, West Germany, Sweden, Luxembourg, Belgium, France, England, Wales, Scotland, Canada.
Mexico, Colombia, Venezuela, Argentina

land for marketing Du Pont products throughout Europe. Canada, Ltd., another Du Pont subsidiary, was also going well, increasing its sales from $56 million in 1954 to $96 million in 1959. Carpenter had also begun plans for expanding the nylon and cellophane production in Argentina, and building a titanium dioxide plant in Mexico.

Du Pont's overseas invasion was now in full swing.

Crawford Greenewalt gave this expansion every encouragement. But the one person most closely involved with overseeing and judging Carpenter's results was Greenewalt's protégé, the chairman of the finance committee, Lammot du Pont Copeland.

By the time he rose to the presidency, Copeland was committed to the concept that the future progress and well-being of Du Pont was greatly linked to its overseas expansion. "The key to success," he told the National Convention of the Foreign Trade Council in November 1963, "lies first with a lively research establishment. But an enterprise must also have an aggressive marketing organization attuned to world markets and able to move as promptly with its new product abroad as it does at home. This is the course we have charted for Du Pont."[62] It was a course that had already produced results. In 1954 only 6 percent of Du Pont's sales were foreign. When Copeland spoke in 1963, foreign sales had risen to over 15 percent.

But more important was the fact that Du Pont's foreign plants were already returning a higher percentage increase in profits each year than Wilmington was able to increase exports abroad. Over 16,000 foreign workers were now working for Du Pont in thirty-five plants in thirteen different countries. Du Pont was no longer tied to mere export trade. Now the race for overseas markets involved open exploitation of foreign labor.

Copeland himself explained this foreign expansion as the result of market competition. "Since there are other potential producers in each of our product lines, a competitor will build a plant there if we don't." And what of the underdeveloped countries of Asia, Latin America, and Africa, the former victims of colonialization and imperialism? "In the developing countries, there are other factors," he elucidated, "close government control of the economy which closes the border to imports when the first local producer is established, tariffs and other trade restrictions. The point is that the export business in both these areas will be lost in any event. But if we build the plant, we lose the market to ourselves." And the profits, of course, are not returned to the local economy, but are forwarded to Wilmington, chemicals' new Rome. Copeland underscored this fact. "In the last ten years," he told the assembled industrialists, "the Du Pont Company's own favorable balance of international payments adds up to the scarcely insignificant figure of $1.3 billion. Moreover, in the future, despite what we anticipate will be continued heavy investment abroad, we expect our balance of international payments will be even more favorable. While the figures are not exactly comparable, the chemical industry as a whole has had a favorable balance of payments of $9 billion in the last ten years, and, in recent years, this balance has been more than $1 billion annually." In some cases, in the advanced industrial countries, Copeland pointed out, increased exports even paid for the new plants. "For example, the announcement of our synthetic rubber and acrylic fiber plant in Europe a few years ago resulted in increased export sales of about $63 million by the time the plants went on steam. This amount far exceeded the cost of the new plant."

But in the underdeveloped countries the situation was far different. Centuries of European colonialism and economic imperialism had prevented the development of indigenous industry. Without these industries, increased buying of Du Pont products could not be stimulated merely by Wilmington's announcing plans to build a local plant. Still suffering from the crippling polio of foreign exploitation, the underdeveloped countries offered only two opportunities for profit: cheap labor and raw and crude resources. But both opportunities were capable of returning a higher yield on plant investment than the United States or Europe, since costs were lower. Accordingly, by 1970 half of Du Pont's overseas plants were in Latin America.

Copeland's extraordinary and frank address in 1963 marked the beginning of a new era for Du Pont, an era of overseas investment. It also marked a change in the family's political policies. Only a decade before, the Du Ponts had been in general opposition to increased U.S. foreign aid to underdeveloped countries. Du Pont director Colgate Darden, later Irénée's son-in-law, had served on the Fairless Committee, named after its chairman, Benjamin Fairless of U.S. Steel. Joining John L. Lewis, Fairless, and the chairmen of Proctor & Gamble, the New York *Herald Tribune,* and the Bank of America, Darden attacked most of the State Department's foreign aid programs.

With Du Pont's personal involvement in overseas investment, Wilmington's foreign policy changed dramatically, accepting the basic arguments of corporate liberalism. U.S. foreign aid was a means to encourage political stability in the revolutionary tempest sweeping the underdeveloped countries, Copeland explained. Corporate investment overseas was now advanced by Wilmington as "humanitarian." But in his entire speech, Copeland devoted only one sentence of lip service to this aspect, before going on to the more important concern of "the eventual development of tremendous, profitable markets. . . . As businessmen, however, we also recognize that, in most of these areas, markets are relatively small, and there is often a high degree of economic and political instability. It seems to me that this presents an opportunity to our government and to other governments which have undertaken programs of economic assistance to the emerging nations. The objectives and the implementation of these programs should be sharpened up to foster political and economic stability so that private capital will be attracted to these areas."

To Du Pont, Washington should use foreign aid as a bludgeon of bribery to force economically desperate governments to maintain law and order in the face of popular uprisings or creeping socialism. ". . . we have the freedom and responsibility to specify the terms on which we will assist, and we should exercise this fully. Once stability or indications of it have been achieved in the developing countries, private capital, both domestic and foreign, will be attracted to the obvious market opportunities. We should make certain that this is well understood because it should act as an additional incentive for the establishment of stability.

"Du Pont already has invested quite substantial amounts in some of the developing countries, and we are prepared to increase investments for profitable projects when we find solid evidence of political and economic stability. Mexico is a good example of what I mean." Mexico, with a so-called "nationalistic" government, was indeed a good example. Although Mexican law stipulated that all foreign companies must be majority-owned by Mexican nationals, a special deal was struck in the case of Du Pont. Three plants, Policrón de México, S.A., Pigmentos y Productos Químicos, S.A., and Tetraetilo de México, S.A., were set up as companies with 49 percent Du Pont control. In exchange, Du Pont Company was allowed to establish two wholly owned subsidiaries, Colorquím, S.A., and Du Pont, S.A., which, with Endo Laboratories, Inc., another Du Pont subsidiary, ran and wholly owned four plants throughout Mexico. This effectively put Mexico's chemical industry under Du Pont domination.

No longer would Wilmington cry "communism!" when Asian, Latin American, or African governments built their own public projects. "We must be prepared to accept the fact that a significant proportion of economic and social progress in the developing countries will be achieved through government initiative," said Copeland. "These nations need roads and dams and schools and health facilities on which a sound economic system can be built. And frankly, I am not concerned by the use of government enterprise in the developing countries if it is limited to these purposes and accompanied by the growth of political and economic maturity. But once the basic facilities exist, the developing nations will have to depend upon private capital to fuel their engines of human progress."

Copeland's own remarks revealed that a new political maturity in the family had been reached, a maturity of class consciousness that understood the use of state power to financially develop political order and the economic preconditions for business expansion abroad. Forty years before, Herbert Hoover had made a similar recommendation regarding the financing of public works abroad, only he had suggested the use of corporate funds. Now the American taxpayer, the bulk of whom were of the middle and working classes, paid the tab for the corporations.

Copeland's address was the most important public statement by the Du Pont family since Lammot du Pont's dramatic offer of reconciliation to FDR in 1937, and in many ways it represented an extension of the Wilmington-Washington détente that had developed since then. It was fitting indeed that Copeland's speech was not to Du Pont stockholders, or even to the chemical industry as a whole, but to a national convention of some of the most sophisticated corporate leaders in the country, gathered to celebrate the fiftieth anniversary of the National Foreign Trade Council, a corporate organization founded just before World War I to promote the first big investment drive of American monopolies overseas. And it was an indication of the political sophistication the family had reached that Copeland had defined the investment problems of particular corporations as a *national* problem. Copeland by then was firmly convinced that not only the destiny of Du Pont, but also of the present system of U.S. government, the country, and capitalism itself, were tied to overseas expansion. "We must certainly take accurate bearings of the vital questions of exports, foreign investments, the U.S. balance of payments deficit, and proposed tariff reductions under the Expansion Act of 1962. And any course that we set obviously must serve the broad, national interest of the United States and the countries with which our foreign trade is conducted as well as our corporate interests." No longer was Du Pont the only concern; now a coordinated *system* of overseas expansion was necessary. "The course we chart in world markets will determine, in part, the profitability of our own enterprises and the economic strength and stature of the United States abroad. . . . If we don't participate in the rapidly expanding markets abroad, we will soon be the victims of economic isolation." Overseas markets, in a general sense for *all* U.S. business, must be protected and extended at all costs.

In this regard, Copeland was particularly disturbed by the Kennedy administration's failure to consult the Du Ponts before negotiating over tariffs with economically revived European capitalism. Those negotiations with west European powers resulted in lower chemical tariffs that hurt Du Pont's markets. "It should be pointed out to the officials responsible for these negotiations that such attrition is not a simple and painless matter for industry and its people. It is not something which can easily be dismissed in high-sounding words about the broader national interest. A few months ago, Du Pont was forced out of the indigo dye business by foreign competition."

Three days after Copeland's speech, President Kennedy was assassinated; the new Johnson administration almost immediately began preparing for massive military escalation in Vietnam. Although Kennedy's tariff agreements with Europe were not reversed, his reservations about fully engaging in an Asian war were. For Johnson, Indochina was the first domino of the Asian market, an opinion ideologically strengthened by the fact that the anti-colonial revolution in Indochina was led by communists who had fought the Japanese and the French.

This "domino" theory and all measures to protect U.S. markets abroad were accepted by the Du Ponts. The CIA-financed military overthrow of President Goulart, who threatened to limit foreign profits to 10 percent in Brazil (where Du Pont had a subsidiary and two large plants), was viewed with relief in Wilmington. So also, Johnson's intervention in 1965 with 20,000 "neutral" marines to crush a popular revolt in the Dominican Republic, the "sugar bowl" replacement for Cuba, was viewed warmly by the family. Significantly, American Sugar & Refining Company, in which the Du Ponts held a substantial interest, used the island as a resource for its sugar production.

That same year, another CIA-backed military coup overthrew Indonesia's President Sukarno. Sukarno had resisted political demands made by the United States in exchange for foreign aid, demands that would have ended his nationalization of U.S. and European corporate properties. Sukarno threatened to found a new United Nations of underdeveloped and exploited countries. He was preparing to replace Indonesia's U.S.-trained army with a people's militia, when the army struck first in 1965. Over one million of Sukarno's followers died in one of the greatest bloodbaths in history. The *New York Times* reported that the carnage was so massive that bodies were even clogging the country's canals. As a result, U.S. corporate properties, including the rubber plantations of Du Pont-controlled U.S. Rubber Company, were saved from public ownership.

But that was not all. The new regime of General Suharto put political prisoners to work on the rubber plantations. NBC news, on February 19, 1967, at 6:30 P.M., captured the scene of political prisoners working American corporate-owned rubber fields in Sumatra and Borneo as slave labor under the guns of Suharto's soldiers. The two biggest American corporations on those islands were Goodyear and the U.S. Rubber Company. Two years later Alex Campbell, managing editor of the *New Republic,* upon visiting the "New Order" of Indonesia, reported, "The government plans to send some 60,000 [political prisoners] to forced labor on rubber plantations in Borneo. Perhaps 10,000 have already gone there. They are said to be dying like flies. Meanwhile those still in the camps may be slowly dying of starvation."[63] Among the rubber plantations reportedly involved were those of U.S. Rubber Company, which owns 44,000 acres in Indonesia, and a subsidiary, U.S. Rubber Sumatra Plantations.

In July 1969 President Nixon, who in *Foreign Affairs* magazine, October 1967, termed Indonesia, "containing the region's richest hoard of natural resources," as "the greatest prize in the Southeast Asian area," personally flew to Indonesia to endorse the "progress" of General Suharto. Today, in violation of the same international accords that were used at Nuremberg to convict Alfred Krupp for using Nazi concentration camp prisoners in his munitions plants, U.S. Rubber (now Uniroyal) is allegedly benefiting from the use of thousands of political prisoners as slave labor in the rubber fields of Indonesia. It is unlikely that J. Simpson Dean, brother-in-law of Irénée du Pont, Jr., is unaware of the source of this plantation labor. Dean, a director also of Wilmington Trust, the Du Pont family's bank, sits on the board of Uniroyal with a loyal family lieutenant, J. W. Chinn, Jr., chief executive officer of Wilmington Trust and a director of Irénée du Pont, Jr.'s Greater Wilmington Development Council. Other Du Ponts who are major stockholders in Uniroyal are Lammot du Pont Copeland, Pierre S. du Pont III (Lammot du Pont's eldest son), George P. Edmonds and Colgate Darden, Jr. (Lammot and Irénée du Pont's sons-in-law), and until his death in 1970, Henry B. du Pont. Congressman Pierre S. du Pont IV also owns over $140,000 worth of Uniroyal common. All together, the family holds a controlling block of 18 percent of Uniroyal stock.

The Indonesian coup may have been lucrative for the Du Ponts, but the return would have been minuscule compared to the immediate financial gains won through U.S. intervention in Indochina.

During the 1964 presidential campaign Barry Goldwater's call for the bombing of North Vietnam won him $71,000 in Du Pont family donations, his third largest contribution.[64] Polly Buck, daughter-in-law of Alice du Pont, even called the roll of states at the national convention in San Francisco's Cow Palace that led to Goldwater's nomination. Polly, in fact, was the secretary of the Republican National Committee.

When the "liberal" alternative, President Johnson, carried out Goldwater's threat the following year, Wilmington applauded with enthusiasm. In the heat of the 1965 escalation, the American Conservatives Union pushed for full invasion of North Vietnam and the overthrow of its government. The president of the ACU was Lammot du Pont Copeland, Jr., who was also national treasurer of the archconservative Young Americans for Freedom from 1962 to 1966.

Most of the Du Ponts quietly shared young Copeland's enthusiasm for intervention, but steered clear of the publicity hazards of open promotion. The pro-war leaders in the family were Lammot du Pont Copeland, Jr., his father, Lammot du Pont Copeland, Sr., R. R. M. (Bobby) Carpenter, Jr., and P. S. du Pont III, who was a member of the ultra-conservative Freedoms Foundation. The Du Ponts well understood that Vietnam was the controlling hub of an area—as Secretary of State John Foster Dulles put it in 1954, the first year of direct U.S. intervention—"rich in many raw materials such as tin, oil, rubber, and iron ore. The area has great strategic value."[65]

A year before, on August 4, 1953, President Eisenhower himself had told a conference of the U.S. state governors in Seattle: "Now let us assume that we lost Indochina. . . . The tin and tungsten that we so greatly value from that area would cease coming. . . . So when the United States votes 400 million dollars to help that war, we are not voting a give-away program. We are voting for the cheapest way that we can to prevent the occurrence of something that would be of a most terrible significance to the United States of America, our security, our power and ability to get certain things we need from the riches of the Indochinese territory and from Southeast Asia."

By 1965, Henry Cabot Lodge, Ambassador to the U.S.-installed Diem dictatorship in southern Vietnam, addressed the exclusive Middlesex Club of Cambridge in similar terms. "Geographically," he was reported saying by the Boston *Sunday Globe* on February 28, 1965, "Vietnam stands at the hub of a vast area of the world—Southeast Asia—an area with a population of 249 million persons. . . . He who holds or has influence in Vietnam can affect the future of the Philippines and Formosa to the east, Thailand and Burma with their huge rice surpluses to the west, and Malaysia and Indonesia with their rubber, ore, and tin to the south. . . . Vietnam thus does not exist in a geographical vacuum—from it large storehouses of wealth and population can be influenced and undermined."

But an aspect of more concern to the Du Ponts was the potential Indochina held for capital investment. As Jules Henry explained in the *Nation*: "The establishment throughout Southeast Asia of industrial complexes backed by American capital is sure to have a salutary effect on the development of our foreign involvement: the vastland's cheap labor pool will permit competition with the lower production costs of Chinese and Japanese industry, which have immobilized our trading capabilities in Asia for many years. . . . The destruction of the Vietnamese countryside is the first, and necessary, step to the industrialization of Vietnam and the nationalization of its agriculture."[66]

"After the war," asserted Arthur Tunnell of the Saigon branch of Investors Overseas Services, "there is going to be a big future for American businessmen here."[67] First National City's vice-president Henry M. Sperry agreed. "We believe we're going to win this war," he said, ". . . Afterwards, you'll have a major job of reconstruction on your hands. That will take financing, and financing means banks."[68] That was in 1965. Within five years Du Pont established Du Pont Far East, Inc., with branch offices in Hong Kong, Bangkok (Thailand), Taipei (Taiwan), and Tokyo (Japan). In Chiang Kai-shek's Taiwan, where labor receives very low wages, Wilmington also set up Du Pont Taiwan, Ltd., with a plant busily turning out "Myler" polyester film. In Japan Du Pont had already bought 50 percent interest into two Mitzui Chemicals subsidiaries and established 50 percent interest in two other companies, Showa Neoprene KK and Tokyo Products Company, Ltd. In addition, Du Pont was just expanding its market in Australia, where a subsidiary manufactured and sold pigments, photographic products, and urea herbicides.

These investments all underscored the Du Pont's growing stake in the Asian labor market and hopes for future expansion. Other family interests were also looking to the East. Uniroyal then owned (and still does own, under "perpetuity" leases) some 30,000 acres of crude rubber plantations in Malaysia, a former British colony directly below Vietnam. Uniroyal also owns plants in India and Japan, where it also has controlling interests in Kaisha Company and Sumitomo Naugatuck Kabushiki Company.

Du Pont Company lent itself well to the Vietnam war effort, again, as in previous wars, for a price. The escalation years of 1965 and 1966 resulted in the highest earnings ever achieved by the company, and dividends of $6.00 and $6.75 per share. As Vice-President Henry B. du Pont once put it while addressing the Virginia State Chamber of Commerce, "National Security must not be auctioned to the lowest bidder. . . . There are no bargains in the safeguarding of our freedom."[69]

There were especially no bargains from Du Pont for GI's in Vietnam. Du Pont IMR ("improved military rifle") powder made at the Carney Point, New Jersey, plant was linked to the infamous jamming of M-16 rifles during combat. The Du Pont powder left a residue in rifles which caused the lethal jammings. Finding a higher rate of malfunction with Du

Pont powder in tests in Panama, where conditions are similar to those in Vietnam, Secretary of Defense Robert McNamara reluctantly ordered a switch to Olin Mathieson in 1968.[70] But the Du Ponts were not hurting. Other war contracts, totaling $171 million for 1968 alone, soon found their way to Wilmington. Again, as in the past, it helped to have a friend in Washington. Johnson's new Secretary of Defense was none other than former Du Pont lobbyist Clark Clifford.

Although Wilmington has not released figures of its profits from the Vietnam War, its own 1966 *Annual Report* confirmed that "the Department of Defense military buildup has resulted in the increased use of Du Pont commercial products." Here are the products specifically mentioned: textile fibers, packaging films, photographic films, plastics, dyes, methanol and formaldehyde, elastomers, Freon fluorocarbon products, protective fabrics and finishes, and petroleum chemicals. In addition, the company noted that "increased demands for military explosives and related specialties have resulted in accelerated schedules for increased quantities of products."[71] That year Du Pont's sales scored a new record: $3.19 billion. There is little doubt that the Pentagon's spending had much to do with stimulating the economy, which had recently been stagnating for lack of markets. Du Pont itself received a massive injection of military adrenaline, scoring $161 million in war orders in 1966, up from $69 million in 1964.[72]

The following year, 1967, Du Pont announced it was furnishing the U.S. Army ordnance plant at Parsons, Kansas, with engineering services and production management. Du Pont itself reaped $23 million in war orders, and its subsidiary, Remington Arms, another $156 million.[73] In addition, the company was continuing its operation of the Atomic Energy Commission's Savannah River plant and laboratory. "The major objective of the work," Wilmington reported, "was the production of nuclear materials for national defense, but a substantial effort was devoted to other AEC programs of national interest."[74]

In 1968 a slight breeze from the barren sands of Utah's desert blew in over pasture lands. Silently and swiftly, it passed over some 6,400 sheep peacefully grazing on warm green grass. Within seconds, all were dead, the pasture suddenly resembling a battlefield littered with corpses. And, in fact, that was just what it was.

The sheep were the hapless victims of one of the U.S. Army's newest weapons: XV nerve gas. Produced by the Army using chemicals procured from chemical companies, including Du Pont, the invisible death had escaped from tests at the Army's Dugway Proving Grounds, carried on something as innocent as a breeze. Now the word was out. The U.S.

government was secretly producing chemical weapons in flagrant opposition to most international accords, including the Geneva Convention. As Vice-President Henry B. du Pont had put it just five years before, to suggest "that science and technology serve ends which differ from the common purpose seems to me as fallacious as it is dangerous."[75]

The incident triggered a public outcry, and the Pentagon, first denying then admitting secret research, hurriedly set up a Permanent Chemical Safety Committee. Except for establishing standards for preventing another embarrassing occurrence, this committee resolved nothing. Du Pont's production of internationally outlawed chemical warfare bombs continued, assisted (under independent defense contracts) by Dr. William A. Mosher and Dr. James Moore of the University of Delaware, who also procured rare chemicals for use in the CIA's secret mind-control experiments at some 80 hospitals, prisons and universities around the country. Significantly, the Permanent Chemical Safety Committee was chaired by Du Pont's own production manager, Jake T. Nolen.

Du Pont developed other weapons for the Department of Defense in violation of the Geneva Convention, which the U.S. has conveniently never signed. Besides storing VX nerve gas at its Newport, Indiana, plant, Du Pont had a defense contract for "research and development of a Micro-Gravel concept" for anti-personnel mines similar to small "letter bombs": the mines were to be dropped from overhead planes. This contract, awarded to Du Pont in 1968, contributed to the record $212 million in war orders scored by Du Pont in 1969.[76]

Other Du Pont family interests did as well in 1969. Du Pont-controlled Uniroyal grossed $174 million from the Defense Department that year. Hercules Chemicals, the Du Pont spin-off in which the family held a substantial interest, collected over $179 million for rocket propellants and anti-personnel weapons, including the infamous burning jelly, napalm. Boeing Aircraft, over which former Du Pont chairman Crawford Greenewalt served as a director, raked in over $653 million for its production of B-52's and other aerial weaponry. Henry B. du Pont's North American Aviation, which merged with Rockwell family interests in 1967 to form North American Rockwell, took in $674 million for its production of OU-10 "Bronco" counterinsurgency aircraft, homing optical bombs (TV-guided), F-100's, Condor air-to-surface missiles, and liquid rocket fuels for ICBM's and a score of other missiles. General Motors, in which the family retained an estimated 17 percent holding, collected $584 million for tanks, aircraft engines, rocket launchers, and M-16 rifles. Indeed, Du Pont stockholder ties in G.M. were still so strong that chairman Lammot du Pont Copeland found it important enough to stress at the annual meeting in May 1969 that "Since the divestiture, the G.M. dividends have been paid directly to Du Pont stockholders who retained the G.M. shares distributed to them. Our dividend on common last year was $5.75 and the G.M. dividend was $4.55 per share."[77]

The beneficial effect the Vietnam War had on Du Pont interests can be easily seen by noting the various percentages of total sales the Pentagon's military orders represented for 1969 alone.

For Du Pont Company and its subsidiaries, Pentagon orders in 1969 amounted to 6.8 percent of total sales, or $212 million out of a total $3,078 million.

For Henry B. du Pont's North American Rockwell, Pentagon orders amounted to 28 percent of total sales, or $674.2 million out of a total $2,438 million.

For Uniroyal, Pentagon orders amounted to 14 percent of total sales, or $174.1 million out of a total $1260 million.

For Hercules, Inc., 27 percent or $179.6 million out of a $642 million total.

For Boeing Aircraft, 22 percent, or $653.6 million out of a $2,880 million total.

For Newport News Shipbuilding and Dry Dock Company (a Tenneco subsidiary which has Irénée du Pont's son-in-law, Colgate Darden, as a major stockholder), 13 percent, or $236 million out of a Tenneco total of $1.7 billion.

It is interesting to note that North American Rockwell, which in 1969 was the eighth largest Pentagon contractor, employed 104 high-ranking retired officers. Boeing, which was the ninth largest, employed 169 retired officers. Retired generals and admirals are very useful in contract negotiations with the Pentagon, since 90 percent of all military contracts are personally negotiated rather than awarded on a formally advertised competitive basis.[78]

With their G.M. diversification funds, many Du Ponts also invested in new firms utilizing the latest scientific technology, including computers, which worked on military contracts during the Vietnam era. William H. du Pont, the son of William du Pont, Jr., set up Sci-Tek, Inc., a computer-based operation which took in $15,000 in Navy contracts in 1971, $80,000 in 1972.[79] Emile F. du Pont's Dukane Corporation grossed $20,744 on one Navy contract in 1972 for developing a locater system in jet planes.[80] Reynolds and Richard C. du Pont's All-American Engineering raked in $1.6 million in 1972, bringing its Vietnam era (1964–1972) total to $11 million.

All told, the family's varied corporate interests grossed over 15 billion in

DEFENSE AWARDS (rounded to millions of dollars)*

	1964	1965	1966	1967	1968	1969	1970	1971	1972	Total
E. I. du Pont de Nemours & Co. (including Remington Arms)	64	82	161	180	170	212	162	96	105	1,232
North American (Aviation) Rockwell (Henry B. du Pont, director)	1,000	746	520	689	669	674	707	477	702	6,184
Uniroyal (U.S. Rubber Co.) (J. Simpson Dean, director)	—	—	74	217	154	174	115	66	80	880
Boeing Aircraft (Crawford Greenewalt, director)	1,300	583	914	912	762	653	474	731	1,170	7,499
Hercules, Inc. (J. H. T. McConnell, Christiana Securities)	136	104	119	193	171	179	125	115	112	1,254
All American Engineering**(a) (Reynolds du Pont, R. C. du Pont, Jr., director)	3.4	1.5	.6	1.3	.7	NA	.6	.5(b)	1.6(b)	10.2

TOTAL = 17 Billion

*100 Companies and Their Subsidiary Corporations (1965–72), (a) 500 Contractors Listed According to Net Value of Military Prime Contract Awards for Research, Development, Test, and Evaluations, U.S. Department of Defense; (b) Defense/Aerospace Contract Quarterly, op. cit.

** Figures are rounded to nearest one tenth of a million.

war contracts between 1964, the year of the first arms buildup, and 1972. Of the top ten war contractors, three (North American Rockwell, Boeing, and General Motors) represented large investments of the Du Pont family. Of the top forty Pentagon contractors, eight (North American Rockwell, Boeing, General Motors, Newport News Shipbuilding, Du Pont, Hercules, and Uniroyal), or one-fifth, were Du Pont interests. Du Pont Company alone reaped over $1 billion in war contracts. One Du Pont enthusiast recently became very flustered at the suggestion of war profiteering by his favorite family. "I challenge anyone to show proof of any money made off this tragic war!"

Thirteen

THE CRISIS YEARS

1. GUARDING THE HOMEFRONT

On a warm starless night in the summer of 1968, a tense quiet hung over the city of Wilmington. Nearby, like a sleeping giant, rested the Delaware River, its black waters still simmering from the heat of the day. Across the river, along the New Jersey banks, the Du Pont Chamber Works could be seen in the distance, flaring orange and yellow against the night. From that vast city of yellow lights spewed forth the tall, bright-blue arc that traced the Delaware Memorial Bridge rising to span the river, then reaching down to touch the shores of the state of Delaware. Over the blue arc, a long steady stream of yellow auto lights quietly flowed. But only a few got off at the Wilmington exit.

Du Pont Highway, the main artery leading into Wilmington, carried little traffic beyond an occasional army jeep passing by on patrol, enforcing the 10:00 P.M. curfew. The capital city of chemicals was silent that night, its skyline dark and somber. No lights radiated from Du Pont Company's Nemours Building, nor from the Du Pont family's Bank of Delaware nor their Delaware Trust Building. Even the lobby of their Hotel Du Pont was dimly lit, expecting few visitors. Only the police headquarters in City Hall a block away betrayed any sign of life.

There were only a few policemen inside, all murmuring complaints about the heat and none bothering to look busy. They all looked very much alike in their uniforms, having the rough look of men who had reached middle age prematurely. Like chicks around a hen, they gathered around the desk sergeant, a big man with drooping jowls and small eyes reddened with fatigue. Like most of the men, he hadn't had much rest since the curfew was imposed four months before. It wasn't that the work was so challenging. Hardly, especially with the National Guard on hand to help. It was just the boring nightly routine of endless arrests and bookings that was tiring.

The sergeant had just finished checking the night's list of arrests when a thin, unimpressive-looking man walked quietly through the entrance and approached the desk. The man, a Caucasian, was slight of figure, with a dark suit that hung loosely about his slender shoulders. His short black hair was plastered down in that conservative, no-nonsense style of a small businessman in his mid-forties who has already lost his youthful flair. He had a quiet manner about him as he spoke with thin, weak lips, his small eyes peering timidly behind light-rimmed glasses.

The policemen scratched their heads and looked questioningly at each other as their visitor stated his desire to post bail for four young Black prisoners. The sergeant knew the case: the four were part of a party of seven Black men charged with illegal entry. They had claimed they were fleeing from unknown assailants and were forced to take refuge in an occupied home. Police, on the scene on a supposed tip-off, and National Guardsmen reported hearing gunshots and discovered the van the men were driving was peppered with bullet holes, but they were unable to find anyone but the seven Blacks. So the seven were arrested and charged with illegal entry.

The sergeant looked up at the man, not sure he wanted to be bothered, and told him to sit down. The visitor sat patiently for half an hour or so and then rose and quietly approached the sergeant again about bail.

"Bail's pretty high, you know," warned the sergeant.

The man seemed undisturbed. "I'll put up my yacht as collateral," he answered.

The sergeant was startled for a moment. Then he broke into a large infectious smile that caught on the other policemen's faces.

"Your yacht, eh?" he said. "Sit down please." The visitor again complied. After a while he nervously began casting glances at his watch. Finally, after the sergeant had left, he got up and approached the other policemen.

"I'm sorry," he said quietly, "I really can't stay here all night, so I'll just have to let my lawyer handle this." He took out a card from his wallet. "When you know how much the bail is set for, please contact me."

The policemen's eyes widened as they read the card:

IRÉNÉE du PONT, Jr.

The four prisoners were released within half an hour.

This incident, hitherto unpublished, may well shock some readers, for direct involvement by Delaware's richest family in the personal trials of Black Delawarians has indeed been rare. That the four young Blacks involved were all leading political activists, in fact, makes Irénée's actions unprecedented in the family's 200-year history. Yet these were unprecedented days for the Du Ponts, days of mounting defeat abroad in the most unpopular war in the country's history, days of social disintegration, upheaval, and mounting rebellion at home, even in Delaware.

Irénée Jr.'s providing bail for these four Black activists, an event so completely without precedent in the affairs of the Du Ponts, was the inevitable culmination of the family's attempt to control social discontent in Wilmington, the capital city of their empire. The discontent had been sharpening in response to underlying economic and social trends that were transforming cities everywhere in the country. But now some members of the family were aware of what was taking place in Wilmington and were actively trying to head off a social explosion.

Indeed, since World War I, when agricultural mechanization and northern urban industrialization spurred the first rural migrations to Delaware's only real city, Wilmington, the Du Ponts had been involved in trying to cool the smoldering coals of social fusion, openly fearing the revolt against established order that might someday be kindled. In the Twenties Pierre du Pont initiated the state's extensive school building program, financed by first himself, then a graduated income tax (which he initiated as Tax Commissioner), while Alfred I. du Pont led a drive to pass state social security legislation for the elderly. Both projects, although accomplishing their goals, did little to uplift the lives of Wilmington's growing Black population.

With the Depression, Wilmington was hit with its second great influx of rural migrants, as well as hordes of unemployed transients from other cities. Once again Pierre was on hand, worriedly serving on Delaware's Unemployment Relief Commission. But it was not until World War II that white workers began deserting Wilmington in growing numbers, moving to that automobile-created milk-white culture called the suburb. Meanwhile the Black influx into the city continued at its usual steady rate. Again, Pierre du Pont donned his governmental garb in 1944 and watched over the state's financial development as Tax Commissioner until 1949.

Pierre's leaving the Tax Commission renewed what can be termed Wilmington's "era of neglect" by the Du Ponts. Preoccupied with their own company's hectic expansion in the South and overseas, and smug about the economic prosperity in the suburbs, the family as a whole ignored the increasing decay of Wilmington's central residential area, exactly at a time when influx into the city by poor southern Blacks and outflow to the suburbs by working-class whites were greater than ever. Of the five Du Ponts who were the most politically active during the Fifties, Francis V. du Pont (the state's leading Republican), Alexis du Pont Bayard (the state's leading Democrat), J. H. Tyler McConnell (Democratic nominee for governor in 1956), E. I. du Pont (Republican State Committeeman) and Reynolds du Pont (Republican legislator), none showed any real recognition of, much less active concern for, Wilmington's economic disintegration and the subsequent hardships befalling its Black residents.

In fact, four Du Ponts—Nicholas R., son of Eugene du Pont, Jr.; Pierre S. III, son of Lammot du Pont; Lammot du Pont Copeland, Sr.; and George T. Weymouth, an in-law—were identified before the Senate Finance Committee in 1954 as sharing in a $549,375 "windfall" profit off construction of the Clifton Park Manor housing project in Wilmington. Later, investigators raised the "swindle" figure to $898,000 on a paid-in capital investment of $7,325. It seems the Clifton Park project was given a guarantee on an FHA-approved mortgage of $5,980,000, but the actual cost of construction allegedly came to only $5,082,000.

By 1960, Blacks, according to official statistics, made up 26 percent of Wilmington's population,[1] a conservative estimate. This population, made up mostly of unskilled laborers and unemployed poor, was concentrated in an overcrowded area where over 37 percent of the housing was substandard and still rapidly deteriorating.[2] In the Black area monthly rents had risen 95 percent since 1950, from a median $37.30 to $72.60, while white areas of the city endured a rent increase of "only" 36 percent, from $52.40 to $71.10.[3] This Duchy of Du Pont—until the 1950's a segregated state *de jure,* and until the late 1960's *openly* practicing segregation (it is still a segregated state *de facto,* but covertly through income lines)—offered Wilmington Blacks a median income of only $3,813 a year in 1960; white median income, on the other hand, boosted by Du Pont's army of highly paid chemists, was $6,190.[4]

Of all the Du Ponts, only Henry B. du Pont, scion of North American Aviation, and J. H. Tyler McConnell, Hercules director and son-in-law of William du Pont, Jr., seemed to have some sense of the impending economic disaster—and social danger—in Wilmington's decay. This does not mean that urban decay was not noticed by other Du Ponts; in 1960 that would have been an impossible task for any resident of the Wilmington area. However, Henry and McConnell were clearly the first Du Ponts to try to initiate a change in the family's policy of neglect—but it was a change clearly based on the business ethic and built on the need for a proper social climate for both the family and Du Pont's international headquarters.

On October 4, 1960, Du Pont Company led twelve of Delaware's other leading employers in sponsoring a slide show, "Which Way Wilmington?" Out of the meeting came the Greater Wilmington Development Council, brainchild of Joseph Chinn, Jr., chairman of Wilmington Trust, Edwin P. Neilan, president of the Bank of Delaware, and two other Du Pont executives. Henry and McConnell, meanwhile, advised and consented as GWDC's chairman and president respectively.

GWDC's motives were obvious to everyone right from the start. "The Development Council's power base is among the community's top business leaders and professional people," editorialized the Du Pont-owned Wilmington *Evening Journal,* "who have drawn together out of enlightened self-interest as much as anything. Predictably, this approach will be hardheaded and economic."[5] And narrow-minded. While developing working papers that showed the high proportion of jobless among Blacks, the GWDC could only conclude that "unemployed labor is an economic waste, and an economic waste is a drain on the economy"[6] through the loss of purchasing power. The *human* misery involved in joblessness went unobserved. GWDC's employment program, token at best, met dismal failure.

In programs directly affecting corporate interests, however, GWDC was more successful. Henry, after all, was one of the more farsighted members of Delaware's State Goals Commission and State Planning Commission, personally shaping the lives of half a million Delawarians. In November 1961 GWDC announced a fifty-year redevelopment plan for the city, including a Midtown Wilmington Plan, a Pilot Plan, and an elaborate design envisioning Wilmington as a major metropolitan center connecting New Jersey, Pennsylvania, and Maryland. Then, as now, it was a vision dear to the hearts of many leading Du Ponts. One Du Pont, in fact, William Winder Laird, Jr., son of Mary Belin du Pont, became so excited about Wilmington's redevelopment prospects that he began making speeches to the Chamber of Commerce on "Urban Renewal Through Private Initiative—Dream or Reality?" Laird was also determined to make it his own profitable reality by buying up over $1 million worth of center-city properties.[7] Involved in Laird's real estate speculation was another Du Pont in-law, George T. Weymouth, also a member of GWDC, and Eleuthère I. du Pont, son of Francis V. du Pont and grandson of Senator T. Coleman du Pont.

Another speculator was former Lieutenant Governor John W. Rollins, owner (with his brother) of Rollins, Inc., a company in which Eleuthère I. du Pont's Sigma Capital Shares held a 5,000-share investment. In late 1966 Rollins even submitted a proposal to turn the west city center commerical area into a $100 million complex, offering to work closely with the GWDC.

In 1965 Henry B. and William du Pont ushered Block Blight, Inc., under GWDC's wing. Founded in 1956 for the purpose of buying, rehabilitating, and reselling slum housing, Block Blight could claim only 166 finished homes by 1965. Strapped to the ideology that possession of private property is the first step toward urban renewal, Block Blight tried unsuccessfully to bring middle-class families, that all-important tax base for Wilmington's powerful, back into the city. Among its directors were state Senator Reynolds du Pont and banker C. Douglas Buck, Jr., another grandson of Senator T. Coleman du Pont.

GWDC's interest in Block Blight, however, reflected a growing concern about the restlessness of Wilmington's poor, who were already living in overcrowded, dilapidated housing. Rents had increased in the Black community, and inflation in general had reached intolerable levels, so that even President Johnson was urging surtaxes to cool the economy. Yet Wilmington's poor saw corporate and banking interests in the state thriving, imbued with elaborate plans for the state's future, including the future of the Black community.

Also, there was the Vietnam War, with draft boards dipping into the cream of Black and poor white youth and offering no ear for legal challenges to a draft for an undeclared war. In fact, for thousands of Wilmington's Black youth, awakened to political consciousness by the civil rights movement, the Vietnamese represented no "enemy," despite the ominous exhortations of drum-beating white cold warriors. Moreover, the Vietnam War had produced few jobs for Black Delawareans. Even in the peak year of 1969 the war brought only $55 million in defense business into the state.[8]

For the poor, Wilmington was a city of coordinated frustration. Discrimination in housing was rampant. Blacks who tried to move out of the center city into the better homes of the suburbs were often subjected to harassment. In previously all-white Collins Park, a Black home was bombed twice, the first time being damaged, then destroyed. Blacks justifiably felt their rights were seldom protected by state, county, or city police. As for the courts, many Blacks felt they had found little justice but plenty of Du Pont "presence," carrying the judicial traditions of James M. Tunnel of Wilmington Trust Company, former judge of the Superior Court and U.S. senatorial candidate in 1966, and G. Burton Pearson (who married Lammot du Pont's daughter in 1968), former judge on the State Supreme Court and past president of the Delaware Bar Association.

Liberal lawyers were few and far between in Delaware, and again the Du Pont domination of the legal system was all too obvious: William S. Potter, a Du Pont in-law, was, like Pearson, past president of the Delaware Bar Association; Edmund N. Carpenter, nephew of Margaretta L. du Pont, was also a top member of the Delaware Bar, as well as a former deputy attorney general, a member of the Delaware Law Enforcement and Planning Agency, and former chairman of a state commission to reform jury service. As for juries, Irénée du Pont, Jr., was foreman of the Grand Jury, and

W. Laird Stabler, a Du Pont relative, prosecuted as deputy attorney general from 1961 to 1964, was Master of the Family Court from 1964 to 1965, and served as a Republican state representative until his election as attorney general in 1968.

Both parties in the state offered no avenue for reform. The Republican Party was totally dominated by the Du Ponts, the outstanding leaders having been Francis V. du Pont, Reynolds du Pont, state Senate majority leader, Eleuthère I. du Pont, treasurer of the Republican State Finance Committee from 1953 to 1964, and A. Felix du Pont, Jr. The Democratic Party, with William S. Potter and Alexis I. du Pont Bayard dominating the state chairmanship since 1956, offered little in the way of relief for Blacks; the weight of Dixie Delawarians, led by former U.S. Senator J. Allen Frear, Jr., V. B. Derrickson, and Charles Terry, was also felt. As governor, Terry had even worsened the plight of Black civil rights in Delaware.

Wilmington saw its first civil disturbance in the summer of 1967. Although it was a minor outbreak of anger in the frustrated Black community, minor especially when compared to the scores of cities burning from Black rebellions at that time, the flooding of the area with shotgun-toting state and city police revealed Terry's "overkill" policy. On Terry's urging, the legislature on August 4 passed the Emergency Riot Act, giving the governor sweeping powers.

Although there is no doubt that the Emergency Riot Act was approved by GWDC members, Terry's crudity and openly racist posture ran head on against GWDC's more sophisticated recommendations and policies. The southern Delawarian's feeble response to the future prescriptions of northern Delaware industrialists and financiers gathered in the GWDC, stirred a grumble of dissatisfaction in the mansions along the Brandywine. The futile efforts to move Terry on the GWDC path—efforts on the part of Du Pont in-laws like G. Burton Pearson, Jr., chairman of Terry's State Goals Commission, C. Douglas Buck, Jr., member of the State Human Relations Commission, and Richard P. Sanger, member of Mayor Babiarz's Advisory Committee on Urban Renewal—convinced many Du Ponts, especially Henry B., that the occupant of the governor's mansion had to be changed. Henry began looking for a Republican candidate, and he didn't have to look far. In fact, he didn't even have to look beyond his own company.

Many are called, but few are chosen in Delaware. Russell B. Peterson was one of the chosen. A $70,000 Du Pont executive, Peterson was among Henry's intimate circle who had risen with the GWDC into the upper ranks of the Republican machine. Having harbored designs on high political office for years, Peterson had worked hard developing his liberal reputation, even at a threat to his business career. In 1959 his modest plan for the upgrading of only four Blacks in Du Pont Company was rejected by Du Pont's management as too radical. This temporary setback, however, turned out to be a boost for Peterson the following year when the Du Ponts, responding to President Eisenhower's personal appeal for their support of racial integration in industry (since many of their plants were in the South), adopted the "Peterson plan."

Peterson's first step toward the governor's mansion came in 1966, when Henry appointed him head of the GWDC's Neighborhood Improvement Program. This $750,000 "experiment" aimed at developing a dialogue between Wilmington's power elite and the Black community. Local residents were hired as street workers to contact their neighbors, identify problems, and recommend solutions. "Those of us who are involved in operating this program," Peterson explained to his fellow GWDC members early in 1967, "and those residents who are to be assisted by it are virtually in two separate worlds. . . . We're going to place heavy emphasis on the job problem this year in an attempt to involve local business and industry." To Peterson, the GWDC would "become the dominant force in the solution of social problems."

Although Peterson's "job program," the GWDC-sponsored Job Opportunities Center, failed to produce more than twenty-six jobs in an area (East Side, West Side, and Northeast Wilmington) where unemployment officially topped 17 percent, his smooth style of operating impressed many younger Du Ponts, including Irénée du Pont, Jr., and Pierre S. du Pont IV. The appearance of reform, rather than results, was what the family endorsed.

Of the two, Irénée undoubtedly carried more weight in family circles. He had moved up since taking his father's chair on the board of directors in 1959 at the age of 39. He succeeded 80-year-old Donaldson Brown on Du Pont's finance committee in 1965, and rose to the executive committee as a vice-president in 1967. By then, as one of the richest Du Ponts, Irénée was also a director of Wilmington Trust and Christiana Securities, and a trustee of the Longwood Foundation, the $60 million philanthropy set up by the late Pierre S. du Pont II.

To a great extent, Irénée was Henry B.'s protégé in business and community affairs. In business, although certainly wealthy enough to stand on his own, Irénée usually followed Henry's approach in Du Pont Company, Christiana Securities, and Wilmington Trust. In community affairs, Irénée followed his cousin's lead in the Longwood Foundation and GWDC. This in no way implied that Irénée did not have a mind of his own. He did, and a rather sharp one at that. It merely meant Irénée essentially agreed with Henry's general outlook on life.

As old Henry's health steadily deteriorated, Irénée took over more and more of his cousin's tasks and eventually his posts. He also took up Henry's enthusiasm for Russell Peterson, who by 1967 was a member of the Republican state finance committee.

Peterson's unannounced candidacy was not without its trials, however, and interestingly enough, some of his most potent opposition came from Lammot du Pont Copeland, Sr., president of Du Pont.

In both domestic and foreign policy, conservative Copeland did not share Peterson's liberal posture. In fact, Copeland had found Charles Terry likable enough for him to accompany the governor to the National Governors' Conference that year in order to urge high textile tariffs to fight the Kennedy Round's proposed reduction.

Lammot made his first open move against Peterson's bid on October 20, 1967, when he announced, as Du Pont president, that "An employee of the Du Pont Company who becomes governor or lieutenant governor should resign."[9] The statement was made on the pretext of preserving Du Pont from political charges of openly dominating the state, and it was pointed out to Lammot that New Castle County Executive William T. Conner was on "leave of absence" as a Du Pont attorney while governing about two-thirds of Delaware's population. Conner, as well as many company officials in the state legislature, had not been asked to resign. Copeland could only respond to the charges of unfairly pressuring Peterson by weakly assuring, "We encourage employees to take an active role in public affairs"[10]—in Peterson's case, at the price of his job.

A month later, in a speech before the American Petroleum Institute, Copeland made it clear just how different his approach to social problems was from Peterson's. "There are some people today who ignore a law if they don't happen to approve of it," he asserted. "I haven't heard any loud expression of public outrage when this happens—on a picket line, for example, but such tolerance has never been extended to business."[11]

Copeland's ideology was certainly no different from Henry B. du Pont's, but his methods for dealing with current community problems were. While Copeland raged against the rebellions, Henry's GWDC gave $166,000 to the Wilmington Youth Emergency Action Council (WYEAC), an organization of local "gang" youth with the goal of changing "the relationship between the official establishment of Wilmington and the youth who believe that Wilmington does not care for them and in turn don't give a damn for Wilmington." Copeland was effectively pitting himself in the political arena against policies and plans then being developed by the GWDC leadership.

Unfortunately for Copeland, his political stance came at a most inopportune time in his business career. Under his leadership, Du Pont had entered a period of very real crisis, one endangering the entire family fortune.

Most of Du Pont's ailments had little to do with Copeland personally, resulting more from congenital diseases of big business. Since the nineteenth century, the Du Ponts had always been guided by the rule of thumb of a 10 percent return on invested capital. "I would rather have a $3 billion business at 10 percent return than a $6 billion business at a 5 percent return or even a 6 percent return,"[12] Crawford Greenewalt had once said. This was entirely possible during the years Du Pont was still expanding horizontally and vertically as a product innovator. From World War I through the Twenties and Thirties Du Pont expanded into chemicals, rubber, artificial fibers, and automobiles (General Motors). In 1955 Crawford managed to score the company's postwar high, a yield of 13.8 percent. But after that Du Pont's troubles began.

First, Du Pont was by then a growing giant of assets, and maintaining a 10 percent yield on so huge an amount of invested capital required a constant expansion of sales to match the company's increase in assets. Meanwhile, technological developments were eroding costs—and prices at the same time. This need for increased sales was translatable into a need for increased markets. Here Du Pont met an unfamiliar problem—competition.

In the United States two dozen other companies were now producing nylon and other artificial fibers, often at lower prices than Du Pont because their plants were newer and used more efficient cost (labor) saving technology. "We are probably better than ever," commented chairman Crawford Greenewalt in 1967, "but there is no doubt about our competitors' technical sophistication. We have lost some of our competitive margin."[13] In 1961, the year Du Pont's earnings fell to 8.1 percent, Celanese Corporation even produced a plastic superior to Du Pont's Debrin acetal resin, successfully beating back a Du Pont patent suit while also introducing an acetate rayon to compete with Du Pont's viscose rayon.

Abroad, in Europe and Japan, labor costs were even lower, and revived indigenous industries were moving to capture their native markets and even those beyond their borders. Both Crawford Greenewalt and Lammot du Pont Copeland tried to meet this second challenge by expanding Du Pont abroad, even buying into some Japanese firms. But stiff competition from European and Japanese companies continued to grow.

The Kennedy Round tariff cuts only exacerbated this dilemma. Designed to open overseas markets for American farm produce, tobacco, and aluminum, the new tariffs cut down the legal walls that had previously protected the American chemical corporations. Copeland played a low-key role in the early tariff battles in Washington, sending only one or two letters to

Congress while Monsanto, Westinghouse, and other smaller companies were very aggressive. This may be because Copeland recognized that Du Pont was not one industry, but many industries. While the rayon and dyes departments definitely encountered difficulties, the paints and finishes departments were not affected, and film and cellophane departments, which were not into exports, were not immediately influenced by imports. And cushioned by Vietnam War orders, the explosives department felt nothing. In fact, the 1961–1965 chemicals boom hid Du Pont's mounting crisis. Only after Du Pont was deprived of 30 percent of its earnings through the G.M. divestiture in 1965, and only after foreign textiles began entering the American market, did Copeland finally launch an aggressive opposition to reciprocal trade in an attempt to save and expand Du Pont's foreign and domestic textile markets.

This was only one example of Copeland's personal leadership failings. There were others, but all of them were coupled with the albatross of Du Pont's own size. The problem of bigness was one of the main reasons for Du Pont's loss of reputation as the leading innovator in the industry. As Crawford Greenewalt observed in 1967, "one of the penalties of size is that it's now hard to develop a product that can make such a big impact."[14] A new product would simply not bulk enough to greatly affect Du Pont's earnings, which by then had slipped from 13.7 percent in 1955 to 7.9 percent, far below the family's traditional 10 percent rule of thumb.

Ironically, Copeland tried to answer the problem of bigness with even further bigness. During his first year as president he increased capital expenditures by 50 percent, from 1962's $245 million to $370 million in 1963. In 1964 he eased off to $290 million, but by the following year capital expenditures were on the rise again to $327 million. In 1966 Copeland spent a colossal $531 million on plant and equipment, reducing Du Pont's net cash and marketable securities from $624 million to $432 million in one year. By midsummer of 1967 Du Pont's liquid assets had dropped to $227 million.

The reason for Du Pont's drop in liquid assets was Copeland's rigid adherence to another Du Pont tradition—the financing of all expansion out of earnings on hand. This practice allowed Du Pont to be free of debt and bankers, the clan jealously preserving its control of the company's destiny and board of directors. As Russell Pippin, Du Pont vice-president and director, explained to the New York Society of Securities Analysts, "The Du Pont Company down through the years has been noted for conservative financial management; we do not take exception to these views."[15]

Much of Copeland's construction expenditure went to finance overseas plant expansion, but most went to expand domestic operations. Unfortunately for Du Pont, and for Copeland in particular, it appears not enough went into modernizing existing production lines. Rather than improving what he already had by installing the most advanced, cost-saving technology, Copeland made his giant bigger. This produced disastrous results when the economy slowed up in 1966: Copeland had expanded Du Pont's fiber plants exactly when sales were declining, creating huge surpluses.

Through the Kennedy Tariff Round cuts, the textile industry had been sacrificed for foreign markets needed in other industries. This resulted in a flood of foreign imports which hurt Du Pont's textile customers, on whom Du Pont depended for one-third of its sales volume. Orders for Du Pont products declined by as much as 6 percent in 1966. This decrease in sales was made worse by domestic competition. Armed with new patents and those released by Du Pont to avoid anti-trust prosecution, domestic competitors were giving Du Pont a run for its profits. These included the giant oil corporations, who were going into petrochemicals and plastics. A lack of markets caused overproduction and excess inventories in textiles; prices dropped in synthetic textiles around the country, also forcing Du Pont's prices down even further, as much as 17 percent in nylon and 40 percent in Dacron.

In these price wars, Copeland, following the postwar tradition of evading charges of being a trust that underpriced competitors (and a longer tradition of maximizing profits), didn't lead any reduction in prices. And glued to this tradition, Du Pont lost the initiative—and some markets with it. Furthermore, the price erosion reduced Du Pont's dollar income from sales, and the sales volume was unable to increase fast enough to keep pace with the cost of the chemical giant's output, even though Du Pont was now functioning at only 70 percent of capacity (this left 30 percent of the company's machinery idle while depreciating). Capital costs thus rose, aggravated by the inflation which the Vietnam War was heating to a boil. Here again, Copeland's traditionalism crippled his reign. Instead of shifting research funds to existing production processes in order to find ways of lowering costs and raising productivity, he maintained the traditional heavy investment in basic research for long-term development. This approach lacked the flexibility to shift quickly into new markets or even to retain old ones. With dollar sales down and production costs up, Du Pont's profits fell 4.4 percent, depressing earnings. Accordingly, the attractiveness of Du Pont stock to investors also fell: the market value of Du Pont common declined by more than 100 points, or $4.6 billion. In one year, Delaware's richest family saw 40 percent of the value of their Du Pont stock disappear.

Copeland's ominous tidings in April 1967 that market problems "can well be with us for at least another year" proved an understatement in subsequent years. But 1967 was bad enough for the besieged president. Profits fell 24 percent in the first quarter. By June Du Pont's stock had fallen 50 percent from its 1964 high of $293.75; now a share was worth only $153.23. Moreover, the plunge of the big stock pulled down the market's entire bellwether index, leaving Du Pont still the highest priced blue chip stock on the Dow-Jones industrial average.

To add to Copeland's woes, Corfam, Du Pont's new artificial leather for shoes, had not panned out after an investment of over $60 million. "Get set to be swept off your feet," Du Pont ads announced in newspapers across the country in 1964, "Du Pont invites you to 'step into tomorrow.'" Potential buyers were swept off their feet, all right, but by the prices. Corfam shoes were just as expensive as leather, selling for $40. At that price a customer could buy instead top-grain leather. To make matters worse, one of Corfam's supposed attributes, shape retention, backfired: customers complained Corfam shoes never felt "broken in." And while Copeland was unable to reduce its manufacturing costs, Goodrich introduced a cheaper "Aztran" competitor that was already finding a market among brand-name shoe makers.

Corfam's monumental failure—a financial loss of $80 million to $100 million—was only a reflection of the general failure of Copeland's campaign to develop a direct consumer market. Throughout its long history, Du Pont had sold over 95 percent of its products to other businesses. The consumer was generally left untouched, and the Du Pont identity of its products was lost along the retailing way. Copeland, believing that here lay an untapped resource for needed liquid capital, strove to change Du Pont's traditional policy, explaining that the company was "making a more concentrated effort to get to the customer."[16] "Everybody who is anybody at Du Pont," noted *Business Week* in November 1963, "is said to be on notice to submit any consumer product ideas for consideration."[17] Copeland established a Consumer Products Division in his first year in office, placing it under the auspices of the Fabrics and Finishes Department, and moved lawn and garden products and "Zerex" antifreeze there from the Industrial Biochemicals Department. He also moved the new division into electronics, cellulose springs, and Duco mending cement, and poured immense amounts into plants to make old and new chemicals for chain and department store products.

This move into the slippery consumer market was Copeland's only break with family business tradition, and ironically, it proved to be his greatest failure. While the direction was economically sound in principle, considering that competitors like Monsanto were using similar diversified marketing techniques to achieve flexibility in gathering liquid earnings and greater profit margins, it was unwise in the light of the concrete economic situation at *that time,* a time of beginning economic contraction. As the 1967 *Annual Report,* commenting on a 3 percent drop in sales and a 20 percent decline in earnings per common share, summed up, "the year 1967 was disappointing for Du Pont."

Yet Copeland stubbornly plowed on, refusing to abandon projects like Corfam, pouring more and more money into new products for markets that were not there, frantically spending $60 million in advertising in 1967 to try to create the markets that would not appear, announcing another $20 million construction project for the new Brandywine Building in downtown Wilmington to house some 2,000 Du Pont employees and commercial tenants by 1971, expanding out of reserves and earnings, helping to reduce stock value, and refusing to borrow.

Copeland even had still newer products ready for production—Zeset (which shrinkproofs woolen fabrics), nylon shutters and plastic vanity tops, curtains that change color and density when the sun hits; fiber that screens out salt and other impurities from water; ski jackets—when his political opposition to the GWDC's candidate, Russell Peterson, broke the final straw and ushered in the confrontation of December 1967.

Copeland's opposition to Peterson's ambitions inevitably brought him into opposition with the concern of other members of the family for banking the fires of social discontent in Wilmington. The point of this concern was to maintain a climate for, as *Business Week* so aptly put it, "the smooth functioning at the top of Du Pont [which] contributes to its efficiency."[18]

The rebellion of the oppressed Black community in July 1967 made GWDC members believe the implementation of their policies was even more urgent. In November, the same month Copeland was denouncing lawbreakers, Henry B. du Pont as president of the Longwood Foundation granted $500,000 to the GWDC Housing Corporation for renovation of the Asbury Heights area of Wilmington. But the unnoticed details of GWDC's plans revealed Henry's true intent for the poor Black community. Of some eighty dwelling units, the GWDC contracted for thirty, being permitted by Section 221-d-3 of the federal housing code to rent the renovated homes for $90 to $140 per month and also receive federal assistance. Relocation, not betterment, was GWDC's plan for Wilmington's poor Blacks. It was part of a conscious effort to force the poor out of the city and lure the stable (and taxpaying) middle-class to return. This was the corporate reason behind the GWDC's support for "open housing." "As the GWDC has pointed out," editorialized the *News-Journal* in late 1966, "there is the economic and social health of the community. Industries in New Castle County are already having difficulty hiring qualified Negroes because of lack of housing opportunities." The economic and social health of Du Pont and their top management necessitated replacing the racist crudity of Charles Terry with the subtlety of a reliable Du Pont executive, Russell Peterson.

In view of his poor performance at the Du Pont helm, Copeland put himself in a most unfavorable situation by obstructing the GWDC candidate. There were few family members who subscribed to his methods politically or businesswise. Among the family elders who installed Copeland into office, Crawford Greenewalt, George P. Edmonds, and W. W. Laird, Jr., all supported the GWDC's policies and may well have been disillusioned with Copeland's reign. Walter Carpenter, Jr., and Henry F. du Pont, both over 80, were inactive in the company's affairs, and W. Sam Carpenter III, and GWDC members Emile F. du Pont and H. Rodney Sharp, Jr., offered little enthusiasm for Copeland's policies. Irénée du Pont, Jr., although maintaining his personal friendship with Copeland, was quietly at odds with him concerning political and economic style. Copeland was clearly isolated in the family hierarchy.

Copeland's public statement attacking Peterson's job was in October 1967. His attack on the rebellious "who ignore a law" came in November. A month later, in the last week of December, Copeland attended the Du Pont board meeting which all but ended his active career.

Whatever negotiations or possible demands may have been made preceding or during the meeting went unrecorded in the official minutes and it may be true that no record was even needed. But one thing is clear: when the family leaders emerged from the large board room, Lammot du Pont Copeland, Sr., was no longer president of Du Pont. To the shock of most business leaders across the country, the Du Ponts released an announcement that Copeland had resigned the presidency and was assuming the semi-retirement spot of the chairmanship from Greenewalt, who also stayed on as a director. And replacing Copeland was an experienced and able vice-president who had risen to active leadership within Henry B.'s GWDC that year: Charles Brelsford McCoy.

Bald, lean, 58-year-old "Brel" McCoy was billed as "the first real outsider" president of Du Pont. Walter Carpenter's brother, R. R. M. Carpenter, it was pointed out, had married into the family and so Walter could not be considered a real outsider. McCoy's brother, on the other hand, only became a Du Pont production manager. His sister only married the company's secretary, Henry Bush, and his father, John W. McCoy, was only a former Du Pont director, vice-president, and member of the executive committee. Du Pont never mentioned, however, that McCoy's brother-in-law, Henry Bush, was actually a Du Pont. Bush's mother was Joanna (du Pont) Bradford, daughter of Eleuthera du Pont and sister-in-law to both Henry B. du Pont and Alfred I. du Pont. But even that does not tell all. McCoy's own son had married a Du Pont. McCoy's daughter-in-law was the former Carol V. Kitchell. Her maternal grandmother was Margaretta du Pont, sister of Irénée, Pierre, and Lammot du Pont and wife of Ruly Carpenter. Carol's mother, Irene du Pont Carpenter, had married William J. Kitchell before going on to plow through two more marriages with Richard P. Morgan and J. Avery Draper III. Carol was the offspring of her mother's first marriage. Her father, William J. Kitchell, was a leading director of the family's Blue Ridge Mutual Fund, of which E. I. du Pont, Emile F. du Pont, and Donald F. Carpenter were also directors. Clearly, Charles McCoy was no outsider to the Du Ponts.

McCoy's first three months in office coincided with the first rise in the company's sales and earnings since the second quarter of 1966, and some of the family saw this as a hopeful sign for the future. During these first three months of 1968 progress also seemed to be underway on their political front as well. Peterson continued his unofficial campaign, quietly resigning from positions which could become a magnet for charges of Du Pont domination. He withdrew from the Republican State Finance Committee, Reynolds du Pont taking his place, and also resigned from the GWDC leadership, Irénée du Pont, Jr., replacing him there.

Irénée also began playing a more active part in Wilmington affairs. In February 1968 he hosted a dinner for Jackie Robinson held by the Delaware chapter of the National Conference of Christians and Jews. "It may come as a surprise to you, as it did to me," Irénée told the gathering, "to read in the classified ads that traditional organizations of racial hate are still advertising for members."[19] Some of the Ku Klux Klan ads Irénée was referring to, however, had appeared in his family's own *News-Journal* papers.

Three years later, when Irénée was himself a director of the *News-Journal*, Klan ads were still being smeared across its pages. Yet Irénée pursued his goal of restoring Wilmington's calm climate and, as one family historian put it, "disciplined populace," with unmitigated gall. "A major target for our work with these official groups," he explained as Robinson and others looked on, "is to further develop two-way communication between community factions and the police."[20] Tensions between the Black community and the front-line hired guardians of the Du Pont "order," the police, were smoldering.

Irénée realized that the fire hose of diplomacy was needed if the community-oriented climate of Wilmington that contributed to the effectiveness of Du Pont management was to be maintained and GWDC plans for the city furthered.

Two months later, in April, the GWDC formally announced the creation of Downtown Wilmington, Inc., to centralize business leadership for the final drive to implement GWDC's plans for the downtown area. Wilmington's corporate leaders realized these plans offered immense benefits for the business community and only marginal benefits for the Black ghetto. In fact, some of the Black residents had already been forced out and their homes razed to make way for corporate planning. With the control of redevelopment not in the hands of the people of the inner city, but in the hands of those such as Du Pont director George P. Edmonds (husband of Reynolds du Pont's sister Natalie), Henry B. du Pont, Irénée du Pont, Jr., and Joseph W. Chinn, Jr. (chairman of Wilmington Trust and Henry B. du Pont's appointee to the GWDC's New Firm Recruitment Committee), it was only a matter of time and circumstance before Wilmington's Black community exploded in anger. And significantly enough, the announcement of Downtown Wilmington occurred squarely in the face of that explosion.

On April 4, 1968, while supporting the wage demands of Black sanitation workers in Memphis, Tennessee, Dr. Martin Luther King was assassinated. Many Blacks saw this as the result of King's increasing shift of emphasis from religion to economic demands of Black workers and his recent statements against the Vietnam War; most Blacks simply saw it as a manifestation of white racism in America, and in cities throughout the country Black communities expressed their bitterness and grief by taking to the streets.

One of the mildest outbreaks was in Wilmington, Delaware. While whole blocks of Black ghettos in other cities burned, in Wilmington property damage was estimated at less than $250,000. Contrary to other areas where insurrections flared at the time, Wilmington endured no deaths and no major injuries. In fact, not the rebellion, but the reaction of government officials was probably the most extreme happening in Delaware that month.

On the morning of April 9 Governor Terry responded to Mayor John Babiarz's call for 500 National Guardsmen to quell a small disorder involving fewer than 100 Blacks. But for Terry, even 500 troops were too small in number. For the first time in the state's history, the governor ordered the mobilizing of the entire Delaware Army and Air National Guard, and 3,500 armed, mostly white, troops soon entered downtown Wilmington. They were to stay nine long months, the longest armed occupation of any American city in peacetime history.

By Easter Sunday, April 14, when Mayor Babiarz lifted the citywide curfew and declared the situation under control, over 370 persons had been arrested. Most had been picked up for curfew violations, but some arrests fell under the 1967 Emergency Riot Act that made the mere urging of property destruction liable for the same full penalty as the actual act. Terry, however, citing "intelligence reports" predicting violence the next day, refused to withdraw the troops. The next day passed quietly. But on April 29 there was violence—by the National Guard. On that day Douglas Henry, Jr., a Black man accused by police of burglary, was shot and killed *in the custody of police* by a Guardsman. Quickly, the state legislature passed and Terry signed a bill making the Guard exempt from any civil or criminal action resulting from any such atrocities "performed in the line of duty" while under the governor's mobilization orders.

Many Du Ponts were concerned that future incidents like the Henry killing could trigger further protests by the Black community as well as worsen Wilmington's already tarnished reputation for tranquility. Some quietly supported Mayor Babiarz's formal ending of the city emergency on May 1 and his withdrawal of city police from joint patrols with Terry's Guardsmen. The governor's continued insistence on retaining the Guard and backing up its patrols with state police began the Du Pont family's complete disaffection with his reign. Many Du Ponts who had previously held reservations about supporting Peterson now joined the long line to his campaign treasury led by Irénée du Pont, Jr.

Irénée replaced the ailing Henry B. du Pont as chairman of the GWDC that month. "We're beginning to see solutions not only to the physical problems but the human problems of the urban environment," he asserted. The GWDC, he contended, is "hacking its way through the jungle of urban problems."[21] The machete Irénée used to cut up the Black community was "moderate-income" housing. With Irénée's ascension to Henry's chair, the GWDC made housing a top priority. The result was a "pilot" plan for middle-income housing in northeastern Wilmington which Black residents living in the area could not afford. For the rest of the Black community, the GWDC set up the Neighborhood Improvement Association to sponsor "sweep-up" campaigns and beautification projects to try to gild the ghetto's dilapidated housing under the ominous shadow of the bulldozer. Meanwhile, Downtown Wilmington, Inc., began formulating final plans for an elaborate shopping mall.

Still, Terry's troop occupation hindered the attractiveness of Wilmington as a business opportunity. No Du Ponts were heard protesting the arrest of antiwar demonstrators on April 27 for violating an "emergency" city ordinance prohibiting assembly by ten or more persons, or Terry's crushing of a Black student protest at the Delaware State University on May 16 with state police and National Guardsmen armed with automatic weapons, gas, and dogs, or the warrantless arrest on June 6 of twenty-seven Blacks by police and the stripping and macing of young Black girls in jail. But the family's alarm that their state was becoming a national scandal was undoubtedly mounting.

"He has kept them too long,"[22] said state Senate majority leader Reynolds du Pont of the Guard in June. Reynolds explained he had no quarrel with Terry's original calling out of the Guard; it was only that the Guard had now gone overboard. By the following February, when Terry had been safely disposed of, Reynolds would be more candidly calling the governor's troop occupation a "keystone comedy approach."[23]

Terry, meanwhile, continued his ravings about imminent revolution. Independence Day, he assured the state's whites, would see a terrible Black rebellion. None occurred. In August came the shooting incident which caused four leaders of the Wilmington Youth Emergency Action Council to take refuge in a nearby home, resulting in their arrest. Privately, Irénée du Pont, Jr., bailed out the WYEAC leaders, who were nevertheless convicted later, by a city judge, of unlawful entry. The judge claimed there was no evidence of a shooting, while the *News-Journal* reported ten bullet holes in the WYEAC van, eleven empty cartridges on the lawn of the house where the WYEAC leaders had sought refuge, a crowd of 120 people at the scene, and sounds of gunfire heard by National Guardsmen and police who arrived at the scene.

This frame-up was only the beginning of a long campaign by Terry against the GWDC-financed Black youth organization. In September the arrest of six Black youths at the Cherry Island firing range was associated with WYEAC by the governor, who announced that he would block any further money from the Office of Economic Opportunity designated for the organization. The GWDC repeated its support of WYEAC, only to learn that U.S. Senator McClellan was coming to the aid of Democratic Party brethren with an official investigation of WYEAC by the Senate Internal Security Committee. On October 1, OEO stated it would not renew its grants to WYEAC, and from October 8 to 11 McClellan's committee held hearings in Wilmington, relying solely on reports of their own investigators and on witnesses sympathetic to Terry and hostile to WYEAC. No present or former members of WYEAC were even called to testify. Publicly Irénée opposed McClellan's investigation. But privately, he authorized GWDC cooperation in police investigation of WYEAC. Finally, Irénée rescinded GWDC's own funding of WYEAC, effectively dissolving the youth organization.

Terry had been counting on McClellan's hearings to generate an atmosphere of hysteria conducive to his reelection. But the governor had forgotten who actually ruled the state. When Du Ponts in the Democratic Party began eroding his own party's following, he became even more extreme, publicly accepting the support of Wallacites. It was in this atmosphere that the White Vigilantes of North America held organizational meetings in Delaware urging the use of arms. Wilmington policeman Ralph Prior headed the revived Ku Klux Klan, and a state legislature committee recommended sterilization of welfare mothers who gave birth to two illegitimate children. Eugene D. Bookhammer, Peterson's running mate, was reported to have made a similar proposal.

Bookhammer's suggestion was par for the Republican course—a steady drift to the right. As election day drew nearer, Peterson became more and more conservative in his "Three-S" (Shrink crime rate, Salvage dollars, Save the people) campaign, urging more police, an end to "political interference" with police, and better pay for police. Although his electoral package had definite reforms in it, the keynote of his campaign, like most other state and national campaigns that year, was "law and order."

Peterson's shift to the right cut into Terry's lead, as did Du Pont money. In the last few days before the election Terry suffered three successive blows: on November 1, sixty clergymen released a statement attacking the Guard occupation; on November 3, white liberals and radicals successfully sponsored a demonstration, in violation of the city's "assembly" law, "against fears in the white community and the Guard occupation"; on November 4, Terry suffered a heart attack.

The next day Russell Peterson was narrowly elected governor.

Peterson had a plentiful supply of members of the Du Pont circle on his winning slate. On a federal level he had the newly elected Republican Congressman William V. Roth. Roth's sojourn to the pinnacles of power was lighted along the way by his marriage to Jane K. Richards, daughter of Robert H. Richards, Jr., a director of Du Pont Company and Wilmington Trust. Jane's grandfather, Robert H. Richards, Sr., was the "guiding genius" secretary of Pierre du Pont's Christiana Securities, the family holding company, as well as former deputy attorney general of Delaware.

On a state level Peterson would also have many a helping Du Pont hand. Reynolds du Pont was elected president pro tem of the state Senate, where two other senators of the seventeen-member body, Dean Steele and Everette Hale, were Du Pont Company employees, and two more senators, Margaret R. Manning and Louise Conner, were the wives of present or former Du Pont executives. In the state House of Representatives Pierre S. du Pont IV, who had run unopposed in 1968, joined seven other Du Pont employees and Clarice U. Heckert, the wife of a Du Pont employee. There also, reigning as House majority leader, was W. Laird Stabler, Jr., a Du Pont relation whose father had also been high in the company hierarchy. On the powerful Joint Legislative Finance Committee, which passes on all budget requests from state agencies, sat Representative Herbert Lesher (chairman), Senator Steele (chairman of the Senate Finance Committee), Senator Everette Hale, and Representatives John Billingsley and Marie Pagano, all Du Pont employees.

Peterson filled his own "chemical cabinet" with Du Ponters. For the post of executive assistant he chose Christopher Perry, former *News-Journal* employee and member of the State Republican Committee; his father, Glen Perry, had been the architect of Du Pont's propaganda in the General Motors anti-trust case and retired only later that year as Du Pont's public relations director. For the post of press secretary, Peterson picked Jerry Sapienza of the *News-Journal*. To head the State Highway Commission, Peterson named Charles L. Eller, a veteran of twenty-seven years with Du Pont who in 1968 supervised the company's $300 million construction program. Eller replaced Frank Mackie, a recent Du Pont retiree. "We can't have two Du Ponters on the commission,"[24] Peterson told reporters, whereupon he appointed the wife of Alex De Dominics, a Du Pont employee, as the commission's first female member. The Du Pont situation was not much different in the State Treasury. There, Daniel J. Ross, a Du Pont retiree, watched over the state's fiscal books, recording the disbursements signed by Peterson and his lieutenants.

But the whole reason for Peterson's campaign had been Wilmington. There in the surrounding suburbs, C. Douglas Buck, Jr., son of Alice du Pont and grandson of Senator T. Coleman du Pont, presided over the New Castle County Council. William Conner, a Du Pont executive, administrated as County Executive. And in Wilmington itself, a new mayor had been elected—Harry G. Haskell, Jr.

Harry Haskell, Jr., owed his political life to the Du Ponts. His father, Harold Haskell, Sr., and uncle, J. Amory Haskell, had both been Du Pont vice-presidents and directors. Although his father had organized Du Pont's Explosives Department and was eventually made general manager of all of Du Pont's high explosives interests, Harry, Jr., felt no compulsion to fit into the available niches in the company hierarchy. Instead, Harry invested in non-Du Pont holdings: Garrett Miller & Co., Brown & Scott Packing Company, Fable Brands Corporation, and Shur-Whip Company. Harry served on the boards of all these companies and was also a director of Gurt Hill Farm, nationally famous for its Guernsey cows. In 1955 he became a member of the Delaware State Chamber of Commerce.

But Haskell's real love was Republican politics. A delegate to the 1952 Republican Convention, which nominated Eisenhower, Harry was appointed in 1954 as secretary of the departmental council in the U.S. Department of Health, Education, and Welfare, where he was first associated with Nelson Rockefeller, then HEW undersecretary. As secretary of the departmental council, Harry was responsible for the development of secretarial and international relations of HEW. He stayed there for one and a half years until appointed by Eisenhower in August 1955 to the special presidential committee headed by Rockefeller "to help in winning the minds of men throughout the world for the cause of freedom and democracy."[25] Translated, that meant Radio Free Europe, which Harry believed was "America's mightiest weapon in this ideological battle."[26]

In 1956, backed by "Veterans for Haskell," Harry ran for Congress as a cold warrior opposed to ending hydrogen bomb tests or the peacetime draft. As for his domestic policies, Harry summed it all up in one sentence: "Labor can only progress as our economy progresses."[27] Supported by most Du Ponts and the *News-Journal,* Harry was a shoo-in.

After completing his two-year term in 1958, Harry turned toward deeper involvement in business, reportedly owning over thirteen companies in Europe and becoming a director of ARAD, a subsidiary of a far-flung development corporation in Israel, RASSCO. A firm believer in corporate-controlled education as a panacea for social ills, Haskell took on trusteeships of Fisk University, Hobart College, and William Smith College; as a Congressman he had been one of the sponsors of the Defense Education Act of 1958, the law designed to meet American capitalism's need for highly skilled labor as part of "national defense." He was also treasurer of Unidel Foundation, the exclusive financial conduit founded by his father that controls most of the Du Pont family's grant money to the University of Delaware.

By 1966 Haskell was a director and chairman of the finance committee of Abercrombie & Fitch, one of the country's largest sporting goods retailers. Owning all of Ray Evans Properties, Haskell also held a considerable interest in Peoples Bank and Trust Company (of Wilmington). That year he also joined the board of Wilmington's TV station, WHYY, which had been started with a $150,000 grant from Henry B. du Pont's Longwood Foundation. But it was through another Du Pont, W. W. Laird, Jr., that Harry found the road back to active politics. Joining in Laird's Rockland Corporation to speculate in Wilmington real estate, Haskell found political complement to his deals in Block Blight, Inc., and Irénée du Pont's Downtown Wilmington, Inc., boards of which he became a sterling member.

Through this business association, solidified by Haskell's directorship on Wilmington Trust and his family's long Du Pont history, GWDC circles in the Republican Party were encouraged to support the former Congressman as the mayoral nominee on Peterson's "law and order" slate.

With Haskell's election, the GWDC planned for better days, but during the remaining six months of Babiarz's lame duck administration the GWDC continued to function as practically a parallel city government, led by Irénée du Pont, Jr.

Irénée's role during this period in many ways paved the way for Haskell's administration. An example of this occurred only two weeks after Haskell's election. On November 18, police were attempting to question a group of Black youths about a gas station robbery when one of the youths panicked, ran, and was shot in the neck. When parents and white sympathizers heard about the shooting and came to the police station, the police refused to provide information and they were subjected to harassment from Guardsmen.

This incendiary provocation was even worsened when the Guard and city and state police entered the Black community en masse and surrounded the home of a local Black leader, William Hallman, on the pretext of searching for the robbery suspect. Six White Coalition members went to the scene to confront the police on their lack of a search warrant. The police balked long enough to give Irénée time to work behind the scenes, pressuring city officials to obtain a warrant and withdraw the Guard from around Hallman's home. According to Hallman, Irénée worked until 3:00 A.M. in the morning on a crisis "that could have touched off a tinderbox."[28] Eventually, Irénée's efforts, combined with the determination of the Black community and its white allies, was enough to convince the city to obtain the warrant and pull back the Guard.

Two days later Irénée asserted to grateful white GWDC members that their organization had had "very limited, very superficial and very stereotyped" contacts with Blacks. The GWDC must break through "the roadblock of racial attitudes," he stated. "The white community must understand the reality of being Black, of having another skin color."[29] Harlan W. Roberts, staff associate for the Methodist Action Program, attested to just one aspect of that Black experience in Wilmington. "It is more dangerous for a Black man in the Wilmington police lockup than it is in the jungles of Vietnam."

Terry left office amid mounting criticism and demonstrations against the Guard occupation. Irénée and Peterson were not happy about the demonstrations, however, as they included more radical groups, such as the

University of Delaware chapter of Students for a Democratic Society (SDS) and the New York-based Youth Against War and Fascism, both of which could be expected to open broader questions of class control. To discourage just such a planned demonstration, Peterson on January 2, 1969, threatened to extend the period of Guard occupation if SDS or other groups protested in Wilmington.

Pressure by the business leaders was also brought to bear, and some members of the White Coalition were threatened with the loss of their jobs if they participated. Haskell and Peterson pressured Black organizations to hold back support, a tactic particularly successful with the local NAACP. The Committee of 39, whose president was a Du Pont executive, came out in opposition to the demonstration, and the Wilmington Council of Churches, which had privately favored the protest and mounted its own clerical criticisms, had its GWDC financing cut off by Irénée. Even Irénée's former allies, WYEAC, came under attack as one of its organizers, Ned Butler, was fired from the Catholic Inner City because of his role in planning the demonstration and he was replaced by an Atlas Chemical efficiency expert.

Despite this concerted campaign, the demonstration went off as planned, while Peterson, now inaugurated, stepped up his own plans and hurriedly announced the withdrawal of the Guard. The longest armed occupation of any American city in peacetime was at last over. Hundreds of people had been arbitrarily arrested by the Guard and police, and four people killed. But more important to the Du Ponts, over a thousand newspapers across the country had recorded the sordid event. Most of those reports were sketchy and referred to "Black rioting" that had long before been crushed by the military. And since the larger issues of democracy versus corporate control had seldom been raised, the experiment in military repression had in fact succeeded. Only Terry's blunt style and prolonged fascination with armed power had marred the military experiment which most Du Ponts had initially endorsed. And now a new governor, Russell Peterson, could restore the city's tarnished image and pursue the GWDC programs that would attract other firms and taxable middle-income families.

With Haskell's ascension to office, the GWDC ceased being a parallel city government. Instead, it moved into City Hall itself, shedding its executive director in the process as Haskell's administration took over its housing program. To run the show, and the city, Haskell hired a top GWDC staff member, Allan Rusten, as his administrative assistant. Rusten, the *News-Journal* reported, "has been responsible for administration of all of GWDC's social action programs."[30] Formerly, Rusten was in charge of

GWDC's public relations, a post he also held with the Republican State Committee and for Goldwater's National Republican Platform Committee in 1964. Now, in City Hall, he had direct supervision over all activities of ten of the thirteen city departments. For the next four years, while Harry Haskell traveled around the country wearing his mayoral ribbon, it was Rusten, and through him Irénée du Pont, Jr., who held the keys to the city.

With obstacles in local government removed, Irénée hoped to pursue his GWDC program in 1969, successfully crippling the GWDC's Black rival, the Urban Coalition, through Du Pont control of 30 to 40 percent of its treasury. Two years later the Urban Coalition would still be smarting under Irénée's charge that the Black organization's proposed $161,000 budget was "unrealistic." "Either the Urban Coalition is here to do business," answered Roosevelt Franklin, president of the NAACP, "or let's close up shop and quit game playing; $161,000 is no money for this business community." Franklin, however, was mistaken. If anyone was playing games, it was not Irénée. His business motives and plans for Black removal to make way for the GWDC's new civic center were by then frank and obvious. Only the political and economic climate of Wilmington had stalled their implementation for two years.

Much of Wilmington's unfavorable business climate had been the legacy of the Guard occupation; but some aspects were generated by the Du Ponts' political enemies. One such Democratic gladiator was Dr. C. Harold Brown, director of the University of Delaware's Division of Urban Affairs. In May, Brown released a three-year investigatory study into GWDC's $750,000 program establishing three neighborhood centers in Wilmington. "The centers are tragic failures," the study reported, citing evidence that 84 to 96 percent of area residents never received any help, two-thirds to three-fourths of the residents had never attended their meetings, two-thirds had never been in contact with the centers, and 10 to 20 percent had never even heard of them. Irénée's angry response came swiftly. "I don't understand why he made public his results before showing them to us," the GWDC chairman said. "I think it was unwise. There are a great number of dedicated people working at these centers. When they read this, it cuts the feet out from under them."[31]

For a while that year it looked like Irénée's family would also share that fate. Worsening economic conditions around the country threw a pall over Wilmington's economy and GWDC's plans. By the end of 1969 American capitalism had entered its greatest crisis since 1929, a crisis which threatened to pull the stock market, and with it the Du Ponts, down to ruin.

2. THE FALL OF THE HOUSE OF DU PONT

In Wall Street's competitive world of stocks and bonds, few brokers had a stronger reputation than Edmond du Pont. From his prestigious 1 Wall Street offices on the nineteenth floor of the Irving Trust Building in New York or from his Wilmington office, Edmond, as senior partner of F. I. du Pont & Company, made decisions on which whole fortunes depended, sometimes so quickly that associates were left breathless.

But Edmond's neat, conservative appearance and cool manner betrayed no signs of a rash man. Rather, crew-cut Edmond looked the model of efficiency, his trim 155-pound frame smoothly dressed in the traditional pinstripe suit which accentuated his bushy-browed, darkish good looks. "We're not interested in our rank," he once exclaimed. "We're interested in doing business in an efficient manner."[32]

That was in 1963, when Edmond's own past record seemed to bear him out. Edmond had joined his father, Francis I. du Pont, in 1932, a year after the founding of the firm and the same year he married Averell Adelaide Ross, the daughter of the founder of the prestigious accounting firm of Lybrand, Ross Bros., and Montgomery. A year later, in the grip of the Depression, his father made him a partner of the firm.

Those were drab days for the market, when the Dow-Jones industrial average limped below 42. With stubborn determination, Francis and his son held on, their fortunes not really made until the bonanza of World War II. As John Kenneth Galbraith once remarked, "The Great Depression of the Thirties never came to an end. It merely disappeared in the great mobilization of the Forties,"[33] and with the mobilization also disappeared the brokerage house's troubles. Francis, however, did not see the full bloom of his dreams. He died at the age of 69 in 1942, when the market was just beginning to boom again. Edmond assumed the helm.

Edmond's reign was synonymous with expansion. Merely four years after his father's death, Francis I. du Pont & Company took over the entire nineteenth floor of 1 Wall Street. By 1953 the firm had 62 branches and 575 salesmen, and it merged with J. E. Bennett the following year to form the second largest brokerage house in the country.

By 1963 F. I. du Pont & Company had 110 offices and 1,300 registered representatives. That year Edmond continued his diet of smaller companies by absorbing A. C. Allyn Company of Chicago and some assets of A. M. Kidder of New York. When Kidder went under, he took over its offices on the eighteenth floor of 1 Wall Street.

In the bull market of the Sixties there seemed no end to F. I. du Pont's growth. Like his favorite character, Tom Jones, Edmond found himself with strange bedfellows, including formerly estranged relatives. With two other family brokerage firms, Laird Inc. and Laird, Bissell, & Meeds, Edmond underwrote 7,602,285 shares of Royal Dutch Petroleum stock in 1958. In 1963 he participated with Laird and Company and Laird, Bissell, & Meeds in a group of investors led by Morgan Stanley & Co., underwriting $200 million worth of $4\frac{1}{4}$ percent 30-year debentures offered by Socony-Mobil Oil Co. (Rockefeller family interests). These same firms also joined Edmond in 1962 in underwriting the privately owned Mid-Center Parking Center in Wilmington, and in 1964 Edmond, Laird Inc., and a Dallas firm made a joint bid to purchase the Pure Oil Company for more than $700 million.

All these ventures, as well as time itself, helped breach the rifts created in the family by Alfred I. du Pont's famous feud with Pierre S. du Pont. Edmond's father had sided with Alfred against Pierre's allies but soon after reached a truce and a $30 million investment by the family. Now, through Laird, Bissell, & Meeds, Edmond was rubbing shoulders with Garrett Van S. Copeland, older son of Du Pont President Lammot du Pont Copeland, Henry Silliman, son-in-law of old Irénée du Pont, Edward Newbold Smith, son-in-law of Henry B. du Pont, and Alfred Bissell, who married the niece of Eugene du Pont, Jr. Through Laird Inc., Edmond was also in touch with George Weymouth, another in-law, Silliman, Smith, and Alfred du Pont Dent, grandson of Alfred I. du Pont.

Assisting along the way also was Edmond's brother Emile, whose sharp mind had propelled him to a vice-presidency and directorship in Du Pont Company. Emile was brought into the family's Blue Ridge Mutual Fund by Eleuthère du Pont, as was Edmond. There, Edmond also joined Donald F. Carpenter and James Q. du Pont in stock speculation, while Emile in 1967 joined Eleuthère and Reynolds du Pont in another fund, Sigma Capital Shares Corporation. Eleuthère also made Edmond treasurer of his Delaware Chemical Engineering Corporation. These growing ties were also reflected in the Continental American Life Insurance Company, where Eleuthère, as treasurer, put Edmond's knowledge of mutual funds to profitable use. Edmond even served as a director of Continental American for a period with George P. Edmonds, son-in-law of Lammot du Pont, and Francis V. du Pont, son of T. Coleman du Pont. With this economic rise came the social laurels of a directorship in old Henry F. du Pont's Winterthur Corporation and, in 1965, trusteeship of the University of Delaware.

That year Edmond reportedly joined other Du Ponts in buying out the president of Waddell & Reed, Cameron K. Reed, securing control of over 24 percent (145,440 shares) of the investment firm's voting stock and $12\frac{1}{2}$

percent of Class A nonvoting stock quoted at $43.25 a share. In keeping with Edmond's own interest in mutual funds, Waddell & Reed was an investment adviser to mutual funds and owned 80 percent of United Investors Life Insurance Company, of which Edmond was a director. Moreover, Waddell & Reed also managed the huge $2.1 billion United Funds, Inc., and United International Fund; Edmond also served as director of these companies. To complement this tidy affair, Wilmington Trust was made direct custodian over United Funds' $400 million science fund.

All seemed to be going well for Edmond in the Sixties. He had also involved himself in two other stock investment companies: the $398 million Delaware Fund and the $100 million Decatur Income Fund, where he joined Lammot du Pont Copeland's other son, Lammot du Pont Copeland, Jr. His own younger son, Edmond Rex du Pont, Jr., was now securely niched in F. I. du Pont & Company, while his elder son, Anthony, had graduated from Yale and taken an engineering job with Douglas Aircraft Company.

Most of these days Edmond spent at F. I. du Pont's ground floor office at the Du Pont Building in Wilmington, where he lived in a modest ten-room house. Once a week, until her death in 1967 at the age of 92, Edmond's mother would stop by the office to chat about her many investments. Edmond's brother, A. Rhett du Pont, was also making quite a name for himself. Despite a reputation as a drinker (he was, for example, fined $200 for drunken driving and a hit-and-run accident in 1959), A. Rhett knew how to make money. He had even won recognition from David Rockefeller's Downtown Lower Manhattan Association in 1961 and was a member of the board of governors of the American Stock Exchange.

In 1967 F. I. du Pont & Company was generating close to $100 million in income from its own operations, and had become a major stockholder in such corporate giants as A.T. & T. Other Du Ponts, led by Lammot du Pont Copeland and Emile F. du Pont, by then had invested heavily in F. I. du Pont & Company, and Garrett Van S. Copeland, Lammot's son, and Peter R. du Pont, Emile's son, had even become partners.

Then came the deluge of 1968–1969. The market was swept by a flood of calls as investors feared the drought of domestic capital caused by antiinflationary taxes and the decline in earnings. Edmond had sensed this danger in 1967 when, commenting on Johnson's wartime surtax on corporate and personal income, he warned that "it would seem prudent to await action on any tax increase in order to be sure that business adjustments that have been under way for more than a year have run their course."[34]

But time was late for American capitalism, and Johnson knew it. The huge return of capital from export sales that Lammot du Pont Copeland in

1963 had expected would outweigh the loss of capital spent abroad for overseas plant construction had been hindered by the use of that capital in still further huge investments abroad. Moreover, this overseas economic empire required a military shield, especially in Europe, the Mediterranean, the Pacific, and in later years particularly, in Southeast Asia. This meant dollars flowing abroad not only for U.S. corporate investments, but also for U.S. military presence.

During the first two decades after World War II, European and Japanese financiers and their governments welcomed the dollar as a valuable source of needed capital for reconstruction and as a currency basis for international trade. For those two decades the U.S. dollar had reigned as the undisputed lord of world capital, the foundation of the postwar international monetary system in the "Free (Enterprise) World."

With European and Japanese reconstruction completed in the Sixties and their economies revived, however, the accumulated dollar overflow lost much of its glow and became increasingly exchanged for U.S. gold (gold being the accepted arbiter among currencies). This deficit in the U.S. balance of payments grew into a deeper and deeper problem for the U.S. government. Its gold stocks were becoming depleted at the same time that the federal treasury, financing a huge arms buildup, continued to turn out annual deficits, further undercutting the real value of the dollar. The crisis was only aggravated more by the Vietnam War. The U.S. corporate war machine consumed even more foreign goods and raw materials, spent even more dollars abroad, and chalked up ever higher deficits in the domestic and international balance sheets.

Key to all this was the mounting crisis of U.S. productivity. The dollar's value had been undermined also by the domestic effects of overseas investment: the flow of U.S. capital abroad dried up the financial sources for most domestic capital investment, leaving the domestic field neglected. It was this that was one of Du Pont's chief problems when McCoy assumed office late in 1967. And Du Pont was not unique: with the exception of computers and reproduction machines industries, this stagnation of domestic investment had put a brake on technological innovation in many key areas of production (auto, appliances, etc.). To make matters worse, the federal government's open commitment not to permit another 1929 collapse only encouraged investors further to avoid capital investment in industry and steer their capital into more speculative, riskier, but more quickly profitable waters, often with unsound business practices.

By 1967 the U.S. economy was suffering a crucial decline in its productivity differential with European and Japanese companies. Some of these companies were jointly owned by American corporations which saw fit to reinvest much of their profits in foreign plants and develop foreign consumer markets. In a few cases, foreign management, backed by a majority of foreign directors and their governments, reinvested in their own countries despite American grumblings; in those cases, concern over short-run profits for their investments outweighed the broader economic interests of the American corporate class as a whole.

As a result, U.S.-made goods were steadily being underpriced and driven out of the world market. Eventually, in 1971, the U.S. would add to its balance of payments deficits *the first trade deficit in a century*. By the following year this trade deficit would increase *threefold*.

The Vietnam War, however, played not only an economic role in undermining the dollar, but also a crucial political role. The Vietnamese's smashing Tet offensive in 1968 seriously eroded what foreign confidence still existed in a U.S. victory and the dollar's market prospects in Asia and the rest of the underdeveloped world. If the Vietnamese could prevent American corporations from establishing plants to use cheap labor and the raw materials of Southeast Asia, perhaps other underdeveloped nations could do likewise. The continuing rush on U.S. gold mounted, soon triggering a "gold crisis." Then, as the United States sought to protect its gold reserves by restricting and eventually ceasing gold payments, challenges were raised in the world's money markets to the exchange value of the dollar itself, thus spurring the selling of dollars and the pressure for devaluation. That devaluation, only the official adjustment to the decline in the dollar's buying power, played an important role in the subsequent worsening of inflation in the United States, popping many a balloon among the American people.

In a desperate attempt to cut into the mounting war deficit and slow down inflation, President Johnson had imposed the surtax. Even Edmond du Pont had to admit in 1967 that "In view of the federal deficit for the past fiscal year and the much larger deficit looming this year, it would appear essential to enlarge federal revenues through a tax increase that would have the effect of stemming any new inflationary tide."[35] But Edmond felt business was slowing on its own, and encouraged Johnson to wait until it started up again. Johnson, openly fearful of Black rebellions sweeping the country over inflation, unemployment, and the draft, and equally alarmed about the speculation frenzy boosting stock prices above their earnings justification, warned of a future overheating of the economy and wanted to nip the problem in its credit bud by raising prime interest rates.

In this, Johnson succeeded, only to frustrate dreams of immediate profits and drive the marketeers into a selling frenzy. Millions of these shares that were bought on margin, often by mutual funds employing leverage, were suddenly dumped on the market; and as mutual funds—the modern counterpart of the speculative investment trusts of the golden Twenties—had been Edmond's specialty, he also inherited their debacle.

Throughout 1968 F. I. du Pont & Company was swamped with a flood of selling and speculative buying, most often on margin. Edmond's back office became one of the messiest in the brokerage business. Orders being processed by hand were backed up in long lines, snarled in paperwork. The result was a 100 percent increase in Edmond's costs: increased personnel, massive overtime, and, following the national inflation, a general rising trend in all expenses. Although F. I. du Pont raked in a record $119.6 million in total income from operations in 1968, its net income available to the partners (before taxes) fell to $8.9 million, down 26 percent from the $12 million net income a year before. After federal taxes, du Pont scored only a $4.7 million profit, far below 1967's $5.9 million.

With its liquid capital reserves falling, du Pont did not present a pretty picture to other houses on the Exchange who were aware that some of du Pont's problems were the result of its own doing. Despite Edmond's claim of a heavy reliance on research, by 1968 this was simply not the case. Edmond's persistence in paying low wages for research personnel had caused a high turnover in du Pont's research staff, weakening its capabilities. This lack of an adequate research department hurt the marketing ability of du Pont's salesmen and diminished the company's attractiveness to new institutional clients. Consequently, du Pont salesmen were willing to accept innumerable small orders, which only contributed further to the backlogging problem.

Thousands of orders for selling and buying were delayed in du Pont's backwaters. Yet, these and even more orders were accepted by du Pont. This was in violation of the antifraud provisions of the securities laws, which prohibit sales by a dealer when he has reason to believe he will be unable to deliver the securities promptly. Hundreds of complaints were sent to du Pont by investors, but for the most part Edmond and his long-time managing partner, Charles Moran, Jr., ignored them. For this, both were fined $25,000 each by the Exchange and the firm was hit with an additional $50,000 fine. If Edmond was to avoid this unhappy occurrence in the future and meet the Exchange's audit of his capital reserves backing his business, he realized, he would have to raise additional capital and modernize the firm's research, accounting, and even its organizational structure.

Edmond tried to deal with this problem by taking the first step toward incorporating the partnership, a maneuver other brokerage houses were also employing to modernize their organization, exploit corporate tax loopholes, and have a stronger legal basis for acquiring needed loans, floating bonds, and selling stock to raise capital. Edmond's plan called for a board of seventeen directing partners with himself as chairman; it probably would have been implemented had time permitted. But the crush of ensuing events robbed Edmond of his opportunity—and his company.

The deluge came in mid-May 1969, when the market broke badly, suffering a 10 percent decline in stock prices across the board. In the heat of mass selling, calls went out for more capital behind margined stock, but frantic stock owners found credit scarce in an apprehensive money market. Overloaded commercial banks were unable to accommodate the flood of demands for loans, and banks in general feared a contraction of available resources for commercial paper. In an attempt to buoy their stock values, corporations flooded the money market with I.O.U.'s, ballooning the market to $24.4 billion by June. With the unavailability of an expanding overseas market diminishing the dollar's value in contrast to foreign currencies, and the resultant inflation further tightening credit, brokerage houses had to accept $6.9 billion in notes the following year, $709 million in one month.

Saddled with many speculative mutual funds and small investors as customers, F. I. du Pont was particularly hard-hit by the selling, and operational costs triggered a $7.7 million deficit in 1969. At that point the New York Stock Exchange, suspecting that Edmond and Moran had accepted too much business on margin without adequate liquid capital as insurance, in June 1969 asked for an audit of F. I. du Pont's capital reserves to see if it met the board of governors' rule of 20 to 1, the required ratio of total indebtedness to net capital.

The Exchange also asked F. I. du Pont to reduce its loans. Such demands proved Moran's management so incompetent that in September he was forced out of the firm.

To attract additional capital, in 1970 Edmond merged F. I. du Pont with Glore Forgan Staats, Inc., one of the country's leading underwriters. With twenty offices, it was one of the largest consolidations in Wall Street history, and Edmond hoped Glore Forgan's trade would answer questions about du Pont's capital reserves. But to lay the question to rest once and for all, at the very same time du Pont absorbed Hirsch & Co. Although this was designed as another "partner" acquisition to improve du Pont's capital picture, it also charged du Pont with 50,000 to 60,000 new accounts, a huge intake of business which du Pont was not yet prepared to handle.

To cope with this mounting problem of back office snares and gather additional capital at the same time, Edmond shopped around for a computer company willing to provide capital in exchange for a huge computer operations contract. Just a week before Edmond's group finally found their solution in Texas, they approached one computer company for a contract on back office business with one condition: a $4 million to $5 million capital injection into F. I. du Pont. The company refused.

The following week Edmond found what he thought was an easy mark in the lean, crew-cut Texan, H. Ross Perot. Perot owed a lot to the brokerage houses of Wall Street. When the market crisis first developed, Perot's computer firm, Electronic Data Systems Corporation, looked so handy that investors gave it a price-earnings ratio of 500 to 1; brokers were convinced that the new computer service had tremendous growth potential. Perot's stock, which went public in 1968 at $16.50 a share, skyrocketed to a high of $161 by 1970, suddenly transforming Ross Perot into a billionaire—on paper.

Perot's first big contract was handling Medicare claims in Texas for Blue Shield, and he soon landed other Medicare contracts in nine other locales. According to a General Accounting Office report released in 1973 by Congressman L. H. Fountain, chairman of the House Intergovernmental Relations Subcommittee, Perot's firm made a 100 percent profit on Medicare contracts, a 200 percent profit from the Texas contract alone.

In July 1970 Perot made his first real break into Wall Street through the F. I. du Pont contract, purchasing the firm's computer operation with 100,000 shares of Electronic Data Systems stock worth $3.8 million. Edmond granted Perot both back- and front-office paperwork, and the Texan took little time in making himself felt. First, Perot moved his own personnel on the scene. Then he suggested "bank balances" to replace the old cumbersome stock certificates. But other, less beneficial things arrived with Perot—rumors.

Almost immediately, F. I. du Pont was hit with rumors about a lack of capital. "Almost by definition," recalled Wallace C. Latour, Edmond's new managing director, "the rumors circulating about us had to be false. No one knew what kind of shape we were in, including ourselves. We knew that we weren't comfortable in capital, but we thought we had enough."[36] But rumors are considered a way of life on the Stock Exchange, and despite du Pont's claims, this time they were reflecting the truth of the situation. "We have had some customers ask for their securities," Latour admitted, and the American Stock Exchange even had to severely censure two floor members and fine them $1,000 each for spreading false rumors. Edmond had his accountants audit the books and dutifully pronounce the firm financially "sound," but the New York Stock Exchange, suspecting

Edmond's figures were unreliable, remained uncertain. Felix Rohatyn, partner of Lazard Freres & Company and chairman of the Exchange's surveillance committee, insisted Edmond provide more funds.

As most of their own funds were tied into the precarious mutual funds sector, Edmond's partners elected to sell the 100,000 EDS shares they had received from Perot. Originally they had wanted those shares as an investment in what they considered "a great growth situation," but now they were resigned to the sale to raise the necessary capital to cool the Exchange's heated concern. For its part, in November the Securities Exchange Commission asked Perot to remove his previous two-year restriction on the sale of that stock. It was then, Perot later claimed, that he first found out about F. I. du Pont's capital problems.

Perot already had a deep stake in F. I. du Pont & Company. If F. I. du Pont could not meet the Exchange's legal requirement and was forced to close, Perot's Electronic Data Systems would lose $8 million in du Pont business annually, or up to 20 percent of its revenue. Its stock, and Perot's billion dollar personal worth, would then be worth substantially less. F. I. du Pont's collapse would also hurt his plans to capture the computer business of other brokerage houses, which would be jeopardized by the fall of the market's second largest firm.

But the Texan industrialist was also aware that if he needed the Du Ponts, they, and all of Wall Street, needed him even more. Merrill Lynch, which had avoided a heavy commitment in the margined mutual funds, was about to rescue another failing giant, Goodbody & Company, but only if no other firm collapsed before the deal was completed in December. If both F. I. du Pont and Goodbody failed, over half a million investors might lose their securities and cash, since the Exchange had already exhausted its reserves indemnifying customers of other firms. At the time, there was no Securities Investor Protection Corporation to use taxpayers' money to insure private speculators, and if two such leading firms failed, public confidence in Wall Street would shatter, and possibly Congress would be prompted to shy away from passing the SIPC bill the Street so desperately needed.

Perot grasped the crisis probably better and more candidly than any federal official would have dared. "I realized," he explained, "that you'd have to nationalize the airlines and other capital-intensive industries quick if they couldn't get money out of the Street. You'd have to nationalize the utilities—quick. You couldn't sell public school bonds."[37] And getting the money for such public necessities as schools, Perot realized, would eventually mean nationalizing the private banks (including his own Republic National Bank of Dallas), which controlled the country's money. To a capitalist like Perot, the interest of private capitalism was synonymous with the national interest. "I feel strongly that everyone ought to make every contribution he can to the country."[38]

Despite his patriotic stance, however, Perot put his own profit first. When the partners first tried to sell their 100,000 EDS shares, Perot, Edmond later charged, delayed their registration. Then, when Edmond approached the billionaire Texan to invest $5 million in the firm, Perot still hedged, playing his cards. The White House, by this time alerted to the immense economic danger, then intervened.

Perot was well known in conservative Republican circles since his unsuccessful propaganda stunt of attempting to jet tons of Christmas gifts to American prisoners of war in North Vietnam. He had been a large contributor to Richard Nixon's 1968 campaign, and he knew the President personally, so the calls he now received from Attorney General Mitchell, Treasury Secretary John Connally, and Presidential Assistant Peter Flanigan urging his investment in F. I. du Pont, while pleasing, were not surprising. It may have fired Perot's patriotic embers, but his stance in the negotiations remained imperturbably cool.

Meanwhile, the pressure built on Edmond. In September the Big Board conducted its annual surprise audit of F. I. du Pont. The following month the Exchange's accounting firm released figures showing a $17.7 million deficit for F. I. du Pont in 1970. Most of these operating losses were the result of write-offs and the recommended 1/to 16.45 reserves required because of the back-office mess Perot's computer had yet to clear up. In desperation, Edmond asked Perot to raise his loan to $10 million to create a better than 10 to 1 ratio for the firm.

Edmond du Pont found that Ross Perot drove a hard bargain. When the final deal was reached on December 15, Edmond had been forced to agree to a number of concessions in exchange for Perot's $10 million investment. He promised to incorporate the firm, whereupon Perot would have the right to convert $1.5 million of his investment into 51 percent of the firm's stock. This would give control of F. I. du Pont to someone outside the Du Pont family for the first time in its forty-year history. F. I. du Pont would also have to issue $8.5 million worth of debentures to Perot, and arrange for a loan collateralized by a Chicago partner, John W. Allyn, owner of the Chicago White Sox baseball team. Edmond agreed to all this for the loan, and promised Perot high preference in the event of forced liquidation. Finally, Edmond was not only to obtain the signature of all general partners and lenders on a statement promising to keep their funds in the firm, but also to raise an additional $15 million. "I don't want to be in the position of putting my money into the top of a funnel," Perot asserted, "and having others pulling it out the other end."[39] If Edmond failed, Perot's 51 percent investment would automatically become 91 percent.

Edmond failed.

It may seem a mystery that Edmond du Pont was unable to gather the necessary funds from such wealthy brethren as his. After all, $15 million does not seem much for the richest family on earth to raise, and the Du Ponts then held more personal wealth than any single family.

The key to the Du Pont riddle had much to do with the general state of the economy at the time, a looming crisis which inspired smaller, but crucial dramas within the story of Edmond's fall.

First was the drama unfolding within Du Pont Company itself. Since the 1965 G. M. divestiture, Du Pont's stock had declined well over 100 points. Like most combines, Du Pont had the problem of providing big enough earnings after the giant stage had been reached. "It's a case of having to run faster just to stand still,"[40] commented Standard and Poor's *Outlook*. Sales were still rising, well over $3.5 billion, but earnings per share were not matching the 1965 high of $8.63. Du Pont's competition had grown in recent years from diversified and expansion-minded oil companies and foreign concerns, while its factories were plagued by overcapacity, which was true of the entire chemical industry for that matter.

Although Du Pont had friends (and relatives) in the investment world (*Poor* still recommended Du Pont stock, pointing to its low price-earnings ratio), institutional investors saw problems and began to reduce their holdings in chemicals. Investment companies and mutual funds reduced their chemical and drug stock portions of their portfolios from the 8.4 percent of March 1964, to 4.2 percent in 1969. Such selling drove Du Pont stock down to 160 in January 1969, a far cry from its 261 high only four years before. The deluge of May only made matters worse for the Du Ponts as they saw their stock tumble to 131 by June, joining 417 other new lows on the New York Stock Exchange.

The continued fall in earnings put tremendous pressure on the Du Ponts. The family's holdings in the company were now worth one-half of their 1965 value, a tremendous blow to the family coffers. And to make matters worse, in the midst of this economic storm, one young member of the family now found he couldn't keep his head above troubled financial waters. Among the many paper empires starving for credit in those precarious days was that of Lammot du Pont Copeland, Jr. Using the credit of his famous name, Copeland had built a house of cards over recent years, and now it came tumbling down with a reverberation heard round the world.

Motsey's Paper Empire

Since his graduation from Harvard in 1954, young Lammot Copeland, Jr.—or "Motsey," as he is called in family circles—had had a passion for right-wing politics, associating himself with the ultra-conservative Young Americans for Freedom. Buoyed by many personal trust funds (of which four alone were valued at a cool $11 million) and by his father's ascension to the Du Pont presidency, Motsey became a bigwig in conservative political circles, being national treasurer of YAF from 1962 to 1966. Following Goldwater's defeat in 1964, Motsey also became a director and treasurer of the American Conservative Victory Fund, and president of the American Conservative Union.

Although some of these facts were mentioned earlier, they are worth repeating as they are what took Motsey on the road to financial disaster. To acquire a forum for his right-wing ideas, Motsey began purchasing newspapers in southern California, an area dominated by aerospace and defense industries and renowned for its political conservatism. He began these purchases in 1963, the year his father became president of Du Pont.

Within a few years, Motsey bought the Currier News Corporation, Graphic Productions Corporation, the San Fernando Valley *Times,* the *Standard Register,* and Great Western Publishing Company, extending his newspaper holdings into northern California as well. His Citizen-News Company, which operated a chain of newspapers in the Los Angeles area, including the *Citizen-News* of Hollywood, was his biggest stake, the revenues of the two dailies and twenty-seven weeklies running close to $9 million a year when he took them over.

Motsey's problems, like those of his father and most of his Du Pont relatives, began around 1967. That was the year when growing public concern over an unwinnable Vietnam War began causing a shift to the left in the political temper of the country's population, a shift that took on momentum over the next three years as the prospects of victory became dimmer and the occasions of social upheaval greater and more frequent. This political shift cut into the attractiveness of Motsey's right-wing politics, and the readership of his papers suffered accordingly. By mid-1970 their annual revenues had fallen to about $5 million.

But in 1967 Motsey saw only roses, and through his West Coast dealings he was introduced to the man who was to play a key role in his downfall, Thomas A. Shaheen. A heavyset, outgoing promoter, Shaheen was then based in Chicago as "financial adviser" to the Pension Fund of the Journeyman Barbers, Hairdressers, Cosmetologists and Proprietors International Union of America—the Barber's Union. He had left California in

1965 following an unsuccessful attempt to develop supermarkets, and had been declared bankrupt by a Chicago court the following year. But he left behind a hustler's legend in California, and one money broker there became the medium for Shaheen's meeting Motsey.

If the Du Ponts gave their version of what followed, Motsey would be described as the next victim of Shaheen's operation. But Motsey's own deals through Winthrop-Lawrence Corporation, the "hard-money" loan and investment firm he established with Shaheen in 1967, suggested otherwise. There were victims, all right, but none by the name of Lammot du Pont Copeland, Jr.

The first victim was the Barber's Union, many of whose members are elderly and have only future pensions standing between them and old age pauperism. Under Shaheen's advice, union officials lent $12 million in pension funds to various ventures of which $4.5 million later became delinquent, including a $1.3 million loan to Copeland's own northern California newspaper operations. Some of these loans from the Barber's Union were also used to finance Copeland and Shaheen's other deals.

The next victim was the Dean Van Lines, a West Coast trucking company. Dean's search for capital, in the credit squeeze of 1966, eventually led it to Winthrop-Lawrence. According to sources quoted in the *Wall Street Journal,* Motsey and Shaheen agreed to arrange a quick $1.6 million bank loan for Dean. But Dean's treasury didn't see that loan for almost a year. To keep things afloat, Shaheen arranged for the Barber's Union to advance interim loans of about $700,000. Finally the $1.6 million loan came through, allegedly minus some $600,000 in "fees." Motsey arranged for additional loans which finally forced Dean's owners to sign over control to Winthrop-Lawrence. In September 1969 Dean, its profits now drained away, filed a Chapter 11 bankruptcy petition, whereupon Motsey and Shaheen sold off eight of Dean's affiliates for $500,000 at a profit of nearly 300 percent.

Another hapless case was that of Edmund C. Giusti, a California real estate speculator whose plan for a country club also led him to Winthrop-Lawrence—and trouble. According to a deposition filed by Giusti in California superior court, Shaheen agreed to arrange a $1.1 million loan, but at a very high cost: a $97,000 fee to Shaheen, a $35,000 fee to Motsey, $106,000 in fees and commissions, and 100 acres of Giusti's 1,500-acre plot, worth $400,000. After it was all over, Giusti still needed money, and another $1.2 million loan was allegedly "approved" by Shaheen. This loan never materialized, but $500,000 in pension funds from the Barber's Union did—to Winthrop-Lawrence, which then channeled the money to Giusti. Again, the cost was steep: $20,597 in "fees" to Shaheen, and 200 more acres of land valued at $740,000. Shaheen, meanwhile, received a large fee also from Winthrop-Lawrence for arranging the loan.

Motsey was riding high these days, making loans with New York banks to finance new acquisitions. He got Winthrop-Lawrence involved in an abortive attempt at franchising Mexican foods under the name of "Taco Boy," and steered the firm into setting up the Pleasure Petroleum Corporation and financing college dormitories in Kentucky, Louisiana, Georgia, and Mississippi. On his own, he invested in Calumet Publishing Company, a Chicago-based newspaper chain, and speculated in Texas, Arizona, Maryland, and California real estate. One Los Angeles tract, worth $2.2 million, proved a disaster, its steep hill discouraging development construction. With another tract, a $1.8 million Sacramento shopping center, Motsey was more fortunate. Observing that its occupancy rate never rose above the break-even stage, Motsey simply sold the shopping center to Super Stores, Inc., a Mobile, Alabama, store chain haplessly controlled by his own Winthrop-Lawrence.

But Motsey's biggest venture was in Transogram Company, a New York toy manufacturer founded in 1915 and listed prominently on the American Stock Exchange. "Transogram had everything we needed," Shaheen recalled, "a listing, a history and a problem."[41] Transogram's problem was an operating deficit which had grown since the death of its chief executive, Charles Raizen, in 1967. By January 1969, when Motsey and Shaheen opened and successfully closed negotiations for acquisition, Transogram's owners had suspended payments to creditors and the workers' pension plan.

Motsey had expected this acquisition to proceed quickly, but it was not until mid-October that it was finally approved by Transogram's stock owners. Meanwhile, Motsey had overextended himself, accumulating a tidal wave of debts that were now close to catching up with him.

To ease the burden, Motsey and Shaheen surrendered a 25 percent interest in Winthrop-Lawrence to MacDonald Lynch, a Texas financier, in exchange for his $1 million certificate of deposit. This certificate Motsey placed in the vaults of the Royal National Bank of New York in exchange for a line of credit from the bank which was quickly exhausted.

Motsey and Shaheen next turned to Transogram. At a board meeting attended by Copeland, Transogram's directors loaned Shaheen $250,000 in spite of their own financial problems. The money was supposed to be used to acquire the Yellow Cab Company of Philadelphia and Connie Mack Stadium; in exchange, Shaheen promised Transogram a 20 percent interest in each. Neither company, however, was ever acquired.

In December Motsey moved to take over Transogram, planning to buy

250,000 shares (25 percent of the company's stock) then held by the Raizen estate. Motsey put $500,000 down and signed notes for $4 million, again using the advantage of his name to buy credibility. At the last minute, however, an unknown party who had agreed to pick up $1 million worth of the Transogram notes suddenly backed off, jeopardizing Motsey's whole scheme.

To save the day, Motsey made an appeal to Dad.

Lammot du Pont Copeland, Sr., had already been involved in his son's deals. Already he held a $3.6 million note from Winthrop-Lawrence convertible into 35 percent of the firm's stock. Only the previous April he had put up $3.35 million worth of his own blue chip stock to partly collateralize a $3.7 million loan for his son from Wilmington Trust, the family bank, and only in October he had loaned two more $500,000 advances to his son. Now Motsey was back for more, and his father, growing concerned, once again dipped into his pocket. This time the Du Pont chairman arranged a $3 million loan from Chemical Bank and Trust Company of New York, of which he was a director. Copeland, Sr., again backed the loan with his own stocks.

It was a high price to pay, but Copeland's son was finally chairman of a large industrial corporation, Transogram. And there were immediate spoils. Winthrop-Lawrence paid 80,000 Transogram shares worth $6 apiece to Shaheen's personal holding company, the Columbia Financial Corporation, "for services rendered . . . in the negotiations." Motsey also was able to trade off the lavishly equipped, air-conditioned dormitories of Southwestern Louisiana University to Transogram. Subsequently, the toy company took a $183,000 operating loss off these dormitories the following year.

Transogram continued to suffer an operating loss, and only by juggling accounts was it able to show a mere $189,000 profit for 1969. Yet Motsey's ambitions knew no bounds, directing Transogram to acquire two profitable companies, Quaker Masonry Company of Hollandale, Florida, and Southern Precision Industries, Inc., of Harrison, Arkansas. To pay the former owners, Motsey gave them Transogram stock, promising to buy it back in the future.

The use of Transogram stock now became Motsey's chief bargaining tool for more capital. By January 1970 his other debts were also catching up. His favorite project, the *Citizen-News,* was losing $60,000 every month. To head this company Motsey had hired Richard Horton, a former San Quentin Prison inmate. Horton had been jailed in the mid-Sixties for his role as a member of a confidence ring which drove the bank of Brighton, Colorado, to bankruptcy within twenty-one months through forgery and phony accounting. Now, as Motsey's lieutenant, he strove to keep the *Citizen-News* afloat by cutting costs, firing half the staff, and shifting the paper's politics to a more liberal stance in keeping with the new political trends. But his efforts failed; they were no doubt hampered by Motsey's $13,000-a-month "consulting fee" (which Copeland claimed to have collected for only one month) and by his siphoning off of *Citizen-News* revenue to finance other newspapers in northern California.

To stave off the debts being called on his marginal empire, Motsey began approaching smaller banks outside New York which the name of Du Pont could entice into loans. To paint a sound picture, Motsey's unaudited personal financial statement on April 30 showed liabilities of only $9 million and boasted assets of $29.5 million. Buried in the report, however, was a tiny footnote that "Mr. Copeland has personally guaranteed obligations of companies he owns. There is, in each instance, security considered ample for the obligation so guaranteed."[42] Within three and a half months it would be revealed that that little footnote had $50 million in liabilities lurking behind it.

In these latest of late hours Motsey increasingly used Transogram's stock to shore up his paper empire. For collateral he pledged 20,000 Transogram shares at the Missouri State Bank and Trust Company in St. Louis; 10,000 Transogram shares at Peoples Bank in Aurora, Colorado; 17,000 shares at the Houston Bank and Trust Company; 10,000 shares at the Madison National Bank in Washington, D.C.; 40,000 shares at Louisiana National Bank in Baton Rouge; and $300,000 worth of Transogram notes at the Huntington National Bank in Columbus, Ohio.

Some banks didn't even ask for security. One Midwest bank, for example, gave Winthrop-Lawrence a $450,000 loan with almost no questions asked. All told, forty-three banks were induced into becoming Motsey's creditors.

Still that was not enough. Motsey's last hope, to buy his own bank, was yet unrealized. Over a year earlier Transogram had attempted to acquire the Mountain Savings and Loan Association of Denver, but federal savings and loan authorities stepped in, refusing to grant approval.

The first crack in the veneer covering Motsey's empire appeared in mid-June 1970 in the person of Motsey's father. Copeland, Sr., was plagued by his own financial problems as Du Pont's stock continued to flounder in the market's storm. Apparently by this time he saw Motsey's empire as unsalvageable and, probably urging his son to abandon a sinking ship, cut the financial lifeline. To smooth the blow for his son and at the same time protect his own high position in Chemical Bank, Copeland quietly arranged a final $5.5 million loan for Winthrop-Lawrence through that most secretive of world capitalism's institutions, a Swiss bank.

Motsey used the advance from the Union Bank of Switzerland to pay off Chemical's $3 million loan (freeing his father's collateral) and his father's own $1 million loan. This left Motsey with $1.5 million, and after returning a compensating balance of $500,000 to the Swiss bank and paying a discount of $165,000, his final holding came to only $800,000. Meanwhile, Copeland, Sr., was still in the hole to the tune of $3.5 million worth of blue chip stock left with the Swiss bank as collateral. Copeland probably expected soon to kiss that goodbye, but he undoubtedly considered his reputation with Chemical Bank more important. Significantly, Motsey had also made one of his few repayments of debts to First National City Bank, another bank in which Du Pont Company had large deposits and of which Du Pont president Charles McCoy was a director. Motsey's repayment of that $150,000 loan may well have been consistent with his father's effort to protect his own and *Du Pont*'s reputation.

Having covered his son's tracks in New York, Copeland, Sr., then turned to cleaning house in Wilmington, immediately disclosing his son's precarious position to the family bank, Wilmington Trust. At the instructions of Copeland's attorney, William S. Potter (himself a director of Wilmington Trust and a Du Pont in-law), a $3.4 million judgment was secretly taken by Wilmington Trust against Motsey's $3.7 million debt on the loan granted him the previous year. In return, Wilmington Trust held off liquidating Motsey's and his father's collateral, possibly to give Motsey time to better arrange his affairs before filing for bankruptcy.

Events closed in on Motsey the rest of that summer. In July one of Motsey's smaller bank creditors, angered over his failure to repay a $250,000 six-month note when due on March 25, threatened to blow the whole lid off the Copeland empire by throwing Motsey into involuntary bankruptcy. "The thing I resented most," recalled an officer of the Worthen Bank and Trust Co. of Little Rock, Arkansas, "was all those guys telling us that we didn't dare to go up against the Du Ponts. So we went up to Wilmington armed with the necessary papers. The next day we got our money."[43]

No sooner had Motsey bought off the Arkansas bank than more trouble broke out in California. In Hollywood a finance company seized the *Citizen-News* Building with security guards in lieu of $450,000 owed by Motsey. Motsey's *Citizen-News* lieutenant, Richard Horton, after a scuffle with the guards, repossessed the building with the aid of local police, only to see the finance company then take the case to the Internal Revenue Service for the *Citizen-News*'s failure to pay employee withholding taxes. Two weeks later the *Citizen-News,* thrown into bankruptcy proceedings, ceased publication.

With the death of his newspaper, Motsey was in a real sense signaling the coming of his departure from the world of high finance. That month he told an associate "that sooner or later he was going to have to file for bankruptcy. I passed the word around, but nobody believed me. From beginning to end in this thing, nobody could believe a Du Pont could go bankrupt."[44]

Whatever plans Motsey might have had for filing bankruptcy papers, he kept them secret from his Winthrop-Lawrence associates, never mentioning them or Wilmington Trust's recent judgment against him, to Shaheen. He even spent a good deal of time in August and September in London, where Shaheen was sheltering his family—and himself—from a Chicago Federal Grand Jury investigation into delinquent Barber Union loans made while he was the union's pension fund adviser. Shaheen was using his presence there in typical fashion, setting up a closed-end offshore fund and obtaining the distribution rights from London Screenplays Ltd. to five movies, including "The Virgin and the Gypsy." Never emotionally strong enough to say no to Shaheen, Motsey signed notes for the films and was to be chairman of the mutual fund; then another bomb was laid on Wilmington.

A few years back, Joseph Keenan, president of the International Brotherhood of Electrical Workers, approved a $2.7 million loan to some of Motsey's California newspapers. The inappropriateness of union officials providing pension funds for right-wing antilabor newspapers would have been enough to raise rank-and-file ire, but the IBEW leadership even allowed Motsey to persuade them later to surrender a $700,000 trust deed on some of his newspaper properties that the millionaire scion had put up as part collateral. Motsey simply paid them $44,000 and then used the deed to obtain another $400,000 loan from the Maccabees Mutual Life Insurance Company of Southfield, Michigan.

Motsey failed to pay back the union's loan when it came due in the spring of 1970. Apparently, paying back millions to financial brethren at Chemical Bank and First National City Bank meant more to Motsey than paying back a loan from a union's pension fund for its elderly workers. In July the union began pressing Motsey to repay his debt. Finally, on September 11 and 18, the union's Wilmington attorney notified Motsey and Wilmington Trust that it intended to take possession of the collateral still due them: 18,187 shares of Christiana Securities common worth about $2 million. There was only one catch: Motsey's stock was safely locked away in the vaults of Wilmington Trust.

On September 28 Wilmington Trust's counsel, Richards, Layton, & Finger, informed the union that its request was "not timely." An additional twenty-five days were required for normal bank procedures to be fulfilled. Exactly twenty-two days later Motsey filed papers for voluntary bankruptcy under Section 10.

Motsey's move came as a complete shock. "I couldn't believe it," said Shaheen. "We were all ready to go with this mutual fund and boom— Lammot flies back to Wilmington and files for bankruptcy."[45] One of the accountants closest to Motsey expressed similar surprise. "I was with Lammot the day before he filed bankruptcy and he never mentioned a word of it. The first I knew about it was in the papers."[46]

With Motsey went the keystone to the entire Copeland empire. Having received only $200,000 out of $4 million in notes pledged by its chairman, Transogram stock plummeted from its 1970 high of $15.25 down to $3.62, cutting the stock value held by all those small banks nearly 80 percent. One Midwestern bank president was forced to resign, and the former owners of Transogram's new acquisitions, Quaker Masonry and Southern Precision Industries, were left holding devalued stock with little hope of ever seeing Motsey's promise to buy their shares come true. London Screenplays, holding Motsey's notes, had their credit line cut off by Morgan Grenfell & Co., the big British banking concern. Over 100 banks across the country saw their loans, and their credibility, jeopardized.

Winthrop-Lawrence was forced into bankruptcy as well. In turn, Massey Junior College in Atlanta, Georgia, and a trade school at Pascagoula, Mississippi, both had to turn students out of their rooms and put their dormitories up for sale. Meanwhile, Motsey's California newspapers had gone into receivership.

Overnight, 38-year-old Motsey became a national figure, although not the way he had originally intended. Over a dozen suits were launched against him by famous associates charging fraud, and Motsey, in turn, sued his Winthrop-Lawrence associates, secure in the knowledge that Delaware law protects "spendthrift" trusts from litigation. Apparently, Motsey was a big spender. His trusts amounted to over $13 million. Despite his $50 million in debts, Motsey to this day enjoys a $311,000 yearly income from these trusts, which allows him to live in a style proper for any self-respecting Du Pont, bankrupt or not.

On November 24 Lammot du Pont Copeland, Jr., made his first public appearance in Wilmington's federal court. Accompanied by his New York lawyer, David Griff, Motsey appeared somewhat nervous as he entered the packed courtroom to face his creditors, of which there were over 100. But as he spoke in answer to questions put by the federal bankruptcy referee,

Murray C. Schwartz, it became only too clear that the tall, reserved heir was well-informed on the details of his financial empire. Copeland, moreover, found himself even smiling shyly at photographers.

The Barber's Union found nothing to smile about, however. They were awarded the 9,000 shares of Christiana Securities Motsey had put up as $900,000 collateral. This still left the union's pension fund short $400,000 by Copeland, and about $4 million more owed through loans arranged by Shaheen.

The Electrical Workers Union was also not happy. The IBEC had received only $1.8 million worth of Christiana Security collateral, leaving its pension fund short by $700,000.

But perhaps the unhappiest of all was Lammot du Pont Copeland, Sr. Copeland's $3.5 million collateral with the Union Bank of Switzerland was liquidated on the stock market. With Wilmington Trust, he got a somewhat better deal. Although it quickly liquidated Motsey's $410,000 collateral, it spared Copeland, Sr.'s $3.35 million block of blue chip stocks. Instead, it sold the stock to a syndicate headed by former business associates of William Potter, Copeland's attorney.

But even more important was the damage done to Copeland's name among Du Pont Company stockholders and the family. Motsey had committed a grave sin against the family's financial mores—he had lost Christiana stock in his personal speculations instead of preserving its traditional use as a family trust. About $2.7 million worth of Christiana had subsequently fallen into the hands of outsiders—labor unions, at that. The following April, before hundreds of stockholders gathered in Hotel Du Pont for Du Pont's annual meeting, Copeland would be called upon by one irate stockholder to resign his chairmanship because of his son's dealings. He would refuse then, only to resign the following year, as one company official put it, because of "personal troubles relating to his son."

Motsey's was one of the greatest personal bankruptcies in American history, and for the economy and Edmond du Pont, it came at precisely the wrong time. First, it put a damper on the family's willingness to bail out private ventures by any one member or group in the clan. Second, it undermined Lammot du Pont Copeland, Sr.'s ability to help with Edmond's problems in F. I. du Pont even if he wanted to. With Du Pont stock still in trouble, and millions in blue chip stocks that were posted as collateral for Motsey now disappearing or in jeopardy, Copeland had to fend for himself. It was not surprising, then, that when Edmond desperately called for more capital for F. I. du Pont in December 1970, only one month after Motsey's bankruptcy hearings, Copeland turned him down.

In fact Copeland and the rest of the family were considering pulling out of F. I. du Pont altogether. No doubt Edmond's own misfortunes and the company's losses were the main reasons for this decision. But the final impetus may well have been growing rumors of an impending suit soon to be filed against him for allegedly practicing some of the same "milking" techniques ascribed to Motsey. The following June these rumors were indeed confirmed when a complaint was filed in Philadelphia's District Court claiming F. I. du Pont's involvement in a conspiracy which allegedly had brought about the bankruptcy of the largest railroad in the country— the Penn Central.

The Great Train Robbery

The Du Ponts had been involved with the Pennsylvania Railroad ever since Pierre S. du Pont II joined the railroad's board in 1930. Becoming a member of its finance committee two years later, Pierre advised the railroad on the refinancing of its capital structure throughout the grim days of the Depression and right up until 1953, less than a year before his death.

At that time Lammot du Pont Copeland donned Pierre's mantle and also assumed a leading position on the board of the Philadelphia, Baltimore, and Washington Railroad, a Pennsylvania Railroad subsidiary which had as board members two other Wilmington Trust directors, W. Stradley and H. Morris. Fusing these Du Pont ties to the Pennsylvania Railroad was the family's long-standing close relation to Morgan interests, which held 7.2 percent of Pennsylvania's stock and were probably its biggest shareholders.

It was this Du Pont association with Morgan interests that led to crucial negotiating activities concerning Pennsylvania Railroad soon after Pierre's death. The focus of these negotiations was the Toledo, Peoria, and Western Railroad, a valuable "bridge carrier" line that linked the Santa Fe Railroad in the west with the Pennsylvania Railroad in the east. Morgan interests, represented by J. P. Morgan & Company and Guaranty Trust Company, owned large controlling blocks of stock in both the Santa Fe and the Pennsylvania and therefore had a vested interest in the status quo of profits.

This interest was threatened in 1954 when Ben Heineman acquired control of the Minneapolis and St. Louis Railway. Heineman sought to link the T.P. & W. and another line, the Monon Railroad, with his own line to form an "outerbelt" line connecting east and west by bypassing the traditional Chicago and St. Louis gateways. Such a bypass, by avoiding those cities' traffic congestion and the accompanying loss in shipping time and cost to shippers, would pose a serious competitive threat to the old Santa Fe-Pennsylvania lines which used the gateway cities. Heineman's bid for the T.P. & W. in the spring of 1954, then, presented a challenge to the Pennsylvania's and the Santa Fe's profitable operations. Both railroads responded to this challenge by offering their own bid to the T.P. & W.'s owners.

Unfortunately for Heineman, the T.P. & W. was controlled by the Du Ponts through the trust department of their Wilmington Trust Company, which owned 82 percent of T.P. & W.'s stock. Although Wilmington Trust had run the T.P. & W. profitably since 1947, it suddenly took an interest in selling the line when both the Santa Fe and the Pennsylvania management expressed concern that the T.P. & W. should not fall into "unfriendly hands."[47] From then on, although Heineman made repeated offers to bid competitively (and even made one bid 33 percent higher), Wilmington Trust officials, particularly President George P. Edmonds, son-in-law of Lammot du Pont, Vice-President Joseph Chinn, and Vice-President J. Sellers Bancroft—who served as a director of the T.P. & W. and co-trustee of the estate of the late president of the railroad, George P. Mc-Near—consistently steered the T.P. & W. into the hands of their friends and actually, through the Pennsylvania, themselves.

On April 15, 1955, Wilmington Trust agreed to sell to the Santa Fe and Pennsylvania each a 26 percent holding. On April 29, however, the other co-trustee of the McNear estate heard of Heineman's offer and requested that the bid be reopened, but to no avail. This violation of trust gave the estate's beneficiaries the angry fuel to demand an acceptance of Heineman's offer, and on May 26 Wilmington Trust reopened the bid. Subsequently, Santa Fe had to better Heineman's offer and quickly bought all of the trust's T.P. & W. stock and resold half of it to Pennsylvania Railroad. As a sidelight, Lammot du Pont Copeland, representing Du Pont interests on the Pennsylvania board, also later became a director of Wilmington Trust.

The T.P. & W. deal illustrated not only the cooperation between "friendly hands," but also served as a further move by the Du Ponts into the Pennsylvania Railroad. A year later, in 1956, Copeland and the two Wilmington Trust representatives on the Philadelphia, Baltimore, and Washington Railroad board approved the absorption of the Pittsburgh, Cincinnati, Chicago, and St. Louis Railroad by the Pennsylvania subsidiary. A few years later, when the Pennsylvania merged with the New York Central to form the largest railroad network in the country, the Du Ponts did not sit on the Penn Central board, probably to keep the railroad from being implicated in their court-ordered divestiture of control of General Motors, the Penn Central's biggest customer and another link in the Du Pont-Morgan community of interests. But they did keep their stock interest in the new $4.4 billion combine.

Size, however, brings its problems in the areas of both generating high enough earnings and operating efficiently. This is especially true of railroads, as they have borne the brunt of automotive trucking competition with particularly disastrous results. The T.P. & W. deal exemplifies what problems ensue for railroads when short-run profits are placed above efficiency. The T.P. & W. acquisition by Pennsylvania Railroad and Santa Fe did not result in cost-saving efficiency, but greater cost-generating congestion in St. Louis and Chicago. Heineman's bypass plan, which would have cut costs in the long run by avoiding traffic snarls, was scrapped in the interest of the status quo of the Pennsylvania's immediate profits.

The Du Ponts, in taking steps to destroy Heineman's plan and hand the T.P. & W. over to the Pennsylvania, as well as in their leadership role in the Pennsylvania Railroad itself, directly contributed to the inefficiency of the country's rail system and to the Penn Central's inability to compete with the trucking industry, an inability which, along with other problems, was a key factor in the Penn Central bankruptcy. Translated into the effects on most of the country's population, the Du Ponts' complicity in the T.P. & W. affair resulted in higher prices for goods shipped and cutbacks on less profitable passenger service (to cut costs to compensate for lost freight business). It represents just one example of profiteering which is costly to the people of this country; as long as mass transit is privately owned, the people may be deprived of any chance of a viable (and much needed) transportation system between cities.

Above and beyond these functional dilemmas of capitalism and its profit motive, Penn Central also became afflicted with increasing management negligence. What was neglected was Penn Central's needs; what was not neglected was Penn Central's financial reserves.

According to a June 1971 suit filed in Philadelphia's Federal District Court by Penn Central, F. I. du Pont & Company and top Penn Central management had been involved over the years in a lucrative conspiracy to exploit the railroad's resources for their own private investments and profits, a violation of the Federal Securities Law.

F. I. du Pont was the principal investment adviser to Penn Central and approved the railroad's major investments in other firms. For these investments, the railroad's Supplemental Pension Plan, with a book value of $278 million and a real value of $331 million, and the $11.5 million Contingent Compensation Fund were used. The Supplemental Pension Plan represented the present and future income of 21,000 active and 15,000 retired railroad workers. The Contingent Compensation Fund was designed as deferred compensation for company officers. Two other source funds, the Pennsylvania Company and the Employee Benefit Funds of the Buckeye Pipeline Company, were also employed.

All of these funds were under the control of Penn Central directors David C. Beven, Richard King Mellon's hand-picked vice-president in charge of finance, and General Charles J. Hodge, erstwhile partner in F. I. du Pont and former business partner of Maurice Stans, Nixon's Commerce Secretary. All were used to invest in the Penphil Company, of which Hodge was a promoter and Beven was founder, secretary, and treasurer. Another Penn Central director, General O. F. Lassiter, owned 20 percent of one of Penphil's subsidiaries, Florphil Company, a firm involved in Florida investments.

F. I. du Pont's overt involvement in Penphil was through one of its vice-presidents, Hobart C. Ramsey, in 1963. Ramsey and Alphonso Manero, who became a du Pont partner in 1968, were among Penphil's thirteen original shareholders. Later, another du Pont partner, Mrs. Marie L. Hodge, also became associated with Penphil as a stockholder. But the big du Pont force in Penphil's growth was the chairman of Edmond du Pont's executive committee, Charles Hodge.

During the Sixties, Beven, Hodge, and F. I. du Pont & Company allegedly used Penn Central's pension fund "to build Penphil into a large worldwide conglomerate."[48] The record does indeed show that Penphil was becoming a conglomerate, buying 30,488 shares of Kaneb Pipeline Company, 10,000 shares of Tropical Gas Company, 5,000 shares of National Homes Corporation, 30,000 shares of Continental Mortgage Investors, 10,000 shares of the Great Southwest Corporation, 21,280 shares of the First Bank and Trust Company of Boca Raton, 51,000 shares of Holiday International Tours, and 4,668 shares of the University National Bank of Boca Raton.

All these firms, with the exception of Holiday International Tours and the Florida banks, were controlled by Beven and Hodge; Holiday International was established by Penphil to hook up and use Penn Central funds invested in another company, Executive Jet Aviation, Inc., to establish a worldwide competitor to Pan Am.

This last scheme, the brainchild of General Lassiter, involved—according to testimony in December 1970 before the House Banking and Currency Committee—everything from corporate pimping of women employees to holdings in International Air Bahama, before Pan Am tipped off the Civil Aeronautics Board about its new competitors. Apparently, the Federal Aviation Act prohibits railroads from running air carriers. In January 1969 the CAB laid the second largest fine in its history on Penn Central, $70,000, and ordered the railroad to turn over control of EJA to a Detroit bank, causing a loss to Penn Central of $22 million.

The EJA disaster was only one of many Penn Central losses from investments recommended by Beven and Hodge. On December 1, 1969, Penn Central bought 90 percent of Great Southwest Corporation, costing it $92 million. By June 1971 the stock was worth only $40 million. Meanwhile, Penphil had already dropped 10,000 GSC shares in 1965 at a net profit of 130 percent, its owners obviously intending to shift to Penn Central for resources. This same ruse was used for Tropical Gas, in which $2.2 million of Penn Central funds were invested, and was repeated again in September 1968 before Tropical Gas was merged in 1969 with the U.S. Freight Company, Beven and Hodge selling out. By then, Penphil's worth had increased 200 percent since 1967, while Penn Central funds were also steered into Arvida Corporation (58 percent), a resort in Boca Raton, Florida, where Penphil picked up 26,000 shares of Bancshares of Florida in exchange for its bank holdings.

This incredible wild scenario was only brought to an end when Penn Central, caught in Nixon's credit squeeze, had its lawyers finally file for reorganization under bankruptcy laws in June 1970. This left $82 million worth of Penn Central I.O.U.'s practically worthless, contributing to an already capital-short market's woes. Additionally, in December, the very month Edmond du Pont was hurriedly calling on relatives in Wilmington to invest in his brokerage firm, the House Banking and Currency Committee released its "Executive Jet Aviation" report, exposing the shady behavior of one of Edmond's top executives and partners, Charles Hodge, in financially advising the now bankrupt Penn Central. Such alleged swindles revealed that more than back-office snarls was wrong with F. I. du Pont & Company and must only have further discouraged the family's willingness to help resolve Edmond's need for capital.

Less than a year later Penn Central's lawyers would sue F. I. du Pont & Company, charging the brokerage house with having been a "co-conspirator" with Beven, profiteering off commissions and fees for investments in Penphil and other related companies, exploiting the resources of Penn Central to benefit Penphil, trading on Penn Central's credit lines for Penphil, hurting the railroad's credit, and causing a loss of the use of funds for its own railroad needs.

These were charges that could destroy the reputation of any brokerage house as an investment adviser, and what was worse, Penn Central's bankruptcy seemed to confirm them. Chemical Bank had given preferential loans to Penphil based on the Penn Central and F. I. du Pont luminaries involved, and other large New York banks had given loans to Penn Central, some of which ended up in Penphil or its subsidiaries. The railroad's pension fund was now depleted, and in January 1972 Philadelphia District Attorney Arlen Spector would obtain indictments against Hodge, Beven, and Lassiter, charging them with causing monetary damages of $66 million which, it was claimed, triggered off the bankruptcy.

More than anyone else, Lammot du Pont Copeland, Sr., probably knew the falsity of that latter charge. As this former Pennsylvania Railroad director well knew, $66 million did not account for Penn Central's losses of up to $400 million a year. Much of the answer lay instead within Penn Central's own mounting inefficiency and the failure of most large railroads to generate enough profits to keep investors from straying into more lucrative diversification.

But the damage done to F. I. du Pont's reputation by the Penn Central fiasco was irreparable, and the reputation and fortune of the family as a whole, especially among banks on which the family in its own investment trend had increasingly relied, had to be protected—even at the cost of one of its favorite sons. Copeland, for one, had his own directorship (and Du Pont's reputation) with Chemical Bank to preserve. This, compounded with his son's bankruptcy and his own losses, were no doubt the key factors behind his refusal to Edmond's plea for capital assistance. These were also the main reasons why Edmond's plea fell on deaf ears throughout the Du Pont mansions along the Brandywine.

Having failed to obtain the signed promises of all general partners and lenders to keep their funds, and failing to raise the $15 million he pledged, Edmond was removed from the chair he had occupied for almost thirty years, and his father for ten before him. On December 29, 1970, at a meeting of the general partners, he "resigned" and was replaced by another partner favored by the Perot group, John W. Allyn. Managing director Wallace Latour, always loyal to Edmond and his own job, opposed yielding to the Perot forces. He, too, was replaced. Perot's holding in the brokerage firm now automatically rose from 51 percent to 91 percent. As one of his associates put it, "It was a *great* deal."[49]

Other Du Ponts, led by Lammot du Pont Copeland and Edmond's older brother Emile, didn't think so, and they continued their plans to withdraw their $30 million from the firm, giving their six-month required notices. This threat and an additional audit revealing that the firm needed another $30 million to $40 million for a 1 to 10 capital-debt ratio, infuriated the Texan.

"They knew I wanted to do this thing in the national interest," Perot claimed. "They would have been wiped out if I hadn't come in, but when I did they looked on me as someone pouring money into a funnel so they could take it out at the bottom." Perot made no bones about his *nouveau riche* resentment for "those people who have never worked." "When something happens to their trust fund, they're traumatized."[50]

Perot's mentioning of the family's concern for its trust funds probably was an accurate description of what was most on Du Pont minds at the time. It also revealed how important the trust funds' ability to flexibly buy, sell, and diversify in general had become to the family, keynoting the clan's increasing move from industrial to financial preoccupations.

For their part, the Du Ponts claimed that Perot had "stolen" the firm. Although Edmond was incommunicado and reported ill, his elder son, Anthony, had taken up the Du Pont banner. Thirty-seven-year-old Tony had a $1 million investment of his own in his father's firm and also headed a small aerospace defense plant in Torrance, California. Helping him through the negotiations was one of Edmond's former general partners, 57-year-old Morris Goldstein. Together, they represented twenty investors, mostly Du Ponts, who had made an investment of $25 million to $30 million.

On February 10 Tony and Goldstein arrived in Dallas for a meeting with Perot. As the meeting progressed, Tony insisted that the partners' December agreement giving Perot control didn't have the approval of the investors they represented. Perot's claim on the firm, he explained quietly, would result in a deluge of lawsuits. Having played his ace, Tony then made his offer, suggesting that Perot buy the family out or search for a third party to buy *him* out.

The bluff didn't work. Perot simply turned the tables and agreed. "I want out," he said, and then made it clear that he also wanted hard conditions: his $10 million returned, a 25 percent ownership for $750,000, all the firm's data processing and bookkeeping contracts, and a guarantee by the family that they would raise another $30 million to give the firm a solid 1 to 10 ratio.

Tony was astounded. "We explained that if the investor group had that kind of money, we wouldn't be having conversations with him in the first place."[51] The meeting ended with nothing resolved.

At this point the New York Stock Exchange and the Securities Exchange Commission intervened, frightened of the economic consequences if the second largest brokerage house in the country were forced to close its doors for lack of capital. Felix Rohatyn, chairman of the Exchange's surveillance committee, became a mediator for the Perot group, while the Exchange's vice-chairman, Ralph De Nunzio, became the mediator for the Du Ponts. The Exchange's chairman, Bernard Lasker, acted as the go-between.

The pressure built on the Du Ponts. On March 8 and 10 the board of governors of the Securities Investor Protection Corporation, only recently created by Congress, stated they wanted some plan worked out by March 11 to be presented before a joint meeting of the SIPC and the SEC. March 11 passed, as did March 15, the deadline for Perot's $10 million loan if no agreement had been reached. Perot agreed to extend the deadline three more days, after which F. I. du Pont would have to close its doors. That threat finally brought direct intervention from the White House.

In the age of Watergate, it is worth recalling that the Nixon administration, in the persons of Attorney General Mitchell, Treasury Secretary John Connally, and Presidential Assistant Peter M. Flanigan (a former vice-president of Dillon, Reed), had already violated the law by encouraging Perot's $10 million investment. The Exchange's own rules, adopted under the self-regulatory auspices of the Securities Exchange Act of 1934, stipulated that "the major business of an outsider buying a member firm has to be securities transactions."[52] Perot's business was selling computer services, not stocks. Furthermore, there is serious question as to whether the Nixon administration also violated the Banking Act of 1933, which forbade commercial bank officers from being officers of investment banking houses. At the time, Perot was a director of the Republic National Bank of Dallas. Nevertheless, the White House, and the Exchange itself, ignored the law and invited this personal friend of Richard Nixon to take control of a major investment house.

Following Perot's extension of his deadline, Lammot du Pont Copeland, Sr., received a call from the White House. It was Peter Flanigan. Would the Du Ponts come to Washington for a conference?

On March 16 Copeland, Anthony du Pont, and Goldstein arrived in the capital and were confronted by Attorney General Mitchell, Flanigan, and two SIPC board members, Donald Regan, chairman of Merrill, Lynch, and Bruce MacLaury, an undersecretary of the Treasury Department. But the Du Pont family has a long history of resisting government pressure. They still refused to keep their funds in the firm, although the meeting may well have succeeded in impressing upon the Du Ponts the seriousness of the situation.

The next afternoon the Du Ponts again met with Perot's negotiators in New York, Stock Exchange officials acting as mediators and also applying last-minute pressure. After several fruitless hours the meeting was adjourned. During this interval, the Exchange's president, Robert Haack, privately addressed the Du Ponts on the danger of their losing their entire $30 million investment if F. I. du Pont was forced to close its doors and be liquidated. The Du Ponts were simply courting disaster. Having cordially laid down his bomb, Haack left the Du Ponts to ponder their fate.

When the meeting was reconvened, a new flexibility was noted emanating from the Wilmington group. It took several hours more, proposing and counterproposing into the night, but at 1:00 A.M. an agreement was finally reached. The family would keep their money in the firm in return for a 20 percent holding and warrants, subordinated debentures, and preferred stock. This meant that if the firm earned $20 million each year in the next five years, the Du Ponts would receive $20 million on top of their $30 million holding. If all went well, their $30 million investment could return as much as $60 million within fifteen years.

Perot, holding 80 percent, would make much more, but most of the responsibility for raising needed capital would fall on him. He would get assistance, of course. The Exchange agreed to indemnify $15 million of his investment and provide assistance for customers of Perot's Electronic Data Systems. The Federal Reserve Board also came through, approving a $55 million loan to Perot from Chase Manhattan and nine other banks. Although Perot had put up only $78.5 million worth of EDS stock as collateral, the FRB waived the usual $157 million stock requirement for a loan of that size. In return, Perot agreed to inject $30 million more into F. I. du Pont to give it a 1 to 10 ratio.

Everyone seemed content with the St. Patrick's Day agreement. "If du Pont had failed," appraised Bernard Lasker, "Merrill Lynch would not have taken over Goodbody, and if both these leading firms had gone down at once, there's no question that the effect on the country, the industry, investors, and the economy would have been severe, if not disastrous. . . ."[53] "As long as there is a Wall Street we will owe a tremendous debt to Ross Perot. I for one will be, as long as I live, forever grateful."[54]

Only one party was neither content nor grateful—Edmond du Pont. In April Edmond broke his silence and announced he was thinking of suing the firm, claiming that $3.1 million in bank loans drawn over his signature during 1970 was not for his personal behalf, but the firm's. He remained steadfast in holding out as F. I. du Pont's largest investor, refusing to sign any agreement.

Faced with Edmond's stubbornness, the general partners simply "retired" him from the firm on April 27, thereby avoiding any need for his signature. On March 14, the firm was incorporated as Du Pont, Glore, Forgan, Inc., and the Perot take-over was completed. A. Rhett du Pont's and Emile du Pont's sons, A. Rhett du Pont, Jr., and Peter R. du Pont, remained as vice-presidents.

Edmond was not through fighting, however. In December he sued Perot for $6 million in damages, charging that Perot had taken advantage of his computer firm's intimate knowledge of F. I. du Pont to drive a hard bargain and force the du Pont partners into signing the agreements that surrendered control to him. Actually, Perot's knowledge of the Du Pont family's financial woes may have been even more intimate; Perot's own bank, the Republic National Bank at Dallas, of which Perot was a director in 1970, was listed by Lammot du Pont Copeland, Jr., that year as one of his many creditors. Edmond also asserted Perot had deliberately delayed the registration of 100,000 EDS shares which Edmond had planned to use to bolster the capital position of the firm.

Perot described Edmond's charges as "pathetic." The plausibility that Edmond's claims amounted to more than that simplistic characterization, that they may have even been true, was undoubtedly hurt by the picture Edmond had been painting of himself. To the press, he described himself as a man who had lost $8 to $10 million—"Everything I had"[55]—and was now forced to live on a monthly Social Security check of $257. That grim picture of dire poverty simply did not fit the plush reality of a Du Pont who was still a director of the Continental American Life Insurance and the Rockland Corporation, who owned sizable blocks of stock in other companies, and who continued to live in a fashionable home near close relatives all of whom were millionaires.

Meanwhile, every day Perot called his chief lieutenant at F. I. du Pont, Morton Meyerson. "Found it yet?" he would ask, only to hear the same negative reply from New York. Over $86 million was missing in securities recorded on Edmond's books, and many investors feared the drain on EDS stock, which, valued at $1 billion a year before, had plunged to $300 million. By June 1972 Perot had soaked over $64 million into du Pont, while the mansions along the Brandywine buzzed with chuckles tempered with a few gulps of genuine concern for the family's own interest still in du Pont. Within two years, Perot's salvaging job of F. I. du Pont finally took hold, but at the cost of $100 million, the milking of Walston & Co. for capital and the abandoning of the merged brokerage business, Du Pont Walston. Perot claimed he was leaving Wall Street and closed Du Pont Walston, its bills paid. Along the Brandywine the gulps subsided but the chuckles continued, even as Perot's computer firm chalked up new lucrative contracts with government agencies in Washington, D.C., Albany (where he also managed to be the top bidder), Sacramento, and, yes, even with a chemical firm founded by one E. I. Du Pont.

3. PICKING UP THE PIECES

On a cold winter night in January 1971 a well-heeled crowd of people filed into Wilmington's deserted City Hall and mounted the long winding staircase and elevators that led to the city council chambers. Inside the paneled chambers they filed in quietly between rows, cheerfully greeting their many fellow Republicans, and politely took their seats. In front of them, beyond the railing, was the city council in full session, also sitting quietly, awaiting the arrival of Mayor Harry Haskell and the beginning of the annual "State of the City" show.

Few of these people had noticed the two plainclothes policemen at the entrance to the council chambers, and even those probably would not have, had the policemen not tried to stop one person from entering.

That person, Ramón Ceci, was a local longshoreman with a history of opposing the powers that be in Wilmington. Returning from a hitch in the Navy, Ceci had attended the University of Delaware and, in the heat of the antiwar upsurges of the time, became a leader of the local chapter of Students for a Democratic Society. As student government president, he made life difficult for the Du Pont-controlled administrators before finally resigning and graduating to the docks of Wilmington. Fired by a zeal for justice in his home town, Ceci had long been involved in supporting the plight of its Black community and was active in the white opposition to the National Guard occupation and "the drafting of poor and working people in an undeclared, immoral, and imperialist war against the people of Vietnam." By 1970 Ceci was known to some of the politically active Du Ponts, and the Du Ponts, in turn, were known and opposed by him and his friends.

Probably for this reason, Wilmington authorities were concerned about reports that Ceci would show up that night to publicly mar Harry Haskell's moment of glory with a leaflet attacking Haskell's $1\frac{1}{2}$ percent wage tax and his real estate speculation in the city through the Rockland Corporation. During the day, police came to both Ceci's home and his place of work to arrest him for a parking violation over a year old, but workers on the docks hid Ceci while detaining police.

That night Ceci showed up at City Hall with other young friends from the community, determined to be allowed to attend the mayor's public address. When the two plainsclothesmen stepped forward and attempted to stop him at the chambers' doors without identifying themselves, Ceci quickly pushed their arms aside and began loudly shouting about being attacked by two unknown men who refused to identify themselves. The commotion forced the policemen to retreat into the shadows as Ceci and his friends entered the chambers, gave out leaflets to those who would take them, and sat down.

Finally Haskell appeared, looking unworn after his two years in office, his body trim and dressed impeccably, his mouth creased in a smile, but his eyes always darting about anxiously from behind their steel-rimmed glasses.

508

Slowly, to the applause of the Republican faithful turned out for the occasion, he walked down the center aisle, his aides flanking him on both sides.

For the next half hour, Haskell delivered his State of the City address, claiming that he had halted Wilmington's "downward rush" by firing sixty municipal workers, beefing up the police force (and doubling the number of minority policemen), installing 1,400 new powerful sodium lights that glared down on the Black community at night, establishing a "neighborhood" Model Cities Council (with little control by neighborhood people), and last but not least, imposing a city wage tax to "keep the property tax as low as possible."[56]

In a city where the Du Ponts own over $10 million worth of property and where most of the skyscrapers are Du Pont skyscrapers, such a statement by a Du Pont-supported mayor and son of a Du Pont vice-president might raise anyone's temperature. It raised Ceci's. As Haskell returned down the aisle to a standing Republican ovation, Ceci shouted a remark to the mayor about his real estate speculation. Embarrassed, Haskell hurriedly left the chambers, leaving Ceci to angry Republicans, a curious press, and eager police. That night Ceci was arrested—for his parking ticket, of course.

The mayor's attempt to bury the facts with a shrug and an arrest didn't work this time, however, for Ceci's public charges and his friends' calls to the *News-Journal* were too blatant to ignore. The next day the *News-Journal* carried a large article on Ceci's charges and his subsequent arrest.

Such embarrassing scenes were what the Du Ponts had to face frequently in those days. Merely a month later antiwar Wilmingtonians brought before the common council a demand for an end to all drafting in the city for "the undeclared war in Vietnam." Some weeks after that Haskell was caught permitting police to hide an electronic eavesdropping device at the site of an impending antiwar demonstration. The bugging was reported in the press around the country and drew some uncomplimentary comments. To add to Haskell's angry embarrassment, the city council censured the mayor; one Democratic member even sent him a copy of George Orwell's *1984*.

No sooner was this incident past when over 300 residents, mostly youths, took to the streets on March 20 to protest the Vietnam War. Following a rally in front of Du Pont headquarters at Rodney Square, the demonstrators, led by the local chapter of Youth Against War and Fascism, began marching down Wilmington's Main Street chanting, "Du Ponts get rich! GI's die!" receiving open support from shoppers along the way. The march was stopped only by a phalanx of police moving up Main Street from the opposite direction, resulting in four arrests. But the damage to Wilmington's "disciplined" image had already been done.

This last scene was particularly disquieting to the Du Ponts, but 1971 had even more to offer. On September 2, inmates in Governor Peterson's new "model" prison at Smyrna rebelled against the poor food and the behavior of the guards. Three guards were taken hostage, but were released after the press was allowed to see the prisoners, and negotiations ended the revolt. Afterwards, guards beat the prisoners severely, sparking sympathy protests in Wilmington. Angry over the rebellion and its exposure of conditions in his model prison, Governor Peterson put part of the blame for the revolt on the "meddling" prison reform activities of William H. du Pont's wife. William became so angry about Peterson's charges that he resigned from the Republican Party. Many other Du Ponts—some of whom had been involved in setting up the new prison for mostly poor Black Delawarians—also believed the governor's remarks were unwarranted. Some cooled their support for Peterson's national political ambitions, an important factor in Peterson's electoral defeat the following year.

Peterson was not the only Republican incumbent to incur Du Pont anger. Many Du Ponts were becoming disillusioned with the Vietnam War policies of President Nixon as well.

Richard Nixon became associated with the Du Ponts after World War II, when he served on the witch-hunting House Un-American Activities Committee (HUAC). (He was also an OPA co-worker with Du Pont Chairman Irving Shapiro in wartime Washington.) The Du Ponts, applauding his part in the inquisitions, fully endorsed Nixon's vice-presidential candidacies in 1952 and 1956 and donated $125,000, the highest contribution, to his unsuccessful bid for the presidency in 1960.

During his tenure on Wall Street, Nixon often came in contact with associates of F. I. du Pont & Company, and although there seems some evidence that many Du Ponts were less than enthusiastic about his decision to run for the 1968 Republican nomination (A. Felix du Pont, Jr., for example, openly organized in behalf of Nelson Rockefeller's campaign), the clan fully backed his campaign once his nomination was secured. In fact, Nixon's running mate, Maryland Governor Spiro Agnew, was well known to his Delaware neighbors. Some Du Ponts, including Samuel F. du Pont, had supported Agnew's rise through Baltimore politics, Sam du Pont even serving on Agnew's State Law Enforcement Commission.

Walter Carpenter's son, Edmund N. Carpenter II (whose wife Edna was also a former Republican national committeewoman), chaired the "Delaware Citizens for Nixon-Agnew Committee." Edmund, a past president of the New Castle County Young Republicans, and deputy attorney general and a director of the Bank of Delaware, was a member of the National Republican Finance Committee. Apparently, Edmund was quite successful in helping finance Nixon's campaign. He raised over $14,000 from Lammot du Pont Copeland alone. Henry B. du Pont gave $3,000 to Nixon's cause.

Helping Edmund's efforts was State Representative Pierre S. du Pont IV, also a member of the National Republican Finance Committee and the Republican National Committee.

Young "Pete" du Pont had become a force in Republican circles over the years. From 1964 to 1965 this tall, spectacled Harvard Law graduate served well enough as assistant legal counsel for the Republican State Committee to be elected vice-chairman of the powerful Brandywine Hundred Republican Committee and he was elected to Delaware's House of Representatives unopposed. From 1966 to 1968 Pierre was chairman of the Republican Program Development Committee, and he developed an image as an "idea man," a reputation that some of his associates reportedly believe was undeserved.

In January 1968 Pierre replaced his uncle, State Senator Reynolds du Pont, on the National Republican Finance Committee and was catapulted to national political prominence.

Following Nixon's election, Pierre latched onto the President's coattails to be carried to his goal—national office. In April 1969 he organized the twentieth annual Booster Luncheon at the Hotel Du Pont. Along with the usual entourage of Delaware's Republican hierarchy, Pierre's fund-raising luncheon was attended by Maryland's Rogers C. B. Morton, the new Republican National Committee chairman and director of Atlas Chemicals (a Du Pont spin-off), Florida's Senator Edward Gurney, and Ohio Congressman Robert Taft, Jr. There, in the citadel of the Du Pont empire, Morton and the Du Ponts discussed Republican strategy for the 1970 election, strategy which included Pierre's campaign for Delaware's only Congressional seat.

To Pierre, destiny was clearly beckoning. "As in other times in our history, our government is being challenged," Pierre asserted on announcing his candidacy. "I believe I can help meet that challenge by moving from the House of Representatives in Dover to the House of Representatives in Washington." To help move him along, in June Nixon appointed the Congressional candidate to the Federal Air Quality Board, emphasizing Pierre's national political attributes. During his well-financed campaign, Pierre sought to push a liberal image and play down his family name, choosing to call himself "Pete." In November, just a few days after easily defeating his Democratic opponent at the polls, "Pierre" suddenly reappeared, shaking hands and expressing his warmest thanks to Du Pont executives as they left the company's Wilmington headquarters.

Pierre had political beneficiaries in Washington as well. In an act of generosity that had few precedents in American history, Congressional leaders felt Pierre's name and connections were important enough to merit his appointment to the House Foreign Affairs Committee, even though he did not apply for it. "It's unusual for a freshman Congressman to be assigned this important committee," Pierre admitted with all due humility. "I'm delighted."[57]

This first Du Pont in Congress in over forty years was also appointed to the Committee's most important subcommittees, Foreign Economic Policy and Asian Affairs (of particular import in light of the Vietnam War, then raging). To round out his duties, Pierre was assigned to the Merchant Marine and Fisheries Committee as well, serving on the Coast Guard, Merchant Marine, and Oceanography subcommittees. The last subcommittee, oceanography, has much prominence in political circles, being concerned with "oceanographic industrial development," including off-shore oil exploitation by corporations.

Yet, for all these weighty appointments, Delaware's laureled Congressman had his problems. In fact, Pierre had difficulty even getting to his first meeting of the Foreign Affairs Committee, wandering through the tunnels under the Capitol, totally lost. Pierre analyzed the situation. "The first step in any Congressional Committee work," he concluded, "is learning how to find your way to the meeting!"[58]

One meeting that Pierre did manage to get to was his first White House briefing. This success was marred afterwards, however, when Pierre, lost again, stumbled into the office of Henry Kissinger.

Despite these bloopers, the impact of a Du Pont presence in Congress was clearly felt. Once, when Senator Edward Kennedy was testifying before the Foreign Affairs Committee on emergency foreign aid to the bankrupt Pakistani government, Pierre used the occasion to debate with the famed New Englander on whether the Republicans or Democrats were responsible for suggesting foreign aid be broken down into examinable categories. But the significance of the political leaders of two of the country's most powerful and wealthy families squaring off was not lost on their colleagues. "I must say," commented Representative Cornelius Gallagher, chairman of the subcommittee, "it was very interesting to hear a Kennedy and a Du Pont discuss bankruptcy."

Others, representing a poorer segment of the population, were not so impressed. In May 1972 Pierre's Washington, D.C., office was attacked by some fifty angry youths. Desks were turned over and papers rifled. Soon after, Pierre's stance in the House took a decisive swing away from his previous conservative voting pattern. After riding the Nixon landslide to reelection, he became more of an outspoken opponent of Nixon's environmental policies, opposing the President's plan for shore oil terminals. The "energy crisis" is really a "planning crisis" of some seventy agencies, Pierre explained.

But like so many of his family, it was with the immensely unpopular Indochina War that Pierre showed his greatest opposition to the President's policies. In May 1973 he publicly opposed Nixon's bombing of Cambodia in support of the Lon Nol dictatorship, claiming that "we have no commitment to the Cambodian government."[59] A month later Pierre described Watergate, the corporate liberal's trump card against Nixon's continuation of the war, as "perhaps the worst scandal in history."[60]

With Vietnam, Pierre was only following the path already taken by other Du Ponts.

As early as 1970 Du Pont Company had made clear its opposition to the inflation-generating (and thus economically recessive) Indochina War. Even before that, Du Pont's top economist, Ira T. Ellis, had participated in a fifteen-man committee for the U.S. Chamber of Commerce to study the economic effects of peace in Vietnam. Whatever reservations there were to coming out against the continuation of the war dissolved in May 1970, when the U.S. invasion of Cambodia was met with a wave of massive protests across the country, the shootings of students at Kent State University and Jackson State College, and even larger protests which tied up whole cities and threatened to spread to some sympathetic labor unions.

"The Vietnam War is tearing at the whole fabric of our social and political and economic life," declared Du Pont president Charles McCoy on June 4. "The events of recent weeks have emphasized how deeply the war is dividing our country. It has taken a terrible toll in human life and raised questions about the preservation of democratic values. . . . Confidence in our economy, as well as the social stability of the United States, is being seriously strained. Major domestic needs are not getting the attention they should have. The inflationary trend is continuing."[61]

McCoy's remarks were not made in a vacuum. Other bankers and corporate executives had expressed similar alarm. Only two days before, for example, on June 3, Thomas J. Watson, Jr., president of IBM, had told a Congressional committee that the Vietnam War presented "a major obstacle" to the economic health of the country. Now the president of Du Pont was telling the annual meeting of the Manufacturing Chemists Association, "It is hard to see how we can apply adequate resources to domestic needs and restore a feeling of national unity and confidence, until we reach a settlement of this conflict in Southeast Asia."

Overcapacity (or overproduction), McCoy told the chemists, was the greatest problem confronting the chemical industry. And inflation, as it spurred a reduction in the volume of consumer purchases and inevitably Du Pont's own sales to other manufacturers, had to be stopped. One of the key ways was to cut back on deficit spending that only contributed to undermining the value of (and purchasing power of) the dollar. And one of the key spending items then causing so much social strain was the military spending for the Indochina War.

Yet, for all his concern about inflation, one of McCoy's own policies contributed to inflation. To finance $480 million worth of capital expenditures, Du Pont borrowed $190 million worth of European currencies for further overseas expansion. This speculation was deliberately done in anticipation of the decline in the dollar's value and the accompanying rise in value of foreign currencies. Joined also by other American corporations, Du Pont's foreign exchange speculation only exacerbated the deficit in the balance of payments and brought sooner the inevitable devaluation of the dollar.

More significant to the company itself was the fact that McCoy's taking loans from European banks represented a major shift away from Du Pont's traditional policy of funding investments out of its own internal resources. "We have no policy for or against," McCoy explained of any future reliance on banks. "Given the opportunity with good potential investments, we're going to use our credit as we have in Europe."[62] McCoy's statement was the heralding of a dramatic new shift in company policy, and the closing of 170 years of Du Pont financial tradition. Du Pont had shed its "sound" classical economics garb and joined the rest of the country in the mortgaged age of Keynes's deficit spending.

Outside funding was not the only change McCoy initiated. He also scrapped the family's traditional rule-of-thumb formula of 10 percent return on invested capital. Du Pont, he reasoned, had already passed up opportunities for new lucrative projects, including Xerography and Polaroid Land cameras, that did not fit into the old formula's mold. The company's earnings policy, according to Du Pont economist Charles Reeder, had to be "redefined every so often to accept reality,"[63] and the reality of 5.8 percent earning was imposing. An openness to discuss new projects must be put into effect, McCoy decreed, projects that before would never have made the executive committee's agenda.

To make this policy work, McCoy revamped the executive committee itself, making each of the eight $250,000 vice-presidents a liaison to a department to improve the "connection between the operating groups and the policy level, and to give us better understanding of our problems."[64]

One of these problems inherited from the Copeland reign was Corfam, a product without a market. Already the company had lost $100 million on this plastic leather. McCoy simply resolved the matter by declaring the product a failure. As one executive summed it up to the press, "There really isn't much to tell."[65]

Other Copeland projects, including nylon window shutters, a photo-copier, and a $250,000 color previewer, also got the axe. So did marginal operations such as cleaning agents and the family's holy of holies, black powder. Thus the first Lammot du Pont's original pre-Civil War plant at Moosic, Pennsylvania, joined its founder in history.

In one way, however, McCoy followed family tradition, and that was in his labor policy—he fired 10 percent of the payroll, cutting the lifelines of 12,000 families. The only significant resistance to these layoffs and accom-panying speedups on the assembly line came from an electrochemical plant at Niagara Falls, New York. The Niagara strike was the first major strike in over forty years at Du Pont. It became the longest strike in the com-pany's history.

It began in October 1970, after Wilmington categorically refused to bargain, responding to only one of the union's twenty contract proposals. Some of these proposals tried to speak directly to the decline in real earn-ings as compared to workers in other companies. A Du Pont mechanic in 1967, for example, made 9 cents more an hour than a G.M. mechanic. By 1970 he was making $1.52 less. To help rectify this, Niagara workers asked for a 20-cent per hour average wage increase, a 4-cent per hour increase in wage differential, one more yearly holiday from work, and a new grievance procedure to protect them from the company's fantastic speedups and authoritarian shop practices. On September 21 Du Pont made its characteristic "final offer." No average wage increase, only 2-cents per hour increase in wage differential and hardly any change in the grievance procedure. The 1,100 workers voted to strike.

At first Wilmington thought the union would fold quickly. But when bundled workers continued to walk their picket line through snow and cold, Du Pont headquarters set into gear a series of attacks. First the company announced it was cutting back the number of jobs available at the plant in the future. Then it stopped its Blue Cross and Blue Shield pay-ments, a crucial blow to the workers, many of whom were middle-aged and needed the medical care. To keep their families insured, each worker now had to pay another $30 a month from his dwindling savings. Then McCoy flew in supervisors and research scientists from the Chamber Works and other research facilities in the Wilmington area to work as scabs in the Niagara plant. There, protected by local police, these strikebreakers worked in two-week shifts for extra pay and vacation benefits—often under threat of losing their own jobs if they did not comply.

The situation exemplified well the weak position of a local in a decentralized, fragmented company-union—The Federation of Independent Unions, Du Pont System—pitted against a centralized corporate power like Du Pont with close ties to a host of other corporations and banks. Yet in the midst of this struggle, that reality and the revelation of Du Pont's Achilles' heel—its dependency on labor—inspired other Du Pont locals around the country. In Wilmington, workers from the Newport plant staged a brief picket line in support, but no work stoppage. "The Du Ponts have run this state for a long time," one picketer explained, "but things are going to change. Things are finally coming down." Something had already come down. Embarrassed by the demonstration, Du Pont officials chose that day to take down the "Du Pont" sign from the plant entrance for the first time in twenty-five years "for cleaning."

For a while local leaders at the Newport and Edgemore plants talked about a demonstration of support for Niagara at the annual stockholders' meeting, and Niagara talked of busing workers down to join. Students and labor militants in the area also offered support, but there was hesitation from the local leaders—fatal hesitation, as it turned out. In March the whole alliance began melting away as the Niagara workers, threatened by Wilmington with the closing of the plant, voted in a new management-endorsed president and two other officials. The new president, whose own brother was in management, quickly dissolved the negotiating committee and on April 7 settled the strike himself on the company's terms. The sweetheart contract was signed on April 12. The strike, which had lasted six months, was betrayed.

That very same day, hundreds of Du Ponts and their allies and lieutenants gathered in the Grand Ballroom of Hotel Du Pont to hold their annual stockholders' meeting. The Niagara workers were not mentioned once.

Instead, the *Annual Report* for 1970 was distributed with a poignant last line from Charles McCoy: "Its able and dedicated employees continue to be the company's most valuable resource."[66] Only three years earlier Du Pont had dared to quote the words of one of McCoy's predecessors, Walter S. Carpenter, Jr., that "it has been my observation in industry that no decision or policy is made which, in the vernacular of the marketplace, can be adjudged 'good business' which cannot also be reconciled with our fondest concept of man's brotherhood."[67] Carpenter, too, had enforced a no-strike policy during his wartime tenure.

McCoy continued his revamping of Du Pont. Not only workers, but also managers fell under the blows of McCoy's axe. About sixty senior executives were reassigned or "retired" early. Twenty of Du Pont's twenty-five department heads were changed and even four members of the executive committee were replaced. The shake-up resulted in a breaking down of huge departments, pinpointing responsibility in each area. Each Wednesday the executive committee met to hear reports from department managers. Everything was now under top management's close observation, perhaps more so than since the Du Ponts left powder for finance after World War I. Gone now, also, were Donaldson Brown's renowned overhead trolleys. From these had hung Pierre du Pont's financial charts rigidly focusing on how a department's return-on-investment measured up to the minimum 10 percent yield rule. "The old system looked backward rather than forward," noted Vice-President Edwin A. Gee. "Now, the thrust is to the future."[68]

Gee himself represented that future as one of the company's new stars rising with developments in nonwoven fabrics, where a 20 percent to 40 percent annual growth was forecast. Another rising star was Edward R. Kane, since 1969 in charge of overseeing textile fiber and European operations. These two fields, in a real sense, represented Du Pont's immediate future. Textiles made up one-third of the company's total sales, while the profits of European operations had jumped 21 percent since Kane's taking office, to $443 million. "That," said one associate, "in a year when Du Pont sales dropped $16 million and earnings were off 8 percent, makes Kane look awfully good."[69]

Apparently, others agreed. In April 1971, when Lammot du Pont Copeland resigned over, among other things, his son's bankruptcy, McCoy assumed the board chairmanship. But Irénée du Pont, Jr., did not step into the presidency, as most expected. Instead, McCoy retained the helm, the first man in fifty-two years, since Pierre du Pont, who held both positions. And even more significant, not Irénée, but Edward Kane, was elected vice-chairman. "Since this is the normal route for Du Pont presidents," commented *Business Week*, "the question is whether Irénée du Pont now still has a chance for the presidency."[70]

Whatever Irénée's own thoughts were on the matter, he wisely kept them to himself, observing appreciatively McCoy's investment in new, more competitive technology in Du Pont plants. McCoy expected an 8 percent average rate of growth on earnings through 1975. "I think the five-year goal is reasonable," he asserted. It was.

By diversifying into pharmaceutical, medical instruments, and electronics, Du Pont's instrument sales skyrocketed from 1967's $200,000 to $20 million in 1972. A single clinical analyzer was expected to gross $50 million annually by 1976. Twenty-four new products, designed for quick profits, were approved in all. By diversifying capital into varying, faster growing fields each year, following the shifts of the market from 1970's polyester to 1971's nylon, for example, McCoy gained a new flexibility for the muscle-bound giant from Wilmington. Du Pont's enormous research resources were shifted from long-term basic research to less theoretical aspects and applied to production processes already existing; development time was speeded up to regain market initiative.

But the key to scoring the profit margins that could cushion losses each year lay in the cheap labor markets of the underdeveloped countries abroad and the consumer sales markets of the industrialized countries. McCoy expanded Du Pont's investment abroad from $950 million when he took office to $1.5 billion in 1972. By then, 18 percent or $680 million worth of the company's business was abroad, not counting the $300 million taken in from unconsolidated subsidiaries, mostly in Canada.

This increase in foreign holdings and trade, as well as its foreign currency speculation, were the main reasons Du Pont's stock suddenly jumped 5¼ points on December 21, 1971. Seventy-eight thousand shares were traded, mostly to foreign institutional investors, that is, banks and financiers, who well recognized that the dollar's devaluation would lead to a boost in sales for a company so well hedged in world markets as Du Pont. By Christmas Du Pont's stock had risen over 100 points in two years, from 1969's low of 92½ to 199. The reason was given by Robert Stovall, vice-president of Reynolds Securities. "We expect a 12 percent earnings improvement in 1972."[71]

McCoy did better—a 16 percent increase in earnings to $414 million, resulting in the first increase in dividends, to $5.45 a share, since McCoy's first days in office. Key to this was the 18 percent increase in foreign business, to $800 million, and a 13 percent increase in total sales, now reaching an incredible $4.4 billion.

McCoy laid down some of the reasons for success. "Du Pont is investing increasingly large sums to build new plants and to install new technology at older plants,"[72] he explained.

But always the issue of sales brought back the question of inflation-generating war, of Indochina war. "The increasing emphasis in the economy on civilian goods benefits our markets, and the conclusion of the war in Vietnam will accelerate this trend."

Indeed, the de-escalation of direct involvement by American ground troops had already brought vast dividends in restoring social calm in the

United States and an improvement in sales at home and abroad. This de-escalation had begun since the defeat of the U.S.-backed invasion by Saigon forces of Laos. That debacle was the final crushing blow to Nixon's war policies, and, coupled with mounting popular and corporate pressures at home, forced his shift to the negotiating table.

For this reason, as well as for the general alarm George McGovern caused among the more conservative larger corporations, almost all the Du Ponts supported Richard Nixon for reelection in 1972. As early as January 1971, Du Pont ties to the Nixon campaign were strengthened by the appointment of Delaware's Thomas B. Evans, Jr., as co-chairman of the Republican National Committee. Evans, top Republican and associate of Governor Peterson, had headed a dinner for Vice-President Agnew in October 1970, which was the target of an antiwar demonstration by residents and college youths. Significantly, at the time of his appointment, Evans made it a point of assuring the press that he firmly believed President Nixon was getting American troops out of Southeast Asia.

No doubt Evans was believed in Du Pont circles, for Nixon's scandalous campaign received sizable Du Pont donations.

Delaware Trust director John E. du Pont, son of William, Jr., donated a whopping $141,125.

Reynolds du Pont, who tried to keep Republican donations out of CREEP's hands, gave $49,000.

Lammot du Pont Copeland, Sr., gave $22,500.

Du Pont Vice-President Hugh R. Sharp, Jr., whose father married Irénée du Pont's sister Isabella, gave $9,900.

His brother, Bayard Sharp, gave a total of $14,000: $9,000 to the Committee to Reelect the President, $2,000 to the Republican National Finance Committee, and $3,000 to the Republican Convention Gala.

Mrs. Henry B. du Pont, widow of Henry, who died in 1969, gave $1,000.

W. Sam Carpenter, an in-law and Du Pont director, gave $18,000.

Eugenia du Pont Carpenter, daughter of Walter Carpenter III and Henry B. du Pont's daughter, E. Murton du Pont, gave $1,000.

Walter S. Carpenter, Jr., her grandfather, gave $9,000.

Edmund N. Carpenter II, her uncle, gave $2,500.

Irénée du Pont, Jr., gave $3,000.

Crawford Greenewalt gave $5,000.

Charles McCoy gave $4,650.

George P. Edmonds gave $5,000.

Du Pont executives gave another $47,736, including $3,000 each from

Shapiro, Kane, Gee, Dawson, and Dallas, and $2,000 each from Swank and Harrington.

This brought the total Du Pont contribution to Nixon to well over half a million dollars.

Interestingly enough, one year later, in December 1973, a reelected President Nixon named Du Pont's chief patents attorney as U.S. Patents Commissioner, an important position in an age of competitive challenges to Du Pont's exclusive patents.

Du Pont commitment to Nixon's campaign can probably best be illustrated by a comment Elise, wife of Congressman Pierre du Pont, made during protest demonstrations at the Nixon 1973 inauguration. "Isn't this just like a football game?" she asked one Delaware reporter. When the newsman looked puzzled, she clarified: "No, I mean it's *us* against *them.*"

Additionally, William F. Raskob, trustee of the estate of Pierre du Pont's friend, the late John J. Raskob, gave $7,000.[73]

According to all known records, there was only one Democratic Du Pont donation, $13,000 from Mrs. Thomas F. Bayard. The family's contributions to the Peterson reelection campaign were also reportedly slimmer than in 1968, a factor that probably contributed to the Republican governor's defeat and his subsequent transfer as an aide to Harry Haskell's and Irénée du Pont, Jr.'s old political ally, the lord of Pocantico Hills, New York Governor Nelson Rockefeller.

New York is not the only state with growing political ties to Delaware's ruling family. Other states, including Maryland and South Carolina, listen attentively to residing Du Ponts (such as Samuel F. du Pont and A. Rhett du Pont, Jr., respectively). Du Pont influence can also be seen in Pennsylvania, Missouri, and California, all of which will be examined later. But the state that endures the strongest Du Pont ties outside of Delaware lies a thousand miles to the south. There, in the balmy air of the land of sunshine, Du Ponts reign as the most powerful political and economic force in the state. For unknown to most Americans, Florida is second only to Delaware in Du Pont influence. In fact, Florida is the family's hidden empire, an empire with a history of its own.

Fourteen

FLORIDA—THE HIDDEN EMPIRE

1. ALFRED THE CONQUEROR

On a warm autumn day in September of 1970 a line of mourners quietly filed across the manicured grounds of Nemours, the Delaware estate of the late Alfred I. du Pont. Slowly they approached the tall stone bell tower that loomed overhead.

Beneath that carillon rested the remains of the man who, in his struggle with Pierre du Pont, had torn the Du Pont clan asunder over five decades ago. The greatest "rebel" in Du Pont history, Alfred I. du Pont, had died in Florida in 1935. Now his family and friends gathered to place next to him the remains of his third and last wife, Jessie.

While Jessie Ball du Pont was being entombed next to her husband in Delaware, mourners also gathered a thousand miles to the south, in the state of Florida. There, in Jacksonville, Florida's busiest port, flags flew at half mast in her honor, and bankers and politicians by the score expressed their feelings of loss. Florida had lost not only its richest resident, with a personal estate valued at over $100 million; Florida had lost its queen.

As the reigning monarch of a vast multibillion dollar Du Pont empire, and the state's leading dispenser of philanthropic grace, Jessie du Pont was truly the Queen of Florida. Aided and guided by the guardian of her throne, brother Edward Ball, the Du Pont estate controlled Florida's largest bank, Florida's government, and Florida's most important railroad, and owned outright the largest chunk of Florida's real estate held in private hands. In Florida Jessie's word was golden; her brother's word was law.

How this came about is the untold story of the Du Pont family's hidden empire in the land of sun and sand. It is an epic that spans half a century, marking Florida's long climb out of the murky swamps to the playland we now call the sunshine state. And above all, it is the story not only of a queen, but of a king and the regent who became what many Floridians called "the emperor."

The Du Pont empire in Florida was literally born under the shadow of ruin, ruin of Florida's economy, and ruin of the personal fortune of Alfred I. du Pont.

In 1923 Alfred's feud with his Wilmington brethren and his narrow escape from financial disaster prompted him to look for greener fields beyond the stone fences of Delaware. His search ended a thousand miles away, in the whirlwind of southern Florida's land boom.

"In those days," Jessie recalled of Alfred's winter visits to Florida, "everyone dressed for dinner. We were staying at the Royal Palm. We would dine, then change to street clothes and go out to mingle with the crowds. My brother and I had been through the southern California booms, and it was exciting.

"Mr. du Pont and I would walk down to Flagler Street weaving through the crowds. The binder boys were busy on every hand. The air was electrified, charged and surcharged. It would take us ten minutes to walk two blocks."[1]

Alfred anticipated well enough the coming financial collapse during his visits to the Miami area, but he also knew northern Florida well enough to recognize the enormous potential fortune which was beckoning. While Jessie dabbled in her own real estate speculation, buying two Miami Beach lots for $33,000 in 1923 and selling them for $165,000 in 1925 just before the boom deflated, Alfred pursued more long-range interests. In 1924 he sent Jessie's shrewd but "pigheaded" brother, Ed Ball, to inspect land values in northern Florida, in what is now called the panhandle.

Here was an area yet untouched by the boom, with land prices still bargain-rate. Once, great cotton plantations had flourished in this area, generating the warped old-time southern culture of huge, white elegant mansions standing beside rows of miserable pens for human slaves. Fine towns had sprung up along the Old Spanish Trail then and the cotton and lumber trade made the Gulf port of St. Joseph one of the liveliest cities in Florida.

All this had long since passed, succumbing to the cause for human freedom and the ravages of the boll weevil. Now, as Ed Ball drove along the Old Spanish Trail and over rutted backwoods roads from Tallahassee to the Alabama line in his little battered Chevrolet, he saw only wilderness growing over decayed vestiges of the past. But it was in the wilderness that Ball saw gold, the gold of valuable pine timber and rich, fertile soil. After poring over technical volumes on lumbering and wood pulp industries, Alfred du Pont accepted Ball's report as ample reason to buy 66,081 acres of western Florida's vast timberland. That was in 1924.

A year later, anticipating the coming real estate crash and predicting its effect on the state's banks, Alfred had Ball buy stock in three northern Florida banks, the Barnett National, the Atlantic National, and the Florida National. All were located in Jacksonville, the state's biggest deep-water port and financial center. It was Alfred's first step into Florida banking, and his first real step toward his empire.

In 1926 the expected crash arrived, bringing with it financial upheaval. Land went begging, tourists stayed away, and banks, short of cash, succumbed beneath the tidal wave of depositors' demands for their money. But into this tumult came literally millions of envied dollars—in the person of Alfred du Pont.

Alfred decided to close his Nemours estate in Wilmington and sail his huge yacht south, entering the St. Johns River just below Jacksonville. It was almost like a military operation. Like an admiral commanding a beachhead invasion, Alfred lived aboard his ship while he directed the opening of offices in the city, securing the fifteenth floor of the brand new eighteen-story headquarters of the Barnett National Bank. Thus was born Almours Securities, Inc., to which Alfred transferred most of his Delaware and Florida land and stock holdings, worth about $40 million, making the newly consolidated investment company one of the most powerful—and quiet—in the state.

In February 1927 Alfred and Jessie moved into their luxurious new estate three miles south of the city on the St. Johns River. Epping Forest, named after the Virginia plantation of Mary Ball, mother of George Washington and one of Jessie's ancestors, was (and is) one of Florida's most beautiful estates. Rising two stories above the banks of the river, this massive Spanish, hacienda-style mansion, roofed with Spanish tiles, had six master bedrooms and windows gilded with wrought iron grills. The entire estate was deeply shaded by pine- and moss-draped hickory and oak. From this princely residence Alfred du Pont issued commands to his front man, Ed Ball, to make the moves which would carve his empire out of Florida's misfortune.

Du Pont's first move was to gain control over the Florida National Bank of Jacksonville. Alfred chose the Florida National over the others for one basic reason—it was the easiest to capture. Unlike the Barnett National and the Atlantic National, Florida National's stock was spread out among many hands, and with banks around the state tottering and cash reserves drying up, the original owners were in no position to turn down Alfred's magic name and ready cash.

Alfred's partnership with William du Pont in the Delaware Trust Bank had given him and Ed Ball invaluable banking experience, even though he had been forced to sell his share of Delaware Trust to Willie over management disagreements. Alfred used this financial experience well. He used his political experience also, organizing his first political campaign in Florida in 1928 by allying with the Ku Klux Klan to deliver the state to

Herbert Hoover. "Hoover's prosperity" never reached Florida, however, and by April 1929 over eighty Florida banks, or one-fourth of the state's total, had closed. And into this banking vacuum, Alfred marched his green legions.

Du Pont's strategy met its first real test on July 12, 1929. On that day the Citizens Bank of Tampa failed and took fifteen other banks down with it. A panic broke out across the state, hitting Florida National with $3 million in withdrawals in ten days. Desperately, Ed Ball cabled Alfred and Jessie, then vacationing in Europe, for permission to place $15 million worth of Du Pont common in the bank to be used as collateral for a loan from New York banks. "Use your own judgment," Alfred replied, "but pull our bank through."[2] The next day cheerful tellers greeted long lines at the windows with the news that Alfred du Pont had put $15 million at the bank's disposal. The run was over by noon.

With this victory under his belt, Alfred began to expand his holdings across Florida. In September 1929 Du Pont cash was seen at work in Lakeland, where three out of four banks had closed. That month Ed Ball bought up the charter and building of the defunct First National and opened the new Florida National at Lakeland.

Later that year Alfred's third Florida National Bank opened at Bartow, where both of the city's banks had closed. In 1930 Alfred bought one of the two banks still operating in Orlando and opened his fourth Florida National Bank. He opened still a fifth bank at Daytona Beach, where four out of six banks had failed, and a sixth bank in St. Petersburg, where he stopped a run by having money piled high and clearly visible in windows as it arrived from other Florida National banks. That year Alfred came to the fore and openly assumed the presidency of his Jacksonville bank. Newspapers around the country took note. The Du Pont empire in Florida was now clearly emerging.

In mid-1931 Alfred completed his financial conquest of the state by capturing its southern capital, Miami. Welcomed in newspapers by his only competitor, First National, Alfred's forces entered the Magic City and took over the failing Third National, establishing the Florida National Bank and Trust Company of Miami. Alfred celebrated this victory by crowning himself chairman of the board. Miami was now an occupied city and probably would have remained so had Alfred lived longer.

Through the pursuit of his own goals, Alfred had also managed to keep capitalism alive in Florida, even during the storm-tossed days of the early Depression. His seven banks provided a wide range of loans, from small consumer and personal loans to million-dollar loans to the state's major corporations. Fueled by this capital, the business life of Florida endured

DU PONT EMPIRE IN FLORIDA

(Estate of Alfred I. du Pont)

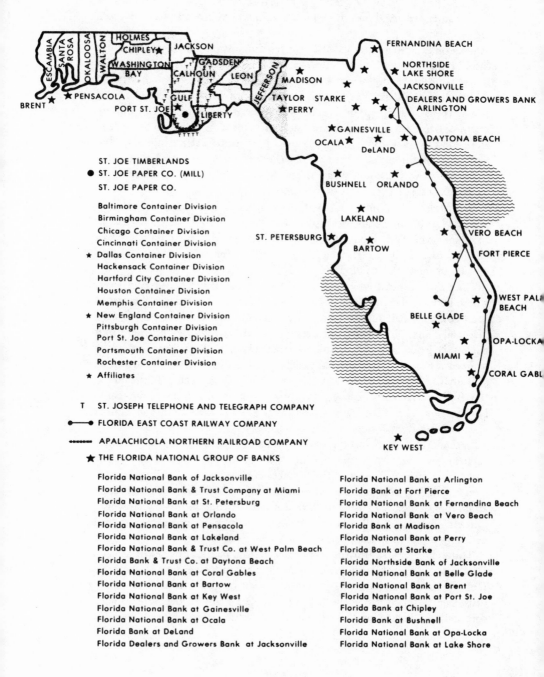

ST. JOE TIMBERLANDS
● ST. JOE PAPER CO. (MILL)
ST. JOE PAPER CO.

Baltimore Container Division
Birmingham Container Division
Chicago Container Division
Cincinnati Container Division
★ Dallas Container Division
Hackensack Container Division
Hartford City Container Division
Houston Container Division
Memphis Container Division
★ New England Container Division
Pittsburgh Container Division
Port St. Joe Container Division
Portsmouth Container Division
Rochester Container Division

★ Affiliates

T   ST. JOSEPH TELEPHONE AND TELEGRAPH COMPANY

●—● FLORIDA EAST COAST RAILWAY COMPANY

········ APALACHICOLA NORTHERN RAILROAD COMPANY

★ THE FLORIDA NATIONAL GROUP OF BANKS

Florida National Bank of Jacksonville
Florida National Bank & Trust Company at Miami
Florida National Bank at St. Petersburg
Florida National Bank at Orlando
Florida National Bank at Pensacola
Florida National Bank at Lakeland
Florida National Bank & Trust Co. at West Palm Beach
Florida Bank & Trust Co. at Daytona Beach
Florida National Bank at Coral Gables
Florida National Bank at Bartow
Florida National Bank at Key West
Florida National Bank at Gainesville
Florida National Bank at Ocala
Florida Bank at DeLand
Florida Dealers and Growers Bank at Jacksonville

Florida National Bank at Arlington
Florida Bank at Fort Pierce
Florida National Bank at Fernandina Beach
Florida National Bank at Vero Beach
Florida Bank at Madison
Florida Bank at Perry
Florida Bank at Starke
Florida Northside Bank of Jacksonville
Florida National Bank at Belle Glade
Florida National Bank at Brent
Florida National Bank at Port St. Joe
Florida Bank at Chipley
Florida Bank at Bushnell
Florida National Bank at Opa-Locka
Florida National Bank at Lake Shore

and grew. Cattle ranches in the north, citrus in the central area, truck farming in the marshy south, home construction all over the state, even the first ventures in appliances and electronics—all were recipients of loans from Florida National. By 1935 Florida National Bank had over $45 million in deposits, one-tenth of that always kept on hand as capital reserve, the other 90 percent collecting interest as loans.

Alfred was active on other fronts as well. His plans to exploit his vast timberland holdings in western Florida would eventually culminate in the founding of the St. Joe Paper Company in 1936. In preparation for building the paper plant at St. Joe, an ideal deep-water port for ocean-going freighters, Alfred turned the fishing village into a company town. In 1933 Ed Ball bought out a bondholders' group in St. Louis, Missouri, giving Alfred absolute control over St. Joe's five major companies: the Apalachicola Northern Railroad Company, the St. Joseph Telephone and Telegraph Company, the St. Joe Dock and Terminal Company, the St. Joseph Land and Development Company, and the Port of St. Joe Company. Thus, St. Joe's communications system, its only railroad, its docks and warehouses, and most of its real estate came under Alfred's thumb. The only thing left in St. Joe that he did not own outright was its people, and in an economic sense he actually owned them too. Later the St. Joe Paper Company even erected homes for their workers to buy on installments. The only thing missing was the company store.

With the St. Louis transaction, Alfred also received a bonus—another 240,000 acres of timber. This raised Alfred's total timberland holdings to over 300,000 acres, making him the timber baron of Florida.

In a very real way, Alfred's growing stake in Florida was based on a very old trend in American social thought—the belief in a new conquerable frontier over the horizon. "There is no power on earth that can stop the growth of Florida," he told a Virginia supreme court justice in 1931. "It is the nation's last frontier."[3] Alfred firmly believed this, and was determined to back his convictions—and his timber and banking stakes—by expanding Florida's commercial life.

In this vein, he launched the Gulf Coast Highway Association to promote a vigorous road-building program. The target of this lobbying group was public funds. Its object was put by Alfred himself as "good roads and more good roads," chiefly through western Florida, the site of Du Pont timberlands and Alfred's hopes for industrial development.

No main arteries existed in Northwest Florida when Alfred established the Association (with himself as president) in the early Thirties. But, fueled with Du Pont money, the Association soon became the most energetic road lobbyer in the South. Ultimately, federal and state funds built three truck highways for corporate activity: U.S. 90, from Pensacola to Lake City by the inland route; U.S. 98, covering the same area via the Gulf coastline; and U.S. 19, connecting Tallahassee with Tampa and the southern part of the state.

Today, if you ride along U.S. 98 into Panama City, you will pass over a long bridge spanning St. Andrew's Bay. It is not by accident that its name is the Alfred I. du Pont Bridge.

Alfred's passion for commercial arteries was not limited to roads. It also extended to railroads.

The most important railroad in Florida is the Florida East Coast Railroad. The line, which spurred the founding of Miami, runs along some of the most valuable real estate in Florida, the eastern "Gold Coast," linking Jacksonville with St. Augustine, Daytona Beach, Vero Beach, West Palm Beach, Fort Lauderdale, and Miami. The railroad also has a spur into the agricultural markets around Lake Okeechobee, and until the Labor Day storm of 1935, also ran across the Florida Keys to Key West. Later, the Keys section was sold to the state for the Miami-Key West Highway, returning the Du Pont estate a handsome profit on an abandoned mass of twisted wreckage and flooded real estate.

Du Pont's interest in the Florida East Coast Railroad began with its bankruptcy in 1931. Beset by increased demands for service during the Twenties and by threatened competition, the railroad had floated a $45 million bond issue to finance the double-tracking of its line between Jacksonville and Miami and a widening of the existing tracks to handle larger and heavier carloads. All might have gone well for these plans had not the Florida collapse and Wall Street's own troubles in 1929 intervened, slicing into business activity. The railroad's earnings dropped dramatically, and as they were not enough to maintain operations and meet its $45 million debt to bondholders at the same time, corporate law forced the line into receivership in 1931.

It is significant that Jessie Ball du Pont was appointed to the State Bond Board in 1934, for that period not only coincides with Florida National's growing financing of the purchase of government bonds, and the estate's purchase of municipal bonds, but also her brother's growing interest in the railroad's defaulted 5 percent first and refunding mortgage bonds. Ed reasoned that control of the railroad's bonded debt was control of the railroad itself. By 1941 the Du Pont Estate, through St. Joe Paper Company, controlled 56 percent of these bonds with a face value of $23,250,-000.

2. THE REGENT RULES

The year 1935 represents a milestone in the history of the Du Pont empire in Florida. In April of that year, Alfred returned to Epping Forest from vacationing in Miami rather earlier than usual. He was not feeling well. On Sunday, April 28, he suffered his second heart attack within a week, and a few minutes after midnight Alfred du Pont died.

Newspapers throughout Florida flashed the news in banner headlines that the state's wealthiest citizen and largest landowner was dead. With awe, millions of Depression-racked Floridians read the list of chief beneficiaries of his $100 million estate: Jessie, his wife; Edward Ball, his brother-in-law; his four children by his first marriage: Mrs. Madeleine du Pont Ruoff (then living in Germany, effused like her children, with enthusiasm for Adolf Hitler); Mrs. Bessie du Pont Huidekoper; Victorine du Pont Dent; and Alfred V. du Pont (whose legal claims were diminished by his earlier disinheritance). Each received 5,000 shares of Almours Securities, worth about $750,000. Ed Ball's sisters, Isabella Ball Baker and Elsie Ball Bowlez, and his brother Thomas, got 1,000 shares each, worth about $150,000. Denise du Pont, Alfred's foster child by the tragic Alicia, was put under Jessie's guardianship and was to receive an annuity beginning at $5,000 and increasing to $30,000 as she grew older, crowned with a $100,000 birthday gift when she reached 21. Two nephews, Maurice du Pont Lee and Cazenove du Pont Lee, as well as their children, received annuities for the rest of their lives.

Alfred's funeral was treated with the pomp of royalty. Returned to his Nemours estate, his coffin was carried by the seven presidents of his Florida National Banks. Accompanying them, bearing official resolutions of praise, were Tallahassee's representatives and senators. Among the national dignitaries was Secretary of War George Dern. Delaware Du Ponts, with the notable exceptions of Pierre du Pont and Alfred's first wife, Bessie, were also on hand to ease Jessie's sorrow. But over the whole affair, the man in command was the short, bald eighth pallbearer leading the line of bankers, industrialists, and politicians to Alfred's grave—Edward Ball.

Ed Ball emerged from Alfred's demise as the single most powerful man in Florida. This was no sudden unexpected rise, but the expressed wish and plan of Alfred du Pont. Alfred had named Ed a trustee of his estate. Jessie and Colonel Reginald Huidekoper, Alfred's son-in-law, were also trustees along with Florida National Bank of Jacksonville, but Ed was the one in charge.

As a fulfillment of Alfred's will, Ed set up the Nemours Foundation in September 1936, with the same trustees as for the estate. This foundation was to be the humanitarian side of the Du Pont estate. In March 1937, eight of the country's leading hospital administrators met at Epping Forest and formulated the policies that would guide the Alfred I. du Pont Institute for crippled children. Two years later, ground was broken on a 22-acre tract of the Nemours estate near Wilmington, and construction began on the three-story hospital that has since become world renowned. By 1963 over half a million patient-days had been spent by the hospital in providing free care, and in many cases cures, for crippled children.

The hospital became Jessie's major concern. This activity, combined with her $55 million in gifts to colleges, universities, and right-wing causes such as the Strom Thurmond Fund, became the Du Pont estate's "human" face. Gruff and abrupt Ed Ball provided the business face. In fact, Ball's business deals were the financial bedrock on which Jessie's charity depended.

The estate's main holding was its Florida National bank. In 1938 Ed opened the Alfred I. du Pont Building in Miami. One of the city's largest commercial buildings, it featured shops and arcades of the Du Pont Plaza, a second-story bank office, and walls capable of withstanding 250-mile-an-hour hurricane winds. It was then one of the showplaces of Miami.

Ed continued collecting banks for the estate. "Banking is a cinch," he once explained. "Now a drugstore—that takes some running." By 1944, when he bought the American National Bank of Pensacola, the Du Pont estate had absorbed fifteen banks with total resources of $259 million.

Ed also continued Alfred's timber program, establishing the St. Joe Paper Company in 1936 with a well-known paper maker, Mead Corporation. Mead provided the experienced know-how to begin the mill's operation in 1938 and to operate its 300-ton-a-day capacity for producing tough craft paperboard. Southern pine was brought in by 100 pulpwood cars of the restored Apalachicola Northern Railroad; the St. Joe Dock and Terminal Company and the St. Joseph Land and Development Company, absorbed as subsidiaries of St. Joe Paper, rehabilitated Port St. Joe so ocean-going ships could enter the Gulf Harbor, come up to St. Joe's back door, and tie up at the docks and load the huge paper rolls. After operations were successfully underway, Ed's insulting remarks to the Mead management about "inefficiency" drove them out of the company in 1940, when Ed bought out Mead's holdings.

The next year, Ed used St. Joe Paper to expand the Du Pont empire still further. By paying only 20 percent of their par value, Ed bought up 56 percent of the bonded debts of the Florida East Coast Railroad. To Ed, the railroad was a tremendous opportunity for profits. Since it had gone into receivership in 1931, the F.E.C. had managed not only to meet its interest payments to bondholders, but also to gather a $1.3 million surplus. In

FLORIDA DU PONTS

(Major beneficiaries of the Estate of Alfred I. du Pont)

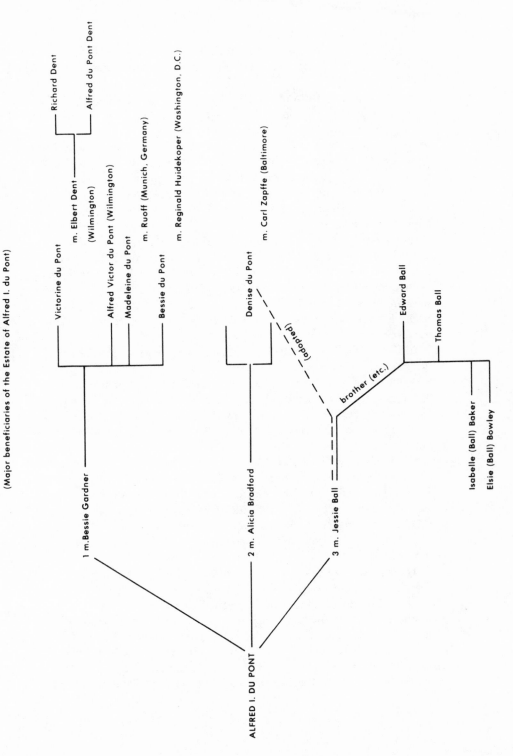

1941, armed with his majority control over the line's debts, Ball submitted a plan for reorganization which would have given him absolute control over the railroad.

Ed's judgment was confirmed with the coming of World War II. Like his in-laws in the North, Ed found the god Mars a bearer of good fortune. As passenger traffic tripled overnight with mobilization, the F.E.C.'s gross operating revenue skyrocketed from under $10 million to an average of over $25 million during the war years. In 1943 the F.E.C. scored a $10 million profit, making it one of the most profitable lines in the country.

Ed was not alone in recognizing the F.E.C.'s potential, however. In 1944, in an attempt to secure control over the line for themselves, the owners of the large Atlantic Coast Line Railroad submitted their own proposal for F.E.C.'s reorganization which won the Interstate Commerce Commission's approval. Ball, irate over losing control and having to accept A.C.L. bonds for F.E.C. bonds, took his case to federal courts in Florida. For ten more years his plans were frustrated by legal battles that cost both sides an estimated $5 million. By 1954, when the A.C.L.'s case finally went to the Supreme Court, the F.E.C. held every American record for drawn-out receiver and bankruptcy proceedings.

While the F.E.C. may have held the records, Ed Ball held the bonds, and his majority holding, worth some $33 million, carried great weight in the Supreme Court's deliberations over a railroad which, although profitable, had accumulated over $100 million in combined debts. Only Ed was in a commanding position to reorganize the line under existing property laws. Predictably, the Court rejected the A.C.L.'s prosposal. Ed thought the battle was now over.

He was wrong. Two years later, in 1956, the A.C.L. came back with another proposal, this one in alliance with the estate of the founder of the F.E.C., Henry Flagler. The Flagler estate held most of the railroad's common stock. Although lower federal courts in Florida had repeatedly ruled that the stock had no equity, the A.C.L. insisted on its right to merge with the F.E.C. by swapping its bondholders' A.C.L. stock, bonds, and some cash.

The A.C.L.'s position was weak, however. The courts had ruled in the past that the bondholders, not the stockholders, were the only real property owners of the F.E.C. And probably more important, major political forces in the now powerful and prosperous Miami area were throwing their weight behind Ball. It seems Ed had openly promised to relocate the F.E.C.'s Miami passenger station from its downtown site, the scene of incredible traffic congestion. The A.C.L. hedged on this, and Miami's corporate and financial leaders, already close to the Du Pont estate through the Florida National Bank, swung their political forces behind Du Pont's bid.

By 1958 the A.C.L. recognized the inevitable and struck a bargain with Ball, agreeing to withdraw from the fifteen-year-long wrestling match in return for a seat on the board of Florida National Bank of Jacksonville. "We expect to cooperate in every way with A.C.L. and other railroads serving Florida," Ball announced, "and we were happy to have [A.C.L. president] Mr. Rici accept our invitation to go on the board. We think he will make a very valuable addition."[4]

Ed had other valuable additions to the estate as well. With assets peaking $500 million, the Florida National group of banks was then the largest bank group south of Philadelphia. Twenty-eight banks dotted the Sunshine State, the biggest at St. Petersburg, Miami, and Jacksonville (over $50 million in deposits in each), the rest at Fernandina Beach, Madison, Perry, Starke, Arlington, Gainesville, Ocala, Daytona Beach, De Land, Orlando, Bushnell, Lakeland, Bartow, Vero Beach, Fort Pierce, West Palm Beach, Belle Glade, Coral Gables, Key West, Pensacola, Grant, Chipley, and Port St. Joe.

This last bank served the company town of the estate's St. Joe Paper Company. Ed had expanded St. Joe's landholdings to over one million acres, mostly in Bay, Gulf, Liberty, Franklin, Gadsden, Jefferson, Calhoun, Leon, Wakulla, Walton, and Taylor Counties of the Florida panhandle. In an itemized property report to the Interstate Commerce Commission, Ed gave St. Joe's vast landholdings an assessed value of $56.69 million including almost $10 million in counties served by the Florida East Coast Railroad, which also owned considerable tracts of land.

To even further underscore this interlocking of real estate interests of the Du Pont estate, half a dozen Florida National banks also owned real estate in cities served by the F.E.C. railroad. The Jacksonville bank, for example, owned ten plots of land in the city and one plot in the surrounding area, assessed, with buildings, at $490,000. The Daytona Beach bank owned three plots worth $142,000; Fort Pierce bank's property was worth $68,000; the Belle Glade bank's, $102,000; the Miami bank owned two plots and the Du Pont Plaza, assessed at $2.4 million. And to complement this whole setup in eastern Florida real estate, Du Pont also set up the Silver Glen Springs Company, Jacksonville Properties, Inc., and Florida National Realty with combined assets topping $2 million.

But it was in western Florida that Du Pont had its greatest stake in land. Besides St. Joe's $46 million assessed holding in panhandle timberland, its affiliates also owned properties. The St. Joseph Land and Development Company had an inventory value of $49,000, and Port St. Joe Dock owned property with a market value of $494,000. As Governor Fuller Warren once explained, "It's hard to find a road anywhere in the state that hasn't some Du Pont property adjacent to it." And roads, the pet project of Alfred du Pont, increased property values.

Ed also increased the worth of St. Joe Paper's own plant facilities. In 1943 he installed its first corrugated containerboard equipment, injecting still another corrugator in 1945. In 1950 he built an entire new box plant, and by 1954 he had tripled St. Joe's output. To provide more water for production, St. Joe tapped the Chipola River eighteen miles away and built a canal to the plant that turned the public's water into private profits.

While St. Joe Paper expanded within Florida, it also grew outside the state. In 1946 St. Joe acquired a half-interest in New England Container Company at Chicopee, Massachusetts. In 1947 it scored the same deal with a box plant in South Hackensack, New Jersey, buying up the other half in 1950. In 1947 also Ed opened a third plant at Houston, Texas, and by 1963 St. Joe had acquired box plants in Rochester, New York; Pittsburgh, Pennsylvania; Hartford City, Indiana; Birmingham, Alabama; Cincinnati, Ohio; Baltimore, Maryland; Memphis, Tennessee; Portsmouth, Virginia; and Dallas, Texas. Over half of these plants were nonunion, floating cheerily in the South's cheap labor pool.

In 1958, the same year Du Pont Company was making a similar move, Ed decided to slip behind the tariff walls of the new European Common Market. In May of that year, he bought into the National Board and Paper Mills, Ltd., located at Waterford, Ireland, and became chairman of the board. Du Pont was now international.

The estate of Alfred I. du Pont now owned some $227 million in direct holdings. Through these, it controlled the $81 million St. Joe Paper Company, the $37 million Apalachicola Northern Railroad, and the $2 million Reynolds Bros. Lumber Company. It owned $200 million worth of Alfred's E. I. du Pont de Nemours stock, $2.9 million worth of General Motors stock, $600,000 in Nemours real estate, $509,000 in other stocks and notes, $3.5 million worth of government bonds, $33 millon worth of Florida East Coast bonds, $968,000 of tax-free municipal bonds, and it had a $36 million stake in the Florida National Bank group.

But the real worth of the Du Pont estate was in the big assets controlled by these investments: $530 million in deposits in the Florida National Bank group; the $200 million assets of the St. Joe Paper Company; and the $80 million Florida East Coast Railroad.

In building this empire, Ed Ball found few obstacles besides the Atlantic Coast Line. Florida officials, only too happy to see the color of Du Pont money in their state, seldom gave Ball anything but praise. When, for example, Ed opposed the state's yielding part of its gasoline tax to pay off municipal bonded debts from the boom of the Twenties, Tallahassee stopped fulfilling its pledge. Roy E. Crummer, one of Florida's biggest municipal bond dealers, charged that the Du Pont estate had fraudulently concealed a conspiracy to destroy his multimillion-dollar bond refunding operations, and sued the estate for $30 million. Tallahassee's federal judge, Dozier De Vane, dismissed the charges as having no legal bearing. Crummer appealed to the Fifth District Court of Appeals in New Orleans, which reversed De Vane's opinion and sent the case back to him for a trial. Again, De Vane ordered the jury to acquit the estate.

Eight months later, for a handsome profit, De Vane sold property which was eventually transferred to the estate's St. Joe Paper Company. The property, a 39-acre tract in Leon County, had been bought by the judge for $15,000, was appraised at $30,000, but sold for $50,000, a 330 percent profit.

Probably the only real thorn in Ed Ball's side during all these years was Senator Claude Pepper. Ball had originally supported Pepper in the Thirties, but as the Senator stuck by his allegiance to the New Deal, Ball's anger grew, especially when Roosevelt's Justice Department lawyers spent three unsuccessful years during the Forties trying to bring an anti-trust rap against the estate.

Ball counterattacked on two fronts. First, he tried to build an image of the estate as chiefly a charity among media professionals by establishing in 1942 the Alfred I. du Pont Awards in Radio-Television. Second, he decided to burst Roosevelt's "trial balloon" in the South, Florida Senator Claude Pepper.

In 1944 Ball summoned together a secret meeting in Jacksonville to purge the South's most eloquent spokesman for liberalism. To oppose Pepper, Judge Ollie Edmunds was chosen, backed with $68,000 from the Florida Association of Industries, the local offspring of the National Association of Manufacturers. "I told Ollie he couldn't follow the Marquis of Queensbury rules in a barroom brawl," Ball once recalled, "but he wouldn't listen."[5] Edmunds, who insisted on fighting fair, lost.

This didn't end Ball's determination to unseat Pepper. Ed Ball wasn't one usually to finance elections, but he was quite willing to use money to crush any politician who crossed him—and Claude Pepper had crossed him.

Pepper's downfall was the result of Ball's ambition to capture the Florida East Coast Railroad. Ball bought $23 million worth of the F.E.C.'s bonds at bargain prices—about 20 percent of their par value. A bill was before Congress designed to (1) benefit holders who purchased bonds in the speculative market for far less than their face value, and (2) permit the lumber industry to treat income from timber as a capital gain rather than an income tax advance. Roosevelt vetoed the bill, and Pepper supported the President, refusing to vote to override him. In those days of a growing Republican and conservative Democratic coalition, it was a futile gesture; the Senate voted 72 to 14 to override.

With that display of courage, Pepper indelibly wrote himself into Ed Ball's little black book. Ball selected Dan Crisp, Jacksonville public relations expert, to begin a concerted campaign of race hatred and political reaction that included, among other activities, great infusions of money into the media. "Ball gave some of the money," Crisp recalled, "but his genius is in collecting. He collected money from lots and lots of big businessmen, big industrialists, oil men like H. L. Hunt [who was Ed Ball's partner in a Dallas box plant] in all parts of the country."[6] Both the U.S. Chamber of Commerce and the National Association of Manufacturers joined in the right-wing cause, and the AMA even assessed members up to $25 each.

The Florida Democratic Club handled some news releases, but most of the organizing was done by the Democratic Club of Duval County and the Anti-Pepper Campaign Committee of Volusia County. The "county" designations were intentionally misleading. Actually, they were statewide organizations. They accused Pepper of being a communist, of favoring racial equality, and of backing labor racketeering, the universal smear against the CIO's postwar organizing drive in the South.

Pepper saw the steamroller coming and tried to zero in on the driver, Ed Ball. He warned the Interstate Commerce Commission that if the Du Pont estate gained control over the Florida East Coast Railroad, the line would become just another cog "in one great machine which he operates and manipulates. . . . Everything which controls this vast empire runs right to the fingers of Mr. Edward Ball. . . . I feel that if the operation of the railroad is given to the Du Pont interests, my friends among the workers will regret it to the end of their lives."[7] Pepper's words were later to prove prophetic but, like his support of Roosevelt, futile.

To oppose Pepper in the 1950 Democratic primary, Ball picked George Smathers. Although Smathers was a former friend and protégé of the Senator, he was no Ollie Edmunds. Quickly, the "Order of Smathers Sergeants" was set up, composed of rabidly anti-communist youth, to "keep order on Election Day." That this was an openly extra-legal fascist trend was confirmed by Smathers' own embracing of McCarthyism. "Florida will not allow herself to become entangled in the spiralling spider web of the Red network. The people of our state will no longer tolerate advocates of treason."[8] The CIO, likewise, was denounced as "carpetbaggers." In fact,

Smathers was in many ways more violent in his slander than even the infamous witch-hunter from Wisconsin.

The *coup de grâce* came merely a week before the primary. A little book suddenly blanketed Florida, nine tons of them being shipped to Miami alone. It was titled, "The Red Record of Senator Claude Pepper." Predictably, Pepper was soon out of his job.

A short while later, Pepper's campaign manager met Ball for the first time and, finding the old financier likable enough after a few drinks, he asked: "Now that the election is over, wouldn't you like to bury the hatchet?"

"I'll bury it," Ball replied, "right in Claude's thick skull."[9]

The transition from Pepper to Smathers was like day to night. If anything, George Smathers was at least consistent in his politics—consistently reactionary. A drummer of the Cold War, racism, and antilabor legislation, this pride of Du Pont often raged against revolutionary Cuba and, according to documents in the J. F. Kennedy Library, had frequent talks with President Kennedy discussing ways to overthrow its socialist government.[10] This particularly tickled Ed Ball's fancy, not only because of his own ultra-conservative views, but also because American-owned industry in Cuba under the hated Batista dictatorship had used the Florida East Coast Railroad as their closest rail link on the mainland.

After the failure of the CIA-backed Bay of Pigs invasion, Smathers aided in getting back the citizenship of one counterrevolutionary, Frank Sturgis. Sturgis, a self-styled mercenary, joined the forces of Fidel Castro in 1958 at the behest of the Batista regime, only to defect in 1960. Years later, in 1972, Sturgis joined Bay of Pigs invaders James McCord (CIA), Eugenio Martinez, Virgilio Gonzales, and ex-CIA agent E. Howard Hunt in breaking into Democratic Party Headquarters at the behest of Nixon's Re-election Committee, in what has since become known as the Watergate affair.

Smathers was helpful in other matters as well. When it came to the Du Pont-G.M. divestiture, the Florida Senator (along with Senator Harry Byrd of Virginia, an associate of former Virginia governor Colgate Darden, Irénée du Pont's son-in-law) was a major spokesman for the 1962 amendment to the Internal Revenue Code. This tax windfall not only benefited the Delaware Du Ponts but also the Florida Du Ponts' vast holdings in General Motors and Du Pont Company. In fact, the Alfred I. du Pont estate owned over one million shares in Du Pont (worth over $200 million) and some 445,000 shares in General Motors (worth over $33 million).

Later, in 1966, Smathers also voted against legislation aimed at the Du

Pont estate's control over the Florida National banks. Since then, he has left the Senate floor for its darker wings, where he lobbies for southern wealth and large corporations.

Indeed, Smathers has been acquiring a whole new set of very interesting friends in Florida. Smathers was the guest of honor at the ground-breaking ceremony of the Key Biscayne Bank, in which Richard Nixon held savings account No. 1. This bank was largely controlled by Charles G. (Bebe) Rebozo, a close friend of Nixon and of right-wing Cuban counterrevolutionaries in Miami. Another director was Robert Abplanalp, another millionaire friend of Nixon, owner of a Bahamas island frequently used by President Nixon as a retreat, and landlord of one of the rented houses in Nixon's official Florida White House compound at Key Biscayne.

It was this same Bebe Rebozo who joined Senator Smathers' own brother, Frank Smathers, and Donald Berg, a personal friend and business associate of Lou Chesler, front man for Meyer Lansky, chairman of the "National Crime Syndicate," in forming the Cape Florida Development Company. Nixon had also invested in this firm and even visited its office in 1967 to pose for promotion pictures, in return for which Cape Florida arranged for his purchase of two lots of Key Biscayne real estate. In addition, Rebozo's bank allegedly gave several six-figure loans to Nixon before the 1968 election. Senator Smathers also had investments in another firm associated with organized crime, the Major Realty Company of Florida, founded in 1959. Smathers served on the board of directors with a member of the National Crime Syndicate: Ben Siegelbaum, a Lansky front man, with a $100,000 holding in the firm.

Today Smathers' lobbying efforts for the shipping industry have been particularly successful, scoring the largest government subsidies in history under the Nixon administration.

But none of this would ever have been possible had not Ed Ball picked him out to run against Claude Pepper. Undoubtedly, the new senator had his debt, and he soon paid it. Smathers' greatest gift to the Du Pont estate came in 1956. That year he sponsored an amendment to the Bank Holding Act that specifically exempted personal trusts from the law's prohibition against banking institutions engaging in commercial interests outside the banking fields. Ostensibly, this was done to allow trusts to function as charities. But had Smathers' amendment not been made, the Du Pont estate would have been prohibited from controlling the Florida National banks and the Florida East Coast Railroad (as well as the St. Joe Paper Company) at the same time. Two years later Ball secured control over the Florida East Coast Railroad.

At about the same time there was a flurry of renewed interest in the proposed cross-Florida canal. That proposal, made during World War II in fear of German U-boats' marauding oil tankers, had been scrapped when a pipeline was deemed more efficient. Now the proposal was being resurrected. "All these navigation projects are purely political," explained Army Engineer Corps economist Clyde Thompson. "The corps is under extreme political pressure in Florida and always has been."[11] From whom? Some said Ed Ball, since the chief economic beneficiary of the canal would be the pulpwood interests on the Florida Gulf Coast, most of which were controlled by St. Joe Paper Company. Jacksonville, the seat of Du Pont power, would also be the port most likely to prosper from the barge traffic. Significantly, the estate's Florida East Coast Railroad was the only railroad not opposed to the barge canal.

During his campaign in 1960, Senator John F. Kennedy pledged to support the canal. In return, Ed Ball pledged to support and vote for Kennedy. Ball lived up to his pledge, and Kennedy did likewise, granting the first $145,000 of federal funds to study the canal's feasibility. Only years later, after the hazards to Silver Springs' water purity by potential oil barge spills were apparent, and ecological disaster imminent, did President Nixon finally halt construction. By then one-third of the canal was completed, 13,000 acres of forest destroyed, and $70 million of public money spent. The money, however, went to some good use. Out of the little cypress wood that was salvaged, the public, for $70 million, got six picnic tables with covered barbecue pits.

3. DU PONT'S PINE CURTAIN

Between 1951 and 1962 the Du Pont estate reaped a $74 million income. Despite its claims about Jessie's generosity, the estate donated only 12 percent (or $9 million) to the Nemours Foundation's charities for crippled children and the elderly. On the other hand, $67 million went to the estate's beneficiaries; Jessie du Pont alone raked in $59 million.

This exemplifies well the ability of the estate to provide decent wages for its employees. Yet in 1962, when 192 railroads agreed to provide their workers with a 10-cent-an-hour raise, only one railroad in the country balked—the Florida East Coast Railroad.

It wasn't that the F.E.C. was in financial trouble. Hardly. It was worth over $92 million and it paid cities and counties, as chairman Ed Ball put it, "what taxes we thought right." In fact, Ball was claiming that the F.E.C.'s local assessed property taxes were too high and pledged he would pay only a small fraction of its taxes until his court suit was resolved. Thus, Ball rejected the F.E.C.'s $75,000 tax in Miami, agreeing to pay only $20,000.

"The spineless regulatory agencies of the State of Florida will not clamp down on an organization which is inherently powerful financially," commented the Miami *Herald,* "and which wields in several guises a tremendous political clout."[12] One Tallahassee member of the Florida State Road Board explained his problem frankly: "Sure, we could condemn Mr. Ball's property in Dade County [that is, Miami]. . . . But he plays a game of checkers, with the whole state for a board. I can hit home in Dade County, but he'll clobber me in west Florida. You can't build a road two miles long up here without running into Ball property . . . he'd also force us in condemnation proceeding for the land we need everywhere else in the state. We'd never get a road built without a costly battle."[13]

This was the same bourbon-sipping old millionaire who flatly rejected railway workers a 10-cent-per-hour raise. After repeated attempts at negotiations had failed, the 1,300 nonoperating employees struck and the 650 operating employees respected their picket lines. The date was January 23, 1963. The longest railroad walkout in history had begun.

Two weeks later Ball withdrew his last offer, used supervisory personnel to resume some freight services, and began recruiting strikebreakers. In an ironic twist, one of these "scabs" was William L. Calley, later to win infamy as the Army lieutenant in Vietnam who personally supervised the mass murder of some 300 old men, women, and children, including infants, at My Lai.

In March 1963 the chairman of the National Federal Mediation Board visited Jacksonville in a personal attempt to resolve the strike, only to angrily leave when Ball refused to stop taping his words.

In April Ball met with union leaders but refused to make any wage offer whatever. The meeting failed.

In May the Secretary of Labor wired both sides urging voluntary arbitration. The unions agreed. Ball refused.

In July still another meeting was met by Ball's unwillingness to bargain.

Meanwhile, the Cape Canaveral space complex was paralyzed by the strike. The F.E.C. was the only railroad that brought in supplies to the base and NASA's industrial area. Alarm was also spreading in Washington about the loss of so vital a rail link if another crisis such as the 1962 Cuban missile crisis should require another mobilization.

On September 24 President Kennedy voiced his "increasing concern" because of the strike's "current and potential impact upon vital defense and space programs."[14] The President set up a federal inquiry board, which heard Ball propose in October that President Kennedy imitate President Grover Cleveland's action in the Pullman strike by sending in troops to forcibly put down the workers. The inquiry board was not impressed with

Ball's prescription. Instead, it recommended that NASA put an embargo on the F.E.C.

Whatever hope the workers had of legally winning their strike ended when Lyndon Johnson assumed the presidency after Kennedy's assassination. In February 1964 Johnson approved NASA's authorization to Ball to move F.E.C. freight trains into the launch area with strikebreakers. Angry rail workers picketed the Cape in protest, and construction workers at the Cape threatened to close down the complex in solidarity. Meanwhile, federal court injunctions and one contempt order had been served on the railroad for Ball's breaking of collective bargaining processes guaranteed by the Railway Labor Act.

Unperturbed, Ball calmly continued one of his favorite pastimes—munching lime Lifesavers. "Whatever happens to this strike," he said of the scabs, "they are not going to be out of their jobs." Johnson concurred, sending FBI agents to protect the strikebreakers from "lawlessness."

"Consider how it feels," said G. E. Leighty, chairman of the Railway Labor Executives Association, "spending over twenty-eight months on strike simply and solely to gain equal treatment with all other railroaders.

"Consider how it feels losing your home because of it, exhausting your savings, facing your wife and kids and their needs. . . .

"Consider how it feels after twenty-eight months of strike, when you know this man's power comes from a huge financial empire that would have been split up years ago—except for its special exemption from a banking law."[15]

The mounting pressure on the now renamed Cape Kennedy finally broke ice on February 5, 1964, when Senator Wayne Morse of Oregon delivered a speech attacking "the grave abuses of power by the Du Pont estate. . . . The obvious, simple, and effective way to end that abuse, of which this estate is guilty—by splitting up the power—is to bring the Du Pont estate under the Bank Holding Company Act and to keep it there."

Subsequently, Congressman Wright Patman's Banking and Currency Committee opened hearings the following May on proposed legislation. Four times Patman's committee asked Ball to furnish annual reports, beginning with 1951, for the F.E.C. and St. Joe Paper Company. Four times Ball arrogantly refused, submitting only the reports for 1963. But this time Ball would not be left to his bourbon and Lifesavers. In June he was served with a subpoena ordering him to personally appear before the House Committee.

"This is one more step toward total government control," the angry financier told the committee in Washington, "and one more step away from the individual's right to acquire and hold private property." Looking every one of his 77 years, Ball warned of the destruction of the American way of life "by certain groups of our society who believe that this country owes them a living and that the way to get the necessary money is deficit financing or the forced sale of private property from those who have worked for it."[16] Ball failed, however, to mention that he himself had inherited control of Alfred du Pont's millions and had not earned its original "seed money." In fact, these were odd words from a man whose property was built on underpaying the labor of others.

Before the hearings as well as after them, Congressman Patman was the least impressed by Ball's allegations about benefiting Florida's business life. "Would a Du Pont bank," he asked pointedly, "loan money to put up a building in competition with some of the city property owned by the Du Pont empire?"[17]

Ball countered that making the estate give up part of its holdings would be "ridiculous," "communistic," and an act of a "police state." "You will be happy to know," he told the Committee, "that I am not going to live forever."[18] Perhaps Ed Ball wouldn't, but a "perpetual trust" does.

It took Ed seventy-four pages to give the Congressmen a piece of his mind, but it left few onlookers with any new impression. Leon Keyserling, chairman of the Council of Economic Advisors under Truman, had earlier held that the Du Pont estate was "still operating in an aggressive, vigorous, competitive, expansionary business enterprise gigantic in size and exhibiting customary business ruthlessness in its objectiveness." Ball's testimony did little to change Keyserling's mind.

More deadly were other revelations brought forth in the course of the hearings, among them the exposure of St. Joe's land deals with Judge De Vane only eight months after he dismissed the Crummer suit against the estate. Low property assessments on St. Joe's 76,000 acres in Franklin County were also exposed. The land was assessed an average of only 30 cents per acre, while it was worth anywhere from $50 to $30,000 an acre. In another deal Gulf County commissioners bought—for $84,000, or $1,900 per acre—43.8 acres of Du Pont land as the site for their courthouse and jail; it was assessed at only $10 an acre. Miami Mayor Robert K. High testified his belief that the estate had two sets of books. This was denied by Ball. "We keep books in the way everybody else keeps them,"[19] he asserted, only to have to admit later that the St. Joe Paper Company had indeed undervalued its stocks and bonds for 1962–1964 tax purposes by over $90 million. That admission came only after the state's first investigation of Du Pont's books. Florida Comptroller Ray Green, who had originally resisted the investigation and sided with Ball, his partner in an

Alfred I. du Pont, wintering at Miami Beach in 1933 as the aging "Count" of Florida. During his ten-year residence in Florida, Alfred du Pont became the Sunshine State's largest landowner and built the foundation of a multibillion-dollar empire that includes the state's largest bank chain, largest paper company and most lucrative railroad. (UNITED PRESS INTERNATIONAL)

THE FLORIDA DU PONTS

Jessie Ball du Pont, wife and heir of Alfred I. du Pont and "Queen of Florida" (c. 1951). (WIDE WORLD PHOTOS)

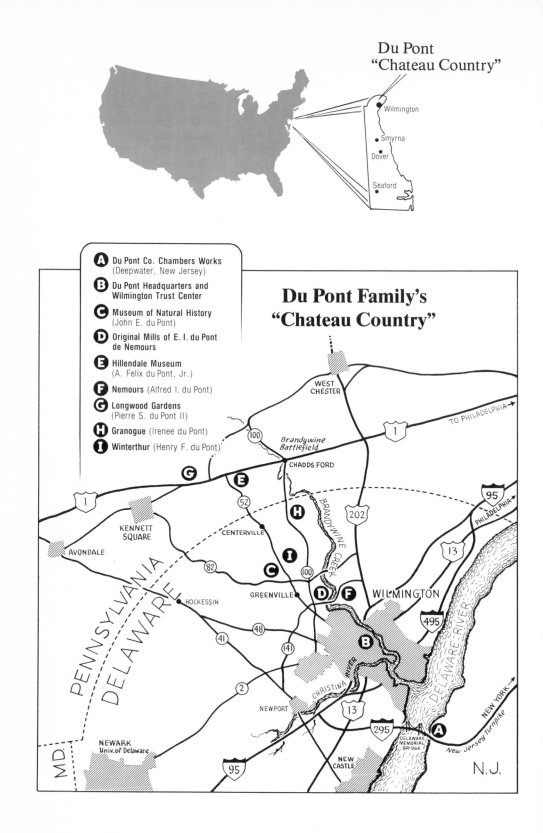

Du Pont
"Chateau Country"

- Wilmington
- Smyrna
- Dover
- Seaford

A Du Pont Co. Chambers Works
(Deepwater, New Jersey)

B Du Pont Headquarters and
Wilmington Trust Center

C Museum of Natural History
(John E. du Pont)

D Original Mills of E. I. du Pont
de Nemours

E Hillendale Museum
(A. Felix du Pont, Jr.)

F Nemours (Alfred I. du Pont)

G Longwood Gardens
(Pierre S. du Pont II)

H Granogue (Irenee du Pont)

I Winterthur (Henry F. du Pont)

Du Pont Family's "Chateau Country"

Granogue, the 514-acre estate of multimillionaire "farmer" Irénée du Pont, Jr., has a 70-room mansion. (GERARD COLBY)

Nemours, the princely estate of "the Count," Alfred I. du Pont. Nemours cost Alfred $2 million when he built it for himself and his second wife, Jessie, just before World War I, with operating costs, including a small army of servants, yearly costing a small fortune. (NEMOURS MANSION AND GARDENS)

Winterthur, the 196-room mansion-turned-museum of Henry F. du Pont, was named for the Swiss home of its original owner, James Antoine Bidermann, son-in-law of the first E.I. du Pont. To house his growing obsession for American antiques, Henry added wing after wing on to the mansion. (WINTERTHUR MUSEUM AND GARDENS)

Mt. Cuba, the 1500-acre estate of the late Lammot du Pont Copeland, Sr., former chairman of Du Pont, contains the above large mansion as well as an 18th-century-design garden complete with swimming pool built in the shape of a Maltese Cross. (GERARD COLBY)

Longwood Gardens, the estate of the late Pierre S. du Pont II, has illuminated fountains that jet 130 feet into the air. The main greenhouse, seen in this photo, was the scene for a 1950 family reunion covered by *Life* magazine. It is now open to the public as another tax-free foundation controlling over $100 million in assets. (LONGWOOD GARDENS)

Du Pont's Crawford Greenewalt (at right, upper row), brother-in-law of Irénée du Pont, Jr., began his rise to power in Du Pont as head of Du Pont's involvement in the making of the first atomic bomb. Greenewalt is photographed here with other leaders of the secret Manhattan Project, including physicist Enrico Fermi (seated, third from left) and General Leslie Groves (seated left).

Du Pont built and runs the Savannah River Plant, the only producer of nuclear weapons-grade plutonium in the Western Hemisphere. Photo shows the plant's reactors used to produce nuclear materials on a 300 square mile reservation in west central South Carolina. (DEPARTMENT OF ENERGY)

Edmond du Pont, head of the country's second largest brokerage house, F. I. du Pont & Company, until the 1969–71 crisis on Wall Street. (WIDE WORLD PHOTOS)

Lammot du Pont Copeland, Jr. ("Motsey"), left, the first Du Pont to go bankrupt. The collapse of Copeland's paper empire shook the financial world. The $50 million lost was the largest personal bankruptcy in U.S. history. (WIDE WORLD PHOTOS)

insurance company, described the $90 million discrepancy as only "an honest mistake."[20]

It is interesting to note that two large newspapers steadfastly loyal to Ball were also connected to the estate. One was the Pensacola *Journal*, controlled by the chain of John H. Perry, a director of the Florida East Coast Railroad, which also had on its board Braden Ball, a director of the St. Joe Paper Company. The other paper was the Panama City *Herald,* also part of the Perry chain.

The hearings before the Senate Banking Committee were just as embarrassing for Ball as were the House hearings. One newspaperman, who was cited by Senator Paul Douglas for his courage to testify against Du Pont, was Joseph Maloney, publisher of the weekly Apalachicola *Times.* Maloney described the Du Pont estate's reign over the panhandle as like being ruled by a "feudal lord." St. Joe, he charged, boycotted the small businessmen of Calhoun County when local officials would not cancel the firm's tax bill. The company's vast timber holdings held back land development for other uses, such as beachfronts, retarding the panhandle's economic development. "The Big Bend area is rich in natural resources. It is a sleeping giant, anesthetized by the power of the Du Pont estate," said Maloney. "It is my belief that the part of Florida where I live cannot fend for itself and prosper behind Mr. Ball's pine curtain."[21] Indeed, much of Maloney's argument did have a striking resemblance to those of the rising bourgeoisie fighting feudalism's landed aristocracy centuries before.

Miami Mayor Robert High, however, was considered a greater threat to Du Pont. Rumors circulating around Port St. Joe had it that if High's ambition to be elected governor were fulfilled that year, the paper mill would close down, throwing over 3,000 residents out of work. Nevertheless, High's appearance before the Senate committee exposed the F.E.C.'s cutbacks in passenger trains between Jacksonville and Miami and the railroad's failure to eliminate many dangerous, unautomated grade crossings.

On June 10, 1965, the House Committee on Banking and Currency approved by a vote of 25 to 3 a bill designed to eliminate the Du Pont estate's exemption under the Bank Holding Act of 1956. Ball, on hearing the news, was described as "not happy," but he did have his compensation. Jacksonville's Congressman Charles Bennett attached to it an amendment which included labor unions and churches in the removal of exemptions. "Why do you want to put all this in and kill the bill?" committee chairman Patman asked the Floridian.

Patman got his answer in September, when the bill reached the House floor. There, watching the debate from the gallery, was crusty old Ed Ball. Like a general observing the movements of his troops, Ball looked down on every Congressman from Florida as all, save one who could not even bring himself to vote, endorsed Bennett's amendment. After it passed, the old multimillionaire openly broke out in a broad grin and gave the fighter's traditional victory sign—clasped hands—to the assembly below. As if that were not blatant enough, observers were then treated to the spectacle of a long line of Congressmen filing up to the gallery for the privilege of shaking Ed Ball's hand. To each, Jovial Ed had just two words: "I'm delighted."[22]

The Du Ponts of Delaware now laid aside their worries, convinced the bill would be rejected because of Bennett's amendment. For his part, Bennett denied it was a torpedo amendment. "I did it for the purpose of making the bill better,"[23] he contended.

Surprisingly, labor unions persisted in their support for the bill, promising to endorse senators who voted for it. The liberal Democratic coalition held together, joined even by some conservatives who saw such legislation as an open door to attacking the bank holdings of such unions as the United Mine Workers. Other economic power blocs, such as New York's Chase Manhattan Bank and Atlanta's Trust Company of Georgia (with its $39 million control over Coca-Cola International) generally abstained from the fight, correctly estimating that the law would be enforceable only with regard to the Du Pont estate. Ball's maverick stranglehold on Florida, not their own monopolies, was the target. It was not surprising, then, that a joint letter by Emmanuel Celler, chairman of the House Judiciary Committee, and Florida Congressman L. F. Sikes urging the bill's defeat was met by less than enthusiasm.

Before Ed Ball could even act on this turn of events, in 1966 the bill was enacted into law, giving the Du Pont estate five years to surrender its control over the Florida National banks.

But Ed Ball was not through fighting yet. Ed knew the law defined "control" as an interest of 25 percent or above, so he waited; he waited for almost the full five years, biding his time by sipping Jack Daniels, trying to implement an evasive scheme for mergers with two other Florida holding companies, hiring 900 scabs for the Florida East Coast Railroad, and taking care of Jessie, who had broken her leg in 1966 and then moved to her Wilmington mansion and began to deteriorate.

Finally, just two weeks before the five-year deadline of June 30, 1971, Ed ended the suspense. He suddenly sold 3,213,103 shares of the estate's stake in Florida National Banks of Florida, Inc., the holding company he set up in 1970. And even in this deal, Ed Ball kept it all within the family, having most of the $60.6 million sale managed by F. I. du Pont & Company.

Ed's sale reduced the Du Pont estate's holding from 59.6 percent to 24.9 percent, just below the technical ceiling of ownership and just beyond the grips of Federal Reserve investigators. But the reality of power lurking behind economic appearance was not what the sale would imply. Ed personally owned another 602,645 shares of Florida National, a 6.4 percent holding, and Jessie had held another 424,787 shares, a 4.5 percent holding, for a combined additional holding of almost 11 percent. While Ed's sale technically removed the estate's designation as a bank holding company and pleased Federal Reserve Chairman Arthur Burns, it still kept Ed in charge. The octogenarian millionaire resigned the chairmanship of Florida National Banks of Florida, Inc., but the preliminary prospectus for the sale of the shares pointed out that "for the immediate future, the operation of the constituent banks will be directed by the coordinator's office of the Florida National group of banks. This office includes the following individuals: Edward Ball, coordinator. . . ."

Ed well knew that the striking railway unions had expected him to sell his personal holdings in the Florida banks, not just the estate's. With control over the banks maintained, Ball would keep his vast capital resources to hold out indefinitely against the strikers. Reading the lurid handwriting on the wall, the strikers surrendered after almost a decade of struggle. The longest railway walkout in history was over, but the men were never to return to their jobs.

"It can be seen," an irate Congressman Patman wrote Federal Reserve Chairman Arthur Burns, "that Mr. Ball through his various connections will, after distribution to the public of over three million shares of this holding company, still maintain control of more than 35 percent of the outstanding shares."[24] But the railway was now running, and the government's biggest concern was the space project and defense program, not the livelihood of strikers. Patman's plea fell on deaf ears; the government did nothing.

Beyond the obvious point that very few of "the public" could ever afford to buy Ed's stock, Patman also missed the essence of the case: the victor was not just the very visible Ed Ball, but the descendants of Alfred I. du Pont who, if they have their way, will reign forever through Alfred's "perpetual trust."

Undoubtedly, some of the clarity of this gruesome reality was clouded by the death of Alfred's closest link to the world of the living, Jessie Ball du Pont. For years Jessie had been visible in Jacksonville as the state's leading philanthropist, every year giving away a million, while tucking away several more million in her purse. From 1935 to 1966 Jessie raked in over $119 million in cash from the estate, while the Nemours Foundation, supposedly the reason for the estate's special tax breaks, got only about $15 million. A host of other beneficiaries, all Du Pont or Ball relatives, took in another $2.4 million.

For years, though, Jessie played good samaritan, and Floridians were only too glad to see the color of her money, no matter what the amount. A grateful Stetson University, for example, gave her its third honorary degree to a woman, having Jessie share the honor with the wife of China's former dictator, General Chiang Kai-shek. Seven other southern colleges and universities also showered her with honorary degrees.

Most of Jessie's personal contributions over the years went to milk-white colleges and universities throughout the South, bolstering that region's "traditional" segregation and racism. A list of her contributions of $50,000 or more, published at her death,[25] reveals that out of 100 such donations not one was made to a Black college or university. In fact, during the Fifties Jessie served on the Florida State Board of Control (Regents), the state agency which controlled public education and grants to professors and was notorious for its prejudice, tacitly endorsing the open practice of racial segregation in the state's school system.

Yet Jessie always managed to preach to others to "Do good, for good is good to do. . . ."[26] Every morning at Epping Forest the little lady would rise early and walk about her Spanish hacienda, which she called "the shack," observing the thousands of azaleas and other blossoms on the grounds. By 10:00 A.M. she was in her office at the Barnett Bank Building in Jacksonville, reviewing the stacks of pleas that covered her old rolltop desk. That sums up Jessie's whole life—every day reviewing, like some absolute monarch, desperate pleas for her pity and *noblesse oblige*.

In 1966 Jessie's thirty-year routine was broken by a splintered leg, and with her routine went her spirit. She became a frail invalid, secluding herself at Alfred's huge mansion at Wilmington, lounging on an estate that was gated and kept safely locked from the nearby hospital, the Alfred I. du Pont Institute.

Almost immediately, things began to change. Her working relation with the hospital staff became strained, her "bossy old ways," as one former staff member put it, too much to endure. Finally, Ed, who had moved in with her, fired Dr. Alfred Shands, the hospital's director since its founding. Shands had built the hospital's excellent reputation over thirty long years. Now, with the divine right of private wealth to rule over administrative talent, the 70-year-old physician was turned out of the hospital in which he had invested so much energy and so many years.

There were other changes in Jessie's charities. One was with the famed Alfred I. du Pont Radio-TV Awards. For the first eight years of their existence the awards had been under the administration of the Florida National Bank of Jacksonville, meaning Ed. They suffered accordingly. In 1950, however, the awards began almost two decades of quality selections. This was chiefly the result of the autonomy of the new curator, Professor O. W. Riegal of Washington and Lee University. Riegal attracted judges from the *New York Times*, the *Washington Post*, the *Christian Science Monitor,* the Federal Communications Commission, and the National Association of Educational Broadcasters. Awards went to such commentators as Eric Sevareid, still expectedly conservative, but at least of far better quality than former examples of Ed's tastes.

In 1963 the judges gave the commentator award to a liberal, Howard K. Smith. A right-wing protest demonstration was held at the awards site in Washington, and Jacksonville angrily swung into action. The new bank trustee hired a public relations man to investigate the incident, a man who subsequently took all advice from conservative New York broadcasting company officials. Soon Ed's bank was making demands that broadcasting corporate executives be among the judges to avoid any chance of another politically embarrassing incident. All this was done without Jessie's knowledge, as she was ill. Finally, in 1967 Washington and Lee protested, terming the loss of its autonomy "an absurdity." With Jessie now holing up at Nemours, Ed terminated the arrangements with the university. Eventually, publicity in *Saturday Review* spurred him to hand the awards over to Columbia University's School of Journalism, but the reputation of the Du Pont Awards had by then suffered a damaging blow.

Ball's switch to Columbia did not signify any political move toward corporate liberalism during this period of his sister's deterioration. If anything, Ed swung further to the right, reputedly backing the South's archsegregationist, George Wallace, in the 1968 contest for the presidency. Ed's bedfellows in this support for the American National Party included over fifty oil magnates (including Ed's box plant partner, H. L. Hunt) from Dallas, the site of the Kennedy assassination only five years before.

Jessie's death at 86 in September of 1970, and Ed's own advancing years, raised questions among some observers as to who was next in line to control the multibillion dollar Du Pont estate. Most of these questions remain unanswered, primarily because the nature of a trust is traditionally more shrouded than Ed Ball has led many to believe. To unravel the present, it is necessary to reveal the past.

Alfred du Pont's estate had many beneficiaries. By 1964, however, there were only two major annuitants besides Jessie. They were Maurice du Pont Lee, Alfred's nephew, who received a $15,000 annuity, and Denise du Pont, Alfred's foster daughter by Alicia. Denise's annuity was $30,000.

Of these two, only Denise collected a good chunk of Jessie's $100 million to $200 million fortune. She now lives in Baltimore with her husband, Carl Zapffe. Far from the active affairs of the estate, Denise must be dismissed as a successor for control.

Most of Jessie's personal estate went to the Alfred I. du Pont Foundation, increasing its income overnight from $1.2 million to $50 million. In order to avoid the 1969 tax reform act's 4 percent excise tax and regulations on foundations, the foundation asked the IRS to renew its classification in 1971 as a "hospital." As a result, the foundation acquired a $35 million surplus by 1973. Of this, only 20 percent went to the crippled children's hospital and nothing was spent on the elderly; $600,000 per year was spent, however, to keep up the 250-acre Nemours estate, which still barred the public. This led to a federal probe in 1974 into alleged technical violations of Alfred I. du Pont's original will. At a March 21 board meeting, the foundation took the legal steam out of the probe by announcing an expansion of medical services and plans to open the Nemours estate to the public. Through this concession, the foundation has managed to keep its "hospital" classification with the IRS—as well as $500,000 it would otherwise have to pay annually in federal excise taxes.

Jessie left much of the rest of her estate to one Richard Dent. According to Ball's submission of estate records before the House Banking and Currency committee in 1964, Dent is not an annuity-receiving beneficiary of the estate. If this is true, it is only a technical point. Richard's mother, Victorine du Pont, was a major beneficiary of her father's will, receiving 5,000 shares of Almours Securities (worth $750,000 at the time). Living in Wilmington, Richard's family still managed to become actively involved in not only benefits from the estate, but also its control: his father, Elbert Dent, succeeded to the trustee seat of Colonel Reginald Huidekoper (husband of Victorine's sister Bessie) in 1943 on the latter's death. Elbert took quite an interest in the business side of the estate, serving not only as trustee of the estate and Nemours Foundation, but also as a director of the St. Joe Paper Company, the National Board and Paper Mills in Ireland, the Florida National Bank of Jacksonville, and the Florida National Bank and Trust Company at Miami. Dent's career was abruptly ended when he died in the Sixties, and he was replaced by Ed Ball's energetic lieutenant, Roger L. Main. Richard du Pont Dent, in contrast to his father, takes little active interest in the affairs of the estate of his grandfather and cannot be considered in the line of succession for control. His brother, Alfred du Pont Dent, however, has become a director of the foundation's hospital and probably carries the most weight of the Delaware beneficiaries. But

Alfred's lack of activity in the estate's Florida holdings rules him out as any pretender to the Jacksonville throne. In fact, if it were left to him, the estate would sell its Florida holdings and return to Delaware and the mandated job of taking care of crippled children.

Ironically enough, the one Du Pont who stood out in Florida for years was not a descendant of Alfred du Pont, but the son of Alfred's famous cousin, Lammot du Pont. Of all his cousins, Alfred respected Lammot the most because of his capabilities. Yet it was a twist in the family's history that it was the very branch that kicked Alfred out of Du Pont Company and prompted his desertion to Florida that later threatened to return in this saga as a major power in one of his banks.

Young Willis Harrington du Pont was one of a large brood of heirs to the fortune of his father, Lammot du Pont, former chairman of General Motors and Du Pont Company. Perhaps for this reason, and because of the death of his younger brother David in 1955, Willis decided to leave the competitive world of the Du Ponts in Delaware to his older stepbrothers, Reynolds du Pont and Pierre S. du Pont III. Willis came to Florida and dabbled in citrus, cattle, and aviation investments. To celebrate his newfound playground, he built an $800,000 mansion for his wife, a dark, beautiful aristocrat from Franco's fascist Spain named Miren de Amezola de Balboa.

Willis's new home, located at 3500 St. Gardens Road in leafy Coconut Grove, was one of the most luxurious dwellings in Florida. It took thirty-five carloads of sandstone from Ohio quarries just to construct his dream house. Named Baymere, an Old English word meaning near-the-swamp, the massive three-story mansion featured thirty-three beautifully furnished rooms, including nine bedrooms, nineteen bathrooms, elevator service between the floors, and a basement with assorted recreation rooms. One of these was a Ping-Pong room complete with a robot player which pitched Ping-Pong balls so Willis could play alone if he had to.

Closed-circuit TV allowed Willis and his wife to keep an eye on the antics of their young children, imaginatively named Willis Victor, Lammot, and Miren. Underwater windows for the swimming pool served the same purpose, besides appealing to Willis's aesthetic tastes, as did the gushing fountain on the first floor. From the back door, a well-tended green lawn swept down to Miami's balmy Biscayne Bay. If you could take your eyes off that beautiful spot for a moment, you might have noticed (and, if your name was du Pont, even use) the lighted tennis court, or the golf putting green, or the large swimming pool with a number of wading pools all connected by a bridge. And in the large garage and parked about the mansion waited seven cars, all new, shiny, and very expensive.

One night in October of 1967, just after they had come home from a party and gone to bed, Willis and his wife were awakened by the yapping of their two Yorkshire terriers. Because his home is so big, Willis had installed his closed-circuit TV for sweeping inspections of the estate, but he never got a chance to use it that night. Within seconds, the bedroom door crashed open and five masked men, waving pistols in black-gloved hands, rushed in and rounded up the du Ponts, four-year-old Victor, and their servants. Lammot, age one, was left in the nursery. "We'll keep an eye on him," one gunman assured Mrs. du Pont as he motioned them all downstairs.

"I was so nervous," recalled Mrs. du Pont, "I couldn't remember the combination."[27]

One of the men waved a gun in front of her. "Maybe this will refresh your memory."

It did.

Or at least it refreshed Willis's memory, and he opened the safe, a special walk-in model with a burglar alarm supposedly designed for just such an occasion. Since Willis was using the combination, the alarm didn't go off.

Inside was $1.6 million.

Unfortunately for the robbers, only $100,000 was in cash and jewelry, including 1,000 silver dollars, five men's watches worth a total of $3,000, Miren's diamond-studded watch worth $5,000, and other jewelry valued at $25,000. But the big haul, besides some $500,000 in U.S. coins, was the famed Prince Mikhailovich collection of Czarist coins.

Quickly, the gunmen tied everyone up with Willis's stylish neckties and prowled the house in fruitless search for other treasures. Intermittently, however, they would interrupt their professional work to meet the creature comforts of their host.

Willis complained of an itch in his leg. Willis was scratched.

Willis complained of being cold, and he was given a blanket to snuggle up to.

Finally, one of the intruders, realizing the rare coins were worthless to him, told Willis he would contact him for a $200,000 ransom, and admonished the millionaire for not "working to earn a living like everybody else." To compensate, the group's leader reassured Willis in a thick New York accent that "This is my first day on the job." Then he and the others left, driving off in Mrs. du Pont's big red Cadillac. Later, Willis had still another complaint: the robbers, he explained disgustedly, had "bad grammar."

Willis apparently learned one lesson from his family's ordeal: "I'll never keep valuables in the house again." He did manage to recover one $10,000 bill, apparently dropped on the bedroom floor by the thieves in their haste. But the total haul of his unwelcome visitors still exceeded $1.6 million.

Willis wanted his coins back. Having little faith in the efficiency of the local police, he hired a private detective to act as a middleman. Newspapers around the country cooperated by printing the detective's phone number. In January 1968 Willis had his first nibble in Philadelphia. It cost him $50,000 in ransom, but he got back sixteen rare gold American pieces worth $250,000. Two additional attempts for the remaining coins failed before Philadelphia police swept down on two local "fences." In July, another police raid in Miami netted two more middlemen and Willis's 1785 Brasher doubloon, worth $100,000.

Willis survived his losses handsomely, enjoying his mansion—minus any valuables—and using the membership privileges of a number of exclusive clubs for the rich: the Jockey Club in Miami; the La Gorce Country Club in the same city; the Riviera Country Club at Coral Gables; the Palm Bay Club; and, of course, the Wilmington Country Club.

Willis expanded his citrus, cattle ranch and aviation holdings and was a large stockholder in Continental Aviation and president of the Dumod Corporation in Florida. He was also a partner of C.B. Richard, Ellis & Co. in New York. But more important, Willis succeeded the late Elbert Dent as a director of the Florida National Bank and Trust Company at Miami. As Edward Ball was also a director of that bank, it can be assumed that Willis's appointment was endorsed, and may even have been encouraged, by the large stockholder from Jacksonville. This development was an important one economically in the Du Pont family, raising the specter of a possible future merger of these two once diverse branches of America's richest family.

While it is true that Willis's roost was still hundreds of miles from the Jacksonville throne, he was nonetheless the most powerful Du Pont in Florida. Yet few in the upper circles of Miami or Jacksonville believed that Willis was in a position to step into Ed Ball's shoes, or even that he could if he were in such a position. Willis du Pont, one heard repeatedly in Florida, had little direct connection with Alfred du Pont's estate and no experience with Ball's select managerial staff. Moreover, it was claimed, much of his prestige was owed to his inherited wealth and name rather than any dynamism or outstanding achievements of his own.

Whether or not these claims are true, Willis du Pont at 47 is still a young man, and a young man with the name of Du Pont moving so easily in Florida's highest circles is one to watch.

There are other Du Ponts in Florida, of course. William K. Carpenter, 64, worth about $200 million, lives in Boca Raton. Bayard Sharp, 70, worth $225 million, spends time running an exclusive resort in Boca Grande. Alice Francis du Pont Mills, worth $275 million, lives in Hobe Sound. Her father A. Felix du Pont, Sr., also had bought large amounts of timberland in northern Florida about the same time as Alfred's first venture, but neither he nor his sons were ever seen among Florida's power elite. Another Wilmington Du Pont, reportedly one William du Pont, is speculating in beachfront real estate and retail food industry in southwestern Florida along the Gulf, allying with certain Clearwater and Tampa interests. If this is so, it will be the first Du Pont family penetration of the Tampa area.

For years, another pristine part of southwestern Florida was also the winter roost of another branch of Lammot du Pont's family, that of H.R. Sharp, who married Lammot's sister. The 113-acre estate on Gasparilla Island, however, including its miles of beachfront property, was recently donated to the state by the Sharp sons for a handsome tax write-off.

In Miami Springs lives S. Hallock du Pont, Jr. "Hal" has followed his father and brother, Richard S. du Pont, into aviation, founding two companies, Orlando Aviation Services and du Pont Aero Finance, Inc. These curious little firms seem to keep this Du Pont scion busy flying about in his Lear jet. But Hal keeps a very low profile. In fact, he uses a Spanish-sounding alias, John Aragones, which he explains helps him keep the price down when pursuing his passion for old Du Pont gunpowder cans. He is, no doubt, a crack shot, winning championships as a skeet shooter. He is also a brigadier general and former National Commander of the Civilian Air Patrol, an important position within the Defense establishment in a state famous for its past CIA-directed Cuban exile raids on Cuba and illegal arms shipments to dictators like Nicaragua's deposed generalissimo "Tacho" Somoza.

Most of the major cities in Florida abound with other Du Ponts. Only some of these, mostly owners of winter homes, are descended from the Wilmington branch. The great majority trace their lineage to Abraham du Pont (the great-uncle of the Wilmington branch's founder, Pierre Samuel du Pont de Nemours); Abraham settled his roost in Georgia in 1695 and his descendants have now spread throughout the South and, lately, the rest of the country.

In 1972, for example, the Jacksonville City Directory listed seven Du Ponts in Volume I and ten Du Ponts in Volume II. Most of these have working-class occupations and none seem to be relatives of Alfred's branch. Jacksonville's telephone directory, on the other hand, shows many more Du Ponts who live in upper-class neighborhoods, some in luxurious mansions, but, again, any connections they may have to Alfred or his Wilmington brethren remain obscure.

In searching for Du Pont power in Florida, then, all roads lead back to Jacksonville. Here, in a small unpretentious office, Ed Ball confounded his enemies by refusing to die. Old, bald and cantankerous, he was still the most powerful man in Florida, retaining the chair of the Florida East Coast Railroad and the St. Joe Paper Company, and directing the Jacksonville Properties, Inc., Port St. Joe Dock and Terminal Company, Apalachicola Railroad, Wakulla Edgewater Co., Almours Securities, St. Joseph Land and Development Company, Silver Glenn Springs Co., Ballynahinch Castle, Inc., the Nemours Foundation, and the Alfred I. du Pont Foundation.

Despite his divestiture in 1971 of some three million shares of the estate's holding in the Florida National Bank group (now thirty-one banks), the *1972 Dun & Bradstreet Million Dollar Market Directory* listed Ball as a director of the Florida National Bank of Orlando, as did *Poor's Register of Directors,* while *Moody's 1972 Finance Manual* listed Ball also as a director of the Florida National Bank of West Palm Beach. *Who's Who in America* listed him as a director of the Florida National Bank of Jacksonville and the Florida National Bank and Trust Company at Miami, although this source may have just been in want of updating.

Ball's personal ownership of hotels in Wakulla Springs, Florida, and Biloxi, Mississippi, bring their own colorful tales. When he took over the swanky Edgewater Gulf Hotel near Biloxi, a story goes, Ball's policies even affected the many tin cans being thrown away as garbage. He had the tops removed and camellias planted in the cans, and sold each one for 35 cents. Today you can still buy these cans. The sight of thousands of them heaped along the road is, this writer can confirm, indescribable.

One could still phone Ed Ball at his Jacksonville office, as this writer did in 1972, but you would be lucky if you got past his able personal secretary and close friend, Irene Walsh. Irene served as a director of all the Du Pont subsidiaries, continuing the secretarial role for Ball that she began under Alfred du Pont. Irene was elderly then, like most of Ball's few surviving friends. It was obvious that a new generation would soon have to administer the affairs of Alfred du Pont's multibillion-dollar empire.

In his eighties, Jessie's brother remained unconvinced, still the crusty older schemer. A couple of years before, Ed, as chairman of the Florida East Coast Railroad, announced that a large block of the railroad's valuable first mortgage bonds would be offered for public sale. The Securities Exchange Commission, however, caught wind of rumors of foul play and launched an investigation. Ed refused to answer queries put forth by the SEC investigators, and the SEC finally had to take its case to a federal court in Washington, filing suit requesting the court to order Ball to answer questions.

Soon the SEC began receiving mysterious phone calls from the Pentagon. Two calls were made by a Pentagon aide specifically at the request of Nixon's

Defense Secretary, Melvin Laird, asking about the SEC suit against Ball and the F.E.C. The Pentagon warned the SEC investigators to "stop harassing Mr. Ball, because he was an old man."[28]

The SEC continued pressing the case and on January 24, 1973, publicly announced that charges were being brought against the Du Pont estate and F.E.C. president Thornton for fraud. The F.E.C. had allegedly filed false statements to the SEC, failing to report that the estate had bought $18.8 million worth of the F.E.C.'s first mortgage bonds for 752,384 shares of F.E.C. common, reaping a substantial premium in the process. It was F.E.C. chairman Ball selling bonds below face value to estate trustee Ball. But even worse, the SEC charged that the reason the F.E.C. had not reported this sale to the Du Pont estate was because Ball had secretly arranged to buy up the F.E.C. bonds before the railroad had even made a public announcement of its intention to sell the bonds, allowing Du Pont to buy the bonds below face value before they were even offered to the public. Translated into economic reality, "the public" the SEC was referring to were other financial speculators who might want to get a piece of Du Pont's action.

Ball's problems with the SEC probably contributed to the Du Pont estate's losing control of a sizeable chunk of its empire. The thirty-one Florida National banks, worth some $1.3 billion, were slated for even bigger things when, in 1969, Ball announced a proposal to link up the Florida National group with two other Florida bank groups: A. L. Ellis, with fourteen banks, including some in Sarasota and Tarpon Springs; and Raymond Mason's Charter Bankshares, which controls eleven banks, including the First National Bank of St. Petersburg.

"In a capital-short area such as Florida," Ed commented, "this additional strength would be very helpful."[29] It would be particularly helpful to the trustees of the Du Pont estate, as it would technically lower their percentage of the total stock (thereby avoiding renewed charges of being a bank holding company), while retaining internal control and expanding their control over Florida into the promising southwestern Gulf area. Florida National would then outpace in capital even the giant Citizens and Southern Banks of Georgia.

It was more than the Federal Reserve Board could take. Dominated by New York banking interests, the Fed again hauled out the 1966 amendment to the 1956 Bank Holding Act and in 1973 repeated its argument that the estate, because it also controlled an industrial company (St. Joe), should own no more than 5 percent of a bank holding company. The Fed now demanded that the Du Pont estate get rid of *all* its holdings in the Florida National group. Ed obliged by simply putting the shares into a trust controlled by friends, with the bank's directors and employees having purchasing rights for three years. Ed, meantime, retained his own 10 percent personal holding in the bank.

As the September 1977 deadline approached, Florida Associates, Inc., headed by Ball's protegé, bank president John Manry, Jr., had been unable to get Florida National's directors to buy the estate's stock. This was exactly what the Fed had hoped for when it insisted Ed reduce the Du Pont holding to 24 percent, with a commensurate reduction in Ball's influence on the bank's board. If the deadline was not met, a secondary offering would likely occur and the estate's representative on the Florida National's board might have to resign. Ball would certainly lose control then.

But Ball knew his contenders from the North were playing for even greater stakes. It was not just the bank they wanted. It was the estate itself.

The proof, to Ed, could be found in the outside bidders. One was Duke University, once a beneficiary of Jessie's largesse. Duke's trustees were willing to pay $18 per share. The fact that Florida National's stock was worth only $14 per share did not ease Ball's worries over why Duke wanted it so badly. The promise by Duke President Terry Sanford, the former North Carolina governor with ties to the liberal Carnegie Corporation, that he would not try to exercise control over the bank did not impress the Florida Associates. Manry made it clear they wanted to keep outsiders out.

There was good reason. Opening the bidding to outsiders legally meant other outside offers would also have to be considered. And the only other bidder at that point was Combanks Corporation. Combanks, ominously, was offering $18.50 per share, 50 cents more than Duke. And even more worrisome was the fact that Combanks was controlled by Hugh Culverhouse.

Behind Culverhouse's bid, Ed knew, was his law partner, William B. Mills. Mills had been an old friend of Jessie and was a trustee of the estate. But when Ed decided to evade the Federal Reserve's demand by putting the shares in the Florida Associate's trust, Mills had tried to stop him. He failed, and earned Ed's everlasting enmity, but had won the trust of a formidable ally, the only man Ed Ball probably ever feared: Alfred du Pont Dent.

Looking at Dent was like seeing the ghost of Alfred I. du Pont. The specter of his grandfather looked out from Dent's eyes and it clearly shook the old man's confidence, if not his conscience. Du Pont's will had instructed the trustees of his estate to pay out any money earned by the businesses they invested in to charity. Since the death of Jessie in 1970, the estate had raked in over $70 million in earnings from stocks and the forced sale of the bank securities alone. In 1975, St. Joe, which Ball used as the estate's holding company, earned $187 a share, but Ed could not bring himself to part with more than a miserly $4 in dividends. The hospital for crippled children, which Alfred ordered to be the main concern of his estate after Jessie's passing, was given only $200,000 or .13 of 1 percent on its investment in St. Joe. In terms of the object of Alfred's will, the tail was obviously wagging the dog.

Instead of honoring the terms of the will, Ed Ball kept plowing the estate's money back into other money-making investments, just as he had for over thirty years.

St. Joe, for example, had grown to 23 plants around the country, with more plants in Northern Ireland, where U.S. income taxes and decent wages need not be paid, and are not. The Florida East Coast Railroad still enjoyed a virtual monopoly in transporting fresh produce from the rich agricultural region of Lake Okeechobee and the Indian River citrus region, and reaped over $2 million a year in profits from the Kennedy Space Center. It bought a 50 percent interest in the Atlantic and East Coast Terminal Company, made a $193,000 investment in Railway Express Agency, Inc., a $59,000 stock investment in the Pullman Company, a $542,000 investment in the Fruit Growers Express Company and set up the Florida East Coast Highway Dispatch Company. By 1974, the F.E.C. had over $91 million in assets, and enjoyed greater profits after Ball chopped the maintenance crews from 757 in 1960 to 139 in 1971, transportation employees from 880 to 254, maintenance of way crews from 364 to 142, and the professional and clerical staff from 540 to 230. The F.E.C.'s total payroll declined from $15.6 million in 1962 to $4.7 million in 1968; Ball did not bother to report figures after then. As practically all the workers were employed originally as strikebreakers, they were without a union, took in lower pay than most other railroad workers, did twice as much work because of the layoffs, and were now at the mercy of Ed Ball's charity, not much to hope for from a man worth $100 million who tipped with quarters.

And what of the railroad workers who were on strike for so many years for railroader equality? Ball refused to even rehire them. They, too, had seen the cruel, but real, face of Du Pont "philanthropy."

The mounting scandals surrounding his grandfather's name and the Scrooge-like obstinancy of Ball in ignoring the mandate of the Du Pont will to care for crippled children finally moved Dent to action. As the estate moved into the crucial 1977 year, he flew to Jacksonville to join Mills in a fateful confrontation with Ball.

This was a new role for Dent. Tall, lean and rumpled in appearance, he had been regarded by many in Wilmington as a lazy youth wasting his years deciphering the secrets of backgammon. Inherited wealth, it is said, often robs people of a meaning in life otherwise gained through struggle, makes them less imaginative and narrows their focus to neurotic obsessions and narcissism. The rich's fascination with gambling and games like backgammon are seen in this context, and some took Dent's concern for crippled children as newfound, a case of grandstanding to win respect in his home town. It was probably an unfair assessment of a man who was going through the search for some meaning in life typical of middle-age. And just as typical for the rich, he had found it in his grandfather's money and what it could do for others as well as himself. That did not take imagination. But beating Ed Ball did.

Here, too, Dent's critics had underestimated him. Backgammon requires intelligence and subtlety, and it seems his training in it now served Dent well. He had reasoned that his grandfather's will was Ed's Achilles' heel and his move now over the issue of expanding his case for crippled children was an example of exquisite timing. Ed, to evade the 1969 Tax Reform Act's requirement that a foundation disburse 5 percent of its assets each year in charitable bequests, had managed to classify the estate's Nemours Foundation as a hospital. As the 1977 deadline for the Florida National divestment put the estate into the national limelight, Dent used the media's attention to put added pressure on Ball. When he arrived at the estate's sparse headquarters at the Florida National Bank building for his conference with Ball, the press was on hand watching every move.

Ed walked into the meeting and gave Mills and opposing attorneys a courteous "Good morning" mantled in frost. Towards the gray-haired Dent, whose features strongly resembled those of his grandfather's, from the eyes and nose right down to the familiar Du Pont cleft in the chin, Ball could not help but extend a warmer tone. He was like Montezuma seeing Cortes on his horse for the first time, the living embodiment of an ancient legend portending the return of a god-like lord from the past to reclaim his throne. Like the Aztec emperor, Ball saw physical signs that could not be denied and had to be embraced even as he sensed they augured his doom. "I'd like to get this unpleasantness cleared up before I cross the creek," he had said, using the Du Pont family's expression for death employed since the days their gunpowder mills, exploding, would literally blow men and machines across Brandywine Creek. It was his own testament to how deeply Alfred du Pont's life on the Brandywine with other Du Ponts in an era long gone by had pervaded his own life, possessed his soul, even though he had never actually shared Alfred's experience.

The spell was soon broken. His bald brow lowered into a hawkish frown when Dent and Mills, saying it was time to cease hoarding, proposed liquidating Ed's empire and investing the proceeds in securities that would yield at least $20 to $50 million each year to the children's hospital. That meant the Wilmington hospital could expand beyond its pitifully small service of 950 in-patients a year. But it also meant the sale of 702,880 shares of Du Pont, 1,100,000 shares of General Motors, a recently acquired 23 percent interest in Jacksonville's Charter Oil Company, another 23 percent of the Florida National Banks of Florida, Inc., 100 percent of the Florida East Coast Railroad with all its assets, including the Apalachicola Northern Railroad, the Apalachicola Telephone and Telegraph Company with over 20,000 subscribers, and over 1,100,000 acres of Florida and Georgia pinelands, and, of course, the estate's 74 percent interest in the holding company which controlled all this, the St. Joe Paper Company, the jewel in Ed Ball's crown.

Ed exploded. He called for the bank's security guards. He insisted they forcibly throw the other trustees' lawyers out of the room. When Florida National Banks officials balked, Ed walked out, decreeing the meeting adjourned over protests, and charged down the hall to the refuge of his personal office. When the trustees followed, Ed threw his frail five foot six inch frame across the door, insisting they leave their lawyers outside. Behind him, Dent and Mills could observe the chiffon-scarved Mrs. Walsh, Ed's secretary for 40 years, her powdered face white with dismay. They accepted Ed's terms, hoping to end his tantrum. But once inside they discovered they had, like so many before them, underestimated the little man. Ball's own lawyers were there, waiting for them. They objected. Ed insisted. At that point the trustees wisely left.

Ed, seated behind his plain wooden desk next to a small picture of himself flanked by crossed miniature U.S. flags, tried to appear confident as he put the blame on Mills.

"The grapevine told me that Mr. Mills is just waiting for me to cross the creek," he said. "Then he will try to disqualify the other board trustees, leaving only him as trustee." Ever the Caesar, he tried to divide and conquer, insisting "Dent is under the influence of Mills."

"It looks to me like Mr. Dent is trying to keep one foot in Mr. Mills' stirrup and one foot in the stirrup of the rest of the board."[30]

Ed's argument was lame, and he knew it. Dent's legitimacy as grandson was unquestionable and it would have been all but impossible for Mills to ever have challenged it even if he entertained the malevolent designs attributed to him by Ball. Dent understood this and knew who his ally was and who Ed Ball was. "You have to understand that Ed Ball likes to get money," he explained frankly, "control it and hang on to it."[31] It wasn't that Ed wanted luxury. He had not taken a penny of the estate's money for himself since 1951. "I've got a couple of acres of good old Florida mud and sand," he offered, "a few shares of General Motors, Du Pont and St. Joe Paper."[32] Such comments reached the heights of disingenuity. With St. Joe shares valued at $5,000 each, his "few shares" of 5000 were alone worth $25 million. But if Ball used his control over the estate's enormous assets as leverage in attracting deals and secret information that built his own $100 million fortune, his daily life was culturally deprived. He lived like a pauper in two simple rooms in Jacksonville's Robert Meyer Hotel originally rented at $49 a room. His one routine was his evening gathering with close aides around a small bar in his room, sipping bourbon "to ward off heart attacks" (he had had four serious coronaries and did not hear or see well), toasting, "Confusion to the enemies!" Once, when he saw a reporter giving news on his television he turned to the set and lifted his glass. "And confusion to you, too!"[33]

Ed, rather, was simply the Sorceror's Apprentice gone mad, no longer able to distinguish himself from his magic capital broom. He had, in fact, become its appendage.

Two years later, the Wilmington newspapers got word that Ed Ball had flown from Jacksonville by chartered plane, landed at Philadelphia International Airport and motored to the 300-acre Nemours estate of his dead brother-in-law and sister. He had come, it was reported, to pay a surprise visit to inspect the new 180-bed hospital being constructed as a concession to the IRS, Mr. Dent, and a suit launched against him and his aides by the attorneys general of both Delaware and Florida. It was his first sojourn since 1974 to the high-walled compound, and security guards obeyed his wish to be protected from inquiring reporters or photographers. Even Dent was not informed of his presence.

Ed inspected the first floor of both the new hospital and the old 60-bed one. He toured Alfred and Jessie's mansion, preserved, like its surrounding formal garden, for 40 years with Foundation money, a source of controversy that led Ed to recently open the grounds to the public to justify the expenditure. It is a vast mausoleum, an American Taj Mahal devoted not to the living, but to the memory of the dead.

Ed was described as "pleasant and very courteous" by the staff and seemed in good spirits as he was left to pay his respects to the graves of his sister and brother-in-law beneath the carillon tower. But he was not. Only the year before a bout of pneumonia had confined him to St. Vincent's Medical Center in Jacksonville. Now, at 91, he had come to say goodbye.

He was pugnacious and tart-tongued to the end. In 1977, for example, the new administration of Governor du Pont in Delaware had decided to add to Dent and the Federal Reserve's pressure on Ed by suing the trustees to get Ed to give more than the meager 1 percent of the estate's asset value that he yearly paid out. Delaware was confident because the trust, since it was supposedly dedicated to the handicapped, became subject to state regulations governing tax-free charitable institutions. By 1980, however, the du Pont

Administration, exhausted by Ed's legal maneuvers, agreed to settle for only 3 percent. At which point Ed, smelling blood, leaped to the offense, paying an outside auditor to lower the estate's conservative 1979 value of $1.1 billion on an average price of St. Joe stock to $642 million, arguing a fall in St. Joe price. Instead of $33 million being paid out, only $19 million was accepted as due, and Ed insisted there was not enough cash on hand to pay even that amount. Delaware's State Solicitor expressed that he was "very concerned." "The trustees are not trying to rip off the company," he volunteered. "They are honorable men, but they don't have a philosophy consistent with acting as fiduciaries for crippled children. They are into income appreciation instead of income distribution."[34] The state would continue its suit with Florida to remove Ball and his Florida cronies. The deathwatch began once again, as it had for twenty years.

Then, in June, 1981, almost to the surprise of everyone, it ended. Ed had entered Ochsner Foundation Hospital in New Orleans for surgery to repair an abdominal aneurysm. For two months he fought his body as its condition steadily deteriorated. Finally, at age 93, Ed Ball, the man *Forbes* called "the king of northern Florida,"[35] was dead.

The enemy was as confused as ever.

"Ed Ball would have appreciated this," joked St. Joe's 65-year-old president Jacob C. Belin. He reported calls "almost daily by international oil companies, paper companies, chemical companies and tobacco concerns to buy up all or part of St. Joe's assets."[36] It was like the chaotic last scenes in *Zorba the Greek* when the villagers pillaged the home of the local rich woman whose body was barely cold.

Jake Belin kept them all at bay. This comely, greying man was Ed's heir apparent, and he was not about to surrender so easily a throne he had waited so long to inherit. Joining forces with president Winfred Thornton of the Florida East Coast Railroad, he fought off threats of raids and insisted that "We don't anticipate any change in the direction of the trust which Mr. Ball has influenced for so many years." His spokesman, Stanley Fraser, said the Florida trustees would elect someone from among themselves to replace Ball.

Belin is faced with Florida's and Delaware's suit to remove him, Thornton, and their friend, Thomas S. Coldeway, as trustees for conflict of interest in managing companies while short-changing crippled children and the elderly. The latter new emphasis was Ed Ball's last innovation, and was such a sharp shift in focus from Alfred du Pont's order that his estate care for crippled children that it was originally included in the suits by Florida's Attorney General Jim Smith and Delaware Attorney General Richard Gebellin. The 1980 settlement allowed Ball's diversion from the will to proceed, but only on the provision that Delawareans be given first consideration as beneficiaries of the estate. In November of that year, the Foundation purchased an office building in Wilmington for a new optical and dental clinic for the elderly, and the project has gone ahead despite the renewal of the suits caused by Ball's downward revaluation of the estate.

The new hospital, which was to eventually house the clinic, has been caught in the struggle between Belin's allies and Delaware. To many in Delaware, Belin has been making moves that not only jeopardize the hospital but also threaten to shift the focus of its charity to the Jacksonville area. As evidence, they point to Belin's opening of a small hospital for crippled children in Jacksonville and the changes his architects and designers have made in the hospital's steam-sterilizing and fire-fighting systems that might make it impossible to operate safely. The contractors have sued the Foundation for $6 million, charging that the changes were made without adequate plans or specifications and that Belin and Company are refusing to pay the cost of finishing construction in the way the Foundation originally requested. Significantly, one of the contractors is Ernest DiSabatino & Sons, which has been closely associated in deals with the Wilmington Du Ponts, constructing a factory for Henry B. du Pont's All-American Industries, serving on one of Governor du Pont's commissions, and even marrying one of the DiSabatino granddaughters to Henry Rust, treasurer of the Rockland Corporation and nephew of Irénée du Pont, Jr.

"It's like watching a nuclear war across the ocean," commented an official at the hospital who worries that the legal broadsides being fired between Delaware and Florida will produce fallout that will reach the hospital soon, halting construction.[37] Belin, operating out of Ed's old office, has countersued, but he is clearly worried about his public image. He has recently hired a public relations firm. Unfortunately, they have not advised him that replacing Ed Ball's color portrait of the late Shah of Iran with pictures of his two favorite historical figures, Confederate generals Robert E. Lee and Stonewall Jackson, will not exactly dispel the image Ball created for the estate of being a tool for bigotry against Blacks, unions and liberals.

Nor will Belin's continued expansion of the estate's business empire. St. Joe is now worth $400 million and has a sugar-growing and refining operation near Lake Okeechobee and $50 million worth of Charter Oil stock. "We're working with the St. Joe Port Authority to develop the port," Belin also proudly admits, "which has great potential."[38] Belin hopes a new shipping terminal there will bring "three million tons of coal a year" through the port to electric utility plants. The estate's 100-mile Apalachicola Northern Railroad, of course, will profit from hauling the coal part way, so much so, in fact, that Belin is more than doubling the number of the railroad's cars.

And what of crippled children? Belin, as trustee of Ed Ball's personal estate, is dipping into the $100 million fortune the old curmudgeon left behind. This includes sizeable chunks of real estate near Titusville. "We've sold some to McDonnell-Douglas and some to Hughes Aircraft," he explains. "We've reinvested the proceeds in government securities to produce income. As we continue to liquidate assets of Mr. Ball's estate, the income flow will increase."[39]

That leaves the Alfred I. du Pont estate intact. Ed's personal fortune proved to be his greatest secret weapon, a ready source of cash that Belin could use to protect Ed's empire from the ravages of crippled children. And Ed could rely on Belin as his own apprentice. The estate is the source of Belin's power, for which he received salary of $75,000 per year from St. Joe, plus $10,000 from the two estates as a trustee. "A big salary isn't everything," Jake confesses. "I've had many opportunities to go elsewhere. Mrs. du Pont and Mr. Ball helped us over the years. Mr. Ball made it easy to get in on his personal business deals."[40]

He still is. By leaving his personal fortune in Belin's hands, Ed had found a way of extending his role as sorceror's apprentice beyond even the grave.

The only question is if, once again, he will have his way.

Dent and his allies in the attorneys general offices of Delaware and Florida hope not. They have pressed their suit into court, into Jacksonville, where a Florida judge is now deliberating on the matter.

"We were always a tempting target for politicians trying to get attention," Belin claims. "These attacks always seemed to crop up shortly before elections." His attorney, Fred Kent, warns that removing Belin's aides as trustees would mean "nothing will be left for crippled children in 1999 and beyond. . . . These trustees are reinvesting the income in the assets to fight inflation."

And inflation is a potent word. Ever since the Supreme Court ordered one person-one vote reapportionment in the Sixties, however, northern Florida politics and courts are not as predictably pro-Ball as they were when Ed was known as the power behind the "Pork Chop Gang" of rural businessmen, politicans, and segregationists. Even Belin admits that while "Mr. Ball was a great man," Florida is a different state. "You can't do things like you once did them. One man or a group of people can't manipulate the Legislature or a county commission or do things behind closed doors."[41]

Perhaps. But many in Delaware might not agree. And if Alfred du Pont Dent has his way, and he just may if conflict of interest has any meaning left in American law, the estate of his grandfather will end its 60-year-long Florida exile and return to the bosom of the Brandywine. There, one might easily expect the Du Pont family to exert great influence over Dent, who was once a director of one of the family's securities investment firms, Laird, Inc. Alfred du Pont's vast $2 billion fortune—and with it one of the world's richest foundations—will then be in their hands. And in Delaware, the Company State, decisions are still made behind closed doors. What that could mean for not only Delaware but America is best illustrated in the motives behind Belin's dogged refusal to sell Ed Ball's personal 10.34 percent holding in Florida National Banks. It is now worth $27 million. Within a short time, that could jump to $38 million. The reason is New York, the very financial force that has for so long dominated the same Federal Reserve Board that forced Ed to loosen the estate's hold on Florida National. Chemical Bank of New York has bought an option to buy Florida National. And behind Chemical, among other financial groups represented on the board of directors, are the Du Ponts, represented by Du Pont chairman Edward Jefferson. Chemical, in fact, shares Wilmington Trust's responsibility as registrar of Du Pont stock and has been associated with the Du Ponts for decades.

All that Chemical is waiting for is federal approval of interstate banking that would allow New York banks to expand their control over banks across the country. This will require the overthrow of existing New Deal laws safeguarding the national banking system from such overconcentration. And behind the increasingly successful drive for that approval is the state leading the way with legislative revisions as "the nation's first state in financial services," Delaware.

Leading Delaware, of course, are the Du Ponts, particularly Governor Pierre S. du Pont IV, grandson of Lammot du Pont. Alfred du Pont's arch-nemesis, Pierre, may have won the final battle after all.

It is, perhaps, a strange irony that it should be part of Alfred's estate that will probably feel the first effects of this latest expansion of corporate power inaugurated by the heirs of his greatest rivals. But then Delaware and the Du Ponts have always been historically the greatest innovators of basic changes in the structure of American business law, a fact neglected or ignored, probably because of Delaware's smallness and remoteness, by most Americans, to their everlasting pain. But as millions of Americans begin to feel the impact of what Floridians will probably soon bear, some eyes may turn their focus on Delaware. If they do, they will witness extraordinary and fearful events. If they train their ears on the state as well, they may just hear the carillon above Alfred's grave pealing a familiar protest—and a warning—into the night.

Fifteen

A DYNASTY OF DOUBTS

1. THE CULTURAL CONSPIRACY

The power of the Du Ponts is so extensive that it permeates most aspects of our daily lives.

If we buy high-test gasoline for our cars, we are helping to strengthen the Du Pont empire. If our shirts are made of Dacron, or our frying pans of Teflon, we enrich the Du Ponts. If our car is made by General Motors, or its tires by Uniroyal, we enrich the Du Ponts. If we fly on a Boeing jetliner, buy Conoco or Crown gasoline, drink a Coke, eat a Chiquita banana, or sprinkle Domino sugar over our cereal, we have enriched the Du Ponts. Our ties may well be made of Du Pont rayon and colored with Du Pont dyes. Our cars may be upholstered with Du Pont artificial leather and finished with Du Pont lacquers. If we have an X ray taken at a hospital or buy see-through cellophane packages at the supermarket, spread fertilizer on our lawns or Lucite paint over our walls, take home-movies on vacation or fish with a nylon line or hunt with a Remington rifle, we may have just helped buy some Du Pont his next $600 suit.

Although the Rockefeller, Morgan, and Mellon banking families probably control more corporate assets, the Du Ponts have more personal wealth. In fact, no family in America has been richer longer than the Du Ponts. They are the country's oldest industrial family, producing gunpowder sixty-eight years before Rockefeller was identified with oil, eighty-six years before Carnegie with steel, ninety years before Ford with automobiles.

The Vanderbilts, it is often pointed out, survive as rich people; the Du Ponts survive as a corporation. This may be changing now, but there is little doubt that the survival of the Du Pont family as a cohesive body with a separate identity of its own has been the result of the unique role it played in American economic history *as a company.* It should be emphasized, however, that the company has not ruled the family, as is so commonly suggested; rather, the family has ruled the company. Throughout its history, the main concern of the family has always been the family, not the company. In fact, the main concern of Du Pont Company was always the Du Pont family. The family was never as obsessed with the company as it has been with itself. The family was the object of its own determination and, in the early years, sweat. The company was merely a tool, and once, in 1902, when the company was nearly given up, it was retained only in the family's interest. And now, as we shall see, control may well be surrendered, again in the family's interest. The Du Pont family's profit, it is clear, is its own motivation. On this, Delaware's largest clan has built—and torn down—its greatest customs.

Du Pont history, however, did not occur in a vacuum, divorced from the broader social and economic history in which it thrived. Probably the strongest force aiding Du Pont's rise was the State (polis).

In 1930 the former U.S. ambassador to Germany, James W. Gerard, named fifty-nine people who ruled America. Significantly, the ambassador omitted President Hoover and all federal and state officials. The real nature of the state, he explained, was "the power behind the throne," the men of industry and finance who had little time to spare to hold a political office, but, because of their economic positions, held *permanent* influence, not the temporary influence of an officeholder. Among those fifty-nine, Gerard named six Du Ponts: Pierre du Pont, Irénée du Pont, Lammot du Pont, Henry F. du Pont, Eugene du Pont, Jr., and Eugene E. du Pont.

Gerard's revelations were not news along the Brandywine. Since E. I. du Pont had first built his gunpowder mill on the banks of that creek, the power of government was the keystone of the company's growth. Du Pont's first sale was to the U.S. government, and the 1812 War, the Mexican War, and the Civil War were all timely boosts to Du Pont expansion. The Du Ponts had always used political power to protect and further their interests, but for the first ninety years confined this activity, for the most part, to the immediate area of their economic concern, Delaware.

The organizational problems of the Powder Trust of Henry du Pont (who had literally conquered Delaware during the Civil War with a Union army) required the direct use of state power, and Henry's successor, Eugene du Pont, even had Delaware's constitution changed to legally facilitate Du Pont's adjustment to the more efficient form of business organization, the corporation. From then on, the Du Ponts fully exploited Delaware's lenient tax laws, often being given direct assistance from local judges.

William du Pont's heirs, for example, saved millions in inheritance taxes in the early Thirties when Wilmington's federal court ruled that their father's will, made just two years before his death at the age of 73, was not made "in contemplation of death."

Alfred I. du Pont, by incorporating his palatial Nemours mansion at $1 million, saved through "losses," taxes of $200,000 from 1931 to 1935 alone.

Mrs. Wilhelmina du Pont Ross also incorporated her stables and farms, saving $172,469 in taxes.

Pierre du Pont, Francis V. du Pont, Richard C. du Pont, Paulina du Pont, and Mrs. H. Ethel du Pont all gained large tax savings through personal holding companies.

Most of Lammot du Pont's $75 million estate went to the safe abode of family foundations and trusts for his widow and ten children.

Pierre du Pont's $80 million estate was left to his Longwood Foundation, to be administered by Du Pont relatives in keeping up his flowered dreamworld. The settlement for taxes on this estate carries its own story.

Pierre's Longwood estate, where he had spent weekends and vacations since World War I, was in Pennsylvania. Naturally Harrisburg tried to collect a Pennsylvania residency tax. This, however, would have raised the estate's total tax from $3.8 million under Pierre's Delaware citizenship (Delaware itself only asked for $600,000) to between $28 and $41 million. The Du Ponts fought this, insisting Pierre was a Delaware citizen exempt from Pennsylvania's claims. Finally, the state's tax authorities took the Du Ponts to the local court in Chester County and got a favorable ruling from Judge Ernest Harvey in the second week of July 1955. Pennsylvania had the right, the judge decided, to appeal the granting of ancillary letters of administration in Chester County under which the state could collect on Pierre's property in Pennsylvania. One week later, on July 25, the judge suddenly reversed his decision and said that Pennsylvania had no such right. This, he explained, would give the estate the right to appeal if anything went wrong in the case, "such a close one." Nothing did. Pierre's money stayed in the family.

There are other, similar cases. In 1957 the U.S. Internal Revenue Service claimed that some Du Ponts owed $452,207 in back taxes. The government settled for $158,908. The claims involved Marianna du Pont and her husband Henry H. Silliman, for $70,680, settled for $11,926; Octavia du Pont and her husband, J. Bruce Bredin for $195,585, settled for $98,291; Lammot du Pont Copeland and his wife Pamela for $156,642, settled for $30,953; and the Nemours Corporation for $29,300, settled for $17,738.

In 1962 the Treasury Department's original attempt to collect ordinary income tax on the family's sale of some of its G.M. stock was foiled by lobbyist Clark'Clifford's and Crawford Greenewalt's visits to more than sixty Congressional and government offices, including those of Treasury Secretary Dillon and Attorney General Robert Kennedy. That year, in the instance already cited, a special bill saved the Du Ponts $100 million in taxes, and in 1964 a reversal of a Treasury ruling saved them another $2 billion.

The Delaware General Assembly, encouraged by Governor Carvel, followed suit, passing a bill to deal with the G.M. divestiture as capital gains rather than ordinary cash income. With $1 million of the money the state did manage to collect, the State Park Commissioner bought property along the Brandywine from the 400-acre estate of Mrs. Ellen du Pont Wheelwright, daughter of the late Senator T. Coleman du Pont.

In 1963, as Irénée du Pont approached the end of his octogenarian life, the three trustees of his estate, Irénée du Pont, Jr., Crawford Greenewalt, and Ernest May, employed a Wilmington lawyer, S. Samuel Arsht, to approach Delaware's Supreme Court Chancellor Collins J. Seitz about allowing the guardians to ease the tax burden on Irénée's $200 to $400 million estate by distributing some $33 million among his eight children. Seitz subsequently declared Irénée incompetent two months before his death and allowed the trustees to go ahead with their plans, realizing tax savings of some $10 million. Later, Seitz became Wilmington's U.S. Court of Appeals judge.

Old Irénée du Pont's estate was the recipient of another tax boon. In the interest of "justice" tinged with some old-fashioned prejudice, Senator John Williams, "conscience of the Senate" in the Bobby Baker exposés, introduced an amendment to federal tax codes allowing a $2 million compensation for the seizure of Irénée's luxurious estate in Cuba.

Delaware is probably the most lenient state in the country to corporations, having the lowest business tax percentage in the United States. Delaware's advantages include lower cost of incorporation, out-of-state stockholder and director meetings, and as many classes of stock as a corporation deems fit. Predictably, a majority of the largest American corporations are incorporated in Delaware. For the rich who choose to reside in Delaware, state officials have the house special: total tax exemption on personal property.

Du Ponts receive special benefits on land taxes as well. In the eyes of Delaware law, for example, Irénée du Pont, Jr., the scion of the Du Pont industrial empire, is a farmer. The Delaware Farmland Assessment Act provides tax breaks for landed gentry like Irénée. And Irénée does very well. His 514-acre Granogue estate, worth $1.5 million, would "normally" be assessed at $64,500 or $125 an acre. But since Irénée is a "farmer," tax breaks decrease the value of the estate's land by $1.45 million, leaving only forty "non-farm" taxable acres. For these forty acres, Irénée pays only $1,100—a pro rata tax rate of less than $2.50 an acre for his entire estate.

Multimillionaire Irénée du Pont insists a reassessment would force him to sell Granogue, and wants no part of a park gift plan that would not "reasonably compensate" him for his loss. "It comes down to this," he explains. "If the public wants open space, it will in some manner have to pay for it."[1] So speaks the farmer who is past president of the Kennett Pike Association of landlords, mostly Du Ponts, who own most every open field between Wilmington and the Pennsylvania state line.

Du Pont Company's own official position on taxes is just as blatant: "High taxes, by narrowing the gap between income brackets, threaten to discourage ambition to seek or accept positions of great responsibility."[2] Du Pont does not explain, beyond the time-worn trickle-down theory, how this position reconciles itself to the principle of social responsibility, democratic equality, or any alternative to the arbitrary exercise of power through an exclusive ownership of corporate wealth that prevents democratic control.

This is not to suggest that democratic equality has ever been a Du Pont concern. In fact, the family has developed many ruses for avoiding any public control over its wealth. Besides their eleven personal trusts, the Du Ponts have established thirty-seven tax-free foundations:*

Alfred I. du Pont Awards Foundation, worth $1.5 million.
Alfred I du Pont Foundation, worth $7.8 million.
Averell-Ross Foundation, worth $96,000.
Barbee-Hagley Foundation, worth $425,000.
J. Bruce Bredin Foundation, worth $1 million.
Carpenter Foundation, worth $1.3 million.
Charitable Research Foundation, worth $478,000.
Chichester-du Pont Foundation, worth $10 million.
Christiana Foundation, worth $840,000.
Clifton Center Foundation, worth $199,000.
Copeland-de Andelot Foundation, $385,000
Crestlea Foundation, worth $5.3 million.
Crystal Trust Foundation, worth $24 million.
Curran Foundation, worth $1.1 million.
Dean Foundation, worth $384,000.
du Pont Religious, Charitable and Educational Fund,
    worth $71.3 million.
Ederic Foundation, worth $5.4 million.
Eleutherian Mills-Hagley Foundation, worth $43 million.
Episcopal Church School Foundation (assets not available).

---

*Figures, *Foundation Directory*; 1981, 1972, 1963-7.

Good Samaritan Foundation, worth $1 million.

Irénée du Pont, Jr., Foundation (assets not available).

Kraemer Foundation (assets not available).

Lalor Foundation, worth $2.1 million.

Lesesne Foundation, worth $62,000.

Longwood Foundation, worth $103 million.

Marmot Foundation, worth $10.8 million.

Nemours Foundation, worth $6.1 million.

Red Clay Reservation, worth $4.4 million.

Rencourt Foundation, worth $62,000.

Ross Foundation, worth $64,000.

Sharp Foundation, worth $55,000.

Theano Foundation, worth $25,000.

Unidel Foundation, worth over $1 million.

Welfare Foundation, worth $13.9 million.

Weymouth Foundation, worth $55,000.

Weymyss Foundation, worth $106,000.

Winterhur (Museum) Foundation, worth $41.8 million.

All of these Du Pont foundations are supposedly dedicated to the public and are therefore granted exemption from inheritance and income taxes so long as they annually give away a percentage of their assets. But behind this mask of charity, the foundations effectively serve as tax-free holding companies for the family. At the end of 1966, for example, eight of these foundations held 616,243 shares of G.M. stock valued then at $43 million. Four of the Du Pont foundations held another 753,842 shares of Christiana Securities stock, worth over $112 million. Seven held 112,738 shares of Du Pont common, then worth over $16 million.[3] In addition, the Raskob Foundation, set up by the old family ally John J. Raskob, and administered to Catholic charities by his survivors in Wilmington, has stock worth another $36.7 million.

Delaware law makes setting up a foundation as easy as collecting a stock dividend. With 53 foundations, Delaware is the eighth largest state in terms of foundation assets. But in terms of grants, it ranks twentieth.

Most of the above figures for foundation assets are based on ledger value. The discrepancy between their ledger value and their real market value is fantastic, since most of these foundations have many assets in common stocks, particularly in Du Pont. Furthermore, most of these foundations give away far more each year than the ledger value of their assets. Nevertheless, the given total of the above figures amounts to over $340 million.

The biggest of the Du Pont foundations is the Longwood Foundation founded by the $80 million estate of Du Pont and G.M. chairman Pierre S. du Pont to tend his horticulture wonderland for posterity. Today seven Du Ponts guard over a $103 million fortune, one of the largest foundations in the country. They are Irénée du Pont, Jr., H.R. Sharp III, Edward B. du Pont, Irénée du Pont May, H.H. Silliman, Jr., Garrett Van S. Copeland and Pierre S. du Pont III. As of September 1966 this foundation alone held 274,295 shares of G.M. common, 505,945 shares of Christiana Securities, 204 shares of Christiana preferred, and 11,525 shares of Du Pont common.

The other foundations are controlled by the following Du Ponts or relatives:

Alfred I. du Pont Awards	Alfred du Pont Dent
Alfred I. du Pont	Braden Ball, Alfred I. du Pont Estate
Averell-Ross	Francis I. du Pont II W.W. Laird, Jr.
Barbee-Hagley	H.H. Silliman
Bredin	G. Burton Pearson, Jr. Alfred E. Bissell Robert B. Flint J. Bruce Bredin Irénée du Pont, Jr.
Carpenter	William K. Carpenter Renee C. Draper R.R.M. Carpenter, Jr. J. Avery Draper
Charitable Research	Ernest N. May
Chichester-du Pont	Phyllis Mills Wyeth Katherine du Pont Guhagan James P. Mills Richard C. du Pont Alice du Pont Mills Marka T. du Pont A. Felix du Pont, Jr. Reese E. Timmons
Christiana	C. Lalor Burdick
Clifton Center	W.S. Carpenter III

	Edmond N. Carpenter II
Copeland-Andelot	Lammot du Pont Copeland
	William S. Potter
	Alfred E. Bissell
Crestlea	Edward B. du Pont
Crystal Trust	Irénée du Pont, Jr.
	Willard A. Speakman
Dean	J. Simpson Dean
du Pont Religious, Charitable and Educational Fund	Jessie Ball du Pont Estate trustees
Ederic	Reynolds du Pont
	Mrs. G. Burton Pearson, Jr.
	Philip B. Weymouth
	Natalie Riegel Weymouth
	Richard E. Riegel, Jr.
Eleutherian Mills-Hagley	Edward B. du Pont
	Eleuthère I. du Pont
	Nicholas R. du Pont
	W.W. Laird, Jr.
	Philip J. Kimball
Good Samaritan	W.S. Carpenter III
Irénée du Pont, Jr.	Irénée du Pont, Jr.
Kraemer	not available
Lalor	J. Sellers Bancroft
	Alfred E. Bissell
	C. Lalor Burdick
	Dallas S. Townsend
	Rodman C. Ward
Lesesne	Patricia du Pont
Marmot	Willis H. du Pont
Nemours	Alfred du Pont Dent
Red Clay Preservation	Copeland family, Edward B. du Pont
Rencourt	W.S. Carpenter III

	George T. Weymouth
	Eugene E. du Pont
Ross	Donald Ross family
Sharp	Bayard Sharp
Theano	Jean Foulke du Pont
Unidel	W. Sam Carpenter III
Welfare	J. Simpson Dean
	H.B. Robertson
	Edward B. du Pont
Weymouth	George Weymouth family
Weymyss	W.W. Laird, Jr.
Winterhur	Edmond du Pont
	J. Bruce Bredin
	George P. Edmonds
	Louisa Copeland Duemling

The Du Ponts dismiss the suggestion that control over these foundation millions should really be in the hands of the public and dispensed by a democratically controlled Department of Education. Instead, they insist that distribution of grants from assets (most of which would have gone to the public through taxation if the foundations had not been set up) take the form of *gifts* based on their own personal whims and biases. This is the real power of Du Pont foundations: not simply the money involved, but how they use that money.

Formally, the Du Ponts do not impose their own standards in judging grant applications. These standards were written in the will of the original Du Pont donor, and applicants are free to accept them or not. But the appearance of freedom is a dangerous illusion. The reality is that if the public wants money, it must bend to Du Pont values. And as foundations have become a *permanent* influence on urban community life, the realities of Du Pont power are not lost on potential applicants.

Key to this power is the use of "matching" contributions. Du Pont foundations offer large sums most often only if the recipient can raise an equal sum from other sources. This puts the recipient under great pressure, and puts the Du Ponts in the driver's seat, doubling or tripling the power of their money. As Du Pont foundations are a permanent institution, the recipient is under subtle, but real, pressure to mind its ways.

The focus of Du Pont foundations has for the most part been far less social than that of other super-rich families. The Du Ponts concentrate their tax-free foundations on the Du Ponts, carefully preserving the memorabilia of their ancestors and the elegant estates they modeled after the aristocratic ostentation of prerevolutionary France.

Thus, Pierre's Longwood palace and its 1,000 acres of formal gardens, greenhouses, and dancing fountains are preserved for the family and the visiting public, the latter no doubt impressed by brochures reminding them of Pierre's tax-free generosity.

So, also, Alfred's lordly seventy-room limestone chateau, complete with marble sphinxes, a classic temple of Love, a colonnade and sunken gardens that rival those of Versailles, are preserved by the Nemours Foundation from the ravages of public taxation, although the public until recently was kept out by high fences and a stone wall studded with glass.

E. I. du Pont's original gunpowder mills along the Brandywine have also been restored by the Eleutherian Mills-Hagley Foundation, which operates a museum reflecting the family's particular view of its history and a library that contains everything from a Du Pont's first scribbles in a grammer school notebook to his death notice. Interestingly enough, this "public" library bars enterprising researchers from its potentially embarrassing post-1933 records and manuscripts. Here, the family's view of itself as *an institution* is graphically displayed.

Winterthur, the 500-acre horticultural wonderland of multimillionaire Henry F. du Pont (who once described himself as "the head gardener"), also stands in the shade of a foundation, its blooming azaleas, lilacs, and Asiatic primroses covering sixty acres, its mazelike 180-room mansion filled with priceless colonial antiques and, sometimes, wandering lost visitors.

Most of the Du Pont foundations focus on maintaining similar, but smaller, dreamworlds. As Longwood's coordinator, Dr. Richard Lighty, explained in reporting ornamental horticulture grants to five students, "This program is of vital importance. The need for skilled horticulturists has never been greater."[4]

Lately, however, Longwood has been leading the other foundations increasingly into education, an area over which other foundations have long held sway, financing writers and flooding the libraries of the country with approved texts. In 1969, for example, Longwood gave $200,000 to the expansion project of the Newark Free Library, on a matching basis, of course.

The Du Pont family's interest in education goes back to its founder, Pierre Samuel Du Pont, the French aristocrat. As early as 1800 Pierre wrote a treatise on national education for Vice-President Thomas Jefferson, emphasizing that in primary schools "the State should decide what books are to be used."[5] From the primary schools, only those children "having sufficient private means" or "those suitable" would be "selected" by the State to be sent to the secondary school, where "order" would be maintained not only in classrooms, but in every aspect of private life. Pierre's ideas of centralized education did not coincide with the prevailing values of *laissez-faire* capitalism, and were not used.

The Du Ponts generally confined their educational activities to Delaware, specifically the Brandywine school for their workers' children. They did manage, however, to take an early interest in the scholastic endeavors of the Franklin Institute in Philadelphia, and in fact have dominated the institution's board of managers for over 140 years. Here is the list of Du Pont board members:

Victor du Pont	1824–1825
Charles du Pont	1824–1825
E. I. du Pont	1825–1834
E. I. du Pont II	1856–1877
Francis G. du Pont	1888–1905
Pierre S. du Pont	1892–1953
Irénée du Pont	1912–1963
T. Coleman du Pont	1913–1924
Mrs. Irénée du Pont	1936–1961
E. Paul du Pont	1937–1950
A. Felix du Pont, Jr.	1966–

Irénée du Pont also took an active interest in cancer research. In 1935, however, he effectively destroyed the University of Pennsylvania's Cancer Research Department through his passion for profit. Under Irénée's demands, the university was forced to amputate the department. President Thomas R. Gates stated the separation was due "to no other reason than the inability of Mr. du Pont to accede to the university's official policy in respect to patents that might be accrued on the result of scientific work by the university staff. The trustees [had] approved the recommendations of the faculty that all discoveries should be made available to the public without any profits accruing to the individuals responsible or to the institution."[6] The university faculty simply did not believe in profiting out of human suffering.

Such words were anathema to Irénée's ears. Patent profits and "financial reward" were his rule, and he expressed regret "that the differences of view of an underlying principle should make it advisable to discontinue our formal relationship."[7] Subsequently, Irénée found other takers and continued financing the labs on his terms.

Most Du Pont donations to schools were on an individual level before the 1960's. In 1924 T. Coleman du Pont gave a luncheon for financiers at the Bankers Club in New York. "Education," the former Powder Trust president asserted, was the panacea of the world, the only means of mutual understanding and elimination of war. He proposed an "interchange of studies and credits on the world's leading universities"[8] and international scholarships, and he served as vice-chairman of a committee of educators and bankers for studying practical application of his plans.

Coleman's definition of "education" was abstract, but his own activity in this area revealed the true class nature of his plans and the capitalist biases in his understanding of what "education" was. As early as 1910 Coleman gave $500,000 to his alma mater, the Massachusetts Institute of Technology. M.I.T. has always had an intimate relationship with the Du Ponts, over a score of them having gone there, including Alfred I., Pierre, Lammot, Coleman, Henry B., S. Hallock, Irénée, Jr., Irénée III, Reynolds, and W. W. Laird, Jr. Moreover, many of Du Pont's products had been (and still are being) developed by M.I.T. technicians, providing large dividends to the Du Ponts for their support. Most of Du Pont Company's technicians are M.I.T.-trained, as are those of General Motors.

In 1920 Coleman gave another $1 million to the M.I.T. expansion fund, one-tenth of its total amount. Pierre du Pont, Irénée du Pont, and Lammot du Pont also provided huge sums. David Flett du Pont gave $1 million in his will. M.I.T.'s Guggenheim Aeronautical Lab even has a memorial room to Richard C. du Pont, provided by a $110,000 Du Pont donation. All told, the Du Ponts have contributed about $30 million to M.I.T., but they have been more than compensated. Among the talented M.I.T. graduates who have helped the Du Ponts run their company or breed their family are director Charles B. McCoy, director and in-law George P. Edmonds, former president and in-law Crawford Greenewalt, in-law Ernest May, and vice-president Robert L. Hershey. Irénée III is a recent graduate, and his father, Irénée, Jr., serves as a life member of the M.I.T. (Corporation) board, as does Crawford Greenewalt. George P. Edmonds held the same post from 1960 to 1965, and still serves on its Development Committee, while his son, George, Jr., has worked at the M.I.T. instrumentation lab on the Apollo Space Project.

While M.I.T. may be squarely under Du Pont's thumb, the University of Delaware is under the family's foot. Of fourteen members of the executive committee of Delaware's board of trustees, nine are Du Ponts or Du Pont executives: twenty-three of Delaware's twenty-five chaired professors are endowed by Du Pont foundations. Chief among these, besides the Sharp Trust, is the Unidel Foundation, which gives $1 million yearly. Among Unidel's present overseers are Du Pont director Charles McCoy, Edward du Pont, George P. Edmonds, G. Burton Pearson, Wilhelmina du Pont Ross, Mrs. Alfred du Pont Dent, Alfred Bissell, George Weymouth, John McConnell, Walter S. Carpenter III, Edmund N. Carpenter, J. Edward Dean, and Harry Haskell, Jr.; all except Haskell are Du Ponts or relatives, and Haskell's father began the fund with Amy du Pont. Averell du Pont Ross is one of the university's Library Associates. Among Delaware's present trustees are Edmond du Pont, Robert M. Carpenter, Jr., son of Margaretta du Pont, and J. Bruce Bredin, brother-in-law of Irénée du Pont, Jr. As chairman of the board of trustees in 1983, Bredin became the focus of controvesy by bestowing an honorary doctor of laws degree on a guest of Governor Pete and Elise du Pont, Vice-President George Bush, despite protests that this was tantamount to an academic endorsement of the Reagan Administration's recent invasion of Grenada and escalation of the CIA attacks on Nicaragua. As if to agree, Bush used the occasion to term the U.S. invasion "a fine hour" and to urge both Pete and Elise du Pont to remain active in the national political arena after Pete ends his second term as governor, evoking smiles among the invitation-only audience of some 700 Du Ponts, politicians, businessmen, and professors.

No word critical of the Du Ponts has ever been heard emanating from the administration offices of the University of Delaware, yet history avers that the Du Ponts have not always been the charming benefactors they would have people believe. "The power oligarchy has a university located at Newark," Upton Sinclair wrote in 1922, "and here was a typhoid scandal, exactly as at the University of Oregon, with the local magnates controlling the situation, and a young instructor persisting in telling the facts. It was Ibsen's play, 'An Enemy of the People,' precisely reenacted. On the day that one student was buried, this young instructor published a letter, in which he accused of murder the people who had refused to put in a sewage system. He was threatened with tarring and feathering, and the president of the college [a close friend of T. Coleman du Pont] was very sorry he could not offer this young instructor a raise. But he always did what the treasurer of the college wanted—and the treasurer was the man who had blocked the efforts of the board of health to avoid a typhoid epidemic!"

One former faculty member wrote Sinclair disgustedly that "I think the university needs an awakening to the fact that political and social conditions in the state and nation are proper and necessary subjects of the freest possible discourse. I also believe that, in spite of Pierre du Pont's altruistic attitude the Du Pont wealth stands at the gates of opportunity in Delaware, and that some who enter renounce, consciously or unconsciously, their personal freedom of opinion and action. As to the Du Pont control of politics, it should be fully and forever repudiated by the people of Delaware as an insolent attempt to enslave the state to a single great interest."[9]

Half a century later the same pleas were being made. A state budget director who attempted to force the university to give a detailed accounting of its funds was rebuked by the state legislature which, under the pressure of "Rolls-Royce Day," when Du Ponts flooded Dover, granted the university fiscal autonomy. Again, protests by faculty and students opposing the Vietnam War, as well as the university's chemical warfare research and compulsory ROTC, were met with suspensions, firings, and attacks by the university's public relations director as "kooks . . . all of the ultra-liberals, all of the Communist subversives, or whatever else we have around here. . . ."[10] There was little doubt who was calling the shots. John Perkins, Delaware's former president before he graduated in 1967 to the presidency of Dun & Bradstreet, named the eight trustees most influential in setting policy—six of them were Du Pont executives or family members. Meanwhile, the university concentrated on more serious matters than Vietnam, such as the research project analyzing baseball swings with electronic sensors and computors, financed by trustee Robert Carpenter, Jr., owner of the Philadelphia Phillies baseball team.

Delaware and M.I.T. are not the only universities with which the Du Ponts are associated:

The University of Pennsylvania was graced with the trusteeship of A. Rhett du Pont until his death in 1972.

Princeton's University Fund has W. Sam Carpenter III as a trustee.

Cornell University had Walter S. Carpenter, Jr., on its board for years.

The University of Virginia's past president was Colgate Darden, son-in-law of the late Irénée du Pont. The Virginia Law School Association had William Potter as its vice-president.

Harvard hosts Lammot du Pont Copeland, Sr., who headed up its $5 million library drive. Harvard was also the recipient of $500,000 in the will of Eugene du Pont, Jr.

Wilmington College has Irénée du Pont, Jr., as a trustee.

Wheelock College in Boston has George P. Edmonds as its guardian.

Wesley Junior College came under the watchful eye of Reynolds du Pont.

Sweet Briar College's board of overseers has J. H. Taylor McConnell, son-in-law of the late William du Pont, Jr.

And Bucknell University falls under the jurisdiction of the family's hand-picked president of Remington Arms, Rowland Coleman.

Du Ponts have been trustees of Johns Hopkins University, Fisk University, Hobart College, William Smith College, Drexel Institute, Bennett College, Hampton Institute, and the University of Michigan Development Council. In addition, the late Henry B. du Pont was associated with the University of Rhode Island, and the late Jessie Ball du Pont with Washington and Lee University, University of the South, College of William and Mary, and all of Florida's major universities.

For the Du Ponts, education is seen as an area to pursue not only prestige and self-esteem through *noblesse oblige* contributions, but personal interests as well. Jean du Pont, for example, donor of the chapel organ at Delaware's Smyrna Prison, in 1965 established the E. Paul du Pont endowment fund to the University of Delaware for the study of Delaware's prison system. The Lalor Foundation gives awards to anyone of the non-socialist world who can come up with new advances in the field of fertility and reproduction, particularly marine reproduction.

More fish may be fine, but the Du Ponts, in the tradition of most wealthy families, abhor with Malthusian passion any potentially revolutionary increase in the number of human mouths to feed. Irénée du Pont, Jr.'s Crystal Trust, when it has not been giving grants to Radio Free Europe, has been filling the coffers of the Delaware League of Planned Parenthood to the tune of tens of thousands of dollars. A. Felix du Pont, Jr.'s Chichester-du Pont Foundation has likewise given over $35,000 to the World Population Fund of Planned Parenthood, and Lammot du Pont Copeland's Andelot Foundation gave $75,000 to International Planned Parenthood in 1967 alone. There are many Du Ponts who are involved in pursuing various updated versions of the tired, nineteenth-century line of Malthus that the poor, through their own reproduction, are to blame for the world's problems and their own poverty. They fully accept Malthus' defense of a capitalist class's exclusive right to private control over the production and distribution of goods and services. To the Du Ponts, it is the "overpopulation" of the poor and laboring class, not their own class's defining of the needs of the people through the needs of a profitable marketplace, which is to blame.

The logic of a capitalist Holland, the most densely populated country yet among the highest per-capita income nations, or the logic of a starvationless socialist China versus starvation-racked capitalist India, was lost to the likes of Mrs. Reynolds du Pont, the past president of Delaware's Planned Parenthood who had five children of her own; or Lammot du Pont Copeland, Sr., former vice-chairman of Planned Parenthood who, like Pierre S. du Pont III, another promoter, had three children; or Mrs. Irénée du Pont, Jr., another booster who yet had six children; or former Lieutenant Governor

Bookhammer, who suggested forced sterilization of welfare mothers.

Today, Delaware's League for Planned Parenthood is big on voluntary sterilizations, running clinics in Wilmington, Newark, and the working class suburb, Newcastle. The chairman is Garrett Van S. Copeland, son of the late Du Pont ex-chairman, Lammot du Pont Copeland; Kathleen du Pont is Vice President; the Advisory Committee includes Emily du Pont, widow of Henry B. du Pont and mother of three (including Edward du Pont), and Du Pont in-laws H. Ingersoll Brown and Annette Reese. Recent funding cuts by the Reagan Administration have "forced us to change our procedure for collecting fees," they recently explained in a League leaflet. "We ask that you pay for all services at the time they are provided... We accept WSFS, VISA, Mastercharge and Medicaid." The last applies not to abortion for poor women, of course, but for sterilizations, whereby any question of future choice in having children is irrevocably removed. Meanwhile, Du Pont women caught in a socially embarrassing situation continue to easily afford the choice of an abortion, leaving their child-bearing capacities usually intact.

Yet, for some children, there always seems room in the world, and the Du Ponts continue to find money for these, contributing to education in the finest traditions of the original Père Du Pont. Most of these donations have gone to exclusive private schools for the very rich. Reynolds du Pont, for example, has given $360,000 to the Lawrenceville School, of which he is trustee. T. Coleman du Pont contributed heavily to the endowment of the Hill School, an eastern prep school. W. W. Laird, Jr., son of Mary du Pont, is past president of the Tatnell School, while W. Sam Carpenter III is trustee of the Taft School. J. Bruce Bredin, husband of Octavia du Pont, is trustee of the famous St. Andrew's School, which the Du Ponts helped found. But the family's favorite is their own Tower Hill School, where many a Du Pont received his first social veneer and now takes drivers' education in an $11,000 Mercedes Benz. Over Tower Hill Irénée du Pont, Jr., W. Sam Carpenter III, and G. Burton Pearson lord as trustees. Gordon Rust, husband of Frances du Pont Morgan, even taught there.

Du Pont family foundations have also provided their share to the education of America's economic royalty. In just one year, 1966, Irénée du Pont, Jr.'s Crystal Trust gave $500,000 to the William Penn Charter School in Pennsylvania, $300,000 to Bryn Mawr College, $100,000 to the Dana Hill School in Massachusetts, and $94,000 to the Pilot School in Delaware. Similar gifts by other Du Pont foundations have been made to the Pomfret School and the Ethel Walker School in Connecticut, St. Mary's-in-the-Mountains (New Hampshire), and many, many others.

In Delaware the Du Ponts have also given to Delaware Technical College. Sponsored by Du Pont Company, this college trains young Delawareans for white-collar jobs in the state's chemical industries, and also trains police for maintaining Du Pont order. Richard P. Sanger, son-in-law of Emile F. du Pont, even serves as chairman of the Advisory Committee on Police Science. In many ways, Delaware Technical is merely a training ground for Du Pont, on a lower level than the University of Delaware. As then Du Pont president Lammot du Pont Copeland once put it in a speech at the university, "I am very sure that you, as a production organization, can turn out a product more perfectly adapted to the needs of the user if you know something about that customer and his needs. I suspect that the incentive to do so will be greater if your knowledge of the customer has led you to respect him and, perhaps, even to like him." Whereupon, Lammot supplied the information on Du Pont's needs; Du Pont money supplied the goodwill.

Yet, for all of Pierre du Pont's $12 million for public schools in Delaware, the youth still suffer from a low educational achievement. Much of the key to this riddle can be found in the schools themselves. Lammot du Pont, when he was Du Pont chairman, once emphasized the role of the gifted in modern life from the standpoint of business. All progress in industry, he explained, depended upon the outstanding skills of individuals above the "run-of-the-mill" population in intelligence. To Lammot, intelligence capacity was mainly inherent, not developed by environment over a period of time, and industry, he said, "sorely needs such men to serve not only as specialists but as business managers."[11]

Du Pont's interest in recruiting natural leaders from the laboring and professional classes of Delaware may well fit its own corporate needs, but it leaves education for most Delawareans sorely lacking. According to results of National Merit tests released in 1970, Delaware's better students are among the best in the country academically. In 1969 this intellectual elite had the highest minimum qualifying score of the fifty states. But the average student suffers from an educational program geared only to the gifted. Most Delaware students do not read as well as the national average, and the state ranks thirty-fifth in the percentage of young men passing the Armed Forces Mental Qualification Test. When the State Department of Public Instruction's own tests proved that 75 percent of Delaware's children had scores below the national average, the tests were put under lock and key by the governor, Russell Peterson, a former $70,000-a-year Du Pont executive. Significantly, almost every school board in the northern part of the state is dominated by Du Pont employees who fully identify with the company's general outlook, and it is the school board that controls the selection of texts and teachers.

Another important reason for the low scores was the low economic position to which Du Pont, as the state's major economic and political force, has driven the area. While the Du Ponts smother the state with their wealth's presence, little of it is seen by Delawarians. Thirty thousand of the state's 260,000 people in New Castle County were classified by the federal government's Office for Economic Opportunity as living in poverty.

Private charities have always been the Du Ponts' way of placing Band-Aids over Delaware's gaping wounds. The most active of these charities is the United Fund and Council of Delaware. This fund, to which local Du Pont and G.M. workers are heavily pressured to donate out of their weekly pay checks, is headed by a board of eighty-five directors, of which twenty-eight are Du Pont executives or family members; decisions are made by a thirty-one member executive committee of which twelve are Du Ponters.

Community control is nil; Du Pont control is all.

For obvious reasons, the Du Ponts take great pains to protect their public image in Delaware. Wilmington's only television station, WHYY-TV, was financed by the Longwood Foundation and has former mayor Harry Haskell, Jr., as a director. The city's only newspaper, the *News-Journal,* is controlled by the family holding company, Christiana Securities. The major radio station in Wilmington is owned by John Rollins, a conservative Republican who is very close politically (although not socially) to the Du Ponts. In 1967 the Du Ponts, through just one of their mutual funds, Sigma Capital Shares, owned 5,000 shares of Rollins Inc., which controls Rollins Broadcasting. By 1972 their interest had grown to 28,000 shares, worth $1,029,000.

The Du Ponts even have their finger in Wilmington's suburban pie. Reginald Rockwell, the reactionary owner of the Newark weekly paper, was financed by Reynolds du Pont. Through an alleged Du Pont loan, Rockwell gained control of the *New Castle Weekly & Suburban News.*

In the early Seventies the Du Ponts showed an interest in shedding the *News-Journal,* primarily for three reasons: (1) its declining earnings; (2) public criticism of Du Pont domination, highlighted by the Nader Study Group Report, making difficult their dealing with (3) mounting attempts by the newspaper's staff to show their integrity and independence.

Public image was very important to the president of Christiana Securities, Irénée du Pont, Jr. He well remembered the public anger over his family's reactionary role during the Depression, and might still recall the mysterious burning of garages and barns on his father's estate, Granogue, at the outbreak of World War II. Once, after the war, he was even slighted personally when, giving a sailor and his girl a hitch in New York, his generosity was rewarded by hostility.

"What did you say your name was?" asked the sailor amiably as he got out.

"Du Pont," Irénée replied with a smile. The sailor's face suddenly dropped.

"One of those Delaware Du Ponts?"

Irénée nodded.

"If I'd known that," the sailor said angrily, "I'd never have taken the ride."[12]

Another exposure to publicity came in 1959, when Irénée appeared with his father and son on the front page of *Life* magazine as part of the Du Ponts' publicity campaign during the G.M. anti-trust case. After that—with the exception of a visit in 1960 to the Navy's 2nd Fleet during maneuvers, in support of the arms race—Irénée's public role, like the family's, was now low-keyed. This was especially true when the Vietnam escalation began. Privately they encouraged the intervention. Edmond du Pont even attended the mapping stages in 1964 at the Global Military Strategy Conference. Publicly the family carefully avoided any statements supporting the war, anxious to preserve their plastic image against any possible resurrection of the "Merchants of Death" label.

The Twenties were probably the years when the Du Ponts had their greatest influence in America. Yet within a decade they saw much of that power undermined by social revolt, their own lack of political flexibility, and the Nye Committee's exposés. They did not want that to happen again. Under government pressure, the Du Ponts had shed their cartels after World War II simply because they no longer needed them; Europe was then in no position to offer competition in foreign markets. With those cartels, then, the Du Ponts hoped they had also shed their "Merchants of Death" label. Although they participated fully in the arms race (chiefly through North American Aviation and Remington Arms), they now hoped those charges were dead, drowned in the tidal wave of anti-communism.

But almost inevitably, as the Vietnam War grew more unpopular, the allegations returned, coupled with the 1967–1968 Black rebellion against the clan's domination of Delaware.

2. DECISIVE TIMES

The American intervention in the Indochinese revolution was already an obvious failure when Du Pont president Charles McCoy announced his opposition in 1970. Inflation and competition were swiftly eroding Du Pont's earnings. Du Pont had suffered badly since the 1965 divestiture, which only exacerbated the lack of technological innovation that began in the 1950's when it became apparent how huge an innovation was necessary to increase the chemical giant's earnings. Copeland's expansion into overseas commodities (Europe) and cheap labor (Latin America and Asia) markets became part of the solution; but by drying up revenue for needed capital investment at home, it also became part of the problem.

When McCoy replaced Copeland, he brought changes to Du Pont. McCoy saw the wisdom of Copeland's overseas program, and continued it. But he also used more efficiently what funds were left, cutting wasteful projects that did not have markets, and diversifying, chiefly into pharmaceuticals. To fund the foreign fronts, he broke sharply with family tradition and borrowed $350 million abroad. But money was still needed for a domestic plant overhaul that could increase productivity and reduce costs. Holding down prices by increasing the volume of production, McCoy reasoned, would win back lost markets.

To finance the domestic overhaul, McCoy first tried cutting costs. Over a space of two years, 1970 and 1971, he laid off and retired thousands of workers—over 12,000 of them. McCoy claimed to have relocated most of these men in other jobs or retired them on pensions. The job relocation claim was highly suspect, but even its veracity did not change the problem facing the workers who remained at Du Pont—speedup. This meant one worker was forced to do the work of two in a department, laboring harder and producing more for the same wages; in effect, this was a cut in the value of his labor time and thereby his real wages. McCoy anticipated grumbles from the ranks over this policy, but "the nation needs vast amounts of new industrial investment," he insisted, "to meet growing markets here and abroad, and also to increase productivity.... American workers must not press for excessive wage increases because higher employment costs will inevitably damage our international competitive position,"[13] or rather, Du Pont's competitive position. For the sake of Du Pont and the preservation of American corporate rule throughout the nonsocialist world, Du Pont workers were told to tighten their belts.

But even with this, Du Pont's capital needs for expansion could not be met, and then-Vice-President Irving Shapiro, in charge of finance, expected to borrow again in the near future for foreign and domestic investments. Foreign markets now accounted for 25 percent of Du Pont's sales, and probably 25 percent of its profits. Wilmington expected its foreign sales to double by 1980. But so did other foreign firms, including Du Pont's old friend, Imperial Chemical Industries (I.C.I.). As this market rivalry grew, Americans and foreigners learned to expect to hear a more politically aggressive—and vocal—Du Pont.

This may well have made some Du Ponts uneasy. In some ways the postwar boom had made the Du Ponts soft. Most of the family simply did not want to endure the inevitable rough and tumble of public attacks and counterattacks on which the earlier generation of Lammot du Pont cut its teeth. Added to this was the family's own problems with the company. If the use of state power to force them out of G.M.'s management had taught the Du Ponts anything, it was the rule of diversification. Du Pont Company was now entering its own diversification even into pharmaceuticals and petrochemicals, and the lesson was not lost on the family.

Previously, the family's diversifications into such areas as automobiles and rubber were not a move away from Du Pont, but an expansion of the company. Even Henry B. du Pont's aviation ventures did not lead him out of the company, and he did remain as one of its top directors. As long as the family's main interest was in the company, and as long as its control over its investment was secured through control of the company itself, the Du Ponts would always be Du Pont.

But the G.M. anti-trust case changed all that.

First, it told the Du Ponts that the collective decision of most industrial and financial leaders was that no one group of interests or one family could any longer be allowed to control the country's largest corporation. This position, the Du Ponts sadly learned, was backed by the full power of the government.

Second, it told the Du Ponts that not just G.M., but all of the major corporations were subject to this policy. In fact, most of the biggest corporations had already become multi-group combinations through the natural laws of economic concentration and through bank and market financing, the lubricant for the intermingling of interests. This meant that after G.M. would come Du Pont—not by force, of course, but by the same process as with other major corporations: through finance capital. G.M.'s loss would and did hurt Du Pont's earnings, the earnings that it had for so long used to finance internal investments and ventures into other fields. Thus Du Pont would soon be forced to seek capital from outsiders— namely, banks. And this would bring about a growing influence on Du Pont by the banks and their integrated corporate interests, and eventually some seats on the Du Pont board would be exchanged for an open door to credit.

The Du Ponts tried to avoid this prospect by searching for a large bank which they could take over or develop for the company. For a time, the Chemical Bank in New York looked like it might become the Du Pont bank, but hopes in this area dimmed when the ever-aggressive Rockefeller forces, assisted by their able allies from the 1929 crash, Kuhn, Loeb, succeeded in effecting its merger with their New York Trust Company in

1959. Since then, the Du Ponts have still kept their foot in the door of the bank, which manages one of Uniroyal's employee funds and has three directors who are also Uniroyal directors. Du Pont interests were directly represented on the board of this $15.4 billion bank by Lammot du Pont Copeland, Sr., and now by Du Pont Chairman Edward Jefferson, although W. Sam Carpenter III, once in charge of Du Pont's international department has been an adviser to Chemical's ventures in international financing.

Du Pont ties with the Rockefellers began to increase, strengthened for political reasons as well as economic. With Du Pont's expansion abroad, there was a growing harmony of political views developing between the Brandywine and Pocantico Hills. Rockefeller interests have traditionally dominated the State Department with their experience in foreign affairs. A. Felix du Pont, Jr., became a supporter of Nelson Rockefeller for President, organizing in Delaware on his behalf in the Sixties. Irénée du Pont, Jr., Lammot du Pont Copeland, Sr., and A. Rhett du Pont were all known to have had Rockefeller affiliations, and Irénée's successful candidate for governor of Delaware in 1968, former Du Pont executive Russell Peterson, was after 1972 an aide to Governor Nelson Rockefeller, living on the Pocantico estate. Rockefeller subsequently resigned from New York's highest office to launch his 1976 presidential campaign through his "national priorities" commission, and Peterson was a member of that commission. Then he was appointed by Nixon as chairman of the federal environmental council.

The other wing of the Rockefeller family, that of John D.'s brother, William Rockefeller, has also had long associations with the Du Ponts through Remington Arms. It was as a result of this that the former Du Pont chairman Charles B. McCoy sat for years on the board of the First National City Bank of New York, as Irving Shapiro does today under its Citicorp alias. Citicorp's $34 billion assets in 1974 must have looked very tempting to Wilmington, but the bank was solidly controlled by William Rockefeller's family and the Stillmans. Barring any sudden shift to the Du Ponts, which is considered highly unlikely, Citicorp will undoubtedly continue its long alliance with the Morgan interests.

In the absence of any other openings, the Du Ponts have been drifting closer to their old-time associates, the Morgans. The Du Pont-Morgan relationship has a long history. Du Pont's original World War I expansion was financed by Great Britain through Morgan loans. Pierre, Irénée, and Lammot du Pont had close financial relations with the Morgans through their joint control of General Motors. Du Ponts sat on the boards of many Morgan interests, including Bankers Trust Company. There was a short rift over G.M. and over Pierre du Pont's and J. J. Raskob's political activities during the late Twenties, as well as over Du Pont's attempted entrance into U.S. Steel, but their conservative political alliance during the Depression and their growing harmony in the Pennsylvania Railroad and the U.S. Rubber Company provided soothing balm.

Again in the 1950's there were considerable misgivings between the two groups over General Motors, and no Du Ponts were associated with Morgan banks during this period. But the alliance continued to function where there were coinciding interests, such as with the Pennsylvania Railroad's absorption of the T.P. & W. Railroad, referred to earlier.

With the serious beginning of Du Pont Company's withdrawal from General Motors in 1963, however, Du Pont chairman Crawford Greenewalt joined the board of Morgan Guaranty; that was the first time a Du Pont was elected to the board of that leading Morgan bank. By 1970 this connection had been severed, but in 1972 Howard W. Johnson was elected to the Du Pont board. The presence of this outsider caused a stir, and Du Pont explained that Johnson was a member of the M.I.T. Corporation, an obvious reference to M.I.T.–Du Pont connections and Irénée du Pont, Jr.'s own membership on the M.I.T. board. But Du Pont failed to mention that Howard W. Johnson was also a director of Morgan Guaranty and J.P. Morgan until changes in SEC rules forced the disclosure in annual reports.

This appointment was very significant: for the first time in Du Pont's 170-year history, outside banking interests were being allowed on the Du Pont board. Previous to World War I the Du Ponts had little need of banks, financing their expansion out of the company's internal resources. After 1920 Du Pont used war profits and General Motors dividends to finance its expansion. Now, however, G.M.'s earnings are unavailable to the company, since they are passed on to its stockholders and the family, and the company's need for banks is very real. The Johnson appointment portended the growing future power of Morgan in Du Pont.

For the family, this also meant the eroding of its control over the company. And adding to these woes was a shortage of young Du Ponts in the company's top management. As in finance, the needs of the huge corporation have been felt by the family in the area of management. To run a far-flung empire like Du Pont efficiently, management personnel must be of top quality, and the competition seems to have been too much for many young Du Ponts who entered the firm in the Fifties and early Sixties. While it helps to have Du Pont for a name, this is no longer any guarantee of a top management position. The family's own stake in the company's efficiency cannot allow that any longer.

Some Du Ponts who were passionately involved with the firm earlier, have since lost their enthusiasm; some even surrendered their jobs. The wandering from the family fold of Lammot (Motsey) du Pont Copeland, Jr., is only one hapless example of a general trend among the family's youth. Stellar hopes of the Fifties, such as Henry B. du Pont III and F. George du Pont, have since faded. John E. du Pont has failed to take the seat on the Du Pont board vacated by his father, William Du Pont, Jr., but succeeded in taking up William's interest in banking, as did his brother, William III, and sister Margaret, who remain directors of Delaware Trust. James Q. du Pont, after twenty years with Du Pont's public relations department, left chemicals to join E. I. du Pont's mutual funds ventures. Pierre S. du Pont IV, foresaking his father's role in the firm, has gone into politics.

Most of these ruptures with the traditions of the older generation have been the result of the independence that wealth brings younger Du Ponts. Some departures have been downright embarrassing.

Christopher du Pont was reported to have burned down the fifty-room mansion of his father, A. Felix du Pont, Jr., while Felix and his wife were vacationing at Cape Cod. A story has it that Christopher was partying with two friends when the fire broke out. They escaped, but when Felix returned to Wilmington, he found his Carousel Farm a gutted ruin.

Three years earlier, in 1964, it had been Nicholas du Pont who suffered mortification. Following the Maryland Hunt Cup race, his 20-year-old daughter Genevieve joined eight college men in a motel cottage outside Baltimore for an all-night party. Before long, beer and gin inspired the smashing of lamps, beds, and windows. By the time the police arrived, the cottage and its occupants were drenched in beer. "We're not going to allow this to happen in Baltimore County," bellowed the local judge. "I feel there is a pattern to this, and it is going to stop."[14] It did, just short of Genevieve du Pont. Bailed out the same day as her arrest, she was the only one acquitted.

Such goings-on would have been unheard of from Du Pont youth in earlier times. Only Irénée du Pont III seems to have followed the family's staid path in M.I.T., but a lifelong Du Pont career seems an unlikely prospect for him, especially considering the problems his father is now having.

By 1974 Irénée du Pont, Jr., was the only Du Pont left in the company's day-to-day activities. Only three others, Emile F. du Pont, Lammot du Pont Copeland, Sr., and Hugh R. Sharp, Jr., had anything directly to do with the company's top management. Apparently, after the ugly publicity over his son passed, Copeland was reinstated on the Du Pont finance committee, his overseas expansion program fully appreciated by McCoy and going full blast. Emile, on the other hand, asked to be relieved of his post on the same committee. This may have been because of the near bankruptcy of the firm of his brother Edmond, which may have cast a pall over his name in some financial circles. More likely, however, it was the result of Emile's age. Over 70, he simply wished to spend his last days clipping coupons and leaving the complicated matters of corporate finance to more energetic and perhaps more resourceful younger minds. He died in 1974. Approaching 70, Copeland was also no youngster, and dapper Hugh Sharp, Jr., was also over 60. Irénée, only midway through his fifth decade, was more alone in his ninth-floor office in Du Pont Building than was at first obvious.

To the misfortune of Irénée's presidential ambitions, the lack of young Du Ponts in the company coincided with a lack of older Du Ponts as well. Previous towering figurés of Du Pont wealth, such as Irénée du Pont, Sr., William du Pont, Jr., Henry F. du Pont, and Henry B. du Pont were no longer on hand at monthly board meetings to shower their golden light on his career. Irénée, Sr., died in 1963, leaving behind $200 to $400 million. "Willie the horseman," the English-born gentryman who designed twenty-five racetracks around the world, died in 1965 at the age of 69; an owner of 1.2 million shares of Du Pont alone, Willie had a fortune estimated at $400 million. At about the same time, Donaldson Brown, worth $75 to $100 million, left the company and soon died. In 1969 Henry F. du Pont, the country's leading horticulturist, joined Willie at Sand Hole Woods at the age of 84; a past director of General Motors as well as Du Pont, Henry was worth over $100 million. The year 1970 brought a rash of deaths in the family. Alfred Victor du Pont, son of Alfred I. du Pont, died at the age of 70, leaving behind as monuments half a dozen architectural achievements, including the Delaware Memorial Bridge and the Florida National Bank building in Miami. Then Henry B. du Pont, a major stockholder in Du Pont and North American Rockwell, joined his ancestors; Henry was worth $200 million. Finally, Jessie Ball du Pont died at the age of 86. Jessie had been left $27 million by her husband, Alfred I. du Pont; by 1970, through the skill of her brother, Edward Ball, she reigned over a multibillion dollar empire, including over one million shares of Du Pont common. Her own personal fortune was valued at $100 to $200 million.

With the exception of Jessie, who was not associated with the company, all these deaths diminished Irénée's personal power in Du Pont. Irénée was passed over for the presidency in 1971 when Charles McCoy, in a very irregular move, retained the top executive post even as he took the chair from Lammot du Pont Copeland. "The only explanation," commented one investment analyst, "is that something big is happening in control of Du Pont. The old lines could be crumbling."[15]

They were. Or rather, the family was cutting them. The future growth of the chemical industry, especially its Wilmington giant, was becoming more and more uncertain, and the family was becoming uneasy about risking its fortune in one area of investment. "As you are aware, Christiana's performance is very importantly dependent upon the performance of the Du Pont Company," Irénée told the family at the Christiana annual meeting in April 1971. "Prospects for 1971 are difficult to assess." Such words do not exude confidence, especially in a family that has increasingly been looking beyond the committed concern of their ancestors.

The Du Ponts are no longer an industrial family in the traditional sense. Most of them are inactive in industry, their interest shifted over to the lucrative world of stocks and bonds. "The management of the Du Pont Company," Pierre du Pont once wrote, "having been in the hands of the Du Pont family for more than a century, should be regarded as a sacred trust to be carried on by the coming generation."[16] But even as he wrote those lines decades ago, Pierre, by shifting the concern of his own activities to the financial side of the company, far from the grime of production, was actually setting the course for the family's drift from direct management. This was inevitable, for the overall strategic rule of any ownership group in any giant capitalist organization must come from the top, for efficient and cohesive planning to benefit its own profit interests. To a great extent, the private ownership prerogatives of any major corporation dictate rule from the top, even if that be by management personnel who are themselves owners or are appointed by owners: it is simply a matter of private ownership molding the most efficient organizational structure possible within the limits of their own values and profit needs.

Nevertheless, such an organizational structure in so large and bureaucratic a corporation as Du Pont bred lack of interest among the family's youth who, already wealthy, saw no need to endure the dehumanizing bureaucracy and competitive managerial in-fighting that must be endured for many years if one is to climb to the top of a major American corporation. For the "coming generation" of Du Ponts, Pierre's sacred trust was a stale anachronism. The government's G.M. anti-trust case and the subsequent loss of G.M. dividends had made that clear to almost everyone, even to most of the elders.

Irénée's announcement of plans to dissolve Christiana Securities, then, came as a surprise only to those who thought in the past. The Du Ponts, thinking of the future, did not want $2.2 billion of their $10 billion fortune chained to a company the management of which they soon might not control if outside bankers were allowed on the board, and to an industry that showed a sluggishness in earnings growth. Even if earnings improved, the increasing scarcity of markets would eventually result in another economic contraction; this eventuality underscored the wisdom of selling high while high prices for Du Pont stock still existed. This would necessitate waiting for an earnings gain to drive up prices again to at least their high of the Sixties, regaining whatever value Du Pont's stock had lost since the G.M. divestiture, if possible. Christiana Securities, as a holding company mostly of Du Pont stock, impaired the ability of family members to quickly shift their fortune into other, more promising areas of investment. As the 1969–1971 economic crisis had taught, now more than ever, the Du Ponts needed, and wanted, flexibility, not the rigidity of a holding company tied irrevocably by sheer weight of its holdings to one company.

"The original reasons for establishing Christiana have run their course and no longer prevail,"[17] Irénée explained. In apparent reference to mounting public criticism of their blatant domination of Du Pont Company and the *News-Journal* papers—and perhaps in subtle reference to the family's unwillingness to assume the brunt of attacks by Du Pont's competitors in the coming market-scarce years—Irénée admitted that "the climate for holding companies is just no longer beneficial to the stockholders."

The Du Ponts had another, more immediate reason, of course: taxes. The dissolution of Christiana Securities into Du Pont would save the family from having to pay an intercorporate dividend tax of 7.2 percent on each dividend payment. When one considers that Christiana paid out over $61.8 million in dividends in 1971, mostly to the family, that extra 7.2 percent amounts to a sizable fortune. If the family had held all its Du Pont stock directly that year rather than through a holding company, it would have saved them $4.4 million in taxes. As Irénée put it in one of his classic understatements, the dissolution of Christiana "simplifies rather complex dealings with the Securities Exchange Commission."

The dissolution of Christiana Securities (which once had preferred shares valued in excess of $10,000 each) would not necessarily mean the end of the clan's holdings in the world's largest chemical corporation. If Christiana were dissolved tomorrow, the family would still own 13,417,120 common shares of Du Pont on top of its many millions more already held directly by individuals. But the dissolution of Christiana would facilitate sales of Du Pont common if some of the family so wished, and some apparently do.

And what of the *News-Journal* papers? Irénée's insistence on the publication of a statement by the ownership, entitled "View From The Top," endorsing Nixon in the 1972 elections after the editors had already refused to endorse him or Senator George McGovern was roundly denounced as "undefined usurpation of power by Irénée du Pont, Jr."

Some suggested Irénée's endorsement of an incumbent president in Washington may have been designed to facilitate the SEC's approval of the Christiana–Du Pont merger. Irénée, however, responded that he was a model defender of freedom of the press. The owners of "most papers wouldn't stand for" an editorial position in conflict with its interests, he asserted.

The *News-Journal* papers were not for sale right now, Irénée insisted, but they might soon be. Richard Sanger, executive editor of the papers, righteously demanded the papers be turned over to "employees," meaning the management, which included himself. But it was difficult to picture Sanger in his self-made role of "employee," since he was the son-in-law of Emile F. du Pont. Christiana Securities and Du Pont Company might move out from direct control over the *News-Journal*, observers reasoned, but the Du Pont family influence would remain. It has.

3. THE DU PONTS TODAY

"I'm a pragmatist," Pete du Pont once said. "I admired President Kennedy a great deal. He was a very pragmatic sort of individual."[18]

So is Pete du Pont. Only a few years ago some Du Ponts, including his father, Pierre S. du Pont III, would have raised a storm over Pete's admiration of Kennedy. But times have changed, and Pete du Pont changes with them, not through searching for root causes, but through pragmatic adjustments to popular sentiment or imposing crises.

As Delaware's only Congressman, he opposed President Nixon's bombing in Indochina, but only after it was apparent that the United States could not impose its presence on Indochina and public criticism had grown to tidal wave proportions at home.

As one of a new generation of Du Ponts, he has also adjusted his own personal economics, moving steadily away from the company which has given him fame and fortune. In May 1971 Pete released a statement of his stock holdings. Here are the major listings:

Christiana Securities	4,417 common, worth $558,750
Delfi American Co.	19,431 shares, worth $310,896
Du Pont Company	1,713 shares, worth $246,672
Wilmington Trust	872 shares, worth $34,444
General Electric	625 shares, worth $77,344
Phillips Petroleum	3,240 shares, worth $106,110
General Motors	25,658 shares, worth $241,214
IBM	890 shares, worth $322,180
Uniroyal	6,268 shares, worth $141,688
Standard Oil (New Jersey)	504 shares, worth $45,108
Standard Oil (Indiana)	220 shares, worth $19,140
Amplex Corporation	25 shares, worth $20,625
Millville Manufacturing Co.	204 shares, worth $42,600

In addition, Pete had various trusts which held stock of General Electric, Phizer, Middle South Utilities, General Telephone & Electronics, Gulf Oil, IBM, Polaroid, General Motors, Xerox, and Christiana. Figures for these, which must be quite substantial, were not released. But the fact remains that the value of his admitted stock holdings doubled since he took Congressional office in 1970, when he released an earlier statement.

Of all these figures, one really stands out—Du Pont. At only 1,713 shares, Pete's holding in Du Pont is one of his smaller investments, only $246,672 out of a total $2.2 million. Close to 90 percent of Pete's stock-holdings are in other companies, and if we subtract his Christiana holdings, over 62 percent of his stock portfolio is in other companies than the chemical firm, the traditional stronghold of the family.

Pete du Pont's own figures illustrate what is happening within the Du Pont empire today—diversification.

Some of the Du Ponts have been quite successful at this in the past, appreciating its tax benefits by speculating. Henry B. du Pont's investment in North American Aviation and Eugene du Pont, Jr.'s investment in Phillips Petroleum are outstanding examples. But always the interest of the chemical firm was held in mind, and Henry and Eugene always stayed within the fold of Du Pont Company.

Such is not the case anymore. Since the G.M. divestiture filled family coffers with billions of dollars, many younger Du Ponts have sallied forth into the corporate world beyond Du Pont to begin operations of their own; but unlike past ventures into aviation, for example, these ventures are primarily financial in nature, and seldom involve their participation in industrial management.

This diversification of Du Pont family holdings means that majority blocks of stocks in companies are being replaced by minority blocks which are still large and important enough to exercise some measure of control over a company. Direct control is seldom needed if management is doing its job efficiently and turning out fat dividends. Rather than an Irénée du Pont exercising absolute domination, now the family fortune has been passed on to a number of heirs, even as the family's *total* wealth continues to grow. This splitting up of family stock blocks does not mean that capital no longer tends to accumulate. Just the opposite. It is the very tendency of capital toward accumulation in the form of mergers that is reducing the share held by each individual Du Pont in a company. Emile F. du Pont, for example, might well have held 15 percent of Symington-Wayne when he was a director of that company. When Symington-Wayne merged with Dresser Industries, his holding in the new company may have been reduced in half, to perhaps 7.5 percent. But capital has accumulated; a bigger corporation has been born. These mergers, while reducing controlling stock blocks, actually increase, through the added assets and resource benefits of combination, the Du Pont family's wealth. Thus Du Pont wealth, and the power of their business class as a whole, is not diminishing, but growing.

There are over 100 multimillion dollar companies in which the Du Ponts have a controlling or large interest directly or through Du Pont Company or Wilmington Trust. Here is the list, complete with the names of Du Ponts responsible for overseeing the investment in that company; most of them are directors (D). In some selected cases, assets are given:

Company	Du Ponts (or relatives)
All American (Engineering) Industries	Richard C. du Pont, Jr. (D)
American Guaranty & Trust Co.	E.I. du Pont
Apalachicola Railroad	Alfred I. du Pont Estate
Ardee Oil Company	E. Paul du Pont, Jr. R. Jacques du Pont (D) W.W. Laird, Jr. (D)
Artisans Savings Bank	J. Bruce Bredin (D)
Atlantic Aviation	Edward B. du Pont (D)
Atlas Chemicals	Ernest T. du Pont, Jr.
Bank of Delaware ($930 million)	C. Douglas Buck, Jr. (D), others
Baymond Corporation	J. Bruce Bredin (D) Reynolds du Pont (D)
Block Blight, Inc.	W.W. Laird, Jr (D), others
Boeing Aircraft	C.B. McCoy (former Director)
Bradford, Inc. (Howard Johnson chain in Delaware)	H.B. Bissell (D)
Bredin Realty	J. Bruce Bredin (D)
Broseco Corporation	Donaldson Brown Estate
Chemical Bank New York Trust ($48.2 billion)	Until 1975, Lammot du Pont Copeland Sr. (Current interest through Du Pont Company) represented

by chairman E. G. Jefferson

Claymont Insurance Company	George P. du Pont (D)
Citicorp (Citibank)· ($129 billion)	C.B. McCoy (past D)
Coca-Cola, International	George P. Edmonds (past D)
Coca-Cola Bottling (Maine)	Alfred E. Bissell (D)
Comedy Center	Lammot du Pont Copeland, Jr.
Continental American Life Insurance Co. (Crown Central Petroleum)	E.I. du Pont (D) Edmond du Pont (D) G.P. Edmonds (D)
Continental Aviation	Willis du Pont
Continental Can Corporation	George P. Edmonds (past D)
Crown Central Petroleum ($546 million)	E.I. du Pont (through W.G. Copeland (D))
Decatur Income Fund ($448 million)	Edmond du Pont (past D)
Delaware Fund ($287 million)	Edmond du Pont (past D)
Delaware Importers	Reynolds du Pont (D)
Delaware Park (Raceway), Inc.	Alfred E. Bissell (D)
Delaware Trust ($721 million)	J.H.T. McConnell (D) William du Pont III (D)
Delfi American Corp.	E.I. du Pont (D)
Delfi Capital Sales	E.I. du Pont (D)
Delfi Management	E.I. du Pont (D) W.W. Laird, Jr.
Delmarva Power & Light Co. ($1.4 billion)	Irénée du Pont, Jr. (past D)

Diamond State Telephone
Co. ($388 million)

Charles B. McCoy (past D)

Downtown Wilmington,
Inc.

Irénée du Pont, Jr. (D)
George P. Edmonds (D)

Dumod Corporation
(Florida)

Willis du Pont

du Pont Aerospace

Anthony du Pont

du Pont Aero Finances

S. Hallock du Pont, Jr.

Dutch Village, Inc.

A. Felix du Pont, Jr. (D)

E.I. du Pont de Nemours
($24.3 billion)

Irénée du Pont, Jr. (D)
Louisa Copeland Duemlng (D)
Crawford Greenewalt (D)
C.B. McCoy (D)
H.R. Sharp III (D)

Electric Hose & Rubber
Co.

R.H. Richards, Jr. (D)

Europa Corporation

S. Hallock du Pont

Farmers Mutual Insurance
Co.

C. Douglas Buck, Jr.
Willard A. Speakman

Florida East Coast Railroad

Alfred I. du Pont Estate

Florida National Banks of
Florida, Inc.

Alfred I. du Pont Estate
Edward Ball Estate

Florida National Realty

Alfred I. du Pont Estate

Fox Min Enterprises

John E. du Pont

Garret Corporation
(California)

Anthony A. du Pont

Garrett-Miller Co.

C. Douglas Buck, Jr. (D)

General Precision
Equipment Corporation

George T. Weymouth (D)

Girard Bank of Delaware
($341 million)

Alexis I. du Pont Bayard (D)

Greater Wilmington

Development Council	Irénée du Pont, Jr.
Hercules Chemical Corp. ($1.09 billion)	J.H.T. McConnell (past D) George and Irene Carpenter Thouron
Jacksonville Properties	Alfred I. du Pont Estate
J.E. Rhoads, Inc.	R.H. Richards, Jr. (D)
Keystone Sand Company	Alfred I. du Pont Estate
Kingsford Company	George T. Weymouth (D)
Krieghoff Gun Company (Miami, Fla.)	S. Hallock du Pont
Laird & Company	George T. Weymouth (D)
Laird, Bissell & Meeds	W.W. Laird, Jr. Alfred E. Bissell (D) Garrett Copeland (V.P.)
Laird Inc. ($32 million)	Alfred du Pont Dent (D) George T. Weymouth (D)
Liberty Mutual Insurance Co. (Delaware)	Willard A. Speakman, Jr. (D)
Marine Construction Co. (Wilmington)	Ernest T. du Pont, Jr. (D)
Mavibal International Corporation	George P. du Pont (D)
Metropolitan Merchandise Mart	George T. Weymouth (D)
Metrox Corporation	Nicholas R. du Pont (D)
Mill Creek Oil Company	William Potter family
National Liberty Corporation	John E. du Pont
Nemours Corporation	J. Simpson Dean
New Garden Aviation	Alexis (Lex) I. du Pont; Everett du Pont
Niront Corporation	Nicholas R. du Pont (D)

Northern Delaware Industrial Development Corp.	William H. Frederick, Jr.
Oil Associates, Inc.	Nicholas R. du Pont (D)
Old Brandywine Village, Inc.	Alfred E. Bissell (D)
Orlando Aviation Services	S. Hallock du Pont, Jr.
Rancho San Andreas, Inc.	John E. du Pont
Red Devil, Inc.	Peter R. du Pont (D)
Ridgely, Inc.	Nicholas R. du Pont (D)
Rockland Corporation (Wilmington Trust)	W.W. Laird, Jr. E.I. du Pont
Rockwell International	(Edward B. du Pont) H.B. du Pont family trust
Rodney Real Estate Associates	A. Felix du Pont, Jr. Nicholas R. du Pont
Rollins Inc.	E.I. du Pont
Sigma Capital Shares ($28 million)	E.I. du Pont (D)
Sigma Exchange Fund	E.I. du Pont (D)
Sigma Investment Shares ($50 million)	Francis I. du Pont II (D) H.H. Silliman (D)
Sigma Trust Shares ($23 million)	E.I. du Pont (D) Donald Carpenter
Sigma Venture Fund ($34 million)	E.I. du Pont (D)
Silver Glenn Springs Inc.	Alfred I. du Pont Estate
Speakman Company	Willard Speakman III (Pres.) R.H. Richards, Jr. (D)
St. Joe Paper Company ($400 million)	Alfred I. du Pont Estate

St. Joseph Telephone & Telegraph Co.	Alfred I. du Pont Estate
Summit Aviation	Edmond N. du Pont Richard C. du Pont, Jr. (D) Richard S. du Pont
Swearington Aviation	Willis du Pont
Terminal Warehouses, Inc.	J. Bruce Bredin (D) Reynolds du Pont (D)
Thorton Fire Brick Company	William Potter (D) family
Uniroyal	J. Simpson Dean (past D)
United Foods, Inc.	Pierre S. du Pont III (D)
United Fund (Delaware)	George T. Weymouth (D)
United International Fund (Delaware)	Edmond du Pont (D), others
United Investors Life Insurance	Edmond du Pont George T. Weymouth
Waddell & Reed, Inc.	Edmond du Pont George T. Weymouth
Wakulla Edgewater Company	Alfred I. du Pont Estate
W.H. du Pont Associates	William H. du Pont (H.E.I. du Pont)
WHYY-TV	A. Felix du Pont, Jr. (past D)
Wilmington Research Corporation	John H. Remer (D)
Wilmington Suburban News	Reynolds du Pont
Wilmington Trust Company ($1.4 billion)	Irénée du Pont, Jr. (D) Edward B. du Pont (D) G. Edmonds, others
Wiltruco Realty	George P. du Pont (D)

Total Selected Assets: $210.6 Billion

In addition, the Du Ponts have large blocks of stock in the following companies:

General Motors (about 17 percent)

Crucible Steel (150,000 shares held by Remington Arms, Du Pont subsidiary)

Wilmington Savings Fund Society (Ira Ellis, Du Pont economist, and at least one other Du Pont executive are directors)

Mellon National Bank (about 7 percent)

W.T. Grant (Wilmington Trust director J. Chinn was a director)

American Sugar & Refining Company (Domino Sugar) (TNEC)

United Fruit (TNEC)

Mid-Continent Petroleum

Mulco Products

National Computer Analysts

D. Van Nostrand

Standard Register

Artesian Water Co.

Chanslor-Western Oil Co.

Avondale Shipyards, Inc.

Mergers removed Du Ponts from the boards of three companies: Emile F. du Pont from Symington-Wayne (which merged with Dresser Industries), Anthony A. du Pont from Garret Corporation (merged into Signal Companies), Colgate Darden from Newport News Shipbuilding (merged into Tenneco), and A. Felix du Pont, Jr., from Piasecki Helicopter (which became Piasecki Aircraft). The Du Pont family's investment in North American Rockwell appears intact, despite their failure so far to replace Henry B. du Pont on the board after his death in 1970.

For their multi-billion dollar chemical company, the Du Ponts have continued their search for a large bank, investing in various brand names. Du Pont Company has bought 6 percent of the outstanding preferred stock of the $2.9 billion Girard Trust Company in Philadelphia, including 3.3 percent of its sole voting right stock. Additionally, Girard has interlocking directorships with Diamond State Telephone, over which the Du Ponts until recently shared control with A.T. & T., and American Sugar Refining Company, in which the family once held a large block of stock. Until recently, Du Pont Company's stake in Philadelphia was also reflected in the presence of Walter J. Beadle, a long-time executive and a director of Du Pont of Canada, on the board of Philadelphia National Bank. Another factor to consider in the budding of economic alliances is the marriage of Lammot du Pont Copeland's daughter Louisa to James Biddle of the Philadelphia banking family.

The Du Pont family also reportedly holds about 7 percent of the stock of Mellon National Bank and Trust. The Mellon family's urban redevelopment of Pittsburgh, which provided skyscrapers for the Mellons but no homes for the displaced thousands, was a favorite model for Irénée du Pont's shopping complex plans for Wilmington.

4. ORBITS OF GOLD

There are over 1,500 lineal descendants of that mischievous French aristocrat, Pierre Samuel Du Pont de Nemours. Of these, only about 250 belong to the very rich, and of these, only 53 belong to the central core that holds real power in the family. Within that core, the Du Ponts have still a more select group, their own power elite.

If you traveled around the United States looking for Du Ponts, you would find them in almost every major city. Some of these have lived there for decades and may not even be related to the Wilmington branch. But there are some key areas in the country where the local influence of the Delaware dynasty is clearly felt:

Charleston, South Carolina. For years, the gaslights of Charleston were familiar to one group of Du Ponts headed by Eugene du Pont III and A. Rhett du Pont, Sr.

Eugene lost interest in Delaware after the death in 1954 of his father, Eugene, Jr., and sold Owl's Nest, the family's famous estate which had once housed a visiting in-law, President Franklin Roosevelt. Eugene moved to South Carolina and from there he joined his brother, Nicholas R. du Pont, in heavily investing in Texas, Louisiana, Oklahoma, and Wyoming oil and gas properties. To handle this business, Nicholas set up the $10 million Ridgely, Inc. But in 1965 Eugene filed suit against his brother, who was president of the firm, for improper handling of the properties, claiming $4 million in undue losses.

A. Rhett du Pont's fortunes were tied to those of his brother Edmond, whom he joined to run the large Wall Street brokerage house founded by their father, Francis I. du Pont. In his heyday, Rhett bought properties in Delaware and Pennsylvania before moving to Charleston. There he became associated with the First National Bank of South Carolina, which has administered his estate since his death in 1972. Rhett's last years were marked with bitterness, as F. I. du Pont Company's troubles forced him and his brother out of the management. To make matters worse, a wide rift developed between him and his children by his first wife, Gertrude du Pont, whom he had divorced in 1962. That quarrel became so heated that in November 1971 Gertrude and the boys, A. Rhett, Jr., Thomas, and Francis I. du Pont III, sued Rhett for valuable Pennsylvania properties near Granogue which he had promised to turn over to the boys in his 1962 separation agreement.[19] Three months later, angry and embittered, Rhett died.

Jacksonville, Florida. Here reigns the multi-billion dollar empire of Alfred I. du Pont. The major beneficiaries live out of state, and Alfred du Pont Dent struggles to return the fortune to Delaware by liquidating the assets of his grandfather's estate. He is fought by Ed Ball's appointed trustees.

Miami, Florida. Many Du Ponts vacation here, but until recent years only one called it his home: Willis H. du Pont, son of Lammot du Pont. Involved in citrus, cattle, and aviation, Willis also joined the board of the Miami bank in the Florida National bank group controlled by the Alfred I. du Pont estate. Now he is joined in the Sunshine State by other young Du Ponts, including Tom, son of Reynolds du Pont, and aviator Sam Hallock "Hal" du Pont, Jr., who lives in Miami Springs.

Louisiana. One Du Pont is a force in this area through his directorship on the Bank of Terrebonne and Trust Company. He is Harold Du Pont, who has no connection to the Wilmington branch. But in New Orleans resides Ernest du Pont's daughter Nancy, now married to influential Henry Druns III.

Louisville, Kentucky. For many years in the last century, Alfred V. du Pont was the richest man in this city. With his brother, Antoine Bidermann du Pont, he was involved in everything from streetcars to the First National Bank of Louisville. Bidermann's son, T. Coleman du Pont, maintained an estate in Kentucky and interests in Kentucky coal mines up until his death in 1930 when his son, Francis V. du Pont, took them over. Although Frank did not have many economic ties to this area, the renown of his father and grandfather remains, as do the Coleman in-laws and the liberal reputation of Frank's cousin, Ethel B. du Pont, for years a labor columnist for the Louisville *Times.*

Virginia. Colgate Darden, son-in-law of Irénée du Pont and former governor of Virginia, is a director of many companies in this state, including, until recently, the giant Newport News Ship and Drydock Company.

Michigan. For years the Du Ponts were a power in this state through their control of General Motors and their presence in the Detroit National Bank. Today only two persons by the name of Du Pont hold any local prominence. They are George B. Du Pont, president of the George B. Du

Pont Company, which makes bolts and screws, and director of the Troy National Bank, and his son Kent. They are not, however, members of the Wilmington branch.

Kansas City, Missouri. From 1949 to 1962 Edmond du Pont was a director of Kansas City's United Funds. Today Du Pont Company runs a plant here, but none of the four resident Du Ponts seem to have any connection with the Wilmington family.

California. Jessie Ball was a schoolteacher in southern California when Alfred I. du Pont came to marry her and take her away. For many years Amy du Pont, sister of Eugene, Jr., called California home. Lammot du Pont Copeland, Jr., blanketed this area with his weekly conservative newspapers before going bankrupt in 1970 and forcing the *Citizen-News* papers in Los Angeles into reorganization, while retaining the management of Richard Horton.

Another local Du Pont is young Anthony Averell du Pont, son of Edmond du Pont. Tony, a resident of Pasadena, has been a top executive for the Garrett Corporation, one of the country's largest war contractors. Tony also had $1 million investment in (F.I.) Du Pont, Glore Forgan, and was a negotiator for the family in the F.I. du Pont reorganization talks in Washington and New York.

Blond-haired Michael du Pont, another son of Reynolds du Pont, owned nightclubs in Palo Alto and San Francisco (where he also owns a fashionable restaurant) and has been active in producing motion pictures. One of his pictures was titled *The Answer.* It wasn't. He is now reduced to selling television and stage lighting equipment in Salt Lake City, where he lives with his wife, Elizabeth.

New York. Fun City is only fun for those who can afford it, and it is no wonder that many Du Ponts, including Willis H. du Pont and Paul du Pont, have apartments here. Penny du Pont, cousin of Crawford Greenewalt, is a regular resident of Greenwich Village, an actress, and hosts a show on Cable TV, while F. George du Pont, Jr., lives off Central Park West and David B. du Pont in the fashionable East 50's. Du Pont Company, of course, has a large office complex in the Empire State Building (built by Du Ponts formerly associated with G.M.) and Uniroyal has its own skyscraper. (F. I.) Du Pont, Glore Forgan had its headquarters at Wall Street, and operated four other midtown branches. Across the river, in Elizabeth, New Jersey, James du Pont serves as a director of the Union County Trust Company and is president of Thermoplastic Process, Inc., and the Thermoplastic Equipment Corporation.

Besides Miami, the older Du Ponts use three traditional vacation spots of the Eastern rich: Fisher's Island (New York), Cape Cod, and Block Island. Du Ponts will also be found in Philadelphia (Benjamin B. du Pont, Mrs.

James Biddle, the Riegals), Baltimore (T. Coleman du Pont III, the Zappfes), Connecticut (Benjamin and Stephen du Pont) and Washington (Mrs. Francis V. du Pont). But when we speak seriously of Du Pont power, we speak of Wilmington, Delaware.

Wilmington. Aptly titled the "chemical capital of the world," Wilmington is also a capital contradiction. Inside is mid-twentieth-century urban America; outside, prerevolutionary eighteenth-century France.

Inside its boundaries Wilmington stands like a castle, its tall gleaming towers in the center, surrounded by the poverty and decay of ghettos. The skyscrapers are owned by Du Ponts and their friends; so are the ghettos. Everywhere are the police, speeding along in new patrol cars. Everywhere are Black residents, sullen and quiet, in contrast to the powerful community of the Sixties. Now, alone they face the Du Ponts, the city, and its police and courts, the area's mass movement of white liberals and more radical dissenters having dissolved with the number of U.S. troops in Vietnam.

Outside the city, to the south, open fields become farmland; to the north, open fields become Du Pont estates. This is America's "chateau country," a greater concentration per mile of country estates than anywhere in the world—even in the provinces of France itself. Above all, this is Du Pont country.

Over three dozen Du Pont estates dominate this area, erecting a dream-world of chateaus, formal gardens, fountains, colonnades, even temples of love—all that made prerevolutionary France such a joy for Pierre Samuel Du Pont de Nemours and such an object of anger for French peasants. But today in Delaware there are no peasants, just thousands upon thousands of rolling green hills owned by America's first industrial family. Here the Du Ponts breed their steeds and ride to the hounds, swim in heated pools and take off in planes from private landing strips, and dance at debutante parties held for their daughters with as many as 1,000 very rich guests.

Here Samuel Hallock du Pont bred dogs in the famous kennels of his 1,300-acre Squirrel Run estate near Newark. Sam had quieted down a bit from his knife-throwing days. His second marriage to Virginia Simmons brought old Sam the serenity of aristocracy, and he even had claim to fame as holder of the American Legion Medal of Merit for setting up a $350 per month trust fund for World War I's Sergeant Alvin York. He died in 1978.

Nearby, Samuel F. du Pont and his wife Jan and three children reside at Hexton, a Victorian Gothic mansion surrounded by 55 acres of family playland, complete with a 55-foot yacht, two runabouts, and a sailboat.

The estate of George P. Edmonds and his wife, Natalie du Pont, prevails over Westover Hills, Wilmington's steppingstone to the Du Pont haven of Greenville. Covering an entire block of this exclusive community of rising executives and independent-minded Du Ponts and in-laws, Edmonds' property contains a large, handsome brick mansion and a many-tiered garden of fountains, flowers, and a pool. For neighbors, Edmonds has E. I. du Pont and an assortment of Du Pont in-laws, including John H. Remer and Eve du Pont Remer, W. A. Speakman, Jr., Alfred E. Bissell and Julia du Pont Andrews Bissell, and Alexis du Pont Bayard.

Across the Kennett Pike, on Rising Sun Lane, are the estates of Walter Carpenter, Jr., and Lammot (Motsey) du Pont Copeland, Jr. Carpenter's estate looks as old as its late octogenarian owner, the wooden mansion drab and in need of painting, the gardens needing care. Adjacent, along the Pike, is the stately St. Amours, the former estate of Lammot du Pont. Further down Rising Sun Lane is Motsey's $500,000 modern home with its pool and wide circular driveway. Here, with his camera-shy wife, Motsey publishes newsletters on, among other things, credit unions. They won't be coming after Motsey, however, despite his $55 million bankruptcy. He just inherited his father's $200-400 million estate, shared, of course, with brother and sister. And he collects his $300,000-a-year income from trust funds while contemplating his bankruptcy amid jokes as head of the Comedy Center in Wilmington. He also dabbles in real estate, building $90,000 town houses, destroying park trees and erecting what residents decry as "The Great Wall of Rockford." Perhaps Motsey can sell them another joke, but not soon.

In Montchanin, the area above the old Brandywine gunpowder mills, is Hagley, the estate of H. H. Silliman and Marianna du Pont. Nemours, the estate of J. Simpson Dean, features a formal garden of sixty varieties of tree peonies and old bricks that were originally set in Wilmington side-walks. Nearby are the estates of the late James Q. du Pont and William Potter, an in-law, Ernest du Pont, Jr., and R.R.M. Carpenter, Jr., whose father was Ruly Carpenter and whose mother was Margaretta du Pont. The ducal estate of Alfred I. du Pont, Nemours, is just across the Brandywine, hidden behind trees and a tall stone wall. Mrs. E. Paul du Pont still lives at her vast Montchanin estate above the Brandywine, called Squirrel Run Hill, devoting her efforts futilely to reform a state prison system growing out of control.

Next we come to Greenville, heartland of the Du Pont family. Here, Pierre S. du Pont III doesn't bother with such antics as prison reform, preferring yachts and his Bois des Fosses estate, named after the estate in France of his great-great-great grandfather, the original Pierre Samuel Du Pont de Nemours. Brookdale Farm, the estate of W. Sam Carpenter III, has a multileveled garden constructed from the foundations of old barn extensions. Reynolds du Pont lounges on Randlea, his Greenville estate; F. George du Pont resides at The Hayloft; Mrs. Elsie du Pont Elcick at Louviers; the family of Stephen du Pont at Buck Hill Farm. The late H.R. Sharp, Jr., lived at Harry's Gate; J.H.T. McConnell and Jean du Pont live at Crooked Billet; Richard Reigal at Fishekill; and Governor Pete du Pont IV at Patterns, shunning the modest state mansion with notorious regularity.

Lammot du Pont Copeland's Mt. Cuba estate, where Copeland had entertained such feudal dignitaries as the Belgian King and the Crown Prince of Greece, covers a scenic hilltop of ponds and streams laced with hollies, magnolias, azaleas, and mountain laurel. Mt. Cuba is dominated by Copeland's long, immense brick mansion, with the gate guarded by two stone preying eagles. It boasts a swimming pool built in the shape of a Maltese Cross and a collection of souvenirs from the eighteenth-century French chemist, Lavoisier, friend of Pierre Samuel Du Pont and manufacturer of gunpowder for King Louis XVI, with whom Lavoisier shared the guillotine. His widow, Pamela, still lives there.

H. Allaire du Pont, widow of aviator Richard C. du Pont, resides at Up-the-hill, and she fed chocolate sundaes to Kelso, three-time "Horse of the Year," at her Bohemia Stables on the Delmarva Peninsula. Her stout, amiable son, Richard C. ("Kip") du Pont, Jr., can be seen at the Atlantic Aviation facilities, not far from the Newcastle estate of Mrs. Sarah Townsend du Pont. In Greenville also are the estates 'of Donald P. Ross and Wilhelmina du Pont Ross, J. Avery Draper and Renée du Pont Carpenter Draper, William du Pont Carpenter, G. Burton Pearson and Edith du Pont Pearson, Robert Flint and Lucile du Pont Flint, Crawford Greenewalt and Margaretta du Pont Greenewalt, Alfred du Pont Dent, George Bissell and George T. Weymouth (both Du Pont relations), J. Bruce Bredin and Octavia du Pont Bredin, and C. Douglas Buck, Jr., grandson of T. Coleman du Pont.

Traveling north and west, we find Ellison Downs and Molly Laird Downs's Limerick estate along Lancaster Pike, A. Felix du Pont's estate along the Kennett Pike, and Robert Wheelwright and Ellen du Pont Wheelwright's Goodstay. In Centerville we find the estates of Alexis I. du Pont and R. M. Layton, late son-in-law of Greta du Pont Barksdale Brown and Donaldson Brown. Nearby, on Snuff Mill Road, is the residence of Charles B. McCoy and Nicholas R. du Pont's Ridgely estate. A few miles to the east is Smith's Bridge Road, where E. Paul du Pont, Jr., resides near Irénée du Pont, Jr.

Irénée du Pont, Jr., lives at Granogue, a sprawling hilltop mansion near the Pennsylvania line. The 70-room home is surrounded by three gardens: the Formal Garden, with roses, tulips, magnolias, and dogwoods; the Woodland Garden, with native wild flowers and an artificial spring; and the

Shrubbery Garden, with a path edged with French ivy from the first Du Pont grave at Chevannes, France, where the original Pierre Samuel Du Pont's wife is buried. Irénée seems to have a penchant for such ancestor worship, considering himself the guardian of family legends, including gold coins surrounding the Family Founder. Some of the garden paths have little resting places on the side, looking more like outdoor shrines. One such niche had a strange figurine as the center of attention—a tyrannosaurus rex, ancestor of those cherished pets of Irénée, Sr., the iguanas. On this writer's visit in May 1971, Granogue seemed to have all the other Du Pont trappings, including an enormous greenhouse, tennis court, pool, a pipe organ, and even motorcycling teenagers armed with cans of beer. Since then, the grounds have been the scene of celebration again with the marriage of a charming daughter, Cynthia, amid a "medieval vaudeville" of music and dancers. Indeed, Granogue remains *the* chateau of America's "chateau country."

Still further north, above the Pennsylvania line, are the homes of R. Jacques du Pont in Red Lion and Mrs. Philip F. du Pont in Farville. Not far from the famed and ever-blossoming Longwood Gardens of Pierre S. du Pont II is the estate of John E. du Pont at Newport Square. Named Foxcatcher Farms, this was only one of a half dozen estates which William du Pont, Jr., owned from Virginia to California, Georgia to Delaware (where he had two). Foxcatcher's broodmares were the pride of William, and John has continued this aristocratic hobby, paying $250,000 for a horse named Rose Trader like most youngsters would buy a model airplane. In his pre-banking days John was an obsessive athlete, determined to win the Olympics pentathlon, building a six-lane indoor pool especially for the 1967 national championships which he hosted and participated in, shooting, riding, cross-country running, swimming, fencing—and losing.

One of John's biggest complaints in those musclebound days was the efforts of mothers to marry him off to their daughters. "You'd be surprised how many pushy mothers there are who have a daughter they want me to meet," he once told a *Life* reporter. "Even on the farm, I run in the woods a lot or swim underwater. It's a great way to avoid people." John's desperation may have been a bit exaggerated, but the Du Ponts, notoriously inbred, are also the magnet of amorous attentions from the state's oldest and wealthiest families.

In a fashion typical of ruling houses, the Du Ponts have absorbed Delaware's oldest families of indigenous wealth: the Saulsburys, the Bancrofts, the Holcombs, the Bradfords, the Bushes, the Bayards, the Ridgelys, the Drapers, the Laytons, the Marvels, the Tatnells, the Sellers, the Grays, and the Townsends. This, of course, was no forced absorption or usurpation, but merely the result of the magnetic attraction that an industrial dynasty has for old families with dwindling fortunes.

The specific marriages involved were: Mary du Pont to Willard Sauls-bury; Alfred I. du Pont's daughter Madeleine to John Bancroft, Jr.; Pierre S. du Pont III to Jane Holcomb (a descendant of Charlemagne and of a score of royal houses, including the Bourbons); Eleuthera du Pont to Edward Bradford; Joanna du Pont Bradford to Henry T. Bush; Elizabeth Bradford du Pont to Thomas F. Bayard; Charles I. du Pont to Anne Ridgely; Renée du Pont Carpenter to J. Avery Draper; Greta (du Pont) Barksdale Brown to Rodney M. Layton; A. Felix du Pont, Sr., to Anne Marvel, and Emile F. du Pont to Margaret Marvel; through the Bushes to the Tatnells; through the Bancrofts to the Sellers; through the Thourens (Esther du Pont married John Thouren) to the Grays; and further Du Pont marriages directly into the Townsends and Ridgelys (Eugene du Pont, Jr.)

Du Pont women have provided the clan with many in-laws from other families as well, including the Balls, Bredins, Browns, Bucks, Carpenters, Chandlers, Copelands, Dardens, Davies, Deans, Dents, Donaldsons, Edmonds, Faulkners, Flints, Glasses, Greenewalts, Lairds, Lees, Mays, Pearsons, Peytons, Potters, Remers, Richards, Riegals, Rosses, Rusts, Sangers, Sillimans, Smiths, Springers, Thourens, Weymouths, and Wheel-wrights, to list the first line. The second line of Du Pont in-laws are made up of the families who had the good fortune of seeing a child wed someone whose mother or grandmother was a Du Pont. These include the Curtises, Bissels, Bollings, Brills, Bushes, Denhams, Donohues, Downses, Drapers, Fenns, Goffs, Kimballs, Kitchells, McCoys, Phelpses, Reeses, Robertsons, Thourons and Worths.

Most of the Du Ponts, plus the first line of their in-laws and a few of the second line, make up the 250 "big" Du Ponts. These are the Du Ponts who comprise the richest family in the world, worth about $10 billion.[20] These are the Du Ponts who own more estates, more thoroughbred horses, more yachts, more servants than the Queen of England and the royal family.

Within the inner core of sixty Du Ponts are the eleven Du Ponts who are the clan's power elite. Without touching upon its power elite for the moment, the Du Pont family's inner core is made up of the following forty-nine individuals:

Alexis du Pont Bayard. Long a power in the Democratic Party, Bayard was defeated for the U.S. Senate in 1952, partly due to the efforts of Francis V. du Pont, who urged Delawareans not to vote "for my cousin, Lex." Bayard is the son of Elizabeth du Pont and Thomas Bayard, and the grandson of Alexis I. du Pont. He was a director of the Farmers Bank and partner of Bayard, Brill, and Handelman. His political position, not his wealth, has earned him a prominant place in the family's inner core. But he is a maverick liberal

Democrat and getting on in years.

Alfred E. Bissell. Bissell is the husband of Julia du Pont Andrews, niece of the late Eugene du Pont, Jr. He has been a partner of Laird, Bissell, & Meeds, chairman of Delaware Trust Company, and director of Farmers Bank of Delaware, Delaware Park, Inc., Coca-Cola Bottling (Portland, Maine), Old Brandywine Village, Inc., and the Bredin Foundation; vice-president of Delaware Hospital; and trustee of Tower Hill School and the Winterthur Foundation.

Robert H. Bolling, Jr., married to Joan Ross, daughter of Wilhelmina du Pont and Donald P. Ross and granddaughter of William K. du Pont and niece of S. Hallock du Pont. Bolling is a quiet director of Wilmington Trust, which describes him as "a consulting engineer."

John Bruce Bredin. Bredin is the husband of Octavia du Pont, daughter of Irénée du Pont. He was president of Bredin Realty, and is director of Wilmington Trust, Artisans Savings Bank, Old Brandywine Village, Inc., and Terminal Warehouses, Ltd., and the Baymond Corporation of Toronto. He is a trustee of the University of Delaware, the Bredin Foundation, St. Andrews School, Sweet Briar College, Winterthur Museum, and Wilmington Medical Center. An avid speculator in real eatate, Bredin shares his wife's $150 million inheritance.

C. Douglas Buck, Jr. Buck's mother was Alice du Pont, daughter of T. Coleman du Pont, and his father was Delaware's governor for many years. He has been a director of the Bank of Delaware, Garrett-Miller Company, Farmers Mutual Insurance Company of Delaware, and Block Blight, Inc., and a trustee of the Hampton Institute. A large Delaware landowner, he was president of the Kennett Pike Association in 1966 and was president of the New Castle County Council. His father's estate, Buena Vista, was donated to the state by the former governor and can still be seen along Route 13 (Du Pont Highway).

Robert R.M. (Ruly) Carpenter III. He sold the Phillies baseball team for $30 million after his willingness to pay high salaries bought Philadelphia a winning team, triggering the rise in players' salaries across the nation. Now an avid gardener, he is worth about $50 million.

William K. Carpenter. Only the $200 million inheritance from his mother Margaretta du Pont, sister of Pierre II, has earned William K. a listing in the inner core. Unlike his brother, Bobby, he has remained outside Wilmington, residing in Boca Raton, Florida.

Garrett Van S. Copeland. He is the son of the late Lammot du Pont Copeland, Sr. He was a major holder of (F.I.) Du Pont, Glore Forgan stock and is a director of Laird, Bissell & Meeds and president of Delaware Planned Parenthood. Quietly powerful in Wilmington circles and now very, very rich, he is a man to watch.

Lammot du Pont Copeland, Jr. Motsey was the first Du Pont ever to go bankrupt. Presently, he is living off $13 million in trust funds, courageously enduring his embarrassment in a $500,000 home, constantly showered by the clan's sympathy and a $300,000 annual trust income. A man worth noting since recently inheriting part of his father's $200-400 million fortune, he is now director of the Comedy Center.

Mrs. Constance du Pont Darden. The 79-year-old daughter of the late Irénée du Pont was widowed in 1981. Her husband, Colgate Darden, had been a director of the Newport News Shipbuilding and Drydock Company, Merchants and Farmers Bank of Franklin (Virginia) and Life Insurance Company of Virginia, and was governor of Virginia and president of the University of Virginia. Darden shared Constance's $150 million inheritance.

J. Simpson Dean. Dean's wife was Polly du Pont, sister of S. Hallock du Pont. Dean was a director of Uniroyal and of Wilmington Trust, and is president of the Nemours Corporation, which breeds thoroughbred horses.

Alfred du Pont Dent. Dent and his brother Richard are among the major heirs to the $2 billion Alfred I. du Pont estate in Florida. Dent's mother was Victorine, daughter of Alfred I. du Pont, and his father, Elbert Dent, was for many years a leading trustee of the estate. Alfred Dent is a director of Laird, Inc., and lives in Wilmington.

J. Avery Draper. The third husband of 72-year-old Irénée du Pont Carpenter (who inherited a fortune now estimated at $200 million), Draper is a vice-president of Laird, Bissell, & Meeds.

Edmond du Pont. Although his status has dropped somewhat with his fortune, this former head of F.I. du Pont & Company is looked upon with sympathy in the family. He was a director of the Rockland Corporation and Winterthur Foundation, and Continental American Life Insurance Company. To a great extent, to Edmond's future is tied the future of his son, Edmond R. du Pont.

Eleuthère I. du Pont. He heads the family's Sigma mutual funds group. He is also a director of Continental American Life Insurance Company and of Rockland Corporation, and is president of Delfi Management, Inc. He also heads American Guaranty and Trust Company.

Ernest T. du Pont, Jr. He has been a director of Delaware Trust and Marine Construction Company of Wilmington, and watches over his father's holdings in Atlas Chemicals and other companies. He gives frequent financial advice to his brother, Samuel F. du Pont.

Evelyn Rebecca du Pont. Divorced and remarried, Evelyn, 58, has been somewhat of a recluse since helping auction the furniture of his late father, William du Pont, Jr. He is worth over $125 million.

Francis I. du Pont II. Son of Emile F. du Pont, he has joined E.I. du Pont's Sigma Investment Fund as a director.

John E. du Pont. Athletic son of William du Pont, Jr., he was a director of Delaware Trust until 1981, when he sold his holdings. Forty-eight years old, he is worth about $125 million.

Nicholas R. du Pont. Oil-speculating son of Eugene du Pont, Jr., he is president of Niront Corporation, Oil Associates, and Metrox Inc., and director of Ridgely, Inc.

Pierre S. du Pont III. Politically reactionary member of the Du Pont board, he has never lost his antagonism to union shops. Pierre has also been a director of Delaware Importers, the liquor business owned by his brother Reynolds, vice-president of Christiana Securities, and trustee of the ultraconservative Freedom Foundation.

Peter du Pont. The son of Emile F. du Pont, he is a director of Laird, Inc.

Reynolds du Pont. Reynolds is a son of Lammot du Pont. For 16 years, he combined his activity as a leader in the Delaware state Senate with his directorships in Sigma Capital Shares, Delaware Importers (liquors)— admittedly never abstaining on a bill concerning the liquor industry, All American Engineering Company, Sigma Trust Shares, and Bredin's Terminal Warehouses. Reynolds' immediate family has developed important corporate alliances through marriage. His son, Thomas, married Ruth Lawrence, granddaughter of Murray Becker, director of City Stores, Inc. His daughter, Natalie, married Frank Randolph Lyon III, whose father is a director of Union Carbide. As sixth heir to a $1.25 billion estimated current worth of the surviving children of Lammot du Pont, "Reyn" is probably worth, minus business losses, between $150 to $200 million.

Richard C. du Pont, Jr. Son of the glider hero of the Thirties, he is a director of All American Industries and owner of Summit Aviation. He was also director of Edward du Pont's Atlantic Aviation. Amiable, Kippy nevertheless harbors ultra-right convictions that he believes in acting upon, outfitting warplanes for Latin and Asian dictators while employing a top ex(?)-CIA operator as his aide. A man to beware.

Richard S. du Pont. This elder heir of S. Hallock du Pont has been associated with Richard C's Summit Aviation. Unlike his cousin, however, a trip to Cuba in 1977 convinced him that past U.S. policy was a serious mistake and he recommends an end to the blockade and restoration of diplomatic relations.

S. Hallock du Pont, Jr., is the President of Orlando Aviation Services and du Pont Aero Finances of Florida, where he is also a brigadier general in the Civil Aviation Patrol.

William H. du Pont (now Henry E.I. du Pont). Son of William du Pont, Jr., he was the president of a Delaware-based computer firm, Sci-Tek, until the Crime Syndicate "ruined" him, William has rejected the legacy of his father, but not his fortune.

William du Pont III, another son of William Jr., is a director of Delaware Trust, as is his sister Margaret du Pont Smith, wife of E. Newbold Smith. At 31 years, he and his half sister are both worth over $125 million. William owns a stud farm for thoroughbreds in Kentucky.

Willis H. du Pont. The last child of Lammot du Pont, Willis, 47, has seen his inheritance grow into a $250 million fortune while residing at Palm Beach, Florida, where he has sizeable citrus, cattle, banking and real estate holdings.

Mary Belin du Pont Faulkner. Married to a Bostonian, Mary, 76, has been removed from Wilmington social life, but not her $250 million inheritance from her late father, Lammot du Pont. Mrs. James Faulkner has seven children.

Lucille du Pont Flint. Married to Robert B. Flint of Greenville, Del., Lucille, 67, will leave about $150 million to her five children.

Mary Jane du Pont Lunger. The owner of Christiana Stables is the daughter of Philip du Pont, who left her $50 million in 1928; her fortune is now estimated at $125 million. The 67-year-old widow of a stockbroker, she has five children, one of whom, Brett, races autos in the Grand Prix.

Ernest N. May. Outside of his marriage to Irene, daughter of Irénée du Pont, and his large Christiana stock holdings, May has not been tied into family projects. The only basis for his being listed here is money—lots of it, almost all of it Irene's $150 million.

Irénée du Pont May. The son of Ernest N. May, he is a director of Delaware Trust and is a rising political star among Delaware Republicans. Irénée's brothers, Ernest, Jr., Thomas, and John, can also be expected to rise in Delaware circles.

J.H. Tyler McConnell. McConnell was married to Jean, daughter of William du Pont, Jr. He is president of Delaware Trust and a former director of Hercules Chemical. A power in Delaware's Democratic Party, McConnell has headed the state's highway department and its River and Bay Authority. His former wife, 60-year-old Jean, worth $125 million, was reportedly furious over McConnell's being named president of Delaware Trust instead of her, and has moved to Coral Gables, Florida, where she lives with her third husband, William Mason Shehaan.

Alice du Pont Mills. Married to James Mills of Hobe Sound, Florida, Alice is the sister of A. Felix du Pont, Jr. With a $275 million fortune, she raises horses, collects dividends and has seen her daughter become the wife of a famous painter, Jamie Wyeth.

Bernard Peyton. Husband of Margaret C. du Pont, Peyton was a director of Du Pont Company.

G. Burton Pearson, Jr. In 1968 Pearson married Edith, daughter of Lammot du Pont. Previous to that he was active in politics, rising through the state's judicial system until he graduated to the directorship of Du Pont and Wilmington Trust, where he now chairs the trust committee. That post complements his trusteeship over the Bredin and Unidel Foundations. Holding the strings to such fortune, it is no surprise that he is a trustee also of the University of Delaware and a leading member of its finance, executive and instruction committees. Edith's fortune is estimated at $250 million.

R.H. Richards, Jr. He is the son of Christiana Securities' first secretary, R.H. Richards. He was a director of Continental American Life Insurance, Wilmington Trust, as well as a partner in Richards, Layton and Finger. His son, R.H. Richards III, is married to Marianna du Pont, granddaughter of the late Irénée du Pont.

Donald P. Ross. Ross is a director of Wilmington Trust. His main claim to fame, besides his ownership of Brandywine Stables, is his marriage to Wilhelmina du Pont, daughter of William K. du Pont, who held a large block of Christiana Securities stock and a $125 million fortune.

Senator William V. Roth. The co-author of the Kemp-Roth Act described by Budget Director David Stockman as "the trojan horse" for Reaganomics' tax cuts for the rich, Roth is married to the former Jane Richards, sister-in-law of Marianna du Pont and a daughter of R.H. Richards, Jr.

Eleanor du Pont Rust. This 76-year-old sister of Irénée du Pont, Jr., worth $150 million, resides in Thomasville, Georgia. One of her four children, Henry, has deepened his family's ties to the DiSabatino construction family in Wilmington by marrying one of the daughters, Joan.

Richard P. Sanger. Sanger was the executive editor of the *News-Journal* and director of Delaware Trust. Predictably, he is also married to a Du Pont, Margaret Marvel, stepdaughter of Emile F. du Pont.

Bayard Sharp. Bayard is the very rich son of Hugh R. Sharp, Sr., and Isabella du Pont, sister of Pierre S. Du Pont II. When he was not racing one of his thoroughbreds, he served as a director of Christiana Securities. Now he races stocks, worth some $250 million.

Henry H. Sillman. Sillman is the husband of Marianna du Pont, daughter of Irénée du Pont. Once active in Christiana Securities affairs as a stockholder, he is vice-president of Laird, Bissell & Meeds and sole trustee of the Barbee-Hagley Foundation. Henry rules over Mariannas' fortune, about $150 million.

Edward Newbold Smith. Son-in-law of H.B. du Pont, Smith was also vice-president of Laird, Bissell & Meeds. Although slowing down in appearances at Du Pont social affairs, he remains in touch with the Edward and Richard C. du Pont families.

William A. Speakman, Jr. He is director of Wilmington Trust, Farmers Mutual Life Insurance, and Liberty Mutual Insurance Company, and chairman of the Speakman Company. His son, Willard III, is president of Speakman and husband of Isabella Pearson, stepdaughter of Edith du Pont.

Esther du Pont Thouron. Worth $250 million, Esther, 75, is the wife of John Thouron of Unionville, Pennsylvania, and the daughter of Lammot du Pont. Since her husband was knighted in 1976 for sponsoring U.S.-British student exchanges, Esther has taken to calling herself "Lady Esther," apparently unconcerned that in accepting the status of nobility, she has by law lost her U.S. citizenship.

George T. Weymouth. A Du Pont relative, Weymouth has been a director of Delaware Trust, Laird & Company, United Investors Life Insurance Company, General Precision Equipment Corporation, Kingsford Co., Metropolitan Merchandise Mart, Inc., Rockland Corporation, and Weymouth Properties, which includes Delaware's Twin Lakes. A trustee of the Rencourt Foundation, Weymouth headed a group of Du Ponts owning 145,410 shares in Waddell & Reed. His son, Frolic, is reputed to be among the most amicable Du Ponts alive.

Beyond these, high in the thin air breathed only by the national leaders of American capitalism, rule the power elite of the Du Pont family. These Du Ponts, with the exceptions of George Edmonds and Charles McCoy, once constituted the overwhelming majority of the board of Christiana Securities, for decades the family's focus of power in Du Pont Company.

Here they are in the approximate order of importance in the family hierarchy, starting with the old guard of senior statesmen and then proceeding to the younger activists.

Irénée du Pont, Jr. Irénée is president of Christiana Securities. He is the only son of Irénée du Pont, the $400 million family patriarch who died in 1963. Married to Barbara Batchelder, daughter of Dartmouth National Bank director and past president, Charles N. Batchelder, Irénée is also a director of Du Pont, M.I.T. Corporation, Wilmington Trust, and the Wilmington Medical Center. A trustee of the Longwood Foundation, Irénée also is chairman of the Greater Wilmington Development Council, past chairman of the Delaware Chamber of Commerce, and trustee of the Bredin Foundation, Crystal Trust, Wilmington College, Tower Hill School (his alma mater), and the Mt. Cuba Astronomical Observatory. Irénée's fortune, including family trusts, has been calculated at nearly $200 million.

Crawford Greenewalt. This M.I.T.-trained chemist rose to be Du Pont chairman and president, helped by his marriage to Irénée du Pont's daughter Margaretta. He is a director of Du Pont, M.I.T. Corporation, and the Philadelphia Academy of Natural Sciences, regent of the Smithsonian Institution, and a trustee of the Longwood Foundation. A man with considerable contacts in the United States intelligence agencies through his past association with the Atomic Energy Commission and his chairmanship of the Free Europe Committee, the corporate promoter of the CIA's Radio Free Europe in the 1960's, he has turned over Du Pont's seat on the board of Boeing (Aircraft) Corporation to the former chairman, Irving Shapiro. He is worth about $150 million.

George P. Edmonds. Edmonds is the husband of Natalie du Pont, daughter of Lammot du Pont. Although he was not a Christiana director, his wife held considerable stock and he is honorary chairman of Wilmington Trust, past director of Continental Can and Coca-Cola International, and current director of Du Pont, Continental American Life Insurance, Claymont Insurance, Wiltruco Realty, Inc., Mavibal International Corporation, 100 West 10th Street Corporation, and Downtown Wilmington; he is also trustee of Wheelock College, University of Delaware, the Christiana Foundation, and Delaware Park, past director of Uniroyal, and a member of M.I.T.'s corporation development committee. Edmonds is worth over $200 million.

William Winder Laird, Jr. Laird is the son of Mary Alletta du Pont and W.W. Laird. He was a director of Christiana Securities, Du Pont, and Rockland Corporation, vice-president of Gates Engineering, a trustee of the Averill-Ross and Eleutherian Mills-Hagley foundations, a donor to the Wymyss foundation, and a director of Delfi Management, the investment concern for which he sacrificed his directorship of Wilmington Trust. Laird's fortune has been estimated at $75 to $100 million.

R.R.M. (Bobby) Carpenter, Jr. For the most part, the Carpenter family's interest in Christiana Securities was represented by Bobby Carpenter, the son of Margaretta du Pont and Ruly Carpenter. Besides his ownership of the Philadelphia Phillies baseball team (and his alleged founding of the politically right-wing Delaware Defenders of the Republic), Bobby Carpenter had no business concern other than Christiana Securities. He is personally worth about $200 million. His son, Ruly, brought the Phillies into the World Series, then sold the club for a handsome profit. He now raises vegetables.

A. Felix du Pont, Jr. Felix is the son of a Du Pont vice-president with the same name. He was vice-president of Christiana Securities, the base of his fortune besides his aviation and real estate holdings, and a director of All American Engineering, Dutch Village, and co-founder with Laurence Rockefeller of Piasecki Aircraft. He is a trustee of the Chichester-du-Pont Foundation and the Franklin Institute. His fortune is estimated at about $275 million.

Charles B. McCoy. McCoy's power derived from his presidency and chairmanship of Du Pont, not his personal wealth. He was not a director of Christiana, but had ties to the Du Pont family through his sister, who married Henry Bush (son of Joanna du Pont Bradford, great-great-grandson of Eleuthera du Pont), and his son, who married Carol Kitchell (granddaughter of Margaretta du Pont and a relation to Du Pont in-law William Potter). McCoy was also a director of Citicorp of New York and Remington Arms, and was regional chairman of the National Alliance of Businessmen. He remains on the board of Wilmington Trust and Wilmington Medical Center, as well as Du Pont.

Edward B. du Pont. This is the only serious pretender to the family's crown in the crowd, in his late forties. He is the son of the late Henry B. du Pont II. A fervent yachtsman, Edward served as a director of Christiana Securities, is chairman of Atlantic Aviation, and trustee of the Eleutherian Mills-Hagley, the Crestlea and Longwood Foundations. His worth is about $75 million and he admits sharing beneficial ownership of another $11 million worth of Du Pont with Irénée du Pont, Jr., $41.7 million with H.R. Sharp III, and $4.9 million with C.B. McCoy and the late Lammot du Pont Copeland. As he is involved in Shapiro's financial schemes for Delaware, Edward can be expected to rise in wealth and status.

Hugh R. Sharp III. Sharp is the grandson of Isabella du Pont and H. Rodney Sharp. A thin, amiable person, Sharp is a director of Du Pont and Wilmington Trust, and a trustee of the Sharp and Andelot-Copeland foundations. He runs Du Pont's computer analyzer systems and admits a combined worth, with his family trust and shared voting control with Edward du Pont over another 886,717 shares of Du Pont Common, of $48 million in Du Pont holdings alone. He is actually worth much more. His late father's fortune was estimated at $200 million. He has one sister, H. Dunbar Sharp Plumb, and a brother, William. But he is the heir to power. He will ultimately share in the $225 million fortune of his powerful 73-year-old father, H.R. Sharp, Jr.

Louisa Copeland Duemling. Louisa is the granddaughter of Du Pont director Charles Copeland and Louisa du Pont, sister of Irénée du Pont. Her late father, Lammot du Pont Copeland, Sr., was a vice-president of Christiana Securities, a director of Du Pont, Wilmington Trust, and Chemical Bank New York Trust, a member of the Board of Overseers of Harvard University, and a trustee of the Andelot-Copeland Foundation, and worth between $200 and $400 million, now inherited by Louisa, and her brothers, Garrett and the disgraced Lammot, Jr. ("Motsey"). Louisa only admits to immediate family ownership of $12 million worth of Du Pont, but concedes having beneficial control over another $63 million and sharing control with McCoy and Edward du Pont of $4.9 million, and Irénée, Greenewalt and Heckert of another $44 million, the latter two probably in foundations. She is a director of Du Pont.

Pierre S. Du Pont IV. Son of Pierre du Pont III, and grandson of Lammot du Pont, "Pete" is not one of the richest Du Ponts, but his position as Delaware's chief political promoter of bringing back capital into the state and probable 1988 United States presidential contender has catapulted him into an important position within the top, inner-core of the family hierarchy. All big decisions must now take him into consideration. On the basis of a third share in his father's $175 million (quite below the $250 million estimated by *Forbes*) estate, Pete is worth at least $50 million.

There was one other director of Christiana, Ellison Downs, but his role was insignificant in this powerhouse of Du Pont wealth; he was resigned to taking notes as secretary and watching over the substantial holdings of his wife Molly, sister of William Winder Laird, Jr. His brother is Robert Downs, a big contributor to the Republican Party who married another of Laird's sisters.

Of all these members of the Du Pont power elite, the most outstanding in the 1970's were Irénée du Pont, Jr., Edward B. du Pont, and Governor Pierre S. du Pont IV.

Irénée is an assertive person, having earned a reputation in Wilmington as a hard bargainer when it comes to money. In 1972, for example, the Opportunity School House, existing in what its secretary, Mrs. Marie Di Meglio, described as a "deplorable, unyielding facility," found an opportunity to buy land next to the Wilmington High School for construction of a new Opportunity School for the poor. That the school would be so close to their own Westover Hills was disturbing enough for the Du Ponts. Irénée, along with Reynolds du Pont and W.W. Laird, Jr., blocked the sale through the Delaware School Auxiliary Association, demanding the land be not broken up but used for athletics. "What's more important, a football field or saving those children's lives?" Mrs. Di Meglio asked. Finally, complaining that she couldn't "take on the loving Du Pont family,"[22] she threw in the towel.

One would think that with all his money, this most powerful of Du Pont heirs could afford to be more lenient. In 1971 he personally owned 106,415 shares of Christiana common, worth $15.9 million, and 7,849 of Du Pont common, worth $16.9 million. His immediate family trusts held 22,275 more Du Pont common, and directly held another 3,700 shares. As for Christiana, his trusts held 37,861 shares of common and 251 shares of 7 percent cumulative preferred (valued in 1971 at $18,521 each), and his immediate family owned another 81,200 shares of common, for a grand total of $43.9 million.[23]

Today, he admits being worth more, much more, in fact over $56 million more, for a total immediate family holding of over $100 million in Du Pont alone. In addition, he admits sharing beneficial ownership of another $11.4 million worth of Du Pont with Edward B. du Pont and another $39 million with Greenewalt, Du Pont President Heckert and the late Lammot du Pont Copeland, Sr., quite possibly a reflection of their shared trusteeship over Pierre II's Longwood Foundation.

Regardless of how many more millions Irénée had invested in other blue chip stocks, why, one might ask, should any man who owns $43.9 million worth of Du Pont holdings as just part of his vast fortune have to be such a hard bargainer?

The answer lies in the 170-year history of the Du Ponts. It has been precisely by "hard bargaining," by exploitation of labor at home and abroad, by fat government contracts, that the Du Ponts amassed their $10 billion fortune. Such hard bargaining was the only way that fortune could have been built; and it is the only way it can be protected from more democratic sentiments among the population.

In the 1970's the Du Ponts began taking their first serious steps out of the company of E.I. du Pont de Nemours, to complete their shift from an industrial family to a financial family. But because of that hard-bargaining way of life, protected by present property laws, they continued to enjoy the luxuries of untold wealth.

Mrs. Allaire du Pont, owner of Bohemia Stables and Kelso, history's greatest four-legged money maker, could still boast that "her best news of the week had just arrived from California, where Kelso's half brother, Pure Flight, just won..."[24]

And Mrs. A. Felix du Pont, Jr., could still feel that life really hadn't changed much for her family since she commented some years ago that "We all love to ride and sail and travel, and I devote a great deal of time to my work with the National Association of Mental Health. It is meshing all these activities that makes life so interesting, I think."[25]

And 34-year old John E. du Pont could still count his 250,000 seashells collected from beaches all over the world, or his 5,000 stuffed birds shot from trees around the world, or his 100 beagles, or his stock of $250,000 thoroughbreds, or he could even build another Museum of Natural History to house any more whimsical pastimes that might have come into his law-and-order obsessed head as he swooped over the countryside in search of "baddies" in his helicopter, wearing his police uniform and helmet emblazoned with the insignia of his "Foxcatcher" estate.

"Pete" du Pont could still wander the halls of Congress dreaming the dreams of those who already have inherited power but want more. His wife, Elise, could still explain the meaning of courage in her own unique way: "You have to learn when to stick to your convictions," she once said. "For instance, I planned on the blueprints exactly where I wanted all the light switches. Then one freezing day I had to meet the electrician at the house and go over all my placements with him. He suggested that I put a lot of switches in different places than I had planned. I was uncertain, but all I wanted was to get back home where it was warm, so I gave in. And I shouldn't have. Several of the switches are in very annoying places now..."[26] So now, amid her herb garden, terraces, greenhouses, library, five-wing mansion with its own "Patterns" flag, and glass-walled gallery with cascades of flowering plants, Mrs. du Pont must put up with her light switches.

In a city where 11 percent (mostly Black) of the residents were considered by the federal government to be living in poverty, and where a Wilmington policeman named Ralph Prior could openly organize Ku Klux Klan chapters, Mrs. W. Henry du Pont could still donate more "boys homes" for youth sentenced as criminals, while a few miles to the south, the country's only millionaire sheriff, Samuel F. du Pont, satisfying his own particular urges, could prowl through Cecil County, Maryland, with a gun and a K-9 police dog commenting that "I'm not a trained corrections officer and I don't rehabilitate. I just warehouse human beings,"[27] and still return each day to his 57-acre country estate overlooking the Sassafras River, complete with thoroughbred stables, dog-breeding kennels, a deer herd, swimming pool, a few boats, and two private airstrips.

In a state where one family reigned supreme, state Senator Reynolds du Pont could still answer calls in the legislature for his resignation as Senate president by quipping with a smile that "I'm vain enough to think they don't mean it,"[28] and when he discovered they did, he could even try to cut his opponent Senator's term by two years. Reynolds lost that time and quit politics. But losing his favorite license plate and parking space next to the governor was more of a blow to him than the loss Delaware suffered when an ultra-rightist former lieutenant governor, Sherman Tribbit, entered the governor's mansion as fitting example of the fruit of 100 years of Du Pont rule.

Finally, Irénée du Pont could still pursue his plans to make Wilmington the crossroads of the East with his civic center named Xanadu, after the estate his father owned in prerevolutionary Cuba. Irénée could explain with a straight face that building badly needed housing "would be a disaster,"[29] and then return to his seventy-room mansion. "It is a delicate operation to bring off a commercial venture (like Xanadu) with many different forces which have to be coordinated all to say yes at the right time," said the Greater Wilmington Development Council's maestro. "If a politician or somebody wishes to stop the venture, he can because it's so delicate...You can't permit that to happen if you want to succeed. It's going to succeed. I'll bet a fifth of whiskey on it."[30] Just about anyone in Delaware would, too.

Yet Irénée, stockholder in Diamond State Telephone, director of the *News-Journal,* Delmarva Power and Light Company, GWDC, and Du Pont, Delaware's largest employer, could still claim, "I don't believe there is Du Pont family control of Delaware"[31]—even as he was enriched every time a Delawarean used the phone, read the newspaper, or turned on a light.

5. DU PONTS AT THE CROSSROADS

The Du Ponts reached their zenith of prestige and political power in the Twenties. But as happened with most other American plutocrats, their golden age ended unexpectedly with the crash and the ensuing years of the Depression. In those grim and tumultuous years, the Du Ponts swung politically to the right, fighting the labor movement and the Roosevelt reforms with equal vigor. Even through World War II and its Cold War aftermath, they persisted in consistently dangerous right-wing politics.

There were exceptions, of course, and they should be noted precisely because they were aberrations in the normal behavior of the clan. Ethel B. du Pont, niece of Coleman du Pont, for example, placed newspaper ads to support striking G.M. workers in 1945–1946. Zara du Pont, on the other hand, had a long history of liberal causes. This aged sister of Coleman du Pont was seen regularly on picket lines in Boston throughout the Thirties. Known to family and friends as "Aunt Zadie," this extraordinary woman had friends among union organizers who, although disagreeing with her pacifism, respected her sincerity. When police once attacked a picket line of the National Maritime Union in Everett, Massachusetts, for example, Aunt Zadie responded by showing up the next morning on the line wearing a gas mask. A Du Pont is always news, and pictures of her masked face hit the national press that day and the police and city government were forced, under public pressure, to withdraw their assaults.

Zadie once explained her ideology at a stockholders meeting of Bethlehem Steel. "Bethlehem's present policies," she declared, "are calculated to destroy labor's faith in the devotion of America's industrial leaders to democracy, and so to destroy labor's will to cooperate with them." It was pure New Deal corporatism, in the tradition of Gerard Swope's NRA. Perhaps for this reason, Pierre discouraged the tirades of abuse usually flung at her by others in the clan because of her support of the Socialist Party and the Spanish Loyalists then fighting Franco's fascist armies. In any case, the emergence of any active supporter of labor from such a clan as the Du Ponts must be considered one of the great feats of history. Aunt Zadie was certainly a refreshing exception to the general Du Pont rule.

The only other Du Pont approaching Zadie's liberalism was Ernest May, the husband of Irene du Pont. May was one of the many Americans who opposed the landing of U.S. troops in Korea to support the U.S.-installed Rhee dictatorship, and he even placed a newspaper ad protesting the Korean War and the occupation of postwar (and potentially revolutionary) Europe by U.S. troops. Later, when Fidel Castro overthrew General Batista, May questioned the wisdom of seeking tax relief for the confiscation of the Xanadu estate of his father-in-law, Irénée du Pont.

Although he was effectively barred by Irénée du Pont, Jr., and Crawford Greenewalt, his fellow trustees, from exercising any real control over the estate of his father-in-law, May never bent in his politics. In January 1968 he endorsed the Wilmington NAACP's fight for fair housing. "Where would America be," he wrote to the *News-Journal*, "without the men of the cutting edge? . . . "[32] May has seldom matched his words with activity, but he stands as a political maverick haunting the family.

It is a sad testament, but probably an inevitable one, that these Du Ponts are the only exceptions, besides McGovern-backer Alexis du Pont Bayard, to the Du Pont family's traditional ultraconservatism. In fact, Zadie and Ethel are the only Du Ponts in the family's 170-year history to have ever been known for publicly supporting a work stoppage by labor. "Manufacturing is a true creation of wealth," wrote the original E.I. du Pont. "It is taking cotton which costs 20 cents per pound and making it worth several dollars." But who, Zadie would ask, is doing the manufacturing, the work? "It is the men of our organization," Irénée du Pont explained, "not Lammot du Pont, nor I who do it, but the organization trained to work together."[33] But who, Zadie would ask, gets the rewards?

By 1972 some Du Ponts were asking the same question about their own holdings in Du Pont Company. Since then, the family is moving increasingly in two directions.

The first direction was away from the company that bears their name. Symptomatic of this was the growth of the family's mutual funds. Blue Ridge Mutual Fund, which had $52 million in assets in 1967, had its name changed to Sigma Investment Shares in 1969 by Eleuthère du Pont. Its assets in 1974 were about $72 million. The same held true for Sigma Venture Shares, which Eleuthère began in 1969. Worth $3 million in assets in 1971, it had assets of $6.2 million in 1974.

Involved in Eleuthère's group were James Q. du Pont, Donald F. Carpenter, Emile F. du Pont, R.M. Layton, W.J. Kitchell, Reynolds du Pont, H.H. Sillman, and Francis I. du Pont II.

These were some of the common stocks owned by just one of Eleuthère's firms, Sigma Investment Shares:

Shares	Company
37,000	ELTRA Corp.
15,600	Purolator, Inc.
15,000	Addressograph Multigraph
3,000	International Business Machines
25,000	Sperry Rand
6,000	Xerox Corporation
15,000	Air Products & Chemicals
5,000	E. I. du Pont
40,000	W. R. Grace
17,000	Hercules, Inc.
26,224	Pittston Company
12,000	Abbott Laboratories
25,000	Gillette Company
10,000	Merck & Company
10,000	G. D. Searle
9,000	Warner-Lambert
45,000	Sunbeam Corporation
20,000	Zenith Radio
25,000	Bank of Delaware
30,000	Beneficial Corporation
15,000	Connecticut General Insurance
25,000	Continental Corporation
37,440	Transamerica Corporation
25,500	Quaker Oats
35,000	Mohasco Industries
45,000	Purex Corporation
50,000	Scovill Manufacturing
45,000	Simmons Company

Shares	Company
20,000	Columbia Broadcasting System
7,000	Eastman Kodak
22,000	Briggs & Stratton
20,000	Parker-Hannifin
27,000	Rex Chainbelt
18,000	Sundstrand Corporation
45,000	U.S. Industries
25,000	Universal Oil Products
40,000	VSI Corporation
30,000	Broadway-Hale Stores
27,000	Malone & Hyde
27,000	Melville Shoe

30,000 Skaggs Companies
18,000 Atlantic Richfield
35,000 Continental Oil
20,000 Exxon Corporation
35,000 Texaco, Inc.
35,000 Maryland Cup Company
19,000 Nashua Corporation
30,000 Trans Union Corporation
40,000 Carlisle Corporation
45,000 Phillips-Van Heusen
30,000 V. F. Corporation
70,000 Central Illinois Public Service
17,000 Houston Natural Gas
21,200 Long Island Lighting
50,000 Northern States Power
16,000 Rochester Telephone[35]

Along with mutual funds, E.I. du Pont also steered Continental American Life Insurance toward increased speculation in bonds. In 1968 Continental owned $6.7 million worth of corporate stock (of which $4.4 million was in utilities) and $36 million worth of corporate bonds.[35] By 1974 Continental owned $7 million in corporate stock and $61 million in corporate bonds. Its holdings of federal bonds decreased, while state bonds increased. With assets of $164 million in 1968, Continental in 1974 admitted assets of $203 million.[36]

Within Eleuthère's group, W.W. Laird, Jr., and Edmond du Pont also functioned, although Edmond's problems with (F.I.) Du Pont, Glore Forgan set him back some.

The development within the family of concerted financial speculation independent of Du Pont Company was a harbinger of the future, but it could only find its real flowering through a bank with large resources under their exclusive command. Some Du Ponts had already entered this field, but they were associated with medium-sized banking institutions and, because of legal restrictions, remained as yet separated from Eleuthère's group. In fact, since W.W. Laird had to surrender his directorship of Wilmington Trust in order to keep his position on Delfi Management, the only connections between the mutual funds/insurance group and the medium-sized banking group represented by Du Ponts in Delaware Trust/Wilmington Trust were through the family's traditional meeting grounds, Christiana Securities and Du Pont Company. Here, these two groups were confronted by a minority group who have mostly avoided ventures independent of Du Pont Company.

This last group, represented by Irénée du Pont, Jr., Lammot du Pont Copeland, Sr., R.R.M. Carpenter, Jr., and Hugh R. Sharp, Jr., took the traditional path of reentrenchment into Du Pont, which was currently showing record earnings ($12.04 a share for 1973), but profit margins still lower than those of 1965. Of the four, however, none was opposed to outside speculation or banking, and all were involved in outside interests, as long as they remained auxiliary to Du Pont.

Yet Du Pont's own needs directed a different course. If the Du Ponts remaining in the firm were to exercise effective control, they would need their own bank to offset outside bankers who were able to offer ample funds for needed plant expansion. This required forging an alliance between the various groups within the family, but only New York banks still looked large enough to meet Du Pont's appetite for capital. An external alliance with some group other than the Morgans was needed if the family was to outweigh Morgan influence or, if that was impossible, even survive the loss of Du Pont as a family. The Mellon and Rockefeller families loomed as the Du Ponts' last hope. Some alliance had to be secured, if only as a temporary refuge for capital concentration and a springboard to establishing commanding control over a large bank. If that alliance were not achieved, the family's cohesion would die with its control of Du Pont. Without a bank, the transition of the Du Ponts from an industrial family to a financial family would have failed, and the dissolution of the family as an institution would ensue.

Meanwhile, McCoy, Irénée, Sharp, and Copeland had still to deal with Du Pont's own prospects. Unless productivity of Du Pont workers was increased, the chemical firm would be unable to compete at home and abroad and still return high enough profits to its owners to attract bond buyers, stock investors, and bank loans. This signaled a more aggressive attack by management on the status quo of Du Pont's blue-collar workers—more layoffs and increased speedups, while wages were held down: in effect, reducing real wages. Sooner or later, this would also trigger a response by labor trying to defend itself against inflation and deteriorating (and increasingly dangerous) work conditions, and sparks would fly again as in the past.

With its white-collar workers, Du Pont could expect easier times. Wilmington's new International Design office in Plainview, Long Island, offered a good example. Concerned about retaining good draftsmen and engineers to design plants for the huge foreign expansion it was planning, Du Pont raised salaries 18 percent. But just as important as paying top dollar and fringe benefits is work location. Du Pont found that white-collar workers lost time and energy traveling into New York City every day from their Long Island homes. To make happier, less tired, and therefore more efficient workers, Wilmington decided to set up a new International Design headquarters right in Long Island, where most of the city's draftsmen and engineers lived.

By taking the initiative, Du Pont got a big lead over other corporations in the race to control Long Island's design labor market. By situating their offices in the Plainview industrial area right off the Long Island Expressway, Du Pont brought high salaries to where design workers were already settled with homes and families, a key personal factor in controlling hired labor. Over 100 designers were soon working at this office, and over 200 more slated to be hired. For reasons of security and efficiency (less paper work), most of these designers (as well as those in Houston, Texas) worked without blueprints, using only models based on standards sent to them from Wilmington. As is traditional with Du Pont, few designers, like few Du Pont research scientists, know what their co-workers are working on. The creative impulse and social responsibility were technocratically suppressed to meet organizational pressures. In this sense, little had changed since William H. Whyte wrote in 1956 that "Du Pont men frankly admit their narrowness of approach toward their work, dealing mostly with concrete tasks they are personally connected with, and are seldom worried about this approach. The big picture that cuts across the entire company is left to the executive and finance committees, and the Board."[38] Within that big picture, one of the immediate projects for the Plainview designers was the new plant Du Pont was planning to build in Mexico, Wilmington's favorite source of cheap labor abroad.

Abroad, the situation was tighter, as renewed competition from Europe and Japan meant renewed trade wars and perhaps even a resurrection of those "outdated" cartel agreements of old. To protect Remington Arms, Du Pont was a vigorous member of the Sporting Arms and Ammunition Manufacturers Association (SAAMI). SAAMI is dedicated to fighting U.S. surplus sales in America and preventing foreign importation of arms and ammunition. It was instrumental in securing the 1958 amendment to Section 414 of the Mutual Security Act of 1954, banning reimportation of U.S.-made arms originally exported as military aid. Responding to the lobbying efforts of this group, the Defense Department has banned the sale of U.S. surplus arms in America, and in 1968 the Gun Control Act had the full blessing of Du Pont, as it also carried a ban on the importation of all military surplus arms. By keeping prices up, the SAAMI serves as a trade association similar to General Henry du Pont's Powder Trust in the nineteenth century.

Yet such efforts could only serve as plugs in the dike. McCoy's new slogan for Du Pont, "There's a world of things we're doing something about," did not ease the worries of market analysts in the Wilmington headquarters.

Earnings may indeed have been rising, but the subtle growing crisis of market contraction due to foreign and domestic competition and revolutions by laboring classes abroad remained. Mounting demands for a better life soon forced conservative monarchs in the Middle East to dramatically raise oil prices, causing a shift in petrodollars out of the United States and back to OPEC accounts, many of which were in foreign subsidiaries of New York banks.

To Wilmington, finding financial capital for overseas factories became paramount, underscored by the recent appointment of Irving Shapiro, vice-president in charge of finances, as the new chief executive officer and chairman of Du Pont. Shapiro, of witch-hunting fame during the McCarthy era, was the dark-horse compromise between vice-chairman Edward Kane, who was slated for the job, and Irénée du Pont, Jr., who may have once wanted it but whose appointment in those crucial days of Christiana dissolution might undermine the company's efforts to shed its image of Du Pont family domination then anathema to institutional investors and other banking groups. Irving Shapiro, who watchfully accompanied the Nader team on each of their interviews with Du Pont workers, was the first chairman of Du Pont who was really not related to the Du Pont family, a fact of no minor importance. The same was true of Kane, who became president.

There was a very real symbolic meaning to the boos greeting one stockholder, who showed up at the Annual Meeting in April 1973 wrapped in a "sick" blanket. "If someone is ill, they should stay home!" someone shouted to a rousing cheer. Yet all the cheers he received, and all the boos the stockholder reaped, could not hide the creased brows on more than one face that day.

In 1974 a writer who had studied the Du Ponts closed his book with a prediction that to some seemed extreme: "Labor problems at home and revolution and economic warfare abroad have traditionally inspired a shift of Du Pont politics to the right, and the same can be expected again. Even if this rule doesn't prove to hold true for Greenville's pragmatic Congressman, Pierre S. du Pont IV, the center of the struggle will eventually find its way to the government. As in the past, the "Armorers of the Republic," as the Du Ponts like to call themselves, will be forced out of their seclusion and into the political arena.

"In the past, Du Ponts have responded to political crisis by overreacting. This effect may also be repeated. For above all else, the Du Ponts fear internal revolt." Even as those words were being written, the Du Ponts were already on the move, undertaking political actions that would shake not only Delaware, but America and the world.

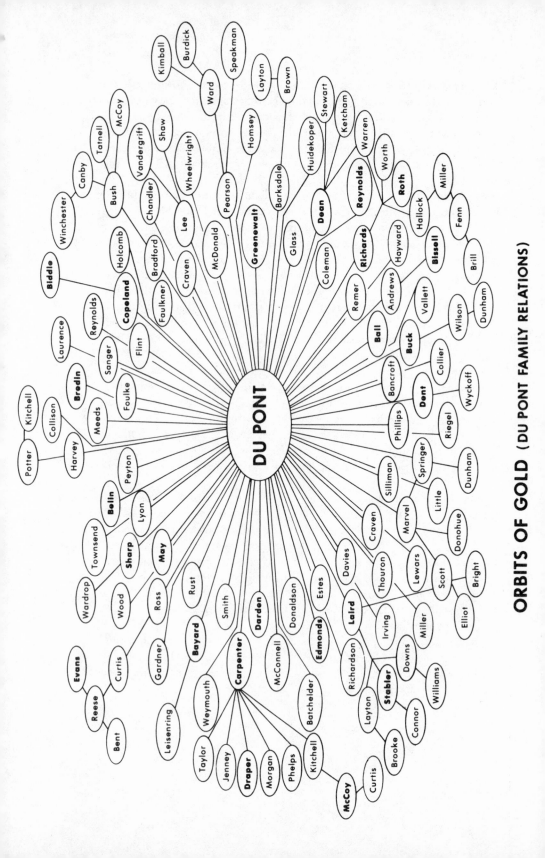

ORBITS OF GOLD (DU PONT FAMILY RELATIONS)

Sixteen

A DYNASTY
IN TRANSITION

1. THE BATTLE FOR THE BRANDYWINE

The dirt cast about during the 1972 national election had barely settled when a group of men gathered in the large home of Reynolds du Pont, Delaware's leading state senator. There was a somber tone to their meeting, odd for a time when most Republicans had cause to celebrate. Their presidential candidate, Richard Nixon, had been re-elected in a landslide that buried George McGovern's protests about being the victim of dirty tricks and a second-rate burglary at his campaign headquarters. No one in this Republican group ever considered the election stolen, then or now. It had been paid for, fair and square, like any other commodity, and the Du Ponts had paid their share, almost half a million dollars if you included the tithes paid by their top employees at the chemical company. John E. du Pont, the largest donor, at $141,125.00, spoke the sentiments of most of his family when he later explained that "If McGovern were elected, he would have started a socialistic trend."[1] To evade just such a socialistic intrusion into his freedom to be generous, namely, the federal gift tax, John had sent 46 separate checks for $3002.67 to such organizations as Florida CREEP and Nebraska TV-Media CREEP. Other family members like Reynolds did likewise, and the results were telling.

Tom du Pont, Reynolds' son, had gotten himself a seat in Delaware's House of Representatives. And Reynolds' nephew, Pete du Pont, had been re-elected as Delaware's sole congressman, and his prospects for taking the governorship in 1976, if he chose to run, looked good.

Except for one obstacle: a rotund, sandy-haired man who was the subject of this solemn gathering, Melvin Slawik.

Melvin Slawik? An obstacle to *any* Du Pont in Delaware? Yet Slawik had just defeated the Republican candidate for New Castle County Executive, William Frederick. Frederick, 37, was a notable in the 1969-70 *Who's Who in American Politics,* a man who counted among his business directorships Pen-Del Equipment Corporation, 222 Building Inc., State Line Machine Corporation, and Joseph Frederick & Sons. An evangelical Protestant, he was president of the Full Gospel Businessmen Fellowship Institute. But his most potent listing was as a Secretary Treasurer of Wilmington Trust Company, the Du Pont family bank.

Understandably, Slawik had been surprised by his election in New Castle, *the* bastion of Du Pont power. "With a name like Slawik," he gleefully told a reporter at his victory party, "I took New Castle County!"[2]

Or, rather, a demographically altered New Castle County took him. To the Du Ponts, it was an ominous sign. Ever since the court-ordered reapportionment of the Sixties, southern Delaware's control over the state legislature had been eclipsed by the rise of industry and population north of the Chesapeake-Delaware Canal that both literally and culturally divides the small state. New Castle County, which encompasses northern Delaware, is the home of the Du Ponts. Both the city of Wilmington, where Du Pont Company has its giant central bureaucracy, and the "chateau country" of mansions in the hills northwest of the city, lie within the county's boundaries. The Du Ponts had always dominated the county government through their Republican Party. Until, that is, Mel Slawik came along.

Although universally acclaimed as an affable fellow, Slawik had never given the Du Ponts a political reason to like him. At a time when Henry B. du Pont was ordering the *News-Journal* papers to play down the civil rights movement, telling the editors that "A continued overplaying of integration in our papers certainly plays right into the hands of the radical element of our population.... Many of the writers on your staff seem to have a degree of dedication to certain causes which would make them appear to be quite far to the left,"[3] and forcing the resignation of its independent-minded editor, Creed Black, by appointing a top Du Pont Public Relations executive, Charles Hackett, to oversee the newspapers, Mel Slawik was engaging in sit-ins at Wilmington lunch counters and arguing for the recognition of human rights.

Like the Du Ponts, Slawik was in many ways the product of his social environment, which was a world away from the Brandywine. He and his mother had been forced on welfare in New York City after his father died in 1947 when Slawik was twelve. Contrary to the Du Ponts' stereotype of welfare recipients, Slawik needed no more incentive to work than the humiliation he felt every day when taking food stamps to the A&P cashier. He worked hard, delivering newspapers, cleaning dishes and cooking in a hospital kitchen, and always reading. His friends told him he'd never make college, but they had underestimated him, as so many would in the future. He not only passed the entrance exam but ended up a *summa cum laude* graduate from Rutgers University. With his personal background and after a brief stint in the New Castle County's welfare department after being fired as a sales trainee for trying to organize a white collar union at Continental Diamond and Fiber company in Newark, Delaware, it was not surprising that he took his master's degree in social work. Mel Slawik, no one doubted, wanted to help people.

Over the next eleven years, he found ample opportunity in Delaware. From 1960 to 1967, he was director of Presbyterian Social Services in the state. People in Delaware still fondly recall his work with poor families in Wilmington. He set up a "Family Camp" for them where he could take them to the beach. He easily related to their yearnings for respect and human dignity, and strong bonds of mutual trust and loyalty were fused.

It was a quality that followed him throughout his career. He was elected national president of the United Presbyterian Health, Education and Welfare Association. In 1968 he founded Delaware's Geriatric Services for the elderly with a small grant from the Bureau of Aging. By then, he had also served four years as a state representative and that year was elected to the state Senate. When he left the Senate in 1972 to run for the office of County Executive, Geriatric Services was a resounding success, its $2 million budget and staff barely able to keep up with the elderly's demands for its services, the only one of its kind in Delaware.

His service in Dover politics had also won national recognition. Rutgers' Eagleton Institute of Political Science named him one of the outstanding legislators in America. The NAACP presented him with its prestigious Award of Special Recognition for Minority Services. His contributions to organized labor won him honors from the United Auto Workers of America and the Delaware State Employees Union. Most Du Ponts, including Senate pro-tem president Reynolds du Pont, may not have appreciated his efforts to help create the DSEU or his civil rights stands, but the voters in his normally "red-neck" district tolerated Slawik's causes because he always supported their own bread-and-butter concerns. This constantly put him at odds with the special interests of the Du Ponts, and he fought Reynolds over a change in Delaware's tax on income from the sale of stocks and bonds. For years, Delaware had taxed these capital gains like any other income. In 1967, however, Wilmington tax lawyers led by Johannes Krahmer drafted a bill that followed the federal setup, which allows a lower tax rate for capital gains. Since wealthy families like the Du Ponts derive most of their income from investments in stocks and bonds, not salaries, Slawick opposed the bill as a proposed special interest legislation favoring the rich.

The mansions of the Brandywine, obviously, were not toasting to the political health of Mel Slawik.

Slawik did not care. To him, the Du Ponts and their allies already had too many tax windfalls. Delaware, unlike 44 states in the Union, has no personal property tax. Most residents owned little personal property anyway beyond their houses and land. But not the Du Ponts. Crawford Greenewalt and his wife, for example, admitted owning stocks, bonds, jewelry and other property worth $20 to $30 million, yet paid property taxes on only 1-2 percent of their holdings.[4] Henry B. du Pont admitted total property holdings—real (land, houses, and improvements thereon), tangible (cars, boats, livestock, cash, etc.), personal and intangible (stocks, bonds, patents, interests in insurance policies, etc.)—of $56 million, yet paid a property tax on only 10 percent of that, the $6.1 million of real property.

Nor does Delaware have a stock transfer tax. This particularly benefits the Du Ponts as the richest stockholders in the state. Most owners of stock do not buy or sell securities in great numbers. The Du Ponts and other wealthy families do.

Nor does Wilmington's wage tax include income from stocks and bonds. In the 1970's it was common for Irénée du Pont, Jr., and H.R. Sharp each to reap between $200,000 and $300,000 in dividends from their shares in Du Pont and Christiana Securities alone. Yet neither paid any taxes to Wilmington on that income; the onus of the wage tax is instead put on the working class.

Nor was Delaware's income tax on wages and salaries really progressive beyond $30,000 when one looked at the loopholes for the rich, including tax-free government securities, deductions, exemptions, and credits. By these means, as Marvin Brams points out in his *Delaware Inheritance and Estate Taxes* (University of Delaware, 1969), the 11 percent tax rate was reduced to 6.8 percent for Delawareans who made $200,000 in 1971; those making $15-17,999 paid 4.3 percent, only 2.5 percent less.

Nor did Delaware have a gift tax until 1971. Even then, the new law allowed a mere six months between the time money was given to an heir and the date of a benefactor's death for the estate to be taxable at rates still below 27 of 36 other states having inheritance taxes.[5] Any gifts received before those six months were exempt. Forty-two states require more time. And heirs of modest estates of $25,000 end up paying a higher tax rate than those heirs of net estates worth $2.5 million and even $5 million.[6] Delaware's trust laws also exempt the beneficiary of a trust from gift taxes; the tax, instead, is paid to the state and federal governments by the millionaire who sets up the trust before his death. As long as the trust's principal is not distributed, four generations of heirs can live off the dividends and interest without paying any Delaware estate taxes. If the trust is in Delaware or other government bonds, the heirs do not pay any federal taxes either.

Slawik had had enough. When the new capital gains bill was introduced he challenged Reynolds du Pont in the Senate. Governor Russell Peterson, a former $70,000-a-year Du Pont executive, threw the executive branch's weight behind the measure in 1970 and it was enacted by legislators terrified by threats that the Du Ponts would move elsewhere. That was unlikely. Even Congressman Pete du Pont conceded that tax rates were only one of a multitude of factors determining where his family members lived.[7] But the threat always worked, and still does.

Conditions in New Castle County had gotten worse by the early 1970's. The uncontrolled construction of new installations by Du Pont and other chemical companies and the lucrative housing developments for the thousands of employees they brought into the area had made a shambles of the county's sewer system. As early as November 1970, the county government, headed by William J. Conner, a member of Du Pont's Legal Department from 1947 to 1966, announced a complete breakdown was imminent.

Part of the responsibility lay with a zoning commission which had for years been steered by a Du Pont family member, Samuel H. Homsey. No intensive studies were undertaken to guide the county in land use. While W.W. Laird and other Du Ponts and the Allied Woodlawn trustees prevented new developments from being constructed in chateau country and kept land prices high by releasing only a few parcels at a time onto the residential market, encouraging overconcentration in selected areas, the county's Levy Court, which controlled the sewer system's construction, built what "it could afford"[8] (which was limited by the county's low tax base) rather than what was needed, resulting in what the Conner Administration admitted in 1970 was a "poorly planned, outdated and polluting sewer system."[9]

Housing was also a big problem, exacerbated for minorities by racial discrimination incorporated in Woodlawn Trustees leases which read: "No lot or part thereof shall be conveyed to, used, owned or occupied as owner or tenant by any person not of the Caucasian race."[10] Meanwhile, in the previous two decades the city had torn down more housing than it put up[11] and the Black community charged that banks denied Afro-Americans home loans for no apparent reason.[12] This was all in violation of the Supreme Court's ruling two decades earlier outlawing racially discriminating covenants in real estate deeds. Until the early 1960's, when fair housing erupted as an issue, Du Pont Company participated in the state's segretation, finding housing for its employees and placing them with selected realtors; then, as controversy rose over this practice, it withdrew altogether, leaving minority employees to fend for themselves. In 1968, Woodlawn struck the offending covenant, but was later caught segregating a Wilmington rental project by the Delaware Human Rights Commission.

With the exception of Slawik's Geriatric Services, medical services for the county's poor were dismal as well, reflected in the high infant mortality rates in Hispanic and Black communities in contrast to the very low rates in the affluent districts.[13] Wilmington Medical Center was the fifth largest voluntary general hospital in the nation and charged the highest fees in the state.[14] In December, 1970, two young boys died enroute to another hospital after being denied emergency care at Wilmington Medical Center. The hospital had practiced racial segregation in its wards until 1957 and a study by Sociometrics, an independent consultant, revealed that Wilmington Center's care to poor patients was of a low quality.[15] When the 1970 incident occurred, the Wilmington *News-Journal* papers reported the boys' deaths, but did not report Wilmington Medical's refusal to treat them, even though a sworn affidavit by the boys' parents was given by a City Hall official to a *News-Journal* reporter.[16] At the time, Du Ponts were directors of both the *News-Journal* and the Medical Center.

Under these circumstances it was not surprising, as the Nader Report on Delaware pointed out, that "the highest incidence of mental illness was in census tracts of poor whites and blacks."[17]

Between 1959 and 1969, the national poverty rate declined from 22.1 percent to 12.3 percent of the population; in Delaware, the rate of decline was one of the lowest in the country, dropping from 16.8 percent to 15.7 percent; in absolute figures, the number of poor Delawarians actually *rose* from 73,000 to 85,000.[18] Yet in 1970 Delaware was making welfare payments to the poor that were consistently below the national average; this included aid to the elderly, to families with dependent children, and to families of the unemployed.[19] That year federal officials ruled that Delaware's legal ceiling on benefits was too low and threatened a court suit; the Peterson Administration then pressed a bill through the legislature raising the ceiling, but only after assuring the Du Pont-dominated assembly of white collar professionals that not one additional dollar would actually go to any family on welfare.[20]

The county administration under William Conner was failing to respond to a mounting crisis that was now extending to Du Pont employees as well. Of seven sites for a 400-unit low-income housing project proposed by the Wilmington Housing Authority to the federal Department of Housing and Urban Development (HUD), the county planning commission vetoed four and failed to approve a fifth. The two other sites were rejected outright by HUD. The County Council, dominated by its president, Du Pont family member C. Douglas Buck, Jr., then established its own housing authority to study the possibility of building 900 units by 1973. About 70 percent of the county's families earned less than $10,000 a year; 50 percent less than

$8,000; 13,000 families had annual incomes below $5,000. In a county where residential properties were inflated by Du Pont family hoarding and speculation and the population influx conveyed by Interstate 95 (promoted by the former leader of the state's highway commission, Du Pont family member H.R. Sharp), new homes were simply beyond most citizens' means. And in the areas already developed, the congestion was so bad that there was not enough land left for recreation. The district called New Castle Hundred,* for example, dominated by the Greater Wilmington Airport that Henry B. du Pont had pressured the county to build, contained only 13 public parks or recreational facilities. Most local residents, of course, could not afford the private clubs that Du Pont executives enjoyed.

These were all issues that motivated Mel Slawik to run for County Executive in 1972. Unions remembered his impressive record as chairman of the House Labor Committee. Minorities remembered his track record on civil rights. The elderly remembered his four years of building Geriatric Services. Polish-American and Italian-American residents in the working-class suburbs of New Castle remembered him as a man who had stood against the Du Ponts' hoarding of over 35 percent of the rural land in Christiana Hundred district, 19 percent in Mill Creek Hundred, and 13 percent in Brandywine Hundred. They listened to his pledge of more parks, more and better educated police, an improved sewer system, a local service tax, and more housing.

The Du Ponts' *News-Journal* papers saw them listening and soon a series of articles appeared by Jack Nolan, admittedly inspired by Republican state representative George Hering. "Why don't you go after Mel Slawik,"[21] Hering had told Nolan after complaining about Nolan's investigation into his law firm's receiving almost $90,000 worth of business from the Peterson state administration.

Nolan did, and on May 16, 1972, the *News-Journal's* attacks on Slawick began. They claimed conflict of interest by Slawick in voting for legislation that benefited Geriatric Services and noted that the agency, which had grown into a million dollar service, had failed a recent audit. Nolan later recalled Slawick being cooperative during his investigation, and insisted, "We weren't trying to hang scalps on anyone's belt. At that time, Slawik was just a minor figure from a blue-collar district." But Nolan's additional comment to the *Delaware Today* Magazine, edited by a son of a Du Pont executive, was equally telling. "Maybe he thought no one would ever look. But they did." It would take two more years for Slawik to prove his innocence. In 1974 the

---

* "Hundred" was a colonial designation for a voting district. The term has survived in Delaware.

state Attorney General exonerated him from any wrongdoing at Geriatric Services. But by then the damage had been done by the *News-Journal*. "He was going big-time," said Nolan.[22]

No one will ever know how many votes the *News-Journal* series cost Slawik, but his campaign survived. Although he pledged to take another look at the assessment of property values, including those of the Du Ponts, he generally kept a low-key tone, building a momentum that was designed to peak on election day. He was trying his best, but he never believed, he later confessed, that he would actually win.

The strategy worked. His Republican opponent, William Frederick, underestimated Slawik. When the returns came in, Slawik had won by 1515 votes.

Now, at Reynolds du Pont's home, the Republican leaders feared the worst. If Slawik made good on his property reassessment pledge, the Du Ponts and their corporate allies were bound to suffer because county assessments were notoriously biased. A small shopping center near Du Pont's Experimental Station, for example, was assessed at $6224 per acre; the Station, which has never paid taxes on its research equipment or industrial fixtures, was assessed at only $699 per acre.[23] In addition, most of the Du Pont mansions and estate grounds were grossly undervalued compared to nearby homes; it was not uncommon for adjacent homeowners to have their properties assessed at two, six, and even 13 times what Du Ponts paid per acre.[24]

The Du Ponts were also worried about what Slawik would do about pollution. In July, 1970, air pollution had gotten so bad that the Conner Administration was forced to declare a state of alert. For a week, 350,000 people in New Castle County, and particularly Wilmington, were subjected to sulfur dioxide levels as high as .4 parts per million, far beyond the .1 part per million considered the safe maximum level. The Peterson Administration in Dover proclaimed a 24-hour pollution watch on July 28, but it limited only open burning and incinerator operations. Under Delaware law, industrial firms, including three of the biggest pollutors, Du Pont's Edgemor and Chambers Works plants and the Delmarva Power and Light plant at Cherry Island, could not be forced to shut down. Delaware's Water and Air Resources Act, it seems, had been amended with Section 8203(b), destroying state-wide standards and allowing different ones for different neighborhoods, despite the fact that northern Delaware industries are usually very near residential areas. The promoter of the amendment was Du Pont's chief environmental lobbyist in the Legal Department, the same William Conner who was Slawik's predecessor as County Executive.

Since the passage of that law in 1966, Delaware's Division of Environmental Control had admitted that the county emitted 200,000 tons of sulfur dioxide every year. New York, with 10 million residents and many industries, put out 400,000 tons. There were only 350,000 people in New Castle County, however. The source of the air pollution was obvious.

The same was true for water pollution. In July, 1971, the *Evening Journal,* in an unusual display of candor, reported that "An analysis of a typical milk bottle full of river water from near the Delaware Memorial Bridge at the mouth of the Christiana River shows dissolved oxygen levels too little to support fish; and certain bacteria counts four times the permissable drinking water standards."[25] Du Pont's Chambers Works and Edgemor plants, which treated their wastes only on a primary level before dumping them into the Delaware River, shared responsibility with other Delaware, New Jersey and Pennsylvania companies. Yet Du Pont opposed water quality standards proposed by the Delaware River Basin Commission. Again, William Conner's amendments for the Water and Air Resources Act provided loopholes in the form of Section 6007's allowance for variance and waiver of public hearings *by the applicant* for a variance. Du Pont applied for the first two variances.

Section 6006, another brainchild of Conner's, called for "conference, conciliation or persuasion" in bringing violators into line. As Peterson's Attorney General, William Laird Stabler, put it, "the old things of conference, conciliation and persuasion should be part of" the state's enforcement efforts.[26] Stabler, a Du Pont in-law, assigned only one lawyer per day each week to work with the state Water and Air Resources Commission, which in 1971 was brought under the control of the governor's Department of Natural Resources and Environmental Control in a major governmental "streamlining" by an Economy Committee made up of 34 corporate executives full time and 18 more part time and financed by corporations and a $20,000 grant from the Du Ponts' Welfare Foundation.

The election of an ultra-conservative Democrat as governor in 1972 did not really concern the gathering at Reynolds du Pont's home. Sherman Tribbitt, after all, had introduced the bill in the General Assembly which granted the Du Ponts special tax breaks during Christiana Securities and Du Pont's court-ordered divestiture of General Motors. He could be expected to continue to respond favorably to Du Pont influence.

What really worried them was Mel Slawik. What if he should take his job seriously and try to do through the county government what no one had been able to get Dover to do?

In a real sense, it was what Slawik symbolized that alarmed the top Republicans that night. He represented a shift of political power that accompanied the movement of new job locations to the suburbs throughout the country, undermining the traditional control of the Republican Party in those areas. Slawik, moreover, was a representative of a blue-collar constituency that threatened to undermine the power of the landed gentry from southern Delaware who had traditionally run the Democratic Party. Du Pont in-laws such as lawyers G. Burton Pearson and William Potter had been big wheels in the Democratic Party, carrying out the family's traditional conciliation with segregationists south of the canal. Now along comes this Slawik, leader of a coalition of not only white blue-collar workers, but Black and Hispanic blue-collar workers to boot.

In such times of crisis, politics are more than the usual diversion for men like Reynolds du Pont and Pete du Pont. They are the major means of protecting their interests and control, the fastest way of getting things that they need done. From now on, the men decided at Reynolds' home, they would not repeat William Frederick's mistake. From now on, they would keep a close watch on Slawik's every move.

In the first few months of his term of office, Slawik confirmed their worst fears. His inaugural speech on January 3, 1973, shook the Brandywine. "I intend to change the image of county government," he said, "from that of a land planner to that of a community problem solver and a responder to citizen desires."

The *News-Journal* stories began to appear again. One charged Slawik with paying off political debts with jobs on the county payroll. Another pointed to a full-time professor being paid $100 a day as part-time consultant. Still another repeated the old charge that Geriatric Services money had been misused by Slawik during his campaign. When a campaign worker, Bayard Austin, hit a police car and refused to take a sobriety test, the *News-Journal* ran stories that pointed at Slawik. Austin had bought the car from Slawik and not changed its title until five months later. "Hell," the County Executive said, "It was as if I had had the accident!"

In some ways, he had. Slawik had trusted the man to change the title, and now the *News-Journal* was raking him over the coals for a minor incident. His own accident was ever trusting Austin.

The attacks grew more serious, however, after Slawik moved to fulfill his campaign pledge about reassessing industrial and residential properties. The crux of the matter was Delaware's Constitution. Article VIII, section 7 states very clearly that "In all assessments of the value of real estate for taxation, the value of the land and buildings and improvements thereon shall be included." There is no provision for any exclusion of industrial property in the constitution. And the constitution is specifically cited as the legal basis for the taxing of residential properties. Yet much industrial property had escaped being included in assessments since the constitution was first passed in 1897, when the only real industrial concentration to speak of was the gunpowder plants of Du Pont. Tax revenues due under the constitution for "state, county, hundred district, school, municipal or other public purposes" were simply never collected.

Slawik decided to enforce the state's highest law. And therein lay his greatest crime against vested interests, and his doom.

Within a month or two of taking office, Slawick's county attorney, Thomas Luce, had called in the representatives of Du Pont's Legal Department, Getty and other companies to express the county's willingness to "phase in" taxation on removable fixtures over a period of years.[27]

The county had already won a case in Superior Court against a group of private water companies which had appealed a decision by a county board of assessment that pipes, mains and conduits laid beneath the ground by the companies and storage tanks above the ground constituted real property and were therefore taxable under the constitution. The companies, led by Wilmington Suburban Water Corporation, held that the agreements they had with landowners had clauses asserting the right to remove the equipment. The question was whether a chattel that was removable was a "fixture" under the common law concept of real property. The Superior Court in 1972 held it was, citing as precedent a 1966 case, *Wilmington Housing Authority v. Parcel of Land,*[28] which determined that removability, while significant, was not a controlling factor. "The ultimate test," wrote Richard Peterson of George Washington University's National Law Center in his review of the decision, "was whether the annexor's *intent* was to provide for a permanent or a temporary annexation purpose." Based on this precedent, the Superior Court held that it was "inconceivable" that Wilmington Suburban "had actually contemplated removal of the items prior to the expiration of their useful life."[29]

In 1973, the judgment was affirmed by the Delaware Supreme Court in *Wilmington Suburban Water Corporation v. Board of Assessment* for New Castle County, 316 A 2d 211 (Delaware Supreme Court, 1973). From then on the county assessors in Delaware were free to apply the constitution and assess all manufacturing machinery and equipment that could reasonably be defined as fixtures, leaving to the assessor much discretion as to what fell within the guidelines.

Delaware was not alone in having a fixtures tax. In fact, all but 11 states in the Union tax fixtures in various ways. Only Delaware, however, had never attempted to collect what was its citizens' rightful due.

According to Slawik, Du Pont, Getty, and the other companies would not hear of it, rejecting the "phase-in" and promising, "You will back up on this." Slawick estimated up to $200 million in taxes were due.[30] Delaware's Citizens Coalition for Tax Reform, a non-profit organization headed by former Du Pont employee Ted Keller, estimates that the county should have received $10.5 million in taxes on the Getty refinery alone in 1982, as compared to the $904,625 it did receive. The major parcel of Getty's refinery at Delaware City is still assessed at only a bit over $15 million, while in 1957 Getty itself stated that the original installation cost "was over $200 million." Construction projects between 1978 and the fall of 1983 amounted to another $324 million, bringing the total value, excluding 20 years of intensive construction between 1957 and 1977, to well over $500 million.[31]

In 1974, the Slawik administration publicly announced that industrial fixtures would be assessed and taxed.

The tax was never collected. Instead, the Slawik Administration quickly found itself fighting for its life.

The first serious rumbles from the Brandywine were felt when Slawik began to move also on his pledge to review existing assessments of real property. An examination of county records revealed that Reynolds du Pont owned a house with 85 acres of property that was assessed for only $71,800, when it had actually been purchased in 1969 from Governor Russell for $130,000; under Delaware law, it should have been assessed for $91,000, or 70 percent of fair market value. Similarly, U.S. Senator William V. Roth, whose wife, the former Jane Richards, is a Du Pont in-law, paid $157,500 for his house and 6.7 acres in 1970; under the law, it should have been assessed for $110,250. The assessor, however, put a value on it that year of only $61,200, leaving $59,050 worth of Roth's property untaxed. Senator Roth ended up paying only $800, or the equivalent of what owners of $40,000 suburban homes had to pay.[32]

The revelation of these facts by the Nader Task Force on Delaware in January 1973 spurred Slawik to action. He and his aides began to look at the outside assessor hired by the previous Connor administration, Cole-Layer-Trumble of Dayton, Ohio, one of the country's largest appraisal companies. First they found that in Cincinnati, CLT's assessments in 1969 had generated some 9000 complaints. Often those who complained simply had their appraisals cut in half, without showing any documentation. Cincinnati paid $2 million for the assessment. In West Virginia, CLT's original $39.7 million figure for Continental Oil Company's subsidiary, Consolidated Coal, was secretly lowered to $28.4 million. When West Virginia discovered the discrepancy, it reassessed Consolidated at $40.6 million and barred CLT from the state, claiming it was "a little too close to the property owners." In St. Petersburg, Florida, the local newspaper uncovered the fact that of all the appraisal firms bidding for the city's contract, CLT had the most assessments thrown out when examined. Outside Cleveland, CLT appraised a chicken coop, described by the *Cleveland Plain Dealer* as "a dilapidated building with a roof falling down and leaking," as having a value of $10,840.[33] In Allentown, Pennsylvania, appraisals there also sparked resident protests. With major companies like U.S. Steel, on the other hand, CLT was charged with giving assessment breaks and a pro-industry bias by the Bucks County Taxpayers Association. In New Jersey, CLT encountered similar charges for its appraisal of U.S. Steel's land for 45¢ per square foot, when homeowners' land across the street had been appraised at $1.70 per square foot.

U.S. Steel had been a client of CLT's sister firm, American Appraisal Inc.[34]

But the worst and perhaps most revealing story came from Westmoreland County in western Pennsylvania, home of the Mellon family which controls Gulf Oil, Alcoa, and Mellon National Bank. There, in the suburbs outside Pittsburgh, CLT was charged with assessments biased in favor of the Mellons. Property values in Ligonier Township, for example, were allegedly increased by about 40 percent, while properties of the Mellon family, who own about 15,000 acres in the town, had been raised only 2 percent. Much of the Mellon land had been valued at less than $100 per acre; in one case, a 312-acre Mellon property was assessed at 64¢ an acre. When this last figure was published and a public outcry arose, Westmoreland County officials claimed a mathematical error and quickly adjusted the figure in par with the other Mellon assessments. Real estate agents, however, placed the real per acre value in the thousands.

Although the chairman of the county assessment board who reported these discrepancies was subsequently fired, County Controller Wayne Gongaware discovered that CLT had hired inexperienced high school and college students at $1.50 an hour to do initial inspection, and then sometimes even disregarded their work in favor of no first-hand evaluation. Instead, Gongaware explained, "They had their employees take the county's books across the street at night where their clerks erased the students' penciled-in writing and replaced it with the county's figures from its property tax cards,"[36] many of which were not even up to date. Gongaware estimated that most homes were increased 25 to 75 percent by CLT, while many industrial and commercial properties and land held by real estate interests had no increases despite state laws requiring uniform assessments. U.S. Steel's assessment was reduced $1 million; Alcoa's, $4 million. "What CLT did was cheating by fraud," Gongaware claimed. "When you deliberately erase records and put in our old records and then sell them back to the county for $1 million, that's fraud."[37] Confirming Gongaware's findings, county District Attorney John Scales petitioned county judge David Weiss to convene a grand jury; Weiss refused.

"It's unheard of for a judge to turn down a district attorney's request for a special grand jury," said Pennsylvania's Deputy Attorney General, Peter Brown.[38] Weiss later claimed he believed Brown and Gongaware were out "to get" county commissioner Jim Kelly; for his part, Kelly claimed that "this controversy is all a bunch of bullshoes."[39] The investigation was frozen. "It's just astounding what went on," Gongaware said. "We revealed it to the county commissioners and they just laughed at us."[40] At that point, Gongaware reversed his earlier refusal to pay CLT its final $121,000 due.

Suburbanite Mrs. Dorothy Shope and farmer Robert Shirey then decided to run for two of the three county commissioner seats in the local elections as candidates of the Association of Concerned Taxpayers (ACT), won, and joined Kelly on the commission. But Shirey's loyalty suddenly began taking a turn toward Kelly and both then excluded Mrs. Shope from executive sessions or failed to attend those she scheduled, even when she was actually the elected chair. Later it was discovered Shirey not only rented a farm from the Mellons but also received some $9000 of his $12,000 in listed campaign contributions from the Mellons. The largest came from Richard Mellon Scaife, who had shared John E. du Pont's penchant for writing $3000 checks to Richard Nixon's CREEP in 1972; in fact, 330 such checks for a total $990,000. Scaife has also given money to Delaware Senator Bill Roth.

Shirey, like many in Delaware who share the same fear about the Du Ponts, warned that "There are great dangers involved in pushing the Mellons too hard on the assessment question. There was once a time when I could pick up a phone and get a grant for a library from the Mellon Foundation, but now it's dried up. . . . You've got to be careful, the family could leave the county."[41] He threatened Mrs. Shope with a legal suit if that happened.

Mrs. Shope was learning that it was one thing to hold office and another to hold power. Whatever doubts she had about this were dissolved when she received an invitation from Pittsburgh's county District Attorney to visit his office. Robert Duggan, a middle-aged man with silver hair, was an old friend of Shirey, who was in telephone contact with him daily. Duggan was also an old friend of Richard Mellon Scaife. In fact, through his close relationship to Scaife's sister, Cordelia, Duggan had risen from Cordelia's private attorney to *consigliore* to Scaife himself. It was Duggan who moved Scaife into the nether world of ultra-right wing politics and backing Barry Goldwater and "the governor from Hollywood," Ronald Reagan. And, of course, Richard Nixon.

Duggan was rumored also to be an old friend of the underworld. When the IRS, investigating Duggan, contacted Cordelia to seek her testimony, she flew to Nevada and Mrs. Cordelia Scaife May became Mrs. Cordelia Scaife Duggan. The District Attorney's wife was thereby shielded by law from having to testify against her husband.

The IRS was thwarted, but other federal officials and reporters tracking organized crime began following a thickening trail of clues that led to the DA's office. In September, 1971, federal indictments began to come down. About this time, Scaife, who had backed Duggan financially in the past, is believed to have cut the DA loose. Juries subsequently convicted three of Duggan's key assistants. According to the U.S. Attorney, they were "in effect franchising all the numbers rackets in the Pittsburgh area."[42] Duggan's Racket Squad chief, Sam Ferrarro, was convicted of seven counts of taking $300,000 in bribes from organized crime figures for protection.

Mrs. Shope was innocent of Duggan's ties when she went to his office. But when, in the absence of her lawyer, Duggan suggested they meet Shirey for dinner "in a place where we won't be recognized," she walked out. "From that day on my life has become a living hell," she told *Harper's* George Criles III, who investigated her story for the *Washington Monthly*. Phone calls followed her to her house, even the courtroom, threatening her children. The brakes on her new car suddenly failed and the accident "totaled" it. Judge Weiss stated he was at last considering convening a grand jury—to investigate Mrs. Shope. "Here she is acting both as chairman of the commissioners and as a private citizen fighting the will of the commission. Who ever heard of such a thing?"[43] County records were then closed to the public. Robert Elston, chair of the Association of Concerned Taxpayers, had his car firebombed; he only barely escaped a second explosion by smelling gas and jumping out of his car. The local newspaper, the *Tribune Review*, concluded a six-part series by arguing that "politics" was behind "largely a contrived tax revolt."[44] the *Tribune Review* was owned by Richard Mellon Scaife.

Scaife ran his newspaper like a dictator, decreeing the end of reports on torture and killings by the Chilean military after the CIA-backed coup against Allende, ordering the destruction of all but smiling photographs of Richard Nixon, interfering with the news and firing editors and reporters alike.

The intervention of Ralph Nader, however, brought national media coverage to ACT's charge against Cole-Layer-Trumble and an investigation by the Senate Subcommittee on Intergovernmental Relations. It took time but CLT came under investigation by the state of Tennessee over the awarding of a major contract. After CLT's president, William Gunlock, was subpoenaed, he resigned.

District Attorney Duggan did not have so easy an exit. An hour before a federal grand jury indicted him for allegedly taking a minimum of $250,000 in bribes, Robert Duggan was found on the lawn of his estate in Westmoreland County, dead of a shot-gun blast into his chest. The weapon lay with the body. The coroner ruled it a suicide.

Even before his death, however, the controversy surrounding CLT in

Westmoreland County had attracted the attention of Slawik's aides. The Mellons had in the past been political and business allies of the Du Ponts, who held large blocks of stock in Alcoa, Gulf, and Mellon National Bank. The Mellons' renewal of downtown Pittsburgh with their "Golden Triangle" had originally been the Du Ponts' inspiration for their plans for downtown Wilmington. But it was Cole-Layer-Trumble, not the similarity of Mellon control over Pittsburgh to the Du Ponts' hold over Wilmington, which interested Slawik. Soon, however, the analogy between the cities became manifest.

As in Westmoreland County, Cole-Layer-Trumble's contract with New Castle County allowed it to use unskilled "listers," including high school students, to inspect properties. New Castle residents paid CLT $1.8 million for the contract, slightly below what Cincinnati had paid. In that city Fred J. Morr, who hired CLT when he was a Hamilton Company auditor, was asked at a county budget hearing why he gave CLT the contract. "Republican headquarters made me do it,"[45] he blurted, so regretting that admission later that he denied it. In New Castle County, Slawik aides found, CLT got its contract from the Republican administration of William Conner without having to engage in competitive bidding.

In March, County Executive Slawik asked Cole-Layer-Trumble to justify the $4 million reduction it had made in assessing Du Pont Company properties. CLT, Slawik had learned, had made the reduction afer negotiating with Du Pont officials who used data from a secret appraisal done by another company hired by the chemical giant, International Appraisal Company of Fair Lawn, New Jersey. International had admitted not knowing of any Du Pont-CLT negotiations which led to the lower valuations and suggested that its own study might show a total valuation actually higher than CLT's. When Slawik asked Du Pont for a copy of International's appraisal, Du Pont refused.

It was then that Slawik sent a mildly worded letter to CLT asking about reductions for Du Pont and other "large industrial and commercial complexes" amounting to a whopping $33 million. Only 132 individuals and firms accounted for this sum, 90 percent of the total $36 million in reduced assessments. "It is most difficult to justify such large reductions," Slawik wrote.[46] It was also expensive to New Castle homeowners. As CLT itself stated in a press release explaining its assumptions to the public before its reassessments were made, "Since a revaluation program does not raise taxes, and since those who have been paying more than their fair share will get reductions, it follows that some people will have to pay a larger tax bill to take up the slack."[47]

One such "fair share" reduction was land used as a parking lot at 1301 Market St. Owned by Du Pont Company, it had been assessed at $126,800.

CLT reduced it to $90,000. The previous figure had been based on 1950 property values that had long since risen. On the other hand, a private house at 726 Madison Street which sold for $700 in 1970 was reassessed by CLT at $2800; next door, another house sold in 1970 for $1200 had its assessment raised to $3200. It was clear who CLT's "some people" were and who they were not.

In the summer of 1973, the secretive headquarters of Du Pont made one of its classic bloopers. Applying to the Securities and Exchange Commission for clearance to purchase industrial property from the Holotron Corporation of Columbus, Ohio, Du Pont filed an appraisal done on a Holotron plant which Du Pont leased in the Delaware Industrial Park on the edge of Newark, the city which houses the University of Delaware. Du Pont had paid for the appraisal by a private Wilmington firm, Appraisal Consultants, Inc. The purchase of the property was being claimed as an investment expense by Du Pont for tax purposes, and cited the $300,000 worth assigned by the Wilmington firm in October 1971.

Under the state's 70 percent rate, that would mean an assessment of $210,000. But Cole-Layer-Trumble's more recent assessment was only $177,800 or 59 percent of the fair market value. At the time, Du Pont claimed an expense of $50,000 a year in leasing the plant from Holotron. And Holotron, it turned out, was itself a joint venture half-owned by Du Pont and half by Scientific Advances, a subsidiary of the research think-tank, Battelle Memorial Institute. Holotron, in fact, had been established to develop experimental photography techniques. By leasing from a company it half-owned, Du Pont could claim rental expense while it tested the new techniques; and its half-owned company, meanwhile, got a tax assessment break by Cole-Layer-Trumble, cutting back still further on taxes to the public sector. Later, when assured that the experimental technique would work and be profitable, Du Pont moved to buy the Newark plant, apparently deducting the purchase price based on the earlier and higher appraisal by the Wilmington firm as an expense also.

It was a neat trick, but what concerned Slawik was that the appraisal submitted to the SEC was the first such document made public, inadvertantly, that indicated a pro-business bias by CLT. The Slawik Administration estimated that over $700,000[48] would be lost to the county treasury that year because of CLT's underassessments of industrial and commercial properties.

Two reporters at the *News-Journal* papers, Robert Hodierne and Robert Frump, conducted their own study of New Castle residential properties and had to agree, to the chagrin of Du Pont elders on the paper's board, that something was rotten in Denmark. They found that non-Du Pont family properties were quite uniformly assessed at about the 70 percent rate due. A former CLT official, David Reed, who joined the Slawik team to head the county's tax assessment division, also uncovered glaring errors. But it was the Du Pont document by the Wilmington firm that indicated just how low were previous estimates of money lost to the county by CLT's appraisals.

That was money that should have gone to the county's public schools; one could only speculate on how much of the money the county had lost to Du Pont Company was instead transferred as dividends to Du Pont family members and ended up written off their taxes as donations to such exclusive non-profit private schools in chauteau country as Tower Hill, Tatnell, Friends, and St. Andrew's, all endowed by the Du Ponts. New Castle's public schools, meanwhile, remained underfinanced, its children culturally deprived in comparison to those offspring of the rich who enjoyed the high, better-financed standards a Tower Hill provided.

In a country like America, where the people put such a high value on education as a means to social mobility, a higher income and fulfillment of the American dream, such an inequitable tax system was a subtle but painful insult to the common citizen's striving for human dignity. Yet there were academicians in such corporate-endowed universities as Harvard or Yale, or even the private prep schools like Philips Andover or Exeter and, yes, even such exclusive primary schools as Tower Hill, who taught only the American dream, and not its reality. It was not surprising, then, that most young Du Ponts so easily took on the ideology of individual self-reliance of their parents, and, often, of their parents before them. Nor that they, in contradiction to that reality of their own lives, could embrace the ideology's attending belief that there are no classes in America, only individuals. Within that context, the average American was soon reduced, at worst, to the image of a ne'er do well, or, at best, the pitied object of *noblesse oblige*. More often than not, the idealized American was the solid respectable image of one's upper class father and mother, assisted, companioned, and ultimately awed by a retinue of upper middle-class professionals who dreamed of sharing such grace that comes from inherited wealth and raw power. That such elitism undermined respect for democracy goes without saying, proving that the children of the rich, too, could be culturally deprived.

Undaunted by such concerns, Mel Slawik moved forward with a $50,000 review of CLT's assessments by a team of professional appraisers. Holcomb and Salter Realty of New Castle handled apartment complexes, tract homes and estates in chateau country. The review concluded gross under-assessments were evident in most cases, averaging 21 percent below fair value. Henry E.I. du Pont's estate, for example, was assessed at $475,800, a full $100,000 below what it should have been. The industrial and commercial sites were checked by John Fortner of Appraisal Consultants, the author of the

Holotron appraisal. Du Pont's past was literally catching up with the company. Fortner did lower assessments for Du Pont's Brandywine Building, Country Club, Chestnut Rise Laboratory and Edgemoor Plant, but still found 43 under-assessments by CLT of the 60 properties checked, including Du Pont's Louvier's Building in downtown Wilmington. Slawik estimated at least $9 million would be added to the county's assessment rolls, producing additional school and county revenues of about $120,000 a year. Prompted by Slawik's review, Wilmington Mayor Thomas Maloney asked the city council for power to require all current exempt properties to reapply for exemption. Meanwhile, Slawik had pressed ahead with his plan to tax industrial and commercial fixtures. It seemed he was about to legally change the power base in Delaware and shift more wealth into the public sector. In 1973, also, a proposal for a 6200-person housing complex for a corridor of Christiana was adopted by the Republican-dominated county council. Another proposal for a shopping center in Greenville made by Daniel C. Lickle was unanimously rejected, 7 to 0. The defeat to Lickle, who is a Du Pont in-law (he is married to Nancy "Missy" Kitchell, daughter of William Kitchill and Irene Carpenter and niece of ultra-conservative "Bobby" Carpenter and second cousin of former Du Pont chairman Lammot du Pont Copeland, Sr.), seemed to signal the beginning of a new era.

To the Du Ponts, things were clearly getting out of control. But to smiling Mel Slawik, the will of the people was finally having its day. He was happily riding the crest of that will, at the peak of his power. He had no premonition of his coming fall.

2. SECURING THE HOMEFRONT

The Du Ponts had other reasons to be unhappy in 1973. OPEC's hike of Middle East oil prices, they knew, would eventually have a disastrous impact on the earnings of their chemical company, which used petroleum as its basic feed stock in the production of artificial fibers. The Watergate investigation was beginning to develop badly for Richard Nixon, their choice for president in 1972, and there was the scent of rebellion in the air. Across the nation, the opponents of everything they held dear—big business, privilege and nationalism—seemed to be rising with a new disturbing boldness.

Robert Vesco's illegal contributions to the president had been dragged into the glare of the media along with his embezzlement of some $200 million from his holding company, International Controls Corporation. This particularly embarrassed some members of the family who had been unable to restrain their lust for new capital and embraced Vesco in 1966 as a partner, then succumbed to his "fan dance," and allowed him to buy 80 percent of

All-American Engineering, the aviation engineering firm originally founded by their most famous aviator, Richard C. du Pont. To some, it was perhaps fortunate that the family hero of World War II had not lived to see their shame. Now it was left to his son, Richard C. du Pont, Jr., to salve the wounds inflicted by Vesco's pilferage and snap the reins to prod the firm beyond its recent losses. In October, "Kippy" had done just that at All-American's annual meeting of just 30 shareholders. "Once again Kippy has topped the ballot," one shareholder·commented. "He has a little clique that works for him, very well."[50]

Kippy's vision, however, extended beyond aviation those days. Like many in his family, some of his hopes centered on Christiana Securities, the family holding company that controlled Du Pont. Christiana's leaders, Irénée and Edward du Pont, were facing stiff resistance from a small group of Du Pont shareholders who had challenged Christiana's petition for dissolution before the SEC at almost the last moment, forcing more public hearings to be scheduled. It was these hearings, subject to the "wild card" of media coverage and political whim, that would determine if Richard's holdings in Christiana, like those of other relatives', could be exchanged for Du Pont without his having to endure either a large tax bite or a sharp plunge in the value of Du Pont's stock. The latter would undoubtedly occur if the family tried to unload its huge $1.7 billion holding on the open market. That was why the deal struck between Christiana's directors and Du Pont's officers was so crucial. Christiana holdings would shield them from the dangers of the public treasury and marketplace and keep their stock within the company, where their 23 percent holding would allow them to retain control. Then, if they wished, individual family members would be freer to unload their stock as they pleased. Diversification of investment beyond chemicals certainly seemed in order, at least for some like Richard who had other immediate concerns. Many in the family were hinting that oil stocks were the answer. Their value was sure to rise with earnings as OPEC provided a great leap in prices.

And then there was, as always, the trusted boon of real estate. Richard had already taken a small step in this direction—a minor financial interest in a condominium project in the lucrative Rockford Park Area of Wilmington, to be named Bancroft Mills.[51] There was only one serious problem for Richard's designs, as for those of real estate speculators J. Bruce Bredin of Bredin Realty and W.W. Laird of Rockland Corporation, two family members with sterling entrepreneurial spirits. And that problem was named Mel Slawik.

Slawik's investigation into New Castle County's tax base had stirred ripples of concern that were now widening throughout the state. Delaware had faced a fiscal crisis in 1971 and Governor Peterson had met it with budget cuts and taxes that put the onus on the consumer, who paid $14 million more each year in taxes and for items such as gasoline; corporations and wealthy individuals, on the other hand, paid only $4.4 million more in income taxes.[52] In 1972, according to Delaware's Controller General, seven Delaware banks, including the Du Ponts' Delaware Trust and Farmers Bank, had paid *no* 1972 income tax by May, 1972, and Wilmington Trust and Bank of Delaware, with combined net profits exceeding $13.5 million, paid only $635,000, less than 5 percent. Some residents, including Citizens Coalition for Tax Reform's cochairman Ted Keller, began to call for an end to the state's exempting of banks from paying taxes on income from dividends, certain classes of interest, and capital gains from intangibles, all important sources of bank profits.[53]

To answer the growing concern, a Delaware Tax Study Committee was formed headed by two leading Democrats, former Governor Elbert Carvel and Senator John Williams. Both men, however, had shown partiality toward the Du Ponts in the past. Williams had introduced the federal legislation that saved the Du Ponts a fortune in federal taxes during the GM divestiture. And Carvel, whose first term (1949-53) as governor was marked by anti-Du Pont opinions, had long since mellowed during his second term (1961-65), appointing H. B. du Pont to the state planning council, Mrs. A. Felix du Pont to the ad hoc goals committee, R.R.M. (Bobby) Carpenter, Jr., to the racing commission, and two other Du Pont lieutenants to the highway commission and his Administration of Justice. In fact, Carvel's administrations had helped cause Delaware's fiscal crisis. H.B. du Pont's influence in the planning council did much to help keep non-Du Pont heavy industry out of the state. The reason was blatantly political: the Du Ponts did not want the growth of blue-collar industries that could undermine Du Pont's control of state politics through its own white-collar bureaucracy and research force. But as a result, an important source of revenue was lost to the state treasury. As an alternative source of funds, Delaware followed the fiscal philosophy of a sister state, New York, then under the governorship of Nelson Rockefeller, and had begun mortgaging the state's future to bankers and private bond buyers, by 1963 raising its long-term state and local outstanding debt to the second highest in the nation. Within four years, further borrowing had given Delaware twice the debt of the average state in the union.[54] The Du Pont family's traditional fear of federal statutory and regulatory involvement in their companies and estates also levied a heavy toll on Delaware's ability to get its fair share of the federal treasury; its representatives in Congress were blatantly lackadaisical in seeking federal assistance. This pattern of behavior goes back to the Du Ponts' hostility to the New Deal of President Franklin Roosevelt. In 1942, for example,

Delaware received less federal money than any other state; the same was true for 1953 and 1957; all three years were chosen as representative by a U.S. Department of Commerce study of intergovernmental revenues. By 1967, Delaware was still below the national $77.68 per capita average with $72.87.⁵⁵ Clearly, Elbert Carvel was not part of the solution, but part of the problem.

Former Du Pont executive Russell Peterson only made the problem worse. Delaware's share of federal revenues declined still further during his first year in office, slipping to $78 per person as compared to the $100 per capita national average; by 1970, when Pete du Pont was elected the state's sole representative in Congress and William Roth was elected to the U.S. Senate, Delaware lagged behind even further in revenue-sharing, getting only $93 compared to the $119 average among states.⁵⁶ Peterson continued the Du Pont's traditional opposition to new blue-collar industries coming into the state, and brooked no opposition. When Emily Womack won the Democratic Party's only statewide office in 1970 as a state treasurer, replacing ex-Du Pont employee Daniel Ross, she soon found herself stripped of most of her functions by Peterson's newly reorganized state government. Under the governor's new "streamlined" executive, most of her power went to a new position, appointed by the governor—the director of the Division of the Treasury, for which Peterson chose Daniel Ross. Bank borrowing continued. In June 1971, Peterson was forced to call in an emergency session of the legislature and tell them that the state faced a $30 million deficit.

New Castle County Executive Slawik's approach, therefore, represented a new local alternative source of revenues for needed public services. As the second most powerful officeholder in the state, Slawik, with a mostly blue-collar constituency, also represented a serious threat to not only the Du Ponts' traditional rule over Delaware but also their plans for its future as a white-collar based headquarters for corporations and banks. Especially banks, if the family was to move successfully into finance after Christiana Securities' dissolution freed it of its 180-year-old industrial ties. In January, 1974, the president of Christiana Securities, Irénée du Pont, Jr., was named chairman of Delaware's State Chamber of Commerce. It was a measure of how much the family leaders saw Delaware as key to the clan's future. Only a year before, Irénée had underscored his commitment to preserving chateau country from changes. "I want to make sure this area remains a nice place to live," he said, "even if I do nothing else in my life."⁵⁷

With his new position, Irénée was indisputably the most powerful businessman in the state. He was already chairman of the Greater Wilmington Development Council which had already altered the face of Delaware's only real city. Residents who also wanted the city to remain a nice place to live but stood in the way of GWDC's plans for I-95 had been evicted. A similar fate met residents who had once lived where now a widened Delaware Ave. hosts a park, suitably named after GWDC's former chairman, Henry B. du Pont. Throughout the Sixties and early Seventies, GWDC, with its 66 board members representing Wilmington's major industries and banks as well as the Roman Catholic Diocese and University of Delaware, had been the state's powerhouse. Its executive vice president, Peter Larson, was Wilmington's city planner when most of the major urban renewal programs were formulated. Former Mayor Haskell's top assistant, Allan Rusten, had come from GWDC. On a state level, GWDC was behind the establishment of planning departments in both the county and state governments, as well as the Delaware Authority for Regional Transit. The chairman of one of GWDC's most active committees, Russell Peterson, even became governor. Yet, for all its power, and probably because of it, the GWDC refused to make policy suggestions on such crucial social issues as school desegregation.

The election of Democrats in 1972 to the top offices in Wilmington, New Castle County and the state shook the Republican establishment. Although GWDC still provided Mayor Thomas Malooney with his city planner, Malooney needed to assert his independence from the Du Ponts and chose as a developer for the city's planned civic center a company which was outside GWDC's charmed circle. Downtown Wilmington Inc., the GWDC subsidiary that had pushed the project along as the city's paid coordinator, lost its city funding and was obliged to finance the work itself in order to keep its coordinating role. The project, meanwhile, remained incomplete, with blocks of downtown real estate still empty. Then came Slawik's tax reassessment throughout the county, inspiring Malooney to seek a reexamination of the city's tax exemptions as well. The Du Ponts, led by Irénée, looked upon these moves as dangerous intrusions into their traditional prerogatives; if "they" were to be stopped, it would have to start with Slawik. Since he enjoyed popularity, loyalty and power on the county level, the assault would have to be made from above, on the state or federal level.

Irénée du Pont's assumption of the top office in the State Chamber of Commerce reflected this. His title, chairman, was a new one, part of the Chamber's reorganization along the lines of corporate management, with vice-chairmen and a president as well; the new treasurer, significantly, was from the Du Ponts' own bank, Wilmington Trust. Under Irénée's leadership, the Chamber began a concerted lobbying effort at the state capital in Dover to challenge New Castle's County Executive.

Slawik soon found himself confronted on a number of fronts. Questions were raised by the *News-Journal* papers about Slawik's relationship with contractor Mario Capano. The *News-Journal* emphasized the short time it took the county planning department to approve Capano's housing project, Taylortowne, and pointed to his friendship with Slawik and his remodeling of Slawik's home.

The remodeling, however, was no gift; Slawik had paid for it. Capano, a successful businessman who had been in the construction business for a decade, did give his friend a break, charging Slawik what it cost. But it was not free.

Nor were the 39 days it took the county planning department to approve Capano's project so quick when one considered the five months Capano had spent with county engineers and planners perfecting his plan. It was a wise investment in time, considering the Transportation Department's previous concern about traffic congestion in the area. Nor was Taylortowne a surprise to the council members. It had been talked about for months and the area had already been slated for development by the Republicans. Nor did Slawik take part in the final approval by the council. As County Executive, he did not have a vote on the council; in fact, he was not even present at the meeting. Nor did his party have control over the council. The Republicans did, and it was a Republican-majority council that approved Capano's project.

Yet, because Du Pont in-law Lickle's proposal for a shopping center was rejected by the council at the same meetings, and the Transportation Department did not oppose Capano's well-prepared plan, the *News-Journal* hinted at corruption and pointed at Slawik.

County officials were surprised when the State Attorney General's office announced it had actually begun an investigation. It seemed too blatantly political to be taken seriously. Slawik had long been at odds with Governor Sherman Tribbitt and had fought the Du Pont old guard in the state's Democratic Party. This cabal was led by former nominee for governor John H.T. McConnell and lawyer William Potter. McConnell, who married William du Pont's daughter, Jean, had headed up the Delaware River and Bay Authority and the State Highway Department, besides being president of Delaware Trust, an executive of Hercules Chemicals, and president of GWDC. Potter had also married a Du Pont, Alice Harvey, granddaughter of Victor du Pont and second cousin to H. B. du Pont's wife, Emily. He was president of the Copeland-Andelot Foundation, sharing trusteeship with Henry B. du Pont, Hugh R. Sharp, Jr., Lammot du Pont Copeland, Jr. and Alfred E. Bissell. Potter, 69, the senior partner of one of the Du Ponts' favorite law firms, Potter, Anderson and Corroon, had for years represented Delaware on the Democratic National Committee. He also represented

Copeland Jr. during his bankruptcy negotiations and, before that, had interceded with former House Speaker Sherman Tribbitt to push through the bill that allowed the Du Pont family to save about $48 million in state taxes during Christiana Securities and Du Pont's divestiture of GM stock.

But the investigation was serious, indeed. After all the fanfare given it by the *News-Journal,* its exoneration of Slawik seemed an anticlimax.

No sooner had the State Attorney General dropped this investigation than a new one was launched, this time on the federal level. It was ordered by the local U.S. Attorney, Ralph Keil, who had been appointed by Richard Nixon at the behest of Du Pont in-law Senator William Roth. Soon FBI agents were looking into every aspect of Slawik's life.

At the same time, Irénée had marshalled lawyers from the State Chamber of Commerce against Slawik's plan to tax industrial and commercial fixtures as mandated by the state constitution. Ordered by Irving Shapiro and Irénée, Du Pont Company attorneys also lent their talents to the cause, drafting a bill that would, according to Bruce Ralston, the Chamber's director of governmental affairs, modify the impact of "the State Supreme Court's decision through legislation."[58] The Chamber kept the drafting session secret, however, because of the state-wide elections. "The taxation of fixtures is an immensely complicated issue," Ralston said, "and we would have been in a real donnybrook if it had become an election issue."[59]

3. THE CASE OF THE MISSING RECORDS

Delaware's local elections in 1974 were indeed devoid of issues except one, thanks to Watergate: corruption in government. Pete du Pont had moved to distance himself from the fallen Republican vice-president and president by announcing in January 1974 that he would not accept campaign contributions over $100. The National Information Center on Political Finance did disclose that Pete had been among those Congressmen on the House Agriculture Committee who received campaign contributions from the same dairy industry associations that had made heavy contributions to Nixon's CREEP after he overruled the Secretary of Agriculture and ordered an increase in milk price subsidies. But Pete avoided any hint of scandal in the press. Likewise, in May, when he disclosed stock holdings of $2.5 million, including shares in a number of oil companies, no one asked if federal conflict-of-interest laws had been violated when he voted in Congress on oil-related bills. Nor did the press point out the contradiction between Pete's posing as an advocate of full disclosure and his failure to disclose the amount of his stockholdings in oil and other interests held in a beneficial trust.[60]

His Democratic opponent, University of Delaware professor James Soles, did criticize Pete for using his franking privilege with the federal mails right up until September, but federal law allows the privilege to extend to a month before an election.

Only when Soles raised the question of secret contributions to Pete's first campaign for Congress in 1970 did the state awake from its slumber. After the 1970 race, according to Soles, du Pont was quoted as saying if everything were known about the finances of the campaign, he and every other politician would have to go to jail.[61] Soles challenged du Pont to prove his campaign finances were aboveboard.

Pete balked. In a curious twist of the law's intent, Pete claimed that the old Corrupt Practices Act then in effect kept him from knowing or making public the details of his 1970 campaign finances. The Nader Report on Delaware, however, charged that "in the 1970 Congressional race, Pierre S. du Pont IV intentionally remained ignorant of the exact amount raised by his campaign committees to take advantage of a loophole in the federal law.... A candidate need only report monies raised directly for him, or funds which he knew about. Therefore, a candidate can purposely remain ignorant of money raised for him by committees and none of that money need be reported anywhere."[62]

Pete's 1970 campaign was financed by a number of such committees headed by his campaign manager, Glenn Kenton, his campaign treasurer, Henry H. Silliman, Jr. (Pete's cousin and Irénée du Pont, Jr.'s nephew) and his general campaign chairman, Edmund Carpenter II, partner of the powerful Richards, Layton and Finger law firm, and one of two sons of former Du Pont chairman Walter Carpenter. Edmund is well connected. He is married to E. Francis du Pont's daughter, F. Carroll (she had been married to a News-Journal reporter and Du Pont family author John Gates). He is also brother-in-law of Henry B. du Pont's daughter, E. Murton du Pont, cousin of Bobby Carpenter, and second cousin of Nancy, wife of Daniel Lickle of respected shopping center fame.

Of the three, 53-year-old Carpenter was the obvious political heavyweight. Kenton, a tall, shrewd and ambitious young man, had risen on Pete's star. Silliman's claim to fame, besides his $100,000 18-acre estate, was his mother's large holdings in Christiana Securities; as an "inner core" family member, he could be relied upon to keep a tight lip about the books he kept. Carpenter, on the other hand, was well known in national Republican politics, almost as much as William Potter was in Democratic circles. Edmund's $2,500 donation to CREEP was buttressed by another $27,000 donated by his father and brother W. Sam Carpenter. He had also chaired Delaware Citizens for Nixon-Agnew in 1968. As a fellow of the American Bar Association, former chairman of the state commission to reform jury service, past deputy attorney general of Delaware, and member of the Governor's Crime Commission and the Delaware Law Enforcement and Planning Agency, Carpenter had a reputation that the Du Ponts and many Delawareans considered unimpeachable.

It was probably for that reason that Carpenter, the titular finance chairman, and not Silliman, the actual treasurer, was given custody of the records of secret contributions after the 1970 campaign was over. Challenged by Soles four years later to produce the books, Pete replied that the old Corrupt Practices law required his keeping campaign financial records for only two years. Some had probably been thrown out, he said, "in the normal course of housecleaning."[63]

Soles refused to be put off. Pete had made a big deal out of his limiting contributions to $100, Soles argued, but the Congressman enjoyed the advantage of incumbency only because of a campaign based on unknown financing practices of four years earlier. If Pete had already been elected by big money, it would be hard to believe his newfound populist line was not merely an exploitation of Watergate and the public's hope for a restored political integrity.

Du Pont now fired back that Soles was "foolish and desperate." He attempted to demean the issue by calling it "silly," but the heat of public pressure would not fade. He acted as if insulted, protesting that "There was nothing illegal about the 1970 campaign."[64]

Perhaps, but Soles emphasized that the voter was being asked to take Pete's word for it, not exactly an uncompromised source. When Soles's charges made page one headlines on October 28, Pete called a press conference that morning and announced he was reversing his earlier refusal to open the books. It was "the ultimate triumph of rhetoric over substance," he argued, but conceded that he needed to maintain the confidence of voters. He admitted that about $150,000 had been raised in 1970, and although the records might be incomplete, the list of contributors could be "reconstructed" from them. Carpenter promised reporters that he would disclose the records later in the day.

He did not. Instead, that afternoon Carpenter admitted that the records had been burned.

How did that happen? Carpenter concluded that he had failed to circle them as files over three years old that were to be kept. He hadn't realized their fate until his personal secretary had informed him. No, he did not keep the records at his office, but in his home. He explained that it was possible that they were burned by his household staff during the spring. It was just as Pete had foreseen earlier: destroyed "in the normal course of housecleaning."

Soles was not about to challenge Carpenter's integrity. He was "a man of principle," he said of the powerful attorney, then asked, "Do you really think a candidate does not keep a list of donors and how much they give?"[65] There were, of course, other possible sources, including bank records of the campaign and donors or records of companies that did business with the campaign. But Carpenter claimed to have no knowledge of other records and no authority to look into the matter.

A list of donors was compiled by Pete from "general recollection." His father, Pierre S. du Pont III, gave over $3000, as did his uncle, Reynolds du Pont. Elise, his wife, gave from $3,000 to $5,000, and the Republican Boosters Club gave $10,000. Smaller donations were made by Irénée du Pont, Jr., Richard S. du Pont, J. Bruce Bredin, Richard C. du Pont, Edward B. du Pont, and his Texan brother-in-law Baron Kidd.

Many of these had been individually contacted by Carpenter and Kenton after Carpenter threw a quiet luncheon for them at Hotel Du Pont's Georgian Room in the fall of 1969.

4. SILENCING THE CRITICS

If the disappearance of the donors' records had any impact on voters, it was not discernable in New Castle County. The *News-Journal* papers treated it cautiously, and down-played Pete's connections to the Du Pont family, as it had in his last two elections. But the downstate newspaper, the *Delaware State News*, prided itself on its independence and had gained a nationwide reputation as a feisty, courageous hornet buzzing the Du Pont giant with a journalistic integrity rare for Delaware. For 25 years, first under its founding editor, Jack Smyth, then his successor, son Joe Smyth, the *State News* breathed freedom, purpose and outrage, attracting awards and many young idealistic reporters. It also attracted the ire of the Du Ponts and their *News-Journal* papers, whose salesmen threatened to withdraw their papers from any newsstand which stocked it when it first appeared, distributed grossly understated statistics on the *States News's* circulation to advertisers, and tried unsuccessfully to throttle the small downstate daily.[66] But the *State News* survived in Dover, pricking at the consciences of some journalists at the *News-Journal* who did have qualms about their papers' exploitation by the Du Ponts. One editor, Les Cansler, even bared his shame to the *State News's* Jack Smyth, writing that "I fear that our city editor pays little attention to releases, except when they come down from the Du Pont Building. Then he quivers with awe and follows instructions to a 'T'."[67] Under Joe Smyth, the *State News* moved to the offense, scoring *News-Journal* biased coverage of Governor Peterson and the University of "Delapont" repeatedly in editorials during the early Seventies. In 1974, it levelled a barrage of criticisms at Pete du Pont and the management of the Farmer's Bank. Joe Smyth was toying with the idea of expanding the *State News's* distribution into northern New Castle to challenge the *News-Journal's* monopoly over the area, and in 1972 had taken out a $630,000 ten-year loan to finance the paper's operations and growth, using its plant and equipment as collateral.

It may have been his greatest mistake. In October, 1974, when his reportage and anti-Du Pont coverage were at their heady zenith, the Farmers Bank served notice it would not renew the *State News's* loan unless a 10.5 to 12 percent interest was paid instead of the 7.5 per cent it had originally agreed to. Although the State of Delaware owned 49.3 percent of the stock of Farmers Bank, a system of scaled voting left the Tribbit government with little say on the board of directors; the real power lay with directors like chairman O.H.R. Baldwin, a director of E.I. du Pont's Continental American Life Insurance Company, Mulco Products, Wilmington Medical Center and Rollins Leasing; Alfred E. Bissell, chairman of Delaware Trust and partner of Laird, Bissell & Meeds, a trustee of J. Bruce Bredin's foundation and husband of Eugene du Pont, Jr.'s niece, Julia du Pont Andrews; J.R. Johnson, director of Hercules Chemicals; J.R. Horsey of the trust department of Wilmington Trust (he was also attorney for the state House of Representatives); and H.K. Dugdale and Alton F. Hillis, directors of Artesians' Savings Bank, in which J. Bruce Bredin, Irénée du Pont's brother-in-law, had a large interest and was also a director. Liberal Democrats such as Alexis du Pont Bayard and the late James G. Smith joined the Townsends in presenting another view, but Dixiecrats like former Lt. Governor Eugene Bookhammer undermined any solid front by the party of Jefferson.

Smyth remained uncowed. On October 27 he announced the *State News* was endorsing Democrat James Soles for Congress; Pete du Pont, he editorialized, "should be removed from office on November 5. The trouble with Pierre du Pont is that he's slippery, clever and ambitious at a time when the country needs members of Congress who are forthright, thoughtful and dedicated. Du Pont has developed an annoying habit. When questioned about an issue on which he should take a stand, du Pont politely refuses to do so.... That's clever and slippery, and the mark of a too-ambitious man. ...When you cut through the rhetoric and get to the gut issues, you find that Pierre du Pont has been a leader who doesn't lead, a talker who doesn't act, a profile without courage."[68] Smyth criticized du Pont for standing by "a corrupt president" until "in the end, even the nation's number one Nixon puppet, Charles Sandman of New Jersey, deserted the Good Ship Corruption ahead of du Pont." He scored du Pont's "vacillation" on Nelson Rockefeller's nomination for the vice-presidency. "If du Pont stays in character,

Rockefeller's brothers will come out against him before du Pont will.... To du Pont, 'election reform' is a program which allows him to spend two-and-a-half times as much money as his challenger." James Soles, "an obscure professor," on the other hand, "seems to know what he's talking about, and he seems willing to honestly share his opinions with Delawareans."

In that same issue, Smyth also began serializing a 600-page unflattering biography of the Du Pont family and history of Du Pont Company, *Du Pont: Behind the Nylon Curtain*. The series ran for six Sundays, making the exposé the state's top-selling book and one of the Du Ponts' biggest headaches. The reaction from Du Pont loyalists was immediate. Jack Costello, a white-haired 42-year-old former *State News* columnist fired by Smyth, dispatched a letter the next day suggesting Smyth delay the serialization until after the election and launch an investigation of the author. Smyth, citing his contract with the publisher, Prentice-Hall, calling for a certain number of articles before the official November 14 publication date, refused, but printed Costello's letter in the *State News* when the second installment appeared on the front page on November 3, just two days before the election. Neither installment mentioned the Congressman. But by then, Costello had already filed charges against Smyth before the Delaware News Council, accusing the editor of attempting to influence Congressman du Pont's chances for re-election.

The Council decided to meet with Costello on Halloween night. Smyth declined attending. "I have a feeling they're going to be getting into a question of prior censorship, and I don't want to be party to that." But he found the date "entirely appropriate." "The recklessness of his [Costello's] witchhunting and ghost-visions make the timing perfect."[69]

It took the News Council over three months to clear the *State News* of bias, and then only after its consultant, Robert Shaw, manager of the Minnesota Press Council, warned the Delaware Council that their consideration of Costello's demand that they request Smyth to suppress the serialization even temporarily until after the du Pont-Soles contest was over was a case of prior restraint endangering the freedom of the press. By then, some Council members' efforts "to prevent a similar case of 'poor taste'" in the future had come to naught.

Or almost. Du Pont, for his part, hastily called a final press conference before the election. He disclaimed any concern about the book and publicly disassociated himself from Costello's effort to halt the serialization or his charges before the News Council. He did make Smyth's editorials the focus of his anger, however, and singled out Smyth and news editor Charles Elliott for a "Tantrum of personal attacks" and "petulant raging against my name, my heritage and my family." Du Pont was furious at Elliott's poor rating of the Congressman's press party at his "Patterns" mansion and description of the "tent-like" dress his wife, Elise du Pont, was wearing. "He comes to my house, drinks my whiskey and insults my wife," du Pont said of Elliott. The *Delaware State News,* despite admittedly fair news coverage edited by Elliott, had fallen "far below the standards of decent journalism." But he had "no strong feelings" about the book, despite Costello's accusations.[70]

Then it was revealed that du Pont had met and talked privately with Costello on October 24, three days before the serialization began. Elliott knew this because he had seen them talking at an annual high school journalists workshop at Seaford High School on that date.[71] Du Pont and Costello admitted talking, but denied they discussed Costello's complaint. "I've never discussed that question with Jack," said du Pont. "I don't even recall it."[72] Costello charged that Elliott had claimed he had a "secret" meeting with du Pont rather than an open workshop, but only conceded that he spoke to du Pont in his capacity as a journalist. "Any newsman worth a damn will talk to the state's lone congressman whenever the opportunity arises," he wrote, and called Elliott's editorial about their private conversation "premeditated libel." He insisted that "the Seaford meeting, coming as it did, on Thursday, October 24, was three days before the first excerpt of the book was printed and therefore I had no knowledge of its contents until I read it the following Saturday."[73]

Yet, when informed in 1979 that du Pont had been subpoenaed by the author to answer questions about the meeting, Costello, a conservative, confessed discussing the book with du Pont and knowing enough about its contents to denounce its author as a "radical." "I simply stated it the way I saw it," he told the *State News.* "They ran this radical's book right at the moment he was running [for re-election] and I thought it was a coincidence. As I recall, he [du Pont] said he thought it was, too."[74] But Costello maintained it was he, not du Pont, who brought the book up, even though he had earlier stated in 1974 he had not had knowledge of its contents at the time. Members of both Pierre's family and Du Pont Company's hierarchy, on the other hand, did, thanks to their access to a leaked manuscript. Costello, rather, was peeved at du Pont for publicly brushing off Costello's efforts on Pete's behalf after it had caused such flack. "I took exception to that," he recalled. "I thought he [du Pont] could have said something a little more weighty about it."[75] He denied Pete had pressured him, but then Pete needn't have; Costello was only too eager to find some means of service. Later, backed by local Republicans, Costello launched his own Dover weekly, *News Week,* billed as "Dover's oldest weekly" in 1979. It was five years old.

The election of 1974 did not help the Du Ponts in Dover. The number of Du Pont affiliated memberships in the legislature dropped from 11 to 5 in the House and from 5 to 4 in the Senate. Among those defeated was

Reynolds du Pont's son, Thomas (who has since moved to Florida). Reynolds did not choose to run for re-election, but he did see his nephew, Pete, get re-elected to Congress, a necessary victory if the young scion was to fulfill his ambition to run for governor in 1976, as predicted in the exposé biography.[76] Pete never admitted hearing of the book or its author before 1974, although federal court documents show the author requested interviews in 1973 of both him and Reynolds, and that Reynolds, instead of replying, contacted Du Pont Company headquarters.[77] For there, on the 9th floor, a more serious and ultimately successful campaign than Costello's had been launched against the book.

It began as a secret investigation of the author, initiated when Irénée du Pont, Jr., was contacted in 1973 and asked to submit to an interview.[78] His decline was actually drafted by company officials. At the same time, the company found through the services of the Eleutherian Mills-Hagley Historical Library an informant by the name of Marc Duke who had been an acquaintance of the author and shared with him a common literary agent, Oscar Collier.[79]

In June, 1974, Du Pont Chairman Irving Shapiro was alerted that the book was to be published that fall. Du Pont's officials then sought backgrounds on the members of the board of directors of the book's publisher, Prentice-Hall, and "to reach out," if necessary, "through other sources."[80] Public Relations Director Thomas Stephenson wrote a memo: "Let's arrange to obtain and review a copy as soon as possible."[81] They did, within 24 hours, in fact. A Prentice-Hall salesman recalled receiving an "unorthodox" order[82] to drop a copy of the original unedited manuscript to Wilmington's Greenwood bookstore, "but what's a poor salesman to do when his boss tells him to do something?"[83] The bookstore had once been owned by William W. Laird, Jr., a cousin of Pete du Pont and uncle of Pete's future lieutenant in state government, Nathan Hayward III. A director of Du Pont, Laird was one of the most powerful members of the Du Pont family, a heavy speculator in New Castle County real estate and a large investor in E. I. du Pont's Sigma Trust Shares mutual funds. He was also a director of the holding companies, Christiana Securities and Wilmington Trust. In the last few years, the bookstore's ownership had passed to Colwyn Krussman, whose father was a Du Pont employee. It wasn't long before the manuscript found its way into the hands of another Du Pont family member and real estate speculator, J. Bruce Bredin.

Bredin, the dapper husband of Octavia du Pont, wore many hats over the years. Since leaving Du Pont Company in 1950 and later graduating to the board of directors, he had concentrated on real estate, the Artisians Savings Bank, Canadian companies (Terminal Warehouse, Ltd., and Baymond Corporation, in association with Reynolds du Pont) and had been vice-president of a secret Du Pont family front for investments around the world (including Germany) named Penas de Hicacos, based in Cuba until General Batista's fall to Castro's revolution. Because he had financed many scientific expeditions for the Smithsonian to tropical colonies like the Belgian Congo (1955) and the Caribbean isles, often using his own yacht, he was named a Fellow by the institution; similar bequests by his tax-free foundation won him a seat on the board of trustees of the University of Delaware. But if there was anything that marked Bruce Bredin it was his loyalty to his adopted clan. It was Bredin who allowed his eight-month-old baby girl, Alleta, to be used in a Du Pont publicity stunt, photographed in her crib with the caption "Fingered by Uncle Sam" in an attempt to discredit the federal government's GM divestiture suit.

Bredin's reaction to the manuscript of *Behind the Nylon Curtain* was predictable: after a cursory review, he decided it was "unfriendly"[84] and delivered it to the Public Affairs Department of Du Pont, where Vice-President Thomas Stephenson sent it on to Irénée du Pont, Jr., Bredin's brother-in-law and fellow stockholder of Christiana Securities and director of GWDC and Wilmington Trust. Du Pont's lawyers also gave it a closer inspection and concluded there was nothing the company could do at that time; no immediate action was recommended.[85] Within a month, however, word came to Du Pont through its informer, Marc Duke, that the book had been selected for distribution by a subsidiary of Book-of-the-Month Club, Fortune Book Club.[86] This meant the book would be widely distributed throughout the nation. Irénée and A. Felix du Pont noted "concern"[87] and, after Irénée left the country on an inspection of Du Pont operations in Latin America, the Public Affairs Department swung into action, reversing its earlier wait-and-see strategy. Phone calls were made—not to Prentice-Hall, the publisher, as would be expected if there were to be demands for "corrections" in the text—but instead to an old contact, Robert Lubar of Time, Inc. (whose *Fortune* magazine Du Pont mistakenly believed still controlled Fortune Book Club) and then to Book-of-the-Month Club warning that the manuscript had been reviewed around Wilmington by "family members and lawyers" and been found "actionable" and "scurrilous."[88] Book-of-the-Month Club officials quickly reversed the earlier selection by its editors, while Du Pont over the phone denied Prentice-Hall's accusations that the chemical giant had threatened litigation. After a hasty trip by Du Pont lawyers to New York to confer with BOMC officials the following week, this denial was finally put in writing in a letter to Prentice-Hall, although it did not rule out a suit "if and when the book is published."[89]

The ruse apparently worked; a "chill" of the First Amendment's freedom of press and speech settled in. Without informing the author of Du Pont's interference for over three months, Prentice-Hall secretly cut the print run by one-third so that the book could "not price profitably according to any conceivable formula"[90] and slashed the advertising budget in half. When rave reviews and the *Delaware State News* serialization (arranged by the author with a reluctant Prentice-Hall) nevertheless stimulated such sales that the first print run of 10,000 copies was virtually sold out within six weeks, Prentice-Hall's delay in printing another 3,000 copies allowed many orders to go unfulfilled for weeks. Meanwhile, according to at least two sources from within the company, Du Pont sent an official with a helper to buy up and remove copies from bookstores.

It was all too much for either the book's editor, Bram Cavin, or Prentice-Hall's own legal counsel, William Daly, to take, and they bolted, cooperating in an investigation by the *New York Times* of Du Pont's interference. The *Times's* subsequent article, "Club Withdraws Book on Du Ponts," in January, 1975, again stimulated orders that went unfulfilled, some in Delaware, until as late as March; by that time interest in the unavailable book had waned and Prentice-Hall refused to print any further copies, spend any more money on advertising, or to return the rights to the book to the author. (Although the book was quietly categorized as "out of print" by Prentice-Hall in 1976, rights were not formally returned in writing until legal pressure was exerted by the author in 1982.) Du Pont, meanwhile, encouraged unfavorable reviews by circulating an internal company critique of the book among sympathetic media outlets; at least in one case, however, Du Pont told the reviewers not to give Du Pont any public attribution. Du Pont's opinions then ended up in reviews with readers unaware of Du Pont's hand behind the scenes.

With the *New York Times* (which had printed a rave review of the book, calling it "something of a miracle,"[91]) Du Pont took a hard line. It launched an investigation of the reviewer, Robert Sherrill, similar to the one it had earlier undertaken of the author.[92] It also pressured the *Times* directly, requesting a meeting with Sunday editor Max Frankel not only to detail its distress, but to discuss, in broader context, the problems of "reviewing books about business."[93] Frankel asked Du Pont to "not wait for a visit here" and to explain "what problems" Du Pont exactly had in mind first to "help me in terms of sharing your thoughts with my colleagues."[94] Du Pont then responded that "it would be a futile exercise to confront the reviewer with a list of the errors and distortions in his review or to debate the merits of the book," and offered copies of two unfavorable reviews by the *Philadelphia Inquirier* and the former Philadelphia bureau of the *Wall Street Journal* as substitutes, commenting that "a major problem with reviews of books about business is that the reviewers often have little or no knowledge of the way business enterprises actually function, or have an insurmountable bias against business."[95] Du Pont chose not to pursue a meeting, and whether the *Times* accepted Du Pont's charge that most reviewers of books on corporations were either ignorant or biased, Frankel in his reply denied as "untrue" the *Wall Street Journal* reviewer's claim that the book was "merely a rehash and amalgam of a previous published work." But he did ominously concede that Du Pont had prompted the *Times* to "think some more" on "the expertise of our reviews of business books."[96]

Du Pont was pleased. "We achieved partial success," noted Public Relations Director Stephenson. "This is as good as we could have expected," agreed Du Pont lawyer Richard E. Manning. Stephenson would eventually be subpoenaed for questioning by the author during his federal suit against Du Pont for inducing breach of contract and Prentice-Hall for breach of contract. It would ultimately take eight years since the book was first published for the author to have his day in court (and, then, deprived of a jury because of a technical omission by the author's first attorney, William Standard of Rabinowitz, Boudin & Standard of New York; Standard was subsequently replaced by Ronald De Petris, former U.S. Assistant District Attorney, who was well qualified for the case: he had headed up the Justice Department's Fraud and Criminal Division in New York), and for Prentice-Hall to be convicted of killing off the book for "no legitimate business reason." But by then the book was quite dead, if not forgotten, and Prentice-Hall had fired for "non-productivity" the book's editor, Bram Cavin, who subsequently left publishing altogether in disgust. Du Pont, on the other hand, was let off the hook by a conservative Nixon appointee, Federal Judge Charles Brieant, its admitted attempt to limit the book's distribution with references to Book-of-the-Month Club about "lawyers" and "actionable" excused as an exercise of *Du Pont's* First Amendment right to freedom of speech. Brieant's decision on Du Pont, by removing the argued cause (Du Pont's phone calls) behind the effect (Book-of-the-Month Club's cancellation and Prentice-Hall's cutbacks in distribution and advertising) and his expressed sympathy with Du Pont's reaction to such an exposé, opened the way for Prentice-Hall to attempt a reversal with the one court in the entire country that the New York-based publishing industry considers the most important to its interests: the United States Court of Appeals for the Second Circuit, which includes New York.

In 1983, almost a year after hearing oral arguments, a federal appellate panel of three conservative judges appointed by recent Republican presidents reversed even Prentice-Hall's conviction. When it came to Brieant's letting off Du Pont, they agreed. Then, using that decision, the judges held that no motive had been proven for Prentice-Hall's action. Brieant, however, had held that his inability to discover Prentice-Hall's motives for acting as it did did not negate the hard facts of what it still did: kill the book off. The appeals judges arbitrarily chose to ignore that point and simply asserted that it had not been proven that Prentice-Hall had shown bad faith in its business judgment, and awarded the decision to the publisher, laying aside the book's promising sales record and the expert testimony by simply branding the book "a Marxist version of history" that "would not appeal to mainstream readers" but only a few ("presumably Marxists," as *Nation* magazine chided the judges).

The decision was, nevertheless, a testament to just how far the country had slipped since 1974 back into the McCarthyite climate of the Fifties favored by the ultra-conservative forces (including the Du Ponts) backing the Reagan Administration. "The Court of Appeals, in clear violation of Rule 52(a), did its own fact-finding," argued the American Civil Liberties Union (ACLU) and the Massachusetts Civil Liberties Union to U.S. Supreme Court Justice Thurgood Marshall in representing the author in 1984. "Such discrimination based on the content of a literary work is 'the essence of . . . forbidden censorship' under the First Amendment."

Predictably, the *News-Journal* repeated the political damnations in its news account and the column of Bill Frank, who joyfully titled his piece "The Perfect Ending," predicting "I can wager . . . that no publisher is going to issue another so-called 'exposé' of the Du Pont Co. or the family for a long, long time."

Whatever Frank's handicaps as a soothsayer, there were broader constitutional concerns that affected even him as a citizen. The problem was that the appeals judges had broken their own federal court rules, specifically Rule 52(a) of the Federal Rules of Civil Procedure. An Appellate Court is bound by a lower court's findings of fact unless the Appellate Court shows they are clearly erroneous. If the correct legal standards, in this case "bad faith," are applied, and the lower court finds the facts in favor of the plaintiff, the plaintiff wins. If there is some confusion about the lower court's findings in light of possibly wrong standards being applied, then the case must be remanded back to the District Court for further finding under the correct standards. The Appellate Court cannot simply ignore those findings and enter judgment for the defendant where the District Court's factual findings are in the plaintiff's favor.

Yet that is exactly what the appeals judges, led by an ultra-conservative Reagan appointee, Ralph Winter,* did. Although both the Appellate Court and the District Court agreed that "bad faith" in business dealings was an

---

*The other two judges concurring in Winter's decision were Sterry Waterman, an aging Eisenhower appointee, and L. W. Pierce, brother of Reagan cabinet member Samuel Pierce, the same head of Housing and Urban Development (HUD) currently being asked by Governor Pete du Pont to subsidize the construction of Chase Manhattan Bank's new $36 million credit card headquarters in Wilmington, Delaware, with a $10 million federal grant.

applicable legal standard, and no specific factual errors were cited in Brieant's decision, the Appellate Court did not remand the case back to Judge Brieant, but simply dismissed his findings of facts. Nor was it interested in seeing this case ever reviewed by the Supreme Court. To remove this possibility, the judges simply ignored also Brieant's decision for Du Pont under the First Amendment, and instead narrowed their own decision to New York law, agreeing with Brieant's finding that Du Pont's conduct was not coercive on Book-of-the-Month Club or Prentice-Hall's actions and therefore not a tort under New York law.

By violating their own federal court rules, a matter of law, and ignoring the plaintiff's right to have his favorable award against Prentice-Hall remanded back to the District Court for review, as well as by removing the federal constitutional issue through ignoring the First Amendment ruling by the District Court in favor of Du Pont, the appeals judges designed their decision in such a way as to lock up the case forever in their court and bar the author from further legal efforts to assert his rights.

Corporate censorship was now effectively upheld as the law of the land, with ominous national implications for the constitutional guarantees of freedom of speech and press. Once again, as with its lax 1897 incorporation law for corporations around the country, the Du Pont family had led America into a fundamental change in the structure of American law.

A similar local victory was won over the *Delaware State News*. In 1975, Smyth filed suit against the Farmers Bank, seeking $100,000 in compensatory damages and charging the bank with a "willful and malicious effort to retaliate" for articles printed in 1973 and 1974. The bank, according to Smyth, had attempted to "coerce" a higher interest payment in October, 1974, and then arbitrarily terminated the loan altogether in December.[97] Smyth managed to get refinancing through Baltimore's Maryland National Bank and the Wilmington Savings Fund Society, but it wasn't long before *State News* reporters observed that Smyth's independent character had gone through a dramatic change, becoming noticeably more conservative. Within a few years *News* editor Charles Elliott and investigative reporters Rolf Rykken and Don Glickstein had seen the handwriting on the wall and left. "What once was a bold, feisty and sometimes outrageous newspaper has lost its spirit, its soul, its guts," wrote one hold-out, reporter Jack Croft, in 1981, shortly before he, too, resigned. "A few years ago, owner Smyth decided to stop being a newsman and [became] a businessman. Shortly thereafter, the *State News* stopped being a newspaper and started becoming a business. . . . Downstate Delaware has lost what could have been a great little newspaper."[98]

Apparently, most of the news staff agreed. Four days earlier, they had filed into Croft's apartment to offer condolences to a stack of issues lying in wake in a borrowed baby casket. Twenty-three year veteran Jim Miller, the paper's first city editor, looked mournfully into the casket and said, "Doesn't it look natural?"[99]

Natural or not, the death of the *State News's* crusading spirit has been sorely felt in Delaware. "Now, it's an ordinary, respectable small-town paper," says the *Philadelphia Inquirer's* Delaware editor, Rick Edmonds, "without much impact."[100] Joe Smyth has resigned as editor and moved to Phoenix, Arizona, where his father's Independent Newspapers, Inc., has its corporate headquarters. Jack Costello's weekly, meanwhile, now called *The Sentinel,* is still in business.

5. THE THURSDAY NIGHT MASSACRE

The taming of such media storms as the *State News* and *Behind the Nylon Curtain* was still underway in November 1974 when the Du Ponts were confronted by yet another rebellion, this time at the heart of their control over northern Delaware's press: the *News-Journal* papers. During the previous year, reporters for the papers had confirmed New Castle County Executive Mel Slawik's charge of property tax underassessments, including homes of Du Pont family members, and although editors continued their disparaging coverage of Slawik, the papers also poked fun at such Du Pont family affairs as the annual Holly Ball, a Christmas-time party for the debutantes of chateau country, with proceeds going to charity in the true fashion of *noblesse oblige.*

The reason for all this was John Craig, a veteran *News-Journal* reporter and Wilmington native who had worked his way up to replace Du Pont Company's Chick Hackert as Executive Editor after the latter's death in 1970. Craig was backed for the job by Du Pont in-law Richard "Dixie" Sanger, who was Christiana Securities' uneasy appointment as president of the *News-Journal.* The board was reluctant to give Craig control of the papers, but Sanger insisted that Craig's independence would help the papers shed their image as Du Pont organs. Seeing the public-relations usefulness of this to win needed SEC approval if the desire of many family members to dissolve Christiana Securities was ever to be realized, Christiana's chairman, Irénée du Pont, Jr., threw his support behind Sanger and the board's resistance summarily collapsed, although Robert Carpenter, Jr., continued his criticisms.

Craig took his job seriously and wanted to put out the best newspapers possible. He brought bright young reporters and editors into the staff from outside Delaware, including three veterans from *Pacific Stars and Stripes,* John

Baker, Curtis Wilkie and Bob Hodierne. Some of the older staff members resented the newcomers, but the *News-Journal,* for the first time in its history, had begun to win many national awards. Wilkie was praised for his stories during the 1972 presidential campaign and the paper won the Public Service Award of the Associated Press Managing Editors Association. Although Irénée du Pont, Jr., forced the editors to print an endorsement of Richard Nixon by the owners (Christiana Securities) as a "View from the Top," Craig's insistence on independent news coverage reaped a harvest of controversial stories, including stories on the Nemours Foundation and Ed Ball's use of the Alfred du Pont estate, an analysis of serious problems at the family's brokerage firm of Laird, Bissell and Meeds, changes in Du Pont's pension plan, real estate dealings by Delaware Chief Justice Daniel Herrmann, and articles by investigative reporter David Walsh suggesting that Irving Shapiro had risen to power because no Du Pont family member, including Irénée, was capable of doing the job.

It seemed a dramatic, refreshing change.

Delawareans, accustomed to reading Philadelphia papers for news on their own state, were not used to it.

Nor were the Du Ponts. Irénée, Edward, Robert Carpenter, Jr., and others were pursuing their plan to dissolve Christiana Securities into Du Pont. This would mean that Du Pont Company would inherit the *News-Journal* papers. At first, Du Pont had every intention of retaining ownership, using a board of trustees of trusted academicians, "public" representatives, clergymen, and others to act as an advisory news council. But when the Nader Study Group on Delaware in 1971 criticized the pro-Du Pont bias of the papers in their book and recommended the sale of the *News-Journal,* the family, according to the *Philadelphia Inquirer,* was moved "to accept a fact they had already become painfully aware of—that control of the papers sometimes resulted in more bad publicity than it was worth—and they have had them for sale ever since."[101] If so, the family must have been aware of the Nader Team's criticisms during their stay in Delaware (Irving Shapiro personally accompanied the team during their formal interviews with Du Pont employees), because the decision to sell the papers was made in April, 1971, a full seven months before the Nader team had its report ready for publication. At any rate, in the summer of 1971, Irving Shapiro and Irénée du Pont met with in-law Rodney Layton of the family's top law firm, Richards, Layton & Finger, and *News-Journal* president Sanger and devised the trustees' plan. "The idea was to put it into effect as soon as possible," a Du Pont source told the *Philadelphia Bulletin,* "and definitely prior to the publication of the Nader report."[102]

The plan never came off because the Du Ponts could not decide how the trustees would be appointed or by whom. Whatever inclinations they might have had to pursue the plan, however, were overwhelmed by fears of loss of control during the following year's presidential campaign, when the editors refused to endorse candidates Congressman Pierre du Pont, Richard Nixon or Senator J. Caleb Boggs and even ran an unflattering cartoon of Richard Nixon. Although Craig was placated for the owners' "View from the Top" endorsement of Republicans by a board resolution that made him a vice-president with expanded powers, a strike that idled the *News-Journal* during the campaign did not impress the Du Ponts on the papers' board of directors. One of those was Irénée, who had just joined the board. Irénée took the line that the newspapers' assets were in danger. In early 1973, Christiana Securities intervened, according to Irénée, "in an effort to preserve the asset. We placed an experienced manager in charge of the board of the papers with the understanding he would use the office to provide financial and business leadership that was obviously lacking at the paper as it existed prior to that time."[103]

Yet the assets were so large, $24.2 million, that when Du Pont Company first learned of its size from appraiser Vincent Manno, the executive committee was shocked. The company agreed to pay the family that amount when the Christiana merger went through. From that moment on, the company's stake in preserving a financially lucrative operation for future prospective buyers ultimately outweighed all considerations about the paper's journalistic quality. Irénée, too, had the same stake in "preserving the asset," so it could be sold to Du Pont at the agreed-upon price. Business speculation, then, replaced journalism as the highest priority. The freedom of the press was soon for sale also.

"Maybe it's time we bit the bullet and sent one of our people over there,"[104] Shapiro told Sanger. The man they sent was David H. Dawson, 66, a senior vice-president and director who was scheduled to retire in September, 1973. In January, Dawson was asked to spend one-third of his time on the *News-Journal* "problems" as chairman of its board of directors, representing the owner. To help him in his new task, Du Pont Company provided the talents of two new employees, assessor Vincent Manno and Edward W. Barrett, former Dean of Columbia's Graduate School of Journalism. Armed with Manno's statistics on industry averages for editorial costs and Barrett's advice on production costs, Dawson quickly used budget cutting as his axe in attacking Craig's news operation.

The newsroom was particularly vulnerable. Its editorial costs were 46 percent above the national average and its employees had never formed a newspapermen's guild or union. Some of those costs were for machinery, including a $1.5 million photo composition system designed to reduce the number of employees. Dawson was committed to this expense. That left only salaries and operating budgets. *News-Journal* photographers were winning a host of awards, but Dawson considered that the outstanding ones were art, rather than news. The number of photographers would have to be cut. The travel budget would also be slashed; Delaware, it was argued, did not have to follow national stories like the 1972 election so closely, awards notwithstanding. Craig resisted the reduction in news coverage. "I think that attitude is patronizing of the community," he argued. "The people here have as high an income and intelligence level as the people in New York or Washington. They want the same kind of information."[105]

But it was precisely information that was being targeted. Dawson was particularly peeved about the stories on Irving Shapiro's rise and Irénée du Pont, describing them as "unforgivable."[106] Dawson put the blame on the editors. "I'd contact Dixie [Sanger], saying here's another example of poor editing," he later recalled. "I recognize that it's good to have reporters who are aggressive, but editors are there to restrain them."[107] Dawson claimed that "the board and many people in Wilmington" severely criticized Craig for slanted news, bad taste and liberalism.

Craig offered to compromise, but pointed to the board's Du Pont composition as the problem; he suggested a larger board, reflecting the community. It was his undoing. When earnings fell off in early 1974 with the general economy, his news department was set upon by Dawson's demands for another 10-15 percent cut. Craig had already vacated 16 editorial positions, reduced its portion of revenues from 14.8 to 13.9 percent and cut news coverage in the paper by almost 20 percent. Dawson's demands meant that more employees would have to be retired early or laid off.

Craig then made blunder number two. He convened a group of his five "best people" at the Red Fox Inn in nearby Pennsylvania on November 3, 1974, and set up a reorganization plan that called for ten job eliminations, including some of the Old Guard and one of Dawson's neighbors. On November 22, Craig and his team met Dawson at the Wilmington Country Club and presented their plan. Five hours of debate ensued, with Dawson resisting the forced retirements and lay-offs and raising Barrett's criticism of the time spent in compiling news from wire services, arguing that more time could be spent editing. "With all respect, Mr. Dawson," replied Hodierne, "that's bullshit." Dawson, used to the gentility of life at Du Pont's executive suites, was not used to being talked to like that. He disliked Hodierne, 29, who as the youngest fully accredited journalist in Vietnam and a winner of journalism awards had been called a "traitor" by an Army information officer for his *Stars and Stripes* articles. "It was John's first mistake," Dawson later said of Craig's choosing the newcomers over the Old Guard, "and led to effectively putting him under the control of the *Stars and Stripes* people. He was more and more entrapped."

It was an "outside agitator" line Dawson would use repeatedly in his campaign to reassert control over the papers. Although the *News-Journal* had run an unfavorable review of *Behind the Nylon Curtain* by a University of Delaware professor, Carol Hoffecker, which repeated false claims (about the author's supposedly rare visit to the family's manuscripts museum) identical to those made by Du Pont's Public Affairs Department in its secret internal critique of the book, the news editors' loyalty to the family was still questioned when a five-part series appeared during the week of December 9 on financial control of the University of Delaware, a Du Pont sacred cow. For Dawson, the series was "the last straw"; he confronted Sanger, reviewed the remaining articles yet to be run, and discussed firing Craig. The situation worsened when Lammot du Pont Copeland, Jr.'s *Commuter News Digest* ran a story by an ex-*News-Journal* reporter, Charles Wilson, indicating that Craig's newcomers were pushing aside older employees. But this was not news to Dawson. He had already learned from Sanger that second week of December that Craig had appointed Baker managing editor, Hodierne metropolitan editor, and Wilkie associate editor. What probably allowed Dawson to vent his furies was the decision handed down by the SEC the same day the Wilson article appeared, Friday the 13th. The Du Pont family, the SEC ruled, would be allowed to swap its Christiana holdings for Du Pont stock.

Dawson then countermanded Craig's promotions, even though Craig had been given power to make such appointments since his vice-presidency in 1972. Craig was now in an untenable position and wrote Dawson on Monday informing him that he still believed the promotions should proceed.

Desperate for a compromise, Wilkie and Sanger tried to enlist support from Du Pont Company's Public Affairs Department. Vice-President Thomas Stephenson, busy at the time in drafting his own secret letter of protest against the *New York Times* review of *Behind the Nylon Curtain,* listened politely and the newsmen left thinking Du Pont might come to the aid of freedom of the press. It didn't. Shapiro had endorsed their plan subject to a later independent study, and may have spoken once to Dawson, but he knew that the real power in the company resided with the family. He could only go so far without jeopardizing his own position, which he had no intention of doing.

Negotiations collapsed again with another Dawson refusal to compromise and on Monday, December 23, Irénée and Carpenter Jr. led the *News-Journal* board in vetoing Craig's promotions. The vote was 7 to 1, with only Sanger casting the opposition vote. On Tuesday, Christmas Eve, Wilkie sent another desperate plea in writing to Stephenson through columnist John Gates, an ex-Du Pont in-law who had married Stephenson's daughter. Wilmington Mayor Tom Malooney, hoping to save Craig's valued independent editorship, also called Irving Shapiro. But Du Pont officials refused to stop the confrontation. "It all hinges on who should run a newspaper," Wilkie summed up at a staff meeting on December 28, "chemists or journalists."[108] On December 30th, 64 people, including half the newsroom, registered their protest against interference in a petition to the board. Dawson replied on January 3, disingenuously claiming that "the only issue in dispute was a plan to proliferate the number of supervisory positions."[109] "Lies, lies, lies," Wilkie sadly concluded.[110] In fact, Dawson had himself admitted his concern about stories that "reported shortcomings of the Du Pont Company or various Du Pont family members."[111] In Dawson's view, the recent series on University of Delaware finances constituted the type of story that "the board would like to know about."[112] The board, in effect, wanted to review sensitive news articles before they were published. "Stories about company and family tax assessments, institutions such as the Holly Ball for Du Pont debutantes, the University of Delaware, and unionization of Du Pont plants," the editors later said, "were in the future to be handled with kid gloves or not handled at all."[113]

The blocking of their promotions forced Hodierne and Baker to do some hard thinking about their careers. Hodierne had turned down a higher-paying job in Louisville because of the promised promotion; Baker felt his professional reputation had been damaged. They sought legal counsel, who then wrote Dawson of their concerns and suggested that the editors had oral contracts for promotions. Dawson then moved to axe both men from the payroll. As chairman, he convened an emergency meeting of the board on the evening of Thursday, January 2, 1975. Du Pont in-law Robert Richards, Jr., who was the only member unable to attend, wired a recommendation the gist of which was that Craig should be fired. Dawson moved that Craig be stripped of the powers conferred on him in 1970 so that any editorial restructuring would have to first be approved by the board. The board passed the resolution and asked Craig to fire Baker and Hodierne. Craig did, allowing both men to be eligible for severance pay after the board refused any severance pay to those who quit. Then Craig himself resigned. The board refused to fire Wilkie, who had asked Craig to inform them he wanted to be fired by a chemist because no journalist would fire him. Wilkie forsook his severance pay and also quit.

The *News-Journal* staff, informed by Craig, was stunned. Baker, in one of his last official acts, turned to reporter Jack Murray: "Cover this," he said. Murray did, determined to be as objective as possible, including background material Craig had given him off the record, as well as statements Dawson made on the condition that they not be printed. Murray judged them to be of vital news importance to the community, and the next day Delawareans learned that Dawson said that henceforth the board would be "advised and consulted" before any articles were published that might be "particularly argumentative and disturbing to the community."[114] Baker, Hodierne and Wilkie were also barred from entering the *News-Journal* building after they left.

"The sacred cows are grazing more peacefully in Delaware today,[115] Hodierne stated after urging sympathizers to stay on and continue the fight for an independent daily in New Castle. But Assistant Metropolitan Editor Shaun Mullen, asked to write biographical sketches of the award-winning journalists he had just seen fired, could not go on. He resigned the next day. So did Special Projects Editor Jay Harris, whose articles (with staffer Ralph Moyed) exposing heroin traffic in Delaware had won first place awards from the Associated Press Managing Editors and the Greater Philadelphia Chapter of Sigma Delta Chi, the professional journalists' society. The Newark bureau's crack woman reporter, Marti Steward, also quit. "I wouldn't want to be part of a newspaper where the board controlled a newspaper over the objections of the editors,"[116] said Mullen. Hodierne understood. "For me," he agreed, "it got to the point where we couldn't put out an honest newspaper. And I couldn't put up with that."[117]

Eleven of the Old Guard, led by Public Editor Cy Liberman, leaped to the board's defense. It was an odd role for a journalist ostensibly representing the interests of the public, not management, to champion owners who sought to control the news, but then Liberman, a veteran of 33 years, was one of those whom Craig had slated for early retirement. "The situation has been misrepresented elsewhere," Liberman and his ten allies said in a circulated statement, "as part of an attack on the integrity of the *News-Journal* papers being made by former staff members whose ambitions for fast personal advancement have been thwarted."[118] Liberman followed that up with a similar echoing of Dawson in his "Public Editor" column on January 4. Some reporters who disagreed with Liberman, like Hugh Cutter, nevertheless could not bring themselves to follow the lead of Craig and the other editors. "We are caught between our own idealism and the reality of having a job before resigning,"[119] said the young reporter. But Cutler never did' resign. He remained, eventually settling into a niche in the newsroom.

The "Thursday Night Massacre" caused an uproar in Delaware. Governor Sherman Tribbitt, whose own top aide had been indicted as a result of *News-Journal* investigations, stated he was "gravely concerned that these actions could hamper the continued development of a free and independent press in Delaware." Hailing the "ever burgeoning aggressiveness" of recent reporting, he urged the formation of a citizens group to "preserve the intellectual and journalistic integrity of the *News-Journal* papers."[120] The presidents of the Delaware Bar Association and State Labor Council also expressed worries, as did the American Association of University Women, and a Concerned Faculty for a Free Press was formed at, of all places, the University of Delaware, defending the series on the university's financing as "factual reporting of information which is common to other states."[121] By January 6, the entire nation was aware of what had happened in Delaware when the *New York Times* ran a story on the upheaval, headlined "Du Pont Newspapers in Delaware Shaken by News-Control Dispute." On that night, some 250 Delawareans gathered to discuss the issue and set up a steering committee to offer to act as mediator.

Their offer was not accepted. In fact, some Du Ponts actually seemed quite surprised by all the commotion. Dawson denounced the governor's statement as "just politics"[122] while Irénée's brother-in-law, board member Henry Silliman, claimed, "This is just a case of sacking a guy who asked for it— Craig. This is not a case of Du Pont influence. It's plain ordinary people making the decision to get rid of Craig."[123] University of Delaware President E.B. Trabant rejected the governor's suggestion that he serve on the proposed citizens committee. It was "an internal management problem," he insisted. "I didn't read that any reporter has been dismissed for any reporting on any topic."[124] Then Dawson made matters worse on January 6. He "strongly urged" that the editors print his reply to the governor denying any interest in controlling the news. Wilkie called the statement "a deceitful document," and ended by reiterating Joseph Welch's rebuke of Senator Joe McCarthy, "Have you no decency left, sir?" Sanger, ever the tactician, labelled Dawson's action "a damn fool thing to do."[125]

Apparently, Irving Shapiro agreed with Sanger. Shapiro quickly fired off a press release denying any Du Pont Company involvement in the intervention. "The company maintains a hands-off policy with respect to the papers' treatment of news and editorials," he stated, "And will continue to do so. . . . Allegations have been made in the current controversy that the Du Pont Company has intervened or wishes to intervene in the editorial processes of the Wilmington newspapers. This is emphatically not true, and there are no solid facts which would support a contrary inference."[126] He did not reveal his part in sending Dawson, a Du Pont vice-president and director, over to the *News-Journal,* or his lending Barrett, a Du Pont consultant, to Dawson to advise him.

To some degree, it was true that the family, and not the company, were the prime movers. And this was precisely what Craig had in mind when he told *Newsweek* magazine that "people who suggest that the board is trying to protect the Du Pont Company interests are missing the issue. Many of the board members have no connection to the company. It was never a question of particular stories or sacred cows. They just didn't like the tone of the paper."[127]

This rings true in one sense. "Tone" is a matter of perspective, whether in art, music or politics. And families like the Du Ponts, observing from high in the upper realms of American society, are especially sensitive of any hint of corruption of democracy that may point in their direction or to their corporate managers; expressions of outrage are considered totally intolerable. "Tone," for example, was the identical complaint given by Irénée du Pont, Jr., and Du Pont Company officials in explaining to a federal judge their hostility toward a book contemporary to the *News-Journal* dispute, *Behind the Nylon Curtain.*

Yet Dawson's claim to the press that the issue at the *News-Journal* was really "the financial soundness of the papers"[128] and Sanger's insistence that his dispute with the board was over "essentially a business matter"[129] were not merely a ruse; they were also a paradox. For their very arguments underscored the symbiotic relationship between Christiana Securities and Du Pont Company; or, more precisely, between Irénée du Pont, Jr.'s drive to "save the asset" owned by Christiana by cutting costs exactly where most desirable from the Du Pont's own conservative political point of view—the news and editorial department—and Irving Shapiro's concern that the newspapers he had already agreed to purchase from Christiana as part of the merger would, in turn, be a financially lucrative property capable of easily attracting bidders when Du Pont put the paper up for sale as planned.

This obvious financial tie was the answer to Wilkie's puzzlement over Du Pont Company's behavior during the dispute. "I don't understand how the situation got out of hand," the young reporter later confessed. "For what happened is not in the best interest of either party. Du Pont either chose not to believe or didn't care. I'm surprised and disappointed they didn't step in to call off the dogs."[130] Wilkie, it seems, never understood that it was the family, not the company, which was master. Expecting the opposing general's hired army, in this case Du Pont executives, to be willing to play the role of cavalry coming to the rescue was a basic flaw in judgment resulting from a classic case of poor reconnaissance before the battle. It reflected the degree to which the disarming illusion of books like James Burnham's *Managerial Revolution,* with their promise of powerful independent corporate managers, has penetrated American society, including its journalists who normally pride themselves in professional skepticism. Wilkie's innocence was in his belief in a free press and that neither party gained from what happened. Du Pont Company did gain, despite the bad publicity; it was having its future property beefed up on the balance sheet. And the family gained also: the controversy killed off a move led by Sanger to turn the paper over to its employees, while cooling the interest of more liberal buyers who might well have felt, as Christopher Perry adduced, that "their offers will not be well received by a conservative seller."[131] With such economic and political stakes, the Du Ponts were not about to back down to Craig and his liberal *Stars and Stripes* group.

If there was any confusion about that, it was Wilkie's, not the company's. The family and the company understood exactly what their interests were; Wilkie's comments reveal that the editors were either ignorant of those interests or did not give them enough weight. Not understanding power and the willingness of those who wield power to use it if threatened, the editors were predictably shocked by the vehemence of the counterattack and their ensuing isolation. Wilkie's claim that the purging of him and his allies did not serve "either party" was at best naïve, for the immediate battle, while clearly provoked by Dawson, was ill-prepared; and that left Delaware's press vanquished and the Du Ponts triumphant. Wilkie's battle, therefore, was more valiant than his analysis was accurate. His statements, in fact, were strikingly reminiscent of those in the 1920's who, not aware of the economic and political stakes involved, bewilderedly ascribed an accidental quality to the First World War even as the system of rivalries for economic and political power which gave it birth prepared to deliver to them yet another terrible offspring, another wasteful and mutually destructive "impossibility" shaped by its origins into necessity. Power, itself, is seldom an accident; only its immediate exercise may be. With the Du Ponts and Shapiro behind the scenes, Dawson's appearance and his immediate attacks on Craig's method of operations was no accident.

Craig, contrary to Wilkie, seemed to understand where power really lay in this struggle, perhaps because he had lived so many years in the Du Pont fiefdom. But being a native Delawarean also has its handicap of illusions. Craig's comments to *Newsweek* about there never being a question of "particular stories or sacred cows," for example, obviously contradicted most of what he and the other editors had earlier stated, and was probably explainable as not only an effort to distance himself from the fired editors, but also as a manifestation of the naïveté characteristic of many Americans about financial power and those who hold it. "I'm absolutely convinced that what we tried to do here is in the best interest of the Du Pont family," he told Christopher Perry, son of a retired Du Pont public relations executive and publisher of *Delaware Today* magazine. "They're nice people. I've known many of them all my life. They're not robber barons. For the papers to be independent is in their own best interest, as irritating as it might be occasionally. It's in the company's best interest, too."[132] It was straight native Wilmingtonese, but it was Wilmingtonese of an earlier age, when smiling patronage reaped the rewards of good feelings for both the dispenser and the receiver, when innocence reigned before the challenge. But when the challenge came, an iron fist was revealed beneath the velvet glove.

The *Delaware State News's* Joe Smyth poignantly reminded Craig of his naïveté, publishing a letter Craig had written him four years earlier urging the *State News* to "give up that crap about the 'Du Pont house organ.'" Smyth, at the time facing his own mounting Du Pont pressure, pointed out that the source of Craig's dangerous naïveté was right under his nose. "The *News-Journal* newspapers are the prime source of information for thousands of Delawareans. Having those papers edited by the Du Ponts is like allowing the White House to run the *Washington Post*.

"But edit they do. Because, by God, this is their state. And in Wilmington, freedom of the press belongs to the family that owns it."[133]

It was not really surprising that Craig, one of those "thousands of Delawareans" whose consciousness was early shaped by the Du Pont-controlled "prime source of information" could develop such a blind spot, particularly when he was so involved in the actual *News-Journal* operation on a daily basis for so long. Nor was it any shocker that he defended his naïveté. That is true of all whose desire to do a good self-respecting job creates a need to believe in what they are doing and in those who entrusted them with the responsibility to do it. Such is especially true of many working journalists who must learn to seek the story while being sensitive not to tread on the toes of their wealthy publishers or the top editors they have hired. In a state like Delaware, Craig could be forgiven his innocence; his only real crime, after all, was taking his job seriously. For that he was cast from the tower of success, hopefully into the light.

But even if Craig insisted on not opening his eyes, Irving Shapiro, unencumbered by such native reflexes, recognized that others outside Delaware would not be so blind, especially after Dawson conducted a disastrous meeting with the newsroom staff—his first. Dawson began with assurances he was not there to dictate and ended with a reiteration of his demand to review "especially sensitive" stories for his suggestions and a warning that an editor who consistently rejected suggestions and showed poor judgment could face dismissal.[134] Ralph Moyed, who reported the meeting, raised the spectre of Watergate then haunting the nation in order to pinpoint the danger to the citizenry. "I am confident that the loss [of Craig and his top lieutenants] is especially appreciated because of what happened in Washington during the Nixon administration. I don't think, on balance, that many newspapers distinguished themselves in the early stages of the unraveling of the Watergate outrages. But they recovered. And in the process, they helped uncover the Nixon-Agnew plot to discredit the press so that the two men would be free to accomplish their goals."[135] He titled the column "Many Are Watching."

Many were, indeed, and not just in Delaware, but throughout the nation. There were already speculations that the scandal over Christiana's control of the newspapers might hinder its planned merger with Du Pont. When the Democratic governor made his call for a citizens committee, Shapiro could smell politics in the air. He knew that the proposal was not acceptable to the Du Ponts, and probably shared Dawson's feeling of being "heartened" by a group of Du Ponts and their political allies who seized the initiative from the Democratic governor and met at the home of Hallie and Alton Tybout, relatives of the former Emily Tybout, widow of H.B. du Pont, to discuss the issue and plan a public meeting the following night which launched their own "citizens committee." It would only be a matter of time, however, before this committee would no longer be able to hold at bay such groups as the Concerned Faculty for a Free Press, which had also endorsed Governor Tribbitt's proposal. Statements of gratitude for their concern would not be enough. An alternative would have to be introduced, and fast.

Charges such as columnist Norm Lockman's that Dawson might be insensitive to the professional responsibility of newsmen to report the news and the stain on their careers if they do not and other reporters subsequently do, underlined the need for an immediate change in image if not in substance.

This became even more urgent when the *Philadelphia Bulletin* pursued Tribbitt's question of a guiding committee of community leaders that would likely "take the form of a press council." Clearly, something new was needed on the scene. But while a *State News* might allow itself to be scrutinized by the Delaware News Council, as in the case of the serialization of *Behind the Nylon Curtain,* the Du Ponts would have none of that for their *News-Journal.* In fact, they ignored the Delaware News Council altogether, as did their critics, even though the charges against the Du Ponts about accuracy and fairness in news reporting were much more serious than in the *State News's* case.

The grand solution came, as it often does in modern Du Pont history, from New York, and its name was Norman Isaacs. A colleague of Edward Barrett's at the Columbia School of Journalism, Isaccs had once been courted by Charles Reese, a member of the *News-Journal* board, to come to Wilmington as executive editor more than a decade earlier. And for good reason. Isaacs was not only an editor but also travelled in the right circles among experts in what was blatantly called during the Fifties "cold war

674

propaganda" and "psychological warfare."* Isaacs was well acquainted with the Radio Free Europe crowd. In 1959, he had served on the State Department's "public affairs mission" to Yugoslavia (whose feud with Stalin had long inspired futile solicitation by British and American intelligence agencies) and also served on a task force on "Government and the Press" for the 20th Century Fund, a liberal think-tank directed by, among others, Adolf Berle. A key figure in intelligence circles, Berle had set up the intelligence division in the State Department during the Roosevelt Administration and after the war helped Allen Dulles and others set up Radio Free Europe and a host of other CIA propaganda operations focused on Eastern Europe and Latin America. Isaacs, like Berle, was both a liberal and a cold warrior, a political hybrid that flourished in the hothouse of the McCarthy era (Berle, in fact, was chairman of the Liberal Party), often shamelessly trying to prove its loyalty by out-Righting the Right in domestic politics while criticizing it for over-reliance on repressive dictatorships, military solutions and a lack of sophistication in foreign affairs. Eastern Europe, one of Berle's great concerns, became also Isaac's focus, and Radio Free Europe brought many a liberal together with ultra-conservatives they might otherwise have shunned.

This strange alliance included the Du Ponts. At the time Reece was trying to recruit Isaacs for the Wilmington papers, Du Pont's chairman, Crawford Greenewalt, was also chairman of the Free Europe Committee, Allen Dulles's organization of corporate sponsors for Radio Free Europe.[136] Collaborating with Dulles and Greenewalt was Harlan Wendell of Du Pont's Public Relations Department.[†] Nor was Isaacs a lone editor among these charmed circles; other liberals included Peter Grenquist,** the secretary of the

*Harry Haskell, later Delaware's sole congressman, Wilmington's mayor, and a confidante of the Du Ponts (his father was a Du Pont executive) also travelled in these circles during the Fifties. In 1955 he was assistant to President Eisenhower's Special Assistant on Psychological Warfare and Cold War Strategy, Nelson Rockefeller, who had succeeded Time-Life's C.D. Jackson at the post. In January, 1975, Haskell, in probably his last performance, took to the air waves in New York on the Long John Nebel Show to deliver an attack on the book, *Behind the Nylon Curtain*, that was so vehement that Nebel felt obliged to offer the author equal time.

†Subpoenaed records indicate Wendell was also involved in Du Pont's campaign against the 1974 Prentice-Hall edition of *Behind the Nylon Curtain*.

**Years later, as head of Prentice-Hall's Trade Books Division, testifying in the *Behind the Nylon Curtain* case, Grenquist would deny ever having met or heard of Harold G. Brown, the Du Pont official who made the phone calls that resulted in Book-of-the-Month Club's cancelling its contract with Prentice-Hall to have its Fortune Book Club subsidiary distribute the book. John Kirk, Prentice-Hall's Trade editor-in-chief, who suppressed press information on Du Pont's interference and subsequently with Grenquist fired the book's editor for "non-productivity," had also worked for Radio Free Europe's publishing arm, Free Europe Press, and two other publishing houses identified as CIA conduits before joining Prentice-Hall.

Columbia University-sponsored think tank, the American Assembly, who went on to become acting secretary of the President's Commission on National Goals where, at White House conferences, he "served coffee" to Crawford Greenewalt and Harold G. Brown of Du Pont's Public Relations Department; joining him there was also Dave Amerman of Prentice-Hall, publisher for the Assembly and the Commission. Prentice-Hall was also the secret incorporator in Delaware of the CIA's Pacific Corporation, parent of Air America. Editors and publishers, the record shows, had a big hand in the intelligence operations of the Fifties and Sixties, and probably still do.

Isaacs, obviously, was no lightweight when it came to managing the news. The *News-Journal* "board has delegated to me complete power," he announced on his arrival in Wilmington, and he vowed there would be "no more public fights between the news staff and the board of directors.... I've been delegated to operate the newspapers and if there are to be quarrels, they will be with me."[137] This took the heat off the Du Ponts and put the spotlight on a hired troubleshooter. Isaacs was accordingly named publisher, president and member of the board of directors of the *News-Journal*, while Dick Sanger was demoted to the hotseat of executive editor where he would have to put his friendly relations with the staff to a direct daily test.

The *News-Journal*, of course, hailed the change. The *New York Times* carried the announcement of Isaacs's appointment on the same day and same page that carried also its article revealing Du Pont's interference with *Behind the Nylon Curtain*, quoting the charge of Prentice-Hall's lawyer, William Daly, that Book-of-the-Month Club had "knuckled under" to Du Pont.[138] For Isaacs, however, there was only praise. He appeared the ideal choice, as associate dean of a school whose own magazine, the *Columbia Journalism Review*, had once run an article by a writer who called the *News-Journal* "no more than house organs of the Du Ponts."

The *Times* also quoted Craig's statement to the newsroom that Isaacs's appointment was "as welcome as it was dramatic." Impressed by Isaacs's Columbia credentials, Craig said, "I cannot conceive of these papers being edited under his leadership, except in the most professional manner."[139]

The manner was immediately evident. Isaacs consolidated his position with respect to the staff by naming Shaun Muller assignments editor, encouraging the young reporter to withdraw his resignation. To replace John Baker as metropolitan editor he named a 31-year-old native Wilmington resident, John Taylor, Jr., who had been with the *News-Journal* for eight years. Isaacs also quickly met with the "Public Committee on the *News-Journal* Controversy" and assured them he would report to the board only on "significant matters of business."[140] Any newspaper, he explained, is "a quasi public institution... a public utility in private hands." He suggested the group create a press council independent of newspapers and politicians to monitor regional news; the committee included former New Castle County Council President C. Douglas Buck, Jr., a Du Pont family member; a former special assistant to Governor Russell Peterson; Ernest S. Wilson, Jr., an attorney associated with the Du Ponts in the Northern Delaware Industrial Development Corporation; Du Pont family attorney L. Coleman Dorsey; the wife of future Republican Congressman Thomas Evans; a Du Pont marketing executive; and Rosamond du Pont. The Committee members announced they were satisfied.

Issacs, meanwhile, had told the *Times* he considered himself "a tough editor who will tolerate no outside interference."[141]

None was needed. According to Mullen, who subsequently left Wilmington and joined the *Philadelphia Inquirer*, the *News-Journal* coverage of the Du Pont company and family "tapered off to a trickle"[142] after Issacs was named publisher. This did not mean "investigative" journalism was cut out entirely; Issacs seems to have agreed with Dawson's urging that "the sooner we can get some good investigative stories in the papers the better" in order to restore the paper's credibility.[143] Under a two-year contract with Christiana Securities, Issacs's responsibilities included reviewing controversial articles. Soon it became apparent who was the target of a "restored" investigative journalism in the *News-Journal*: Melvin Slawik.

6. THE TRIALS OF MEL SLAWIK

When the *News-Journal* controversy first erupted, New Castle County Executive Slawik had been one of the first to express his concern for the integrity of the newspaper, even though it had made him, as Christopher Perry acknowledged, "a frequent target of *News-Journal* probes and articles."[144] Perry himself had run a slanted cover article against Slawik in his August, 1974, issue of *Delaware Today* in which some 106 negative comments overwhelmed 30 positive statements, and most of these were concentrated in the beginning and at the end to lend the article some credence to the unsophisticated reader. Until then, it was the *News-Journal* which had led the onslaught against Slawik's reputation. "I have never hated anyone in my life," Slawik was quoted by *Delaware Today*. "But I hate the *Journal* now. I suppose if you can learn to live in a concentration camp, you can learn to live with the *Journal*." After the *Delaware Today* article, however, the *News-Journal's* editors began to back off, and concentrated on other, more powerful targets, including the family which would ultimately fire them. Coverage of Slawik's efforts to pursue his plans to tax industrial and commercial fixtures took on a more balanced tone in the area's press as an ex-*News-Journal* reporter, Bob Frump, now working for the *Philadelphia Bulletin*, quoted Slawik's concern that "we don't want to drive anyone out of business with the changes. We don't want to hurt anyone too badly," but added his comment that "Taxes would be kept low with the new assessments, though, and that's a good thought."[145] The Frump article was a rarity in that it analyzed Slawik's planned fixtures tax with thoroughness and fairness, pointing out that "The plan could...dramatically lower property taxes paid by homeowners by shifting a heavier load of the tax burden to business and industry."[146] It also recorded Du Pont's opposition and its drafting of legislation in conjunction with Irénée du Pont's State Chamber of Commerce to attempt to set aside the state constitution with a piece of legislation.

That was on November 17, 1974. Five days later, the *News-Journal* entered its crisis when Craig's editorial team met with Christiana Securities' agent, Du Pont retired vice-president David Dawson. On December 7, the *Evening Journal's* Dover Bureau ran an article that confirmed that Delaware's tax and workman's compensation rates for corporations were the lowest of the Eastern industrial states studied by Ernst and Ernst accounting firm for the New Jersey Manufacturer's Association.[147] If the article was a surprise to Delawareans and a delight to the Slawik Administration for its exposure of facts that supported Slawik's plans, it was also short lived. Before another week had passed, Craig's editors were fighting for their jobs and their integrity. Mel Slawik, however, did not know his stakes would be even higher: his freedom.

When the *News-Journal* dispute hit the headlines, Slawik had reason to sit it out as a bystander happily wishing plagues on both houses. Instead, he spoke for the integrity of the newspaper. He was also wise enough to realize that no matter how much he disliked the way Craig had treated him, whatever the DuPonts put in Craig's place would probably be worse.

It was. Within a little over a year Mel Slawik, surrounded by *News-Journal* headlines screaming about corruption, would be sentenced to a year in prison for a crime of which he was never convicted.

Slawik's downfall was planned in the offices of Senator William Roth's handpicked U.S. Attorney, Richard Keil. The U.S. Attorney's office had spent thousands of dollars and hundreds of hours of FBI agents' time in an exhaustive investigation of Slawik's life. In the summer of 1974, Keil finally found a weak spot, a loose thread that could unravel the fabric of Slawik's whole career. What was so surprising was that it took the U.S. Attorney's office so long, for that same human thread had already tripped Slawik once and was well known as a problem for Slawik: Bayard Austin. In fact, Austin was such a disreputable and obvious weapon that his lack of credibility may account for why Delaware's federal prosecutors probably hesitated to use him; that they eventually did may also be a measure of their desperation. But it worked.

That summer, Slawik received a strange phone call. It was from his erstwhile friend, Bayard Austin, calling from his new home in Florida where he had gone to live after making such a mess of his life—and Mel Slawick's reputation—in Delaware. Austin was frantic. FBI agents had been swooping around, he said, and he had been subpoenaed to present himself before a federal grand jury in Delaware. They were apparently investigating him as part of a general sweep of friends of Slawik and Capano, the contractor for the Taylortowne housing project. Austin didn't want to go. He was scared by their claims that he was being made a "fall guy" and he might say something foolish, maybe anything to get them off his back. Mel had to come down and give him some advice, he pleaded.

Slawik was immediately apprehensive. "Bardie" Austin had already betrayed his trust. He had worked for Slawik in previous campaigns and Slawik had given him a job at Geriatric Services. Then came the 1972 race, uphill all the way, and campaign workers were not easy to come by. "Bardie worked hard for me doing odd jobs when I was running for County Executive," Slawik told Detroit radio host Lou Gordon in 1976, "but after I was elected Bardie evidently got carried away and did nothing but cause trouble for me. He drank too much, talked and lied too much, and was always getting in trouble and getting his name in the paper—and they always mentioned his connection with me. One incident involved his crashing into a County Police car while he was drunk; he proceeded to tell the Police Chief that he was a friend of mine and he'd have him fired. Finally I couldn't take any more so I had a job in Florida arranged for him by a friend, and Bardie and his family moved to Florida."[148]

Yet all that only underscored the fact that Austin was irresponsible to his friends and was capable of lying to them or about them. And Slawik was convinced Austin was now genuinely upset. Austin just might say anything he thought some overeager FBI agents might want him to say, especially if they could compromise him through possible legal problems, such as taxes. Slawik was unaware of how far the FBI might go to entrap its prey;* that would take the power of a Special Investigating Committee of the U.S. Senate to reveal, and that would not happen until 1976.

But Slawik did know that FBI agents had already spun some tales to alarm Austin. "He was typical of the kind the government manages to come up with," Slawik recalled to Lou Gordon, not attempting to hide his bitterness, "completely unstable, heavy drinker, and easily brainwashed. They told him

---

*The Church Committee revealed a wide range of FBI abuses of authority, including the keeping of files on congressmen's personal lives, illegal wiretaps, and false derogatory "leaks" about such civil rights leaders as Martin Luther King. The smear operations were carried on under the code name "Cointelpro" (counter-intelligence-project) and excused as national security concerns.

I planned to make him the 'fall guy' for all my crimes—whatever they were."[149] What was being insinuated was corruption of office, involving Slawik's relation to Capano's construction of the Taylortowne housing project.

Slawik decided to fly down to Florida. It was precisely because he didn't trust Austin's judgment that he brought along a friend as a witness as well as Capano to answer any questions Austin might have. They met at a hotel and the men carried out a rambling conversation reassuring Austin there was never any intention to set him up, that nothing illegal had been done, that Capano had never received any favors or kickbacks, and advising Austin to tell the Grand Jury the truth and that he had the right to invoke the Fifth Amendment if he was genuinely scared about something. Slawik believed that if Austin did decide to immunize himself Austin might feel freer to then speak the truth. The County Executive also warned Austin not to lie about anyone.

Slawik was apparently not suspicious that Austin dragged the conversation on for five hours, but he should have been. Austin had allowed the FBI to hide a tape recorder on his body. In fact, his phone call to Slawik had been bugged also and was actually an FBI ruse to draw Slawik into meeting with Austin in Florida in order to later charge him with "interstate racketeering."

A judge later threw that charge out of court. The fact that the tape showed that not one word had been uttered by Slawik about any illegal activity or corruption throughout the five hours of conversation must have caused some consternation among the FBI agents, if merely because of the quandary it put the U.S. Attorney's office in to justify the enormous expenses it was building up (they would ultimately reach an alleged $2 million). Slawik, meanwhile, returned to Delaware convinced that the issue was resolved, although U.S. Attorney Keil's earlier statement that he was "going to get Slawik" still gave him some cause for concern.

Slawik resumed his battle to enforce the state constitution's provision for a tax on industrial and commercial fixtures. Lawyers for Du Pont, Getty, Delmarva Power and Light, Diamond State Telephone, and Irénée du Pont's State Chamber of Commerce had been unable to pressure him to back down and had decided to mount a massive lobbying campaign to push a bill through the legislature in June that not only excluded manufacturing machinery and equipment from property subject to county taxation, but also some items already taxed.[150]

The *News-Journal* all but ignored the scandal of this attempt to lay aside the constitution by simple statute, and Bill 416, sponsored by Greenville's John McKay and Elsemere's Robert Byrd, passed the legislature and was signed into law by Governor Tribbitt on July 8. Bill 416 became 60 *Laws of Delaware* Chapter 194.

There was only one problem, which apparently Irénée du Pont and others at the Chamber of Commerce hoped no one would notice: the law violated the state constitution and a decision by Delaware's Supreme Court affirming the taxability of industrial fixtures.

Mel Slawik, of course, noticed the contradiction and he quickly had his county prosecutor, Thomas Luce, prepare a legal suit to test the law before the Superior Court. He intended to seek a declaratory judgment against the Chamber of Commerce's leading promoters of the bill: Du Pont, Getty, Delmarva Power and Light, General Motors, Chrysler, and the Northern Delaware Industrial Corporation.

Slawik soon found himself fighting a two-front war. *News-Journal* publisher Norman Isaacs, in the course of reviewing "controversial articles" before they went to press, had been approving stories that alleged corruption in the office of the New Castle County Executive. The headlines were sensationalist enough not only to sell newspapers but also severely damage the reputation of Mel Slawik. As the County Executive would soon learn, it could also prejudice any jury from the community, disclaimers notwithstanding.

So it happened that in the midst of this *News-Journal* campaign for honesty, law and order, Slawik was suddenly subpoenaed and hauled before a federal grand jury of solid well-heeled citizens investigating "corruption." For over five hours, Slawik was subjected to an interrogation by the U.S. Attorney's prosecutors. The questions were often vague. Did he, for example, advise Austin to tell the truth to these grand jurors? Yes, he had, answered Slawik. The prosecutor did not ask Slawik, however, if he had ever advised Austin on the Fifth Amendment. Nor did he ask Slawik if he had requested Austin to take the Fifth. Nor did he tell Slawik that his conversation with Austin had been taped or even inform the grand jury of the secret recordings.

Instead, the federal prosecutor simply left this grand jury and went to a second one that had been convened. There, in a scene reminiscent of a medieval Star Chamber, he revealed the existence of the tapes and argued that Slawik, in counselling Austin on the Fifth, had been attempting to obstruct justice and had lied to the first grand jury when he testified that he had told Austin to cooperate and tell the truth. Without ever questioning Slawik or giving him any opportunity to confront his accuser or explain his purpose in counselling Austin on the Fifth Amendment, the second grand jury handed the prosecutor the indictment he sought: 13 counts of obstruction of justice, conspiracy, and perjury. Three years of FBI investigations into charges of corruption headlined by the *News-Journal* had been unable to prove one instance of corruption involving Slawik. Yet the New Castle County Executive was now faced with the prospect of a ruined reputation and being jailed for years.

The *News-Journal* trumpeted its war against corruption. No investigation, however, was ever launched into the activities of Irénée du Pont or other members of the Chamber of Commerce then wantonly conspiring to break the highest law in the state, the constitution. Despite the pressure of an impending trial and lack of media support, Slawik pressed his case against the Du Ponts anyway, bringing a civil action against the six aforementioned sterling members of the State Chamber of Commerce. Of the six, three had Du Ponts on their boards of directors: Irénée du Pont, Jr., chairman of the Chamber, was a director of two, Du Pont and Delmarva Power and Light. The other, Northern Delaware Industrial Development Corporation, was billed as a "non profit" corporation and had among its directors Bernard Isaacson, a director, like Irénée, of Wilmington Trust and Irving Shapiro's closest friend, and William H. Frederick, son-in-law of Crawford Greenewalt and nephew by marriage of Irénée. Getty, General Motors and Chrysler were all companies in which Du Pont family members or their mutual funds owned large blocks of stock.

From the list of directors, however, one name stood out for its frequency: Irénée du Pont, Jr. Mel Slawik may not have realized it, but he was taking on probably the most powerful Du Pont of all.

November 10, 1975, is a significant date in Delaware's history, for on that day there appeared some manifestation of the furies descending upon the second most powerful elected official in Delaware. County prosecutor Luce announced the filing of the Slawik Administration's suit against the State Chamber of Commerce's leading industries. And Pierre S. du Pont IV, Delaware's sole Congressman, announced that the Labor Department of Republican Administration of President Gerald Ford and Vice-President Nelson Rockefeller would begin an investigation the following Monday into alleged "problems" at the Delaware labor department's unemployment office. Democratic Governor Tribbitt, the most powerful elected official in Delaware, suggested that the federal probe was politically motivated, a reference to Congressman du Pont's gubernatorial ambitions. The two biggest obstacles between Pete du Pont and the governor's mansion, both Democrats, were now tainted by federal investigations.

Norman Isaacs ran these stories together in the *News-Journal,* but continued parading the corruption issue around Slawik's name. When Slawik raised questions in 1975 about Greenville's zoning practices effectively restricting public low-income housing, the paper headlined that Slawik was charging Greenville with being unfair to Mario Capano, the Taylortowne developer indicted along with Slawik. The County Executive confronted Isaacs directly, pointing out that he had never mentioned Capano. Isaacs simply replied that the headline conveyed what the *News-Journal* believed Slawik actually meant.[151] There was no retraction.

But there was room for Delawareans to enjoy another folksy portrait of Irénée du Pont on November 30 by John Gates. "I was down in the basement trying to fix the oil burner," Irénée was quoted. "My wife started hollering. I knew the oil burner hadn't exploded. I was standing right there." Irénée's wife, it seems, had been startled by a pair of balloons drifting over the Granogue estate at about treetop height and one had settled in Granogue's long winding driveway. "We got in the VW," Irénée chuckled, "and drove down to see what was going on." Finding the balloon already tethered to a ground support car that had come onto the estate's grounds, Irénée was offered a ride. He couldn't resist. But he was no man's fool. Instead, he sent his daughter up first, "to test the thing perhaps," offered Gates, "and when they emerged safe and sound, Irénée ventured up himself." Delighted by the adventure, Irénée blossomed into rare magnanimity and invited everyone into the mansion for coffee, toast and juice. "We were out of eggs and bacon by then," the heir remarked.[152]

Slawik, meanwhile, was running out of time. The fixtures tax was still tied up in court by Irénée's lawyers, and as Christmas approached, New Castle County's poorest families, deprived of some assistance by Du Pont's decision in 1974 to sever its donations to the Urban Coalition,[153] paid a property tax that was 12.4 times as great a percentage of family income as that paid by the county's richest families, including the Du Ponts.[154]

At the end of February, 1976, Mel Slawik surrendered himself into the hands of the federal court for trial on the perjury charges. For two weeks, the *News-Journal* ran daily stories on Slawik and the prosecution's charges of corruption. The judge was James L. Latchum, formerly of the Potter, Anderson, Carroon law firm of William S. Potter, the Du Pont in-law whose domination of the New Castle Democratic Party Slawik had dared to challenge. Latchum, himself, had had his conflict with the County Executive, Slawik having been instrumental in defeating Latchum's bid for the lieutenant governorship.

Latchum did not step down, as the state's conflict-of-interest laws might have suggested. Instead, he proceeded to allow anything into testimony that made Slawik look bad, including unrelated allegations of corruption for which Slawik had never been indicted. Keil was not on hand, however, having stepped down from office during allegations about his part in a possible obstruction of justice; he was not indicted like Slawik. His replacement as U.S. Attorney was the former state attorney general under Governor Russell Peterson, W. Laird Stabler, a Du Pont in-law. Stabler, in fact, was brother-in-law to Nancy Kitchell, wife of Daniel C. Lickle, the real estate promoter whose proposed shopping center had been rejected by the County Council at the same meeting Capano's Taylortowne was endorsed. Stabler, therefore, had a potential conflict-of-interest, but he sat in on the trial conducted by his assistant and later participated in Slawik's ill-fated plea bargaining.

On March 9, 1976, the jury found Slawik guilty of three counts of perjury. Three days later, Governor Tribbitt removed Slawik from public office. On April 21, Latchum imposed a needlessly harsh sentence: four years in prison, more time as a first offender than most of the Watergate criminals received. Slawik's only break was that the sentences were to run concurrently.

The impossible had happened, and Slawik was warned he could expect little different in his coming trial for obstruction of justice under Judge Murray Schwartz. He was broke, with no job and little means to continue to fight for his exoneration. Predictably, his lawyer then suggested the second trial be "negotiated" out of court. Slawik considered the trauma a second trial would place on his wife and three children and thought it over. Laird's office, sensing what Slawik's lawyer did not, actually initiated the plea bargaining negotiations, however, and on June 11 Slawik agreed to enter a technical plea of guilty (but with no admission of guilt) to one count of obstruction in exchange for the dismissal of the remaining counts, the dropping of the charges against his friends, and a maximum sentence of one year and a day to run concurrently with the four-year sentence and not to commence until his appeals on that sentence were concluded.

"I don't feel that I am guilty of any federal violation," Slawik said to District Judge Stapleton, "but at the same time I've just gone through a long trial for perjury, and I wasn't guilty of that either, I really wasn't. But I got convicted anyway. My lawyer advises me that I have a substantial risk of, you know, being convicted on this one. And facing, you know, another trial, the time and so on, the long investigation, frankly, I just surrender, Your Honor. You know, I just want to get it over with....Again, I feel in my heart and my mind that I'm not guilty of these charges."[155]

The Third Circuit Court of Appeals agreed with Slawik on January 3, 1977, and reversed the perjury convictions. The court held that all three perjury counts of the indictments should have been dismissed; the case should never have gone to trial. The court specifically cited the U.S. Attorney's vague and ambiguous questioning of Slawik before the grand jury "which would trap an unwary, assenting witness 'in perjury.'"[156] Slawik petitioned to withdraw his plea bargain and requested a trial. But there still would be no justice for Slawik in Delaware. Judge Stapleton held that the technicalities of the law and Slawik's "voluntary" and sane decision required that the bargained guilty plea on the obstruction count must remain. Mel Slawik was sent to Allenwood Federal Prison.

By then, the political reform movement in New Castle County that Slawik had led was disheartened and shaken by the power of a single family and all but collapsed. County attorney Joseph Bernstein did continue to press the county's suit for a declaratory judgment that 60 *Delaware Laws* Chapter 194 was unconstitutional. In November, 1976, he succeeded in getting a motion for dismissal made in May by Du Pont and the other companies denied by the Superior Court. Getty, significantly, was represented by the law firm which bears the family name of the wife of Senator William Roth, *Richards,* Layton and Finger.

The movement's political momentum, however, had already been stopped by the 1976 elections. Those elections painfully demonstrated how Delaware, under Du Pont domination, had become such a queer political phenomenon. In most other states, the Republicans were hurt by Watergate; but in Delaware, in a bizarre reversal orchestrated by the Du Ponts, it was the Democrats who suffered. What Mel Slawik had lost because of the atmosphere against corruption generated by Watergate, Pete du Pont gained. Running on a campaign that made much of his voluntary ceiling on campaign donations and even more of contributions to Governor Tribbitt's race by high-level state employees, du Pont was swept into the governor's mansion under a slogan that seemed a deliberate answer to the *Delaware State News's* "no leader" charge during his 1974 congressional campaign: "*PETE du Pont, Leadership . . . for a change.*" Even one of Slawik's last supporters, Ted Keller of the Citizens' Coalition for Tax Reform, was lured from his previous endorsement of Tribbitt by the governor's refusal to tax Getty's fixtures and by Pete's implied promise that he would. "I'd look for an increase in business income taxes first, if an increase is needed," du Pont wrote to Keller, specifically citing Getty. "Perhaps surprisingly, Delaware's business taxes are among the lightest in this region and our personal income tax is the highest."[157] Keller was so beguiled by Pete's charm and his anger at Tribbitt that he released Pete's letter along with his own letter effectively endorsing du Pont to the press shortly before the election.[158] It was a move Keller would later regret.

A Republican, Mary Jornlin, replaced Mel Slawik's administration in New Castle County that year. After securing her control over county agencies, the new County Executive soon hoisted her true colors up the flagpole in front of the County building. In January, 1978, Assistant County Attorney Catherine Mulholland raised the unconstitutional nature of 60 *Delaware Laws* to her superior, County Attorney Joseph Farnan, Jr. "The statute clearly conflicted with the State Constitution; the problem then became how to proceed. Should the County tax fixtures, it would violate the statute; if it did not, it would continue to violate the Constitution." In reviewing the county's suit, she noted that "we are getting nowhere. Even if the Supreme Court finds in our favor, we merely go back to the Superior Court and begin at the beginning. We have already missed at least two tax years . . . due to the passage of time and the defendants' real interest in prolonging this suit as long as possible. I would suggest the County 'gear up' the assessment division, tax fixtures (in violation of the statute) and defend our tax thereafter based on the Constitution."[159] Her suggestion was rebuffed. Instead, in May, Farnan, acting for the Jornlin administration, withdrew the county's suit. Mary Jornlin subsequently married Vincent Theisen, an associate of the Du Ponts and treasurer of Hotel Rodney, and accepted a seat on the board of the Du Pont family holding bank, Wilmington Trust Company, where she now reigns in sublime bliss.

The Du Ponts' smashing victory over Slawik and the state constitution did not mean, however, that compromises were no longer needed in the post-Slawik era. They would be, at least until the Christiana Securities merger in Du Pont was finalized. The bill to cut the state's capital gains tax by 50 percent, for example, had to wait until the closing minutes of the 12th General Assembly before it was finally pushed through in July, 1976, by Irénée's State Chamber of Commerce, justified as a means of luring the wealthy to take up residence in Delaware. Although the law ended up costing the state some $10 million a year, it was championed by the Chamber's lobbyist, Bruce Ralston, as a cost effective attempt to stop a $3 to $5 million a year tax drain caused by "economic exiles who are forced into exile by these confiscatory rates. They won't stand for it because they don't have to."[160]

There was more than a touch of arrogance in that remark, and Democrat Representative John Ferguson resented the bill as a handout to the rich. "It's about time we did something for the little man,"[161] he said. But Pete's uncle, former senator Reynolds du Pont, would have none of that. "There are all kinds of reasons for going to Florida," he warned. The capital gains tax "makes it a little bit expensive to live here."[162] Reynolds, of course, was a multimillionaire.

By April, 1977, some legislators, seeing the cut as responsible for 25 percent of the state's projected deficit of $40 million, began to have second thoughts. At the same time, the Citizens Coalition for Tax Reform, involved in the effort to restore the capital gains tax to its original status, also wrote Governor du Pont asking if he had taken any steps to request an IRS audit of Getty Oil International's books. The FEA, Coalition chairman Ted Keller noted, had three weeks before included Getty in a group of 20 companies that had been accused of overcharging subsidiaries for crude oil.[163]

Asking the IRS in (it had earlier expressed a willingness to assess Getty's refinery in Delaware) was the last thing that Governor du Pont's corporate backers wanted. There were big plans for Delaware, and taxing business was not one of them. Financial power on an international level was. So was political power on a national level. There was no point in reviving any populist threats to those plans when so much time had already been lost crushing them. The Du Pont homeland was just settling back into its dull routine of acquiescence to powerlessness and apathy. The feisty *Delaware State News* had been brought to heel. The Wilmington *News-Journal* revolt had been smashed. An embarrassing exposé biography on the family had "disappeared" because, as Irénée du Pont put it, it simply was "a bad book." Pete du Pont's New Castle County Republicans had thrown the downstate Democrats out of the governor's mansion. And populist Mel Slawik, the troublesome County Executive who had raised the greatest threat to the clan's power in its 170-year history, was now locked up in a federal prison, smeared with disgrace.

Humbled and chagrined, the county government could be counted again as one of the fold. The family's control over the county's public libraries, its private Wilmington Free Library Institute, for example, was reaffirmed, despite the scandals of the embezzlement of $80,000 in mostly county funds by its director, Dr. Jack Bryant, and a law suit brought by an employee, Patricia Trivits. Trivits claimed she had been fired in 1972 because she "knew too much" and had resisted bookkeeping changes that discontinued keeping certain financial records on book purchases and invoices. When the *American Librarians Association Journal* charged the Institute with violations of due process, citing its failure to give her prior notice, probation status, or a fair hearing, Institute president Edward du Pont answered with a letter claiming Trivits had been fired for being insubordinate and incompetent. Trivits sued for defamation, only to see her case thrown out of court in 1976 by the ever-reliable Judge James Latchum, presider of the Slawik trial of the same year.

Edward, meanwhile, reaffirmed his ideological belief in the special qualities that wealthy private citizens and their private corporations bring to public institutions when they and only they decide, for example, how to spend the 90 percent of the Wilmington Free Library's budget provided by the county's taxpayers. In the midst of mounting criticism, Edward remained serene. "I still have the fundamental feeling," he decreed, "that the private sector can run things better than the public sector."[164]

Nor was this opinion shaken when the Newark and Greater Wilmington Leagues of Women Voters protested that county residents were not given equal access to library service and wrote letters to the Institute urging it to open its meetings. Edward's response was again regal. He simply ignored them. Until, that is, the Leagues in March 1976 released a report charging his Institute with an "independent, insular attitude" while taking county money, and urged more county government and citizen representation on its board as voting members. Edward then merely opened the Institute's meetings, leaving the board's original voting membership intact and the Leagues with a hollow victory.[165]

7. A CAPTAIN'S ODYSSEY

A similar "containment" strategy had been employed with problems surrounding Du Pont Company, such as charges that toxic chemicals were causing cancer among Delaware, New Jersey and West Virginian workers and that freon gases were destroying the earth's ozone layer.[166] Those issues would ultimately have to be dealt with on a national level. For the immediate, however, the main line on the 9th floor of Du Pont headquarters was one of non-controversy; a quiescent image of a willing listener to social concerns was what was needed to steer Du Pont through unchartered legal seas to its safe berth with Christiana Securities.

The captain, of course, was Irving Shapiro. Never before had Du Pont been placed in abler hands when it came to politics. Shapiro had proven his loyalty to the family for over two decades, ever since he had taken the antitrust expertise he had learned at public expense in the Justice Department and defected to the Du Ponts to help them battle Justice's efforts to force them to give up their monopoly over some of General Motors' purchasing accounts. It was this obsequious deferral to all things Du Pont, even more than his growing knowledge of how to manipulate the law in the interest of high finance, that led to Shapiro's sudden rise in the firm as the family's *consigliore*. He guarded their interests when Nader's investigators came around in 1970, sitting in on all their official interviews with Du Pont employees. He was the first to notify the company in June, 1974, of *Behind the Nylon Curtain's* imminent publication.[167] He deferred to their demands for the removal of the *News-Journal* editors and did not intervene. And in the Christiana merger negotiations he gave them the sweetest of sweetheart contracts.

"The deal is a windfall for the Du Pont family," said Du Pont shareholder Lewis Murtaugh, "and bad news for ordinary shareholders in E.I. du Pont de Nemours."[168] The deal called for an exchange of 1.123 shares of Du Pont for every one share of Christiana. This saved the Du Ponts enormous capital gains taxes they would have had to pay if Christiana had liquidated and turned its Du Pont stock over to its shareholders. It also allowed the family to escape paying double taxes on its Christiana dividends as well as its Du Pont stock; now only Du Pont dividends would be taxed, while the family could retain its direct 23 percent control. Furthermore, Christiana stock was discounted at a mere 2.5 percent of the price of the Du Pont stock it owned, instead of the 10 to 20 percent discount Christiana stock had traditionally sold at. The profit for Du Pont was a mere $55 million, far less than the amount Christiana would have been forced to pay if it had sold its shares on the market.

Shapiro remained unperturbed by the loss. He insisted that the lower profit was "the kind of money I like to see."[169] It was also the kind of money the Du Ponts wanted to pay, although no Du Pont would admit it to the press, anxious to protect Du Pont Company officials from charges of collusion and conflict of interest. Edward du Pont, for example, who helped Irénée negotiate for Christiana, claimed he had yielded to ultimatum. C.B. McCoy, who represented the company as chairman, said he had driven a hard bargain; he did not mention having any conflict-of-interest as a Du Pont in-law. Shapiro projected less bluster than McCoy. If he had tried to drive a harder bargain, he claimed, the deal would have slipped off the hook, as if it was he, not the Du Ponts, who had landed the prize catch. He did hook his own reward, however, even if the shareholders he was supposed to be legally representing did not. With unprecedented rapidity in a company normally known for its long executive climbs, he rose in four short years from assistant general counsel to senior vice-president, then chairman.

Shapiro had to pay a price for this in human companionship. After his appointment as chairman, he noticed that lunch conversations with old friends became more cautious. His weekly poker games, which he had enjoyed for 20 years as an escape from office tensions, were suddenly transformed into an extension of that strain. "I knew I had become a restraint on everyone else," he later recalled, "so one day I invented a fiction and I dropped out."[170] He attributed the breakdown in friendships that attend fears for promotion in the corporate hierarchy as "human nature." "I've probably built some walls around myself," he conceded. "But I simply must be in a position to make a decision based on merits. You don't want to be trapped and unable to move because the person involved is a friend."[171]

What exactly "merit" was, however, seemed to be dictated by Du Pont's profit concerns, and his subordinates, accepting this standard in their own lives as well, understood that their old friend was no longer playing the role of Du Pont Personified just in the courtroom, but now in daily life. "One of the trade-offs in a job like mine is that you have a lot of acquaintances but not a lot of friends," he told John Taylor of *Delaware Today.* "Anybody in a job like this lives in splendid isolation. It's a little lonely at the top."[172]

He compensated by immersing himself even deeper in Du Pont's tasks. "He's a workaholic," complained his wife, Charlotte, a shy, quiet trim woman who admitted her own conformity to the traditional conservative image of the corporate wife. "My main consideration is him. I feel I'm a part of what he's doing and I want to make it as easy as I can. I'm not a woman's libber as you can see."[173] Charlotte did not really share much of her husband's doings, however. As a young lawyer he was often gone for weeks at a time. "It was tough on the little children," she recalled, and Irving himself calls

that time "one of the most painful experiences of my life. My family has paid
a price for the fact that I've been occupied on a full-time basis with these
kind of responsibilities."[174] Even as chairman, when things were supposed to
be easier, Irving would come home and spend his evenings in the den,
poring over reports, while Charlotte would quietly sit next to him, reading
novels.

Diversions for the couple were rare: an occasional party with friends, a
quiet dinner, a baseball game played by the Du Pont family-owned
Philadelphia Phillies. They hadn't seen a movie in years.

It is a portrait of a man who was probably always a workaholic, racing to
outpace the ghost of early poverty and fulfill the dream of a father who
always wanted his son to be a lawyer rather than heir to a small dry cleaning
business. "I dreaded it," he said of his childhood years at his father's shop.
"You took the dirty clothes and had to mark each garment with a number. I
found it very distasteful to handle other people's dirt. I ducked out as soon as
I could."[175] His father was happy for him. "I think my father always had a
sense of frustration that he wasn't involved in intellectual pursuits," he said.
"My going to law school was a great vicarious experience for him. When I
was admitted to the bar, he visualized it as his being admitted to the bar."[176]
It was the first step in Shapiro's long odyssey in search of recognition and
acceptance.

It was a quest marked by a shrewd adjustment of his arguments to fit the
opinions and prejudices of more powerful men in order to lead them to his
own conclusion. "One of the things I did," he spoke of his time at the
Supreme Court as a young attorney for the Justice Department, "was analyze
how each of those justices functioned, what kind of approach each took,
what kind of arguments appealed to him and how that showed up in the
opinions he wrote."[177]

He had his own mind, of course; he realized that otherwise his usefulness
and value would be limited. But his method was the classic lawyer's
penchant for compromise and persuasion, rather than confrontation.

It was not a style the elder Du Ponts were used to in the early 1950's,
when an offer of an $11,000 salary brought Shapiro to the company to help
the clan fight his former employer's efforts to end their control over the
nation's largest corporation, General Motors. "When I came to Du Pont,
lawyers were treated like outsiders,"[178] he once remarked. And they were
outsiders. No lawyer had ever occupied the chairman's seat at Du Pont;
rather, they were seen as hired guns, legal mouthpieces, and occasionally,
advisors, but never as business or social peers. This was especially true for
Jews, the Du Pont family's anti-Semitism being legendary. Shapiro decided
to challenge that image by making himself indispensable, not only in the

GM litigation, but throughout the vast corporate subculture that is called Du Pont Company. He began attending sales and staff meetings to learn how the business operated and to convince the Du Ponts that early consultation with him could save them many headaches later. Over a period of time, he became their *consigliore* against the government and ultimately won their acceptance into the company's inner sanctum. But he was not invited to the family's intimate social gatherings or their exclusive clubs. In the real world of power, Irving Shapiro remained a hireling, an outsider still knocking at the mansion door.

He never showed resentment. Instead, he played the role of a wise Talleyrand before the Du Pont throne: he was competent, intelligent, useful, everyone's friend, a man one could confide in and be sure he would keep a tight lip. And a man who, in turn, seldom confided in anyone, a loner, even to some extent with Charlotte. His social discrimination only reinforced his sense of his Jewishness and he found some outlet for his frustration and fear of future holocausts in a political loyalty to Zionism's concept of an exclusively Jewish state in Palestine, becoming a leader in B'nai B'rith, the United Jewish Appeal, and a founder of the Jerusalem Institute of Management.

At Du Pont, he emphasized the personal approach, the mark of a man who wanted to be liked, and was. This, combined with his expertise in government negotiations, was exactly the quality the Du Ponts were looking for during the turbulent era of the Sixties and early Seventies, when companies like Du Pont were being challenged to accept some of the responsibilities and not just the privileges and rights of legally recognized "citizenship." Appointed assistant general counsel in 1965 during the last stages of the GM divestiture, he was nominated as a director, vice-president and executive committee member in 1970. "Shapiro has as high a level of admiration and acceptance by the departments as any man in the company," Chairman Charles McCoy told the Du Ponts. "It would be a popular choice which would give the organization added confidence in the flexibility of the present management and our merit system."[179]

Three years later, when he was named chairman, his promotion was billed as the corporate essence of the American dream come true, an image embraced by not only Du Pont's public relations office but also his own family. "When he told me he was going to be vice-president, I was so nervous, so shocked that I couldn't believe it," Charlotte said. "It just had never occurred to me that he might get an administrative post." Their son, Stu, himself a corporate lawyer, agreed. "A Jew simply does not become chairman of the Du Pont Company. In fact, a lawyer doesn't become chairman of Du Pont."[180]

But it was precisely because he was a lawyer savvy in the ways of government and public relations that he had been selected. "I had been doing these things (more accountability and work in community affairs) in my other capacities within the company, and I had prior experience with government matters of public affairs," Shapiro acknowledged, "so it wasn't a great transition for me. I think the people who chose me for chairman had the perception that the world was changing and Du Pont had better change if it was going to stay on top."[181]

The "people" he was referring to were the Du Ponts, represented by Irénée and other elders of Christiana Securities. Articles in the business section of the December 15, 1974, issue of the *State News* reflect just some of the problems confronting the Du Ponts. One article titled "Merger Faces Major Obstacle" describes how the SEC approval for the tax-free merger would require additional approval by the IRS; it also recounts the court struggle of Du Pont shareholder Lewis Murtaugh to block the merger on the grounds that Shapiro and McCoy's deal with Irénée and Edward du Pont was a profits "windfall" for Christiana. Another article that same day pointed out how Du Pont was one of eight companies convicted of price-fixing in selling dye and that scientists of the Environmental Protection Agency had testified that a Du Pont product, freon, was destroying the thin layer of ozone gas in the earth's atmosphere which keeps out some of the sun's strongest and cancer-producing rays.[182]

8. A DIRTY WORD CALLED CANCER

Cancer was a word Irving had been hired as chairman to disassociate from Du Pont's good name. Bad publicity for Du Pont might easily mushroom into a major obstacle for the Christiana merger. Irving's approach was two-fold: 1) express concern and the need for more studies and thus show signs of being a responsible corporate citizen while delaying a government ban; 2) threaten the nation with massive unemployment if it insisted on protecting its health at cost to Du Pont's profit margins.

The two tactics were employed simultaneously. Shapiro ran a series of full-page ads called "discussions by Du Pont to offer a perspective," that were classics of corporate propaganda. "You want the ozone question answered one way or the other," one ad was headlined, "so does Du Pont," whereupon a list of "Assumptions" were answered by "Fact" and "Research" drafted by the company's public affairs department. "Independent research," much of it financed by the company, was cited along with a list of the prestigious names of the universities with which the researchers were affiliated to back up Du Pont's assertion that there was "no conclusive evidence" that fluorocarbons were a world health hazard. "Should the theory be proven correct after all the evidence is in, Du Pont, as we have stated, will stop the manufacture and sale of the offending compounds. In the meantime, we believe that to act without the facts—whether it be to alarm consumers, or to enact restrictive legislation—is irresponsible. Final decisions cannot be made with only the information at hand."[183]

Charges that it was Du Pont that was being irresponsible were answered with threats. A Du Pont spokesman testified in Washington that a production ban could mean a loss of $8 billion to the U.S. gross national product and a loss of jobs for a bulk of 200,000 workers in various companies throughout the country.[184]

Before the public, however, Shapiro presented the image of responsibility. "We in industry can't do everything we might like to do," he told young businessmen at Junior Achievement's National Business Leadership Conference in Chicago in January 1975. "We must make intelligent choices from among our alternatives, and we are going to have to crank in much more than bottom-line effects to those decisions. How such decisions affect people, communities, resources and the environment is a factor that grows bigger by the day—and the sensitivity of industry leadership must rise with it."[185] Emphasizing people as investments by society and business who have a "replacement cost" of about $45,000 for high school graduates and $65,000 for college graduates, Shapiro championed "greater individuality and better utilization of human potential" before his youthful audience, stating "we have to recognize this increasingly by giving people not just pay but more say."[186]

Shapiro's speech was not just a call for sensitivity training for top corporate executives, however; it was also a challenge to them to "develop leaders to meet further government intervention with statesmanship and objectivity. It is time to end the historic confrontation between business and government." Shapiro wanted corporate leaders to take the initiative of leading America away from "politicians" and government. "Surely business leadership can read public concerns and evaluate them as well as the politicians. We should increasingly seek to take affirmative actions on our own in areas of justified public concern—and not wait until we are forced to action by legislation and bureaucratic decree. If business leadership comes up with more positive proposals for sound reform on its own, we should have a stronger voice in our own future, limiting the possibility some see that our economic system might someday become 'free' and 'enterprise' in name only."[187]

Shapiro's speech proved to be his debut in national politics. It was also to prove to be the debut of a new aggressiveness by top corporate leaders that would ultimately culminate in "the Reagan Revolution" against environmental, safety and health regulations.

It was a "Shapiro phenomenon" whispered only on the 9th floor of Du Pont headquarters but one which went overlooked in the over-confidence of liberals after the fall of Richard Nixon. Dazzled by Nixon's spectacular descent and the thunderous applause of self-congratulations, most reformers concentrated on the 1976 elections and paid scant attention to the design behind Irving Shapiro's Chicago speech and the subterranean currents of corporate power that were being stirred by his words. It was not until the middle of the election year, when Shapiro was elected chairman of the powerful Business Roundtable by the country's biggest industrialists, that labor and liberals began to see the danger.

Nevertheless, there were harbingers of the future to see in 1975, including Shapiro's failure to fully inform stockholders or Du Pont workers about incidences of bladder cancer at Du Pont plants. The issue was first raised in early 1974 by the National Cancer Institute's report that Salem County, New Jersey, between 1950 and 1969 had the highest rate of bladder cancer for white males in the entire United States. In January, 1975, *New York Times* reporter Mary Churchill learned from Du Pont that 330 employees at the Chambers Works, one of the world's largest chemical plants and located in Salem County, had contracted bladder cancer since 1919. One of the products Du Pont started making at Chambers that year was beta-nephthylamine (BNA), a chemical used in dye bases; within ten years, Du Pont workers began getting bladder cancer, and the company started sending a long line of patients to Johns Hopkins Hospital in Baltimore. In 1931, researchers identified links between cancer and BNA and benzidine, also produced at the Chambers Works. The Du Ponts continued to authorize its production. By 1938 Switzerland, a leading chemicals producer, banned BNA. The Du Ponts still authorized production. In 1949 the Manufacturing Chemists Association, an industry lobbying group, admitted "there is no known safe, allowable exposure. The only safe method of handling must be on the basis of no exposure whatever."[188] Still no ban by the Du Ponts. In 1952 and 1954, benzidine's carcinogenic potential was positively identified and confirmed. The Du Ponts continued production, and workers continued to die.

In 1955, the Du Pont Company ceased making BNA, but it was not until 1965 that the Du Ponts dropped the production of benzidine. By then, scores had died since 1950, 73 in fact, between 1950 and 1969.

In all those years since 1929, Johns Hopkins Hospital had made no public announcement warning of the dangers of working at Du Pont's Chambers Works. Dr. Hugh J. Jewett, who handled the cases sent in by Du Pont and was identified by Du Pont spokesman James P. Reynolds in 1975 as "the country's leading urologist when the bladder tumor cases were recognized as employment connected,"[189] refused comment. But in 1973, in a similar situation involving another company, Jewett had been quoted by the *Washington Post* saying, "It's none of my damn business to tell them how to run their plants."[190]

No one, of course, tells the Du Ponts how to run their plants. That is one of the main reasons they have been intent on keeping out national labor unions. In 1973, it was revealed that the Du Ponts were exposing their Chambers employees also to two other chemicals identified by the U.S. Department of Labor as cancer-causing: alpha-nephthylamine (alpha) and 4.4' Methylenebiso 2—chlorobenzenamine, an agent used to cure rubber and known by its trade name, MOCA. A petition was brought to the Labor Department and courts by the Oil, Chemical and Atomic Workers Union (OCAW) and the Health Research Group, founded by Ralph Nader. The Labor Department, hit with Shapiro Tactic Number One (insisting there was no evidence yet linking MOCA and alpha to human cancer, and asking for further studies), refused their petition for a ban on exposure. Du Pont production of MOCA and alpha was allowed to continue, although on a much lower level of exposure to workers. In December, 1974, the OCAW and HRG's appeal to federal judges in Philadelphia was thrown out of court.

The Health Research Group's and the union's actions did stir concern among Du Pont workers, however. Shapiro's executives had never informed the Chambers workers that the OCAW and HRG had asked for a *zero* tolerance, and the workers, while continuing to work under the Labor Department safety standards, warned they would refuse if the chemicals were proven to cause cancer in humans. Du Pont officials only admitted alpha and MOCA were "cancer-suspects." "How many dead workers do you have to have before you take action?"[191] asked HRG researcher Bertrand Cottine.

Workers at the Repauno plant ten miles north of Chambers were also concerned and asked Du Pont if OCA, which they make and sent to Chambers as a component of MOCA, could cause cancer. "We knew what kind of answer we were going to get," commented Bob McIlvaine, the local union's safety and health representative. "They assured us it was not." He persisted, requesting permission for the workers to shower before leaving the plant. "Our people work in it all day long and get it all in our skin and all in our clothes." Showers were already in effect at Chambers, but Du Pont refused. "Their argument," said McIlvaine, "is, 'What are you after? A paid shower?'"[192]

As the alarm was raised by information Du Pont denied the value of, company researchers began worrying about chloroprene, a chemical similar to vinyl chloride, a known carcinogen that Du Pont had been making since 1931. In December, 1974, they found two studies by Soviet health scientists suggesting links between skin and lung cancer and chloroprene. Some 3000

Du Pont workers had already been exposed. In March, 1975, a team of Du Pont scientists arrived in the Soviet Union to supposedly talk with the Soviet scientists who conducted the studies. They never met them. Instead, the Du Pont team talked with chemical industry representatives, complained about alleged vagueness in the studies, and returned to Wilmington. Company officials decided to give the chemical's profits, rather than workers' lives, the greater benefit of doubt. Chloroprene production continued at plants in Louisville, Kentucky, Texas, Louisiana and Northern Ireland. "Exposure is kept to the lowest practicable level,"[193] assured Du Pont's Reynolds. But Dr. Joseph Wagoner, director of the National Institute for Occupational Safety and Health's Division of Field Studies, was unhappy. "If I want to know about a health problem, I go to the health people."[194] Meanwhile, the president of the Louisville Du Pont union, Dudley Lacy, reported that company officials told him, "The Russian study didn't prove anything."[195] He was not told of Du Pont's failure to speak to Soviet health officials.

Queried at the annual meeting in 1975, Chairman Irving Shapiro repeated the official line. "They discovered nothing in Russia which changes our thinking," he told the stockholders and the public. "When all the data is in, a judgment will be made."[196]

Shapiro Tactic Number One. Tactic Number Two was already in effect in the minds of the Louisville workers. "You can smell fumes," Lacy remarked. "Whether it's chloroprene or not, I don't know. It appears to us that there's a large amount of death due to something. There appears to be a little too much of it." Then he added his fear that if chloroprene production was stopped, "all the jobs would be gone." He then retreated to Shapiro's position. "There's a big question, yes, but it should be studied more."[197]

Dr. John Zapp, director of Du Pont's Haskell Experimental Laboratory, admitted that his lab never tested chloroprene for its cancer-causing potential before Du Pont authorized its production and marketing.

Of the 800 chemical reports the Haskell Lab did prepare yearly, very few detailed studies were released. "They keep us uninformed on a lot of things," one local union official in Philadelphia told reporter Don Glickstein of the *Delaware State News*. "People don't know the full hazards of the kind of work they're involved in." Hazards were left to supervisors to reveal. "They're very safety-minded," commented the president of the Repauno local, H. Van Etten, "except when safety interferes with production. They say, 'We have the facilities, the experimental laboratory, we are very careful.' If we say we want independent testing, they block it."[198]

The director of the new Delaware Tumor Registry was Dr. Reuben Teixido. His computers, however, were not programmed to do an intensive analysis of cancers by geographic area, and Teixido not only held that researching victims by jobs and materials they worked with was far in the future, but that determining work-related conditions for even those cancer deaths already compiled by federal investigators for Delaware between 1950 and 1969 was an "enterprise frought with dangers of misrepresentation." Teixido worked at the Wilmington Medical Center, a position not to be envied when one considered that among the Center's trustees were Joseph Dallas, Norman Copeland, Robert L. Richards, Hugh R. Sharp, Jr., Crawford Greenewalt, and Charles B. McCoy, all Du Pont Company directors at the time.

It was these same directors who sanctioned Shapiro's efforts to undermine the Toxic Substances Control Act. Du Pont led the fight to weaken the bill through the Manufacturing Chemists Association (MCA), chaired by Du Pont president Edward R. Kane. Du Pont sought to strike from the bill a key provision which would have given the EPA the power to require testing before a new chemical is marketed.

Under federal law, any food or drug suspected of containing a chemical which might be carcinogenic must be removed from the market. For the sake of the health of the public, the chemical is guilty until proven innocent. The Toxic Substances bill, introduced by California's Senator John Tunney, sought to apply the same protection to workers on the job and to the public exposed to other chemicals. "The American public ends up being the guinea pig for these chemicals," Tunney's legislative assistant, Daniel Jaffe, pointed out. "Any kind of chemical can be put on the market with no testing. We're playing Russian roulette, and one of these days, the chamber might be full. You're putting the whole population at risk."[199]

Nevertheless, Du Pont insisted that profits derived from the chemical again be given the greater benefit of doubt. "The EPA administration [should] provide justification for any pre-market testing," argued a company position paper. Du Pont also wanted a provision forbidding the EPA from regulating a chemical if its manufacturer is regulated under law by other federal agencies. It insisted that this would prevent duplication and make the law more effective.

Jaffe saw this reasoning as nonsense and a ploy to escape EPA regulation. In the name of lowering government costs and inflation, Du Pont's provision would actually require an increase in government expense by forcing the law to be administered in a round-about manner; it would "really be socking it to the American public." Enter Shapiro Tactic Number Two: The MCA threatened that the bill's passage might mean an "excessive cost in complying with new regulations";[200] if so, the consumer could expect higher prices.

No one on the 9th floor of Du Pont headquarters could see any alternative. Certainly executive salaries and dividends could not be reduced. Charles McCoy, for example, only made $487,000 during 1975, his last year as chairman; and in 1974, he made only $701,000. Granted, it might take a typical chemist earning, according to the Labor Department, $34,476 a year, or an average engineer with an annual salary of $31,464, over 20 years to accumulate what McCoy made in that one year, but then these were hard times for everyone. Even the biggest Du Pont stockholder, Lammot du Pont Copeland, Sr., made only $1,526,989. Lammot might have been consoled, however, by the $116,000 in compensation he received as a Du Pont director and another $1,000,000 paid to his immediate family because of their Christiana and Du Pont stockholdings.[201]

9. A QUESTION OF CREDIBILITY

Holding the line against any further governmental interferences of these hard-working leaders of free enterprise was Irving Shapiro, the recipient in 1974 of a paltry $216,300 salary, another $85,000 in incentive compensation, and a $25,278 bonus on dividend units awarded previously. "Only a small mind would suggest" that he was motivated in the Du Pont-Christiana negotiations by a desire to protect and prolong his position with Du Pont, Shapiro testified in May, 1975, during Lewis Murtaugh's court suit against the merger. "I can't conceive of anything else I could possibly have done as one of the architects of this transaction."[202]

Many—on both sides of the dispute—agreed with him, and Shapiro acted indignant with those who did not. "I assume they're calling Mr. McCoy and myself liars," he said. Shapiro had learned that the best way to deal with any impugning of one's motives was to confront it directly, with feeling, if possible. During his 75-minute testimony at the week-long trial before Judge Murray Schwartz, Shapiro acted as if he was hurt, insulted, outraged; but he was always fully in charge, rattling the plaintiffs' attorney, Joseph A. Rosenthal, early in his cross-examination by challenging, "Are you suggesting we tried to deceive the Securities and Exchange Commission?"[203] If so, the lawyer was "wrong." Case ended. In December, Judge Schwartz made it official, approving the merger.

"The single overriding demand is credibility," Shapiro explained years later. "People won't follow you if you're not credible or they don't understand what you're doing and why you're doing it. You can't make anything happen unless people believe you are someone who speaks the truth."[204]

Du Pont lawyers were apparently not so successful when it came to their legal fight against government charges of discrimination. In June, 1975, their motion for dismissal against claims brought by the Equal Employment Opportunities Commission (EEOC) was rejected. The EEOC had found that a pattern of discrimination based on sex, race, and national origin existed in the higher job levels at the Chestnut Run and Christiana Laboratories. After two years of trying to reach an out-of-court settlement with Du Pont officials, the EEOC filed suit in November, 1972, charging Du Pont had violated the 1964 Civil Rights Act.

To hear Du Pont's public relations officers tell it, the mere presence of Shapiro, a Jew, in the chairman's seat at Du Pont seemed to provide enough of an answer to the charge. Irv Shapiro, after all, was a lawyer, an officer of the court, who studied the finer points of the law with a respect bordering on devotion. "To me," he would say later of the Supreme Court, "the justices were the great wise men." And the Supreme Court's rulings and the Civil Rights Act were the law of the land.

Irv Shapiro was also an honorable man. "When you ask Irv a question, you'd better be ready for a truthful, down-to-earth response," Bernard B. Isaacson once remarked. "He doesn't sugarcoat anything and his word is his bond." Isaacson, a director of the Northern Delaware Industrial Development Corporation which sought to stop New Castle County Executive Melvin Slawik's attempt to tax industrial and commercial fixtures, should have known. He was Shapiro's closest friend. As a homeowner in exclusive Greenville, Shapiro, of course, had his own reasons for opposing Slawik's plan to reassess the homes and estates of chateau country.

Yet, when a woman who was exposed to a Du Pont toxic gas leak wanted answers to what were the possible effects of exposure to the gases, how harmful the gas was to public health, and whether the company had paid the medical costs of any of the other gas leak victims, her queries were viewed as "irrelevant," "vague and unspecific."[205] She had to take Shapiro's lawyers to court to get her answers. Du Pont countered that the $2000 fine it paid for violating Delaware's clean air laws was irrelevant to her personal injury suit. The woman, Jacqueline Evans, was one of 21 people rushed to Wilmington area hospitals on the night of April 22, 1975.

A month earlier, the independent union at the Edgemoor plant had warned Du Pont officials about a chlorine leak. The workers were so concerned they filed a formal complaint with the federal Occupational Safety and Health Administration (OSHA), charging an immediate threat of death or serious physical harm. "The company has been disregarding safety precautions."[206] On March 2, according to the complaint, a pipefitter, James Bradley, was forced by Du Pont management to work for three days in the area where the gas was leaking, an "abnormally dangerous condition." On April 3 and 4, an OSHA inspector, one of seven working out of the local Wilmington office to inspect an estimated 12,000 places of business, visited the facility but issued no citation. On April 14, another worker was rushed to the plant hospital because of a gas leak and given oxygen for 20 minutes.

Then, at around 8 p.m. on April 22, a poisonous gas was released for a half an hour from the plant. Slowly, a cloud of titanium tetrachloride and chlorine gas, both listed by the federal government as Toxic Substances causing death in laboratory animals and/or man, passed over areas north and east of the city of Wilmington. Police rushed in to evacuate a movie theatre and seal off the area, while ambulances raced to hospitals carrying people vomiting, choking and coughing.

When questioned by newsmen about reports that companies are tipped off of pending "surprise" visits, OSHA officials denied such was the case and stated that their lack of staff did not hurt the quality of inspections. "What we do, we do thoroughly," said local OSHA director Alonzo Griffin. As for the small $140-$160 average fine rate levied since 1972, "We're not here to issue heavy fines against the employer or drive him out of business," Griffin said. "The main thing is to see that action is taken."[207] Then what happened with the April 3 and 4 inspections of the Du Pont Edgemoor leaks? Why were there no citations? Mark Durham, another OSHA official, asked the press to put the questions in writing. OSHA claimed its concern was balancing requirements of the federal freedom of information laws with its desire to maintain confidentiality with Du Pont.

Du Pont's response to what it had done about the employee warnings and complaint to OSHA completed the neat circle of argument: "There was no citation issued,"[208] explained Don Kasha, Edgemoor's employee relations officer. Apparently OSHA eventually overcame its fear of driving Du Pont out of business and fined the company $2000. Nevertheless, Shapiro's Legal Department rejected Ms. Evans's claim for $300,000 in damages, asserting a "mechanical defect" was not "gross negligence" and even if there was negligence, it was not a public nuisance.[209]

It was precisely such arrogance that sparked a new interest in national unions by Du Pont workers. Gathering in Philadelphia in June, 1975, 36 representatives from three independent Du Pont unions, including workers from Delaware's Edgemoor and Newport plants and Christina Laboratories, shared common tales of harassment by company officials. The harassment, they claimed, was a deliberate effort to stop the organizing drive of the United Steelworkers of America.

Out of some 84,000 Du Pont workers, there were only 32 independent unions of more than 100 members each; most of the plants had no union at all. The Steelworkers' drive, led by Elmer Chatak, had been successful in getting the endorsement of the executive boards of 13 of the independent unions, and Du Pont Headquarters was clearly getting worried. The rave reviews the Steelworkers paper, *Steel Labor,* gave *Behind the Nylon Curtain* and the Nader Report, *The Company State,* in September, 1975, was equally unwelcome, as was the publicity given in October to charges that Du Pont's laying off of two union officials in Richmond, Virginia, who had been critical of company policies was, according to one of the leaders, George Cobb, "a political move to try to stop the biggest movement against the Du Pont Company in the last 20 years."[210]

But what really concerned Shapiro and other managers were the growing ties between Du Pont workers and consumer/community advocates like Ralph Nader. In January, 1976, over 300 dissident Du Pont workers representing 30 to 40 plants rallied in Richmond under the chairmanship of a laid-off worker, Frank H. Eastman. The rally was an attempt to get workers to use their ownership of stock to vote for a proxy resolution which asked for improved pension benefits for Du Pont's blue-collar workers. At the previous annual meeting, Chairman Shapiro had ruled an employee pension proposal out of order, insisting that pensions were not an issue for a national Du Pont decision but should be worked out at local plants. The workers, who argued that the current pension plan allowed management to raise benefits for white-collar workers while offering a token and unequal raise for blue-collar pensioners, knew that Shapiro's ruling was an attempt to shatter the negotiating strength of the workers into scores of different local plant fragments. When the Richmond local union took the lead in organizing nationwide Du Pont workers' opposition, Wilmington headquarters handed the Richmond workers an unusual Christmas message: their plant was to be closed down, allegedly because of declining cellophane sales.

Undeterred, the Richmond workers the following month hosted representatives from Du Pont plants as far away as Indiana, Iowa, Alabama and Massachusetts in what one organizer called "the biggest movement in the labor field since John L. Lewis led them out of the coal mines."[211] Ralph Nader gave a two-and-one-half hour speech and question-and-answer session, charging Delaware with being "a political and corporate plantation. They got the whole system rigged against you," he said. "To call it paternalism is to be too charitable." Delaware law protected the Du Ponts from reforms, and he urged the workers to lobby for new laws that would guarantee stockholder rights, more worker control over company practices and policies which affected them, and strict disclosure requirements that would reveal how managers and directors of large corporations use depreciation and investment credits to hide their real profits from workers and stockholders. "It's ridiculous that an international corporation like Du Pont is chartered by the State of Delaware."[212]

Nader encouraged the workers to resist "divide and rule" tactics that separate one plant's workers from another's and workers from their natural allies among consumers, environmentalists, students and other people being

Wilmington today, dominated by Du Pont and family controlled banks. Broad building at left is Du Pont Company's Brandywine Building; Wilmington Trust and former Farmers Bank (now Girard Trust) are seen at center; tall building at right is the Bank of Delaware. (GERARD COLBY)

Du Pont Building, international headquarters for the world's largest chemical company. (GERARD COLBY)

Rodney Square, Wilmington's central park, is surrounded by City Hall, post office, library, and Du Pont Building and Hotel. View from the City Hall includes, left to right, Delaware Trust building (behind library), built by Alfred I. and William du Pont, Bank of Delaware, former Farmers Bank and Du Pont Building, all except Farmers controlled by the Du Pont family. (GERARD COLBY)

Crowned by the logo of the Du Pont family's bank, the new Rodney Square Club, perched atop the Wilmington Trust Center, enjoys a commanding view of northern Delaware, the capital of the Du Pont empire. (GERARD COLBY)

Du Pont's Reach Into the Caribbean Basin

━━━ DU PONT COMPANY SUBSIDIARIES

- - - - DU PONT FAMILY R. C. du Pont & Summit Aviation;
Ambassador Robert Duemling; Senator William Roth

★ LOCATION OF XANADU former Cuban estate of Irénée du Pont, Sr.

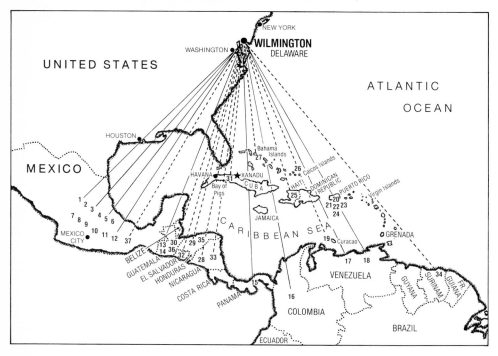

DU PONT CO. SUBSIDIARIES:

MEXICO
1 **Cartuchos Deportivos de Mexico, S.A. (40%)**, ammunition factory of Remington Arms

2 **Colorquim, S.A., de C.V.**, pigments and dyes factories

3 **Du Pont S.A. de C.V.**, explosives, finishes, agricultural chemicals and resin factories

4 **Du Pont Farmaceuticos de Mexico**, drug factory

5 **Du Pont Sistemas de Interconexiones**

6 **La Dominica, S.A. de C.V. (49%)**, acid and fluorspar factory

7 **Mexicanos, S.A. de C.V.**, electronic connectors factory

8 **Mexofina, S.A. de C.V. (100%)**, exploration for oil and gas in conjunction w. Pemex

9 **Nylon de Mexico, S.A. (40%)**, synthetic fiber factory

10 **Pigmentos y Productos Quimicos, S.A. (49%)**, titanium dioxide pigments factory

11 **Quimica Fluor, S.A. de C.U. (32.8%)**, hydrofluoric and sulfuric acids factory

12 **Tetraetile de Mexico (49%)**, gasoline additives factory

GUATEMALA
13 **Quimica Du Pont Centroamerica, S.A.**, markets Du Pont products

14 **Continental Oil Co. of Guatemala (100%)**, explorer for oil

PANAMA
15 **Refineria Panama S.A. (50%)**, refines petroleum products

COLUMBIA
16 **Du Pont de Colombia**, agricultural chemicals factory

VENEZUELA
17 **Du Pont de Venezuela (100%)**, agricultural chemicals and finishes factory

18 **Continental Oil Co. ov Venezuela (100%)**, drills for oil; controls producing oil field

CURACAO
19 **Du Pont Overseas Capital N.V. (100%)**, financial company for worldwide operations

PUERTO RICO
20 **Du Pont Agrichemicals Caribe**, agricultural chemicals factory

21 **Du Pont Electronic Materials, Inc.**, electronics film factory

22 **Du Pont Pharmaceuticals Caribe**, drug products factory

23 **Du Pont Pharmaceuticals, Inc.**, drug products factory

24 **Du Pont Pharmaceuticals Pan America, Inc.**, sales company

DU PONT FAMILY HOLDINGS AND BUSINESS RELATIONS

25 **Haiti:** Hotel owned by Richard C. du Pont; warplane sales by du Pont's Summit Aviation.

26 **Providenciales (NE of Haiti, in Caicos Islands):** Real Estate project owned by Richard C. du Pont

27 **Bahamas:** Refinery 50% owned by Charter Oil; largest stockholder is the Alfred I. du Pont Estate.

28 **Nicaragua:** Warplane sales by Richard C. du Pont's Summit Aviation to Somoza dictatorship before Sandinista Revolution.

29 **Honduras:** Warplane sales by Richard du Pont's Summit Aviation

30 **Guatemala:** Warplane sales by du Pont's Summit Aviation

31 **Cuba:** Before 1958 Revolution led by Castro, large sugar holdings through United Fruit, American International Corporation, American Sugar and Refining Co.; Xanadu estate of Irénée du Pont at Varadero Beach, east of Havana.

DU PONT FAMILY POLITICAL INFLUENCE

32 **Senator William Roth:** Chairman of powerful Senate Special Investigating Committee; Co-Chairman of U.S. Observer Delegation, 1984 El Salvador elections. Supports Reagan policy of growing U.S. military presence in area.

33 **Richard C. du Pont:** Modifies warplanes used by CIA in bombing attacks on Nicaragua.

34 **Ambassador Robert Duemling:** Husband of Du Pont director Louisa du Pont Copeland Duemling, he is ambassador to bauxite-rich Surinam, whose leftist government has been a target of 4 coup attempts allegedly organized by CIA station in Duemling's embassy.

35 **Gov. Pierre S. du Pont IV:** Committed Delaware National Guard units to 1983 U.S. military maneuvers in

36 Honduras along Nicaraguan border; has toured Guatemala and Mexico on official visits as Delaware governor, noting oil in area as an important issue. Shandoah

37 Oil, one of the largest holders of oil leases in Guatemala's northwest Mayan Indian highlands, was targetted for purchase by Du Pont in the 1970's.

Irénée du Pont (center in white), the lord of Xanadu, hosting friends at his huge Cuban estate before the 1958 Revolution led by Fidel Castro. Du Pont was alleged by some to be the most powerful American in Cuba next to the U.S. ambassador.

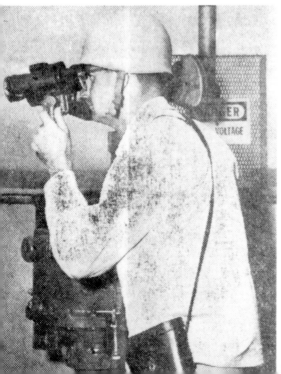

As a special guest of the Defense Department, Irénée du Pont, Jr., observes naval target bombing as part of November, 1960 U.S. naval maneuvers in Atlantic and Caribbean that were prelude to Atlantic Fleet's participation in CIA's Bay of Pigs invasion less than five months later. (U.S. NAVY)

The son of Lammot du Pont, Pierre S. du Pont III (right), as head of the committee that erected the museum at the base of the Statue of Liberty during the Eisenhower (second from left) - Nixon Administration. Pierre lived to see his only son, Pierre IV, rise 30 years later as a serious aspirant to the White House, where this photograph was taken in 1954. (KING FEATURES)

Irving S. Shapiro used the experience he had gained as a Justice Department prosecutor against his former employer to help the Du Ponts attempt to retain control over General Motors' business. Although the Supreme Court ordered divestiture, Shapiro's legal powers on behalf of the family's enterprise led to his being named the first Du Pont Chairman who was Jewish and without any Du Pont family relatives. (COURTESY OF DELAWARE *State News*)

William Roth, co-author of the Kemp–Roth Act described by Reagan budget director David Stockman as a "trojan horse" for tax cuts for the rich. Married to a Du Pont in-law, Roth overcame his status when he first ran for the U.S. Senate by wearing a button that told voters "I am Bill Roth." (COURTESY OF DELAWARE *State News*/GARY EMEIGH)

Vice President and former CIA director George Bush (center), receiving University of Delaware's honorary doctorate of laws in 1983 from trustees chairman J. Bruce Bredin (right), a brother-in-law of Irénée du Pont, Jr. At left (sitting) is Governor Pete du Pont, rumored to be Bush's first choice as a running mate. (REVIEW/Dennis Sandusky)

UNIVERSITY of DELAWARE

DuPont Company
and the
NUCLEAR WEAPONS INDUSTRIAL COMPLEX

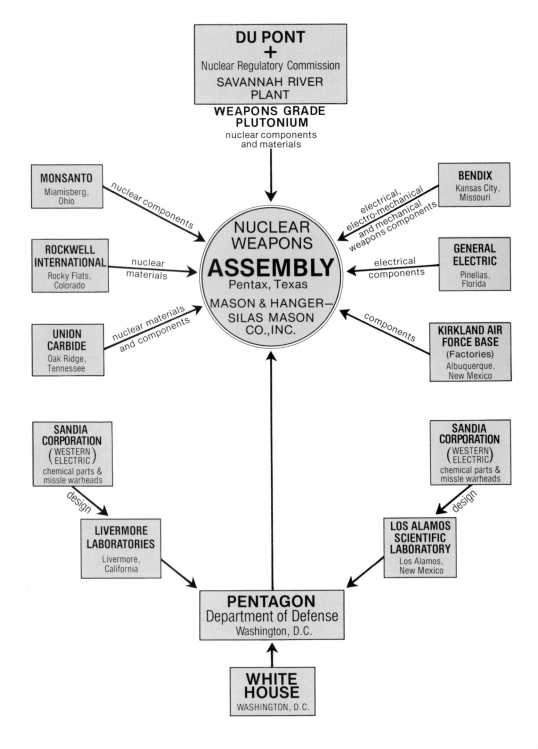

Richard du Pont and the CIA's Illegal War on Nicaragua

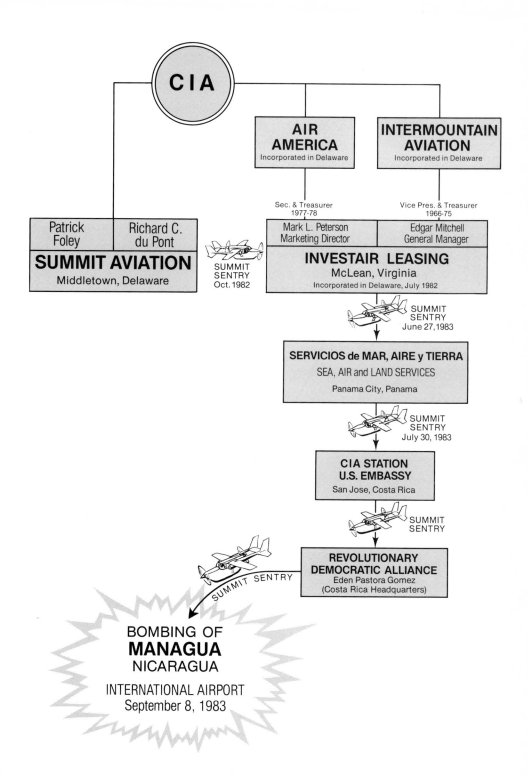

THE DU PONT ELDERS, former chairmen C.B. McCoy (left) and Crawford Greenewalt (center) and George P. Edmonds, all relatives of the Du Ponts. (COURTESY OF DELAWARE *State News*),

Pierre S. ("Pete") du Pont IV (center) and wife Elise (left) celebrate his induction as governor of Delaware in 1977. (COURTESY OF DELAWARE *State News*).

exploited by Du Pont. "You can't possibly represent your interests by yourselves." To avoid Du Pont's ability to "brainwash" local media and use unfair labor practices against local plants, contract negotiations should be moved to a "central location of high visibility." He scored Du Pont's alleged control of inventions by employees on their own time outside of work as "suppression of freedom of speech." He warned against "a spate of lies" by top management that told workers that stricter consumer safety and environmental controls will endanger jobs. The company knows workers are really consumers, he said, and that the high prices Du Pont hopes can be sustained actually exploit consumers. As for Du Pont's propaganda about helping the environment, "the worst pollution in the country is in the plants."[213]

Dr. Sidney Wolfe also spoke, warning that a disproportionate number of the over 100,000 deaths from job-related diseases each year were those of Du Pont employees, and he condemned Du Pont for conducting "human experimentation" rather than stop a chemical's use when it first becomes suspicious. Nader also charged that Du Pont and other large corporations, instead of fighting reforms, were large enough and had the financial resources and technical capability to make blue-collar jobs safe "rather than breeding places for lung disease and cancer." It was criminal to force a worker to have to choose between having a livelihood and working at certain risk to his health.

Nader suggested Irving Shapiro work as a $300,000 a year neoprene worker. "It's clear he might have an added sensitivity, despite the salary."[214]

An unlikely scenario. "The plain fact is that I can't do anything with my hands,"[215] Shapiro once confessed. Talking, rather, was his expertise, and while spokesman Jack Conmy played a subdued role before reporters inquiring about the Richmond rally— "We feel fine... if that's what they want to do"[216]—Irv Shapiro began to prepare for the Cobb resolution at the April 12 annual meeting, and for what he did best.

"We have to convince the American people they ought to be satisfied with what's going on," he told John Gates of the purged and reborn *News-Journal.* "You do that by going public and asking to be judged on the merits.... Industry has traditionally played its cards close to the chest and treated the public as an outsider. The public doesn't know the facts."[217]

Irving Shapiro did, or at least enough facts to "show that you're making tough choices and making them in a rational way." But what values lay behind the logic, the "rational" arguments? Logic, like computers, can be taught to serve many different masters. Here, too, Shapiro had an answer. "History says the profit system works better than any other that's been devised so far." But there must be social responsibility, since corporations owe their existence to public tolerance. "Corporations are a useful way to bring together people and capital for getting a job done.... They exist," he claimed, "because they serve the public interest."

It was as if money and power had nothing to do with it. Instead, in Shapiro's view, enormous corporate power came about by consent of the public it served. And it was a premise the *News-Journal* no longer questioned. Only once, after commenting on the luncheon as being "subtly impressive, elegant without being lavish," did Gates the student venture forth once again as Gates the reporter, noting that Shapiro's "off-the-record answer to a question"—complete with a direction to close the service kitchen door "to foil eavesdroppers"—was "nothing extraordinary, but the impression of confidentiality has been made." Shapiro, the reporter seemed to be hinting, was extremely skilled at public relations, the master propagandist.

Then Shapiro made a rare gaffe. After assuring Gates that all political contributions by Du Pont officials were open to public inspection, the chairman made it clear that Du Pont forbids the giving of bribes to foreign sources to promote business. It was a statement that would soon return to haunt Shapiro. Just a little over a month later, a House subcommittee staff report would disclose that Du Pont Company subsidiaries between 1973 and 1975 had made $337,000 in illegal foreign payments. Du Pont officials in Wilmington would be charged with "serious shortcomings" in the voluntary-disclosure program of the Securities and Exchange Commission.[218]

It was perhaps in anticipation of this report that Shapiro raised the issue at the April 12 annual meeting but downplayed it as "nothing of such substance to warrant detailed discussion. Considering the risk that this matter could be misunderstood in foreign countries, we intend to say nothing more."[219]

But the likelihood was that it was not "foreign countries" whose "misunderstanding" would be at risk, since their governments already had knowledge of what they had received and, in the Middle East at least, had greater control over the press. What was really of concern were other listeners: the American public.

A Du Pont annual meeting is always a sight to behold. Some 2,000 shareholders, Du Ponts and critics alike, pack themselves in the Playhouse of the Du Pont Hotel to hear the report of the chairman and, occasionally, complaints. The April, 1976, meeting, however, was extraordinary on many counts. There was a paradoxical blend of confidence and apprehension in the air. It was evident in the picket lines set up outside the hotel by Du Pont blue-collar workers that Du Pont family members were obliged to cross to get into the meeting. It was evident also in Irving Shapiro's joyful report that net income had risen from 39 cents per share from 1975's first quarter to $2.80 a share. And it was evident in the fact that it was not Shapiro's financial report that drew most of the comment, but the Cobb proposal to amend the company's pension plan.

This was understandable—and unfortunate. For buried within Shapiro's finances was an extraordinary story that would ultimately affect everyone in the United States, including Du Pont's workforce.

Ever since the Arab oil embargo that was the Arab world's answer to U.S. support for Israel's seizure of the West Bank during the 1973 Middle East war, Du Pont had been both beneficiary and victim of fluctuating oil supplies. At first, in 1974, when fears ran high that curtailed oil feedstocks for the production of synthetic fibers would mean a polyester shortage, Du Pont's sales soared; for nine months after Shapiro took command, Du Pont enjoyed both inflated prices and such demand that its stock ran short. To meet what was expected to be continued large demand in the immediate future, Shapiro authorized capital expenditures to expand Du Pont's plant capacity.

It was a huge mistake. In 1975, as fears declined with renewed oil supplies and a slump occurred in the fibers market which accounted for 40 percent of the company's sales and earnings, Du Pont's earnings fell 33 percent, plunging profits from 1973's $12 a share to $4.50. "The guts of our business simply came to an end one day," Shapiro said of September 15. "After that, we couldn't give a pound of product away."[220] Plants that had been running at full capacity for months suddenly were idle over 50 percent of the time. It was a disaster, since Shapiro had departed from the Du Pont family's tradition of financing expansion from internal company funds and had gone to New York banks for loans. This meant that the company's "after-break-even" profit margin was much higher than before. In an attempt to meet those margins through an increase in the volume of sales, Shapiro cut prices; but the market was already glutted with fibers. Sales dropped by $200 million and earnings by 72 percent from $2.43 a share to 67 cents. Two more quarters of losses followed. The company, according to Du Pont economist Charles Reeder, "hit percentages of decline that people here simply couldn't believe."[221] Competition was keen as prices tumbled with not only the economic slump, but also technological improvements that had reduced labor costs.

By September, Du Pont common was selling 30 times above its actual earnings, with a growth stock multiple lower than other blue chip shares such as Eastman Kodak, Xerox or IBM. John M. McCarthy of the $1.4 billion Affiliated Fund shook the market when, predicting a fall in Du Pont earnings and stock prices, he sold 16,000 shares in 1975. Other large investors, such as Dallas's First National Bank and Republic National Bank as well as Chicago's First National Bank, also unloaded shares.

The volatility of Du Pont's stock may not have been deserved, but it scared wealthy individual and institutional investors. The deteriorating economic situation gave them little hope for a fibers comeback, and while cyclical stocks like Du Pont do sell more on future earnings than current earnings, there was a question about fibers' future. The excuse of being a seasonal stock simply didn't explain Du Pont's decline.

Du Pont's top economist, Charles B. Reeder, tried to provide a plausible answer. "There's a simple two-word answer to why chemical company earnings vary all over the lot. The words are product mix."[222] Perhaps, but the decline in the industry was broadly affecting plastics and film as well as fiber. Product mix may protect earnings by diversifying markets a company produces for, but it will not protect any firm from the crushing weight on prices that technological improvement bequeaths in a competitive market. Shapiro's executive committee was gripped in crisis. It was fibers, in fact, not film or plastics, that saved Shapiro's head. In mid-1975, fibers began their seasonal rally and by the third quarter there was enough improvement to allow Shapiro in December to admit, "I got my first good night's sleep all year."[223]

Shapiro by then had made a fateful decision, one that would shape Du Pont's future forever. He had decided to move toward backward integration and secure Du Pont's supply of raw materials. He was convinced that oil supplies would steadily decline in the years ahead.

In November, 1975, two deals were struck. The first was with National Distillers and Chemical Corporation, a New York-headquartered firm which had Nelson Rockefeller's distant cousin, Hulbert Aldrich, on its board and was well within the orbit of Morgan banking interests, with Morrow and Co. as its proxy solicitation firm. The selection of National, then, for a deal Shapiro described as "made in heaven,"[224] was not outside Du Pont's traditional reliance on Morgan alliances. The arrangement called for a joint-venture $100-million plant to produce synthetic gas and carbon monoxide, essential for making two key ingredients in plastics and synthetic fibers: methanol and acetic acid. Shapiro was gambling on a shortage of both by 1979.

The second deal, with Atlantic Richfield Oil Company (ARCO), was more of a departure from tradition. Atlantic Refining of Philadelphia had been part of the Rockefellers' Standard Oil Trust when it was set loose by the 1911 Supreme Court dissolution. An eastern company always short of crude, Atlantic Refining was given a new shot of adrenelin when Robert Anderson,

son of a Chicago banker, sold his New Mexico oil holdings to it in 1962 and came on board as chairman in 1965. In 1966, Anderson steered Atlantic into a merger with a West Coast company, Richfield Oil, and in 1968 ARCO discovered the largest oil field yet found in North America, in Prudhoe Bay off Alaska. In 1970, ARCO absorbed Sinclair Oil of Teapot Dome infamy, and two years later Anderson moved his headquarters from New York's financial wellspring to Los Angeles, closer to his 100,000-acre New Mexico ranch. It was with this man, a self-proclaimed liberal, graduate of the Rockefeller-endowed University of Chicago and benefactor of the Aspen Institute for Humanistic Studies at Aspen, Colorado, that the ultra-conservative Du Ponts, thanks to Irving Shapiro, found themselves in alliance.

Shapiro's 50-50 deal with Anderson called for a $500-million refinery to produce 100,000 barrels of oil per day for raw material for petrochemicals. Unfortunately, Du Pont had cancelled a similar project before the oil crisis. "Our suppliers were making more on the feedstocks they sold us than we were getting from the products we made with them," Shapiro explained. "We are spreading our bets.... We will continue to bring in new technology, but now we know that we must also have assured sources of supply."[225]

It did not seem a major diversion of capital from Du Pont's traditional business, just a backward integration to assure feedstock for that business. No one, except perhaps Du Pont family members who were quietly building their oil stock portfolios, could have anticipated that it was a serious harbinger of new directions in the future.

Du Pont's board of directors turned out *en masse* to listen to Shapiro's report at the 1976 annual meeting and offer the chairman a united bloc of support. Sales, they heard happily, were up over 30 percent from the previous year's first quarter of $1.6 billion, and almost a fifth of this $500 million increase was from sales in Europe. There, a 50 percent drop in fibers prices had led to plant closings by European competitors, protests by French workers, and charges that Du Pont was not only dumping its surplus on the market, but also driving natural fibers such as cotton and wool off the market entirely.[226]

"Most of our product lines are doing very well,"[227] Shapiro said to the audience overflowing the Playhouse, and he predicted an increase of textile fiber shipments during 1976 by 15 percent over 1975, and an "even better year" in 1977. Sales of fluorocarbons had been "impacted" by adverse publicity about the ozone layer's destruction, he admitted, and there were still "pockets of weakness" in fibers, but he exuded confidence in the future.

John Toland, an employee from the Philadelphia plant, decided to take Shapiro at his word and mounted the podium during the question period.

Shapiro took a look at Toland's jacket and noticed it bore the insignia of the United Steelworkers of America. Earlier, the chairman had stated that the shareholders gathering was "not the place for employees or their representatives... to make statements about their employee relationships, and had used his control over the sound system of the speaker's microphone to enforce his decree."[228] Anticipating that Toland was about to speak in favor of the Cobb blue-collar pension proposal, Shapiro sought to point out the worker's allegiance to the Steelworkers' organizing drive in order to discredit his statements before the conservative Du Ponts.

"I don't recognize that symbol on your jacket," Shapiro said.

Toland recognized immediately that he was being baited.

"That's what will be representing the workers in the future if you keep shutting us off,"[229] he shot back. But Shapiro, the experienced veteran of earlier post-war witchhunts, had scored with the Du Ponts.

The proponents of the change in the pension fund sensed it, and their pleas reflected their desperation. Sponsor Cobb said that pensioners did not receive enough money to keep up with inflation. His proposal would provide a pension based on the number of years of employment times 1.5 percent of the average annual salary of the highest salary of five years, usually the last five years of employment. June Doble argued for the justice of another part of the proposal which would permit retirement with full benefits after 30 years of service to Du Pont. Her job, she explained, was scheduled to be eliminated with a shutdown of an operation at the Du Pont plant in Spruence, Virginia. She had served Du Pont for 31 years, yet, because she had started work at the tender age of 16, she would be deprived of immediate collection of benefits if and when she was laid off. Ted Keller, a Du Pont employee and Chairman of Delaware's Tax Reform Coalition, said the current pension plan discriminated against lower-paid workers who could not afford the current option involving subtraction of 50 percent of Social Security benefits, and suggested a cut in executives' fringe benefits to remedy the problem.* And Cobb's co-worker, Frank Eastman, warned that if the pension plan wasn't improved soon, the company's local unions, like the 13 colonies

---

*Keller had introduced a proposal to include blue-collar workers in Du Pont's "B" bonus profit-sharing plan in 1974. He had submitted the proposal first in early 1973 to his immediate superior at the Public Affairs Department, Thomas Stephenson, who had offered to transmit it to the Executive Committee. Stephenson's answer did not come back, however, until May 4, 1973, after the 1973 annual meeting was already over. It was a rejection. Undeterred, Keller informed Du Pont's secretary, Henry Bush, on December 19 of his intention to submit his proposal at the 1974 annual meeting. Du Pont general counsel Richard Manning then tried to get the SEC's approval to exclude Keller's resolution from the 1974 proxy statement. The SEC refused. The Du Ponts were then obliged to openly defeat Keller's proposal each time it was raised in 1974, 1977, and 1982, but only after trying to get the SEC to agree to Du Pont's excluding Keller's proposal from each meeting's proxy statement.

before the American Revolution, would have to "form a strong union" to fight the pension plan's "taxation without representation."

Du Pont executives controlled the $2.5 billion pension fund, one of the largest in the country, with $802 million invested in Du Pont stock and a total 66 percent invested in other common stocks, including huge holdings in such predominantly non-unionized companies as IBM, General Mills, Exxon, Standard Oil of Ohio, Digital Equipment, K-Mart, and Halliburton, the last being also an equal employment and OSHA violator. Among companies doing business in apartheid South Africa that Du Pont executives directed pensioners' money into were IBM, General Electric, Exxon, Ford, Deere, Caterpillar, Texaco, Amax, United Technologies (General Al Haig's firm), Owens-Illinois, National Cash Register, and two old friends of the Du Ponts, General Motors and J.P. Morgan Company.[230]

Through its control over the money due to its employees, the Du Pont Company was able to use the pension fund as a giant $2.5 billion holding company, investing in companies it favored. Du Pont had always disclaimed getting any benefit out of the fund, arguing its selection of stocks was made only on the basis of a return on investment for the fund. But neither this argument nor the public relations boon of priding itself as an innovator of private employee pensions in America could explain why such a huge (47 percent) investment of the fund had been concentrated in Du Pont Company stock rather than more safely diversified in other securities. In fact, the employees pension fund owned 5.2 percent of Du Pont's entire common stock, making the employees plan the largest single stockholder; yet the employees had no representative of their own on Du Pont's board of directors, reflecting the separation between their ownership and the company's control of their own pension fund.

Nor were many Du Pont workers ever to live long enough to collect what had been put in the fund for their retirement. This was especially true of blue-collar workers who were forced to endure hazardous work conditions while being exposed to toxic chemicals, fumes, or low-level radiation. The Du Ponts had insisted that workers must wait until the age of 50 to get even reduced benefits, and even then 15 years of service was required. To receive a full pension, 27 years of service and 58 years of age were demanded.

It came as no great shock, then, that President Edward Kane, speaking for management, rose to the podium to voice his opposition to the Cobb pension proposal, just as he had earlier rejected Ted Keller's proposal to include blue collar workers in the Company's profit-sharing plan (which Du Pont admitted using as a "competitive compensation" for managers and white collar employees to improve products, efficiency, and productivity, including that of blue-collar workers). What was surprising was his inadvertent admission that workers who waited until the age of 65 to retire after serving

Du Pont for 35 or more years "typically received net retirement income equal to no more than 85 percent of their net working income,"[231] rather than a full 100 percent. Kane also boasted that 11 percent of the waged employees who had retired as of the end of 1975 were able to take advantage of the pension plan option which involved subtraction of part of their Social Security benefits. But that only proved Keller's point: 89 percent of the retirees were *not* able to do so. Not realizing enough had been said already, Kane added that the Cobb proposal would increase the company's costs by $65 million at 1975 levels, and he asserted that would mean pensions much higher than those offered by Du Pont's competitors.

It was a terribly odd way for Kane to try to prove his point. The March, 1976, proxy report given out to stockholders before the meeting confirmed that the salaries and fees Du Pont paid its top officers and directors alone totalled almost $4 million in 1976; another $1.2 million were received by the same men as dividend units. (In March, 1974, C.B. McCoy exercised his option for 4,000 shares. As a result, the company was forced to sell him the stock at a loss of almost 50 percent, cancelling 3000 dividend units. McCoy made a profit of over $270,000 on this one transaction.) The 1975 Annual Report showed another $40 million had been paid in bonuses, mostly to managers and white collar employees. Christiana Securities common stockholders got an even larger chunk in the form of common stock dividends: $70 million.[232] None of these figures included the $71 million in annual interest and principal payments on the $1.2 billion long-term debt Shapiro had recently accumulated in loans from mostly New York banks. And the myriad ways that large transnational corporations like Du Pont hide their real profits, including depreciation and investment credits and even financial transfers and overcharges to and by subsidiaries, would have to await disclosure by Washington and the United Nations in the future. In 1975, Du Pont reported generating a $51.9 million investment tax credit, for a total deferred investment tax credit of $152 million, and deferred income taxes of another $126.3 million, both listed as liabilities on Du Pont's balance sheet.

Du Pont workers, however, saw none of the money earned by their 5.2 percent holding of Du Pont, and would not until they retired with pensions that Kane had unintentionally acknowledged were only par for the industry. Meanwhile, their pension fund would be used by the company to provide Du Pont with capital that, in turn, would help finance the construction of more plants in the non-unionized Sunbelt. In other words, through company control over their pension fund, Du Pont workers in the North were (and are) financing the loss of their own jobs and the destruction of their own communities.[233] Later, when the Steelworkers' organizing drive reached the final voting stage, Du Pont's northern workers would feel the full impact of this process as Du Pont non-unionized workers in the South cast their ballots with the company.

Nor was this phenomenon of the Du Ponts utilizing workers' pension monies for their own ends limited to the Du Pont Pension and Retirement Plan. Because of its blue-chip reputation, Du Pont Company also attracted investments by other pension funds as well. In 1976 ten pension funds in the private sector controlled either by other companies, including Ford and AT&T, or such unions as the Teamsters, the International Longshoremen's Association or the International Brotherhood of Electrical Workers, invested $25.6 million in Du Pont stock. Fourteen other unions of workers in the public sector, including New York, Texas, and Pennsylvania teachers, invested another $182 million in Du Pont.[234]

Such a huge pool of capital gave the Du Ponts reason enough to oppose any change in how the pension fund operated. Cobb's proposal was quickly drowned by a tidal wave of millions of shares owned by the family.

Ultimately, then, the resolution of all disputes turned on the power of the Du Pont family over the giant company which bore their name.

In a speech in Boston a little over a week later, Irving Shapiro did not contest this. Indeed, he answered the call of Ralph Nader's Corporate Accountability Research Group for federal chartering of big companies with limits on size, diversity and share of market permitted to any one corporation as "a phony issue." The real issue, he explained, "is power."[235] He correctly described Nader's proposal for federal chartering as an attempt at "displacing the states." But he did not explain exactly what it was about Delaware's General Corporation Law, for instance, that he wanted to protect or that Nader wanted to replace. Delaware's law was certainly the corporation law *par excellence,* a classic case of a law drafted by and for a single rich family (in this case the Du Ponts, to permit easy and relatively tax-free incorporation of their monopoly trust of captured gunpowder companies into a single combined corporation). After New Jersey's notoriously liberal governor, Woodrow Wilson, tightened his own state's corporation law in 1911, the sweet legal waters of the Delaware were enjoyed by most of the other large corporations in America as well.

Shapiro, however, wisely chose to avoid details, opting instead to hide the concrete behind an abstract argument for states rights and a warning about the dread of "more centralization, less freedom all around."[236]

Shapiro's words were characteristic of the aggressive advocate of a client, on the one hand stripping away the facade of compromise that made such proposed "restrictions" on corporate size look attractive as a non-confrontational reform and on the other throwing a veil over exactly what it was he was defending in state chartering of corporations. In many ways, his argument had an historical parallel to those which defended another

"American way of life" in an earlier era of the country: In the 1850's the South also discerned the motive behind the seemingly compromising argument of an Illinois politician who likewise called only for restrictions on the size of their mode of production, slavery. Then, too, the proposal to restrict slavery's expansion and prevent it from entering into the new territories of the Western frontier seemed reasonable. But the Southern slaveholder knew it would be the death of his way of life. The Southern plantation system, like the modern large corporation, relied heavily on loans to carry out the extensive cultivation of the system's basic crops, cotton and tobacco, for export; both crops, however, quickly eroded the soil and made expansion into virgin land absolutely vital. The Illinois politician's compromise, while appealing to his Midwestern farmer constituency who wanted to avoid war but also feared losing the western territories to the South's slave labor, would actually throttle the plantation system. That is why the South opposed Abraham Lincoln, laid bare the motive behind his seeming non-confrontational approach, and could never peacefully accept its implementation with his election to the White House.

Whether Shapiro saw the historical parallel is unknown but it is unlikely. It is more probable that he was simply doing his narrow job as an advocate for a client, in this case Du Pont and corporations in general. He probably never dreamed that his exposure of the struggle for power behind Nader's proposal for restrictions and his defense of state rights echoed so loudly down the halls of American history.

The rest of Shapiro's speech repeated the standard homilies of "letting constituent democracy exercise its voice in the marketplace" where citizens are reduced to consumers who can only passively react to others' decisions on products and how they are made, not initiate or take part in those decisions. The ticket of admission to this marketplace was, of course, the dollar. Without it, no admission. Therefore, even participation on this passive level depended on the good will of the owners of the corporation who controlled access to a wage or salary.

The alternative, whether West Germany's co-determination with labor union representatives on corporate boards, or Harvard Professor George Lodge's nationally chartered "community-oriented collectives," would, according to Shapiro, "be a fundamental break with America's past." The absurdity of arguing that there has been no American history but corporate history, no other means of economic organization but that of the corporation, did not disturb Shapiro's line of reasoning. Nor did the obvious impact of highly political biases of the Du Ponts or other conservative corporate leaders on business decisions faze his assertion that "We do not need to remodel and in effect politicize the economic system" or "put miniature governmental structure into the boardrooms of the 500 largest corporations." Americans have a right to criticize and seek governmental action, he said; "none of that, though, constitutes a right to a seat on a board." That was solely the prerogative of the wealthy who could afford to own large blocs of stock. "How many of (these) investors," he asked, "would continue to risk their capital in these 'community-oriented collectives'?...Could they run a chemical business? Could such a board recognize a successful management strategy reaching five to 10 years into the future?" Could they ever learn? Could the Du Ponts ever be interested in teaching them, as they teach their own sons and daughters?

Shapiro did score points in contending against the "smaller is always better" line of reformers who would attempt to return America to an earlier, simpler laissez-faire age of smaller enterprises. Would consumers be better off, he asked, if the auto industry were to become the Big Eight or the Big 16? "Economic theory as well as the history of that industry suggest the opposite. The relative price of automobiles has come down as the size of the manufacturer has gone up. It takes fewer hours of work for a typical person to earn enough money to buy a car now than it did in 1950 or 1920." And, he might have added, thanks to technology that only large enterprise could afford, fewer hours of labor on the assembly line, a basic ingredient in operating costs and thereby price.

But it was when he came to the issue of codes of conduct for executives that Irving again stumbled. "Everyone ought to include prohibitions of certain kinds of conduct which cannot be justified regardless of circumstance," he declared. "Thus, for example, secret bribery of government officials, whether at home or abroad, subverts the governmental process. Similarly, one could not justify shipping to another nation a product that is inherently unsafe regardless of whether that nation has had the wit to preclude such a product."[237]

Yet, Du Pont under Shapiro's captaining did both.

Merely a month later came the embarrassing report from a subcommittee of the House Commerce Committee that between 1973 and 1975 Du Pont officers paid at least $337,000 to foreign government employees. In addition, the report charged, one Du Pont foreign subsidiary acted as a conduit for the payment of $155,000 by a foreign government to a New York export agent. "This payment was a kickback over and above the standard price for supplying a product to a foreign government."[238] The report criticized the SEC for not requiring disclosure of the Du Pont payments despite the conclusion of its own staff that they might "constitute bribery under the laws of the U.S."[239] Shapiro denied that the staff got the facts straight, claiming that the money went to the exporter, not the foreign government, but refused to disclose any more information than to confirm that the payments actually totalled $400,000 and that none of its employees had been penalized. SEC Chairman Roderick Hills criticized the subcommittee's releasing the information, claiming "at Du Pont, the chief officer and the directors knew nothing about it." Yet Shapiro had confirmed at the annual meeting that an audit had turned up such payments; and he had not disclosed full details to the shareholders.

"It seems to me that secrecy in government or corporate operations is to hide incompetence, privilege or corruption," claimed committee member Rep. Henry Waxman of California. "And I think they are not entitled to it." Subcommitee chairman Rep. John Moss of California agreed. "There would have been no disclosure if I hadn't made the determination to disclose it."[240]

He rejected Du Pont and the SEC's claim that $400,000 were, as Shapiro put it at the annual meeting, "nothing of substance."

Over sixty other companies had also admitted "questionable payments" with the understanding that by doing so there was less likelihood of enforcement fines or public disclosure by the SEC. "If trust and respect are lacking," Shapiro had told his Boston audience, "it is not just because of recent, well-publicized misbehavior by some companies; it is also because for years we in business have not taken the public into our confidence.... Going public is not painful and it helps dispel the aura of suspicion."[241]

For people in Latin America, on the other hand, Du Pont's not going public could be very painful, even deadly.

Du Pont, through its pharmaceutical subsidiary Endo Laboratories, sells "Valpirone," Du Pont's market name for dipyrone, a pain reliever and fever reducer. Valpirone is sold in Latin America, but not in the United States. And for a good reason. Valpirone may cause fatal blood diseases, including agranuclocytosis, a severe depression of the marrow of the bone.

Dipyrone has already been taken off the market in Australia, and may no longer be sold in the U.S. as a routine treatment for pain, arthritis or fever. According to the Federal Drug Administration, dipyrone "should be restricted to use for... antipyretic effect in serious life-threatening situations where salicylates or similar drugs are known to be ineffective or are contraindicated or not tolerated."[242]

According to the American Medical Association's *Drug Evaluations,* "no dosage (of dipyrone) for analgesia is justified." The "only justifiable use is as a last resort to reduce fever when safer measures have failed." In Latin America, however, Du Pont does not post such warnings about its Valpirone product, and it is often a first, not last, resort to reduce fever. As stated, Du Pont does not market Valpirone in the United States. But where does that leave Chairman Shapiro's claim that "one could not justify shipping to another nation a product that is inherently unsafe?"

"I've learned that integrity and credibility are the name of the game in this job,"[243] the chairman once said. But for residents of Barrio La Boca on the northwestern coast of Puerto Rico, credibility was becoming more difficult to lend to Du Pont.

There, on the banks of the Manati River that flows placidly into the Caribbean, cows and chickens belonging to local farmers began to die, and the 100 fishermen who knew little else in life but to fish began noticing that the once clear green color of the river was turning black. Fish were dying in mounds. When red sores began showing up on the fishermen's skins, they took their case to the EPA to protest a permit it had given Du Pont's $65 million textile and paper dyes plant upstream to discharge wastes in the river.

Du Pont, which had been attracted to the area by its rich underground spring of pure mineral water, responded with Shapiro Tactic Number One, claiming that it had installed the most modern technology in the world at the plant. "We have tried very diligently to serve the community," said plant manager N.J. Irsch, "yet we are the guys who have gotten into trouble."[244] When local public interest lawyers pointed out that all that technology promised Puerto Rico 76 million gallons of contaminated water rather than purification devices, Shapiro Tactic Number Two was implemented: Du Pont, taking advantage of employment fears while the island was going through a severe economic depression, threatened to shut down and throw 350 residents out of work.

Local officials quickly, and helplessly, charged "blackmail," the bitter fruit of thirty years of intensive industrialization by American corporations celebrated as "Operation Bootstrap." Efforts by the Secretary of Natural Resources, Cruz Matos, to question further reckless projects such as open pit mining of copper reserves and a nuclear power plant were rewarded with firings, while officials in the capital, San Juan, wanted Puerto Rico removed altogether from the "unapplicable" and "costly" EPA's regulatory umbrella. The Puerto Rico Lung Association, the Episcopal Church, and labor unions such as the Amalgamated Meatcutters were opposed. They held that America's concern about health as a human right had just recently dawned. They were not anxious to return to the dark.

10. ATTACK AT DAWN (Earning the Flagship)

The corporate offensive against the EPA which began in 1974 in Puerto Rico was mirrored in the United States by 1976. Du Pont was at the front lines of this attack, led by Irving Shapiro. In June, Du Pont challenged the legal power of the EPA to order reductions in the lead content of gasoline; a lower federal court had already upheld the EPA and the Supreme Court had refused to review the case, but that was not enough for Du Pont. Delay, a key objective in Shapiro Tactic Number One, was the object pursued in continued litigation.

The front was broad. It included resistance against the Food and Drug Administration's efforts to ban fluorocarbons because of their damage to the ozone layer; against the EPA's efforts to protect the air from polluting lead-added gasoline; against the Justice Department's charges of price-fixing of Du Pont's Lucite paint; against the United Steelworkers' attempt to organize Du Pont's workers; and against the Oil, Chemical and Atomic Workers' and Natural Resources Defense Council's warnings about the danger of extended exposure to low-level radiation by nuclear power workers and atomic workers at Du Pont's Savannah River Plant.

Against the National Cancer Institute's warning that New Jersey had the highest incidence of cancer among white males in the nation, and Salem County, the site of Du Pont's Chambers Works, the highest incidence of bladder cancer, Du Pont and other chemical firms fielded a lobbying front, the Chemicals Industry Council. At hearings before a New Jersey senate investigating committee, CIC's vice-chairman, Christian Housen, Jr., simply dismissed the warnings as "scare tactics" and the statistics they were based upon as "highly questionable." The state's 120,000 chemical workers "are healthier than the general populace," Housen claimed, "and have longer life expectancies and lower rates of cancer than the general population. This fact indicates a good job is being done to protect chemical workers." As for the EPA's tests that showed cancer-producing chemicals in the air of seven chemical plant sites, Housen stone-walled it. "We don't think the chemical industry has any uncontrolled or unknown emissions which might be causing the problem.... However, there are many different sources of emissions, from cars, from planes, from power plants, vaporization painting, and so on and on...." Housen asserted that "the number of cancers caused by chemical manufacturing is very small," and while lauding the industry as a "valuable tool in curing and eliminating disease," held that "the contribution of the chemical industry to the overall cancer rate in New Jersey is minute."[245]

The New Jersey senators were astounded at Housen's audacity. "I want to see the basis of those statistics," demanded State Senator John Shevin. "Our figures show that New Jersey has a cancer rate that is 14 percent higher than the national average.... There is no question about the intensity of the problem in New Jersey."[246]

Against the Justice Department's price fixing suit, Du Pont Headquarters expressed a tone bordering on contempt: "I presume the government will be kind enough to send it to us after it released the information in a press conference yesterday."[247] The company defended as "fair and legal" its prohibition against retailers selling Lucite below the price fixed by Du Pont if they wished to participate in a rebate program for advertising they paid for.

Against a "severe personal injuries" suit brought by eight Cyanamid workers and their wives alleging Du Pont's failure to properly warn them of the carcinogenic hazards of alpha-nepthylamine in the pigments and dyes they handled, Du Pont Headquarters simply denied that alpha was carcinogenic.[248]

Against the urging of the National Academy of Sciences that uses of fluorocarbon gases be curtailed, and the proposals of Dr. Alexander Schmidt that non-essential uses in spray cans be phased out, Du Pont headquarters argued for a delay until still more tests it had funded at universities could be completed.

Against accusations before a Congressional committee by top union officials at the Belle, West Virginia, Du Pont plant that working conditions had produced an abnormally high cancer rate among workers, Du Pont released a statement admitting 206 fatal cancers of the eye, throat, skin, brain and face since 1954, higher than 157 cases it expected using company-wide averages; but the company blamed the rate on where the workers lived, Kanawha County, instead of where they worked.[249]

But Ernest A. Woodacre, Du Pont's own director of environmental affairs, called to testify after his presence was identified by Du Pont workers at the Congressional hearing in May, 1976, two months before Du Pont's statement was released with updated figures, admitted that even the 144 cancer cases he knew of was higher than the cancer death rate for the entire Kanawha River Valley.[250]

One of the problems, according to Earl McCune, the local union's safety chairman, was that Du Pont dumped its wastes in the river just 500 feet from where it took water for drinking by its employees. "The plant is the only place along the Great Kanawha River that still takes its drinking water from the river."[251] A month after that statement was quoted by the *Philadelphia Bulletin*, the *News-Journal* assigned Wallace C. Judd, Jr., to report on the plant. Judd wrote on the loyalty Belle Workers felt for Du Pont and how "offended" Du Pont managers were that McCune and his union "chose to make the charges in a national forum instead of working it out in-house."[252] The article, titled EYE CANCER SCARE DOESN'T BOTHER MOST DU PONTERS IN PLANT, quoted one 61-year-old veteran worker, Ozzie Hill, as saying, "I have complete trust with our management, and I'll leave this [cancer controversy] to people more knowledgeable than I. The amount of cash they [Du Pont] have put here merits our trust. They wouldn't be stumbling around with any stupid mistakes." Judd quoted a chemist at the nearby Union Carbide plant who expressed envy at the pride and loyalty of Du Pont workers, and then zeroed in on "the real issue": "A new morality" emerging from "a small but distinct group of workers" who favored a strong union that rejected Du Pont's paternalism. Judd then followed this piece up with an article titled DU PONT BLAMES CANCER RATE ON LOCALE, NOT COMPANY.[253] (Judd has since moved on to the public relations office of Delmarva Power and Light Company, where the company's Salem nuclear plants are likewise vigorously defended.)

The *Philadelphia Bulletin* remained unimpressed. When Du Pont headquarters released a report on August 20 claiming that the cancer rate among its male employees was 21 percent lower than the general U.S. population between 1954 and 1974, the *Bulletin* investigated and found problems. "The report is too well done to attribute its errors to incompetent statistics," Dr. Michael Shimkin of the University of California concluded in a letter to the U.S. House subcommittee after studying the Du Pont report. "Therefore, it is reasonable to surmise that there was a deliberate attempt to mislead. I would classify it as a public relations snow job."[254] Shimkin, 64, a health expert, had been asked to do an independent review of the report by the subcommittee on oversight and investigation of the House Interstate and Foreign Commerce Committee. Two other experts at the National Cancer Institute and the National Institute of Occupational Safety and Health concurred; Du Pont was concocting a "healthy worker" fallacy. Du Pont's failure to use a "cohort" approach—following up on workers, for 15 to 20 years, regardless of whether they retire or leave the company—tended "to minimize or obscure the true cancer rate" at Du Pont's Belle plant, Dr. John F. Finklea, director of the National Cancer Institute, also told the subcommittee. New Jersey's Congressman Andrew Maguire criticized "the faulty methodology employed by Du Pont in its cancer registry" and charged that use of its registry "to publicly congratulate itself on its low cancer rate is not merited, is misleading to the public and is a disservice to workers."[255] He also pointed out that further studies of Chambers Works employees would be difficult. Du Pont had destroyed medical records of workers terminated before 1960.

Dr. Bruce Karrh, Assistant Medical Director for Du Pont, attacked criticisms as "very unfair. . . . They are just looking for a reason to be critical when they make that statement." He defended the report as "the best that could be done" in a short period.[256]

When it came to ocean dumping, however, Du Pont did not have the excuse of a short period to reflect on the effects. Since 1968 it had been dumping off the coast of New Jersey two million gallons of waste every week, and EPA studies had detected higher concentrations of certain metals in clams and scallops near the dump site, 35 miles off the coast. In September, 1976, the EPA held hearings and Ocean City, New Jersey, mayor Harry Kelly objected to Du Pont's earning profits at the possible expense of his townspeople. If Du Pont couldn't find anything better to do with its waste, he suggested the company "send its poisons to its stockholders with their dividend checks."[257]

Du Pont requested a two-year extension on its sea dumping to develop a process of making the wastes into a product it could sell for the treatment of sewage. Otherwise, it warned, landfills would have to be used. The EPA at first refused, then gave in. "We feel very good about the ruling,"[258] said a Du Pont spokesman.

It was not that Du Pont officials felt good about dumping or workplace hazards; it was just the question of cost that probably dictated most of their resistance to reform. And costs were on everyone's minds at Du Pont Headquarters. Irving Shapiro was determined to pull the company out of its slump and restore the high earnings of the 1950's. His strategy was that if demand increased from 75 percent of capacity ($8.5 billion in 1976) to 90 percent ($10 billion) and Du Pont could earn 8 percent on those sales as it did before the post-Vietnam recession, Du Pont could make $800 million, or $15 a share on its 48 million share capitalization. With an improved operating rate and an investment base (capital spending) growing much more slowly, that would mean that Irving could reach the 20 percent return on stock equity that once made Du Pont a legend among American corporations.

In July, 1976, Shapiro was again confronted with a decline in profits for the second quarter. Investors were selling their stock holdings of Du Pont and other chemicals, producing a 15 percent average drop of issues. A decade of doubled sales had generated hardly any increase in demand for nylon and Dacron, the staples of Du Pont's fibers division. Lucite, Freon and Teflon also lagged, shaking the traditional Du Pont confidence. "There was a smugness, a feeling that we're just a little better than anyone else,"[259] Shapiro confessed. He responded by slashing spending for research and development, Du Pont's greatest strength in the past, putting out fewer new products and concentrating on existing products, finding new ways, for example, that manufacturers could use polyester fibers than just for double-knitting materials. "No doubt about it," Shapiro boasted, "we're mean, tough S.O.B.'s"[260]

In October, he announced more of the same for 1977, a second year of cuts in capital spending projecting only $2.5 billion for the years 1977-1980, down from $3 billion from 1973 to 1976. He dismissed worries about new products, Du Pont's greatest winners in the past. "We started our spending earlier than others and therefore we did it at lower construction costs. Now we are peeling off the spending." President Kane, a true team player, chimed in: "We've got a good reservoir of low-cost plant capacity. Now we can live off the hump awhile."[261]

Still, Shapiro could not let go of his hopes for fibers. He dared not. With so much of the company's plant still tied to artificial fibers, he had no choice but to feign optimism in his public stance. "Despite all the pain and agony of the moment, we think the industry will have a shakeout," he insisted. "Long-term, man-made fibers will become the major fiber because they are more economical."[262]

But Shapiro knew better, and his investment plans for the future showed it: a greater emphasis on value-added specialty products, particularly in the photo and pharmaceutical divisions. Agricultural chemicals, industrial chemicals and plastics could also be expected to hold their own. The non-fibers industry had shown a return on sales above 9 percent throughout the first three quarters of 1976. But not fibers. Fibers had again showed a loss in the third quarter. Kevlar, the new lightweight superstrong polyester fiber billed as having five times the strength of steel, was the only exception, its future looking bright for its use in belted tires and even bullet-proof vests.

President Jerry Ford was its most prominent model. The Du Pont family's favorite in the 1976 presidential race had donned Kevlar after a series of assassination attempts in 1975. Shapiro, too, had been threatened, letter bombs having been sent to his office, along with scores of others to top corporate officials, in June of 1976, but he was loathe to wear a vest.

He was opposed to insular attitudes that muffled an ear to public criticism and hurt effective responses. "The chief executive has the same problem Nixon had in the White House," he explained, "if you get yourself closed off in your office, you get cut off from the real world."[263]

Shapiro's "real world" easily slipped into *Realpolitik* when it came to law and power. "You're dealing with events all over the world, and American law can't really enforce it." Prohibiting American corporations from bribing foreign nations was therefore "foolishness." The same applied to fluorocarbons, which gave Du Pont a full 1 percent of its profits and 3 percent of its $7.5 billion sales. "You're not just talking about "banning a product," he warned, "you're talking about putting people out of work."[264] As for "public input" into corporate decision-making, citizens groups could always have close contact with management, but public participation in business decisions was out. This applied as well to suggestions for public representatives on corporate boards. "You don't want to turn industry," he said with a straight face, "into a political instrument."[265]

Du Pont family and management donations that year went mostly to Jerry Ford, although to many it looked like a losing cause from the beginning. The nation, after eight years of Republican rule from Richard Nixon, Spiro Agnew, Nelson Rockefeller and Jerry Ford, wanted a fresh start, one which Democrat Jimmy Carter promised them.

Carter was not an unknown among Du Ponts. William Roth, a Du Pont relative, had known Carter as a fellow member of David Rockefeller's Trilateral Commission, an organization of leaders from the corporate and political establishments of Europe, the United States, and Japan. Both men had endorsed the Commission's report, "Crisis of Democracy," and its call for fiscal austerity in social services spending to meet the economic recession that the decline of American corporations in an increasingly competitive world market had, with armaments spending and the rise in the price of oil, bequeathed to the American people. It was these pressures, both external and internal, that inspired the Trilateralists to assume that "the United States is more likely to face serious military or diplomatic reversal during the coming years than at any moment in its history. If this does occur, it could pose a traumatic shock to American democracy." Most worrisome, was the "adversary culture" among intellectuals "who assert their disgust with the corruption, materialism and inefficiency of democracy and with the subservience of democratic government to 'monopoly capitalism.'" Such intellectuals have an "absence of direct responsibility for practical affairs" and hold values which "tend to be privatistic in their impact and import." It is these "oppositionist intellectuals and privatistic youth" that manifest a "decay in the social base of democracy," and "the imbalances stemming from the actual operations of democracy itself which make the governability of democracy a vital, and indeed, an urgent issue for the Trilateral societies."[266]

The Commission's report on the United States, actually drafted by Samuel P. Huntington, a member of the intelligence community and a top liaison between the academic community and the CIA, identified the problem in Americans taking democracy too seriously. The substantial increase in governmental activity for the goals of equality and freedom, exemplified by the civil rights movement, was accompanied by "a substantial increase in governmental authority." At the same time nondefense expenditures by the government, mostly social services, rose as a percentage of the Gross National Product while defense spending as a GNP percentage declined after the end of the Vietnam War, reflecting a dramatic change not only in attitudes, but also the volume of products with a marketable value. To the Trilateralists, the "Defense Shift" of the 1950's was replaced by the "Welfare Shift" of the 1960's and 1970's.[267]

This was not a theory of the New Right. It was a seriously argued thesis of some of the most respected members of the corporate establishment, a view held widely among members of the Commission's United States counterpart, the Council of Foreign Relations, including the Du Ponts and Irving Shapiro.

Here, to the Trilateralists, was the origin of inflation.[268] Here also was a democracy based philosophically and legally on the sanctity and precepts of private property and ruled by a corporate class that had by the date of the Commission's report used those laws and precepts to accumulate control over most of the industry and financial institutions in the United States and some 80 percent of the nation's wealth; it was predictably also a democracy that showed a marked inability to meet the needs or expectations of all its people. This the Commission readily defined as a "decline in public confidence and trust,"[269] and was behind "the decline in party identification" and "the decay of the party system"[270] that had been dominated since the Civil War by the Republican and Democratic party organizations. "In part, this was the result of what were perceived to be significant party failures: the failure to 'win' the war in Indochina; the failure of the Great Society's social programs to achieve their anticipated results; and the intractability of inflation."[271] Doubts set in among the established leaders, including "doubts about the morality of their rule."

It was to this theme of morality in politics and America that the presidential campaigns of both major candidates repeatedly turned in 1976. Both Ford and Carter understood the yearning of the American people for decency and morality in government. Both, after all, were members of the Trilateral Commission and grasped the meaning behind the Commission's warning that "probably no development of the 1960's and 1970's has greater import for the future of American politics than the decline in the authority, status, influence and effectiveness of the presidency."[272]

And any occupant of the White House, the Commission warned, would have to deal with "the democratic distemper,"[273] manifested by strikes, tax protests, and all the unrest caused by "the democratic surge of the 1960's".[274] "The public develops expectations which it is impossible for government to meet."[275] Education adds fuel to the fire by being "the single most important status variable affecting political participation and attitudes."[276] "The increase in ideological thinking is primarily the result of the increased salience which citizens perceive politics to have for their own immediate concerns: The political events of the last decade, and the crisis atmosphere which has attended them, have caused citizens to perceive politics as increasingly central to their lives."[277] In 1940, less than 40 percent of the American people were educated beyond elementary school; in 1970 the figure was 75 percent; 35 percent had gone to college. "The more educated a person is, the more likely he is to participate in politics, to have a more consistent and more ideological outlook on political issues, and to hold more 'enlightened' or 'liberal' or 'change-oriented' views on social, cultural and foreign policy issues. Consequently, the democratic surge could be simply the reflection of a more highly educated populace."[278]

The problem for the Trilateralists was authority. "A government which lacks authority and which is committed to substantial domestic programs will have little ability, short of a cataclysmic crisis, to impose on its people the sacrifices which may be necessary to deal with foreign policy problems and defense."[279] Property concentrations, while never directly dealt with in the Commission report, also required authority for protection. All this, in turn, necessitated a "moderation in democracy."

"Al Smith once remarked that 'the only cure for the evils of democracy is more democracy.' Our analysis," the Commission countered in its conclusion, "suggests that applying that cure at the present time could well be adding fuel to the flames. Instead, some of the problems of government in the United States today stem from an excess of democracy—an 'excess of democracy' in much the same sense in which David Donald used the term to refer to the consequences of the Jacksonian revolution which helped to precipitate the Civil War."

The analogy to the Jacksonian revolution precipitating the Civil War was accurate. Then, too, farmers, "the common man," had taken democracy so seriously that they challenged vested propertied interests in the name of the people and democracy. Then, too, such populist agrarian laborers called themselves "democrats," and dared to confront the hold that the Southern slavocracy and their allied merchant bankers in the Northeast had on the federal government and their lives. What was not so accurate but equally revealing in the Trilateralist analogy, however, was the blame the Commission put on the "democratic distemper" of the common citizen, and not the intransigence of the large property owners, for the tragedy of the Civil War. It is as if the Trilateralists could not perceive any necessary reason to have to fight to end slavery. Henry Clay and John Bell could both have been Trilateralists.

The appearance of Irving Shapiro on the national political arena, then, came as no great surprise to those who understood the role he had chosen for himself years before. He was the reasonable, lawyerly spokesman for vested corporate interests, and the Du Ponts, historically the self-appointed "guardians of the republic" during such times of crises as these, fully supported his election as chairman of the powerful Business Roundtable that year. Nor, then, did many wonder why he sought a meeting in September, just two months before election day, with the front-running candidate, Jimmy Carter. "Sacrifice" and less democracy were the two top items on the corporate agenda for America. Could Carter muster the courage to carry them out?

Carter begged off Shapiro's invitation to address the Business Roundtable, but he did suggest he join 16 other businessmen, bankers and trade association executives in Atlanta for a four-hour luncheon. When Shapiro arrived, he immediately took a seat near Carter. "I wanted to watch him in operation close up," he later recalled, "judge how he functioned, and come up with a gut reaction." Each participant was given three to four minutes to speak. "I wanted to find out if he was really paying attention. I was very impressed. I came away with a feeling that here was a man of considerable intellect, a careful and precise person. He asked a lot of questions, took copious notes and wanted to understand problems. When he disagreed, he was explicit. On some issues he was inexperienced, and said so."[280]

Some of those issues were those Shapiro himself raised. "I was asked to turn in papers on nine subjects and told to keep them short."[281] He did. The subjects he picked became major issues in the Carter Administration:

1) Capital formation and jobs;
2) Common situs picketing or expansion of the striking authority of building trade locals to an entire construction site;
3) Consumer Protection Agency;
4) Energy problems;
5) Environmental issues;
6) National health insurance;
7) Standby wage and price controls;
8) Taxation of foreign source income;
9) Unemployment.

To Shapiro, Carter "was making a mistake in favoring the Consumer Protection Agency"; environmental issues involved questions of priorities, costs, and a timetable for water quality upgrading. But unemployment, Shapiro knew, was at the heart of any Democratic candidate's concern because it involved his labor constituency. After the election, Shapiro correctly called it the number one issue for the new president. But he tried to temper the Democrat's concern by reminding him of the number one concern of corporation executives who controlled hiring in the private sector and saw employment as a labor cost, and then only within the context of being able to arrange bank loans at favorable interest rates that would finance industrial expansion: "Inflation," he warned, "goes right along with it [unemployment], and we have to deal with both together."[282]

Shapiro's remark was both ominous and accurate. It meant that big business would lower unemployment only when it was profitable for itself to do so. Shapiro was setting the terms for the corporate sector's cooperation with the Democratic administration: if you wish to lower labor's unemployment, you must lower inflation that is eroding the dollar's value and driving up the interest rates for our industrial and commercial loans.

Shapiro was aware that wages did not actually cause inflation, and said so; wages, rather, were an effect of inflation and usually ran after it, trying to keep up with prices. Inflation had a deeper cause rooted in the productivity of American industry and its position in a world marketplace of competing producers; productivity, in turn, rested more on the technological tools labor was given than on the ability or willingness of human labor to simply work harder, faster or longer hours. The latter could be increased, of course, and such an increase could generate more profits that could be used to buy more modern technology. But there was a limit on how far you could push workers, a human limit, if not a political limit. With a Democratic administration, Shapiro knew, the political threshold would be lower and corporate leaders would have to take that into account if they were to really influence the president.

A month before the election, as Ford seemed unable to overtake Carter's lead, Shapiro publicly began to hedge his bets. "Mr. Ford is a better president than he is given credit for," he told the press, "and Governor Carter is a far superior candidate than McGovern. I am reasonably relaxed and feel comfortable with either candidate." Then he added that it was no longer possible for corporate leaders to concentrate solely on producing profits. "We must also produce jobs," he told the *New York Times,* "and products that people need."[283] It was the kind of remark that Democrats more than Republicans needed to hear.

In November, President Gerald Ford, the man who had earlier led the campaign in Congress to impeach Chief Justice Earl Warren, was defeated. The Du Ponts may have been impressed by his conservatism and his naming of Victorine du Pont Homsey to the White House Commission on Fine Arts, but the majority of American voters were not. Ford had received wide Du Pont family support, particularly from Reynolds du Pont. But perhaps Mrs. Rose Hayward MacDonald, mother of Nathan Hayward III, and Crawford Greenewalt more clearly saw the Republican future. They donated to the primary campaign of California's arch-conservative, Ronald Reagan.[284]

Alexis I du Pont Bayward remained the family maverick, contributing to the Carter campaign.

Right after Carter's election, Shapiro spoke on the Democrat's major concern: unemployment. He stated his belief that a stronger economy would take care of male heads of households and female non-heads of households who tended to go in and out of the work force. Then he turned to a deeper structural unemployment problem in American capitalism, one that was to worsen precisely as corporations invested in labor-saving technology that would improve the economy but leave millions of untrained American workers behind. "The third category of joblessness," he explained to the press, "is the most serious. It consists of youth under 20, from the center cities, who are not educated or not equipped to hold a job.... Even with a good economy, none of those youngsters will be employed unless special steps are taken to help them."[285]

This represented a new phenomenon, unprecedented in American history in its scale and qualitative impact on society and politics. In the past, jobs expanded with the economy. Now, for the first time, the opposite was the case: As the economy expanded, the total number of jobs would contract.

Shapiro insisted that government subsidies were needed to aid private companies to educate and train youths. Additionally, a public works program would have to be set up to absorb those not able to get into private programs. Shapiro, however, put the training subsidies within the context of private profit for the companies. "The government ought to subsidize their education and their training for jobs in business, while the business world should pay them only for the work performed."[286] The public taxpayer, in other words, not private corporations, should bear the load of work-time that was not profitable.

He was also opposed to the government paying less than the normal wage. "I don't think you can hire anyone at a marginal rate of pay and satisfy him. You've got to bring these youngsters in and convince them they can do something with their lives. Show them they can earn money to support themselves and be useful in society." Only as "a last resort," should a Civilian Conservation Corps be set up as in the Thirties, and then only with "meaningful tasks, not leaf-raking."

Then he made his appeal to Carter and the nation for a partnership with corporate rule over the economy: "I hope for a state of mind that recognizes no administration can be successful unless the economy of the United States is working well. There is a great need for industry and government to work together to make the economy work that way. We wouldn't then be adversaries."[287]

It was a new image for Du Pont, one of social responsibility, and the press was not used to dealing with Shapiro's shift in gears. "The head of Du Pont has always been a powerful influence in American industry by virtue of the company's vast operations in the industrial, chemical, fiber, fabric, photographic, plastic and other fields," noted the *New York Times*. But the Du Pont chairman was now even a bigger power. He also headed the blue-ribbon Business Roundtable of 160 corporate executives. As such, he was probably "the one person who might be considered the principal spokesman for private business."[288]

Never in 50 years had the Du Ponts wielded such political clout, not since the late Twenties when their treasurer, John J. Raskob, was head of the Democratic National Committee. Norman Isaacs and Dixie Sanger celebrated the event in the *News-Journal*. DU PONT'S SHAPIRO EMERGES AS KEY BUSINESS SPOKESMAN ran the headline, and the article below recounted the chairman's rise to national prominence through his speeches before Boston's Commercial Club, New York's Conference Board, and the Business Roundtable. "Is it a bird, a plane, or Superman?" asked the *News-Journal*. "No, it's Irving Shapiro, spokesman for U.S. private industry."[289]

That Shapiro was also the spokesman for the Du Ponts was obvious. "Perhaps one-third of my time is occupied with issues not directly related to decisions" involving running the chemical company, but "in my definition, everything I do is company business." Public opinion affects regulations, he explained, which affects Du Pont's sales and earnings. "Industry exists with the concurrence of the American public; you ignore it at your own cost." Shapiro ignored nothing, and favored chief executives pounding the marbled halls of Washington over company lobbyists. He was convinced from his own experience that congressmen and senators took a company's view more seriously when they were confronted by the powerful head of a corporation rather than hired lobbyists. He was right. Elected politicians know what large corporations can do for campaign coffers—their own or their opponent's. And a chief executive, more than a lobbyist, is a man not to cross without peril, a man who can indeed speak for all the power he represents. Only the previous year, Shapiro recalled, the Business Roundtable mobilized 70 chief executives to confront elected politicians in Washington over a measure. One congressman, he noted, could not help but remark, "I've never seen so many $300 suits."[290] The congressman was revealing more his own lower standards of wealth than any accurate appraisal of clothing; $700 suits, rather, were more common among corporate leaders. Shapiro apparently was wise enough, however, not to correct him.

By December, the chairman was settled into his new role. "A society which thinks poorly of its businessmen and deeply distrusts their motives is not a great society," he had argued two years earlier, "but a society in trouble. We are in danger of demolishing our own house and hanging the carpenter."[291] In April, 1976, he had answered Nader and Professor George Lodge's call for public representatives on corporate boards by accepting that "The burden of proof now falls on us in business and the jury we must convince is some 220 million Americans, not self-appointed pressure groups and not a small number of theoreticians, however erudite they may be, who wish to restructure the economic system to suit biases the public does not share."[292] Now, as chairman of the Business Roundtable and with rumors that he was being considered for Secretary of the Treasury by Carter, Shapiro tempered his remarks, calling for an improvement in communications between business, the people, and government.

But there was no doubt about his sense of mission: in the years ahead he would launch a wide offense against regulatory safeguards passed since the New Deal; at the same time he would mount a public relations campaign to "educate the people."

His targets were those of Spiro Agnew: the media and liberal activists. In December, he delivered a speech in Los Angeles criticizing the media for failing to educate the American people as to the business point of view. "One reason why the public doesn't understand economic issues," he told the *Philadelphia Inquirer* a week before, "is that they're not getting much of an education—from businessmen, from the media or from government...."[293]

He also laid into people, "various activist groups particularly," who would like the government to "seize" a lot of the power that corporations enjoyed. "I don't think that in government itself there is, at this point in time, the state of mind that would contemplate seizing power from corporate boards, for example, and all the rest of it. There are people who are advocating that point of view, and unless they're met head-on with facts, the odds can be that at a future point in time their argument will carry the day because there is no response."

Shapiro was not only apprehensive about the future under the new Democratic administration; he was also worried about how his own efforts would be interpreted; it would be "the kiss of death," he warned, "when you say it's a PR campaign. I go at it a different way and say that, as a practical matter, the objectives of business and society are not different. The problem is that the public doesn't perceive some of this, and so it's necessary first for business to carry its story to the public, second for business to carry its story to the government, because the government ultimately will be responding to what it thinks the public wants.

"Now you may think that's PR, but I think it's more substantial than puffery. What it's saying really, I think, is that the world ahead is a different world than the one we've lived in in the past. Business has a role to play in that world, but it has to get out of its offices and go to the public in the same way that public officeholders go to the public...the intelligent businessman is going to see himself much like a United States Senator, who's got a constituency that he has to satisfy and he has to communicate with. So

I can go at this as a strictly self-interest proposition, and say a man in my kind of job in industry today can't be successful if he simply stays in his office and tends to the production quotas, the sales quotas, hiring and that sort of thing."

It went without saying that most U.S. Senators *were* businessmen already; what was significant in Shapiro's remarks was its design of a mobilized corporate class directly confronting liberal reformers. It required making corporate officers into publicized political activists.

"You're considered a little bit unique in this belief," questioned Charles Layton of the *Philadelphia Inquirer.* "I don't think that there is yet a great uprising among your colleagues to get together and do this."

But there would be.

In his advocacy of the politically active corporate official, Shapiro was also careful to protect the sovereignty of corporation boards from the public. "I think business has to draw a very careful line so that it doesn't overstep its role and start assuming political responsibilities," he strategized. "Because once it does that, then it really is part of the state. And then the arguments for public elections and all the rest have substance. So business has to recognize a sharp distinction between people who hold public office in the public interest and the role of business. But within those limits there's plenty of room for activity."

Was there a model toward which America's corporate leaders could point and emulate?

Yes, there was.

The Du Ponts.

Using Wilmington as his example, Shapiro concluded that "it's in business's self-interest to create something like the GWDC (Greater Wilmington Development Council) to help do the planning, to help some of the things come into being."[294]

11. SAFE HARBOR FOR CHRISTIANA

In Wilmington, GWDC chairman Irénée du Pont, Jr., was indeed doing some planning, and one of the things that was finally coming into being was the merger of Christiana Securities into Du Pont. There were still some sharp rocks to avoid, including Lewis Murtaugh's stubborn case that the company's management, including Shapiro, was in thrall to the Du Ponts. The Supreme Court had agreed to review in December, delaying the scheduled hearing from January to early March. But the SEC was now on the side of the Du Ponts. It was a sign of how far the federal government had come from the stormy days of the New Deal, and, helped by some 50 lawyers and five million words of legal argument, the clouds of contention broke by early spring.

Forbes magazine, perhaps not understanding what was at stake, trivialized Murtaugh's case as well as the Du Pont's motives. "Those five million words are the best legal thought that money can buy. But their whole purpose is ultimately to obscure the basic issue, to disguise the fact that it is a simple feud between two greedy families over the price to be charged for the use of the can opener [Du Pont Company]. Who's right? In spite of the unevenly matched antagonists, the case could be decided either way."[295]

Hardly. The high court's decision was predictable. This might have been clearer to *Forbes* had it known that the authorized legend of the origins of Christiana which Du Pont now revived (and *Forbes,* like the *New York Times,* repeated) had been used in an earlier but similar financial ruse some 60 years before by the same wing of the Du Pont family. Pierre du Pont, the story goes, had been upset over rumors in 1915 that his cousin T. Coleman du Pont was thinking of selling his $14 million interest in the chemical firm, and the German war machine, acting through Kuhn Loeb, was feared to be making a move to grab the stock. Pierre, prompted by concern expressed by the British, did the only patriotic thing and bought Coleman out and locked the stock up in a "tin can" called Christiana Securities, in the process of cutting out his erratic cousin Alfred, whose loyalty to Pierre, at least, was questionable. Now, 60 years later, Pierre's nephew, Irénée du Pont, Jr., had told C.B. McCoy that it was time to open the can, now worth $1.7 billion; Du Pont Company would provide the can opener: Its own stock.

A quaint legend, based on stories told by Pierre's side of the family. The fact that it was a rationale for Pierre's seizing control of the firm (he did not buy the stock for the company, but himself and his allies) and that Pierre used unfounded fears by the British to hurry Coleman out the door, and then Alfred, has been buried by Du Pont's public relations office.* Nevertheless, that the legend was being repeated now, at the same time that Irving Shapiro was offering a new revised updated version about mysterious "black sheep Du Ponts" and strange visitations in Wilmington by robed apparitions said to resemble Arab sheiks, made *Forbes's* gullability all the more intriguing.

Chairman Shapiro, according to *Forbes,* "comes close to implying that one reason [for the SEC support for the merger] is the fear that a yet unborn black sheep Du Pont scion might get his hands on Christiana and wreck the chemical company. Black sheep Du Ponts are not exactly in short supply;

---

*See Chapter 7, "Du Pont Civil War."

Lammot du Pont Copeland, Jr., has recently filed the largest personal bankruptcy in history, for example. The SEC's imagination is stimulated."[296]

Perhaps. But if that most imaginative use yet of an individual's fiscal disaster was the basis for the SEC's decision to okay the merger, it did not explain why an ostensibly neutral government agency so aggressively took on an advocacy role in favor of Christiana and Du Pont and *against* Lewis Murtaugh, especially when it was clear Murtaugh's figures about how much Christiana stockholders were gaining were virtually incontestable. McCoy and Shapiro, by accepting Du Pont's low 2.5 percent discount of Christiana stock instead of the normal 10 percent minimum it was usually discounted for, were costing Du Pont shareholders a million shares of Du Pont, or some $200 million. Murtaugh's fears may have been wrong that the value of Du Pont stock would decline because Du Pont, by giving its own stock for Christiana's, would effectively be increasing the total number of its shares on the market; but his fears about the discount rate were right on the mark and should have elicited SEC concern.

It did not, perhaps because there were other, larger fears. Shapiro had used fear once before to win a big case, in the 1940's, when in the midst of a national hysteria he perfected the legal argument that American Communists were not members of a legitimate political party but agents and spies of a foreign power. Now, once again, he offered the same spectre of foreign intrigue to sell the Christiana merger, speaking of Arab investors who were said to have shown an interest in buying into Du Pont. "Anyone who gets control of Christiana Securities gets control of Du Pont." After the 1974 oil price hike, he warned darkly, "we had some fellows who said they represented Saudi Arabian interests nosing around Christiana."[297] There were no Saudi buyers, however, and apparently no Du Ponts willing to sell, although there were a few eyes cast furtively at the look-alike grandson of Pierre's arch enemy "rebel" cousin, Alfred du Pont Dent, who had recently launched his own struggle to wrest control over his grandfather's estate's 702,000 Du Pont shares from Ed Ball. Dent has never claimed being approached, and suggestions that he may have been the "black sheep Du Pont" was no doubt a continuation of the smear his grandfather also suffered at the hands of his family.

Another line taken by Shapiro, if not as misleading, was at least as presumptuous: that the Du Ponts were poor managers.[298] But if his negotiations with the Christiana leaders should have proved anything, it was that the Du Ponts who had guided Du Pont for 170 years through eleven generations were very good managers indeed, and very shrewd bargainers. Shapiro's 7.4 percent return on shareholders' equity had still to match the Du Ponts' 20 percent return in the 1950's or even their 12 percent in the 1960's.

It was as unfair for Shapiro to claim poor management as it would have been to charge all the problems now confronting Du Pont as a result of accumulated internal problems and external interferences (the loss of GM dividends, the post-Vietnam recession, the Arab oil price hike, technology's depression on prices, revived European and Japanese competition) on Shapiro.

The family was probably not angry with Shapiro. Undoubtedly, they saw some merit in what he was saying about them and publicly, at least, agreed with him. "I would have been terribly surprised if anyone had asked me to be president," Irénée said in 1973. "I know my limitations. Besides, I as a stockholder would have objected to me as president."[299] Such self-effacing illusions of incompetence served the family's immediate interests. It helped to diffuse the clan's formidable political reputation and made them seem less important and therefore less of a threat to any possible public interest. Shapiro's claim, then, that "The Du Ponts have run out of managerial talent. Irénée is the last of the old breed,"[300] while totally inaccurate (a number of Du Ponts held managerial positions, including H.R. Sharp III, who headed the company's Computer System Section of the Finance Department, and Pierre Coleman du Pont, a supervisor in the fast-growing photo-products plant at Glasgow, Delaware) was not contested.

Christiana was contested, but not by Shapiro or the SEC. Richard J. Collins, a St. Louis attorney, and Lewis Murtaugh representing themselves and other Du Pont shareholders, defended their case against the SEC's approval before the Supreme Court. Before 8 of the 9 Justices (William Rehnquist was absent because of a back injury), Collins and Murtaugh argued that the SEC should have considered the Christiana shares' fair market value as well as the firm's net asset value in deciding if there was indeed an "exchange of equivalents" as Du Pont and Christiana held. If it had, the SEC would have been forced to concede that the 10 percent discount would have been far more fair than the proposed 2.5 percent. Instead, the SEC evaluated the holding company solely on the basis of net asset value, and held that the effect on Du Pont shareholders was not relevant. The 8th Circuit Court in St. Louis had disagreed and reversed the SEC. Now it was up to the Supreme Court.

Representing Du Pont, Daniel Gribbon spoke more in his 15 alloted minutes, but said less. His argument boiled down to emphasizing the fairness and reasonableness of the merger, rather than defending it as the best Shapiro and McCoy could have gotten. While conceding that Christiana shares normally sold for 20 to 25 percent below that of Du Pont common stock, he praised the executives for getting what they did get, saying that some Du Ponts had even tried to get a premium on their Christiana stock. It was quite an admission and one that should have added weight to Collins's claims. But Gribbon had an ace, a political ace. The merger, he explained, removed any threat that Christiana's shareholders could control or harm the chemical giant. Again, fear of unknown and nonexistent parties became the issue.

The SEC, represented by David Farber, also admitted that the St. Louis court had used fair market value in determining the value of Christiana, but in his 20 minutes Farber reminded the Justices that federal law dictates the use of net asset value in order to prevent a diluting of the holding company's "intrinsic value." "No one has been injured by this merger."[301] He denied there was any "overreaching" by either party.

The questions by the Justices, who often left the bench amid proceedings and followed Chief Justice Burger to lunch in the middle of an argument, were few, so few, in fact, that Murtaugh was surprised. Collins was not. Justice Lewis Powell had singed Collins's feathers midflight when he asked him if he would object if Christiana would merge with IBM. Collins answered "no"; his arguments, he said, had been based on Christiana using its power over the Du Pont executives to get ultra-generous terms. Then he realized his mistake. His negative answer had undermined his whole previous argument about valuation methods. He quickly tried to escape by saying he would also insist on getting a price above IBM's net asset value, but Powell had sprung the trap. "The betting in Wall Street," the *New York Times* reported, "appeared to be that the court would allow the merger to go through."[302]

The decision came rolling down heavy and fast only three months later. Chief Justice Warren Burger, delivering the majority opinion, backed the SEC and said the 8th Circuit Court had exceeded its authority. The decision was 7 to 1. Only Justice William J. Brennan, Jr., dissented. Du Pont's directors were in a classic "conflict of interest situation," because of Christiana's position as "controlling shareholder" of Du Pont, he protested. They had entered a transaction that "handsomely benefited Christiana without extracting the price for Du Pont that an arms-length negotiator would have demanded and received."[303] Both Shapiro and C.B. McCoy, the Appeals Court had noted, were appointed as Du Pont's negotiators by the Du Pont board, which was controlled by Christiana.

Shapiro was "very pleased." The Du Ponts were "pleased." Murtaugh was not, but there was little else he could do. Delaware's Federal Judge Murray Schwartz had also decided against him. He could have appealed that also if Schwartz's final order had not been held in abeyance. All that was left to

Murtaugh was to wonder why the Supreme Court's dissenting vote was not larger. His argument that Du Pont shares would be depressed in value by putting onto the open market more Du Pont stock to exchange for Christiana's assets was rejected by Chief Justice Burger. There was no evidence, Burger held, that the Du Ponts in Christiana, who for so long had been indirect investors in Du Pont, would now change the essential nature of their investment.

On the previous Friday, Du Pont's stock had fallen ⅜ths to $116.25. On the following Wednesday, it was down to $114.50. "Obviously," said John E. Baynum, manager of the Wilmington branch of White, Weld and Co. investment firm, "the feeling on the street was that Du Pont had a pretty good case."[304] Which, ironically, was why investors had sold Du Pont but not Christiana, which remained unchanged at $116.50. The market had spoken louder than the Court as to who the real winner was.

In the hills north of Wilmington, glasses were lifted in quiet toast to victory. All that remained was the convening of a special meeting of the stockholders of Du Pont and Christiana. The Du Pont meeting had been deliberately postponed because the company was, Shapiro admitted, "reluctant to ask stockholders to deal with this subject while the integrity of its management was under attack."[305] Now both were scheduled for October.

12. MURDER ON THE BRANDYWINE

As the meetings approached, absences in the family roster became more painfully noticeable, a result of that nagging reminder of the human condition, death, of which some visitations were the normal end of the family's characteristic logevity, while others were disturbingly irregular.

One "crossing of the creek" had been expected, that of 88-year-old Walter Carpenter, Jr. To his last day in March, 1976, Carpenter enjoyed the odd geneological distinction of being a Du Pont in-law still incorrectly trumpted by the press as "the first person outside the Du Pont family to be elected president." (C.B. McCoy was, and is, another such public relations phenomenon). He had been a titan in family lore, the youngest man (at 32 years of age) to be elected a director; a General Motors director for 32 years, the captain who had guided Du Pont through the lucrative waters of World War II toward its rising atomic star over Japan as the principal contractor of the Manhattan Project) and one of the few honorary chairmen in the company's history, a true Du Pont laureate. He had also been a recipient of the Order of Alphonso the Wise, in recognition of his outstanding cultural and charitable support for Franco's fascist Spain.

The death of Henry B. du Pont III, elder brother of Edward du Pont, in September, 1976, on the other hand, sent shock waves through the family. The great-great-great-grandson of the founder of Du Pont Company, Henry had a long thin face that, with the exception of his eyes, resembled more his grand-uncle, Lammot du Pont, than his father, Henry B. du Pont II. He lived in Westport, Connecticut, near the Bridgeport plant of Du Pont's subsidiary, Remington Arms, where he served as a top executive. At 44, Henry was considered a rising power in the family when his life was suddenly cut down in a freak accident. He had just arrived at Block Island airport in a private single-engine Beechcraft Bonanza airplane with his father-in-law and co-pilot, Dan Wheeler, planning to meet a family sailboat en route from Newport, Rhode Island. Both men were guilty of the serious safety violations of leaving the engine idle while Henry disembarked and Wheeler left the controls to climb into the back seat. Wheeler was handing suitcases to Henry, who was standing on the wing, when the passenger door swung shut. Wheeler leaned forward to reopen the door and the front seat fell forward against the power controls. The propeller churned and the plane shot forward and began circling wildly in front of the airport's terminal, threatening at one point to smash right through the window of the terminal's restaurant. Henry clung desperately to the door handle, but it broke away and he was hurled into the air. As he tumbled some 20 feet, he struck his head. Bleeding profusely, Henry was rushed to Lawrence and Memorial Hospital, where he died three days later. He left behind a wife, Joan, and a nine-year-old son, Henry B. IV. The following Tuesday, a shocked and bereaved family once again gathered at Christ Church above the Brandywine where so many had been baptized and married and, like Henry, sent to the grave.

But undoubtedly the most bizarre and frightening demise was that of Christiana Securities' long-time treasurer, Theodore E. House, in the summer of 1977. Only the year before, House had been elected to join Irénée du Pont on the board of trustees of Wilmington College. Ted House, 56, was a friend of Irénée as well as his personal financial secretary; as Christiana's only full-time employee and treasurer for 24 years, he handled Christiana's taxes and other financial matters and knew the inner workings of the family's fortune like no one else. House, however, maintained an air of mystery about himself. Irénée was one of the few Du Ponts on Christiana's board who actually knew House well. "He took care of all the routine financial problems," was all that Lammot du Pont Copeland could offer later. "I know very little about him myself."[306] Ellason Downs, a Du Pont in-law on the Christiana board, likewise described having "a very fine business relationship" with House, "not a close personal relationship."[307] House, most agreed, was a very private fellow.

On Thursday, September 1, Irénée du Pont's normally tranquil morning at Granogue was interrupted by a phone call. It was from Nadine, House's slim, attractive 41-year-old wife. Ted had not returned home to their apartment last night or reported for work that morning at Christiana's small office. She was worried. Could Irénée check in to see if he was alright? Irénée said he would and drove over to the two-story, brick house in the fashionable suburb of Alapocas shortly after noon. He was totally unprepared for what he found. There, lying face down on the floor on the screened porch, was Ted House, his skull fractured by repeated blows.

The police immediately found discrepancies in stories surrounding the murdered man. There were no signs of a burglary, nothing missing, no forced entry, although Nadine reported that burglars broke in the previous year and they had never repaired the back door where the robbers got in. There were no signs of struggle, although House had been struck many times, probably with a heavy wine bottle used as art decor on the porch. A burned out cigarette on an ashtray indicated he was not dozing when he was attacked and was probably sitting in a chair when struck from behind. He was a reformed alcoholic and director of the Limen House for Men, a rehabilitation program for alcoholics; yet he had been drinking a cocktail when he was killed. His house was in an affluent suburb and filled with antiques; but his financial records showed he had little money. Police first reported he was separated from Nadine; she said he was living with her at the apartment. She had seen him last the night of his death, at the house. He was playing old records on the porch when she left about 6 p.m. The record player had been turned off when the police arrived.

Why was he drinking again? No one knew. The neighbors were of little help. "Especially around here," one said. "You don't get to know your neighbors that well."[308] But someone anonymously offered a $1000 reward for information. Irénée denied it was he.

As the investigation into clues proceeded, police found themselves in two worlds, one of high finance, the other of Wilmington's underworld of sex and crime. House, it seems, had kept records of the financial and sexual dealings of his business and social contacts. It was these notes that led detectives to both mansions and the seamier streets of Wilmington's inner city. Why should Christiana's treasurer keep such records? No one knew or was willing to say. But on October 7 Nadine filed a legal petition demanding that the police return the records and a cashier's check for $3646, claiming House's safety deposit box had been seized illegally without a court order.

The murder of Christiana's treasurer hung like a pall over the firm's name as its last shareholder's meeting, scheduled for Oct. 17, approached. House's name continued to haunt the headlines as a series of events struck, one by one, in the week before the meeting. The first occurred on the night of October 13. A security guard at the Brandywine 100 luxury apartments off Faulke Road where the Houses had a penthouse suite heard a horn blowing in the basement garage. When he got there, he found Nadine visibly shaken. She had just returned from visiting the House home at Apolacas which was being fixed up for sale, "the first time I've been out at night since Ted's death," she said, and had parked her green-grey Continental Mark IV in the regular space when she heard a "popping sound," like a car backfiring. "I felt a jolt ... then it dawned on me that someone was shooting at me."[309] Terrorized, she had sounded the horn.

The guard and a neighbor quickly took Nadine to her penthouse suite on the 7th floor and called police. By the time her attorney arrived, police had roped off the area. Heel marks had been found in the ground some feet outside the garage and a dent had been found notched in the vinyl roof of Nadine's car less than three inches above the windshield, but police acted skeptical. "We're not even positive there was a shooting," Capt. Edward Mowdas told the press. "The damage to the roof could have been done by something else.... She's the only one who saw or heard anything."[310] The police left Nadine in the care of her two sons by a previous marriage, Mark, 22, and Scott, 17. "I'm really scared," Nadine, shaking, whispered. "Someone must think I have information about Ted's death.... Not at all.... Don't you think I would have told [the police] by now? I wish to hell they'd find him."[311] She said she was hiring a bodyguard because the police didn't have the money to pay for her protection. Questioned by the press, the police disputed Nadine's statement, claiming, "She doesn't even want to talk to us much ... She doesn't want anything to do with us."[312]

The next day, October 15, the *News-Journal* reported that a police source had stated that Nadine had also reported being fired at on September 30, two weeks before, and that five .22 caliber shell casings had been found the next day in a small stream about 25 feet from her parking spot and a few feet from where the heel marks had been found the night of October 13. It was also reported that Nadine and House had been separated but had recently reconciled, and that House periodically spent the night at the couple's old home nearby where he was murdered. Nadine, the *Journal* stated, had continued to refuse to take a lie detector test.

Nadine was furious. She charged that the police had manufactured this latest story and denied ever saying there was a shooting two weeks ago. The detectives under chief prosecutor Charles M. Oberly III had "lied and committed illegal acts,"[313] while bumbling the investigation. She had voluntarily submitted to questioning four times and had declined to allow the police to use their polygraph only because her doctor had advised her not to because of a severe adrenal ailment that caused her blood pressure to rise under strain, often causing black-outs. When she had herself tested anyway by an out-of-state polygraph expert, "they asked me my name, and, zip, it went off the chart." Now, she said in tears, the police were pointing at her, and smearing House's name. "They asked me if I thought he was a bisexual. They asked me did he have any dealings with Puerto Ricans or Blacks." She sighed. "I know he made love to me every night. What else he did I couldn't tell you." She knew nothing of any other sexual encounters. The police had also questioned her about her own private life during her six-year marriage; she had never dated, except during her one-year separation, and "they were simple two-date things." House had started drinking again two years ago, after Christiana's dissolution was approved by the SEC. "When Ted was drinking he did some very unreal things," she conceded, but insisted that the motive for his murder was probably robbery. He had had a wallet "stuffed with cash" that she had seen the night of his death when he gave her some money, and he also carried a pistol, and she had told police of this. She believed someone had frightened him enough to make him carry the gun.

The next day, Sgt. Wayne Merritt admitted Nadine had not said anything to police about an earlier September 30th shooting. But he disputed her claim of denied police protection, and said she had not wanted bodyguards. The police had found no wallet with cash and no pistol. Although they had taken the safe deposit box under a subpoena signed by the Attorney General, they denied removing anything from it.

About the same time, the most powerful Du Ponts gathered to hold their last meeting as Christiana Securities. Du Pont Company had just held its own special meeting and officially approved the merger, the Du Ponts, of course, voting their millions of shares in favor of the deal despite an obvious conflict of interest. Now, as Irénée, Lammot du Pont Copeland, Sr., and Crawford Greenewalt stood together in the back of the room, watching, the last cast of the die was made, loaded, no doubt, but no less satisfying. The merger was now legal.

Irénée, accompanied by Ellason Downs, met Irving Shapiro at the 9th floor of Du Pont Headquarters. There, as Du Pont ancestors peered down from portraits on the walls, Irénée and Shapiro signed the historic documents that opened "the tin can," freeing the richest family in the world from its tethers to the chemical firm of their forebears. Only years later would it be clear that what had been opened was a Pandora's box.

And what of Nadine House? As the weeks went by, her life was plunged deeper into the bizarre. The police had turned to mysticism for a solution to the murder. They had contacted Peter Hurkos, the mystic involved in the

Boston Strangler case. When he reportedly asked for an $8000 fee for three days, they balked. Whereupon the anonymous donor raised his reward to $5000.

On October 19, two days after Irénée had officially dissolved Christiana Securities, *News-Journal* reporter Ralph Moyed joined a friend of Nadine's, two detectives, and four of House's children at the House home to hold hands in an effort to contact the murdered man. A white-haired spiritualist had phoned the family after hearing of the shooting incident at Nadine's car and reported having a vision of a man standing by a bike outside the house the night of the shooting. The family and police were startled. They had known, but not released to the press, that a bicyclist had been seen driving between House's home and Nadine's apartment about 15 minutes before the alleged shooting.

The spiritualist, who asked not to be identified, held the seance for no money. Just a few feet from the French doors to the porch where House's body was found, the participants gathered in a circle, bathed in the red glow of a single lightbulb suspended from a movie screen stand, and heard the mystic eerily describe how a young six-foot man named "John" had accidentally killed House with a single blow for rejecting his demand for over $75,000. The children were excited, but it all predictably came to naught. And the police kept looking at Nadine.

Two weeks later Nadine reported being attacked in her apartment by a man. Rushed by county police to a hospital, she was treated for an inch-long gash in her head and neck injuries. "Police wouldn't say whether Mrs. House might have gotten her injuries as a result of a fainting spell," reported the *News-Journal*.[314] But Nadine immediately agreed to undergo hypnosis for the police. "I want to clear this up," she said. "I'm not going to spend the rest of my life getting choked and hit over the head....I can't believe he was trying to kill me. If he wanted to, he could have." She explained that she had volunteered for hypnosis because "They say I might know some things that I am blocking out."[315] At Delaware State Hospital, Nadine went through a two-hour session. "She was not faking," said psychologist Cono Galliani.[316] She freely answered questions. The police were still not satisfied.

"There was a great deal of harassment,"[317] reported Cheryl Fetkenher, sales representative at the Brandywine Hilton, where Nadine worked. She reported that House and Nadine had been getting along; he used to call her at work. Since the murder, Nadine was losing weight and suffering blackouts from her high blood pressure. "She was so thin and worn-looking." The police, Ms. Fetkenher said, were again at the hotel asking personal questions. "It seemed they weren't trying to find out anything but were just harassing her."[318]

Nadine apparently agreed. Taking her doctor's advice, she took a leave of absence a few days later after collapsing in the Wilmington office of the Delaware Department of Justice just before another scheduled interrogation. Although two witnesses placed her in the apartment at the time House was killed, "the police were saying she did it but couldn't prove it," said her son, Mark. "I can't see her coming back. She has very few friends here."

Nadine fled Delaware. The next month, the *News-Journal* reported the police were "winding down" their probe.

Theodore House's murderer has never been found.

* * *

Whatever Irénée felt about all this, he did not express it publicly. He was by nature a very personal man, like his slain friend, and he did not easily share grief in front of prying reporters. But House's murder, including the discovery of his body, deeply shook Irénée, who had once unsuccessfully attempted to open a rehabilitation center for alcoholics in Wilmington with House slated to be director; local residents had unfairly rejected it as a "drunk tank for the rich."[319]

House's death had a symbolic meaning also, for with him went the only non-Du Pont in the inner circle of Christiana Securities. Now, with both the corporate shell and House gone, all that was left was what, after all, it had always really been: the family. Signing the dissolution documents with Irénée, Irving Shapiro spoke for the future as well as the past. "It is the end of an era," he said, "and the beginning of a new one."[320]

With the homefront secure, and freed of all but voluntary ties to the chemical giant which bore their name, the Du Ponts could now stretch their wings and venture forth beyond Delaware into the most serious political quest of their 180-year adventure in America. They were about to embark on what some would call the most dangerous experiment with American democracy since the New Deal. They would ultimately join Ronald Reagan in calling it "New Federalism". But while Reagan's strong opposition had prevented him from implementing his philosophy of austerity while governor in California, no such restraints existed in Delaware by 1976. The Du Ponts, in fact, would anticipate Reagan's presidential efforts to strike down New Deal safeguards and reforms by at least four years in their state. Led by Governor Pete du Pont in Delaware and assisted on the national level by the able Irving Shapiro, the Du Ponts would now begin to mobilize their allies to remold America in their own ultra-conservative image.

Seventeen

A DYNASTY REBORN

1. PRELUDE TO REAGANOMICS

The large colonial chamber in Delaware's capitol, though packed with people, was hushed, the delegates to the General Assembly showing respect for the man who stood before them. He was tall, lean, and impeccably dressed, his brown hair carefully groomed above a long attractive face bearing thin dark glasses and the cleft chin of his famous family. He was very rich, and now, as governor, very powerful. Yet, in this first major address of his new administration, Pete du Pont was troubled.

Delaware, he told the startled delegates, was "bankrupt," a pauper "living day-to-day on borrowed money."[1] It's debt would climb to $171 million by 1978, ill tidings for a state with a shrinking tax base and depressed industrial growth. In other states, he claimed, many programs are financed by cities; but in Delaware the state has had to bear the burden. There was only one solution: austerity. He would have to cut $40 million out of the state's budget, with public education paying the greatest toll.

Democrats, when they recovered, charged that du Pont was exaggerating, another case of "Champagne Pete" overblowing a crisis to justify insensitivity to the average citizen he had derided as "Joe Six-Pack" during his election campaign. Pete later did admit his bankruptcy charge was not a "legal definition" of the word, but by then it had served its purpose; it made headlines, putting the blame for his proposed cuts on the previous Democratic administration of Governor Sherman Tribbitt.

The cuts read like a scenario of Reaganomics: $14.6 million from public education; an $11.3 million suspension in cost-of-living increases that had been scheduled for inflation-burdened state employees; welfare costs would essentially be disavowed, and shifted to the backs of county governments. There would also be a huge cutback in highway construction, a transfer of some highway maintenance costs to counties, and a closing of one of the campuses of the Delaware Technical and Community College, the state's only public two-year institution of higher education and the only source of further education that many high school graduates from the working class could afford.

There was no doubt who would suffer most. Glenn Kenton, Pete du Pont's long-time aide who had been appointed Delaware's Secretary of State, acknowledged that the education reductions would fall hardest on the poorer school districts. But he had a solution: Delaware's first sales tax. "The problem is that in Delaware we have no sales tax and the 49th lowest property tax in the country. We cannot continue, in my judgment, to support the kind of state services we're supporting with no sales tax and with the second lowest property tax in the country. The income tax just will not take the load any longer."[2]

Kenton was merely repeating what Pete had claimed, that Delaware had the highest personal income tax and highest per capita debt in America.[3] Pete's figures, however, ignored the *total* state tax paid by Delawareans. When low county and local taxes were plugged into the equation, according to the private, non-profit Tax Foundation, Inc., of New York, Delawareans' tax bills fell well below the average for all 50 states and ranked eleventh in state and local taxes paid per capita. New York's $1023 per capita in 1975 was almost 30 percent higher than Delaware's $727. Delaware, in fact, was in tune with its geographic neighbors: New Jersey at $725 and Maryland at $728. Pennsylvania had a lower annual tax tab of $636, yet many of its residents crossed into Delaware each weekend to shop at its malls. As for personal income taxes, Delaware ranked 26th on the basis of *collections* per $1000 of personal income, reflecting the many tax-loopholes enjoyed by the rich in the state, which had one of the nation's highest per person income levels.[4] Throughout the United States, there was an average of one official millionaire for every 300,000 people; in Delaware, there was one millionaire for every 40,000 people, eight times the national average.[5] Obviously, moving vans were a rare sight in Greenville.

So were registered Democrats. But that did not hinder Governor Tribbitt from endorsing a cut in the capital gains tax, or former Governor Elbert Carvel from endorsing a state sales tax. Nor did it prevent Tribbitt's Delaware Revenue Study Committee from cutting from the draft of its final report a telling point made by its acting chairman, David N. Williams, that individual taxes had increased much more since 1968 than corporate income taxes.[6] It was, perhaps, understandable that the Delaware Oil Men's Association were opposed to a legislative act that placed a 1¢ per gallon tax on refined oil, and that Governor Tribbitt so easily bent to J. Paul Getty's threat to close his only U.S. refinery in Delaware City by vetoing the measure. It was also understandable that the Delaware Association of Realtors opposed an attempt to increase the state real estate transfer tax. But it was difficult to understand why Eleanor Craig, chair of the Delaware Economic and Financial Advisory Council, and Weston Nellius, state secretary of finance, two close economic advisors to Governor du Pont, would now lobby so strongly for sales tax legislation when du Pont had pledged during his campaign to oppose any sales tax. Unless, of course, there was more afoot.

And there was.

The first warning of a drastic change for Delaware had been sounded by the governor himself when he loosely used the term "bankruptcy." He proposed a $56 million, 30-month bond issue to meet the crisis. But the full meaning of that move toward greater indebtedness to private financial interests was lost in the fanfare surrounding the sales tax.

The campaign was led by Irénée du Pont's State Chamber of Commerce, and, to be sure, it was earnest. The Chamber wanted to raise $40 million to help meet the $50 million deficit Pete was facing that year. "We are extremely serious about the proposal," assured Chamber President Ross Amerson. "We feel it is the most practical approach for putting Delaware on a sound financial basis."[7]

It was not a new line. It had been tried before, by Du Pont Chairman Charles McCoy in 1974, for example. McCoy, in an important speech titled, "An Approach to Delaware's Future," argued that a sales tax "makes sense for Delaware and should be put into effect promptly."[8]

It was not, and for very good reasons. It was not fair, David Williams argued, to levy a state sales tax when taxes under existing tax laws were not collected, when there were numerous other untaxed sources of revenue, when the state had no overall fiscal policy, when the division of revenue couldn't even produce the data necessary for fiscal forecasts, when business taxes were going to be reduced or repealed, and when the state was already being said to be "unattractive" to business.[9] But fairness alone, unfortunately, is no criterion for political practice in Delaware, or in any state. Power is, and it was power that Pete du Pont understood. The opposition of retailers, represented by the small business chambers of commerce of Newark and Dover, had demonstrated that big business was usurping the role of speaking for all "business" interests. The mayor of Delmar, frightened that the sales tax would kill plans for a mall expected to draw Maryland residents across the state border, also voiced his opposition. So did the head of the state AFL-CIO, John Campanelli. And L.V. Crose of the United Auto Workers presented petitions bearing the names of 2000 workers at a public hearing of the House Revenue and Taxation Committee requested but not attended by Governor du Pont.

But he heard the message. A sales tax was inherently regressive, opponents pointed out, despite the State Chamber of Commerce's suggested exemptions on necessities such as food and medicine. They did not believe the exemptions would last very long or that the tax rate would remain low. Moreover, a good part of the gross receipts tax, which the State Chamber's proposal would eliminate, was not paid by Delawareans because much of what was manufactured and wholesaled in Delaware was sold outside the state; a sales tax, on the other hand, would be paid mostly by Delawareans and would discourage out-of-state shoppers. Despite a *News-Journal* endorsement of the sales tax and Kenton's claim that du Pont was "softening" his earlier opposition to a sales tax, Governor du Pont wisely deferred and proposed an adjusted gross income tax instead. But he warned the Greater Dover Chamber of Commerce that unless the legislature gave him the $40 million budget cuts he wanted, a sales tax was inevitable. He also said, "We're going to become ugly, mean and vindictive"[10] about collecting back taxes. Needless to say, Governor du Pont got his cuts.

The State Chamber of Commerce, however, refused to yield on the sales tax. They were for the cuts, but they also wanted the sales tax. They simply wanted the whole pie, and it was a sign of the times that they thought they could get it. "I think the opposition is a lot more vocal," said Anderson, "but I don't think there is that much opposition. It's real close."[11] Anderson was banking on the influence of his corporate supporters, particularly his biggest, Du Pont Company, represented by Vice President Irénée du Pont, Jr.

Du Pont's campaign mounted steadily from chief counsel C.E. Welch's testimony before the legislature on April 21. On May 16, 1977, the Public Affairs Department was geared up by Thomas Stephenson to acquaint its members with Delaware's financial "plight." The next day, textile fibers vice-president Robert Forney sent a letter to over 2500 employees urging them to "consider this problem and make your *individual* views known to your state representative, state senator, Governor du Pont and Lieutenant Governor Mc Ginnes."[12] Forney denied Du Pont was pressuring its employees. "If you read the letter, you can see that the only word I underlined is individual," he said. Similar notices were sent out to other du Pont employees in the state. As the legislative session's adjournment neared, Chairman Irving Shapiro threw his own formidable weight into the fray. On the night of June 28, he sent off Western Union mailgrams to targeted employees.

There was no denying now that Shapiro was pressuring his employees to support the sales tax. "Introduced last Friday in Dover was H.B. 544 which would restructure personal income taxes and enact a 2.9% sales tax," Shapiro wired. "This bill is consistent with our views. As we understand it, there is significant underlying Democratic support for this measure which may not be forthcoming unless the governor personally endorses the sales tax/ piggybacking concept. I urge your support and ask that you telephone or send a telegram to the Governor and your state legislators today so that they will know of your personal concern before they adjourn June 30."[13]

Shapiro's willingness to act as "point-man" on the unpopular issue served the interests of the governor. Retreating from Kenton's "softening" description, Pete now seemed the personification of independence from his family's company. The state tax issue would be used occasionally for other such displays of supposed friction between Pete and the company during his first term of office, as in December 1978 when Shapiro took to television to describe Pete as a "highly intelligent, articulate, attractive gentleman" who was nevertheless wrong to oppose a "modest" sales tax. He was withholding judgment on the governor's stewardship, he said, as "it remains to be seen" whether du Pont planned to merely "tinker" with Delaware's tax system or propose "strong remedial action."[14] Hercules Chemicals president, Alexander Giacco, accompanying him on the "Perspective Delaware" WPVI-TV show, could not help but refer to himself, tongue in cheek, as "an intruder in the Pete and Irv show."[15]

While Delawareans were dazzled by the flying sparks, however, Pete was moving to jettison another campaign pledge, one which affected the very basis for any future discussion of Delaware's financial health. During his first year in office, du Pont dodged his previous commitment to limit capital improvement bonds to no more that $30 million a year[16] by introducing three issues of a new "various purpose" bond that put Delaware under another $48 million debt load and another $40.7 million the following year.[17]

If the governor really had any differences with Shapiro, they did not extend to one of Shapiro's greatest concerns: anti-pollution costs. "Du Pont makes a couple of good cases,"[18] Pete said after addressing 200 members and guests of the Delaware branch of the American Chemical Society at the Du Pont Country Club. He said Congress should consider weakening federal water pollution control laws and told the press and listeners that he foresaw no political problems advocating the same position as Du Pont.

Du Pont Company was then resisting installation of the "best available" water pollution control technology by the July 1, 1983, deadline set by law in 1972. The Company claimed that eliminating the last amounts of pollution did not significantly improve water quality and was too expensive. Pete agreed.

But residents along the South River at Waynesboro, Virginia, and the south fork of the Shenandoah River were not so sympathetic. A Du Pont plant along the river used mercury in production from 1929 to 1950; by 1977, the mercury that the company had found in local fish was still in evidence, four times the permissible level of .4 parts per million. The fish were so poisoned that Governor Mills Godwin imposed a ban in June 1977 on human consumption, and State Health Director Dr. James Kenley confirmed the ban might have to be maintained for years.[19]

To Irving Shapiro, however, the demands of environmentalists were strident, resulted in wasted resources, and delayed creation of new jobs. In a speech before the Southern Governor's Conference at San Antonio, Texas, in August 1977 he decried that "government simply responds to pressures applied by one-sided public thinkers." As if he were an elected public executive speaking for "all the people," Shapiro asserted that "advocacy does not require a balance scale.... Activists speak only to issues that interest them, leaving the other dimensions of the human condition for others to worry about." As an example, he cited Du Pont's five-year effort to build a plant on the Gulf Coast of the state of Mississippi. Lawsuits filed by a group of 11 people, "a substantial number of whom do not even reside in Mississippi," had delayed the project, and "many more years may pass" before construction could proceed. "Who has been the loser in the meantime?" he asked the governors, referring to the 500 to 600 jobs promised for the area.[20]

Shapiro's comments revealed more about Du Pont's own anti-environmental control campaign than the facts behind the De Lisle, Mississippi, controversy. What was at stake was not simply a lawsuit by a group of outsiders, but the Mississippi Air and Water Pollution Control Commission's legally mandated responsibility to protect the waters of the Bay of St. Louis. Save the Bay, Inc. was an organization of state residents backed by environmentalists from nearby New Orleans. What had made Shapiro angry was that they had upset Du Pont's plan to start construction of a pigments plant without having to face legally conducted public hearings as required by law.

Despite testimony by a scientist from the Gulf Coast Research Laboratory that laboratory tests indicated that the brownish gel effluent from the proposed plant would kill shrimp, a vital source of the Gulf's fishing industry,[21] the state Commission had gone along with Du Pont and allowed construction to proceed. Environmentalists brought suit in court and were fought all the way to the Supreme Court by Du Pont and the Commission. At the high court, new hearings were ordered. Shapiro was furious, not just because of De Lisle itself, but what it represented. "Opposition by groups such as Save the Bay, Inc., points up a growing problem for the company" (Pigments Vice-President Arthur H.) Geil said, noting that "there could be some objection to any site the company picks."[22]

Mississippi, however, was not just any site. It was part of a grand strategy of shifting plants to the non-union South. In February 1977, *Du Pont News* printed a list of 15 new construction projects authorized for start-up in 1977 or later; of the fifteen, 13 were in Southern states. The state of Mississippi "rates among the very top choices,"[23] Vice President Irénée du Pont, Jr., had told delegates to Mississippi's first annual Governor's Conference on Economic Development in 1973. In the past, Mississippi had "ended up as a bridesmaid instead of a bride," he said. Now Du Pont was marrying the state to northern industry, citing taxes as one of Du Pont's top criteria for expansion site selection. Mississippi's government, unlike Delaware's, has comparatively little overhead in the way of public services to its citizens, ranking among the nation's lowest in per capita taxation as well as per capita service expenditures. Irénée apparently did not mention wages and workman's compensation benefits as being among Du Pont's 84 selection criteria; there, too, Mississippi ranks among the lowest in America, with a standard of living that leaves much to be desired.

To Wilmington, the state was the vital southernmost link in its "Mississippi Connection," a system of 24 Du Pont plants and terminals along the Mississippi watershed that used the mighty river and its tributaries as a superhighway, shipping more than 10 products and a variety of supplies between factories and then to markets with a fleet of towboats and over 40 huge barges, all controlled by the company's Transportation and Distribution Department.[24] The Mississippi also provided free water for the company's manufacturing plants, and it was the efforts of the federal EPA to restore and protect its quality and the nation's environment as a whole that had drawn Shapiro's ire. Du Pont was being forced to spend another $3 billion to meet federal water, air and noise standards, when, the Chairman claimed, only $750 million was needed to guarantee measurable improvements.[25]

This new assertiveness by Shapiro against environmental laws accompanied Jimmy Carter's taking of the presidential oath. By that time, Irving Shapiro had reason to feel the worst was behind him. The appearance at Du Pont Headquarters in November 1976 of picket lines in sympathy with 35 workers who had been reprimanded for walking off their jobs at the Newport pigments plant over management's refusal to deal with their grievances had caused some embarrassment, but the issue had sputtered out. Likewise, the outbreak of a mysterious intestinal illness that struck more than 300 Chambers Works employees in September, while making headlines for a brief while, was arrested. The United Steelworkers organizing drive was also being undercut by a rival International Association of Du Pont Employees Union that, as of July, included the Chambers Works local union. Charges that the "legionnaires disease" may have been linked to leaks of DuPont's F-11 fluorocarbon refrigerant used in the Bellevue Stafford Hotel's air-conditioning system (the heat of a cigarette could cause a chemical breakdown of F-11 into deadly phosgene gas, and 80 percent of 21 legionnaires surveyed by the Natural Resources Defense Council smoked; the theory being that the leaks may have found their way through an opening in an air shaft on the second floor of the hotel, where the legionnaires met in hospitality rooms) had been successfully refuted as "unfounded and irresponsible" by Du Pont's director of Research and Development, Dr. Theodore Cairas. The Franklin Institute of Philadelphia found no evidence that the F-11 leak had taken the suspected route. The disease was subsequently attributed to a virus.

There were a few reversals, including Du Pont's F-22 replacement for its fluorocarbon aerosols. The same day Du Pont announced F-22's introduction, three federal agencies—the EPA, the Food and Drug Administration, and the Consumer Products Safety Commission—also established an unusual joint program to regulate fluorocarbons, declaring that F-22 was also a health hazard. Left without a replacement, Shapiro had to endure the elation of competitors.

But the greatest problem continued to be fibers. By the April 1977 annual meeting, fibers had made what Shapiro called a "nominal but very welcome profit" to raise first quarter earnings above 1976's last quarter, but keep them still below that of the first quarter of 1976. Fibers' ten cents a share earnings were less than nominal; they were disastrous, down from its low of 70 cents of a year before. This continued the pressure on Shapiro, who had leveraged Du Pont for the first time in its 174 year history. Since 1973, Du Pont's long-term debt had risen from $250 million to $1.5 billion. Capital spending had outpaced the sales volume by 33 percent, and Shapiro's cuts in this area, while helping, had not been enough.

This was what was behind Shapiro's new aggressiveness against government regulations that increased costs.

In February 1977, Shapiro launched the offensive in a policy statement issued by the Business Roundtable calling for "great restraint in the future extension of government regulations into American life." The statement urged that "business leaders bring this special experience, knowledge and competence to the formulation of national policy," and then "accept the decisions of democracy."[26] The Roundtable warned against any form of national economic planning for the corporate sector, including wage and price controls, and came out against the Carter Administration's stimulative package then being debated by Congress. Public spending programs should be replaced by permanent tax cuts, the statement argued, which would spur investment and offset inflation. All available energy resources should be developed, and big oil companies preserved from anti-trust actions.

The Carter White House was stung. Shapiro was thought to be an ally.

2. CARTER'S "POINT MAN"

After his tacit endorsement of Carter just before the election, Carter had named Shapiro as a member of his transition team that recommended high-level appointments and screened other recommendations. He had even been considered for a cabinet post, but begged off, convincing his key contact banker, Bert Lance, and Vice-President Walter Mondale that he wanted to remain in the private sector.

Now they knew why. Du Pont's chairman wanted to remain a critic outside the Administration, keeping the Democrats in line and challenging federal regulatory laws. Whatever doubts Carter may have had on this score were put to rest when, on the same day Carter named him to head a nine-member panel to search for a successor to FBI Director Clarence Kelley, Shapiro publicly attacked the president's economic program as an unnecessary consumer tax rebate after a meeting of the Business Council. The economy doesn't need stimulating, said Shapiro, and "the Social Security job credit does not contribute to capital formation." He wanted less taxes and a bigger break for big business to stimulate capital investment. Businesses didn't have the capital to invest, he asserted, and prices didn't provide an economic justification for constructing factories. "It is inconceivable to me that anyone would invest a dollar in more man-made fiber plant facilities," he said, "because the selling prices are so low that the investment can't be justified."

It was a problem that high technology had bequeathed to most industries, not just man-made fibers; higher productivity and lowered labor costs per product had, through competition, driven prices so low that the volume of sales was not able to keep up with the volume of production; because of the high productivity of labor with new technology and the fixed cost of the machinery anyway, it cost little extra to allow the volume of products available for sale in the market to grow in the hope of bringing in more total revenue with sales. The result was a classic case of overproduction; the market was glutted; as prices dropped further, Du Pont could only hope to either artificially buoy prices by withholding products and idling factories and laying off workers, or use its size to absorb the loss in order to drive competitors out of the market. In the United States and Europe, it did both.

Shapiro's complementary *cause célèbre*, therefore, became tariff protection and reduction of inflation that caused interest rates to climb. "When you depreciate a plant," he explained, "you are depreciating on the basis of the original cost of the plant. When you replace that plant you now face an investment that may be twice as much as the original cost." With technology and competition working to drive down prices, glutting markets, and lowering total profits, "the retained earnings in the business don't give you enough to make up for that differential [in new plant costs]."[27]

A week later the Supreme Court ruled against Du Pont's claim that the EPA didn't have the authority to issue industry-wide regulation on the discharge of pollutants. In a unanimous decision, the Court held that the Water Pollution Control Act authorized the EPA's enforcement of the mid-1983 standards to which Du Pont had objected. The EPA could give variances for individual plants, but was not required to do so for new plants.[28] This, Shapiro had calculated, meant an increased cost of $2.2

billion above the $750 million he considered reasonable. When inflation was added in, the increased costs of new plants were a death knell to his dream of returning Du Pont to the 20 percent earnings of the Fabulous Fifties.

Whatever the merits of his arguments about less environmental controls, Shapiro's complaints about the increased costs of plants due to inflation could not be dismissed as simply a case of corporate propaganda for tax and regulatory relief. They had a real basis in fact, and it was a problem that sophisticated analysts could discern beneath Shapiro's public posture of projecting a "good" outlook for Du Pont at the annual meeting in April 1977.

Inflation affected not simply a company's earnings but also eroded its net assets. To obscure how a company fared under inflation, earnings were reported much higher than warranted. This was made clearer when earnings were adjusted for replacement costs of inventories and depreciable plant and equipment. If the distributable income dropped, so often did the stock, even if the earnings were reported up; the replacement adjusted profits, i.e., the distributable corporate profits after taxes, were often much lower than clever accounting revealed.

Du Pont's management was guilty of this deception in 1975. Shapiro reported a $272 million profit that year. Why then did Shapiro that year (1974-75) leverage the company for the first time in its history and borrow heavily in the bond market? Because, according to William S. Easman of the prestigious Faulkner, Dawkins and Sullivan research firm, Du Pont, after adjusting for the impact of inflation on its replacement costs, had actually "lost" $100 million. [29]

It certainly explained why some members of the family were so anxious to dissolve Christiana Securities and diversify their stockholdings beyond Du Pont.

The SEC requirement in 1976 that all annual reports footnote replacement costs also explained Shapiro's sudden candor. He was only revealing in February 1977 what the 1976 annual report was already admitting to those analysts with enough savvy to understand what those curious little footnotes really meant. Now, with distributable income figures available, investors could better judge how well Du Pont would be able to cover current dividends in the future or even increase them. If the situation looked bleak, the stock's price might well suffer from investors' unloading. Shapiro, then, had nothing to lose by admitting the problem and attacking the one area always more vulnerable to acts of will than a glutted market: government.

The key to the heart of any Democratic administration is organized labor, and it was here that Shapiro, as head of the Business Roundtable, exerted pressure. At issue was the AFL-CIO's legislative package of proposed reforms in the laws that had governed the American labor movement since the postwar witchhunts had decimated its militancy. Du Pont and the Business Roundtable had been instrumental in defeating the common situs bill to extend union picketing rights in the construction industry, and George Meany, head of the AFL-CIO, was anxious to avoid another defeat. Insisting that "ideology is baloney," Meany withdrew the labor movement's 30-year-old demand for the repeal of section 14b of the Taft-Hartley Act, the so-called right to work section the Du Ponts had championed in 1947 that had since allowed 20 states to outlaw union shops and compulsory union membership. Gone also was a proposal to put American workers on a par with Canadian workers' right to get automatic union certification with the signing up of 55 percent of the workers in a shop, as opposed to the current law requiring supervision by federal agents of a secret ballot. "We feel we have proven that all we want are more dependable guarantees of speedy, foolproof elections and stronger deterrants to chronic defiance of labor laws,"[30] said AFL-CIO press spokesman Albert Zack.

Success, however, hinged on getting the cooperation of the big corporation representatives on the labor-management group organized by Carter's Secretary of Labor, John T. Dunlop, to voluntarily control wages and prices. Meany's counterpart in this group was General Electric chairman Reginald Jones, but the real power, he knew, was a new member, Du Pont's Irving Shapiro, chairman of the Business Roundtable.

Du Pont's efforts to resist the Steelworkers' organizing drive made it the company to watch. The *New York Times* in June 1977 noted that Shapiro was "likely to be a crucial decision-maker on what posture important elements in management take toward the measure."[31] Meany knew this and sought to convince the Business Roundtable that labor was not seeking any unfair advantage in organizing campaigns or any disruption of established relations with companies already organized. George Meany was not a naïve man. His appeal to the Roundtable, then, was correctly interpreted as a sign of weakness, and the Roundtable let him know it. "From industry's viewpoint, this [proposed labor law reform] is nothing more than a tool for organizing," said a Roundtable management official. "It would make it vastly easier for unions to move into the Sunbelt and take over employees in textiles and chemicals where in election after election the workers have shown they don't want unions. We accept unionism if it's a matter of free choice, but we're not going to help railroad workers into a union. That's as fundamental as motherhood."[32]

Meany's retreat was being turned into a rout. "In our opinion," complained his executive assistant, Thomas Donahue, "these proposals would only be opposed by those employers who seek to thwart the legitimate desire of their employees for organization."[33]

"Those employers" never needed to be flushed out of the bush. Since the federal legalization of union collective bargaining during the Depression of the Thirties, Du Pont family members had backed "right-to-work" groups. The same groups that had defeated Meany on common situs were now arrayed against the labor law reform bill. Chief among these was a shadowy organization called the National Action Committee, an outgrowth of the construction industry. It had no formal offices, no permanent address, not even a fixed name. Yet it was the nucleus of a powerful coalition of some 100 major corporations and their trade associations.

Its power ironically lay in labor's weak representation in government on all levels—in Congress, in the Supreme Court, in the White House. Labor unions represented only 17 percent of the American workforce, one of the lowest percentages in the advanced industrial world; its failure to organize the unorganized worker extended from the workplace to the political arena, where few union members actually ran for federal office, abdicating political leadership to the professional self-employed middle class. Without its own representatives, the nation's workforce had sunk into the apathy of the powerless, while labor unions, despite their small membership relative to the working population, were presented by the media as "Big Labor" symbolized by a cigar-chomping George Meany.

Big Business fully exploited this situation to launch its anti-union drive. As Harold Coxson, director of labor law for the National Chamber of Commerce put it, "a public mood of antipathy toward the labor movement had encouraged the business community."[34] Under the sway of campaign donations and pro-business ideology, pliant congressmen had been given a bill to introduce as an alternative to the labor law reform legislation: a proposed ban on union shops throughout America.

Allied with National Action was the National Right to Work Committee, with a subsidiary whose name more accurately reflected its political view: Americans Against Union Control of Government. With a budget of $5.5 million, this ultra-conservative organization was dedicated to what its president Reed Larson called "the damaging effect of excessive union power."[35]

Like the Liberty Lobby of the 1930's, these groups served as a front for Du Pont and other large corporations, and labor was not fooled. "As far as the business community is concerned, the respectable business community, these groups are a windfall blessing," charged Lane Kirkland of the AFL-CIO. "They do all the dirty work, slanderous advertising, the name-calling, and the business community keeps its hands clean and gets the job done."[36]

Du Pont's hands were not always so clean, however, especially when it came to its own workers. Officials of the National Institute for Occupational Safety and Health (NIOSH) charged the company with hindering a federal probe of the high-cancer rate at the Belle, West Virginia, plant. Dr. Joseph Wagoner, chief of NIOSH's industry-wide studies branch, first made the issue public in January 1977, when he said Du Pont management had refused to allow the agency's investigators to examine the medical and employment records of cancer victims. Du Pont's Assistant Medical Director, Dr. Bruce Karrh, held that NIOSH had no "legal authority" to review the records; Du Pont claimed it was protecting its employees' right to privacy.

"I think the situation speaks for itself," Dr. Wagoner said. "They handed us a study which demonstrated there is a cancer problem at Belle and the methods they used minimized the extent of the hazard. That can only be ascertained with a full epidemiological study as suggested by Dr. Karrh to Congress."[37] Although Karrh claimed Du Pont was "fully cooperating," Wagoner said the company's actions were "not consistent" with "cooperation in any way."[38]

Nor was this the only snag. According to Dr. Betsy Egan, NIOSH's epidemiologist who headed a five-member team of investigators that collected data at the Belle plant, Du Pont's record keeping was actually replete with "errors" and "a lot of problems"; she rated the company's records "very poor." In most cases, Du Pont officials refused to provide such necessary information as health insurance data and doctors' certificates for disability wage payments; and what files they did photostat for NIOSH were often incomplete, leaving out death certificates and parts of work history. "They don't have full medical records," Dr. Karrh admitted, "[but] they can do a study on cancer with what they have. These are our employees. We have a responsibility to protect them and we are probably more concerned than NIOSH is concerned."[39]

Such paternalism in the case of one of the two highest cancer incidences among Du Pont's 80 plants nationwide was presumptuous if not suspect. NIOSH accordingly did not accept Du Pont's excuse for withholding the data, pointing out that Du Pont regularly broke their workers' right to privacy by making such "confidential" medical data available to management for their employment files. "This medical information shouldn't be contained there because people other than the plant physician had access to it," Dr. Egan said.[40]

Shapiro would not bend. His refusal to honor NIOSH's subpoena escalated into a test of national law involving ACLU executive director Aryeh Neier, who was sufficiently swayed by Du Pont's claim of protection under the constitutional right of privacy to draw analogies to the case of Dr. Daniel Ellsberg, whose leak of the Pentagon Papers inspired the Nixon White House to send the Watergate burglars to break into his psychologist's offices to secure Ellsberg's personal medical records. For some it was an odd twist, indeed, to see a reputedly liberal organization such as the ACLU use the case of a liberal *cause célèbre* like Ellsberg's to shield a conservative company management from having to release information that might prove a relationship between the workplace conditions it imposed and cancer among its workers. It was difficult for many at NIOSH to see how Neier's legal abstraction of a patient's right to control access to his or her own medical files had any relevance to the reality of Du Pont's own violation of the doctor-patient confidentiality it claimed to be protecting, or that Neier's argument served anyone but the Shapiro management. "Corporations know precisely what is in their employees' medical records," said Dr. Egan, and use them to demote, transfer, and dismiss workers that company doctors discover have chronic ailments. Without identifiable records it was impossible to contact the workers and their families for follow-up information. Du Pont's insistence on providing only records with coded numbers was clearly inadequate, as were the 7700 waivers sent back out of the 3600 it sent out to current and past employees. "We can't stand behind the results of studies of anonymous workers," said Egan.[41]

Similar delaying tactics bought Du Pont two additional years for its "Freon" 11 and 12 fluorocarbon propellants. When Oregon banned the sale of the aerosol gases, Du Pont's C. Edward Lorenz, chairman of the Organics Chemicals Department task force handling the controversy, termed the state's move "premature and unnecessary." Instead, he endorsed the EPA and FDA's announced agreement with Du Pont on a plan for a two-year phase-out. By not recalling any aerosols on the market, Du Pont was effectively indemnified from possible legal suits by its manufacturing customers or retailers.

With acrylonitrile, Shapiro decided to take the initiative. Despite Du Pont's previous denials of its carcinogenic capacities, medical evidence had been piling up to the contrary and after OSHA began questioning the chemical's impact on workers, Du Pont in May, 1977, confirmed that its own studies indicated an "excess cancer incidence and cancer mortality"[42] among workers exposed to acrylonitrile at a Du Pont textile fibers plant in Camden, South Carolina. Principally used in the manufacture of acrylic fibers and synthetic rubber, the chemical was also suspected by the Food and Drug Administration of migrating into beverages in plastic containers made with acrylonitrile.[43] The FDA had already closed three Monsanto plants that made such plastic bottles. Some 120,000 workers in the United States were exposed to acrylonitrile in manufacturing.[44] When the number of consumers who used plastic bottles made with the chemical were also included, the figure ran into the millions, with incalculable long-term effects.

Such attempts to head off suits or a bad press did not extend to rebellion among employees. Here, on the basic question of power over the company's direction, operation and policies, Du Pont was willing to take a fall. And the results of such a hard-nosed strategy were impressive. A profit-sharing proposal introduced by Ted Keller to extend bonuses beyond management was soundly beaten at the 1977 annual meeting. Du Pont paid $45 million in bonuses in 1976 to 10.7 percent of its employees, mostly managers. "Stop taking so damn much money for yourselves," employee Henry Wright told Shapiro and other managers, "and start giving some to the little guy."[45] Another employee from Virginia agreed that profit sharing would "make us feel more part of the company," and Keller asked if "the company would win more brownie points with an incentive plan for the few or for the many?"

"The issue is not public relations," Shapiro quickly responded. "It is management and the best use of our money to reach our potential."[46]

Such "best use" included $171,000 in bonuses to Shapiro in 1976, boosting his total pay to $457,000.

Shapiro's biggest employee challenge, however, continued to be those workers who had affiliated with the United Steelworkers organizing drive. The Delaware Valley plants had been particularly responsive, with the Philadelphia, Edgemoor, Newport, Repauno and Carney's Point plants all pledging to join. But the areas' three largest worksites, the Chambers Works with 6,500 workers, the Seaford plant with 3,000 and the Experimental Station with 2,000 laboratory technicians and scientists had remained outside the Steelworkers, Chambers disaffiliating to join the independent rival International Association of Du Pont Employee Unions, better known as the Southern Association for its stronghold beneath the Mason-Dixon Line. Blocked by the Southern Association and set back in 1977 by workers' rejection at the Potomac River Works in Martinsburg, West Virginia, the momentum of the Steelworkers seemed to have been halted. "We don't see any situation different from what we read and heard two years ago,"[47] said Carl De Martino of Du Pont's employee relations department, which was running a program of having plant managers assign supervisors to "assay" workers' attitudes.

At the Newport, Delaware, pigments plant it was not hard to tell what attitudes persisted. The workers there had been denied a contract since 1974. When 32 of them finally staged a walkout in 1976 over grievances, plant manager Ralph Fortney negotiated a return to work, and then placed "progress reports" in the files of those who participated in the job action. The local union alleged Fortney had violated a pledge that there would be no reprisals, which Fortney denied, saying such reports were standard in cases of "disruptive" and "insubordinate" behavior. The union filed a protest with the National Labor Relations Board, but the company remained unfazed.

At the Chambers Works, employees were cautious, and sicker. Twenty-four suspected carcinogens were still being used at the plant. "Cancer is very real down here," said Mrs. Mildred Lang, director of the Salem County division of the American Cancer Society. "It touches a lot of lives." But the victims were quiet. "You can't find one of them to bitch. You accept things. You have to. If it weren't for Du Pont in Salem County this whole place would just fold up and jump in the river."[48]

The workers' passivity was fully exploited then, as it had been for decades. Dr. Wilhelm Hueper, former assistant director of Du Pont's Haskell Laboratory in Wilmington, confirmed that Du Pont headquarters had been fully aware of the dangers of just one carcinogen, betanaphthylamine, decades before its production was stopped in 1955. In 1938, he and several other scientists wrote a study which warned of the dangers of the chemical. "Before the report on the chemical was published, I was disgusted," he said. "They [Du Pont] didn't want to know any more—at least not from me."[49]

Beguiled by the company's paternalism, the workers fatalistically accepted their lot. "You lose a lot of people who were close to you," admitted plant manager Paul Humanick.[50] "Most people seem grateful the company was looking after them," commented cancer specialist Dr. Robert Freilich of the Wilmington Medical Center. "It's sort of surprising."[51]

Of the 283 workers who contracted cancer, 220 died; most lived until 55, the youngest died in his early thirties. Paternalism also proved uneconomical in the long run. Besides workman's compensation, health bills and usual pension benefits, Du Pont had made no other payments to the victims or their families.

Relying on government seemed as ineffective as relying on Du Pont, and things didn't change whether the administration was Republican or Democrat. That applied as well to Jimmy Carter.

Carter came in tow after September 1977, when Shapiro and other Roundtable corporate officials "pushed our way into the White House."[52] Carter was then confronted with the aftershock of his first serious scandal, that of Bert Lance. Shapiro had been close to Lance, using him as his conduit to the president.[53] But "knowing the facts he knew" about his banking problems, Lance should never have accepted a job that required Senate confirmation, Shapiro believed. "Anybody with that set of facts would face certain problems in Washington. With the wisdom of hindsight, he [Carter] made a bad call."[54] After Lance was finally "let go," Shapiro saw his opportunity, one similar to that which helped him rise at Du Pont. The boss had made mistakes. It need not have happened. "He has a chance of being a great president but he has to avoid some of these self-inflicting wounds." Enter advisor Irving Shapiro, ever the useful *consigliore*. He and other corporate leaders arranged a personal meeting with the shaken Carter. They told him they were tired of not being able to get by his aides. He needed to listen to their concerns. "It had an impact on his thinking," he later recalled. "He began to make himself available personally to the business community. He appeared before the Business Council . . . . He had his picture taken with everybody and then sent autographed pictures and letters."[55] Shapiro and other corporate leaders rallied behind Carter and when Lance's successor was chosen by Carter, Shapiro was sufficiently aware of who would replace him that Du Pont's public relations staff issued Shapiro's congratulatory statement 24 hours prematurely.

Shapiro survived the embarrassment to thereafter be referred to as Carter's "point man" to the corporate community. It was a familiar role for the lawyer, one he had played for the Du Pont family for years, and he liked the part. "It would be a mistake to infer that nothing happens in government without calling Wilmington," Shapiro chided a reporter in January 1978 when asked about his role in selecting the new Federal Reserve Board chairman; but the usual self-effacement could not hide the fact that his recommendation of G. William Miller had indeed been accepted by the president. "We've had access to [Carter's] staff," he admitted. "On important issues, we've had access to the president. We've been able to present our point of view."[56]

Their views seemed to coincide more and more. Du Pont's endorsement of Carter's energy program was deeply appreciated. "It is high time the nation had a comprehensive energy policy," stated Senior Vice-President Edward C. Jefferson, head of the company's key Energy Committee, "and it is encouraging to see the president take strong leadership to define the problem." Du Pont urged deregulation of domestic oil and natural gas, "market mechanisms" always being preferable to raise prices to world levels and "true value" than taxes: "We do not believe it is in the national interest to raise petroleum prices above world market levels . . . many industrial uses of energy are not amenable to conservation or conversion to non-oil energy sources. For example, feedstock and many process uses from a practical standpoint are non substitutable. Taxing such uses will be inflationary and place us at a competitive disadvantage."[57]

Shapiro had already guided Du Pont into alliances with domestic energy producers such as ARCO and National Distillers. ARCO pulled out of its deal with Du Pont, forecasting an improvement in oil supplies, but Shapiro found a suitable replacement with CONOCO. Continental Oil Company had been the western states subsidiary of the Standard Oil Trust and the

Rockefellers still held a considerable block of stock in the company and a representative on the board of directors, Nancy Hanks of Rockefeller Brothers, Inc., an aide of Nelson Rockefeller. Shapiro's decision in June, 1978, then, to join CONOCO in a $130 million joint exploration drilling venture in Texas, where Du Pont's five plants are the company's principal consumers of natural gas—found no opposition from the Du Pont board. Du Pont family members had been moving in the direction of the Rockefellers for years, ever since A. Felix du Pont and Laurence Rockefeller jointly founded Piasecki Aircraft Company. Felix had headed up the Delaware section of Nelson Rockefeller's drive for the 1968 Republican presidential nomination, and ex-Governor Russell Peterson, a former Du Pont executive, had even worked briefly for the Rockefellers in the early 1970's, staying at their Pocantico estate.

The full implications of Shapiro's alliance with CONOCO, however, was not perceived in the Carter days. It was seen rather as an attempt to secure petroleum feedstock, which it surely was. What was more important to the Democratic Administration was Du Pont's political support for its new Department of Energy. Du Pont, seeing the emergence of a comprehensive energy program as a means to facilitating deregulation of domestic oil and gas as well as more nuclear power, did not hesitate to give Carter what he wanted. "We regard the formation of the Department of Energy as a very constructive step," said Jefferson. "We are also encouraged by the president's initiatives on development of domestic oil and gas and speedier licensing of nuclear power."[58]

Shapiro was in the White House when, in October 1977, the president "was raising hell with the oil industry" before a press conference. After Carter finished, Shapiro turned off the television in Hamilton Jordan's office and the two men began "doing our business." Irving Shapiro, counsel to the rich and powerful, had finally arrived thanks to the Du Ponts.

In February 1978, Shapiro threw a large party at the Wilmington Country Club. Several Du Ponts came, as did 300 of Delaware's leading citizens. Politicians, lawyers, federal and state judges, corporate officials, religious and civic leaders, all gathered to welcome the *News-Journal* papers' new owner, the Gannett Company, amid rumors that Gannett had included a buy-back clause in the purchase agreement, as once suggested by Du Pont's Charles Reece to Lammot du Pont Copeland to pressure any non-Du Pont owner to collaborate in preserving a flattering image of the company and the family. Norman Isaacs was not there; he had left Wilmington in July 1976, his task completed. Mel Slawik was not there either; he was in jail. But Isaacs' replacement, Andy Fisher, was, and no one doubted he was telling the truth when he assured the happy crowd that "not once have I experienced or witnessed an attempt by the Du Pont Company or Christiana Securities Company to influence the context of news or editorial columns.... The papers have been, are, and will be free to report all the news, without fear or favor." It was "public testimony," columnist Bill Frank wrote, "contrary to what the Nader cult may think."[59] The arrangements for the party were made by Harold G. Brown, of Du Pont's Public Affairs Department.

3. PASSING A MILESTONE

That month, Du Pont's board of directors welcomed a new member, Edward B. du Pont. Edward had worked for the company from 1960 to 1967; but it was apparent to all that it was his father's name, not his experience, that won him his seat at the helm of the world's largest chemical company. Edward was a vice-president of the family holding bank, Wilmington Trust; and his succession to a seat on the Du Pont board was more symbolic of the new era the Du Pont family had entered than simply a continuation of the clan's control over the chemical firm.

The Du Ponts, granted, still held the largest block of stock in the company, but Edward's presence was not the result of any particular expertise in chemical manufacturing or management. Rather, Edward was there as both heir to his father's huge shareholding and as head of the family bank's trust department, now more than Du Pont Company the repository of the Du Pont family's present and future fortune. As such, Edward du Pont was the living personification of a new financial power emerging on the national scene.

In 1972, Wilmington Trust was already listed as the 20th largest institutional investor in the United States by the Senate Committee on Government Operations.[60] Its assets were then $7 billion. On the following page are just some of its 1974 stockholdings.[61]

To quietly buy these stocks, Wilmington Trust used two "street names," Dean & Davis and Hirs & Haney.

In addition, Wilmington Trust managed Du Pont's Pension Trust Fund, worth $2.5 billion by the time of Edward's ascension to the Du Pont board. The Du Pont Pension Trust Fund was then the fifth largest stockholder in three companies: Continental Illinois Corporation (with a 1.54 percent holding), Northwest Airlines (3.7 percent) and Florida Power and Light (1.39 percent).

The small size of the percentage of total outstanding voting shares owned or controlled by Wilmington Trust in each of the listed companies was reflective of the growing power of minority shareholders over modern corporations with thousands of stockowners. In most cases, no longer do one

	shares	percentage of outstanding stock
United Aircraft	300,000	2.5
CPC International	85,000	.4
R.J. Reynolds	140,000	.3
Caterpillar Tractor	744,100	1.3
Litton Industries	210,358	.6
Westinghouse Electric	512,200	.6
United Air Lines	377,120	1.8
Northwest Airlines	417,100	2.0
Norfolk & Western Rlwy.	70,000	.7
Long Island Lighting	312,440	1.5
Ford Motor	285,300	.4
CPC International	87,000	*
CONOCO	189,080	.4
Mobil Oil	433,400	.4
Pacific Southwest Airlines	49,000	1.3
Rollins, Inc.	109,327	.9
Interstate Stores	69,500	1.3
Potomac Electric Power	100,000	.5
General Telephone & Electronics	779,037	.7
Southern Railway	100,000	1.4
Seaboard Coast Line Industries	125,380	.9

*For Decatur Income Fund, managed by Eleuthère du Pont's Delfi Management.

or two families own the bulk of a large corporation's stock; in fact, the Du Ponts were one of the few families in mid-20th century America to retain such a large holding of a major corporation. Most wealthy families had already made ample use of the ladle of public stock offerings to dip into the vast ocean of America's wages and salaries. Millions of average Americans, attracted by the corporate illusion of a magically self-expanding capital, and unaware of the source of that expansion in the market value of goods produced by labor each day beyond what it cost an employer to pay for a given day's wage, found themselves inside the corporate system as simultaneously employee, consumer, and shareholder, yet holding little power over their lives or stock ownership. Instead, as Berle and Means describe in their classic *The Modern Corporation and Private Property,** "in the corporate system, the 'owner' of industrial wealth is left with a mere symbol of ownership while the power, the responsibility and the substance which have been an integral part of ownership in the past are being transferred to a separate group in whose hands lies control."[62]

"The rapid rise in number of shareholders, both directly and indirectly through stockholdings of insurance companies, mutual funds, and pension funds," noted Julius W. Allen for the Library of Congress, "has diluted the power of most shareholders and has given management or minority shareholders the possibility to obtain and exercise control."[63]

"As a result," wrote Berle and Means, "we have reached a condition in which the individual interest of the shareholder is definitely made subservient to the will of a controlling group of managers even though the capital of the enterprise is made up out of the aggregated contributions of perhaps many thousands of individuals. The legal doctrine that the judgment of the directors must prevail as to the best interests of the enterprise, is in fact tantamount to saying that in any given instance the interests of the individual may be sacrificed to the economic exigencies of the enterprise as a whole, the interpretation of the board of directors as to what constitutes an economic exigency being practicably final."[64]

"Everyone keeps talking about the Family," said Irénée du Pont, Jr., on his retirement from Du Pont company management two months after Edward became a director, "and the family is not an entity."[65] The *News-Journal* noted that "he added that even when some family members do get together they don't talk business."[66]

Which might have led many Delawareans to ask what exactly it was that 10 Du Pont family members discussed when they met each month as directors of the Wilmington Trust Company.[67] Or when eight Du Pont family members met each month as directors of Du Pont;[68] or when four

---

*An interesting sidelight to the story of this book was the alleged role of the then-Du Pont-controlled General Motors in attempting its suppression in a manner similar to Du Pont's own campaign against Book-of-the-Month Club's carrying of *Behind the Nylon Curtain* some 40 years later. On June 27, 1947, Berle wrote in his memoirs that "A Mr. Darr of the West Publishing Company had related how 'one of the large corporation clients of the Corporation Trust Company (Darr believes the General Motors Corporation) read a review of the book and then called on the Corporation Trust Company explaining that in the view of that corporation no such book ought to be published. The Corporation Trust Company agreed that they would require CCH [the Corporation Clearing House, publisher of the book controlled by the Corporation Trust Company] to drop it at once. This the CCH did. That was in 1932. It would be interesting to know whether a corporation of that size and standing would do the same thing in 1947." (Berle papers, Memoires, FDR Library, Hyde Park, NY)

members of the Du Pont family met each month as directors of Atlantic Aviation, and five other Du Ponts met each month as directors of Delaware Trust Bank; or when three members of the Du Pont family met each month as directors of Continental American Life Insurance Company,[69] or when four members of the Du Pont family met each other each month as directors of Sigma Trust mutual funds;[70] or when at least two dozen members of the Du Pont family met each month as trustees of some 30 family foundations or even the University of Delaware.

Yet the "independent" Gannett *News-Journal* spoke openly of the "waning of the family's influence"[71] as if it were fact. No reports were seen, however, of the *spread* of the family's influence since the Christiana dissolution into oil (Crown Central Petroleum, for example, now has a representative of E.I. du Pont's CALICO group on its board as the result of a merger).[72] (Another curiosity is Beneficial Corporation, worth $6.7 billion; now headquartered in Wilmington, this insurance giant includes among its directors former governor and People's Bank director Elbert Carvel and E. Norman Veasey of the Du Pont family law firm of Richards, Layton and Finger.[73])

Yes, everyone keeps talking about the Family.

But for Irénée, a career was over. "I think I've done about as much as I can," he confessed. "One becomes less inventive in that capacity as time goes by."[74] Irénée liked to evaluate his contribution as being that of an individual, but he acknowledged that his name "must have been an enormous advantage. It would be highly unusual for a B.S. chemical engineer to reach the level I did without pull."[75] And being heir to a $250 million fortune from a former president and chairman of the company could indeed be called "pull." There was perhaps more symbol than irony in the fact that the *New York Times* when announcing Irénée's retirement accompanied its article with a picture not of him, but of his long departed father.

As if to mark the end of an era, Du Pont also announced that the Carney's Point plant which made smokeless powder and nitrocellulose, two products of the turn of the century that launched Du Pont into unprecedented profits and the chemicals industry, would soon close. Dynamite, the other product that had been the bridge in the 19th century between the firm's first product, black powder, and the later explosives of World War I, had been discontinued the year before.

Irénée had told Shapiro he wanted to step down right after the Christiana merger had been completed. But he would remain as a director and, because of his enormous stockholding, a member of the all-powerful Finance Committee. Still dark-haired and young looking at 58 years of age, Irénée ventured that his particular vice-presidency might be eliminated rather than filled, but he had nothing but praise for the man who had been chosen as chairman rather than he. "I supported the line of reasoning that said you get the best operator you have who is familiar with public affairs and governmental affairs and you say 'go for it,'" he recollected of the 1973 chairmanship sweepstakes. "That was Irving Shapiro. And there wasn't any argument to the contrary."[76] Shapiro reciprocated. "Irénée du Pont has didicated his entire company career to looking out for the interest of Du Pont employees. In the fields of employee relations and safety and in the fair treatment of individuals he has played a unique leadership role."[77]

With Irénée went the last Du Pont in senior management of the chemical firm. More might come, but for the time being his passing from the scene was a milestone. It was the first time in 178 years that a Du Pont was not active in the company's top management.

Only two years before, at the groundbreaking ceremony for Wilmington College's new library, Irénée had spoken of the last great *consigliore* to the family before Shapiro, John J. Raskob. But he had been unable to offer anything more to some 50 members of Raskob's family other than to simply say that "a man of such genius flourished in this country at the time he was most urgently needed."[78] More should have been said of the "Wizard of Wall Street" and closest business and political ally of Irénée's powerful uncle, Pierre du Pont. Raskob and Pierre had built the empire Irénée had inherited, and Irénée's family had maintained close ties to the Raskobs; one Raskob daughter was even bridesmaid to Irénée's daughter, Cynthia.

Ironically, it had been Pierre's insistence on modern managerial expertise and the incorporation of non-family members into the inner sanctums of power that made Du Pont, in its success, the corporate giant whose awesome responsibility could no longer be entrusted merely on the basis of filial love. "When I started training young kids and they wound up being my boss," commented Henry E.I. du Pont, "I said, 'bye, bye to that.'"[79] "It has become so vast that you might as well be working for IBM," said Alfred du Pont Dent, whose brother and several cousins resigned "when they realized they were just knocking their heads against a wall."[80] As early as 1944 E. Paul du Pont could see it coming. He warned his older brother Felix that "I am convinced the Du Pont Company should not have lost these young men," but Felix would only reply that "The subject . . . is being studied."[81] By the time Felix looked up from his studies, E.I. du Pont had led a whole group of Du Pont young heirs into a venture of financial speculation that would bloom by the sixties into the $100 million Sigma Group of mutual funds. By then it was too late; some of the family's best talent had pioneered into the same green valleys of high finance in which the rest of the family would ultimately have to settle.

Eleuthère's group, in fact, had drawn the early support of such local family celebrities as Reynolds du Pont and Pete du Pont, both of whom had left the company for a career in Delaware politics. Henry B. du Pont's sons had tried to follow their father into Du Pont, but by the time of the Christiana dissolution, Henry III was dead and Edward had left the company to pursue his father's interests in aviation at All American Engineering and Atlantic Aviation. Similarly, the namesake son of Richard C. du Pont, who had founded All American, had neven gone into the chemical firm but followed the legend of his father into All American and Summit Aviation. Richard's brother, A. Felix du Pont, Jr., another aviation buff, also failed to inspire his children to follow him into Du Pont; likewise the sons of his uncle E. Paul spurned Du Pont careers, Alexis I. (Lex) also going into aviation while R. Jacques went into real estate and oil, and Stephen, F. George, E. Paul, Jr., and Benjamin B. went essentially into themselves. The wing of E. Paul's other brothers went their own way, too, with Ernest's family watching over Atlas Chemicals or, in the case of Sam F., delving in sheriffing, and Francis's sons and grandsons revelling in their father's lucrative field of stocks and bonds, Emile being the only serious exception as a Du Pont executive. Only James Q. du Pont's son, Pierre Coleman, seemed to take the family name's presence in the chemical company seriously. "I have a little man in me that keeps saying I have to keep the Du Pont name important," he explained.[82]

Edward du Pont's return to Du Pont, then, represented a new development. In the past, other Du Ponts had been elected to the board also after having left the company's management. What made Edward's ascension unique was that it came when his position as vice-president in charge of the trust department of Wilmington Trust held a particular importance for the family; Christiana Securities' dissolution had shifted the focus of the bulk of the Du Pont fortune from the holding company (and Du Pont) to the trust department of the bank. This applied not only to the interest of individual Du Ponts to use the bank to pursue their own particular interests in other fields, contributing to the expected growing diversification of the family fortune, but also to the former Christiana leadership and those Du Ponts who retained most of their holdings in the chemical firm in the form of blind trusts for their heirs. This supplemented Wilmington Trust's role as custodian of the stockholdings of the Du Pont Pension Trust Fund. Thus Wilmington Trust was identified in Du Pont's 1978 proxy statements after the Christiana dissolution as holding an aggregate of over 25 million shares of Du Pont common, or 10.6 percent of the company's total voting stock.

Edward, therefore, was well positioned at the center of Du Pont family power. He had, of course, other investment ties to Du Pont Company, including the $3 million in business his Atlantic Aviation did with the chemical company in airplane charter service and maintaining, operating and storing Du Pont's own airplanes,[83] a business, incidentally, that would grow to over $7 million by 1983.[84] And he was also a principal stockholder in Du Pont. But his growing power in the family, while derived from his father's Du Pont Company fortune and his own role in the Christiana-Du Pont negotiations, was now based on his key position at Wilmington Trust.

Edward was also a director of All American Engineering (Industries), which put him regularly in touch with Richard C. du Pont's group (a reciprocating tie with Richard's serving once on the board of Edward's Atlantic Aviation). Wilmington Trust was also custodian of stocks controlled by Eleuthère du Pont's Sigma mutual funds, and shared interlocking directorships through two Du Pont family members, George P. Edmonds and Rodney Layton, with Eleuthère's Continental American Life Insurance Company (CALICO).

What affected any of these companies, then, was felt by all, a business community of mutual interests that found expression in the Delaware State Chamber of Commerce, chaired by Irénée du Pont, Jr., and the Delaware Business Roundtable, the state section of Irving Shapiro's nationwide Business Roundtable, chaired by William G. Copeland, board chairman of Eleuthère's CALICO and director of the Bank of Delaware and Diamond State Telephone.

The CALICO chairman became a powerful voice for the united front of big business. Democratic legislators, for example, attempted to pass a tax on life insurance proceeds over $10,000 that would have prevented large inheritances from being "sheltered" from state inheritance tax collection. Copeland publicly derided their bill as "just another piece of goofy Delaware legislation" effectively raising the tax exemption from inheritance tax from $70,000 to a surviving spouse to a maximum of $80,000. He said the 2.5 percent gross sales tax on premiums paid by his customers was already "a hell of a good source of income" for the state, and warned that even if the bill were passed, it "won't affect our companies at all. Our agents will simply recommend that people move their assets out of the state."[85] The bill was not passed.

4. STEERING TOWARD THE RIGHT

Irving Shapiro, who joined the CALICO board, lent his voice as well. Since his August 28, 1977, speech before the Southern Governors Conference, Shapiro had been mounting a broad attack against federal and state corporate and upper income taxes, environmental laws, and welfare payments, using inflation and lack of investment as the cutting edges of his financial argument. "Thirteen of the 30 companies that comprise the Dow

Jones industrial average are trading below book value," he had told the governors. "The last time this happened was shortly after World War II when investors were fearful of a depression. . . . Fixed business investments account for less than 10 percent of our gross national product—the lowest rate in any industrial country. Rates elsewhere range from 12 percent (Italy) to more than 25 percent (in Japan). In the United States, the consequences of underinvestment have been severe. The rate of growth in worker productivity is below the historic trendline, and promises to get worse before it gets better. . . . During the next 10 years the available labor force will increase by 16 million; it will be necessary to create about 1.6 million new jobs a year simply to keep the number of unemployed from growing. It will be difficult to accomplish this at the current rate of investment . . . higher unemployment but limited gains in productivity. It is a mixed bag at best; we can live with some of it, but not, for long, with all of it."[86]

Shapiro knew that labor was not the cause of inflation; lack of investment in high-tech machinery was, causing international trade and balance of payments deficits that eroded the value of the dollar on the world's money markets. Government spending, draining the nation's privately controlled credit markets, was driving up interest rates that made investment loans impossible. That, in turn, only deepened the productivity and inflation crisis that had come to be known as "stagflation" (for stagnation-inflation).

The Carter Administration had attempted to arrest the effects of inflation by merely resurrecting Nixon's wage-price controls, but on an even less effective voluntary basis. It was, of course, incorrect for Carter to measure wage gains against productivity for a number of reasons. First, there is an absolute limit to a worker's output per hour with a given machine. Second, if a machine is outdated, it will not produce goods as cheaply as another machine in, for example, West Germany; that means American industry will lose out on export markets and the resulting trade deficit creates a payments deficit that weakens the dollar; that hurts the real wages of working people first, the unemployed hardest of all. And all Americans end up paying out more dollars to buy even the less expensive goods from abroad. Third, in such a situation the worker is forced to fight to increase wages. Wages, therefore, should not be measured against productivity, but against inflation. Fourth, if you want to increase productivity, buy or invent new, more productive technology, tools and machinery. That has always been the key to the success of the American economy, not turning workers into slaves. The United State's productivity, likewise, should be measured against other nations' productivity, not wages. You only measure productivity against wages, apples against pears, when you want to create a false image against workers and are planning to get your profits, not by earning them on the competitive international market, but by forcing workers to work harder with speedups which cause an increase in job-related injuries and "givebacks" of previously negotiated benefits, including, of course, medical benefits.

Shapiro knew the social instability that can develop from such nationwide policies and scored Carter's program accordingly. "Too often in recent years," he said, "people—particularly people in government—have pointed at labor and management and blamed the wage-price spiral as the root of inflation. That spiral is an effect of inflation, not a cause."

Shapiro's analysis, however, cringed before the political implications of a labor theory of value that was implicit in his pointing at the lack of technological investment as being behind the productivity lag and trade deficits that eroded the dollar.

He quickly emerged from the depths of serious analysis and beat a fast retreat to the surface of illusory appearances, swimming in the safer, more accepted currents of monetary theory. "The cause is rooted in government deficits and in the fact that the money supply has risen faster than real economic activity," he offered. "Too much money chasing too few goods is the fundamental cause of inflation." From there, it was only one more short step backwards to Reaganomics, and he took it. "It is strange," he said, "that a nation that has concerned itself so deeply with the management of demand—stimulating or restraining consumption according to the needs of the moment—has assumed that adequate supplies, and adequate capital investment to meet future needs will somehow take care of themselves." Irving Shapiro, the national spokesman for American corporate leaders, had announced that the Age of Keynes and its liberal New Deal was over. Although it would not be clear until much later, the social and political mentality of big business was retreating into an earlier, darker age.

In this mind-set, Shapiro had his agenda. "The place to start in balancing the supply side of the equation is the energy area. I hope that when you gather at tomorrow's general session to consider President Carter's energy program, you will think hard about the supply side." In the vulnerable field of energy, he knew he would hit home. The oil crisis had put fear and desperation back in the hearts of Americans. Energy was the one issue that could be used as a wedge against a wide range of environmental regulations that liberals had promoted. After paying credibility's wages by giving due recognition to the "sense of limits...keener sense of mortality" and "awareness" of "the laws of ecology," he applied the cost-effective techniques of the balance sheet to measure the worth of both pollution control and human control (welfare). "The job creation ratio between a dollar spent on production equipment and a dollar spent on pollution control is at least two to one. Even those who prefer other sets of numbers will not argue with the principle that if we want more jobs we had better put our money where the jobs come from. We can also agree, without argument, that what is consumed today is not available tomorrow... When we spend, we should seek to solve problems, not merely to postpone them... Witness today the tragedy of our welfare system, which spends some $45 billion annually so that the poor can subsist from day to day, but does almost nothing for the future. We spend, but do not invest... we are trading economic growth for current consumption—in the name of 'Quality of Life.' I ask you: Whose life? Without economic growth, the disadvantaged have no chance at all."

Confronted by the need for social adjustment, American corporate leaders such as Shapiro retreated to their traditional emphasis on an expanded marketplace. In the name of growth, of promoting private investment, all things would become increasingly possible. What was once rejected as affronts to Americans' traditional beliefs in equality, justice and democracy, would now, as in earlier times of crisis, become reluctantly acceptable by hard-nosed "realists" who embraced the system they profited by as inevitable and immutable. It was the classic pose of a statesman for the status quo who sought a "proper balance" between the demands for social justice and the future health of the corporate economy upon which the viability of those demands were forced to rest.

"Advocacy does not require a balance scale," Shapiro explained, "it is somebody else's responsibility to use wise judgment in making the critical choices." He bemoaned the "consumerists, environmentalists, and other ists, including industrialists. Each is a single-minded specialist, fulfilling a separate obligation to think in a single dimension." Ever the wise judge of human nature, Shapiro offered that such behavior was "human," rather than socially conditioned by the competitive individualism of the marketplace. He did hold that such attitudes were "perilous," but only because they inspired governmental inefficiency, forcing government to "simply respond to pressures applied by one-sided thinkers ... it is no wonder, then, that we have real trouble establishing priorities that reflect wise judgments."

Speaking for all Americans, Shapiro then got to his agenda. He warned that "the United States is unlikely to create the necessary minimum 1.6 million new jobs per year if its capital budgets are burdened by tens of billions of dollars of unnecessary or ineffective spending to make clean water cleaner." Then he moved onto the regulatory agencies and the courts which enforce the laws, labelling them "an administrative and judicial maze the likes of which the world has rarely seen" and blaming them on "one-dimensional thinking." As his prime example, he lashed out at the "group of 11 people" who "incorporated themselves and began to litigate in the name of a clean environment" creating delays that have cost Mississippians on the

Gulf "a $20 to $25 million annual loss to the community in payrolls and plant purchases."[87] When all the arguments for statemenship were said and done, Shapiro had ended up just another spokesman for a special interest— Du Pont.

Whatever doubts the Southern governors may have had on that score should have been laid to rest when Shapiro put his alleged concern about jobs in a bluntly corporate context on the front page of the *Wall Street Journal*. "If a friend of mine in industry," he said, "calls up and says, 'Irv, we've had a presentation that says we ought to build a plant in Delaware, what do you say?' I couldn't in good conscience invite a fellow chief executive to come to Delaware and subject himself to a 19.8 percent [state personal income] tax rate."[88] Shapiro's conscience about his "fellow chief executive's" income was not fairly balanced by his concern for the average Delawarean's income or the true state of Delaware's tax system. As Allan Marvel commented in *Tax Notes,* "That 19.8 percent figure does sound pretty drastic, and Shapiro could cite it, correctly, as the highest marginal rate of state income taxation in the nation. In fact, most income-taxing states apply schedules that do not go above a maximum rate of ten percent. Unlike Delaware, however, most income-taxing states also impose general sales taxes, and in most of them, as well, property tax rates are far higher than in Delaware. Any business executive seriously interested in comparative economics of industry location would surely want to consider the total tax climate, and not just the level of state individual income taxation.

"But even looking at the Delaware state income tax, one finds the 19.8 percent figure gives a grossly misleading impression ... the actual tax burden imposed by the Delaware tax upon taxpayers receiving up to $300,000 a year is likely to be less than five percent of their total income ... 1) the high percentage cited by Shapiro is the rate that applies only to taxable income in excess of $100,000; even for taxpayers well above that level, much income is taxed at lower rates, ranging upwards from 1.6 percent; 2) the high percentage also refers only to taxable income, while the 'less than five percent' rate relates tax liability to total income, allowing deductions and exemptions; and 3) for high-income taxpayers, a very large fraction of state tax liability is offset by a reduction in Federal income tax, due to the deductibility provision of the Federal law."[89]

Shapiro, who made well over $300,000 each year, knew this. But his statement was part of a general assault on the state's tax system that he was kicking off, and even the Du Pont administration in Dover was forced to defend its revenue base.

Pete du Pont's secretary of state, Glenn Kenton, tried to "get some of the facts straight" when he spoke to financial analysts in Wilmington in

October, 1978. "As Mr. Ratledge of the University of Delaware pointed out quite accurately to Mr. Shapiro in a recent letter to the editor of the *News-Journal* papers, while 19.8 percent is the top marginal rate for taxable income over $100,000, the effective rates are far, far less." For a $111,000 income, in fact, the rate was really 4.7 to 6.1 percent; for $230,000, actually a lower minimum, 4.3 percent, to a high 7.1 percent, hardly unfair or even very progressive. In terms of state or local taxes per $1000 of personal income, Delaware stood 32nd from the top.[90]

Shapiro would not be deterred. "Tax reform must come to Delaware some day and we don't intend to back off from that message," Du Pont's general counsel Charles Welch told the State Bar Association in January, 1979. "The kind of tax reform I consider essential to bring new industry and new jobs to Delaware may not be just around the corner, but I feel strongly that we must have some tax program to keep the people we now have."[91] He then explained exactly what he meant: exclude all pension income from taxation, double the deduction for federal taxes paid, increase the exclusion for dividend income for Delawarians over 60 by 1000 percent (from $100 to $1000), set up a special 10-year income averaging for lump sum payments from profit sharing and retirement plans, and hike the inheritance tax exemption on transfers between husbands and wives from $70,000 to $250,000. "I realize that in some quarters these proposals will be pegged as benefiting the 'fat cat,'" Welch admitted. "My answer is simple. Who gets hurt most in Delaware: those without jobs and those who cannot afford to leave." He once again reiterated the claim of wanting to "minimize the self-imposed exile of retired Delawareans." He also endorsed a sales tax.

"How do we stabilize our revenue if, as one consequence of a sales tax, we chase out-of-state shoppers back home?" answered Du Pont employee Ted Keller of the Citizens Coalition for Tax Reform. He cited the Brookings Institution report that federal deductions on state taxes actually burdened the middle and working classes and benefitted the rich. Inheriting $250,000 put you in the top one percent of the population, he also pointed out, and he questioned why a $200,000 pension should be excluded from taxation or given the benefit of a 10-year income averaging. "I get tired of hearing that the only cures for Delaware's problems are more taxes for most of us and fewer taxes for the rich."

Tired or not, Keller was treated to more such statements as the State Chamber of Commerce joined in the attack. Chamber President William Wyer testified before a state legislative committee considering a bill to reduce taxes for higher incomes that Pete Rose, the Phillies baseball star, paid a whopping $800,000 by owner and Du Pont heir Robert Carpenter, could not afford Delaware's tax; Wyer said the superstar would owe $111,000 even with exemption. Democrat Gerard Cain countered that Rose, at the real 5.2 percent rate, would only pay $33,600, but by June 1979 resistance had collapsed. The *News-Journal* papers refused to print a tax schedule based on the real effective rates prepared by Washington, D.C., tax expert Thomas Field, and instead used the rates cited by the Chamber. That month, the state Senate passed (with the backing of AFL-CIO state president John Campanelli) and Governor du Pont signed HB334, giving a 31 percent cut in the tax on the highest incomes; Delawarians making $7,000 to $25,000 got an average tax cut of only 6.8 percent. It was a measure of the Democrats' weakness that one of the sponsors was Representative Gerard Cain. For his leadership, Keller's tax coalition awarded Cain the celebrated "Dooh Nibor" award—that's Robin Hood spelled backwards—for taking from the poor to give to the rich.

But perhaps the most severe blow felt by Delawareans was the effective nullification of some of the most important provisions of Delaware's nationally lauded Coastal Zone Act. The law limited industrial development along Delaware's coastline, forbidding heavy industry along a two-mile strip from the coast. It was designed to prevent the coast's degradation. Du Pont Company had not seriously objected to the law when it was passed during the Peterson administration; the Nader Study Group pointed out that the law complemented Du Pont's concern that Delaware's workforce remain heavily white-collar in orientation with the state's reputation as a corporate headquarters; Mel Slawik's election showed that blue-collar loyalties to the status quo were less reliable than commonly assumed. Potential industrial competitors for the state's blue-collar workforce, including the possibility of higher wages that often results from such competition, was also discouraged by the law.

Du Pont reversed its position, however, as plans for Christiana Securities' dissolution began to be implemented.

Previous to then, Du Pont's opposition was limited. But in 1978, as the Du Ponts began to consider Delaware's future within the context of new opportunities for diversified investments—including oil—the company went beyond Charles McCoy's previous recommendations for "restrictions based not on the type of economic activity, but on environmental and other standards,"[92] and launched a full-scale assault.

Du Pont's Charles Welch, testifying before the state House Revenue and Finance Committee, coupled his attack on Delaware's tax structure by telling of a bumper sticker he had seen recently in Texas which read "Let the Yankees Freeze in the Dark."

"What Texans are telling us is that Delaware's Coastal Zone Law speaks loud and clear—Delaware wants all the benefits without taking any of the risks. Delaware cannot achieve a viable industrial program so long as the Coastal Zone Law remains in effect in its present form."[93] He warned that "Without some immediate legislative action on the coastal zone, we simply will not be in a position to be credible with industry in asking them to locate in Delaware and expand our ever shrinking tax base."[94] The Du Ponts' Wilmington Trust bank agreed. Vice-President Paul Shipley said the law and the state's taxes on higher personal income, bureaucratic "red tape" and "management by crisis" was similar to a "beware sign" at the state borders.

5. PETE'S MAGICAL MYSTERY TOUR

Pete du Pont, while campaigning for governor, had pledged to keep the Coastal Zone Act intact. After taking office, he reversed his position in alignment with amendments proposed by Du Pont and Wilmington Trust. The reason was obvious: oil. Studies had indicated the possibility of large deposits of oil under water in the Baltimore Canyon off the northeastern coast.

"We hope to get the coastal zone legislation that is in the Senate through so we can take advantage of the offshore oil situation,"[95] the governor said during a trip to New York to consult with Wall Street investors about Delaware's financial situation. By January 1979, the *Delaware State News* was reporting that Du Pont "also called on the General Assembly to amend Delaware's Coastal Zone Act to allow pipelines on shore and support facilities along the state's coast."[96]

There was only one problem: Pete was breaking the law.

Title 29, Section 5851, Subsection 1 of the Delaware Code read that "In our democratic form of government, the conduct of officers and employees of the State must hold the respect and confidence of the people. They must, therefore, avoid conduct which is in violation of their public trust or which creates a justifiable impression among the public that such a trust is being violated."

There was no question that Governor du Pont, by pressing for a change in the Coastal Zone Act, was creating an impression that he was violating the public trust. Two of the successful bidders for Lease Sales 40 and 49 were Exxon and Texaco. According to the financial report the governor filed in April 1978, Pete held 1120 shares of voting stock in Exxon, worth over $50,000 as well as additional non-voting Exxon stock held in an income-producing trust the value of which du Pont refused to disclose other than to admit they were worth in excess of $5,000.[97] He also owned 222 voting shares in Texaco worth $5758 and 3280 shares in Phillips Petroleum worth over $97,000, and 440 shares in Standard Oil of Indiana worth over $20,000.

All of these companies were involved in bidding for Lease Sales 40 and 49. Governor du Pont recorded that his $160,000 holdings in oil companies only brought in a gross income of over $8,000, but there is no way of knowing how much more he received from the Exxon stock in his trust which, considering the huge size of most Du Pont family trusts, might easily have been quite a lot. According to *Forbes* magazine, Pete's father, Pierre III, reportedly has a $250 million fortune. Considering his age, 72, much of this probably has already been passed on as trust accounts to his three heirs, including his only son, Pete. This would include oil stocks worth millions of dollars, and Pete acknowledges that his trust account holds shares in Exxon and Gulf Oil. Pete's trust number at Wilmington Trust is 4980, but the total worth of its assets remains undisclosed. By 1983, however, Pete's admitted shareholdings in Exxon had doubled to 2240 shares.[98] These, like his other admitted holdings, were not put in a blind trust by Pete as other officeholders, such as President Carter, had done.

Oil's role as a feedstock for Du Pont also compromised the governor's promotion of oil exploration off the Delaware coast. From 1978 to 1979, the Governor's admitted stock in Du Pont rose in value from over $626,000 to over $891,000, a gain of almost 30 percent in one year alone.

Title 29, Section 5855 of the Delaware Code is specific: "No employee shall have any interest, financial or otherwise, direct or indirect, or engage in any business or transaction or incur any obligation of any nature which is in substantial conflict with the proper performance of his duties in the public interest."

But this was not the first time du Pont had a conflict of interest. He had owned oil stocks as a congressman,[99] too, when, as a member of the Oceonography subcommittee of the Merchant Marine and Fisheries Committee, he took an active role in scuttling the Outer Continental Shelf Lands Act. He was opposed to provisions that restricted drilling to government-owned operations, insisting that private oil corporations could do a better job. Conservationists and environmentalists thought no drilling at all was the best way to protect some of the world's richest fishing waters from pollution. "I just feel Pete has sold us down the river to the oil companies,"[100] said Delaware's Grace Pierce. The League of Conservation Voters, which had previously given him high marks, also noticed the subtle change in his votes, and his score declined from a 90 percent rating on "critical issues" to a low 36 percent during his last year in Congress. But no one noted Pete's oil holdings or asked if any federal conflict-of-interest laws were being violated. Instead, environmentalists were puzzled.

"He feels his constituency is revolving more and more around the major energy industries,"[101] conjectured Delaware Audobon Society president John Shields.

It was not a bad guess.

In mid February, 1978, Governor du Pont flew to Louisiana to discuss Delaware's potential for oil companies there. In April, as reports of dry wells being drilled offshore grew, Pete told local business leaders not to be discouraged; over 200 wells were drilled in the North Sea, he said, before oil was struck. He predicted that if oil was found off the coast the Port of Wilmington would rival Philadelphia as the number one port on the Delaware River. He had potential boons for other parts of Delaware also. Lewes, for example, could become an important port and Sussex County Airport, he explained, would be an ideal base for helicopters servicing the oil industry. It was enough to make any small businessman swoon.

May found the governor happily touring Shell's drilling rig offshore. One year later, he had amendments to the Coastal Zoning Act introduced in the state house, HB447, and HB448. "The Governor says he needs the amendments to the Coastal Zone Act as a pro-business signal," fumed former Governor Russell Peterson. "Yes, Big Oil would be pleased. They have always resented the people of Delaware stopping their plans for despoiling our coastal zone."[102] Even the *News-Journal* was opposed to rushing to amend the law.

HB447, allowing a Getty pipeline, passed the House on June 12, 1979, but was bottled up in a Senate committee. HB448, allowing onshore support facilities, almost met the same fate, but escaped the committee bottleneck when it was amended to exclude all tank farms and was passed by the Senate, modified, and returned to the House, where it was not expected to be voted on before the Assembly's session ended at the end of the month.

On the next to the last day of the legislative session, Majority Leader William Gordy, realizing that defenders of the Coastal Zone Act were absent from the House chambers, suddenly asked that House Bill 448, containing the governor's proposed amendments, be considered even though it was not on the agenda. House Speaker John Ferguson quickly moved for an immediate roll call vote on the bill, ignoring amendments that had been proposed and were properly supposed to be considered first. Some representatives rose to object. Ferguson simply ignored them, and the bill was passed. Delaware's famed Coastal Zone Act had been gutted right on the floor of the House amidst shameless procedural violations.

In an uncustomary move, the bill was then immediately taken to the governor's office. There, Pete du Pont signed it into law.

"Governor du Pont and his legislative allies are sending a message all right," said an angry Peterson, "a clear anti-environmental signal to the country that will drive away existing and potential businesses and lose more jobs than Big Oil would ever provide. The anti-business image was concocted by the oil companies, their partners in the petrochemical industry and the law firms in Wilmington that represent them."[103]

Four months later a jet owned by Getty Oil company landed at Tulsa Oklahoma's airport and careened to a stop. Out stepped Pete du Pont, accompanied by his wife, Elise, and Secretary of State Glenn Kenton, fresh from the Southern Governor's Conference in New Orleans. Pete and his party climbed into a car and were driven to the Oklahoma Petroleum Council, where he was to address 250 oilmen and their wives on energy.

"The atmosphere in the room, before his talk, was less than electric," Theodore Barrington, senior editor of the *Oil and Gas Journal,* recalled. "He started late; before a group sated with food and drink and panel sessions. Most chins, including mine, were propped up by elbows. We had heard it all before, so many times, and yet here was one more politician about to assault us with the energy word."[104]

But Pete was not simply "one more politician." In July, he was one of the few Northeastern governors to join oil state governors at the National Governors Conference in opposing the use of a portion of a proposed windfall profits tax on deregulated oil to assist the poor in meeting their heating bills. Pete said he wanted the money to finance the search by private companies for new sources of energy. Not many politicians from up north were willing to back the oil companies like Pete was.

If Barrington did not know this, the introduction Getty Oil's Jack Jones gave du Pont should have been a clue. Jones praised Pete's "strong leadership" in improving Delaware's attitude toward business interests, and noted that the changes in Delaware "have been noticed in our industry and around the country. He understands the need for business and government to work together. We have worked closely with the du Pont administration."[105]

Barrington noticed the audience shaking off its stupor about 15 minutes into Pete's speech. "People's eyes opened," he wrote. "Everybody sat up straighter. Soon, no one wanted to miss a word."[106]

"All you representatives of the big, bad oil industry don't look so bad to me," said Pete. He heaped praise on Getty for forging a working alliance with his administration, and pointed out the changes in the Coastal Zone Act as proof of how Delaware's business image had improved. He encouraged the oil men to bring their business to Delaware and criticized government regulations and "the belief in Washington that it can be solved with conservation alone." He blamed bureaucracy for the failure of power plants to switch from oil to coal, and attacked President Carter's curbs on foreign oil imports. He speculated about an oil shortfall by 1985 which could produce "terrible shortages, massive unemployment, and a crippling of American industry's competitiveness on the world market." The only solution, he argued, was to "start producing energy just as fast and just as hard as we know how. Stop moaning and groaning about how tough it is to work with the government and get out and do it. . . . I'm going to count on you all to drill, take risks, invest a little more and find us some more oil."[107]

The banquet hall rocked with applause.

"Get smarter," he exorted. "Get the government off your back."

He was given a standing ovation.

"He talked our line," said CONOCO's Assistant Controller Thomas Pickerell.

"I am amazed that he is so knowledgable," said another oil man.[108]

Barrington was impressed with Pete's speaking style. "Had he not gone beyond energy, this could easily be written off as the result of a good speaker addressing a sympathetic audience. . . . This was not the case. Rather, it was one of a stunning, overwhelming speaker capturing an audience. . . . With barely a reference to his notes, without the slightest break in his logic, he spoke with that sincerity which jaded journalists almost never hear, and when they do, are perhaps overly impressed.

"As, perhaps, am I. But I don't think so. The irony of hearing du Pont is that regarding energy or anything else, I have barely heard of him. Scion of a famous family, well into his 40's, he prompts one to ask: Will he one day be running for higher office?"[109]

As if to answer that question, Pete took the Getty jet to Washington, where he visited the offices of GOPAC, the Republican fund-raising outfit he helped launch to finance Republican legislative candidates—and, of course, future national convention delegates. But first he stopped off at the Getty headquarters in Tulsa to discuss the Baltimore Canyon drillings and the company's consideration of Delaware for a planned $90 million methyl alcohol plant. He also raised the question of Getty's proposed pipeline from its Delaware City refinery to Marcus Hook, Pennsylvania. Later that month, the state Department of Natural Resources and Environmental Control, over the protests of Delaware Citizens for Clean Air, granted Getty a state variance to allow its refinery to operate a malfunctioning catalytic cracking unit that was violating air control standards. Repairing the cracker would have given jobs to up to 1000 skilled workmen. Not repairing it allowed small particles of pollution to be emitted that are more easily inhaled in human lungs.

"I consider myself an environmentalist," said Pete, back in Delaware, "a person who is very concerned about developing our energy resources from a national economic point of view and someone who's a friend of bringing jobs here."[110]

Jobs, in fact, became Pete's rationale for about every major change he made in Delaware law. It also was his excuse for logging 27,000 miles in out-of-state trips in the first 14 months of his administration. Because the oil and banking contacts on Pete's itinerary were often kept secret, Dover legislators dubbed the trips a "Magical Mystery Tour," borrowing the title of a Beatles album. "It always fascinated me that he says he is going out of state to drum up jobs," commented Senate President Pro Tem Richard Cordrey, a Democrat, "but these trips always involve a small political speech. I believe he gets invited to the political speeches and then arranges (state business) on the side."[111] Ten of the 30 trips were openly for political appearances at GOP fund-raisers, even delivering the keynote guest speech at the New York Republican Convention, an event that underlined his continuing alliance with Rockefeller interests which dominated New York Republican politics. But Pete was obviously also wooing the oil-rich Sunbelt. In Oklahoma, GOP chairman Harold Hunter, responding to "glowing reports" from oilmen about du Pont's Tulsa speech, asked Pete to do some fundraising on behalf of his state's Republican legislative candidates. Texas also called on the governor to raise money among oilmen. In November, he returned to Texas to attend the Republican governors conference.

His entourage was impressive; it included his energy adviser, two cabinet officials, his press secretary and an aide. There, at Austin's enormous University of Texas Special Events Center, du Pont strolled up the aisle bathed in spotlight as the university's 200-piece band struck up "Our Delaware" as part of Gov. William Clement's $200,000 three-day extravaganza featuring Henry Kissinger, fireworks flashing the outline of Texas near the ceiling, and shouting and hooting Texans—all paid for by corporations, including Du Pont Company.

During that trip, Pete, Kenton and their aides also visited Guatemala, where State Police Sergeant Andy Stayton reluctantly surrendered his pistol before entering the well-guarded office of the dictator, and Mexico, where President Pedro Diaz made a point of playing host wearing a tie from Hagley, the Du Pont Company's ancestral home on the Brandywine. "Did you see his Hagley tie?" Pete asked repeatedly. "That made me feel at home." So did the Du Pont plant he toured. "You'd have known you were in a Du Pont plant," he said to an accompanying Delaware reporter. "They have all the pollution controls in."[112]

Why Guatemala and Mexico?

"Both nations are rapidly developing and are particularly interested in Delaware's technological prowess in poultry production," Pete later explained. But more was involved than chickens. The Guatemalans hoped "to become self-sufficient in oil and food," a task easier in the case of oil as Shanendoah Oil of Fort Worth, a company Du Pont Company had considered buying, drilled in the western highlands where Indians fought expropriation and some joined leftist guerrillas.

Oil also held Pete's fascination in Mexico. "The largest single factor in

Mexico's sudden growth is its large reserves of oil and natural gas ... it is important that we work closely with Mexico and Canada in the future.... It would be best—and I have said it many times—if we could reduce our foreign oil imports and rely solely upon production in this nation. However, we must forge closer links and stronger cooperation with Mexico and Canada to bring economic prosperity to our hemisphere."[113]

Du Pont, in both his courting of conservative domestic oil producers and his perspective on Mexican, Guatemalan and Canadian oil providing some replacement for the volatile Middle East's, was beginning to sound more like a national office holder than a governor of a small state, and others had taken notice.

"Someone with national ambitions would naturally consider them (oilmen) a political ally," analyzed former Governor Peterson. "There is a possibility a northeast governor would conceivably be looking for that support in the long run. I don't want to attach any motive to what Governor du Pont is doing, but it seems to me pretty obvious anyone with national ambitions would find support from the major financial interests very inviting."[114]

The *News Week* of Jack Costello, the former *State News* reporter, also noted that du Pont would be "rapping both President Carter and Ted Kennedy, until he knows for sure who will be the Democratic nominee. A few days ago he popped Ted as the 'classic liberal' going off in another direction while the country is going conservative. No doubt the Governor said all that with a straight face, figuring most people would swallow it without ever wondering when Du Pont became a conservative." *News Week* noted that "Du Pont has set up a GOP Political Action Committee to find GOP legislative candidates around the country. Now why would the governor of little Delaware do anything like that? Because he's building up a bankful of IOU's when he makes his national move in '84."[115]

Although Pete disclaimed any national ambitions, commentators noted his visits to half the nation's states since taking office, charming Orange County's conservative kingmakers of the Lincoln Club, who launched both Richard Nixon's and Ronald Reagan's rise, as well as the corporate bigwigs of the exclusive Bohemian Club in California. His GOPAC, thanks mostly to his speeches, had raised $200,000 in one year and helped Republicans win control of the legislative houses of two states, one of them Delaware. By now, Republicans around the country were taking the hint. "Du Pont for President!" shouted the New Jersey host of a $75-a-head cocktail party, and Pete's dodging of controversial issues such as abortion and right-to-work and his chameleon pragmatism had served him well in all surroundings. "Pete strikes me as a conservative," said Texas GOP chairman Chet Upham. "He comes across to Texans extremely well. I think he'd do real well." Wisconsin GOP leader Paul Swain happily called him a "moderate Republican, rather than being a conservative." But a political aide to Iowa Governor Robert Ray spoke for the consensus: "Du Pont was in Iowa last year" and "he went over very well ... I'm sure Pete du Pont has some political ambitions."[116]

That the support was wide was evident, ranging from Tennessee's Charles Overby, administrative assistant to Governor Lamar Alexander ("Very attractive. If he wanted to pursue the presidency, he'd have some friends in Tennessee") to Michigan's former GOP chairman Bill McLaughlin ("Governor du Pont and his philosophy is a saleable philosophy in Michigan. He would have a good image and would do well. Among organization Republicans, Pete du Pont would be well received in Michigan").[117]

And the top presidential contenders knew it. "Du Pont," reported Sam Walty of *Delaware Today,* "is frequently mentioned on most lists of potential vice-presidential candidates. He also remains the most prominent of Delaware's politicians still uncommitted to any presidential camp."[118]

Texas's John Connally and George Bush both visited Pete in Delaware, angling for his support. The message was about the same: more oil, more coal, less government spending, less government regulations, helping big business in helping America. Only the style was different, Connally's sounding like Oral Roberts, Bush's like a Harvard professor.

Pete seemed inclined toward Bush, and the former CIA director reciprocated, calling Pete "a man of total, total integrity ... the hope of the Republican party lies in people like Pete du Pont."[119]

"I gather du Pont wants to be president too," Bush had told a reporter in New Hampshire after a Wilmington visit, "but not this time. I think he's trying to broaden his base."[120] Du Pont was certainly in the running as a possible Bush running mate. Bush was not put off by the similarity of their well-heeled backgrounds, stating, "I wouldn't look for philosophical balance, (though) to some degree you have to have regionalism."[121]

The ex-CIA chief was also the favorite of the Brandywine. In contrast to his runner-up fund-raising position nationwide to Connally, Bush was the Du Pont family's first choice. Bayard Sharp, long a Republican funding angel, threw a party for the Texan from Connecticut which won Bush thousands of dollars from such Du Ponts as Hugh Sharp, Jr., Mary Sharp, Ruly Carpenter, C.B. McCoy, George Weymouth, Mrs. Henry B. du Pont, Du Pont Vice-President Charles Harrington and Richard C. du Pont.

6. RICHARD'S CARIBBEAN CAPERS

Richard was then also involved in more clandestine operations. He was fuming over President Carter's lack of support of Nicaragua's besieged dictator, General Anastasio Somoza. He had met Somoza over the years during his frequent sojourns to the Caribbean and felt that Somoza, whose family had ruled Nicaragua since U.S. Marines had crushed the rebellion of General Sandino in the Thirties, was owed his due as a U.S. ally no matter how bad the State Department ranked his human rights record. Federal law prohibited arms sales to Somoza because of his regime's flagrant violations of human rights. So Richard turned to his private air fleet, Summit Aviation.

Summit was the multi-million-dollar airplane charter and overhaul company that Richard had founded shortly after the failure of the CIA's invasion of Cuba's Bay of Pigs. Growing up with the name and legend of his father, Richard had always been a flying bug. As a boy he went to St. Andrew's, the exclusive elementary academy founded by his uncle, A. Felix du Pont; there, amidst other Du Ponts, he studied at the Irénée du Pont Library and walked the grounds listening to the bells of the carillon dedicated to his father's memory. Richard C. du Pont had been the champion glider flier who died testing a glider for the army during World War II. A pioneer in aviation, he had founded Delaware's Civil Air Patrol, and after his death the Du Pont family continued leading the wing in honor of their hero, Hugh Sharp becoming its second commander.

Richard's legend grew over the years. In 1946 the first Delaware Air Show was dedicated to him, and his only son, who had flown with his father in a makeshift airborne cradle, must have felt the pull to follow his father's calling. The insecurity of being a fatherless child was evident in his problem with his weight, but Richard, known as "Kippy" to the family, developed a jovial personality that was genuinely amicable. And he kept his eyes focused on his goal. By the time he entered Emery Riddle College in Miami in 1955, he had already flown solo and was the 1000th member of the Delaware Civil Air Patrol. At Riddle, he majored in aviation business administration. "I'm just naturally interested in it,"[122] he said. It was probably at Riddle, named for the man who founded Riddle Airlines, a CIA asset later active in mounting the Bay of Pigs operation, that young Richard first came in contact with the CIA. This, too, may have seemed "natural." He was young, fatherless, impressionable, patriotic, all the classic characteristics for recruitment as an "asset." Whether he was witting or not was not as important as the pro-CIA feelings that predominated among his ultra-conservative family.

In December 1960, Richard announced he was going to develop Baker Field off Delaware's Route 896. Baker had become an available option after the closing in January of that year of the Piasecki Airport, named after the company founded by uncle A. Felix du Pont, Jr., and Laurence Rockefeller.

Within a year Richard had founded Summit Aviation, apparently with the help of a friend, Patrick J. Foley. Foley, however, was no ordinary chum. According to Washington sources, he was an operative for the Central Intelligence Agency.[123]

The following year the Du Ponts gathered at their Vic Mead Club for a special event. Richard had married a pretty young woman named Caroline Johnstone. The wedding party was made up of young Du Ponts: George Weymouth, Robert H. Robinson, Anne Canby, Natelle Riegel, Julie Smith, Laura du Pont and Richard's cousin, Richard S. du Pont, son of Sam Hallock du Pont.

Cousin Richard S. soon emerged as one of Kippy's closest business partners. In March 1965, the *News-Journal* ran a photograph of both young men together; Richard S. was named vice-president of Manor Aviation, a charter service company that had held a Cessna franchise since its 1960 founding. The following year Summit was named as a sales outlet for Lear executive jets. Richard had also ventured into other fields, buying the Chesapeake Inn on U.S. 213, a quarter of a mile from the Chesapeake City Bridge, and taking his seat on the board of the aviation company his father had founded and uncle Henry B. du Pont effectively ran, All American Aviation, now called All American Engineering. That year another man was also elected to All American's board by the Du Ponts—Robert Vesco.

Richard was by then considered one of the most informed men in Delaware on aviation products. His employees often won aviation mechanics safety awards. He was a respected man, owner of a new company, Delaware Air Freight (DelAir), and named by J. H. T. McConnell, a family in-law and head of Delaware Trust, as a member of the bank's local advisory board at Middletown, Delaware, where Summit was headquartered. He was also a happy man, living contentedly with his wife at Great House Farms at Chesapeake City, just over the Maryland border, where his mother also resided, raising such horses as Kelso and the filly Me at her famous Bohemia Stables.

Richard lived the good life, and looked it, sporting a rotund figure and beard during his frequent fishing trips to the Caribbean, where he hobnobbed with rich Americans and their not infrequently Latin dictator allies and business partners. Richard showed little regard for the "natives of the Caribbean." On one such expedition, in 1970, he and his wife took their small diesel-powered yacht, the "Yellow Dot," some 1500 miles through the Bahamas, catching marlin, tuna, albacore, and dolphins. Pulling in at the dock of the Diamond Salt Company on Long Island in the Bahamas, Richard gave some fish to natives while he took on fresh water and plugged into an electrical outlet.

"They were really excited," he said later. "This was like somebody giving us steak. They love fresh fish, but are too lazy to go after them. When you toss one on the dock, they'll do handstands."[124]

But with other Americans, it was as clubbish as anything one would find among colonialists of an earlier, British empire. Pulling into French Cay, the

Du Ponts found a sailboat anchored belonging to an old friend, Dr. Gifford Pinchot of Baltimore. "Here we had gone all the way down the Bahamas chain and see a boat just 30 miles from home. But that wasn't all. It was owned and skippered by Dr. G.B. Pinchot and the other day at Summit I went into the coffee room and there he was. He has an airplane and gets it serviced at Summit." In the balmy air of what was then still the playground of the American rich, it was a small world indeed. That night, as if to demonstrate how casually Americans like the Du Ponts took themselves as heirs to empire—was World War II really the war for British succession?— Richard and his wife dined at the Pan American Club with Robin Wainwright, British Commissioner of Grand Turk. Strictly Kipling.

It is, perhaps, too easy to see how Richard, lost in this relaxed and privileged world of fronds and beaches and leaping marlin, would see the Cuban Revolution. Its sweaty desperation and rising outrage simply made no sense amidst the tinkling crystal of chilled Margueritas and hushed, civilized white-tie conversations. It could only seem an aberration, some evil visitation from afar, where bandits schemed to steal what is rightfully ours and enslave a people, first with dreams of the impossible, then with guns.

So it came to pass that Jimmy Carter opened a window and Richard S. du Pont looked out at the world with fresh eyes and called upon his cousin to join him in a great adventure. They would go to Cuba.

Richard and his wife met their cousin and *Newsday* publisher William Attwood and his family in Florida. Attwood had long been invited to come to Cuba by the head of the Cuban mission to the United Nations, Teofilio Costa. From Florida, they flew by private plane to Havana, where they were met by members of the Cuban Foreign Service.

They toured the giant island widely, visiting a school, a factory, the Revolutionary Museum with its artifacts describing the history behind the 1958 revolution, a youth camp, even a 45,000-acre dairy cooperative managed by Ramon Castro, brother of President Fidel Castro. In Havana, the former waterhole of vacationing Americans and gambling den of Florida mobster Meyer Lansky, they met with intellectuals and several government ministers. It was a far cry from the days when their cousin, Irénée du Pont, Sr., held sway over the island with an influence second only to the U.S. Ambassador, if not the dictator General Batista. They found that Cuba was still a poor country by U.S. standards, but its people were no longer starving and could read and write, attend free school and have a right to a job and medical care. If the individual freedoms and conveniences Americans were used to were not in evidence, they never had been available to most Cubans, who now had more than under the Batista regime.

Richard S. du Pont was visibly impressed. What he saw shook his political biases to the marrow. "God knows, we're not pure along these lines, but Cuba has us whipped hands down when it comes to turbulent development. So anyone trying to understand Cuba today must first appreciate what they've gone through. To me it's no surprise that Cuba got behind Castro and, when we failed to extend our help in any meaningful way, that Fidel went the Marxist-Leninist route. What other choice did he have?"[125]

Richard S., or "Dick" as the family called him, was no communist or even a socialist. He was an unabashed believer in capitalism. But to him, U.S. policy had played a role in preventing capitalism from ever having a chance to really develop an internal market in Cuba. "I do not believe that Cuba became a Communist country because socialism prevailed over capitalism. I believe the change was directly attributable to the failure of capitalists to practice good capitalism ... our system works only when successful individuals maintain the self-discipline to consider the less fortunate, and do something about their problems. It works only when our government is truly responsive to the majority of its constituency.

"Today's Latin American countries bear striking resemblances to pre-revolutionary Cuba. What course they choose will depend largely on how we handle ourselves and on an accurate and enlightened understanding by the United States of these countries."

Dick du Pont explained the placement of Soviet missiles in Cuba and the sending of Cuban troops to fight CIA-backed UNITA and South African troops invading Angola as a quid-pro-quo of Cuban reliance on Soviet aid, and termed it "naive" for Americans "to think Cuba wouldn't respond." On the other hand, "we have by no means compiled a record we can brag about. It is an indisputable fact that we organized, equipped and launched the Bay of Pigs invasion, based on amateurish and unreliable data collected by our CIA ... we have used our 'good' offices to pressure other American countries, through the OAS, often against such countries' wishes, to support the blockade.... The recent CIA hearings chaired by Senator Church have revealed that the CIA has attempted on eight separate occasions to assassinate Fidel Castro. These are not bits of Communist propaganda. These are just plain facts—hard things to accept about ourselves; but this we have done! It is little wonder, therefore, that the Cubans see us as imperialists. We've given them every reason to do so."

It was an extraordinary admission for any American of the business class, much less a Du Pont. Apparently Dick du Pont felt chagrined by what had been done in the name of the American people. He certainly seemed angry at being deceived for so long. "Whether the CIA got out of hand or whether a government sponsored these maneuvers is an important question, but I cannot believe the majority of Americans would condone any of these moves if put to popular ballot. Therefore I say it is high time we as citizens of the United States put some pressure on our representatives to conduct themselves in a manner worthy of the American people. We don't think of ourselves as imperialists or expansionists or aggressors. Let's see that our officials conduct themselves accordingly."

Dick seemed particularly embarrassed about having to answer for illegal CIA operations when confronting Cubans. He and his cousin had a three-hour conversation with Fidel Castro, and meeting face to face the man who had been billed as an arch villain by the American government and media for so long was an unsettling experience. "I for one didn't like apologizing for my government's abuses in Cuba," he fumed. "I would have preferred to look President Castro squarely in the eye and say, 'We have only tried to help,' but I couldn't, because we clearly hadn't."

As if to ward off any suggestion that a Du Pont could be harboring sympathies for socialism or for the communist form of government, Dick was also quick to affirm that he did not have any use for their system. "I believe that capitalism, despite its many imperfections, has clearly proven the best means to the universal end of all forms of government—namely, the *funding* of the goods and services requisite to an orderly society." Dick held onto the fundamental tenet of capitalism since the system emerged out of medieval Europe: the essential "fallen" nature of man. Once this view of human nature was accepted, one could more wisely structure checks and balances into government to protect individual rights from abuse by other individuals or government.

Whatever merit one gave to such a pessimistically weighted view of human desires, the competitive marketplace's need for individual freedoms balanced by some order had undoubtedly given birth to concerns for individual political rights which may prove to be capitalism's greatest contribution to social theory and government. The fact that this contribution was often undermined by the economic side of capitalism's competitiveness, however, seemed to escape du Pont in his praise of the "funding" the system generated. For that funding was also based on the acceptance of humanity's "fallen" nature, and the extraordinary belief that the best way to meet the needs of all the people was to accept and appeal to the worst side of human individual selfishness. Through the individual acquisition of wealth, held and owned exclusively, society was indeed advanced beyond the backwardness of rural life, but at terrible human cost. It was this cost that Dick du Pont recognized as what the majority of working Cubans had been unwilling any longer to accept and had backed Castro's revolution, much to the CIA's shock at the Bay of Pigs.

But to those on the other side of the tracks like Dick du Pont, scion of

America's richest family, capitalism had more good than pain to offer. The misery of Cuba under a U.S.-sponsored Batista dictatorship and the excessive abuses of corporate exploitation was, to him, an aberration, an exception. That the celebration of individual selfishness in the name of "funding" had naturally resulted in a wealthy elite in Cuba and in the control of its economy and government by American business interests, including those of his own family, was simplistically seen as merely a "mistake," just as the CIA's analysis was merely "amateurish and unreliable" and its invasion, like the U.S. policy which promoted the intervention and continued the economic blockade, were also only "mistakes." Dick du Pont, for reasons obviously of his own background's "blindspot," had been unable to see any better purpose for government and economic organization than "funding"; in spite of his humanitarian and democratic impulses, he had ultimately, like Irving Shapiro and Irénée du Pont, reduced politics to a question of private financial investments.

Still, Dick earnestly told readers of the *News-Journal* that "Cuba has achieved a great deal since the revolution. It is truly amazing to see the high degree of employment, the very strong work ethic, the national pride and the greatly improved standard of living, education and productivity which those people have attained, particularly when compared to the rest of Latin America." To ideologues among his family who read such a rebuke of their life-long assumptions that work ethic, national pride, and productivity can only exist in an atmosphere of selfish accumulation of money and wealth, such words must have seemed to border on treason.

But Dick du Pont appealed to reason and history, to the "long-standing ties" of culture and trade that existed in the Americas, and begged his readers to remind themselves that Cubans were culturally more like Americans than Russians and that they should not allow themselves to lose sight of that in their phobia of the Soviets. "It seems absurd that we now espouse a policy of mutual open hostility," he concluded. "I cannot see why the U.S. supports an economic blockade against Cuba, but does nothing of that sort with Romania, Bulgaria, East Germany and the like. Why wouldn't it be a simple matter for us to curtail the CIA nonsense, lift the blockade and have the kind of 'normal' arms-length policy with limited trade, etc., that we espouse with all the other Communist countries?"

His cousin, Richard C., provided the answer. It was impossible for Kippy to conceive of socialism or revolution in Latin America as being anything but an extension of Soviet subversion, of "outside agitators" from whom Latin Americans, much like Du Pont workers with respect to the Steelworkers Union, had to be protected, often despite themselves.

That meant arms, and Kippy had myriad ties to the military industrial complex through his All American Industries. In May 1974, for example, All American joined ILC Company of Dover and Du Pont Company in a $65,000 study funded by the Navy to develop an "Aerocrane," a lighter-than-air craft using helicopter engines and dirigibles made with Du Pont's Revlar 29 fabric, for logging, ship loading and earth-moving. In 1975, the Air Force awarded All American a $2 million contract to produce launchers for unmanned drones for target practice at Florida's Tyndall Air Force Base. In 1977, the navy awarded Richard a $1.5 million contract for landing aids for military helicopters, an extension of All American's business of producing arresting gear made of Du Pont nylon tape attached to the ends of cables for aircraft carriers and Navy and Marine land-air bases since World War II. By the 1980 elections, All American had climbed out of the $13.5 million net loss left in 1973 by a fleeing Robert Vesco (who had been allowed to buy 75 percent of the stock in exchange for needed capital) and was registering net sales of $17.5 million and building a new $1.6 million plant near South Chapel Street to produce such new products as the Nissley wind turbine and rotary hydraulic arresting gear.

The practicalities of such business affairs with the Pentagon and the accompanying regular associations with the military mind, combined with an upbringing molded by family expectations and the fatherless boy's characteristic need to identify with authority symbols, probably contributed much of the explanation for why Kippy's mind remained more closed than his cousin's.

Given the ultra-conservatism of his family, that was not surprising. What was extraordinary was Dick's ability to break out of the ideological mind-set of his brethren, a feat no doubt aided by his relationship to the better-informed publishing family of his fiancée, Janet Attwood.

In May 1977, some 700 guests gathered in Philadelphia to honor eighty-one-year-old Jimmy Doolittle at the Spirit of St. Louis Dinner. Dick flew up a party of seven to the Friday night banquet, including his fiancée and his mother, Mrs. S. Hallock du Pont. It was a testament to the high regard with which Dick and his family were held in aviation circles that he shared the speakers' table with actor and aviation buff Cliff Robertson and Montana rancher Land Lindbergh, son of the famed aviator who had died three years before. Also at the table was Dick's aunt, Mrs. A. Felix du Pont; her title as honorary chairman averring the key role the Du Pont family had played in the development of American aviation. The Spirit of St. Louis dinners were named for the airplane in which Lindbergh had flown the first trans-Atlantic flight a half-century ago. They were held across the country by the Lindbergh Memorial Fund Committee, chaired by astronaut Neil Armstrong, to raise money for special projects. The project this year was the reconditioning of the original B-25 that Jimmy Doolittle had flown over Tokyo in the first of America's air raids over Japan.

Dick had been chosen to escort Doolittle to the reconditioned bomber at Philadelphia International Airport's TWA hanger, another symbol of Du Pont presence in aviation, Henry B. du Pont having been TWA's chairman. Doolittle was now old and frail, a mere wisp of the man who had once commanded thousands, been a director of Shell Oil, and during the Fifties, President Eisenhower's personal inspector of secret CIA operations and assets throughout Latin America. The moment was magic with nostalgia, harkening to the days when American leaders openly analogized their nation with the young Roman Republic, when a courageous "lone eagle" named Lindbergh carried the nation's banner back to a war-exhausted Europe and another young ace named Doolittle struck at the Pacific heart of an opposing Axis. Now it seemed that the Republic had aged with its warriors, its institutions straining under the mighty burden of militarily defending the unique empire it had molded as Europe's uneasy heir.

In many ways, Dick du Pont as an heir to America's richest dynasty and his family's proudest days, the son of aviation pioneers and a patrician uncomfortable in the purple robes of an "imperialist," symbolized the American Republic as it approached what the Trilateralists had called the "crisis of democracy" and what others whispered were its last days. There were those who disagreed, of course, and held that like the dark 1850's, these days too would pass and the American Republic, through trial and struggle, would enter a new stage in its life and again offer hope for humanity.

But there were others who felt that no metamorphosis was needed; no fundamental change was being urged by history, that America, like they, had grown too old of mind to change, or need not, indeed, must not. And then there was Richard C. du Pont, who, while his cousin wondered about the future America beside the shoulder of an aging Doolittle, confidently gave tours of the DC-3 he flew against Caribbean revolutions, and time.

"He has a place in the Caribbean. And he often flies down there," Steve Seningen, manager of Summit Aviation's charter operation, said of Richard C. "Sometimes he flies supplies, too. Big stuff he might need. You know."

Richard owned a hotel in Haiti and a project in Providenciales, an island in the Turks and Caicos northeast of Haiti. His Summit Aviation had cargo planes which moved "hazardous materials" in small batches out of Delaware for various chemical firms.[126] Summit also had a fleet of Cessna and Piper single- and multi-engine airplanes. Some of these were converted into sophisticated warplanes and sold to dictatorships in the Caribbean basin, including Haiti, Honduras, Guatemala and Somoza's Nicaragua.

Richard was not happy with President Carter's ban on military sales to the

Somoza regime. Neither was the CIA. Patrick Foley, the Summit executive Washington sources identified as a former CIA operative, insisted that all of Summit's sales abroad, including the modified Cessna Skymaster he and du Pont called the "Summit Sentry," had been approved by the U.S. Government. But when News-Journal reporter Phil Mildford and Joe Trento asked to see copies of export permits, Foley and du Pont refused. Nor could the State Department locate them.[127]

It was illegal to ship arms to Somoza or the Guatemalan dictatorship, and whether reports of automatic arms being flown out of Summit's airport to those countries were true or not, there was no question that the Summit Sentry was outfitted with switches, controls, wiring and mountings for machine guns, bomb racks, rocket launchers, spy cameras, aerial loudspeaker systems and devices for dropping propaganda leaflets. Foley at first had denied the modifications were done at Summit, but later confirmed that they had been done since at least 1976. The conversion, which hikes the cost of the Skymaster from $100,000 to as high as $500,000 when it leaves Summit's hangers, turns the civilian plane into a miniature attack-fighter-bomber that has the military designation 02-337. This "civic action" aircraft was used extensively in Vietnam for counterinsurgency operations. It was also used to protect the illegal southeast Asia heroin connection by which the CIA funded mercenaries while avoiding Congressional appropriations and committee oversight.

"I can tell you emphatically," said an international arms dealer who knew Foley when he was operating openly as a CIA officer, "that these planes have been used by high-ranking members of the Thai military in northern Thailand to protect illegal drug operations along the Cambodian border. They are perfect for that sort of action. You can move some drugs with them, but better, you can keep out intruders with them."[128] A Thai Royal Navy source confirmed current sales. "We have been promised by Summit . . . further military conversions," he said. "We have made the arrangements with Summit,"[129] using airframes made in France, to which Cessna had shifted Skymaster production to avoid stringent export laws.

Foley also identified two airplanes he said were being modified "for the State Department" for use along the Vietnam coast.

However deeply Kippy was involved, and reports of automatic weapons being fired from the direction of du Pont's Maryland farm suggest he is very deeply enmeshed, it appears that Foley is the one who actually runs the operation, assisted by Clifford C. Barry. Both men refused to give News-Journal reporters details of their backgrounds (although Foley admitted being also a 747 freighter pilot for Flying Tiger Airlines, the firm founded by General Claire Chennault of the China Lobby of the 1950's, who in turn was linked to Robert Dix of the CIA's Civil Air Transport and Air America). At one point, Barry attempted to prevent Kippy from answering reporters' questions about Summit's military conversion.

The CIA operation apparently worked like this. Cessna manufactured the airframes in France. These were classic bush planes, short-take-off-and-landing (STOL) aircraft capable of a take-off in only 538 feet, and having a ceiling of 10,000 feet, 28,500 feet for the pressurized model.

A Swedish company made the machine-guns and flew them to the U.S. Army's Aberdeen Proving Grounds in Maryland for test-firing. Then the guns were shipped across the Delaware border in violation of federal law. Foley denied purchasing any machine guns, but later, according to the *News-Journal*, "complained about the exorbitant prices the Swedes charge for equipment."[130] One source told the reporters that at least one machine gun system had been installed at Summit. Another source later told this author that automatic weapons were also being shipped out of Summit Airport to Somoza's Nicaragua.[131] Still another source said that ultra-light aircraft were being outfitted for spraying such materials as crop defoliants and were being shipped to Guatemala.[132] A visit to Summit in August 1983 found the company still outfitting planes for at least one Latin American regime, probably Guatemala.

From Summit, the planes were flown to Florida for an expedition, filing papers with customs before being flown out of the country. Theodore Roosevelt III, grandson of the president by the same name and a stockbroker in Philadelphia with the Delaware Fund, flew Summit Sentries down to Haiti in 1978, despite Richard du Pont's claim that he used commercial ferry services. Roosevelt is known in intelligence circles. Members of his family have been top members of the intelligence agencies, including Kermit Roosevelt, who organized the 1953 CIA coup against Prime Minister Mossadegh that returned Shah Muhammed Pahlevi to power in Iran. Theodore confirmed flying the planes first to Palm Beach, Florida. This is the state, it will be recalled, where Dick du Pont's brother, Sam Hallock du Pont, Jr., also runs an airline charter service out of Orlando and a company called Aero Finances, Inc., as well as a firm which imports West German firearms, Krieghoff Gun Company.

Another Du Pont aviator said to have favored Somoza was Alexis I. du Pont. "Lex" owns New Garden Aviation and an airfield at Toughkenamon, Pennsylvania. Bearded, trim, with dark hair despite his 50 years, Lex and his son Everitt promote business reliance on general aviation and had ties to Air Force personnel in 1979 and 1980, including Upper Darby's Major General Mike Bohanick and Philadelphia's Paul Heintz and airline owner Charles Ludington.

7. A THORN CALLED HUMAN RIGHTS, ABROAD...

President Carter's human rights policy also clashed with the Du Ponts' over South Africa. Under apartheid, or segregation, non-whites, comprising 83 percent of the country's population, receive only 33 percent of the national income. The average African family income is less than the officially defined poverty level, while white per capita income exceeds that of Africans by over 1000 percent. Whites get a free education; Africans must pay. And only whites are legally entitled to vote; Africans are made foreigners in their own country, denied citizenship and forced to live in arid "Bantustans" and carry official passbooks when travelling or working in white areas or living in segregated housing compounds. Black trade unions are subjected to terror and refused recognition. Predictably, the infant mortality rate for Africans is over four times that of whites. Amnesty International documents over 10,000 political prisoners.

At first the controversy centered around the University of Delaware, which holds some $49 million worth of common stock in American companies with investments in South Africa. Four of these companies, Exxon, IBM, Caterpillar Tractor and Minnesota Mining and Manufacturing played a key role in the apartheid economy, accounting for some $140 million worth of investments. The university also held shares of Chase Manhattan and Citicorp, whose loans had kept the apartheid regime afloat after a world financial boycott following the Sharpville massacre in 1960 and the Soweto uprising in 1976. Students and faculty, accordingly, petitioned the university's board of trustees to divest their holdings in these companies, as scores of other universities, colleges and other religious institutions and trade unions had done. A chapter of the national Coalition Against Investment in South Africa (CAISA), backed by Clergy and Laity Concerned, presented a detailed 47-page documented report on South African conditions and the American corporations involved.

The trustees, including many Du Ponts, gathered to deliberate. Irving Shapiro assured the trustees that Du Pont Company had no investments, branches or offices in South Africa and does no business there; therefore, the university's holding of over $2 million worth of Du Pont stock should be immune from any projected sale. He did not tell the trustees, however, that Du Pont does do business in South Africa through distributors. In Johannesburg, for example, are Du Pont Cellulose Film, S.A., and the E.I. du Pont de Nemours Photo Products Department; both distributors are openly listed in the city's telephone directory.[133]

In any case, the Du Ponts refused CAISA's proposal, and the trustees kept their lucrative investments.

So did Governor Pete du Pont. Pete owned stock in AMAX (which operates mines in South Africa and Namibia, the former German colony now militarily occupied by South Africa in violation of UN accords), Armstrong Cork, General Electric, Exxon, IBM, General Motors and Texaco, all with heavy investments in South Africa.[134]

Pete's cousin and state director of economic development, Nathan Hayward III, was even more blatant in his support of apartheid. Hayward owned stock in a South African mining company, Vaal Reefs Exploration and Mining Company.[135]

Behind the continuation of American corporations to refuse to honor international sanctions was also another Du Pont-supported Republican politician, Thomas B. Evans, who had replaced Pete as Delaware's sole congressman. Before entering Congress, Evans had represented the Du Pont family's enormous financial clout in the Republican Party as co-chairman of the Republican National Committee. He had followed the political thrust of most of the family in endorsing Richard Nixon's campaign for the presidency in early 1968 and had been an enthusiastic supporter of Maryland's Spiro Agnew's attacks on the media and liberals. "He deserves respect for what he says and stands for,"[136] Evans said in January, 1971. Working under Kansas's conservative senator, Robert Dole, Evans claimed to have a direct line to the Nixon White House. In 1976, Dole joined Nixon's hand-picked successor, Jerry Ford, on the Republican presidential ticket, while Evans was carried into Congress by a Du Pont-financed campaign.

The Soweto uprising and its brutal crushing by the South African army that year moved millions of Americans to reconsider their nation's economic ties to the apartheid regime, but not Evans. On May 1, 1978, the House Committee on Banking, Currency and Housing by a vote of 28-16 reported out an amendment to its Export-Import Bank financing bill that had been sponsored by Massachusetts Congressman Paul Tsongas and passed by the Subcommittee on International Trade, Investment and Monetary Policy. The Tsongas amendment called for the ending of all Bank financing to South Africa.

By early June, however, the mood in Congress had been changed by frightening statements by Carter's National Security Advisor (and Trilateralist) Zbigniew Brzezinski about the dangers of Cuban involvement in Angola and the use of American military planes to supply the efforts of the Mobutu dictatorship in Zaire to crush an invasion by Zairean rebels into Shaba province from across the Angolan border.

Seeing that the atmosphere in Congress had become more frightened, Evans seized the opportunity to circulate a "Dear Colleague" letter on May 31 saying he intended to offer "a vehicle for positive social change in South

Africa but (which) would not impair our exports to that country with which we enjoy a one-half billion (dollar) surplus." Evans's new amendment reflected the position of his friend, Leon Sullivan, a General Motors director and Baptist minister who developed a Code of Ethics for U.S. companies in South Africa which called for continued investments as long as the particular company implemented reforms for integration at the workplace. The Evans amendment, which was passed, struck out Tsongas's ban on Export-Import Bank financing and substituted the Sullivan code, giving the apartheid regime, in the words of Florida's arch-conservative Representative Richard Kelly, "a whack in the shins rather than a kick in the head." Exports by American banks and corporations of capital and goods to South Africa continued, giving the regime a vital lifeline of financial and technological support.

Twenty-six Du Ponts, including Dick du Pont, flocked to Evans's support in his 1980 reelection bid, donating $22,525. In a small state like Delaware, such a contribution carries inordinate weight. Du Pont Company's Edward Jefferson and retired vice-president Charles H. Harrington gave another $1000, while Wilmington Trust retired director W.A. Worth wrote out a check for $250. Over $3000 was donated to Evans in 1979 before his campaign even began; among those donors to the Republican was former Democratic gubernatorial candidate John H. Tyler McConnell.[137]

George Bush got a similar amount for his primaries, $21,175 from 33 Du Pont family members; Du Pont Company officials Jefferson, Heckert and Harold E. May gave another $1000, and Worth, $500. Texas's John Connally attracted only $5,600, plus another $1000 from Du Pont's C.H. Harrington. Tennessee's Senator Howard Baker received the least, $1750; Harrington seems to have spread his bets here also, giving $1000.

Ronald Reagan was not favored, perhaps because he was widely considered too conservative to be electable. W. Laird Stabler was the only Republican family member in Wilmington who gave to his run for the nomination, and then only $500. Philadelphia's James Biddle, married to Lammot du Pont Copeland's daughter, Louisa, gave $500, while Florida's Coleman Walker, an in-law of the Andrew and Bissell families, got up $250. After the election, Ronald Reagan apparently inspired John H.T. McConnell to again show his capacity to cross party lines if the Republican candidate is conservative enough. On November 21, 1980, he donated $1000 to the Reagan/Bush Committee.

Reagan seems to have inspired little confidence at Du Pont Headquarters. No executive except retired C. H. Harrington ($250) gave to his primaries, although he was clearly the front-runner. This undoubtedly reflected Du Pont's concern that the Republicans needed a candidate with wide appeal to beat an incumbent Democratic president. And Wilmington clearly wanted Jimmy Carter out of office.

This was not just the average big businessman's preference for a Republican president. Carter had, in Wilmington's view, bungled foreign policy while proving unreliable on domestic issues such as regulatory relief and organized labor. Du Pont was struggling to free itself of its traditional dependence on artificial fibers and was hoping to recoup losses by further investing in cheap labor factories in the Third World and by moving away from the bulk commodities end of petrochemicals in the United States and moving "downstream" to specialty chemicals and high value-added thermoplastics, X-ray films, pharmaceuticals and agricultural chemicals. "Fibers isn't the business of the future as it was of the past,"[138] Chairman Shapiro had finally admitted in October 1978.

Abroad, the big loss was Iran. The sheikhs and shahs of the Middle East had told American companies that if they wanted to ensure their access to oil supplies, they should build petrochemical plants in the Middle East. When oil shortages eased in the West, many American and European companies cancelled their plans for Middle East plants. Shapiro, however, had already pushed Du Pont's new polyester plant in Iran to completion. When civil strife broke out in that country in late 1978, Du Pont was stuck with its 40 percent investment in a large factory that had just started production that year.

As protests in Iran grew into revolution, private entrepreneurs fled the country with $3 billion and production shutdowns forced the Shah to cut $10 billion from his $47 billion budget because of lost tax revenues. He had planned to borrow $4 billion from American and European banks to mitigate the financial crisis, but the potential instability had also hurt Iran's credit standing in the West.

The Du Pont plant became expendable. The Shah backed off from the guaranteed subsidies he had promised Du Pont, including exemption from import duties on raw materials. Amid mounting unrest, the Shah suddenly became a titan of humanitarian concern for Iran's laboring classes, the rural peasants and industrial workers, and waxed gloriously nationalistic. "It will be unconscionable to extend such protection to this (Du Pont) venture which favors some wealthy people," stated one of his officials, "and to take the money from basic needs at home." When the smoke cleared, the Shah, too, had fled with billions of dollars, the Carter administration was confronted by the Ayatollah Khomeini's withdrawal of billions of dollars in Iranian assets from Chase Manhattan and other New York banks, and Du Pont was out $40 million. After the CIA and U.S. military officials, working out of the Teheran embassy, failed to repeat their 1953 success in fomenting a military coup and the Iranians seized the embassy, President Carter froze Iran's assets in U.S. banks. Du Pont was among the first American companies and banks to apply for a cut of Iran's money to recover its $40 million loss. Iran, meanwhile, held the embassy's personnel as hostages for its seized assets. The stalemate would last exactly a year, fatally hurting the presidential campaigns of both Carter and his major Democratic challenger, Senator Edward M. Kennedy.

As a result of media coverage which all but ignored the key issues of Iran's assets until the hostages' impending release, and the growing frustrations of a misinformed public, and the ensuing public anger, American political opinion took a sharp turn to the right, benefitting mostly the one man the Du Ponts had thought unelectable: Ronald Reagan.

By the time the presidential campaigns were underway, Du Pont Company had other reasons to dislike the Carter Administration. Carter's severing of diplomatic relations with Taiwan cast a shadow over Du Pont's expanding Pacific operations. The company had just opened a new "Tovex" water gel explosives plant in Hong Kong and owned two subsidiaries in Taiwan. At the Neili industrial district in the capital of Taipei, Du Pont Taiwan Ltd. employed hundreds of Taiwanese to manufacture electronic connectors for slitting and packaging "Mylar" polyester film and made paste compositions and components for Du Pont's new automatic clinical analyzer. And more was on the agenda. Du Pont Taiwan Ltd. was then in the middle of constructing a plant near Lung Tang to produce its "benlate" fungacide and "Lamate" insecticide. In addition, its Pacific marketing subsidiary, Du Pont Far East, Inc., had a branch office in Taipei. Of 650 Du Pont employees, all but seven were Taiwanese. In Wilmington, the International Department uneasily announced Du Pont expected to continue its activities on the island.

Du Pont then had 26 percent of its capital invested abroad, and Shapiro had plans to increase this to 33 percent. Behind this move was not only the lure of cheap labor but the worry that consumer spending in the United States would continue to drop as the economy slipped deeper into expected recession. But foreign competition was stiff and expected to get tougher, especially as the socialist countries began to increase exports. In Eastern Europe, 60 modern petrochemical plants were on the drawing boards or under construction, and Third World markets were expected to dry up as those countries developed their own industries. Libya already had a $2-billion petrochemical industry, Iran a $4-billion complex, and Saudi Arabia had four world-scale ethylene crackers.

In Europe, where oil feedstocks were higher priced than in the United States, synthetic fibers continued to operate at a loss compounded by price cuts resulting from a lack of demand and a glutted market. Du Pont's

European headquarters at Geneva, faced by the third straight year of losses, phased out its acrylic fibers plants in Holland, and looked with relief when eleven European competitors established a fibers cartel to fix prices; Du Pont had already seen its prices decline 15 percent since 1974 and hoped the cartel would stabilize prices while it reduced output. The Europeans, meanwhile, charged Du Pont with dumping its surplus on the market.

In the States, Du Pont made the same charge against Japan, threatening to unleash a politically dangerous trade war by filing an official request for a Justice Department investigation. Pressured by a worried White House and the Tokyo government, Japanese firms agreed to raise their price for yarns by as much as 30 cents per pound, and Du Pont, satisfied, dropped its charge in Washington, ignoring the protests of consumer federations.

Although Du Pont's $545 million earnings on 1977's $9.4 billion sales was a lower performance than, for example, Eastman's $643 million earnings on only $5.9 billion in sales, Shapiro had not given up his goal of restoring the company to the 20 percent earnings it had scored in the legendary Fifties. "Our gamble is that with the largest R&D (research and development) budget in the chemical industry we will create enough products each year to keep our momentum going."[139] He downplayed the lag in the industry and the 30 percent excess capacity during the summer of 1978, claiming "our greatest strength is we can go worldwide every time we invent a product." He was banking on his newer "high-tech" ventures in electronics, photo products, agricultural chemicals and pharmaceuticals, and analysts noted that they now produced 25 percent of Du Pont's total sales. "I hope I'm not selling myself to you," he said, "but I would rather be around for the next ten years than the last ten years."[140] Shapiro was then 62 years old and scheduled to retire in 1981.

Despite such displays of optimism and a relative increase of profits from the bottom Du Pont had reached in 1975, there were disturbing signs that most of Du Pont's problems were out of its control. The worldwide recession had hurt sales of new houses and cars, big users of Du Pont plastics. The ARCO deal had fallen through, and Shapiro tried to compensate with joint ventures with CONOCO in 1978 and Shell Chemical in 1979, the latter designed to provide Du Pont with about one-third of its ethylene, propylene and butaliene needs for at least ten years. But oil prices were not expected to decline during that period. In fact, they would probably rise even higher.

The impact of this had been felt by Du Pont in more diverse ways than simply increased costs in feedstocks. Sometimes it was felt in public relations. Conservationists charged that synthetic fibers were a waste of fossil fuels when natural fibers were available. Du Pont, however, had led the conquest of the natural fibers market with its low-priced synthetics, and was criticized in both Europe and the States for doing exactly what Shapiro had lauded.

Rising oil prices, on the other hand, had eroded the value of Du Pont's cash reserves. European countries using much more imported oil than the United States were soon forced to use the price of a barrel of oil as a barometer of gold's market value rather than the U.S. dollar. The higher values set on gold reserves in turn affected the value of paper money they backed. To make the diminished value of currency palatable and avoid a tight money market, more paper money was printed to keep up credit lines for business. The value of gold began to rise.

The International Monetary Fund, dominated by American banks, had attempted to defend paper currency against gold, insisting on valuing gold at the traditional $35 per ounce, but when it auctioned some of its gold reserves, it was forced by the soaring price to abandon its own principle and take the $275 per ounce others would have profited by if it had not. European demand for gold increased even more, draining reserves held by the U.S. Treasury from 1971's 70 percent of American gold reserves to 1979's 25 percent; 75 percent, or roughly 1 billion ounces, were held in the vaults of the nation's private central banks. Three billion ounces of gold were in circulation in the world that year and only one billion ounces were estimated left to be mined. With production held at a steady 50 million ounces per year, mostly by South Africa, that meant that the gold supply would be exhausted within 20 years, or the year 2000. In the long run, then, gold prices could be expected to continue to rise. In the short run, gold could be expected to be very volatile, responding to political events that, for example, might increase the price of energy; anything that stymied production from the wells of the Middle East, such as Iran's revolution, would increase gold's value in oil importing countries such as Europe and Japan, eroding the value of paper money held by American banks and corporations, including Du Pont. And as long as American industry's productivity lagged behind that of Europe and Japan, creating deficits in trade and payments, the value of the dollar would in the long run decline more than the value of European or Japanese currencies. Measured against each other, the U.S. dollar would be worth less than Swiss francs, deutsche marks and Japanese yen.

Du Pont, like other American banks and corporations, tried to mitigate the impact of this loss in the dollar's value by speculating in the world money markets, but currency fluctuations cut deeply into Du Pont's earnings, costing 13 cents per share in the last quarter of fiscal year 1977 alone. Yearly improvements in earnings, therefore, became even more crucial to Shapiro—if his 20 percent goal was ever to be reached. And he tried to salvage their value by struggling daily "to maintain a favorable balance in other currencies," using the computers run by H.R. Sharp III of the Finance Department. "Manipulating foreign currencies is the closest thing we do to shooting craps,"[141] Shapiro assured a concerned stockholder at the April 1978 annual meeting.

In his modest, wood-panelled office with its unusual, neo-impressionist portrait of the famous three Du Pont brothers who made Du Pont into the world's largest chemical firm, Shapiro insisted: "We've regained the momentum. Now we can restore ourselves as the premier company in this industry," but the fibers division still lagged at only a 4.4 percent net profit on its huge capital investment of plants and debt service.

8. ...AND AT HOME

The Du Ponts on the board were placing much of the blame on the president. Carter had lowered the chemical industry's rating for priority allocations of oil. He had also not thrown enough support, they believed, behind the company's struggle to keep up tariff duties against foreign fiber imports. Nor had he stopped the Federal Trade Commission's suit against alleged anticompetitive pricing by Du Pont, NALCO chemicals, PPG Industries and Ethyl Corporation for antiknock gasoline additives.

The FTC had charged that the four companies which controlled 80 percent of the $600 million a year titanium dioxide pigment market had signalled price changes to each other well in advance through press releases, "eliminating uncertainty about each other's willingness to follow an upward price lead," according to FTC's Alfred Dougherty, and "not overreact to downward momentum." The Justice Department concurred, stating that the practices, while not showing evidence of collusion, constituted anticompetitive action. Shapiro accused the FTC "of seeking to impose on industry the personal social views" of Carter's FTC chairman Michael Pertschuk, and held that any of thousands of price decisions routinely announced to the business press could at any time be alleged illegal at the FTC's whim. But the Justice Department denied that. "This kind of communication may have anticompetitive effects only in certain well-defined circumstances."

Shapiro developed a legal strategy that he would use in other circumstances, including the *Behind the Nylon Curtain* suit, resting his case on the Bill of Rights and stating that Du Pont, as a "corporate citizen," had the right of free speech. He filed suit in Wilmington Federal Court to block the FTC complaint, knowing that the Supreme Court under Chief Justice Warren Burger and other Nixon-era appointees were now opposed to broad readings of enforcement powers of federal regulatory agencies. On September

18, 1979, the deadline for compliance, administrative law judge Miles Brown dismissed the FTC's case, holding that Du Pont's advantage had resulted from "intelligent planning" and the company was not required to be less aggressive in capitalizing on its advantage. Shapiro was elated, but large problems still loomed. That day, as the Iran crisis grew, wild trading soared gold to $377.

Shapiro, in his desperation, tried many tacks. To cut costs, he closed Du Pont's dyes factories, surrendering back to the Germans the business the Du Ponts had stolen in the 1920's when they took over the dye patents seized from German companies during World War I. One of the plants affected was the controversial one in Puerto Rico's Manati River, where 300 workers were employed.

Shapiro also continued to restrict research, and overhauled the company's time-honored committee structure founded by Pierre du Pont. The star of former President Edward Kane fell with fibers. "It was a management failure,"[142] Shapiro said of the decision to expand fiber plants and absorb the $1 billion in shipping cost increases with OPEC's price rise, forcing the whole fibers industry to follow Du Pont into disaster. Kane took the fall.

On the other hand, the star of Robert C. Forney, vice-president of plastics products and resin which had 21 percent net earnings, rose. Forney, who had enough courage to foresee the end result of 27 years in fibers and act on it to join the photoproducts department in 1977, came onto the board as a senior vice-president in January 1979. His successor, Roger Drexel of biochemicals, signalled the rewards accruing to those who found themselves part of Du Pont's shift to specialty products and genetic engineering; Drexel had emerged in the hierarchy with agrichemicals and followed that development into biochemicals when the latter department was established in 1972, underlining the close affinity between the chemistry involved in insecticides and drugs for humans. Drexel, in turn, was succeeded by Dale Wolf, one more rising star out of agrichemicals into biochemicals. Another winning division was pharmaceuticals. Endo Laboratories' business in anticoagulants and painkillers was grossing $75 million a year in sales. By 1979, Du Pont admitted it was on the lookout for a $400 million pharmaceutical company.

In Photo Products, another money-maker, Shapiro placed John Metzger, Jr., an ambitious young executive who had managed to escape the Polymer Intermediates Department in late 1974 and latched onto the growing new field. Photo Products offered much promise, particularly in X-rays, Du Pont's largest contribution to the growing health-care field.

But perhaps the most significant personality to emerge out of all this was Edward Jefferson. A native of England, Jefferson represented everything Shapiro admired; he was calm, decorous, charming, well-educated (he had a doctorate from the University of London), reserved—and very effective as a manager. Jefferson had joined Du Pont in 1960 and used his English schooling to successfully run the research program of the plastics division. Soon he had been promoted to assistant general manager of two departments and then was running the entire division. In 1972 he was appointed vice-president and general manager of the film division and in 1973 was made a senior vice-president and member of Du Pont's six-member executive committee under the new chairman, Irving Shapiro.

In January 1979, Shapiro reorganized the Central Research and Development Department, the company's fundamental research and long-range development arm, to respond directly to Jefferson, who was given responsibility for "the broad direction and coordination" of all other research and development activities in Du Pont. Industrial and staff departments were effectively stripped of their liaison representative in the Executive Committee. Shapiro acknowledged Jefferson's appointment as "an important departure from past practice."[143] Jefferson would now act as liaison for both the Corporate Plans Department and the Engineering Department as well as for all research and development matters. Shapiro, in making the appointment, cited "the changing availability and cost of energy and raw materials, environmental considerations and government regulation, as external elements affecting the course of research and development."[144]

Jefferson had been particularly adept at grasping Shapiro's points about manipulating mass media and influencing congressmen. Shapiro had launched Du Pont's Governmental Affairs Action Program (GAAP) as his complement to his broader Business Roundtable program of mobilizing corporate executives into political involvement. He had the Public Affairs Department draw up a GAAP handbook encouraging sales managers and plant managers to "become aggressively and constructively involved in the workings of government at every level and to participate in the well-directed and coordinated effort to disseminate information on legislation being considered in government."[145] "Lobbying used to be based on 'whom you know,'" senior vice-president and director William Simeral told one audience of 100 executives. "Now it has become a means of providing factual information to government decision makers."[146] To explain exactly what this "factual information" was and how it should be presented *en masse* to congressmen and local lawmakers, Shapiro conducted GAAP seminars for his executives. To buttress this with local workplace propaganda, he called in 63 company newsletter editors and communicators from over 50 worksites to a conference. "If the First Amendment makes sense in a political structure," he told them, "it also makes sense in an industrial structure."[147]

Now here was a man who knew how to make use of the potential of his organization. "The people who work for Du Pont are intelligent, they're knowledgeable, they want to know about their jobs, they want to know about their company," he said, smiling reassurances. "And they have a right to know. I think that's fundamental. This isn't an act of grace by management. People who work for Du Pont have a right to know what's happening in their plants, what's happening at the management of the enterprise, where our problems are, and what risks there are that ought to be disclosed."[148]

These plaudits to corporate responsibility did not extend, however, to standards set by the federal Occupational Safety and Health Administration (OSHA) for exposure to acrylonitrile, a toxic chemical used in the making of synthetic fibers. A *Du Pont News* article headlined how "Du Pont informs employees of TSCA 'substantial risk' reporting responsibilities," outlining how the company theoretically responded to the guidelines of the Toxic Substances Control Act (TSCA), although a hint of what was at play was found in the article's comment that of the average one report per week that reached Wilmington, it was "still too early to decide what fraction routinely will contain information that should be sent to the EPA," according to Du Pont's director of environmental affairs, James Reilly.[149] Paul Harding of the Du Pont-funded Society of Plastic Industry was more specific. He called OSHA's exposure standard of two parts of acrylonitrile per million parts of air in any eight-hour period "totally uncalled for in the case of acrylonitrile since the industry is already operating with plant levels considerably lower than the existing standard of 20 parts per million," or 1000 percent higher. "It is impossible at this point for the industry to determine if it can comply," he asserted, "because OSHA has not established adequate testing procedures."[150] Nevertheless, Du Pont confirmed that through engineering changes and other means, the OSHA level could and would be met that year.

It was a perfect example of what Chairman Shapiro meant when he told the site editors that "good communication is good management," especially since Du Pont's own studies showed that workers exposed to acrylonitrile at its Camden, S.C., plant had contracted three times the "expected" cancer rate among Du Pont workers. As the *Du Pont News* headline that ran below the site editors' conference article explained, "Du Pont's industrial hygienists help protect your on-the-job health."[151]

The conference was addressed by David Broder, associate editor of the *Washington Post,* which for years had Du Pont in-law Colgate Dardin on its advisory board.

In June of 1979, Du Pont again demonstrated good communications when the White House lifted the federal ban on MMT, a gasoline additive used to raise the octane level of unleaded gasoline. Extensive tests by the

Coordinating Research Council on behalf of auto producers and gasoline companies had confirmed that MMT resulted in an increase in emissions of hydrocarbons, a major component of smog. In addition, MMT eroded catalytic reactors in automobiles and for that reason was opposed by General Motors. Finally, the National Institute of Health had found that MMT releases manganese oxides and chlorides into the atmosphere, which, even in small doses, impair people's nervous system and has been suspected of brain damage "indistinguishable from Parkinson's disease." As Dr. Ellen Silbergeld explained, "the symptoms, signs, prognosis and treatment are the same."[152]

Carter's lifting of the ban for summer driving until October 1979 may explain why Irving Shapiro was reluctant to disavow the president, but it did not placate the Du Ponts. The outlawing of MMT and tetraethyl lead in the oil refining process was laid at the White House's doorsteps along with Iran's oil cutoff and Saudi Arabia's cutbacks to 65 percent of its total light crude output. All of that had resulted in an increase in the price of naptha, which was made from light crude oil, from 1973's $22 per ton to 1979's $250 per ton. And naptha, as any good artificial fibers chemist knows, is necessary for creating benzene, a basic ingredient in the production of nylons.

Here, again, Shapiro saw reason to be soft on Carter. Carter's price controls had allowed domestic oil purchases to be made below the world market price. The European Economic Commission had accordingly charged Carter with unfairly subsidizing Du Pont and other synthetic fibers producers such as Dow, and publicly warned it might brand U.S. oil price controls an unfair subsidy in violation of international trade agreements signed by the U.S. Du Pont, the Europeans claimed, was able to undercut continental producers by as much as 30 percent on certain acrylic and polyester yarns. There was no questioning the fact that the American corporate share of Britain's market for polyester filament yarn had risen in less than one year from 4 percent to 1979's 20 percent. Furthermore, American corporations were charging low prices for oil-based chemicals, including vinyl acetate, used in the manufacture of plastic products. If it didn't stop, additional tariffs would be imposed on the American companies' booming exports of synthetic fibers and oil-based chemicals to the Common Market. Article 20(1) of the Geneva Agreement on Tariffs and Trade allowed protection "during periods when the domestic price of such materials is held below the world price as part of a Government stabilization program."

Carter was worried about the Commissioner's report to Europe's foreign ministers, and he knew that the British and the Italians, as well as the French, were under considerable pressure from companies and unions hit by layoffs. He knew he was in violation of the trade rules. His administration had held that such price controls were designed precisely for the reason enunciated in Article 20(1), namely to stabilize the U.S. economy by keeping prices down while encouraging trade unions to keep their wages down. The fallacy, again, of blaming inflation on wages and of measuring productivity (the real cause of inflation) against wages—apples against pears—was clear enough to Shapiro. But Du Pont won European markets by Carter's price controls.

The Du Ponts were not happy when Carter bent to European pressure. He was anxious to save the Tokyo Round tariff reductions of the previous summer, which had hurt Du Pont's fibers market. Article 20(1) had never been used, and for the Common Market to now do so would mean a historic departure from the Atlantic alliance that was the cornerstone of the international trade and military strategy of the Trilateralists who dominated Carter's cabinet.

Shapiro, however, realized Carter's dilemma and sought to adjust Du Pont's gears. If domestic oil was to be deregulated, perhaps Du Pont would best move in that direction. It was this logic, at least partly, that led Shapiro down the path to CONOCO, one of the nation's largest holders of domestic oil and gas reserves.

But if there was anything that infuriated the Du Ponts to the breaking point with Carter it was his acquiescence to his labor constituency as reelection time approached. Concern had earlier been expressed during the long ten-day coal strike, when some Du Pont plants, particularly the Washington Works in Parkersburg, West Virginia, were forced to cope with 30 percent reductions in electricity by March 1978. In the hard-hit Southeast and Mid-Central regions, where power companies depended on coal, Du Pont gratefully noted that strike-breakers had provided non-union coal to utilities to keep its plants going. At the height of the strike in February, Shapiro sent a telegram to the president urging him "to obtain an equitable solution to the strike as soon as possible," and warned that some Du Pont plants "will be forced to begin closing about March 1,"[153] a totally misleading and incorrect assessment. In fact no plants were closed.

But what really concerned both Shapiro and the Du Ponts most was the United Steelworkers' continued efforts to organize Du Pont Company. At Seaford, the world's largest nylon plant, a four-year effort to unionize its 3200 employees, backed by a 1975 NLRB ruling ordering management not to further interfere, was making steady progress, with several hundred already signed up by March 1978. Du Pont's favorite local, the Seaford Nylon Employees Council, argued that under the current system workers did not have to pay union dues. "But our Blue Shield coverage is $7.15 a month that we have to pay out of our own checks," countered Russell Shockly, head of the 38-member organizing committee at the plant, "plus $1 dues to the council, and $100 deductible on Blue Shield—that works out to $192 a year. With the Steelworkers, you pay $144 a year to have them represent you ... you'd get sick days and have the bargaining power the Steelworkers have."[154] When Du Pont gave the Seaford workers only an 8 percent wage increase in 1979, hardly enough to keep up with inflation, more employees there began signing up with the Steelworkers.

Seaford, according to the Steelworkers, was one of "six large independent unions (that) hold the key to moving ... to the bargaining table in Wilmington."[155] All of those six, except the Chambers Works, were in the union-resistant South. In May, a majority of the 600 workers at the Florence, South Carolina, textile plant signed Steelworkers cards, prompting national organizer Elmer Chatak to predict "we may be closer than we think." At Newport, Delaware, another victory was scored. "Things are coming together," said the Steelworker's Peter Vaccarella to 50 Du Ponters in Wilmington. "I have the feeling that it's starting to break."[156] But the four Du Pont-controlled industrial fortresses remained: Richmond, Virginia; Waynesboro, Virginia; Seaford, Delaware; and, of course, the Chambers Works in Deepwater, New Jersey.

The Steelworkers helped laid off workers at Carneys Point, New Jersey, to get special federal aid through a program under the Trade Act of 1974 for workers who suffered unemployment because of foreign imports, in this case nitrocellulose. Production there had been slated for phase-out when an explosion ripped through the gunpowder plant and killed three workers, terminating production completely. Du Pont area supervisors blamed the Steelworkers' drive for Carney's closing. Local workers blamed the plant's losses on excess management overhead, namely the promotion of unqualified employees to supervisory positions in order to undermine union organizing. In fact, the local union wrote Shapiro warning that the plant would end up closed. "Each and every answer," said employee Robert Wygand, "was that it was plant management's responsibility.... Beware Chambers Works, you are in the same boat as Carneys Point Works was. Until Du Pont Wilmington management converts the system they now have, Chambers Works will continue to decay and finally die. Here, it is too late. So let's put the blame where it belongs, on the shoulders of Du Pont management and not the unions as Mr. Gatanis stated."[157] Gatanis was a former vice-president of the Chemical Workers Association, the Chambers' local union, who had been promoted to management. In June 1978, Chambers had also suffered an explosion, setting fires in several areas and injuring seven workers. Just a week before, the plant had been told it had won a New Jersey Governor's Safety Award.

Promotions were just one way Du Pont tried to undermine blue-collar solidarity. Du Pont had a conscious policy of dividing its work force by discriminating between blue and white collars with differentiated benefits, including profit sharing. It had been seen at annual meetings, when proposals to bring blue-collar benefits on a par with white-collar were drowned in a sea of millions of shares voted by Du Pont family members or when pleas extending beyond the time allotted by the chairman were suddenly silenced by Shapiro's flick of a switch that cut the speaker's microphone dead.

With federal agencies, Shapiro found the going rougher. During the Carter Administration, up until February 1980, Du Pont was hit with 65 citations for violations of national workplace standards by the Occupational Safety and Health Administration.[158] Another gadfly was the National Labor Relations Board. Du Pont was charged by the board with threatening and coercing United Steelworkers' supporters at its Martinsville, Virginia, plant[159] and was found guilty of unfair labor practices during an unsuccessful Chattanooga organizing effort in 1979 by the Teamsters Union. In the later case, Judge James M. Fitzpatrick held that Du Pont had shown a tendency to violate the National Labor Relations Act and "has engaged in widespread misconduct demonstrating a general disregard of employee statutory rights."[160]

In September 1980, Du Pont also fired a steelworker activist at the Seaford plant. "Any small thing that would come about, they would write it down," said the discharged worker, Robert Hooper. "They can get at anyone at any time. I was more or less a scapegoat." William Gaylor, the Seaford plant manager, disputed the charge. "We're not aware whether he was an organizer or not," he said. "His discharge was solely because of his performance."[161] Hooper had been actively organizing for the Steelworkers for four years.

Some of the most serious incidents, however, occurred at the Newport pigments plant. In December 1978, the NLRB cited Du Pont for violating federal law by keeping employees under photographic and videotape surveillance during a strike over the same issue that triggered a walkout two years before and the company's reneging on promises to negotiate any vacancies with the local union. Then, like now, Du Pont was convicted by the NLRB of unfair labor practices for refusing to discuss the workers' grievances until they returned to work.

But more important, perhaps, was Du Pont's own 1979 study that showed that Newport workers between 1957 and 1977 had a lung cancer death rate 75 percent higher than the general Du Pont work force, and a fatal heart disease rate 27 percent higher.[162] The only material at Newport that was a known cause of cancer was asbestos, used for pipe insulation. Two other suspected carcinogens, chromium dioxide and perchlorolthylene were also used. In 1980, six Repauno and Chambers workers suffering with asbestosis, a fatal lung cancer, sued Du Pont for "willful and wonton" misconduct in not telling them about the general danger of asbestos or about health problems that four Du Pont doctors allegedly knew were developing in the workers' lungs. Just the previous year, OSHA had fined Du Pont $63,000 for asbestos health violations at the Repauno plant.

Shapiro's lawyers were contesting the fine, but there was no contesting a 1964 Du Pont internal memo from G.J. Stoops, chief of the physiology section of the Haskett Laboratory to Dr. C.A. D'Alonzo, of Du Pont's Employee Relations Department. That memo, written on official Du Pont Company stationery, confirmed that Du Pont had known about the asbestos danger it was exposing its workers to for at least 16 years before the New Jersey workers filed suit.

"The Du Pont Company spends between 3 to 7 per cent of the cost of new construction on insulating materials, much of which contains asbestos," Stopps wrote. "Roughly 200,000 pounds of pipe insulation are used every year and approximately 70 percent of this insulation is asbestos. With figures of this magnitude it is not difficult to visualize a real health hazard existing just in this one use of asbestos.

"Because of the long time lag from first exposure to diagnosis (the mean period is about 40 years), the potential respiratory disease problem is liable to grow in size. This is particularly true of the nylon plants which are big users of asbestos insulation on their "Dowtherm" lines, all of which have been installed in the last 26 years. The compensation aspects of this problem speak for themselves and point to the need for adequate pulmonary function studies on all workers exposed to a definite risk of respiratory damage."[163]

Stopps warned of legal suits and disability allowances and suggested that "for less money than would be involved in the loss of a single court suit an effective pulmonary function testing program can be set up and operated for a trial period of five years."[164]

Stopps's proposal was effectively ignored. Even x-rays, the afflicted workers charged, were inadequately done.[165] The pride of Du Pont's Photo Products Division, the x-ray, was never seriously put to work by Du Pont to help its own workers.

Asbestos-related claims were common in many states, but not Delaware. In fact, OSHA's senior safety officer in Wilmington, Paul Tackett, said his office had never investigated a claim involving Du Pont. "Unfortunately, the unions representing the Delaware Du Pont workers are independent," said former state Representative Thomas Little, who was the lawyer for the Edgemoor workers. "They don't have the communications network the other, larger national unions have used to educate their workers about asbestos.

They're just catching up here." Asbestos existed at the Chambers Works, the Edgemoor plant, and the Newport pigments plant, where two afflicted workers also filed suit.

Du Pont lawyers asked the court to dismiss the Newport case also, claiming that it was irrelevant because the plant did not use asbestos in the manufacturing process and had stopped using it for insulation in 1970 and had begun to replace it with non-asbestos material. Some workers, meanwhile, needing Du Pont's compensation for medical bills, dropped their suits against the chemical company in order not to delay the payments. Litigation continued against 23 other corporations identified as manufacturers and suppliers of asbestos insulation to Du Pont; the corporate defenders merely split most of the legal costs; the workers, however, had few financial resources to fall back on. By 1983, according to Wilmington labor lawyer Jacob Kreshtool, at least one of them was approaching death as the corporate lawyers continued their delaying tactics in the courts.[166] Meanwhile, Du Pont, thanks to the state's workers compensation law, once again managed to evade responsibility, this time, the Stopp memo indicated, getting away with what might well be criminal negligence.

9. THE $550 QUESTION

"Are large corporations substances or are they running out of control?" Shapiro rhetorically asked while debating Carter's SEC chairman, Harold Williams, on corporate accountability at Carnegie Mellon University in October 1979. "Where I come out is, there is room for improvement, but a lot of changes have been made. Corporate directors are watching the store more closely today than at any other time in our industry. It doesn't correct past mistakes.... But there is no need today for fundamental changes.... There is no system in view that is demonstrably better."

But Williams warned the Du Pont Chairman of overconfidence. "Arrogance is bred in the corporate board room by handpicked insider directors who rely on the chief executive for promotions and are anxious to keep the atmosphere amiable; and by outside directors whose social and professional connections may overlap. They often do business together and are involved in the same community charitable and social organization." Nothing better described the insular community of the Du Ponts and Shapiro's executives, and Williams probably knew it. He argued that the chief executive officer should not be the chairman. "The role of the chairman and CEO are not the same. The chairman's role is to create the kind of open, contributing and questioning environment which I have discribed. The CEO's role is to speak for management. These roles are not the same and can conflict."

No one was shocked that Shapiro did not agree, but the fervor of his response was unsettling. He insisted that tension has no place in the boardroom and inside directors who know the business are indispensable. Besides, being a director requires "experience and perspective" that no amount of sincerity or independence can replace. Williams would not be put off. "Over time, no activity can flourish if the public takes a dim view of it. Over a longer term, no activity can continue unaltered if public apathy or distrust becomes public antagonism." He cautioned about the "accountability gap." "There can come to be a growing sense that business no longer attempts to balance its interest and the public's but rather focuses entirely on its narrow objectives." Without accountability, "the institution becomes an end unto itself, out of touch with its relationship and its responsibilities to the rest of society. . . . If the mood—the social ethic—is one of disinclination to criticize, if directors are expected to ratify management decisions and if inquisitiveness is interpreted as distrust of the chief executive and a violation of good corporate manners or protocol, that system breeds a tendency to rubber stamp management, make comfortable decisions and avoid confronting significant issues as long as possible."

"Two centuries of national experience," Shapiro retorted, "have shown that the United States has been uncommonly successful at meeting economic needs through the reliance on private initiative." He opposed reliance on government and held at the same time that public perceptions had no place in business decisions. "I don't think that's any way to run a business. . . . If corporations succumbed to that pressure, and in effect declared the public's work to be their own, the next step would be to turn them into institutions accountable to the public in the same way that units of government are accountable."

How Shapiro perceived reconciling the refusal to take seriously public perceptions when making decisions of substance and the avoidance of making public intervention through government accordingly inevitable was revealed by his conclusion, said in words almost identical to those he offered to the *Philadelphia Inquirer* three years earlier when launching the public relations campaign he disliked calling "PR": "For many years, corporations have played their cards too close to the vest. The relative silence and anonymity of leadership has hurt business," contributing to "distrust and fear." It had been said many times, in many speeches, but Shapiro always made it sound as if he were saying it for the first time. It was a measure of his performance that Williams ended the debate by praising the Du Pont chairman as "an honest man and good citizen" and commenting that if all chief executives were like him his agency, the Securities and Exchange Commission, would soon be out of work.[167]

But what if all, or at least most, chief executives *were* like Irving Shapiro.

There had to have been some consensus for Shapiro to be elected chairman of the Business Roundtable in 1976, and chairman of Du Pont in 1973. Some of the reasons had to be Shapiro's capacity for leadership, to dare to take initiative, and he showed it again at Carnegie-Mellon when he proposed that "corporate leaders have no choice but to state the standards by which they intend to play the game. A code of ethics needs to come from the board."[168]

A month later, not a code of ethics, but an heir apparent came from Du Pont's board. Shapiro had elevated, with the Du Ponts' concurrence, Edward Jefferson to the presidency. Jefferson was the ideal choice. Ever the courteous English gentleman, Jefferson was liked by the Du Ponts and respected for his capacity to manage men as well as ideas. He was also very much in line with the Shapiro philosophy that Du Pont's top executive must be accessible to the mass media and public opinion shapers, serving as both the company's lightning rod for public concern and the spokesman for the board of directors. "We have to continue what Irv Shapiro has already handled so effectively," said Jefferson upon his appointment, "upgrading our communications with the public, press and Government. We need to be more available to people who have questions about us."[169]

The questions were certainly mounting.

The EPA wanted to know what Du Pont intended to do about "Benlate," a fungicide it made out of benomyl, one of 26 pesticides which laboratory evidence indicated, according to EPA pesticides chief Edwin L. Johnson, "unreasonable health or environmental risks." Benomyl has been shown to cause birth defects among research animals; one of its breakdown products, MBC, also causes gene mutations. The fear was for farmers, housewives, gardeners, and contamination to fish, wildlife and crops such as rice, fruit, peanuts, and beans. Du Pont made Benlate at the Hermitage Island, Georgia, plant for the Biochemicals Division, headed by Dale. The product was claimed by Du Pont to be "biodegradable."[170]

Likewise, West Virginia's Department of Natural Resources wanted to know what Du Pont intended to do about anitine hydrochloride and composite plant waste spills by the Belle, West Virginia, plant into the Kanawah River in violation of Water Pollution Control Permit No. 5302. The Department termed the violation "inexcusable."[171] The state's Air Pollution Control Commission also recorded 11 releases of pollutants into the air by the Belle plant between 1976 and January 1979.[172]

But perhaps the biggest controversy surrounding Du Pont in 1980 was the company's practice of screening of employees from ethnic minorities for "defective" genes. Workers in the chemical industry found to have a "hypersusceptibility" to industrial poisons were often arbitrarily transferred.

Du Pont admitted to conducting thousands of these genetic tests, but had no systematized data on the results or conclusions about which tests were better than others.[173] There was therefore no way to measure how results might be applied in the workplace. Nor could Du Pont Headquarters provide specific information to the *New York Times* on how its workers might be benefitting from the tests.

Why, then, did Du Pont even conduct the tests?

Irving Shapiro tried to provide an answer. "In 1972, at the request of Black employees who wanted the information for their own personal benefit, the company began testing Black employees and Black job applicants for the sickle-cell trait."[174] He did not acknowledge that the original request asked for tests for sickle-cell *anemia* which affects 2 percent of American Blacks, not the *trait*, which affects up to 10 percent of America's Black population. Du Pont's program had been expanded beyond the original request, affecting, at least at the Chambers Works, job placement. But there was a riddle even in Shapiro's line of argument. Why thousands of tests anyway? At such costs to a company infamous for its OSHA and EPA violations, for its reluctance to establish health safeguards for the workplace and the environment? And with a management committed in every other instance to cutting costs?

Costs, however, were precisely the reason the program was set up. Du Pont was attempting to decrease the number of future workers' compensation drives and negligence suits by workers who were fatally poisoned or bore deformed children. With individual records proving such tests, the company would be able to build a stronger legal case that it had attempted to safeguard the health of those workers who did bring suit. As Shapiro confirmed, "when the results have been positive, the individuals have been told."[175]

Shapiro was affronted by charges of scientific racism. "Du Pont does not discriminate against Blacks on the basis of sickle-cell blood tests.... Without qualification, Du Pont does not use sickle-cell tests to screen for employment, job placement or promotion.... The effect of the (*New York Times*) articles suggesting scientific racism by Du Pont is offensive to a management that has worked diligently to foster an end to racism in this country and has about 11,000 Black employees. The implication of the articles was especially unfortunate since the tests for the sickle-cell trait were simply part of a long-established program for the welfare of employees using medical resources to protect their health and safety."[176]

The *Times* article, written by Richard Severo, quoted the director of Du Pont's Haskell Laboratory, Dr. Charles Reinhardt, who had written an article in 1978 for the *Journal of Occupational Medicine* affirming that anemic Black workers at the Chambers Works, where he was instrumental in starting a genetic-screening program, were "restricted from work involving the fondling of nitro and amino compounds."[177] The Shapiro statement, however, was printed without comment by the *Times* and a subsequent letter by Du Pont President Edward Jefferson accompanied by a copy of the original 1972 tests request by Dr. Meade of the Black Du Pont Employees Association, prompted a hasty retraction by the *Washington Post,* claiming "our sources were wrong" although they were quite right.

Nevertheless, by admitting that Du Pont merely "informed" the workers with the trait and insisting it did not use the tests to transfer them from jobs, Shapiro was acknowledging that Du Pont had put the onus on the workers to have information on just how badly chemicals at the worksite could affect his or her genes. Instead, the worker was left in place exposed.

That, in turn, raised a broader question. Why, if Du Pont was genuinely concerned for "the welfare of employees," did it not simply clean up the worksite or provide adequate protection? Or, just as the EPA has done in the case of the environment, ban such highly dangerous chemicals from workplaces which cannot be cleaned up or workers adequately protected?

The answer was obvious. Some of those chemicals are highly profitable. Neil Holtzman, associate professor of pediatrics at Johns Hopkins Medical School, was not impressed by that corporate ethic. It forced humanity to endanger its own gene pools that were created, defined and redefined over thousands of generations of pastoral life, long before the industrial revolution or Du Pont's claim on life. These gene pools are precious and "go to the skein of life itself," said Holtzman. "It is only in the last half dozen generations that man has come into contact with these new chemicals."[178]

The Du Ponts have been in the center of introducing these chemicals to humanity. Of 40,000 to 90,000 chemical compounds currently used by American industry and 35,000 chemicals now on the market, most have been introduced only since the end of World War II, many by Du Pont Company and without testing for what their long-term effects might be on life and the environment.[179]

"Essentially, what we're doing is imposing the human gene pool to an environment that is quite different from the environment in which man evolved," said Dr. Holtzman. "We don't know how many of man's genes that predominate today are predominant because of natural selection. Regardless of that number, the fact is that man's genetic constitution did not evolve in an atmosphere filled with chemicals that fill it today."[180]

Nor can humanity's continuing biological evolution outpace the risks in being exposed to many of the 1000 new industrial chemical compounds invented every year that reach the market. The 700,000 Americans now recorded by the U.S. Department of Labor as permanently and totally disabled with workplace-related diseases and the 400,000 new cases of workplace-related diseases estimated to develop annually by the President's Report on Occupational Safety and Health in 1974 have already borne grim testimony.[181]

The United States, governed by parties since the Civil War that have admittedly championed, if not been dominated by, business interests, has lagged behind Europe in the field of industrial medicine and providing social safeguards for labor. As Alice Hamilton, pioneer in the field in America, noted to her chagrin when attending the International Congress on Occupational Accidents and Diseases in 1910 in Brussels, Belgium, "For an American it was no occasion for national pride. There were but two of us on the program.... It was still more mortifying to be unable to answer any of the questions put to us: What was the rate of lead poisoning in such and such an industry? What legal regulations did we have for the dangerous trades? What was our system of compensation? Finally, Dr. Gilbert, of the Belgian Labor Department, dismissed the subject: 'It is well known that there is no industrial hygiene in the United States. Ça n'existe pas.'"[182]

But Americans, culturally isolated by oceans from the rest of the industrial world, did not know that. The absence of labor representation in Congress levied its toll on workers' health, and workers paid dearly for their non-participation in politics. It was not until 1970, with the passage of the U.S. Occupational Safety and Health Act, that America showed it was awakening to an enormous "quiet crisis" that had for decades been denied by Du Pont as the leader of the chemical corporations.

So then, two years later, Du Pont initiated genetic testing. At issue supposedly was thalessimia, a deficiency of the enzyme glucose-6-phosphate-dehydrogenase (G-6-PD), which manifests itself in blood as an anemia. Of two million American Blacks estimated to have a single gene for the trait, fewer than 50,000 have actual anemia, a debilitating disease; the other 1,950,000 cases are relatively harmless. To get the disease seriously one must have the gene from both parents.

Sickle-cell anemia affects not only Afro-Americans, however, but also people with hereditary roots in the Mediterranean and in the Middle East: Italians, Greeks, Yugoslavs, Spaniards, Portuguese, Arabs, Jews. Similar traits can be found in Chinese, Filipinos, and East Asians as well. People from central and northern Europe, particularly Swedes, Danes, and Norwegians, also have a deficiency of serum alpha called antitrypsin; exposure to certain chemicals can trigger chronic bronchitis and emphysema.

"What if you do, in fact, demonstrate that a certain group is more at risk than another subgroup," said Dr. Nicholas Ashford, associate professor of technology and policy at MIT. "You could eliminate them from those jobs or you could make the workplace safe for everybody, including the most sensitive members of the population. I believe the latter is the only sensible policy."[183]

Du Pont, or rather its profits, did not agree. If so, there was more than hyperbole, then, to charges that Du Pont was practicing scientific racism, despite Shapiro's protestations about feeling personally wounded or affronted. Such statements smacked, at best, of self-deception; at worst, of psychological tactics remarkably similar to Gestalt's projection of guilt from oneself onto one's accusers. For by expanding a request by Afro-American workers into a major program of thousands of tests in search of "defective" genes, Du Pont had, perhaps inadvertently, singled out a particular ethnic group; that done, Du Pont management chose to lock the attention of its genetic testing program on a single ethnic group. Conscious or not, its program was racist precisely because its focus on reducing work compensation and negligence suits ended up concentrating on that ethnic minority least able to defend its legal rights; Black Americans were being singled out if not in the workplace today, then ultimately in the courtrooms tomorrow. How, also, would these people be regarded when treated as "inferior," when they were really the proverbial canaries of the mines, the living guinea pigs of future illnesses that broke down even the healthiest of their fellow workers years later.

Anthony Mazzochi, an official of the Oil Chemical and Atomic Workers Union, recognized the implications immediately of Du Pont's focusing on the genetic "hypersusceptibility" of ethnic minorities rather than removing the hazards of work conditions. "1984 is already here," he portended. "I think that in the 1980's we are going to see a lot of victim-blaming. The emphasis will not be so much what you work with; it will have to do with who your mother and father are."[184]

While Shapiro would insist again and again there was no racism, no discrimination based on ethnic background, he would still authorize the transfer of women workers from a worksite where genes could be affected by chemicals, perhaps stubbornly mindless of the connection to the central issue at dispute: a protected, healthy environment for *all* workers. Such transfers, like such genetic testing, was really, in the words of MIT's Dr. King, "a major effort to deflect the issue." To King, "From the point of view of the whole work force it [ethnic genetic testing] is an extraordinary waste of social resources. Most of those genetically linked problems are very rare. But the benefits to the company are immense. Testing switches the locus of the problem from the company to the worker, it gets the company out of having to start a cleanup program, it is a forum of social and intellectual propaganda, it may protect management later against legal claims, and it deflects attention from the real problems. It costs a lot more to lower cadmium levels than to screen."[185] Beyond that was the psychological impact on the person tested. "I don't want someone telling me that the chronic anemia I may suffer because of benzene that has been dumped illegally is really that my genes aren't adequate," Dr. King said. "I have as much right to be healthy as anyone else. But some in industry are saying that because you have less G-6-PD you do not have the same rights as other Americans to be employed and to be healthy."[186]

There were disturbing implications here in the chemical industry. On October 9, 1971, OSHA charged that a Du Pont competitor (or ally, if one took the Federal Trade Commission's complaint on monopoly pricing at its word), had initiated a formal employment policy that effectively required women to be sterilized in order to hold jobs in areas where certain toxic substances were exposed. The government imposed a paltry $10,000 fine which American Cyanamid, "surprised and shocked," said it would fight "with all the resources at its command." The charges, brought by 13 women, including four who had been unquestionably sterilized, were held as "absolutely false" by American Cyanamid.

Du Pont transferred women workers out of a similar dangerous area, replacing them with men. The labor movement and feminists, however, argued that chemical poisons were just as dangerous to men, and the company was using women and potential pregnancies discriminatorily as a rationale for conditions dangerous to all workers; "It's not even clear what the relation is between the worker's blood level and the blood level of the fetus or the embryo," said Dr. Jeanne Stillman, Executive Director of Columbia University's Women's Occupational and Health Research Center. "There is not one clear-cut experiment establishing that lead is a terotogen. If it is going to be the policy òf this society to ban fertile women from working with terotogens, let's not talk about it with lead—let's talk about it with x-rays. We know x-rays have a tremendous terotogen effect. I haven't heard anyone suggest that we eliminate all fertile women from the health-care industry where they can be exposed to radiation."[187] Male sperm, she pointed out, is at least as susceptible to environmental hazards as the ovum.

It went without saying in Wilmington that 75 percent of all women have finished their child-bearing by 35 years of age. The ban on women without even taking their age into account or their consent could easily be considered as Du Pont's effort to keep women out of an overcrowded and therefore politically volatile labor market.

Although the issue was allowed to subside during the 1980 election, after the Reagan victory Du Pont boldly moved forward. In testimony before the subcommittee of the House Committee on Science and Technology in

October 1981, Bruce Karrh, Du Pont's medical director, insisted that genetic screening was voluntary and for employees' "personal use" and their "education and edification."[188] Subcommittee chairman Albert Gore questioned Du Pont's revealing such personal records to at least two federal agencies dealing with occupational safety without the employees' consent. Access to the employees' records, Karrh blurted out, were on a "need to know" basis, and he then acknowledged under questioning that Du Pont had no national program to counsel or educate Black employees on what the results of the genetic tests really meant. The only criterion for their selection for the tests was skin color and facial features. Obviously the incentive for the tests came from Du Pont, not the workers.

In the course of Karrh's testimony, in fact, it was revealed that the original inspiration for the testing was President Nixon. The president in 1972 signed a bill providing $115 million to find a "cure" for the anemia. That was not such a whimsical task, however, because the trait may well have been, ironically, a genetic boon: the immunizing of African slaves from the ravages of malaria in the swampy rice plantations of the South, another case of human adaptation to environment and natural selection not easily or wisely tampered with. What was equally revealing was that the initiator of the request for the testing was not rank and file Black Du Pont "employees," as Shapiro had previously led the press to believe, but a Du Pont white-collar worker, Dr. Alston Meade, a senior research biologist and president of the Black Du Pont Employees Association. Meade had responded to Nixon's allocation of funds and his own sense of concern about the anemia. What was originally requested as a study of the anemia, became a broader study of the trait and a wider basis for job displacement or denial of work with certain chemicals by Blacks who carried the broader trait.

The National Academy of Sciences had warned, however, that specific symptoms in ethnic minorities resulting from exposure to chemicals was based on inconclusive research; drawing conclusions too fast, the Academy warned, might result in unnecessary and harmful stigmatization of that ethnic minority. The fact that Mediterranean whites also susceptible to the trait were not tested by Du Pont did not go unnoticed, nor did the barring of women from working with hexafluoroacetone and six other compounds. Laboratory tests with male animals had shown that the chemicals also affected the production of sperm, and Du Pont did not differentiate between what it considered safe for men (1 per million exposure) and what it held safe for women. Why then were women barred? The answer, from Du Pont's Karrh, was a classical case of sexism; pregnancies occur with women, he explained, despite the best of intentions.

Representative Gore probed Karrh's biases further. Had there ever been an unexpected pregnancy of a Du Pont employee in an area of risk? Dr. Karrh replied as if on cue. He had no knowledge of such an instance, he said, but he was sure there must have been some.

Whether Karrh was just an example of how corporate life, particularly in Du Pont Company, could insulate a man from the progress in social values that had occurred all around him, or whether he was, more darkly (and less possibly), a naïve goat for more machinating minds in Du Pont's upper hierarchy, the medical director's testimony obscured the cost-cutting goals involved in Du Pont's genetic screening.

Shapiro's letter to the *New York Times,* like Jeffersons' to the *Washington Post,* was typical of the kind of response Du Pont gave to criticism. On October 9, 1976, when columnist Jack Anderson reported about the aforementioned confidential Congressional report by a California doctor labeling Du Pont's cancer study as "misleading" and a "public relations snow job," Du Pont denied the report and claimed that Anderson's charges were politically motivated. The insinuation was that holding political beliefs to the left of the Du Ponts' own conservative values discredited a historian's or reporter's facts; such tactics had been applied by the Du Ponts over the decades in attempts to discredit facts by smearing their reporter. In the 1970's and 1980's, the Du Ponts proved in the cases of Jack Anderson and the book *Behind the Nylon Curtain* that time had neither mellowed their views nor given them reason to alter a strategy that had been allowed to succeed for so long.

The same applied to the EPA's report in April 1980 that Du Pont was among the nation's top 20 carcinogen emitters. The mass media, which received millions of dollars in advertising revenue from the listed 20 companies, mostly ignored the report. In northern Delaware, where the Chambers Works' emissions of carbontetrachloride, chlorobenzene, toluene and D-diochlorobenzine into the area's atmosphere was certainly worthwhile local news, only Newark's *Delaware Alternative Press* carried it.

Likewise, when the *Delaware Today* magazine ran a two-part series on the poisoning of the Potomac Aquifer, the major source of water for northern Delaware, specifically citing EPA studies that criticized leaks of radioactive materials, dangerous pesticides and other dangerous chemicals from the Newport pigments plant as being responsible for endangering the aquifer's survival,[189] Du Pont's L.L. Hash fired off a memo to the Newport management staff claiming the articles were "highly inaccurate and misleading." While not denying the presence of radioactive waste at Newport's landfill, Du Pont's Hash issued a broad refutation of the charges, then advised the staff in a handwritten afterthought that "If anyone calls for info on this article tell them someone will be able to answer any questions on

Monday. Give them the guards' number if they ask for a phone number. P.S. Do not answer any questions."[190] He did not remind his staff that Newport had already been identified by a Congressional report on the 3383 worst waste-dumping sites in the United States. The report also cited the Du Pont Edgemoor plant's Cherry Island Industrial Landfill near Wilmington, the Du Pont Experimental Station's Central Research and Development Department, and two other landfills, Tybouts Corner and Llangollen, used by Du Pont. Kenneth Weiss, a resource engineer in the state's solid waste section, acknowledged the fouling of underground water wells. "It's probable something hazardous must have gone in there," he said.[191]

Who, if not top management and the board of directors, was responsible? In 1979, the Hart-Scott-Rodino Antitrust Improvements Act attempted to deal with that question. Irving Shapiro successfully pressured Senator Joseph Biden to drop his support for the bill. Shapiro also involved himself in personal negotiations to revise the proposed Criminal Code Bill (S.1. and S.1437), getting provisions holding corporate management criminally liable for failure to prevent a subordinate manager's felonies struck from the bill, along with another statute criminalizing "reckless endangerment" when anyone, including a corporation, placed innocent people "in danger of imminent death or serious bodily injury."[192] The subject of corporate responsibility was the focus of 1980's Big Business Day convened by Ralph Nader and sponsored by scores of trade unions and environmentalist and religious organizations. Part of the event was a meeting of "shadow boards of directors" made of public representatives who had monitored what were claimed to be some of the worst violators, including Du Pont. Shapiro failed to send a spokesman, but Du Pont did have two executives present at the Du Pont shadow board, quietly taking notes for the home office.

But the sharpest answer Shapiro gave critics was also his most clandestine. It was directed at the United Steelworkers and involved attitude surveys (with only selected answers communicated to the workers) to identify "trouble spots," a 156-page mimeographed book originally prepared for the Old Hickory plant managers on strategy and tactics of psychological warfare at the workplace, covering psychological profiles and a wide range of situations and optional approaches to manipulating workers.[193] Additionally, a 141-page mimeographed volume on strategy and tactics for defeating union organizing efforts across the country circulated among Du Pont managers in the Southern plants. Titled "The Way to Win," its own introduction describes it as "an anti-union book." "We are convinced that an organization known as a labor union serves no positive function in our society."[194] Its recommended attitude toward fair labor practices ordered by law was like a page out of the "dirty tricks" that the Nixon White House and the CIA's

Clandestine Operations Division had visited upon the nation, bequeathing Watergate and CIA-mobster scandals and a growing cynicism about corruption that gnawed at the heart of America's body politic: "All of us are familiar with the idea 'It's not whether you won or lost but how you played the game.' That sentiment may be fine for football games, but it doesn't apply to union campaigns. The late Vince Lombardi had the more proper approach: 'Winning isn't the important thing, it's the *ONLY* thing.'" If such lack of ethics could be preached by a coach to young athletes and win wide approval in corporate America, corruption was less exceptional in the corporate suites than probably most Americans believed or public relations offices would have them believe. But it had already been evident in politics and the vehemence with which unions were attacked had scored growing victories in elections. The significance of the fact that the authors of "The Way to Win" were editors of the New Right's *Labor Analysis and Forecast* newsletter and allies of the National Right to Work Committee was probably not lost on those Du Pont managers who read the mimeographed copies circulating in the offices.

Du Pont's own "Employee Relations Venture Plan" may have been actually the more formidable of the two books because its less strident anti-unionism was a much more subtle and therefore effective means of influencing workers. It reflected the company's official paternalism and its endorsement of the local "councils" Du Pont had originally set up in the Thirties as bulwarks to unionism. It also confirmed Du Pont's long-standing practice, since Ruly Carpenter first set up a labor spy network in Du Pont plants during World War I, of keeping secret files on Du Pont employees. Now called "The Know Your Employee Program," the files were compiled by floor supervisors and office managers and delved into such personal areas of a worker's life as his prejudices, outside interests, relatives and friends, health problems, and his general psychological make-up.[195]

"Do you know of any personal problems an employee is having?" was one of 24 typical questions supervisors were to answer for an "employee analysis." "Does the employee have any relatives, friends, etc. who may have an influence over employees?"[196] Designated "Personal and Confidential," neither the results nor even the existence of the files were revealed to the workers. It was not "personal" or "confidential" for the workers, but for management, a blatant violation of the American worker's right to privacy and the confidentiality of his personal records. Ironically, it was exactly this right that Du Pont used as grounds to deny medical records to NIOSH during its investigation of cancer-related diseases in Du Pont plants.

Du Pont supplemented this with video displays at "high traffic" areas in the plants, speakers, films (produced at $50,000 each) and leaflets purporting to show how the Steelworkers had misled the workers on facts; the latter were compiled by Employee Relations into working "Facts Books" used by managers in talks on the plant floor. One film, made at High Point, North Carolina, backfired. It was so obviously slanted that it regularly received boos at showings. The Employee Relations Department was not discouraged. As it geared up for action, "fact sheets" began appearing more frequently in plants, one-on-one conversations increased between supervisors and workers, and the company emphasized top union executives' salaries, ignoring its own incentive compensation bonuses in 1980 alone of $478,000 to Shapiro, $354,000 for Kane, $260,000 for Jefferson, Sineral, Heckert and Forney, and $5.3 million for all directors and officers as a group. Another $1.8 million was paid to them in dividend units, and another $126,000 under Du Pont's Thrift Plan.[197]

What propaganda could not succeed in accomplishing, other tactics did. In Philadelphia, where the Steelworkers enjoyed local Du Pont worker support and had set up their regional organizing headquarters, the local Du Pont paint plant was struck by Headquarters' announcement of its closing. The company rejected a city offered tax subsidy and proceeded to plan a shift of its production to Front Royal, Virginia, telling 350 workers they were now out of a job. In Camden, New Jersey, union supporters charged that work assignments and close supervision had become so discriminatory as to constitute "intimidation." In early 1980 Billy Holden distributed 30 Steelworkers' baseball hats to eager takers at the plant. By July the climate had worsened. "Right now," he said then, "if you put a $100 bill on these hats, they would not wear it. The supervisors scared these guys."[198]

Grievances mounted in Du Pont plants across the country, driving up legal costs for the locals, 20 of whose executive committees had endorsed the Steelworkers. "Du Pont keeps these guys broke,"[199] said John Kitchen, organizer for Virginia and North Carolina. Not only was the organizing drive stymied, but some plants had followed the Chambers Works and reversed their earlier endorsement of national unions. Such was the case in Florence, South Carolina, where the International Brotherhood of Electrical Workers was ousted after Du Pont refused to bargain in good faith. By the time the IBEW's charge to that effect was upheld by the NLRB and a Federal Appeals Court, the union's momentum had been lost. In Waynesboro, Virginia, a similar situation resulted in the decertification of the Steelworkers as collective bargaining agent for the plant's workers. Both reversals convinced John Oshinski, successor to Elmer Chatak as the Steelworkers' national organizing director for Du Pont, that holding certification elections piecemeal, as the campaign in each plant peaked, was folly. He tried to put on the brakes. "We've restrained quite a few locations from rushing into an election," he explained. "We will move in concert when we have a majority of plants going."[200] It was an all-or-nothing strategy, requiring great skill to control the tempo of organizing in each plant in order to crescendo in unison. The key question was whether Oshinski had the organizing capacity to be such a maestro.

When one considered Du Pont Headquarters' financial resources, ironically generated by the labor of the very workers the Steelworkers hoped to organize, and the long administrative training of Shapiro's crack team of executives and lawyers, most analysts put their bets on Du Pont. Oshinski simply did not seem much of a match against Shapiro, who had decades of experience in manipulating men and ideas and was a master propagandist who easily commanded the attention of mass media to put forth the company's best profile while he organized less savory tactics behind the doors of the Headquarters' 9th floor.

Shapiro, however, spurned overconfidence. Gold had hit $718 an ounce on February 7, undermining the company's cash reserves. Inflation could not only drive workers against Du Pont management, but influence votes in the 1980 election. Usually, an increase in workers' voting benefited the Democratic Party. But now the Democratic incumbent in the White House was catching the blame, and he was a president to whom Shapiro had developed close ties.

Shapiro's honeymoon with the Carter White House had been over a long time ago, and relations had become strained as the 1980 election approached. The issue of contention was predictable enough: labor. The American workers who constitute over 80 percent of the population and cast the great bulk of its votes had in fact been the underlying issue behind not only Du Pont's friction with the Occupational Safety and Health Administration and the National Labor Board but also the EPA, the FDA, and other regulatory agencies. Shapiro's Business Roundtable had advocated cost-benefit accounting for measuring the value of health standards, and calculated the value of human lives at $550 apiece.[201] Most Americans understandably put a higher value on their lives, and it was this sense of self-preservation that had been behind most of the checks on industry that had been legislated over the last 80 years. Labor had been at the forefront of the movement for these reforms, usually pressuring liberal members of the professional class who sat in Congress as Democrats, rather than electing to Congress members from their own ranks. But as long as Labor could deliver the votes and campaign contributions, the laws were passed, the regulatory agencies were set up, and the Du Ponts fought back, bankrolling political opposition, most often Republicans.

To get reelected in 1980, Jimmy Carter was expected to rely on the coalition of labor, ethnic minorities, and liberal urban professionals that had traditionally dominated the Democratic Party since Roosevelt's New Deal. His growing acquiescence to the needs of organized labor, then, came as no jolt for Shapiro. The chairman nevertheless had his duty to do for Du Pont.

Carter's Achilles' heel was inflation, a problem industry had created but he was expected to cure. He focused his economic program against that aspect of inflation most felt by the vast majority of voters, consumer prices, which were rising at an annual rate of 13 percent in 1979. To lower that to a targeted 9 percent by 1980, 8 percent by 1981, and 6.5 percent by 1982, he had to induce the continued cooperation of organized labor. He hoped to keep labor costs down so corporations would be encouraged to take advantage of tax credits and invest in the expensive new technology needed if industrial productivity was to increase and restore America's competititive edge on the world market. To keep labor in line meant keeping the largest labor unions in line, including the Steelworkers. His wage and price guidelines may have shown, as Shapiro charged, a fallacious wage-price spiral theory of inflation, but the retarding of wage demands was still useful to Du Pont and other corporations, and their representatives joined the AFL-CIO union leaders on the President's Guidelines Board. By 1979, however, the standard of living of millions of workers had declined to such an extent that rank-and-file pressure on the union leaders forced them to demand some relief from the president in his guidelines and board representation which had been decidedly weighted in favor of the corporations.

In the fall of 1979, Carter finally granted more flexibility on pay guidelines and gave labor a more powerful role on the new Pay Advisory Board. Shapiro quickly attacked the president. The Pay Board, he said, was nothing more than a "forum for showboating and playing to constituent groups and not a way to conduct government policy."[202]

"This is a plan designed to line up the AFL-CIO," Shapiro objected. "It does not reflect industry's thinking. Our views were solicited and rejected. As Election Day draws closer, we can expect more of this, and that is not necessarily good news for the nation."[203] Shapiro's friend, General Motors' chairman of the Business Roundtable, was a bit more restrained but the message was the same. "The Government sets the nation's basic fiscal and monetary policies and has been responsible for the nation's energy and regulatory policies," he told reporters on the "Meet the Press" television show. "These are the fundamental causes of inflation; and restraint and discipline must be applied in these areas as well as by business and labor."[204] He did not, of course, volunteer to take a cut in his six-figure salary to set an example.

Publicly, at least, Shapiro kept his iron in Carter's fire, stating he supported .him for reelection. Contrary to popular impressions, though, Shapiro was not a Democrat. "I'm not registered for any party," he once admitted. "I really haven't been involved in partisan politics."[205] And he proved it when Carter named him as co-chairman of his proposed Economic Revitalization Board two months before the election. Shapiro accepted and at the same time expressed doubts about Carter's plan to encourage pension funds to invest in industry, in areas affected by economic dislocation or industrial bottlenecks. Du Pont's pension fund was then approaching $5 billion, and Shapiro was not about to deprive Du Pont of the use of the bulk of that capital by shifting the Plan's holdings in Du Pont to any potentially risky ventures urged by government no matter how much Carter promised to guarantee a minimum return. If an industry or an urban area were unable to attract new investment with its own profit-making potential, it was doubtful "that pension financing being available is the answer."[206] Du Pont enjoyed its control of the pension fund and was not about to voluntarily surrender it.

The chairman had other reservations about Carter, namely his future. To make that point perfectly clear, he accepted the co-chairman's role and then declined to invite any corporate representatives. "I have talked to some of my friends in the business community," he explained, and "timing will affect who you can get to serve." Some business leaders were backing Ronald Reagan and would be unwilling to act as if Carter had their support. "You don't want just Democrats," he said, adding that "If the president is not re-elected, this thing is academic."

It was, and he probably knew it. Reagan had attracted the support of most corporate leaders when he demonstrated that his folksy style and Hollywood charisma outweighed many Americans' concerns about his reputation as an arch-conservative.

For many corporate officials, it was a delightful surprise and an indication of just how far the country had come from Barry Goldwater's disastrous 1964 campaign. But it was also a sign of the weakened position of organized labor in America. Unions represented fewer Americans and were no longer able to deliver the vote that made the New Deal coalition, on which Carter relied, viable. Once the primaries showed that an arch-conservative was electable, the corporate money poured into Reagan's coffers. Corporate political action committees (PAC's) and individuals gave $10 million through individual donations not subject to any contribution or spending limits, over 382 times the $27,773 Carter's re-election received. One man, Cecil Hadin of Houston, Texas, gave $143,221, and that was after having already spent $182,176 on Connally's campaign. Arch-reactionary Senator Jesse Helms's Congressional Club spent $4.6 million on conservative candidates. The Fund for a Conservative Majority spent $2 million. The National Conservative PAC spent $3.3 million, of which $1.8 million went to support Ronald Reagan. It also spent $1 million financing media attacks on Democratic senators, some 78 percent of all the money spent in 1980 to influence the senatorial races.[207]

It was all defended before the Supreme Court on grounds Shapiro had pioneered for Du Pont in his cases against the FTC and the book, *Behind the Nylon Curtain:* the constitutional right of freedom of speech. And it was all designed to influence the American voter.

The Du Ponts were among the nation's largest contributors to the Republican campaign that culminated in the election of Ronald Reagan and George Bush, later, significantly, also chairman of the President's Commission on Deregulation. They gave over $215,000; Du Pont Company executives gave another $37,900 for a total Du Pont contribution of over $250,000.

Most of these contributions went through the Republican National Committee. A few went to such far-right organizations as:

Fund for a Conservative Majority
Committee for the Survival of a Free Congress
National Conservative Political Action Committee
Americans for Constitutional Action

Only Alexis I. du Pont Bayard and Jamie Wyeth gave to Democrats. Wyeth donated to Senator Kennedy's doomed campaign. Bayard, as if trying to balance the rest of his family's Republicanism, gave $32,500 to the Democrats.

Here is the list of Du Pont family contributions to the Republican party presidential campaigns as reported to the Federal Elections Commission:

Edward Ball	3000	J. Simpson and Mrs. Dean	2500
James Biddle	1000	Alfred du Pont Dent	1250
Robert H. Bolling, Jr.	8500	Ellason Downs	4500
J. Bruce Bredin	1000	Robert N. and Mrs. Downs	1000
C. Douglas Buck, Jr.	125	A. Felix du Pont, Jr.	7350
Donald F. Carpenter	1000	Eugene du Pont III	1250
Edmund N. Carpenter, Jr.	2000	Ewel S. du Pont	200
R.R.M. Carpenter III	1950	Francis I. du Pont III	250
Garret Van S. Copeland	2000	Mrs. Henry B. (Emily)	
Lammot and Mrs. Lammot		du Pont	500
du Pont Copeland	47500	Mrs. Marka T. du Pont	750
Colgate Dardin	500	Mrs. Martha V. du Pont	1000

Mr. and Mrs. Pierre S. du Pont III	4000
Pierre S. du Pont IV	1500
Reynolds and Mrs. du Pont	17250
Mr. and Mrs. Richard C. du Pont	400
Richard S. du Pont	1605
Sam Hallock du Pont, Jr.	500
Thomas L. du Pont	750
William F. du Pont	250
William K. du Pont	11000
Willis H. du Pont	1500
George P. Edmonds	250
Lucille Flint	500
Robert Flint	500
Mr. and Mrs. Baron Kidd	4600
W. Frederick Laird	500
Walter J. Laird	250
Rodney Layton	1000
Jane D. Lunger	500
Mr. and Mrs. Ernest May	5850
Mrs. Irénée Sophie du Pont May	5500
John H Tyler McConnell	1200
Charles B. McCoy	2900
Mrs. George B. Pearson, Jr.	2000
William G. Reynolds	1355
Donald P. Ross	3000
Jane Richards Roth	250
Mr. and Mrs. Philip G. Rust	3250
Bayard Sharp	25500
Hugh Rodney Sharp	5750
Henry H. Silliman	950
W.A. Speakman III	450

(Republican candidates and Business Industry PAC)	10144
Mr. and Mrs. William Laird Stabler, Jr.	2750
Mr. and Mrs. Coleman Walker	1250
George and Betsy Weymouth	8575
Du Pont Company	
David K. Barnes	1100
Richard E. Emmert	300
Charles J. Harrington (Retired)	31750
Mr and Mrs Richard E. Heckert	1530
Edward Jefferson	700
Harold E. May	250
William Simeral	1750
Dale Wolf	200
Wilmington Trust	
Bernard Isaacson	250
William Worth	4200

Following the Reagan - Bush victory, the Du Ponts, as if startled by the enormity of the Republican victory, rushed forward with donations totalling an amount unparalleled for a non-presidential year:

$183,600	Du Pont family donations plus
40,850	Du Pont executives
224,450	Total

Perhaps this had all been anticipated by the alliance between Delaware's U.S. Senator William V. Roth, who is married to a Du Pont in-law, and conservative New York Congressman Jack Kemp. They had joined in bequeathing America the Kemp-Roth Tax Act which gave 17 percent of all its benefits to the wealthiest 1 percent of the population, and 35 percent to the wealthiest 5 percent. Later, in a December, 1981, *Atlantic Monthly* interview, the Reagan Administration's budget director, David Stockman, would admit that the Kemp-Roth Act was a "Trojan horse" for tax cuts for the rich.

But the most intriguing sign that the Du Ponts were moving into new political and financial alliances was the unexpected election to the Du Pont Company board of Margaret P. MacKimm. Described in the 1979 Annual Report as a "Vice-President and Director of Public Relations for Kraft, Inc.," the food processing conglomerate, Margaret MacKimm's title was changed in 1980 to vice-president of Dart and Kraft. During the election year, Kraft had merged with Dart Industries, the $2.4 billion sales giant of Tupperware and Duracell batteries, founded by Justin Dart, a key financial force behind the rise of Ronald Reagan.

Eighteen

A DYNASTY IN WAITING

1. AN ARISTOCRAT MEETS THE BANKERS

Wilmington, despite its smallness and relaxed atmosphere, is not a town where pinstripe suits are noticed. There are too many business visitors to Du Pont's headquarters for that to happen. But if there was ever a time when it would have behooved Delawareans to know of the arrival of a certain group of men, it was on June 11, 1980. On that day, Irving Shapiro hosted some powerful visitors. They were all bankers from New York, from one bank, in fact—Chase Manhattan. They had travelled without notice or fanfare to the small city beside the Delaware to hold an extraordinary conference that would affect the lives of millions of Americans, and perhaps the future of the nation.

Irving Shapiro, now grayed by his 65 years and about to retire as chairman of Du Pont, had convened this meeting. He was a director of Citicorp, a bank with Rockefeller oil origins similar to Chase's, and a board member of the Bank of Delaware, a local bank with sizeable Du Pont Company deposits.

But he was not the man of the hour. That man, rather, was walking into the room with an entourage of his own lieutenants. His name was Pierre S. du Pont IV.

Pete du Pont was then in the middle of his campaign for re-election as the governor of Delaware. He was not worried about his chances. He had easily met his campaign budget of $232,000, almost $140,000 having been raised the previous year at a single event, a $500-a-head cocktail party and dinner featuring the deceased Nelson Rockefeller's ex-aide and former Secretary of State, Henry Kissinger. Pete's opponent was no serious match. Bill Gordy was a fourth-generation dirt farmer who had risen in Delaware politics through the creaking patronage system of downstate Democrats. He did not expect to raise more than $75,000 for his campaign, and could not even afford a poll to gauge voter concerns.

Du Pont, of course, had already hired professional pollsters and would conduct several more polls. He had learned to expect some criticism, for example, on his delay in erecting new prisons. He had opposed a policy of warehousing people rather than striking at the economic roots of crime when he first ran in 1976. But since winning the governor's mansion by the largest margin in Delaware's gubernatorial history, he had reversed his position as his fiscal austerity was accompanied by a rising crime rate. Only his delay in constructing new prisons had inspired jibes, especially when overcrowding caused such abysmal conditions that inmates risked their lives to engage in protests. But no one, it seems, questioned the wisdom of his reversal when it did come, or why so many Blacks were held in pretrial without being able to meet bail, or how much the construction of new jails would really cost. Nor did many challenge the contradiction between his concern about warehousing and his bringing back the gallows soon after taking office. "There is an appropriate place for the death penalty in Delaware's criminal justice system,"[1] he had said, listing 19 circumstances that could end in hanging.

There were the usual misgivings of liberals to endure, well-meaning folk who nagged with studies proving that capital punishment failed to deter murder or crimes. Most killings were acts of passion, done in the heat of the moment without premeditation. Those that were premeditated were seldom done by people who were discouraged by the existence of capital punishment. Repression also did not remove the economic and social origins of crime. If anything, the death penalty aggravated an atmosphere of violence and disrespect for human life, and made law breakers even more desperate if someone had been hurt or taken hostage. It burdened judges and strained the whole judicial system with appeals. The ethic was likewise self-contradictory. "Is it not absurd to be killing people who kill people in order to teach people that killing is wrong?"[2] said Henry Schwarzchild of the American Civil Liberties Union. That logic and judicial studies convinced the English population and Parliament to reject any following of America's lead in restoring the death penalty.

And there was another more serious social matter. Of the over 700 people on death row in American prisons by 1981, 46 percent were from minority groups, mostly Blacks. Only nine were women. In cases where the victim was white, Blacks stood ten times the chance of being sent to death as convicted whites facing the same penalty. Schwarzchild dared to say what many white Americans did not want to hear: "We very arbitrarily and discriminatorily pick out some individual people, not even those who commit the most heinous crimes. But we virtually never execute white middle class people, especially women."

Schwarzchild was a Nazi refugee who had seen personally how discriminatory executions, if allowed, began to steadily spread from minorities, to communists, to socialists, to labor leaders, to liberals, then to anyone who opposed the status quo and its ruling group. "It comes very directly," he warned. "In Berlin we were 'Jewishly' and politically conscious and active ... we escaped in just barely enough time." In Germany, one of Europe's most civilized countries, with a democracy also under economic and political stress, it was said it could never happen there, too. But it had. It had been allowed, and the promoters were often the most respected members of society, businessmen and professionals, all men who thought themselves honorable and civilized pillars of law and order. It was precisely because of the broad political implications of the death penalty falling most on impoverished minorities that the Supreme Court was so often moved to stay executions during the 1970's, holding that the Constitution's 8th Amendment with its ban on cruel and unusual punishment had been violated by discretionary sentencing based on race and socio-economic class.

Pete du Pont was not moved, as New York's Governor Hugh Carey had been in refusing to sign similar bills passed by the Albany legislature. But the governor was forced to deal with one aspect of discrimination as a legacy of Delaware's earlier days of segregation. In November, 1978, after years of delay by white school officials, a federal court suit begun in 1971 by Black students reached the Supreme Court, which affirmed that a desegregation plan was needed for Wilmington area schools and asked Delaware's Federal Judge Murray Schwartz for details. Pete attempted to keep control of the process, but his efforts to have the legislators in Dover draw up a plan was so bogged down that Schwartz ordered the busing of Wilmington students to the better-equipped schools in the suburbs for nine years; he also ordered suburban students to be bused to Wilmington schools for three years to force an upgrading of Wilmington facilities by the white-controlled state and local governments and to foster more racial mixing and hopefully, in time, tolerance.

Pete remained ambiguous about busing as a final resort to end *de facto* segregation, a position that, considering the anger by which busing was greeted in the white community, would lose him few votes. By 1980, meanwhile, as the governor lauded his administration's educational "achievements" during his re-election campaign, public state colleges and universities would still be unconstitutionally segregated, inspiring another Federal Court order the following January. By then, however, Ronald Reagan was expected to change the criteria for the acceptable level of desegregation, delaying matters still more in the courts.

Du Pont, it was clear to the Chase bankers, had Delaware well under control and was a "safe environment" for their activities. They therefore proposed to the governor on that mild day in June that he consider "liberalizing" the state's banking laws. New York's legislature, they explained, was unwilling to remove ceilings on the amount of interest banks could charge for loans and pay for deposits and time accounts. They also needed a revised banking code "flexible" enough to allow them to export these interest charges to depositors or charge account customers in other states. If the governor could enact such legislation, Chase and other banks would set up offices in Delaware and move credit operations and sizeable chunks of capital into the state.

Pete had been fully aware of what they wanted. Since imposing his austerity measures and budget cuts, he had been able to keep up the state's debt payments to New York banks and had won back enough of Wall Street's confidence that they forgave his alarmist speech about "bankruptcy" and restored the state's credit rating that they had lowered after that blooper. Since then, Pete's financial team, led by cousin Nathan Hayward III, had paid friendly visits to the Big Apple and had heard Wall Street's impatience with Albany legislators in September, 1979. "We found it interesting," said Hayward, Pete's former director of Delaware's Office of Management, Budget and Planning, "and we tucked it away."[3]

But not too deeply. The Du Ponts had always been eager for a large bank to give them the financial flexibility they needed for investment diversification. That was especially true now that "the tin box," Christiana Securities, had been opened, freeing the family fortune of its traditional chain to the chemical company founded by their family. Wilmington Trust had proven inadequate. Despite their huge deposits in the trust department, the bank was a newcomer in the world of high finance. Its relative underdevelopment of business connections and the Delaware area's limited commercial market had left Wilmington Trust far behind in the running as big banking's business exploded in the 1970's. In 1972, Wilmington Trust ranked 20th of the 32 largest institutional investors in the nation with assets under management of $5 billion and over;[4] by 1975, it had slipped to 25th, and in 1976 to 26th.[5]

The other major Du Pont family bank, Delaware Trust, fared no better, slipping from 229th place in 1975 to 295th in 1976. And it had only $597 million under management.[6] Bank of Delaware also fell from 218th in 1974 to 293rd in 1976, with $544 million.[7]

Wilmington Trust was the nation's 12th largest equity holder in 1977, controlling portfolios worth $4.9 billion. (Delaware Trust and Bank of Delaware were not even among the top 100.) Yet it was easily dwarfed by Chase's $6 billion, Manufacturer Hanover's $7 billion, U.S. Trust's $7.6 billion, Citibank's $13.6 billion, Bankers Trust's $14 billion, and Morgan Guaranty's $19 billion. There was no doubt that in the world of high finance, Wilmington was a pygmy next to the New York giant. If Wilmington was ever to grow and join the big time, new capital was needed in the state. What the Chase bankers were proposing was just that, and to

Shapiro and the Du Ponts it was seen as a godsend. Du Pont Company's traditional alliances with J.P. Morgan would help. Du Pont Company already had interlocking directorships with Morgan and its commercial bank, Morgan Guaranty. With other interlocking directorships with Chemical Bank and Citibank, representing Du Pont's large deposit accounts in those banks, the basis for developing reciprocal relations existed. That would give the Du Ponts access to huge amounts of capital for leverage in moving into other corporations and financial institutions. Wilmington as a result could become a financial center in the Eastern United States.

Pete's approach was to the point. "We basically said, 'What would it take for you to make an investment in Delaware?'" Hayward recalled.[8] A lifting of the ceiling on interest rates? Granted. Reciprocal hikes in interest for credit cards? Granted. Variable interest rates? Granted. Unlimited fees for credit card usage? No problem. Legal rights to foreclose on homes to collect card debts? Delighted. Lower tax rates? Of course.

Pete appointed a secret task force headed by his trusted lieutenant, Glenn Kenton. O. Francis Biondi, a prominent Democratic lawyer, set to work reviewing the statutes of South Dakota, which had passed similar legislation, and began writing drafts. It was unclear if Biondi was working for the state or the banks until, very late in September, according to Bank of Delaware lawyer Richard Eckman, another member of the task force, it was revealed that Biondi had become Chase's lawyer in Delaware.

Shapiro joined the lawyers from Chase and J.P. Morgan in drafting the legislation. There were no written analyses by any Delaware officials. Kenton later claimed giving only "oral evaluations."[9]

It was all kept "very quiet," said Eckman. "Nobody was talking. It wasn't in the papers."[10] Delaware's division of consumer affairs, which receives complaints and statistics on credit collection abuses and practices, would have had something to say if it was contacted by the governor. It was not. It was never shown the drafts. Consistent with recommendations of the American Bankers Association for revising state laws, the public was kept in the dark.

Did Pete du Pont violate the public trust of his office? The Delaware criminal code stipulates that it is a misdemeanor for a public office holder to deliberately fail to perform a delegated responsibility. But Glenn Kenton didn't see it that way. He freely admitted that he and the governor had a "bias" that "banks should charge what they want in fees" and "I didn't see any sense in running that fundamental principle by anybody who doesn't agree with it."[11]

A participant in the drafting was more candid. Secrecy was necessary because "it was before the election."[12]

Pete, Shapiro, and Biondi worked quietly on key legislators and in

September assured Chase of passage. The bill was by then drafted, still with no public knowledge. Shapiro later offered a Catch-22 in defense. "The people who had an interest in the bill were involved."[13] If the public did not know about it, however, how could they ever develop an interest in the bill? Shapiro, as usual, was speaking for other people's interests; he would define what those interests were and who should therefore be involved in decision-making. Otherwise, someone might be given a chance to voice an objection. "You couldn't afford to scare the banks away,"[14] he acknowledged.

On October 30, Pete ran into his first public confrontation over his possible violation of conflict-of-interest laws—but the issue was not the secret banking bill; it was his oil stock holdings. The scene was the gubernatorial debate. Delaware's *State News* reporter Jack Croft noted that the Governor had taken expense-paid trips via a Getty jet, opposed a barrel tax on incoming crude, pushed through the amendment to the Coastal Zone Act that allowed pipelines and oil rig supply stations to come ashore into the zone. Considering Pete's substantial oil stock holdings, Croft wondered if that did not constitute a conflict of interest.

Pete's reply was simple.

"I don't think so, Jack," he said.

End of issue.

Croft asked if Getty was paying its fair share of taxes, an interesting question in light of Getty's refusal to pay the fixtures tax required by the state constitution. Pete's response was again matter-of-fact. "I hope they are," he said.

An answer like that might have cost any politician votes in any other state. But not Pete du Pont and not in Delaware. Pete was re-elected in November, the first time in over 20 years that an incumbent governor had been returned to office in Delaware.

After the results were in and champagne again popped at "Patterns," Croft drafted a column in the *State News* asking about Getty and its due taxes. "It's a simple question of fairness," he wrote. "Of justice."[15]

But justice in Delaware, as in many states, was not a simple question.

On January 14, 1981, Pete invited key legislators to breakfast, but it was Irving Shapiro who presided. After Pete disclosed the proposed banking bill, the Du Pont Chairman addressed the legislators on its importance to Delaware's economy. The emphasis, wisely, was put on the benefits to the state, not the Wilmington area, which would be the real beneficiary. It was titled the Financial Center Development Act. It would, according to Shapiro, make Delaware "the first state in finance."

The Democrats looked at the complex 61-page bill and did not even read it before agreeing to sponsor it. "I confess I have no expertise in the banking area," Senate Majority Whip Harris McDowell III later explained. "I am mystified by the bill; in fact, I'm sure it is designed to do that."[16]

The next day the press was called by the governor to a special press conference, held not in his office, as usual, but in the large conference room of the capital's Townsend Building. There, reporters found Governor du Pont flanked by New Castle County's new Executive, Richard T. Collins, and the Democratic mayor of Wilmington, William McLaughlin. "Delaware has a unique opportunity to modernize its banking laws to better reflect the changing patterns of the banking industry and to help make our state one of the financial centers of the nation," du Pont told the press. "Enactment of this legislation would enhance our state's reputation for financial stability and for a conducive business climate and it will reaffirm our desire to expand job opportunities for our citizens."[17]

Whereupon, officials from Chase Manhattan and Morgan Guaranty pledged they would open banks in Delaware. Hearings were held a week later—for three hours. Since the Senate was in session, no Democratic senators attended; probably none had enough legal training to question the bill anyway, since none were lawyers. Shapiro and Biondi were both scheduled as witnesses, however. At 7 P.M., consumer attorney Douglas Schactman was allowed to testify. He had only been given a few hours to read the bill, but could understand enough to speak eloquently against it. It didn't matter. Most of the legislators had gone by then; the "rules," he said, "were stacked against me."[18]

The Consumers Federation of America also objected. Jim Boyle, its director of governmental relations, asked the legislators to "consider some of the things this bill would do. It would allow foreclosure on a homestead when it is used as collateral in a credit card transaction. It would allow a bank to retroactively increase the interest rate on a credit card holder's outstanding balance." The legislation was "anti-free enterprise."[19]

"My impression is that the State of Delaware is forward looking,"[20] said J.P. Morgan vice-chairman James Botsi. Such forward-looking behavior by the Delaware State Chamber of Commerce included blocking bills that would have given unemployment benefits to workers locked-out or on strike, requiring industries to give the public a year's notice before moving out of state or closing, and introducing deposits on bottled beverages to encourage returns rather than waste.

"Is that blackmail?" one influential businessman was quoted by the *State News*. "God damn right, it is. It's about time. Eighty-two percent of the jobs are generated by business."[21]

"Delaware is a conservative, pro-business state," said State Chamber of Commerce president William Wyer. "It always had been. We're trying to renew that tradition. We're just starting back."[22]

"In the good old days," Shapiro said of business-government cooperation, "it was just a natural relationship. Delaware's a small state and people knew each other on a first-name basis. Everybody was together. That tended to fall apart in the Peterson administration and with his successor."[23] Now things were back together again. Republican House Speaker Charles Hebner was exuberant. "There's a growing realization that business is not a group of robber barons under the J.P. Morgan era."[24]

Two days later, on February 3, the state senate, without a hearing, debated and passed the Financial Center Development Act. "One day we will regret firing this little cannon," warned State Senator Harris McDowell. Eighteen amendments were attempted. They all failed.

"That bill got as good a hearing as I've heard in four years,"[25] said Governor du Pont, and on February 18 he signed it into law.

Irving Shapiro, said Bank of Delaware's Eckman, was the first to anticipate the national and historical implications of the act before it was even finally drafted. He compared it to Delaware's 1899 corporation law, which the Du Ponts drafted to enable them to centralize their vast gunpowder holdings into a single corporation. That law changed the structure of American law and American history. Delaware succeeded in pressuring many other states to follow suit and, more important, effectively established a nationwide corporation law by allowing out-of-state corporations to incorporate in Delaware and be protected by its lenient statutes for businesses. Now, again thanks to the Du Ponts, Delaware was doing the same with the nation's banking laws.

Banks immediately began threatening the legislatures of New York, New Jersey, Pennsylvania and Maryland with desertions to Delaware unless similar legislation was enacted. Maryland hedged, raising its usury ceiling to 24 percent from its previous rate of 12 to 21 percent for various loans. That didn't satisfy four banks, which promptly committed themselves to Delaware. Pennsylvania got the message and in 1982 passed legislation granting banks expansion privileges within the state. In New York, legislators and Governor Carey hurriedly tacked amendments onto bills that temporarily lifted interest ceilings to hold off Manufacturers Hanover and Marine Midland's threats to leave. Meanwhile, credit card holders in other states were beginning to feel the impact of what had gone unnoticed in little Delaware. The Provident National Bank of Philadelphia, one of ten banks that began moving credit operations into Delaware, notified some 100,000 customers that their Master Cards would now cost them $20 per year and a higher rate of interest. Other banks did likewise to millions of credit card holders. Accordingly, New York bankers urged Governor du Pont to travel the country to encourage banks to come to Delaware to increase their profits. Pete did so, addressing bankers in Chicago and California, pledging his state's "political stability and predictability" and "hospitable climate."[26] Pete was not just interested in helping the banks scare changes in state laws. He wanted bank capital in Delaware. He even sent Lt. Governor Michael Castle as far as London, Frankfurt and Stockholm to present the glories of his statutes.

The influx of capital into Wilmington was astounding. Morgan Bank of Delaware, setting up shop in the Delaware Trust Building, alone brought in $1.65 billion. Citibank brought in $50 million, with more promised. This bank's great significance was its interest-free checking deposits, one of its greatest profit-making operations, averaging $5.1 *billion* a day during the financial week of July 29, 1981. Deposits would be used to finance loans, which, at 22 percent interest, would bring in before-tax profits of about $1 billion a year. Maryland National Bank capitalized Delaware at $194 million; First (Maryland Bankcorporation's) Omni Bank, $107 million; Provident National, $125 million; Philadelphia National, $150 million; Chemical New York Corporation, $618 million; Equitable Bankcorporation of Maryland and Suburban Bank (of Bethesda, Maryland), $10 million each. Manufacturers Hanover would eventually capitalize in Delaware at $100 million and Girard Bank of Philadelphia in 1981, backed by Pete du Pont, Shapiro and J.H.T. McConnell of Delaware Trust, simply bought the venerable Farmers Bank from the State of Delaware; the skyline of Wilmington lost a landmark as the giant letters spelling the bank's name were taken down from atop its 19-story downtown building. Later, it too would be devoured by Pittsburgh's Mellon National Bank. Mellon had launched an interstate network of "Cash Stream" automatic tellers in over two hundred 7-Eleven stores, including 41 stores in Delaware.

All this undermined the legal safeguards against bank over-centralization that had been passed during the New Deal in the wake of nation-wide bank failures that swept the nation. Now, in the interest of deregulation, the banking industry seemed to be recreating the very dangers that the New Deal had sought to avoid. Ominously, many of the banks that had moved to Delaware were seriously overextended in loans to Third World nations that now threatened to default. In May, 1982, the following New York banks, all of which have subsidiaries now in Delaware, were listed among the 23 weakest banks in the United States: Chemical, Manufacturers Hanover, Chase, Citibank, Morgan Guaranty, and Bank of New York.[27]

The Du Ponts, however, were giddy with their success.[28] Nathan Hayward was "thrilled." Pete said it meant more jobs. Citibank Delaware president Earl Glazier agreed. "We're not going to replace Wilmington Trust. No way. But we may provide some career opportunity for some people that might not have happened."[29]

The Du Ponts also agreed, and not just about jobs. To make sure no bank replaced Wilmington Trust or their control of it, they amended the bank's charter to stagger the terms of directors to delay any outsiders' ability to elect a majority by at least a year. One million preferred shares were authorized to block the chances of a hostile offer to buy the bank. And to seal it all up, any future bylaw amendment or sale of assets worth $1 million or more required not just a majority vote by shareholders, but a two-thirds vote, including management; unless the board agreed. The board owned 13.4 percent of the common stock.

The Du Ponts knew that the bank's stock was attractive, priced at 41 percent below book value and only four times earnings. So they made clear in the proxy statement their willingness to merge into "a regional organization of sufficient size." But it would be on their terms, for a price that would "reflect the bank's true potential."

Under the 1981 law, special tax breaks were established for financial institutions and organizations when profits exeeded $20 million. This benefited such financial services corporations as the Beneficial Corporation, which expanded into a multi-billion-dollar operation under a board of directors that now included Du Pont family lawyer E. Norman Veasey and former governor Elbert Carvel. Du Pont family banks also benefited.

Du Pont family real-estate interests in Wilmington focused on the promise of vacant downtown lots that were christened the "Christina Gateway." As GWDC began laying off employees, Irénée du Pont, Jr., promoted the Gateway's potentials for the new financial immigrants, although the planned Citicorp building remained stalled. Nevertheless, both Wilmington Trust, with Edward du Pont now a senior vice-president, and Du Pont Company celebrated the bounties of Wilmington, Du Pont by producing a special slick brochure, and the bank by beginning construction on a new headquarters for some 1100 personnel. Called the Wilmington Trust Center, the tower was constructed literally on top of the city's old Romanesque post office; and on its top floor, plans were underway for a new exclusive social club for the corporate elite.

Eleuthère Irénée du Pont expanded his mutual funds operations also. As the money markets began to heat up with inflation, Eleuthère survived the loss of Theodore Ashford and his $125 million investment portfolio by securing a contract for his Delfi Management with the $222 million state pension fund. In October, 1979, he launched his Sigma Tax Free Bond Fund with a modest capitalization of $1.1 million. The following year, in 1980, he launched three more operations, Sigma Government Securities Fund, Sigma Money Market, and Sigma Special Fund, the last two with $10 and $9.2 million capitalization. In 1981, he set up his Sigma Tax Free Fund, which had 4.6 percent of its holdings in Pete's Delaware state bonds, "selling a high level of current interest income." Only Massachusetts, Florida, New York and Washington outranked Delaware as selected states.

That year its stock yielded 9.9% earnings, and Eleuthère's ten funds had portfolios worth well over $130 million. Yet *William E. Donoghue's Money Fund Report*, surveying investment results for the 12 months ending in October, 1982, found that Sigma Government Securities had one of the lowest rate of returns among funds investing in seven-day and 30-day U.S. Treasury notes; Sigma Money Market ranked second lowest of 54 funds in the domestic prime market in yields from seven-day notes, third lowest in yields of 30-day notes, and ranked 42nd of 44 of 12-month notes reported as of August, 1982.[30] While such yields vary from market to market over time, these were figures that could not be discounted when evaluating the performance of Eleuthère's management of two of his new Sigma funds.

Eleuthère's other major concern, Continental American Life Insurance, fared better. Backed by Du Pont family directors George P. Edmonds, Rodney Layton, and Eleuthère, as well as by Irving Shapiro and former Du Pont P.R. executive Harold Brayman, Continental American was steered by chairman W.G. Copeland into an eventful merger in January, 1980, with Crown Central Petroleum, a middle-Atlantic and Southeastern states oil refiner and retailer with about 4100 wells in Texas, Louisiana, California and the Rocky Mountain and mid-continent areas. For the merger, CALICO received 774,152 shares of convertible preferred shares in Crown and a seat on its board. Crown was significant not only for its domestic infrastructure of terminals, and a pipeline connected to the Houston-to-New York Colonial Pipeline System, but for its continued drilling in Texas and Oklahoma and working wells in Nigeria. The investment signalled a shift of Du Pont family investment into mostly domestic oil, a harbinger of what was to come the following year: the largest corporate merger of all time, again into domestic oil, supplemented by recent strikes in the North Sea.

2. THE LORD OF DELAWARE MARRIES

There were signs of it coming: in the 1975 deal with National Distillers and Chemicals to jointly produce synthesis gas and carbon monoxide as feedstocks for methanol production; in the ARCO deal to refine oil for petroleum feedstock; in the 1978 deal with CONOCO (Continental Oil Company, hereinafter called Conoco) to jointly explore for oil and natural gas in Texas; in the 1979 deal with Shell Chemicals to obtain one-third of Du Pont's ethylene, propylene and butadiene.

But they were signs, not reasons.

The reasons were more subtle and historical. They involved U.S. foreign relations and oil holdings abroad; they involved the Du Pont family's own motives, now beyond concerns merely for the chemical firm; they involved the move of the Du Pont fortune into the lucrative energy field, particularly oil and nuclear power; and they involved the family's new use of the chemical firm as leverage to achieve their financial goals.

It is difficult to assess how many of Du Pont's top management understood this. Life at Du Pont is also life *in* Du Pont, with the Wilmington suburbs being an extension of that subculture. If there is questioning, it is either absorbed into the matrix of the organization, defined within its needs, or it is necessarily expelled. The pressure to conform is enormous, especially when it appears benevolent. "It is easy to fight obvious tyranny," wrote sociologist William Whyte in his 1956 classic, *The Organization Man*, "it is not easy to fight benevolence, and few things are more calculated to rob the individual of his defenses than the idea that his interests and those of society can be wholly compatible....Like the good society, the good organization encourages individual expression....But there always remains some conflict between the individual and The Organization. Is The Organization to be the arbiter? The Organization will look to its own interests, but it will look to the individual's only *as The Organization interprets them*."[31]

As Shapiro exemplified so often over the previous decade, Du Pont has had a penchant for interpreting the interests of the individual, of all American individuals, for a very long time, probably from its birth as a company. It has long been given a name: paternalism, practiced in the name of progress, of efficiency, of *community*. "De Tocqueville made a prophecy," recalled Whyte. "If America ever destroyed its genius it would be by intensifying the social virtues at the expense of others, by making the individual come to regard himself as a hostage to prevailing opinion, by creating, in sum, a tyranny of the majority. And this is what the organization man is doing. He is doing it for what he feels are good reasons, but this only makes the tyranny more powerful, not less. At the very time when the pressures of our highly organized society make so stringent a demand on the individual, he is himself compounding the impact."[32]

Ironically, it was the quintessential organization man, Irving Shapiro, who intensified this process in a company where it had already gone to extremes.

He did so by further centralizing authority in Du Pont's corporate structure, undermining the careful balance between individual initiative and organizational needs that Pierre S. du Pont had taken such pains to attempt in his committee structure.

What was left was the company mold, and a hierarchy more steeply structured than what had been easily felt and seen among top management in the past as a sense of importance, of even belonging to an elite within Du Pont, and therefore within Wilmington, Delaware, what Shapiro admitted as "a feeling that we were just a bit better," a narrow egoism that made true cooperation and its key component of individual independence lacking when, in 1981, it was most needed.

For central to Du Pont's corporate image, emblazoned even on the cover of its 1975 Annual Report in the image of Thomas Jefferson's letter to E.I. du Pont, was the family. And if the rest of management took Shapiro at his word about the importance of being a professional manager, of being a team player and Organization Man, it also saw his deference in practice to the needs of the family, even, in the case of Christiana Securities, their self-interested desires.

The problem, perhaps, flowed from the pragmatic approach of American business, too often seen and denounced as merely amoral. "Aside from the fact that the managerial group is open to all comers, there is another fact which disqualifies its members as a ruling class," wrote Whyte. "They have no collective sense of direction. They have none because their organizations have none. Owing to its essential differences in functions and goals, and not unimportantly, the American inability to put things together into a doctrine until after it's all over, our many different hierarchies are not so comparable as might appear. Like the union man who becomes an industrial-relations executive, the ex-government lawyer turned a corporation counsel, the erstwhile blue blood who becomes a sales trainee, many organization men have a conflict in loyalties they must resolve."[33] If there was anything obvious to Shapiro, it was that he was not a member of a true ruling class. It showed in his stockholdings even more than his deference to the family's needs. He was, clearly, not a Du Pont. He was and remained always an outsider. Thus his alliance was "more to The Organization itself than to any particular one, for it is in the development of their professional techniques, not in ideology, that they find continuity—and this, perhaps, is one more reason why managerial people have not coalesced into a ruling class. 'They have not taken over the governing functions,' Max Lerner has pointed out, 'nor is there any sign that they want to or can.'"[34] Shapiro often pointed this out himself. He was probably the first Organization Man at the helm of a company that had been ruled for so long by a family self-conscious of its role in business and in history, possessed of an ideology. And it was precisely this that made him seem unique for Du Pont.

But is was also his greatest weakness. Such men "concentrated on the fact of their skills rather than on the uses to which their skills are put. The question of the *cui bono* the technician regards as beyond his technical competence."[35] Ultimately, they retreat to the bosom of the Organization, allowing it to interpret in the name of the common good.

Whyte said this was "premature" behavior. "To preach technique before content, the skills of getting along" —Shapiro's "communication is good management" — "from why and to what end the getting along is for, does not produce maturity. It produces a sort of permanent prematurity, and this is true not only of the child being taught life adjustment but of the Organization Man being taught well-roundedness."[36]

The reaction of the call for buying Conoco was not mature; it was acquiescence to a more confident and permanent human force confronting the managers—the Du Pont family. It was this that explained why they made the momentous decision that was immediately questioned by analysts—and now, in whispers along the corridors of the Headquarters, among themselves.

It was a testament to the fact of their cohesion as functional, rather than one based on basic kinship ties, that there was no unity of opposition, indeed, perhaps any opposition, to the Conoco purchase. Shapiro may have served as retired elder statesman, but it was only as consigliore, awarded prestige with no rights by birth and always revocable.

So it came about that executives who had become used to seeing their chairman leverage their company, unlike family members who had a kinship stake in not mortgaging their heirs' future, were encouraged in the summer of 1981 by the ultimate Organization Man, the individual who probably most personifies the bloodless abstraction of capital, the banker. A property, with familiar and friendly management, was up for sale, and J.P. Morgan had selected Du Pont from a list of companies it thought could help the targeted management keep their jobs secure from hostile bidders.

The property contained, of course, what Du Pont could use: oil, lots of it, over 1.5 billion barrels, much of it in the western United States and the North Sea, readily available and safe from foreign repossession, with extensive distribution in Europe where Middle East oil is expensive. And coal, 44.9 million tons of it, one of the largest reserves in America. And natural gas, 2.6 trillion cubic feet, and 38 processing plants recovering gas liquids including ethane, an important chemical feedstock. And, finally, uranium, 61 million recoverable pounds in the United States and 32 million pounds in Niger, Africa.

The Morgan bankers, who were in agreement with Concoco Chairman Bailey's offer to sell out to Du Pont, thought it was a good buy.

There were many reasons why it was not, at least for Du Pont Company. First, there were formidable competing bidders: Mobil Oil and Seagram, both billion dollar operations with cash on hand, were already driving up the price of Conoco's stock, and Du Pont's entry would drive it up further. The winning bidder would surely have to pay a premium on the stock's value. Most take-over bidders paid that kind of money in order to get rid of management, not to save it. Why should Du Pont want to help Conoco's managers? Were Conoco's assets really worth it? Du Pont would not even be able to use all the oil and gas that Conoco had. Why should Du Pont, already in debt to banks, pay for what it could not use?

The solution to the riddle was, as usual in most human dilemmas, found in history, in this case the history behind the competition for Conoco's stock. The battle over Conoco actually had its origins in Canada in mid-1980. Prime Minister Pierre Trudeau wanted to regain for Canadian financial interests the 70 percent of Canada's oil and gas reserves that were owned primarily by American corporations. He established tax levies on foreign firms and investment tax credits for Canadians with the stipulation that their companies engage in oil exploration. Canadian banks feverishly agreed to back the companies with loans. Toronto's new energy policy, therefore, made oil exploration in Canada more lucrative if ownership of the exploring companies was in Canadian names. American firms accordingly began selling some of their reserves to Canadian concerns.

Conoco was one of those firms. It had a controlling 53 percent interest in Hudson's Bay Oil and Gas Company, owner of 265 million barrels of Canadian oil and 3.4 trillion cubic feet of natural gas. Morgan Stanley, Conoco's broker, valued the Conoco stockholding at about $1.7 billion. Conoco's directors wanted more, $900 million more, in fact.

One of the possible Canadian buyers Morgan had listed was Dome Petroleum. Dome contacted Ralph Bailey, the bulky, sandy-haired engineer who had risen to Conoco's chair, and offered to make a $1.7 billion bid through a tender offer for 20 percent of Conoco stock that would then be swapped for Conoco's share in Hudson Bay. This arrangement, Dome explained, would allow it to avoid paying capital gains taxes.

Bailey was cryptic, but did not refuse. Dome's executives believed Bailey was only trying to avoid any personal direct negotiations with them before beginning their bid so the IRS would not question the swap on possible charges of collusion.

When Dome's tender offer was announced on May 5, Conoco and Morgan Stanley acted shocked. They claimed Bailey had been worried about the legal implications of the tender offer and made no deal. If Bailey had, it was a terrible mistake. Dome's offer of $65 for each Conoco share was well above the $50 it fetched on the New York Stock Exchange, and Dome's offer drew a favorable response from Conoco's institutional investors. The reason was not just the price. Conoco had a reputation as a company with solid roots in the old Standard Oil Trust and as a firm with promise, but it always seemed just that, promise. Although it was a large company, it never seemed able to make it to the top ten where the chips were decidedly bluer. It had never exploited its huge domestic oil or gas reserves on the scale many thought it could; instead, its exploration and development program appeared sluggish, its directors, including the representatives of Rockefeller Brothers, Inc., acting more like keepers of a holding bank or some national security energy reserve in the American homeland, than the voracious profit-seekers many investors would have preferred. Its management, accordingly, suffered a reputation as not being very aggressive, even though Consolidated Coal, its subsidiary, had a tough reputation among miners dying of lung diseases. Moreover, Conoco now had problems abroad. Its holdings in Libya were jeapordized by the nationalism of its leader, Col. Qaddafi, and the new Reagan Administration's open hostility to Qaddafi for his support for Arab nationalists in northern Africa and the Middle East did not make Conoco's position any less worrisome.

The response by investors to Dome's offer was overwhelming: 52 percent of Conoco's shares came in, instead of just the 20 percent it had asked for.

It was the first tip-off that Conoco's directors lacked the confidence of shareholders and that Conoco was susceptible to a take-over.

That caught the sharp eye of Edgar Bronfman, the handsome, polished 52-year old playboy chairman of Seagram, the world's largest liquor distiller and a Canadian firm, although its headquarters were on 5th Avenue in Manhattan. Seagram had $2.3 billion in cash on hand from its sale the previous year of oil and gas properties to SUNOCO, the oil firm controlled by the Pew family of Philadelphia. Only in April, Bronfman had been foiled in attempting a hostile take-over of St. Joe Minerals. Now the dapper Canadian saw another opportunity. He knew Dome was too small to arrange credit to buy the 52 percent offered to it. Assuming it bought the 20 percent it wanted, that left 32 percent available to the highest bidder.

Bronfman quickly put in a call to Conoco management and said he wanted to talk. Conoco's Bailey conditioned it on Bronfman's pledge that his bid was a friendly one, and not hostile to management. "Of course," said Bronfman, who then arrived at Conoco's Stamford, Connecticut, headquarters with a negotiating team. There they worked out what Bronfman thought was a deal with Bailey to buy 35 percent for cash and a standstill agreement—which bars voting stock against management—for a certain number of years yet to be negotiated. In the middle of the negotiation, however, Bailey cut off the talks, agreeing to meet the next day. Unknown to Bronfman, Bailey had a private jet waiting to fly him to Oklahoma to conclude merger talks with Cities Service, then also fighting a Canadian raider, Nu-West.

Was this a sign of bad faith? Bronfman later said it was, and his charge was somewhat supported by what happened the next day. Bronfman arrived with his brother, Charles, and this team was shown into Bailey's office. While there, the limousine of Dome's president, William Richards, pulled up the Conoco driveway. Bailey then began his shuttle negotiations, keeping the Bronfmans upstairs while the Dome people were put in a small conference room downstairs, their isolation ensured by security guards. Bailey later said he was worried that if Richards and Bronfman crossed paths, Dome might just as soon sell its Conoco shares to Bronfman as trade them in to Bailey for Hudson's Bay. That was unlikely. Dome wanted Hudson's Bay badly, and would end up proving it by buying up complete control.

After Bailey, assisted by the legendary merger lawyer Joe Flom of Skidder Arps Slate Meager & Flom, worked out his deal with Richards, Richards was then brought before the waiting directors of Conoco, who approved the exchange of Hudson's Bay for Dome's 20 percent of Conoco plus $245 million. Only then was Bronfman brought in to make his offer.

Bronfman explained he was interested in an investment for his grandchildren, not control. He would like to buy 35 percent for cash and a standstill agreement. But the Conoco directors wanted him to sign the agreement for beyond the 15-year period he had agreed to. By now, Bronfman was wary. Flom had been getting tenacious with the Bronfmans that afternoon while, they later claimed, misleading them about how well the Dome negotiations were going. As late as 3:30 P.M. Flom had allegedly told Charles that "nothing is going to happen with Dome."[37]

"Ralph," Charles Bronfman later testified saying to Bailey just before going into the Conoco boardroom, "I am convinced Joe Flom is trying to sabotage this deal."[38] When they learned that the Dome exchange had just been approved, the Bronfmans felt burned. The situation had changed. The Conoco directors had gotten back the stock Dome had bought and felt more confident than Bronfman had anticipated. His $73 per share might attract institutional shareholders, but it did not impress the Conoco directors. The $8 more per share he was offering only reflected the increase in Conoco's price since Dome made its offer; it didn't even match that: Conoco was now selling at $60, $10 above its May 5th listing.

They rejected Bronfman's offer and proceeded to prepare to announce their merger with Cities Service, while putting out calls to see what large company could be lined up as a White Knight if a raider showed up.

That was on June 17.

The next two days the Bronfmans bought 143,000 shares of Conoco on the open market, and the Exchange suspended trading and told Bailey to put out some statement to explain the unusual activity. Bailey's statement did not mention Seagram by name, referring only to a foreign company; and it reported an offer to purchase 25 percent, not the true 35 percent. Canada, meanwhile, worried about its own sinking dollar on the world money markets, tried to halt its bankers from backing up any more oil purchases from Americans. But by now it was too late. Bronfman was not to be stopped. On June 22nd he filed a pre-merger notice with the Justice Department. On June 25th, he overrode the Conoco board's rejection and made a public unfriendly bid for Conoco shares.

Undoubtedly, some of the blame for the merger mania must be laid at the White House. Since President Reagan had appointed William Baxter as head of the anti-trust division of the Justice Department, it had been evident that in the name of efficient economics of scale the Administration would not block most large corporate mergers even though the FTC study in 1979 had held that there were "on average no economic benefits from large mergers." In fact, it was questionable whether large mergers were not antithetical to efficiency.

Northwestern University's Frederich Scherer conducted interviews with executives of acquired companies and found that in automobiles, for example, a clubbish attitude had blinded executives to trends toward smaller, more fuel-efficient cars. Inflation also made companies' assets spiral in value. That attracted mergers, but did not reflect any real growth in earnings because the sales market, especially during a recession, was usually slow in absorbing the inflated value of the assets with an increase in sales revenue. The gap between a company's revenue from sales, on one hand, and the value of its assets on the other, would show up as a *decline* in earnings that could affect the attractiveness (and therefore price) of a stock, and the company's ability to raise capital to finance debt payments to banks or even operations.

"I think it is ironic that the Reagan Administration is worried about bureaucracy in the government," commented Dennis Mueller, an economist who studied mergers in Europe and the U.S., "but encouraging it in business."[39] A Carter hold-over in Baxter's anti-trust division was equally alarmed. "The views of the agency's head seem to be antithetical to the agency's purpose and it makes a lot of people around here nervous,"[40] he said.

When Bronfman made his unfriendly bid, Bailey knew that Conoco's days as an independent firm were limited. He had been caught with his hand in the stocks jar. While claiming to have balked at Dome's offer because of possible legal problems, Bailey had actually been negotiating with another oil company, Cities Service, for a merger. He later argued that this merger would have given Conoco a higher percentage of U.S.-based income, ostensibly to ease worries about its troublesome Libyan holdings. Cities Service had a strong exploration program in the U.S.

But that didn't answer why Bailey had not simply strengthened the domestic programs of Conoco itself, which had huge U.S. reserves. It also didn't explain why Bailey's directors were going along with a merger with a company which not only had its own problems but was actually smaller. That would only dilute the value of their Conoco stocks, the very factor they gave on June 27 in excusing their refusal of Seagram's June 25 offering. They were also aware that under SEC rules, Bronfman would have to prorate his purchases. That meant that even if he attracted 100 percent of the shares (which was unlikely), he could purchase only 35 shares of every 100 that came in, turning back 59 shares. Those 59, the directors claimed, might fall as low as $40 a share on the market, dragging down the value of the other 41 shares. When the $73 shares and the $40 shares were prorated, that meant Bronfman's $73 price would really be worth about $53 a share to Conoco's shareholders, too low, they insisted, to be in the company's interest.

The usual answer has been to criticize Bailey for lack of boldness in not buying Conoco's outstanding stock. More likely, however, Bailey was attempting to exchange shares in Conoco's treasury for an interest in another company. Bailey, like the Du Ponts, was probably trying to diversify.

Morgan realized it was a marriage made in a broker's heaven, if not for the independent-minded Conoco executives or for the Du Pont executives devoted to chemicals, then certainly for the major interested parties, Bailey's directors and the Du Pont family.

It may have seemed surprising, in this context, that Bailey's directors failed to purchase more of their own stock even though they knew a raid was coming that would drive up prices. But there were two probable reasons they did not. One was that Conoco's stock had not yet shown clear evidence of rising. When Dome's exchange took 22 million shares off the market, for example, Conoco's stock still did not rise very far, to $56 at most. Laying out cash to buy shares to discourage a raid might raise the price, but Conoco would be financing its own rise in shares. The increased price might accomplish just what it would be designed to do—discourage other bidders—and prevent a further gain in the value of the stockholdings of the controlling investors they represented.

These investors were not necessarily loyal to management. Eleven of the 14 were "outsiders," representing large investors. While most of them were professional corporate managers themselves, their fundamental loyalty was not to other executives but to the interest of a Conoco they saw through the eyes of the corporate investors they represented. Particular interests become defined as the common interest. It was stunning evidence that the "outside directors" model championed by reformers for corporate boards was too vague; if the outsiders are profit-seekers first and citizens second, then their motives may be no more conducive to industrial democracy than that of management insiders.

Joe Flom's failure to lock down in writing Bronfman's promise to keep his bid friendly and not pursue the bidding unilaterally leaves a big gap in comprehension. It has been excused on the grounds that for men in high places their word is their bond. If so, there would be little need in the world for lawyers. No one knew this better than Joe Flom, a veteran of many nasty take-overs.

It is very possible, then, that Bronfman inadvertantly had taken the bait. While his bid killed the Cities Service merger, destroying any real chance Bailey's team had to remain independent, it also meant Morgan and Flom would have to bring in someone new, someone with enough financial clout to play White Knight. That someone might even have close ties to both Morgan and Flom.

The Conoco directors, meanwhile, saw the value of their holdings double in two weeks of heated bids. Mobil jumped in, and Bailey threw fuel on the fire by agreeing to talk with Texaco about a merger. He claimed to be favoring one oil giant over another because of "very serious anti-trust and public policy issues."[41]

Meanwhile, some unknown investors on the Philadelphia Stock Exchange had been wise enough on the week of June 19th to June 25th to speculate in call options to buy 100 Conoco stocks at a "striking price" of $70 per share by July 17. At the beginning of the year, Conoco's call options had languished near 0. On June 19, they were selling for $\frac{1}{16}$ or a "steenth," as low as an option can get. Over the next few days, 5 options were quietly traded. It is possible, someone might have been fishing for a long-shot gain, or closing out a profitable short position in the call, which had been as high as 10½ in the final quarter of 1980; or had purchased the call as insurance to minimize a loss if Conoco stock that he had sold late the previous year now rose.[42] Or, just as possible, someone had a tip about what was going on inside Conoco's headquarters. It is interesting that someone knew enough to suggest that a reporter make a phone call to Du Pont Company on June 22 and inquire if Wilmington was engaged in talks with Conoco. Du Pont Headquarters denied being in touch with Conoco, and the disclaimer was printed in the back pages of the *New York Times* on June 23. Two days later, Bronfman made his offer to purchase 35 million shares at $73 per share. Over the next ten days, the Conoco call rose 124 times in value. A

Manhattan broker called it "unreal."[43] But for some investor, the profits were very real indeed. The purchase of one Conoco call on June 19, when some of Conoco common was selling for $56.25, would have cost the buyer $6.25; by July 6, when 2159 contracts turned over, the call, minus brokerage commission, was worth $775.

That day Du Pont Company made a cash bid of $87.50 per share for 40 percent of Conoco's common stock, and offered 1.6 Du Pont shares for each remaining Conoco share.

Securities analysts were stunned. It was a huge premium to pay over Conoco's market price which even two days later, when Conoco was the most active issue on the New York Stock Exchange, was much lower, at 76⅜. Conoco's big shareholders represented on its board may have been happy; Conoco common, the competitive bidding Bailey was promoting, had appreciated over 35 percent in value since June 19. But, usually a bidder is only willing to pay a premium over market price if he believes he can do a better job of managing the targeted company's assets, which he must assume have been undervalued by the stock market. Du Pont obviously believed Conoco's huge gas and oil reserves had been undervalued and was banking on their worth rising in an energy-scarce future. But it did not plan to replace the Conoco executives. So why was it willing to play White Knight for them against Seagram's Villain?

3. BEHIND THE MATCHMAKERS

The answer was in how Du Pont got involved in the first place. The chemical company's executives had come to know Conoco's executives through their joint oil and gas exploration venture in Texas. Bailey's maneuvering for a merger was driving up Conoco stock, but it was a dangerous game. The Conoco top brass were confronted by take-over threats from all sides in late June and early July; the Bronfmans were known to like to control what they owned and could now be expected to have little regard for Bailey; and Mobil had oil executives who were every bit as experienced and competent as Conoco's. Du Pont's chemical engineers, on the other hand, had shown they knew little about the oil business. Conoco's top management would be safe.

Morgan Stanley, Conoco's broker, apparently agreed. Morgan was the perfect matchmaker. It had command of the lines of credit needed to both finance Du Pont's purchase and protect Conoco's managers from hostile bids. Bailey, with Morgan's assent, picked up the phone and called Wilmington. Exactly when the first contact was made is unclear, but Edward Jefferson, chairman for only two months, admitted calling Bailey on June 24, two days after Bronfman filed hs pre-merger notice with the Justice Department, and about the time Conoco and its New York hirelings were making calls to line up a White Knight. Jefferson acknowledges only to getting assurances from Bailey that no other chemical company like Dow had been approached. That would have been highly irregular. Dow was heavily leveraged. It was not even on Morgan's list of prospects. Lee Smith pointed out, "By making the call, Jefferson encouraged hopes that Du Pont might be a White Knight."[44]

Jefferson could not recall what prompted him to contact Baily other than rumors about Dow being approached or what he may have read while vacationing in Colorado in the middle of June.

While he was in the wilds, however, Irving Shapiro was in Wilmington. He was now chairman of Du Pont's finance committee and, since the April stockholders' meeting, had been spending more time at his new law office a block away. Behind his desk hung a reproduction of the new impressionist painting of Pierre, Lammot and Irénée du Pont that still adorned the Du Pont chairman's lair. Shapiro was still representing Du Pont as a member of the law firm of Skadden, Arps, Slate, Meagher and Flom ... Joe Flom, the lawyer for Conoco that Charles Bronfman had warned Bailey about; the same Joe Flom who at the time also headed the law firm Shapiro now worked for. In fact, Shapiro's son, Stu, was a partner in the firm. As Shapiro put it, "We would be careful not to let any personal activity affect the proper choice of law firm."[45] Or the proper destiny for Conoco.

Shapiro led the Du Pont finance committee in approving a merger with Conoco, as well as the terms that were then endorsed by the entire Du Pont board which already had a direct interlock with Conoco through Gilbert E. Jones, a director of both companies. Jones also sat on the board of IBM with Shapiro, and with another Conoco director, C.W. Buek, on the board of U.S. Trust Company. Du Pont director and Trilateralist Andrew Brimmer, likewise, sat on the board of United Air Lines with Conoco director Lauris Norstad.

Morgan-related First Boston Corp. was picked as Du Pont's broker for the tender offer, reflecting the company's long ties to Morgan interests. Du Pont director Howard Johnson was on the Morgan board. Du Pont then owed about $22.1 million to J.P. Morgan's commercial bank, Morgan Guaranty Trust Company.[46]

Morgan in June had arranged a $1 billion credit line for Conoco to ward off any hostile offers. It now arranged a $4 billion loan for the Du Ponts.

The total price tag when Du Pont made its July 6 bid was $7.3 billion.

That was a lot of money that now would not go into Du Pont's promising new array of specialty products, and analysts had to wonder. This was another reason not to make the deal, and Shapiro knew it. He had been the one who steered Du Pont through the fibres rapids to the smoother waters of value-added specialties downstream. True, the Du Ponts had allowed the restructuring of the company to begin years before, when Lammot du Pont Copeland, the last direct Du Pont heir to occupy the captain's chair, stepped down from the helm and McCoy, a relative, but not an heir, took over. Shapiro had only continued this process, but at a break-neck pace, spurred on by the rise in oil prices. By 1979, he had directed 35 percent of Du Pont's business into high technology products. The Photo Products Department was expanding into electronic sound and video recording tapes, penetrating the printing industry with printing plates, and made 25 percent of the world's X-ray products and most of Polaroid's film. Its electronics connectors, growing with the exploding market in telecommunications and data processing, expected a 20 percent annual growth. The Biochemicals Department's agricultural chemicals generated 10 percent of Du Pont's earnings making pesticides, fungicides, and herbicides. An expansion into the brave new world of genetic engineering also looked promising, with wide application in everything from pollution control to pharmaceuticals. Electronic machines capable of analyzing blood 35 different ways automatically were also a rising business.

Much of this was questioned by environmentalists and health experts for its impact on the declining quality of food through spraying of carcinogenic chemicals or the rising costs of medical care or the ethics and morals relating to human evolution and the lack of government protection from potential abuses in gene-splicing. But for Du Pont these ventures represented a money-saving move away from the older lines of synthetic fibres that were heavily dependent on petroleum. It also was an escape from the stagnant paint market, which had not responded well to poor ratings. And it would not get better. By 1982, *Consumer Reports* labelled Du Pont's "Easy Care" Latex Flat and "Lucite" wall paints as the worst of 32 paints tested, charging they "lacked the qualities you should expect in expensive paint."[47]

The automobile industry was still a billion dollar market for Du Pont, consuming plastics, artificial fibres, paints and lacquers, and electronic connectors, but the federal safety and environmental laws that encouraged plastic sales to make cars lighter had also required more concentrated, less volatile auto paints which increased costs. The new "value-added" products, on the other hand, required less capital investment to set up shop and, as new industries, were poorly unionized, allowing Du Pont Headquarters to pay cheaper wages and run shops without interference from organized labor representatives.

So now, analysts asked, why the move back *into* oil? Would not the Conoco purchase retard development of these promising new lines of products? Would it not delay Du Pont's search for a $400 million pharmaceutical company? Why did the finance committee recommend the purchase? What really was going on?

Edgar Bronfman decided not to wait for the answer. On July 12, he bid $85 a share for 51 percent of Conoco. Three days later, Du Pont responded with a $95 a share offer, and raised its stock offer for 1.6 shares per Conoco share, to 1.7 shares.

It was a terrible mistake. Shapiro and Jefferson, by not closing the deal with a solid cash offer, allowed Bronfman to keep on bidding—and buying—while the Justice Department reviewed Du Pont's stock for its anti-trust merits, as required by law.

Mobil came in with a $90 offer in cash for just over 50 percent on July 17 and pledged securities worth an equal amount to Conoco's remaining stock. Mobil was obviously eyeing the same thing as Du Pont: Conoco's vast oil reserves could be bought for less than $12 a barrel. John S. Herold, Inc., the reputable oil analysts, valued Conoco's assets at about $160 a share, much higher than anyone was bidding.

Bronfman shot back with $92 a share in cash for 51 percent on July 23. Three days later Mobil countered with a $105 per share offer for 51 percent, but lowered the value of the securities it was offering for the rest of Conoco to the equivalent of $85 a share.

In Wilmington, the Du Ponts realized the mistake they had made. They tried to rectify it by increasing their cash purchase of Conoco from 40 percent of its shares to 45 percent. Mobil responded by raising its cash offer to $115 a share on August 3.

Edgar Bronfman responded another way on that day; he began buying the 15.5 million shares his strictly-cash offer had attracted. Wilmington groaned, quietly.

The Reagan Administration offered them some relief. On that same day, Assistant Attorney General Baxter weighed in with his approval of the Du Pont-Conoco merger. It had been expected, and was probably the reason Bronfman began buying that day. He knew his head start would not last long. Mobil had not been denied Baxter's approval. It was still pending, despite the fact that under the Reagan Administration oil companies had been given license to purchase each other following the general line of Reagan's SEC Chairman John Shad who blessed mergers as "facilitating capital formation"—as well as fees for such merger and acquisitions specialists as E.F. Hutton and Company of which Shad was vice-chairman. But Mobil was not favored by Baxter, and his delay gave Du Pont the decided edge. Questions were raised about the merger's profitability for Mobil shareholders, since the purchase would probably have pulled down its

14 percent yield to 11 percent. The Reagan Justice Department, however, had not ruled Mobil out, signalling a willingness that other corporate giants quickly picked up.

Thirteen huge corporations, mostly oil companies, lined up $46 billion in credit that month. Mobil raised $6 billion, as did Gulf Oil. Texaco raised $5.5 billion. Marathon $5 billion. Cities Service took on $1 billion to ward off raiders, then $3 billion more. Pennzoil set up a $2.5 billion credit line; Allied Corporation, $2 billion; Phillips Petroleum, $1 billion. North West Industries and U.S. Steel loaned $4 billion more for working capital needs, but they were the exception. Most of the other credit lines were set up for acquisitions, exactly what President Carter had feared the oil companies would do rather than invest in research on non-fossil fuel sources of energy.

Shapiro had made headlines defending such oil company mergers when he testified against Senator Edward Kennedy's bill to restrict them; the testimony ended up in a personal confrontation between the Du Pont Chairman and the Massachusetts Senator. Now, at Skadden, Arps, Shapiro was joined by four Carter officials: Carter's Deputy Secretary of Energy, Lyn Coleman; his Assistant Secretary of Energy for International Affairs, Leslie Goldman; the Special Assistant to the Secretary of Energy, Douglas Robinson; and Carter's Associate General Counsel for the Environmental Protection Agency, James Rogers. "They practice the type of law that I tried to practice as a lawyer," Shapiro said of Skadden, Arps. "I wanted to be associated with a man like Joe Flom."[48] Flom, the merger king. Now Flom was advising Conoco, which borrowed $3 billion; his friend and ally, Shapiro, was having Du Pont borrow $4 billion. And their rival for Conoco, Edgar Bronfman, had borrowed $3.9 billion. All to buy Conoco's shares.

The huge borrowing that month may have helped the giants, but it didn't make life easier for the average American. Small businesses and housing were "near collapse" because of the severe shortage of capital, charged Rhode Island Congressman Ferdinand St. German, chairman of the House Banking Committee. The big borrowers were causing tight money in the credit lines, "a shortage clearly not shared by the huge oil companies who desire funds for an international game of monopoly."[49]

This, in its essence as a movement of capital, was nothing new in the history of American business. Such "games" of monopoly were always played during times of international economic contraction when overproduction exhausted markets and triggered recessions, even depressions. In those bleak times, horizons looked darker for smaller companies whose capital reserves or markets were too limited to offer a view beyond the crisis of the next fiscal period. Smaller firms have not the capacities of giant corporations to absorb the punch of a deep recession, and this vulnerability often translates into bankruptcy or selling out. That is why recessions are often also periods of mergers that result in greater combinations of industrial and retail capital, larger corporations extending their control over industrial and retail markets. Large banks, too, unhappily foreclose on customers or demand more say over a company which must reschedule its debt payments; this applies to companies which are dangerously high-wiring their profit-margins as well as to those giants which must borrow from banks to consume what others' ruin has offered. More bank representatives thus are seen on industrial boards, or even in troubled governments such as New York, furthering the process of what has become known as the growth of finance capital. Even small banks, hit by defaults on loans, become prey.

The problem, however, is that it further stretches the liquidity of banks, small and large alike, which have already overextended themselves during the earlier days of heady expansion. The crisis of payments rendered the banks by customers no longer able to meet their interest, much less their principal, on loans reduces the number of areas where high finance can respond with flexibility. So any one area of crisis threatens all, and the true domino theory emerges from nightmare into reality. When that point has been reached, there is no turning back. There is only hope in going forward, trying to contain the crisis by extending it with more loans, more mergers, larger combinations of capital, now dubbed corporate "conglomerates."

This explains more rationally than simplistic charges of greed why super-banks like Chase Manhattan were willing to make so many loans in the first half of 1981. Chase made 70 such loans totalling $15.1 billion during those six months; Citibank 68 totalling $13.3 billion; Manufacturers Hanover 56 totalling $11.1 billion; Bank of America 52 loans amounting to $10.8 billion; J.P. Morgan & Co. 39 loans totalling $10.7 billion.[50] Nor are Americans alone. All large bankers seem to act alike. In the same period, for example, Barclays of London made 37 loans totalling $11.2 billion; Banque Nationale de Paris 30 loans worth $11.1 billion; Bank of Tokyo 50 worth $10.8 billion; Arab Banking Corporation (London) 34 worth $9.5 billion; Bank of Montreal 27 loans worth $8.3 billion. All seem to agree on the strategy of more loans, more rescheduled debt payments, more mergers. It underscores the interdependency of Western banking, especially of American banking, which is required to seek foreign partners for big loans because U.S. law prohibits a bank from lending over 10 percent of its capital and surplus. Foreign banks, to non-bankers' dismay, are not so restricted. Thus, in any great financial crisis for a single large bank, there is no place in the Western world to hide. There are no safe refuges.

This also accounts for the decline in American banks' earnings even as the assets of the giants grow, and why bigness is not necessarily a sign of good health. Since 1950, American banks' equity as a percentage of their total assets slipped from 9 percent to 6 percent in 1968, 4.1 percent in 1973, 3.7 percent in 1978, down to 3.6 percent in 1980.[51] Some of this is also the result of a loss of loan business to the commercial paper market and the new money market funds that have sought to exploit the declining value of money and volatile interest rates by offering higher yields for "deposits," or money put in their hands. To compete, the banks have had to raise their own interest rates, narrowing the previously lucrative gap between rates paid to depositers and rates received from borrowers. That meant a growing squeeze on bank profits and bankers' agitating for a removal of New Deal laws that prevented them from interstate banking, interstate mergers, and charging outlandish interest rates for loans or credit lines.

It also explains why the financial community worries when articles appear about their liquidity crisis, citing its own statistics. Working from material submitted by banks to the Federal Reserve, J.T. Holt & Co. of Westport, Connecticut, analyzed the banks' equity-to-asset ratio, loan loss reserves ($298 million), percentage of the total loan portfolio that was accounted for by real estate construction and development loans (especially vulnerable during a recession), percentage of loans accounted for by borrowings from less-developed countries ($96 billion to non-OPEC countries); percentage of loans accounted for by commercial and industrial loans (some were as high as 80 percent, 30 percentage points above the 50 percent considered normal); purchased liability ratio (inter-bank short-term borrowing, usually overnight). Morgan Bank of Delaware ranked as the strongest bank in the U.S. but its parent, Morgan Guaranty, ranked as one of the 25 weakest, as did Manufacturers Hanover, Bank of America, Chemical Bank, Bank of New York, and Citibank,[52] all with or planning to have Delaware subsidiaries under Pete du Pont's new bank law. Du Pont Company had interlocking directorships and/or deposits with five of these banks.

This desperate inter-dependency between big banks and conglomerates also clarifies why the financial community was so hard put to admit the role its lending and the conglomerates' borrowing played in increasing interest rates. It was far more convenient to claim that in a money market where $1 trillion exchanges hands every day, 13 corporations borrowing $46 billion in the single orgiastic month of July, 1981, had little affect on the nation's financial resources or on interest rates, and was actually not a withdrawal of money from circulation but a recirculation of money back into the economy. A neat formula if one could believe that the multiplier effect of money in circulation was actually an expansion of real value simply because the same money exchanges hands many times. But the reaction in the moneymarkets and the Federal Reserve Board betrayed the truth. Yes, said the Fed, there was a $51 billion rise in the money supply, some of which was the result of bank loans extended to the conglomerates. But simply because some of the loan proceeds were put into bank deposits and counted in the money supply did not mean a real expansion of goods and services in the economy. Too much money chasing too few goods is a classic monetary symptom (not cause) of inflation from international productivity differentials and a depressed dollar value. To try to keep that symptom of inflation under control, the Fed contracts the money supply made available to the central banks. And, sure enough, when the week of August 5, 1981, ended with a huge $3.7 billion increase in business loans over just the previous week and it was announced that there had been a large $5.1 billion gain in what the Fed calls the M-1B money supply (covering currency, interest and non-interest-bearing checking and other checkable deposits in banks and savings institutions), to a total $433.7 billion, most interest rates edged higher in anticipation that the Fed would make bank reserves scarcer to reduce excessive growth in the money supply. No wonder there were few bankers indeed with the courage of Fiduciary Trust Bank of Philadelphia's Lacy Hunt to admit that the conglomerates' huge loans "are an adverse development for the money and bond markets." With such interlocking interests and the debt crisis so sharp, who wanted to concede that such loans crowded out other borrowers and raised interest rates in the short- *and* long-term markets?

This growth in the money supply perplexes monetarists, who myopically hold that money supply is the source of inflation, rather than productivity lag and resulting trade and payments deficits. Yet it is clear that the growth of money market funds such as Eleuthère I. du Pont's were part of a "revolution" in cash management that resulted from inflation and high interest rates. These funds surged ahead by $74.6 billion in August, 1981, alone to a total $142.7 billion, spurring the growth of the second important money measure, M-2 (which includes M-1B as well as savings deposits, money market funds and certain short-term bank borrowings in domestic and "offshore" [meaning Bahamas and other tax-havens] money markets). Monetary economists base their theory on the premise that there is some "connection" between changes in the money supply, inflation and economic activity. Before the mid-1970's they were quite satisfied that M-1B was an accurate measure of the amount of money available for spending in the economy. But M-2 in some cases just diverted money from government securities (mainly tax-exempt Treasury bills, large negotiable certificates of deposit and other financial instruments). That meant M-1B might actually underestimate the money supply, playing havoc with their forecasts.

If what existed in the economy could not be understood by the monetarists, at least it could be reacted to. So the Securities Industries

Association letter to the White House endorsing the Reagan program was inevitable. Controlled money-supply growth, reduced taxes, deregulation of business, reduced federal spending all "enjoy overwhelming support in the stock brokerage and investment banking community."

So, therefore, did the Reagan Administration's approval of Metro-Goldwyn-Mayer's purchase of United Artists, and Caterpillar Tractor's purchase of International Harvester's solar turbine division. Chemical Bank's interest in taking over the deceased Ed Ball's favorite bank, Florida National Banks of Florida, Inc., was not discouraged. At about the same time, the Administration dropped the Federal Trade Comission's 1973 anti-trust suit against Exxon, Texaco, Gulf, Standard Oil of California, Standard Oil of Indiana, Shell, Atlantic Richfield and Mobil as being "not in the public interest."

It is no accident, therefore, that Du Pont's expenditure of $7 billion to take over Conoco coincided with President Reagan's signing of a bill giving $60 billion in tax cuts to American industrial corporations for "stimulating new investment in plant and equipment and creating jobs." Du Pont's acquisition of Conoco, however, "created no new productive capacity or directly productive (as compared with managerial) employment, whatever Du Pont chooses to do with its new property later on."[53] Du Pont's burgeoning Headquarters in this regard reflected only what had been happening in American business as a whole for the last thirty years. The ratio of overhead personnel to all employees in American manufacturing rose from 18 to over 30 percent between 1950 and 1980, a huge increase which contributed significantly to the productivity decline of the 1970's. According to economist David Gordon, bureaucratic control accounted for over 85 percent of the measured retardation in labor productivity between 1954 and 1973, and 1974 and 1978."[54]

Such mergers, therefore, contributed to deindustrialization, rather than ameliorated it. This was especially true in the area of finance, where from 1975 to 1980, over $100 billion in cash reserves were diverted toward supporting tender offers alone.[55] Yet Wall Street could self-righteously criticize Mobil's seizure of U.S. Steel as a case of diversifying rather than modernizing. Mobil, incidentally, had been prevented by Asst. Attorney General Baxter from competing with U.S. Steel for control over Marathon Oil; whereupon Mobil simply took over U.S. Steel. The cover of different industries now in place, the administration felt free to render its blessings.

Du Pont also had worried about Mobil's intentions during the Conoco bidding. Wilmington questioned whether Mobil's willingness to pay $8.8 billion for Conoco was not simply the first in a series of steps that would make Du Pont also a target for take-over. Did Conoco, in other words, offer such a reasonable rate of return to warrant that kind of money? As Robert Metz of the *New York Times* speculated in his "Market Place" column, Du Pont may have been the actual target, but Mobil had been prevented from buying Conoco shares by the Reagan Administration. Mobil's mistake was in waiting until July 17, eleven days after Du Pont filed its first bid. The time factor in getting clearance from Asst. Attorney General Baxter put Mobil at a distinct disadvantage with Conoco's shareholders. "No one thought that Mobil would get anti-trust clearance," said Joseph Perella of First Boston Corporation, which Du Pont chose as dealer manager for the tender offer.

Mobil was probably not alone with such designs, and the Bronfmans had not made Mobil's mistakes. On August 4, Mobil raised its bid again to $120 per share, but it tied Conoco shareholders to its securing of 51 percent and their accepting securities Mobil was offering. The lack of confidence Conoco investors showed was soon evident; Mobil attracted only 735,000 shares; eventually Mobil would have to get rid of these on the open market. The Bronfmans, on the other hand, had attracted 15.5 million shares; after returning 2.2 million tenders to their owners, they had at least 18 percent of Conoco. Then they even extended the deadline for their $92 a share offer, knowing they would collect more from shareholders who did not want to see their stock decline on the market after the bidding was over and turn-backs settled down the market for Conoco stock.

At Du Pont Headquarters, the approval of the Justice Department on August 4 put the gears in full throttle. Tenders were recorded and tallied and soon the figure was apparent: 37.9 million shares had been bought for $18 each; 9.4 million shares for 1.7 Du Pont shares each. After midnight, Jefferson threw a party downstairs at Hotel Du Pont's Du Barry Room, an ornate banquet room with a high carved white ceiling overwhelmed by a huge crystal chandelier. A trio of musicians played soft music as Du Pont executives were served hors d'oeuvres on fine china and offered tinkling glasses filled with Dom Perignon 1970. Five cases of champagne were consumed as the 50 to 70 members of Jefferson's team talked about their roles, exuding confidence. "Everyone just kind of accepted that if we got all these things done, we would do it," said spokesperson Faith Wohl. Jefferson gave a brief speech of praise and headed for home. The affair, after only an hour, duly broke up. Upstairs, at 3:45 A.M., the formal buying began.

Beneath the confidence, however, concern was growing. How would Du Pont explain it? "Du Pont's strength," as Thomas Peters and Robert Waterman correctly noted the following year in their *In Search of Excellence*, "had been in downstream innovation and value-added to products in specialized market niches those innovations had created."[57] Now, suddenly, $7.3 billion for an oil company?

But there had been worries about the specialized markets. In the new field of life sciences, for example, Du Pont did not enjoy an exclusive role as *the* innovator, as it once had in fibers and plastics. Competition, particularly from Dow and Revlon, was tough. Shapiro and Jefferson anticipated the really big returns only in the distant future, when Du Pont's enormous research resources and marketing capital could produce the difference, in a new product that would create new industries and do for Du Pont in biochemistry what Carothers' nylon did for fibers. They had entered the field because, as Jefferson put it, "The business is moving and if you want a ticket you'd better get with it now." By 1990, they hoped to increase revenues from 1980's $1.4 billion to $5 billion, and Jefferson's academic and practical training as a researcher would help. Specialty fibers and plastics were targeted to grow from a $4.6 billion business to a $9.5 billion one, and electronics from $450 million to $2 billion. This would increase the downstream share of Du Pont's business to 55 percent.

But all this rested on being able to phase out Du Pont's huge dependence on bulk fibers and chemicals, which represented 55 percent of Du Pont's business. This was certainly a marked improvement over the previous decade, but it would have to be lowered by another 10 percent if revenues were to increase from 1980's $14 billion to 1990's projected $30 billion.

Cutbacks in primary research could also hurt Du Pont in genetics, a new field less amenable to Shapiro's preference for applied research. Du Pont's desire to repeat the big find nylon once represented also led it to continue its penchant for secrecy and going alone, rather than involving itself in joint ventures or purchases of other firms, as Monsanto did by buying into Genetech.

The DNA research efforts were late in start-up, its director, Dr. Ralph Hardy, only having been recruited in 1979. Two P-3 containment labs were constructed between 1978 and 1980, with special security precautions to prevent the escape of deadly bacteria. If Du Pont's record in other areas of toxic chemical contamination of workers is any guide, these labs bear watching. As its workplace and environmental policies have demonstrated, Du Pont has not been known to be above the temptation to "play God," as religious leaders have warned about companies that might use the Supreme Court's June 1980 approval of patents for new forms of life for private profit. "Who is going to control these things, who will benefit, who will bear any adverse consequences," President Carter was asked in July, 1980, by 350 scientists and clergymen convened by Bishop Thomas Kelly of the U.S. Catholic Conference, Rev. Clare Randell, Executive Secretary of the National Council of Churches, and Rabbi Bernard Mandelbaum of Synagogue Council of America.

Du Pont has given a $100,000 grant to California Institute of Technology, which has probably the nation's most sensitive equipment for analyzing samples of pure interferon, the living substance which is the basis of the genetics industry. Du Pont has probably already synthesized interferon; it was the first to purify one of the known human interferons, fiberblast interferon. It is zeroing in on the drug and medical areas, where Wilmington already has production and marketing capacities of its pharmaceutical subsidiary, Endo Laboratories, and where it expects the first commercial application will make big money. But that will require a capital investment in Endo to handle the business, and research, meanwhile, is dependent on profits from Endo's relatively small market for funding. The problem there is that, with pharmaceuticals as a whole, Du Pont was a late-comer. Endo Laboratories, purchased only in 1969, commanded a sales market of just $100 million, tiny compared to giants such as Merck or Eli Lilly or Johnson & Johnson. And plans called for the purchase of only a medium-sized $400-million firm, a weak candidate to sponsor in a field of heavy competition. It is small wonder that Hardy confirmed that his team was "focusing on a fewer number of things."[58] In agricultural chemicals the prospects for quicker returns looked better. Du Pont applied its genetics research as both a defensive and offensive strategy against displacement of herbicides by environmental laws. In this field, its $42 million research in nitrogen fixation had only one real competitor, Allied Chemical with a $30-million research budget, although Dow has also put $5 million into Collaborative Genetics of Waltham, Massachusetts.

Specialty fibers also had limitations, as innovators. This was fully recognized by Jefferson. Explaining Du Pont's genetics research, he said, "In 20 years these specialties will not be advanced products. You've got to have your year 2000 vision."[59]

The same vision, Jefferson claimed, guided Du Pont to Conoco. "If you can't see where we're going," the 60-year-old chairman said, "it's because you don't know where we've been. Du Pont has changed all through its history. It started out as an explosives business, it matured into a chemical business which got into plastics, paints and fibers. If you look back a little more than a decade, it set its sights on diversification, into electronics and pharmaceuticals. Now we are adding energy. What we can do is to bring some of the talents of our engineering department and our research labs to the problems and opportunities that exist in the energy field. The current management have got to run what they've got well, and they've got to do something for the future management. This is our tradition. I suspect that my successors in the 1990's will be very glad we acquired Conoco."[60]

Perhaps, but the analogies to Du Pont's earlier transitions were lacking. The Du Ponts never leveraged their company the way Shapiro and Jefferson had. Nor could Du Pont's engineering really better Conoco's when it came to experience in drilling, laying pipelines, or recovering residue oil by pumping chemicals or high-pressure gases underground. In fact, Du Pont had to call on Exxon for advice on integrating and digesting the Conoco organization.

And as for Du Pont management having a "tradition" of doing something for future management, the entire 180-year history of the Du Pont family, who *were* the top management, suggests otherwise. The tradition, rather, was rivalry and feuds and *lack* of preparation for future managers to such a degree that the company was almost lost once (in 1904) and, despite Pierre's introduction of professional managerial techniques, ultimately left with a floundering company in the early 1970's and no family top managers by 1978. If anything held the Du Ponts to the company, it was not a tradition for preparing for the future but the traditions of the past; not preparing for management, but preserving for the *family* the source of its wealth. The family's enrichment, not the company's management, was the traditional goal, and it was these kinship ties, more than merit, which for so long led to top management and bound the company to the family's destiny and vice versa. The elders understood this, even if family youth believed a meritorious career was as important as family tradition and wealth. Jefferson, it seems, was projecting the goals of the Organization Man that he held onto the history of the Du Pont family and their company.

But even if the family's history were unknown, the evidence of the Conoco purchase itself was at hand to belie Jefferson's claims. Conoco was bought at a premium, deeply indebting the company, at a time when the price of oil was steady, and, because of a world glut, not expected to rise, at least for a while. Du Pont itself had acknowledged this only two days before Jefferson made his fateful phone call to Conoco's Ralph Bailey: "The biggest effect of the oil surplus on us so far is that we're guessing this element of costs will go up at a lower rate than we were previously forecasting."[61]

Equally telling was Du Pont's announced plan at that time to continue its program to use more coal as a plant power source. This plan did not change after the merger. Harry Flavin of Merrill Lynch confirmed that Du Pont was still scheduled to move its 17 percent dependence on coal to 70 percent in 1990.[62] Yet Du Pont, after purchasing Conoco, began plans to sell much of Conoco's coal reserves.

4. THE HIDDEN DOWRY

Jefferson at first denied it. "We have no plans to sell the coal," he said on August 9, right after the tender offer succeeded. "You know, back in the time when nylon was being presented to the world, it was described as coming from coal, air, and water. It wasn't until the mid-1950's that cheaper petroleum appeared to replace coal. There is a great deal of coal-based chemistry, and its time will come again. We have a competence to reign in that field."[63] Bailey said pretty much the same on August 2. Speculation that Du Pont would sell off Conoco's coal subsidiary was "utter nonsense.... The coal company is a very important part of the new Du Pont, and it will not be sold."[64]

But by August 10, Bailey was forced to change his line. He admitted that Du Pont would sell some of Conoco's coal reserves, especially those which had a high asset value but low earnings potential.[65]

The description was apropos. High asset value. By December 8, Jefferson was acknowledging to 200 securities analysts and portfolio managers that "a sizeable piece" of Conoco's $2 billion natural resources would be sold the following year.[66] The executives of Consolidated Coal, the Conoco subsidiary, were not happy. "Do you want me to answer in oil-field language which you won't be able to print?" one executive vice-president told a reporter who asked for his reaction. "You don't work with a company for 32 years and have it branded on your back and walk away feeling good from something like this."[67] Other oil executives crowded around the table during lunch at the Du Pont Headquarters agreed with him.

Accepting the transition from being an executive of one of the largest oil companies in the United States to being an employee of a wholly owned subsidiary must have been hard to take. So also must have Jefferson's acknowledgement that Du Pont management would now be stretched (to cover Conoco). Jefferson, however, pointed out that Du Pont made some of its greatest innovations when it held a major stake in General Motors. The comparison was again a poor one. General Motors seldom actively drew Du Pont's management staff into its day-to-day operations, but instead was guided by the organizational experience of Du Pont's directors, led by Pierre du Pont, John J. Raskob, and Donaldson Brown. There was reorganizing of GM along Du Pont's committee lines and introductions of charts, yes, but seldom of Du Pont executives on an operating level. That was left, wisely, to GM's Alfred Sloan.[68]

This leads to the question of Ralph Bailey's role in the whole affair. Unlike many of his executives, Bailey was quite content with his new home in Wilmington, to where the Conoco staff moved from Connecticut. His public statements echoed Jefferson's. "Du Pont is a company that has grown through the products of the lab," he said, "and Conoco has been successful through discovery. I look upon the combined company as one that is being built for the next century. It is the kind of company that will have its growth almost assured because of the very natural fit."[69]

Jefferson also talked of Conoco's oil as if he intended to use it for Du Pont. "If you don't get a very high percentage of oil out of the ground with the pressure methods of recovery, then there are opportunities for new approaches, particularly at today's prices of hydrocarbons." He spoke of such use as if it were a mark of patriotism in the struggle against OPEC. "The thing that is going to happen in the next decade, and already is happening, is that more and more chemicals and plastics will be made by the resource-producing countries. You'll find polyethylene, for example, is already made by Middle Eastern oil producers. Conoco gives us a position to compete against the producing countries."

The argument was flawed on several accounts. First, Third World countries were still in a primary stage of developing their chemical industries; world-wide recession tends to arrest further development by drying up demand (more correctly defined as markets *capable of paying*) and thereby lines of credit. Second, Du Pont could hardly expect to compete in developing countries that have petrochemical industries owned by the state; few of such governments would allow it. Coups are by no means impossible feats, as the CIA's overthrow of Iran and its nationalized oil demonstrated in 1953; but a long series of such coups is unlikely in today's world, where the U.S. does not enjoy the hegemony it had in the Fabulous Fifties. There could be isolated cases, of course, but a multi-continental roll-back of Third World nationalism and state ownership of industries, while undoubtedly sought by the Reagan Administration and AID's new Bureau of Private Enterprise (headed by Elise du Pont, the governor's wife) is highly improbable. Third, most developing countries' petrochemical industries are incapable of winning markets from Du Pont outside their borders; they simply lack Du Pont's powerful marketing capacities, including its huge business contacts network, command of capital and advertising, and transportation apparatus. Fourth, Du Pont's real competition is from European and Japanese firms, not developing nations, and those firms rely much more on oil than Du Pont. Fifth, Du Pont uses natural gas, not oil, for 70 percent of its feedstock. Furthermore, as stated earlier, Du Pont planned to further its move away from oil by expanding its reliance on coal. The prospect, therefore, of Du Pont spending $7 billion for an oil company in order to "compete" with the Third World was ludicrous.

What then could be Du Pont's use for Conoco's oil, especially if other chemical companies followed Du Pont's lead to greater reliance on coal? That would lower demand for domestic oil, and its price. And also the value of Conoco's oil assets.

There, of course, was the solution to the riddle: assets.

But for what purpose?

Dome Petroleum, ironically enough, provided an example. Dome had bid for the rest of Hudson Bay's shares held by the Thomson family. That revealed that Dome wanted not just Hudson Bay's valuable properties in Canada and abroad, but the cash flow from Hudson Bay's subsidiaries. Without complete control, Dome was entitled only to dividends from Hudson Bay. With complete control it could use the subsidiaries' revenue to service the $2.2 billion debt, 35.3 percent of its equity, that it had taken on the previous December. Hudson Bay's subsidiaries, in other words, were targeted for milking. If enough capital were not put back into the subsidiaries, the milk would turn to blood.

Du Pont, of course, had a huge debt. Longer term borrowings arranged through Morgan Stanley amounted to over $1 billion in the beginning of 1979, up from $241 million in 1972 when the company was still chaired by C.B. McCoy. By 1974, under Shapiro, it had been raised three-fold, to $793 million. That year Shapiro consolidated all majority-owned subsidiaries into Du Pont's accounts. Thereafter, Remington Arms and Du Pont of Canada's financial conditions were subsumed within Du Pont's accounting, and their past financial statements were no longer restated. These changes had no effect on Du Pont's net income, but increased Du Pont's reported sales revenue as a base for credit. In 1975, Du Pont's long-term debt was up again to $888 million, and in 1976, to $1.2 billion.[70]

Through this entire period, the Du Ponts, who were no outsiders with little experience in managing Du Pont and therefore quite wise to Shapiro's every step, authorized an increase in special compensation awards to his executives from $786,344 in 1973 to $1.4 million in 1974, $1.1 million in 1975, $1.1 million in 1976, $1.1 million in 1977, and $1.3 million in 1978.[71] It is odd for management to be so rewarded when a company's performance is so poor (net earnings from 1974 to 1977 were below that of 1973). It is intriguing that such amounts would be paid when the $1 billion debt incurred is equivalent to the $1 billion management alleged was absorbed as shipment losses because of OPEC price increases, especially intriguing when it is remembered that the Shapiro management claimed that it did not pass on these OPEC increases for fear of alienating or losing customers, a decision Shapiro himself acknowledged as "a management failure."[72] The mystery gets even deeper (but less puzzling?) when one considers the findings of the Secretariat of the United Nations Conference on Trade and Development that out of the 1973 and 1979 increases in prices triggered by OPEC, "the subsequent spiraling of the prices was magnified by the pricing strategies of the chemicals majors through their extensive control of all phases of processing, marketing and distribution."[73] The inter-relationships between oil companies producing oil and gas and the chemical companies in Western Europe and North America had allowed the chemicals majors to penetrate many traditional markets of natural commodities, including natural rubber, cotton, metals and wool, systematically eliminating or eroding demand for competing primary commodities, irrespective of prices, which were sometimes three times higher than the natural commodities, as in cotton in the 1960's. This penetration, then, went "beyond the neo-classical economic notion of 'interfiber competition' and theory preaching the primacy of price in supply and demand."[74] Research and development allowed creation and control of knowledge that was a vital pre-condition for aggressive marketing, introducing new products and reducing manufacturing costs. Shapiro, in fact, used some of his loaned funds to allow Edward Kane to introduce new manufacturing processes that increased productivity from 69 pounds per employee in 1974 to 104 pounds in 1979.[75] He then, like the other majors, applied the techniques in the blending of fibers and "components of various properties corresponding to more complex and demanding cloth formation and diversified fiber end-uses"[76] for texture, color, dyeability, durability, and tensile strength. Marketing techniques psychologically conditioned brand recognition in the apparel-consuming public, with Du Pont concentrating on "market guidance" for the textile industry based on its technical and marketing know-how and the stagnation of natural fibers, with emphasis "that individual corporate growth was now only possible through the use of synthetic fibers."[77] Du Pont's Textile Marketing Division promoted Dacron, mobilizing 300 sales outlets in retail promotions by the end of 1977, and 60 television commercials during peak viewing times.[78]

All this was designed to protect Du Pont from too many losses in its vulnerable synthetic fibers market, offsetting the decline in demand by an offensive marketing and production strategy. This was one of the reasons the Common Market filed complaints of "dumping," when actually Shapiro was quite correct in arguing that he got a higher price in Europe for his synthetics than in America. But the aggressive marketing in Europe was nevertheless there. "Our immediate need," Shapiro conceded, "was to stop the bleeding before we could think about the future."[79]

So he bled others, first his own pure research program, then his European workforce (4000 fired). While earnings continued to drop, he kept up dividend payments to shareholders to generate cash on the stock market, and through more loans advanced new product divisions, such as biochemicals and photo products. Still it was not enough.

The UN found that the chemicals majors also indulged in other practices to survive the 1970's, including transfer pricing—that is, arbitrarily assigning prices to the transfers of goods and services, technology or loans between their related enterprises in various countries.[80] That included shipment losses.

One-third of all world trade is conducted between affiliates of transnational corporations, and Du Pont did over 30 percent of its business abroad, particularly in Europe.

The UN report cites overpricing through the manipulation of intracorporate transactions to lower taxation rates. Du Pont was found guilty of just such a practice by the Internal Revenue Service in the past. The IRS asserted that Du Pont sold products to its wholly owned Swiss subsidiary at unrealistically low prices as a means of cheating on U.S. taxes by diverting to the Swiss subsidiary income that ordinarily would have been taxable in the United States. The IRS reallocated the incomes, taxing most of the Swiss subsidiary's income as if earned by Du Pont in the U.S. Du Pont paid under protest and then did only what the rich can do: it sued for a refund in the Federal Court of Claims. The Court upheld the IRS. In 1980, so did the Supreme Court.

The chemicals majors inflated prices and eroded competing natural fibers that might have more effectively competed in the marketplace and forced a sharper lowering of prices for synthetics than occured. But for Shapiro, prices were low enough. What is more important was the interdependency of the chemical companies with the oil majors for oil and gas feedstocks and the expansion and protection of the synthetic fibers market. Du Pont's chemical companies' alliances with ARCO, Conoco, and Shell were replicated by other chemical companies. "It is the interactions of these oil and chemical oligopolies," found the UN report, "and not the unfettered operation of the laws of supply and demand which largely determine the fiber mix that is used in the textile market."[81]

This conquest by synthetic fibers was pioneered by the Du Pont family, not Shapiro, and the huge revenues it brought the company put the Du Ponts on the boards of major banks with intimate relations with the oil majors. These banks included Citibank (C.B. McCoy was a director), Chemical Bank (Lammot du Pont Copeland, Sr., was a director), Morgan Guaranty (Crawford Greenwalt was a director). "On the surface," the UN report stated, "it appears industrial companies use banks for their own ends—true, but the real qualitative change in the power structures of capital is that banks raise the industrialists to the level of financiers."[82] By the time the family had decided to move their investments beyond Du Pont and dissolve Christiana, many Du Ponts were thinking of themselves as being on that level.

Wilmington Trust is not known to be a bank with oil ties. Yet it was a sign of the Du Pont family's move away from its previous concentration in chemicals and aviation and into energy that by 1976 Wilmington Trust held 1.1 percent of Kerr-McGee, 2.2 percent of Gulf Oil, and 1.3 percent of Diamond Shamrock.[83] Bank of Delaware also held 1.4 percent of Amerada Hess.[84]

In 1977, Du Pont Company purchased the assets of the Du Pont family's Christiana Securities, making a book profit of $55 million. In 1978, profits were up 29 percent in the first half of the fiscal year, plants were running high and there was an upswing in prices and earnings for Du Pont. "When I look at our recent earnings," said Shapiro, "I'm confident we're on the right track."[85] So the directors felt confident enough to return $200 million in long-term obligations. That still left a huge $1 billion debt. That year, Du Pont stock sold for ten times its earnings and well below the price it had commanded as recently as 1976. With the market prospects looking brighter, there was reason to believe there would be an appreciation in value. In 1979, as profits continued to improve with earnings, the Du Pont board decided in May to authorize the splitting of each common share three for one, increasing the total number of common shares from 65 million to 195 million and reducing the par value from $5 a share to $1.66 ⅔. The hope appeared to be that sustained growth would draw in more capital through stock sales that would in turn raise the stock's price and appreciate the value of shares held in the company's treasury for future loans if needed. It seemed reasonable, and significant in that the Du Pont family members were showing their willingness to dilute their controlling share of the company in exchange for an appreciation in value and some expected profit-taking. At the same time, however, there was growing alarm about oil giants moving into chemicals majors' traditional markets. Exxon Chemicals already had sales of $4 billion, and Shell was competing in the ethylene market. There was also the pestering fear that consumer spending might drop sharply with the recession.

It did. Du Pont's plastics in 1980 saw a slash in profits from 1979's $435 million to $272 million; fibers, from $509 million to $324 million. Overall operating profits in the U.S. plunged almost $400 million and in Europe was halved to $124 million. Earnings dropped badly. Interest payments to mostly banks, meanwhile, remained a huge $17 million.[86] The crunch was on.

The first move was in February, 1980, as things began to slip. Remington Arms, of which Du Pont owned 69.5 percent, was merged into Du Pont; the minority shareholders, mostly associated with William Rockefeller family interests, were bought out. This meant that Remington's cash flow, and not merely its dividends, was available for tapping if need be. Another $192 million in long-term borrowing was taken on, up from $52 million in 1979,

$13 million in 1978; Du Pont also increased short-term borrowing by $163 million.[87] Some of this was used to retire other debts and pay interest. Total long-term debt held steady at $1,068,000,000.

Enter Conoco. Conoco earned $716 million on $13.6 billion in revenues; Du Pont earned $1.02 billion on $18.7 billion. But Conoco's assets included tangible properties that would appreciate over time, not depreciate. They could be used by Du Pont to remove some of the volatility in Du Pont's earnings. And they could be sold.

"Chemical companies in recent years have been increasingly worried about oil companies using their oil reserves to develop into the petrochemical business," commented Kidder, Peabody's Paul Christopherson. "Du Pont will be the one chemical company in the whole world that has put all those concerns behind it."

Ralph Bailey also put it all behind him, settling comfortably into his new office in Wilmington. Questions were raised about an inside deal. Why, if he had been serious about the Texaco merger, hadn't he stalled Du Pont while testing the Reagan Administration on its anti-trust position? Because, some conjectured, Du Pont had assured Conoco's top management they could keep their jobs.

Ralph Bailey seemed able to shrug off the anguish of Conoco's second level managerial team. He denied he had made any deal in order to save his job or income, which in 1980 was $637,710. He also owned 29,699 shares of Conoco common with an option to buy 79,000 more at an average price of $39.70.[88] Du Pont, of course, was paying $98. Bailey ended up owning 50,671 shares of Du Pont common, with the right to acquire another 144,098 shares. He was also made a director of Morgan Guaranty, J.P. Morgan, Du Pont, and became vice-chairman of Du Pont's board. He now owned more Du Pont common stock than Shapiro (16,891) and Jefferson (12,038) combined.[89]

The Conoco directors were also pleased. They represented the largest shareholders—financiers, not oilmen. And they made a killing. In 1976, Conoco's admitted major stockholders held 16 percent of its outstanding shares and were represented by six Street names, Cede, Cudd, Lerche, Pace, Pitt and Salkeld. Behind three of these were Chase Manhattan (Cudd), Bank of New York (Lerche), and Bankers Trust (Pitt). Conoco's largest debt holder was Chase, followed by Citibank, Morgan Guaranty, Mellon and the pension funds of New York State Employees and California State Teachers.[90] Conoco had strong ties to the Rockefeller family interests, represented by Nancy Hanks. Chase Manhattan also had three secondary director interlocks with the Conoco board through C.W. Buek (Equitable Life Assurance), Archie McCardell (American Express, General Foods) and Gilbert Jones (IBM).[91] It was not surprising that Conoco gave Chase the bulk of its loan business, much to Morgan's displeasure. But it was a sign of growing ties between Du Pont and the Rockefellers, as well as of Du Pont's legal discretion about having a Morgan banker on its board, that Chase was also given the business of arranging Du Pont's $4 billion line of cash credit. Thirty-seven banks participated, including three which had Du Pont board members as executives, Chemical (which lent $27.2 million), Citibank ($39.3 million) and Morgan Guaranty ($50 million). Chemical, in fact, was chosen as the forwarding agent.[92]

The big winner, however, turned out to be Edgar Bronfman. Edgar kept buying and buying. When his deadline expired, he had extended it and went back to buying more. Seagram ended up with 28 million Conoco shares, or 32.6 percent. Turning it in to Du Pont, he collected 47.6 million Du Pont shares, or 20.2 percent of 236 million shares outstanding.

It came as quite a shock in Wilmington. "I almost stopped drinking V.O. for a couple of weeks,"[93] Governor du Pont later said with a smile. The family had owned 46.8 million shares, 30 percent of the old company. But in the new Du Pont, 236 million new shares had been issued. That reduced the family's holding to 19.8 percent, with the Wilmington Trust group owning about 11 percent. Except for the latter group, the Du Ponts would find it difficult to vote as a bloc quickly—unless the Wilmington Trust group organized them.

That was exactly what Bronfman was wary of, especially when he heard rumors of rebellion along the Brandywine.

At Du Pont Headquarters, the worry was of another caliber. "Are they going to buy another 20 percent and kick us all out?"[94] Jefferson and other executives wondered. It was the typical concern of management: their own jobs come first.

Jefferson was alleged to also have the Du Ponts to worry about. "It doesn't take much imagination," said one close source, "to see some of the Du Pont family members on the board going to Jefferson and saying: 'You've taken on $4 billion of debt to buy Conoco, depressed the stock price, and now we have to contend with the Bronfmans. What are you going to do for us next?'"[95]

Someone must have said something or planned something because Jefferson was soon on the phone to the Seagram Building, inviting Edgar and Charles down to Wilmington.

The Bronfmans arrived with an air of confidence, but not so much to be unimpressed by all the signs of Du Pont wealth around them. After all, there are not many families in America that control an entire state and have not just a building but streets, highways, parks, schools, hotels, even governors named after them. Jefferson wined the Bronfmans with plenty of Seagram's best and implored them not to buy any more stock. Edgar and Charles listened, smiled, and ate an elegant lunch at Du Pont Hotel. Then they left. "You know," said Edgar, "they are very classy people."[96]

Class means something to a Jewish family anxious to move beyond what they consider the borderline respectability of liquor. And the Du Ponts are the very model of WASP elite in America. No one understood this better than Irving Shapiro. Shapiro did it the right way. He went to *them*. He took Jefferson up to the Seagram Building in Manhattan and there he did what he does best—compromised. Shapiro and Bronfman knew each other well. In 1977, as leader of the Business Roundtable, Shapiro had struck another deal with Bronfman, who was then representing the World Jewish Congress in trying to get Washington's opposition to the Arab boycott against companies doing business with Israel. Bronfman wanted no boycott, and Shapiro wanted no fight. A struggle on the floor of Congress could bust the reputation of Du Pont and other corporations which did business with both Israeli and Arab.

Now Shapiro proposed another deal. A limit of a 25 percent holding and a standstill agreement for 15 years, exactly the terms Bronfman had been willing to accept from Conoco. If Seagram wants to cut the term to ten years, fine, only it must let Du Pont know within the first six years. Meanwhile, the Bronfman brothers can sit on Du Pont's board and Jefferson and Shapiro will sit on Seagram's; that way both sides can keep an eye on each other.

Bronfman agreed, on one condition. If any other group, such as the Du Ponts, moved to grab 20 percent or more of Du Pont stock, he wanted the freedom to act. "Frankly," said Jefferson, "the Du Ponts are more likely to sell stock than buy more."[97] It had been said. Precisely what Shapiro had assured the SEC would not happen when the commissioners expressed concern that the family would unload their holdings and devalue the stock.

Edgar misunderstood, or at least shared Jefferson's misunderstanding. He thought of the idle rich who sell their stock for spending money. "I have relatives like that too,"[98] he said, then treated them all to a lunch of oysters on the half shell with a 1968 Chablis, saddle of venison with a 1959 Mission-Haut-Brion, and apricot souflée with "a great Sauterne," Chateau d'Yquem.

Edgar Bronfman did not have relatives like the Du Ponts. Whatever thoughts he had along those lines were straightened out when he walked into his first director's meeting at the Du Pont boardroom. There, surrounded by portraits of eleven grim generations of Du Ponts, Edgar and Charles gazed across the giant polished mahogany table into the faces of Du Pont elders staring back, all managing, at one moment or another, to smile.

The smiles were probably genuine, not merely cordial. For although the Bronfmans now held at least 21.3 percent, the Du Ponts still dominated the board. They also had gotten what they wanted. They had used the chemical firm's leverage to branch out into oil, coal and uranium. And now, with management and the Bronfmans obliged by their standstill agreement to follow that management, Conoco, too, could be auctioned off piece by piece to settle Du Pont's debt, or used as leverage for a still larger acquisition, perhaps even a bank.

For that, they would not have to rely on the good graces of an outsider. One of their own was in place. His name was Pete. And he had even bigger ambitions.

5. THE PRINCE AND THE PAUPER

He arrived unnoticed, looking older, more worn, and walked the streets of Wilmington like a rejected lover. It had been five years since he held a job here, five years in which he had seen friends turn their backs, employers refuse to see him, prison. But Mel Slawik was back.

He had never left Delaware. After spending six months at Allenwood Federal Penetentiary, he returned to look for work as a social worker. There was no question about his credentials. He still held his masters degree in social work from Rutgers and no one could take twenty years of experience from him. But no one would hire him; social agency executives have it difficult enough in a conservative state like Delaware; they did not need the possible bad publicity. His family still had his tavern near the town of Bear, "Mel's Place" it had been called, and he kept up the business as best he could. He applied for social work across the river in New Jersey, and finally located work at an anti-poverty agency in Bridgeton, New Jersey.

A month or so after Pete du Pont's re-election in Delaware, the Bridgeton agency had visitors. Representatives of the Community Action of Greater Wilmington (CAGW), one of the city's largest anti-poverty agencies, were scouting for a new director to help them survive the budget cuts promised by President-elect Ronald Reagan. The head of the Bridgeton agency, William Hallman, had been recommended by state Representative Herman Holloway, a member of the CAGW board. They met Hallman, liked him and asked him to join. When he came, he brought Mel Slawik as his deputy director.

"He has the capabilities I need at this junction," Hallman told an incredulous *News-Journal*, "and he has the background, no doubt about it." The CAGW had been criticized for a lack of competent staff. "Having people like Mel around will at least compensate for that lack."

Mel Slawik was good copy, and the reporters seemed to know what they were expected to write. They ran a story on "The Surprising Return of Slawik," picturing the former county executive standing behind his desk, looking earnest and hopeful.

"Slawik was forced to leave the county executive post in 1976 after being convicted for lying to a federal grand jury investigating corruption in county government," wrote reporter Charles Farrell. "His jury conviction was eventually overturned, but he spent more than six months in jail for obstruction of justice." Hallman was immediately put on the defensive. "We couldn't very well deny Mel Slawik a position because of a previous conviction. That's in the regulations. And he was never convicted of malfeasance. You shouldn't beat a dead horse. He should have the opportunity for employment like everybody else." Slawik, too, was apologetic, and made the mistake of saying that the way he returned to public service in Delaware was "sort of like coming in the back door." He admitted he had some general detractors, but said that, in general, "the reception has been good. Most people are happy to have me back."

Not most people along the Brandywine. They may well have shuddered at his pledge to "develop a better community relationship with a political base. This has to become a viable community agency—supported by the community or it's going to go out of existence." "For this," the reporter wrote, "he said he will be earning around $19,000 a year. CAGW's greatest priority, according to Slawik, is to 'affirm its role in the whole greater Wilmington area. It's thought of as just for Wilmington and there are areas in the suburbs that could use some advocacy.'"

Suburbs? New Castle County? This sounded too much like the old Mel Slawik, and he spoke openly of politics. "I know a lot of politicians," he said, "and have good relations with some, and some not so good relations. But I'm going to have to show the political structure, both Republican and Democrat, that this agency is not partisan. We have to work with everybody." The News-Journal then reported that "Slawik recalled that while he was county executive, he obtained some revenue sharing money that 'kept CAGW alive.' Asked if he missed politics, Slawik said he maintains ties with those in office. 'You're never really out of politics.'" The paper printed his disclaimer of any intention of running for elected office and the U.S. Attorney's assurance he could not because of his felony conviction.[99]

Eleven months passed, during which Slawik worked hard by all accounts, helping Hallman meet the 50 percent slash in federal aid that President Reagan's budget cuts were imposing on poverty agencies across the nation. He secured a new headquarters for CAGW at 2nd and Market Streets, property sure to appreciate in value as part of the area adjoining the Christina Gateway, the focus of GWDC plans for downtown real estate development, including a projected new building for the new Delaware branch of Citibank. And he avoided getting involved in the renewed controversy over County Executive Richard Collins's refusal to tax industrial and commercial fixtures.

The issue had resurfaced due to the efforts of the Citizens Coalition for Tax Reform led by Ted Keller and Mark Haskell of the University of Delaware's College of Urban Affairs. It was a replay of the Slawik days, with the same battle lines drawn between the same contenders, with one notable absentee—Mel Slawik. Pressured by the State Chamber of Commerce, Collins confirmed that his "administration is not considering and has not ever considered imposing a fixtures tax in New Castle County."[100] Councilman James Farly introduced a protective resolution that became the subject of objections by the Citizens Coalition, but the *News-Journal* failed even to report it, although a reporter was present. Meanwhile, a $2 million contract for property value reassessments was about to go to a familiar name, Cole-Layer-Trumble, since 1975 under new ownership, Day and Zimmerman, Inc., a Philadelphia engineering firm. "This isn't the old CLT," said vice-president Joseph La Sala. The new CLT, however, had shown a novel way of winning friends: When Ted Keller, testifying for the County Council, associated the new CLT with the old CLT's reputation of "deception, incompetence, and favoritism to the affluent and large industrial property owners,"[102] it threatened to sue him and the Coalition.[103] Keller was obliged to make a retraction, but a storm of protest by property owners and real estate agents sent the CLT contract down to defeat in November, 1981, by a Council facing reelection.

Through it all, Slawik had been concentrating instead on plans for CAGW to buy a grocery store to provide food at low prices, an apartment building for low-income housing, and a policeman's lodge for conversion into a half-way house for released prisoners. Many of the participants in these programs would be Hispanics or Blacks; the latter alone made up 50 percent of Wilmington's population and endured a high rate of unemployment. Slawik, as an associate of one of the state's principal Black leaders, Rep. Herman Holloway, would be organizing programs that could give CAGW his proposed "political base" among a community living in an area slated for real estate development. The contradiction with Irénée du Pont's plans for the Christina Gateway or lawyer Irving Shapiro's call for a "financial center" or even Governor du Pont's program to make Delaware "the Luxembourg of the United States for banking and finance" need not be emphasized. Suffice it to say it was not the kind of activity in downtown Wilmington that fit a conservative white-collar image.

The attack, nevertheless, came from an unexpected place: the office of the CAGW. But its deliverer was familiar enough: the *News-Journal*.

A little more than a month after CLT's bid for property reassessments was rejected, a story appeared in the paper about Community Action of Greater Wilmington, the anti-poverty agency responsible for administering federal money for residential weatherproofing that winter, and Head Start pre-kindergarten and community nutrition programs. It cited financial records that allegedly showed the agency had only $5600 left of a $118,000 federal Community Service Administration grant to run programs through December. The records were "released after a six-hour meeting of the executive board and read publicly by treasurer Elmer Fitchett." "How could this happen?" one of CAGW's board members was quoted saying.

The situation was reported as scandalous: over $145,000 in debts, including $45,000 due since November; misappropriated funds; overspending. Identifying his source as "a member of the committee at the meeting," reporter Michael Jackson, a recent young arrival from Philadelphia, wrote that a request had been made that Hallman resign, but the motion had been defeated. He also reported that as soon as the report was read, "the board went into executive session that may have been in violation of the state Freedom of Information Act."[104] Meanwhile, Jackson kept his own source secret.

Later it was revealed to be CAGW's comptroller, Richard Thompson, a man who as a vice-president of Delaware Trust had pleaded guilty in 1970 to embezzlement and was given psychiatric care in lieu of jail. Slawik had collided with Thompson over the latter's absenteeism and wanted him to resign or dock his pay. Thompson thought that unfair, especially since Hallman, the director, was often absent from the office for days of the week, keeping in touch by phone and making decisions. Slawik had not been happy with Hallman, either, and proposed he take a leave of absence. Hallman refused, insisting on making key decisions that undoubtedly led to mismanagement. Thompson, however, had no sympathies for Slawik, and began feeding reporter Jackson stories about huge financial deficits and wild spending. In fact, there were no huge deficits.

The next article, on December 18, was more focused. Headlined SLAWIK HAD ANTI-POVERTY AGENCY PLACE STORM WINDOWS ON HIS HOME, the article began by reporting that Slawik "ordered" employees of CAGW to install storm windows on his home "in apparent violation of federal regulations that required documentation that the home was eligible for the program." The article was completely misleading. Slawik had asked Robert Hall, director of planning, to inquire if it would be proper for him to give several employees work by hiring them out of his own pocket for the job; he ordered no one. Later Hall affirmed it was all right. The federal regulation, of course, applied only to homes which were weatherized with federal funds. Jackson did not point that out; nor did his editors; but the article did point out Slawik's removal from office in 1976 "after his conviction on federal perjury charges." It also failed to mention the reversal by the appeals court, but did not fail to mention his serving time in prison, and repeated the charges of wild spending. Unidentified "sources" were alleged to have said both Hallman and Slawik had lost their hiring and firing powers because of "the financial woes."[105]

Slawik by now had grimly realized that not only was Jackson's reportage inaccurate, but the *News-Journal* editors were apparently allowing it to happen. He also suspected that he was being made the goat for the destruction of not only his programs, but the CAGW itself.

A week later, the *News-Journal* unleashed another salvo, picturing CAGW's Richard Thompson rubbing his eyes as Slawik addressed a meeting. Hallman and Slawik were reported allowed to "cling" to their posts by a tie vote during a meeting "called because immense financial problems at the agency have led to a deficit of more than $100,000."[106]

Slawik's corrections on Jackson's stories, submitted later in a formal complaint to the National News Council in New York, were by now as voluminous as the articles, and others in the Wilmington community shared his concern, contacting the paper. On December 27, Public Editor Harry Themal, holding a post that is supposed to represent the public, not management, responded that "those friends must be hard-pressed to defend Slawik and his associates when the anti-poverty agency where he is second in command has overspent its available funds by more than $100,000." After repeating the false charge, Themal then recounted Slawik's jailing "after pleading guilty to obstruction of justice in a federal probe of county government corruption. Some people in the community," Themal conceded, "and Slawik himself, felt the newspapers had hounded the government into pursuing him. That contention was and is ridiculous because prosecutors and judges are influenced by evidence, not newspaper stories."[107] Which, of course, was why the prosecutor and the judge and an inflamed jury in Slawik's only trial were ultimately reversed.

What happened next was predictable. Five days after Christmas, County Executive Richard Collins halted all payments of federal aid to CAGW. The money suspended included not only a $60,000 grant for weatherproofing poor people's homes in the community that winter, but also $30,000 to train unemployed residents in the weatherproofing skills. The staff, including Slawik, was laid off.

Governor du Pont's Administration also stepped in to halt any payments of a $260,000 federal grant scheduled to be funneled through the state Office of Economic Opportunity. Wilmington Mayor William McLaughlin also froze funds.

Governor du Pont established a task force of the three levels of government, headed by cousin Nathan Hayward, to investigate. The *News-Journal,* encouraged, froze minds with a chilling editorial charging that "squanderers" had "spent thousands of unbudgeted dollars on fancy meals, travel, personal phone calls and the hiring of good buddies." A "comfortable surplus of $150,000" had "in just a few months" become a $100,000 deficit. "The director and his assistants abused the public trust," and the editorial questioned "how they were able to get away with this abuse month after month." Praising the funding freeze, the *News-Journal* insisted that authorities "place the agency in federal receivership. Do that at once."[108]

MORE HEADS ROLL AT CAGW[109] ran the headline the next day, although no one had already been fired to account for the "more." That, however, did not stop Jackson from mistakenly reporting the establishment of a committee to oversee operations that had already existed, or the *News-Journal* from printing a photo of Slawik and Thompson, their hands to their faces, with a caption alleging they were in a "huddle at back of meeting room." The insinuation was obvious. Slawik was somehow in cahoots with Thompson, who had just been fired along with Hallman. In reality, Slawik was not fired, nor were he and Thompson talking to each other at the time. The photograph actually shows Slawik standing in front of Thompson, his back to him, his hand on his chin, while Thompson is adjusting his glasses. Neither is acknowledging the other. But Mel Slawik's reputation and career had once again been ruined.

On January 11, the *News-Journal* cartoonist imaginatively drew a carton of eggs labeled "Community Action of Greater Wilmington" and the caption, "You start with a couple of bad ones, then you have to throw them all out." By February, CAGW's new headquarters on Market Street was under attack; the paper charged it had apparently been bought illegally. But comments by lawyers quoted in the article, CAGW boardmember Gary Hindes wrote *News-Journal* Executive Editor Sydney Hurlbert, indicated that was a groundless charge. Hindes asserted that the *News-Journal's* "Jackson and (Hugh) Cutler are continuing to malign CAGW."[110] Yes, Hugh Cutler had never left after the Thursday Night Massacre of 1975. He had indeed found his niche.

"This is a story of how a newspaper destroyed an agency," wrote the President of the New Castle County Council on March 7, 1982. An audit of CAGW showed a surplus of $49,000. "Unfortunately, the damage has already been done: CAGW has lost all credibility in the community; staff people have been fired; reputations have been ruined; and vital services to the poor and needy have gotten lost in the shuffle."

"Freedom of the press is a right we hold sacred; but with this right is the obligation to print the truth."[111]

It was the first time that the *News-Journal* had done so—as a letter to the editor.

Mel Slawik had less luck with his June, 1982, letter of complaint to the National News Council. Associate Director of the Council Richard Cunningham wrote back suggesting Slawik avail himself of the good services of Public Editor Harry Themal. Cunningham had called the *News-Journal* for background and concluded Themal's columns, acknowledging unfairness, had given "you your day in court."[112] Slawik pressed his complaint, asking the newspaper to acknowledge it was wrong and apologize, asking Themal for the memo of concern he told Cunningham he had sent to the paper's editors (Themal refused on the grounds of confidentiality) and asking three more times for help from the News Council.

But Mel Slawik had indeed had his day in court, the National News Council repeated.

Only then did Slawik notice the name of the Council's Chairman and now "Senior Advisor": Norman Isaacs, the former president of the *News-Journal*.

On December 16, 1982, the Governor's Task Force filed its report on CAGW. It expressed its concern about the CAGW staff's "lateness of the (CAGW) board notification of the proposed acquisition and impending purchase" of the Market Street property, and admonished the CAGW for poor management and "the substantial investment of time and money it has taken to help identify and alleviate the problem which this agency has encountered...."[113]

The Market Street property charge bothered CAGW board member June Eisley the most. "I can't help but wonder what kind of job the Task Force did if it could make a statement like that," she wrote its chairman, Nathan Hayward III. "On what information was this statement made? I know it wasn't true when I read it so I went back through all my old minutes and am enclosing parts of the minutes from February, March, May and June of 1981, which document that the Board had been in on the entire transaction starting at that time." She took offense at the report's admonition about money and time spent by its members. "If anyone had *listened* to those of us who knew what had happened and tried to explain it at the very beginning, no one would have had to spend money or your time on a task force.... Gary Hindes said, basically, last January what it took a whole year of audits and investigations to prove. The problem was, in my opinion, that too many people in authority wanted to believe the allegations; and many, in fact, wanted the agency to die."[114]

Eisley represented the President of the New Castle County Council on the CAGW board, which barely survived the ordeal without funding. She was furious over what had been done to the agency and, after waiting two months to hear from Hayward, let the governor know it, sending him a copy of her correspondence to his representative on the Task Force, asking him to read it. "I always had the feeling that politics was involved in the Task Force," Eisley wrote du Pont, "and its final report, along with the aggravation that CAGW encountered because of the needless, held-up funding by the State for months upon months, reinforced my suspicions. It was very discouraging for me to see political game-playing when the survival of New Castle County's official anti-poverty agency, whose business is helping poor people, was involved."[115]

But the governor had other people on his mind that month. Earlier, in his January "state of the state" address he had already made his gesture to the poor. He spoke with compassion before the legislature when he announced increased state aid to families with dependent children would begin in January, 1984. Real compassion, some argued, would not allow those needy to starve another year before granting them relief. And his solemn tone contrasted with an administration that had, in fact, done little for the plight of the needy in six long years. Social Services still suffered from his budget cuts, while he continued to press for tax breaks for upper incomes and corporations. Since the year of his reelection, 1980, the percentage of the state's general fund contributed by corporate income taxes also declined by 20 percent, from 1979's $50.2 million to 1982's $40.4 million.[116]

Pete's ally—or rather, mentor—in this effort was Irving Shapiro. Since chairing his last Du Pont annual meeting in April, 1981, Shapiro had been turning his attention to Delaware. This was no conflict with his role as chairman of Du Pont's finance committee. After helping Jefferson with the Conoco merger and settling the Bronfman affair, he found the Du Ponts shared his interest in other mergers and fields of investment beyond the chemical company, and their views on Delaware's future had long coincided.

"I want to make Delaware a financial services center," he said, and saw his captaining of Du Pont's finances, including the huge capital represented by Du Pont and Conoco's combined assets, as, in league with the Du Ponts, a powerful tool to shape Delaware to their latest perspective. He found his allies among the family not to have changed: Irénée du Pont, Jr., still represented the family's major voice in the affairs of the company as well as Delaware's business community through the State Chamber of Commerce. Eleuthère du Pont remained the guardian of the family's thrust into the money markets and its fledgling interest in Crown Central Petroleum; Irving retaining his seat on Continental American Life Insurance's board; Edward du

Pont maintained his role as quiet keeper of the keys to the family treasure, the trust department of Wilmington Trust; and Pete du Pont continued expanding his reach over the family's political networks, succeeding to the power of his uncle, Reynolds du Pont, in state affairs and now easily reaching beyond.

At Du Pont, Conoco's fiercely independent oilmen proved more troublesome to absorb than the more powerful Bronfmans. The latter quietly took their seats at Du Pont's board and watched, were pleasant; and at the finance committee, Edgar or Charles would listen carefully, ask questions, and learn—always learn. With the oil men, however, it was rough at first; resentments had to be soothed, self interests appealed to, curiosity stoked. The Steelworkers aroused everyone's interest, although their organizing efforts seemed a faint rumor, a whisper in the night. The ram horns of an earlier age of labor were simply not heard within Jericho. Occasionally a small legion would be assembled at Employees Relations and dispatched to do battle with video displays, lectures, a leaflet of facts, a dark word of advice, but the local garrisons were doing well in the provinces. All seemed secure, especially if the windows were kept shut, the cries not heard, the fear not felt. Just DU PONT...Better things...Du Pont...There's a whole world...Du Pont. The organization predominant.

"We have no arbitration. That's what kills us," said Glen Ferguson. He was the grievance chairman of his union at Du Pont's Newport pigments plant. He filed 147 grievances in 1981 and was surprised now, in June of 1982, that management refused to come to an agreement on safety. He already had won his test case. A supervisor could not order a woman to perform a job she believed unsafe. Yet the "symbol put on automatic shutoff equipment had come down, replaced by restraints, then locked barriers ordered by upper management," he said. Recently, he had been barred from bringing his union files into the lunch room as usual; to do his grievance filing, he now had to miss lunch. "I'm not allowed to go on the plant to solicit or investigate grievances," he charged, "but when I'm at work, I'm not allowed out of my area without permission. That stops the union cold."[117]

Plant manager Frank Bredemus could not understand. "We attempt to deal fairly and responsibly with the union. If we are not responsive, then we're not doing our job." Ferguson, he insisted, was allowed three hours per week for grievance work. "Perhaps Glen is not typical of how the employees view the system."[118]

Carl De Martino, Jefferson's vice-president for employee relations, assured that the system of 3300 national union members out of 25,000 workers meant Du Pont and the worker were spared the "open charade" of national unions. "Du Pont doesn't bargain like the national unions. Our method is that we talk and take all the inputs . . . and we make an offer, but our offer is a reasonable one."

"We just have to like what is given," affirmed Ferguson.

"It isn't that we don't want unions," explained De Martino. "We don't want anybody in the middle of that [employee-supervisor] relationship. Our goal is to start them non-union and maintain them non-union."[119]

Two years before Edward Escue took issue with De Martino on the need for unions. "As a Du Pont employee of 16 years and arbitrator for the local independent union at the Old Hickory, Tennessee, plant, I have been involved in four discharge cases within the last two years. An impartial arbitrator ruled those employees were discharged unjustly. Two of these people had over 13 years with the company. Had there not been a union to protest and arbitrate, these Du Ponters would no longer be with the company. How would they get their share of this 'fair and equitable treatment?'"[120]

It had been the rallying cry, but not in harmony; pro-union highs at plants lowered; others which had been low, rose. There was unity of purpose, but not of motion or pace; no orchestra, just a small band of organizers racing to play in tune against the cacaphony around them, missing a beat here, a note there, and almost always met with a deafening silence in the South, where high local wages lulled one to sleep, numb to conditions and strange things called unions. When there seemed to be an awakening, bolts of fear sufficed for reason, raising spectres of long lines of grim payless strikers, enslaved by "labor bosses." And there was always the (Du Pont) family company or the company (Du Ponter) family, or flattery to youth too schooled to accept, at least for now, the leaders of "big labor," rejecting organizers for being too political or not political enough.

But always the result was the same, and when the vote was finally called, the defeat was worse than expected: Chattanooga, 1146 against, 961 for; Kingston, North Carolina, 1183 against, 681 for; and on it went, 14 plants in all, most of them in the South, with a Carl De Martino who could say, "I don't think geography makes any difference."

It was a decisive moment in the history of American labor and an encouragement to an anti-union White House. For as long as the South remained the bastion of cheap labor, all job security would be threatened, all labor cheapened. The Du Pont defeat broke the stride of recent union gains in the South, and broke the back of labor's most significant organizing drive in a generation. "We granted the Du Pont workers," said the National organizer John Oshinski, "the opportunity to throw off Du Pont's total control of their working lives. The majority chose to turn down the opportunity. This hard-fought campaign has now been concluded."[121] It was all he had to offer the vanquished; for the victor, this, too, was a feast.

Later, there would be calls for continuing, and Oshinski would waver before dropping away, leaving the Du Pont workers to their fate.

It was swift in coming.

"We're working under worse conditions now than we have in years," said Fred Durham, vice-president of the Newport local, as he and other off-duty workers picketed in front of Du Pont Headquarters. "We decided our only action is to go public."[122] Funeral leave had been reduced to a day. Union activities were being considered in work evaluations, they charged, in violation of federal labor law. Asbestos in the plant's insulation was causing sickness, cancers. Workers handing out handbills about labor rights were filmed and surveilled by Du Pont, also in violation of federal labor protection laws.

"When you think about it, if you don't believe the individual counts," Jefferson told a *Delaware Today* writer, six months before the Steelworkers' vote, "then things get very defeatist. There's no reason for even trying."[123]

"They've done everyone in," Fred Durham reported just two weeks later of an exposure of 30 employees at the Newport plant to deadly high-level polychlorinated biphenyls (PCBs). The production of PCBs had been banned by federal laws several years ago. But on December 1, 1982, six weeks after one of seven trial runs to produce a yellow pigment that looked like dry pancake matter, "one of our chemists, in looking at the process that we were running, got the idea that we could be making PCB."[124] The dust from the batter had been inhaled by the workers in concentrations of just over 50 parts per million, the EPA limit, to almost 700 parts. Even 50 parts were dangerous, according to Philip Bierbaum of the National Institute for Occupational Safety and Health in Cincinatti. "We believe that the PCB's based on animal studies are very toxic,"[125] causing cancer, liver damage, reproduction problems and skin diseases. Nevertheless, Du Pont manager David Willete insisted that calculations indicated the workers had not been exposed to any health hazards. None of the men were wearing respirators.

There were also reports of direct contact with the material in liquid form during clean-ups. Willete denied any attempt was made to dry out the PCB from its original liquid form or to shovel it out. But Ara Histed, who attended the grievance meeting, said workers involved in the contamination cleanup described attempts to dry out the remaining four batches of liquid matter. "After it plugged the machine, they tried to liquify it again and that's when it spilled out.... So they had to shovel it.... It spilled on the men's shoes.... They still wear the same shoes." The PCBs sloshed out of 55-gallon drums and spilled onto about 30 workers. Supervisors told them it was PCB, "but they did not explain to them what it was." A laundry worker at the plant stated that "as far as I'm concerned anybody that washed their clothes in the plant laundry has been exposed to the stuff." The worker asked that his name not be used because he feared losing his job.[126]

"The Occupational Safety and Health Administration has been a disaster," asserted Irving Shapiro. "You don't create a safe environment for workers by having inspectors going around and fining factories. By the time he left the office, I had the Secretary of Labor [under Carter] pretty well convinced that he was on the wrong track. I wouldn't quarrel with a suitable program that focused on education, not penalties."[127]

Shapiro was working hard to remove such penalties, and he was getting paid very well for doing so. At Du Pont, for example, his legal counsel on regulations, finance and other matters grossed an income between May, 1981, and December, 1981, of $70,000.[128] Each day he stopped off at Du Pont Headquarters and then walked the block and a half to his new office at Skadden, Arps's Wilmington offices. Skadden had a team of 14 lawyers there, but Shapiro was the star. He liked and admired merger-master Joe Flom. Skadden, with an army of 300 lawyers, was in the vanguard of law firms adopting business practices and Shapiro had already gotten the firm to set up a corporate-style chief executive to administer the firm rather than practice law, examining data on office expansion, long-term planning for areas of practice, day-to-day operations, and hiring needs. In the last category, Shapiro was opposed to wasting talent and time invested by laying off failed prospectees for partnership after seven years, which is traditional in law. Both Flom and Shapiro declined the executive position, there being more interest and money in practicing law. And Shapiro practices it well, representing such clients as Occidental Petroleum and Mead Corporation.

Shapiro was now trying to jettison English common law, the backbone of American law. For Mead, for example, Shapiro lobbied senators with Griffin Bell to push through a bill freeing corporate clients from the threat of huge fines levied for fixing prices. The law currently stipulates triple damages on total damages by all conspirators, a time-honored common-law doctrine of the "joint and several liability" of co-conspirators.[129] The bill, sponsored by arch-conservative Senator Strom Thurmond (whose seniority has secured for him the chair of the powerful Senate Judiciary Committee), would permit a "right of combination" whereby a company can sue for damages another conspirator who has not settled a claim, or damages only in proportion to their share of the sales at issue, effectively eliminating triple-damage. Even a 100 percent damage, then, would be limited by the share of the market affected.

Shapiro, said Joe Flom, "is especially good at figuring out what kind of government reaction we might get to a particular business action, whether it is in energy, anti-trust or securities. I think it's been an easy transition for him."[130]

In energy, Shapiro was Du Pont's architect, steering the company into a series of alliances with energy companies. He had no use for Carter's energy policies, although he liked the step toward a concerted national energy program. "On the energy issue," he once remarked sharply, "I must say that if we ran this business the way the President and Congress have tried to deal with this problem, we'd be tossed out pretty quickly."[131] Whether he meant that literally for Carter, despite his public support for his re-election, is unknown. But more than one political analyst noted the presence of Shapiro's heir apparent, Edward Jefferson, on candidate Reagan's energy advisory team during his race against Carter.

The snaring of Conoco for the Du Ponts was not Shapiro's only great achievement in energy, although it is probably the crowning one. He also is a legal adviser to Bechtel Corporation, a leading constructor of nuclear power plants. In May, 1982, at the Annual Meeting, Shapiro faced one of his only public moral dramas as chairman when he was confronted by ten church groups calling for an end to Du Pont's running of the government's Savannah River Plant, the country's only producer of plutonium for atomic weapons.

The origins of the SRP go back to the Manhattan Project, the secret program to make the first atomic bomb, which involved Du Pont Company and particularly family in-law Crawford Greenewalt. Du Pont's performance during the war involved, incidentally, the Chambers Works in Deepwater, New Jersey, where radioactive residue is still embedded in buildings, raising some serious legal damages questions about the health of workers exposed there to long-term radioactivity. Du Pont had not informed post-war workers of the potential dangers of working at certain sites in Chambers. But it is probably indemnified from damages of lawsuits by the contract it signed with the U.S. Government during World War II, which specifically stipulates that the Du Pont Company will be free of all obligations and that everything will fall on the shoulders of Washington. President Roosevelt, in fact, signed a special executive order to this effect under the First War Powers Act protecting Du Pont from the laws of the United States.

It was President Harry Truman's reluctance to do likewise, documents show, that delayed Du Pont's participation in the Savannah River Plant.

Contrary to the publicity that Du Pont's public relations office has put out for over thirty years, Du Pont did not patriotically jump to the president's call to help set up the SRP. In fact, there was quite a delay, from July 2,

1950, when President Truman first wrote Du Pont, to October 17, 1950, when Greenewalt deemed to respond after Du Pont had gotten out of the president what it wanted. This delay came despite the inflated sense of urgency about developing the hydrogen bomb during those days of the Korean War and the first Soviet atomic explosion.

The search for a site for the new atomic plant was still going on by the Atomic Energy Commission when its chairman, Gordon Dean, wrote President Truman on September 27, 1950, and informed him that Du Pont Company insisted on having the president's personal approval. This was not merely for corporate propaganda purposes, but for protection of Du Pont from any suits by individuals or corporations.

"In view of the hazards and uncertainties in the work and the fact that the Company will perform the work for a fee of one dollar, the Company feels that it must have any additional protection which might be afforded by specific action of the President pursuant to section 12(b) quoted above."[132]

The section referred to the Atomic Energy Act which had an exemption, Dean noted, "similar in many respects to the exemption provided in the First War Powers Act."[133] The statute exempts, by presidential order, "any specific action of the Commission in a particular matter from the provisions of law relating to contracts whenever he determines such action is essential in the interest of the common defense and security." Du Pont's cooperation was considered essential for the nation's defense and security. If the only way the government could get it was to sign a special presidential exemption of provisions of contract law for the AEC's contract with Du Pont, the president had no choice. He had to sign. The Du Ponts knew this when they insisted he do so.

The key provision, as Dean wrote White House Counsel Frank Murphy, had to do with such matters as storage and spills or other accidental releases of radioactive materials, including even a nuclear accident. During the Manhattan Project, "The contract contained an indemnity clause holding the Company harmless against any losses, expenses, or liabilities of any kind except caused directly by bad faith or willful misconduct on the part of some corporate officer or officers of the company."

"... The Company feels that it can be assured of substantially this kind of protection only by action of the President..."[134]

The AEC attempted to convince the Du Ponts that the AEC had full powers to enter the cost reimbursement contract and that no other company on the project had insisted on the extraordinary presidential exemptions.[135]

Furthermore, Du Pont's real concern was money.... "It is clear," wrote Dean to White House Counsel Frank Murphy, "that the principal legal problem raised by the Du Pont Company is the problem of the legality of a commitment contingent in nature but necessarily unlimited as to amount which may involve future appropriations."[136] The question was the extent of the government's obligation if any legal action should ensue from Du Pont's work. Du Pont wanted to be absolutely sure that it had no obligations; everything would be borne by the taxpayer.

Du Pont selected the Savannah River site. From the beginning it was expected that "the new AEC plant, while having a primarily military purpose at this time, will add to the nation's capacity for producing fuels which someday will be needed to utilize atomic energy for useful power. If the new facilities are not needed for defense, they can produce fuel for industry."[137] Two hundred sixty million dollars was initially appropriated. Families living there were moved out.

Workers who were moved in were not adequately protected. Du Pont, according to Dr. William Norwood, a former Chambers Works employee, was the only one of five major nuclear production facilities that would not cooperate with the National Transuranium Registry in Hanford, Washington, a clearinghouse and research center for the health of nuclear workers. Du Pont was not informing its workers that the Registry wanted to perform autopsies on their bodies when they died, and was refusing to give adequate information to Norwood so the Registry could identify people poisoned by plutonium. Du Pont's plant manager admitted to Allendale (S.C.) *County Citizen* reporter Patrick Tyler that Du Pont was not informing workers of all the dangers of plutonium. Du Pont, the manager conceded, "Should not have been as positive" in telling workers their health was not threatened by minute quantities of plutonium, as long-term effects are unknown. About 350 Du Pont workers had traces of plutonium in their urine, the "great majority" with traces less than five percent of the permissible federal level.[138]

Du Pont's amoral position on plutonium production contrasts strangely with its confidence in SRP's waste disposal system. By 1988, a new plant is scheduled to be in operation to solidify high-level waste; it will be subsequently shipped to a federal mined geologic repository. Hydraulic mining of wastes from existing tanks will also be provided by the new plant. The seepage basins were originally constructed assuming only shallow migration of radioactive wastes. Since then it is shown that seepage continues downward into acquifers and does not "seep out" into shallow groundwater only. How much contamination has already occurred is unknown, but the Tuscaloosa aquifer's contamination has already been confirmed by the SRP.[139] The SRP reactors do not have containment covers to prevent massive amounts of contamination from entering the air. The Three-Mile Island release would have been much more serious if civilian reactors had not been required to have domes. Already releases of krypton 85, a fission product, from SRP have contributed to changes in the electrical properties of the atmosphere that affect weather.[140] Furthermore, the arms race and increase in military spending for nuclear weapons has increased plutonium production and radioactive waste at SRP.[141] Millions of gallons of this waste are stored at the facility, awaiting a federal decision on how and where to store them permanently.[142] The Reagan Administration has authorized the rehaul of an old L-reactor which was scheduled to pump radioactive wastes into the Savannah River until environmentalists won a temporary restraining order.[143] Senator Strom Thurmond, an advocate of increased defense spending, is a frequent visitor to Du Pont's SRP. The SRP is the sole producer of all weapons-grade plutonium made in the western hemisphere.

Jefferson leaped to the SRP's defense in September, 1982, to attack a *News-Journal* report by Joe Trento on a blood disease, polycythemin vera, that has struck the town of Ellenton, S.C., at 500 times the national rate. The town's disease, Jefferson pointed out, has never been known to be triggered by radiation. But Trento's article revealed a dislike of Du Pont's power by area residents almost as potent as the disease, as well as a statement by Dr. Carl J. Johnson, a Denver expert on nuclear illnesses, who said he was privy to a secret report on radiation emissions at Savannah River and claimed, "they have been much greater than reported to the public. . . ."[144]

Du Pont's involvement in the secrets of atomic warfare probably had much to do with its advanced security consciousness and played a role not only in Greenewalt's rise in the company but in his contacts within the intelligence community through Radio Free Europe's board of corporate sponsors, the Free Europe Committee, of which he was chairman in the early 1960's.[145] One unfortunate sidelight to the work of this committee of respected businessmen was its use of Boy Scouts to distribute the "Truth Broadcasting" pamphlets of the CIA-controlled Radio Free Europe in home towns across the nation. Out of the Manhattan Project also came James Moore, assistant professor of chemistry at the University of Delaware. Moore was involved in the CIA's mind-control drug research, known as Project MK-ULTRA. Moore was a key contact for the CIA with a prominent chemical company president who supplied the CIA with drugs.[146]

In 1967, Greenewalt joined in ceremonies in Chicago marking the 25th anniversary of the first self-sustained nuclear chain reaction, which he had witnessed when Enrico Fermi pulled the rods that changed human destiny. By 1979, Du Pont was the second largest AEC contractor, with $124.9 million in contracts.[147]

The SRP, according to its external affairs officer, James Gaver, has sold heavy water (D_2O) for the past 25 years to a number of foreign countries, including Argentina, Brazil, Taiwan, India, Pakistan, Spain, West Germany, Israel, and the kingdom of apartheid, South Africa.[148] Other SRP products, including radioisotopes, amercium (for oil exploration and home smoke detectors), plutonium-238 (used in the space program and cardiac pacemakers), Californium-252 (cancer therapy, natural resource exploration), uranium-233, cobalt-244 and cobalt 60,[149] end up being used by private companies. Du Pont used to disclaim having any significant commercial relations to SRP products, but in light of the increased use of radioactive materials in so many of its specialty lines, and now by New England Nuclear and Conoco, an update in its brochures is obviously needed. The relations, if not primary, are surely secondary. When Conoco's large uranium reserves are plugged in, the cycle from ore to product is complete. Conoco has one of the largest uranium holdings in the United States, with sizeable holdings in Niger, Africa, as well, Does Conoco sell uranium to the SRP. The SRP denies it. But it does admit that New England Nuclear sells products to the SRP. SRP thereby becomes a market for Du Pont.

The Du Pont family owns holdings in companies like Long Island Lighting Company (a favorite of Eleuthère I. du Pont's Sigma Trust Shares for years) and Delmarva Power and Light (which had large stocks in the Peachbottom and Salem nuclear plants of the Delaware-Southeastern Pennsylvania-Southern New Jersey areas and more scheduled at Summit) made nuclear power an irradiated apple in the family's eye. Irving Shapiro, furthermore, had joined in Pete du Pont's promotion of nuclear plants in the area, titling one major speech before he retired, "We Need *More* Nuclear Power," while quietly, in August, 1983, taking an advisory post for Bechtel, one of the nation's largest builders of nuclear power plants, including Salem.

Everyone at the 1982 Annual Meeting, then, showed courtesy to the speaker and a somberness at his words when a Du Pont chemist backed the proposal of the ten clergy groups and deplored "a policy of actually laying plans which could incinerate several hundred million people." It was a sobering moment. So was the next when over 15,000 shares for the resolution were squashed by 180,000,000 shares cast by the family and guests. Jefferson had by then passed the ultimate test as chairman of a Du Pont annual meeting. Evelyn Davis, perennial gadfly, suggested the Bronfmans "throw out the whole top management of Du Pont. It couldn't be any worse."

"Thank you, Mrs. Davis," Jefferson replied in his English baritone, and cut the time to three minutes on each matter to a sustained and appreciated applause. Before it was over, W.W. Laird and Rodney Sharp, Jr., had announced their retirement from the board, and more than one stockholder commented that now there were just two Du Ponts to every Bronfman.

Edgar and Charles Bronfman had definitely emerged out of the wars as the charmed princes. There had to be admiration for any brothers' family who managed in just two years to double the assets of their business, especially when the figures were from $2.8 billion to $6 billion. Seagram's net income had swollen from $145 million to $1.6 billion, all because Seagram had shed its Texas Pacific Oil Company, booked at $500 million, for $2.3 billion in cash and Sunoco notes, then borrowed $2.6 billion against the notes to acquire 32 percent of Conoco and then traded that in for 20 percent of Du Pont. That 20 percent tucks away some of Du Pont's earnings into Seagram's books and allows the Bronfmans to enjoy a steady $120 million diet. And the Bronfmans were not put off from taking their 25 percent by Du Pont's drop to $35 from the $54 a share they had paid. Such tendered tithes, they believed, are seldom wrought from heaven.

The Du Ponts knew what that meant. Edgar could borrow against ten years of cash flow and confront them at the end of his standstill with another $1 billion.

If so, the Du Ponts might not resist; such Cheshires are hard to bag. For with each acquisition the Du Ponts made for stock, Edgar's share would fall. And if it fell enough, below 20 percent, he would have to come hat in hand to the Brandywine merely to hold on to the equity accounting of his holding. So they will digest and divest, but not as much as they had planned, for the ace is Du Pont, and they have a winning hand—if only they hold on to it. Meanwhile, they will continue to diversify, but use the company to do it. Par the debt and secure the pension until a prospect comes by. And always, always, watch for the bank which can be lured into the lair.

For that task, they had Irving and Pierre. Irving might end playing Kissinger to Pete's Rockefeller. But it would have to be an austere Rockefeller, smiling and compassionate, but cheap. For the longest postwar period of expansion was over with Carter and Iran, and now the deficits must be met.

Pete's speeches were appropriate for such times, never too far ahead to scare, or too far behind to bore. Twenty-two million dollar deficits persuade one to lay off, to make cuts to match the recession's decline in revenues. As interest rates decline, borrow to keep afloat, and even a bonded raft takes off like a speedboat when an economy surges.

The key was productivity, and Pete knew it. He wrote a speech on it, "Retooling the Workforce," delivered before curious members of the National Press Club. He satiated their curiosity with points so accurate you would think they were written by an Irving Shapiro. Even the monetarist's cautions were there, warning against "Congress's attempts to throw money" at the problems "with extended unemployment benefits that cushion the blow rather than offering a hope for a better job." Jobs were the central theme, based on retraining and retooling. But remembering his wife at AID's* new Bureau of Private Enterprise, he wisely avoided mention of reconquering markets.

Elise, too, had a role to play, and her Wawa chain store fortune and her raised children assured it would no longer be confined to the home. She had dabbled in real estate, then was accepted into the University of Pennsylvania, and ignored the crude comments that she could only have gotten in through her husband's family. True, Du Ponts had bequeathed endowments and sat as trustees of the University. And true, she was only one of 25 admitted under a new policy that looked upon intellectual ability as based on "achievements" and "potential" rather than test scores. Yes, she had mediocre grades at Bryn Mawr and poor scores in her law school entrance exam. But it had been 20 years since she had done undergraduate work and left her home in Wawa, Pennsylvania, for Delaware. Dean Louis Pollak understood. So did Assistant Dean Arnold Miller. And that was that.

A year or so in a Wilmington law firm likewise shows experience and potential, enough to be appointed as head of a new federal agency designed to reflect the Reagan commitment "to increased opportunities for the private sector in AID programs," said AID's M. Peter McPherson, the author of "Altruism Pays Dividends." If Elise was confused about her role or lack of experience in development matters, the name could always help: "Bureau for Private Enterprise." "Before I resigned," said Dr. Eugene Babb, AID's former top agricultural development official, "I had a number of meetings with Elise. She was very noncommittal. She had no clear idea of what she wanted to do or what the Administration wanted to do."[150] Babb had resigned along with Dr. Stephen Joseph, AID's top health official, and many others who refused to go along with Ronald Reagan's decision to go ahead and give away baby formula that causes death when mixed with the water of many developing countries. The Reagan Administration had been the only government to vote against the World Health Organization's proposed code for marketing baby formula. The code had been opposed by the Grocery Manufacturers of America and the baby-food corporations. Moved by the fact that millions of infants could die, McPherson tried to get the State Department and the Department of Health and Human Services to abstain, "but the White House demanded a no vote,"[151] Dr. Babb said. He and Dr. Joseph then did the only thing they felt in human decency they could do. They officially exposed the facts and were forced to resign. Many joined them

---

*Agency for International Development.

in protest. Elise du Pont, like McPherson, decided to stay on. To Elise, more was at stake than the lives of children.

What exactly that was was hard for many to fathom. The stakes must have been very high, or perhaps many wanted to think so. In August, 1983, however, there was a glimpse into the future. Elise was being asked to run for Congress. Against an incumbent Democrat. In Delaware.

The incumbent's name is Thomas Carper, and in 1982 he did what many considered impossible. He rode the wave of popular dissatisfaction with Reaganomics right over the wall of $13,500 in Du Pont family donations that Representative Tom Evans had built. The wall was half as high as usual, no doubt dismantled by Evans's own indescretions with an ex-Playboy bunny moonlighting as a rather successful lobbyist for agricultural interests. Now, perhaps, a Du Pont in the flesh, or at least in name, could win back Delaware's lone seat in Congress for the Republicans.

"She is an exceptionally qualified person," said Republican state chairman Jerome Herliky. "I like the idea of her very much."[153]

"A lot of people have been calling Elise," agreed GOP national Committeewoman Priscilla Rakestraw, "sending notes, and calling us about Elise du Pont."[154]

The name has magic in Delaware, like a drug dose for an addict. And Delawareans have been mainlining Du Pont Company, Du Pont wealth, Du Pont family for years.

Could Tom Carper break the spell?

If not, the name of Du Pont will be given national limelight, attracting perhaps even those feminists who believe feminism is voting for a woman, any woman, over a man. It would not be the first time a politician exploited a special interest. And it would help a brand name with instant national recognition in the headlines, while her husband, no longer governor, quietly worked the circuit of contacts he had developed through his chairmanship of GOPAC, established for Republican legislative candidates—and future convention delegates.

An unknown governor from Georgia had done the same, choosing to step down from state office in order to serve the Democratic National Committee, dispensing funds and contacts and endorsements—and winning friends.

To do it right, the candidate must be able to say he has accomplished most of his goals as governor. He must be able to stand on his record, and in American pragmatism, or opportunism, in normal times that means victories more than principles. Pete du Pont never claimed he wanted to be another Lincoln. He just wants to be president.

The speech before the National Press Club on "Retooling the Workplace" was designed to show off presidential qualities. So were Pete's speeches before oil men in Oklahoma, Louisiana and Texas. So were his trips to Chicago, Cleveland, San Francisco and New York to make speeches to bankers. As many Delawareans noticed and commented about in the local press, it seemed whenever the governor was going somewhere on a business trip, he was also making political speeches.

His family, as campaign contributions attest, support him. Most are proud of him. And they like what he has done for—and to—Delaware, and the nation.

Probably the most important accomplishment of Pete du Pont's Administration was what was openly described as the slow gutting of the Glass-Steagall Act. That is the law passed during the New Deal to stop banks from consuming each other in mergers and market raiding across state lines or outside their particular form of banking; it drew a line between commercial banks which take in the public's deposits and give out commercial loans, and investment banks which borrow and lend on credit, underwrite offerings and buy and sell insurance.

Beneath the move for change was the growing liquidity crisis among large banks which had overextended their foreign lending, and were constantly threatened with defaults from the developing countries of the Third World. In the second quarter of 1981, the top ten banks took an 8.1 percent loss on earnings. Mergers by industrial conglomerates also tightened money.

Commercial banks wanted broad powers to become financial conglomerates like American Express and Prudential Insurance and General Electric's multi-billion-dollar finance business. The United States, meaning the American consumer, "is (commercially) overbanked,"[155] claimed Bankers Trust President John Hannon, Jr. Small businesses were succumbing. The American wanted more investment banking, commercial bank giants argued, including fee banking, developing loans to be sold to outside investors, and loans for corporations who were desperate to change federal New Deal laws that prohibited commercial banks from underwriting public securities or corporate securities. By March of 1983 bank lobbyists had handed out $3,425,000 to campaigning congressmen over the previous two years. Four hundred eighty-two senators and representatives received an average $7107 each.[156] Large banks were beginning to more openly skim their customers' accounts. Citibank in May, 1979, for example, offered only 4½ percent annual interest on passbook savings accounts. Inflation was eating dollars nearly twice as fast as regular savings interest. The banks were shortchanging the interest their customers were entitled to by law. The New York State Banking Board's new regulation, based on implementing a 1978 state law, still allowed banks not to tell their depositors of maximum available interest rates.[157]

Likewise, offshore banks "shielded" assets from creditors or competitors and the Internal Revenue Service. "Brass-plate" banks were sold to persons who foolishly bought them in the Bahamas or the Verdes for "status" or "prestige." Jerome Schneider, President of the WFI Corporation of Los Angeles, sold 157 such "banks," 120 for $35,000 each. "Many of the owners alleged that WFI Corporation, reported Associated Press, had misrepresented the potential uses of brass-plate banks. They were unable to make use of these banks because they had neither the extensive bank experience required nor the tremendous financial resources necessary to enter into the sophisticated and complex world of off-shore banking. "We have determined that illegal uses abound and legitimate uses are extremely limited."[158]

Even large "legitimate" banks were suspect. One such case was Citicorp. "In 1982, the SEC's Enforcement Division recommended a civil suit against *Citicorp,* the bank of which *Irving Shapiro* is a director, for failing to disclose to shareholders that $46 million, or 2 percent of pretax earnings between 1974 and 1978, came from *questionable foreign exchange practices.*" (Emphasis added.)[159]

One of these questionable practices is called "parking." It involves transfering foreign exchange positions to shift profits to tax havens such as the Bahamas. Citicorp was involved in this, according to Citicorp executive David Edwards, through its Paris branch, ordering sham transactions of buying, for example, $40 million in French francs, then selling the francs back to Paris at 2 percent higher rate, netting the Bahamas branch a $200,000 profit. Coded messages and postdated trading tickets with artificial exchange rates were just some of the cover-ups used. A Citibank manual warned bankers to be careful about it: "The parking of foreign exchange positions should be kept as inconspicuous as possible."[160]

This way banks, using "offshore" subsidiaries, can cheat the American taxpayer and the IRS. "The IRS allows American corporations like Du Pont to deduct foreign taxes from their U.S. tax liability. But since taxes in Europe were often higher than in the U.S., Citicorp could end up paying more overseas than it could deduct in the U.S. Parking enabled it to manipulate the origin of its profits so that the excess would be shifted to Nassau and taxed at the lower tax rate."[161]

A confidential Management Information System, computerized, measured Citicorps' branches' real performances. Straight out of a Chicago gangland scenario, a second set of books was set up called the Management Profit Report which barred its foreign bank examiners.

Irving Shapiro, it will be recalled, put Governor Pete du Pont and New York bankers together in 1980 during du Pont's re-election campaign to draft the Delaware Financial Center Development Act. By 1983, a host of out-of-state banks and credit card operations had set up in Delaware (mostly in the Wilmington area) to the delight of the governor and his aides, Glenn Kenton and cousin Nathan Hayward III. Among them were E.F. Hutton and Citibank of Delaware. Irving Shapiro ended up representing both.

In July, 1982, E.F. Hutton was running into friction with Delaware bankers who objected to its coming into the state. Although the Financial Center Development Act required out-of-staters to set up small offices with no displays and encouraged them to conduct their financial interstate transactions quietly and not take business away from Delaware banks, many Delawarean bankers feared there would be banking through the back door.

E.F. Hutton called on Shapiro, who warned Hutton not to try to ram its way into Delaware with anything so foolish as a lawsuit. He suggested what he usually suggests: a deal. Through his high political contacts in the state, Shapiro had a bill passed, allowing "limited-purpose trust companies" into Delaware if the pay-off in Delaware is cheap—namely, jobs. One hundred employees would have to be taken on within three years. There was, however, no requirement that they had to have been Delaware residents. Hutton and others who wanted to bring their IRAs, Keoghs and employee-benefit plans for small businesses into the state could also bring in their own employees. To placate the local wardheelers, however, this was not advised. Discretion was expected and assumed.

Taxes, of course, made it all click. New York State and City had combined taxes on basic net income of 24.2 percent in 1983. They refused to play Russian Roulette with Delaware. The "First State," meanwhile, was saddled with Pete du Pont's sliding scale—downwards—of 8.7 percent to 2.7 percent of income, about as regressive as possible. The fact that more banks didn't move down from New York as expected underscored that there were other factors than taxes that encourage a bank to choose a cultural and commercial capital like New York over the Wilmington of the Du Ponts. But that was hard for many Du Ponts, just emerging from their isolation in chateau country, to understand. They believed they had everything they needed. Banks, however, need customers. Delaware was simply too small a market.

The strategy, therefore, was for Wilmington Trust and GWDC to foster a gradual growth, focused on the Greater Wilmington Airport area for the county and Christina Gateway for the city. Young Irénée du Pont May, Jr., joined County Executive Collins in the county end of the endeavor.

In February, 1982, Governor du Pont hosted a "Defense Task Force" where 25 federal agencies joined major armaments producers at the Radison Hotel

Ballroom in Wilmington. "This conference will give you the tools and the background to become aggressive," du Pont declared, "to go out there and get the contracts and do the job."[162]

Represented were 150 companies, including Boeing (which had Shapiro as a director), Edward du Pont's Atlantic Aviation, Richard C. du Pont's All American Industries and Du Pont Company. "I personally am not happy with growth in the defense sector," said a University of Delaware political scientist, "but it is an obligation to make information available to people."[163] As the arms spending grew along with deficits, Pete du Pont endorsed President Reagan's call for not just cutbacks but givebacks. To Pete, New Federalism was "a return of the decision-making process to the people," and represented " 'the will of the majority' to see budgets balanced and taxes held down."[164] In the true tradition of Jeremy Bentham, who in the 19th century in Britain first argued for large-scale contracting of government services to private companies, Medicare was contracted out to private doctors, doubling costs; and the National Alliance for Businessmen's job training program was not very successful. Now, under Reagan, more such ventures were underway, while the disappearing tax base due to unemployment undermined government services, which also began to be contracted out at higher cost to the consumer. But then Bentham's own Scotland had endorsed his contracting out of road building, only to discover scandals and road collapses which led to the movement for civil service reform.

Turning Delaware into a corporate tax haven had to have its impact somewhere. Reporting an expected $4.5 million deficit, New Castle County was preparing to raise property taxes on homes and small businesses, while artfully dodging the constitutionally mandated fixtures tax that with Getty alone would have raised $10 million and wiped out the deficit. The tax haven was felt in education also. Governor du Pont was asking state-subsidized schools to return money. Finally, because Governor du Pont refused to decouple from the Reaganomics of the Accelerated Cost Recovery System that accompanied the 1981 Reagan tax cut, Delaware lost an estimated $8 million in 1982, $9.4 million in 1983. "The estimated loss," said the Citizens Coalition for Tax Reform, "grows to total an estimated $84.2 million for years 1983 through 1987.

"Late last Spring the Governor told us there was no possibility of a tax cut, yet he is protecting a large state tax cut for big business, and a few individuals . . . on top of the big federal tax cut they've already received."[165]

Other, poorer Delawareans had it even rougher than the working middle class. These were the unemployed, with the "last hired–first fired" employment practice for Blacks still rampant in Delaware. Blacks suffered a 50 percent unemployment rate in Delaware. As the cutbacks worked their way into the white sector, crime rose across the staté. Pete was surprised, but he encouraged swift "justice" and courts "untethered" by the language of the Constitution.

"We put people in jail faster in this state than in any other jurisdiction in the country in similar circumstances,"[166] said Corrections Commissioner John L. Sullivan in 1983. One hundred fifty out of every 100,000 people in Delaware were in jail. The new 336-bed Gander Hill prison, opened in Wilmington the previous year to alleviate overcrowding, was itself overflowing by June 1983. By December, 1984, Gander Hill was expected to pack in some 700 prisoners, putting two or three prisoners in every cell designed for one person. When du Pont came into office, there were about 1000 prisoners, now there were an expected 2500 by January, 1985. In August, 1983, inmates struck for better conditions, including being served hot instead of cold food. The strike was settled temporarily. Du Pont's bafflement finally found an answer. The construction of two new prisons was made the state's top priority.

Then Irving Shapiro again appeared with three new bills he wanted to see passed in Dover. It had been five years since he made his major address to Dover legislators, in June, 1978, telling them how to boost economic development by lowering corporate and high-income taxes. Since then, Shapiro had developed a good, if not close, working relationship with Governor du Pont. The governor had listened to Shapiro call for lower taxes on higher incomes and moved increasingly in that direction as the 1980 elections approached. He had always held to fiscal conservative views, but in 1980 he revealed just how patrician they were when he joined Shapiro in the Financial Center Development Act. Du Pont needed to create more jobs in order to be re-elected and he seemed fascinated by the world of mergers and high finance, and saw each such development in his state as a sign of growing economic power, almost of modernity itself. Du Pont-Conoco was the zenith of signs. "This is the first time I remember something as complex and distant as a corporate merger—which is not your man-in-the-street kind of issue—being the topic of conversation everywhere in the city," Pete said. "The community feeling was, we're really going someplace. People here have so much confidence in the Du Pont management, that if this is what it desires to do, then it must be right."

Pete also understood Shapiro's role, even with the Bronfmans. "It does of course reduce the proportion of the company shares held by the family. But I think the family crossed that bridge a long time ago. It really ceased to be a family company fifteen or twenty years ago. This is all just part of the trend of the company becoming a large corporation, with professional managers and a whole range of investors."[167]

It was within that context—as a professional manager and consigliore to him as he had been to other Du Ponts—that Pete regarded Shapiro. Irving was a man who was useful in politics as in business because of his capacity to command facts when needed and, more important, his marvelous ability to get people to make a deal. Shapiro was, if anything, overconfident in his negotiating skills. "He thinks he can negotiate anything," remarked Champion International Chairman Andres Sigler, "and he probably can, but there are times when you really need to go to the wall, and Irv is not likely to do it."

Nor was Pete du Pont. But with a new package of bills, they both showed an unusual tenacity. It marked a new strength of character, or a new ambition, and as the values held were consistent with the social myopia displayed in the past, no doubt the latter was the case.

The International Banking Development Act would allow offshore banking in Delaware. It would effectively turn the state of Delaware *into* an offshore bank by bringing into Delaware high-volume bank transactions floated through such tax havens as Cayman Islands and the Bahamas. There are 262 banks in the Bahamas, one for every 1,000 inhabitants.[168] Fourteen states had already passed similar legislation, but Delaware would allow money flowing through the state to remain untaxed. In the Bahamas, tight bank secrecy laws protected bankers from leaks to the IRS. There might be some Eurobond investments by a major corporation that would make interest payments into a private offshore bank—such as the Du Pont family or company might use. This bill, then, was admittedly "not going to be a big employer" or attract much business. So why pass it? So those already in the state can use it, including its drafters. Yet the potential for scandal from "parking" or other activities Citicorp made infamous was enormous. Irving Shapiro, at any rate, was Citicorp's lawyer in Delaware.

The second bill, the Consumers Credit Act, allowed smaller banks to form subsidiaries as part of a "qualifying association" already located in the state. There were also exemptions from a $25 million capitalization and from having to employ 100 people within a year of setting up shop. Most important, it allowed the issuing of credit cards with no ceiling on the cards' interest rates. This law, Hayward offered, encouraged "non-bank banks" to move into Delaware as small associations.

The association would be required to hire 250 employees, not just 100, within a year. It allowed banks to issue consumer loans and credit cards in states with ceilings on rates or fees. "The purpose basically is to broaden the market through services nationally." Both laws put prohibitions or restrictions on doing consumer business in Delaware. And one provided jobs. No one seemed to object that the jobs would be poorly paid, unlike industries where "real" money can be made by an unskilled worker.

Both bills were easily steered through the legislature. Within 24 hours of the Senate's passage of the Consumer Credit Act, the Computer Corporation of America, operating the credit card business of 90 banks in the Midwest, voted to move to Wilmington.

The last bill drafted by Shapiro was called the Financial Services Development Act. It allowed a bank to sell insurance in violation of the Glass-Steagall Act.

Because Wilmington Trust and the Bank of Delaware were already given insurance powers in their state charters, the Delaware Bankers Association stayed on the sidelines and did not help Shapiro. Nor did the State Chamber of Commerce. Pete did, however, repeating the litany about "jobs" and enhancing Delaware's reputation as a financial center. But 100 jobs could not compare to a family's need to keep an insurance shop going. Insurance is one of the few small businesses with a low overhead. For that reason there are a lot of licensed brokers who see their business as their first step toward the status of being self-employed, or the last step down if their small business couldn't compete with a bank.

The governor proceeded without the support of Irénée, Edward, and Eleuthère (Eleuthère, after all, was on the board of the largest insurance company in the state, Continental American Life Insurance). Perhaps CALICO was too big to be affected, perhaps not, but Eleuthère abstained. So did J. Tyler McConnell of Delaware Trust.

Had Shapiro done his political homework? Most likely, unless he had that arrogance referred to earlier—his certainty that he could negotiate anything.

He couldn't.

Pete was out on a limb, all alone.

It was Pete's first true crusade. Some people crusade for people, others for ideas. Pete crusaded for victory. He was in too deep now to withdraw.

For the first time since the 1977 budget fight and the Financial Center Development Act, Pete took the lead in lobbying for a piece of legislation. But what he found dismayed him. Insurers said they were fighting for their lives.

"There's a real fear down there (in Wilmington) that things are out of control,"[169] said one. Others called it a slap on the face of small business. There were fears of other states retaliating against Delaware for stealing banks. Perhaps they would pass similar legislation, too. Did not William H. Kennedy, Jr., President of the American Bankers Association, not audaciously state that "With the payment of interest on checking accounts and such, banks are in a position now where they're going to have to figure out new ways of making money. And if they can't do it on a national basis— and that'll be decided in a year or so—then it's fair game to go at it from state to state."[170]

That was exactly what the Federal Reserve Board did not want. Already about a dozen states had followed Delaware and South Dakota's lead and, urged by the White House's new federalism, deregulated banks in the last few months. But the variety of laws was disturbing as the break with precedent. (Congress in the 1950's had lifted Glass-Steagall's outright prohibition and allowed states to decide for themselves. All had opted for stability. Now it was coming apart, and in different directions.) South Dakota allowed banks to own insurance companies; Washington allowed banks to own anything of a financial nature; California allowed sponsorship of mutual funds investment companies; Arkansas said banks could give the same services as Savings & Loan Associations, credit unions, investment companies, farm credit companies or other financial service suppliers; New York and Connecticut eased the setting up of state-chartered institutions out of federally chartered banks and savings associations.

What had Pete started? That's what Senate Majority Leader Thomas Sharp was hinting. "We really don't know what the end result is going to be."[171]

Investment bankers and brokers charged that the commercial banking giants were singling out vulnerable states like Delaware. Commercial bankers retorted that brokers were moving into banking, too, with money market schemes.

This was not just hypocrisy on all sides, but part of a general financial consolidation from the centrifugal force of a market spinning in disarray and convulsing with mergers and reorganizations that made fortunes for sharp lawyers like Shapiro and Flom. It was a sign of the general merging of capital, making the corporate groups that fused in the center and held together an unprecedented conglomeration of power. Others may first be thrown out from this center by desperate counterbalancing alliances, but they can never be as strong and must, like a pulsar, be attracted again to the central group simply by the density of its interrelated capital.

It was left to the Federal Reserve, the only agency with a clearly mandated network of majors barred from selling, distributing or underwriting securities, to step in and discipline its own house. It also slapped Pete on the wrist.

The slap came on April 13, when Pete's Insurance Commissioner David Elliott received a letter from Paul Volcker, chairman of the Federal Reserve Board. Elliott had earlier sent Shapiro's drafted bill to Volcker for review. The Fed chairman's response was strong, saying he was "seriously concerned about the possibility of widely divergent and inconsistent laws governing both bank and thrift powers, with deposit-taking organizations shopping for the most permissive rules, and states competing to pass such laws in order to enhance local employment. The Secretary of the Treasury has stated that 'this kind of deregulation—haphazard and without consistency or an underlying concept of what is appropriate for an insured institution—is obviously unsatisfactory,' and I agree with him fully... the implication has not been that a single state, or group of states, should set the nationwide pattern."[172]

That should have been enough.

Not for Pete. It was as if he were more afraid of losing this battle' than wreaking havoc on the nation's financial structure.

"As Yogi Berra said, it ain't over until it's over,"[173] Pete said. But it was. Pete just refused to believe it. Until, perhaps, he got a warning from another, overconfident loser. Ex-Representative Tom Evans, of Playboy bunny and crop bill fame, phoned Pete to let him know how grim it all looked. Even the brokers, he said, do not like your bill.

Pete decided to begin "putting on the full-court press."[174] Not since 1977 had the governor gone formally before all four party caucuses to lobby for a bill. "It's clearly perceived as an administration bill, what the administration wants," said Pete's press secretary. "And that's what it is."[175]

Governor du Pont lobbied meetings, receptions, caucuses of the 132nd General Assembly, carried a slick booklet put out by Shaprio and his Citibank crew, and called the bill "the most important legislation of my administration."[176]

Everyone wondered why. Was he so impressed by the Christmas card he had gotten from Morgan Delaware showing 100 signatures to prove the bank had met its employment requirements? Did Shapiro convince him it was that important to his career? But for Pete, the state-paid trips around the country to see unnamed bankers and oilmen had earned a rebellion among lawmakers and a whimsical name; the "Magical Mystery Tour," as one legislator dubbed it, was over.

On June 8, Governor du Pont announced he was withdrawing the bill. It was his first, and probably, as Governor, his last, major defeat.

Irving Shapiro compounded his loss of face later that month when he was embroiled in charges of duplicity—and violations of federal laws forbidding compliance with the Arab boycott of Israel. Ironically, it had been he who put together another of his classic compromises with Edgar Bronfman to avoid a clash in Washington between the American Jewish Congress, of which Bronfman was a director, and Du Pont and other large corporate sellers in the Middle East. The first sign of future shame came just a few months later, at the April, 1977, annual meeting, when William Marlow, general counsel to the American Jewish Congress, submitted a resolution calling on Du Pont to cease complying with the Arab boycott and accused Du Pont of betraying the very principles Shapiro had urged Congress enact as chairman of the Business Roundtable. Speaking of "negative blacklisting and similar exclusionary certificates," Marlow charged, "these very prohibitions which the chairman of Du Pont urged President Carter to be enacted into law are ignored by Du Pont in its business practices and rejected by Du Pont's management in opposing our resolution."[177]

"The Israeli government itself required many of the same negative certificates," Shapiro had replied as chairman of the meeting. "There is no problem at Du Pont. This is a political issue, really.[178]

But Federal Judge James Latchum, again ironically the man who had tried and sentenced Mel Slawik, only to see his court reversed, now felt there was indeed a problem at Du Pont, a serious legal problem, and he demanded Du Pont turn over the documents that it had so far refused to surrender.

The trading incidents which the Commerce Department suspected were in violation of law took place between 1979 and 1980, when Mr. Shapiro was chairman, and involved Du Pont's European subsidiaries. Shapiro at first told reporters on June 21, 1983, that he knew nothing about the violations or the Commerce Department investigation. But former Commerce Secretary Phillip Klutznick then revealed the next day that Shapiro, "an old friend," had discussed it with him when he was a member of Carter's cabinet. "I remember Irv talking to me about it and I asked my people to look into it," Klutznick said. "He came to me because of some controversy. But I disqualified myself for obvious reasons. I am a former president of major Jewish organizations....It was handled at a lower level." He said Shapiro approached him with an "open hand," asking what Du Pont had to do to get the controversy settled.[179]

The next day Shapiro's memory had returned. "I mentioned the dispute," he admitted. "It seemed like they were harassing us over the matter. Someone later called for the secretary and said he had talked to his people and thought there was a legitimate basis for their action."[180] Commerce wanted the documents to decide if the company, and possibly Shapiro, should be prosecuted for more than 400 "apparent violations." As chairman of the Business Roundtable, Shapiro had argued unsuccessfully for an exemption of foreign subsidiaries of American companies. Commerce's request centered on records of Du Pont's subsidiaries in Switzerland, West Germany, Belgium and the United Kingdom, and some sales by Conoco.

"My view of it," offered Shapiro, "was that they [the Commerce Department] were going after Du Pont because it was newsworthy because I was instrumental in formulating the [antiboycott] law."[181]

A little over a week later, one of Shapiro's closest predecessors at the Du Pont helm died. Lammot du Pont Copeland, Sr., had been the last direct heir of the founder of Du Pont, serving as its 11th president and chairman during its great expansion abroad, from 1967 to 1971, when his son's bankruptcy drove him into retirement. In many ways he had symbolized the pre-Shapiro era, when he was a director of General Motors as well, and with his father, Charles Copeland, and his uncles, Pierre and Irénée, had reigned at a younger E.I. du Pont de Nemours where one could never forget that it was your great-great-grandfather who had founded the firm on the banks of the Brandywine.

Lammot du Pont Copeland, a direct but shy man, was 78 years old when he died of a heart attack at his Mount Cuba estate in the hills north of Wilmington. He was survied by his sons, Lammot Jr., who had settled his debts, Garrett, and his daughter Louisa, a new member of the Du Pont board and the wife of Robert Duemling, ambassador to Surinam for Ronald Reagan, to whose party the deceased and his immediate family in 1979-80 gave $45,500.[182]

That the weight of such heavy private donations on the body politic would have been balanced somewhat by public financing of campaigns was precisely the threat of the bill put before the governor just three weeks later. Du Pont had let the bill sit on his desk for two weeks. Now, with a carefully prepared statement, he vetoed it. His reason for killing the bill was simple: now was not the time to be giving taxpayers' money away. Then he prepared for what was to him a more momentous decision. That night, in a small private gathering of friends, he announced his retirement from elected office in Delaware. The constitution forbade his holding the governorship for a third term. Nor would he run, as President Reagan had asked, against the popular young Democratic Senator, Joseph Biden. He was breaking tradition. Republican governors are expected to run for the Senate, usually a shoo-in. But Biden was a tough contender, who enjoyed wide support and an unbroken lead over du Pont in the polls. "Obviously, his not running for the Senate against me is welcome news," said the senator. "I'm not kidding anyone. If he had run, I believe it would have been a toss-up."[183]

Glenn Kenton would not concede even that. "Biden's support is a mile wide and an inch deep...he is eminently beatable, in our judgment, by a good candidate."[184] Du Pont agreed. "We basically start even,"[185] he insisted, dismissing suspicions that he was afraid to lose. "I'd have enjoyed the campaign. It would have been a challenge, it would have been fun, and it would have been winnable."[186] Pierre S. du Pont IV was just not tied down to tradition. "You should never get to the point in life that you run for office because it's there, or because it's the traditional thing to do."[187] Besides, if he wanted to be senator, he would have challenged Biden in 1978.

That would have been quite irregular. Governors usually do not resign after only two years in office to run against a popular senator. Pete was unfazed by the obvious. When he did not run against Biden in 1978 people should have known that once he selected the executive side of government, he would not run against Biden. "Being a United States Senator is a high honor and an important responsibility," he explained, "but...my interests and my talents lie much more in the executive branch of government where I have enjoyed eight years of service as governor for more than the time which I served in the legislative branch of government."[188]

Biden saw the water boiling, and assumed a fire was burning in du Pont. "If I were Pete du Pont," he offered, "and I wanted to be a candidate for the presidency, the last thing I'd want is to be a defeated candidate for the Senate or a winning freshman senator. You have no forum as a freshman senator. You have to wait in line to go to the bathroom there."[189]

Kenton had the same opinion. Pete would have been Senator du Pont, he insisted, but that might not have been wise for his ambitions. "The governors [elected to the Senate] who have gone down there by and large have disappeared. You just get consumed. You lose control of your own destiny. If you really want to help set the agenda and control your own destiny, the last place you want to go is the United States Senate."

Kenton pointed out that the last three elected presidents—Reagan, Carter and Nixon—were not holding other offices when they ran and won. "The next generation of leaders is not coming from the United States Senate.[190] It's coming from the governorships, in spite of the fact that Carter nearly poisoned the well."[191]

The obvious was emerging. Pete had big plans for himself.

The goal and the strategy were clear. Like Carter, Pete du Pont would continue to work his national party network as funder and endorser, only now he would do it full-time. Through his Jobs for American Graduates, a national extension of his private job counselling program in Delaware funded by federal grants and criticized for its claim to success by getting "jobs" at McDonald's and in the U.S. Armed Services, Pete has placed a cadre of supporters in at least eight key states around the country working with state and local education departments and spreading the good name of du Pont. Then, in 1988, when the Republican party was ready for a return to the "moderate" center, Pete du Pont would be waiting—and cashing in his IOU's.

"I want GOPAC to continue," he confirmed, "perhaps even expand the role in supporting local candidates and Republican organizations.

"Beginning in 1985, I will have the opportunity, the interest, and the time to consider and prepare for America's agenda for 1988 and beyond. It will take a full-time commitment unconstrained by the current agenda of the U.S. Senate, because working on the next agenda is a full-time challenge."[192]

Du Pont said he could take a cabinet post or a position on the Republican

National Committee or work independently on issues such as education and job training, two achievements he claims for his governorship in Delaware. Recently, Pete had been named chairman of the Education Commission of the States.

"What title you have after your name isn't important. What is important is that everything is going to change."[193] In 1983, the issues were arms control, the economy, budget deficits, social security reform, the Middle East peoples, Central American problems. "By 1984, however, the issues will be much different than they are today, and I believe the leaders will be different, too.

"If the Republican Party is to once again capture, and dominate, the national agenda in 1988 and beyond as it did in the 1980's, it will need to identify those issues early and come forward with sound practical solutions to address them. And it will need new leaders with the time and energy to devote to appraising America's future needs rather than today's problems."[194]

It was a line consistent with how he had run Delaware, focusing not on today's problems, but on what he—and other Du Ponts and people who shared their views—believed America should be.

Some of 1988's issues, to Pete, "seem clear: Retooling and retraining the American workforce to meet international competition, and educational reform—improving the quality, quantity and focus of the training of the next generation of Americans. Dealing with a vastly different, younger, post-Stalin Soviet leadership will be a challenge. So, too, will a strong, affordable national defense during times of technological explosion and the demand for more sophisticated and costly weapons."[195]

To Senator Biden, Pete du Pont sounded like he was announcing for the presidency five years before the election. Pete's capacity to fund such a long campaign was not to be underestimated. Biden knew du Pont could command vast resources and attract others he could not command. That was why Biden had already raised over $555,000 to defend his Senate seat from a Du Pont family onslaught. When told of Pete's decision, he confirmed that "the main place it takes the pressure off is dollars."[196] While he warned his staff not to take his re-election for granted and "remember a guy named Biden in 1972 who won"—Biden, at 29, had defeated former Republican Governor Caleb Boggs in a startling upset—he did concede that whoever the Republicans ran against him, "I don't think he will have as much money as the governor would have had."[197]

He may have been wrong. One of the names most mentioned in Republican circles was Governor du Pont's personal lawyer, Edmund Carpenter, the Du Pont in-law whose maid was said to have burned Congressman du Pont's campaign finance records.

Democratic Congressman Thomas Carper was also advised not to believe his seat in Washington was safe. Just two weeks after Pete's announcement, word came that another Du Pont was seriously considering taking him on: Elise du Pont, wife of the governor. Elise had already met with top Republicans, including Francis Di Mondi, and "I think she's giving it full, serious consideration,"[198] said national committeewoman Priscilla Rakestraw. "I think the biggest thing is, how would she be perceived by the press," said former state Rep. John Burris, "how much fun would they have with it if she were a candidate?" But after two months of campaigning, she would be seen as independent, assertive, and deeply knowledgeable about federal government, he predicted, certainly not a wild assumption for the *News-Journal*. "Then all of a sudden it's Elise du Pont," he said, "not Mrs. Pete du Pont."[199]

And as Elise du Pont, she would attract the attention of many women across the country to the family name. When 1988 came around, Elise might well have done for Pete in the national media what he could not do in public but would quietly be doing among key members of the Republican national organization: convincing them that the time had come for a Du Pont in the White House.

If so, America may truly have reached the point described by Pete as "a revolutionary moment in its political governance." Speaking to Delaware lawyers on the "Kafkaesque nightmare" of liberal federal judges who have committed "heresy" and "strayed from the original federalist blueprint for a constitutional democracy . . ." and are "infusing their own political vision into the Constitution," du Pont arrayed himself against those who take moral principles into the courts for "the transmutation of transcendental principles into constitutional rights." As examples of judges becoming "increasingly involved in areas of decision-making traditionally regarded as the province of other branches of government," he gave "reorganized school systems, reapportioned legislatures, restructured public and private employment practices, fixed minimum standards for prisons and mental health facilities, and established guidelines for everything from public housing projects to the system of political patronage." In other words, the New Deal. He endorsed the attack on environmentalists and other legal reformers as "a small group of fortunately situated people in a roving commission . . ." made by Nixon's most conservative appointee to the Supreme Court, William Rehnquist, opponent of desegregation and alleged sympathizer of the notoriously reactionary John Birch Society. Du Pont took some hope in "recent decisions of the Supreme Court suggesting that it may be heeding the changing political sentiments . . . even discover encouraging signs of a proper respect—however grudging—for the legitimate role of state governments in the federal system." But he insisted, "It's time we try to save the courts from themselves" and "emphasize the tradition of restraint in articles and books, in legal brief and oral arguments. Time is running short." Otherwise, he warned, "Draconian proposals" will be enacted, including legislative curtailments of judicial power, restrictions on their jurisdiction, or constitutional amendments reversing particular decisions or altering vestiges of judicial office such as life tenure or methods of selection or removal.[200]

It was certainly debatable whether judges have written laws or in most cases simply responded to citizens' petitions and attempted to enforce federal laws in states where local powers have refused to abide by them. And the du Pont Administration, at least in the area of desegregation of the University, has not had a record above reproach. But the general tone and direction of du Pont's remarks, including his warning of "Draconian proposals" if the courts do not come around to his way of thinking and "restrain" themselves, offered broader implications and left little doubt as to what would be the intentions of a President du Pont. "I submit," he said, referring to the American Revolution, the Civil War, and the New Deal, "that the republic has arrived—as it has every so often in its history—at a revolutionary moment in its political governance."[201] There was no question as to what end of the political spectrum a President du Pont would ally himself with; there was little doubt in what direction his revolution would lead: it would be a revolution to the Right.

In some ways it has already begun. Perched high above Wilmington, on the 12th floor of the new Wilmington Trust Center, there is a bronze plaque, first displayed in June, 1983, with the names of the club's new board of governors. They include much of Delaware's business establishment, financiers, lawyers, politicians, all dedicated to making Delaware, as Shapiro and the governor had put it, "the nation's first state in financial services." And all dedicated, admittedly, to making themselves richer than they already were. Irving Shapiro was listed. So was John Tyler McConnell, Edmund Carpenter, and Jane Roth, wife of Senator William Roth who had been reelected the previous year with $25,250[202] in Du Pont family donations. So was Mary Jornlin Thiesen, who succeeded Mel Slawik as County Executive and has now gone on to her rewards as a director of Wilmington Trust. Edward du Pont's name was there too.

But not Pete du Pont's. That may change soon, but in June, 1983, he was still governor of all the people, and didn't need to be included. His efforts to put Delaware at the vanguard of the revolution of New Federalism had already won him a place in spirit, if not in name. It had been Pete du Pont and the Du Pont family with their small group of allies at the Rodney Club who had led the way in changing America's law. The terror of unemployment had been invoked in a state where they controlled private employment, and the laws they had pushed through a willing legislature would, through their impact on the quest for corporate profits, encourage other states to invoke states rights to pass similar laws. In the end, states would rush to Congress to push the deregulation promoted by the Reagan program if for no other reason than to have at least some national standard by which to live and profit in a corporate marketplace called America. Guided by a strategy resting on states rights, the Republic of the New Deal would be systematically dismantled. And, as exemplified by the sky patrol of helicopters requested by Wilmington bankers, there would be more police, more prisons. There would be no chaos. There would be order, a new law and a new order.

To those who saw nothing wrong with this, opposition would be resented as both unfair and privileged. But to the wisest opponents, in Delaware and without, the Du Ponts and their state would remain the barometer of the corporate class. To some, such a perspective would seem a prism offering only distorted visions. But to others, it would explain why the same state, the same family, that had already changed American corporate law once in the 1890's and led the opposition to the New Deal some 40 years later, would come forth again to change American law in the 1980's. To some it would always seem an accident. To others, a powerful family whose members had once called themselves "the Armorers of the Republic" and the "Guardians of the Republic," now re-emerging on the national stage, so soon after Vietnam and Watergate had caused America to re-examine itself and its leaders as never before, is no accident, but a sociological and anthropological phenomenon rooted in the family's past as part of its living history. Its institutional means may change in form, from industry to finance, just as may the commodity whose use the Du Ponts sell, from gunpowder to paper money. But the family remains, its fundamental loyalties, campaign donations reveal, undisturbed by changing surnames.

Their methods of rule also remain: control over information, political organization, law, means to a livelihood, police and, as Wilmington affirmed in 1968, an army. Perhaps soon America will be ready to break from its passive reliance on the market and its fatalistic views about money, human nature and the Right, and choose once again to take up the fight for a prosperity based on equality, justice and democracy, the real American dream. But if it should, America will have to pass by Pete du Pont, who will be waiting, in the "moderate" political center. "Candidate Reagan correctly perceived that the majority of Americans felt the pendulum had swung too far in one direction," the governor concluded in his statement on his future. "It was time that it swung back toward the center."[203]

It left one wondering what Pete du Pont would consider the Right. But if Theodore Barrington, senior editor of Tulsa's *Oil and Gas Journal* is correct, America may soon find out. "By the time I shook his hand after the speech," wrote Barrington, "I had a strange feeling—one I've never had before—that I had just heard a future President of the United States."[204]

APPENDIX

DU PONT WORLD EMPIRE 1984
$13.5 billion in foreign sales*
$ 6.3 billion in foreign assets (27% of total Du Pont as
34,562 employees

★ Du Pont International Headquarters: Wilmington, Delaware

▲ Du Pont International Design & Engineering Offices—Houston, Texas; Plainview, Long Island, N.Y.

■ Du Pont Plants (including subsidiaries)—Canada, England, West Germany, Belgium, Holland, Luxembourg, Sweden, Spain, Puerto Rico, Mexico, Colombia, Venezuela, Brazel, Chile, Argentina, Australia, Taiwan, Japan, Hong Kong, Singapore

◯ Du Pont Foreign Sales Offices—Bangkok, Thailand; T'aipei, Taiwan; Lima, Peru; Paris, France; Milan, Italy; Geneva, Switzerland; Tokyo, Japan; Buenos Aires, Argentina; Guatemala City, Guatemala; Manila, Philippines; New Zealand; Ireland; London, England; Marsta, Sweden; Madrid, Spain; Michelin, Belgium; Montreal, Canada

⋔ UNIROYAL Plantations—Indonesia, Malaya, Liberia

▢ UNIROYAL Plants—India, Malaya, Indonesia, Japan, Australia, South Africa, Liberia, Turkey, Italy, West Germany, Sweden, Luxembourg, Belgium, France, England, Wales, Scotland, Canada, Mexico, Colombia, Venezuela, Argentina

◉ Marine Transportation and Tanker Fleet Home Port (Monrovia, Liberia)—1.6 million deadweight tons

Ⓕ Conoco Oil Operations—Dubai, United Arab Emirates (107,612 barrels/day [b/d]); Great Britain (35,603 b/d); Norway (12,211 b/d); Libya (107,000 b/d); Indonesia (62,240 b/d; exploration leases in Java Sea and Northern Sumatra); Egypt (exploration leases in Gulf of Suez and Bitter Lake); Holland (North Sea exploration); Italy (Tyrrhenian Sea exploration); Central Africa Republic (reserves; exploration); Australia (exploration; reserves)

☼ Conoco Uranium Reserve (Niger, Africa)

★ WILMINGTON

* $11 billion foreign operations' sales
  2.5 billion U.S. plant sales abroad
  $13.5 billion total sales abroad

ⓒ Conoco Carbon Black Project (South Korea; Yugoslavia)

[C] Conoco Mining Project (Chad, Africa; Alberta, Canada)

Holdings: 350 million tons of coal in Canada
94.5 million acres of *undeveloped* petroleum acreage (mostly in Africa and Indonesia)
670 million barrels of proved oil reserves already developed
417 billion cubic feet of proved natural gas reserves already developed (Europe)

Sources: Du Pont 1982 *Annual Report*; *International Petroleum Encyclopedia—1983* (Pennwell Publishing Co., Tulsa, Okla.); *Moody's Industrial Manual—1983*; *European Offshore Oil and Gas Yearbook* (Kogan Page, London); *Who Owns Whom in America—1983*.

Du Pont's $1 Billion Biomedical Business

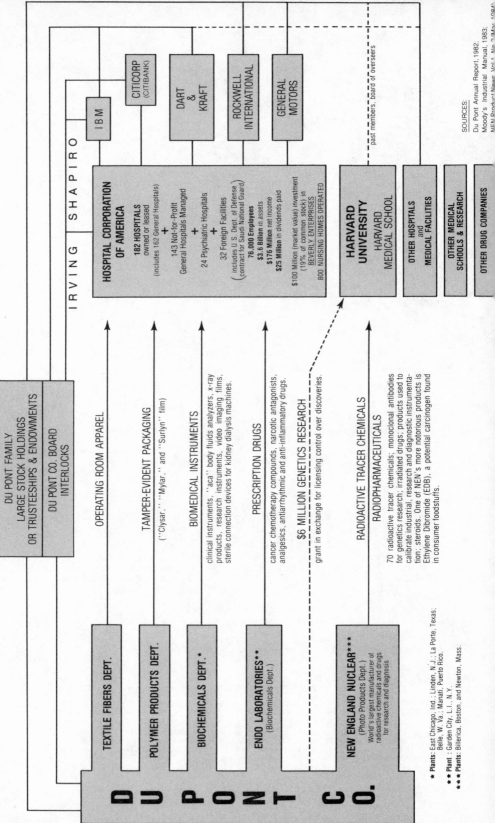

IRVING SHAPIRO

IBM

CITICORP (CITIBANK)

DART & KRAFT

ROCKWELL INTERNATIONAL

GENERAL MOTORS

DU PONT FAMILY LARGE STOCK HOLDINGS OR TRUSTEESHIPS & ENDOWMENTS

DU PONT CO. BOARD INTERLOCKS

HOSPITAL CORPORATION OF AMERICA

182 HOSPITALS owned or leased
(includes 162 General Hospitals)
+
143 Not-for-Profit General Hospitals Managed
+
24 Psychiatric Hospitals
+
32 Foreign Facilities
(includes U.S. Dept. of Defense contract for Saudi National Guard)
76,000 Employees
$3.6 Billion in assets
$176 Million net income
$25 Million in dividends paid
$100 Million (market value) investment (19% of common stock) in BEVERLY ENTERPRISES
800 NURSING HOMES OPERATED

HARVARD UNIVERSITY
HARVARD MEDICAL SCHOOL

OTHER HOSPITALS and MEDICAL FACILITIES

OTHER MEDICAL SCHOOLS & RESEARCH

OTHER DRUG COMPANIES

OPERATING ROOM APPAREL

TAMPER-EVIDENT PACKAGING
("Clysar," "Mylar," and "Surlyn" film)

BIOMEDICAL INSTRUMENTS
clinical instruments, "aca" body fluids analyzers, x-ray products, research instruments, video imaging films, sterile connection devices for kidney dialysis machines.

PRESCRIPTION DRUGS
cancer chemotherapy compounds, narcotic antagonists, analgesics, antiarrhythmic and anti-inflammatory drugs.

$6 MILLION GENETICS RESEARCH
grant in exchange for licensing control over discoveries.

RADIOACTIVE TRACER CHEMICALS
RADIOPHARMACEUTICALS
70 radioactive tracer chemicals; monoclonal antibodies for genetics research; irradiated drugs; products used to calibrate industrial, research and diagnostic instrumentation; steroids. One of NEN's more notorious products is Ethylene Dibromide (EDB), a potential carcinogen found in consumer foodstuffs.

TEXTILE FIBERS DEPT.

POLYMER PRODUCTS DEPT.

BIOCHEMICALS DEPT. *

ENDO LABORATORIES ** (Biochemicals Dept.)

NEW ENGLAND NUCLEAR *** (Photo Products Dept.)
World's largest manufacturer of radioactive chemicals and drugs for research and diagnosis

DU PONT CO.

past members, board of overseers

* **Plants** : East Chicago, Ind.; Linden, N.J.; La Porte, Texas; Belle, W. Va.; Manati, Puerto Rico.
** **Plant** : Garden City, L.I., N.Y.
*** **Plants** : Billerica, Boston, and Newton, Mass.

SOURCES:
Du Pont Annual Report, 1982;
Moody's Industrial Manual, 1983;
NEN Product News, Vol.1, No.2 (May, 1984)

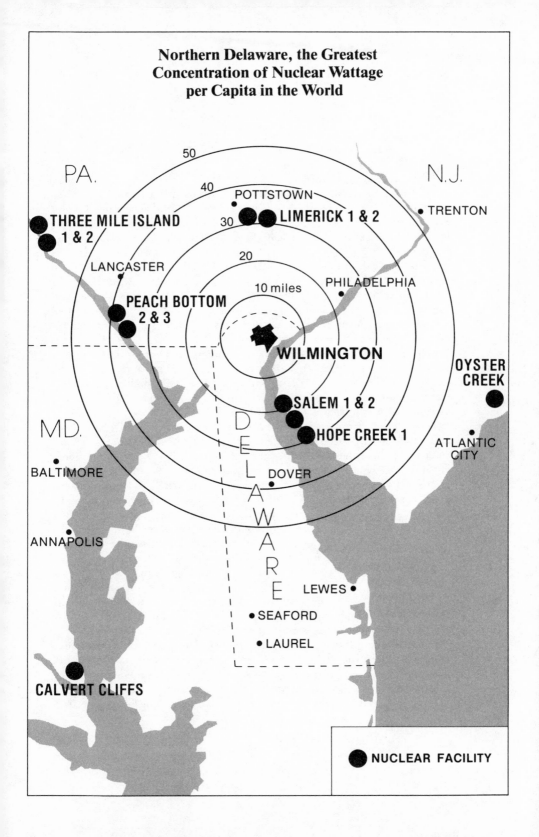

Northern Delaware, the Greatest Concentration of Nuclear Wattage per Capita in the World

PA.

N.J.

50

40

POTTSTOWN

TRENTON

THREE MILE ISLAND 1 & 2

30

LIMERICK 1 & 2

LANCASTER

20

PHILADELPHIA

10 miles

PEACH BOTTOM 2 & 3

WILMINGTON

OYSTER CREEK

MD.

D
E
L
A
W
A
R
E

SALEM 1 & 2

HOPE CREEK 1

BALTIMORE

DOVER

ATLANTIC CITY

ANNAPOLIS

LEWES

SEAFORD

LAUREL

CALVERT CLIFFS

● NUCLEAR FACILITY

THE 1984 RACE FOR GOVERNOR OF DELAWARE

Like the great cities throughout the union, Wilmington, Delaware, with the rise of an immigrant-based Democratic Party and Black Democratic politicians, now too has its own modern non-discriminating social club (the Rodney Square Club on top of the Wilmington Trust Building) with an identifiable presence as an institution of an "enlightened" corporate class subtly extending its influence into Democratic as well as Republican political circles. All that remains are the deals to be cut, and there are signs that some have already been made. Former Wilmington Trust executive William T. Quillen, the Democrat whom Republican Governor du Pont had surprisingly appointed a state supreme court judge, is now making a well-financed drive to capture the Democratic nomination for governor and has chosen as his campaign finance co-chairman former Du Pont chairman Irving Shapiro and Chase Manhattan lawyer O. Francis Biondi, promoters and drafters of Governor du Pont's new banking legislation. Quillen is trying to steal the nomination from David Levinson, a director of Delaware's privately funded Blood Bank. Levinson's story is symptomatic of what independent Delawareans have been forced to face in what Ralph Nader called "The Company State."

Levinson is a rarity in Delaware history. He is a native of Delaware who became financially successful while owing nothing to the Du Ponts. He accomplished this remarkable feat in the only way possible: he made his money outside of Delaware. Levinson is the son of a well-respected Middletown veterinarian whose own political aspirations as an independent-minded six-term Republican mayor (his town-owned utility company, for example, provided power at cheaper rates than the establishment's Delmarva Power & Light Company, yet made enough profits to help finance the town budget) were victimized by Du Pont-backed Republican leaders and downstate Dixicrats who were susceptible to anti-Semitic tactics. In return for a pledge of loyalty by Democrat Tip Webb, Republican leaders cut Louis Levinson's name off of some 500 paper ballots when the elder Levinson ran for State House Representative. Webb subsequently voted Republican so often in the House that fellow Democrats forced him to move his seat to the Republican side of the aisle, the only time that has happened in Delaware's history.

It was a searing lesson for young David Levinson. After he left Delaware to study at Harvard University, where he earned his bachelor and law degrees, he landed a job in 1960 with a Tucson company developing Midwestern and Southwestern real estate before going into business with a partner in St. Louis in the mid-Sixties building moderate income housing, while keeping his legal residence in Delaware.

Since moving back to Middletown, Levinson has proven to be a serious challenger to Du Pont power in the state. His financial independence has immunized him from the usual pressures and temptations that have led other contenders into the fold of the Brandywine; and since his business activities have all been outside of Delaware, he has kept free of financial or political debts to the Du Pont establishment, continuing to try to break through the Du Pont stranglehold over Delaware politics despite a setback in 1982 that would have encouraged many others to throw in the towel. That year he ran for the U.S. Senate against incumbent William Roth, co-author of the Kemp-Roth Tax Act and the powerful chairman of the Senate Permanent Investigating Subcommittee that made Joe McCarthy infamous during the Fifties. Roth, backed by Wilmington's *News-Journal* newspapers and a campaign war-chest of over one million dollars in donations from the Du Pont family and their business allies (including Richard Mellon Scaife of Pittsburgh), was still worried enough to refuse to debate Levinson. Roth won his third term, but Levinson did not give up. He was sufficiently encouraged by a post-election poll which showed him leading Michael Castle, Pete du Pont's heir apparent, to decide to run for governor, shaping a program calling for new high-tech industries to create jobs, better vocational training and better-paid teachers in schools, half-way houses for non-violent offenders to alleviate prison overcrowding, replacement of landfills with solid waste conversion into fertilizer for sale to farmers, and delivery of human services "to restore human values to government." His criticism of the Reagan era's commitment to business values in government, while being a proponent of business methods, has won him few friends along the Brandywine.

No Democratic candidate in Delaware who has been forced into a primary battle has ever been able to go on to victory in the general election, at least so far.

Quillen, on the other hand, is currently a member of a law firm long associated with the Du Ponts and major corporations: Potter, Anderson & Carroon; in fact, the firm was founded by a recent deceased Du Pont family in-law, William Potter, who was a director of Wilmington Trust and a leader of the family's Old Guard in northern Delaware Democratic politics. If Shapiro, Biondi and Topel's illegally elected (by state committee instead of convention) successor as Democratic state chairman, Sam Shipley, succeed in using money to steamroll Quillen's nomination, Delaware's Democratic party may well have been delivered to the Du Ponts. Whether Quillen or Republican Michael Castle, the suitor of European banks for Wilmington, succeeds Governor Pierre S. du Pont IV will be quite irrelevant to the Du Ponts. But for Democrats and independent Delawareans, a Quillen victory will mean control by the Du Ponts of the state's Democratic Party for at least the rest of the decade, and quite possibly longer. Delaware will effectively have become a one-party state: the Du Pont Party.

NOTES

Chapter 1

1. *New York Times,* March 17, 1981, Sec. 4, p. 11.
2. Wilmington *News-Journal,* April 19, 1977.
3. *Ibid.*
4. See "An Analysis of Evacuation Time Estimates Around 52 Nuclear Power Plant Sites," Division of Emergency Preparedness, Office of Inspection and Enforcement, U.S. Nuclear Regulatory Commission (Document NUREG/CR-1856, PNL-3662 Vol. 1), Washington, D.C. May 1981, pp. A-44, B-44, 82, 83.
5. Pierre S. du Pont, "To Neighbors of Salem Generating Station," Brochure on Radiological Emergency Response Plan for Salem Generating Station, Delaware Division for Emergency Planning, Delaware City/Dover 1983.
6. Theodore Keller, Chairman of Citizens Coalition for Tax Reform, before Delaware Public Service Commission, March 31, 1981.
7. Wilmington *News-Journal,* August 4, 1983.
8. Wilmington *News-Journal,* October 7, 1974.
9. See "The Structure of the U.S. Petroleum Industry—A Summary of Survey Data," Special Subcommittee on Integrated Oil Operations, Committee on Interior and Insular Affairs, U.S. Senate, Serial No. 94-37(92-127), U.S. Government Printing Office (Washington, D.C. 1976), p. 86; Norman Medvin, *The Energy Cartel,* Vintage Books (New York, 1974), p. 34; "Petroleum Industry Involvement in Alternative Sources of Energy," Committee on Energy and Natural Resources, U.S. Senate; U.S. Government Printing Office (Washington, D.C., 1977).
10. See "An analysis of Evacuation Time Estimates Around 52 Nuclear Power Plant Sites," Nuclear Regulatory Commission, *op. cit,* p. 82.
11. "Criteria for Preparation and Evaluation of Radiological Emergency Response Plans and Preparedness in Support of Nuclear Power Plants," U.S. Nuclear Regulatory Commission/ Federal Emergency Management Agency (Washington, D.C., 1980), Document NVREG-0654, FEMA-REPA-1, Rev. 1; see pages 16, 49, 50, 63, 1-4, 1-8, 1-9, 4-6, 4-9.
12. See Delaware Air Regulation, No. XIV, Section 3, allowing variances even if mass emission and capacity standards are violated; in addition, the du Pont Administration, through the State Department of Natural Resources and Environmental Control, is considering even more liberal revisions in the code and as of August, 1983, has scheduled hearings. See also Regulation No. VIII, Sec. 1-3, specifically exempting oil refineries (there is only one, Getty) from sulfur emission standards.
13. Constitution of the State of Delaware (1897), Article VIII, Section 7 ("In all assessments of the value of real estate for taxation, the value of the land and

buildings and improvements thereon shall be included"). Fixtures were ruled as taxable under Delaware Constitution by the Delaware Superior Court in 1972 in *Wilmington Suburban Water Corporation v. Board of Assessment* for New Castle County (291 A.2d 293), and by the Delaware Supreme Court in 1973 (316 A,2d 211). For legal analysis of the definitional issues around Delaware's real property and a survey of other states' taxing codes with respect to fixtures, see Richard Peterson, "Real Property—Definitional Issues," unpublished manuscript, George Washington University National Law Center, July 9, 1975.

14. See Pierre S. du Pont IV, "Financial Disclosure Report," for years 1976, 1978, 1983, on file at the office of the Delaware Secretary of State.

15. See Delaware Criminal Code, Title 11, Sections 1211, 1212, 1213; and Title 29, Section 5851, Subsection I and Section 5855.

16. *New York Times,* October 24, 1981, p. 48.

17. Robert S. England, "Slow Death from the Poison Wasteland," *Delaware Today,* August 1980, p. 18.

18. *Ibid.,* pp. 15, 17, 19; see also England, "Where the Poison Rivers Flow," *Delaware Today,* October 1980.

19. Wilmington *News-Journal,* July 8, 1978.

20. *Ibid.*

21. Ferdinand Lundberg, *The Rich and the Super-Rich* (New York: Lyle Stuart Inc., 1968), p. 169.

22. March, 1983, Proxy Statement, E.I. du Pont de Nemours & Co., p. 13-14. Computations are based on the July 8, 1983, market value of $47.125 per share of Du Pont common as listed by the New York Stock Exchange at the end of that day of trading.

23. *Ibid.,* p. 7.

24. Paraphrase by Wilmington *Evening Journal,* September 7, 1966, of speech made that day by Irénée du Pont, Jr., at Howard High School, Wilmington, Delaware.

25. See Chapter 8, "Merchants of Death."

26. See Chapter 9, Sec. 5, "Irénée's Secret War".

27. See Chapter 11, Sec. 3, "The War of Wars"; Chapter 12, Sec. 1, "The Iceman Cometh," and Sec. 4, "The Young Charlemagnes."

28. See Chapter 10, Sec. 5, "The MacGuire Affair" and Sec. 6, "Rearming the Wehrmacht"; Chapter 11, Sec. 2, "Defending the Economic Frontier" and Chapter 14, "Florida, The Hidden Empire," Section 2, "The Regent Rules."

29. See Chapter 10, "Decade of Despair," Sec. 5, "The MacGuire Affair."

30. See Chapter 9, Sec. 9, "The Crash of the House of Cards"; see Chapter 10, Sec. 4, "Deserting the Ship of State," and Sec. 8, "A Climactic Defeat"; Chapter 11, Sec. 1, "Roosevelt Comes to Terms"; Chapter 13, "The Crisis Years."

Chapter 2

1. John K. Winkler, *The Du Pont Dynasty* (Baltimore: Reynal & Hitchcock, Inc. 1935), p. 21.

2. Wilmington *Evening Journal,* December 16, 1930, article by Raymond Gynot, Professor of History, Sorbonne, Paris.

3. As author William Carr notes, family accounts differ as to whether Père Du Pont left behind a gold coin. The earliest family history by Bessie Gardner du Pont makes no reference to the incident at all. The first published reference to a

coin is in 1942, 150 years later, by a Du Pont public relations executive, William Dutton, who drew on family legend. Later, Marc Duke in his *The du Ponts*, repeating the official version, notes that Du Pont did not await the return of the homeowners but quickly moved his family beyond Newport to a safe country inn. If this is true, one can understand why. As Judge Charles Brieant once put it (ironically in sympathy with the Du Ponts' official version), colonial families were not likely to take intruders kindly. To Brieant, the fact that the Du Ponts were not beset upon by angry Americans was proof that a gold coin must have been left behind. There is another obvious possibility, one inadvertently provided by Duke, an apologist for the family and alleged informer for Du Pont Company: the Americans simply did not know who to look for and Père Du Pont had decided not to wait around to tell them.

4. William H. Carr, *The Du Ponts of Delaware* (New York: Dodd, Mead & Co., 1964), p. 48.

5. B. G. du Pont, *Life of E. I. du Pont*, VI, 63.

6. Du Pont de Nemours to Thomas Jefferson, September 8, 1805, cited in Dumas Malone, ed., *Correspondence between Thomas Jefferson and Pierre Samuel Du Pont de Nemours* (Boston: Houghton Mifflin Company, 1930), p. v.

7. Pierre S. Du Pont de Nemours to Nicholas Bidermann, December 1, 1800, *ibid.*, p. 173.

8. B. G. du Pont, *Life of E. I. du Pont*, p. 379.

9. Winkler, *The Du Pont Dynasty*, p. 55.

10. B. G. du Pont, *Life of E. I. du Pont*, VI, 64.

11. Malone, *Correspondence*, p. 30.

12. *Ibid.*, p. 47.

13. William A. Williams, *The Contours of American History* (Cleveland: The World Publishing Company, 1961), p. 179.

14. Ross M. Robertson, *History of the American Economy* (New York: Harcourt, Brace & World, Inc., 1964), p. 107.

15. William A. Williams, *The Tragedy of American Diplomacy* (New York: Dell Publishing Co., Inc., 1962), p. 16.

16. Williams, *Contours*, p. 149.

17. *Ibid.*, p. 180.

18. *Ibid.*, p. 148.

19. Williams, *Tragedy*, p. 20.

20. Malone, *Correspondence*, p. 47.

21. Thomas Jefferson to Robert Livingston, April 25, 1802.

22. *Correspondence of Jefferson and Du Pont de Nemours*, with introduction by Gilbert Chinard (Baltimore: Johns Hopkins Press, 1930), p. xxiii.

23. *Ibid.*, p. xxxiv.

24. Williams, *Contours*, p. 183.

25. *Ibid.*, p. 184.

26. *Annals of Congress*, 7th Congress, 2nd Session, p. 1105.

27. Chinard, *Correspondence*, p. xliii.

28. An outstanding example of this practice was the contract of powderman François Parant, whose unhappy story is related, from Irénée du Pont's point of view, by B. G. du Pont in Volume VI of her *Life of E. I. du Pont*. Irénée, fearing that Parant, if he left the company, might become a neighboring competitor with his powder-making skills, had the powderman

thrown in jail for two months after he quit and finally had him driven out of Delaware.

29. B. G. du Pont, *Life of E. I. du Pont,* IX, 228.
30. Winkler, *The Du Pont Dynasty,* p. 77.
31. *Delaware Gazette,* May 2, 1814 (on microfilm at the library of the University of Delaware).
32. B. G. du Pont, *Life of E. I. du Pont,* IX, 169.
33. Dutton, *Du Pont,* p. 61.
34. B. G. du Pont, *Lives of Victor and Josephine du Pont* (Wilmington: privately printed, 1930), p. 203.
35. Alfred V. du Pont to William Kemble, February 7, 1841, Papers of E. I. du Pont de Nemours & Co., Series A, Part II, Eleutherian-Mills Library.
36. Alfred V. du Pont to William Kemble, July 12, 1842, Papers of E. I. du Pont de Nemours & Co., Series A, Part II, Eleutherian-Mills Library.
37. Alfred V. du Pont to Moorison, Di Carrick & Co., May 20, 1846, Papers of E. I. du Pont de Nemours & Co., Series A, Part II, Eleutherian-Mills Library.
38. Samuel F. du Pont to Sophie du Pont, May 7, 1848, *Letters of Captain S. F. du Pont, 1846–48* (Wilmington: privately printed, 1885), p. 393.
39. S. F. du Pont to Sophie du Pont, June 6, 1848, *Ibid.,* p. 409.
40. Carr, *The du Ponts of Delaware,* p. 150.
41. Article from the London *Echo,* Papers of Samuel F. du Pont, Series E, W 9–35018, Eleutherian-Mills Library.
42. Henry F. du Pont Collection of Winterthur Manuscripts, Group 9, Mrs. Samuel F. du Pont, Series E-General File, Box 176, W 9–39865, Eleutherian-Mills Library.

Chapter 3

1. William H. Carr, *The du Ponts of Delaware* (New York: Dodd, Mead & Co., 1964), p. 162.
2. *Ibid.*
3. *Records of the Office of the Chief of Ordinance,* U.S. Department of War, 352. RG156, Microfilm Accession 352, Reel 4, Eleutherian-Mills Library.
4. Robert A. Thompson, "Samuel F. du Pont and the William B. Reed Mission to China" (Master's thesis, University of Delaware, June 1965), p. 11.
5. *Ibid.,* p. 2.
6. Henry A. du Pont, *Rear Admiral Samuel F. du Pont* (New York: National American Society, 1926), p. 88
7. *Ibid.,* p. 94.
8. *Ibid.,* p. 95.
9. John A. Harrison, *China Since 1800* (New York: Harcourt, Brace & World, Inc., 1967), p. 27.
10. *Official Records of the Union and Confederate Navies,* Series I, XII, 260.
11. H. A. du Pont, *Rear Admiral,* p. 120.
12. *Ibid.,* p. 135.
13. Captain Charles H. Davis, U.S.N., *Life of Charles Henry Davis, Rear Admiral* (Boston: Houghton Mifflin & Co., 1899), p. 165.

14. Gideon Welles, *Diary*, CXI, 217.
15. H. A. du Pont, *Rear Admiral*, p. 139.
16. *Ibid.*, p. 138.
17. *Official Records*, Series I, XIII, 503.
18. H. A. du Pont, *Rear Admiral*, p. 143.
19. *Ibid.*, p. 167.
20. *Ibid.*, p. 173.
21. *Official Records*, Series I, XII, 820.
22. *Ibid.*, Series I, XIII, 503.
23. *Ibid.*, XIV, 571.
24. *Ibid.*
25. H. A. du Pont, *Rear Admiral*, p. 191.
26. *Ibid.*, p. 192.
27. *Ibid.*, p. 201.
28. *Ibid.*, p. 194.
29. *Ibid.*, p. 208.
30. *Ibid.*, p. 195.
31. *Official Records*, Series I, XIV, 5–8.
32. *Ibid.*, p. 132.
33. H. A. du Pont, *Rear Admiral*, p. 225.
34. *Official Records*, Series I, XIV, 59.
35. *Ibid.*, pp. 63–64.
36. H. A. du Pont, *Rear Admiral*, p. 179.
37. *Official Records*, Series I, XIV, 61.
38. *Ibid.*, pp. 139–40.
39. *Ibid.*, p. 300.
40. H. A. du Pont, *Rear Admiral*, p. 286.
41. *Ibid.*
42. Stephen E. Ambrose, "West Point in the Fifties, The letters of Henry A. du Pont," *Civil War History*, X, 1964, p. 296.
43. Henry A. du Pont, *The Campaign of 1864 in the Valley of Virginia and the Expedition to Lynchburg* (New York: National Americana Society, 1925).
44. *Ibid.*, p. 5.
45. Carr, *The du Ponts of Delaware*, p. 181.
46. Henry du Pont to Secretary of War Edwin Stanton, September 28, 1862, Correspondence of the Department of War, No. 630, *National Archives*.
47. Henry du Pont to Edwin Stanton, August 13, 1862, Correspondence of the Department of War, No. 796, *National Archives*.
48. *Records of the Office of the Chief of Ordinance,* U.S. Department of War, 352. RG156, Microfilm Accession 352, Reel 4, Eleutherian-Mills Library.
49. Richard O. Boyer and Herbert M. Morais, *Labor's Untold Story* (New York: United Electrical, Radio and Machine Workers of America, 1970), p. 21.
50. *Ibid.*
51. *Records of the Office of the Chief of Ordinance, loc. cit.*
52. Boyer and Morais, *Labor's Untold Story*, p. 20.
53. *Ibid.*, p. 19.
54. William S. Dutton, *Du Pont—One Hundred and Forty Years* (New York: Charles Scribners' Sons, 1942), p. 98.
55. *Ibid.*, p. 100.

Chapter 4

1. John K. Winkler, *The Du Pont Dynasty* (Baltimore: Reynal & Hitchcock, Inc., 1935), p. 119.
2. Richard O. Boyer and Herbert M. Morais, *Labor's Untold Story* (New York: United Electrical, Radio and Machine Workers of America, 1970), p. 23.
3. Foster Rhea Dulles, *Labor in America* (New York: Crowell & Co., 1947), quoted in Boyer and Morais, *Labor's Untold Story*, p. 34.
4. Correspondence of E. I. du Pont de Nemours & Co., March 17, 1877, Eleutherian-Mills Library.
5. Alfred V. du Pont to Charles McKinney, December 1843, Papers of E. I. du Pont de Nemours & Co., Series A, Part II, Eleutherian-Mills Library.
6. Bessie Gardner du Pont, *E. I. du Pont de Nemours & Co.—A History* (Boston: Houghton Mifflin Company, 1920), p. 129.
7. Winkler, *The Du Pont Dynasty*, p. 104.
8. William S. Dutton, *Du Pont—One Hundred and Forty Years* (New York: Charles Scribner's Sons, 1942), p. 109.
9. Winkler, *The Du Pont Dynasty*, p. 128.
10. Dutton, *Du Pont*, p. 116.
11. *Ibid.*
12. *Ibid.*, p. 131.
13. Winkler, *The Du Pont Dynasty*, p. 133.

Chapter 5

1. Allan J. Henry, ed., *Francis G. du Pont—A Memoir* (Philadelphia: William F. Fell Co., 1951), p. 267.
2. Alfred V. du Pont to Frederick Wright, November 2, 1842, Papers of E. I. du Pont de Nemours & Co., Series A, Part II, Eleutherian-Mills Library.
3. *Ibid.*
4. Henry, *Francis G. du Pont*, p. 54.
5. William H. Carr, *The Du Ponts of Delaware* (New York: Dodd, Mead & Co., 1964), p. 127.
6. Casualty Records, 1815 to 1907, Miscellaneous Papers Concerning E. I. du Pont Company, Treasurer's Office, 1802–1945, Accession 621, Eleutherian-Mills Library.
7. Marquis James, *Alfred I. du Pont—Family Rebel* (Indianapolis: Bobbs-Merrill Company, Inc., 1941), p. 77.
8. Cincinnati *Enquirer*, May 18, 1893.
9. Louisville *Courier-Journal*, May 19, 1893.
10. *U.S. vs. Du Pont* (1907), Brief of the United States, II, 14.
11. *Ibid.*, Testimony of F. J. Waddell, Brief of the United States, II, 60.
12. *Ibid.*, pp. 60ff.
13. *Ibid.*, p. 130.
14. See William S. Stevens, "The Powder Trust—1872 to 1912" (Doctoral thesis, University of Pennsylvania, Philadelphia, 1912).
15. *U.S. vs. Du Pont*, Government Exhibition No. 119, "European Agreement," Petitioner's Record Exhibits, II, 1124–25.
16. William A. Williams, *The Tragedy of American Diplomacy* (New York: Dell Pubishing Co., Inc., 1962), p. 26.

914

17. *Ibid.*
18. *Ibid.*, p. 27.
19. *Ibid.*, p. 16.
20. *Ibid.*, p. 17.
21. *Ibid.*, p. 26.
22. *Ibid.*, p. 31.
23. *Ibid.*, p. 30.
24. *Ibid.*, p. 36.
25. Julius W. Pratt, *Expansionists of 1898: The Acquisition of Hawaii and the Spanish Islands* (Gloucester, Mass.: P. Smith, 1959) [c. 1936], p. 207.
26. Williams, *Tragedy*, p. 39.
27. William A. Williams, *The Contours of American History* (Cleveland: The World Publishing Company, 1961), p. 346.
28. C. S. Olcott, *Life of William McKinley* (Boston: Houghton Mifflin Company, 1916), II, 108–11.
29. Williams, *Tragedy*, p. 38.
30. *Ibid.*
31. *Ibid.*
32. Walter Lord, *The Good Years* (New York: Harper & Brothers, 1962), p. 34.
33. James, *Alfred I. du Pont*, p. 118.
34. *Ibid.*, p. 104.
35. R. S. Waddell, "Brief on Smokeless Powder," February 1907 (sent to all members of U.S. Congress), *Selections from the National Archives*, File No. 4480, "Complaints Against the Powder Trust by Buckeye Powder Company," Eleutherian-Mills Library.
36. James, *Alfred I. du Pont*, p. 47.

Chapter 6

1. *U.S. vs. Du Pont*, Defendant's Record, Testimony of Francis I. du Pont, II, 964.
2. *Ibid.*, Testimony of Alfred I. du Pont, I, 446.
3. Marquis James, *Alfred I. du Pont—Family Rebel* (Indianapolis: Bobbs-Merrill Company, Inc., 1941), p. 145.
4. *U.S. vs. Du Pont*, Testimony of Alfred I. du Pont.
5. *Ibid.*
6. Charles Wertenbaker, "Du Pont," *Fortune*, November 1934, p. 180.
7. James, *Alfred I. du Pont*, p. 147.
8. John W. Donaldson, *Caveat Venditor—A Profile of Coleman du Pont* (Wilmington: privately printed, 1964), p. 8.
9. James, *Alfred I. du Pont*, p. 149.
10. *Ibid.*
11. *Ibid.*
12. John K. Winkler, *The Du Pont Dynasty* (Baltimore: Reynal & Hitchcock, Inc., 1935), p. 160.
13. Walter Lord, *The Good Years* (New York: Harper & Brothers, 1962), p. 299.
14. See "The Industrial Replacement of Men by Women," Industrial Commission of New York, March 1914.
15. Survey, U.S. Bureau of Labor, April 17, 1920.

16. Lord, *The Good Years.*
17. *Ibid.*
18. See John Spargo, *The Bitter Cry of the Children* (New York: The MacMillan Co., 1907) and J. Van Vorst, *The Cry of the Children* (New York: Moffat, Yard & Co., 1908).
19. See "Child Labor in Canneries," Child Labor Bulletin, Vol. I, No. 4, February 1913.
20. Lord, *The Good Years,* p. 76.
21. *Ibid.,* p. 51.
22. Donaldson, *Caveat Venditor,* p. 11.
23. *U.S. vs. Du Pont,* Petitioner's Record Exhibits, IV, 1788, Government Exhibit No. 166, "Resolution of the Directors of the Delaware Investment Company": also *Ibid.,* p. 1756, "Resolution of the Directors of the Delaware Securities Company."
24. *Philip du Pont vs. Pierre S. du Pont,* Petitioner's Brief, II, 330–33.
25. *Records of the Department of Commerce and Labor,* Interview with R. S. Waddell, President of Buckeye Powder Company and former General Sales Manager of Du Pont Company; August 28, 1907, *Selections from the National Archives.*
26. *Ibid.*
27. Chicago *Chronicle,* January 2, 1907.
28. See Leonard Leopold, "The Growth of American Foreign Policy and American Imperialism," *Problems in American Civilization* (Boston: Heath & Company), 1969.
29. *Ibid.*
30. *Ibid.*
31. Chicago *Chronicle,* January 2, 1907.
32. *U.S. vs. Du Pont, et al.* Petitioner's Record, Government Exhibit No. 212, IV, 1959.
33. *Ibid.,* I, 206.
34. *Ibid.,* IV, 2106.
35. *Selections from the National Archives,* File No. 4480, "Complaints Against the Powder Trust by Buckeye Powder Company," Eleutherian-Mills Library.
36. *Ibid.*
37. Chicago *Chronicle,* January 2, 1907.
38. *Ibid.*
39. R. S. Waddell, "More Facts on the Powder Trust," June 1906, *Selections from the National Archives,* File No. 4480, "Complaints Against the Powder Trust by Buckeye Powder Company," Eleutherian-Mills Library.
40. *U.S. vs. Du Pont,* Petitioner's Record, Government Exhibit No. 212, IV, 1959.
41. R. S. Waddell, "More Facts on the Powder Trust," January 1907, *Selections from the National Archives,* File No. 4480, "Complaints Against the Powder Trust by Buckeye Powder Company," Eleutherian-Mills Library.
42. R. S. Waddell to Herbert Smith, Records of the Federal Trade Commission, Bureau of Corporations, *National Archives,* File No. 0–40–7, Record Group 122.
43. Calendar No. 6435, House Joint Resolution 224, 59th Congress, 2nd Session.
44. Chicago *Chronicle,* January 2, 1907.

45. See Richard Hofstadter, *Social Darwinism in American Thought, 1860–1915* (Philadelphia: University of Pennsylvania Press, 1945).

46. See Sigmund Diamond, *The Reputation of the American Businessman* (Cambridge: Harvard University Press, 1955).

47. T. Coleman du Pont, "The Powder Case Briefly Stated," Du Pont Company memorandum to employees, October 5, 1911.

48. "Du Pont—The Powder and the Glory," *Fortune*, January 1935, p. 125.

49. Henry A. du Pont to Benjamin Harrison, July 11, 1892, Papers of Benjamin Harrison, pp. 31754–55, Library of Congress (photo print), Accession 825, Eleutherian-Mills Library.

50. Wilmington *Every Evening*, May 11, 1895.

51. Philadelphia *Public Ledger*, May 19, 1895.

52. *New York Times*, May 18, 1896.

53. Papers of H. A. du Pont, Series B, Box 38, Eleutherian-Mills Library.

Chapter 7

1. Marquis James, *Alfred I. du Pont—Family Rebel* (Indianapolis: Bobbs-Merrill Company, Inc., 1941), p. 214.

2. *Ibid.*, p. 193.

3. *Ibid.*, p. 201.

4. Philadelphia *North American*, October 31, 1909.

5. New York *World, December* 5, 1909.

6. New York *Sun*, October 31, 1909.

7. James, *Alfred I. du Pont*, p. 227.

8. Papers of H. A. du Pont, Series B, Box 38, Eleutherian-Mills Library.

9. Taft's visits were on May 11, 13; December 1, 1910.

10. Selected Papers of E. I. du Pont de Nemours & Co., Accession of letters from W. H. Taft, 442,665, R. 973, Library of Congress.

11. New York *Evening Post,* November 14, 1910.

12. Robert G. Houston to Congressman W. H. Heald, Selected Papers of E. I. du Pont de Nemours & Co., Taft letters, *op. cit.*

13. W. H. Taft to H. A. du Pont, September 8, 1910, *Ibid.*

14. *Ibid.*, November 25, 1910.

15. Linda Diane Vollmar, "T. Coleman du Pont's Correspondence, 1907–12" (Master's thesis, University of Delaware, June 1969), p. 48.

16. *Ibid.*, p. 50.

17. *Ibid.*, p. 57.

18. *Ibid.*, p. 60.

19. *Ibid.*, p. 48.

20. *U.S. vs. Du Pont, et al.*

21. Vollmar, "T. Coleman du Pont," p. 92.

22. *Ibid.*, p. 94.

23. *Ibid.*

24. George W. Wickersham to T. C. du Pont, October 20, 1911, Vollmar, "T. Coleman du Pont," p. 95.

25. T. C. du Pont to C. P. Taft, October 26, 1911, *Ibid.,* p. 103.

26. J. F. Alee to A. I. du Pont, July 13, 1921, Papers of A. I. du Pont, quoted in James, p. 244.

27. Wilmington *Morning News,* February 14, 1912.

28. Papers of H. A. du Pont, Series B, Box 38, Eleutherian-Mills Library.

29. James, *Alfred I. du Pont*, p. 245.

30. W. H. Taft, Selected Papers of E. I. du Pont de Nemours & Co., Taft letters.
31. *Ibid.,* W. H. Taft to Charles Taft, June 2, 1912.
32. John K. Winkler, *The Du Pont Dynasty* (Baltimore: Reynal & Hitchcock, Inc., 1935), p. 167.
33. This fact remains to disprove William S. Dutton's claim in his *Du Pont— One Hundred and Forty Years* (New York: Charles Scribner's Sons, 1942) that "Today, as diversified chemical manufacturers as well as producers of explosives, Hercules and Atlas rank among Du Pont's most aggressive and respectful competitors" (p. 197). The modern interlocks between both firms and the Du Ponts persist for Hercules just as strongly today as they did in 1912, if not more strongly. It is of little surprise that Dutton, himself a Du Pont executive, described his own book as "the Du Pont Company as seen by Du Pont men. It is an 'inside' view" ("Introduction," p. vii).
34. W. H. Taft to George W. Marshall, June 12, 1912, Taft letters.
35. William H. Carr, *The Du Ponts of Delaware* (New York: Dodd, Mead & Co., 1964), p. 268.
36. John W. Donaldson, *Caveat Venditor—A Profile of Coleman du Pont* (Wilmington: privately printed, 1964), p. 4.
37. *Ibid.*
38. Carr, p. 279.
39. Winkler, *The Du Pont Dynasty,* p. 296.
40. U.S. Federal Trade Commission, Records of the Bureau of Corporations, Entry 1, Department of Commerce, Social and Economic Branch. Selections: 1903, 1906–8, 1912–13, 1915. File No. 4480, M–62.11, R.G.122, Reel 1 (microfilm), Eleutherian-Mills Library.
41. *U.S. vs. Du Pont,* Answer of E. I. du Pont & Co., *et al.,* Pleadings, p. 108.
42. *Ibid.,* p. 319.
43. Wilmington *Sunday Star,* June 17, 1906.
44. Wilmington *Every Evening,* October 30, 1916.
45. Milford *Chronicle,* October 13, 1916.
46. Wilmington *Every Evening,* September 19, 1916.
47. Wilmington *Morning News,* October 18, 1916.
48. Donaldson, *Caveat Venditor,* p. 17.
49. *Ibid.,* p. 18.
50. *Ibid.,* p. 20.
51. *Du Pont vs. Du Pont,* Testimony of William du Pont.
52. *Du Pont vs. Du Pont,* I, 97.
53. *Ibid.,* Testimony of P. S. du Pont, VIII, 19.
54. *Ibid.,* I, 100.
55. *Ibid.,* VI, 104.
56. *Ibid.,* p. 114.
57. *Ibid.,* p. 118.
58. *Ibid.,* p. 126.
59. *Ibid.,* p. 130.
60. James, *Alfred I. du Pont,* p. 259.
61. *Ibid.,* Testimony of P. S. du Pont, VII, 25.
62. *Ibid.,* Testimony of Francis I. du Pont, IV, 83–86.
63. *Ibid.,* Testimony of Francis I. du Pont, VII, 89–92, 134.

64. James, *Alfred I. du Pont,* p. 281.
65. *Ibid.,* p. 282.
66. Wilmington *Morning News,* May 20, 1916.
67. James, *Alfred I. du Pont,* p. 296.

Chapter 8

1. W. J. Reader, *Imperial Chemical Industries—A History* (Oxford, England: Oxford University Press, 1970), Vol. I, "The Forerunners—1870–1926," pp. 212–15. Quoted also by Alfred D. Chandler and Stephen Salsbury, *Pierre S. du Pont and the Making of the Modern Corporation* (New York: Harper & Row, Publishers, 1971), p. 299. (Purported to be an objective historical account, this book is highly complimentary to Pierre du Pont, possibly because Chandler's grandmother was a Du Pont; in fact his middle initial "D" stands for Du Pont.)

2. William S. Dutton, *Du Pont—One Hundred and Forty Years* (New York: Charles Scribner's Sons, 1942), pp. 225–26.

3. John K. Winkler, *The Du Pont Dynasty* (Baltimore: Reynal & Hitchcock, Inc., 1935), p. 223.

4. Chandler and Salsbury, *Pierre S. du Pont,* p. 369.

5. P. S. du Pont to T. Coleman du Pont, February 5, 1915, *United States vs. E. I. du Pont de Nemours, General Motors, U.S. Rubber, Delaware Realty & Investment Corporation, Pierre S. du Pont, Lammot du Pont, Irénée du Pont,* U.S. District Court for Northern District of Illinois, Pierre S. du Pont Deposition, Exhibit No. 30.

6. Colonel Edmund G. Buckner (Du Pont vice-president in charge of military sales), "On the Relations of Du Pont American Industries to the War," Speech at Du Pont General Sales Convention, June 19, 1918. (Cp.v.3061 at the New York Public Library, Fifth Avenue.)

7. *Ibid.*

8. Testimony of P. S. du Pont, September 12, 1934, Nye Investigating Committee, United States Senate.

9. *New York Times,* October 11, 1915.

10. Senator R. M. La Follette, *La Follette's Magazine,* September 1915.

11. William A. Williams, *The Tragedy of American Diplomacy* (New York: Dell Publishing Co., Inc., 1962), p. 52.

12. William A. Williams, *The Contours of American History* (Cleveland: The World Publishing Company, 1961), p. 412.

13. Richard O. Boyer and Herbert M. Morais, *Labor's Untold Story* (New York: United Electrical, Radio and Machine Workers of America, 1970), p. 193, also, Williams, *Tragedy,* pp. 80–81, p. 75.

14. *Ibid.,* p. 194.

15. Williams, *Tragedy,* p. 52.

16. Boyer and Morais, *Labor's Untold Story,* p. 193.

17. U.S. State Department, Foreign Publications, 1917, supplement 2, I, pp. 516–8.

18. Woodrow Wilson, Speech at St. Louis, Missouri, September 5, 1919, reprinted in *Congressional Record,* Sept. 8, 1919, p. 5006.

19. Wilson, *The New Freedom* (New York: Doubleday & Company, Inc., 1913), pp. 57–58.

20. Wilson, Speech before Congress, *Congressional Record,* April 2, 1917.
21. Senator Morris, Speech before U.S. Senate, *Congressional Record,* April 4, 1917.
22. Quoted in Boyer and Morais, *Labor's Untold Story,* p. 23.
23. Buckner, Speech at Du Pont General Sales Convention, June 19, 1918.
24. Dutton, *Du Pont,* p. 209.
25. *Annual Report,* 1918, E. I. du Pont de Nemours & Co.
26. Philadelphia *Public Ledger,* July 21, 1916.
27. *Ibid.,* July 27, 1916.
28. *New York Times,* November 28 and 29, 1916.
29. Wilmington *Sun,* November 1, 1919.
30. Alfred I. du Pont to Maurice du Pont, December 10, 1932, quoted in Marquis James, *Alfred I. du Pont—Family Rebel* (Indianapolis: Bobbs-Merrill Company, Inc., 1941), p. 315.
31. House Report No. 998, 66th Congress, 2nd Session.
32. *Ibid.*
33. *Ibid.*
34. Dutton, *Du Pont,* p. 249.
35. Ferdinand Lundberg, *America's Sixty Families* (New York: Vanguard Press, 1937), pp. 154 and 156.
36. *Ibid.,* p. 172.
37. Buckner, Speech at Du Pont General Sales Convention, June 19, 1918.
38. *Ibid.*
39. Chandler and Salsbury, *Pierre S. du Pont,* p. 429.

Chapter 9

1. Irving Bernstein, *The Lean Years* (Baltimore: Penguin Books, Inc., 1966), p. 54.
2. Harry Jerome, *Mechanization in Industry* (New York: National Bureau of Research, 1934), pp. 122–25.
3. Bernstein, *The Lean Years,* p. 54.
4. *Ibid.*
5. *Ibid.,* p. 65.
6. William A. Williams, *The Tragedy of American Diplomacy* (New York: Dell Publishing Co., Inc., 1962), p. 145.
7. Bernstein, *The Lean Years,* p. 54.
8. Hugh Grant, *An Australian Looks at America* (London: Allen & Unwin, 1928), pp. 117–18.
9. William S. Dutton, *Du Pont—One Hundred and Forty Years* (New York: Charles Scribner's Sons, 1942), p. 288.
10. The Foundation years later sued Du Pont in an attempt to regain its patents. It failed. (*New York Times,* November 20, 1928, p. 16).
11. John K. Winkler, *The Du Pont Dynasty* (Baltimore: Reynal & Hitchcock, Inc., 1935), p. 265.
12. *New York Times,* September 25, 1923, p. 9.
13. *Ibid.,* also, *Report* of the Special Senate Committee to Investigate the Munitions Industry, 1936, p. 266, and Munitions Hearings, Exhibit 4874–C.
14. Munitions Hearings, Part 4, p. 2573, Exhibit 920.
15. *Report* of the Munitions Committee, pp. 266–68.

920

16. Munitions Hearings, Part 11.
17. *Ibid.*
18. *Ibid.*, p. 2559, Exhibit 910.
19. *Report*, p. 270; also Munitions Hearings, Part 11, Testimony December 6, 7, and 10, 1934.
20. Munitions Hearings, Part 11, Exhibit 928, p. 2581.
21. *Ibid.*, Exhibit 929.
22. *Ibid.*, Part 11, pp. 2578–80, Exhibit 926.
23. *Ibid.*, p. 2571, Exhibit 918.
24. *New York Times*, May 9, 1920, p. 1.
25. *Ibid.*
26. *Ibid.*
27. *Ibid.*
28. *Ibid.*, June 15, 1920, p. 2.
29. Ferdinand Lundberg, *America's Sixty Families* (New York: Vanguard Press, 1937), p. 153.
30. *Ibid.*, p. 156.
31. Munitions Hearings; *Report* of the Munitions Committee.
32. William G. Johnson, *"The Life and Political Career of Henry Algernon Du Pont"* (Master's thesis, University of Delaware), p. 100.
33. *New York Times*, October 17, 1920, p. 3.
34. Williams, *Tragedy*, p. 105.
35. Edward Earle Purinton, "Gunpowder for Peace," *The Independent*, August 21, 1920.
36. *New York Times*, February 22, 1921, p. 15.
37. Marquis James, *Alfred I. du Pont—Family Rebel* (Indianapolis: Bobbs-Merrill Company, Inc., 1941), p. 336.
38. *Ibid.*, p. 327.
39. *Ibid.*, p. 336.
40. *Ibid.*
41. *Ibid.*, p. 343.
42. *Ibid.*
43. *Forum*, December 1920.
44. T. C. du Pont, "Does America Want Immigration or Emigration," *Current Opinion*, Vol. LXIX, No. 2, August 1920.
45. *Ibid.*
46. T. C. du Pont, "Better Treatment for the Immigrant," *Forum*, December 1920.
47. Upton Sinclair, *The Brass Check, A Study of American Journalism* (Pasadena, Calif.: the author, 1920).
48. *New York Times*, July 8, 1921, p. 5.
49. *Ibid.*, March 15, 1922, p. 5.
50. Munitions Hearings, Exhibit 4873–Z; also *Report*, p. 273.
51. *Report*, pp. 265–66.
52. *New York Times*, December 20, 1963.
53. Bernstein, *The Lean Years*, p. 10 (citing a report of the Bureau of Labor Statistics).
54. Winkler, *The Du Pont Dynasty*, p. 268.
55. "The Du Pont Story" (film), E. I. du Pont de Nemours & Co., Advertising Department, Wilmington, Delaware.
56. Winkler, *The Du Pont Dynasty*, p. 272.

57. Report by J. J. Raskob to the Du Pont Finance Committee, *New York Times*, February 18, 1953, p. 41; Winkler, *The Du Pont Dynasty*, p. 257.
58. *1917 Annual Report*, E. I. du Pont de Nemours & Co.
59. *1918 Annual Report*, E. I. du Pont de Nemours & Co.
60. *New York Times*, June 4, 1957, pp. 23–24.
61. Winkler, *The Du Pont Dynasty*, p. 261.
62. James, *Alfred I. du Pont*, p. 341.
63. *Ibid.*, p. 346.
64. *Ibid.*, p. 352.
65. Wilmington *Sunday Star*, August 27, 1922.
66. Winkler, *The Du Pont Dynasty*, p. 299.
67. *Report*, Parts 3 and 5.
68. Munitions Hearings, Part 12, p. 2846, Exhibit 1056.
69. *Report*, p. 273.
70. *Conference on Limitation of Armaments*, November 12, 1921–February 6, 1922 (Washington, D.C.: Government Printing Office).
71. Richard Sasuly, *I. G. Farben* (New York: Boni & Gaer, Inc., 1947), p. 81.
72. Munitions Hearings, Part 6, p. 1596, Exhibit 597.
73. *Ibid.*, Part 9, p. 2138.
74. *Ibid.*, p. 2143.
75. *Ibid.*, p. 2146.
76. *Ibid.*, p. 2143.
77. *Ibid.*, p. 2140.
78. *Ibid.*, p. 2242.
79. *Ibid.*, p. 2158.
80. *Ibid.*, p. 2254, Exhibit 837.
81. *Report*, p. 250.
82. *New York Times*, November 19, 1934, p. 1.
83. *Ibid.*
84. *Ibid.*
85. *Report*, Part 3, p. 16.
86. *New York Times*, November 16, 1946, p. 10.
87. *Ibid.*, October 31, 1924, p. 6.
88. Silas Brent, "Deep Water Runs Still," *The Nation*, July 8, 1925.
89. *Ibid.*
90. *New York Times*, November 3, 1924, p. 6.
91. Bent, "Deep Water."
92. Anti-trust suit by Department of Justice, 1937, Equity No. E–84–321, District Court of the United States, Southern District of New York, *U.S. vs. Ethyl Gasoline Corporation, Carle L. Webb and John Cord Taylor;* plaintiff's petition filed February 19, 1937.
93. Bent, "Deep Water."
94. *New York Times*, January 4, 1924, p. 2.
95. *Ibid.*
96. *Ibid.*
97. James, *Alfred I. du Pont*, p. 349.
98. *Ibid.*, p. 381.
99. Winkler, *The Du Pont Dynasty*, p. 301.
100. *New York Times*, April 17, 1924, p. 20.
101. *Ibid.*, May 11, 1924, Sec. IX, p. 11.
102. Wilmington *Sun*, November 1, 1919.

922

103. *Outlook*, October 14, 1925.
104. Winkler, *The Du Pont Dynasty*, p. 304.
105. *New York Times*, April 6, 1926, p. 10.
106. James, *Alfred I. du Pont*, p. 401.
107. *Ibid.*, May 13, 1925, p. 2.
108. *New York Times*, January 8, 1928, Sec. IX, p. 5.
109. Milton Lamask, *Seed Money—The Guggenheim Story* (New York: Farrar, Straus & Company, 1964), p. 142.
110. *Ibid.*
111. *Ibid.*
112. *Ibid.*
113. Alfred D. Chandler and Stephen Salsbury, *Pierre S. du Pont and the Making of the Modern Corporation* (New York: Harper & Row, Publishers, 1971), p. 583.
114. "America's Answer to the Rubber Monopoly," *American Review of Reviews*, November 1928, p. 522.
115. TNEC study (1937) Cited by Ferdinand Lundberg, *The Rich and the Super-Rich* (New.York: Lyle Stuart, Inc., 1968), p. 171.
116. *Ibid.*
117. *Federated Press*, March 20, 1930, article of Harvey O'Conner.
118. *New York Times*, July 29, 1927, p. 1.
119. *Ibid.*, July 31, 1927, p. 23.
120. *Ibid.*, March 19, 1928, p. 1.
121. *Ibid.*, March 24, 1928, p. 30.
122. Henry F. Pringle, "John J. Raskob—A Portrait," *Outlook*, August 22, 1928.
123. "Chemistry's Tremendous Tomorrow," an interview with Irénée du Pont, *Literary Digest*, November 3, 1923, p. 23.
124. Bernstein, *The Lean Years*, p. 48.
125. *Ibid.* (Department of Agriculture figures).
126. *Ibid.*, p. 49.
127. David Weintrub, "Unemployment and Increasing Productivity," *Technological Trends and National Policy* (Philadelphia: National Resources Committee, 1937. Originally submitted to U.S. Works Project Administration, National Research Project on Reemployment Opportunities and Recent Changes in Industrial Techniques, as Report 6, No. 7.
128. Bernstein, *The Lean Years*, p. 60.
129. *New York Times*, November 2, 1928, p. 18.
130. William H. Carr, *The du Ponts of Delaware* (New York: Dodd, Mead & Co., 1964), p. 304.
131. *Ibid.*, p. 305.
132. *Ibid.*
133. *Ibid.*
134. *New Republic*, July 25, 1920.
135. *Ibid.*
136. *New York Times*, June 4, 1957, pp. 1, 23, and 24.
137. *Ibid.*, January 9, 1953, p. 29.
138. *Ibid.*, August 10, 1928, p. 2.
139. J. J. Raskob to P. S. du Pont, May 15, 1923 (*New York Times*, January 7, 1953, p. 33).
140. Chandler and Salsbury, *Pierre S. du Pont*, p. 587.

141. John Kenneth Galbraith, *The Great Crash* (Boston: Houghton Mifflin Company, 1955), p. 20.
142. Chandler and Salsbury, *Pierre S. du Pont*, p. 586.
143. P. S. du Pont, "18th Amendment Not a Remedy for the Drink Evil," *Current History*, April, 1928.
144. *American Review of Reviews*, August 1928, p. 125.
145. *World's Work*, Vol. LVI, No. 5, September 1928.
146. Lundberg, *America's Sixty Families*, pp. 179–82.
147. *New York Times*, July 13, 1928, p. 3.
148. Munitions Hearings; *Report*, p. 1406.
149. *New York Times*, August 28, 1928, p. 2.
150. *Report*, p. 1406.
151. *Ibid.*
152. Lundberg, *America's Sixty Families*, 179–82.
153. James C. Young, "Raskob of General Motors," *World's Work*, Vol. LVI, No. 5, September 1928.
154. *Ibid.*
155. Quoted in Bernstein, *The Lean Years*, p. 75.
156. James, *Alfred I. du Pont*, p. 410.
157. *Ibid.*, p. 422.
158. *New York Times*, November 9, 1928, p. 2.
159. Winkler, *The Du Pont Dynasty*, p. 312.
160. *Ibid.*, p. 317.
161. *Ibid.*, p. 213.
162. *New York Times*, September 7, 1926.
163. *Ibid.*
164. See M. S. Rukeyser, "Du Pont: A Story of Industrial Genius," *Review of Reviews*, LXXVII, 371–79, April 1928; *Outlook*, CXLIX, 662, August 22, 1928.
165. *Commonweal*, May 29, 1929, p. 90.
166. John J. Raskob, "What Next in America?" *North American Review*, Vol. 228, No. 5, November 1929.
167. See John K. Galbraith, "Financial Genius Is Before the Fall," *Economics, Peace, and Laughter* (Boston: Houghton Mifflin Company, 1972), pp. 105–24.
168. Lundberg, *America's Sixty Families*, p. 221.
169. *Ibid.*, p. 237.
170. James, *Alfred I. du Pont*, p. 420.
171. Richard O. Boyer and Herbert M. Morais, *Labor's Untold Story* (New York: United Electrical, Radio and Machine Workers of America, 1970), p. 249.
172. *America's Capacity to Produce* (Washington, D.C.: The Brookings Institution, 1934).
173. Williams, *Tragedy*, p. 123.
174. *Ibid.*, p. 123.
175. *Ibid.*, p. 133.
176. Galbraith, "Financial Genius," p. 114.
177. James, *Alfred I. du Pont*, p. 440.
178. *New York Times*, October 30, 1929.
179. Quoted from Galbraith, *Economics, Peace, and Laughter*, p. 122.

180. *New York Times,* January 10, 1936.
181. *Ibid.,* December 8, 1929, p. 21.
182. James, *Alfred I. du Pont,* p. 427.

Chapter 10

1. Marquis James, *Alfred I. du Pont—Family Rebel* (Indianapolis: Bobbs-Merrill Company, Inc., 1941), p. 473.
2. *Ibid.*
3. Irving Bernstein, *The Lean Years* (Baltimore: Penguin Books, Inc., 1966), p. 77.
4. *Ibid.,* p. 252.
5. James, *Alfred I. du Pont,* p. 474.
6. *Ibid.,* p. 478.
7. Murray N. Rothbound, "The Hoover Myth," *For a New America* (New York: Random House, 1970), p. 178.
8. James, *Alfred I. du Pont,* p. 479.
9. New York *World-Telegram,* October 17, 1931.
10. *New York Times,* April 14, 1930, p. 2.
11. *Ibid.*
12. *Literary Digest,* April 26, 1930, p. 7.
13. *Ibid.*
14. Robert Cruise McManus, *North American Review,* January 1931, p. 14.
15. *Literary Digest,* March 21, 1931, p. 8.
16. *Ibid.,* April 25, 1931.
17. *Outlook,* April 15, 1931, p. 517.
18. *Literary Digest,* December 12, 1931.
19. *Ibid.*
20. *New Republic,* March 2, 1932.
21. *Ibid.*
22. *Ibid.*
23. *Ibid.*
24. Ferdinand Lundberg, *America's Sixty Families* (New York: Vanguard Press, 1937), p. 454.
25. *Ibid.,* p. 455; also *Report* of the Special Senate Committee to Investigate the Munitions Industry, 1936, p. 1403.
26. William Leuchtenburg, *Franklin D. Roosevelt and the New Deal* (New York: Harper & Row, Publishers, 1963), p. 39.
27. Richard O. Boyer and Herbert M. Morais, *Labor's Untold Story* (New York: United Electrical, Radio and Machine Workers of America, 1970), p. 271.
28. *Washington Star,* July 29, 1932.
29. *New York Times,* November 10, 1931, p. 8.
30. Munitions Hearings; *Report,* pp. 1403–8.
31. Leuchtenburg, *Franklin D. Roosevelt,* p. 13.
32. "The Man Who Saved Democracy," *Commonweal,* January 18, 1933, p. 315.
33. *New York Times,* January 17, 1953, p. 25.
34. *Ibid.,* January 14, 1953, p. 39.
35. F. I. du Pont Co., "The Chemical Industry" (New York: E. I. du Pont

Co., 1935), p. 14.

36. *New York Times,* September 1, 1963, Sec. III, p. 3.
37. *Ibid.,* January 26, 1934, p. 6.
38. *Ibid.*
39. *Ibid.,* August 27, 1933, Sec. IV, p. 5.
40. *Ibid.,* March 12, 1933, p. 4.
41. Munitions Hearings; *Report,* p. 1406.
42. *New York Times,* November 24, 1933, p. 1.
43. B. C. Forbes, "The Salaries that Are Paid in Various Lines," *American Magazine,* Vol. 89, January 1920.
44. F. I. du Pont, Inc., "The Chemical Industry."
45. *Ibid.*
46. *Ibid.*
47. *New York Times,* January 26, 1934, p. 6.
48. Albert E. Kahn, *High Treason* (New York: Lear Publishers, 1950), p. 129.
49. *New York Times,* January 31, 1934, p. 25.
50. *Business Week,* September 15, 1934, p. 20.
51. Frederick Rudolph, "The American Liberty League, 1934–40," *American Historical Review,* LVI (1950), 19–33; also *New York Times,* December 21, 1934.
52. *Ibid.*
53. Raskob to Shouse, *Shouse Manuscripts;* quoted also in Leuchtenburg, *Franklin D. Roosevelt,* p. 92.
54. *Congressional Record, Senate,* January 15, 1935, p. 450.
55. *New York Times,* December 20, 1963, p. 1.
56. *Ibid.*
57. La Follette Senate Investigating Committee, *Report,* February 8, 1937.
58. *New York Times,* March 10, 1937.
59. Munitions Hearings; *Report,* 1937, Schedule B and p. 1400.
60. *Ibid.*
61. Dickstein-McCormick Special Committee on Un-American Activities, House of Representatives, 73rd Congress, 2nd Session, Testimony of Major General Smedley D. Butler, November 20, 1934, pp. 8–114, DC 6 II.
62. *Ibid.*
63. *Ibid.*
64. *Ibid.*
65. *Ibid.*
66. *Ibid.*
67. *Ibid.*
68. Lundberg, *America's Sixty Families,* p. 179.
69. Dickstein-McCormick Committee, *loc. cit.*
70. *Ibid.*
71. *Ibid., III, Report* (No. 153), Union Calendar No. 44, 74th Congress, 1st Session, House of Representatives, "Investigation of Nazi And Other Propaganda," p. 111; DC 6 II in testimony).
72. *Ibid.,* Testimony of Paul Comly French.
73. *Ibid., Report.*
74. Kahn, *High Treason,* p. 204.
75. *New York Times,* August 25, 1934, p. 12.

76. *Time*, December 3, 1934, pp. 1–2.
77. *Time*, Statement of Ownership, October 1, 1935.
78. Dickstein-McCormick Committee, *Report*, 1935.
79. *New York Times*, February 2, 1930, p. 21.
80. *Ibid.*
81. *Ibid.*
82. Congressional Record, Senate, January 15, 1935, p. 457.
83. *Ibid.*
84. *Ibid.*
85. *Ibid.*
86. *Ibid.*
87. Alfred D. Chandler and Stephen Salsbury, *Pierre S. du Pont and the Making of the Modern Corporation* (New York: Harper & Row, Publishers, 1971), pp. 570 and 703.
88. Munitions Hearings, Exhibit No. 483.
89. William A. Williams, *The Tragedy of American Diplomacy* (New York: Dell Publishing Co., Inc., 1962), p. 133.
90. *Ibid.*, p. 154.
91. *Ibid.*
92. William A. Williams, ed., *The Shaping of American Diplomacy* (Chicago: Rand McNally & Co., 1960), p. 723. (Remarks to cabinet.)
93. For a treatment of Hoover's interpretation of his nonrecognition policy see Professor Richard N. Current's article in the American Historical Review, LIX, No. 3 (April 1954), pp. 513–42.
94. Williams, *Shaping*, p. 706. (Memorandum to Secretary of State Simpson.)
95. Munitions Hearings, Part 5, p. 1368, Exhibit 512.
96. *Ibid., Report*, p. 253.
97. See U.S. Senate, Committee on Military Affairs, Monograph 1, "Economic and Political Aspects of International Cartels," 1944, p. 6; also Munitions Hearings, 1934, Exhibit 512.
98. Munitions Hearings, pp. 1208–15.
99. *Ibid.*, Part II, p. 2561, Exhibit 911.
100. *New York Times*, September 15, 1934, p. 1.
101. Nye Committee, *Report*, 1936, p. 249.
102. William L. Shirer, *The Rise and Fall of the Third Reich* (New York: Simon and Schuster, Inc., 1960), p. 203.
103. Munitions Hearings, Part 5, p. 1197, Exhibit 506.
104. *Ibid.*, pp. 1197–98, Exhibit 507.
105. *Ibid., Report* of the Special Senate Committee, Munitions Hearings, p. 261.
106. *New York Times*, September 15, 1934.
107. Munitions Hearings, Exhibits 519 and 520, Part V, pp. 1236, 1377, and 1379.
108. Munitions Hearings, Part 5, pp. 1243–44.
109. *Ibid.*, pp. 1246–47.
110. *Ibid.*, p. 1199, Exhibit 508.
111. *Ibid.*, Exhibit 1103, Chart A: "International Relations War Materials or Processes."
112. *Ibid.*
113. *New York Times*, August 31, 1933.

114. See *Report.*
115. *Ibid.*
116. *New York Times,* September 18, 1936, p. 26.
117. Shirer, *Third Reich,* p. 389.
118. Congressional Record, Senate, January 15, 1935, p. 456.
119. *Ibid.,* p. 448.
120. *Ibid.*
121. See *New York Times,* December 5, 1934.
122. Congressional Record, Senate, January 15, 1935, p. 457.
123. *New York Times,* September 15, 1934.
124. John K. Winkler, *The Du Pont Dynasty* (Baltimore: Reynal & Hitch-cock, Inc., 1935), p. 330.
125. *New York Times,* September 16, 1934, p. 30.
126. *Ibid.,* December 6, 1934, p. 4.
127. *Ibid.*
128. Munitions Hearings, Testimony of Irénée du Pont.
129. *Ibid.*
130. *New York Times,* September 15, 1934.
131. Munitions Hearings; *Report,* p. 256.
132. *Ibid.*
133. Munitions Hearings, Part V, pp. 1266–67.
134. James, *Alfred I. du Pont,* pp. 541–42.
135. *New York Times,* December 7, 1935, p. 19.
136. *New York Times,* August 23, 1934, p. 4.
137. Special Committee to Investigate Lobbying Activities, U.S. Senate, 74th Congress, 2nd Session, *Report,* 1936, and *Digest of Data.*
138. Winkler, *The Du Pont Dynasty,* p. 321.
139. Martin Lipset, *The Politics of Unreason* (New York: Harper & Row, Publishers, 1970), p. 201.
140. Senate Lobbying Committee, *Report,* 1936.
141. *New York Times,* April 16, 1936, p. 2.
142. Kahn, *High Treason,* p. 195.
143. *New York Times,* April 16, 1936, p. 2.
144. Senate Lobbying Committee, *Report,* also *Digest of Data,* 1936.
145. *Ibid.*
146. *New York Times,* December 7, 1935, p. 19.
147. *Ibid.,* January 4, 1936, p. 1.
148. Lundberg, *America's Sixty Families,* pp. 480–83.
149. UPI dispatch, January 9, 1935.
150. *New York Times,* January 13, 1936, p. 4.
151. *Ibid.,* January 14, 1936, p. 15.
152. *Ibid.,* January 26, 1936, p. 1.
153. Cordell Hull to FDR, January 22, 1938, PPF 473, FDR Memorial Library.
154. *New York Times,* January 31, 1936.
155. New York *Post,* April 18, 1936.
155. New York *Post,* April 18, 1936.
157. Lundberg, *America's Sixty Families,* p. 484.
158. George W. Ziegelmueller, "A Study of the Speaking of Conservatives in Opposition to the New Deal" (Doctoral thesis, Department of Speech,

928

Northwestern University, 1962), p. 64.

159. *New Republic,* September 2, 1936; also Senate Lobbying Committee, 74th Congress, 2nd Session, *Digest of Data.*

160. New York *World-Telegram,* March 10, 1938.

161. Special Conference Committee, *Annual Report,* 1936.

162. Kahn, *High Treason,* p. 166.

163. Henry Kraus, *The Many and the Few* (Los Angeles: The Plantin Press, 1947), p. 9.

164. New York *American,* May 30, 1936.

165. *New York Times,* May 26, 1936.

166. Forrest Davis, "Labor Spies and the Black Legion," *New Republic,* June 17, 1936.

167. Kahn, *High Treason,* pp. 210–11.

168. New York *World-Telegram,* August 8, 1936.

169. *New Republic,* January 20, 1937, p. 340.

170. *Henderson Report* for the National Recovery Administration, January 23, 1935.

171. Congressional Record, February 8, 1937, *Preliminary Report,* La Follette Committee.

172. *Ibid.*

173. *New York Times,* August 15, 1939, p. 5.

174. Saul Alinsky, *John L. Lewis, An Unauthorized Biography* (New York: G. P. Putnam's Sons, 1949), p. 130.

175. *Daily Worker,* January 21, 1937.

176. Wyndham Mortimer, "History of the UAW," *March of Labor,* March 1951, p. 29.

Chapter 11

1. Ruth du Pont to Eleanor Roosevelt, November 12, 1934, FDR Memorial Library, Papers of Eleanor Roosevelt, File 100.

2. Eleanor Roosevelt to Ruth du Pont, November 20, 1934. Papers of Eleanor Roosevelt, File 100.

3. Ruth du Pont to FDR, May 24, 1935. FDR Memorial Library, Papers of Franklin D. Roosevelt, Box 348, D-Folder 2.

4. FDR to Ruth du Pont, May 24, 1935, *Ibid.*

5. FDR to P. S. du Pont, May 27, 1935, *Ibid.*

6. Stephen Birmingham, *The Right People—A Portrait of the American Social Establishment* (Boston: Little, Brown & Co., 1958), p. 70.

7. *New York Times,* January 31, 1934, p. 25.

8. *Ibid.,* December 8, 1937, p. 1.

9. *Ibid.,* December 31, 1937.

10. Harold Ickes, *Secret Diary,* II (New York: Simon & Schuster, 1953), p. 326.

11. *New York Times,* December 28, 1937, p. 4.

12. *Ibid.,* June 27, 1938, p. 2.

13. *Christian Century,* July 27, 1938, p. 910.

14. Robert Engler, *The Politics of Oil* (Chicago: University of Chicago Press, 1961), p. 175.

15. *Fortune,* December 1937, p. 85.

16. *Ibid.*
17. "Du Pont," Script of "The Cavalcade of America," May 25, 1938, Eleutherian-Mills Library.
18. William S. Dutton, *Du Pont—One Hundred and Forty Years* (New York: Charles Scribner's Sons, 1942), p. 377.
19. William H. Carr, *The du Ponts of Delaware* (New York: Dodd, Mead & Co., 1964), p. 317.
20. *Associated Press,* March 24, 1938.
21. *New York Times,* January 25, 1940, p. 28.
22. William A. Williams, *The Tragedy of American Diplomacy* (New York: Dell Publishing Co., Inc., 1962), p. 170.
23. *Ibid.*
24. *Ibid.,* p. 178.
25. *New York Times,* September 28, 1936, p. 8.
26. Williams, *Tragedy,* pp. 191–192.
27. *Ibid.,* p. 193.
28. *Time,* March 7, 1938; also Williams, *Tragedy,* pp. 160–61.
29. Williams, *Tragedy,* p. 195.
30. *Ibid.*
31. *New York Times,* July 21, 1939, p. 2.
32. *Ibid.,* October 31, p. 16.
33. Congressional Record, June 21, 1944, p. 6480.
34. See Frederic R. Sanborn, "Design for War: A Study of Secret Power Politics, 1937–41," in William A. Williams, ed., *The Shaping of American Diplomacy* (Chicago: Rand McNally & Co., 1960). ·
35. *New York Times,* October 30, 1938, Sec. III, p. 9.
36. Testimony of Assistant Attorney General Wendell Berge, September 7, 1944, Kilgore Senate Committee.
37. *Ibid.*
38. Senate Committee on Military Affairs (1944), "Economic and Political Aspects of International Cartels," Monograph 1, pp. 62–64.
39. *Ibid.*
40. *New York Times,* February 12, 1940, p. 11.
41. See Admiral Robert Theobold, *The Secret of Pearl Harbor: The Washington Contribution to the Japanese Attack,* With Corroborative Forewords by Fleet Admiral William F. Halsey and Rear Admiral Husband E. Kimmel (New York: Devine-Adair Company, 1954).
42. *New York Times,* December 12, 1946, p. 1.
43. Speech by Lammot du Pont at Resolutions Committee, National Association of Manufacturers, Hotel Pennsylvania, New York, New York, September 1942.
44. Special Committee on Post-War Economic Policy and Planning, U.S. Senate, 1943, *Report,* pp. 16–17.
45. Carr, *The du Ponts of Delaware,* p. 330.
46. Dutton, *Du Pont,* p. 374.
47. *New York Times,* May 9, 1943, p. 9.
48. *Ibid.*
49. Dutton, *Du Pont,* p. vii.
50. *New York Times,* May 9, 1943, p. 9; June 4, p. 29.
51. *Ibid.,* September 23, 1943, p. 27.

52. *Ibid.*, September 13, 1943, p. 21.
53. Moody's *Industrials*, 1945 (Du Pont Company).
54. *Ibid.* (N.A. Aviation).
55. Williams, *Tragedy*, p. 203.
56. See John Bagguley, "The World War and the Cold War," *Containment and Revolution* (Boston: Beacon Press, 1967), pp. 76–124.
57. Williams, *The Shaping of American Diplomacy*, p. 946.
58. Williams, *Tragedy*, p. 203.

Chapter 12

1. *New York Times*, December 20, 1963.
2. Temporary National Economic Commission (TNEC), Monograph 29, p. 119.
3. John R. Carlson, *The Plotters* (New York: E. P. Dutton & Co., Inc., 1946), p. 248.
4. United Press, October 19, 1946.
5. Karl Schriftgiesser, *The Lobbyist* (Boston: Little, Brown & Co., 1951), p. 198.
6. Congressmen O'Toole, Klein, Sabath, Lesinski, Holifield, Buchanan, Norton, and Blatnik, statements in *Congressional Record*, April 14–16, 1946.
7. Merwin Hart to Lammot du Pont, *Hearings*, Part 4, p. 76, House Select Committee on Lobbying Activities, 81st Congress, 2nd session.
8. *Hearings, Ibid.*, p. 78.
9. *Ibid., General Interim Report* (1950), pp. 11 and 20.
10. Albert E. Kahn, *High Treason* (New York: Lear Publishers, 1950), p. 336.
11. *Ibid.*
12. Du Pont, *The Autobiography of an American Enterprise* (Wilmington: E. I. du Pont de Nemours & Co., 1952), p. 176.
13. "Latest Facts About Candy Purchases in Super Markets," pamphlet published by E. I. du Pont de Nemours & Co. (Wilmington: 1954).
14. *New York Times*, June 4, 1951, p. 41.
15. *Ibid.*
16. *Ibid.*
17. *Congressional Record*, April 5, 1947.
18. *New York Times*, March 3, 1953.
19. Joseph P. Morray, *From Yalta to Disarmament* (New York: Monthly Review Press, 1961), p. 186.
20. *Du Pont Autobiography*, p. 131.
21. National Science Foundation, *Funds for Research and Development* (Washington, D.C.: Government Printing Office, 1960), pp. 9 and 12.
22. *Fortune*, July 1958.
23. Committee on Armed Services, "Employment of Retired Military and Civilian Personnel by Defense Contract Industries," *Hearings*, 1959, pp. 163 and 166.
24. *New York Times*, March 22, 1969.
25. NEC, Monograph 29, p. 116.
26. *New York Times*, November 18–20, 1948.
27. *Ibid.*, June 4, 1957, pp. 1, 23, and 24.

28. *Ibid.*, July 12, 1949, p. 37.
29. H. B. du Pont, "That No Man Shall Be Poor," *Vital Speeches*, XIV (July 15, 1948), 587–90.
30. Associated Press, March 21, 1952, Chicago.
31. *New York Times*, March 6, 1952, p. 38.
32. *Ibid.*, January 7, 1953, p. 33.
33. *Ibid.*
34. *Ibid.*
35. *Ibid.*, February 18 (p. 39), 19, and 28 (p. 25), 1953.
36. *Ibid.*, February 26, 1953, p. 37.
37. *Ibid.*, February 17 (p. 35), 19, 20 (p. 29), and 27 (p. 31), 1953.
38. *Ibid.*, December 4, 1953, pp. 1 and 12.
39. L. L. L. Golden, *Only By Public Consent* (New York: Hawthorn Books, Inc., 1968), p. 307.
40. *New York Times*, December 20, 1965, p. 26.
41. Robert Engler, *The Politics of Oil* (Chicago: University of Chicago Press, 1961), pp. 172–73.
42. *New York Times*, June 4, 1957, pp. 1, 23, and 24.
43. *Ibid.*, September 14, 1958, p. 1.
44. *Ibid.*
45. *Ibid.*, October 14, 1958, p. 26.
46. *Ibid.*, October 3, 1959, p. 1.
47. *Ibid.*
48. *Ibid.*, May 23, 1961, p. 1.
49. Senator Albert Gore, *Congressional Record, Senate*, May 26, 1965, pp. 11399–903; also *I. F. Stone's Weekly*, July 26, 1965, p. 3.
50. Recounted in David Walsh and David Horowitz, "Attorney at Law," *Ramparts*, VII, No. 10 (January 25–February 7, 1969), 134.
51. *New York Times*, February 4, 1962, p. 46.
52. Ferdinand Lundberg, *The Rich and the Super-Rich* (New York: Lyle Stuart, Inc., 1968), p. 255.
53. "Commercial Banks and Their Trust Activities: Emerging Influences on the American Economy," Staff *Report*, Subcommittee on Domestic Finance, House Committee on Banking and Currency, 1967.
54. Walsh and Horowitz, "Attorney at Law."
55. *Ibid.*
56. *Ibid.*
57. *New York Times*, April 13, 1965, p. 49.
58. *Life*, February 25, 1957, p. 145.
59. *Ibid.*, August 19, 1957, p. 108.
60. *New York Times*, September 23, 1962, Sec. III, p. 3.
61. *Ibid.*, September 29, 1951, p. 1.
62. Lammot du Pont Copeland, "World Trade—the National and Corporate Interests" (November 19, 1963), reprinted in *Vital Speeches*, XXX (February 15, 1964), 264–67.
63. Alex Campbell, "Indonesia—The Greatest Prize," *New Republic*, CLX (April 19, 1969), 18.
64. *Congressional Record, Senate*, May 26, 1965, pp. 11399–903; also *I. F. Stone's Weekly*, July 26, 1965, p. 3.
65. "Why the U.S. Risks War in Indochina," *U.S. News and World Report*,

April 4, 1954.
66. Jules Henry, "Capital's Last Frontier," *Nation*, April 25, 1966.
67. *Ibid.*
68. *Ibid.*
69. Speech by H. B. du Pont before the Virginia State Chamber of Commerce, April 8, 1954.
70. *New York Times*, January 30, 1968, p. 5.
71. E. I. du Pont de Nemours & Co., *Annual Report*, 1966, p. 20.
72. Figures from *100 Companies and Their Subsidiary Corporations Listed According to Net Value of Military Prime Contract Awards*, U.S. Department of Defense, 1964 and 1966.
73. Department of Defense, *100 Top Contractors*, 1967.
74. E. I. du Pont de Nemours & Co., *Annual Report*, 1967, p. 26.
75. *New York Times*, April 1, 1963, p. 43.
76. Department of Defense, *100 Top Contractors*, 1969.
77. Wilmington *Evening Journal*, May 12, 1969.
78. *New York Times*, March 22, 1969.
79. *Defense/Aerospace Contract Quarterly*, DMS Computer Systems (Company sequence) (1971–73 quarterly reports).
80. *Ibid.*, Contract No. 421 72–c–6790.

Chapter 13

1. Charles Tilly, Wagner Jackson, and Barry Kay, *Race and Residence in Wilmington, Delaware* (New York: Columbia University Press, 1965), p. 11.
2. U.S. Census of Housing, 1960, Bulletin HC (1) Part 9, Tables 12 and 38.
3. *Ibid.*, Tables 17 and 39.
4. *Ibid.*, Bulletin PC (1), part 9C, Tables 76 and 78.
5. Wilmington *Evening Journal*, December 9, 1960.
6. Greater Wilmington Development Council, *The Long-Term Unemployment in Wilmington, Delaware*, 1961.
7. As president of the Rockland Corporation, W. W. Laird had acquired twenty-one center-city properties by June 1967, bounded by Fifth, Sixth, Market, and Orange Streets, between the Artisans Savings Bank and the Bank of Delaware, for $1,069,111.
8. *Prime Contractors Which Received Awards of $10,000 or More—Delaware, Fiscal Year 1969*, Department of Defense, Deputy Controller for Information Services.
9. Wilmington *Evening Journal*, October 20, 1967.
10. *Ibid.*
11. Wilmington *Evening Journal*, November 15, 1967.
12. *Fortune*, November 1967, p. 138.
13. *Ibid.*
14. *Ibid.*
15. Transcript of meeting of the New York Society of Securities Analysts, 1960.
16. *Business Week*, November 9, 1963.
17. *Ibid.*
18. *Ibid.*, September 21, 1968.

19. Wilmington *Evening Journal*, February 29, 1969.
20. *Ibid.*
21. *Ibid.*, May 2, 1968.
22. *Ibid.*, June 20, 1968.
23. *Ibid.*, February 25, 1969.
24. Delaware *State News*, March 4, 1969.
25. Wilmington *Evening Journal*, August 27, 1955.
26. *Ibid.*, October 31, 1955.
27. *Ibid.*, October 9, 1956.
28. *Ibid.*, November 19, 1968.
29. *Ibid.*, November 20, 1968.
30. *Ibid.*, November 21, 1968.
31. *Ibid.*, May 10, 1969.
32. *New York Times*, September 1, 1963, Sec. III, p. 3.
33. John Kenneth Galbraith, *American Capitalism* (Boston: Houghton Mifflin Company, 1936), p. 69.
34. *New York Times*, July 9, 1967, Sec. III, p. 12.
35. *Ibid.*
36. *Business Week*, December 5, 1970, p. 78.
37. *Fortune*, July 1971, p. 90.
38. *Ibid.*
39. *Business Week*, March 27, 1971, pp. 74–76.
40. *New York Times*, June 22, 1969, Sec. III, p. 2.
41. *Wall Street Journal*, November 23, 1970, p. 1.
42. *Ibid.*
43. *Ibid.*, November 17, 1970.
44. *Ibid.*, November 23, 1970.
45. *Ibid.*
46. *Ibid.*
47. *Pennsylvania Co., Wilmington Trust Co. vs. J. Russell Coulter, Elizabeth M. McNear, et al.* (opinion of) Delaware Court of Chancery, 186 Atl. 2d 751. For a summary of the case, see also "Commercial Banks and Their Trust Activities—Emerging Influences on the American Economy," Vol. I, U.S. Congress, House Committee on Banking and Currency, Subcommittee on Domestic Finance, 90th Congress, 2nd Session (New York: Armo Press and *New York Times*, published privately, 1969), pp. 775–79.
48. *Penn Central Company vs. F. I. du Pont Company*, U.S. District Court, Eastern District of Pennsylvania, 71–1506, Plaintiff's brief, November 18, 1971.
49. *Fortune*, July 1971.
50. *Ibid.*
51. *Ibid.*
52. Christopher Elias, *Fleecing the Lambs* (Greenwich, Conn.: Fawcett Publications, 1972), p. 174.
53. Philadelphia *Sunday Bulletin*, March 28, 1971, p. 36.
54. *Business Week*, March 27, 1971, pp. 74–76.
55. *Forbes*, June 15, 1972, p. 26.
56. *State of the City Address*, Harry G. Haskell, Jr., January 21, 1971.
57. "Pete du Pont Reports," April 1971.
58. *Ibid.*
59. Wilmington *Morning News*, May 11, 1973.

60. *Ibid.,* June 4, 1973.
61. *New York Times,* June 5, 1970, p. 45.
62. *Business Week,* September 12, 1970, pp. 40–41.
63. *Ibid.*
64. *Ibid.*
65. *Newsweek,* March 29, 1971, p. 84.
66. *1970 Annual Report,* E. I. du Pont de Nemours & Co., p. 16.
67. *This Is Du Pont,* No. 31, "Company and Community," p. 33.
68. *Business Week,* September 12, 1970, pp. 40–41.
69. *Ibid.,* April 24, 1971, p. 21.
70. *Ibid.*
71. *New York Times,* December 22, 1971, p. 52.
72. *1972 Annual Report,* E. I. du Pont de Nemours & Co.
73. Courtesy of Citizens Research Foundation, Princeton, N.J., as of March 22, 1973.

Chapter 14

1. *Suntime,* August 29, 1953, p. 6.
2. Booklet published by Estate of Alfred I. du Pont, 1963, p. 15.
3. *Suntime,* August 29, 1953, p. 7.
4. "Du Pont in Florida," *Florida Trend,* July 1958.
5. *Fortune,* November 1952.
6. Robert Sherrill, *Gothic Politics in the Deep South* (New York: Grossman Publishers, 1968), p. 144.
7. *Ibid.,* pp. 145–46.
8. *Ibid.,* p. 149.
9. *Business Week,* August 27, 1960.
10. *New York Times,* August 17, 1970.
11. *New York Times,* February 28, 1971, p. 23.
12. Miami *Herald,* December 20, 1963.
13. *Labor* (Railway), February 15, 1964.
14. Washington *Post,* May 30, 1965.
15. *Congressional Record,* February 5, 1964.
16. *Florida Times Union,* June 25, 1964.
17. *Associated Press,* April 7, 1964.
18. *Florida Times Union,* June 25, 1964.
19. *Ibid.,* May 5, 1964.
20. *Nation,* July 19, 1965, p. 30.
21. *Florida Times Union,* April 1, 1966.
22. *Ibid.,* September 24, 1965.
23. *Ibid.*
24. *Ibid.,* July 11, 1971.
25. See *Florida Times Union,* September 27, 1970.
26. *Suntime,* August 29, 1953, p. 12.
27. *New York Times,* October 6, 1967, p. 1; also *Newsweek,* October 16, 1967, LXX, 36.
28. *Ibid.,* June 20, 1973.
29. *Ibid.,* August 13, 1969, p. 59.
30. *Forbes,* February 15, 1977, p. 66.

31. *Ibid.*, pp. 63-65.
32. *Ibid.*
33. *Ibid.*, p. 66.
34. *New York Times,* June 24, 1981.
35. *Ibid.*
36. *Forbes,* February 15, 1977, p. 63.
37. See Wilmington *News-Journal,* April 7, 1983, p. B3.
38. *Miami Herald,* February 13, 1983, pp. 1F, 6F.
39. *Ibid.*
40. *Ibid.*
41. *Ibid.*

Chapter 15

1. Wilmington *Evening Journal,* June 4, 1973.
2. *Du Pont, The Autobiography of an Enterprise* (Wilmington: E. I. du Pont de Nemours & Co., 1952), p. 138.
3. Sources are *Foundation Directory, 1964, 1967; Tax Exempt Foundations and Charitable Trusts: Their Impact on Our Economy,* Select Committee on Small Business, March 26, 1968, pp. 13, 33.
4. Delaware *State News,* May 26, 1969.
5. Du Pont de Nemours, *National Education* (Newark, Del.: University of Delaware Press, 1923).
6. *New York Times,* November 23, 1935, p. 20.
7. *Ibid.*
8. *Ibid.,* January 18, 1924.
9. Upton Sinclair, *The Goose Step* (Pasadena, Calif.: the author, 1922), p. 345.
10. Philip M. Boffey, "Du Pont and Delaware: Academic Life Behind the Nylon Curtain," *Science,* May 10, 1968, p. 630.
11. *New York Times,* December 14, 1940, p. 11.
12. W. H. Carr, *The Du Ponts of Delaware* (New York: Dodd, Mead & Co., 1964), p. 324.
13. *1972 Annual Report,* E. I. du Pont de Nemours & Co.
14. *New York Times,* June 12, 1964.
15. *Business Week,* April 24, 1971, p. 21.
16. *U.S. vs. Du Pont,* Exhibit No. 53.
17. *News-Journal,* November 1972.
18. Wilmington *Morning News,* May 1, 1971.
19. U.S. District Court, Eastern District of Pennsylvania, No. 71-2811, filed November 18, 1971 (as of March 1974 this case still awaits decision).
20. This figure is arrived at by totaling the assets of those family holding companies and foundations not referred to by Ferdinand Lundberg in his *The Rich and the Super-Rich* (New York: Lyle Stuart, Inc., 1968), then adding them to Lundberg's calculations (which are accurate on the whole), and adjusting for changes in stock values in August 1973.
21. Stock holdings taken from *Notice of Annual Meeting,* "Proxy Statement," E. I. du Pont de Nemours & Co., March 12, 1971, pp. 3 and 8. The 1971 stock values taken from *Moody's Bank and Finance Manual, 1973,*

936

p. 1352, were Du Pont common-average OTC, $141; Christiana common, $150; Christiana preferred, $18,521.

22. *Ibid.*
23. *News-Journal,* November 17, 1972.
24. *Notice, op. cit.*
25. New York *Post,* August 11, 1973.
26. *Ladies Home Journal,* April 1959, p. 94.
27. *House & Garden,* March, 1970, CXXXVII, p. 16.
28. *New York Times,* September 4, 1970.
29. *News-Journal,* March 3, 1971.
30. *Ibid.,* July 9, 1971.
31. *Ibid.,* July 15, 1971.
32. *Time,* December 13, 1971, p. 80.
33. *News-Journal,* January 23, 1968.
34. *Congressional Digest,* November 1934, p. 281.
35. *Moody's Bank and Finance Manual,* 1973, p. 1184.
36. *Best's Insurance Reports, Life-Health,* 1968.
37. *Ibid.,* 1972.
38. William H. Whyte, Jr., *The Organization Man* (New York: Simon and Schuster, Inc., 1956), p. 140.

Chapter 16

1. Wilmington *News-Journal,* October 5, 1973.
2. David Hoffman, "Our Man Mel," *Delaware Today* (August 1974), p. 25.
3. Ben Bagdikian, "Wilmington's Independent Newspapers," *Columbia Journalism Review* (Summer, 1964), p. 16.
4. James Phelan and Robert Pozen, *The Company State* (New York: Grossman, 1973), p. 345.
5. *Ibid.,* p. 340. The sixth maximum rate on bequests to child heirs, in fact, was lower than in 31 of those 36 states.
6. *Ibid.,* Appendix 3 and 4.
7. *Ibid.,* p. 343.
8. Wilmington *Evening Journal,* March 8, 1971.
9. *Ibid.*
10. Phelan and Pozen, *op. cit.,* p. 265.
11. *Ibid.,* p. 224.
12. *Ibid.,* p. 148.
13. See *New Castle County, Neighborhood Environmental Analysis* (1968); also, Phelan and Pozen, pp. 353-355, 125-126.
14. *Ibid.,* p. 109.
15. *Ibid.*
16. *Ibid.,* p. 214.
17. *Ibid.,* p. 355.
18. Office of Economic Opportunity, "Poverty in 1959 and 1969 by State and OEO Region," *Technical Note 1;* January 3, 1971, Washington, D.C.
19. Delaware Division of Special Services, June, 1970, *Bulletin.*
20. Wilmington *Evening Journal,* June 26, 1970.
21. *Delaware Today, op. cit.,* p. 24.
22. *Ibid.,* p. 25.

23. Phelan and Pozen, p. 269.
24. See Phelan and Pozen, Chapter 12; Table 12-1, for example, on page 289, shows just such a ratio in comparing William du Pont, Jr's estate with the properties of four adjacent homeowners.
25. Wilmington *Evening Journal,* July 2, 1971.
26. Interview with Melvin Slawik, August, 1983.
27. *Ibid.*
28. See *Wilmington Housing Authority vs. Parcel of Land,* 219 A 2d 148 (Del. Supr. Ct., 1966).
29. See *Wilmington Suburban Corporation vs. Board of Assessment for New Castle County,* 291 A 2d 293 (Del. Super., 1972). The quote is from Richard Peterson's text of his unpublished July 9, 1975, analysis of the case, to which the author is grateful.
30. Slawik interview, *op. cit.*
31. Getty Oil Company, Tour Brochure for the Delaware City Complex; also interview with Ted Keller, Chairman, Citizens Coalition for Tax Reform, August, 1983.
32. *Delaware Spectator,* January 31, 1973. See Phelan and Pozen, p. 295.
33. *Delaware Spectator,* February 28, 1973.
34. *Taxes and People,* Spring 1974, citing figures from New Jersey Public Interest Research Group.
35. George Crile III, "The Mellons, the Mafia, and a Colonial County," *The Washington Monthly* (June, 1975), p. 50.
36. *Ibid.*
37. *Ibid.,* p. 51.
38. *Ibid.,* p. 52.
39. *Ibid.*
40. *Ibid.,* p. 52-53.
41. *Ibid.,* p. 54.
42. *Ibid.,* p. 66.
43. *Ibid.,* p. 57.
44. *Ibid.,* p. 58.
45. *Delaware Spectator,* February 28, 1975.
46. *Delaware Spectator,* March 14, 1973.
47. *Delaware Spectator,* January 31, 1973.
48. *Delaware Spectator,* August 9, 1973.
49. Wilmington *Morning News,* September-October, 1973.
50. Wilmington *News-Journal,* October 10, 1973.
51. *Ibid.,* August 9, 1973.
52. Phelan and Pozen, p. 340.
53. Wilmington *Evening Journal,* August 23, 1973.
54. 1967 Census of Governments, State Report #8, Delaware, p. 8.
55. U.S. Department of Commerce, *State and Local Government Study* #43; "State and Local Government Finances in 1942 and 1957" (Government Printing Office, 1958) p. 16.
56. *Congressional Quarterly,* July 9, 1971, p. 1489.
57. John Gates, *The du Pont Family* (New York: Doubleday, 1979), p. 175.
58. *Philadelphia Sunday Bulletin,* November 17, 1974.
59. *Ibid.*
60. See *New York Times,* January 24, 1974, p. 22; May 7, 1974, p. 28.
61. *Delaware State News,* October 28, 1974.

62. *Phelan and Pozen, op. cit.*, p. 306.
63. *Delaware State News*, October 28, 1974.
64. *Ibid.*
65. *Delaware State News*, October 29, 1974.
66. See Phelan and Pozen, Chapter 9, "The Du Pont Dailies."
67. Cansler to Smyth, November 23, 1960.
68. *Delaware State News*, October 27, 1974.
69. *Delaware State News*, November 1, 1974; see also Joseph Smyth to John W. Jardin, Jr. (Delaware News Council), October 31, 1974.
70. *Ibid.*, November 3, 1974.
71. *Ibid.*, November 7, 1979; Nov. 20, 1974.
72. *Ibid.*, November 18, 1979.
73. *Delaware State News*, November 26, 1974.
74. *Ibid.*, November 16, 1979.
75. *Ibid.*
76. See Chapter 15, p. 571
77. *Gerard Colby-Zilg vs. E.I. du Pont de Nemours & Co. and Prentice Hall Inc* (hereinafter referred to as *Colby-Zilg vs. Du Pont*), Deposition of Governor Pierre S. du Pont IV, Exhibit: Gerard Colby-Zilg to Congressman Pierre du Pont, June 26, 1973. Also Colby-Zilg to Reynolds du Pont, June 26, 1973.
78. *Ibid.*, Deposition of Irénée du Pont, Jr.
79. *Ibid.*, Depositions of Irénée du Pont, Jr., Thomas Stephenson and Oscar Collier.
80. *Ibid.*
81. *Ibid.*, Thomas Stephenson to Public Affairs Dept., Du Pont Co., June 12, 1974.
82. Robert Sherrill, "The Book That Du Pont Hated," *Nation*, February 14, 1981, p. 174.
83. *Ibid.*
84. *Ibid.*; see also *Colby-Zilg vs. Du Pont*, Deposition of J. Bruce Bredin.
85. *Colby-Zilg vs. Du Pont*, Richard Rea to Public Affairs Dept., Irénée du Pont, Jr., June 17, 1974.
86. Bettina Sargeant to Stephenson (Du Pont Co. memo), July, 1974.
87. Stephenson memo, July 7, 1974.
88. Brown to Stephenson, July 25, 1974 (Du Pont Co. memo).
89. Rea (Du Pont Co.) to Daly (Prentice-Hall), August 8, 1974.
90. Memo to Peter Grenquist, head of Trade Book Division, Prentice-Hall, Inc., September , 1974.
91. *New York Times*, December 15, 1974, IV, p. 5.
92. *Colby-Zilg vs. Du Pont*, see Deposition of Clinton Archer, Harold G. Brown and Thomas Stephenson, Du Pont memo on Robert Sherrill (December, 1974); also Wilmington *Morning News*, November 15, 1979; *Philadelphia Daily News*, November 16, 1979.
93. Stephenson to Frankel, December 20, 1974.
94. Frankel to Stephenson, December 30, 1974.
95. Stephenson to Frankel, January 17, 1975.
96. Frankel to Stephenson, February 10, 1975.
97. *New York Times*, April 13, 1975.
98. *Delaware State News*, February 16, 1981.
99. Rolf Rykken, "The Lingering Death of the *Delaware State News*," *Delaware Today*, June, 1981, p. 27.
100. *Ibid.*, p. 27.

101. *Philadelphia Inquirer,* January 5, 1975.
102. *Philadelphia Bulletin,* January 12, 1975.
103. Christopher Perry, "The Thursday Night Massacre," *Delaware Today,* February, 1975, p. 28b.
104. *Ibid.*
105. *Ibid.*
106. *Ibid.*
107. *Ibid.,* p. 28d.
108. *Ibid.,* p. 283.
109. David B. Dawson to News and Editorial Department Employees, June 3, 1975.
110. Wilmington *Morning News,* January 4, 1975.
111. *Philadelphia Sunday Bulletin,* January 5, 1975.
112. Wilmington *Evening Journal,* January 3, 1975.
113. *Philadelphia Sunday Bulletin,* January 5, 1975.
114. Wilmington *Evening Journal,* January 3, 1975.
115. Perry, *op.cit.,* p. 28f.
116. *Editor and Publisher,* January 11, 1975.
117. *Ibid.*
118. Perry, *op. cit.,* 286.
119. *Ibid.*
120. *New York Times,* January 6, 1975.
121. Wilmington *Morning News,* January 6, 1975.
122. *Philadelphia Bulletin,* January 5, 1975.
123. *Ibid.*
124. Wilmington *Evening Journal,* January 4, 1975.
125. Christopher Perry, *Delaware Today,* February, 1975, pp. 56 and 28h.
126. *New York Times,* January 7, 1975; Wilmington *Morning News,* January 7, 1975.
127. *Newsweek,* January 13, 1975.
128. Wilmington *Morning News,* January 7, 1975.
129. Richard P. Sanger, "Memorandum to the News and Editorial Department Staff," January 8, 1975.
130. Perry, *op. cit.,* p. 57.
131. *Ibid.*
132. *Ibid.*
133. *Ibid.,* p. 28h.
134. Wilmington *Morning News,* January 7, 1975.
135. Wilmington *Evening Journal,* January 8, 1975.
136. See papers of Free Europe Committee in the John F. Kennedy Presidential Library for Dulles's collaboration with Greenwalt and Harlan Wendell of Du Pont's Public Affairs Dept.
137. Wilmington *News Journal,* January 21, 1975.
138. *New York Times,* January 21, 1975.
139. *Ibid.*
140. Wilmington *Morning News,* January 23, 1975.
141. *New York Times,* January 21, 1975.
142. Interview by Charlotte Dennett of Shaun D. Mullen, September, 1981.
143. Wilmington *Morning News,* January 7; 1975.
144. Perry, *op. cit.,* p. 28h.
145. *Philadelphia Sunday Bulletin,* November 17, 1974.
146. *Ibid.*
147. Wilmington *Evening Journal,* December 7, 1974.

940

148. Mel Slawik to Lou Gordon, October 8, 1976.
149. See Special Senate Committee on Intelligence Abuses, Report on FBI "Cointelpro," including illegal operations against Martin Luther King, Jr., and the civil rights and anti-war movements. Government Printing Office (Washington, D.C., 1976); See also Sanford J. Unger, *The FBI* (Boston: The Atlantic Monthly Press, 1976); and Public Broadcasting's 1982 exposes of FBI's harrassment of actress Jean Seberg, who was driven to suicide.
150. House Bill No. 416, as amended by House Amendment No. 4, 128th General Assembly, Delaware. See particularly Section 1, amendment to S 8101, Chapter 81, Title 9, Delaware Cole, "Property subject to County taxation," section (c) and (e) (2).
151. Interview with Melvin Slawik, *op. cit.*
152. Wilmington *News-Journal*, November 30, 1975.
153. *The Delaware Spectator*, December 26, 1974.
154. Delaware Revenue Study Commission (1973), p. 92-93.
155. *United States vs. Slawik*, 427F Supp. 824(1977), p. 828.
156. Wilmington *News-Journal*, October 21, 1977.
157. Pierre S. du Pont IV, to Ted Keller, September 10, 1976.
158. Wilmington *Morning News*, October 20, 1976; also, Ted Keller to Pierre du Pont, August 13, 1976.
159. Catherine S. Mulholland to Joseph J. Farnan, Jr., January 27, 1978.
160. Wilmington *Evening Journal*, July 1, 1976.
161. *Delaware State News*, July 1, 1976.
162. Wilmington *News-Journal*, January 1, 1977.
163. Ted Keller to Pierre du Pont, May 26.
164. Wilmington *News-Journal*, July 3, 1975.
165. See *News-Journal* articles, March 26, April 20, 1976.
166. Wilmington *News-Journal*, September 2, 1977.
167. Deposition of Thomas Stephenson and Harold G. Brown, *Colby-Zilg vs. Du Pont, op. cit.*
168. *New York Times*, April 11, 1977, p. 43.
169. *Ibid.*
170. John Taylor, "Irving Shapiro, The Man," *Delaware Today*, October 1979, p. 13.
171. *Ibid.*, pp. 44-5.
172. *Ibid.*, p. 14.
173. *Ibid.*, p. 16.
174. *Ibid.*
175. *New York Times*, August 8, 1982, Sec 3, p. 15.
176. Taylor, *op. cit.*, p. 14.
177. *Ibid.*, p. 45.
178. *New York Times*, August 8, 1982, Sec. 3, p. 15.
179. Taylor, *op. cit.*, p. 16.
180. *Ibid.*, p. 17.
181. *Ibid.*
182. *Delaware State News*, December 15, 1974.
183. *New York Times*, September 31, 1975.
184. *Delaware State News*, December 15, 1974.
185. Irving Shapiro, "Leadership for America: Whose Responsibility?" Speech before National Business Leadership Conference, Chicago, Illinois, January 23, 1975.
186. *Ibid.*
187. *Ibid.*

188. *Delaware State News,* June 8, 1975 (see this excellent series of articles by reporter Don Glickstein).
189. *Ibid.*
190. *Ibid.*
191. *Ibid.*
192. *Ibid.*
193. *Ibid.*
194. *Ibid.*
195. *Ibid.*
196. *Ibid.*
197. *Ibid.*
198. *Delaware State News,* June 1, 1975.
199. *Delaware State News,* May 18, 1975.
200. *Ibid.*
201. *Delaware Spectator,* April 24, 1975.
202. Wilmington *Morning News,* May 22, 1975.
203. *Ibid.*
204. Taylor, *op. cit.,* p. 47.
205. *Delaware State News,* December 7, 1975.
206. *Ibid.,* April 23, 1975.
207. *Ibid.,* May 18, 1975.
208. *Ibid.,* April 23, 1975.
209. *Ibid.,* December 7, 1975.
210. *Ibid.,* October 23, 1975.
211. *Ibid.,* February 1, 1976.
212. *Ibid.*
213. *Ibid.*
214. *Philadelphia Inquirer,* February 1, 1976.
215. Taylor, *op. cit,* p. 47.
216. *Delaware State News,* February 1, 1976.
217. *Sunday News-Journal,* March 28, 1976.
218. Wilmington *Evening Journal,* May 25, 1976.
219. *Ibid.,* April 13, 1976.
220. *Business Week,* December 1, 1975, p. 77.
221. *Ibid.*
222. *Ibid.*
223. *Ibid.,* p. 78.
224. *Ibid.*
225. *Ibid.*
226. See "Fibres and Textiles: Dimensions of Corporate Marketing Structures," Secretariat, United Nations Conference on Trade and Development (N.Y.-Geneva, 1981) TD/B/C.1 219; 245 pages. For a brief account in the United States on European developments as related to Du Pont, see *Forbes,* November 1, 1976, p. 34.
227. Wilmington *Evening Journal,* April 13, 1976, p. 9.
228. *Ibid.*
229. *Ibid.*
230. Pension Investments—A Social Audit, Corporate Data Exchange, Inc. (New York, 1979), Chart B, page B-9.
231. Wilmington *Evening Journal,* April 13, 1976, p. 9.

942

232. Figures on officers' and directors' compensation are from pages 8 and 9 of 1976 Proxy Statement of E.I. du Pont de Nemours & Co. Figures on Christiana Securities' income from Du Pont common dividends are based on Proxy Statement's identification of Christiana Securities' holding of Du Pont common at 13,417,120 shares (ftn. p. 9) multiplied by $5.25 total dividends paid in 1976 reported on page 22 of 1976 *Annual Report*.

233. For a broader and more detailed study of this process, see Jeremy Rifkin and Randy Barber, *The North Will Rise Again: Pensions, Politics and Power in the 1980's* (Boston: Beacon Press, 1978).

234. *Pension Investments, op. cit.*, Chart A, p. A-16.

235. Irving Shapiro, "Corporate Reform: What's the Real Issue?" Speech before the Commercial Club of Boston, April 20, 1976.

236. *Ibid.*

237. *Ibid.*

238. Wilmington *Evening Journal,* May 25, 1976.

239. *Ibid.*

240. *Philadelphia Bulletin,* May 30, 1976.

241. Shapiro, "Corporate Reform," *op. cit.*

242. Robert J. Ledogar, *Hungry for Profits: U.S. Food and Drug Multinationals in Latin America,* 1 DOC/North America (New York, 1975) p. 32.

243. Taylor, *op. cit.,* p. 47.

244. *New York Times,* April 9, 1976, p. 13.

245. *New York Times,* October 2, 1976, p. 2.

246. *Ibid.*

247. Wilmington *Evening Journal,* June 8, 1976.

248. *Chemical Worker,* July, 1976.

249. Wilmington *Morning News,* July 7, 1976.

250. *Philadelphia Bulletin,* May 30, 1976.

251. *Ibid.*

252. Wilmington *News Journal,* June 27, 1976.

253. Wilmington *Morning News,* July 7, 1976.

254. *Philadelphia Bulletin,* October 10, 1976, Section 1C.

255. *Ibid.*

256. *Ibid.*

257. *Philadelphia Inquirer,* October 31, 1976.

258. Wilmington *News-Journal,* November 25, 1976.

259. *New York Times,* August 2, 1976, p. 55.

260. *Ibid.*

261. *Forbes,* November 1, 1976, p. 34.

262. *New York Times,* October 1, 1976, IV, p. 1.

263. *Philadelphia Bulletin,* October 1, 1976.

264. *Ibid.*

265. *Ibid.*

266. See Trilateral Commission, *Crisis of Democracy: Report on Governability of Democracies to the Trilateral Commission* (New York: New York University Press, 1975).

267. See *Crisis of Democracy,* Chapter Three: "The United States"

268. *Ibid.,* p. 73.

269. *Ibid.,* pp. 76-85.

270. *Ibid.,* pp. 85-91.

271. *Ibid.,* p. 93.

272. *Ibid.*
273. *Ibid.*, p. 102.
274. *Ibid.*, p. 106.
275. *Ibid.*, p. 104.
276. *Ibid.*, p. 110.
277. *Ibid.*, p. 112.
278. *Ibid.*, p. 110.
279. *Ibid.*, p. 105.
280. *New York Times*, November 12, 1976, IV, p. 1.
281. *Ibid.*
282. *Ibid.*
283. *New York Times*, October 1, 1976, IV, p. 1.
284. Wilmington *News-Journal*, August 25, 1976.
285. *Ibid.*, November 12, 1976, IV, p. 12.
286. *Ibid.*
287. *Ibid.*
288. *Ibid.*
289. Wilmington *News-Journal*, November 16, 1976.
290. *Ibid.*
291. *Philadelphia Inquirer*, December 5, 1976.
292. *News Journal*, April 28, 1976.
293. *Philadelphia Inquirer*, December 5, 1976.
294. *Ibid.*
295. *Ibid.*
296. *Ibid.*
297. *New York Times*, April 11, 1977, p. 43.
298. *Ibid.*
299. *Wall Street Journal, May 24, 1979.*
300. *New York Times*, April 11, 1977.
301. Wilmington *News-Journal*, March 3, 1977.
302. Wilmington *News-Journal*, June 17, 1977.
303. *Ibid.*
304. *Ibid.*
305. Wilmington *Morning News*, May 22, 1976.
306. Wilmington *News-Journal*, September 2, 1977.
307. *Ibid.*
308. *Ibid.*
309. Wilmington *News-Journal*, October 14, 1977, p. 3.
310. *Ibid.*
311. *Ibid.*
312. *Ibid.*
313. Wilmington *News-Journal*, October 16, 1977.
314. Wilmington *News-Journal*, November 1, 1977.
315. *Ibid.*
316. *Ibid.*, November 4, 1977.
317. *Ibid.*, January 8, 1977.
318. *Ibid.*
319. Wilmington *News-Journal*, May 27, 1973.
320. *Ibid.*, October 18, 1977.

Chapter 17

1. *Newsweek,* April 11, 1977, pp. 45-46.
2. Wilmington *News-Journal,* February 27, 1977.
3. *Hercules News,* May 27, 1977.
4. *Delaware State News,* June 8, 1977.
5. *Delaware Spectator,* December 13, 1973.
6. Letter to the Wilmington *News-Journal,* February 1, 1977, by Ted Keller for Citizens Coalition for Tax Reform.
7. *Delaware State News,* April 14, 1977.
8. C.B. McCoy, "An Approach to Delaware's Future." Speech before Wilmington Rotary Club, January 3, 1974.
9. Wilmington *News-Journal,* June 8, 1977.
10. *Ibid.,* April 21, 1977.
11. Memo from T.W. Stephenson to members of Public Affairs Dept., Du Pont Company, May 16, 1977.
12. *Delaware State News,* May 26, 1977.
13. Irving Shapiro, mailgram sent 8:01 P.M., June 28, 1977, to selected employees of Du Pont Company.
14. Wilmington *News-Journal,* December 10, 1978.
15. *Ibid.*
16. Wilmington *News-Journal,* February 27, 1977.
17. *Moody's Government and Municipal Manual,* 1983. Moody's Investors Service, Inc. (New York, 1983), p. 715.
18. Wilmington *News-Journal,* September 22, 1977.
19. *Washington Post,* June 7, 1977.
20. Wilmington *Evening Journal,* August 29, 1977.
21. *Mississippi Sun,* July 22, 1977.
22. *Du Pont News,* Vol. 6, No. 5, May, 1977.
23. Wilmington *Evening Journal,* November 14, 1973.
24. Du Pont *Context,* Vol. 9, November 1, 1980.
25. Wilmington *Evening Journal,* September 22, 1977.
26. *New York Times,* February 10, 1977.
27. *Financial News Service,* February 18, 1977; *Daily News Record,* February 18, 1977.
28. *E.I. du Pont de Nemours & Co. vs. Train;* Petition Nos. 75-978, 75-1473, 75-1705.
29. *Forbes,* March 1, 1977, p. 70.
30. *New York Times,* June 15, 1977, p. D7.
31. *Ibid.*
32. *Ibid.*
33. *Ibid.*
34. *Ibid.,* June 24, 1977, p. F9.
35. *Ibid.*
36. *Ibid.*
37. *Philadelphia Bulletin,* January 30, 1977.
38. *Ibid.*
39. *Ibid.*
40. *Ibid* .
41. *Business Week,* October 31, 1977, p. 38.
42. *Du Pont News,* Vol. 6, No. 6, June, 1977.

43. *Wall Street Journal,* March 14, 1977.
44. *New York Times,* June 29, 1977, IV, p. 1.
45. *Delaware State News,* April 12, 1977.
46. *Ibid.*
47. *Philadelphia Bulletin,* March 13, 1977.
48. *Ibid.,* March 7, 1978.
49. *Ibid.*
50. *Ibid.*
51. *Ibid* .
52. Wilmington *News-Journal,* February 5, 1978.
53. *New York Times,* October 19, 1977, IV, p. 7.
54. Wilmington *News-Journal,* February 5, 1978.
55. *Ibid.*
56. *Ibid.*
57. *Du Pont News,* Vol. 6, No. 6, June, 1977.
58. *Ibid.*
59. Wilmington *Morning News,* March 2, 1978.
60. "Disclosure of Corporate Ownership," U.S. Senate Committee on Government Operations, Subcommittees on Intergovernmental Relations and Budgeting, Management and Expenditures, Government Printing Office (Washington, D.C., 1974), p. 1. Hereafter known as the (Sen.) Metcalf Report.
61. Stockholdings taken from Metcalf Report.
62. Adolf Berle and Gardiner Means, *The Modern Corporation and Private Property,* Macmillan (New York, 1932), p. 68.
63. Julius W. Allen, "The Exercise of Voting Rights by Large Institutional Investors," *Voting Rights in Major Corporations,* Staff Study of Subcommittee on Reports, Accounting and Management, Committee on Governmental Affairs, U.S. Senate, Government Printing Office (Washington, D.C., 1978) p. 616.
64. Berle and Means, *op. cit.,* pp. 277-278.
65. Wilmington *News-Journal,* May 31, 1978.
66. *Ibid.*
67. See *Annual Report,* 1978, Wilmington Trust Co.
68. See *Annual Report,* 1978, E.I. du Pont de Nemours & Co.
69. See *Annual Report,* 1978, Continental American Life Insurance Co.
70. See *Moody's Investment Manual,* 1978.
71. Wilmington *News-Journal,* May 31, 1977.
72. *Moody's Industrials,* 1982, p. 2712.
73. See *Best's Insurance Manual; Moody's Finance Manual*—1980.
74. Wilmington *Evening Journal,* May 31, 1978.
75. *New York Times,* May 31, 1978, IV, p. 2.
76. *Ibid.*
77. *Du Pont News,* Vol 7, No. 6, June, 1978.
78. Wilmington *News-Journal,* May 23, 1976.
79. *Wall Street Journal.*
80. *Ibid.*
81. Wilmington *News-Journal,* June 21, 1979.
82. *Wall Street Journal,* 1980.
83. Du Pont Proxy Statement, March, 1978, p. 9.
84. Du Pont Proxy Statement, March, 1983, p. 7.
85. Wilmington *News-Journal,* March 23, 1977.

946

86. Irving Shapiro, "The American Economy: How Sound?" Speech at Southern Governors Conference, San Antonio, Texas, August 28, 1977, *Vital Speeches,* Vol. 43., No 24, October, 1977, pp. 738-741.
87. *Ibid.*
88. *Tax Notes,* April 24, 1970, p. 460.
89. *Ibid.*
90. Data from College of Urban Affairs, University of Delaware.
91. Wilmington *Evening Journal,* January 3, 1979.
92. Charles McCoy, "An Approach Toward Delaware's Future," Speech before Rotary Club of Wilmington, January 3, 1974.
93. *Delaware State News,* April 22, 1977.
94. Wilmington *Morning News,* April 22, 1977.
95. *Delaware State News,* December 27, 1977.
96. *Delaware State News,* January 18, 1979.
97. Pierre S. du Pont IV, Financial Disclosure Report, filed April 29, 1978, pp. 4-5. (On file at the Offices of the Delaware Secretary of State; a copy is possessed by the author.)
98. Pierre S. du Pont IV, Financial Disclosure Report, filed April .
99. See Pierre S. du Pont IV, Financial Disclosure Report, filed in 1972 and 1977; both show substantial holdings in Exxon and Phillips Petroleum, among other oil companies.
100. Wilmington *News-Journal,* October 28, 1979.
101. *Ibid.*
102. *Ibid.*
103. *Ibid.*
104. *Oil and Gas Journal,* November 5, 1979.
105. Wilmington *News-Journal,* October 28, 1979.
106. *Oil and Gas Journal,* November 5, 1979.
107. Wilmington *News-Journal,* October 3, 1979; October 28, 1979.
108. *Ibid.*
109. *Oil and Gas Journal,* November 5, 1979.
110. Wilmington *News-Journal,* October 28, 1979.
111. Wilmington *News-Journal,* June, 1978.
112. Wilmington *Evening Journal,* November 29, 1979.
113. *County Post,* November 28, 1979.
114. Wilmington *News-Journal,* October 28, 1979.
115. Wilmington *News Week,* November 15-21, 1979.
116. Wilmington *News-Journal,* December 2, 1979.
117. *Ibid.*
118. *Delaware Today,* January, 1980, p. 8.
119. Wilmington *News-Journal,* October 29, 1979.
120. *Ibid.*
121. *Ibid.*
122. Wilmington *News-Journal,* January 18, 1981.
124. Wilmington *News-Journal,* May 29, 1970.
125. Wilmington *News-Journal,* March 9, 1977.
126. Wilmington *News-Journal,* October 30, 1977.
127. Wilmington *News-Journal,* January 18, 1981.
128. *Ibid.*
129. *Ibid.*
130. *Ibid.*

131. Interview, Wilmington, Delaware, August, 1983, #52.
132. Phone Interview #11, Wilmington, Delaware, August, 1983.
133. 1978 Witwatersrand vicinity telephone directory, Republic of South Africa, p. 150.
134. Pierre S. du Pont IV, Financial Disclosure Report, filed April, 1978, at the Office of Delaware Secretary of State, Dover, Delaware.
135. Nathan Hayward III, Financial Disclosure Report, filed April, 1978, at the office of Delaware Secretary of State, Dover, Delaware.
136. Wilmington *Morning News*, January 19, 1971.
137. All figures for 1979-80 campaign donations are from the Federal Elections Commission, as released to the author.
138. *Forbes*, October 2, 1978, p. 37.
139. *Ibid.*
140. *Ibid.*
141. Wilmington *Morning News*, April 18, 1978.
142. *Fortune*, September 10, 1979, p. 74.
143. *Du Pont News*, Vol. 7 No. 12, December, 1978.
144. *Ibid.*
145. *Ibid.*, Vol. 7, No. 5. May, 1978.
146. *Ibid.*
147. *Ibid.*, Vol. 7, No. 10, October 1978.
148. *Ibid.*
149. *Ibid.*, Vol. 8, No. 1, January, 1979.
150. *New York Times*, January 17, 1978, p. 15.
151. *Du Pont News*, Vol. 7, No. 10, October, 1978.
152. *New York Times*, June 6, 1979, Sec. IV.
153. See *Du Pont News*, Vol. 7, No. 4, April 1978, p. 2, and No. 3, March 1978, p. 1.
154. *Delaware State News*, March 5, 1978.
155. *Ibid.*
156. Wilmington *News-Journal*, May 14, 1978.
157. *Today's Sunbeam* (Salem County), December 14, 1978.
158. Figures provided by computer data services of federal Occupational Safety and Health Administration, February, 1980.
159. Wilmington *Evening Journal*, September 11, 1979.
160. *Delaware State News*, September 30, 1981.
161. *Ibid.*, September 14, 1980.
162. Wilmington *News-Journal*, May 26, 1979.
163. G.J. Stopp to C.A. D'Alonzo, November 2, 1964, p. 1.
164. *Ibid.*, p. 2.
165. Wilmington *Evening Journal*, February 1, 1980.
166. Interview, Jacob Kreshtool, August, 1983.
167. *Du Pont Context*, Vol. 9, No. 1, 1980, "Opening the Boardroom Windows," pp. 8-14; also Wilmington *News-Journal*, October 28, 1979.
168. Wilmington *News-Journal*, October 29, 1979.
169. *New York Times*, November 4, 1979.
170. *Environmental News*, Environmental Protection Agency, December 6, 1977, "Farm and Home Fungus-Killing Pesticides Being Reviewed by EPA"; Du Pont Corporate News, Release January 26, 1979; "Resume of Conference with Du Pont Representatives, January 26, 1979, Jekyll Island (Ga)."

171. David Callaghan, Department of Natural Resources, West Virginia, to F.H. Winterkamp, Du Pont plant manager, Belle, West Virginia, March 19, 1977.
172. List of Emergency Air Pollution Releases by Du Pont Belle plant from files of West Virginia Air Pollution Control Commission.
173. *New York Times*, February 3, 1980.
174. *Ibid.*, February 7, 1980, p. A22.
175. *Ibid.*
176. *Ibid.*
177. *Nation*, September 20, 1980, p. 244.
178. *New York Times*, February 3, 1980.
179. Silver, K. and Seixas, N., "Occupational Health," *Toxics Briefing Book*, Conference on Alternative State and Local Policies (Washington, D.C., 1983), p. 1.
180. *New York Times*, February 3, 1980.
181. Silver and Seixas, *op. cit.*
182. Hamilton, Alice, *Exploring the Dangerous Trades*, Little Brown and Co. (Boston, 1943), cited in Silver and Seixas, p 1-2.
183. *New York Times*, February 3, 1980.
184. *Ibid.*
185. *Ibid.*
186. *Ibid.*
187. *Ibid.*
188. *Ibid.*
189. See Rolf Rykken and John Taylor's excellent articles, "Slow Death from the Poison Wasteland" and "Where the Poison Rivers Flow," *Delaware Today*, August and October, 1980.
190. Hash to Newport Plant staff, August 1, 1980.
191. Wilmington *News-Journal*, November 3, 1979.
192. Mark Green and Andrew Buchsbaum, *The Corporate Lobbies* (1980), p. 145.
193. *Employee Relations Venture Plan—Old Hickory, E.I. du Pont de Nemours & Co.*, June 30, 1980 (marked "Personal and Confidential"). Various 1979 and 1980 revisions identified and included. A copy is in the author's possession.
194. Robert Pearlman and Richard Buse, *The Way to Win.* (One of the xeroxed copies that circulated Du Pont offices is in the author's possession.)
195. Employee Relations Venture Plan, *op. cit.*, "Know Your Employee," Attachment #2-VII-A, 2 pages, November 29, 1979.
196. *Ibid.*
197. E.I. du Pont de Nemours & Co., Proxy Statement, March, 1980.
198. *New York Times*, July 13, 1980, p. 13.
199. *Ibid.*
200. *Ibid.*
201. *New Republic*, August 22-29, 1981, p. 9.
202. *New York Times*, October 1, 1979, IV, p. 1.
203. *Ibid.*
204. *Ibid.*
205. Wilmington *News-Journal*, February 5, 1978.
206. Wilmington *Morning News*, September 5, 1980.
207. *New York Times*, November 29, 1981, p. 33.

Chapter 18

1. *New York Times,* May 15, 1977, p. 26.
2. *Ibid.,* March 28, 1981, p. 23.
3. Sharon Fitzgerald, "The Charge of the Bank Brigade," *Delaware Today,* July, 1981.
4. Metcalf Senate Report, 1974, *op. cit.,* p. 1.
5. "Voting Rights in Major Corporations," Senate Subcommittee on Reports, Accounting and Management, 1978, *op. cit.,* p. 474.
6. *Ibid.,* p. 486.
7. *Ibid.,* p. 486.
8. Fitzgerald, *op. cit.,* p. 25.
9. *New York Times,* March 17, 1981, p. D11.
10. *Ibid.*
11. *Ibid.*
12. *Ibid.*
13. *Ibid.*
14. *Ibid.*
15. *Delaware State News,* November 16, 1980.
16. *New York Times,* March 17, 1981, p. D11.
17. *Ibid.*
18. *Ibid.*
19. Fitzgerald, *op. cit.,* p. 41.
20. *Delaware State News,* February 1, 1981.
21. *Ibid.*
22. *Ibid.*
23. *Ibid.*
24. *Ibid.*
25. *New York Times,* March 17, 1981, p. 1.
26. *Ibid.*
27. Wilmington *Morning News,* May 8, 1982.
28. *Delaware State News,* February 4, 1982.
29. Wilmington *News-Journal,* August 8, 1982.
30. *William E. Donoghue's Money Fund* (Holliston, Maryland), October, 1982.
31. William H. Whyte, Jr., *The Organization Man* (New York: Simon and Shuster, 1956), p. 440.
32. *Ibid.,* pp. 438-9.
33. *Ibid.,* p. 308.
34. *Ibid.*
35. *Ibid.*
36. *Ibid.,* p. 439.
37. *The American Lawyer,* November 1981.
38. *Ibid.*
39. *New York Times,* July 9, Sect. IV, p. 10.
40. *Ibid.*
41. *Ibid.,* August 11, 1981, p. D4.
42. *Ibid.,* July 9, 1981; these speculations were offered by the *Times* analyst Vartaniz Vartan.
43. *Ibid.*
44. *Fortune,* September 7, 1981.

950

45. *New York Times,* February 11, 1981, IV, p. 2.
46. E.I. du Pont de Nemours & Co., Proxy Statement, March 6, 1981, p. 7.
47. *Consumer Reports,* February, 1982, pp. 74-75.
48. *New York Times,* February 11, 1981, IV, p. 2.
49. *Ibid.,* August 10, 1981, p. D3.
50. *New York Times,* July 14, 1981, p. D6.
51. *Ibid.,* August 9, 1981, Sec. 3, p. 1.
52. Wilmington *News-Journal,* August 22, 1982.
53. Barry Bluestone and Bennett Harrison, *The DeIndustrialization of America* (New York: Basic Books, 1982), p. 159.
54. David Gordon, "Capital-Labor Conflict and the Productivity Showdown," *American Economic Review,* Papers and Proceedings, Vol. 71, No. 2 (May, 1981) pp. 30-35.
55. *Ibid.,* p. 158.
56. *New York Times,* August 6, 1981.
57. Thomas J. Peters and Robert H. Waterman, Jr., *In Search of Excellence: Lessons From America's Best Run Companies* (New York: Harper & Row, 1982). p. 193.
58. *Business Week,* November 24, 1980, p. 96.
59. *Ibid.*
60. *New York Times,* August 10, 1981, p. D8.
61. *Ibid.,* June 21, 1981, p. F15.
62. *Ibid.,* December 9, 1981, Sec. 4, p. 4.
63. *Ibid.,* August 10, 1981, p. D8.
64. *Ibid.,* August 3, 1981, p. D1.
65. *Ibid.,* August 11, 1981, p. D4.
66. *Ibid.,* December 9, 1981, Sec. 4, p. 4.
67. *Ibid.*
68. See Alfred D. Chandler and Stephen Salisbury, *Pierre S. du Pont and the Making of the Modern Corporation, op. cit.,* billed by corporate spokesmen and their press allies as "the best business history yet written."
69. *New York Times,* August 11, 1981, p. D4.
70. *Moody's Industrial Manual,* 1978, p. 581.
71. *Ibid.,* p. 580.
72. *Fortune,* September 10, 1979, p. 74.
73. United Nations Secretariat, United Nations Conference on Trade and Development, "Fibers and Textiles, Dimensions of Corporate Marketing Structure," (Geneva/New York, 1981), p. 165.
74. *Ibid.,* p. 151.
75. *Business Week,* November 24, 1982, p. 92.
76. *Fibers and Textiles,* p. 153-4.
77. *Ibid.,* p. 154.
78. *Textile World,* April, 1977.
79. *Business Week,* November 24, 1980, p. 92.
80. *"Fibers and Textiles, op. cit.,* p. 155. See also "Transfer Pricing and Multinational Enterprise, Report of the OECD Committee on Fiscal Affairs (Paris, 1972), par. 2.
81. *Ibid.,* p. 165.
82. *Ibid.,* p. 162.
83. "The Structure of the U.S. Petroleum Industry," Special Subcommittee on Integrated Oil Operations, Committee on Interior and Insular Affairs, U.S. Senate, Government Printing Office (Washington, D.C., 1976), pp. 344, 392.

84. *Ibid.*
85. *Forbes,* October 2, 1978, p. 37.
86. *Du Pont Annual Report,* 1980, pp. 48-49, p. 42.
87. *Ibid.,* p. 41.
88. *The New Yorker,* September 7, 1981, p. 114.
89. Du Pont Company *Proxy Statement,* May 3, 1982, p. 5.
90. *Structure of U.S. Petroleum Industry, op. cit.,* p. 342.
91. *Interlocking Directorships,* Committee on Governmental Affairs, U.S. Senate, *op. cit.,* pp. 464-67.
92. Du Pont Company Proxy Statement, July 20, 1981, Exhibit A, May 3, 1982, p. 11.
93. *New York Times,* August 10, 1981, p. D8.
94. *Fortune,* November 16, 1981, p. 75.
95. *Ibid.,* p. 76.
96. *Ibid.*
97. *Ibid.*
98. *Ibid.*
99. Wilmington *News-Journal,* November, 1980.
100. Wilmington *Morning News,* August 28, 1981.
101. Wilmington *News-Journal,* September 27, 1981.
102. Statement by Ted Keller, Citizens Coalition for Tax Reform, before New Castle County Council.
103. Letter, Richard Sarano, General Council, Cole-Layer-Trumble, to Theodore Keller, October 7, 1981.
104. Wilmington *News-Journal,* December 15, 1981.
105. *Ibid.,* December 18, 1981.
106. *Ibid.,* December 23, 1981.
107. *Ibid.,* December 27, 1981.
108. *Ibid.,* January 4, 1982.
109. *Ibid.,* January 5, 1982.
110. Gary E. Hindes to Sydney Hurlbert.
111. Wilmington *News-Journal,* March 3, 1982.
112. Richard Cunningham to Melvin Slawik, August 3, 1982; also June 12, 1983.
113. Report of CAGW Task Force, December 16, 1982.
114. June Y. Eisley to Nathan Hayward III, January 20, 1983.
115. June Y. Eisley to Governor Pierre S. du Pont IV, March 14, 1983.
116. Figures from Delaware State Revenue Division, Dover, Delaware.
117. Wilmington *News-Journal,* June 9, 1982.
118. *Ibid.*
119. *Ibid.*
120. *New York Times,* August 17, 1980, Sec. 3, p. F16.
121. *New York Times,* December 13, 1981, Sec. 1, p. 31.
122. Wilmington *News-Journal,* February 24, 1983.
123. *Delaware Today,* June, 1981, p. 41.
124. Delaware *News-Journal,* March 11, 1983, p. A1.
125. *Ibid.*
126. *Ibid.*
127. *New York Times,* August 8, 1982, Sec. 3, p. F15.
128. Du Pont Company Proxy Statement, March 18, 1982, p. 11.
129. *Fortune,* September 7, 1981, p. 104.
130. *New York Times,* August 8, 1982, Sec. 3, p. F15.

131. *Delaware Today,* October, 1979, p. 14.

132. Gordon Dean, AEC, to Harry Truman, September 27, 1950, p. 2, White House Central Files, 692-B; Harry S. Truman Presidential Library, Independence, Missouri.

133. *Ibid.*

134. Gordon Dean, AEC, to Charles Murphy, White House Counsel, p. 1.

135. *Ibid.,* p. 2.

136. *Ibid.,* p.

137. Atomic Energy Commission Release 322, November 28, 1950.

138. *Delaware State News,* June 8, 1975, p. 3.

139. *State/Columbia, S.C.,* April 17, 1983, p. 13-C.

140. *New York Times,* July 4, 1980.

141. *Atlanta Constitution,* August 22, 1982.

142. *Ibid.,* September 8, 1982.

143. *Ibid.,* October 22, 1982,; *Science,* Vol. 218, No. 4574, November 19, 1982, p. 774.

144. Wilmington *News-Journal,* September 12, 1982; see also Jefferson's reply, September 26, 1982.

145. See files on Free Europe Committee and Greenwalts' role with CIA Director Allen Dulles in the John F. Kennedy Presidential Library outside Boston.

146. Moore's MKLULTRA Subprojects were f1-46, April 8, 1963; 51-24, August 1956; 51-B, 52-94, February 20, 1963; 52-19, December 20, 1962; 52-17 March 1, 1963; 52-23, December 6, 1962; and 52-64, August 24, 1959. See John Marks, *The Search for the Manchurian Candidate* (New York: Times Books, 1979), pp. 108, 112, 116, 200n, 222.

147. *News-Journal,* October 7, 1974.

148. Letter from James Gaver, August 29, 1983.

149. E.I. du Pont de Nemours, *Savannah River Plant 25th Anniversary* (brochure).

150. Ronald Brownstein and Nina Easton, *Reagan's Ruling Class* (Introduction by Ralph Nader), The Presidential Accountability Group (Washington, D.C., 1982), p. 609.

151. *Ibid.,* p. 610.

152. Federal Elections Commission,

153. *Delaware State News,* August 11, 1983.

154. *Ibid.*

155.

156. Wilmington *Morning News,* March 18, 1983.

157. *New York Times,* May 8, 1979.

158. *AP,* May 25, 1983.

159. Roy Dowan, "The Maverick Who Yelled Foul at Citibank," *Fortune,* January 10, 1983, p. 46.

160. *Ibid.,* p. 118.

161. *Ibid.*

162. Wilmington *News-Journal,* February 19, 1982.

163. *Ibid.*

164. *Du Pont Context,* Vol. 11, No. 1, 1982, p. 9.

165. Citizens Coalition for Tax Reform, Statement to Christina School Board members, January 8, 1983.

166. *Philadelphia Inquirer,* June 22, 1983.

167. *New York Times,* August 10, 1981.

168. *New York Times,* March 3, 1977.

169. Wilmington *News-Journal,* May 1, 1983.
170. *New York Times,* March 25, 1983, D1.
171. *Delaware State News,* May 29, 1983.
172. Paul Volker to David Elliott, March 17, 1983.
173. Wilmington *News-Journal,* May 1, 1983.
174. *Delaware State News,* May 15, 1983.
175. *Delaware State News,* May 15, 1983.
175. *Ibid.*
176. Wilmington *News-Journal* (column by Ralph Moyed), April 29, 1983.
177. *New York Times,* April 12, 1977, p. 43.
178. *Ibid.*
179. Wilmington *News-Journal,* June 23, 1983.
180. Wilmington *News-Journal,* June 25, 1983.
181. *Ibid.*
182. Federal Elections Commission,
183. Wilmington *News-Journal,* July 27, 1983.
184. *Ibid.*
185. *Ibid.*
186. *Philadelphia Inquirer,* July 28, 1983.
187. Wilmington *News-Journal,* July 27, 1983.
188. *Ibid.*
189. *Philadelphia Inquirer,* July 28, 1983.
190. *Ibid.*
191. Wilmington *News-Journal,*
192. Statement by Pierre S. du Pont IV, Governor of Delaware, July 27, 1983.
193. Wilmington *News-Journal,* July 27, 1983.
194. Statement, Pierre S. du Pont IV, July 27, 1983.
195. *Ibid.*
196. *Philadelphia Inquirer,* July 29, 1983.
197. *Ibid.*
198. Wilmington *News-Journal,* August 11, 1983.
199. *Ibid.*
200. Pierre S. du Pont IV, "The Proper Role of the Federal Judiciary—Judges Are Tethered to the Language of the Constitution." Speech delivered to the Delaware Law School Moot Court Honors Society, Wilmington, Delaware, November 11, 1981, *Vital Speeches,* p. 167-171.
201. *Ibid.*
202. Federal Elections Commission,
203. Statement, P.S. du Pont IV, July 27, 1983.
204. *Oil and Gas Journal,* November 5, 1979.

Index